D1483637

In this book Christian Gourieroux and Alain Monfort provide an up-to-date and comprehensive analysis of modern time series econometrics. They have succeeded in synthesising in an organised and integrated way a broad and diverse literature. While the book does not assume a deep knowledge of economics, one of its most attractive features is the close attention it pays to economic models and phenomena throughout. The coverage represents a major reference tool for graduate students, researchers and applied economists.

Section one, *Traditional methods*, provides a detailed treatment of classical seasonal adjustment or smoothing methods, giving a central role to empirical analysis, a subject which is often ignored in textbooks. Section two, *Probabilistic and statistical properties of stationary processes*, gives a thorough coverage of various mathematical tools (in particular Box-Jenkins methodology). Section three, *Times series econometrics: stationary and nonstationary models*, is the heart of the book. It is devoted to a range of important topics including causality, exogeneity shocks, multipliers, lag structure, structural forms, error correction models, cointegration, and fractionally integrated models. The final section, *State space models*, describes the main contribution of filtering and smoothing theory to time series econometric problems.

Time Series and Dynamic Models

Themes in Modern Econometrics

Managing editors
PETER C.B. PHILLIPS, *Yale University* and
ADRIAN PAGAN, *Australian National University*

Advisory editors
CHRISTIAN GOURIEROUX, *CREST and CEPREMAP*, *Paris*
MICHAEL WICKENS, *University of York*

Themes in Modern Econometrics is designed to service the large and growing need for explicit teaching tools in econometrics. It will provide an organised sequence of textbooks in econometrics aimed squarely at the student population, and will be the first series in the discipline to have this as its express aim. Written at a level accessible to students with an introductory course in econometrics behind them, each book will address topics or themes that students and researchers encounter daily. While each book will be designed to stand alone as an authoritative survey in its own right, the distinct emphasis throughout will be on pedagogic excellence.

Titles in the series

Statistics and Econometric Models: Volume One
CHRISTIAN GOURIEROUX and ALAIN MONFORT
Translated by QUANG VUONG

Statistics and Econometric Models: Volume Two
CHRISTIAN GOURIEROUX and ALAIN MONFORT
Translated by QUANG VUONG

Time Series and Dynamic Models
CHRISTIAN GOURIEROUX and ALAIN MONFORT
Translated and edited by GIAMPIERO M. GALLO

Time Series and Dynamic Models

Christian Gourieroux
CREST and CEPREMAP, Paris
Alain Monfort
CREST-INSEE, Paris
Translated and edited by Giampiero M. Gallo

CAMBRIDGE
UNIVERSITY PRESS

330.0151955
$G71t$

PUBLISHED BY THE PRESS SYNDICATE OF THE UNIVERSITY OF CAMBRIDGE
The Pitt Building, Trumpington Street, Cambridge CB2 1RP, United Kingdom

CAMBRIDGE UNIVERSITY PRESS
The Edinburgh Building, Cambridge, CB2 2RU, United Kingdom
40 West 20th Street, New York, NY 10011-4211, USA
10 Stamford Road, Oakleigh, Melbourne 3166, Australia

Originally published in French as
Séries Temporelles et Modèles Dynamiques by Économica 1990
$\mathcal{M}$ © Ed. ÉCONOMICA 1990

First published in English by Cambridge University Press 1997
as *Time Series and Dynamic Models*

Printed by Bell and Bain Ltd., Glasgow

Typeset in 10/13 Computer Modern

A catalogue record for this book is available from the British Library

Library of Congress Cataloguing in Publication data are available

ISBN 0 521 41146 7   hardback
ISBN 0 521 42308 2   paperback

TAG

Contents

Part III: Time-series Econometrics: Stationary and Nonstationary Models

Part IV: State-space Models

List of Adopted Notations

x_t the value of a variable at time t, or the variable itself.

$\{x_t\}$ a sequence or a stochastic process indexed by t.

$\mathbf{y}$ a (column) vector.

$\mathbf{A}$ a matrix.

$\mathbf{A}'$ a transposed matrix.

$\det \mathbf{A}$ the determinant of a matrix.

$\varrho(\mathbf{A})$ the rank of matrix $\mathbf{A}$.

$\operatorname{tr}(\mathbf{A})$ the trace of matrix $\mathbf{A}$.

$\mathbf{A}(L)$ a matrix polynomial in the lag operator L.

$\operatorname{degree}(B)$ the degree of a (matrix) polynomial.

$\xrightarrow{\mathrm{p}}$ convergence in probability.

$\xrightarrow{\mathrm{d}}$ convergence in distribution.

$\xrightarrow{a.s.}$ almost sure convergence.

$\operatorname{plim}_{T\to+\infty}$ probability limit.

$\mathbf{E}$ expectation operator.

var variance operator.

avar asymptotic variance operator.

cov covariance operator.

acov asymptotic covariance operator.

$\boldsymbol{R}^m$ the set of real numbers in the m-dimensional space.

$\mathbf{W}$ the n-dimensional Brownian motion.

$\mathbf{1}$ the indicator function.

Preface

The analysis of the evolution of one or more time varying phenomena has long been the domain of interest of experts in various fields. Probability theorists have built an impressive mathematical construction, the theory of stochastic processes, which allows one to study in great detail the properties of a set of random variables indexed by time. Statistical theorists have suggested a number of approaches to the problems of estimation, of hypothesis testing, of forecasting, of filtering, of smoothing for the stochastic processes. Empirical analysts in many fields (physics, engineering, economics...) have developed suitable techniques to solve their own problems, thus creating a wide array of analytical tools which are not always rigorously linked to the theoretical literature.

Confronted with this huge variety of suggestions in time series analysis, the interested students and researchers find themselves somewhat at a loss. The goal of this book is to help them in their training. In order for this help to be effective it was important to avoid too much abstraction or alternatively a mere support to practitioners without any theoretical content. We have tried our best to navigate between these two courses, granting ourselves some freedom from mathematical formalism when it became too cumbersome, but also highlighting the weak theoretical support of certain practices.

Mostly, we have tried to present a variety of aspects of time-series analysis in a synthetic manner: statistical problems, such as seasonal adjustment and forecasting; econometric problems, such as causality, exogeneity, cointegration, and expectations; and some engineering

problems, such as Kalman filtering and smoothing. In deciding on the
boundaries of the exposition, we were obviously forced to cut out many
aspects of time-series analysis, mainly those related to nonlinearities.

The book is made of four main parts:

Part I: Traditional Methods – chapters 2 to 4 In these first chapters we describe a number of techniques, which have been very important
from an historical point of view, and which still play a central role in
empirical analysis: seasonal adjustment by linear regression methods
(chapter 2), seasonal adjustment by moving averages (chapter 3), and
exponential smoothing methods (chapter 4). It was important for us to
recall these classical methods in a detailed fashion, since they are sel-
dom presented in the most popular time-series books, even if they are
included in the econometric packages available to the practitioners.

**Part II: Probabilistic and Statistical Properties of Stationary
Processes – chapters 5 to 9** This part is devoted to a self-contained
presentation of the main properties of the stationary processes both from
a probabilistic and a statistical point of view, without making any specific reference to particular fields of application. Chapter 5 contains an
analysis of the properties of the univariate stationary processes; chapter
6 analyzes aspects related to prediction based on ARMA and ARIMA
processes; extension to the multivariate processes is included in chapter
7, whereas their various representations are suggested in chapter 8. Finally, chapter 9 describes estimation and testing for the univariate and
multivariate stationary processes.

**Part III: Time-series Econometrics: Stationary and Nonstatio-
nary Models – chapters 10 to 14** This part is more closely related
to the concepts, models, and methods employed in econometrics. Thus,
the notions of causality, exogeneity, shock, and multiplier are analyzed in
chapter 10, while the ideas behind cointegration, error correction models,
and fractional processes are presented in chapter 11. Chapter 12 is
devoted to the role and treatment of expectations in econometrics, in
particular rational expectations: the cases of expectations of current and
future variables, of multiple expectations, and of multivariate models
are analyzed. In chapter 13 the attention is focussed on the problem of
specification search, where a general to specific method is proposed when
testing for causality, predeterminedness, exogeneity, structural form, lag
structure, rational expectations, etc. Finally, chapter 14 introduces the
statistical methods suitable for nonstationary models: methods based

on the empirical moments, unit root tests, regression with nonstationary regressors, cointegration tests (limited- and full-information methods), and determination of the integration order.

Part IV: State-space Models In this last part we look at the contributions of filtering theory to time-series econometrics. Chapter 15 contains Kalman filtering and smoothing, and chapter 16 suggests a number of applications: linear models, ARMA and ARIMA models, unobserved component models, missing data, rational expectation models and learning.

We are very grateful to Martine Germond, who graciously took care of typing the French edition. We would like to extend a special thanks to Giampiero M. Gallo, who not only translated the French edition into English, but also suggested some improvements in the presentation of the topics.

Finally, we would like to gratefully acknowledge the financial support for the publication of the French edition of this book and for its translation into English received, respectively, from the French Ministry of Research and Technology, and from the Ministry of Culture.

C. Gourieroux

A. Monfort

1

Introduction

1.1 Definition of a Time Series

The goal of empirical economic analysis is to highlight economic mechanisms and decision making: a number of observations on the relevant variables are thus required to study the existing links among them. The impossibility of controlled experiments in most economic fields has, as a consequence, that these observations can be obtained only through surveys or resorting to existing databases. These data may be available, for example, once a year or once a quarter and thus come from repeated observations, corresponding to different dates. The sequence of observations on one variable $(y_t, t \in \mathcal{T})$ is called *time series*.

The observation dates are usually equally spaced: this is the case with monthly, quarterly series, etc. One year contains an integer number s of intervals separating two subsequent observation dates: $s = 12$ for a monthly series, $s = 4$ for a quarterly series, and so on. The equally spaced dates are henceforth indexed by integers $t = 1, \ldots, T$ where T indicates the number of observations.

Note that in other domains different from economics, certain characteristics (temperature, humidity, etc.) are observed continuously in time by means of mechanical instruments. The index t is then valid in an interval of $\mathbf{R}$. The latter case is very different from the previous, since an infinity of observations is available. The closest economics can get to continuous data are the tick-by-tick observations recorded for price or

Table 1.1 *French Monthly Consumer Price Index (July 1970 = 100)*

	Jan.	Feb.	Mar.	Apr.	May	June	July	Aug.	Sep.	Oct.	Nov.	Dec.
1970	97.9	98.2	98.5	99.0	99.4	99.8	100.0	100.4	100.8	101.2	101.6	101.9
1971	102.5	103.0	103.4	104.0	104.7	105.1	105.6	106.0	106.5	107.1	107.5	108.0
1972	108.3	108.9	109.4	109.8	110.4	111.0	111.9	112.5	113.2	114.2	114.9	115.5
1973	115.5	115.8	116.4	117.2	118.3	119.2	120.2	121.0	122.1	123.4	124.5	125.3
1974	127.4	129.1	130.6	132.7	134.3	135.8	137.5	138.6	140.1	141.8	143.1	144.3
1975	145.9	147.0	148.2	149.5	150.6	151.7	152.8	153.8	155.1	156.3	157.3	158.8
1976	159.9	161.0	162.4	163.8	164.9	165.6	167.2	168.4	200.2	171.8	173.2	173.8
1977	174.3	175.5	177.1	179.4	181.1	182.5	184.1	185.1	186.7	188.2	188.9	189.4
1978	190.3	191.7	193.4	195.5	197.4	198.9	201.5	202.5	203.8	205.7	206.8	207.8

quantities exchanged on the financial markets. The peculiarities linked to continuous data will not be studied in what follows.

The observations can correspond to flows or stocks. The monthly oil consumption is a flow; each observation corresponds to a period. In order for these observations to be directly comparable, we would need the time periods to be the same. In the case of monthly consumption, this time period is 28, 29, 30, or 31 days, and it may be necessary to correct the raw series. A simple way of doing this consists in calculating the average daily consumption for each month. In the case of a stock, the observations correspond to specific dates. The daily value of a US dollar in terms of French francs at the opening of the foreign exchange market is an example of a stock. Note that a flow can always be considered as the difference between two stocks.

1.2 Examples of Time Series

In tables 1.1 and 1.2 we give the values of two time series which will be used in what follows as examples to illustrate the different methods analyzed. The first refers to the monthly French Consumer Price Index (July 1970=100) the second to the monthly French National Railroad Company passenger traffic.

1.3 Graphical Representation

The series are usually presented in a Cartesian plan with the observation values on the y-axis and the corresponding dates on the x-axis. The

Table 1.2 *Passenger Traffic*

	Jan.	Feb.	Mar.	Apr.	May	June	July	Aug.	Sep.	Oct.	Nov.	Dec.
1963	1750	1560	1820	2090	1910	2410	3140	2850	2090	1850	1630	2420
1964	1710	1600	1800	2120	2100	2460	3200	2960	2190	1870	1770	2270
1965	1670	1640	1770	2190	2020	2610	3190	2860	2140	1870	1760	2360
1966	1810	1640	1860	1990	2110	2500	3030	2900	2160	1940	1750	2330
1967	1850	1590	1880	2210	2110	2480	2880	2670	2100	1920	1670	2520
1968	1834	1792	1860	2138	2115	2485	2581	2639	2038	1936	1784	2391
1969	1798	1850	1981	2085	2120	2491	2834	2725	1932	2085	1856	2553
1970	1854	1823	2005	2418	2219	2722	2912	2771	2153	2136	1910	2537
1971	2008	1835	2120	2304	2264	2175	2928	2738	2178	2137	2009	2546
1972	2084	2034	2152	2522	2318	2684	2971	2759	2267	2152	1978	2723
1973	2081	2112	2279	2661	2281	2929	3089	2803	2296	2210	2135	2862
1974	2223	2248	2421	2710	2505	3021	3327	3044	2607	2525	2160	2876
1975	2481	2428	2596	2923	2795	3287	3598	3118	2875	2754	2588	3266
1976	2667	2668	2804	2806	2976	3430	3705	3053	2764	2802	2707	3307
1977	2706	2586	2796	2978	3053	3463	3649	3095	2839	2966	2863	3375
1978	2820	2857	3306	3333	3141	3512	3744	3179	2984	2950	2896	3611
1979	3313	2644	2872	3267	3391	3682	3937	3284	2849	3085	3043	3541
1980	2848	2913	3248	3250	3375	3640	3771	3259	3206	3269	3181	4008

Data for the SNCF Passenger Traffic (French National Railroad Company) in 2nd class, expressed in millions of passengers per kilometer. The monthly observations refer to the period 1963-80.

evolution of the monthly consumer price index between the months of January 1970 and December 1978 (table 1.1) is given in figure 1.1.

The chosen scale for time (a relatively small unit such as a month) allows us to show the medium-term evolution of the series. In this case, it seems to present a break-point at the end of 1973, on the occasion of the first abrupt increase in oil prices.

We define the growth rate of the index between the dates $t - 1$ and t as

$$\delta I_t = \frac{I_t - I_{t-1}}{I_{t-1}},$$

where I_t is the value of the index in month t.

The numerical values of this growth can be derived from the values appearing in table 1.1.

This new series shows more changes in variation than the initial series I_t; an abrupt increase in the index is often compensated for by a weaker

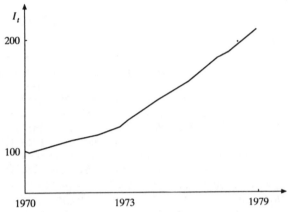

Figure 1.1   Monthly Consumer Price Index

Table 1.3 *Monthly Growth Rates of the Consumer Price Index between February 1970 and December 1978 (percent)*

	Jan.	Feb.	Mar.	Apr.	May	June	July	Aug.	Sep.	Oct.	Nov.	Dec.
1970		0.31	0.31	0.51	0.40	0.40	0.20	0.40	0.40	0.40	0.40	0.30
1971	0.59	0.49	0.39	0.58	0.67	0.38	0.48	0.38	0.47	0.56	0.37	0.47
1972	0.28	0.55	0.46	0.37	0.55	0.54	0.81	0.54	0.62	0.88	0.61	0.52
1973	0.00	0.26	0.52	0.69	0.94	0.76	0.84	0.67	0.91	1.06	0.89	0.64
1974	1.68	1.33	1.16	1.61	1.21	1.12	1.25	0.80	1.08	1.21	0.92	0.84
1975	1.11	0.75	0.82	0.88	0.74	0.73	0.73	0.65	0.85	0.77	0.64	0.95
1976	0.69	0.69	0.87	0.86	0.67	0.42	0.97	0.72	1.07	0.94	0.81	0.35
1977	0.29	0.69	0.91	1.30	0.95	0.77	0.88	0.54	0.86	0.80	0.37	0.26
1978	0.48	0.74	0.89	1.09	0.97	0.76	1.31	0.50	0.64	0.93	0.53	0.48

growth one or two months later. This is an explanation for the various "peaks" and "troughs" displayed in figure 1.2.

Once we have eliminated the "peaks" and the "troughs" in the very short period, we can see a medium-term evolution including four main phases: the first, until October 1973 corresponds to an almost fixed growth rate close to 0.4% monthly. This growth has increased rapidly until mid 1974, then showing a decrease, and since 1976 has stabilized at a level close to 0.7%, higher than the one in the initial period.

The almost stability of δI_t over the period 1970–72 can be highlighted by showing the series I_t in semi-logarithmic scale (with $\ln I_t$ on the y-axis, and t on the x-axis). In fact, the series corresponds to the ap-

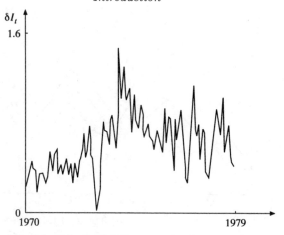

Figure 1.2 Monthly Growth Rates in the Consumer Price Index

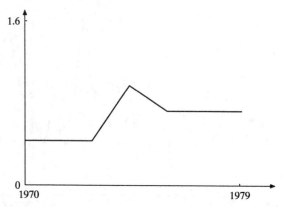

Figure 1.3 Medium-Term Evolution in the Growth Rate of the Price Index

proximated relationship

$$\frac{I_t - I_{t-1}}{I_{t-1}} = \delta_0,$$

where δ_0 is a constant and therefore approximately satisfies the relationship $I_t = I_1(1 + \delta_0)^{t-1}$. Taking the logarithm of this relationship, we can see that the medium-term evolution for the period 1970–72 will be almost linear on a semi-logarithmic scale.

The previous series presents other regularities: in fact the growth rate of the index for August is always less than for July and for September. This peculiarity is clearly explained by the "slumber" of the economy during summer holidays. The effect of this month on the value of the index (seasonal phenomenon) is however less pronounced on the price index series than on other series (e.g., the series in figure 1.5).

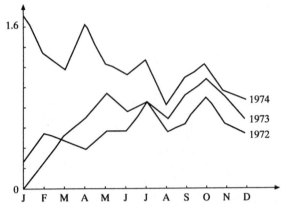

Figure 1.4 Price Index Growth from January 1972 to December 1974

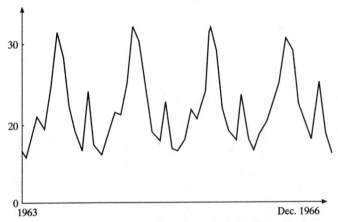

Figure 1.5 Passenger Traffic from January 1963 to December 1966

If we want to highlight this periodicity graphically, we can easily compare the data for one month for different years. This can be done by
showing on the same graph the data for each year, having time (months)
on the x-axis.

This graphical representation highlights the similarities in the shape
within the year. In fact, between May and December, the three years
show peaks for the same months.

Similar remarks can be made for the other series. The graph for
the data relative to the SNCF (French National Railroad Company)
traffic (figure 1.5) shows a medium-term evolution approximately constant and a definitely stronger periodicity of 12 than the previous series.

1.4 Some Problems in Time Series

1.4.1 Forecasting

The problem of forecasting consists in evaluating the future values y_{T+h} $h \geq 1$ of a variable starting from the observation of its past values y_1, $y_2, \ldots, y_T$. The *forecast* denoted $\hat{y}_T(h)$ or $_T\hat{y}_{T+h}$ derived from these observations will generally be different from the value that the variable will take at time $T + h$. For this reason we often prefer to suggest a forecast interval $[\hat{y}_T^1(h), \ \hat{y}_T^2(h)]$, likely to contain the unknown value y_{T+h}.

The quality of the forecast will depend upon the way in which the series evolves. The more the series is a "regular" function of time, the easier it will be to forecast it. For example, the forecasts will be good for most economic variables in growth periods, when the general behavior of the series is linear or exponential. On the other hand, the various forecast methods do not allow to forecast a change in the evolution due to a modification of the economic structure, when nothing in its past suggested it could happen.

The quality of the forecast depends on the *horizon h* and is generally better when h is small.

The methods used for forecasting can be used to compute the past value of a variable as well. We use then the term *backcast* instead of forecast. This can be useful, for example, in the case of missing data and can therefore allow the reconstruction of a time series. These backcast values can also be used to measure the effects of an accidental phenomenon (strike, exceptional weather conditions). The backcast gives an idea of the value which the variable could have taken had that phenomenon not occurred.

1.4.2 Trend Removal

During a growth period, many economic variables have similar medium-term evolutions (*trend*). These variables are therefore strongly correlated with each other, even if this does not translate into the existence of an explanatory link among these variables. To see whether such links exist, it may be useful to remove this trend.

1.4.3 Seasonal Adjustment

When we introduced the series for the SNCF traffic we remarked that the values observed for a certain month were generally on the same side with respect to the annual mean: for example, the values for August

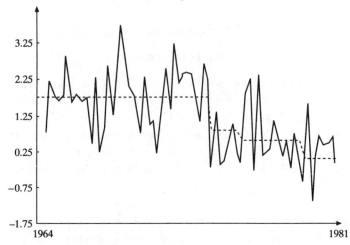

Figure 1.6 GNP Growth Rate – Spain

are always below it. We define the series obtained after having removed the seasonal effect from the initial series *seasonally adjusted series* or *de-seasonalized series*, noted as y_{SA}.

This series, adjusted for the seasonal variations, is of great interest for the interpretation of time series. Let us assume, for example, that an economic policy decision is made in July to reduce the price increase. Does the observation of a lower growth rate in the price index in August allow one to judge the effect of that measure? There is the danger of too quick a conclusion: observation of the raw series shows that a decrease in the growth rate was present every year, therefore the question becomes whether this decrease was stronger or weaker than usual. Observation of the values in the seasonally adjusted series, where seasonal variations have been eliminated, allows one to answer this question directly. Note also that seasonal adjustment may be needed before looking for explanatory links among variables, for the same reasons presented above.

1.4.4 Detection of a Structural Break

Following changes in economic policy or deep changes in the structural relations among variables, the series can show breaks, both in the level or in the slope. We present here two series. The first (figure 1.6 – growth rate of Spanish GNP) shows a sudden fall in its level in correspondence with the several oil crises.

The second (figure 1.7) gives the evolution of the growth rate of the

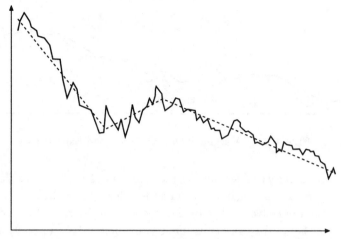

Figure 1.7 British Pound/US Dollar Exchange Rate

British Pound/US Dollar exchange rate. We can observe various breaks in the slope.

It is clearly important to try and forecast these breakpoints, or, if this is impossible, to detect their existence as early as possible in the analysis.

1.4.5 Causality – Time Lags

The simultaneous observation of several variables in time can allow one to address some questions about *causality*. For the period 1975-79, are the oil prices formed on the basis of the observed prices for gold? Or, rather, is it the latter which follows the former? Once the direction of causality is determined, if possible, we need to know with what lag and during which period the explanatory variable influenced the explained variable (assessment of the *time lags*).

1.4.6 Distinction between Short and Long Run

It takes more or less time for the influences among variables to exert their effects and these influences are persistent to a greater or lesser extent. One of the important problems in macroeconomics is to separate the persistent relationships (defined as long term) from those which are not. The latter are often interpreted in terms of adjustment to the long-run relationship.

1.4.7 Study of Agents' Expectations

Time-series analysis also allows one to study how agents react with respect to time. In fact, we often have data both on the values taken by

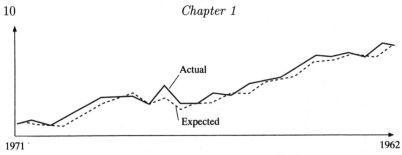

Figure 1.8   Machinery Orders: Actual and Expected

certain economic variables and on the forecasts of these values formulated by company managers three months before (figure 1.8).

We can ask ourselves if they predict the level of the variable correctly, or its evolution. We can try to understand how they implicitly form their expectations, and so on.

1.5 Properties of the Methods Used

Various methods have been devised to solve the problems previously mentioned. The optimal character of each of these methods depends on the problem at hand, for example, seasonal adjustment or forecasting, but at the same time on the available series. There is no single method which can be used to treat all time-series data in a satisfactory way. To illustrate this statement, we can consider three criteria proposed by Lovell (1963) which an acceptable seasonal adjustment method needs to satisfy:

$$(i) \quad x_{SA} + y_{SA} = (x+y)_{SA}, \quad \forall\, x, y,$$

$$(ii) \quad \lambda x_{SA} = (\lambda x)_{SA}, \quad \forall\, x, \, \forall\, \lambda \in I\!\!R^+,$$

$$(iii) \quad x_{SA} y_{SA} = (xy)_{SA}, \quad \forall\, x, y.$$

The first of these properties will be very important in practice, since it will allow to obtain the aggregate seasonally adjusted series from the seasonally adjusted primary series. By the same token, it will allow to obtain the seasonally adjusted series of a stock starting from the associated flow and conversely.

The second property expresses the independence of the seasonal adjustment method with respect to a change in units: a series for oil consumption expressed in cubic meters or in barrels should lead to the same result.

The third property will allow to obtain, for example, the unemployment rate taking the ratio of the seasonally adjusted number of unemployed to the seasonally adjusted work force.

Although they may sound trivial, these three properties nevertheless translate into methods which cannot be used in practice. The first two properties imply the linearity of the seasonal adjustment process. That is, there exist some real numbers $a_{t,\tau}$ such that

$$x_{SA,t} = \sum_\tau a_{t,\tau} x_\tau.$$

If we write the third property

$$\left(\sum_\tau a_{t,\tau} x_\tau \right) \left(\sum_\tau a_{t,\tau} y_\tau \right) = \sum_\tau a_{t,\tau} x_\tau \, y_\tau \quad \forall \, x_\tau, y_\tau,$$

we conclude that there exists a value t_0 such that

$$\forall \, \tau \neq t_0 \quad a_{t,\tau} = 0$$

and

$$a_{t,t_0} = \begin{cases} 0 \\ 1 \end{cases}$$

which implies that the seasonally adjusted value will be equal to either a lagged value or to zero, not such an appealing result!

In spite of the fact that each method will not possess good properties for all existing series, it will always be possible to find acceptable methods for each series studied. Generally, the usual methods are derived from a model describing the time series. They will possess certain "optimality" properties for the series responding to the model. The farther the series is from the assumed model, the worse the adopted method will be, and the more the results will be affected by serious biases.

1.6 Time-series Modeling

The solution for the various problems mentioned rests on some models describing how the series evolves. It is useful to distinguish among three types of models: *adjustment models*, *autopredictive models*, and *explanatory models*. We now present these three types of models briefly, and, in due course, we will point out how they will be used in the rest of the book.

1.6.1 Adjustment Models

The Principle The observation of real data generally shows several regularities. If, for example, we consider the series for passenger traffic between January 1963 and December 1966 (figure 1.5), we can observe that the medium-term movement (trend) is approximately constant. If we remove this trend from the initial series we obtain an approximately periodic curve with a zero mean. Thus, we can formulate the hypothesis that the series was generated by a model of the type

$$y_t = a + s_t + u_t,$$

where a is an unknown constant representing the trend, and s_t is a periodic function of time (e.g., sine) with period 12, zero mean, which we will call the *seasonal component*; u_t, called *irregular component*, will be a zero mean random variable. Note that this irregular component is often small relative to the other two, even if this is not to say that it is negligible. On the contrary, this component often contains the most interesting fluctuations from an economic point of view.

The previous decomposition is classic; sometimes a fourth component is added called *cycle*, which represents periodic medium-term movements.

More generally, we can formulate a model of the type

$$y_t = f(t, u_t),$$

where f is a function characterized by a finite number of unknown parameters and u_t is a zero mean random variable about which various hypotheses can be formulated. Such a model is called an *adjustment model*.

Global and Local Adjustment The hypotheses made about the random variable u_t translate into estimation methods for the function f, chosen on the basis of optimality properties. In fact, in chapter 2, we will propose an optimal estimation method (called the ordinary least squares method) for the case when u_t have the same variance and are uncorrelated. We will also propose a method for the case when u_t have the same variance and are correlated. These methods let each observation play the same role, so that we can say that they lead to global adjustment. The results of the obtained estimation can be used in different ways and, in particular, for seasonal adjustment and forecasting.

In certain cases we may want to base the models and the estimation methods on criteria which allow a different contribution for each observation. In chapter 3 on moving averages we will define series which *locally* behave as low degree polynomials, that is they are invariant with respect to a local polynomial adjustment involving a small number of observations. This definition allows us to introduce an important class of methods of seasonal adjustment.

Chapter 4 is devoted to forecasting methods by smoothing. In it we will see also that these methods can be justified by a *local adjustment* of several functions (polynomials, periodical functions, exponentials, etc.)

around the current value. In these adjustments, the observations play an exponentially decreasing role as we go back in the past, hence the name of exponential smoothing given to these methods.

Additive or Multiplicative Adjustment The adjustment function $f(t, u_t)$ is often additive, that is it can be decomposed in

$$f(t, u_t) = g(t) + u_t.$$

In this case we say that the model is an *additive* adjustment model.

If the function $f(t, u_t)$ can be written as

$$f(t, u_t) = g(t) \cdot u_t$$

we say that the model is a *multiplicative* adjustment model.

Note that, when the various variables are positive, we can transform a multiplicative model into an additive one using the logarithmic function.

Deterministic and Random Adjustment We have seen that an additive adjustment model can be written as

$$y_t = g(t) + u_t,$$

where $g(t)$ is an unobservable, but deterministic function of time.

It is equally possible to assume that $g(t), t$ integer is a stochastic process independent of the process u_t, t integer. A specific class of this kind of model, called the *unobserved component model*, is studied in chapter 15.

1.6.2 Autopredictive Models

In an autopredictive model, we suppose that y_t is a function of its past values and of a random disturbance u_t

$$y_t = f(y_{t-1}, y_{t-2}, ..., u_t).$$

A class of these models, particularly useful for prediction, are the ARIMA models studied in chapter 5 and beyond, first for the univariate case, then for the multivariate case. As we shall see, this class allows for a variety of models by means of a relatively limited number of parameters. Moreover, it is possible to propose the so-called identification methods, which allow the choice of the model from among a set of these models which seems the most suitable for the available data. Once the model is chosen, we can estimate its parameters and determine optimal predictions.

Among the methods of forecasting we find in particular the methods of exponential smoothing. The main advantage of the identification–estimation–prediction method based on the ARIMA models (sometimes called Box–Jenkins method) is that it allows for the selection of the optimal forecasting method from a large set of possibilities, whereas the classical methods (global adjustment or smoothing) involve a greater arbitrariness in the choice of function chosen for the adjustment.

Moreover, we shall see that in the multivariate case these models allow us to give answers to causality related problems, to the distinction between short and long term, and to the agents' expectation behavior (chapters 10 to 13).

1.6.3 Explanatory Models

In this model category, the variable y_t is expressed as a function of a vector of observable variables, called exogenous, x_t and of a random disturbance u_t

$$y_t = f(x_t, u_t).$$

x_t is either deterministic or random; in the latter case the processes $\{x_t\}$ and $\{u_t\}$ have certain properties of independence or uncorrelation.

We consider this class of basic econometric models to draw a connection between them and the autopredictive models.

Static Explanatory Model In a static explanatory model the variables x_t do not contain past values of y_t, and u_t are mutually and serially independent. For example, a model of this type will be

$$y_t = a + b x_t + u_t, \quad t = 1, \ldots, T,$$

where the x_t are independent of all the u_t's, and the u_t's have zero mean and are independent of each other.

Dynamic Explanatory Model An explanatory model can be dynamic both because the u_t are autocorrelated, and because x_t contains past values of y_t, that is some variables called "lagged endogenous".
Autocorrelated Disturbances A useful way of taking into account the autocorrelation of u_t is to assume that the series u_t follows an autopredictive model. The autopredictive approach allows therefore to suggest a class of models for the disturbances, that is for the unexplained component, and appears complementary to the formalization which links y and x, the latter being based on the knowledge of economic mechanisms.
Lagged Endogenous Variables Economic theory often gives indications about the nature of the variables to include in a model. In turn, it rarely gives suggestions about the appropriate temporal lags. The autopredictive approach can also be useful, as we will see in chapter 10, to make this choice.

These dynamic explanatory models will be studied in detail in what follows. We will analyze stationary and nonstationary models (chapters 11, 13, and 14), we will consider dynamic models based on rational expectations (chapter 12) and we will link dynamic models to the Kalman filter theory proposed by engineers (chapters 15 and 16).

I
Traditional Methods

2

Linear Regression
for Seasonal Adjustment

2.1 Linear Model Setup

We suppose that the raw series x_t is the sum of two deterministic components (the trend z_t and the seasonality s_t) and of a random component (the disturbance u_t)

$$x_t = z_t + s_t + u_t.$$

In order for the model description to be complete, we need to specify the functional forms of the deterministic components and to make some assumptions about the distribution of the disturbances u_t, $t = 1, \ldots, T$. Each deterministic component is written as a linear combination of known functions of time

$$z_t = z_t^1 b_1 + z_t^2 b_2 + \cdots + z_t^k b_k = \sum_{i=1}^{k} z_t^i \, b_i,$$

$$s_t = s_t^1 c_1 + s_t^2 c_2 + \cdots + s_t^m c_m = \sum_{j=1}^{m} s_t^j \, c_j,$$

where $b_1, \ldots, b_k, c_1, \ldots, c_m$ are unknown constants to be estimated from the observations.

The disturbances u_t are chosen to have zero mean $E(u_t) = 0$, $\forall \ t$, the same variance $\text{var}(u_t) = \sigma^2$, $\forall \ t$, and are not correlated $\text{cov}(u_t, u_\tau) = 0$, $\forall \ t \neq \tau$.

Table 2.1 *Industrial Production Index.*
Housing and Public Works Sectors

Year	Q1	Q2	Q3	Q4
1966	84	96	87	92
1967	88	99	89	95
1968	91	94	90	95
1969	91	103	94	97
1970	94	108	96	102
1971	91	104	95	102
1972	99	105	92	101
1973	99	105	93	98

Source: INSEE.

Summarizing, the model can be written as

$$x_t = \sum_{i=1}^{k} z_t^i b_i + \sum_{j=1}^{m} s_t^j c_j + u_t \quad t = 1, \ldots, T, \tag{2.1}$$

with $E(u_t) = 0$, var $(u_t) = \sigma^2$, cov $(u_t, u_\tau) = 0$, if $t \neq \tau$. The deterministic part appears as a linear function of the $k + m$ parameters b and c, hence the name of linear model given to (2.1).

This model may be written in vector form. Let us define $\mathbf{x}, \mathbf{z}^1, \ldots, \mathbf{z}^k$, $\mathbf{s}^1, \ldots, \mathbf{s}^m, \mathbf{u}$ as the vectors in $\mathbf{R}^T$ the components of which at time t with $t = 1, \ldots, T$ are, respectively, $x_t, z_t^1, \ldots, z_t^k, s_t^1, \ldots, s_t^m, u_t$. The system of equations (2.1) means that the random vector $\mathbf{x}$ allows the decomposition

$$\mathbf{x} = \sum_{i=1}^{k} \mathbf{z}^i b_i + \sum_{j=1}^{m} \mathbf{s}^j c_j + u,$$

with $E(\mathbf{u}) = \mathbf{0}$, var $(\mathbf{u}) = \sigma^2 \mathbf{I}$, a scalar matrix.

The trend $\sum_{i=1}^{k} \mathbf{z}^i b_i$ is an element of the vector subspace $\mathcal{Z}$ spanned by the vectors $\mathbf{z}^1, \ldots, \mathbf{z}^k$. This subspace has size k since these vectors are linearly independent. By the same token, the seasonal component $\sum_{j=1}^{m} \mathbf{s}^j c_j$ is an element of the subspace $\mathcal{S}$ spanned by $\mathbf{s}^1, \ldots, \mathbf{s}^m$. The size of this subspace is m since the vectors $\mathbf{s}^1, \ldots, \mathbf{s}^m$ form a basis. From now on, we will assume that these conditions on the size of $\mathcal{Z}$ and $\mathcal{S}$ are satisfied.

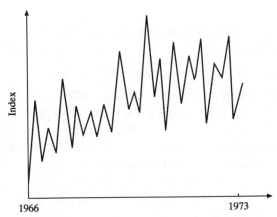

Figure 2.1   French Industrial Production Index

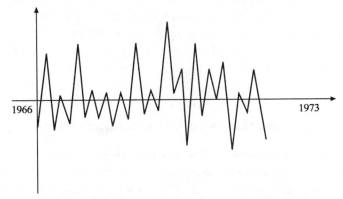

Figure 2.2   Detrended Industrial Production Index

The functions z^i and s^j depend on the way the variable x varies with time. Let us consider, for example, the quarterly series of an industrial production index (figure 2.1 – the data are reproduced in table 2.1). The medium-term growth for the period considered is approximately linear: we can then approximate the trend with a line of the type: $z_t = b_1 + b_2 t$. The subspace $\mathcal{Z}$ of size 2 is spanned by the series $z_t^1 = 1$ and $z_t^2 = t$. If we remove this medium-term movement from the raw data, the resulting series (figure 2.2) shows peaks and troughs of comparable amplitude at regular intervals (in this case four observations – corresponding to one year). A four-period periodic function can be chosen for the seasonal component s_t which will take each of four values (called *seasonal coefficients*), c_1, c_2, c_3, c_4. Thus, $s_t = c_j$, according to which quarter j corresponds to the date t. We can then write $s_t = s_t^1 c_1 + s_t^2 c_2 + s_t^3 c_3 + s_t^4 c_4$ where s_t^j is the indicator function for the quarter j taking the value 1 if the date t corresponds to this quarter and the value 0 otherwise.

As a first approximation to describe this particular series we can propose a model of the type

$$x_t = b_1 + b_2 t + s_t^1 c_1 + s_t^2 c_2 + s_t^3 c_3 + s_t^4 c_4 + u_t. \qquad (2.2)$$

Generally speaking, we can choose a smooth function (one showing little variation in the rate of change) for the trend, oftentimes a low degree polynomial. The simplest model for the seasonal component is one in which the seasonal effect is fixed, as in the previous example. Other types can be proposed: a slow variation in each seasonal coefficient can be described by choosing them as polynomial functions of time. The coefficients of the polynomial are then different from one subperiod to another (cf. exercise 2.6).

The extraction of the seasonal component can also include some variables showing nonzero values for more than one subperiod. For example, one of such variables could be the number of working days in the considered subperiod. Holiday effects, as well as strikes or weekend effects can be represented in the same manner.

2.2 Uniqueness of the Decomposition

The representation chosen for the deterministic components has to be such as to produce a unique decomposition of the raw series between trend and seasonal component. In other words, we may not have two distinct couples $(\mathbf{z}, \mathbf{s})$ and $(\mathbf{z}^*, \mathbf{s}^*)$ such that $z_t + s_t = z_t^* + s_t^*$, or $z_t - z_t^* = s_t - s_t^*$ $\forall t = 1, \ldots, T$. Therefore, only the null function can be interpreted at once as trend and seasonal component. In other words, we need $\mathcal{Z} \cap \mathcal{S} = \{0\}$. In order for this condition to be satisfied, we need the system $\mathbf{z}^1, \ldots, \mathbf{z}^k, \mathbf{s}^1, \ldots, \mathbf{s}^m$ to be a basis. Let us reexamine model (2.2) from this point of view. The subspace $\mathcal{Z}$ is spanned by $\mathbf{z}^1 = (1, 1, \ldots, 1)'$ and $\mathbf{z}^2 = (1, 2, \ldots, T)'$; the seasonal component subspace is spanned by

$$\mathbf{s}^1 = (1, 0, 0, 0, 1, 0, 0, 0, 1, 0, \ldots)',$$

$$\mathbf{s}^2 = (0, 1, 0, 0, 0, 1, 0, 0, 0, 1, \ldots)',$$

$$\mathbf{s}^3 = (0, 0, 1, 0, 0, 0, 1, 0, 0, 0, \ldots)',$$

$$\mathbf{s}^4 = (0, 0, 0, 1, 0, 0, 0, 1, 0, 0, \ldots)'.$$

The uniqueness of the decomposition is not satisfied. In fact, the six vectors, $\mathbf{z}^1$, $\mathbf{z}^2$, $\mathbf{s}^1$, $\mathbf{s}^2$, $\mathbf{s}^3$, $\mathbf{s}^4$, are related to each other by the relationship $\mathbf{z}^1 = \mathbf{s}^1 + \mathbf{s}^2 + \mathbf{s}^3 + \mathbf{s}^4$. In order to establish the uniqueness of the decomposition, one suggestion is to impose a constraint of the type

$$c_1 + c_2 + c_3 + c_4 = 0 \qquad (2.3)$$

on the seasonal effects, so that they cancel each other out within one year. Therefore the subspace of seasonal components $\mathcal{S}^*$ includes all functions s, such that

$$s_t = s_t^1 c_1 + s_t^2 c_2 + s_t^3 c_3 + s_t^4 c_4 \quad s.t. \quad c_1 + c_2 + c_3 + c_4 = 0.$$

Replacing c_4 with $(-c_1 - c_2 - c_3)$, we get

$$s_t = (s_t^1 - s_t^4)c_1 + (s_t^2 - s_t^4)c_2 + (s_t^3 - s_t^4)c_3.$$

The subspace of seasonal components $\mathcal{S}^*$ of size 3 is spanned by

$$\mathbf{s}^{1*} = \mathbf{s}^1 - \mathbf{s}^4, \quad \mathbf{s}^{2*} = \mathbf{s}^2 - \mathbf{s}^4, \quad \mathbf{s}^{3*} = \mathbf{s}^3 - \mathbf{s}^4.$$

Model (2.2)–(2.3) is called *Buys-Ballot's quarterly model* (Buys-Ballot, 1847).

2.3 Transformations for the Raw Series

The simplicity of the linear model makes it interesting to describe the characteristics of a series since it is possible to study its analytical mathematical properties. Even if the linear assumptions seem restrictive, they are less strong than one may think. In fact, several models can be written in a linear form after a transformation of the raw series

$$f(x_t, x_{t-1}, \ldots, x_{t-p}) = \sum_{i=1}^{k} \mathbf{z}^i b_i + \sum_{j=1}^{m} \mathbf{s}^j c_j + \mathbf{u}. \qquad (2.4)$$

These models are of the same type as (2.1) by choosing a new variable x^* as dependent variable defined as

$$x_t^* = f(x_t, x_{t-1}, \ldots, x_{t-p}).$$

2.3.1 Examples

The Multiplicative Model The quarterly model

$$\ln(x_t) = b_1 + b_2 t + s_t^1 c_1 + s_t^2 c_2 + s_t^3 c_3 + s_t^4 c_4 + u_t, \quad x_t > 0, \quad \forall \ t,$$

where s_t^j is the indicator function for the quarter and the seasonal coefficients satisfying $c_1 + c_2 + c_3 + c_4 = 0$ are of the type (2.4). The series derived from the original series is $x_t^* = \ln(x_t)$. It is a multiplicative model, since each component describing the original series can be highlighted by a straightforward application of the exponential function. We have $x_t = z_t^* s_t^* u_t^*$, with $z_t^* = \exp(b_1 + b_2 t)$, $s_t^* = \exp(s_t^1 c_1 + s_t^2 c_2 + s_t^3 c_3 + s_t^4 c_4)$ and $u_t^* = \exp(u_t)$.

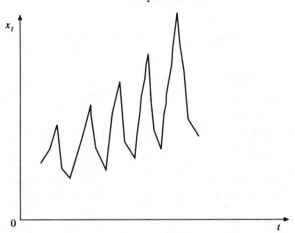

Figure 2.3   Multiplicative Model: Case $b_2 > 0$

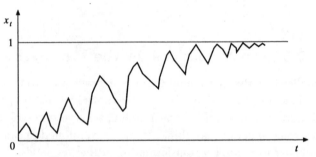

Figure 2.4   Logistic Model: Case $b_2 < 0$

The medium-term trend shows an exponentially increasing shape if $b_2 > 0$ (cf. figure 2.3), decreasing otherwise. Moreover, if $b_2 > 0$ the seasonal effects grow in absolute value as t grows.

The Logistic Model   Let us consider the model given by

$$\ln\left(\frac{1 - x_t}{x_t}\right) = b_1 + b_2 t + \sum_{j=1}^{4} s_t^j c_j + u_t, \quad 0 < x_t < 1, \quad \forall \ t.$$

The variable x_t can be written as

$$x_t = \frac{1}{1 + \exp(b_1 + b_2 t + \sum_{j=1}^{4} s_t^j c_j + u_t)}.$$

Its behavior is depicted in figure 2.4 for the case where b_2 is negative.

This model is called *logistic* and proved itself suited to study households' durable-good consumption behavior, among other phenomena. In this case, x_t would represent the proportion of households owning a certain good at time t.

2.4 Ordinary Least Squares Estimator

Let us consider the linear model (2.1)

$$x_t = \sum_{i=1}^{k} z_t^i b_i + \sum_{j=1}^{m} s_t^j c_j + u_t, \quad t = 1, \ldots, T.$$

The ordinary least squares (OLS) method consists in choosing as estimators of the parameters b_i, c_j the values $\hat{b}_i$, $\hat{c}_j$ minimizing the square of the distance between the series and its deterministic part

$$\sum_{t=1}^{T} u_t^2 = \sum_{t=1}^{T} \left(x_t - \sum_{i=1}^{k} z_t^i b_i - \sum_{j=1}^{m} s_t^j c_j \right)^2.$$

Let us denote $\hat{\mathbf{b}} = \left(\hat{b}_1, \ldots, \hat{b}_k \right)'$, $\hat{\mathbf{c}} = (\hat{c}_1, \ldots, \hat{c}_m)'$ the estimators of the parameter vectors and $\mathbf{Z}$, $\mathbf{S}$ the $(T \times k)$, respectively $(T \times m)$, matrices, the columns of which are $\mathbf{z}^1, \ldots, \mathbf{z}^k$, respectively $\mathbf{s}^1, \ldots, \mathbf{s}^m$. The solutions $\hat{\mathbf{b}}$ and $\hat{\mathbf{c}}$ of this minimization problem satisfy the system of $k + m$ *normal equations*

$$\begin{cases} \mathbf{Z}'\mathbf{Z}\hat{\mathbf{b}} + \mathbf{Z}'\mathbf{S}\hat{\mathbf{c}} = \mathbf{Z}'\mathbf{x}, \\ \mathbf{S}'\mathbf{Z}\hat{\mathbf{b}} + \mathbf{S}'\mathbf{S}\hat{\mathbf{c}} = \mathbf{S}'\mathbf{x}. \end{cases}$$

This system can be written as

$$\begin{pmatrix} \mathbf{Z}'\mathbf{Z} & \mathbf{Z}'\mathbf{S} \\ \mathbf{S}'\mathbf{Z} & \mathbf{S}'\mathbf{S} \end{pmatrix} \begin{pmatrix} \hat{\mathbf{b}} \\ \hat{\mathbf{c}} \end{pmatrix} = \begin{pmatrix} \mathbf{Z}'\mathbf{x} \\ \mathbf{S}'\mathbf{x} \end{pmatrix}.$$

Since the vectors $\mathbf{z}^1, \ldots, \mathbf{z}^k, \mathbf{s}^1, \ldots, \mathbf{s}^m$ are linearly independent, the first matrix on the right-hand side is nonsingular and can be inverted; the system admits the unique solution

$$\begin{pmatrix} \hat{\mathbf{b}} \\ \hat{\mathbf{c}} \end{pmatrix} = \begin{pmatrix} \mathbf{Z}'\mathbf{Z} & \mathbf{Z}'\mathbf{S} \\ \mathbf{S}'\mathbf{Z} & \mathbf{S}'\mathbf{S} \end{pmatrix}^{-1} \begin{pmatrix} \mathbf{Z}'\mathbf{x} \\ \mathbf{S}'\mathbf{x} \end{pmatrix}. \tag{2.5}$$

The expressions for $\hat{\mathbf{b}}$ and $\hat{\mathbf{c}}$ can be derived from the system of normal equations. We have

$$\hat{\mathbf{c}} = (\mathbf{S}'\mathbf{S})^{-1}\mathbf{S}'\mathbf{x} - (\mathbf{S}'\mathbf{S})^{-1}\mathbf{S}'\mathbf{Z}\hat{\mathbf{b}}.$$

Substituting in the first k normal equations we get

$$\left(\mathbf{Z}'\mathbf{Z} - \mathbf{Z}'\mathbf{S}(\mathbf{S}'\mathbf{S})^{-1}\mathbf{S}'\mathbf{Z} \right) \hat{\mathbf{b}} = \mathbf{Z}'\mathbf{x} - \mathbf{Z}'\mathbf{S}(\mathbf{S}'\mathbf{S})^{-1}\mathbf{S}'\mathbf{x},$$

or

$$\hat{\mathbf{b}} = \left(\mathbf{Z}'\mathbf{Z} - \mathbf{Z}'\mathbf{S}(\mathbf{S}'\mathbf{S})^{-1}\mathbf{S}'\mathbf{Z} \right)^{-1} \left(\mathbf{Z}'\mathbf{x} - \mathbf{Z}'\mathbf{S}(\mathbf{S}'\mathbf{S})^{-1}\mathbf{S}'\mathbf{x} \right). \tag{2.6}$$

By the same token we have

$$\hat{\mathbf{c}} = \left(\mathbf{S}'\mathbf{S} - \mathbf{S}'\mathbf{Z}(\mathbf{Z}'\mathbf{Z})^{-1}\mathbf{Z}'\mathbf{S} \right)^{-1} \left(\mathbf{S}'\mathbf{x} - \mathbf{S}'\mathbf{Z}(\mathbf{Z}'\mathbf{Z})^{-1}\mathbf{Z}'\mathbf{x} \right). \tag{2.7}$$

Remark 2.1: In the absence of seasonal components ($m = 0$), we need to discard the block relative to $\mathbf{S}$ and to $\mathbf{c}$ in the system of normal equations; equation (2.5) will then read $\hat{\mathbf{b}} = (\mathbf{Z}'\mathbf{Z})^{-1}\mathbf{Z}'\mathbf{x}$.

Remark 2.2: The method just described is based on the hypothesis that the vectors $\mathbf{z}^1, \ldots, \mathbf{z}^k, \mathbf{s}^1, \ldots, \mathbf{s}^m$ form a basis, therefore it may not be applied to the Buys-Ballot model directly. We will see in section 2.5.2 how it can be modified to suit this model.

2.5 Applications

2.5.1 The Multiplicative Model

Let us consider the multiplicative model without seasonal component defined as

$$\ln x_t = b_1 + b_2 t + u_t, \ \ t = 1, \ldots, T.$$

The matrix $\mathbf{Z}$ has two columns equal to

$$\mathbf{z}^1 = (1, \ldots, 1)' \ \text{and} \ \mathbf{z}^2 = (1, 2, \ldots, T)'.$$

The estimators $\hat{\mathbf{b}}_1$ and $\hat{\mathbf{b}}_2$ are given by

$$\begin{pmatrix} \hat{b}_1 \\ \hat{b}_2 \end{pmatrix} = (\mathbf{Z}'\mathbf{Z})^{-1}\mathbf{Z}'\mathbf{x}^*, \quad \text{with } \mathbf{x}^* = \begin{pmatrix} \ln(x_1) \\ \vdots \\ \ln(x_T) \end{pmatrix},$$

$$\begin{pmatrix} \hat{b}_1 \\ \hat{b}_2 \end{pmatrix} = \begin{pmatrix} T & T(T+1)/2 \\ T(T+1)/2 & T(T+1)(2T+1)/6 \end{pmatrix}^{-1} \begin{pmatrix} \sum_{t=1}^{T} \ln(x_t) \\ \sum_{t=1}^{T} t \ln(x_t) \end{pmatrix}.$$

Hence

$$\hat{b}_1 = 6\left(-\sum_{t=1}^{T} t \ln(x_t) + \frac{2T+1}{3} \sum_{t=1}^{T} \ln(x_t) \right) / (T(T-1)),$$

$$\hat{b}_2 = 12\left(-\sum_{t=1}^{T} t \ln(x_t) + \frac{T+1}{3} \sum_{t=1}^{T} \ln(x_t) \right) / (T(T^2-1)).$$

2.5.2 Buys-Ballot's Quarterly Model

Recall Buys-Ballot's quarterly model

$$x_t = b_1 + b_2 t + s_t^1 c_1 + s_t^2 c_2 + s_t^3 c_3 + s_t^4 c_4 + u_t, \quad t = 1, \ldots, T,$$

where the seasonal coefficients verify $c_1 + c_2 + c_3 + c_4 = 0$. In this case, OLS must be applied by considering the constraint explicitly. The estimators $\hat{b}_1$, $\hat{b}_2$, $\hat{c}_1$, $\hat{c}_2$, $\hat{c}_3$, $\hat{c}_4$ are obtained as solutions of the constrained minimization problem

$$\min_{b,c} \sum_{t=1}^{T} \left(x_t - b_1 - b_2 t - \sum_{j=1}^{4} s_t^j c_j \right)^2$$

$$s.t.\ c_1 + c_2 + c_3 + c_4 = 0.$$

Since $\sum_{j=1}^{4} s_t^j = 1$, $\forall\ t$, this problem can be formulated as

$$\min_{b_2, \delta_j} \sum_{t=1}^{T} \left(x_t - b_2 t - \sum_{j=1}^{4} s_t^j \delta_j \right)^2,$$

with $b_1 = \frac{1}{4} \sum_{j=1}^{4} \delta_j$ and $c_j = \delta_j - \frac{1}{4} \sum_{j=1}^{4} \delta_j$ $\forall\ j$. This last minimization problem shows that the estimators $\hat{b}_1$, $\hat{b}_2$, $\hat{c}_j$, $j = 1, \ldots, 4$, can be calculated in a two-step procedure. First, we solve the minimization of

$$\sum_{t=1}^{T} \left(x_t - b_2 t - \sum_{j=1}^{4} s_t^j \delta_j \right)^2,$$

for $\hat{b}_2, \hat{\delta}_j$, $j = 1, \ldots, 4$, that is, applying OLS *without intercept* and regressing x_t on $z_t^2 = t, s_t^1, s_t^2, s_t^3, s_t^4$. Then, we can obtain $\hat{b}_1$ and $\hat{c}_j$ using the identities

$$\begin{cases} \hat{b}_1 = \frac{1}{4} \sum_{j=1}^{4} \hat{\delta}_j, \\ \hat{c}_j = \hat{\delta}_j - \frac{1}{4} \sum_{j=1}^{4} \hat{\delta}_j & j = 1, \ldots, 4. \end{cases} \tag{2.8}$$

As a first step, therefore let us determine the values of $\hat{b}_2, \hat{\delta}_j$. In order to simplify computations, let us assume that the number of observations T corresponds to an integer number of years N, that is: $T = 4N$. The observation corresponding to the j-th quarter of the n-th year is indexed by $t = 4(n-1) + j$, $n = 1, \ldots, N$, $j = 1, \ldots, 4$.

Let us also denote with

$\tilde{x}_n$ = the mean of the observations on x relative to the four quarters of year n;

$\bar{x}_j$ = the mean of the observations on x relative to the j-th quarter;

$\bar{x}$ = the overall mean of all observations on x.

Note that

$$\bar{x} = \left(\sum_{n=1}^{N} \tilde{x}_n \right) / N = \left(\sum_{j=1}^{4} \bar{x}_j \right) / 4.$$

The estimators of the parameters (cf. exercise 2.9) are

$$\hat{\delta}_j = \bar{x}_j - (j + 2(N-1))\,\hat{b}_2, \quad j = 1, \ldots, 4 \qquad (2.9)$$

and

$$\hat{b}_2 = 3 \frac{\sum_{n=1}^{N} n\tilde{x}_n - \frac{N(N+1)}{2}\bar{x}}{N(N^2-1)}. \qquad (2.10)$$

We can then obtain the estimators $\hat{b}_1$ and $\hat{c}_j$ using the formulae in (2.8)

$$\begin{cases} \hat{b}_1 = \frac{1}{4} \sum_{j=1}^{4} \hat{\delta}_j = \bar{x} - \left(\frac{5}{2} + 2(N-1) \right) \hat{b}_2, \\ \hat{c}_j = \hat{\delta}_j - \hat{b}_1 = \bar{x}_j - \bar{x} - \hat{b}_2(j - \frac{5}{2}). \end{cases} \qquad (2.11)$$

Note that the estimators $\hat{b}_1$ and $\hat{b}_2$ of the trend parameters can be obtained running a simple regression of the annual averages $\tilde{x}_n$ on the index representing the middle of the year in quarterly units: $\tilde{t}_n = 4(n-1) + \frac{5}{2}$ (cf. exercise 2.1).

2.6 Statistical Properties of the Estimators

The estimators of the parameters derived in section 2.4 are random variables approximating the true unknown values **b** and **c**. Their statistical properties need to be investigated, in particular to get an idea of the error contained in these approximations.

2.6.1 First-order Moments

Under the hypothesis $E(u_t) = 0$, the OLS estimators are unbiased, that is, their mean is equal to the values to be estimated. We have that $\forall\ b_i, c_j,\ E(\hat{b}_i) = b_i,\ i = 1, \ldots, k$, and $E(\hat{c}_j) = c_j,\ j = 1, \ldots, m$. In other words, on average, there is neither overestimation nor underestimation of the unknown values.

Moreover the values

$$\hat{z}_t = \sum_{i=1}^{k} \hat{b}_i z_t^i \quad \text{and} \quad \hat{s}_t = \sum_{j=1}^{m} \hat{c}_j s_t^j,$$

are unbiased estimates of the unknown values of the trend and of the seasonal component at time t.

2.6.2 Second-order Moments

A linear function of the estimators $\hat{d} = \sum_{i=1}^{k} \beta_i \hat{b}_i + \sum_{j=1}^{m} \gamma_j \hat{c}_j$ (where the β_i and the γ_j are known numbers) is an unbiased estimator of the linear function of the parameters $d = \sum_{i=1}^{k} \beta_i b_i + \sum_{j=1}^{m} \gamma_j c_j$.

The error made in approximating d with $\hat{d}$ can be measured by the mean square error $E(\hat{d} - d)^2$. Since $d = E(\hat{d})$, this error is equal to the variance of $\hat{d}$, denoted by var $(\hat{d})$. Let us write this variance in an explicit way

$$
\text{var}\,(\hat{d}) = \text{var}\,\left(\sum_{i=1}^{k} \beta_i \hat{b}_i + \sum_{j=1}^{m} \gamma_j \hat{c}_j \right)
$$

$$
= \sum_{i=1}^{k} \beta_i^2 \text{var}\,(\hat{b}_i) + \sum_{j=1}^{m} \gamma_j^2 \text{var}\,(\hat{c}_j) + 2\sum_{i=1}^{k}\sum_{j=1}^{m} \beta_i\gamma_j \text{cov}\,(\hat{b}_i,\ \hat{c}_j)
$$

$$
+ 2\sum_{i=1}^{k}\sum_{i'=1}^{i-1} \beta_i\beta_{i'} \text{cov}\,(\hat{b}_i,\ \hat{b}_{i'}) + 2\sum_{j=1}^{m}\sum_{j'=1}^{j-1} \gamma_j\gamma_{j'} \text{cov}\,(\hat{c}_j,\ \hat{c}_{j'}).
$$

The computation of this variance assumes the estimator variances and covariances as known. These quantities are generally presented in matrix form in the variance–covariance matrix var $(\hat{\mathbf{b}},\ \hat{\mathbf{c}})'$. This is a square, symmetric matrix of order $(k+m)$, which can be partitioned as follows

$$
\text{var}\,\begin{pmatrix} \hat{\mathbf{b}} \\ \hat{\mathbf{c}} \end{pmatrix} = \begin{pmatrix} \text{var}\,(\hat{\mathbf{b}}) & \text{cov}\,(\hat{\mathbf{b}},\hat{\mathbf{c}}) \\ \text{cov}\,(\hat{\mathbf{b}},\hat{\mathbf{c}})' & \text{var}\,(\hat{\mathbf{c}}) \end{pmatrix}.
$$

The matrix var $(\hat{\mathbf{b}})$ is a square matrix with k rows and columns which has the covariance between $\hat{b}_i$ and $\hat{b}_{i*}$ as a generic term of order (i, i^*); in particular, the diagonal elements are just the variances var $(\hat{b}_i)$. The other blocks, cov $(\hat{\mathbf{b}},\ \hat{\mathbf{c}})$ and var $(\hat{\mathbf{c}})$, are of size $(k \times m)$ and $(m \times m)$, and have generic terms equal to cov $(\hat{b}_i,\ \hat{c}_j)$ and cov $(\hat{c}_j,\ \hat{c}_{j*})$.

Denoting $\boldsymbol{\beta} = (\beta_1,\ldots,\beta_k)'$ and $\boldsymbol{\gamma} = (\gamma_1,\ldots,\gamma_m)'$, var $(\hat{d})$ can be written as

$$
\text{var}\,(\hat{d}) = (\boldsymbol{\beta}'\ \boldsymbol{\gamma}')\,\text{var}\,\begin{pmatrix} \hat{\mathbf{b}} \\ \hat{\mathbf{c}} \end{pmatrix}\begin{pmatrix} \boldsymbol{\beta} \\ \boldsymbol{\gamma} \end{pmatrix}. \tag{2.12}
$$

If the disturbances are zero mean, homoskedastic and noncorrelated, we can easily show that the variance–covariance matrix of $\left(\hat{\mathbf{b}},\hat{\mathbf{c}}\right)'$ is given by

$$
\text{var}\,\begin{pmatrix} \hat{\mathbf{b}} \\ \hat{\mathbf{c}} \end{pmatrix} = \sigma^2 \begin{pmatrix} \mathbf{Z'Z} & \mathbf{Z'S} \\ \mathbf{S'Z} & \mathbf{S'S} \end{pmatrix}^{-1}. \tag{2.13}
$$

Let us recall also that the main justification for the ordinary least squares method is the Gauss–Markov theorem which shows that $\hat{d}$ is the best (i.e., minimum variance) unbiased estimator of d, as a linear function of the observations x_t.

Example 2.1: Let us consider the Buys-Ballot model introduced in (2.2) above. We have

$$\text{var} \begin{pmatrix} \hat{b}_2 \\ \hat{\delta} \end{pmatrix} = \sigma^2 \begin{pmatrix} \mathbf{z}^{2'}\mathbf{z}^2 & \mathbf{z}^{2'}\mathbf{S} \\ \mathbf{S}'\mathbf{z}^2 & \mathbf{S}'\mathbf{S} \end{pmatrix}^{-1}.$$

The expression

$$\text{var}(\hat{\delta}) = \sigma^2 \left(\mathbf{S}'\mathbf{S} - \mathbf{S}'\mathbf{z}^2(\mathbf{z}^{2'}\mathbf{z}^2)^{-1}\mathbf{z}^{2'}\mathbf{S} \right)^{-1}$$

allows us to compute the variances and covariances of the estimated seasonal coefficients $\hat{\mathbf{c}}$.

2.6.3 Estimation of the Random Disturbance Variance

The matrix in (2.13) cannot be evaluated numerically since its expression depends on the unknown parameter σ^2. In order to obtain an unbiased estimator of σ^2, let $\hat{u}_t$ be the estimation residual at time t, that is $\hat{u}_t = x_t - \hat{z}_t - \hat{s}_t$. $\hat{u}_t$ is a random approximation to the disturbance u_t. The quantity

$$s^2 = \sum_{t=1}^{T} \hat{u}_t^2/(T - k - m) \tag{2.14}$$

is an unbiased estimator of σ^2. The variance–covariance matrix is then estimated by

$$\widehat{\text{var}} \begin{pmatrix} \hat{\mathbf{b}} \\ \hat{\mathbf{c}} \end{pmatrix} = s^2 \begin{pmatrix} \mathbf{Z}'\mathbf{Z} & \mathbf{Z}'\mathbf{S} \\ \mathbf{S}'\mathbf{Z} & \mathbf{S}'\mathbf{S} \end{pmatrix}^{-1}. \tag{2.15}$$

By the same token, the variance of a linear combination of the estimators

$$\hat{d} = \sum_{i=1}^{k} \beta_i \hat{b}_i + \sum_{j=1}^{m} \gamma_j \hat{b}_j$$

is estimated by

$$\widehat{\text{var}}(\hat{d}) = (\boldsymbol{\beta}' \ \boldsymbol{\gamma}')\widehat{\text{var}} \begin{pmatrix} \hat{\mathbf{b}} \\ \hat{\mathbf{c}} \end{pmatrix} \begin{pmatrix} \boldsymbol{\beta} \\ \boldsymbol{\gamma} \end{pmatrix}.$$

2.6.4 Confidence Intervals

Rather than referring to a point estimation $\hat{d}$ of d, it is often preferable to provide an interval of the type $\hat{d}_1 < d < \hat{d}_2$. The confidence interval

$(d_1, \; d_2)$ is random and is such as to include the true parameter d with a certain probability. If we assume independent and identically distributed $N(0, \sigma^2)$ disturbances, an interval which includes the true value d with 95% probability is given by

$$\left(\hat{d}_1 = \hat{d} - \tau \sqrt{\widehat{\text{var}}(\hat{d})}; \; \hat{d}_2 = \hat{d} + \tau \sqrt{\widehat{\text{var}}(\hat{d})} \right), \tag{2.16}$$

where the probability of the absolute value of a Student's t random variable with $(T - k - m)$ degrees of freedom being greater than τ is 2.5%. If T is large, τ is approximately equal to 2.

2.7 Applications of the Regression Analysis

2.7.1 Outlier Detection

Some observations do not look compatible with the rest of the sample. It is therefore important to investigate whether they are true outliers, i.e., not generated by the same mechanism as the other data; in fact, there is even a chance that neglecting their nature may impair the whole analysis. These atypical data can occur due to several reasons:

(i)   They could be ascribed to measurement, transcription, or calculation errors. In such a case, we can hope to correct them by reexamining the way in which the data were collected and processed.

(ii) They can reflect occasional phenomena (a strike, for instance). The corresponding dates can be traced back easily. For example, outliers appear often in French economic time series for 1963 (miners' strike) and for 1968 (general strike). These occurrences, foreign to the evolution of the series, are customarily eliminated.

We can possibly consider as outliers certain data generated by the same mechanism as the others but drawn from the tails of the distribution. In fact, if we sample every year a group of individuals, we could find at any point in time a billionaire. The treatment of such a case is not clear-cut, but often the corresponding data are discarded and the analysis is carried out on the remaining sample.

Method 1 Until now we have considered a decomposition of x_t of the type

$$x_t = z_t + s_t + u_t \quad t = 1, \ldots, T, \tag{2.17}$$

with no outliers. Assuming that the model (2.17) is well specified to describe the series x_t, and that the disturbances are normally distributed,

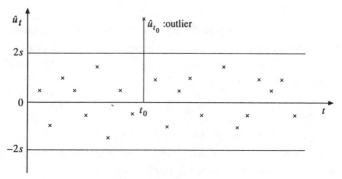

Figure 2.5 Outliers

u_t is included between -2σ and $+2\sigma$ in 95% of the cases. Using all the available approximations, we can say that $\hat{u}_t$ should be included between $-2s$ and $+2s$ most of the time. The dates pertaining to residuals outside this interval could correspond to outliers (cf. figure 2.5). This approach can be easily improved upon, taking into consideration the distribution of the residuals. Let us denote by $\mathbf{A}$ the matrix

$$\mathbf{A} = \mathbf{I} - (\mathbf{Z},\ \mathbf{S}) \begin{pmatrix} \mathbf{Z'Z} & \mathbf{Z'S} \\ \mathbf{S'Z} & \mathbf{S'S} \end{pmatrix}^{-1} \begin{pmatrix} \mathbf{Z'} \\ \mathbf{S'} \end{pmatrix}.$$

The residuals have mean zero and variance–covariance matrix

$$\mathrm{var}\,(\hat{u}) = \sigma^2 \mathbf{A}.$$

The *studentized* residual is given by

$$\frac{\hat{u}_t}{s\sqrt{a_{tt}}},$$

where a_{tt} is the t-th diagonal element of $\mathbf{A}$. If there are no outliers, the studentized residuals follow a standard normal distribution and are less than 2 in 95% of the cases. Then we can reject the null hypothesis of no outliers (i.e., detect an outlier) if

$$\left| \frac{\hat{u}_t}{s\sqrt{a_{tt}}} \right| > 2$$

and accept it otherwise.

Method 2 Another approach includes the possibility of the existence of an outlier at time t_0 by including an indicator variable for such a date

$$x_t = z_t + s_t + \alpha \mathbb{1}_{t=t_0} + u_t, \tag{2.18}$$

where $\mathbb{1}_{t=t_0} = 0$ if $t \neq t_0$, and 1 otherwise. The absence of an outlier can be formulated as $H_0 : \{\alpha = 0\}$, a test of which can be performed by the usual Student's t-test.

Under the general hypothesis, the OLS estimator of α is just the expression $(x_{t_0} - \hat{z}_{t_0} - s_{t_0})$. We can see that for the unrestricted model, the residual sum of squares is just the one obtained by running OLS on the model (2.17) using x_t, $t \neq t_0$. Let us denote it by $RSS_{(-t_0)}$. Under the null hypothesis, the residual sum of squares for the restricted model is obtained by running OLS on the complete set of data. The absolute value of the Student's t-statistic is then

$$\left((RSS - RSS_{(-t_0)})/ \frac{RSS_{(-t_0)}}{(T - k - m - 1)} \right)^{1/2} = |\hat{\alpha}|/\sqrt{\widehat{var}\,(\hat{\alpha})}.$$

A value of this statistic higher than the critical value (at 95% confidence level) of the Student's t-distribution leads to the rejection of the null hypothesis of no outliers and, hence, to the detection of an outlier at time t_0.

2.7.2 Seasonal Adjustment

The series without the seasonal component $x_t^{SA} = x_t - s_t$ can be estimated by

$$\hat{x}_t^{SA} = x_t - \hat{s}_t = x_t - \sum_{j=1}^{m} s_t^j \hat{c}_j. \tag{2.19}$$

The mean square error of approximating x_t^{SA} by $\hat{x}_t^{SA}$ is estimated as

$$\hat{E}(x_t^{SA} - \hat{x}_t^{SA})^2 = \hat{E}(\hat{s}_t - s_t)^2$$

$$= \widehat{var}\,(\sum_{j=1}^{m} s_t^j \hat{c}_j)$$

$$= (s_t^1, \ldots, s_t^m)\, \widehat{var}\,(\hat{c}) \begin{pmatrix} s_t^1 \\ \vdots \\ s_t^m \end{pmatrix}.$$

2.7.3 Forecasting

The estimators $\hat{b}_i$, $\hat{c}_j$ can be used to forecast a value of x yet unobserved, say, $x_{T+h}, h \geq 1$. Assuming that the model specification is still valid at time $T + h$, we have

$$x_{T+h} = \sum_{i=1}^{k} z_{T+h}^i b_i + \sum_{j=1}^{m} s_{T+h}^j c_j,$$

with $E(u_{T+h}) = 0$, $var\,(u_{T+h}) = \sigma^2$, $cov\,(u_{T+h}, u_t) = 0$, $t = 1, \ldots, T$, and the value $\hat{x}_{T+h}$ being approximated by

$$\hat{x}_T(h) = \sum_{i=1}^{k} z_{T+h}^i \hat{b}_i + \sum_{j=1}^{m} s_{T+h}^j \hat{c}_j. \tag{2.20}$$

It can be shown that $\hat{x}_T(h)$ is the best unbiased forecast (with respect to a mean square error criterion) which is a linear combination of the observed values $x_1, \ldots, x_T$ of the variable x. In fact, it satisfies the condition

$$E(\hat{x}_T(h) - x_{T+h}) = 0.$$

Thus, the estimated variance of the forecast error is

$$\hat{e}_h = \hat{E}(\hat{x}_T(h) - x_{T+h})^2$$

$$= \widehat{\text{var}} \left(\sum_{i=1}^{k} z_{T+h}^i \hat{b}_i + \sum_{j=1}^{m} s_{T+h}^j \hat{c}_j - u_{T+h} \right)$$

$$= \widehat{\text{var}}(\hat{d}) + s^2,$$

where $\hat{d}$ is the estimator of

$$d = \sum_{i=1}^{k} z_{T+h}^i b_i + \sum_{j=1}^{m} s_{T+h}^j c_j.$$

Under the normality hypothesis, we get a 95% forecast interval for x_{T+h} considering

$$\left(\hat{x}_T(h) - \tau \hat{e}_h^{1/2}, \ \hat{x}_T(h) + \tau \hat{e}_h^{1/2} \right),$$

where τ is defined as in (2.16).

2.8 Autocorrelated Disturbances

In the previous examples we have assumed that the disturbances were not correlated. Nevertheless, it is possible that the values taken by a time series at contiguous periods be linked to each other. Such links can be taken into account by formulating a few hypotheses about the disturbances.

2.8.1 First-order Autocorrelation

Let us assume that the disturbances follow

$$u_t = \rho u_{t-1} + \epsilon_t, \tag{2.21}$$

where the variables ϵ_t are i.i.d. $N(0, \sigma^2)$ and ρ is a real number included between -1 and $+1$ (cf. chapter 5 for more general models including

(2.21) as a special case). For the sake of simplicity, we will assume that the relationship (2.21) is valid for $t \in (-\infty, \ldots, -1, 0, 1, \ldots, +\infty)$, that is, valid for unobserved values corresponding to indices not included between 1 and T. The model for the disturbances can be written as

$$u_t = \rho u_{t-1} + \epsilon_t$$

$$= \epsilon_t + \rho \epsilon_{t-1} + \rho^2 u_{t-2}$$

$$= \epsilon_t + \rho \epsilon_{t-1} + \ldots + \rho^i \epsilon_{t-i} + \ldots$$

$$= \sum_{i=0}^{\infty} \rho^i \epsilon_{t-i}.$$

From this notation we can see that the moments of u_t can be expressed as

$$E(u_t) = \sum_{i=0}^{\infty} \rho^i E(\epsilon_{t-i}) = 0,$$

and

$$\text{var}\,(u_t) = \text{var}\left(\sum_{i=0}^{\infty} \rho^i \epsilon_{t-i}\right)$$

$$= \sum_{i=0}^{\infty} \rho^{2i} \text{var}\,(\epsilon_{t-i})$$

$$= \sigma^2 \sum_{i=0}^{\infty} \rho^{2i}$$

$$= \frac{\sigma^2}{1 - \rho^2}$$

and for all $h > 0$

$$\text{cov}\,(u_t, u_{t-h}) = \text{cov}\left(\sum_{i=0}^{\infty} \rho^i \epsilon_{t-i}, \sum_{j=0}^{\infty} \rho^j \epsilon_{t-j-h}\right) = \sigma^2 \frac{\rho^h}{1 - \rho^2}.$$

(Cf. the justification for the interchange of the expectation and the summation operators given in the appendix to chapter 5.)

The variance–covariance matrix of the disturbances is nonscalar, and can be represented as

$$\text{var}\,(\mathbf{u}) = \frac{\sigma^2}{1 - \rho^2} \begin{pmatrix} 1 & \rho & \cdots & \rho^{T-1} \\ \rho & 1 & \cdots & \rho^{T-2} \\ \vdots & \ddots & \ddots & \vdots \\ \rho^{T-1} & \cdots & \rho & 1 \end{pmatrix} = \sigma^2 \mathbf{\Omega}. \qquad (2.22)$$

Let us consider the linear model again

$$\mathbf{x} = \sum_{i=1}^{k} \mathbf{z}^i b_i + \sum_{j=1}^{m} \mathbf{s}^j c_j + \mathbf{u}, \qquad (2.23)$$

where we will assume that the vectors $\mathbf{z}^i$ and $\mathbf{s}^j$ are linearly independent, and that the disturbance term $\mathbf{u}$ follows (2.21); the OLS method described in the previous section provides unbiased estimators, but these estimators are not the "best" (i.e., minimum variance) ones. The accuracy can be improved upon by using the generalized least squares (GLS) estimator, defined as

$$\begin{pmatrix} \tilde{\mathbf{b}} \\ \tilde{\mathbf{c}} \end{pmatrix} = \left((\mathbf{Z}, \mathbf{S})' \mathbf{\Omega}^{-1} (\mathbf{Z}, \mathbf{S}) \right)^{-1} (\mathbf{Z}, \mathbf{S})' \mathbf{\Omega}^{-1} \mathbf{x}.$$

The matrix $\mathbf{\Omega}$ can be easily written in its inverse form as

$$\mathbf{\Omega}^{-1} = \begin{pmatrix} 1 & -\rho & 0 & \cdots & 0 \\ -\rho & 1+\rho^2 & -\rho & \cdots & 0 \\ 0 & -\rho & 1+\rho^2 & \cdots & 0 \\ \vdots & \vdots & & \ddots & \vdots \\ 0 & 0 & \cdots & & -\rho & 1 \end{pmatrix}.$$

This GLS estimator coincides with the OLS estimator applied to the model

$$\mathbf{H}\mathbf{x} = \sum_{i=1}^{k} \mathbf{H}\mathbf{z}^i b_i + \sum_{j=1}^{m} \mathbf{H}\mathbf{s}^j c_j + \mathbf{v},$$

where $\mathbf{H}$ is such that $\mathbf{H}\mathbf{\Omega}\mathbf{H}' = \mathbf{I}$, or $\mathbf{H}'\mathbf{H} = \mathbf{\Omega}^{-1}$, and can be written as

$$\mathbf{H} = \begin{pmatrix} \sqrt{1-\rho^2} & 0 & \cdots & 0 & 0 \\ -\rho & 1 & \cdots & 0 & 0 \\ 0 & -\rho & \ddots & 0 & 0 \\ \vdots & & 0 & \ddots & 1 & 0 \\ 0 & 0 & \cdots & -\rho & 1 \end{pmatrix},$$

and $\mathbf{v} = \mathbf{H}\mathbf{u}$.

Let $\mathbf{H}^*$ be the $(T-1 \times T)$ matrix obtained by deleting the first row of $\mathbf{H}$. The GLS estimator is slightly different from the OLS estimator applied to

$$\mathbf{H}^*\mathbf{x} = \sum_{i=1}^{k} \mathbf{H}^* \mathbf{z}^i b_i + \sum_{j=1}^{m} \mathbf{H}^* \mathbf{s}^j c_j + \mathbf{w},$$

that is, the estimator obtained by regressing $(x_t - \rho x_{t-1})$ on $(z_t^i - \rho z_{t-1}^i)$ and $(s_t^j - \rho s_{t-1}^j)$, for $t = 2, \ldots, T$. This approach was first suggested by Cochrane and Orcutt (1949).

These two estimation methods, generalized least squares and Cochrane–Orcutt, cannot be applied straightforwardly because they assume that the parameter ρ is known; since, in general, ρ is unknown, we need to apply a two-step procedure:

(i) in the first step we estimate the parameter ρ. This parameter can be interpreted as the correlation between u_t and u_{t-1}; it can be estimated as the empirical correlation between the residuals $\hat{u}_t$ and $\hat{u}_{t-1}$ derived by OLS

$$\hat{\rho} = \frac{\sum_{t=2}^{T} \hat{u}_t \hat{u}_{t-1}}{\sum_{t=1}^{T} \hat{u}_t^2}.$$

(ii) in the second step, we can use the GLS or the Cochrane–Orcutt estimator by replacing the unknown parameter ρ with its estimated value $\hat{\rho}$.

2.8.2 Testing for First-order Autocorrelation

Before specifying a time-series model with autocorrelated disturbances, it is necessary to establish if such a model is appropriate. To do that, we need to test the hypothesis $\rho = 0$ (absence of serial correlation – hence appropriateness of OLS) against an alternative hypothesis (correlation – hence use of GLS).

Durbin–Watson Test The most commonly used test is performed according to the procedure suggested by Durbin and Watson (1950, 1951), based on the statistic

$$DW = \frac{\sum_{t=2}^{T} (\hat{u}_t - \hat{u}_{t-1})^2}{\sum_{t=1}^{T} \hat{u}_t^2},$$

where $\hat{u}_t$ is the estimated residual from OLS.

If the number of observations is large, we have

$$DW \approx 1 + \sum_{t=2}^{T} \hat{u}_t^2 / \sum_{t=1}^{T} \hat{u}_t^2 - 2 \sum_{t=2}^{T} \hat{u}_t \hat{u}_{t-1} / \sum_{t=1}^{T} \hat{u}_t^2$$

$$\approx 1 + 1 - 2\hat{\rho} = 2(1 - \hat{\rho}).$$

The distribution of such a statistic under the hypothesis $\rho = 0$ depends on the values of the variables z^i and s^j. However, it is possible to relate DW to two statistics, the distribution of which does not depend upon

Table 2.2 *Distribution of Signs*
for First-order Autocorrelation

| | | Sign of $\hat{u}_t$ | |
		$+$	$-$
Sign of	$+$	T_{11}	T_{12}
$\hat{u}_{t-1}$	$-$	T_{21}	T_{22}

these variables. This leads to a test involving the two critical values $d_l < d_u$ as a function of the number of observations T and the number of the explanatory variables k' excluding the constant (cf. table 6 reported at the end of the book). Thus, in model (2.23), $k' = k + m + 1$. When we want to test no autocorrelation versus positive autocorrelation, we reject the null hypothesis of no autocorrelation if $DW < d_l$, we accept it if $DW > d_u$; if $d_l < DW < d_u$ we are in the inconclusive region. This way of setting up the test presents the nuisance of not always allowing a choice between the two hypotheses.

The same procedure can be applied to test no autocorrelation versus negative autocorrelation by considering $4 - DW$ instead of DW. If $(4 - DW) < d_l$ we reject the null hypothesis of no autocorrelation; if $(4 - DW) > d_u$, we accept this hypothesis. Again, we are in the inconclusive region if $d_l < (4 - DW) < d_u$.

Sign Test   Another method to test the hypothesis $\rho = 0$ versus the alternative $\rho \neq 0$, can be based on the sign comparison of the residuals $\hat{u}_t$ and $\hat{u}_{t-1}$, $t = 2, 4, \ldots$. The different combinations of signs and the number of times they appear can be arranged as in table 2.2. The sum of the elements in the table is equal to the integer part of $T/2$.

The hypothesis of no autocorrelation could be tested by applying a χ^2 test to this 2×2 contingency table. Whenever the sign test leads to the acceptance of independence, OLS can be applied; if this hypothesis is rejected, we should use the GLS or the Cochrane–Orcutt estimation method.

2.8.3 Forecasting

If the disturbances are autocorrelated, the forecasting expressions (2.20) have to be modified to take into consideration the links between the observations at two different dates. For example, let us assume that we have available the observations x_1 up to x_T, and that we want to forecast the corresponding value at time $T+1$

$$x_{T+1} = \sum_{i=1}^{k} z_{T+1}^i b_i + \sum_{j=1}^{m} s_{T+1}^j c_j + u_{T+1},$$

where $u_{T+1} = \rho u_T + \epsilon_{T+1}$, with ϵ_{T+1} independent of $\epsilon_1, \ldots, \epsilon_T$ and normally distributed with zero mean and variance σ^2.

We have

$$x_{T+1} = \rho x_T + \sum_{i=1}^{k} (z_{T+1}^i - \rho z_T^i) b_i + \sum_{j=1}^{m} (s_{T+1}^j - \rho s_T^j) c_j + \epsilon_{T+1}.$$

The optimal forecast of x_{T+1} (when the parameters are known) is equal to the deterministic part

$$\rho x_T + \sum_{i=1}^{k} (z_{T+1}^i - \rho z_T^i) b_i + \sum_{j=1}^{m} (s_{T+1}^j - \rho s_T^j) c_j.$$

When the parameters are unknown, a forecast of x_{T+1} will be

$$\begin{aligned}
\hat{x}_T(1) &= \hat{\rho} x_T + \sum_{i=1}^{k} (z_{T+1}^i - \hat{\rho} z_T^i) \hat{b}_i + \sum_{j=1}^{m} (s_{T+1}^j - \hat{\rho} s_T^j) \hat{c}_j \\
&= \sum_{i=1}^{k} z_{T+1}^i \hat{b}_i + \sum_{j=1}^{m} s_{T+1}^j \hat{c}_j + \hat{\rho} \hat{u}_T,
\end{aligned} \qquad (2.24)$$

with $\hat{u}_T = x_T - \sum_{i=1}^{k} z_T^i \hat{b}_i - \sum_{j=1}^{m} s_T^j \hat{c}_j$.

2.8.4 Higher-order Autocorrelation

In a linear model, the disturbance represents mainly the effects of omitted variables. If these variables contain a seasonal component themselves, this will appear as autocorrelation. For example, let us consider a quarterly series. It may be preferable to introduce the autocorrelation between disturbances as $u_t = \rho u_{t-4} + \epsilon_t$, $-1 < \rho < 1$. In this case, the procedure described in the case of first-order autocorrelation can be easily generalized.

Let us assume that we have $4T$ observations available. The variance–covariance matrix of $\mathbf{u}$ is

$$\text{var}(\mathbf{u}) = \sigma^2 \mathbf{\Omega} \otimes \mathbf{I},$$

where $\boldsymbol{\Omega}$ is the matrix described in (2.22), $\mathbf{I}$ is an identity matrix of order 4, and $\otimes$ is the matrix Kronecker product. *
Hence

$$(\operatorname{var}(\mathbf{u}))^{-1} = \frac{1}{\sigma^2}\boldsymbol{\Omega}^{-1} \otimes \mathbf{I}$$

and the GLS estimator is given by

$$\begin{pmatrix} \tilde{\mathbf{b}} \\ \tilde{\mathbf{c}} \end{pmatrix} = \left((\mathbf{Z},\mathbf{S})'(\boldsymbol{\Omega}^{-1} \otimes \mathbf{I})(\mathbf{Z},\mathbf{S})\right)^{-1}(\mathbf{Z},\mathbf{S})'(\boldsymbol{\Omega}^{-1} \otimes \mathbf{I})\mathbf{x}.$$

This estimator can be approximated by the OLS estimator obtained by regressing $(x_t - \rho x_{t-4})$ on $(z_t^i - \rho z_{t-4}^i)$ and $(s_t^j - \rho s_{t-4}^j)$, for $t = 5,\ldots,T$.

These estimation methods assume ρ known, therefore, as a first step we will always need to estimate it. Again, a possible estimation procedure for ρ is

$$\hat{\rho} = \sum_{t=5}^{T} \hat{u}_t \hat{u}_{t-4} / \sum_{t=4}^{T} \hat{u}_t^2.$$

Finally, we can notice that:

(i) Hypothesis testing for $\rho = 0$ based on the signs is immediately generalized to this case under the condition of comparing the signs of u_t and u_{t-4}.

(ii) The forecasting technique is the same as before if we consider $x_{T+1} - \rho x_{T-3}$.

2.9 Two Shortcomings of OLS

Difficulties in Updating The estimators $\hat{\mathbf{b}}$ and $\hat{\mathbf{c}}$ depend upon the available number of observations; in this section we denote by $\hat{\mathbf{b}}^T$, $\hat{\mathbf{c}}^T$ their expressions relative to the sample $1,\ldots,T$. As soon as we have an

---

* If $\mathbf{A} = \{a_{ij}\}$ is a $(p \times q)$ matrix and $\mathbf{B}$ is a $(g \times h)$ matrix, the Kronecker product between $\mathbf{A}$ and $\mathbf{B}$, $\mathbf{A} \otimes \mathbf{B}$, is the $(pg \times qh)$ matrix which can be written as

$$\mathbf{A} \otimes \mathbf{B} = \begin{pmatrix} a_{11}\mathbf{B} & \cdots & a_{1q}\mathbf{B} \\ \vdots & \ddots & \vdots \\ a_{p1}\mathbf{B} & \cdots & a_{pq}\mathbf{B} \end{pmatrix}.$$

When $\mathbf{A}$ and $\mathbf{B}$ are square, nonsingular matrices, $\mathbf{A} \otimes \mathbf{B}$ is a square, nonsingular matrix with

$$(\mathbf{A} \otimes \mathbf{B})^{-1} = (\mathbf{A})^{-1} \otimes (\mathbf{B})^{-1}.$$

extra observation available, say, x_{T+1}, these estimators become $\hat{\mathbf{b}}^{T+1}$, $\hat{\mathbf{c}}^{T+1}$. Note, however, there is no simple relationship between $(\hat{\mathbf{b}}^{T+1}, \hat{\mathbf{c}}^{T+1})$ and $(\hat{\mathbf{b}}^T, \hat{\mathbf{c}}^T)$ (cf. exercise 2.7).

Structural Change The desirable statistical properties of OLS stem from the assumption that the linear model

$$x_t = \sum_{i=1}^{k} z_t^i b_i + \sum_{j=1}^{m} s_t^j c_j + u_t, \tag{2.25}$$

gives a proper description of the original series. However, it may happen that the functional form relating z^i, s^j, and x changes within the sample period. Then, a more appropriate model may be

$$x_t = \begin{cases} \sum_{i=1}^{k} z_t^i b_i + \sum_{j=1}^{m} s_t^j c_j + u_t, & \text{if } t \leq t_0, \\[2mm] \sum_{i=1}^{k^*} z_t^{*i} b_i^* + \sum_{j=1}^{m^*} s_t^{*j} c_j^* + u_t, & \text{if } t > t_0. \end{cases} \tag{2.26}$$

In this case, a seasonal adjustment made using model (2.25) leads to the wrong results. It is therefore necessary to detect a structural change by observing how the series x_t behaves. If found, it must be taken into consideration in the estimation process. Let us consider, for example, model (2.26) corresponding to a structural change; let us denote by a_t the variable assuming the value 1 if $t \leq t_0$, and 0 otherwise. We have

$$x_t = \sum_{i=1}^{k} z_t^i a_t b_i + \sum_{i=1}^{k^*} z_t^{*i} (1 - a_t) b_i^* + \sum_{j=1}^{m} s_t^j a_t c_j + \sum_{j=1}^{m^*} s_t^{*j} (1 - a_t) c_j^* + u_t.$$

Model (2.26) can be written as a linear model where the explanatory variables are $(z_t^i a_t)$, $(z_t^{*i} (1 - a_t))$, $(s_t^j a_t)$ and $(s_t^{*j} (1 - a_t))$. The parameters can be estimated by OLS or by GLS applied to this new model.

2.10 An Application

Let us take as an example the monthly series of the train passenger traffic, choosing the most classical model with a linear trend $b_1 + b_2 t$ and a 12-period seasonal component $\sum_{j=1}^{12} c_j s_t^j$ with $\sum_{j=1}^{12} c_j = 0$. The parameters b_1 and b_2 relative to the trend component and the twelve seasonal coefficients c_j were estimated by OLS over the sample period 1963-79. The last twelve observations relative to 1980 were not used for estimation purposes. This will allow us to evaluate the quality of the forecasts obtained for this year with the estimated model.

Table 2.3 *Unconstrained Coefficient Estimates*

$\hat{b}_2$	$\hat{\delta}_1$	$\hat{\delta}_2$	$\hat{\delta}_3$	$\hat{\delta}_4$	$\hat{\delta}_5$	$\hat{\delta}_6$
6.2	1552	1444	1639	1893	1809	2210

	$\hat{\delta}_7$	$\hat{\delta}_8$	$\hat{\delta}_9$	$\hat{\delta}_{10}$	$\hat{\delta}_{11}$	$\hat{\delta}_{12}$
	2579	2262	1728	1645	1483	2122

Table 2.4 *Estimated Seasonal Coefficients*

Jan.	Feb.	Mar.	Apr.	May	June	July	Aug.	Sep.	Oct.	Nov.	Dec.
-310	-420	-225	29	-55	346	715	398	-136	-219	-381	258

The unconstrained estimates of b_2 and $\delta_j = b_1 + c_j$, $j = 1, \ldots, 12$, are reported in table 2.3.

Averaging the δ_j's, we get an estimate of $\hat{b}_1 = 1864$. By differencing, then, we estimate the seasonal coefficients $\hat{c}_j$, the values of which are reported in table 2.4.

Note that the sum of the seasonal components is equal to zero. As one would expect, the seasonal coefficients for the vacation months (April, June, July, August, and December) are positive, since more people travel in these months. The quality of the seasonal adjustment can be analyzed by reporting on the same figure the observed values of x_t and the adjusted values $\hat{x}_t$ (figure 2.6) or examining the behavior of the estimation residuals (figure 2.7). The latter shows that the evolution of the residuals does not correspond to a sequence of uncorrelated random variables with zero mean and a constant variance, leading us to the conclusion that the fit is unsatisfactory. In particular, figure 2.7 gives the impression that the time trend may be convex. This could be taken into consideration by adopting an additive model (time trend modeled as a second-order degree polynomial), or a monthly version of the multiplicative model described in section 2.3. Note also that even the hypothesis of seasonal coefficient stability could be questioned by inspection of figure 2.6.

The seasonally adjusted series can be obtained by subtracting the estimated seasonal coefficients from the original series. Both original and

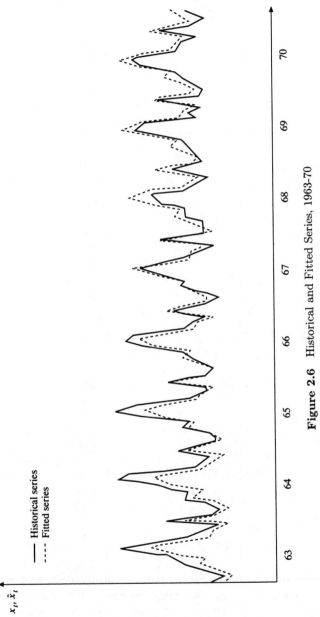

$x_t, \hat{x}_t$

—— Historical series
---- Fitted series

Figure 2.6 Historical and Fitted Series, 1963–70

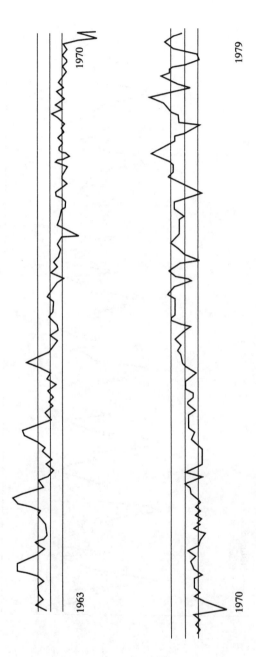

Figure 2.7 Estimated Residuals (1963-79) with 95% Confidence Bands

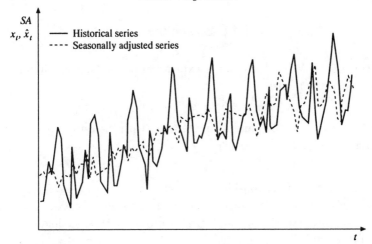

Figure 2.8 Historical and Seasonally Adjusted Series, 1972-79

seasonally adjusted series are represented in figure 2.8. We can notice that the seasonal adjustment has the effect of smoothing the peaks and troughs of the original series.

Finally, the square root of the mean square error between actual and forecasted values for the twelve months outside the sample (corresponding to 1980) is equal to 6.9%.

2.11 Exercises

Exercise 2.1: Write the explicit expression of the OLS estimators of b_1 and b_2 in the model

$$\tilde{x}_n = b_1 + b_2 \tilde{t}_n + u_n, \quad n = 1, \ldots, N,$$

with $\tilde{t}_n = 4(n-1) + 5/2$ and compare them with the estimators $\hat{b}_1$ and $\hat{b}_2$ obtained in (2.10) and (2.11).

Exercise 2.2: Let us consider the model $x_t = z_t + s_t + \alpha \mathbb{1}_{t=t_0} + u_t$ introduced in (2.18). We regress x_t on the z_t^i's and the s_t^j's in order to get estimators of the b_i's and c_j's. Verify that these estimators are biased if $\alpha \neq 0$.

Exercise 2.3: In order to estimate the seasonal component we may think that it is better to extract the time trend first. For example, in Buys-Ballot's quarterly model, we can compute $x_t^* = x_t - 2x_{t-1} + x_{t-2}$, $t = 3, \ldots, T$. Verify that the deterministic part of x_t^* is a linear function of the c_j's. How would you estimate the c_j's?

Exercise 2.4: Describe the evolution of the mean square forecast error e_h as a function of the horizon h in Buys-Ballot's model. What conclusions can you draw?

Exercise 2.5: Let us consider two quarterly series satisfying

$$x_t^1 = b_1 + b_2 t + s_t^1 c_1 + s_t^2 c_2 + s_t^3 c_3 + s_t^4 c_4 + u_t,$$

$$c_1 + c_2 + c_3 + c_4 = 0,$$

$$x_t^2 = b_1^* + b_2^* t + s_t^1 c_1^* + s_t^2 c_2^* + s_t^3 c_3^* + s_t^4 c_4^* + u_t^*,$$

$$c_1^* + c_2^* + c_3^* + c_4^* = 0,$$

where s_t^j is the j-th quarter indicator variable and the disturbances are intertemporally independent, but may be contemporaneously correlated, i.e.

$$\text{cov}\,(u_t, u_\tau^*) = \begin{cases} 0, & \forall \ t \neq \tau, \\ \sigma_{12}, & \text{otherwise.} \end{cases}$$

Using the properties of stacked regressions (cf. Johnston, 1972, p. 240), verify that it does not matter whether you estimate the regressions for x_t^1 and x_t^2 separately or simultaneously.

Table 2.5 *Variance–Covariance Matrix for Exercise 2.8*

0.056											
-5.54	2904										
-5.59	542	2915									
-5.65	548	553	2926								
-5.71	553	559	565	2938							
-5.76	559	565	570	576	2949						
-5.82	564	570	576	582	588	2961					
-5.88	570	576	583	588	593	600	2973				
-5.94	575	581	588	594	599	605	611	2984			
-5.99	581	587	593	599	605	611	617	623	2996		
-6.05	586	592	599	605	611	617	623	629	635	3008	
-6.11	592	598	605	610	617	623	629	635	641	647	3020
-6.16	598	604	610	616	623	629	635	641	647	653	659	3033

Note: Only the lower half of the matrix is given, since it is symmetric.

Exercise 2.6: Let us consider a quarterly model where the seasonal coefficients are a linear function of time

$$x_t = b_1 + b_2 t + \sum_{j=1}^{4} (c_j + d_j t) s_t^j + u_t.$$

Verify that there exist two independent relationships among the explanatory variables. Show that the mean of the seasonal coefficients cannot be zero for four consecutive quarters, unless $d_j = 0$, $j = 1, \ldots, 4$. How does this result change when we impose that the mean of these coefficients be zero over the four quarters of the same year?

Exercise 2.7: Verify that

$$\begin{pmatrix} \hat{b}^{T+1} \\ \hat{c}^{T+1} \end{pmatrix} - \begin{pmatrix} \hat{b}^{T} \\ \hat{c}^{T} \end{pmatrix} = \mathbf{A} \begin{pmatrix} \vdots \\ z_{T+1}^i \\ \vdots \\ s_{T+1}^j \\ \vdots \end{pmatrix} (x_{T+1} - \sum_{i=1}^{k} z_{T+1}^i \hat{b}_i^T - \sum_{j=1}^{m} s_{T+1}^j \hat{c}_j^T),$$

where $\mathbf{A}$ is a matrix which will be determined (cf. section 2.9 for the notation).

Exercise 2.8: Let us consider the train passenger example of section
2.10. The estimated disturbance variance is $s^2 = (200.6)^2$, and the
variance–covariance matrix of α, δ_j, $j = 1, \ldots, 12$ is given in table 2.5.

(i)   Calculate the variances of the estimated seasonal coefficients $\hat{c}_j$,
      $j = 1, \ldots, 12$.
(ii) Calculate the 95% forecast interval width as a function of the hori-
      zon.

Exercise 2.9: Let us consider Buys-Ballot's model once again.

(i)   Determine $\sum_{t=1}^{T} t^2$, $\sum_{t=1}^{T} t s_t^j$, and express $\sum_{t=1}^{T} t^2$ and $\sum_{t=1}^{T} t s_t^j x_t$
      as a function of $\tilde{x}_n, \bar{x}, \bar{x}_j$.
(ii) Using the formulae

$$\hat{\delta}_j = \frac{1}{N}(s^{j\prime}x - s^{j\prime}z^2\hat{b}_2),$$

and

$$\hat{b}_2 = \left(z_2'z_2 - z_2's(s\prime s)^{-1}s'z_2\right)^{-1}\left(z_2'x - z_2's(s\prime s)^{-1}s'x\right),$$

with $z_2 = (1, \ldots, T)'$, derive formulae (2.9) and (2.10).

3

Moving Averages for Seasonal Adjustment

3.1 Introduction

Let us consider a series $x = \{x_t\}$, allowing for an additive decomposition of the type

$$x_t = z_t + s_t + u_t, \quad t = 1, \ldots, T.$$

A simple way of determining each component of this series, for instance the trend z_t, is to apply a linear transformation f to the series, such that the trend is left unchanged and the other components are set to zero. More precisely, let us denote by $x_t^*, z_t^*, s_t^*, u_t^*$ the t-th components of the series x, z, s and u after having been transformed by f. Since f is linear, we have $x_t^* = z_t^* + s_t^* + u_t^*$; moreover, $s_t^* = 0$, $u_t^* = 0$ since f sets the seasonal and disturbance components to zero while keeping the trend unchanged $z_t^* = z_t$. Hence the transformed series x^* is just the trend component.

Evidently, the difficulty of such a method rests in the choice of the transformation f. Since the very definitions of the various components are fairly vague, we cannot reasonably expect to build a transformation which exactly saves the trend component while exactly deleting all seasonal and random effects. At most we can try to determine these properties in an approximate fashion $z_t^* \approx z_t$, $s_t^* \approx 0$, $u_t^* \approx 0$, and in an exact fashion only for particular forms of the components. Thus, the choice of a function f is not automatic and has to be based on a preliminary inspection of the series and on an explicit formalization of the various components. The choice of such a function allows one to avoid certain shortcomings of the regression analysis already mentioned, we must have:

(i)   simple computations;
(ii)   easy updating, as T increases;
(iii) no sensitivity to structural change.

The transformations customarily used are the moving averages where x_t^* is by definition a weighted sum of values of x corresponding to dates around t

$$x_t^* = \theta_{-m_1} x_{t-m_1} + \theta_{-m_1+1} x_{t-m_1+1} + \ldots + \theta_{m_2} x_{t+m_2}$$

$$= \sum_{i=-m_1}^{m_2} \theta_i x_{t+i}, \tag{3.1}$$

where m_1, m_2 are positive integers and $\theta_{-m_1}, \ldots, \theta_{m_2} \in \mathbb{R}$. The number of periods $m_1 + m_2 + 1$ intervening in the transformation is called *order* of the moving average.

It is possible to formulate a moving average value x_t^* only when

$$m_1 + 1 \leq t \leq T - m_2,$$

so that we need to find a different notation for the boundary values $x_1^*, \ldots, x_{m_1}^*$ and $x_{T-m_2+1}^*, \ldots, x_T^*$ in terms of the values of the original series. As a first step it is better not to consider this difficulty. We could, for example, assume that the observed series is indexed by an integer t; t can vary between $-\infty$ and $+\infty$ and there are no boundary values.

Let us denote the lag operator by L which is such that if applied to the original series $\{x_t, t \text{ integer}\}$ the new series is $\{x_{t-1}, t \text{ integer}\}$. The series transformed by the moving average can by written as

$$x^* = Mx = \left(\sum_{i=-m_1}^{m_2} \theta_i L^{-i} \right) x.$$

We can derive the following definition of a moving average.

Definition 3.1: *A moving average is a linear transformation which can be written as a finite linear combination of positive and negative powers of the lag operator*

$$M = \sum_{i=-m_1}^{m_2} \theta_i L^{-i}.$$

The moving averages are oftentimes chosen as centered such that $m_1 = m_2 = m$. The operator M can be written as

$$M = L^m \left(\theta_{-m} + \theta_{-m+1} L^{-1} + \ldots + \theta_m L^{-2m} \right).$$

Let us denote the lead operator by $F = L^{-1}$ and Θ the polynomial such that

$$\Theta(x) = \theta_{-m} + \theta_{-m+1}x + \ldots + \theta_m x 2m.$$

We have

$$M = L^m \Theta(F).$$

The degree of the polynomial Θ characterizes the centered average M. We know both the order of this average, since $2m + 1 = \text{degree}(\Theta) + 1$, and its coefficients, as they are the same as those of the polynomial Θ. The techniques based on moving averages are mainly used for seasonal adjustment. Customarily the series is adjusted using an iterative procedure. We start by applying a first moving average aimed at keeping the trend and deleting the two other components. By doing so we get a first estimation of the trend and hence, by differencing from the original series, of the sum $s + u$. The seasonal component is estimated from $s + u$ (which is easier than from $z + s + u$) applying a moving average which, in turn, aims at isolating s and eliminating u.

Subtracting the estimate of s from the original series, x, we get an estimated value for $z + u$. This can be used as a basis for a new, more precise, trend estimation and so on. This iterative approach allows one to build satisfactory seasonal adjustment procedures by simple steps. Note that the averages used isolate the trend and eliminate the seasonality, or the other way round, but all have to eliminate the disturbance or, at least, to reduce it.

3.2 The Set of Moving Averages

3.2.1 Composition of Moving Averages

Definition 3.2: *The composition (or product) of two given moving averages $\tilde{M}$ and $\tilde{\tilde{M}}$ is the transformation M which generates the new series $MX = \tilde{M}\tilde{\tilde{M}}x$ from any series x.*

It is easy to see that the application $M = \tilde{M}\tilde{\tilde{M}}$ is still a moving average. This result is very important in practice since it allows one to define moving averages starting from simpler moving averages of a smaller order. It also shows that the iterative procedure proposed in the previous chapter is still a moving average method. The composition of moving averages is clearly associative; it is also commutative: $\tilde{M}\tilde{\tilde{M}} = \tilde{\tilde{M}}\tilde{M}$, that is to say, that the moving averages can be applied to the original series in any order.

Theorem 3.1: *The composed average of two centered moving averages is still a centered moving average.*

PROOF: Let us consider two centered averages

$$\tilde{M} = L^{\tilde{m}}\tilde{\Theta}(F) \text{ with degree}(\Theta) = 2\tilde{m},$$
$$\tilde{\tilde{M}} = L^{\tilde{\tilde{m}}}\tilde{\tilde{\Theta}}(F) \text{ with degree}(\Theta) = 2\tilde{\tilde{m}}.$$

Their product is equal to

$$M = \tilde{M}\tilde{\tilde{M}} = L^{\tilde{m}+\tilde{\tilde{m}}}\tilde{\Theta}(F)\tilde{\tilde{\Theta}}(F).$$

Since the degree of $\tilde{\Theta}(F)\tilde{\tilde{\Theta}}(F)$ is equal to $2\tilde{m} + 2\tilde{\tilde{m}}$ the average is centered. Its order is equal to the sum of the orders of $\tilde{M}$ and of $\tilde{\tilde{M}}$ minus 1

$$2m + 1 = (2\tilde{m} + 1) + (2\tilde{\tilde{m}} + 1) - 1.$$

$\square$

Note that a centered moving average can be obtained as the product of two noncentered moving averages. Let us consider, for example, the two "first-difference" operators

$$\Delta = I - L \Leftrightarrow \Delta x_t = x_t - x_{t-1} \quad \text{Backward difference,}$$

and

$$\nabla = F - I = F\Delta \Leftrightarrow \nabla x_t = x_{t+1} - x_t \quad \text{Forward difference.}$$

Their composition, $\Delta\nabla = (I - L)(L^{-1} - I) = L^{-1} - 2I + L$ is a centered moving average of order 3.

3.2.2 Symmetric Moving Averages

Definition 3.3: *A moving average is symmetric if it is centered and if the coefficients having symmetric indices with respect to 0 take the same values*

$$\theta_i = \theta_{-i} \quad i = 1, \ldots, m.$$

The characteristics (order and coefficients) of such a moving average are denoted as $\{[2m + 1] \; ; \; [\theta_m, \theta_{-m+1}, \ldots, \boldsymbol{\theta_0}]\}$; the central term $\boldsymbol{\theta_0}$ is from now on written in bold face.

Theorem 3.2: *A moving average is symmetric if and only if the associated polynomial Θ is symmetric.*

PROOF: This follows directly from the condition $\theta_i = \theta_{-i}$, $i = 1, \ldots, m$.
□

The symmetry condition of the polynomial Θ can be written as

$$\Theta(L) = \theta_{-m} + \theta_{-m+1}L + \ldots + \theta_m L^{2m}$$
$$= L^{2m}[\theta_{-m}F^{2m} + \theta_{-m+1}F^{2m-1} + \ldots + \theta_m]$$
$$\Leftrightarrow \Theta(L) = L^{2m}\Theta(F).$$

Theorem 3.3: *The set of symmetric moving averages is closed with respect to composition.*

PROOF: Let us consider two symmetric averages $\tilde{M}$ and $\tilde{\tilde{M}}$. Their associated polynomials satisfy

$$\tilde{\Theta}(L) = L^{2\tilde{m}}\tilde{\Theta}(F) \text{ and } \tilde{\tilde{\Theta}}(L) = L^{2\tilde{\tilde{m}}}\tilde{\tilde{\Theta}}(F).$$

On the basis of theorem 3.2, the composed average $M = \tilde{M}\tilde{\tilde{M}}$ is centered and has an associated polynomial $\Theta = \tilde{\Theta}\tilde{\tilde{\Theta}}$. Since

$$\Theta(L) = \tilde{\Theta}(L)\tilde{\tilde{\Theta}}(L) = L^{2(\tilde{m}+\tilde{\tilde{m}})}\tilde{\Theta}(F)\tilde{\tilde{\Theta}}(F) = L^{2m}\Theta(F),$$

we conclude that the polynomial is symmetric. □

3.2.3 The Vector Space of Moving Averages

The set of moving averages forms a vector space on $\boldsymbol{R}$ of infinite dimension; it is the smaller subspace containing the powers of the lag operator L^i, i integer. The same space can be spanned by other generators in particular those formed by the first difference operators

$$\{\nabla^i, \; \Delta^i, \; i \text{ positive integer}\}$$

(cf. exercise 3.7).

This system can be interesting from a computational point of view since the first differences of a series x are generally smaller (in absolute value) than the series itself. Finally we can notice that the set of symmetric moving averages forms a vector subspace of the moving average space.

Recalling known results about symmetric polynomials we can show that this subspace is generated by the system $\{(L + F)^i, i \text{ positive integer}\}$ or, equivalently, by the system

$$\{\delta^i = (\nabla\Delta)^i = (L + F - 2I)^i; \ i \text{ positive integer}\}.$$

3.3 Eigenvectors of a Moving Average

A moving average is a linear application of the $I\!\!R^\infty$ space onto itself. We can analyze some of its characteristics such as its eigenvalues and its eigenvectors. In what follows, we consider centered averages even if the results can be easily generalized to any averages.

3.3.1 Solution to a Linear Difference Equation

In this section we recall some established results on the sequences $(x_t, t$ integer) satisfying any equation of the type

$$a_0 x_t + a_1 x_{t+1} + \ldots + a_{2m} x_{t+2m} = 0, \quad \forall \ t, \tag{3.2}$$

called the *linear difference equation* of order $2m$.

The solutions of equation (3.2) form a vector subspace in $I\!\!R^\infty$ of dimension $2m$. In order to define this subspace we need to find $2m$ independent solutions to (3.2). We start by conjecturing the existence of a solution $x_t = \lambda^t$ with λ complex. The value λ must satisfy the characteristic equation

$$a_0 + a_1\lambda + \ldots + a_{2m}\lambda^{2m} = 0. \tag{3.3}$$

The Distinct Roots Case If this equation admits $2m$ distinct roots

$$\lambda_1, \ldots, \lambda_j, \ldots, \lambda_{2m},$$

we get $2m$ independent solutions of equation (3.2)

$$x_{1t} = \lambda_1^t, \ldots, x_{jt} = \lambda_j^t, \ldots, x_{2mt} = \lambda_{2m}^t.$$

The solution of the linear difference equation is given by

$$x_t = \sum_{j=1}^{2m} c_j x_{jt} = \sum_{j=1}^{2m} c_j \lambda_j^t, \tag{3.4}$$

with c_j complex. The roots λ_j can be real or complex. If λ_j is real, the corresponding solution $x_{jt} = \lambda_j^t$ follows an exponential pattern according to the value of λ_j (cf. figure 3.1).

When $\lambda_j > 0$ the series can be interpreted as a trend; when $\lambda_j < 0$ the series can be interpreted as the seasonal component of period 2. When the root λ_j is complex

$$\lambda_j = \rho_j e^{-i\omega_j},$$

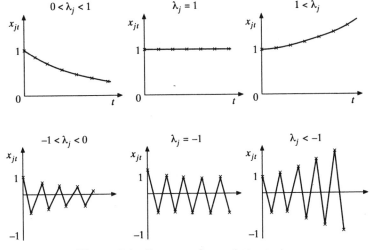

Figure 3.1 Patterns of x_{jt} relative to λ_j

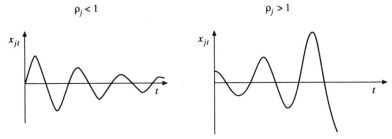

Figure 3.2 Patterns of x_{jt} relative to ρ_j

with

$$\rho_j = |\lambda_j| > 0,$$

and $\omega \in [0,\ 2\pi)$, the real coefficient characteristic equation admits the conjugate root

$$\lambda_{j'} = \bar{\lambda}_j = \rho_j e^{i\omega_j}$$

as a solution. The real combinations of x_{jt} and $x_{j't}$ can be written as

$$x_t = \rho_j^t (c_{1j} \cos \omega_j t + c_{2j} \sin \omega_j t).$$

These series have a sine-wave shape with convergent behavior if $\rho_j < 1$ or explosive behavior if $\rho_j > 1$ (cf. figure 3.2).

Such a function can be interpreted as a seasonal component when its period (equal to $2\pi/\omega_j$) corresponds to a natural periodicity of the original series. If the period is large (ω_j small) such a series can be interpreted as a trend (or as a cycle).

The Multiple Roots Case In the general case, some of the roots of
the characteristic equation can be repeated. If there are J distinct roots

$$\lambda_1, \ldots, \lambda_j, \ldots, \lambda_J,$$

each with multiplicity

$$\alpha_1, \ldots, \alpha_j, \ldots, \alpha_J,$$

the general solution to (3.2) can be written under the form

$$x_t = \lambda_1^t(c_{11} + c_{12}t + \ldots + c_{1\alpha_1}t^{\alpha_1-1}) + \ldots + \lambda_J^t(c_{J1} + \ldots + c_{J\alpha_J}t^{\alpha_J-1}), \quad (3.5)$$

with c_{jk} complex $j = 1, \ldots, J, \ k = 1, \ldots, \alpha_j$.

Equation (3.5) can be written even keeping separate the real roots
from the complex roots. Let us assume that the real roots are the
first J_0 ones. Since the characteristic equation has real coefficients, if
$\lambda_j = \rho_j e^{i\omega_j}$ is a complex root with multiplicity α_j, so is its conjugate $\bar{\lambda}_j$
with the same multiplicity α_j. We can group the complex roots pairwise,
so as to isolate sine and cosine functions. In the more general case the
real series solutions to the nullspace can be written as

$$x_t = \sum_{j=1}^{J_0} \lambda_j^t(c_{j1} + c_{j2}t + \ldots + c_{j\alpha_j}t^{\alpha_j-1})$$

$$+ \sum_{j=J_0+1}^{(J+J_0)/2} \rho_j^t[\cos(\omega_j t)(a_{j1} + a_{j2}t + \ldots + a_{j\alpha_j}t^{\alpha_j-1})$$

$$+ \sin(\omega_j t)(b_{j1} + b_{j2}t + \ldots + b_{j\alpha_j}t^{\alpha_j-1})].$$

3.3.2 Nullspace of a Moving Average

Definition 3.4: *The nullspace of a moving average M (denoted by
$\mathcal{N}(M)$) is the set of time series x such that Mx is equal to zero*

$$\mathcal{N}(M) = \{x : Mx = 0\}.$$

This condition can be written as

$$Mx_t = \theta_{-m}x_{t-m} + \ldots + \theta_m x_{t+m} = 0, \quad \forall\, t,$$

or

$$\theta_{-m}x_t + \ldots + \theta_m x_{t+2m} = 0, \quad \forall\, t.$$

The elements of the nullspace are therefore solutions to a linear difference
equation and can be derived following the procedure described previously
in (3.3.1).

Theorem 3.4:

$$\mathcal{N}(\tilde{M}\tilde{\tilde{M}}) \supset \mathcal{N}(\tilde{M}) + \mathcal{N}(\tilde{\tilde{M}}),$$

where $+$ indicates the sum of subspaces.

PROOF: If $x \in \mathcal{N}(\tilde{M})$, we have $\tilde{M}\tilde{\tilde{M}}x = \tilde{M} \, 0 = 0$. Hence $\mathcal{N}(\tilde{M}\tilde{\tilde{M}}) \supset \mathcal{N}(\tilde{M})$. By the same token, for symmetry reasons, it has to be that $\mathcal{N}(\tilde{M}\tilde{\tilde{M}}) = \mathcal{N}(\tilde{\tilde{M}}\tilde{M}) \supset \mathcal{N}(\tilde{\tilde{M}})$; since $\mathcal{N}(\tilde{M}\tilde{\tilde{M}})$ is a vector subspace the result follows. $\square$

Moreover, since the dimension of $\mathcal{N}(\tilde{M}\tilde{\tilde{M}}) = 2\tilde{m} + 2\tilde{\tilde{m}}$ is equal to the sum of the dimensions of $\mathcal{N}(\tilde{M})$ and of $\mathcal{N}(\tilde{\tilde{M}})$; the two subspaces $\mathcal{N}(\tilde{M}\tilde{\tilde{M}})$ and $\mathcal{N}(\tilde{M}) + \mathcal{N}(\tilde{\tilde{M}})$ coincide if and only if $\mathcal{N}(\tilde{M}) \cap \mathcal{N}(\tilde{\tilde{M}}) = \{0\}$.

3.3.3 Invariance with Respect to a Moving Average

Definition 3.5: *The series x is invariant with respect to the moving average M if and only if*

$$Mx_t = x_t, \quad \forall \, t.$$

The series invariant with respect to M satisfy

$$Mx_t = \theta_{-m}x_{t-m} + \ldots + \theta_m x_{t+m} = x_t, \quad \forall \, t,$$

or

$$\theta_{-m}x_t + \ldots + \theta_m x_{t+2m} = x_{t+m}, \quad \forall \, t.$$

They are solutions to a linear difference equation of order $2m$ and, in particular, they form a vector subspace $\mathcal{J}(M)$ of size $2m$. These solutions are determined from the solutions to the characteristic equation $\Theta(\lambda) - \lambda^m = 0$. Among the solutions only those showing little movement in their rate of change (exponential functions or long-term sine wave) can be interpreted as trends.

Preservation of the Polynomials of Degree p The moving average preserves the polynomials of degree smaller than or equal to p, if $\lambda = 1$ is a root of multiplicity $p+1$ of the characteristic equation $\Theta(\lambda) - \lambda^m = 0$. The polynomial $\Theta(F) - F^m$ is then divisible by $\nabla^{p+1} = (F-I)^{p+1}$. In fact, applying the operator ∇, we are able to decrease the degree of any polynomial by one. For instance, if $x_t = t^n$, $\nabla x_t = (t+1)^n - t^n = nt^{n-1} + \ldots + 1$.

Theorem 3.5:

(i)   *A moving average preserves the constants if and only if*

$$\theta_{-m} + \theta_{-m+1} + \ldots + \theta_m = 1.$$

(ii)   A symmetric moving average preserving the constants pre-serves the polynomials of degree 1.

PROOF: Part (i) is straightforward. In order to show (ii) it is enough to consider the series $x_t = t$. We have

$$x_t^* = \theta_{-m}(t - m) + \ldots + \theta_m(t + m)$$
$$= t(\theta_{-m} + \ldots + \theta_m) + m(\theta_{-m} - \theta_m) +$$
$$+ (m - 1)(\theta_{m-1} - \theta_{-m+1}) + \ldots + 0\theta_0$$
$$= t \cdot 1 + 0 = t = x_t.$$

$\square$

Invariants of a Composed Moving Average Recalling that $\mathcal{J}(M)$ represents the set of series invariant to M, let us suppose that M can be written as a composition of two moving averages $\tilde{M}$ and $\tilde{\tilde{M}}$. We have then

$$\mathcal{J}(M) \supset \mathcal{J}(\tilde{M}) \cap \mathcal{J}(\tilde{\tilde{M}}). \tag{3.6}$$

In fact, if $x \in \mathcal{J}(\tilde{M}) \cap \mathcal{J}(\tilde{\tilde{M}})$ then

$$Mx = \tilde{M}\tilde{\tilde{M}}x = \tilde{M}x = x.$$

The composition of two moving averages preserving the polynomials of a degree smaller than or equal to p, preserves also such polynomials.

3.3.4 Transformed Series from a Geometric Series

The elements of the nullspace and the invariant series are special cases of eigenvectors of the moving average M, associated with the eigenvalues 0 and 1. Any generic geometric series provides other examples of eigenvectors.

Let us consider, for example, the series $x_t = \lambda^t$ where λ is real or complex

$$x_t^* = \theta_{-m}\lambda^{t-m} + \ldots + \theta_m\lambda^{t+m}$$
$$= \lambda^t\lambda^{-m}\Theta(\lambda) = x_t\lambda^{-m}\Theta(\lambda).$$

The initial series is multiplied by the factor $\lambda^{-m}\Theta(\lambda)$ appearing also as an eigenvalue. When λ is real, the application corresponds to a homothetic transformation of factor $\lambda^{-m}\Theta(\lambda)$.

Let us consider the general case where λ is complex, $\lambda = \rho e^{i\omega}$. The series $x_t = \rho^t e^{i\omega t}$ is multiplied by a complex number $\lambda^{-m}\Theta(\lambda) = ce^{i\phi}$, with $c = \rho^{-m} \mid \Theta(\lambda) \mid$ and $\phi = arg[\lambda^{-m}\Theta(\lambda)]$. Thus

$$x_t^* = c\rho^t e^{i(\omega t+\phi)}.$$

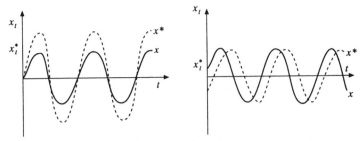

Figure 3.3 Amplitude ($\rho = 1, c > 1, \phi = 0$) and
Phase ($\rho = 1, c > 1, \phi \neq 0$) Effects

Decomposing this complex series according to its real and imaginary parts, and using the linearity of the moving average, we can see that a series appearing in the form $\rho^t \cos(\omega t)$, respectively, $\rho^t \sin(\omega t)$ will be transformed in $c\rho^t \cos(\omega t + \phi)$, respectively, $c\rho^t \sin(\omega t + \phi)$. A twofold effect can be observed for these series:

(i) an amplitude effect by multiplying the modulus of x_t by c,
(ii) a phase effect adding the term ϕ which results in a change of the time origin.

The amplitude effect modifies the height of the peaks in the series. The phase effect is more complex; in fact, it introduces effects interpretable as seasonal components (peaks or troughs) at dates where there were not any (cf. figure 3.3).

When $\rho = 1$, the latter effect can in turn be partially eliminated by choosing symmetric moving averages; hence the importance attributed to them. Let us consider such an average

$$\lambda^{-m}\Theta(\lambda) = \lambda^m \Theta(\lambda^{-1}),$$

given the symmetry of the polynomial Θ; since $\lambda = e^{i\omega}$ we get

$$e^{-im\omega}\Theta(e^{i\omega}) = e^{im\omega}\Theta(e^{-i\omega}) = \overline{[e^{-im\omega}\Theta(e^{i\omega})]}.$$

The eigenvalue associated with the series $x_t = e^{i\omega t}$ is real and the argument ϕ is equal to 0 or to π according to whether this real number is greater or smaller than zero. In the former case, $\phi = 0$, there are no phase effects; in the latter, $\phi = \pi$, there is a phase inversion, peaks become troughs and vice versa. (We will see in what follows that this phenomenon does not have any important consequences.)

Note that the amplitude effect turns out to be

$$\mid \Theta(e^{i\omega}) \mid = \left| \sum_{j=-m}^{m} \theta_j \cos(j\omega) \right|.$$

The application $\omega \mapsto \mid \Theta(e^{i\omega}) \mid$ is called *gain* of the moving average.

Obviously, these results are applicable to real series of the form
$$x_t = a\cos\omega t,$$
or $x_t = a\sin\omega t$ with $a \in \mathbb{R}$.

Even in the case of a symmetric moving average, the other eigenvectors $\rho^t e^{i\omega t}$ with $\rho \neq 1$ are generally associated with complex eigenvalues. Therefore, for these series, there exists a phase effect.

3.4 Transformation of a White Noise by a Moving Average

We turn now to the ways in which the disturbance u can be transformed. We assume that the u_t are zero mean random variables, uncorrelated and homoskedastic. To simplify the notation, we consider a centered moving average
$$u_t^* = \sum_{i=-m}^{m} \theta_i u_{t+i}.$$
These new variables have zero mean since
$$E(u_t^*) = \sum_{i=-m}^{m} \theta_i E(u_{t+i}) = 0.$$

3.4.1 Correlogram of u^*

These variables all have the same variance equal to
$$\sigma^{*2} = \operatorname{var}(u_t^*) = \sigma^2 \sum_{i=-m}^{m} \theta_i^2.$$
The importance of the disturbance is lessened by the transformation if $\sum_{i=-m}^{m} \theta_i^2 < 1$. The residual *variance reduction ratio* is
$$\frac{\sigma^{*2}}{\sigma^2} = \sum_{i=-m}^{m} \theta_i^2,$$
which can be interpreted as the capability of the moving average to reduce the disturbance.

The transformed variables are correlated with each other. Thus, the covariance between u_t^* and u_{t+h}^*, $(h \geq 0)$ is equal to
$$\gamma(h) = \operatorname{cov}(u_t^*, u_{t+h}^*)$$
$$= \sum_{i=-m}^{m} \sum_{j=-m}^{m} \theta_i \theta_j E(u_{t+i} u_{t+h+j})$$
$$= \begin{cases} \sigma^2 \sum_{i=h-m}^{m} \theta_i \theta_{i-h}, & h \leq 2m, \\ 0, & \text{otherwise.} \end{cases}$$

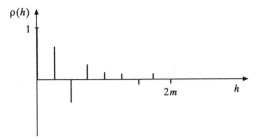

Figure 3.4 Correlogram

Table 3.1 *First Simulation: Values of u_t*

0.4	-0.7	0.8	0.0	-0.9	-0.5	-0.6	0.4	-0.9	0.1
-0.2	-0.9	0.8	-0.1	0.4	-0.7	0.9	-0.5	0.5	-0.9
1.0	-0.3	0.3	0.9	0.8	0.8	0.0	-0.1	0.2	0.5

Note: The values should be read horizontally line by line.

This covariance does not depend on t and becomes zero when $h > 2m$. The previous results may be summarized in the *correlogram* which gives the values of the correlations

$$\rho(h) = \frac{\gamma(h)}{\gamma(0)},$$

as a function of h (cf. figure 3.4). These correlations do not depend on the white noise variance σ^2.

3.4.2 Slutzky–Yule Effect

In this subsection we will propose an intuitive presentation of this effect. The existence of nonzero correlations between adjacent values of the process u^* introduces a spurious effect called *Slutzky–Yule effect*.

The series u^* will present more or less regular oscillations which may suggest the presence of a seasonal component. The outcome would be a wrong estimation of the other components. In order to better understand this phenomenon, in tables 3.1 and 3.2 we consider two simulated series of thirty observations each of a disturbance uniformly distributed on $[-1, -0.9, \ldots, 0.9, 1]$.

If we consider the graphical representation of the evaluation of u_t we obtain a very irregular shape depicted in figures 3.5 and 3.6.

Let us apply to each of these series the moving average defined by

$$u_t^* = [u_{t-2} + 2u_{t-1} + 2u_t + 2u_{t+1} + u_{t+2}]/8.$$

Table 3.2 *Second Simulation: Values of u_t*

-0.1	0.7	0.5	-0.3	0.4	-0.1	-0.2	0.0	0.1	-0.2
0.8	0.6	-0.9	-0.3	-0.1	0.9	-0.1	0.4	-0.5	0.6
0.7	0.9	-0.9	-0.9	0.0	0.6	0.5	-0.5	0.9	-0.7

Note: The values should be read horizontally line by line.

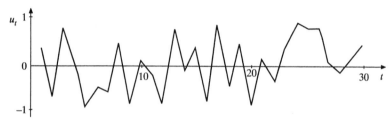

Figure 3.5   First Simulation

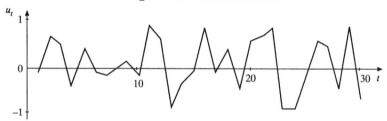

Figure 3.6   Second Simulation

Table 3.3 *First Simulation: Values of u_t^**

		-0.04	-0.16	-0.35	-0.45	-0.40	-0.32	-0.20	-0.20
-0.26	-0.07	-0.01	0.07	0.14	0.07	0.04	0.02	0.01	0.05
0.15	0.25	0.45	0.56	0.66	0.50	0.30	0.19		

Note: Since the moving average is of order 5, we cannot compute u_t^* for the first two and the last two dates.

The values for u_t^* from the simulated series are reported in tables 3.3 and 3.4, with their graphical representations in figures 3.7 and 3.8.

The transformed series u_t^* has a more regular shape than the initial white noise u_t. It shows oscillations which may be mistaken for a seasonal phenomenon. Thus, although the series u_t^* is not strictly periodic, we see cycles appear especially in the second series. The local maxima

Table 3.4 *Second Simulation: Values of* u_t^*

		0.01	0.22	0.04	-0.01	-0.01	-0.06| 0.05	0.25
0.20	0.06	-0.06	-0.14	0.00	0.19	0.22	0.14	0.20	0.36
0.37	0.14	-0.14	-0.26	-0.12	0.01	0.26	0.21		

Note: Since the moving average is of order 5, we cannot compute u_t^* for the first two and the last two dates.

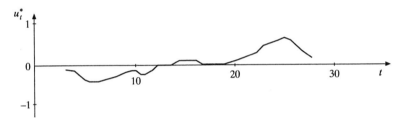

Figure 3.7 First Simulation

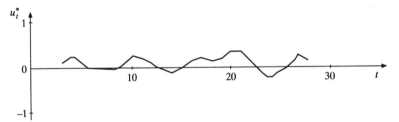

Figure 3.8 Second Simulation

are almost at the same distance from each other (the distance is of 6, 7, 4, and 6 periods). We can try to specify this effect by computing the average period of these cycles. Let us define the average period τ as the average time interval separating two points where the series changes signs, passing from a negative to a positive sign. We have $\tau = 1/\mu$ where μ is the average number of the x-axis crossings per units of time. The quantity $\mu = \Pr(u_t^* < 0, u_{t+1}^* > 0)$ can be easily computed when the disturbances u_t follow a standard normal distribution

$$\mu = \Pr\left(\sum_{i=-m}^{m} \theta_i u_{t+i} < 0, \sum_{i=-m}^{m} \theta_i u_{t+1+i} > 0 \right) = \frac{\alpha}{2\pi},$$

where α is the angle between the two hyperplanes

$$\sum_{i=-m}^{m} \theta_i u_{t+i} = 0 \quad \text{and} \quad \sum_{i=-m}^{m} \theta_i u_{t+1+i} = 0.$$

The cosine of this angle is given by

$$\cos \alpha = \frac{\sum_{i=-m}^{m-1} \theta_i \theta_{i+1}}{\sum_{i=-m}^{m} \theta_i^2} = \rho(1),$$

from which the value of μ can be derived as

$$\mu = \frac{\arccos \rho(1)}{2\pi}.$$

The average distance separating two upward crossings of the x-axis is approximately

$$\tau = \frac{2\pi}{\arccos \rho(1)}. \tag{3.7}$$

The result just given provides a rather vague idea of these spurious cycles. The distance between two crossings of the x-axis is fundamentally random so that the results observed for a certain path can be different from the result derived in (3.8). Thus, in our example

$$\rho(1) = 0.85, \qquad \tau = \frac{2\pi}{\arccos 0.85} \approx 11.3.$$

For the first simulated series these distances τ are around 11 and 15 while for the second around 6 and 10.

It is not possible to avoid this Slutzky–Yule effect. Therefore, one may hope that the average period of spurious oscillations τ be close to the period of the seasonal component since these are strongly reduced in the iterative procedure of the series. On the other hand, we note that these spurious oscillations become negligible when there is a strong reduction of the disturbance amplitude, that is when the residual variance ratio (σ^{*2}/σ^2) is small. This reduction effect is visible when one considers the examples and examines the original and the transformed series.

3.5 Arithmetic Averages

The simplest symmetric moving average example can be obtained assuming that it preserves the constants, that is, assuming that

$$\sum_{i=-m}^{m} \theta_i = 1$$

(recall that it preserves the polynomials of degree 1), and that it minimizes the influence of the disturbance. The coefficients can be obtained as a solution to the constrained minimization problem

$$\min_{\theta_i} \sum_{i=-m}^{m} \theta_i^2$$

$$\text{s.\,t.} \sum_{i=-m}^{m} \theta_i = 1,$$

which results in $\theta_i = 1/(2m + 1)$, $\forall\, i$. Therefore

$$x_t^* = (x_{t-m} + x_{t-m+1} + \ldots + x_{t+m})\,/(2m + 1),$$

which corresponds to the usual arithmetic average. For the first four values of m, these means can be written in the adopted symbolic notation as

$$[\mathbf{1}] = \{[1];\, [\mathbf{1}]\}, \qquad [\mathbf{3}] = \{[3];\, [\tfrac{1}{3}, \tfrac{1}{3}]\},$$

$$[\mathbf{5}] = \{[5];\, [\tfrac{1}{5}, \tfrac{1}{5}, \tfrac{1}{5}]\}, \qquad [\mathbf{7}] = \{[7];\, [\tfrac{1}{7}, \tfrac{1}{7}, \tfrac{1}{7}, \tfrac{1}{7}]\}.$$

3.5.1 Nullspace of the (2m+1) Order Arithmetic Average

The polynomial associated to this moving average is

$$\Theta(\lambda) = (1 + \lambda + \lambda^2 + \ldots + \lambda^{2m})/(2m + 1)$$

$$= \frac{(1 - \lambda^{2m+1})}{(2m + 1)(1 - \lambda)}.$$

The characteristic equation $\Theta(\lambda) = 0$ admits as solutions the $(2m+1)$-th roots different from 1

$$\lambda_j = \exp\left(\frac{i2\pi j}{2m + 1}\right), \quad j = 1, \ldots, 2m.$$

The elements of the nullspace are thus of the form

$$s_t = \sum_{j=1}^{m} \left(c_{1j} \cos \frac{2\pi j t}{2m + 1} + c_{2j} \sin \frac{2\pi j t}{2m + 1} \right).$$

These are the periodic sequences of period $2m + 1$ which are zero on average over their period

$$\sum_{i=-m}^{m} s_{t+i} = 0, \quad \forall\, t.$$

Given a seasonal component made by a zero mean periodic function with an odd period, there always exists an arithmetic average capable of setting it to zero.

3.5.2 Some Series Invariant to the Arithmetic Average

By construction, this average does not alter constant series. Since it is symmetric, it also does not alter the polynomials of degree 1. On the contrary, this property is not maintained for the polynomials of degree 2. As an example, let us consider $x_t = t^2$

$$x_t^* = \frac{1}{2m+1} \sum_{i=-m}^{m} (t+i)^2$$

$$= \frac{1}{2m+1} \left(\sum_{i=-m}^{m} t^2 + 2t \sum_{i=-m}^{m} i + \sum_{i=-m}^{m} i^2 \right)$$

$$= \frac{1}{2m+1} \left[(2m+1)t^2 + \frac{m(m+1)(2m+1)}{3} \right]$$

$$= t^2 + \frac{m(m+1)}{3} \neq t^2.$$

The other invariant series can be determined by solving a difference equation. Thus for a five-term arithmetic average, the characteristic polynomial associated to such a difference equation is

$$\Theta(\lambda) - \lambda^2 = \frac{1}{5} \left(\lambda^4 + \lambda^3 - 4\lambda^2 + \lambda + 1 \right).$$

This polynomial is divisible by $(\lambda - 1)^2$ and

$$\Theta(\lambda) - \lambda^2 = \frac{1}{5} (\lambda - 1)^2 (\lambda^2 + 3\lambda + 1).$$

The roots different from 1 are $(-3 \pm \sqrt{5})/2$ and the corresponding invariant series are

$$x_t = \left(\frac{-3 + \sqrt{5}}{2} \right)^t \quad \text{and} \quad x_t = \left(\frac{-3 - \sqrt{5}}{2} \right)^t.$$

3.5.3 Transformations of a Geometric Series

In order to evaluate the effects of the arithmetic average on other periodic functions, we can compute the gain of such an average $\mid \Theta(e^{i\omega}) \mid$ with $\omega \in [0, \pi)$. The value $\mid \Theta(e^{i\omega}) \mid$ measures the amplitude effect for periodic functions with period $2\pi/\omega$

$$\mid \Theta(e^{i\omega}) \mid = \mid \frac{1}{2m+1} (e^{-im\omega} + \ldots + e^{im\omega}) \mid$$

$$= \frac{1}{2m+1} \mid 1 + e^{i\omega} + \ldots + e^{2im\omega} \mid$$

$$= \frac{1}{2m+1} \frac{\mid 1 - e^{(2m+1)i\omega} \mid}{\mid 1 - e^{i\omega} \mid}$$

$$= \frac{1}{2m+1} \left| \frac{\sin(2m+1)\frac{\omega}{2}}{\sin \frac{\omega}{2}} \right|.$$

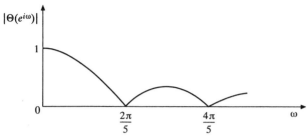

Figure 3.9 Gain Function

This function becomes zero whenever

$$\omega = \frac{2k\pi}{2m+1}, \quad k = 1, 2, \ldots$$

We find again the series belonging to the nullspace of the moving average. The periodic series with a frequency close to $k/(2m+1)$ will be reduced as well, given the continuity of $|\Theta(e^{i\omega})|$. As ω tends to zero, $\Theta(e^{i\omega})$ tends to one; hence the property of preservation of certain trends.

The modification of the amplitude depends on the order of the moving average as well; in particular, we note that as m tends to ∞, $\Theta(e^{i\omega})$ tends to zero, for $\omega \neq 0$. This is a consequence of the fact that if we apply an arithmetic average with a large number of terms to any series, this will tend to make it constant. When $m = 2$ the gain function has the form shown in figure 3.9.

Since the arithmetic average corresponding to $m = 2$ is symmetric, there is no phase effect for sine-wave functions with ω included between zero and $2\pi/5$ or larger than $4\pi/5$ and there is phase inversion if ω is included between $2\pi/5$ and $4\pi/5$.

3.5.4 Transformation of a White Noise Process

The covariance $\gamma(h) = \operatorname{cov}\left(u_t^*, u_{t+h}^*\right) = 0$ whenever $h \geq 2m + 1$. For values of h included between 0 and $2m$, it is equal to

$$\gamma(h) = \sigma^2 \sum_{i=h-m}^{m} \frac{1}{(2m+1)^2} = \sigma^2 \frac{2m+1-h}{(2m+1)^2}.$$

The variance reduction for the disturbance term is therefore

$$\frac{\sigma^{*2}}{\sigma^2} = \frac{\gamma(0)}{\sigma^2} = \frac{1}{2m+1}.$$

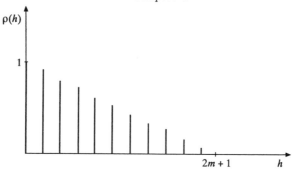

Figure 3.10   Autocorrelation Function

Table 3.5 *Examples of Values of* τ.

m	1	2	3	4	5	6
τ	7.4	9.7	11.8	12.9	14.5	15.7

The autocorrelation function

$$\rho(h) = \frac{\gamma(h)}{\gamma(0)} = \begin{cases} \frac{2m+1-h}{2m+1}, & 0 \le h \le 2m, \\ 0, & \text{otherwise}, \end{cases}$$

corresponds to a straight line as in figure 3.10.

Since the first-order autocorrelation is close to 1, the Slutsky–Yule effect introduces spurious regularities with a large period. This period is approximately given by

$$\tau = \frac{2\pi}{\arccos \frac{2m}{2m+1}} = \frac{2\pi}{\arccos(1 - \frac{1}{2m+1})}.$$

In table 3.5 we give values of τ for different values of m.

3.5.5 How to Cancel Seasonal Components with Even Periods

The arithmetic average with $2m + 1$ terms allows periodic functions of period $2m+1$ which are zero on average over their period to cancel out. Notice that the seasonal components introduced correspond in practice to an even period $2m$. In particular for a quarterly series such a period is 4 and for a monthly series it is 12. If we take an arithmetic average on $2m$ terms, namely

$$x_{1t}^* = \frac{1}{2m}(x_{t-m} + \ldots + x_{t+m-1}),$$

or

$$x_{2t}^* = \frac{1}{2m}(x_{t-m+1} + \ldots + x_{t+m}),$$

it does not involve symmetry around the date t. In order to reintroduce such a symmetry, let us consider the series defined as

$$x_t^* = \frac{1}{2}(x_{1t}^* + x_{2t}^*)$$

$$= \frac{1}{2m}\left(\frac{1}{2}x_{t-m} + x_{t-m+1} + \ldots + x_{t+m-1} + \frac{1}{2}x_{t+m}\right). \tag{3.8}$$

The associated polynomial for this moving average is

$$\Theta(\lambda) = \frac{1}{2m}\left(\frac{1}{2} + \lambda + \lambda^2 + \ldots + \lambda^{2m-1} + \frac{\lambda^{2m}}{2}\right)$$

$$= \frac{1}{2m}\frac{1}{2}(1+\lambda)(1+\lambda+\ldots+\lambda^{2m-1})$$

$$= \frac{1}{2m}\frac{1}{2}(1+\lambda)\frac{1-\lambda^{2m}}{1-\lambda}.$$

This moving average sets to zero all periodic functions of period $2m$ for which the sum of seasonal coefficients is zero and also the series $s_t = (-1)^t t$. Like the arithmetic average, this moving average preserves the polynomials of degree 1. Moreover, to give an idea of the order of magnitude of the variance reduction ratio and the average period of the oscillations induced by the Slutsky–Yule effect, consider that the former is equal to 0.08 while the latter is equal to 15.3, for $m = 12$.

3.6 Averages Derived from the Arithmetic Averages

The arithmetic averages have the advantage of being easy to compute. Combining them allows us to derive a quite large family of moving averages with a simple structure of coefficients and to achieve good approximation to more sophisticated averages.

3.6.1 Composition of Arithmetic Averages

Let us assume that we are interested in constructing a simple moving average which preserves the polynomials of degree 1 and sets to zero the seasonal components of period 4 (quarters) with a linearly varying amplitude of the type

$$s_t = A_1 \sin \pi t/2 + B_1 \cos \pi t/2 + B_2 \cos \pi t$$
$$+ A_3 t \sin \pi t/2 + B_3 t \cos \pi t/2 + B_4 t \cos \pi t.$$

We can consider the composed average of two arithmetic averages of order 4 denoted by **4** chosen in such a way that the resulting moving average M be centered

$$M = \frac{1}{4}(L + I + F + F^2)\frac{1}{4}(L^2 + L + I + F)$$

$$= \frac{1}{16}(L^3 + 2L^2 + 3L + 4I + 3F + 2F^2 + F^3).$$

In symbolic notation

$$M = [\mathbf{4}]^2 = \{[7]; \frac{1}{16}[1, 2, 3, 4]\}.$$

This moving average M sets the function s_t to zero; in fact, the characteristic equation associated to the nullspace is equal to $(1+\lambda+\lambda^2+\lambda^3)^2 = 0$ and allows as solutions the fourth roots of the unity different from 1, each with multiplicity 2. Note that the average is centered, symmetric, and the sum of its coefficients is equal to 1: therefore, it preserves the polynomials of degree less than or equal to 1. Also, the variance reduction ratio for the disturbance is equal to 0.17 and the average period of the oscillations τ is approximately equal to 15.

3.6.2 Spencer Averages of Order 15 and 21

The compositions of the arithmetic averages like the ones examined in the previous section do not preserve the polynomials of a degree larger than 1. We need to modify them if the set of possible trends includes such polynomials. The Spencer averages are an example of such a generalization. Their main characteristics are that they are moving averages which:

(i)   set to zero the seasonal components of periodicity 4 with a linearly varying amplitude;

(ii)   set to zero the seasonal components of periodicity 5 (this last condition allows some flexibility in the period of the seasonal component);

(iii) preserve the polynomials of degree smaller than or equal to 3; and

(iv)   have a relatively simple structure of coefficients.

The first condition on the nullspace is easily satisfied taking the convolution of the arithmetic averages of order 4 and of an arithmetic average of order 5. Let us denote it by $M_1 = [\mathbf{4}]^2[\mathbf{5}]$. This condition will be satisfied by any moving average of the form $M = M_1 M_2$, where M_2 is any moving average, because $\mathcal{N}(M) \supset \mathcal{N}(M_1)$. We know that M_1 preserves the polynomials of degree less than or equal to 1. It does not, though, preserve the polynomials of higher degree. In order to show this, we can write its expression as a function of δ

$$\delta = \nabla\Delta = L^{-1}(I - L)^2 = L + F - 2I$$

so that the arithmetic average of order 5, [5], can be written as

$$[5] = \frac{1}{5}(L^2 + L + I + F + F^2) = \frac{1}{5}(\delta^2 + 5\delta + 5I),$$

and the composition of two arithmetic averages of order 4, denoted by $[4]^2$ can be written as

$$(L^2 + L + I + F)(L + I + F + F^2)/16 = (\delta^3 + 8\delta^2 + 20\delta + 16I)/16.$$

Finally, M_1 can be written as

$$M_1 = I + (180\delta + 156\delta^2 + 65\delta^3 + 13\delta^4 + \delta^5)/80.$$

In order for the average M_1 to preserve the polynomials of the third degree, we need that $L^5(M_1 - I)$ can be divided by $(I - L)^4$, or, equivalently, that the expression of $M_1 - I$ as a function of δ does not contain the first order term. It is easy to obtain this condition by multiplying M_1 by $I - 180/80\delta = I - 9/4\delta$. We can write the new average as

$$M_3 = M_1(I - 9/4\delta) = [4]^2[5](I - 9/4\delta).$$

In order to simplify the moving average coefficients, we attach the term $3\delta^2/4$ to the term $(I - 9/4\delta)$ which still satisfies the conditions about the nullspace and the invariant polynomials. We then get

$$M = M_1\left(I - \frac{9}{4}\delta - \frac{3}{4}\delta^2\right)$$
$$= M_1\left(\frac{-3L^2 + 3L + 4I + 3F - 3F^2}{4}\right),$$

called the Spencer average of order 15. In symbolic notation we can write

$$M = \{[15]; \frac{1}{320}[-3, -6, -5, 3, 21, 46, 67, \mathbf{74}]\}. \tag{3.9}$$

For this average the variance reduction ratio is equal to

$$\frac{\sigma^{*2}}{\sigma^2} \approx 0.19.$$

The average period of the cyclicality induced by the Slutsky–Yule effect is

$$\tau \approx 15.9.$$

Analogously, the twenty-one term Spencer average is given by

$$M = [5]^2[7](I - 4\delta^2 - 3\delta^4 - \delta^6/2)$$
$$= [5]^2[7](-L^3 + L + 2I + F + F^3)/2.$$

In the adopted notation we have

$$M = \{[21]; \frac{1}{350}[-1, -3, -5, -5, -2, 6, 18, 33, 47, 57, \mathbf{60}]\}.$$

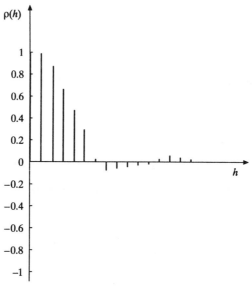

Figure 3.11   Correlogram

The variance reduction ratio is equal to

$$\frac{\sigma^{*2}}{\sigma^2} \approx 0.15,$$

and the average period of the induced cyclicality is

$$\tau \approx 21.3.$$

The correlogram associated to this average has a damped sine-wave shape and becomes zero for $h \geq 21$ (see figure 3.11).

We will not present here the Spencer averages to adjust monthly series for which the reader should refer to Kendall and Stuart (1968).

3.7 Moving Regressions

3.7.1 Local Polynomials

Modeling a trend by low degree polynomials can be very restrictive. The trend which measures the medium- (long-) term evolution has the property of showing little changes of variation over short periods. When this happens, it could be approximated by polynomials. Upon a suitable definition of local polynomial, a better representation could be achieved by choosing functions locally resembling low degree polynomials.

Definition 3.6: *A series* $(x_t, t \in -\infty, \ldots, -1, 0, 1, \ldots, +\infty)$ *can be represented by a polynomial of degree p on any interval of length $2m + 1$*

if fitting a polynomial of degree p on each of these intervals $(t - m, t - m + 1, \ldots, t, \ldots, t + m)$ by the least squares method shows that the estimated and actual values coincide for the central point of the interval, i.e., $\hat{x}_t = x_t$.

The important difference with respect to the fit of a polynomial of degree p for the whole observation period (by the regression method presented in chapter 2) is that the estimated coefficients of the polynomials depend on the interval and therefore are different across intervals.

Let us examine how we can write the condition

$$\hat{x}_t = x_t.$$

The values of the series considered on the interval are

$$x_{t+i}, \quad i = -m, -m + 1, \ldots, m.$$

and the polynomial of degree p can be written as

$$a_0 + a_1 i + a_2 i^2 + \ldots + a_p i^p.$$

The coefficients will be estimated by the method of ordinary least squares, i.e., minimizing

$$\sum_{i=-m}^{m} [x_{t+i} - a_0 - a_1 i - a_2 i^2 - \ldots - a_p i^p]^2.$$

If we denote by $\hat{a}_0, \hat{a}_1, \ldots, \hat{a}_p$ the coefficient estimators of the polynomial, the estimated values of the series are

$$\hat{x}_{t+1} = \hat{a}_0 + \hat{a}_1 i + \ldots + \hat{a}_p i^p.$$

The condition $\hat{x}_t = x_t$ boils down to $x_t = \hat{a}_0$. Since the least squares estimators are linear functions of the observations, $\hat{a}_0$ can be written as

$$\hat{a}_0 = \sum_{i=-m}^{m} \theta_i x_{t+i},$$

where the θ's are real numbers not depending on t.

The series is therefore locally interpretable by a polynomial of degree p if its value at point t, x_t is equal to the quantity $\sum_{i=-m}^{m} \theta_i x_{t+i}$; this quantity can be considered as the value at time t of a centered moving average of order $2m + 1$ with coefficients θ_i. This moving average leaves unchanged the series locally interpretable as a polynomial of degree p. Moreover, it can be shown that this moving average is symmetric (cf. the example below).

Table 3.6 *Characteristics of Some Moving Averages*

p	m	σ^{*2}/σ^2	τ
3	2	0.49	6.5
3	3	0.33	8.4
3	6	0.17	13.0
3	7	0.15	14.3
5	6	0.28	10.3
5	7	0.24	11.5

3.7.2 An Example

Let us apply this procedure, estimating the coefficients when $m = 2$ and $p = 3$. The quantity to be minimized can be written as

$$\sum_{i=-2}^{2} \left(x_{t+i} - a_0 - a_1 i - a_2 i^2 - a_3 i^3\right)^2.$$

The estimators $\hat{a}_0, \hat{a}_1, \hat{a}_2, \hat{a}_3$ are obtained by solving the system of normal equations

$$\hat{a}_0 \sum_{i=-2}^{2} 1 + \hat{a}_1 \sum_{i=-2}^{2} i + \hat{a}_2 \sum_{i=-2}^{2} i^2 + \hat{a}_3 \sum_{i=-2}^{2} i^3 = \sum_{i=-2}^{2} x_{t+i},$$

$$\hat{a}_0 \sum_{i=-2}^{2} i + \hat{a}_1 \sum_{i=-2}^{2} i^2 + \hat{a}_2 \sum_{i=-2}^{2} i^3 + \hat{a}_3 \sum_{i=-2}^{2} i^4 = \sum_{i=-2}^{2} i x_{t+i},$$

$$\hat{a}_0 \sum_{i=-2}^{2} i^2 + \hat{a}_1 \sum_{i=-2}^{2} i^3 + \hat{a}_2 \sum_{i=-2}^{2} i^4 + \hat{a}_3 \sum_{i=-2}^{2} i^5 = \sum_{i=-2}^{2} i^2 x_{t+i},$$

$$\hat{a}_0 \sum_{i=-2}^{2} i^3 + \hat{a}_1 \sum_{i=-2}^{2} i^4 + \hat{a}_2 \sum_{i=-2}^{2} i^5 + \hat{a}_3 \sum_{i=-2}^{2} i^6 = \sum_{i=-2}^{2} i^3 x_{t+i}.$$

All sums of odd powers such as $\sum_{i=-2}^{2} i$, $\sum_{i=-2}^{2} i^3$ and so on, are equal to zero. The system can be rewritten as

$$\begin{cases} 5\hat{a}_0 & +10\hat{a}_2 & & = \sum_i x_{t+i}, \\ & 10\hat{a}_1 & +34\hat{a}_3 & = \sum_i i x_{t+i}, \\ 10\hat{a}_0 & +34\hat{a}_2 & & = \sum_i i^2 x_{t+i}, \\ & 34\hat{a}_1 & +130\hat{a}_3 & = \sum_i i^3 x_{t+i}. \end{cases}$$

We obtain the expression for $\hat{a}_0$ using the first and the third equations

$$\hat{a}_0 = \sum_{i=-2}^{2} (17 - 5i^2)x_{t+i}/35,$$

or

$$\hat{a}_0 = \frac{1}{35} \left(-3x_{t-2} + 12x_{t-1} + 17x_t + 12x_{t+1} - 3x_{t+2}\right).$$

As a general result, $\hat{a}_0$ will be obtained by solving a subsystem the right-hand side elements of which depend on x_{t+i} and x_{t-i} in a symmetric fashion. Therefore a_0 will always be a symmetric moving average.

Moving Averages Preserving Third Degree Local Polynomials
They are given by

$$m = 2 : M = \{[5]; \frac{1}{35}[-3, 12, \mathbf{17}]\},$$

$$m = 3 : M = \{[7]; \frac{1}{21}[-2, 3, 6, \mathbf{7}]\},$$

$$m = 6 : M = \{[13]; \frac{1}{143}[-11, 0, 9, 16, 21, 24, \mathbf{25}]\},$$

$$m = 7 : M = \{[15], \frac{1}{1105}[-78, -13, 42, 87, 122, 147, 162, \mathbf{167}]\},$$

$$m = 10 : M = \{[21]; \frac{1}{3059}[-171, -76, 9, 84, 149, 204, 249, 284, 309, 324, \mathbf{329}]\}.$$

Moving Averages Preserving 5th Degree Local Polynomials.
They are given by

$$m = 6 : M = \{[13]; \frac{1}{2431}[110, -198, -135, 110, 390, 600, \mathbf{677}]\},$$

$$m = 7 : M = \{[15]; \frac{1}{46189}[2145, -2860, -2937, -165, 3755, 7500,$$

$$10125, \mathbf{11063}]\},$$

$$m = 10 : M = \{[21]; \frac{1}{260015}[11628, -6460, -13005, -11220, -3940, 6378,$$

$$17655, 28190, 36660, 42120, \mathbf{44003}]\}.$$

The characteristics of some of these moving averages in terms of their power to reduce the residual variance and the period of the induced cycle are given in table 3.6.

3.7.3 Some Properties of the Averages
Preserving the Local Polynomials

(i)   An average preserving the local polynomials of degree p preserves in particular the polynomials of degree p since the estimated values coincide with the initial series.

(ii) Since the constant series are preserved by these averages, the sum
      of the coefficients is always equal to 1.
(iii) The averages computed for the local polynomials of even degree
      $p = 2q$ are the same as those computed for the polynomials of odd
      degree $p = 2q+1$. This is the outcome of a very peculiar form of the
      normal equations. Let us consider the case $m = 2$, $p = 3$. All that
      is needed for the determination of $\hat{a}_0$ is just the first three normal
      equations, that is those corresponding to the case $m = 2$, $p = 2$.
(iv) The residual variance reduction ratio is easy to compute, since it
      is equal to

$$\frac{\sigma^{*2}}{\sigma^2} = \sum_{i=-m}^{m} \theta_i^2 = \theta_0.$$

Let us show this equality. The fitted series on the interval $(t -
m, \ldots, t + m)$ is obtained from the original series through an
orthogonal projection matrix $\mathbf{P}$

$$\begin{pmatrix} \hat{x}_{t-m} \\ \vdots \\ \hat{x}_t \\ \vdots \\ \hat{x}_{t+m} \end{pmatrix} = \mathbf{P} \begin{pmatrix} x_{t-m} \\ \vdots \\ x_t \\ \vdots \\ x_{t+m} \end{pmatrix}.$$

The matrix $\mathbf{P}$ is square of order $2m + 1$ and its $(m + 1)$-th row
corresponds to the elements $(\theta_{-m}, \ldots, \theta_0, \ldots, \theta_m)$. Since it is symmetric and idempotent, its $(m + 1)$-th column is

$$\begin{pmatrix} \theta_{-m} \\ \vdots \\ \theta_0 \\ \vdots \\ \theta_m \end{pmatrix},$$

and the product of its $(m+1)$-th row and column is the $(m+1)$-th
diagonal element of the matrix $\mathbf{P}$, which can be written as

$$\sum_{i=-m}^{m} \theta_i^2 = \theta_0.$$

(v)   The cancellation of the seasonal component has not been
taken into consideration in the construction of the previous moving
averages. This problem is generally solved *ex-post*, leading to the
choice of particular values of m.

3.8 Moving Averages Derived from Minimizing the Reduction Ratio under Constraints

There exist many moving averages which leave certain trend components unchanged and set to zero certain seasonal components. How can we choose within this set of averages? In the previous sections we have considered either averages with simple coefficients (Spencer averages) or averages whose size was given a priori (moving regression). Other more interesting criteria can be proposed. The customary constraints relate to the trend and the seasonal components. If we want to take into consideration the disturbance term then a possible choice criterion is based on the minimization of

$$\frac{\sigma^{*2}}{\sigma^2} = \sum_{i=-m}^{m} \theta_i^2.$$

In order to express this problem in mathematical terms, let us assume that the set of trend components forms a vector subspace of size k of the space formed by the time-series, generated by $z^1, \ldots, z^k$; by the same token, let us assume that the set of seasonal components be a subspace of size l generated by $s^1, \ldots, s^l$. The linear transformation moving average M must satisfy the conditions

$$Mz^i = z^i, \quad i = 1, \ldots, k$$
$$Ms^j = 0, \quad j = 1, \ldots, l.$$

If these conditions can be reduced to a finite number p of independent affine constraints on the θ_j, the set of moving averages of order $2m + 1 \geq p$ satisfying these conditions forms an affine subspace $\mathcal{M}$ of size $2m + 1 - p$.

This average will minimize the reduction ratio if the coefficients θ_i are solutions to (Bongard, 1962)

$$\min_{\theta_i} \sum_{i=-m}^{m} \theta_i^2$$

$$s.t. \ M \in \mathcal{M}.$$

Thus, we need to minimize the norm of the coefficient vector, knowing that it must belong to $\mathcal{M}$. The solution to this optimization problem is, therefore, the orthogonal projection of the origin on $\mathcal{M}$ (cf. appendix 3.14).

If, for example, we are looking for an average of this kind which sets to zero the seasonal component of period 12 (*l*-11) and preserving the polynomials of third degree (k=4), there are four constraints for the trend

$$\sum_{i=-m}^{m} \theta_i = 1, \quad \sum_{i=-m}^{m} i\theta_i = 0, \quad \sum_{i=-m}^{m} i^2\theta_i = 0, \quad \sum_{i=-m}^{m} i^3\theta_i = 0,$$

and eleven constraints for the seasonal component

$$\sum_{i=-m}^{m} \theta_i \cos \frac{2\pi i j}{12} = 0; \quad j = 1, \ldots, 6,$$

$$\sum_{i=-m}^{m} \theta_i \sin \frac{2\pi i j}{12} = 0; \quad j = 1, \ldots, 5.$$

The average must have at least $2m+1 = 15$ elements. Choosing this order will correspond to a subspace $\mathcal{M}$ containing a single point; that will be the solution and we will not have applied the reduction ratio criterion. If we increase the number of terms of the average to $2m+1 = 19$, $\mathcal{M}$ has size 4; there are four degrees of freedom to better choose the coefficients θ_i.

The obtained average is as

$$M = \{[19]; \frac{1}{4032}[-267, -122, 23, 168, 313, 458, 603, 336, 336, \mathbf{336}]\}.$$
(3.10)

It is characterized by

$$\frac{\sigma^{*2}}{\sigma^2} = 0.13,$$

$$\tau = 12.4.$$

3.9 Distribution of the Moving Average Coefficients

3.9.1 Smoothing [Macaulay (1931)]

Whenever we use a moving average to isolate the trend component, this average must reduce the size of the original oscillations in the series. The transformed series shows a smoother profile. The moving averages preserving the polynomials of degree 1 and having positive coefficients have this property. Actually, in this case, the sequence of coefficients can be considered as a probability distribution and the point

$$[t, x_t^*] = \left(\sum_{i=-m}^{m} \theta_i(t+i), \sum_{i=-m}^{m} \theta_i x_{t+i} \right),$$

is the center of mass for the points

$$[t+i, x_{t+i}], \quad i = -m, \ldots, m.$$

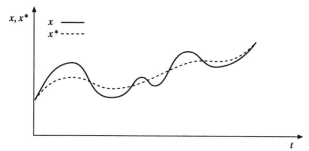

Figure 3.12　Original and Transformed Series

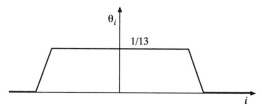

Figure 3.13　Arithmetic Average on 13 Points

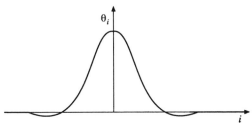

Figure 3.14　Spencer Average on 15 Points

Such an average reduces the size of the concavities and convexities in the original series (cf. figure 3.12).

The transformed series $[t, s_t^*]$ may not always be interpreted as a center of mass. In fact, the moving averages which preserve local polynomials often have some negative coefficients. The problem is now to find another criterion ensuring that the transformed series is smooth.

Let us consider the series

$$x_t = \begin{cases} 0, & \text{if } t \neq 0, \\ 1, & \text{if } t = 0. \end{cases}$$

Its transformation by a moving average is given by

$$x_t^* = \begin{cases} 0, & \text{if } t \leq -m-1, \\ \theta_t, & \text{if } -m < t < m, \\ 0, & \text{if } t \geq m+1 . \end{cases}$$

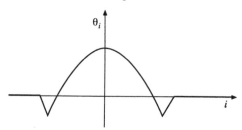

Figure 3.15   Average on 13 Points Preserving Local Polynomials of Degree 2

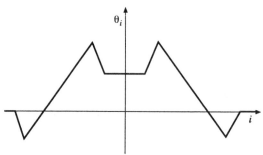

Figure 3.16   Average on 19 Points Obtained as a Minimization of σ^{*2}/σ^2

This transformation is smooth if the function providing the coefficients of the moving average is smooth. We could then see how these coefficients behave as a function of their index. In figures 3.13 to 3.16 we provide the profiles corresponding to some of the moving averages previously studied. Among the four averages presented in the figures, only the Spencer average does not show any discontinuity in correspondence to the extreme values of the coefficients.

Generally, the "smoothness" of the coefficient distribution curve can be measured as

$$Q = \sum_i (\Delta^3 \theta_i)^2.$$

This quantity is zero when the θ_i's are on a parabola; in the general case, Q measures the deviation between the parabola and the actual curve for the θ_i.

3.9.2 Henderson Averages

The suggestion by Henderson was to choose among the moving averages of order $2m + 1$ which preserve the polynomials of degree 2, the one minimizing Q.

The coefficients are obtained as solutions to the constrained minimization problem

$$\min_{\theta_i} \sum_i (\Delta^3 \theta_i)^2$$

$$\text{s.t.} \begin{cases} \sum_{i=-m}^{m} \theta_i = 1, \\[2mm] \sum_{i=-m}^{m} i\theta_i = 0, \\[2mm] \sum_{i=-m}^{m} i^2\theta_i = 0. \end{cases}$$

Making use of the results presented in the appendix, we can see that solving for the coefficients we get

$$\theta_i = \frac{315\left((n-1)^2 - i^2\right)\left(n^2 - i^2\right)\left((n+1)^2 - i^2\right)\left(3n^2 - 16 - 11i^2\right)}{8n(n^2-1)(4n^2-1)(4n^2-9)(4n^2-25)},$$

(3.11)

with $n = m + 2$. These averages are symmetric and the sum of the coefficients is equal to 1 by construction. For example, the Henderson average with fifteen terms ($m = 7$, $n = 9$) is equal to

$$M = \{[15], \frac{1}{193154}[-2652, -3732, -2730, 3641, 16016, 28182, 37422, \mathbf{40860}]\}.$$

Such averages do not, in general, eliminate the seasonal components. A good choice of m may allow a good approximation of this constraint. Thus, a Henderson average with 33 points gets rid of 98.5% of the seasonal component of period 12. An average on 37 points gets rid of 95%. The number of terms needed will be much higher if we decided to impose the elimination of the seasonal components in the minimization problem.

For quarterly series (period 4) we adopt a five-term Henderson average

$$M = \{[5], \frac{1}{286}[-21, 84, \mathbf{160}]\}.$$

3.10 Repeated Moving Averages

3.10.1 Summary of the Properties of the Main Averages

Appealing moving averages must respond to certain criteria, as we have shown: preservation of the trend, elimination of the seasonal component, high capability of reducing the residual variance, smoothness of

Table 3.7 *Synthesis of the Properties of the Various Averages*

Average	Preservation of the Trend	Seasonality Set to 0	Reduction Power	Series Smoothing	Simplicity of the Coefficients
Arithmetic	0	++	+	−	++
Spencer	+	+	+	+	++
Preserving Local Polyn.	++	+	+	−	0
Henderson	+	+	+	++	+
Constrained Minimization	+	+	++	−	0

Note: Properties of the average: (very strong ++); (strong +); (neutral 0); (weak −).

the coefficients, simplicity of the coefficients, elimination of the phase effect, and so on.

Each moving average previously presented was built to satisfy certain criteria, and its behavior with respect to other criteria has been examined afterwards. Each average responds to specific criteria. Combining these averages with each other will allow the derivation of moving averages satisfying a larger number of criteria. Before giving an example of such a combination, we recall in table 3.7 the relevant properties of the main averages.

3.10.2 The Program Census X11

The program Census X11 (Shiskin, Young, and Musgrave, 1965; Laroque, 1977) in its quarterly version is articulated in the following steps.

First Trend Estimation We compute an approximation of the trend applying an arithmetic average eliminating the seasonal components of order 4

$$M_0 = \{[5]; \frac{1}{8}[1, 2, \mathbf{2}]\},$$

so that the first estimate of the trend is

$$\hat{z} = M_0 x.$$

First Estimate of the Detrended Series We subtract the estimated trend from the initial series

$$\widehat{s+u} = x - \hat{z} = (I - M_0)x.$$

First Estimate of the Seasonal Component A five-year moving average of the type

$$M_1 = \{[17]; \frac{1}{9}[1, 0, 0, 0, 2, 0, 0, 0, 3]\},$$

is applied to $\widehat{s+u}$. Then we apply the average

$$I - M_0 = \{[5]; \frac{1}{8}[-1, -2, 6]\}$$

to the series thus obtained so that the sum of seasonal coefficients is approximately zero. The first estimate of s is given by

$$\hat{s} = (I - M_0)M_1(I - M_0)x$$

$$= M_1(I - M_0)^2 x.$$

First Estimate of a Seasonally Adjusted Series We obtain a seasonally adjusted series by subtracting the estimated seasonal coefficients from the orginal series

$$\hat{x}_{SA} = x - \hat{s} = \left(I - M_1(I - M_0)^2\right)x.$$

Second Estimate of the Trend We apply to x_{SA} a five-term Henderson average

$$M_2 = \{[5]; \frac{1}{286}[-21, 84, 160]\},$$

which provides a second estimate of the trend

$$\hat{\hat{z}} = M_2\hat{x}_{SA} = M_2\left(I - M_1(I - M_0)^2\right)x.$$

Second Estimate of the Detrended Series It is obtained by subtracting $\hat{\hat{z}}$ from the original series

$$\widehat{s+u} = \left(I - M_2\left(I - M_1(I - M_0)^2\right)\right)x.$$

Second Estimate of the Seasonality A seven-year moving average M_3 is applied to the seasonal coefficients

$$M_3 = \{[25], \frac{1}{15}[1, 0, 0, 0, 2, 0, 0, 0, 3, 0, 0, 0, 3]\}.$$

The result is transformed by $I - M_0$ so that the sum of the coefficients is approximately zero. We have

$$\hat{\hat{s}} = (I - M_0)M_3\left(I - M_2[I - M_1(I - M_0)^2]\right)x.$$

Table 3.8 *Coefficients of the Average I-M*

i	θ_i	i	θ_i	i	θ_i	i	θ_i
0	0.856	7	0.029	14	0.016	21	0.000
1	0.051	8	-0.097	15	-0.005	22	0.002
2	0.041	9	0.038	16	-0.010	23	0.000
3	0.050	10	0.025	17	0.000	24	0.000
4	-0.140	11	0.012	18	0.008	25	0.000
5	0.055	12	-0.053	19	-0.002	26	0.000
6	0.034	13	0.021	20	-0.030	27	0.000

The seasonal component is a moving average. Its order can be computed using the formula to derive the order of a product

$$order(I - M_0)^2 = 2\,order(I - M_0) - 1$$
$$= 10 - 1 = 9,$$

$$order[I - M_1(I - M_0)^2] = order(M_1) + order(I - M_0)^2 - 1$$
$$= 17 + 9 - 1 = 25,$$

$$order\{I - M_2[I - M_1(I - M_0)^2]\} = order(M_2) + 25 - 1$$
$$= 30 - 1 = 29,$$

$$order\ M_3\{I - M_2[I - M_1(I - M_0)^2]\} = order(M_3) + 29 - 1$$
$$= 25 + 29 - 1 = 53,$$

$$order(M) = order(I - M_0) + 53 - 1 = 5 + 53 - 1 = 57.$$

The average has twenty-eight quarters on each side besides the current quarter. Since all averages involved are symmetric, M is symmetric as well. Table 3.8 shows the coefficients of the average $I - M$ used to pass from the original series to the seasonally adjusted series. The distribution of the coefficients of this moving average can be represented graphically as in figure 3.17.

The troughs of the curve correspond to the quarters of the same type as the current one. The weights are negligible for $i > 16$.

The gain function (shown in figure 3.18)

$$|\Theta(e^{i\omega})| = \left| \sum_{j=-m}^{m} \theta_j \cos j\omega \right|$$

clearly shows the preservation of the trend ($|\Theta(e^{i\omega})|$ is close to 1 at low

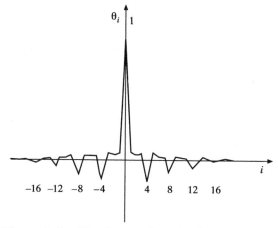

Figure 3.17   Distribution of the Coefficients of $I - M$.

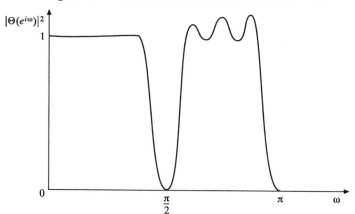

Figure 3.18   Square of the Gain of $I - M$.

frequencies) and the elimination of the seasonal components of period 4 ($|\Theta(e^{i2\pi/4})| \approx 0, |\Theta(e^{i4\pi/4})| \approx 0, \dots$).

Note that there is a monthly version of the program Census X11 and that both versions can be adapted to the multiplicative case. The latter case can be treated by simply applying the additive version to a logarithmic transformation of the series. Also, there exist options allowing the number of working days, the outliers, etc. to be taken into consideration.

3.11 Treatment of the Extreme Points in the Series

When the index of the series under analysis does not span from $-\infty$ to $+\infty$, but can take on a finite set of values $t = 0, \dots, T$, the application of a centered moving average M of order $2M + 1$ allows the derivation of the transformed series just for the dates

$$t = m, \ldots, T - m.$$

In particular, we are not able to derive a seasonally adjusted series for the most recent values. It is therefore necessary to extend the method in order to include the treatment of extreme points in the series. We can think of two approaches.

1 For the recent data x_t, $t = T - m + 1, \ldots, T$, use noncentered moving averages of the type

$$x_{T,0}^* = M_0 s_T = \sum_{i+-m}^{0} \theta_{i,0} x_{T+i},$$

$$s_{T-1,1}^* = M_1 x_T = \sum_{i=-m}^{1} \theta_{i,1} x_{T-1+i},$$

$$\vdots$$

$$x_{T-m+1,m-1}^* = M_{m-1} x_T = \sum_{i=-m}^{m-1} \theta_{i,m-1} x_{T-m+1+i}.$$

These averages M_j which allow the transformed series to be derived, are different from each other in that they involve a different number of terms of the series used in the adjustment but also for the value of the various coefficients. The use of such moving averages will lead to readjust the seasonally adjusted values each time that a new observation is available. Thus the value at time T of the transformed series denoted by x_T^* will be equal to $x_{T,0}^*$ if the data are available up to time T, to $x_{T,1}^*$ if they are available up to time $T + m - 1$. A stable value will be computed only starting from time $T + m$, after which x_T^* will always be equal to $M x_T$.

2 A second approach consists in extrapolating the observed series x_t, $t = 0, \ldots, T$ to obtain some forecast $\tilde{x}_t$ of x_t for $t = T + 1, \ldots, T + m$. Generally, $\tilde{x}_t$ is computed as a linear combination of the observed values x_t, $t = 0, \ldots, T$; we can then apply the centered moving average M to the extrapolated series. The derivation of the extrapolated series must be performed again every time that we have a new observation available. For example, let us consider the transformed value of x_T according to this approach

$$x_T^* = \sum_{i=-m}^{0} \theta_i x_{T+i} + \sum_{j=1}^{m} \theta_j \tilde{x}_{T+j}.$$

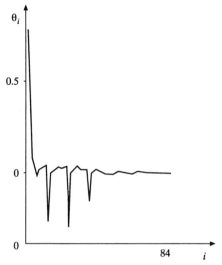
Figure 3.19 Coefficient Distribution for M_0.

The forecast $\tilde{x}_{T+j}$ is defined as a linear combination of the observed values of x; let us consider it as

$$\tilde{x}_{T+j} = \sum_{i=-m}^{0} b_{ij} x_{T+i}, \quad j = 1, \ldots, m.$$

We have

$$x_T^* = \sum_{i=-m}^{0} \theta_i x_{T+i} + \sum_{j=1}^{m} \theta_j \sum_{i=-m}^{0} b_{ij} x_{T+i}$$

$$= \sum_{i=-m}^{0} \left(\theta_i + \sum_{j=1}^{m} b_{ij} \theta_j \right) x_{T+i}$$

$$= \sum_{i=-m}^{0} \theta_{i,0} x_{T+i},$$

from which we see that this second approach is equivalent to applying noncentered moving averages in the same way as the first method proposed.

We could have modified both approaches so as to have all moving averages with the same number of terms. In such a case, x_T^* would be defined as

$$x_{T,0}^* = \sum_{i=-2m}^{0} \theta_{i,0} x_{T+i}$$

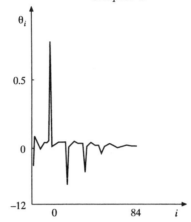

Figure 3.20   Coefficient Distribution for M_{12}

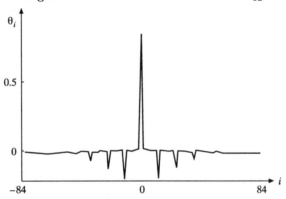

Figure 3.21   Coefficient Distribution for M_{84}

and s^*_{T-m+1} as

$$x^*_{T-m+1,M-1} = \sum_{i=-m-1}^{m-1} \theta_{i,m-1} x^*_{T-m+1+i}.$$

Note that in this case we would need to modify the extrapolation expressions in the second approach.

An important aspect of this methodology is the choice of the various noncentered averages $M_0, M_1, \ldots, M_{m-1}$. In this respect, the second approach seems more manageable because it implies the derivation of optimal forecasts of future values of x with the methods described in chapter 6 (cf. Cleveland and Tiao, 1976; Dagum, 1979). For a given sequence of moving averages, it is possible to study their properties *ex post*; that is how the coefficients, the variance reduction, the gain evolve. We will present such an analysis for the case of the monthly version of the seasonal adjustment program Census X11 (Wallis, 1982). The symmetric

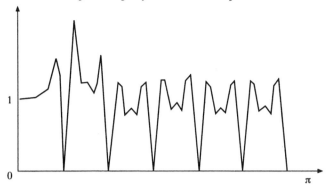

Figure 3.22 Square of the Gain for M_0

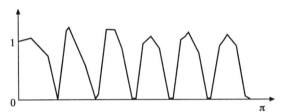

Figure 3.23 Square of the Gain for M_{12}

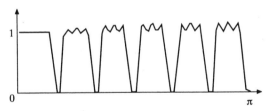

Figure 3.24 Square of the Gain for M_{84}

average of this program computes the seasonally adjusted value using observations spanning over seven years, on each side, that is, eighty-four months. In order to extend the seasonal adjustment we need then to define eighty-four noncentered moving averages. The distributions of the coefficients of M_0, M_{12}, and M_{84} are given in figures 3.19, 3.20, and 3.21. Note that M_{84} is symmetric. The visual inspection of the gain function for these three moving averages is somewhat interesting. We can see that the gain functions of noncentered averages are quite different from the ones of symmetric averages, in particular for frequencies close to the annual cycle.

The ratios for the residual variance reduction are given in table 3.9.

Table 3.9 *Variance Reduction Ratios*

Moving Average	M_0	M_1	M_2	M_3	M_4	M_{12}	M_{24}	M_{36}	M_{84}
σ^{*2}/σ^2	0.93	0.84	0.79	0.79	0.80	0.72	0.74	0.78	0.78

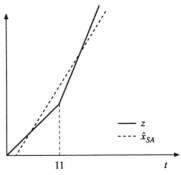

Figure 3.25   Original and Estimated Trend with the Regression Method

3.12 Structural Change

One of the main advantages of the moving average method is that it is better suited than regression to treat abrupt changes in the series. Let us consider a simple example given by the series

$$x_t = \begin{cases} t + (-1)^t, & \text{if } t \leq 11 , \\ 2t - 11 + (-1)^t, & \text{if } t \geq 12 . \end{cases}$$

The trend, defined by

$$z_t = \begin{cases} t & \text{if } t \leq 11, \\ 2t - 11 & \text{if } t \geq 11 , \end{cases}$$

is linear for each of the sub-periods $t \leq 11$ and $t \geq 11$, but it is clearly not linear for the whole period. The seasonal component $s_t = (-1)^t$ retains the same form for the whole period.

Let us assume that we do not suspect the presence of a structural break in the trend and use the regression method with a linear model of the type $x_t = at + b + c(-1)^t$. We would estimate the series free of seasonal components (here coinciding with the trend) as $x_{SA,t} = \hat{a}t + \hat{b}$ (cf. figure 3.25).

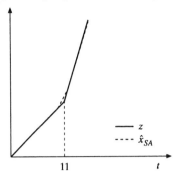

Figure 3.26 Observed and Estimated Trend by the Moving Average Method

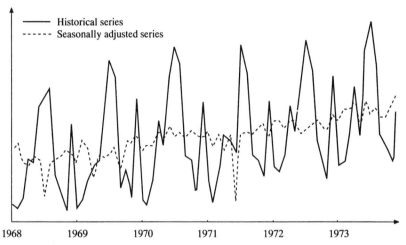

Figure 3.27 Passenger Traffic January 1968–December 1973

If we use a moving average method, for example an average of the type

$$\left\{[3]; \left(\frac{1}{4}, \frac{\mathbf{1}}{\mathbf{2}}\right)\right\}$$

which preserves the polynomials of degree 1 but eliminates the seasonal component $s_t = (-1)^t$. The estimated seasonally adjusted series will be

$$x_{SA,t} = \frac{1}{4}x_{t-1} + \frac{1}{2}x_t + \frac{1}{4}x_{t+1}.$$

$x_{SA,t}$ will be equal to the trend for all values of t except for $t = 11$.

Looking at figure (3.26) it is clear that for this example the latter method gives a better approximation. The choice of a moving period for the computations (rather than a fixed one in the regression) allows one to eliminate the effects of a structural change rapidly.

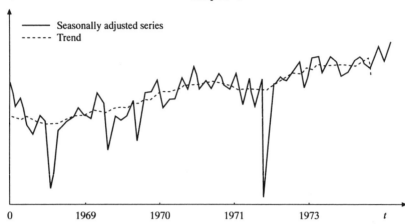

Figure 3.28 Passenger Traffic January 1968–December 1973

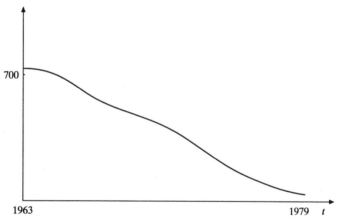

Figure 3.29 Evolution of Seasonal Coefficients for August

3.13 Application to the Passenger Traffic Series

The additive and multiplicative versions of the program Census X11
have been applied to the series for train passenger traffic presented in
chapter 1. The results are fairly close to each other for the two versions,
so that we report here only those of the additive version. In figure 3.27
we present the original and the seasonally adjusted series; in figure 3.28
the seasonally adjusted series and the trend estimated by Census X11
for the period January 1968–December 1973. It is clear that the trend
gives a better idea of the changes in the medium-term evolutions than
in the regression method where the estimated trend was a line.

By the same token, the method leads to a higher degree of flexibility
in the estimation of the seasonal components. In the regression method,

Table 3.10 *Seasonal Coefficients*

	Jan.	Feb.	Mar.	Apr.	May	June	July	Aug.	Sep.	Oct.	Nov.	Dec.
1963	-418	-543	-343	-11	-126	331	988	726	-22	-291	-442	143
1964	-441	-543	-337	-4	-116	332	965	712	-25	-287	-447	146
1965	-400	-530	-330	3	-96	335	919	681	-35	-280	-444	154
1966	-388	-504	-313	17	-79	338	854	632	-52	-264	-438	175
1967	-376	-473	-294	31	-64	339	780	584	-74	-243	-428	197
1968	-362	-450	-266	46	-58	338	714	633	-98	-221	-417	219
1969	-348	-425	-245	60	-53	335	664	491	-117	-208	-404	232
1970	-342	-404	-224	80	-58	339	634	451	-135	-210	-394	248
1971	-338	-386	-212	101	-69	348	621	411	-144	-217	-390	248
1972	-330	-376	-199	114	-76	360	622	363	-144	-225	-390	257
1973	-322	-360	-194	118	-77	373	635	302	-143	-227	-384	271
1974	-316	-350	-189	108	-68	390	647	237	-152	-220	-367	280
1975	-315	-342	-186	98	-52	402	652	171	-163	-206	-344	289
1976	-309	-344	-181	79	-26	410	654	114	-178	-193	-316	291
1977	-306	-341	-176	68	-1	410	651	69	-193	-186	-290	298
1978	-302	-343	-172	59	21	412	644	42	-209	-184	-270	301
1979	-300	-341	-168	55	30	411	637	30	-216	-181	-259	302

they were chosen constants. The moving average approach allows one to get varying coefficients according to the year of reference and to study their evolution.

As an example, we give the values of the seasonal coefficients for the month of August in figure 3.29 and table 3.10. The inspection of the coefficients shows that they are positive (corresponding to a higher than average demand in this period), and that they decrease with time. The growth of traffic in the month of August as a function of time, consequence of both a medium-term growth (in the trend) and of a decreasing seasonal component, is less pronounced than the growth in other months; in fact, between 1963 and 1979 the traffic for the month of August grew at about a 14% rate whereas the average growth had been 60% (cf. table 3.11).

3.14 Appendix
Derivation of the Averages Defined in 3.8 and 3.9

The coefficients of these averages are obtained as a solution to a constrained minimization problem of the type

$$\min_{\theta} \quad \Omega\theta$$

$$s.t. \quad \mathbf{R}'\theta = \alpha$$

Table 3.11 *Seasonally Adjusted Series*

	Jan.	Feb.	Mar.	Apr.	May	June	July	Aug.	Sep.	Oct.	Nov.	Dec.
1963	2168	2103	2163	2101	2036	2079	2152	2124	2112	2141	2072	2277
1964	2121	2143	2137	2124	2216	2128	2235	2248	2215	2157	2217	2124
1965	2070	2170	2100	2187	2116	2275	2271	2179	2175	2150	2204	2206
1966	2198	2144	2173	1973	2189	2162	2176	2268	2212	2204	2188	2155
1967	2226	2063	2174	2179	2174	2141	2100	2186	2174	2163	2098	2323
1968	2196	2242	2126	2092	2173	2147	1867	2106	2136	2157	2201	2172
1969	2146	2275	2226	2025	2173	2156	2170	2234	2049	2266	2260	2321
1970	2196	2227	2229	2338	2277	2383	2278	2320	2288	2346	2304	2289
1971	2346	2221	2332	2203	2333	1827	2307	2327	2322	2354	2399	2289
1972	2414	2410	2351	2408	2394	2324	2349	2396	2411	2377	2368	2460
1973	2403	2472	2473	2543	2358	2556	2454	2501	2439	2437	2519	2591
1974	2539	2598	2610	2602	2573	2630	2680	2807	2759	2745	2527	2596
1975	2796	1770	2782	2825	2847	2885	2946	2947	3038	2960	2932	2977
1976	2976	3012	2985	2727	3002	3020	3051	2939	2942	2995	3023	3016
1977	3012	2927	2972	2910	3054	3053	2998	3026	3032	3152	3153	3077
1978	3122	3200	3478	3274	3120	3100	3100	3137	3193	3134	3166	3310
1979	3613	2985	3040	3212	3361	3271	3300	3254	3065	3266	3302	3239

Note: Seasonal adjustment by the additive version of Census X11.

where $\boldsymbol{\Omega}$ is a symmetric, positive, definite matrix of order $2m + 1$, $\mathbf{R}$ is a $(2m + 1, k)$ matrix, and $\boldsymbol{\alpha}$ is a vector of size k.

Hence for the Henderson averages we have

$$\boldsymbol{\theta}'\boldsymbol{\Omega}\boldsymbol{\theta} = \sum_i (\Delta^3 \theta_i)^2$$

$$\mathbf{R} = \begin{pmatrix} 1 & -m & m^2 \\ 1 & -m+1 & (m-1)^2 \\ \vdots & \vdots & \vdots \\ 1 & -1 & 1 \\ 1 & 0 & 0 \\ 1 & 1 & 1 \\ \vdots & \vdots & \vdots \\ 1 & m & m^2 \end{pmatrix}, \quad \boldsymbol{\alpha} = \begin{pmatrix} 1 \\ 0 \\ 0 \end{pmatrix}.$$

This minimization problem is solved by considering a vector of Lagrange multipliers $2\boldsymbol{\lambda}$ of order k searching for an unconstrained minimum of

$$\boldsymbol{\theta}'\boldsymbol{\Omega}\boldsymbol{\theta} - 2\boldsymbol{\theta}'\mathbf{R}\boldsymbol{\lambda}.$$

The first-order condition can be written as

$$\Omega\boldsymbol{\theta} - \mathbf{R}\boldsymbol{\lambda} = \mathbf{0} \Rightarrow \boldsymbol{\theta} = \Omega^{-1}\mathbf{R}\boldsymbol{\lambda}.$$

Replacing $\boldsymbol{\theta}$ by this expression in the constraint $\mathbf{R}'\boldsymbol{\theta} = \boldsymbol{\alpha}$ we get

$$\boldsymbol{\alpha} = \mathbf{R}'\Omega^{-1}\mathbf{R}\boldsymbol{\lambda} \Rightarrow \boldsymbol{\lambda} = (\mathbf{R}'\Omega^{-1}\mathbf{R})^{-1}\boldsymbol{\alpha}$$

and

$$\boldsymbol{\theta} = \Omega^{-1}\mathbf{R}(\mathbf{R}'\Omega^{-1}\mathbf{R})^{-1}\boldsymbol{\alpha}.$$

3.15 Exercises

Exercise 3.1: Show that the eigenvectors of a moving average are of the type $x_t = P(t)\lambda^t$ where $P(t)$ is a polynomial in t, and λ is a complex number. Is the reverse true?

Exercise 3.2: Verify that necessary and sufficient conditions for a moving average to preserve the polynomials of degree 1 are such that

$$\sum_{i=-m}^{m} \theta_{m+i} = 1 \quad \text{and} \quad \sum_{i=-m}^{m} i\theta_{m+i} = 0.$$

Do they imply that the moving average is symmetric?

Exercise 3.3: Show the expressions of $\Delta^2, \Delta^3, \ldots, \Delta^p$ as a function of the lag operator L.

Exercise 3.4: Verify that a moving average preserving $x_t = t^5$ preserves all polynomials of degree less than or equal to 5 as well.

Exercise 3.5: Which conditions can be imposed on the coefficients to eliminate the phase effect for the series $x_t = 2^t e^{i\omega t}, \ \omega \in \mathbb{R}$?

Exercise 3.6: Derive the smallest order moving averages preserving the polynomials of degree 1 and eliminating the seasonal component of order 4

$$s_t = (-1)^t, (i)^t, (-i)^t.$$

Exercise 3.7: Show that any moving average can be decomposed as a function of the powers of the forward difference ∇ and of the backward difference Δ knowing that $L = I - \Delta$ and that $F = \nabla - I$.

Exercise 3.8: Show that the symmetric moving averages can be decomposed as functions of the powers of the operator $L + F$.

Exercise 3.9: Let $\tilde{M}$ and M be two averages such that $\mathcal{N}(\tilde{M}) \supset \mathcal{N}(M)$. Show that it is possible to find an average $\check{M}$ such that $\tilde{M} = \check{M}M$. Analyze $\mathcal{N}(\check{M})$.

Exercise 3.10: Compute the quantity $Q = \sum_i (\Delta^3 \theta_i)^2$ for a moving average of order $2m + 1$ the coefficients of which are given by

$$\theta_i = \begin{cases} 0, & \text{if } |\,i\,| \geq m + 1, \\ (2m + 1)^{-1}, & \text{if } |\,i\,| \leq m. \end{cases}$$

Show how Q varies with m.

4

Exponential Smoothing Methods

4.1 Simple Exponential Smoothing

4.1.1 Introduction

We have a time series available, that is T real numbers $(x_1, \ldots, x_T)$ indexed by $t = 1, \ldots, T$. Suppose we are at T and we want to forecast the value x_{T+k}; let us denote such a forecast by $\hat{x}_T(k)$ where k is the *horizon* of the forecast.

Definition 4.1: *The value $\hat{x}_T(k)$ given by the simple exponential smoothing method is*

$$\hat{x}_T(k) = (1 - \beta) \sum_{j=0}^{T-1} \beta^j x_{T-j}, \tag{4.1}$$

with β called smoothing parameter $0 < \beta < 1$. *

Formula (4.1) rests on a simple idea: we are assuming that the farther the observations are from the date T at which we compute the forecast, the less they should influence it. Moreover, we consider that this influence decreases exponentially. We easily see that the closer the smoothing parameter is to 1, the more influenced the forecast is by observations distant in time. Also, the forecast is more rigid in the sense that it is

---

* Note that sometimes the smoothing parameter is denoted by $(1 - \beta)$.

not very sensitive to short-term fluctuations. On the other hand, the closer the parameter β is to zero, the softer is the forecast, that is it is influenced by recent observations.

We need to note that, if β is chosen independently of k, $\hat{x}_T(k)$ does not depend upon k; for this reason, from here on, we will use the notation $\hat{x}_T$ rather than $\hat{x}_T(k)$.

4.1.2 Other Interpretations

From formula (4.1) we can deduce that

$$\hat{x}_T = \beta\hat{x}_{T-1} + (1 - \beta)x_T. \tag{4.2}$$

The forecast $\hat{x}_T$ appears as a weighted average between the forecast $\hat{x}_{T-1}$ done at time $(T-1)$ and the last observation x_T, the stronger the weight given to this observation the weaker is β.

Expression (4.2) can be written

$$\hat{x}_T = \hat{x}_{T-1} + (1 - \beta)(x_T - \hat{x}_{T-1}), \tag{4.3}$$

where $\hat{x}_T$ can be interpreted as the forecast at the previous date $\hat{x}_{T-1}$ corrected by a term proportional to the last forecast error. The expression (4.3) is the one used in explanatory linear models to define shifting (or drifting) expectations: once $\hat{x}_T$ is solved for, it implies a distributed lag structure of the Koyck type (expressed in (4.1)).

We can also note that expressions (4.2) or (4.3) provide a simple updating procedure for forecast where the information supplied by the past is summarized in $\hat{x}_{T-1}$.

If we want to use formulas (4.2) or (4.3) we need to initialize the algorithm. The simplest way is to take $\hat{x}_1 = x_1$; however, it is clear that the chosen value for $\hat{x}_1$ has little influence on $\hat{x}_T$ when T is larger.*

The interpretation of such a procedure is useful because it will allow us to propose some generalizations of the method. Let us consider the minimization problem

$$\min_a \sum_{j=0}^{T-1} \beta^j (x_{T-j} - a)^2, \tag{4.4}$$

the solution to which is

$$\hat{a} = \left(\frac{1-\beta}{1-\beta^T}\right) \sum_{j=0}^{T-1} \beta^j x_{T-j}.$$

---

* The computational simplicity has been a strong argument in favor of the simple exponential smoothing for a long time; even with increased computer speed such an argument is still important when the number of series considered is large.

Hence, for T large enough

$$\hat{x}_T \approx \hat{a}.$$

$\hat{x}_T$ can be interpreted as the constant which fits the series the best in a neighborhood of T. The expression "neighborhood" translates the fact that in the expression (4.4) the influence of the observations decreases as we get far from the date T. Note that (4.4) can be interpreted as a weighted regression on a constant, with weights exponentially decreasing with the distance from T.

The latter interpretation shows that the method can be used only when the series can be approximated by a constant in a neighborhood of T. In particular, the method is to be avoided when the series exhibits a nonconstant trend or some fluctuations (these problems will be treated in more detail in chapter 5).

4.1.3 The Choice of the Smoothing Parameter

A further problem to analyze is the choice of β. In practice, the choice of β is oftentimes based on subjective criteria of forecast "rigidity" or of "flexibility" (cf. section 4.1.1). There exists, however, a more objective method which bases the choice of the constant upon the minimization of the forecast error sum of squares at dates $1, \ldots, T - k_0$ for a given horizon k_0

$$\sum_{t=1}^{T-k_0} \left(x_{t+k_0} - \hat{x}_t(k_0) \right)^2.$$

Thus, for $k_0 = 1$ we need to minimize

$$\sum_{t=1}^{T-1} \left(x_{t+1} - (1 - \beta) \sum_{j=0}^{t-1} \beta^j x_{t-j} \right)^2.$$

First of all, it is interesting to note that in general the influence of the choice of β on the results is not too strong for fairly large intervals of β. In order to show this point, we will refer to an example taken from Cox (1961). Let us suppose that x_t is a random variable such that

$$E(x_t) = 0, \ \forall \ \text{integer } t,$$

$$\text{var}\,(x_t) = E(x_t^2) = 1, \ \forall \ \text{integer } t,$$

$$\text{cov}\,(x_t, x_{t+h}) = E(x_t\, x_{t+h}) = \rho^{|h|}, \ \forall \ \text{integers } t, h,$$

with $|\,\rho\,| < 1$. This set of random variables will be treated in detail in chapter 5 as a first-order autoregressive process.

The k-step ahead forecast error with the simple exponential smoothing method can be measured as

$$D_\rho(k, \beta) = E \left(x_{T+k} - \hat{x}_T(k) \right)^2, \ k > 0,$$

where

$$\hat{x}_T(k) = (1 - \beta) \sum_{j=0}^{\infty} \beta^j x_{T-j},$$

which differs from (4.1) because the finite sum has been replaced by its limit; this modification is a minor one if T is sufficiently large.

We have then

$$E \left(x_{T+k} - \hat{x}_T(k) \right)^2 = E \left(x_{T+k}^2 \right) - 2E \left(x_{T+k} \hat{x}_T(k) \right) + E \left(\hat{x}_T^2(k) \right).$$

Postponing to chapter 5 the discussion of why the expectation operator and the infinite sum operator can be interchanged, we can consider the three terms on the right-hand side as

$$E \left(x_{T+k}^2 \right) = 1,$$

$$E \left(x_{T+k} \hat{x}_T(k) \right) = E \left(x_{T+k}(1 - \beta) \sum_{j=0}^{\infty} \beta^j x_{T-j} \right)$$

$$= (1 - \beta) \sum_{j=0}^{\infty} \beta^j \rho^{k+j}$$

$$= \frac{(1 - \beta)\rho^k}{(1 - \beta\rho)}.$$

$$E(\hat{x}_T^2(k)) = (1 - \beta)^2 \ E \left(\sum_{j=0}^{\infty} \beta^j x_{T-j} \sum_{i=0}^{\infty} \beta^i x_{T-i} \right)$$

$$= (1 - \beta)^2 \sum_{j=0}^{\infty} \sum_{i=0}^{\infty} \beta^{i+j} \rho^{|i-j|}$$

$$= (1 - \beta)^2 \sum_{j=0}^{\infty} \beta^{2j} + 2(1 - \beta)^2 \sum_{i=0}^{\infty} \sum_{i>j} \beta^{i+j} \rho^{i-j}$$

$$= \frac{(1 - \beta)^2}{1 - \beta^2} + 2(1 - \beta)^2 \sum_{j=0}^{\infty} \beta^{2j} \sum_{h=1}^{\infty} \beta^h \rho^h$$

$$= \frac{(1 - \beta)^2}{1 - \beta^2} + \frac{2(1 - \beta)^2 \beta\rho}{(1 - \beta^2)(1 - \beta\rho)}.$$

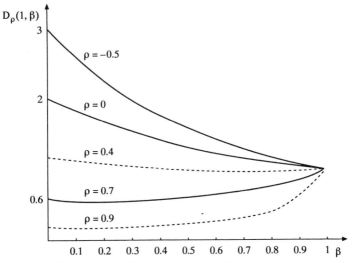

Figure 4.1   Forecast Error as a Function of β and ρ

Hence, we can write

$$D_\rho(k, \beta) = 1 + \frac{1 - \beta}{1 + \beta} + \frac{2(1 - \beta)^2 \beta \rho}{(1 - \beta^2)(1 - \beta\rho)} - \frac{2(1 - \beta)\rho^k}{1 - \beta\rho}$$

$$= \frac{2}{1 + \beta} + \frac{2(1 - \beta)(\beta\rho - \rho^k - \beta\rho^k)}{(1 + \beta)(1 - \beta\rho)}.$$

In particular for $k = 1$ we have

$$D_\rho(1, \beta) = \frac{2(1 - \rho)}{(1 + \beta)(1 - \beta\rho)}.$$

Analyzing this function of β in the interval $(0 \leq \beta \leq 1)$ we note that

$$\frac{d \log D_\rho}{d\beta} = \frac{\rho + 2\beta\rho - 1}{(1 + \beta)(1 - \beta\rho)}.$$

If ρ is in the interval $(1/3, 1)$ the function has a minimum at $\frac{1-\rho}{2\rho}$; if ρ is in the interval $(-1, 1/3)$, the function is decreasing on $[0, 1]$. Therefore, the optimal β noted as $\bar{\beta}$ is

$$\bar{\beta} = \begin{cases} 1 & \text{if } -1 < \rho \leq 1/3, \\ \frac{1-\rho}{2\rho} & \text{if } 1/3 \leq \rho < 1. \end{cases}$$

Representing the function of β on a graph for different values of ρ (e.g., $\rho = -0.5$; $\rho = 0$; $\rho = 0.4$; $\rho = 0.7$; $\rho = 0.9$) we get figure 4.1.

We can see that for negative values of ρ the error is high and that for positive values of ρ (here $\rho = 0.4; \rho = 0.7; \rho = 0.9$), the curve is fairly flat if β is smaller than 0.7 or 0.8. Hence, we have verified on this example that if ρ is negative, the method gives bad results; moreover, if we think that ρ is definitely positive, the best values of β are 0.7 or 0.8. These are the most frequently used values (cf. Brown, 1962, chapter 8).

4.2 Double Exponential Smoothing

4.2.1 Rationale for the Method

In the previous section, we have shown that the single exponential smoothing was suitable for a series which could be approximated by a horizontal line near T. A straightforward generalization can be obtained if we assume that a series y_t can be approximated by a line in a neighborhood of T

$$y_t = a_1 + (t - T)a_2.$$

This suggests we use as a predictor the function

$$\hat{x}_T(k) = \hat{a}_1(T) + k\hat{a}_2(T), \tag{4.5}$$

where $\hat{a}_1(T)$ and $\hat{a}_2(T)$ are the values of a_1 and a_2 minimizing the expression

$$Q = \sum_{j=0}^{T-1} \beta^j (x_{T-j} - a_1 + a_2 j)^2. \tag{4.6}$$

The expressions of $\hat{a}_1(T)$ and $\hat{a}_2(T)$ can be derived by taking partial derivatives of Q. We have

$$\frac{\partial Q}{\partial a_1} = -2 \sum_{j=0}^{T-1} \beta^j \left(x_{T-j} - a_1 + a_2 j \right),$$

$$\frac{\partial Q}{\partial a_2} = 2 \sum_{j=0}^{T-1} j\beta^j \left(x_{T-j} - a_1 + a_2 j \right).$$

Equating these partial derivatives to zero we get

$$\sum_{j=0}^{T-1} \beta^j x_{T-j} - a_1 \sum_{j=0}^{T-1} \beta^j + a_2 \sum_{j=0}^{T-1} j\beta^j = 0,$$

$$\sum_{j=0}^{T-1} j\beta^j x_{T-j} - a_1 \sum_{j=0}^{T-1} j\beta^j + a_2 \sum_{J=0}^{T-1} j^2\beta^j = 0,$$

where replacing finite sums with infinite ones, that is

$$\sum_{j=0}^{T-1} \beta^j \text{ with } \frac{1}{1-\beta},$$

$$\sum_{j=0}^{T-1} j\beta^j \text{ with } \frac{\beta}{(1-\beta)^2},$$

$$\sum_{j=0}^{T-1} j^2\beta^j \text{ with } \frac{\beta(1+\beta)}{(1-\beta)^3};$$

we get

$$(1-\beta)\sum_{j=0}^{T-1}\beta^j x_{T-j} - a_1 + a_2\frac{\beta}{1-\beta} = 0,$$

$$(1-\beta)^2\sum_{j=0}^{T-1}j\beta^j x_{T-j} - a_1\beta + a_2\frac{\beta(1+\beta)}{1-\beta} = 0. \tag{4.7}$$

Denoting the smoothed series by

$$s_1(t) = (1-\beta)\sum_{j=0}^{t-1}\beta^j x_{t-j},$$

and the doubly smoothed series by

$$s_2(t) = (1-\beta)\sum_{j=0}^{t-1}\beta^j s_1(t-j),$$

we see immediately that

$$s_2(T) = (1-\beta)^2\sum_{j=0}^{T-1}\beta^j\sum_{i=0}^{T-j-1}\beta^i x_{T-j-i}$$

$$= (1-\beta)^2\sum_{j=0}^{T-1}\sum_{i=0}^{T-j-1}\beta^{i+j}x_{T-j-i}$$

$$= (1-\beta)^2\sum_{h=0}^{T-1}(h+1)\beta^h x_{T-h}$$

$$= (1-\beta)^2\sum_{h=0}^{T-1}h\beta^h x_{T-h} + (1-\beta)s_1(T).$$

The equations (4.7) can then be written as

$$s_1(T) - a_1 + a_2\frac{\beta}{(1-\beta)} = 0,$$

$$s_2(T) - (1-\beta)s_1(T) - a_1\beta + a_2\frac{\beta(1+\beta)}{(1-\beta)} = 0. \tag{4.8}$$

Solving for a_1 and a_2 we get

$$\hat{a}_1(T) = 2s_1(T) - s_2(T),$$

$$\hat{a}_2(T) = \frac{(1-\beta)}{\beta}\left(s_1(T) - s_2(T)\right). \qquad (4.9)$$

We can also express $s_1(T)$ and $s_2(T)$ as a function of $\hat{a}_1(T)$ and $\hat{a}_2(T)$

$$s_1(T) = \hat{a}_1(T) - \frac{\beta}{(1-\beta)}\hat{a}_2(T),$$

$$s_2(T) = \hat{a}_1(T) - 2\frac{\beta}{(1-\beta)}\hat{a}_2(T). \qquad (4.10)$$

4.2.2 Updating Formulas

In equation (4.9), we have expressed $\hat{a}_1(T)$ and $\hat{a}_2(T)$ as a function of $s_1(T)$ and $s_2(T)$, in order to obtain very simple updating formulas. In fact, from the definition of $s_1(T)$ and $s_2(T)$ we derive

$$s_1(T) = (1-\beta)x_T + \beta s_1(T-1),$$

$$s_2(T) = (1-\beta)s_1(T) + \beta s_2(T-1)$$

$$= (1-\beta)^2 x_T + \beta(1-\beta)s_1(T-1) + \beta s_2(T-1).$$

Using (4.9) we get

$$\hat{a}_1(T) = 2(1-\beta)x_T + 2\beta s_1(T-1) - (1-\beta)^2 x_T$$

$$- \beta(1-\beta)s_1(T-1) - \beta s_2(T-1)$$

$$= x_T(1-\beta^2) + \beta(\beta+1)s_1(T-1) - \beta s_2(T-1).$$

Using (4.10) this expression becomes

$$\hat{a}_1(T) = x_T(1-\beta^2) + \beta^2\left(\hat{a}_1(T-1) + \hat{a}_2(T-1)\right);$$

then, using (4.5) with $k = 1$

$$\hat{a}_1(T) = \hat{a}_1(T-1) + \hat{a}_2(T-1) + (1-\beta^2)\left(x_T - \hat{x}_{T-1}(1)\right).$$

By the same token, for $\hat{a}_2(T)$ we have

$$\hat{a}_2(T) = \frac{(1-\beta)}{\beta}\left(\beta(1-\beta)x_T + \beta^2 s_1(T-1) - \beta s_2(T-1)\right)$$

$$= (1-\beta)^2 x_T + \beta(1-\beta)s_1(T-1) - (1-\beta)s_2(T-1)$$

$$= (1-\beta)^2 x_T + \beta(1-\beta)\hat{a}_1(T-1) - \beta^2\hat{a}_2(T-1)$$

$$- (1-\beta)\hat{a}_1(T-1) + 2\beta\hat{a}_2(T-1)$$

$$= (1-\beta)^2 x_T - (1-\beta)^2\hat{a}_1(T-1) + (2\beta - \beta^2)\hat{a}_2(T-1),$$

where

$$\hat{a}_2(T) = \hat{a}_2(T-1) + (1-\beta)^2\left(x_T - \hat{x}_{T-1}(1)\right).$$

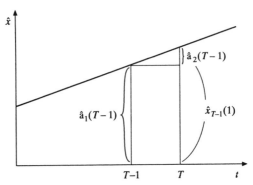

Figure 4.2   Forecast Lines

Finally, we get the updating formulas

$$\hat{a}_1(T) = \hat{a}_1(T-1) + \hat{a}_2(T-1) + \left(1 - \beta^2\right)\left(x_T - \hat{x}_{T-1}(1)\right),$$
$$\hat{a}_2(T) = \hat{a}_2(T-1) + \left(1 - \beta\right)^2\left(x_T - \hat{x}_{T-1}(1)\right).$$
(4.11)

In order to understand these formulas, let us assume that x_T was forecast perfectly at time $T-1$, i.e., that $\hat{x}_{T-1}(1) = x_T$. We have

$$\hat{a}_1(T) = \hat{a}_1(T-1) + \hat{a}_2(T-1),$$
$$\hat{a}_2(T) = \hat{a}_2(T-1).$$
(4.12)

The forecast lines are the same at time $T-1$ and at time T (cf. figure 4.2).

To obtain (4.11), we are adding terms (proportional to the one-step ahead forecast error at the previous date) to the change in the origin implied by the updating terms (4.12). Note that, in order to use formulas (4.11), we need to have initial values for the sequences $\hat{a}_1(t)$ and $\hat{a}_2(t)$. In general, we choose $\hat{a}_1(2) = x_2$ and $\hat{a}_2(2) = x_2 - x_1$.

4.3 The Generalized Exponential Smoothing

4.3.1 Fixed Transition Matrices

Let us try to generalize the methods described in the first two sections fitting a function in a neighborhood of T. In particular we will propose a function, more complicated than an affine one, which may have a periodic component so that it could be applied to seasonal series. We also want to keep an eye on the relative simplicity of the computation involved. This problem was solved by Brown (1962) who introduced the notion of a vector function with a fixed transition matrix.

Definition 4.2: *We define the vector*

$$\mathbf{f}(t) = \begin{pmatrix} f_1(t) \\ \vdots \\ f_n(t) \end{pmatrix},$$

with integer t as a vector function with a fixed transition matrix, if there exists a regular matrix $\mathbf{A}$ *such that*

$$\mathbf{f}(t) = \mathbf{A}\mathbf{f}(t-1), \ \forall \text{ integer } t.$$

The method of generalized exponential smoothing consists of fitting a function $\phi(t - T)$ to the series x_t in a neighborhood of T, with

$$\phi(t - T) = \sum_{i=1}^{n} a_i f_i(t),$$

and to use this fitted function for forecasting purposes

Let us show first that the class of functions $\phi(t)$ so defined includes the most common functions.

Constant Function : $\phi(t) = a$ We get the constant function by posing $f(t) = 1$, and $A = 1$. With such a function the method of generalized exponential smoothing coincides with the method of simple exponential smoothing.

Linear Function : $\phi(t) = a_1 + a_2 t$ We get the linear function by posing

$$f(t) = \begin{pmatrix} 1 \\ t \end{pmatrix},$$

so that

$$\mathbf{A} = \begin{pmatrix} 1 & 0 \\ 1 & 1 \end{pmatrix}, \quad \text{since} \quad \begin{pmatrix} 1 \\ t \end{pmatrix} = \begin{pmatrix} 1 & 0 \\ 1 & 1 \end{pmatrix} \begin{pmatrix} 1 \\ t - 1 \end{pmatrix}.$$

With this function the method of generalized exponential smoothing coincides with the double exponential smoothing.

Polynomials of Degree m We take as a basis the polynomials of the type

$$f_1(t) = 1, \quad f_2(t) = t,$$

$$f_3(t) = t(t-1)/2, \ldots, f_{m+1}(t) = \frac{t(t-1)\ldots(t-m+1)}{m!}.$$

Following the generalization of the Pascal triangle, we have

$$f_k(t) = f_{k-1}(t-1) + f_k(t-1), \quad k > 1.$$

Hence the vector

$$\mathbf{f}(t) = \begin{pmatrix} f_1(t) \\ \vdots \\ f_{m+1}(t) \end{pmatrix}$$

has a fixed transition matrix of the type

$$\mathbf{A} = \begin{pmatrix} 1 & 0 & 0 & \cdots & 0 \\ 1 & 1 & 0 & \cdots & 0 \\ 0 & 1 & 1 & \cdots & 0 \\ \vdots & & \ddots & \ddots & \vdots \\ 0 & \cdots & \cdots & 1 & 1 \end{pmatrix}.$$

Sine-wave Functions The functions $\phi(t) = a_1 \sin \omega t + a_2 \cos \omega t$ can be obtained by taking

$$f(t) = \begin{pmatrix} \sin \omega t \\ \cos \omega t \end{pmatrix},$$

and in this case, we have

$$\mathbf{A} = \begin{pmatrix} \cos \omega & \sin \omega \\ -\sin \omega & \cos \omega \end{pmatrix}.$$

Exponential Function $\phi(t) = ae^{\alpha t}$ is obtained with $f(t) = e^{\alpha t}$; in this case, $A = e^{\alpha}$.

4.3.2 Description of the Method

Fitting the function

$$\phi(t-T) = \sum_{i=1}^{n} a_i f_i(t-T) = \mathbf{f}'(t-T)\mathbf{a}$$

in a neighborhood of T is equivalent to

$$\min_{a} \sum_{j=0}^{T-1} \beta^j \left(x_{T-j} - \mathbf{f}'(-j)\mathbf{a} \right)^2. \tag{4.13}$$

Let us introduce the following notation

$$y = \begin{pmatrix} x_T \\ \vdots \\ x_1 \end{pmatrix},$$

$$\mathbf{F} = \begin{pmatrix} f_1(0) & \cdots & f_n(0) \\ \vdots & & \vdots \\ f_1(-T+1) & \cdots & f_n(-T+1) \end{pmatrix} = \begin{pmatrix} \mathbf{f}'(0) \\ \vdots \\ \mathbf{f}'(-T+1) \end{pmatrix},$$

and

$$\mathbf{\Omega} = \begin{pmatrix} 1 & 0 & \cdots & 0 \\ 0 & \beta^{-1} & \cdots & 0 \\ \vdots & \vdots & \ddots & \vdots \\ 0 & 0 & \cdots & \beta^{-(T-1)} \end{pmatrix}.$$

From regression theory, it is clear that the regression of y on the columns of $\mathbf{F}$, associated with the covariance matrix $\mathbf{\Omega}$ formally leads to the same minimization problem as in (4.13). Therefore its unique solution is

$$\hat{\mathbf{a}}(T) = \left(\mathbf{F}'\mathbf{\Omega}^{-1}\mathbf{F}\right)^{-1}\mathbf{F}'\mathbf{\Omega}^{-1}y.$$

Denoting $\mathbf{F}'\mathbf{\Omega}^{-1}\mathbf{F}$ by $\mathbf{M}(T)$ and $\mathbf{F}'\mathbf{\Omega}^{-1}y$ by $\mathbf{z}(\mathbf{T})$ we have

$$\hat{\mathbf{a}}(T) = \mathbf{M}(T)^{-1}\mathbf{z}(\mathbf{T}). \tag{4.14}$$

The matrices $\mathbf{M}(T)$ and $\mathbf{z}(T)$ can be written as

$$\mathbf{M}(T) = \sum_{j=0}^{T-1} \beta^j \mathbf{f}(-j)\mathbf{f}'(-j),$$

$$\mathbf{z}(T) = \sum_{j=0}^{T-1} \beta^j \mathbf{f}(-j)x_{T-j}. \tag{4.15}$$

From expression (4.15), we can see that, in general, $\mathbf{M}(T)$ converges to a finite matrix $\mathbf{M}$, as $T \to \infty$. If we limit ourselves to the common functions ϕ, the only terms of $\mathbf{M}(T)$ which could pose a problem for convergence are of the type $\beta^j e^{-2\alpha j}$, which are divergent if $\beta \geq e^{2\alpha}$. Notice that, in an economic context, the functions of the type $e^{\alpha t}$ are introduced to express an increasing trend. Therefore, $\alpha > 0$ and $\beta < e^{2\alpha}$. We can then replace $\mathbf{M}(T)$ with its limit, assumed to be a regular matrix, obtaining

$$\hat{\mathbf{a}}(T) = \mathbf{M}^{-1}\mathbf{z}(\mathbf{T}), \tag{4.16}$$

with

$$\mathbf{M} = \sum_{j=0}^{\infty} \beta^j \mathbf{f}(-j)\mathbf{f}'(-j).$$

Recall that the forecast of x_{t+k} made at time T is

$$\hat{x}_T(k) = \mathbf{f}'(k)\hat{\mathbf{a}}(T). \tag{4.17}$$

If we want to update $\hat{\mathbf{a}}(T)$, we have

$$
\begin{aligned}
\mathbf{z}(T) &= \sum_{j=0}^{T-1} \beta^j \mathbf{f}(-j) x_{T-j} \\
&= x_T f(0) + \sum_{j=1}^{T-1} \beta^j \mathbf{f}(-j) x_{T-j} \\
&= x_T f(0) + \beta \sum_{j=0}^{T-2} \beta^j \mathbf{f}(-j-1) x_{T-j-1} \\
&= x_T f(0) + \beta \mathbf{A}^{-1} \sum_{j=0}^{T-2} \beta^j \mathbf{f}(-j) x_{T-j-1} \\
&= x_T f(0) + \beta \mathbf{A}^{-1} \mathbf{z}(T-1).
\end{aligned} \tag{4.18}
$$

Therefore, using (4.16), we obtain

$$\hat{\mathbf{a}}(T) = x_T \mathbf{M}^{-1} \mathbf{f}(0) + \beta \mathbf{M}^{-1} \mathbf{A}^{-1} \mathbf{M} \hat{\mathbf{a}}(T-1),$$

or

$$\hat{\mathbf{a}}(T) = \mathbf{g} x_T + \mathbf{G} \hat{\mathbf{a}}(T-1),$$

$$\text{with } \mathbf{g} = \mathbf{M}^{-1} \mathbf{f}(0), \tag{4.19}$$

$$\mathbf{G} = \beta \mathbf{M}^{-1} \mathbf{A}^{-1} \mathbf{M}.$$

The matrices $\mathbf{g}$ and $\mathbf{G}$ are independent of T, and can be computed once and for all. Expression (4.19) can be written under a different form. In fact

$$
\begin{aligned}
\mathbf{A}^{-1}\mathbf{M} &= \sum_{j=0}^{\infty} \beta^j \mathbf{A}^{-1} \mathbf{f}(-j) \left(\mathbf{A}^{-1} \mathbf{f}(-j) \right)' \mathbf{A}' \\
&= \sum_{h=1}^{\infty} \beta^{h-1} \mathbf{f}(-h) \mathbf{f}'(-h) \mathbf{A}' \\
&= \frac{1}{\beta} \left(\mathbf{M} - \mathbf{f}(0) \mathbf{f}'(0) \right) \mathbf{A}'.
\end{aligned}
$$

We get

$$
\begin{aligned}
\mathbf{G} &= \left(\mathbf{I} - \mathbf{M}^{-1} \mathbf{f}(0) \mathbf{f}'(0) \right) \mathbf{A}' \\
&= \mathbf{A}' - \mathbf{g}\, \mathbf{f}'(1),
\end{aligned}
$$

and

$$\hat{a}(T) = \mathbf{g}x_T + \mathbf{A}'\hat{a}(T-1) - \mathbf{g}\mathbf{f}'(1)\hat{a}(T-1)$$
$$= \mathbf{A}'\hat{a}(T-1) - \mathbf{g}\left(x_T - \hat{x}_{T-1}(1)\right),$$

which generalizes (4.4) and (4.11).

Obviously, an important practical problem is the choice of **f**. The nature of the series (trend, seasonal component) may give some guidelines, but a certain degree of arbitrariness (much less present in the Box–Jenkins techniques introduced in chapter 6) exists.

4.4 The Holt–Winters Methods

4.4.1 The Nonseasonal Method

The methods proposed by Brown, presented in sections 4.2 and 4.3, can be seen as a generalization of the simple exponential smoothing obtained by fitting a horizontal line locally.

Holt and Winters (cf. Winters, 1960) followed a different approach. Like the double exponential smoothing, the nonseasonal Holt–Winters method is based on the assumptions that fitting a line of the type $y_t = a_1 + (t - T)a_2$ in a neighborhood of T, is preferable to fitting a horizontal line. This generalization leads to the updating formula (4.2); more precisely, Holt and Winters propose updating formulas for a_1 and a_2 of the type

$$\hat{a}_1(T) = (1-\alpha)x_T + \alpha\left(\hat{a}_1(T-1) + \hat{a}_2(T-1)\right), \quad 0 < \alpha < 1, \quad (4.20)$$

$$\hat{a}_2(T) = (1-\gamma)\left(\hat{a}_1(T) - \hat{a}_1(T-1)\right) + \gamma\hat{a}_2(T-1), \quad 0 < \gamma < 1. \quad (4.21)$$

Formula (4.20) can be interpreted as a weighted average of two pieces of information on the "level" of the series a_1 at date T, the observation x_T and the forecast made at time $T-1$. Formula (4.21) can be interpreted as a weighted average of two pieces of information on the "slope" of the series a_2 at time T, the difference between the estimated levels at time $T-1$ and T, and the estimated slope at time $T-1$.

In order to use (4.20) and (4.21), we first need to initialize the sequence $(\hat{a}_1(t), \hat{a}_2(t))$. In general, we can take $\hat{a}_1(2) = x_2$ and $\hat{a}_2(2) = x_2 - x_1$. The forecast is then

$$\hat{x}_T(k) = \hat{a}_1(T) + k\hat{a}_2(T).$$

This method is more flexible than the double exponential smoothing method, since it introduces two parameters (α and γ) instead of one

(β). More precisely, the equations (4.11) can be written as

$$\hat{a}_1(T) = (1 - \beta^2)x_T + \beta^2\left(\hat{a}_1(T-1) + \hat{a}_2(T-1)\right),$$

$$\hat{a}_2(T) = \hat{a}_2(T-1) + \frac{(1-\beta)^2}{1-\beta^2}\left(\hat{a}_1(T) - \hat{a}_1(T-1) - \hat{a}_2(T-1)\right),$$

which coincide with equations (4.20) and (4.21) if we take

$$\alpha = \beta^2, \quad \text{and} \quad \gamma = 1 - \frac{(1-\beta)^2}{1-\beta^2} = \frac{2\beta}{1+\beta}.$$

The counterpart to this flexibility lies also, evidently, in the choice of the two parameters, instead of one. This choice is possibly arbitrary through subjective procedures (α and γ close to one imply an extremely "smooth" forecast, since the weight given to the past is very strong); alternatively, we can minimize

$$\min_{\alpha,\gamma} \sum_{t=1}^{T-1} \left(x_{t+1} - \hat{x}_t(1)\right)^2.$$

4.4.2 The Additive Seasonal Method

Let us suppose that the series can be approximated in a neighborhood of T by

$$a_1 + (t - T)a_2 + s_t,$$

where s_t is a seasonal component.

Let us suggest the following updating formulas for a_1, a_2, and s_t

$$\hat{a}_1(T) = (1 - \alpha)(x_T - \hat{s}_{T-j}) + \alpha\left(\hat{a}_1(T-1) + \hat{a}_2(T-1)\right), \;\; 0 < \alpha < 1,$$

$$\hat{a}_2(T) = (1 - \gamma)\left(\hat{a}_1(T) - \hat{a}_1(T-1)\right) + \gamma\hat{a}_2(T-1), \;\; 0 < \gamma < 1,$$

$$\hat{s}_T = (1 - \delta)\left(x_T - \hat{a}_1(T)\right) + \delta s_{T-j}, \;\; 0 < \delta < 1,$$

where j is a constant indicating the number of "seasons," i.e., $j = 12$ for monthly observations, $j = 4$ for quarterly observations. The forecast is

$$\hat{x}_T(k) = \begin{cases} \hat{a}_1(T) + k\hat{a}_2(T) + \hat{s}_{T+k-j} & \text{if } 1 \leq k \leq s, \\[2mm] \hat{a}_1(T) + k\hat{a}_2(T) + \hat{s}_{T+k-2j} & \text{if } s < k \leq 2s, \end{cases}$$

and so on. The expressions (4.22) can be interpreted in the same way as equations (4.20) and (4.21). The main problem is the one of choosing α, γ, and δ, the methods for which are very similar to those mentioned previously.

In order to apply the formulas (4.22), we need to have initial values for the sequences $\hat{a}_1(t)$, $\hat{a}_2(t)$, and $\hat{s}_t$. We can suggest, for example, for the case $j = 4$

$$\hat{a}_1(4) = \frac{1}{8}x_2 + \frac{1}{4}x_3 + \frac{1}{4}x_4 + \frac{1}{4}x_5 + \frac{1}{8}x_6,$$

$$\hat{a}_2(4) = \hat{a}_1(4) - \hat{a}_1(3),$$

with

$$\hat{a}_1(3) = \frac{1}{8}x_1 + \frac{1}{4}x_2 + \frac{1}{4}x_3 + \frac{1}{4}x_4 + \frac{1}{8}x_5,$$

$$\hat{s}_4 = x_4 - \hat{a}_1(4),$$

$$\hat{s}_3 = x_3 - \hat{a}_1(3),$$

$$\hat{s}_2 = x_2 - \hat{a}_1(3) + \hat{a}_2(4),$$

$$\hat{s}_1 = x_1 - \hat{a}_1(3) + 2\hat{a}_2(4).$$

4.4.3 The Multiplicative Seasonal Method

According to this method, the underlying approximation to the series is

$$(a_1 + (t - T)a_2)\, s_t.$$

The updating formulas become, then

$$\hat{a}_1(T) = (1 - \alpha)\frac{x_t}{\hat{s}_{T-j}} + \alpha\left(\hat{a}_1(T-1) + \hat{a}_2(T-1)\right), \quad 0 < \alpha < 1,$$

$$\hat{a}_2(T) = (1 - \gamma)\left(\hat{a}_1(T) - \hat{a}_1(T-1)\right) + \gamma\hat{a}_2(T-1), \quad 0 < \gamma < 1,$$

$$\hat{s}_T = (1 - \delta)\frac{x_T}{\hat{a}_1(T)} + \delta\hat{s}_{T-j}, \quad 0 < \delta < 1,$$

and the forecast

$$\hat{x}_T(k) = \begin{cases} \left(\hat{a}_1(T) + k\hat{a}_2(T)\right)\hat{s}_{T+k-j} & \text{if } 1 \leq k \leq j, \\[2mm] \left(\hat{a}_1(T) + k\hat{a}_2(T)\right)\hat{s}_{T+k-2j} & \text{if } j < k \leq 2j, \end{cases}$$

and so on. In the case $j = 4$, we could take as initial values for $\hat{a}_1$ and $\hat{a}_2$, the initial values of $\hat{a}_1$ and $\hat{a}_2$ previously computed. The initial values of $\hat{s}_1$, $\hat{s}_2$, $\hat{s}_3$, $\hat{s}_4$ can be obtained dividing the observations by the linear trend computed from $\hat{a}_1(4)$ and $\hat{a}_2(4)$.

With the exception of the last one, all the methods examined in this chapter are special cases of the forecasting techniques due to Box and Jenkins (1970). The advantage of these techniques is that they allow to select the most appropriate method for the series under analysis among a

great variety of possible methods, whereas the methods presented here
are suitable only to a specific kind of series. Last, the Box–Jenkins
techniques do not allow an arbitrary choice of the smoothing parameters.
On their part, these techniques require a higher degree of complexity in
their implementation. *

---

*   The optimality aspects of the methods presented in this chapter will be
    discussed later. For the moment, relevant references on this subject are for
    the simple exponential smoothing, Muth (1960); for the Brown techniques,
    Cogger (1974); for the Holt–Winters methods, Harrison(1967), Granger and
    Newbold (1986, p.170), Theil and Wage (1964), and Nerlove and Wage
    (1964).

4.5 Exercises

Exercise 4.1: In the simple exponential smoothing, we can consider that the "mean lag" between the observations and the forecast based on them

$$\hat{x}_T = (1 - \beta) \sum_{j=0}^{T-1} \beta^j x_{T-j},$$

is measurable by

$$\tau = (1 - \beta) \sum_{j=0}^{T-1} \beta^j (T - j).$$

Simplify this expression of τ as a function of β and T. What happens to the expression when $T \to \infty$?

Exercise 4.2: Verify that the functions

$$\phi(t) = a_1 \sin \omega_1 t + a_2 \cos \omega_1 t + a_3 \sin \omega_2 t + a_4 sin \omega_2 t$$

or

$$\phi(t) = (a_1 + a_3 t) \sin \omega t + (a_2 + a_4 t) \cos \omega t$$

can be written in the form

$$\phi(t) = \sum_{i=1}^{4} a_i \mathbf{f}_i(t),$$

where the vector $\mathbf{f}(t)$ has a fixed transition matrix.

Exercise 4.3: Verify that the updating formulas for the simple exponential smoothing, and for the double exponential smoothing are special cases of formula (4.20).

Exercise 4.4: *Simple exponential smoothing – Comparison with the optimal linear forecast.* Let us assume that the hypotheses in Theorem 4.1c are satisfied.

1. Show that the orthogonal projection of x_{T+k} on the whole subspace spanned by $[x_i, \ x_{i+1}, \ldots, x_T, \ 1], \ \forall \ i \leq T$ in a L_2 sense is

$$x_T^*(k) = \rho^k x_T.$$

    Compute $D_\rho^*(k) = E\left(x_{T+k} - x_T^*(k)\right)^2$.

2 Draw on the same graph $D_\rho^*(1)$ and $D_\rho(1, \beta^*(\rho))$ as a function of ρ. Recall that $\beta^*(\rho)$ indicates the optimal value of β, that is

$$\beta^*(\rho) = \begin{cases} 1 & \text{if } -1 \le \rho \le \frac{1}{3}, \\ \frac{1-\rho}{2\rho} & \text{if } \frac{1}{3} \le \rho \le 1. \end{cases}$$

For which values of ρ is there an equality between $D_\rho^*(1)$ and $D_\rho(1, \beta^*(\rho))$? What kind of a process is $\{x_t\}$, then?

Exercise 4.5: *Simple exponential smoothing – Optimality conditions.*
Let us suppose now that

$$x_t = \sum_{i=0}^{t-1} \lambda_i \epsilon_{t-i}, \quad \lambda_0 \ne 0, \ t > 0,$$

where the process $\{\epsilon_t; \text{integer } t\}$ is an independent process such that $E(\epsilon_t) = 0$ and $\text{var}(\epsilon_t) = \sigma_\epsilon^2$.

1 Is the process $\{x_t\}$ stationary? Show that we can always normalize $\lambda = 0$ and that we can put x_t in the form

$$x_t = \sum_{j=1}^{t-1} \phi_j x_{t-j} + \epsilon_t.$$

How can we compute the ϕ_j's as a function of the λ_j's?

2 Compute $E(x_{T+1} \mid x_1, \dots, x_T)$. For which values of λ_i do we have

$$E(x_{T+1} \mid x_1, \dots, x_T) = (1 - \beta) \sum_{j=0}^{T-1} \beta^j x_{T-j}?$$

Compute now $E(x_{T+k} \mid x_1, \dots, x_T)$ and $x_T - x_{T-1}$.

II
Probabilistic and Statistical Properties
of Stationary Processes

5

Some Results on the Univariate Processes

As an introduction to the forecasting techniques suggested by Box and Jenkins (chapter 6), some concepts and results from probability theory and from the theory of stochastic processes need to be introduced. In this chapter, we adopt a simplified presentation of the main concepts, confining ourselves to the univariate case. This will allow us to understand the main aspects of AutoRegressive Moving Average models (ARMA) and AutoRegressive Integrated Moving Average models (ARIMA.) More general results which can be applied to the multivariate case will be discussed in chapter 8 and beyond.

5.1 Covariance Stationary Processes

5.1.1 The Set of Square Integrable Variables

The set L_2 of square integrable variables is analyzed in any standard textbook of probability theory. Rigorously speaking, L_2 can be defined as the set of the equivalence classes of random variables which satisfy $E(x^2) < \infty$ and differ only on a set of probability zero. Here, we will limit ourselves to recalling the simplest properties of this set.

The set of square integrable real random variables $E(x^2) < \infty$, is a normed linear space $I\!R$, the norm of which is equal to $\| x \| = \left(E(x^2) \right)^{1/2}$. For two variables in this space, x, and y, it is possible to compute the expected value of their product $E(xy)$. The mapping $(x, y) \mapsto E(xy)$ defines a scalar product on this space.

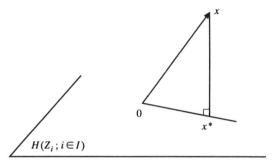

Figure 5.1 Orthogonal Projection

Definition 5.1: *Two variables x and y, such that $E(x^2) < \infty$ and $E(y^2) < \infty$ are said to be orthogonal with respect to L_2 if $E(xy) = 0$.*

Definition 5.2: *A sequence of variables x_n, satisfying $E(x_n^2) < \infty$ converges to a variable x with respect to L_2 (or converges in square mean) if $\| x_n - x \| \to 0$ as $n \to \infty$.*

The existence of a concept of orthogonality and of convergence on a space of square integrable variables allows us to introduce the concept of orthogonal projection. More precisely, let us consider a family of variables z_i, $i \in I$ such that $E(z_i) < \infty$, $\forall\, i$. We will define $H(z_i)$ the smallest closed subspace of square integrable variables containing all the affine combinations of variables z_i (and their limits with respect to L_2), indexed over the integer set.

Given a variable x, $E(x^2) < \infty$, we can look for an element $x^* \in H(z_i)$ which approximates it, that is, satisfies

$$\| x - x^* \| = \min_z \| x - z \|, \quad \text{with } z \in H(z_i). \tag{5.1}$$

Such an element exists. It is called *affine regression* of x on (z_i). x^* is characterized by the fact that $x - x^*$ is orthogonal to all the elements of $H(z_i)$ with respect to the space L_2 (more simply, to the z_i's and to the constant 1

$$E(x - x^*)z = 0, \quad \forall\, z \in H(z_i). \tag{5.2}$$

Although the space of square integrable variables has an infinite dimension, we resort to a representation in $\mathbb{R}^3$ (as in figure 5.1) in order to be able to visualize the orthogonal projection x^*. The orthogonality condition is represented by a square angle.

With a finite number of variables z_i, $i = 1, \ldots, n$, we can write the affine regression in an explicit way by using the orthogonality condition

(5.2). In fact

$$x^* = a_0 + \sum_{i=1}^{n} a_i z_i,$$

which satisfies

$$\begin{cases} E(x\ 1) = E(x^*\ 1), \\[2em] E(x\ z_i) = E(x^*\ z_i), \end{cases}$$

$$\Leftrightarrow$$

$$\begin{cases} E(x) = a_0 + \sum_{j=1}^{n} a_j E(z_j), \\[2em] E(x\ z_i) = a_0 E(z_i) + \sum_{j=1}^{n} a_j E(z_i z_j), \end{cases}$$

$$\Leftrightarrow$$

$$\begin{cases} E(x) = a_0 + \sum_{j=1}^{n} a_j E(z_j), \\[2em] E(x\ z_i) - E(x)E(z_i) = \sum_{j=1}^{n} a_j \left(E(z_i z_j) - E(z_i)E(z_j) \right), \end{cases}$$

for $i = 1, \ldots, n$. The vector of coefficient is given by

$$\begin{pmatrix} a_1 \\ \vdots \\ a_n \end{pmatrix} = \left(\text{var}\,(z) \right)^{-1} \begin{pmatrix} \text{cov}\,(x, z_1) \\ \vdots \\ \text{cov}\,(x, z_n) \end{pmatrix},$$

where $\text{var}\,(z)$ (assumed nonsingular) is the $(n \times n)$ variance–covariance matrix of $(z_1, \ldots, z_n)$, whose (i,j)-th generic term is $\text{cov}\,(z_i, z_j)$. a_0 can then be obtained using the first equality. Finally, we get

$$x^* = E(x) + \text{cov}\,(x, z)(\text{var}\,(z))^{-1}(z - E(z))$$

where $\text{cov}\,(x, z)$ is the row vector whose entries are $\text{cov}\,(x, z_i)$, $i = 1, \ldots, n$.

The concept of affine regression is related to the one of conditional expectation. Under some additional conditions (normality or independence of the innovations in the linear processes), the two concepts coincide (cf. section 6.4.1 and Monfort, 1980, chapter XXII.E). From now on, we will therefore use the notation $x^* = E\,(x|z)$ to indicate an affine regression.

5.1.2 Covariance Stationary Process

A discrete time stationary process is a sequence of real random variables (x_t, t integer). The distribution of such a process is described by the distributions of any finite subfamily $x_{t_1}, \ldots, x_{t_n}$, n positive integer, $t_1, \ldots, t_n$ integers (Kolmogorov Theorem.) In the case when each variable x_t satisfies $E(x_t^2) < \infty$ (second-order process), the distribution of the process can be partially summarized by the expected values of the variables $E(x_t)$ and by their covariances $\operatorname{cov}(x_t, x_{t+h})$. In general, these quantities depend on t.

Definition 5.3: *A process is covariance stationary if*

(i) $\forall$ integer t, $E(x_t^2) < \infty$;
(ii) $\forall$ t, $E(x_t) = m$ *(independent of t)*;
(iii) $\forall$ integer t, h, $\operatorname{cov}(x_t, x_{t+h}) = \gamma(h)$ *(independent of t)*.

In what follows, the term "stationary" will always mean "covariance stationary"; we will omit also the specification that its index belongs to the set of integer numbers. Such a process admits a distribution which is invariant to changes in the indexing of time for its two first moments. In particular, the variables x_t have the same variance equal to $\gamma(0)$ (the property known as *homoskedasticity*).

The function $\gamma : h \rightarrow \gamma(h)$, h integer, is called an *autocovariance function*. This function is:

(i)   even: $\forall$ h, $\gamma(-h) = \gamma(h)$;
(ii)   positive, since

$$\sum_{j=1}^{n} \sum_{k=1}^{n} a_j a_k \gamma(t_j - t_k) = \operatorname{var}\left(\sum_{j=1}^{n} a_j x_{t_j}\right) > 0$$

$\forall$ positive integer n, $\forall$ a_j, a_k real, $\forall$ t_j integer.

Theorem 5.1: *If (x_t) is a stationary process, and if $(a_i, i$ integer) forms a sequence of absolutely summable real numbers with*

$$\sum_{i=-\infty}^{+\infty} |a_i| < +\infty,$$

the variables obtained through the expressions

$$y_t = \sum_{i=-\infty}^{+\infty} a_i x_{t-i},$$

define a new stationary process.

PROOF: The series formed by $a_i x_{t-i}$ is convergent in square mean since

$$\sum_{i=-\infty}^{+\infty} \| a_i x_{t-i} \| = \sum_{i=-\infty}^{+\infty} | a_i | \| x_{t-i} \|$$

$$= \left(\gamma(0) + m^2\right)^{1/2} \sum_{i=-\infty}^{+\infty} | a_i | < +\infty.$$

The expression $\sum_{i=-\infty}^{+\infty} a_i x_{t-i}$ is an element of L^2, and y_t so defined is square integrable. Relying on the results in the appendix for a justification of the interchange between the expected value and infinite sum operators, the moments of the process $\{y_t\}$ can be written as

$$E(y_t) = E\left(\sum_{i=-\infty}^{+\infty} a_i x_{t-i}\right) = \sum_{i=-\infty}^{+\infty} a_i E(x_{t-i})$$

$$= m_x \sum_{i=-\infty}^{+\infty} a_i = m_y \quad \text{(independent of t)};$$

$$\text{cov}(y_t, y_{t+h}) = \text{cov}\left(\sum_{i=-\infty}^{+\infty} a_i x_{t-i}, \sum_{j=-\infty}^{+\infty} a_j x_{t+h-j}\right)$$

$$= \sum_{i=-\infty}^{+\infty} \sum_{j=-\infty}^{+\infty} a_i a_j \text{cov}(x_{t-i}, x_{t+h-j})$$

$$= \sum_{i=-\infty}^{+\infty} \sum_{j=-\infty}^{+\infty} a_i a_j \gamma_x(h+i-j) = \gamma_y(h)$$

(independent of t). □

Example 5.1: An example of a stationary process is given by the *white noise*, a sequence of random variables (ϵ_t) with mean 0, $E(\epsilon_t) = 0$, serially uncorrelated, $\gamma(h) = 0, \forall\ h \neq 0$, and with the same variance var $(\epsilon_t) = \sigma^2 = \gamma(0)$. The path of one white noise can be very different from another. In figures 5.2 and 5.3 we give examples of univariate white noises, where the observations ϵ_t correspond to random draws from the same distribution, discrete in the first case, continuous in the second one.

In figure 5.4, instead, we give an example of a white noise where the variables ϵ_t are zero mean, unit variance, and independent, but are

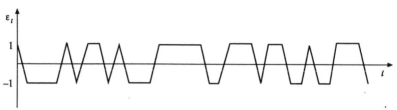

Figure 5.2 Draws from $1/2\delta_{(-1)} + 1/2\delta_{(1)}$ (δ_x Point Mass at x)

Figure 5.3 Draws from the Uniform Distribution [-1,1]

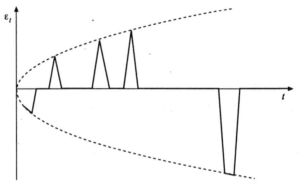

Figure 5.4 Draws from: $\left(1 - \frac{1}{t}\right)\delta_{(0)} + \frac{1}{2t}\left(\delta_{(\sqrt{t})} + \delta_{(-\sqrt{t})}\right)$

drawn from different distributions. They can take values either of 0 or of $\pm\sqrt{t}$. Since we need to compensate for the increasing values $\pm\sqrt{t}$ which the noise can take, we need to assign a smaller and smaller probability to it, namely $1/2t$. Therefore, as t increases, the path often coincides with the t axis, except at rare points where it takes a large value.

Definition 5.4: *If* (x_t) *is a covariance stationary process, we will call* linear innovation *of the process at time* t, *the variable* $x_t - x_t^*$, *where* x_t^* *is the affine regression of* x_t *on* $(x_s,\ s \le t-1)$.

x_t^* can be interpreted as the best affine approximation of x_t which is a function of the past of the process. It is an optimal forecast of x_t based on the information set $I_{t-1} = \{x_{t-1}, x_{t-2}, \dots\}$. We can denote it also by

$$\hat{x}_{t-1}(1) =_{t-1} \hat{x}_t = E\left(x_t \mid I_{t-1}\right).$$

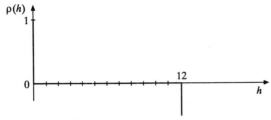

Figure 5.5 Correlogram for the Process in Example 5.2

The linear innovation is the part of x_t uncorrelated with its past; it can be interpreted as the forecast error on x_t, when the forecast is made at time $t-1$. It can be shown that the innovation process $(x_t - x_t^*)$ is a white noise if the process (x_t) is stationary.

5.1.3 Autocorrelation

The autocovariance function gives information on the variability of the series and on its time links. If the only aspect of interest is the latter one, we can limit ourselves to the computation of the successive correlations.

Definition 5.5: *The* autocorrelation function *is defined as*

$$\rho(h) = \frac{\gamma(h)}{\gamma(0)}.$$

$\rho(h)$ measures the correlation between x_t and $x_t + h$, since

$$\frac{\mathrm{cov}\,(x_t, x_{t+h})}{\sqrt{\mathrm{var}\,(x_t)\mathrm{var}\,(x_{t+h})}} = \frac{\gamma(h)}{\sqrt{\gamma(0)\gamma(0)}} = \frac{\gamma(h)}{\gamma(0)}.$$

Like the autocovariance function, the function $\rho(h)$ is also even and positive. Moreover, it satisfies the condition $\rho(0) = 1$. This function is often represented in a graph for positive values of h (since it is even). This graphical representation is called a *correlogram*.

Example 5.2: From a white noise process $\{\epsilon_t\}$ with variance σ^2, let us consider the stationary process $\{x_t\}$ defined as

$$x_t = \epsilon_t - \epsilon_{t-12}.$$

Its autocorrelation function is

$$\gamma(h) = \begin{cases} 2\sigma^2, & \text{if } h = 0, \\ -\sigma^2, & \text{if } h = \pm 12, \\ 0, & \text{otherwise.} \end{cases}$$

We can derive the autocorrelation function as

$$\gamma(h) = \begin{cases} 1, & \text{if } h = 0, \\ -\frac{1}{2}, & \text{if } h = \pm 12, \\ 0, & \text{otherwise.} \end{cases}$$

The correlogram is depicted in figure 5.5.

If we consider m successive observations $x_t, x_{t+1}, \ldots, x_{t+m-1}$ of the process, we can introduce the concept of an *autocorrelation matrix* for the vector $(x_t, x_{t+1}, \ldots, x_{t+m-1})'$ as

$$\mathbf{R}(m) = \begin{pmatrix} 1 & \rho(1) & \rho(2) & \cdots & \rho(m-1) \\ \rho(1) & 1 & \rho(1) & \cdots & \rho(m-2) \\ \vdots & \vdots & \vdots & \ddots & \vdots \\ \rho(m-1) & \rho(m-2) & \rho(m-3) & \cdots & 1 \end{pmatrix}.$$

From the result that the covariance operator is Hermitian positive, we can see that the function ρ is also positive and this implies that any symmetric matrix $\mathbf{R}(m)$ is positive definite. The matrix $\mathbf{R}(m)$ can be written as

$$\mathbf{R}(m) = \begin{pmatrix} & & & \rho(m-1) \\ & \mathbf{R}(m-1) & & \vdots \\ & & & \rho(1) \\ \rho(m-1) & \cdots & \rho(1) & 1 \end{pmatrix},$$

where the upper block diagonal element of order $m-1$ is the matrix $\mathbf{R}(m-1)$. Since a symmetric matrix is associated with a positive quadratic form if and only if its principal minors are positive, we can derive the following theorem.

Theorem 5.2: $\det(\mathbf{R}(m)) \geq 0 \; \forall$ integer m.

The successive autocorrelations are thus subject to a number of constraints

(i) $\det(R(1)) \geq 0 \Leftrightarrow \rho(1)^2 \leq 1$ (which is a classical property of the correlation coefficient).

(ii) $\det(R(2)) \geq 0 \Leftrightarrow (1 - \rho(2))\left(1 + \rho(2) - 2\rho(1)^2\right) \geq 0$. Since $\rho(2)$ is a correlation coefficient smaller than 1 and given the classical property, we have that $\rho(2) \geq 2\rho(1)^2 - 1$. Therefore, if the correlation of order 1 is high, namely close to 1, so is also the correlation of order 2. We cannot have a sudden change of value between $\rho(1)$

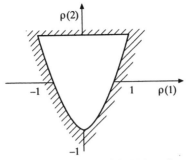

Figure 5.6   Domain of Admissible Values for $\rho(1)$ and $\rho(2)$

and $\rho(2)$, when $\rho(1)$ is high. In particular, the process cannot have a zero autocorrelation of order 2, $\rho(2) = 0$, unless $\mid \rho(1) \mid \leq 1/\sqrt{2}$. The domain of admissible values for $\rho(1)$, $\rho(2)$ is given in figure 5.6.

5.1.4 Partial Autocorrelation

Linear Forecasts as a Function of Memory Size   Let us consider a stationary process x for which the autocorrelation matrices $\mathbf{R}(m)$ are assumed all nonsingular for integer m. We are interested in the best linear affine prediction of x_t based on the K previous values (K is called *memory size*)

$$x_{t-1}, x_{t-2}, \ldots, x_{t-K}.$$

In order to simplify the notation, let us assume a zero mean for the process. The prediction is then

$$E(x_t \mid x_{t-1}, \ldots, x_{t-K}) = a_1(K)x_{t-1} + \ldots + a_K(K)x_{t-K}, \qquad (5.3)$$

where the vector $\mathbf{a}(K) = (a_1(K), \ldots, a_K(K))'$ of the regression coefficients is given by

$$\mathbf{a}(K) = \mathbf{R}(K)^{-1} \begin{pmatrix} \rho(1) \\ \vdots \\ \rho(K) \end{pmatrix}. \qquad (5.4)$$

Theorem 5.3: *The regression coefficients on the past are linked to the regression coefficients on the future in the sense that*

$$E(x_t \mid x_{t+1}, \ldots, x_{t+K}) = a_1(K)x_{t+1} + \ldots + a_K(K)x_{t+K}.$$

PROOF: The vector of regression coefficients is given by

$$\mathbf{R}(K)^{-1} \begin{pmatrix} \rho(1) \\ \vdots \\ \rho(K) \end{pmatrix} = \mathbf{a}(K),$$

using the fact that the autocorrelation function is even. □

We can use this proposition to study the way in which the regression coefficients vary with the memory size K. Let us note first that on the basis of (5.3) we can obtain an expression for the projection of x_t on the past $K - 1$ values

$$E(x_t \mid x_{t-1}, \ldots, x_{t-K+1}) = a_1(K)x_{t-1} + \ldots + a_{K-1}(K)x_{t-K+1}$$
$$+ a_K(K)E(x_{t-K} \mid x_{t-1}, \ldots, x_{t-K+1}).$$

Using the definition of the coefficients $a_k(K)$ and theorem 5.3 we can derive

$$\sum_{k=1}^{K-1} a_k(K-1)x_{t-k} = \sum_{k=1}^{K-1} a_k(K)x_{t-k} + a_K(K) \sum_{k=1}^{K-1} a_{K-k}(K-1)x_{t-k}.$$

The final relationship among the regression coefficients is given by the following theorem.

Theorem 5.4: *We have*

$$a_k(K) = a_k(K-1) - a_K(K)a_{K-k}(K-1), \quad k = 1, \ldots, K-1. \quad (5.5)$$

This formula allows one to get the terms $a_k(K), \; k = 1, \ldots, K-1$ starting from the regression coefficients corresponding to a shorter memory size $K - 1$ once $a_K(K)$ is known. To complete the recursive algorithm, we need to find the expression of the coefficient $a_K(K)$ as a function of the values $a_k(K-1), \; k = 1, \ldots, K-1$. Considering the last line of the expression (5.4) we can write

$$\rho(K-1)a_1(K) + \ldots + \rho(1)a_{K-1}(K) + a_K(K) = \rho(K)$$

$$\Leftrightarrow$$

$$a_K(K) = \rho(K) - (\rho(K-1)a_1(K) + \ldots + \rho(1)a_{K-1}(K))$$

Taking into consideration the recursive formula (5.5) we have

$$a_K(K) = \rho(K)$$

$$- \left(\sum_{k=1}^{K-1} \rho(K-k)a_k(K-1) - a_K(K) \sum_{k=1}^{K-1} \rho(k)a_k(K-1) \right)$$

$$\Leftrightarrow$$

$$a_k(K) = \frac{\rho(K) - \sum_{k=1}^{K-1} \rho(K-k)a_k(K-1)}{1 - \sum_{k=1}^{K-1} \rho(k)a_k(K-1)}.$$

$$(5.6)$$

Definition 5.6: *The recursive system (5.5) and (5.6) is called* Durbin's algorithm, *with the initial condition* $a_1(1) = \rho(1)$.

This algorithm allows for the recursive computation of the various regression coefficients avoiding the inversion of the correlation matrices $\mathbf{R}(K)$ contained in the expression of the regression coefficients (5.4).

Example 5.3: Let us consider the case of a moving average process $x_t = \epsilon_t - \theta\epsilon_{t-1}$, where ϵ_t is a white noise process with variance σ^2, and θ is a real number.

We have

$$\rho(0) = 1, \quad \rho(1) = \frac{-\theta}{1+\theta^2}, \quad \rho(h) = 0, \ \text{if } h \geq 2.$$

Expression (5.6) becomes then for $K \geq 2$

$$a_K(K) = \frac{-\rho(1)a_{K-1}(K-1)}{1 - \rho(1)a_1(K-1)}.$$

On the other hand, from (5.5) we get

$$a_1(K) = a_1(K-1) - a_K(K)a_{K-1}(K-1).$$

These two equations allow the recursive computation of

$$\boldsymbol{\alpha}_K = (a_1(K), \ a_K(K)),$$

i.e., the two regression coefficients at the extremes from which the other values can be derived.

Partial Autocorrelations We can now give a simple interpretation of the central role played by the coefficient $a_K(K)$.

Theorem 5.5: *The coefficient* $a_K(K)$ *is equal to the coefficient of correlation between*

$$x_t - E(x_t \mid x_{t-1}, \ldots, x_{t-K+1})$$

and

$$x_{t-K} - E(x_{t-K} \mid x_{t-1}, \ldots, x_{t-K+1}).$$

It is defined as the partial autocorrelation *of order K, noted as $r(K)$. $r(K) = a_K(K)$ measures the linear link between x_t and x_{t-K} once the influence of intervening variables $x_{t-1}, \ldots, x_{t-K+1}$ has been removed.*

PROOF: Regressing (5.3) on $x_{t-1}, \ldots, x_{t-K+1}$ and subtracting from (5.3) we get

$$E(x_t \mid x_{t-1}, \ldots, x_{t-K}) - E(x_t \mid x_{t-1}, \ldots, x_{t-K+1})$$
$$= a_K(K)(x_{t-K} - E(x_{t-K} \mid x_{t-1}, \ldots, x_{t-K+1}));$$

hence

$$a_K(K) = \frac{\mathrm{cov}\,(\xi, \psi)}{\mathrm{var}\,(\psi)},$$

where

$$\xi = E(x_t \mid x_{t-1}, \ldots, x_{t-K}) - E(x_t \mid x_{t-1}, \ldots, x_{t-K+1}),$$
$$\psi = x_{t-K} - E(x_{t-K} \mid x_{t-1}, \ldots, x_{t-K+1}).$$

The result is derived by noting that

$$\mathrm{cov}\,(x_t - E(x_t \mid x_{t-1}, \ldots, x_{t-K}), \psi) = 0,$$

and that

$$\mathrm{var}\,(x_t - E(x_t \mid x_{t-1}, \ldots, x_{t-K+1})) = \mathrm{var}\,(\psi).$$

$\square$

Theorem 5.6: *The autocorrelation function $(\rho(h))$ and the partial autocorrelation function $(r(h))$ are equivalent.*

PROOF:

(i)   We have already seen how it is possible to compute the regression coefficients $a_k(K)$ (in particular $a_K(K)$) recursively as a function of the autocorrelations. Let us remark that on the basis of formula (5.4), the coefficients $a_k(K)$, $k = 1, \ldots, K$ are just functions of $\rho(1), \ldots, \rho(K)$, and do not depend on higher-order autocorrelations.

(ii)   Conversely, we can show by induction that the correlation $\rho(K)$ is a function of $r(1), \ldots, r(K)$. This proposition is true for $K = 1$, since we have (cf. 5.4) $a_1(1) = r(1) = \rho(1)$. Let us assume that it is true for $K - 1$. From (5.4) we have

$$\mathbf{R}(K-1) \begin{pmatrix} a_1(K) \\ \vdots \\ a_{K-1}(K) \end{pmatrix} + \begin{pmatrix} \rho(K-1) \\ \vdots \\ \rho(1) \end{pmatrix} a_K(K) = \begin{pmatrix} \rho(1) \\ \vdots \\ \rho(K-1) \end{pmatrix},$$

and

$$(\rho(K-1),\ldots,\rho(1)) \begin{pmatrix} a_1(K) \\ \vdots \\ a_{K-1}(K) \end{pmatrix} + a_K(K) = \rho(K).$$

Using the first subsystem, and the induction hypothesis, we can see that

$$\begin{pmatrix} a_1(K) \\ \vdots \\ a_{K-1}(K) \end{pmatrix}$$

is a function of just $r(1),\ldots,r(K)$; the proposition is true also for $\rho(K)$ using the second subsystem. $\square$

Remark 5.1: By analogy to the autocorrelogram, the graph of partial autocorrelations is called *partial correlogram*.

Remark 5.2: We can derive the expression of $r(K)$ as a function of the autocorrelations, using the two subsytems appearing in theorem 5.6. We have

$$\begin{pmatrix} a_1(K) \\ \vdots \\ a_{K-1}(K) \end{pmatrix}$$

$$= \mathbf{R}(K-1)^{-1} \begin{pmatrix} \rho(1) \\ \vdots \\ \rho(K-1) \end{pmatrix} - \mathbf{R}(K-1)^{-1} \begin{pmatrix} \rho(K-1) \\ \vdots \\ \rho(1) \end{pmatrix} r(K).$$

Substituting this in the second subsystem we get

$$r(K) = \frac{\rho(K) - (\rho(K-1)\ldots\rho(1)) \mathbf{R}(K-1)^{-1} \begin{pmatrix} \rho(1) \\ \vdots \\ \rho(K-1) \end{pmatrix}}{1 - (\rho(K-1)\ldots\rho(1)) \mathbf{R}(K-1)^{-1} \begin{pmatrix} \rho(K-1) \\ \vdots \\ \rho(1) \end{pmatrix}}.$$

For example

$$r(2) = \frac{\left(\rho(2) - \rho(1)^2\right)}{\left(1 - \rho(1)^2\right)}.$$

5.1.5 Spectral Density

In this section, we will introduce the concept of spectral density, which will be shown to be equivalent to the autocovariance function.

In what follows, we will consider infinite moving average processes of the type

$$x_t = \sum_{i=-\infty}^{+\infty} a_i \epsilon_{t-i},$$

where $\{\epsilon_t\}$ is a white noise with a constant variance σ^2 and where a_i forms an absolutely summable sequence, that is, such that

$$\sum_{i=-\infty}^{+\infty} \mid a_i \mid < +\infty.$$

The autocovariance function of this process is

$$\gamma(h) = \sigma^2 \sum_{i=-\infty}^{+\infty} a_i a_{i-h}.$$

This function is such that

$$\sum_{h=-\infty}^{+\infty} \mid \gamma(h) \mid < \infty,$$

since

$$\sum_{i=-\infty}^{+\infty} \mid \gamma(h) \mid = \sigma^2 \sum_{h=-\infty}^{+\infty} \left| \sum_{i=-\infty}^{+\infty} a_i a_{i-h} \right|$$

$$\leq \sigma^2 \sum_{h=-\infty}^{+\infty} \sum_{i=-\infty}^{+\infty} \mid a_i \mid \mid a_{i-h} \mid = \sigma^2 \left(\sum_{i=-\infty}^{+\infty} \mid a_i \mid \right)^2 < +\infty.$$

Definition 5.7: *The spectral density of the process $\{x_t\}$ is the real-valued function defined as*

$$f(\omega) = \frac{1}{2\pi} \sum_{h=-\infty}^{+\infty} \gamma(h) e^{i\omega h}, \; \forall \; \omega \; \in \mathbb{R}.$$

This function exists, since the series formed by the terms $\gamma(h)e^{i\omega h}$ is absolutely convergent. Using the evenness of the autocorrelation function, we can verify that the spectral density is a real-valued function

$$f(\omega) = \frac{1}{2\pi}\left(\gamma(0) + \sum_{h=1}^{+\infty}\gamma(h)\left(e^{i\omega h} + e^{-i\omega h}\right)\right)$$

$$= \frac{\gamma(0)}{2\pi} + \frac{1}{\pi}\sum_{h=1}^{+\infty}\gamma(h)\cos\omega h$$

$$= \frac{1}{2\pi}\sum_{h=-\infty}^{+\infty}\gamma(h)\cos\omega h.$$

It is an even, continuous, periodic function with period 2π. Moreover, it can be shown that it is positive (cf. chapter 7 for the intuition behind the proof).

Theorem 5.7: *The autocovariance function and the spectral density function are equivalent. We have*

$$\gamma(h) = \int_{-\pi}^{+\pi} f(\omega)\cos\omega h \, d\omega = \int_{-\pi}^{+\pi} f(\omega)e^{-i\omega h} \, d\omega.$$

PROOF: This equality can be verified by replacing f as a function of γ. The possibility of interchanging $\int$ and $\sum$ is ensured by

$$\sum_{h=-\infty}^{+\infty} |\gamma(h)| < \infty$$

(cf. the appendix).

$$\int_{-\pi}^{+\pi} f(\omega)\cos\omega h \, d\omega = \int_{-\pi}^{+\pi} f(\omega)e^{-i\omega h} \, d\omega$$

$$= \int_{-\pi}^{+\pi} \frac{1}{2\pi}\sum_{j=-\infty}^{+\infty}\gamma(j)e^{i\omega h}e^{-i\omega h} \, d\omega$$

$$= \frac{1}{2\pi}\sum_{j=-\infty}^{+\infty}\gamma(j)\int_{-\pi}^{+\pi} e^{-i\omega(h-j)} \, d\omega.$$

Since

$$\int_{-\pi}^{+\pi} e^{-i\omega(h-j)} \, d\omega = \begin{cases} 0 & \text{if } j \neq h, \\ 2\pi & \text{if } j = h, \end{cases}$$

hence

$$\int_{-\pi}^{+\pi} f(\omega)e^{-i\omega h} \, d\omega = \gamma(h).$$

□

Theorem 5.8: *Let $\{x_t\}$ be an infinite moving average process of the type*

$$x_t = \sum_{i=-\infty}^{+\infty} \alpha_i \epsilon_{t-i},$$

and $\{y_t\}$ the stationary process defined by

$$y_t = \sum_{j=-\infty}^{+\infty} a_j x_{t-j},$$

with

$$\sum_{j=-\infty}^{+\infty} \mid a_j \mid < \infty.$$

The spectral densities of the two processes satisfy

$$f_y(\omega) = f_x(\omega) \left| \sum_{j=-\infty}^{+\infty} a_j e^{i\omega j} \right|^2.$$

PROOF: Let us assume that the process $\{y_t\}$ admits an infinite moving average representation (as will be shown later). It is possible to define the spectral density of y as

$$f_y(\omega) = \frac{1}{2\pi} \sum_{h=-\infty}^{+\infty} \gamma_y(h) e^{i\omega h},$$

since

$$\gamma_y(h) = \sum_{j=-\infty}^{+\infty} \sum_{k=-\infty}^{+\infty} a_j a_k \gamma_x(h+j-k)$$

(cf. theorem 5.1), and

$$\sum_{h=-\infty}^{+\infty} \mid \gamma_y(h) \mid < +\infty.$$

We have that

$$f_y(\omega) = \frac{1}{2\pi} \sum_{h=-\infty}^{+\infty} \sum_{j=-\infty}^{+\infty} \sum_{k=-\infty}^{+\infty} a_j a_k \gamma_x(h+j-k) e^{i\omega h};$$

as the series is absolutely convergent, we can group the summation signs obtaining

$$f_y(\omega) = \frac{1}{2\pi} \sum_{j=-\infty}^{+\infty} a_j e^{-i\omega j} \sum_{k=-\infty}^{+\infty} a_k e^{i\omega k} \sum_{h=-\infty}^{+\infty} \gamma_x(h+j-k) e^{i\omega(h+j-k)}$$

$$= f_x(\omega) \left| \sum_{j=-\infty}^{+\infty} a_j e^{i\omega j} \right|^2.$$

$\square$

Example 5.4: The spectral density of a white noise with variance σ^2 is

$$f(\omega) = \frac{1}{2\pi} \sum_{h=-\infty}^{+\infty} \gamma(h) e^{i\omega h}$$

$$= \frac{\gamma(0)}{2\pi} = \frac{\sigma^2}{2\pi}$$

which is a constant function of ω. Conversely, if x is a stationary process with a constant spectral density $f(\omega) = c$, we have

$$\gamma(h) = \int_{-\pi}^{+\pi} c \cos \omega h \, d\omega = 0, \quad \text{if } h \neq 0.$$

Therefore, such a process is a white noise.

5.1.6 Inverse Autocorrelations

Let us consider a stationary process $\{x_t\}$ with autocovariance function $\gamma(h)$ and with spectral density f. It may well be that the function $1/f$ be interpretable as a spectral density (this is possible if, for example, $1/f$ is continuous). We can then study the properties of a process with spectral density $1/f$.

Definition 5.8: *The* inverse autocovariance function $\gamma i(h)$, *with h integer, is the autocovariance function associated to the inverse spectrum $1/f$. It is defined as*

$$\gamma i(h) = \int_{-\pi}^{+\pi} \frac{1}{f(\omega)} e^{-i\omega h} \, d\omega, \ \forall \, h,$$

$$\Leftrightarrow \frac{1}{f(\omega)} = \frac{1}{2\pi} \sum_{h=-\infty}^{+\infty} \gamma i(h) e^{i\omega h}, \ \forall \, \omega.$$

Evidently, we can introduce the associated concepts of inverse autocorrelation and of inverse partial autocorrelation functions. Hence the inverse autocorrelation function is defined by

$$pi(h) = \frac{\gamma i(h)}{\gamma i(0)}. \tag{5.7}$$

The inverse autocorrelation function can be obtained by applying theorem 5.6 or Durbin's algorithm to the function pi.

Hence, we have

$$ri(K) = \frac{pi(K) - (pi(K-1)\ldots pi(1))\,\mathbf{Ri}(K-1)^{-1}\begin{pmatrix} pi(1) \\ \vdots \\ pi(K-1) \end{pmatrix}}{1 - (pi(K-1)\ldots pi(1))\,\mathbf{Ri}(K-1)^{-1}\begin{pmatrix} pi(1) \\ \vdots \\ pi(K-1) \end{pmatrix}}.$$

Example 5.5: The functions ρ and pi coincide if and only if the functions γ and γi are proportional. In terms of spectral density this condition becomes

$$\exists \lambda > 0 : f(\omega) = \lambda\frac{1}{f(\omega)} \Leftrightarrow \exists \lambda : f(\omega) = \sqrt{\lambda}.$$

This can occur if and only if the process $\{x_t\}$ is a white noise.

Example 5.6: Let ϵ be a white noise and x a first-order moving average process defined as

$$x_t = \epsilon_t - \theta\epsilon_{t-1},\ \mid \theta \mid < 1.$$

If we indicate the variance of the noise with σ^2, we can see that

$$\gamma(0) = \sigma^2(1 + \theta^2),$$
$$\gamma(1) = \gamma(-1) = -\theta\sigma^2,$$
$$\gamma(h) = 0,\ \text{if } \mid h \mid \geq 2.$$

Therefore

$$f(\omega) = \frac{\gamma(0)}{2\pi} + \frac{2\gamma(1)}{2\pi}\cos\omega$$

$$= \frac{\sigma^2}{2\pi}(1 + \theta^2 - 2\theta\cos\omega).$$

It can be shown that

$$pi(h) = \rho(1)^{|h|}.$$

5.2 Lead and Lag Operators

Let us recall the definitions of the lead and lag operators already introduced in chapter 3 before examining how to apply them in this context.

The *lag operator* L transforms the process $\{x_t\}$ into a process $\{y_t\}$ such that $y_t = Lx_t = x_{t-1}$. This operator is linear, it is invertible, and its inverse is defined as $Fx_t = x_{t+1}$. F is called *lead (or forward) operator*. These operators are such that

$$L^n x_t = x_{t-n}, \quad F^n x_t = x_{t+n},$$

and

$$\left(\sum_{i=0}^{n} a_i L^i\right) x_t = \sum_{i=0}^{n} a_i x_{t-i}.$$

The latter equality shows the effect of a polynomial in L on a process.

5.2.1 Series in L

In a more general way, we can define the series in the operator L (or in the operator F). In order to do that, let us restrict ourselves to the set of stationary processes.

Given a stationary process $\{x_t\}$ and an absolutely summable sequence a_i such that $\sum_{i=-\infty}^{+\infty} \mid a_i \mid < +\infty$, we know that the process defined as

$$y_t = \sum_{i=-\infty}^{+\infty} a_i x_{t-i}$$

is a stationary process (cf. theorem 5.6). Let us denote as

$$\sum_{i=-\infty}^{+\infty} a_i L^i$$

the mapping of the stationary process $\{x_t\}$ onto the stationary process $\{y_t\}$. These operator series in L enjoy some properties which allow their manipulation as the original series. In particular, we can sum them and compose them with one another.

Sums of Series in L

$$\left(\sum_{i=-\infty}^{+\infty} a_i L^i + \sum_{i=-\infty}^{+\infty} \alpha_i L^i \right) x_t$$

$$= \sum_{i=-\infty}^{+\infty} a_i L^i x_t + \sum_{i=-\infty}^{+\infty} \alpha_i L^i x_t$$

$$= \sum_{i=-\infty}^{+\infty} a_i x_{t-i} + \sum_{i=-\infty}^{+\infty} \alpha_i x_{t-i}$$

$$= \lim_{\substack{m \to +\infty \\ n \to +\infty}} \left(\sum_{i=-m}^{n} a_i x_{t-i} + \sum_{i=-m}^{n} \alpha_i x_{t-i} \right) \text{(limit in } L_2)$$

$$= \lim_{\substack{m \to +\infty \\ n \to +\infty}} \left(\sum_{i=-m}^{n} (a_i + \alpha_i) x_{t-i} \right)$$

$$= \sum_{i=-\infty}^{+\infty} (a_i + \alpha_i) x_{t-i}$$

$$= \left(\sum_{i=-\infty}^{+\infty} (a_i + \alpha_i) L^i \right) x_t,$$

since the sequence $a + \alpha$ is absolutely summable, given that both a and α are summable. Finally we can see that

$$\sum_{i=-\infty}^{+\infty} a_i L^i + \sum_{i=-\infty}^{+\infty} \alpha_i L^i = \sum_{i=-\infty}^{+\infty} (a_i + \alpha_i) L^i.$$

Analogously, we can show that

$$\lambda \sum_{i=-\infty}^{+\infty} a_i L^i = \sum_{i=-\infty}^{+\infty} \lambda a_i L^i.$$

Product of Series in L

Theorem 5.9:

$$\left(\sum_{j=-\infty}^{+\infty} \alpha_j L^j\right)\left(\sum_{i=-\infty}^{+\infty} a_i L^i\right) x_t$$

$$= \lim_{\substack{n,m\to+\infty \\ r,s\to+\infty}} \left(\sum_{j=-m}^{n} \alpha_j L^j\right)\left(\sum_{i=-r}^{s} a_i L^i\right) x_t.$$

PROOF: Let us denote

$$S_{n,m} = \sum_{j=-m}^{n} \alpha_j L^j,$$

$$S = \sum_{j=-\infty}^{+\infty} \alpha_j L^j,$$

$$\tilde{S} = \sum_{i=-\infty}^{+\infty} a_i L^i,$$

$$\tilde{S}_{s,r} = \sum_{i=-r}^{s} a_i L^i.$$

We have

$$\| S\tilde{S}x_t - S_{n,m}\tilde{S}_{s,r}x_t \|$$

$$\leq \| S\tilde{S}x_t - S_{n,m}\tilde{S}x_t \| + \| S_{n,m}\tilde{S}x_t - S_{n,m}\tilde{S}_{s,r}x_t \|$$

$$= \| S(\tilde{S}x_t) - S_{n,m}(\tilde{S}x_t) \| + \| S_{n,m}(\tilde{S}x_t - \tilde{S}_{s,r}x_t) \|$$

$$\leq \| S(\tilde{S}x_t) - S_{n,m}(\tilde{S}x_t) \| + \left(\sum_{j=-m}^{n} | a_j |\right) \| \tilde{S}x_t - \tilde{S}_{s,r}x_t \|$$

$$\leq \| S(\tilde{S}x_t) - S_{n,m}(\tilde{S}x_t) \| + \left(\sum_{j=-\infty}^{+\infty} | a_j |\right) \| \tilde{S}x_t - \tilde{S}_{s,r}x_t \|.$$

The proposition is then a consequence of

$$Sy_t = \lim_{n,m\to+\infty} S_{n,m}y_t, \qquad \tilde{S}x_t = \lim_{r,s\to+\infty} \tilde{S}_{s,r}x_t.$$

where the limits are taken in L_2. $\square$

Corollary: *The product of two series in L is a series in L.*

PROOF:

$$\left(\sum_{j=-\infty}^{+\infty} \alpha_j L^j \right) \left(\sum_{i=-\infty}^{+\infty} a_i L^i \right) x_t$$

$$= \lim_{\substack{n,m\to+\infty \\ r,s\to+\infty}} \left(\sum_{j=-m}^{n} \alpha_j L^j \right) \left(\sum_{i=-r}^{s} a_i L^i \right) x_t$$

$$= \lim_{\substack{n,m\to+\infty \\ r,s\to+\infty}} \sum_{k=-m-r}^{n+s} \left(\sum_{i=\max(-r,k-n)}^{\min(s,k+m)} a_i \alpha_{k-i} \right) L^k x_t$$

$$= \sum_{k=-\infty}^{+\infty} \left(\sum_{i=-\infty}^{+\infty} a_i \alpha_{k-i} \right) L^k x_t$$

since $b_k = \sum_{i=-\infty}^{+\infty} a_i \alpha_{k-i}$ exists and the series with terms b_k is absolutely summable. The sequence is just the convolution product of the sequences α and a. □

Corollary: *The product of series in L is commutative.*

PROOF:

$$\sum_{i=-\infty}^{+\infty} a_i \alpha_{k-i} = \sum_{i=-\infty}^{+\infty} a_{k-i} \alpha_i.$$

□

5.2.2 Inversion of $(1-\lambda L)$

$(1 - \lambda L)$ is a mapping of the set of stationary processes onto itself. Let us show that this mapping is invertible if and only if $|\lambda| \neq 1$ and derive its inverse when it exists.

Case $|\lambda| < 1$ The real series

$$a_i = \begin{cases} \lambda^i, & \text{if } i \geq 0, \\ 0, & \text{if } i < 0, \end{cases}$$

is absolutely summable, so that the series $\sum_{i=0}^{+\infty} \lambda^i L^i$ can be defined. Multiplying this series by $(1 - \lambda L)$ we get

$$\sum_{i=0}^{+\infty} \lambda^i L^i (1 - \lambda L) = L^0 = 1.$$

$(1 - \lambda L)$ is therefore invertible and its inverse, denoted as $(1 - \lambda L)^{-1}$ or $1/(1 - \lambda L)$, is equal to

$$\sum_{i=0}^{+\infty} \lambda^i L^i.$$

Put in a different way, given a stationary process $\{x_t\}$, the process $\{y_t\}$, defined as

$$y_t = \sum_{i=0}^{+\infty} \lambda^i x_{t-i},$$

is the only stationary process satisfying

$$(1 - \lambda L)y_t^* = y_t^* - \lambda y_{t-1}^* = x_t.$$

This is not the only process satisfying this equation. The other solutions can be found adding to y_t the general solution to the homogeneous equation $y_t^* - \lambda y_{t-1}^* = 0$, that is $A\lambda^t$, where A is a generic random variable. The solutions corresponding to $A \neq 0$ are not stationary.

Case $|\lambda| > 1$ We have

$$1 - \lambda L = -\lambda L \left(1 - \frac{1}{\lambda} F\right).$$

The inverse of $(-\lambda L)$ is equal to $-\frac{1}{\lambda} F = -\frac{1}{\lambda} L^{-1}$. Note that $\left|\frac{1}{\lambda}\right| < 1$ and the series

$$\sum_{i=0}^{+\infty} \frac{1}{\lambda^i} F^i = \sum_{i=0}^{+\infty} \frac{1}{\lambda^i} L^{-i}$$

exists and is the inverse of $(1 - \frac{1}{\lambda} F)$. Therefore $(1 - \lambda L)$, composition of two invertible functions, is invertible as well. Its inverse is given by

$$\frac{1}{1 - \lambda L} = (-\lambda L)^{-1} \left(1 - \frac{1}{\lambda} F\right)^{-1}$$

$$= \left(-\frac{1}{\lambda} F\right) \left(\sum_{i=0}^{+\infty} \frac{1}{\lambda^i} F^i\right)$$

$$= -\sum_{i=0}^{+\infty} \frac{1}{\lambda^{i+1}} F^{i+1}$$

$$= -\sum_{i=1}^{+\infty} \frac{1}{\lambda^i} F^i = -\sum_{i=-1}^{-\infty} \lambda^i L^i.$$

Case $|\lambda| = 1$ In this case, the mapping $(1 - \lambda L)$ is not invertible. Let us assume for example $\lambda = 1$. Any constant process $x_t = m$ is transformed into $(1 - L)x_t = m - m = 0$. The mapping is not one-to-one. By the same token it is not onto either, since integrating out the process $m \neq 0$ does not provide a stationary process. If there existed one, we would in fact have

$$x_t - x_{t-1} = m \Rightarrow E(x_t) - E(x_{t-1}) = m \Rightarrow 0 = m,$$

a contradiction.

5.2.3 Inverse of a Polynomial

Let us consider a polynomial

$$\Phi(z) = 1 + \phi_1 z + \ldots + \phi_p z^p$$

the roots of which, $z_j = 1/\lambda_j$ are greater than 1 in modulus. We know that there exists an integer series

$$\Psi(z) = \sum_{i=0}^{+\infty} \psi_i z^i,$$

such that

$$\sum_{i=0}^{+\infty} |\psi_i| < +\infty \quad \text{and} \quad \Phi(z)\Psi(z) = 1.$$

Being the properties of the series in L (an operator defined on the set of stationary series) identical to those of the power series, we have that

$$\Phi(L)\Psi(L) = 1.$$

Hence the polynomial $\Phi(L) = 1 + \phi_1 L + \ldots + \phi_p L^p$ is invertible and its inverse is $\Psi(L)$.

The coefficients ψ_i can be determined using one of the three following methods.

First Method Make explicit the relationship $\Phi(z)\Psi(z) = 1$. Isolating the coefficients of the terms of the same degree, we get a system of equations in ψ_i which can be solved in a recursive way

$$\psi_0 = 1,$$

$$\psi_1 + \phi_1 = 0,$$

$$\psi_2 + \phi_1\psi_1 + \phi_2 = 0,$$

$$\psi_p + \phi_1\psi_{p-1} + \ldots + \phi_{p-1}\psi_1 + \phi_p = 0,$$

$$\ldots$$

$$\psi_n + \phi_1\psi_{n-1} + \ldots + \phi_{p-1}\psi_{n-p+1} + \phi_p\psi_{n-p} = 0, \quad \forall\, n > p.$$

(5.8)

Second Method Divide 1 by $\Phi(z)$ according to increasing powers of z (cf. the appendix to chapter 7). The coefficients ψ_j will result from

$$1 = \Phi(z)\,(\psi_0 + \psi_1 z + \ldots + \psi_r z^r) + z^{r+1}\lambda_r(z), \ \forall\, r,$$

where $\lambda_r(z)$ are polynomials in z.

Third Method Decompose the fraction $1/\Phi(z)$ in simple elements and write the series expansion of each element of the decomposition. Thus, if all roots of Φ are real distinct, we can write

$$\frac{1}{\Phi(z)} = \frac{1}{\prod_{i=1}^{p}(1 - \lambda_i z)} = \sum_{i=1}^{p} \frac{a_i}{1 - \lambda_i z}$$

$$= \sum_{i=1}^{p} a_i \sum_{j=0}^{+\infty} \lambda_i^j z^j = \sum_{j=0}^{+\infty} \left(\sum_{i=1}^{p} a_i \lambda_i^j \right) z^j.$$

The case of complex or multiple roots can be treated in the usual way (Branson, 1991).

The inverse of the polynomial $\Phi(L)$, an operator defined on the set of the stationary processes, exists as long as the roots of Φ are different from 1 in modulus. Let us assume that the first r roots are greater than 1 in modulus, and the second $p - r$ less than 1 in modulus.

$$\Phi(L) = \prod_{i=1}^{p}(1 - \lambda_i L)$$

$$= \prod_{i=1}^{r}(1 - \lambda_i L) \prod_{i=r+1}^{p} \left(1 - \frac{1}{\lambda_i F} \right) \prod_{i=r+1}^{p} (-\lambda_i L),$$

where, with an obvious notation

$$\Phi(L) = \Phi_1(L)\Phi_2(F)\lambda L^{p-r}.$$

Since Φ_1 and Φ_2 have their roots greater than 1 in modulus, we know that $\Phi_1(L)$ and $\Phi_2(F)$ are invertible. Therefore, $\Phi(L)$ is invertible, and its inverse is given by

$$\frac{1}{\Phi(L)} = \frac{1}{\Phi_1(L)} \frac{1}{\Phi_2(F)} \frac{1}{\lambda} F^{(p-r)}.$$

In this series expansion of $1/\Phi(L)$ the negative powers of L are present if and only if $p = r$, that is if and only if all roots are greater than 1 in modulus.

5.3 ARMA Processes

5.3.1 Autoregressive Processes

Definition 5.9: *We define as an* autoregressive process *of order p a stationary process* $\{x_t\}$ *satisfying a relationship of the type*

$$x_t + \sum_{i=1}^{p} \phi_i x_{t-i} = \epsilon_t, \tag{5.9}$$

where the ϕ_i's *are real numbers and* $\{\epsilon_t\}$ *is a white noise with variance* σ^2.

The relationship (5.9) can be written also as

$$(1 + \phi_1 L + \ldots + \phi_p L^p) x_t = \epsilon_t,$$

or

$$\Phi(L)x_t = \epsilon_t. \tag{5.10}$$

Such a process is denoted AR(p).

Infinite Moving Average Representation This process is defined for the moment in implicit form. In particular, it is not certain that equation (5.9) admits a stationary solution always. In order to study this problem, we can use the results obtained in section 5.2.3.

If the polynomial Φ has all its roots different from 1 in modulus, we can invert the operator $\Phi(L)$ defined on the set of the stationary processes, so that the equation admits a unique solution with an infinite moving average representation of the type

$$x_t = \Phi(L)^{-1}\epsilon_t = \sum_{j=-\infty}^{+\infty} h_j \epsilon_{t-j}, \text{ with } \sum_{j=-\infty}^{+\infty} |h_j| < +\infty.$$

Generally, the present value of the process $\{x_t\}$ depends upon past, present and future values of the white noise at once. Certain of these components may however disappear in the expression of x_t. Thus if the polynomial Φ has all its roots strictly greater than 1 in modulus, the inverse operator $\Phi(L)^{-1}$ admits an expansion which involves only the positive powers of L. We have then

$$x_t = \sum_{j=0}^{+\infty} h_j \epsilon_{t-j}, \text{ with } \sum_{j=0}^{+\infty} |h_j| < +\infty, \text{ and } h_0 = 1.$$

In this case, $x_{t-1}, x_{t-2}, \ldots$ are linear functions of $\epsilon_{t-1}, \epsilon_{t-2}, \ldots$ and are not correlated with ϵ_t. Projecting the autoregressive relationship (5.8) onto the past of x: $x_{t-1}, x_{t-2}, \ldots$, we get

$$\hat{x}_{t-1}(1) = -\sum_{i=1}^{p} \phi_i x_{t-i},$$

$$x_t - \hat{x}_{t-1}(1) = \epsilon_t. \tag{5.11}$$

The white noise can then be interpreted as the innovation process associated with x. When the components ϵ_t are not only uncorrelated, but also independent, $\hat{x}_{t-1}(1) = -\sum_{i=1}^{p} \phi_i x_{t-i}$ is not only the affine regression of x_t on the x_s, $s \leq t - 1$, but also the conditional expectation of x_t based on the x_s, $s \leq t - 1$.

Transformation of the Roots Whenever the roots of $\Phi(z)$ are different from 1 in modulus, it can be shown that we can always assume that these roots are greater than 1 in modulus, even if this entails a change in the associated white noise. It is instructive to start from the spectral density of the process. We have

$$\frac{\sigma^2}{2\pi} = f_x(\omega) \mid 1 + \sum_{j=1}^{p} \phi_j e^{i\omega j} \mid^2,$$

from which

$$f_x(\omega) = \frac{\sigma^2}{2\pi \mid 1 + \sum_{j=1}^{p} \phi_j e^{i\omega j} \mid^2}$$

$$= \frac{\sigma^2}{2\pi \mid \Phi(e^{i\omega}) \mid^2}$$

$$= \frac{\sigma^2}{2\pi \mid \prod_{j=1}^{p} (1 - e^{i\omega}/z_j) \mid^2},$$

where $z_j = 1/\lambda_j$ are the roots of Φ.

Let us assume that the first r roots of Φ are greater than 1 in modulus, and that the last $(p - r)$ are smaller than 1 in modulus. We will denote the polynomial obtained by replacing in Φ the roots smaller than 1 in modulus by their inverses by

$$\Phi^*(z) = \prod_{j=1}^{r} \left(1 - \frac{L}{z_j}\right) \prod_{j=r+1}^{p} (1 - z_j L).$$

Let us consider the stationary process $\{\eta_t\}$ defined as

$$\eta_t = \Phi^*(L)x_t. \tag{5.12}$$

The computation of the spectral density of such a process shows immediately that it is a white noise. In fact

$$f_\eta(\omega) = \mid \Phi^*(e^{i\omega}) \mid^2 f_x(\omega)$$

$$= \frac{\sigma^2}{2\pi} \left| \frac{\Phi^*(e^{i\omega})}{\Phi(e^{i\omega})} \right|^2$$

$$= \frac{\sigma^2}{2\pi} \prod_{j=r+1}^{p} \frac{\mid 1 - z_j e^{i\omega} \mid^2}{\mid 1 - \frac{1}{z_j} e^{i\omega} \mid^2}$$

$$= \frac{\sigma^2}{2\pi} \prod_{j=r+1}^{p} \mid z_j \mid^2,$$

which is independent of ω. Thus $\{\eta_t\}$ is a white noise with variance

$$\sigma^2 \prod_{j=r+1}^{p} \mid z_j \mid^2$$

which is smaller than the one of $\{\epsilon_t\}$. This shows that we can always
assume the roots of an autoregressive process greater than 1 in modulus.
Moreover, the representation of $\{x_t\}$ thus obtained involves a white noise
$\{\eta_t\}$ which can be interpreted as an innovation, the variance of which is
smaller than the variance of the initial white noise.

It should be clear that by taking a root or its inverse we get multiple
representations of $\{x_t\}$ (exactly 2^p if the roots are real) and we need
to choose among them. It should also be clear that the choice of the
representation in which the roots are greater than 1 in modulus (defined
as *canonical representation*) is the best one in the sense that it is the
only one that shows the innovation explicitly. We will retain this choice
in what follows. We have

$$x_t = \sum_{j=0}^{+\infty} h_j \epsilon_{t-j} \quad \text{with} \quad \sum_{j=0}^{+\infty} |h_j| < +\infty, \quad \text{and } h_0 = 1.$$

The various h_j can be obtained by dividing 1 by $(1 + \phi_1 z + \ldots + \phi_p z^p)$
according to increasing powers of z.

Let us remark that if we considered the process $\{\xi_t\}$ defined as

$$\xi_t = \Phi(F)x_t, \tag{5.13}$$

we would have obtained a white noise with the same variance as ϵ_t. ξ_t
may be interpreted as a backcast error of x_t based on the knowledge of
its future

$$\xi_t = x_t - E(x_t \mid x_{t+1}, x_{t+2} \ldots).$$

Then we say that we have obtained a time reversal and equation (5.12)
is called *forward representation* of the process $\{x\}$.

Yule–Walker Equations Let us examine the autocovariance function of $\{x_t\}$. Multiplying (5.9) by x_t we get

$$x_t^2 = -\sum_{i=1}^{p} \phi_i x_t x_{t-i} + \epsilon_t x_t.$$

Taking the expectation

$$\gamma(0) = -\sum_{i=1}^{p} \phi_i \gamma(i) + \sigma^2.$$

Therefore, dividing both sides by $\gamma(0)$ and collecting terms

$$\gamma(0) = \frac{\sigma^2}{1 + \sum_{i=1}^{p} \phi_i \rho(i)}.$$

Multiplying (5.9) by x_{t-h}, $h > 0$, taking the expectation and dividing by $\gamma(0)$, we get

$$\rho(h) + \sum_{i=1}^{p} \phi_i \rho(h - i) = 0, \; \forall \; h > 0. \tag{5.14}$$

The sequence of the autocorrelations satisfies a linear homogeneous difference equation of order p, the coefficients of which are directly related to those of the autoregressive polynomial.

The characteristic polynomial associated with this difference equation is

$$z^p + \sum_{i=1}^{p} \phi_i z^{p-i} = z^p \Phi(z^{-1}),$$

the roots of which, equal to z_i^{-1}, are smaller than 1 in modulus. We know that, as a consequence, the function $\rho(h)$ will be a combination of various components: decreasing exponentials corresponding to the real roots, dampened sine-waves corresponding to the complex roots, with multiple roots introducing polynomial factors (cf. chapter 3).

Writing (5.13) for $h = 1, \ldots, p$ and exploiting the evenness of $\rho(h)$ we get the so-called Yule–Walker equations

$$\begin{pmatrix} \rho(1) \\ \vdots \\ \rho(p) \end{pmatrix} = \begin{pmatrix} 1 & \rho(1) & \rho(2) & \cdots & \rho(p-1) \\ \rho(1) & 1 & \rho(1) & \cdots & \rho(p-2) \\ \vdots & \vdots & & & \vdots \\ \rho(p-1) & & \cdots & \rho(1) & 1 \end{pmatrix} = \begin{pmatrix} \phi_1 \\ \vdots \\ \phi_p \end{pmatrix}.$$

$$\tag{5.15}$$

These equations are bilinear in $\rho(h), \phi_i$. In the form (5.14) they allow to get the ϕ_i's as a function of $\rho(1), \ldots, \rho(p)$ by inversion. We can also express them as a linear system in $\rho(1), \ldots, \rho(p)$ and obtain the expression of these quantities as a function of $\phi_1, \ldots, \phi_p$. The other values of $\rho(h)$ are obtained recursively using (5.13).

The difference equation (5.13) admits just one sequence as a solution, which can be interpreted as an autocorrelation function. In fact, as we have just shown, the initial values $\rho(1), \ldots, \rho(p)$ are determined without ambiguity.

Partial Autocorrelation Function The partial autocorrelation function $r(h)$ can be obtained starting from the correlations $\rho(h)$ using the general methods exposed previously in section 5.1.4. For an AR(p) process, however, we need to stress an important property

$$r(h) = 0, \ \forall \ h > p. \tag{5.16}$$

In fact, $\forall \ h > p$, (5.9) can be written as

$$x_t = -\sum_{i=1}^{p} \phi_i x_{t-i} + 0 \sum_{i=p+1}^{h} x_{t-i} + \epsilon_t,$$

with $E(\epsilon_t) = 0$, $E(\epsilon_t x_{t-i}) = 0$, $i = 1, \ldots, h$. As a consequence, $r(h) = 0$, since $r(h)$ can be interpreted as the coefficient of x_{t-h} in the regression of x_t on $x_{t-1}, \ldots, x_{t-h}$.

Note that $r(p) = \phi_p$, so that $r(p)$ is different from zero if ϕ_p is different from zero, that is if the process is a true AR(p).

Autoregressive Process of Order 1 Let us suppose that we have

$$x_t - \phi x_{t-1} = \epsilon_t, \tag{5.17}$$

where $\{\epsilon_t\}$ is a white noise with variance σ^2.

(i) If $|\phi| = 1$ there is no stationary process satisfying this equation. In fact, let us suppose that, for example, $\phi = 1$. By substitution we would get

$$x_t - x_{t-n} = \epsilon_t + \epsilon_{t-1} + \ldots + \epsilon_{t-n+1}.$$

Therefore

$$E(x_t - x_{t-n})^2 = n\sigma^2,$$

$\forall$ integer n. If $\{x_t\}$ were stationary, we would have

$$E(x_t - x_{t-n})^2 \leq 4\sigma_x^2,$$

since $|\text{cov}\,(x_t, x_{t-n})| \leq \sigma_x^2$, where σ_x^2 is the common variance of the x_t. Hence

$$n\sigma_x^2 \leq 4\sigma_x^2, \qquad \forall \text{ integer } n,$$

which is impossible. An analogous reasoning leads to the same result for $\phi = -1$.

Hence we may assume $|\phi| \neq 1$, and we know that there is a unique stationary process satisfying

$$x_t - \phi x_{t-1} = \epsilon_t,$$

or

$$(1 - \phi L) x_t = \epsilon_t.$$

(ii) If $|\phi| > 1$, we have

$$-\phi L \left(1 - \frac{1}{\phi} F \right) x_t = \epsilon_t,$$

$$x_t = -\frac{1}{\phi} F \left(1 - \frac{1}{\phi} F \right)^{-1} \epsilon_t$$

$$= -\sum_{i=1}^{+\infty} \phi^{-i} \epsilon_{t+i},$$

and the canonical representation is

$$x_t - \frac{1}{\phi} x_{t-1} = \eta_t,$$

where η_t is the innovation at time t.

(iii) If $|\phi| < 1$ we have

$$x_t = (1 - \phi L)^{-1} \epsilon_t$$

$$= \sum_{i=1}^{+\infty} \phi^i \epsilon_{t-i},$$

where ϵ_t is the innovation at the date t.
The forward representation of the process is then

$$x_t - \phi x_{t+1} = \xi_t.$$

We can express the white noise ξ as a function of ϵ

$$\xi_t = \frac{1 - \phi F}{1 - \phi L} \epsilon_t$$

$$= \sum_{i=0}^{+\infty} \phi^i \epsilon_{t-i} - \sum_{i=0}^{+\infty} \phi^{i+1} \epsilon_{t+1-i}$$

$$= -\phi \epsilon_{t+1} + (1 - \phi^2) \sum_{i=0}^{+\infty} \phi^i \epsilon_{t-i}.$$

By the same token, note that

$$x_t = \frac{1}{1 - \phi F} \xi_t$$

$$= \sum_{i=0}^{+\infty} \phi^i \xi_{t+i},$$

and therefore ξ_t is uncorrelated with $x_s, \forall\, s \geq t + 1$.

Finally, we have

$$\rho(h) = \phi \rho(h - 1), \; \forall\, h > 0,$$

from which

$$\rho(h) = \phi^h, \; \forall\, h > 0,$$

since $\rho(0) = 1$ and $\rho(h) = \phi^{|h|} \; \forall\, h$

$$\gamma(0) = \frac{\sigma^2}{1 - \phi^2},$$

$$r(1) = \phi, \; r(h) = 0, \; \forall\, h > 1.$$

The coefficient ϕ can be interpreted as the correlation of order 1. The variance–covariance matrix of $x_t, x_{t+1}, \ldots, x_{t+h}$ can be written as

$$\mathrm{var} \begin{pmatrix} x_t \\ x_{t+1} \\ \vdots \\ x_{t+h} \end{pmatrix} = \frac{\sigma^2}{1 - \phi^2} \begin{pmatrix} 1 & \phi & \phi^2 & \cdots & \phi^h \\ \phi & 1 & \phi & \cdots & \phi^{h-1} \\ \vdots & \vdots & \ddots & \ddots & \vdots \\ \phi^{h-1} & \phi^{h-2} & \cdots & 1 & \phi \\ \phi^h & \phi^{h-1} & \cdots & \phi & 1 \end{pmatrix},$$

for $h \geq 0$.

Graphical Representations of Second-Order Properties

Example 5.7: Let us derive as an example the autocorrelation function for an AR(2) process of the type

$$x_t + 0.9x_{t-1} - 0.8x_{t-2} = \epsilon_t.$$

The polynomial Φ is of second degree; its discriminant is equal to -2.39, hence it is negative. The roots are complex. This explains the sine-wave shape of the correlogram (figure 5.7).

The correlations of order 1, 3, 6 are fairly large in modulus. This property should be reproduced in the paths of the series generated by this process. A large value at a certain date should in general imply a small value after three time periods and a large value six periods after (the size of the values – large or small – depends on the sign of ρ).

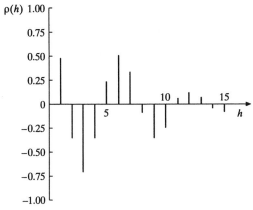

Figure 5.7   Correlogram for the AR(2) process

Figure 5.8   Path for an AR(2) process

In figure 5.8 we report the path of x_t, showing this phenomenon. The presence of the white noise (with variance $\sigma^2 = 4$) implies that the function is not strictly periodical.

Example 5.8: The temporal links can be analyzed through the spectral density. In the case of an AR(1) process, we have

$$f(\omega) = \frac{\sigma^2}{2\pi} \frac{1}{\mid 1 - \phi e^{i\omega} \mid^2} = \frac{\sigma^2}{2\pi} \frac{1}{1 + \phi^2 - 2\phi \cos \omega}.$$

The spectrum implies the graph in figure 5.9 for $\phi > 0$. We see that the largest values of the spectral density correspond to low frequencies, that is to long periods.

This phenomenon becomes more apparent as ϕ approaches 1, since

$$f(0) = \frac{\sigma^2}{2\pi(1 - \phi)^2}, \qquad f(\pi) = \frac{\sigma^2}{2\pi(1 + \phi)^2}.$$

In this case, there is a greater importance of the long-period phenomena (cf. chapter 8). Since the long-period series show a very smooth profile, this characteristic should be found in their paths. These should fluctuate "not much" and without a marked periodic behavior for $\phi \approx 1$. We

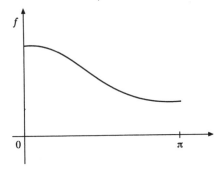

Figure 5.9   Example of the spectrum of an AR(1) process

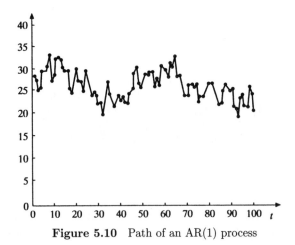

Figure 5.10   Path of an AR(1) process

present in figure 5.10 a realization of a process of the type $x_t = 0.8x_{t-1} + \epsilon_t$ with $\sigma^2 = 4$.

We see clearly that, although the process has a theoretical mean of zero, this property cannot be found in the graph. The fairly strong correlation $\rho(1) = \phi = 0.8$ has the consequence that the first observation, fairly large here, influences the following ones. The various fluctuations due to the white noise are fairly small relative to the value of the empirical mean of x_t. This shows mainly that some AR models can be used in certain cases to approximate time series with a nonstationary profile.

Inverse Autocorrelations   The inverse of the spectral density is given by

$$\frac{1}{f(\omega)} = \frac{2\pi}{\sigma^2} \mid \Phi(e^{i\omega}) \mid^2 .$$

The series expansion of $1/f(\omega)$ as a function of the powers of $e^{i\omega}$ shows that

$$\frac{1}{f(\omega)} = \frac{1}{2\pi} \sum_{h=-\infty}^{+\infty} \gamma i(h) e^{i\omega h} = \frac{2\pi}{\sigma^2} \sum_{j=-p}^{p} c_j e^{i\omega j},$$

where the coefficients c_j can be obtained starting from the polynomial Φ.

We can conclude that

$$\rho i(h) = 0 \quad \forall \, h \geq p+1,$$

$$\rho i(p) = \rho i(-p) = c_p \neq 0.$$

Thus, the order p is such that the inverse autocorrelations become zero starting from $p+1$. This time p is characterized by the values of the inverse autocorrelations $\rho i(h)$. To determine the latter we have

$$| \, \Phi(e^{i\omega}) \, |^2 = \left(\sum_{j=0}^{p} \phi_j e^{i\omega j} \right) \left(\sum_{k=0}^{p} \phi_k e^{-i\omega k} \right)$$

$$= \sum_{j=0}^{p} \sum_{k=0}^{p} \phi_j \phi_k e^{-i\omega(j-k)}$$

$$= \sum_{j=-p}^{p} e^{i\omega j} \left(\sum_{k=0}^{p-|j|} \phi_k \phi_{k+|j|} \right).$$

Hence

$$c_j = \sum_{k=0}^{p-j} \phi_k \phi_{k+j}, \; 0 \leq j \leq p,$$

and $c_j = c_{-j}$. Moreover, since

$$\rho i(h) = \frac{\gamma i(h)}{\gamma i(0)} = \frac{c_h}{c_0},$$

we have the expression

$$\rho i(h) = \frac{\sum_{k=0}^{p-h} \phi_k \phi_{k+h}}{\sum_{k=0}^{p} \phi_k^2}, \quad \text{for } 0 \leq h \leq p. \tag{5.18}$$

This formula is at the basis of the computation of the inverse autocorrelations (Cleveland, 1972).

5.3.2 Moving Average Processes

Definition 5.10: *We call* moving average process *of order* q, MA(q) *a process* $\{x_t\}$ *defined as*

$$x_t = \epsilon_t + \theta_1 \epsilon_{t-1} + \ldots + \theta_q \epsilon_{t-q}, \tag{5.19}$$

where the θ_i *are real numbers, and* ϵ_t *is a white noise with variance* σ^2.

This relationship can be written as
$$x_t = (1 + \theta_1 L + \ldots + \theta_q L^q)\epsilon_t,$$
or
$$x_t = \Theta(L)\epsilon_t.$$
Note that, contrary to the case of an AR(p), the definition of an MA(q) is explicit and does not pose any problems. The process $\{x_t\}$ is completely defined by (5.18) and is automatically stationary.

Infinite Autoregressive Representation Whenever (as we will assume in what follows) $\Theta(z)$ does not have roots equal to 1 in modulus, we can write
$$\sum_{i=-\infty}^{+\infty} \pi_i x_{t-i} = \epsilon_t, \text{ with } \sum_{i=-\infty}^{+\infty} |\pi_i| < +\infty.$$
Moreover, if the roots of $\Theta(z)$ are all greater than 1 in modulus, we have $\pi_i = 0$, $\forall\, i < 0$, and ϵ_t can be interpreted as the innovation of the process. The proof is analogous to the one of section 5.3.2 above. We say then that the process is *invertible*.

Transformation of the Roots As it will be shown, so long as $\Theta(z)$ does not have roots equal to 1 in modulus, we can assume that the process is invertible, but this entails a change in the white noise process. We have
$$x_t = -\sum_{i=1}^{+\infty} \pi_i x_{t-i} + \epsilon_t, \quad \text{with } \sum_{i=-\infty}^{+\infty} |\pi_i| < +\infty. \qquad (5.20)$$
Let us assume that $\Theta(z)$ does not have roots equal to 1 in modulus. Let us denote by $\Theta^*(z)$ the polynomial obtained from $\Theta(z)$ replacing the roots smaller than 1 in modulus by their inverse and let us consider the process $\{\eta_t\}$ defined as
$$x_t = \Theta^*(L)\eta_t.$$
We can easily verify that the spectral density of $\{x_t\}$ is
$$f_x(\omega) = \frac{\sigma^2}{2\pi} \mid \Theta(e^{i\omega}) \mid^2.$$
Computing the spectral density of $\{\eta_t\}$ we can show (following the same procedure as for the autoregressive case) that this process is a white noise with variance
$$\frac{\sigma^2}{\prod_j \mid z_j \mid^2}.$$
The z_j are the roots smaller than 1 in modulus: therefore the variance

of η_t is greater than the one of ϵ_t. More generally, we can get multiple representations of the process $\{x\}$ of this type by inverting any number of roots of Θ (taking the conjugate complex roots in pairs).

In what follows we will avoid this identification problem, imposing that the roots of $\Theta(z)$ be greater than 1 in modulus. This representation will be labelled *canonical representation*: the white noise appearing in such a representation will be called innovation of the process, and the π_i's can be obtained by the long division of 1 by $\Theta(z)$.

Forward Representation Following (5.12), the process $\{\xi_t\}$ defined as $x_t = \Theta(F)\xi_t$ is a white noise with variance σ^2. This provides the *forward representation* of the process. Since Θ has its roots greater than 1 in modulus, ξ_t is uncorrelated with x_s, $s \geq t + 1$.

Autocovariance Function The autocovariance function is given by

$$\gamma(h) = E(x_t x_{t-h})$$

$$= E\left((\epsilon_t + \theta_1 \epsilon_{t-1} + \ldots + \theta_q \epsilon_{t-q})\right.$$

$$\left. \times (\epsilon_{t-h} + \theta_1 \epsilon_{t-h-1} + \ldots + \theta_q \epsilon_{t-h-q})\right)$$

$$= \begin{cases} (\theta_h + \theta_{h+1}\theta_1 + \ldots + \theta_q \theta_{q-h})\sigma^2, & \text{if } 1 \leq h \leq q, \\ 0, & \text{if } h > q. \end{cases}$$

For $h = 0$ we get

$$\gamma(0) = (1 + \theta_1^2 + \ldots \theta_q^2)\sigma^2.$$

The autocorrelation function can be derived as

$$\rho(h) = \frac{(\theta_h + \theta_{h+1}\theta_1 + \ldots + \theta_q \theta_{q-h})}{1 + \theta_1^2 + \ldots + \theta_q^2},$$

if $1 \leq h \leq q$ or equal to 0 if $h > q$.

Note that

$$\rho(q) = \frac{\theta_q}{1 + \theta_1^2 + \ldots + \theta_q^2}$$

is different from zero as soon as θ_q is different from zero, that is, if the process is a true MA(q). The function $\rho(h)$ becomes zero for $h > q$. There exists a sort of "duality" between the autocorrelation function $\rho(\cdot)$ of an MA(q) process and the partial autocorrelation function $r(\cdot)$ of an AR(p) process.

Partial Autocorrelations The partial autocorrelation function $r(\cdot)$ can be computed by the general methods exposed in the autoregressive case, but the formulas are more complicated. Moreover, $r(h)$ does not have the property of becoming zero for h beyond a certain value.

Moving Average Process of Order 1 A moving average process of order 1 is defined as

$$x_t = \epsilon_t - \theta\epsilon_{t-1} = (1 - \theta L)\epsilon_t, \tag{5.21}$$

where ϵ_t is a white noise with variance σ^2.

(i) Correlation We have

$$\rho(1) = \frac{-\theta}{1 + \theta^2},$$

which implies

$$-\frac{1}{2} \le \rho(1) \le \frac{1}{2}$$

and $\rho(h) = 0 \ \forall \ h \ge 2$. A moving average process is not appropriate to describe strong first-order correlations.

(ii) Regression Coefficients The regression coefficients of x_t on $x_{t-1}, \ldots, x_{t-K}$ are such that

$$\begin{pmatrix} 1 & \rho(1) & \cdots & 0 & 0 \\ \rho(1) & 1 & \cdots & 0 & 0 \\ \vdots & \vdots & \ddots & \vdots & \vdots \\ 0 & 0 & \cdots & 1 & \rho(1) \\ 0 & 0 & \cdots & \rho(1) & 1 \end{pmatrix} \begin{pmatrix} a_1(K) \\ \vdots \\ a_K(K) \end{pmatrix} = \begin{pmatrix} \rho(1) \\ 0 \\ \vdots \\ 0 \end{pmatrix}, \quad \forall \ K.$$

Thus, for $k = 2, \ldots, K - 1$, we have

$$\rho(1)a_{k-1}(K) + a_k(K) + \rho(1)a_{k+1}(K) = 0.$$

The regression coefficients satisfy a second-order linear difference equation. The characteristic polynomial of this relationship is

$$\rho(1)z^2 + z + \rho(1) = z\frac{\Theta(z)\Theta(\frac{1}{z})}{1 + \theta^2}.$$

Whenever $|\theta| \ne 1$ the regression coefficients can be written under the form

$$a_k(K) = A\theta^k + B\frac{1}{\theta^k}.$$

The constants A and B are determined using the first and the last relationships

$$a_1(K) + \rho(1)a_2(K) = 0,$$

$$a_{K-1}(K)\rho(1) + a_K(K) = 0.$$

After solving we find

$$A = -\frac{1}{1 - \theta^{2K+2}},$$

$$B = \frac{\theta^{2K+2}}{1 - \theta^{2K+2}}.$$

Hence

$$a_k(K) = -\frac{\theta^k}{1 - \theta^{2K+2}} + \frac{\theta^{2K+2-k}}{1 - \theta^{2K+2}}.$$

In particular the partial autocorrelation of order K is

$$r(K) = a_K(K) = \frac{\theta^K(\theta^2 - 1)}{1 - \theta^{2K+2}}.$$

(iii) Regression Coefficients in the Limit Case $\theta=1$ When $\theta = 1$ the difference equation allowing to determine the coefficients $a_k(K)$ admits a double root $\theta = 1/\theta = 1$. The regression coefficients appear under the form $a_k(K) = A + Bk$. The use of the two relationships at the extremes allows as before to determine the constants A and B. We find

$$a_k(K) = -\frac{K + 1 - k}{K + 1}.$$

Thus we have

$$E(x_t \mid x_{t-1}, \ldots, x_{t-K}) = -\sum_{k=1}^{K} \frac{K + 1 - k}{K + 1} x_{t-k}.$$

(iv) Innovations

(a) When $|\theta| < 1$, the polynomial $(1 - \theta L)$ is invertible and its inverse admits an expansion in positive powers of L. ϵ_t is the innovation at time t.

(b) When $|\theta| > 1$, we need to replace the initial model by inverting the root. The canonical representation is

$$x_t = \eta_t - \frac{1}{\theta} \eta_{t-1},$$

and the innovation is

$$\eta_t = \left(1 - \frac{1}{\theta}L\right)^{-1} x_t = \left(1 - \frac{1}{\theta}L\right)^{-1} (\epsilon_t - \theta\epsilon_{t-1}).$$

(c)   The limit cases $\theta = \pm 1$ are more difficult to deal with. Let us
assume, for example, that $\theta = +1$. Then

$$\hat{x}_{t-1}(1) = E\left(x_t \mid x_{t-1}, \ldots\right)$$

$$= \lim_{K \to +\infty} E\left(x_t \mid x_{t-1}, \ldots, x_{t-K}\right)$$

$$= \lim_{K \to +\infty} - \sum_{k=1}^{K} \frac{K+1-k}{K+1} x_{t-k}.$$

It is apparent that taking the limit coefficient by coefficient would
result in $-\sum_{k=1}^{+\infty} x_{t-k}$, a meaningless quantity since $\sum_{k=1}^{K} x_{t-k} =
\epsilon_{t-1} - \epsilon_{t-K-1}$ does not converge as K goes to infinity. The optimal
forecast in this case, although it exists, does not imply an infinite
autoregressive expression, which means that the process x_t is not
invertible.

The forecast error is

$$x_t + \lim_{K \to +\infty} \sum_{k=1}^{K} \frac{K+1-k}{K+1} x_{t-k}$$

$$= \epsilon_t - \epsilon_{t-1} + \lim_{K \to +\infty} \left(\epsilon_{t-1} - \frac{1}{K+1} \sum_{k=1}^{K+1} \epsilon_{t-k} \right)$$

$$= \epsilon_t - \lim_{K \to +\infty} \left(\frac{1}{K+1} \sum_{k=1}^{K+1} \epsilon_{t-k} \right) = \epsilon_t.$$

Also in this limit case, then, the innovation is ϵ_t.

5.3.3 The Autoregressive Moving Average Processes

The ARMA modeling generalizes at once the pure autoregressive models
and the pure moving average models studied in the previous sections. It
introduces the advantage of a greater flexibility in the applications and
provides a better approximation to real-world series with less parameters
than the pure models.

Definition 5.11: *A stationary process x admits a* minimal ARMA(p,q)
representation if it can be written as

$$x_t + \phi_1 x_{t-1} + \ldots + \phi_p x_{t-p} = \epsilon_t + \theta_1 \epsilon_{t-1} + \ldots + \theta_q \epsilon_{t-q}$$

$$\Leftrightarrow \Phi(L)x_t = \Theta(L)\epsilon_t,$$

$$(5.22)$$

where

(i) $\phi_p \neq 0$, $\theta_q \neq 0$;

(ii) *The polynomials* Φ *and* Θ *have roots strictly greater than 1 in modulus;*

(iii) Φ *and* Θ *do not have roots in common;*

(iv) $\{\epsilon_t\}$ *is a white noise with variance* $\sigma^2 \neq 0$.

Note that we could have chosen a more general representation which would have been allowed had we considered noncentered stationary processes. For example, one possibility is to have

$$x_t + \phi_1 x_{t-1} + \ldots + \phi_p x_{t-p} = \theta^* + \epsilon_t + \theta_1 \epsilon_{t-1} + \ldots + \theta_q \epsilon_{t-q}.$$

We can go back to the case in (5.21) replacing x_t by

$$x_t - E(x_t) = x_t - \frac{\theta^*}{1 + \sum_{j=1}^{p} \phi_j}.$$

An ARMA representation could be studied at first without imposing the constraints on Φ and Θ introduced in the definition 5.11. Such a representation admits a stationary solution if the polynomial Φ has roots different from 1 in modulus. The polynomial $\Phi(L)$ is invertible and the solution is given by

$$\frac{\Theta(L)}{\Phi(L)} \epsilon_t,$$

that is under an infinite moving average form involving past and future values of the white noise. If the roots of Φ are all outside the unit circle, only the past values of the white noise appear in the moving average representation.

A similar step can be followed for the polynomial Θ. Let us assume that this polynomial has all its roots different from 1 in modulus. Then it is invertible and the infinite autoregressive representation can be obtained as

$$\frac{\Phi(L)}{\Theta(L)} x_t = \epsilon_t.$$

If the roots of Θ are all outside the unit circle, this AR(∞) representation involves only the past values of the white noise. ϵ is the innovation process for the process x, if Φ and Θ have roots simultaneously outside the unit circle.

A stationary process admitting an ARMA representation without constraints on Φ and Θ allows for many other representations of the same type. The other possible representations can be obtained examining the shape of the spectral density. If $\Phi(L)x_t = \Theta(L)\epsilon_t$ and $\tilde{\Phi}(L)x_t = \tilde{\Theta}(L)\tilde{\epsilon}_t$

are two representations of the same process, then

$$f_x(\omega) = \frac{\sigma^2}{2\pi} \frac{\mid \Theta(e^{i\omega}) \mid^2}{\mid \Phi(e^{i\omega}) \mid^2} = \frac{\tilde{\sigma}^2}{2\pi} \frac{\mid \tilde{\Theta}(e^{i\omega}) \mid^2}{\mid \tilde{\Phi}(e^{i\omega}) \mid^2}.$$

In addition to the possibility of changing the roots of Φ and Θ with their inverses, we can get the same spectral density by multiplying or dividing Φ and Θ by the same polynomial factor. Among the various representations, we will choose the one in which Φ and Θ have their roots outside the unit circle and for which $f_x(\omega)$ is an irreducible fraction in $e^{i\omega}$. This in turn implies that Φ and Θ do not have common roots. In this representation, the orders p and q are the smallest possible, and they are defined from the spectral density without ambiguity.

In what follows, we will assume that the ARMA representations considered are minimal in the sense of (5.21).

Theorem 5.10: *If x is a stationary process with a minimal* ARMA(p,q) *representation*

$$\Phi(L)x_t = \Theta(L)\epsilon_t.$$

(i) x admits an MA(∞) *representation*

$$x_t = \frac{\Theta(L)}{\Phi(L)}\epsilon_t = \sum_{j=0}^{+\infty} h_j\epsilon_{t-j}, \text{ with } h_0 = 1;$$

(ii) x admits an AR(∞) *representation*

$$\frac{\Phi(L)}{\Theta(L)}x_t = \sum_{j=0}^{+\infty} \pi_j x_{t-j} = \epsilon_t, \text{ with } \pi_0 = 1,$$

(iii) x admits ϵ as innovation.

Remark 5.3: When the polynomials Φ and Θ are not constrained, there might exist a stationary solution to the equation $\Phi(L)x_t = \Theta(L)\epsilon_t$, in spite of the fact that Φ has roots equal to 1 in modulus, so long as also Θ has an equal number of roots equal to 1 in modulus. Thus, the representation

$$(1 - L)x_t = (1 - L)\epsilon_t$$

admits the stationary solution $x_t = \epsilon_t$.

Remark 5.4: The pure processes are special cases of ARMA representations. In fact, an MA(q) process is an ARMA$(0,q)$, and an AR(p)

process is an ARMA$(p, 0)$. The only process which admits both a pure MA representation and a pure AR representation is the ARMA$(0, 0)$ case, that is, a white noise.

Autocovariance

Theorem 5.11: *The autocovariance function of a process $\{x\}$ corresponding to a minimal ARMA representation*

$$\Phi(L)x_t = \Theta(L)\epsilon_t,$$

where the order of Φ is p and the order of Θ is q is such that

$$\gamma(h) + \sum_{j=1}^{p} \phi_j \gamma(h - j) = 0, \ \forall \ h \geq q + 1.$$

PROOF: We have

$$x_t + \sum_{j=1}^{p} \phi_j x_{t-j} = \epsilon_t + \sum_{j=1}^{q} \theta_j \epsilon_{t-j},$$

multiplying by x_{t-h}, $h \geq q + 1$, and taking expectations, we get

$$\gamma(h) + \sum_{j=1}^{p} \phi_j \gamma(h - j) = \text{cov}\left(x_{t-h}, \epsilon_t + \sum_{j=1}^{q} \theta_j \epsilon_{t-j}\right) = 0. \quad (5.23)$$

□

The sequence of the covariances (or of the correlations) satisfies a difference equation of order p starting from $h \geq q + 1$. The characteristic polynomial of this equation is $z^p \Phi(1/z)$.

For example, if Φ has all distinct roots z_j, $j = 1, \ldots, p$, $|z_j| > 1$, the covariances are in the form

$$\gamma(h) = \sum_{j=1}^{p} A_j \frac{1}{z_j^h}, \quad \forall \ h \geq \max(q + 1 - p, 0). \quad (5.24)$$

This relationship, however, does not allow the determination of all values $\gamma(h)$ since initial conditions are needed. These first values of the autocovariance function may be determined starting from the infinite moving average representation

$$x_t = \sum_{j=0}^{+\infty} h_j \epsilon_{t-j}.$$

In fact, if we multiply

$$x_t + \sum_{j=1}^{p} \phi_j x_{t-j} = \epsilon_t + \sum_{j=1}^{q} \theta_j \epsilon_{t-j}$$

by x_{t-h} with $0 \leq h \leq q$ and take expectations, we have

$$\gamma(h) + \sum_{j=1}^{p} \phi_j \gamma(h-j) = \text{cov}\left(\epsilon_t + \sum_{j=1}^{q} \theta_j \epsilon_{t-j}, \sum_{j=0}^{+\infty} h_j \epsilon_{t-h-j}\right)$$

$$= \sigma^2(\theta_h + h_1 \theta_{h+1} + \ldots + h_{q-h} \theta_q).$$

Using these relationships, the difference equations (5.22) and the fact that $\gamma(h) = \gamma(-h)$, we can get all the autocovariances.

Infinite Autoregressive Representation The coefficients of the infinite autoregressive representation are such that

$$\Pi(L)\Theta(L) = \Phi(L).$$

Making this equality explicit we get

$$\sum_{j=0}^{+\infty} \pi_j L^j \sum_{j=0}^{q} \theta_j L^j = \sum_{j=0}^{p} \phi_j L^j,$$

with $\pi_0 = \theta_0 = \phi_0 = 1$ and $\sum_{j=0}^{q} \theta_j \pi_{h-j} = 0, \ \forall \ h \geq \max(p+1, q)$.

Theorem 5.12: *The coefficients of the infinite autoregressive representation satisfy a recurrence relation of order q starting from $\max(p+1, q)$. This equation has a characteristic polynomial $z^q \Theta(\frac{1}{z})$.*

Example 5.9: Let x be an ARMA$(1,1)$ process defined as

$$x_t - \phi x_{t-1} = \epsilon_t - \theta \epsilon_{t-1}$$

with $\phi \neq 0$, $\theta \neq 0$, $|\phi| < 1$, $|\theta| < 1$. The regression coefficients on the past are easily obtained since

$$(1 - \phi L)\frac{1}{1 - \theta L} = (1 - \phi L)(1 + \theta L + \theta^2 L^2 + \ldots + \theta^j L^j + \ldots)$$

$$= 1 - (\phi - \theta)L - (\phi\theta - \theta^2)L^2 - \ldots - (\phi\theta^{j-1} - \theta^j)L^j + \ldots$$

$$= 1 - (\phi - \theta)L \sum_{j=0}^{+\infty} \theta^j L^j.$$

Therefore $\pi_j = -(\phi - \theta)\theta^{j-1}, \ j \geq 1$.

Infinite Moving Average Representation Symmetrically to the autoregressive representation, the coefficients of the moving average representation are such that

$$\sum_{j=1}^{p} \phi_j h_{l-j} = 0, \ \forall \ l \geq \max(q+1, p).$$

They satisfy a difference equation of order p, the characteristic polynomial of which is directly related to the autoregressive polynomial Φ.

Spectral Density

Theorem 5.13: *The spectral density of a stationary process* ARMA $\{x\}$ *is a rational fraction in* $e^{i\omega}$. *It is given by*

$$f_x(\omega) = \frac{\sigma^2}{2\pi} \frac{\mid \Theta(e^{i\omega}) \mid^2}{\mid \Phi(e^{i\omega}) \mid^2}.$$

Canonical Correlations The canonical correlations between the vectors $(x_t, x_{t-1}, \ldots, x_{t-i})'$ and $(x_{t-j-1}, \ldots, x_{t-j-i-1})'$ are by definition the eigenvalues of the matrix

$$\mathbf{A}(i, -1)^{-1}\mathbf{A}(i, j)'\mathbf{A}(i, -1)\mathbf{A}(i, j),$$

where

$$\mathbf{A}(i,j) = \begin{pmatrix} \gamma(j+1) & \gamma(j+2) & \cdots & \gamma(j+i+1) \\ \gamma(j) & \gamma(j+1) & \cdots & \gamma(j+i) \\ \vdots & \vdots & \ddots & \vdots \\ \gamma(j+1-i) & \gamma(j+2-i) & \cdots & \gamma(j+1) \end{pmatrix}. \quad (5.25)$$

The product of the various canonical correlations is

$$\frac{\Delta(i,j)^2}{\Delta(i,-1)^2},$$

where $\Delta(i,j)^2$ indicates the determinant

$$\Delta(i,j) = \det \mathbf{A}(i,j). \quad (5.26)$$

Note in particular that $\Delta(i,j)^2 \leq \Delta(i,-1)^2$. In the next section, we will see that the canonical correlations play an important role for the determination of the order of an ARMA process. At this stage, we just mention a formula allowing a recursive computation of these determinants.

Theorem 5.14:

$$\Delta(i,j)^2 = \Delta(i+1,j)\Delta(i-1,j) + \Delta(i,j-1)\Delta(i,j+1)$$

(cf. Glasbey, 1982, and Pham Dinh, 1984).

5.3.4 Determination of the Orders

The minimal orders p, q have appeared in the previous sections either as indices after which certain sequences become zero, or as orders of linear difference equations. In fact, these different properties provide a way to determine these orders. To show that these properties are peculiar to the series is often difficult, so that we will limit ourselves to mentioning the results without providing a formal proof.

These results are valid for centered regular stationary processes. Such processes have to be such that

$$\lim_{K \to +\infty} E\left(x_t \mid x_{t-K}, x_{t-K-1}, \ldots\right) = E(x_t) = 0,$$

or, equivalently, have to admit an infinite moving average representation

$$x_t = \sum_{j=0}^{+\infty} h_j \epsilon_{t-j}.$$

This equivalence is based on *Wold's Decomposition Theorem* (cf. chapter 7).

Pure Models   The various properties of the pure autoregressive or pure moving average processes show that there exists a certain duality between the two types of models. This is clear from table 5.1 where the different possible definitions of orders are provided. We are assuming that the roots of the autoregressive and moving average polynomials are strictly greater than 1 in modulus.

Mixed Models   In the case of mixed models, we get the following generalizations of these characterizations.

Theorem 5.15: *A regular stationary process for which the autocovariance function satisfies a linear difference equation starting from a certain index admits a minimal* ARMA (p,q) *representation. The autoregressive order p is the smallest possible order of such a difference equation. Considering this minimal order p, the moving average order q is such that $q + 1$ is the smallest index from which such a difference equation is satisfied.*

Theorem 5.16: *If x admits a minimal* ARMA (p, q) *representation:*

(i)   *p is the smallest order of the difference equations satisfied by the coefficients of the* MA (∞) *representation starting from a certain index.*

Table 5.1 *Determination of the Orders for Pure Models*

Autoregressive AR(p)	Moving Average MA(q)
p is the degree of $\Phi(L)$	q is the degree of $\Theta(L)$
$p+1$ is the smallest index from which the partial autocorrelations become zero	$q+1$ is the smallest index from which the direct autocorrelations become zero
$p+1$ is the smallest index from which the inverse autocorrelations become zero	$q+1$ is the smallest index from which the partial inverse autocorrelations become zero
p is the smallest order of the linear difference equations satisfied by the coefficients of the MA(∞) representation.	q is the smallest order of the linear difference equations satisfied by the coefficients of the AR(∞) representation.
p is the smallest order of the difference equations satisfied by the direct autocorrelations.	q is the smallest order of the difference equations satisfied by the inverse autocorrelations.

(ii) q *is the smallest order of the difference equations satisfied by the coefficients of the AR(∞) representation starting from a certain index.*

Theorem 5.17: *A regular stationary process admits a minimal ARMA(p,q) representation if and only if*

$$\Delta(i,j) = 0, \quad \forall\, i \geq p,\ \forall\, j \geq q$$

$$\Delta(p, q-1) \neq 0$$

$$\Delta(p-1, q) \neq 0.$$

In this case we have

$$\Delta(i, q-1) \neq 0, \quad \forall\, i \geq p-1$$

$$\Delta(p-1, j) \neq 0, \quad \forall\, j \geq q-1$$

(cf. Beguin, Gourieroux, and Monfort, 1980; Gourieroux, 1987).

Table 5.2 *Illustration of the Corner Method for an* ARMA *(p,q)*

i \ j	0	1	2	3	...	q-1	q	...
0						:	:	
1						:	:	
2						:	:	
:						:	:	
p-1	...	...	...	...	...	x	x	x
p	...	...	...	...	...	x	0	0
						x	0	0
						x	0	0

$0 \Leftrightarrow \Delta(i,j) = 0$
$x \Leftrightarrow \Delta(i,j) \neq 0$

This theorem leads to the construction of table 5.2 in which the row index is i and the column index is j containing the different values of the determinants $\Delta(i,j)$. The process x admits an ARMA representation if and only if this table contains a lower right corner (or orthant) made of zeros only. This explains why the name *corner method* was given to this way of determining the orders.

For the MA(q) case, the appropriate table becomes table 5.3 where, since $\Delta(0,j) = \gamma(j+1)$, we find the condition $\gamma(q) \neq 0$ and $\gamma(h) = 0$, $\forall\, h \geq q+1$.

The AR(p) case is shown in table 5.4. Recall that the system (5.4) defining the partial autocorrelations implies that

$$r(i) = (-1)^{i-1} \frac{\Delta(i-1,0)}{\Delta(i-1,-1)}.$$

$\Delta(i-1,-1)$ is strictly positive, as it is the determinant of a variance–covariance matrix. As a consequence, examining the first column of table 5.4, we find the condition $r(p) \neq 0$ and $r(h) = 0$, $\forall\, h \geq p+1$.

Table 5.3 *Illustration of the Corner Method for an* MA*(q)*

j	0	1	...	q-1	q
i					
0	$\Delta(0,0)$			x	0
⋮				x	0
⋮				x	0

Table 5.4 *Illustration of the Corner Method for an* AR*(p)*

j	0	1	...
i			
0	$\Delta(0,0)$		
⋮			
⋮			
p-1	x	x	x
p	0	0	0

5.4 ARIMA Processes

It is apparent that for most economic series, the stationarity hypothesis is not appropriate. On the other hand, if we consider, for example, the first differences (or, more generally, differences of order d) of such series, the stationarity hypothesis becomes often more credible. We can then consider the class of processes where the difference of a certain order will correspond to an ARMA representation.

If we denote by $\Delta^d x_t$ the difference of order d of x_t, that is, $(1-L)^d x_t$, we are interested in the process $\{x_t\}$ satisfying

$$\phi(L)(1-L)^d x_t = \Theta(L)\epsilon_t, \qquad (5.27)$$

where the roots of ϕ and Θ are greater than 1 in modulus, and $\{\epsilon_t\}$ is a centered white noise with variance σ^2.

Equation (5.26) can also be written as

$$\Phi(L)x_t = \Theta(L)\epsilon_t, \qquad (5.28)$$

where

$$\Phi(L) = \phi(L)(1-L)^d.$$

Equation (5.27) is similar to the equation defining an ARMA$(p+d,q)$ process with the important difference that the polynomial Φ admits 1 as a root of order d.

The introduction just presented does not suffice; in fact, we may not assume, contrary to the stationary case, that equation (5.27) is valid for any index t and derive x_t by inversion of $\Phi(L)$ since the resulting series in ϵ_t is diverging. To complete the definition, we need to introduce a starting mechanism. In order to help the intuition, we will start with two simple examples.

Let us define a *random walk*, that is a process x satisfying

$$x_t - x_{t-1} = \epsilon_t,$$

starting from a certain date which we will assume equal to 0. If an initial value x_{-1}, deterministic or random, is given, we have

$$x_t = x_{-1} + \sum_{j=0}^{t} \epsilon_{t-j}.$$

The only requirement which may be imposed is that x_{-1} be uncorrelated with future values of the noise. The process $\{x_t\}$ is then unambiguously defined.

By the same token, if we consider a process x satisfying

$$x_t - x_{t-1} = \epsilon_t - \theta\epsilon_{t-1}, \ \forall \ t \geq 0,$$

this process is completely defined by giving the initial conditions x_{-1}, ϵ_{-1}.

More generally, we adopt the following definition

Definition 5.12: *A process* $x = \{x_t, \ t \geq 0\}$ *is an* ARIMA(p,d,q) *process (Integrated Autoregressive Moving Average) if it satisfies a relationship of the type*

$$\phi(L)(1-L)^d x_t = \Theta(L)\epsilon_t, \quad t \geq 0,$$

where

(i)

$$\phi(L) = 1 + \phi_1 L + \ldots + \phi_p L^p, \ \phi_p \neq 0,$$

$$\Theta(L) = 1 + \theta_1 L + \ldots + \theta_q L^q, \ \theta_q \neq 0$$

are polynomials with roots greater than 1 in modulus;

(ii) *the initial conditions*

$$(x_{-1}, \ldots, x_{-p-d}, \epsilon_{-1}, \ldots, \epsilon_{-q})$$

are uncorrelated with $\epsilon_0, \epsilon_1, \ldots, \epsilon_t, \ldots$;

(iii) *the process* $\epsilon = \{\epsilon_t, \ t \geq -q\}$ *is a white noise with variance* σ^2.

Clearly, for certain initial conditions and a given process ϵ, the process x is completely defined, since x_0 is given by the definition equation for $t = 0$, x_1 is given by the equation corresponding to $t = 1$, and so on.

Theorem 5.18: *Let x be an ARIMA(p,d,q) process. The process $\Delta^d x_t$ tends toward a stationary ARMA process.*

PROOF: Let us consider the identity given by the division of 1 by $\phi(L)$ according to increasing powers up to the order t

$$1 = q_t(L)\phi(L) + L^{t+1} r_t(L),$$

where the degree of q_t is t, and the degree of $r_t \leq p-1$. Multiplying the equality $\Delta^d \phi(L) x_t = \Theta(L)\epsilon_t$ by $q_t(L)$ we get

$$\left(1 - L^{t+1} r_t(L)\right) \Delta^d x_t = q_t(L)\Theta(L)\epsilon_t,$$

or

$$\Delta^d x_t = q_t(L)\Theta(L)\epsilon_t + r_t(L)\Delta^d x_{-1}.$$

The terms raised to powers from 0 to t in $q_t(L)\Theta(L)$ are the same as those of $\frac{\Theta(L)}{\phi(L)}$. We have then

$$\Delta^d x_t = \frac{\Theta(L)}{\phi(L)}\tilde{\epsilon}_t + \sum_{j=1}^{q} \tilde{h}_j(t)\epsilon_{-j} + \sum_{j=1}^{q} \tilde{\tilde{h}}_j(t)\Delta^d x_{-j},$$

where

$$\tilde{\epsilon}_t = \begin{cases} \epsilon_t, & \text{if } t \geq 0, \\ 0, & \text{if } t < 0. \end{cases}$$

Since the roots of ϕ are outside the unit circle, we easily see that $\tilde{h}_j(t)$, $j = 1, \ldots, q$ and $\tilde{\tilde{h}}_j(t)$, $j = 1, \ldots, p$ tend to zero as t goes to infinity. Consequently, the difference between $\Delta^d x_t$ and the process

$\frac{\Theta(L)}{\phi(L)}\epsilon_t$ tends to zero in quadratic mean as t goes to infinity. Hence $\Delta^d x_t$ is said to be *asymptotically stationary*. $\square$

Let us turn now to the study of the function $m_t = E(x_t)$, $t \geq 0$.

Theorem 5.19: *If $\{x_t, t \geq 0\}$ is an* ARIMA *(p,d,q) process, the function $m_t = E(x_t)$ is the solution to the difference equation*

$$\Phi(L)m_t = 0, \quad t \geq 0,$$

with initial values $E(x_{-i})$, $i = 1, \ldots, p + d$.

PROOF: Taking the expected value of the definition equations of x_t

$$\Phi(L)x_t = \Theta(L)\epsilon_t, \ t \geq 0$$

with

$$(x_{-1}, \ldots, x_{-p-d}, \epsilon_{-1}, \ldots, \epsilon_{-q})$$

as initial conditions, we get

$$\Phi(L)m_t = 0, \ t \geq 0,$$

with $E(x_{-i})$, $i = 1, \ldots, p + d$ as initial values. $\square$

Since $\Phi(L) = (1 - L)^d \phi(L)$, the characteristic polynomial of the difference equation satisfied by m_t is

$$(1 - z)^d z^p \phi(\frac{1}{z}),$$

the roots of which are 1 of order d and other roots are smaller than 1 in modulus. Hence m_t is asymptotically equivalent to a polynomial in t of degree $d - 1$.

The previous definitions and results can easily be generalized to the case when the second member of the definition equation of x_t contains a constant element θ^*

$$\phi(L)(1 - L)^d x_t = \theta^* + \Theta(L)\epsilon_t.$$

In particular, we can see that $\Delta^d x_t$ is asymptotically equivalent to a stationary ARMA process $\phi(L)y_t = \theta_0^* + \Theta(L)\epsilon_t$ and that $m_t = E(x_t)$ is the solution to $\Phi(L)x_t = \theta_0$ with $E(x_{-i})$, $i = 1, \ldots, p+d$ as initial values. The latter remark implies that, asymptotically, m_t is a polynomial in t of degree d.

5.4.1 Moving Average and Autoregressive Representations

Let us denote

$$\mathbf{z}_{-1} = (x_{-1}, \ldots, x_{-p-d}, \epsilon_{-1}, \ldots, \epsilon_{-q})'.$$

We can express x_t in a moving average form or in an autoregressive form using $\mathbf{z}_{-1}$.

Theorem 5.20: *Let $\{x_t\}$ be an* ARIMA(p,d,q) *process and $\mathbf{z}_{-1}$ the set of initial values.*

(i)   *x_t can be written in a moving average form*

$$x_t = \sum_{j=0}^{t} h_j \epsilon_{t-j} + h^*(t)\mathbf{z}_{-1},$$

where the h_j's represent the coefficients of the long division of Θ by Φ (with $h_0 = 1$), and $h^*(t)$ is a row vector of functions of t.

(ii) *x_t has also an autoregressive form*

$$x_t = -\sum_{j=0}^{t} \pi_j x_{t-j} + \tilde{h}(t)\mathbf{z}_{-1} + \epsilon_t,$$

where the π_j's $j \geq 1$ are the coefficients of the long division of Φ by Θ, and $\tilde{h}(t)$ is a vector of functions of t tending to zero as t goes to infinity.

PROOF: (i)   Let us consider the identity given by the long division of 1 by $\Phi(L)$ up to the order t

$$1 = Q_t(L)\Phi(L) + L^{t+1}R_t(L), \tag{5.29}$$

with degree $(Q_t) = t$ and degree $(R_t) \leq p + d - 1$. Multiplying the definition equation $\Phi(L)x_t = \Theta(L)\epsilon_t$ by $Q_t(L)$ and using (5.28), we get

$$(1 - L^{t+1}R_t(L))x_t = Q_t(L)\Theta(L)\epsilon_t,$$

or

$$x_t = Q_T(L)\Theta(L)\epsilon_t + R_t(L)x_{-1}.$$

Multiplying (5.28) by $\Theta(L)$ we see that the terms raised to powers from 0 to t in $Q_t(L)\Theta(L)$ are the same as those of $\Phi^{-1}(L)\Theta(L)$. Therefore

$$x_t = \sum_{j=0}^{t} h_j \epsilon_{t-j} + \sum_{i=1}^{q} h_{1i}^*(t)\epsilon_{-i} + \sum_{i=1}^{p+d} h_{2i}^*(t)x_{-i}$$

$$= \sum_{j=0}^{t} h_j \epsilon_{t-j} + h^*(t)\mathbf{z}_{-1}.$$

(ii) In a symmetrical manner, we can employ the identity given by the long division of 1 by $\Theta(L)$.

$$1 = Q_t^*(L)\Theta(L) + L^{t+1}R_t^*(L), \tag{5.30}$$

with degree $(Q_t^*) = t$ and degree $(R_t^*) \leq q - 1$. Note that the coefficients of $R_t^*(L)$ tend to zero as t goes to infinity, since the roots of $\Theta(L)$ are outside the unit circle. Multiplying the definition equation of x_t by $Q_t^*(L)$, we have

$$\Phi(L)Q_t^*(L)x_t = \left(1 - L^{t+1}R_t^*(L)\right)\epsilon_t.$$

The same line of reasoning implies as above

$$\sum_{j=0}^{t} \pi_j x_{t-j} + \sum_{i=1}^{p+d} \tilde{h}_{2i}(t)x_{-i} = \epsilon_t - R_t^*(L)\epsilon_{t-1}$$

$$= \epsilon_t + \sum_{i=0}^{q} \tilde{h}_{1i}(t)\epsilon_{-i}.$$

We have seen that $\tilde{h}_{1i}(t)$, $i = 1, \ldots, q$ tends to 0 as t goes to infinity, and, for the same reasons, the same happens to $h_{2i}(t)$, $i = 1, \ldots, p + d$. Finally, as $\pi_0 = 1$ we have

$$x_t = -\sum_{j=1}^{t} \pi_j x_{t-j} + \tilde{h}(t)\mathbf{z}_{-1} + \epsilon_t,$$

where $\tilde{h}(t)$ has the desired property. $\square$

5.5 Appendix

Interchange of E (or $\int$) and $\sum_{i=0}^{+\infty}$

(i)   Let us consider a sequence of random variables u_n in L_2 $(E(u_n^2) < +\infty)$, and let us assume that u_n converges in quadratic mean to u, that is $\lim_{n \to +\infty} E(u_n - u)^2 = 0$. We know that this property implies $\lim_{n \to +\infty} E \mid u_n - u \mid = 0$, and a fortiori $\lim_{n \to +\infty} E(u_n) = E(u)$. Consequently, if the series $\sum_{i=0}^{+\infty} x_i$ converges in L_2, we have

$$E\left(\sum_{i=0}^{+\infty} x_i\right) = \sum_{i=0}^{+\infty} E(x_i),$$

applying the previous result with $u_n = \sum_{i=0}^{n} x_i$ and $u = \sum_{i=0}^{+\infty} x_i$.

(ii) Let us consider two sequences of random variables u_n and v_n in L_2. Let us suppose that u_n, v_n converge to u, respectively, v in L_2. Denoting the norm in L_2 by $\| \cdot \|$ we have

$$E \mid u_n v_m \mid \leq \| u_n \| \, \| v_m \| < +\infty,$$

$$E \mid u v \mid \leq \| u \| \, \| v \| < +\infty,$$

and

$$E \mid u_n \, v_m - uv \mid \; = E \mid u_n(v_m - v) + v(u_n - u) \mid$$

$$\leq \mid u_n(v_m - v) \mid + E \mid v(u_n - u) \mid$$

$$\leq \parallel u_n \parallel \parallel v_m - v \parallel + \parallel v \parallel \parallel u_n - u \parallel .$$

Hence $\lim_{m,n \to +\infty} E \mid u_n \, v_m - uv \mid = 0$, since

$$\parallel u_n \parallel \to \parallel u \parallel, \quad \parallel u_n - u \parallel \to 0, \quad \parallel v_m - v \parallel \to 0.$$

We can conclude that

$$\lim_{m,n \to \infty} E(u_n \, v_m) = E(u \, v).$$

and hence, if the series $\sum_{i=0}^{+\infty} x_i$ and $\sum_{j=0}^{+\infty} y_j$ are convergent in L_2, we get ·

$$E \left(\sum_{i=0}^{+\infty} x_i \sum_{j=0}^{+\infty} y_j \right) = \sum_{i=0}^{+\infty} \sum_{j=0}^{+\infty} E(x_i y_j)$$

by applying the previous result with

$$u_n = \sum_{i=0}^{n} x_i, \quad u = \sum_{i=0}^{+\infty} x_i, \quad v_m = \sum_{i=0}^{m} y_j, \quad v = \sum_{i=0}^{+\infty} y_j.$$

(iii) Let $g_h(x)$ be a sequence of real or complex functions defined on $\mathbb{R}$ such that

$$\sum_{h=0}^{+\infty} \int \mid g_h(x) \mid \, dx < +\infty,$$

then (cf. Rudin, 1966), there exists a function of x, denoted by

$$\sum_{h=0}^{+\infty} g_h(x),$$

such that

$$\lim_{n \to +\infty} \int \left| \sum_{h=0}^{n} g_h(x) - \sum_{h=0}^{+\infty} g_h(x) \right| \, dx = 0.$$

Moreover, this function is such that

$$\int \left(\sum_{h=0}^{+\infty} g_h(x) \right) \, dx = \sum_{h=0}^{+\infty} \int g_h(x) \, dx.$$

5.6 Exercises

Exercise 5.1: Let $\{\epsilon_t\}$ be a white noise. Verify that the processes defined as $x_t = \epsilon_t$ and $y_t = (-1)^t \epsilon_t$ are stationary. Show that their sum

$$z_t = x_t + y_t$$

is not stationary.

Exercise 5.2: Let $y_1, y_2, z_1, \ldots, z_n$ be square integrable random variables. Let us denote by y_1^*, respectively y_2^*, the affine regression of y_1, respectively y_2 on $z_1, \ldots, z_n$. The partial correlation coefficient between y_1 and y_2 with respect to $z_1, \ldots, z_n$ is

$$\rho_{y_1, y_2; z_1, \ldots, z_n} = \frac{\text{cov}\left(y_1 - y_1^*, y_2 - y_2^*\right)}{\sqrt{\text{var}\left(y_1 - y_1^*\right)}\sqrt{\text{var}\left(y_2 - y_2^*\right)}}.$$

Show that the partial correlation coefficient $\rho_{y_1, y_2; z_1, \ldots, z_n}$ between y_1 and y_2 with respect to $z_1, \ldots, z_n$ is equal to

$$\frac{\rho - \rho_{1z}' \mathbf{R}^{-1} \rho_{2z}}{(1 - \rho_{1z}' \mathbf{R}^{-1} \rho_{1z})^{1/2}(1 - \rho_{2z}' \mathbf{R}^{-1} \rho_{2z})^{1/2}},$$

where ρ is the linear correlation coefficient between y_1 and y_2, ρ_{1z}, respectively ρ_{2z}, is the vector of linear correlation coefficients between y_1, respectively y_2, and the z_i's $i = 1, \ldots, n$. $\mathbf{R}$ is the matrix of correlations of the vector containing the z_i's $i = 1, \ldots, n$. Verify also that, if $n = 1$ we have

$$\rho_{y_1, y_2; z} = \frac{\rho - \rho_{1z} \rho_{2z}}{\left(1 - \rho_{1z}^2\right)^{1/2}\left(1 - \rho_{2z}^2\right)^{1/2}}.$$

Exercise 5.3: Show that, if the random vector $(y_1, y_2, z_1, \ldots, z_n)$ is normal, $\rho_{y_1, y_2; z_1, \ldots, z_n}$ can be interpreted as the linear correlation coefficient in the conditional (normal) distribution of (y_1, y_2) given $(z_1, \ldots, z_n)$.

Exercise 5.4: (AR(2) processes) Let us consider the stationary process x_t defined as

$$x_t + \phi_1 x_{t-1} + \phi_2 x_{t-2} = \epsilon_t,$$

where $\{\epsilon_t\}$ is a white noise with variance $\sigma^2 > 0$ and the roots of the polynomial $\Phi(z) = 1 + \phi_1 z + \phi_2 z^2$ are different from 1 in modulus.

(i)   Find the domain D_ϕ for the point $\phi = (\phi_1, \phi_2)$ corresponding to a polynomial Φ with roots strictly greater than 1 in modulus (which will be assumed in what follows).

(ii)   Describe the shape of the autocorrelation function $\rho(\cdot)$. Find the domain of variation D_ρ of $(\rho(1), \rho(2))$. How are these results transformed if we did not assume roots of Φ strictly greater than 1 in modulus?

(iii) Compute the partial autocorrelation function $r(\cdot)$ as a function of ϕ_1 and ϕ_2. Study also the sign of $r(1)$ and $r(2)$.

Exercise 5.5: (MA(2) processes) Let us consider the stationary process x_t defined as

$$x_t = \epsilon_t + \theta_1 \epsilon_{t-1} + \theta_2 \epsilon_{t-2},$$

where $\{\epsilon_t\}$ is a white noise with variance $\sigma^2 > 0$

(i)   The domain D_θ which corresponds to a polynomial $\Theta(z) = 1 + \theta_1 z + \theta_2 z^2$ strictly greater than 1 in modulus can be derived from D_ϕ in exercise 5.4. Compute the function $\rho(\cdot)$ and partition D_θ according to the signs of ρ_1 and ρ_2.

(ii)   Let us consider the process $\{x_t\}$ defined by

$$x_t = \epsilon_t - 2.4\epsilon_{t-1} + 0.8\epsilon_{t-2},$$

where $\{\epsilon_t\}$ is a white noise. Write $\{x_t\}$ in the form

$$x_t = \sum_{i=1}^{+\infty} \pi_i x_{t-i} + \eta_t, \quad \sum_{i=1}^{+\infty} |\pi_i| < +\infty.$$

What is the usefulness of such a representation?

Write η_t as a function of the ϵ_s's and ϵ_t as a function of the η_s's.

Exercise 5.6: (ARMA(1, 1) processes) Let us consider the process defined as

$$x_t - \phi x_{t-1} = \epsilon_t - \theta \epsilon_{t-1},$$

where $\{\epsilon_t\}$ is a white noise with variance $\sigma^2 > 0$.

Let us assume that $|\phi| < 1$ and that $|\theta| < 1$

(i)   Analyze the autocorrelation function $\rho(\cdot)$.

(ii)   Let us consider the process $\{x_t\}$ defined as

$$z_t = \frac{4}{5} z_{t-1} + u_t,$$

where u_t is a white noise with $E(u_t^2) = \frac{9}{50}$. Let us assume that z_t is affected by a measurement error, and that we observe $y_t = z_t + \eta_t$, where η_t is a white noise uncorrelated with u_t (that is, $E(\eta_t u_s) = 0$, $\forall t, s$) and with $E(\eta_t^2) = \frac{1}{2}$. Show that y_t can be written as an

ARMA$(1, 1)$ process. Derive a representation of y_t of the type

$$y_t = -\sum_{i=1}^{+\infty} \pi_i y_{t-i} + \xi_t$$

with $\sum_{i=1}^{+\infty} |\pi_i| < +\infty$ and $\{\xi_t\}$ is a white noise such that
$$E(\xi_t y_{t-i}) = 0, \quad \forall\, i > 0, \ \forall\, t.$$
What is the usefulness of such a representation?

Exercise 5.7: Given two stationary processes $\{x_t\}$ and $\{\tilde{x}_t\}$ defined as
$$\Phi(L)x_t = \Theta(L)\epsilon_t,$$

$$\Phi(L)\tilde{x}_t = \Theta(L)\tilde{\epsilon}_t,$$

where ϵ_t and $\tilde{\epsilon}_t$ are white noises with unit variance. Let us denote the autocovariance functions by $\gamma(\cdot)$, respectively $\tilde{\gamma}(\cdot)$.

(i)   Show that, $\forall\, h \neq 0$, we have

$$\sum_{j=-\infty}^{+\infty} \gamma(h - j)\tilde{\gamma}(j) = 0,$$

and

$$\sum_{j=-\infty}^{+\infty} \gamma(-j)\tilde{\gamma}(j) = 1.$$

(ii) Let us assume that $\Phi(L) = 1$ so that the process x is a moving average process MA(q) with degree $(\Theta) = q$, and that $\tilde{x}$ is an AR(p) process. Let us denote by $\tilde{\boldsymbol{\Gamma}}$ the square matrix of order r the elements of which are
$$\tilde{\gamma}_{ij} = \tilde{\gamma}(j - i), \ i = 1, \ldots, r, \ j = 1, \ldots, r.$$
Show that the elements a_{ij} of $\mathbf{A} = \tilde{\boldsymbol{\Gamma}}^{-1}$ are given by $a_{ij} = \gamma(j - i)$ for $q + 1 \leq i \leq r - q$, $1 \leq j \leq r$.

This result can be used to get an approximated form for the inverse of the variance–covariance matrix of an autoregressive process.

Exercise 5.8: Let us consider the process $\{y_t\}$ defined as
$$y_0 = 0,$$

$$y_1 = \epsilon_1,$$

$$(1 - \phi L)y_t = (1 - \theta L)\epsilon_t, \ \forall\, t \geq 2, \ \phi \neq \theta,$$

where $\{\epsilon_t\}$ is a sequence of zero mean variables, uncorrelated and with the same variance $\sigma^2 = 1$. Describe the conditions under which the process $\{y_t\}$ is asymptotically stationary, that is

$$\exists \text{ stationary } \{x_t\} \lim_{t \to +\infty} E(y_t - x_t)^2 = 0.$$

Compute the limit (when t goes to infinity) of the variance of y_t as a function of ϕ and θ.

Exercise 5.9: Let us consider a stationary process $\{x_t\}$ defined as

$$(1 - 0.5L)x_t = (1 - 4L)\epsilon_t,$$

where ϵ_t is a zero mean white noise with unit variance.

(i)   Compute the innovation η_t of x_t as a function of the ϵ_s's. Provide the standard deviation of η_t.

(ii)   What is the autocovariance function of the sum of the two white noises ϵ_t and η_t?

(iii) Compute the linear regression x_t^* of x_t on the future values x_{t+1}, $x_{t+2}, \dots$ What is the standard deviation of $x_t - x_t^*$?

Exercise 5.10: Let us consider the stationary process $\{y_t\}$ defined as

$$y_t = \epsilon_t - \theta \epsilon_{t-1}, \quad -1 \le \theta \le 1,$$

where $\{\epsilon_t\}$ is a Gaussian white noise with zero mean and variance σ^2. Let us define the process $\{x_t\}$ as

$$x_t = \begin{cases} 1 & \text{if } y_t \ge 0, \\ 0 & \text{if } y_t < 0. \end{cases}$$

(i)   Show that the process $\{x_t\}$ is stationary. What is its autocorrelation function $\rho(\cdot)$?

(ii)   What is the variation domain of $\rho(1)$?

Exercise 5.11: Let

$$\pi_K(z) = a_1(K) + a_2(K)z + \dots + a_K(K)z^{K-1},$$

where the $a_k(K)$'s are the regression coefficients defined in (5.4). Show that

$$\pi_K(z) = \pi_{K-1}(z) + a_K(K)z^{K-1}\left(1 - \frac{1}{z}\pi_{K-1}\left(\frac{1}{z}\right)\right).$$

Exercise 5.12: Show that the expression for $r(K)$ given in remark 5.2 can be manipulated to provide the second equation (5.6) of Durbin's algorithm.

Exercise 5.13: Is the equality

$$\gamma i(0) = \frac{1}{\gamma(0)}$$

possible?

6

The Box and Jenkins Method
for Forecasting

6.1 Description of the Method

Box and Jenkins (1970) have proposed a general forecasting method
for univariate series: such a method is based on the notion of ARIMA
processes. Let us assume that the available observations $x_1, \ldots x_T$ * can
be considered as compatible with an ARIMA model

$$\phi(L)\Delta^d x_t = \theta^* + \Theta(L)\epsilon_t,$$

where degree(ϕ)=p, degree(Θ)=q, and var$(\epsilon_t) = \sigma^2$. We will assume
that the usual hypotheses on the lag polynomials and on the white noise
are satisfied. At time T, the theoretical forecast of a future value x_{T+h}
is given by the linear affine regression of x_{T+h} on $x_T, x_{T-1}, \ldots$. The coefficients of this regression depend on the parameters of the model. Such
a formula cannot be used directly, since these parameters are unknown.
Their estimation is then needed as the first step. This estimation phase
is a fairly delicate one, since the model parameters are subject to various constraints. We usually distinguish the unknown degrees p and q
(which are integer values) from the other parameters, the coefficients
ϕ_j, θ_i of the lag polynomials and the variance σ^2 of the noise. The
latter can take values over a continuous interval, even if they are subject
to a fairly complex set of constraints (for example, those deriving from

---

* In order to simplify the notation we are not distinguishing between the random variables and their realizations.

the requirement that the roots of the polynomial ϕ and Θ be outside the unit circle). The parameter estimation for the integer values is a problem which technically is very close to a problem of testing or of choice among various competing models. The fundamental intuition behind the Box and Jenkins method is to keep separate the phase of the search of the orders (phase of *identification*) from the phase of *estimation* of the other parameters. This method can be summarized as follows

(i)   In a first stage, we will look for plausible values for the orders (p, d, q) using methods not depending on the estimation of the other parameters. This is an *a priori identification*, that is prior to estimation. This stage leads to considering various triplets $(p_j, d_j, q_j, \ j = 1, \ldots, J)$.

(ii) For each of the plausible models, we will search for the corresponding values of the other parameters

$$\phi_1, \ldots, \phi_{p_j}, \theta^*, \theta_1, \ldots, \theta_{q_j}, \sigma^2.$$

This is the *estimation stage*, at the end of which we will have J estimated models: $M_j, \ j = 1, \ldots, J$.

(iii) In the third stage, we will examine whether or not these estimated models are compatible with the hypothesis underlying the model: are the values of the residuals in line with the hypothesis of a white noise? Is it necessary to increase the order p_j, the order q_j, and so on? We will establish a number of requirements which should isolate the models compatible with the data. After this phase (called the *validation stage*) we will generally have a smaller number of estimated models available.

(iv) If the previous phases have been correctly carried out, the retained models show very similar properties in view of their use for forecasting. In the phase of the *model choice* we will keep one M_j of these models. The phases of validation and model choice are called the *a posteriori identification stage*.

(v)   We will be able to produce *forecasts* using the theoretical forecasting formula after having replaced the unknown parameters with their estimates obtained for M_j.

Note that these phases do not succeed one another in a sequential way. In fact, the validation phase could lead to the rejection of all models, requiring a new phase of *a priori* identification. In the latter, what is needed is to retain enough models in order to pass the validation phase, and not too many in order not to have too many parameters to estimate (since estimation is the most costly phase). The method can be summarized with the chart reproduced in figure 6.1.

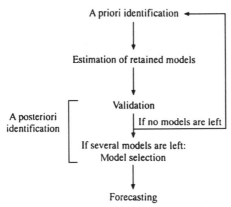

Figure 6.1 Scheme for the Box–Jenkins Method

In the next sections, we will describe in a greater detail these various phases, by stressing the empirical aspects of the method, and by illustrating them with a practical example. Various theoretical justifications about the estimation and testing procedures can be found in chapter 9.

6.2 Estimation of an ARIMA Model

Let us start by illustrating the estimation method which will employ standard statistical techniques. The parameters ϕ_j, θ_j, σ^2 are generally estimated following the maximum likelihood method or a least squares technique. These methods are applied assuming the orders p_j, d_j, q_j as fixed, equal to the values found in the phase of identification a priori.

6.2.1 The Estimation Methods

Let us recall that an ARIMA(p, d, q) model verifies the relationship

$$\phi(L)\Delta^d x_t = \theta^* + \Theta(L)\epsilon_t, \tag{6.1}$$

where the ϵ_t's are nonzero, uncorrelated variables, with the same variance σ^2, and the roots of the polynomials ϕ and Θ have modulus greater than 1. The process $w_t = \Delta^d x_t$ is then (at least asymptotically, given the starting values problem) an ARMA(p, q) process such as

$$\phi(L)w_t = \theta^* + \Theta(L)\epsilon_t. \tag{6.2}$$

Consequently, if we have $x_1, \ldots, x_{T_0}$ as available observations of the process $\{x_t\}$ we can compute the d-th order differences

$$w_{d+1} = \Delta^d x_{d+1}$$

$$\vdots$$

$$w_{T_0} = \Delta^d x_{T_0},$$

and we are back to the estimation of the parameters of model (6.2) starting from these observations. We have previously remarked that we may suppress the constant θ^* so long as we replace w_t by $\hat{w}_t = w_t - \mu$ with $\mu = \theta^* / (1 + \phi_1 + \ldots + \phi_p)$. In what follows we will suppose that $\theta^* = 0$, but the results can be extended to the case $\theta^* \neq 0$ by replacing w_t by $\hat{w}_t$. The additional parameter μ can be estimated in the same way as the others. When there is a constant θ^*, another frequently used method to suppress it is to replace the process $\{w\}$ with the centered process $\{w_t - \bar{w}\}$ and to estimate the other parameters afterwards. Finally, we have to solve the estimation problem of the parameters of an ARMA(p, q) without a constant, that is, of the parameters

$$\phi_1, \ldots, \phi_p, \theta_1, \ldots, \theta_q, \sigma^2,$$

from the information contained in the observations, denoted by

$$z_1, \ldots, z_T, \quad T = T_0 - d.$$

We will assume that the ϵ_t are normal, in order to derive the asymptotic properties of the estimators more easily.

The Case of an ARMA$(0,q) \equiv$ MA(q) Let us start by deriving the likelihood of the model or, which is the same, the joint density of the observations $z_1, \ldots, z_T$. We have

$$z_t = \Theta(L)\epsilon_t, \quad t = 1, \ldots, T,$$

or

$$z_t = \epsilon_t + \sum_{i=1}^{q} \theta_i \epsilon_{t-i}, \tag{6.3}$$

where the ϵ_t are assumed normal. The vector $\mathbf{z}' = (z_1, \ldots, z_T)$ can be expressed as a linear transformation of the vector $\boldsymbol{\varepsilon}' = (\epsilon_{1-q}, \ldots, \epsilon_T)$; therefore it is normally distributed. We could then write a matrix $\mathbf{M}(\boldsymbol{\theta})$ such that $\mathbf{z} = \mathbf{M}(\boldsymbol{\theta})\boldsymbol{\varepsilon}$ and derive from this the density of $\mathbf{z}$. This will be the density of the normal distribution

$$\mathcal{N}\left(0, \sigma^2 \mathbf{M}(\boldsymbol{\theta})\mathbf{M}(\boldsymbol{\theta})'\right).$$

However, this method is not the most suitable to solve the likelihood maximization problem, since it implies the computation of the matrix $(\mathbf{M}(\boldsymbol{\theta})\mathbf{M}(\boldsymbol{\theta})')^{-1}$ the dimension of which is T. Let us follow a different route, starting from the system

$$\epsilon_{1-q} = \epsilon_{1-q},$$

$$\ldots\ldots$$

$$\epsilon_{-1} = \epsilon_{-1},$$

$$\epsilon_0 = \epsilon_0,$$

$$\epsilon_1 = z_1 - \theta_1\epsilon_0 - \ldots - \theta_q\epsilon_{1-q}, \tag{6.4}$$

$$\epsilon_2 = z_2 - \theta_1\epsilon_1 - \ldots - \theta_q\epsilon_{2-q},$$

$$\ldots\ldots$$

$$\epsilon_T = z_T - \theta_1\epsilon_{T-1} - \ldots - \theta_q\epsilon_{T-q}.$$

Let us imagine that we substitute ϵ_1 in the expression for ϵ_2 with a function of $\epsilon_0, \ldots, \epsilon_{1-q}$, then ϵ_1 and ϵ_2 in the expression for ϵ_3 with a function of $\epsilon_0, \ldots, \epsilon_{1-q}$, and so on, obtaining

$$\boldsymbol{\epsilon} = \mathbf{N}\mathbf{z} + \mathbf{X}\boldsymbol{\epsilon}_*, \tag{6.5}$$

where $\mathbf{N}$ is a $(T+q) \times T$ matrix equal to

$$\begin{pmatrix} \mathbf{0} \\ \mathbf{A}_1(\boldsymbol{\theta}) \end{pmatrix},$$

$$\boldsymbol{\epsilon}_* = (\epsilon_{1-q}, \ldots, \epsilon_0),$$

$\mathbf{X}$ is a $(T+q) \times q$ matrix of the type

$$\begin{pmatrix} \mathbf{I_q} \\ \mathbf{A}_2(\boldsymbol{\theta}) \end{pmatrix},$$

$\mathbf{A}_1(\boldsymbol{\theta})$ is a $T \times T$ lower triangular matrix with unit elements along the main diagonal, and $\mathbf{A}_2(\boldsymbol{\theta})$ is a $T \times q$ matrix. Equation (6.5) can also be written as

$$\boldsymbol{\epsilon} = (\mathbf{X} \quad \mathbf{N}) \begin{pmatrix} \boldsymbol{\epsilon}_* \\ \mathbf{z} \end{pmatrix}. \tag{6.6}$$

The square matrix $(\mathbf{X} \quad \mathbf{N})$ is lower triangular, with unit elements along the main diagonal: hence its determinant is equal to one. We can get the density of the random vector $(\boldsymbol{\epsilon}_*' \ \mathbf{z}')'$, by replacing the vector $\boldsymbol{\epsilon}$ by $\mathbf{N}\mathbf{z} + \mathbf{X}\boldsymbol{\epsilon}_*$ in the density of $\boldsymbol{\epsilon}$. We obtain

$$\frac{1}{(2\pi\sigma^2)^{(T+q)/2}} \exp\left(-\frac{1}{2\sigma^2}(\mathbf{N}\mathbf{z} + \mathbf{X}\boldsymbol{\epsilon}_*)'(\mathbf{N}\mathbf{z} + \mathbf{X}\boldsymbol{\epsilon}_*)\right). \tag{6.7}$$

Hence we can refer to the computation of the marginal distribution of $\mathbf{z}$ from the distribution of $\begin{pmatrix} \boldsymbol{\varepsilon}_* \\ \mathbf{z} \end{pmatrix}$. The orthogonal projection of $\mathbf{Nz}$ on the subspace of $\mathbb{R}^{T+q}$ spanned by the columns of $\mathbf{X}$ is given by $\mathbf{X}\hat{\boldsymbol{\varepsilon}}_*$ where

$$\hat{\boldsymbol{\varepsilon}}_* = -(\mathbf{X}'\mathbf{X})^{-1}\mathbf{X}'\mathbf{Nz}.$$

Pythagoras's Theorem allows us to write (6.7) in the form

$$\frac{1}{(2\pi\sigma^2)^{(T+q)/2}} \exp(-\frac{1}{2\sigma^2}((\mathbf{Nz} + \mathbf{X}\hat{\boldsymbol{\varepsilon}}_*)'\,(\mathbf{Nz} + \mathbf{X}\hat{\boldsymbol{\varepsilon}}_*) \\ + (\boldsymbol{\varepsilon}_* - \hat{\boldsymbol{\varepsilon}}_*)'\,\mathbf{X}'\mathbf{X}\,(\boldsymbol{\varepsilon}_* - \hat{\boldsymbol{\varepsilon}}_*))). \tag{6.8}$$

We derive the density of $\mathbf{z}$ by integrating with respect to $\boldsymbol{\varepsilon}_*$. We have

$$L_T = \frac{1}{(2\pi\sigma^2)^{T/2}}(\det(\mathbf{X}'\mathbf{X}))^{-1/2} \\ \exp\left(-\frac{1}{2\sigma^2}(\mathbf{Nz} + \mathbf{X}\hat{\boldsymbol{\varepsilon}}_*)'(\mathbf{Nz} + \mathbf{X}\hat{\boldsymbol{\varepsilon}}_*)\right). \tag{6.9}$$

Denoting

$$S(\boldsymbol{\theta}) = (\mathbf{Nz} + \mathbf{X}\hat{\boldsymbol{\varepsilon}}_*)'(\mathbf{Nz} + \mathbf{X}\hat{\boldsymbol{\varepsilon}}_*),$$

we get

$$\ln L_T = -\frac{T}{2}\ln 2\pi - \frac{T}{2}\ln\sigma^2 - \frac{1}{2}\ln(\det(\mathbf{X}'\mathbf{X})) - \frac{S(\boldsymbol{\theta})}{2\sigma^2}.$$

This log-likelihood can be maximized with respect to the parameters $\boldsymbol{\theta}$ and σ^2 to determine the maximum likelihood estimators. Often we carry out the maximization in two steps, looking for the estimator of $\boldsymbol{\theta}$ by concentrating out the likelihood. Setting to zero the partial derivative of $\ln L_T$ with respect to σ^2, we get

$$\frac{\partial \ln L_T}{\partial \sigma^2} = -\frac{T}{2\sigma^2} + -\frac{S(\boldsymbol{\theta})}{2\sigma^4}.$$

From which we get

$$\sigma^2 = \frac{S(\boldsymbol{\theta})}{T}. \tag{6.10}$$

Substituting it in the log-likelihood, we see that the concentrated log-likelihood is

$$\ln L_T^* = -\frac{T}{2}\ln 2\pi - \frac{T}{2}\ln\frac{S(\boldsymbol{\theta})}{T} - \frac{1}{2}\ln(\det(\mathbf{X}'\mathbf{X})) - \frac{T}{2}.$$

Finally, the function to be minimized is

$$l_T^* = T\ln S(\boldsymbol{\theta}) + \ln(\det(\mathbf{X}'\mathbf{X})). \tag{6.11}$$

At this stage, we can suggest two kinds of method to find an estimator of $\boldsymbol{\theta}$

(i) The *exact methods* aimed at minimizing l_T^* directly, using numerical methods (cf. Osborn, 1976 for an interesting simplification, and section 15.2 for the utilization of the Kalman Filter).

(ii) The *least squares* methods aimed at minimizing $S(\boldsymbol{\theta})$, on the basis that the second term of l_T^* becomes negligible with respect to the first as T increases. The least squares methods are the most used ones. They allow the use of simple algorithms to compute the value of the objective function. These algorithms are generally linked to recursive methods of forecast computations. One of such procedures, proposed by Box and Jenkins, is *backforecasting*.

Equation (6.8) shows that $\hat{\boldsymbol{\varepsilon}}_*$ is the conditional expectation of $\boldsymbol{\varepsilon}_*$ given **z**. Denoting by $\hat{\boldsymbol{\varepsilon}}$ the conditional expectation of $\boldsymbol{\varepsilon}$ given **z**, we can use relationship (6.5) to get

$$\hat{\boldsymbol{\varepsilon}} = \mathbf{Nz} + \mathbf{X}\hat{\boldsymbol{\varepsilon}}_*,$$

and $S(\theta)$ can be written as

$$S(\theta) = \|\hat{\boldsymbol{\varepsilon}}\|^2 = \sum_{i=1-q}^{T} \hat{\epsilon}_i^2. \tag{6.12}$$

This interpretation of $S(\boldsymbol{\theta})$ allows the derivation of a simple computation rule for a given $\boldsymbol{\theta}$. We first determine $\hat{\boldsymbol{\varepsilon}}_*$ by "backforecasting". More precisely, we have

$$\hat{\epsilon}_{1-q} = \hat{z}_{1-q} - \theta_1 \hat{\epsilon}_{1-q-1} - \ldots - \theta_q \hat{\epsilon}_{1-2q},$$

that is

$$\hat{\epsilon}_{1-q} = \hat{z}_{1-q},$$

since $\hat{\epsilon}_{1-q-i} = 0$, $i = 1, \ldots, q$. By the same token, we have

$$\hat{\epsilon}_{2-q} = \hat{z}_{2-q} - \theta_1 \hat{\epsilon}_{1-q}$$

$$\ldots$$

$$\hat{\epsilon}_0 = \hat{z}_0 - \theta_1 \hat{\epsilon}_1 - \ldots - \theta_{q-1} \hat{\epsilon}_{1-q}.$$

Thus, $\hat{\boldsymbol{\varepsilon}}_*$ is known when the forecasts $\hat{z}_i = E(z_i \mid \mathbf{z})$, $i = 1-q, \ldots, 0$ are known. The computation of the $\hat{z}_i$ is easily done by using the forward representation of the process z

$$z_t = \Theta(F)\eta_t.$$

In fact, one may use the forecasting techniques described in section 4.4
by inverting the direction of time

$$\hat{z}_0 = -\sum_{i=1}^{+\infty} \pi_i z_i \approx -\sum_{i=1}^{T} \pi_i z_i,$$

where the π's are the same as the ones used in the forward forecast, that
is the coefficients of the long division of 1 by Θ. The $\hat{\epsilon}_i$, $i = 1, \ldots, T$
are then computed recursively using the expressions (6.4). This fast
computation of $S(\boldsymbol{\theta})$ translates into the possibility of using numerical
optimization algorithms.

The Case of an ARMA(p, q)   The two types of method exist also
under the general case. The exact methods (cf. Newbold, 1974 and
McLeod, 1977) and the least squares methods can be generalized to the
case of an ARMA(p, q) extending the case of an MA(q) process just
described. The basic intuition behind the treatment of an ARMA(p, q)
is that it can be written in a moving average form

$$\sum_{i=0}^{+\infty} \psi_i \epsilon_{t-i},$$

which can be approximated by an MA(Q) process

$$\sum_{i=0}^{Q} \psi_i \epsilon_{t-i},$$

with Q large enough. For all practical purposes we need to solve the
problem of the choice of Q. We have seen that for an MA(q), the $\hat{z}_i$
are 0 for $i \leq -q$. In the ARMA(p, q) case we will stop the backward
forecast when the $\hat{z}_i$'s become negligible. Then we have a simple way of
computing

$$S(\boldsymbol{\phi}, \boldsymbol{\theta}) + \sum_{i=1-Q}^{T} \hat{\epsilon}_i^2,$$

for given

$$\boldsymbol{\phi}' = (\phi_1, \ldots, \phi_p),$$
$$\boldsymbol{\theta}' = (\theta_1, \ldots, \theta_q),$$

which can be minimized numerically.

6.2.2 Initial Values

The optimization algorithms used in the various estimation methods
need initial values for the parameters. The choice of the initial values is

important, since, on the one hand, it reflects on the number of needed iterations to reach the optimum, while, on the other, it results in the attainment of a local or global optimum. In this section we will show that it is possible to compute consistent estimators for ϕ_j and θ_j. These estimators are asymptotically less efficient than those proposed in the previous section, but may provide meaningful initial values.

Use of the Yule–Walker Equations We have seen that the Yule–Walker equations for an ARMA(p,q) imply a link among the autoregressive coefficients and the autocorrelations

$$\begin{pmatrix} \rho(q+1) \\ \vdots \\ \rho(q+p) \end{pmatrix} = \begin{pmatrix} \rho(q) & \cdots & \rho(q-p+1) \\ \vdots & \ddots & \vdots \\ \rho(q+p-1) & \cdots & \rho(q) \end{pmatrix} \begin{pmatrix} \phi_1 \\ \vdots \\ \phi_p \end{pmatrix}. \qquad (6.13)$$

The empirical autocorrelations

$$\hat{\rho}_h = \frac{\frac{1}{T-h}\sum_{t=h+1}^{T}(z_t - \bar{z}_T)(z_{t-h} - \bar{z}_T)}{\frac{1}{T}\sum_{t=1}^{T}(z_t - \bar{z}_T)^2},$$

where $\bar{z}_T = \frac{1}{T}\sum_{t=1}^{T} z_t$ provide consistent estimators of the theoretical autocorrelations (cf. chapter 9). After having replaced the autocorrelations by their consistent estimators we can solve the Yule–Walker system to get consistent estimators of the autoregressive parameters.

Use of the Inverse Autocorrelations The choice of initial values for the moving average coefficients θ_i is a bit more complicated. In fact, we know that, for example, in the case of an MA(q), the $\rho(h)$ are nonlinear functions of the θ_i in such a way that the computation of the θ_i as a function of the $\rho(h)$, $h = 1, \ldots, q$ poses some problems. Evidently, we cannot obtain simple estimators of the θ_i's following this route. The notion of inverse autocorrelation, introduced in the previous chapter (section 5.3.1), allows one to solve this problem. Resorting to these inverse autocorrelations, we have available a Yule–Walker system of the type

$$\begin{pmatrix} \rho i(p+1) \\ \vdots \\ \rho i(p+q) \end{pmatrix} = \begin{pmatrix} \rho i(p) & \cdots & \rho i(p-q+1) \\ \vdots & \ddots & \vdots \\ \rho i(p+q-1) & \cdots & \rho i(q) \end{pmatrix} \begin{pmatrix} \theta_1 \\ \vdots \\ \theta_q \end{pmatrix}. \qquad (6.14)$$

The estimation of the inverse autocorrelations can be obtained by writing the process in an infinite autoregressive form

$$z_t = \sum_{j=1}^{+\infty} -\pi_j z_{t-j} + \epsilon_t.$$

Approximations to the coefficients π_j are obtained by regressing z_t on the past values $z_{t-1}, \ldots, z_{t-P}$ with ordinary least squares, where the index P is chosen large enough. If $\hat{\pi}_j$, $j = 1, \ldots, P$ denote these approximations, the estimators of the inverse autocorrelations can be derived using formula (5.17)

$$\widehat{\rho i}(h) = \frac{\sum_{k=0}^{P-h} \hat{\pi}_k \hat{\pi}_{k+h}}{\sum_{k=0}^{P} \hat{\pi}_k^2}, \tag{6.15}$$

for $0 \leq h \leq P$.

Two-step Regressions Even if it may be not included in the most popular packages, we mention here another approach which presents the twofold advantage of being simple and of providing the simultaneous estimation of the three types of parameters θ_j, ϕ_j, and σ^2. The intuition behind it can be summarized as follows

(i)   We start by regressing z_t on its past $z_{t-1}, \ldots, z_{t-P}$ fixing an order P large enough. We can derive the estimates of the coefficients π_j, $j = 1, \ldots, P$ and of the estimation residuals as well

$$\tilde{\epsilon}_t = z_t + \sum_{j=1}^{P} \hat{\pi}_j z_{t-j}.$$

(ii)   We turn to the ARMA representation of the process by writing it in the form

$$z_t = (-\phi_1 z_{t-1} - \ldots - \phi_p z_{t-p} + \theta_1 \epsilon_{t-1} + \ldots + \theta_q \epsilon_{t-q}) + \epsilon_t.$$

This expression shows that it is possible to regress z_t on

$$z_{t-1}, \ldots, z_{t-p}, \tilde{\epsilon}_{t-1}, \ldots, \tilde{\epsilon}_{t-q},$$

by ordinary least squares. The regression coefficients so obtained provide consistent estimators of $-\phi_1, \ldots, -\phi_p, \theta_1, \ldots, \theta_q$. The sum of the squared corresponding residuals divided by the number of observations corrected by the degrees of freedom is an estimator of σ^2.

6.2.3 Asymptotic Properties of the Estimators

The parameter estimators obtained either by maximizing the exact log-likelihood or by minimizing the approximation $S(\phi, \theta)$ have identical asymptotic properties. Moreover, these properties are very similar to those usually encountered in a sampling framework. More precisely, let us denote by $\boldsymbol{\alpha}$ the vector $(\phi_1, \ldots, \phi_p, \theta_1, \ldots, \theta_q)'$ and $\hat{\boldsymbol{\alpha}}_T$, $\hat{\sigma}_T^2$ the estimators mentioned above. If we assume that the components of the noise are independently normally distributed, it is possible to show that:

Theorem 6.1: *The estimators $\hat{\alpha}_T$, $\hat{\sigma}_T^2$ converge to α, σ^2.*

On the other hand, asymptotic normality holds for the estimators

$$\sqrt{T}\begin{pmatrix} \hat{\alpha}_T - \alpha \\ \hat{\sigma}_T^2 - \sigma^2 \end{pmatrix} \overset{\text{d}}{\to} \mathcal{N}\left(0, \begin{pmatrix} \mathbf{A} & 0 \\ 0 & b \end{pmatrix}\right), \tag{6.16}$$

where

$$\mathbf{A} = \underset{T \to +\infty}{\text{plim}} \left(-\frac{1}{T}\frac{\partial^2 \ln L}{\partial\alpha\partial\alpha'}\right)^{-1},$$

$$b = \underset{T \to +\infty}{\text{plim}} \left(-\frac{1}{T}\frac{\partial^2 \ln L}{\partial(\sigma^2)^2}\right)^{-1}.$$

It is possible (cf. chapter 9) to give various equivalent expressions for these limits, when the noise is Gaussian. The estimators of these expressions can be used to build confidence intervals or to test hypotheses. Note that these asymptotic results are valid whenever the degrees p, d, q are known, without taking into consideration the previous phase of a priori identification.

6.3 Identification

6.3.1 A Priori Identification

Choice of d Let us assume that the process $\{x_t\}$ generating the observations is an ARIMA with $d > 0$. It is clear that, the process being nonstationary we cannot define the autocorrelation function $\rho(h)$. However, the function

$$\rho(h, t) = \frac{\text{cov}\,(x_t, x_{t+h})}{\sqrt{\text{var}\,(x_t)\text{var}\,(x_{t+h})}},$$

is always a meaningful expression, since it can be shown that it tends to 1 as t goes to infinity. Values of the estimated autocorrelation function $\hat{\rho}_T(h)$ close to 1 for a large enough number of values of h are an indication that the series needs differencing to make it stationary. In practice, given the random oscillations due to sampling, it seems that the criterion of proximity to one of the first values of $\hat{\rho}_T(h)$ should be replaced by one of closedness among themselves of these values. In other words, we consider that the series needs differencing if the first $\hat{\rho}_T(h)$ are close to each other, even if $\hat{\rho}(1)$ is fairly different from 1 (cf. Box and Jenkins, 1970, appendix A.6.1). In chapter 14 we will introduce some rigorous tests for nonstationarity. When the decision of differencing a series has

been made, we apply the same criterion to the differenced series, in order
to understand whether a second differencing is needed, and so on. For
economic series the most common values of d are $0, 1, 2$. Higher values
are very rare.

Choice of q (or p) for an MA (or AR) process The guidelines
for the choice of p and q come from the shape of the functions $\hat{\rho}_T(h)$
and $\hat{r}_T(h)$ of the series differenced d times. We can think, for example,
that a tendency of $\hat{\rho}_T(h)$ toward values close to 0 for $h > q$ indicates an
MA(q) or that a tendency of $\hat{r}_T(h)$ toward values close to 0 for $h > p$
indicates an AR(p). In order to decide whether values of $\hat{\rho}_T(h)$ or $\hat{r}_T(h)$
are significantly different from 0, it is advisable to derive their standard
error. We can show (cf. chapter 9) that for an MA(q) we have

$$\operatorname{var}\left(\hat{\rho}_T(h)\right) = \frac{1}{T}\left(1 + 2\sum_{i=1}^{q}\rho^2(i),\right), \quad \forall\, h > q,$$

where T is the number of observations in the series after differencing d
times. As an estimator of the standard error, we can take then

$$\hat{\sigma}(\hat{\rho}_T(h)) = \frac{1}{\sqrt{T}}\left(1 + 2\sum_{i=1}^{q}\hat{\rho}_T^2(i)\right)^{1/2}.$$

By the same token, using a result by Quenouille (1949a), we can take
$\frac{1}{\sqrt{T}}$ as an approximate standard error of $\hat{r}_T(h)$ for $h > p$ if the process
is an AR(p). In order to identify the degree p of an autoregressive process, we can represent the sequence of the estimated partial autocorrelations $\hat{r}_T(h)$ and examine from which value on it stays within the band
$\left(-1.96/\sqrt{T},\ 1.96/\sqrt{T}\right)$. Thus, for the example represented in figure
6.2, we can assume that $p = 3$. Such a step of testing the null hypothesis of zero partial correlation $r(h)$ separately for each autocorrelation
at the significance level of 5% is not strictly rigorous from a statistical
point of view, but provides a useful guideline in practice. By the same
token, in order to identify the degree q of a moving average process we
can represent graphically the sequence of the estimated autocorrelations
$\hat{\rho}_T(h)$ and check after what value of h all $\hat{\rho}_T(h)$ stay within the interval
of bounds

$$\pm\frac{1.96}{\sqrt{T}}\left(1 + 2(\hat{\rho}_T^2(1) + \ldots + \hat{\rho}_T^2(h-1))\right)^{1/2}.$$

In fact, under the null hypothesis that the process is an MA(q) we have

$$\sqrt{T}\hat{\rho}_T(h) \xrightarrow{\mathrm{d}} \mathcal{N}\left(0,\ 1 + 2(\hat{\rho}_T^2(1) + \ldots + \hat{\rho}_T^2(h-1))\right), \quad \forall\ h > q.$$

The program used in section 6.5 below, provides approximate values of

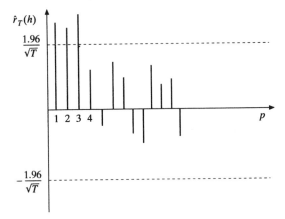

Figure 6.2 Example of Estimated Partial Autocorrelations

these intervals equal to $\pm \frac{1.96}{\sqrt{T}}$ for $1 \le h \le 12$, the values provided by

$$\pm \frac{1.96}{\sqrt{T}} \left(1 + 2(\hat{\rho}_T^2(1) + \ldots + \hat{\rho}_T^2(12))\right)^{1/2}.$$

for $13 \le h \le 24$, and so on.

Choice of p and q for an ARMA Process: the Corner Method A simultaneous identification method for p and q can be derived from the characterization of these orders introduced in theorem 5.17. Let us provide a formulation of this in terms of autocorrelations rather than of autocovariances. Recall that p and q are such that

$$\tilde{\Delta}(i,j) = 0 \quad \forall \ i \ge p \text{ and } j \ge q,$$

$$\tilde{\Delta}(i, q-1) \ne 0 \quad \forall \ i \ge p-1,$$

$$\tilde{\Delta}(p-1, q) \ne 0 \quad \forall \ j \ge q-1,$$

where

$$\tilde{\Delta}(i,j) = \det \begin{pmatrix} \rho(j+1) & \rho(j+2) & \ldots & \rho(j+i+1) \\ \rho(j) & \rho(j+1) & \ldots & \rho(j+i) \\ \vdots & & \ddots & \vdots \\ \rho(j+1-i) & \rho(j+2-i) & \ldots & \rho(j+1) \end{pmatrix}.$$

The values of $\tilde{\Delta}(i,j)$ are unknown, but they can be estimated by the $\hat{\Delta}(i,j)$ obtained by replacing the correlations $\rho(h)$ with their estimators $\hat{\rho}_T(h)$ in the determinant. Since the $\hat{\Delta}(i,j)$ are consistent estimators of the $\Delta(i,j)$, it is likely that we will notice a "break" between rows $i = p-1$ and $i = p$, and between the columns $j = q-1$ and $j = q$ in the matrix with elements $\hat{\Delta}(i,j)$. In practice, since the $\hat{\Delta}(i,j)$ are estimators

Table 6.1 *Identification by the t-ratios
(Critical Value 1.96)*

j	0	1	2	3	4	5
i						
0	7.76	4.99	2.58	0.41	0.58	0.53
1	8.41	3.15	0.91	0.55	0.38	0.48
2	2.53	2.32	0.48	0.13	0.54	0.48
3	2.76	0.80	0.13	0.44	0.72	0.44
4	2.20	0.21	0.85	0.95	0.52	0.43
5	1.56	1.23	0.75	0.99	0.20	0.13

with different variabilities, it is preferable to search for such "breaks" with the aid of the matrix containing the Student t-ratios associated with $\hat{\Delta}(i,j)$. The asymptotic variance of $\hat{\Delta}(i,j)$ can be estimated recalling that $\hat{\Delta}(i,j)$ is a differentiable function of the autocorrelations $\hat{\rho}_T(h)$. The distribution of the latter is normal (cf. chapter 9). Denoting the estimated variance by $\widehat{\text{var}}(\hat{\Delta}(i,j))$, the t-ratio associated with the null hypothesis $\tilde{\Delta}(i,j) = 0$ is given by

$$\frac{\mid \hat{\Delta}(i,j) \mid}{\sqrt{\widehat{\text{var}}(\hat{\Delta}(i,j))}}.$$

Comparing the value of this ratio to 1.96 we get an asymptotic test of the hypothesis $\tilde{\Delta}(i,j) = 0$ at a significance level of 5%. Again, like in the case of the pure processes, such a procedure consists in testing the hypothesis of zero determinants separately, and hence is not rigorous, strictly speaking, from a statistical point of view. It can be improved upon, by testing various determinants to be simultaneously zero, for example $\tilde{\Delta}(i,j)$, $\tilde{\Delta}(i+1,j)$, $\tilde{\Delta}(i,j+1)$. The test is then based on a quadratic form in $\hat{\Delta}(i,j)$, $\hat{\Delta}(i+1,j)$, $\hat{\Delta}(i,j+1)$ which is asymptotically distributed as a $\chi^2(3)$ under the null hypothesis (cf. Beguin, Gourieroux, and Monfort, 1980). In order to illustrate this identification procedure, we have generated 300 observations from the process

$$(1 - 0.5L)x_t = (1 + 0.1L - 0.56L^2)\epsilon_t,$$

where ϵ_t is a Gaussian white noise with unit variance. Table 6.1, containing the t-ratios, shows four possible corners corresponding to the MA(3), ARMA(1,2), ARMA(3,1), and AR(5) processes.

Table 6.2 *Identification by the* χ^2 *(Critical Value 7.81)*

j	0	1	2	3	4
i					
0	*	523.1	853.56	3.34	1.81
1	1221585	73.18	5.67	1.64	0.56
2	22.76	24.95	5.31	0.40	0.90
3	22.95	29.59	1.29	0.99	0.55

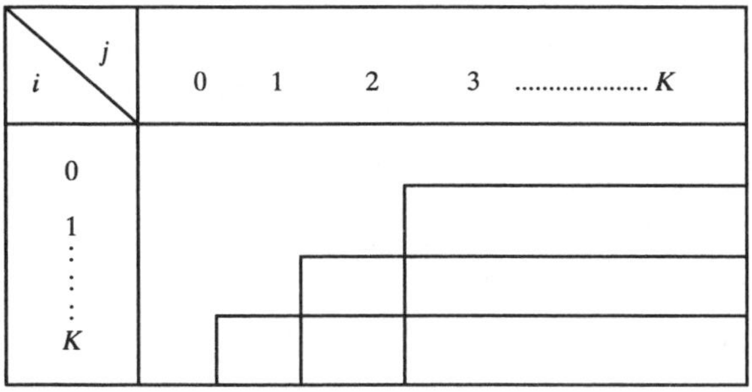

Figure 6.3 Various Orders (p, q) Compatible with the Corner Method

Table 6.2 shows the procedure based on the quadratic forms in $\hat{\Delta}(i, j)$, $\hat{\Delta}(i+1, j)$, $\hat{\Delta}(i, j+1)$. It shows only two acceptable models: MA(3) and ARMA(1,2), the latter being the true model used for the simulation. The data appear compatible with an MA(3) model since the infinite moving average representation of the process

$$x_t = (1 + 0.1L - 0.56L^2) \sum_{k=0}^{+\infty} (0.5)^k L^k \epsilon_t$$

has relatively small coefficients ψ_i for $i \geq 4$. Generally, like in the previous example, the method leads to retain several candidate couples (p, q) as shown in figure 6.3.

For each row, that is for each value of p, there corresponds a possible value of $q = f(p)$. Conversely, for each column, that is for each value of q, there corresponds a value $p = g(q)$. The functions $q = f(p)$ and $p = g(q)$ are decreasing functions of p and q. This empirical regularity can be explained by noting that an ARMA(p_0, q_0) representation can be well approximated by a process ARMA($p_0 - 1, f(p_0 - 1)$) with $f(p_0 - 1) > q_0$, and so on. From this remark, we can derive a simple way of determining the orders by excess. In fact, we can choose the values $g(0)$ and $f(0)$, that is the first values after which the sequence of the estimated partial autocorrelations and the sequence of the estimated autocorrelations can be considered 0. We are thus back to the methods described for the identification of pure AR and MA models. Note, however, that a pure AR or MA representation may require more parameters than an ARMA representation.

6.3.2 Validation

The tests adopted for the model are of two types: the tests regarding the parameters ϕ_j and θ_j of the model and those regarding the hypotheses on the noise ϵ.

Tests on the Parameters In order to compare an ARMA(p, q) representation with an ARMA(p_1, q_1), it is convenient to set up a situation where one of the models is a special case of the other. Let us suppose in what follows that we start from an ARMA(p, q) model and that we examine the tests corresponding to different values of p_1, q_1.

(i) $p_1 = p - 1$, $q_1 = q$. This would be the case where it is possible to reduce the order of lags intervening in the autoregressive part by 1. This is equivalent to testing the significance of the coefficient ϕ_p which can be done by a Student-type test. Let $\hat{\phi}_p$ be the estimator of ϕ_p in the ARMA(p, q) representation, and $\widehat{\text{var}}(\hat{\phi}_p)$ its estimated variance. We will not be able to reject the hypothesis of an ARMA$(p - 1, q)$ (at a significance level of 5%) if

$$\frac{|\hat{\phi}_p|}{\sqrt{\widehat{\text{var}}(\hat{\phi}_p)}} < 1.96.$$

We will accept the ARMA(p, q) representation if the inequality is inverted. Clearly, a similar test holds for $p_1 = p$, $q_1 = q - 1$.

(ii) $p_1 = p + 1, q_1 = q$. This would be the case where it is possible to add an extra lag in the autoregressive part. This can be done by estimating an ARMA(p_1, q_1)=ARMA$(p + 1, q)$ model and testing the hypothesis $\phi_{p+1} = 0$ in this model. This is the same as the procedure described previously.

(iii) $p_1 = p + 1, q_1 = q + 1$. We do not know how to test the need for increasing the orders of the autoregressive and moving average polynomials simultaneously. In fact, a process w with an ARMA representation $\Phi(L)w_t = \Theta(L)\epsilon_t$ admits also ARMA$(p + 1, q + 1)$ representations by multiplying $\Phi(L)$ and $\Theta(L)$ by the same polynomial $1 + \lambda L$. Therefore, within the $\text{ARMA}(p+1, q+1)$ model, the null hypothesis of an $\text{ARMA}(p, q)$ is not identifiable. The usual tests such as the likelihood ratio tests are not usable.

White Noise Tests Their purpose is to verify whether the series of estimated residuals,

$$\tilde{\epsilon}_t = \frac{\hat{\phi}(L)(1 - L)^d}{\hat{\Theta}(L)} x_t,$$

is consistent with the white noise hypothesis for the ϵ_t.

Portmanteau Test This test, very popular, was proposed by Box and Pierce (1970). It is based on the statistics

$$Q = T \sum_{h=1}^{K} \hat{\rho}_h^2(\tilde{\epsilon}),$$

where $\hat{\rho}_h(\tilde{\epsilon})$ is the empirical correlation among residuals h periods apart from each other. Under the null hypothesis of independence of the disturbances ϵ_t, we can show that Q is asymptotically distributed as a χ^2 with $K-p-q$ degrees of freedom. We reject the independence hypothesis at the α significance level if

$$Q > \chi^2_{1-\alpha}(K - p - q).$$

The small sample properties of Q are fairly different from the large sample properties, even for a fairly large T. For this reason, a modified statistics has been proposed in order to correct for this difference

$$Q' = T(T + 2) \sum_{h=1}^{K} \frac{1}{T - h} \hat{\rho}_h^2(\tilde{\epsilon})$$

(cf. Davies, Triggs and Newbold, 1977; Prothero and Wallis, 1976). The number K must be chosen large enough, usually between fifteen and thirty in practice. Once the white noise hypothesis is shown inadequate by the test, we can reexamine the sequence of the estimated autocorrelations to know in which direction to modify the model.

6.3.3 Choice of a Model

It may happen that several models pass the validation phase and that a choice within such a set is needed. The first thing to do is to isolate "twin models," that is to say those corresponding in fact to different representations of the same model (or of close models) and therefore equivalent for forecasting purposes. Once a representative in each class of "twins" is chosen, we may be faced with quite different models, making the choice more difficult. However, there exists a certain number of choice criteria. Some authors even think that these criteria (not very rigorous from a theoretical point of view) allow for the suppression of the identification phase and hence for a completely automatic forecasting procedure.

Predictive Capability Criteria In the case of an ARMA model, the one-step ahead forecast error is such that $\text{var}\,(e_t(1)) = \sigma^2$. We can then propose to choose the model resulting in a fairly small forecast error. Various criteria can be proposed

(i) the estimated variance $\hat{\sigma}^2$;

(ii) the determination coefficient,

$$R^2 = 1 - \frac{\hat{\sigma}^2}{V},$$

V being the empirical variance of the series differenced d times. This second criterion is simply a standardized version of the previous one;

(iii) the modified determination coefficient

$$\bar{R}^2 = 1 - \frac{\hat{\sigma}^2/(T - p - q)}{V/(T - 1)},$$

which allows for the explicit inclusion in the criterion of the orders of the autoregressive and moving average polynomials;

(iv) Fisher's F

$$F = \frac{(V - \hat{\sigma}^2)/(p + q)}{\hat{\sigma}^2/(T - p - q)},$$

introduced by analogy to the linear model case.

The criterion (i) is to be minimized, whereas (ii), (iii), and (iv) are to be maximized.

Information Criteria An approach proposed by Akaike (1969) consists of assuming that the ARMA(p, q) models provide approximations to reality, and that the true distribution of the observations $\nabla^d x_t$ does not necessarily correspond to such a model. We can then base the choice of the model on a measure of the deviation between the true unknown distribution and the proposed model. The common measure is given by the Kullback information quantity. Let $f_0(x)$ be the unknown probability density of the observations, $[f(x), f \in F_{p,q}]$ the density family corresponding to an ARMA(p,q) model. The deviation between the true density and the model is measured by

$$I(f_0, F_{p,q}) = \min_{f \in F_{p,q}} \int \ln \frac{f_0(x)}{f(x)} f_0(x)\, dx.$$

This quantity is always positive, and becomes 0 only when the true density f_0 is a member of $F_{p,q}$. The value of the information quantity $I(f_0, F_{p,q})$ is clearly unknown, but if we have a "good" estimator $\hat{I}(f_0, F_{p,q})$ of this quantity, it could be used as a criterion. The chosen model will be the one corresponding to the smallest estimated value of $\hat{I}(f_0, F_{p,q})$. The proposed estimators for the information quantity are

(i) $AIC(p,q) = \ln \hat{\sigma}^2 + 2(p+q)/T,$

(ii) $BIC(p,q) = \ln \hat{\sigma}^2 + (p+q)\ln T/T,$

(iii) $\phi(p,q) = \ln \hat{\sigma}^2 + (p+q)\, c \ln \ln T/T,$ where $c > 2$.

The first of these criteria was introduced by Akaike (1969) and is by far the most used one. The BIC criterion was proposed by Akaike (1977) and Schwartz (1978), while the third one was introduced by Hannan and Quinn (1979). However, the only consistent estimators of p and q are those from the latter two, and lead to an asymptotically correct selection of the model (Hannan, 1980).

6.4 Forecasting with ARIMA Models

6.4.1 Optimal Forecasts with an ARIMA Model

Let us consider an ARIMA process $\{x_t\}$ defined by

$$\phi(L)(1-L)^d x_t = \Theta(L)\epsilon_t, \quad t \geq 0,$$

or

$$\Phi(L)x_t = \Theta(L)\epsilon_t, \quad t \geq 0,$$

and by the initial conditions

$$\mathbf{z}_{-1} = (x_{-1}, \ldots, x_{-p-d}, \epsilon_{-1}, \ldots, \epsilon_{-q})',$$

uncorrelated with $\epsilon_0, \epsilon_1, \ldots, \epsilon_t, \ldots$. The optimal forecast of x_{t+k}, $k > 0$ formulated at time t is denoted by $_t\hat{x}_{t+k}$ or $\hat{x}_t(k)$ and k is called the *forecast horizon*. This optimal forecast is by definition the affine regression of x_{t+k} on $(\mathbf{z}_{-1}; x_i, i = 0, \ldots, t)$ or, which is equivalent, on $(\mathbf{z}_{-1}; \epsilon_i, i = 0, \ldots, t)$.

Formula Derived from the Moving Average Form The moving average representation of the process (cf. (5.28)) allows to write

$$x_{t+k} = \sum_{j=0}^{t+k} h_j \epsilon_{t+k-j} + h^*(t+k)\mathbf{z}_{-1}.$$

The affine regression of x_{t+k} on $(\mathbf{z}_{-1}; \epsilon_i, \ i = 0, \dots, t)$ is

$$\hat{x}_t(k) = \sum_{j=k}^{t+k} h_j \epsilon_{t+k-j} + h^*(t+k)\mathbf{z}_{-1},$$

or

$$\hat{x}_t(k) = \sum_{j=0}^{t} h_{k+j} \epsilon_{t-j} + h^*(t+k)\mathbf{z}_{-1}. \tag{6.17}$$

We know that this affine regression can be interpreted as a conditional expectation in two cases. The case when the set of variables is normal, and the case when the hypothesis of uncorrelation among the ϵ_i and of $\mathbf{z}_{-1}$ and the $\epsilon_i, \ i \geq 0$ is replaced by an hypothesis of independence. The forecast error $e_t(k) = x_{t+k} - \hat{x}_t(k)$ is obtained as

$$e_t(k) = \sum_{j=0}^{k-1} h_j \epsilon_{t+k-j}. \tag{6.18}$$

In particular, the one-step ahead forecast error is

$$e_t(1) = \epsilon_{t+1}. \tag{6.19}$$

Updating Formulas Formula (6.17) cannot be used directly, since it involves the unobservable ϵ_j's. However, it can be modified into an interesting updating formula

$$\hat{x}_{t+1}(k-1) - \hat{x}_t(k) = \sum_{j=k-1}^{t+k} h_j \epsilon_{t+k-j} - \sum_{j=k}^{t+k} h_j \epsilon_{t+k-j}$$

$$= h_{k-1} \epsilon_{t+1},$$

or

$$\hat{x}_{t+1}(k-1) - \hat{x}_t(k) = h_{k-1} \left(x_{t+1} - \hat{x}_t(1) \right). \tag{6.20}$$

Formula Derived from the Autoregressive Form The autoregressive representation of the process allows to derive a useful relationship

$$x_{t+h} = -\sum_{j=1}^{t+k} \pi_j x_{t+k-j} + \tilde{h}(t+k)\mathbf{z}_{-1} + \epsilon_{t+k}.$$

The term $\tilde{h}(t+k)\mathbf{z}_{-1}$ becomes negligible when t is large enough, so that, approximately

$$x_{t+k} \approx - \sum_{j=1}^{t+k} \pi_j x_{t+k-j} + \epsilon_{t+k},$$

from which

$$\hat{x}_t(k) = - \sum_{j=1}^{t+k} \pi_j \hat{x}_{t+k-j}, \tag{6.21}$$

with

$$\hat{x}_{t+k-j} = \begin{cases} \hat{x}_t(k-j), & \text{if } k > j, \\ x_t(k-j), & \text{if } k \le j. \end{cases}$$

Formula Derived from the ARIMA Form Finally, the expression defining an ARIMA process provides the relationship

$$x_{t+k} = - \sum_{j=1}^{p+d} \phi_j x_{t+k-j} + \sum_{j=0}^{q} \theta_j \epsilon_{t+k-j},$$

with

$$\phi(L) = \sum_{j=0}^{p+d} \phi_j L^j,$$

$$\Theta(L) = \sum_{j=0}^{q} \theta_j L^j,$$

and $\phi_0 = \theta_0 = 1$. We have then

$$\hat{x}_t(k) = - \sum_{j=1}^{p+d} \phi_j \hat{x}_{t+k-j} + \sum_{j=1}^{q} \theta_j \hat{\epsilon}_{t+k-j} \tag{6.22}$$

with

$$\hat{\epsilon}_{t+k-j} = \begin{cases} 0, & \text{if } k > j, \\ \epsilon_{t+k-j}, & \text{if } k \le j. \end{cases}$$

Joint Use of these Formulas Let us assume that we want to forecast up to a horizon K. At time T, we have to compute $\hat{x}_T(k)$, $k = 1, \ldots, K$. At time T+1, we have a new observation available which needs to be considered to modify the forecasts of $x_{T+1}, \ldots, x_{T+K}$, that is to compute $x_{T+1}(k)$, $k = 1, \ldots, K - 1$. We have also to determine a new forecast, that of x_{T+K+1}. These computations can be done by using the expressions presented above in a joint fashion, after replacing the various parameters by consistent estimators.

(i)   We compute $\hat{x}_T(k)$, $k = 1,\ldots,K$ by (6.21) at the first date consid-
      ered T. Once this computation is done we will not use the values
      x_s, $s \leq T$.
(ii) At time $T + 1$, since we know the value of x_{T+1}, we can compute
      $\hat{x}_{T+1}(k)$, $k = 1,\ldots,K - 1$ by (6.20).
(iii) The computation of $x_{T+1}(K)$ can be simply done using (6.22) so
      long as K was chosen greater than q (so that $\hat{\epsilon}_{t+K-i} = 0$, $i =
      1,\ldots,q$) and $K > p+d$ (which allows for not needing to keep track
      of the observations, since $\hat{x}_{t+K-i} = \hat{x}_t(K - i)$, $i = 1,\ldots,p + d$).
      Knowing $\hat{x}_{T+1}(k)$, $k = 1,\ldots,K$ we can repeat the updating phases
      (ii) and (iii) at time $T + 2$ and so on.

6.4.2 Forecast Functions

In the previous section, we have seen how to compute the forecasts $\hat{x}_t(k)$.
It is interesting to study how $\hat{x}_t(k)$ varies as a function of k for fixed t.
This function of k is called *forecast function*. Following (6.22) we have

$$\hat{x}_t(k) - \sum_{j=1}^{p+d} \phi_j \hat{x}_t(k - j) = 0, \ \forall \ k > q, \tag{6.23}$$

with $\hat{x}_t(k - j) = x_{t+k-j}$ if $k \leq j$. Therefore, we have

$$\hat{x}_t(k) = \sum_{i=1}^{p+d} b_i(t) f_i(k). \tag{6.24}$$

The $f_i(k)$, $i = 1,\ldots,p + d$ are the solutions to the difference equation
with characteristic polynomial

$$z^{p+d} - \sum_{i=1}^{p+d} \phi_i z^{p+d-i} = z^{p+d}\Phi\left(\frac{1}{z}\right).$$

The $b_i(t)$ are determined by the initial values, called in this context
pivotal values, namely

$$\hat{x}_t(k), \ k = q, q - 1,\ldots,q - p - d + 1.$$

According to the values of q and $p + d$, the pivotal values are forecasts
and observations, or just observations. In fact:

(i)   if $q > p+d$, the pivotal values are forecasts; moreover, the forecasts
      $\hat{x}_t(1),\ldots,\hat{x}_t(q - p + d)$ do not satisfy (6.24);
(ii) if $q = p+d$, the pivotal values are forecasts and all forecasts satisfy
      (6.24);
(iii) if $q < p+d$, the pivotal values are a mixture of the forecasts $\hat{x}_t(q)$,
      $\ldots$, $\hat{x}_t(1)$ and of the observations x_t, $\ldots$, $x_{t+q-p-d+1}$.
      Therefore, the forecast function will be determined by the polynomial

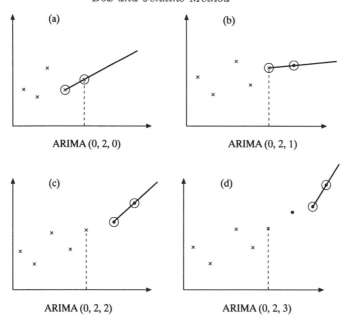

○ Pivotal values   × Observations   • Forecast

Figure 6.4 Pivotal Values for Various ARIMA Models

Φ; in particular, since Φ has d roots equal to 1 and the other roots greater than 1 in modulus, the forecast function admits an asymptotic representation of degree $d - 1$. Also, the way this function is linked to the observations depends upon q. In order to illustrate these outcomes, let us introduce some simple examples. For an ARIMA(0,2,0) (figure 6.4a) the forecast function is a polynomial in k of degree 1, represented by a line. The pivotal values at time t are the observations x_t and x_{t-1}. In the case of an ARIMA(0,2,1) (figure 6.4b) the forecast function is still a line but the pivotal values become $\hat{x}_t(1)$ and x_t. By the same token, for an ARIMA(0,2,2) (figure 6.4c) or for an ARIMA(0,2,3) (figure 6.4d), the forecast function is still a line, but the pivotal values are $\hat{x}_t(1)$, $\hat{x}_t(2)$, respectively, $\hat{x}_t(2)$, $\hat{x}_t(3)$.

If there is a constant θ^* in the definition of the ARIMA process, we need to add to (6.24) a particular solution to the equation

$$\hat{x}_t(k) + \sum_{i=1}^{p+d} \phi_i \hat{x}_t(k - i) = \theta^*.$$

We can choose

$$\frac{\theta^* k^d}{d! \phi(1)}$$

as a particular solution (since the autoregressive polynomial is $(1 - L)^d \phi(L)$). The $b_i(t)$'s are hence derived in a similar fashion as the ones described above. As an example, let us consider the model

$$(1 - L)^2(1 - 0.5L)x_t = 2 + (1 - 0.8L)\epsilon_t.$$

The particular solution here is $2k^2$ and the forecast function appears in the form

$$2k^2 + a + bk + c(0.5)^k.$$

The pivotal values are $\hat{x}_t(1)$, x_t and x_{t-1}. If these pivotal values are respectively equal to 1, 2, and 1, we get

$$2 + a + b + 0.5\,c = 1,$$

$$a + c = 2,$$

$$2 + a - b + 2c = 1,$$

from which $a = 14$, $b = -9$, and $c = -12$. The forecast function is thus

$$\hat{x}_t(k) = 14 - 9k + 2k^2 - \frac{12}{2^k},$$

which shows that this function admits an asymptotic parabola of the type

$$y = 14 - 9k + 2k^2.$$

6.4.3 Forecast Intervals

From the expression of the forecast error (6.18) and from the hypothesis of uncorrelation (or of independence) of the ϵ_t we derive that

$$\text{var}\,(e_t(k)) = \sigma^2 \sum_{j=0}^{k-1} h_j^2.$$

If we assume that the ϵ_t are normal, the forecast error has a normal distribution

$$x_{t+k} - \hat{x}_t(k) = e_t(k) \sim \mathcal{N}\Big(0, \sigma^2 \sum_{j=0}^{k-1} h_j^2\Big).$$

Consequently, denoting $\sigma \sqrt{\sum_{j=0}^{k-1} h_j^2}$ by $s.e.(e_t(k))$, we have that for any value of α between 0 and 1

$$\Pr\big(\hat{x}_t(k) - u_{1-\frac{\alpha}{2}}\, s.e.(e_t(k)) \le x_{t+k} \le \hat{x}_t(k) + u_{1-\frac{\alpha}{2}} s.e.(e_t(k))\big) = 1 - \alpha,$$

where $u_{1-\frac{\alpha}{2}}$ is the $(1 - \frac{\alpha}{2})$-th quantile of the standard normal distribution. The interval with bounds

$$\hat{x}_t(k) \pm u_{1-\frac{\alpha}{2}}\hat{\sigma} \sqrt{\sum_{j=0}^{k-1} \hat{h}_j^2}$$

is a forecast interval of x_{t+k} at the level $1 - \alpha$, with $\hat{\sigma}$ and $\hat{h}_j$ consistent estimators of σ and h. Generally, this interval is chosen at a level $1 - \alpha = 95\%$.

6.5 Some Issues

In the previous sections, we have presented the approach introduced by Box and Jenkins to analyze a series by an ARIMA model. A number of variations can be proposed to this method in order to take into consideration exponential trends, break points, outliers, and seasonal phenomena. Below we present some of these variations. Other types of nonstationarity are studied in chapters 11, 13, and 14 in more detail.

6.5.1 Data Transformation

The goal of the operator $\Delta^d = (1 - L)^d$ applied to x_t is to make the series stationary. However, for some kinds of series this is not suitable.

Logarithmic Transformation For example, if the series x_t has an expected value which is an exponential function of t (exponential trend), no operator Δ^d will set it to 0, since $\Delta^d(e^{\alpha t}) = (e^\alpha - 1)^d e^{\alpha(t-d)}$. In such a case, we could apply a logarithmic transformation to the series x_t, before applying an operator Δ^d. By the same token, if the series is of the type $x_t = (at + b)z_t$, where z_t is stationary, with $E(z_t) = 1$, $\mathrm{var}\,(z_t) = \sigma^2$, $a > 0$, and $at + b > 0$, we have

$$E(x_t) = at + b,$$

$$\mathrm{var}\,(x_t) = \sigma^2(at + b)^2,$$

$$E(\Delta x_t) = a,$$

$$\mathrm{var}\,(\Delta x_t) = \sigma^2((at + b)^2 + (a(t - 1) + b)^2$$
$$- 2(at + b)(a(t - 1) + b)\rho(1)),$$
$$= \sigma^2 \left(a^2 + 2(1 - \rho(1))(at + b)(a(t - 1) + b)\right).$$

Note that the differenced series Δx_t has a constant expected value and an increasing (with t) variance. If we take logarithms, however, we have

$$\Delta \ln x_t = \ln \frac{at + b}{a(t - 1) + b} + \Delta \ln z_t$$

$$\approx \Delta \ln z_t.$$

If z_t is strictly stationary, $\Delta \ln x_t$ will be asymptotically stationary. The logarithmic transformation can be useful. The conditions most generally accepted for its application are either an exponentially growing trend, or a growth of the variability of Δx_t together with a constant mean. Assuming that the series $y_t = \ln x_t$ is an ARIMA process, we can apply the techniques of the previous chapters to it, thus obtaining an estimation of

$$\hat{y}_t(k) = E\left(y_{t+k} \mid y_t, y_{t-1}, \ldots\right).$$

The problem is then to get a forecast $x_t^*(k)$ of x_{t+k} from the forecast $\hat{y}_t(k)$. The first suggestion is to consider

$$x_t^*(k) = \exp\left(\hat{y}_t(k)\right).$$

It is clear however that $x_t^*(k)$ is different from the optimal forecast

$$\hat{x}_t(k) = E\left(x_{t+k} \mid x_t, x_{t-1}, \ldots\right).$$

On the basis of Jensen's Inequality we have

$$\hat{x}_t(k) = E\left(\exp(\ln x_{t+k}) \mid x_t, x_{t-1}, \ldots\right)$$
$$> \exp E\left(\ln x_{t+k} \mid x_t, x_{t-1}, \ldots\right) = x_t^*(k).$$

Assuming that y_t is normal (or x_t log-normal) we have

$$\hat{x}_t(k) = E\left(\exp(y_{t+k}) \mid y_t, y_{t-1}, \ldots\right)$$
$$= \exp\left(E(\hat{y}_t(k))\right) \exp\left(\frac{1}{2}\mathrm{var}\left(y_{t+k} \mid y_t, y_{t-1}, \ldots\right)\right),$$

since the expected value of the log-normal distribution associated with a normal distribution $\mathcal{N}(m, \sigma^2)$ is

$$e^{m+\frac{\sigma^2}{2}}.$$

Hence

$$\hat{x}_t(k) = x_t^*(k) \exp\left(\frac{1}{2}\mathrm{var}\left(y_{t+k} \mid y_t, y_{t-1}, \ldots\right)\right).$$

In order to compute the correction factor, note that

$$\mathrm{var}\left(y_{t+k} \mid y_t, y_{t-1}, \ldots\right) = \mathrm{var}\left(y_{t+k} \mid \epsilon_t, \epsilon_{t-1}, \ldots\right)$$
$$= \mathrm{var}\left(\sum_{j=0}^{k-1} h_j \epsilon_{t+k-j}\right)$$
$$= \sigma^2 \left(\sum_{j=0}^{k-1} h_j^2\right),$$

where ϵ_t is the white noise associated to y_t. Finally, the forecast function of x_{t+k} is

$$\hat{x}_t(k) = \exp\left(\hat{y}_t(k) + \frac{\sigma^2}{2}\sum_{j=0}^{k-1} h_j^2\right).$$

In practice, however, the parameters will be replaced by their estimators.

Box–Cox Transformation The logarithmic transformation is undoubtedly the most used one for economic time series. However, this transformation is an element of a more general class (called *Box–Cox transformation*) defined as

$$T_\lambda(x_t) = \frac{x_t^\lambda - 1}{\lambda}, \quad 0 \le \lambda \le 1, \tag{6.25}$$

where x_t is assumed positive. The parameter λ can be estimated at the same time as the other parameters of the model by the maximum likelihood method. The apparent advantage of the Box–Cox method is that it lets the most appropriate type of transformation be chosen by the data. The identity transformation is included in this class (translated by -1) for $\lambda = 1$, and the logarithmic transformation corresponds to $\lambda = 0$. Obviously, there is a noticeable increase in the computing time (cf. Ansley, Spivey, and Wrobleski, 1977a and 1977b, for a better suited algorithm from this point of view).

6.5.2 Seasonal Models

We know that, for example some monthly series have a marked seasonal profile, that is the data relative to the same month for different years tend to be related in the same way to the yearly average. This would suggest we introduce some sort of a shift at intervals which are multiples of 12. Theoretically, we could just choose p and q large enough as to include these lags. However, it is clear that this would involve increasing the number of parameters, making it practically impossible to estimate them. In order to avoid inflating the number of parameters, Box and Jenkins suggest a particular type of models, called seasonal ARIMA. These are models of the multiplicative type

$$\Delta^d \phi_p(L)\Delta_s^D \phi_P(L^s)x_t = \Theta_q(L)\Theta_Q(L^s)\epsilon_t, \tag{6.26}$$

where s is the period of the seasonal component ($s = 12$ in the previous example, $s = 4$ for quarterly series, ...); $\Delta = 1 - L$; $\Delta_s = 1 - L^s$, ϕ_p, ϕ_P, Θ_q, Θ_Q are polynomials of degree p, P, q, Q the roots of which are greater than 1 in modulus, and ϵ_t is a white noise. A process x_t satisfying this relationship is called SARIMA$_s((p,d,q), (P,D,Q))$. The intuition behind this model is that, starting from x_t, we can obtain s series (one for each month in the example) by applying the same transformation

$$\frac{\Delta_s^D \phi_P(L^s)}{\Theta_Q(L^s)}.$$

We can then assume that the resulting series

$$\alpha_t = \frac{\Delta_s^D \phi_P(L^s)}{\Theta_Q(L^s)} x_t, \qquad (6.27)$$

does not have a seasonal component, and can be expressed as an ARIMA (p, d, q) with small values of (p, d, q)

$$\Delta^d \phi_p(L)\alpha_t = \Theta_q(L)\epsilon_t. \qquad (6.28)$$

Combining (6.27) and (6.28), we get (6.26). The seasonal series can be recognized by examining the estimated autocorrelation and partial auto-correlation functions. In fact, both take large values in correspondence to indices which are multiples of s. The identification of the parameters P, D, Q of the seasonal factors can be done by methods similar to those previously described, and keeping the values of h multiples of s in $\hat{\rho}(h)$ and $\hat{r}(h)$ (cf. Hamilton and Watts, 1978, for a detailed study of $\hat{r}(h)$). The phases of estimation and validation can be carried out by the same procedures as the nonseasonal models.

6.5.3 Intervention Analysis

Box and Tiao (1975) proposed models to take into account breaks in the mean or in the trend. Their idea is to present these breaks as a consequence of exogenous shocks on the series. These shocks may have a permanent or a transitory effect. The model studied in detail is

$$y_t = \sum_{i=1}^m \frac{\omega_i(L)}{\delta_i(L)} x_{it} + \eta_t,$$

where ω_i, δ_i, $(i = 1, \ldots, m)$ are polynomials, η_t is an ARIMA process. The variable x_{it} can assume one of three characterizations:

(i)

$$x_{it} = J_{T_i}(t) = \begin{cases} 0, & \text{if } t < T_i, \\ 1, & \text{if } t \geq T_i, \end{cases}$$

so that x_{it} is a *jump variable*, used to describe the influence of a phenomenon starting at T_i, for example, a change in regulation.

(ii)

$$x_{it} = I_{T_i}(t) = \begin{cases} 0, & \text{if } t \neq T_i, \\ 1, & \text{if } t = T_i, \end{cases}$$

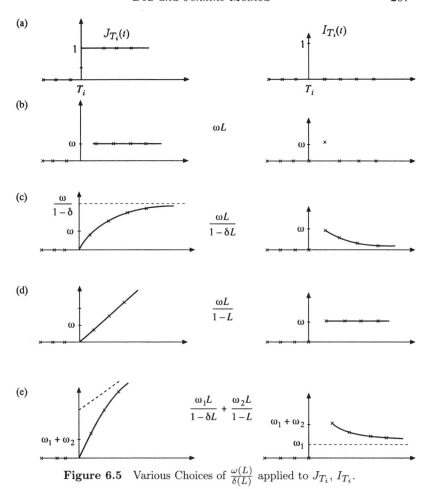

Figure 6.5 Various Choices of $\frac{\omega(L)}{\delta(L)}$ applied to J_{T_i}, I_{T_i}.

so that x_{it} is an *impulse variable*, used to describe the influence on y_t of a phenomenon which happened just in T_i, for example, a strike.

(iii)

$$x_{it} = S_{T_i}(t) = \begin{cases} 0, & \text{if } t < T_{1i} \text{ or } t > T_{2i}, \\ 1, & \text{if } T_{1i} \le t \le T_{2i}, \end{cases}$$

so that x_{it} is a *step variable*, used to describe the influence on y_t of a transitory phenomenon happening between T_{i1} and T_{i2}, for example, a temporary change in regulation.

When the form of the polynomials ω_i and δ_i is chosen, that is when their degree is chosen, and possibly the number of unit roots in δ_i is

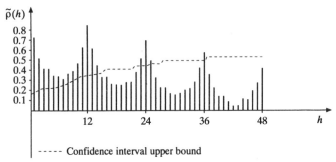

Figure 6.6   Correlogram of x_t

detected, we can estimate the various parameters by least squares or maximum likelihood methods.

Transforming the elementary functions J_{T_i} and I_{T_i} by rational fractions $\frac{\omega(L)}{\delta(L)}$ we get a sizeable set of functions within which we can choose according to the situation. Figures 6.5a to 6.5e show various examples of the possible functions.

6.6 Application to the Passenger Traffic Series

In this section, we will apply the Box–Jenkins forecast method to the monthly series of passenger traffic (number of passengers/kilometer) corresponding to second-class travel on the French main railroad network for the period 1963–79 (cf. 1.2.2).

6.6.1 Model Identification

An inspection of figure 2.5 shows an approximately linear trend and, with all likelihood, we will need to difference the original series. As noted before, the series presents a seasonal component of period 12 which can be taken into consideration by using lag polynomials in L^{12}. Finally, we note that there is no noticeable evolution of the variability, nor a need for a Box–Cox transformation. The estimated autocorrelation function $\hat{\rho}(h)$ in figure 6.6 is clearly positive for the first values of h (at least for $h \leq 12$). There is room for first differencing the series as the visual inspection of the original series suggested. The corresponding values of $\hat{\rho}(h)$ are reported in table 6.3.

The correlogram of the differenced series $(1 - L)x_t$ appears in figure 6.7, showing strong autocorrelations for values of h multiples of 12. The corresponding values of $\hat{\rho}(h)$ are reported in table 6.4. This implies that we need to apply the operator $(1 - L^{12})$ to the series $(1 - L)x_t$ at least once.

Table 6.3 *Estimated Autocorrelation of x_t*

h	$\hat{\rho}(h)$	h	$\hat{\rho}(h)$	h	$\hat{\rho}(h)$	h	$\hat{\rho}(h)$
1	0.726	13	0.615	25	0.493	37	0.375
2	0.523	14	0.431	26	0.323	38	0.222
3	0.421	15	0.341	27	0.241	39	0.153
4	0.421	16	0.339	28	0.242	40	0.157
5	0.353	17	0.272	29	0.187	41	0.106
6	0.335	18	0.249	30	0.171	42	0.084
7	0.338	19	0.256	31	0.172	43	0.084
8	0.400	20	0.319	32	0.228	44	0.140
9	0.400	21	0.320	33	0.226	45	0.140
10	0.481	22	0.392	34	0.301	46	0.206
11	0.645	23	0.535	35	0.432	47	0.317
12	0.854	24	0.724	36	0.595	48	0.459

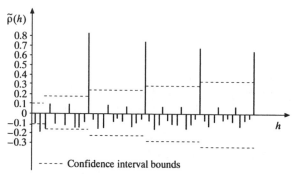

----- Confidence interval bounds

Figure 6.7 Correlogram of $(1-L)x_t$.

The correlogram of the series $(1-L)(1-L^{12})x_t$ does not present systematically large autocorrelations for small values of h or for h multiples of 12 (cf. figure 6.8 and table 6.5). Therefore, we can assume that the series $(1-L)(1-L^{12})x_t$ is generated by a stationary process.

Note that figure 6.8 shows large values of $\hat{\rho}(1)$ and of $\hat{\rho}(12)$. This suggests we introduce into the moving average polynomial a term of the type $(1-\theta_1 L)(1-\theta_2 L^{12})$. The choice of a moving average representation is confirmed by the shape of the estimated partial autocorrelation function of $(1-L)(1-L^{12})x_t$ (figure 6.9 and table 6.6). An autoregressive

Table 6.4 *Estimated Autocorrelation of* $(1 - L)x_t$

h	$\hat{\rho}(h)$	h	$\hat{\rho}(h)$	h	$\hat{\rho}(h)$	h	$\hat{\rho}(h)$
1	-0.124	13	-0.085	25	-0.099	37	-0.115
2	-0.191	14	-0.179	26	-0.173	38	-0.160
3	-0.179	15	-0.162	27	-0.143	39	-0.136
4	0.109	16	0.117	28	0.092	40	0.098
5	-0.106	17	-0.094	29	-0.079	41	-0.070
6	-0.011	18	-0.035	30	-0.011	42	-0.019
7	-0.114	19	-0.099	31	-0.101	43	-0.094
8	0.105	20	0.094	32	0.097	44	0.093
9	-0.149	21	-0.145	33	-0.150	45	-0.132
10	-0.159	22	-0.126	34	-0.105	46	-0.088
11	-0.090	23	-0.075	35	-0.050	47	-0.045
12	0.836	24	0.775	36	0.705	48	0.649

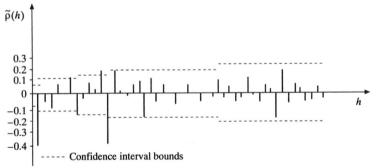

Figure 6.8   Correlogram of $(1 - L)(1 - L^{12})x_t$

representation would need a larger number of parameters, since the partial autocorrelations, especially the first five, are significantly different from 0.

A moving average, of the type

$$(1 - \theta_1 L)(1 - \theta_2 L^{12})\epsilon_t = \epsilon_t - \theta_1 \epsilon_{t-1} - \theta_2 \epsilon_{t-12} + \theta_1 \theta_2 \epsilon_{t-13},$$

admits autocorrelations $\rho(h)$ different from 0 for $h = 1, 11, 12, 13$. This is compatible with the values assumed by $\hat{\rho}(11)$ and $\hat{\rho}(13)$. Finally, the empirical mean of $(1 - L)(1 - L^{12})x_t$ is equal to -0.16 and the empirical variance is 28527. The asymptotic variance of the empirical mean of a

Table 6.5 *Estimated Autocorrelation of*
$(1 - L^{12})(1 - L)x_t$

h	$\hat{\rho}(h)$	h	$\hat{\rho}(h)$	h	$\hat{\rho}(h)$	h	$\hat{\rho}(h)$
1	-0.401	13	0.178	25	0.039	37	-0.054
2	-0.048	14	0.007	26	-0.008	38	0.046
3	-0.116	15	-0.023	27	0.049	39	0.007
4	0.056	16	0.051	28	-0.030	40	-0.194
5	0.010	17	0.069	29	-0.096	41	0.185
6	0.131	18	-0.185	30	0.133	42	-0.072
7	-0.171	19	0.134	31	-0.044	43	0.062
8	-0.012	20	-0.085	32	0.037	44	0.036
9	0.069	21	0.078	33	-0.074	45	-0.043
10	0.013	22	0.007	34	-0.043	46	-0.034
11	0.179	23	-0.107	35	0.134	47	0.037
12	-0.394	24	0.025	36	-0.017	48	-0.028

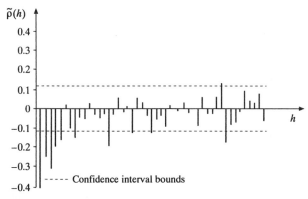

Figure 6.9 Estimated Partial Autocorrelation of $(1 - L)(1 - L^{12})x_t$

moving average $(1 - \theta_1 L)(1 - \theta_2 L^{12})\epsilon_t$ is given by (cf. chapter 9)

$$\frac{1}{T}\gamma(0)\left(1 + 2\rho(1) + 2\rho(11) + 2\rho(12) + 2\rho(13)\right),$$

where T is the number of observations of $(1 - L)(1 - L^{12})x_t$. This
variance is estimated as

$$\frac{1}{204 - 13}28527\left(1 + 2(-0.4)\right) + 2(0.18) + 2(-0.39) + 2(0.18)) = 21.$$

Table 6.6 *Estimated Partial Autocorrelation of*
$(1 - L^{12})(1 - L)x_t$

h	$\hat{r}(h)$	h	$\hat{r}(h)$	h	$\hat{r}(h)$	h	$\hat{r}(h)$
1	-0.401	13	-0.041	25	-0.057	37	-0.018
2	-0.249	14	0.022	26	-0.037	38	0.057
3	-0.306	15	-0.195	27	-0.099	39	0.134
4	0.215	16	-0.030	28	0.016	40	-0.189
5	-0.172	17	0.059	29	-0.007	41	-0.081
6	0.037	18	-0.019	30	-0.007	42	-0.074
7	-0.117	19	0.011	31	0.035	43	-0.015
8	-0.155	20	-0.131	32	-0.012	44	0.095
9	-0.049	21	0.055	33	0.005	45	0.034
10	-0.051	22	0.033	34	-0.086	46	0.017
11	0.250	23	-0.027	35	0.060	47	0.077
12	0.249	24	-0.131	36	-0.009	48	-0.041

The empirical mean is smaller (in modulus) than twice its estimated standard error, so that the process can be considered centered around a mean of 0.

6.6.2 Estimation of the Model

The retained model is a SARIMA$_{12}$ $(0, 1, 1)(0, 1, 1)$

$$(1 - L)(1 - L^{12})x_t = (1 - \theta_1 L)(1 - \theta_2 L^{12})\epsilon_t$$

with $E(\epsilon_t) = 0$ and var $(\epsilon_t) = \sigma^2$. Therefore, there are three parameters to estimate, $\theta_1, \theta_2, \sigma^2$. The estimation method is least squares with "backforecasting." The estimated values of θ_1, θ_2 are reported in table 6.7 with their estimated standard errors. The estimated variance of the white noise is 15100.

6.6.3 Validation

Tests on the Parameters The t-ratios associated with θ_1 and θ_2 are, respectively, 21 and 7. Since they are greater than 1.96 the two coefficients are significantly different from 0.

Table 6.7 *Estimated Parameters*

	θ_1	θ_2
Estimated value	0.84	0.51
Estimated st. error	0.04	0.07

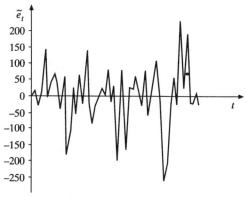

Figure 6.10 Estimated Residuals

White Noise Tests

(i) Series of Estimated Residuals A first step consists of inspecting the sequence of estimated residuals graphically to see whether they show some tendencies or regularities which would lead to the rejection of the white noise hypothesis. In figure 6.10 the series seems compatible with such a hypothesis.

(ii) Portmanteau Test The values of the statistics Q' are reported in table 6.9, corresponding to $K = 12, 24, 36$, together with the critical values of a χ^2 distribution associated with 10, 22, 34 degrees of freedom. Since the estimated statistics fall in the acceptance region, the Portmanteau Test leads to the acceptance of the white noise hypothesis.

This model passes the most common tests. However, it could be improved upon by trying to take into consideration the outliers corresponding to the residuals of period 54 and 89. These exceptional phenomena

Table 6.8 *Portmanteau Test*

K	12	24	36
$Q'(K)$	15.5	25.4	36.8
Critical values ($\alpha = 5\%$)	18	34	46

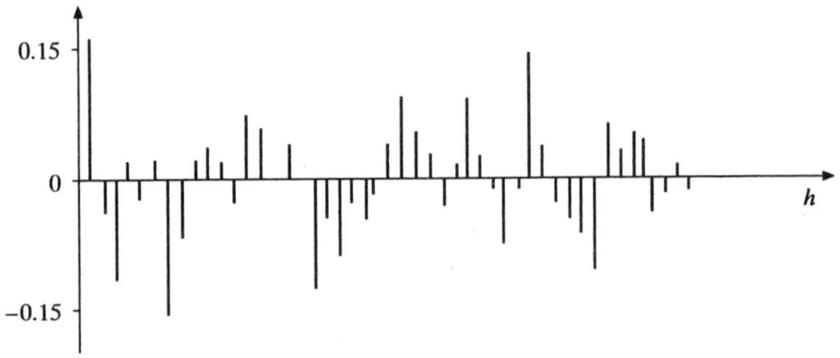

Figure 6.11   Correlogram of the Estimated Residuals

could be taken into consideration by inserting variables for structural breaks (cf. 6.5.3). Another improvement can be achieved by studying the behavior of the estimated autocorrelations of the residuals in more detail than by the Portmanteau Test. The graphical representation is given in figure 6.11 for values reported in table 6.9.

6.6.4 Forecast

The forecasted values for the twelve months of year 1980 are compared with the actual values (not included in the estimation period) in table 6.10. The mean of the relative deviations between the actual values and the forecasts, equal to 4.4%, is much smaller than the one (6.9%) obtained by a regression method. Like in the case of the Buys-Ballot's regression model, the forecast function is equal to the sum of a first-degree polynomial and of seasonal coefficients equal to 0 on average over one year. The improvement in the quality of the forecast comes from the closer adequacy of the forecast function to the characteristics of the series. Note that the pivotal values are the first thirteen forecasts.

Table 6.9 *Autocorrelation of the Residuals*

h	$\hat{\rho}(h)$	h	$\hat{\rho}(h)$	h	$\hat{\rho}(h)$	h	$\hat{\rho}(h)$
1	0.16	13	0.08	25	0.09	37	-0.03
2	-0.04	14	0.06	26	0.05	38	-0.05
3	-0.12	15	-0.00	27	0.02	39	-0.07
4	0.02	16	0.04	28	-0.03	40	-0.11
5	-0.02	17	0.00	29	0.01	41	0.06
6	0.02	18	-0.13	30	0.09	42	0.03
7	-0.16	19	-0.05	31	0.02	43	0.05
8	-0.07	20	-0.09	32	-0.01	44	0.05
9	0.02	21	-0.04	33	-0.08	45	-0.04
10	0.04	22	-0.05	34	-0.01	46	-0.02
11	0.02	23	-0.02	35	0.14	47	0.02
12	-0.02	24	0.04	36	0.03	48	-0.01

Table 6.10 *Realized Values and Forecasts*

Horizon	Realized value	Predicted value	Lower bound	Upper bound	Forecast error
1	2848	3180	2939	3420	-332
2	2913	2845	2602	3088	67
3	3248	3116	2870	3362	131
4	3250	3361	3112	3610	-111
5	3375	3382	3130	3634	-7
6	3640	3733	3478	3988	-93
7	3771	3977	3719	4235	-206
8	3259	3379	3118	3640	-120
9	3206	3041	2777	3304	165
10	3269	3159	2893	3426	109
11	3181	3092	2823	3361	89
12	4008	3666	3394	3938	342

6.7 Exercises

Exercise 6.1: Let us consider an ARIMA process of the type $(1-L)(1-L^4)x_t = \delta + \epsilon_t$, where $\{\epsilon_t\}$ is a zero mean white noise, interpretable as the innovation on x_t. Provide the expression for the forecast function as a function of five parameters. Indicate which are the pivotal values.

Exercise 6.2: Let us consider an ARMA process $\{x_t\}$ defined as

$$\Phi(L)x_t = \Theta(L)\epsilon_t,$$

where $\{\epsilon_t\}$ is a zero mean white noise with variance $\sigma^2 > 0$. Assume that Φ and Θ have roots greater than 1 in modulus. Show that, for any fixed t,

$$\lim_{k \to +\infty} \hat{x}_t(k) = 0$$

in L_2.

Exercise 6.3: Let us consider the process defined by some initial condition (without a need to specify them), and by the condition $(1 - 2L\cos\omega + L^2)x_t = \epsilon_t$, where $\{\epsilon_t\}$ is a zero mean white noise with unit variance σ^2, interpretable as the innovation of x_t. We observe the process at time $t = 1, \ldots, T$. The values for $T - 1$, respectively T, are $x_{T-1} = 0$ and $x_T = 1$.

(i)   What is the forecast function for the process?
(ii) What is the forecast error variance at the horizons $k = 1, 2, 3$?

Exercise 6.4: Let us consider the stationary process $\{x_t\}$ defined as

$$(1 - 4L)x_t = 3 + (1 - 0.5L)\epsilon_t,$$

where ϵ_t is a zero mean white noise with variance $\sigma^2 = 1$.

(i)   Express x_t as a function of the ϵ_{t-i}'s What is the covariance between x_t and ϵ_{t-i}?
(ii)   What is the one-step ahead forecast error variance?
(iii) What is the autocorrelation function of the process?

Exercise 6.5: *Optimality of the Double Exponential Smoothing* We have seen that the double exponential smoothing leads to the forecast function

$$\hat{x}_t(k) = \hat{a}_1(t) + k\hat{a}_2(t), \quad \forall \, k > 0, \tag{1}$$

and to the updating formulae

$$
\begin{aligned}
\hat{a}_1(t) &= \hat{a}_1(t-1) + \hat{a}_2(t-1) + \left(1 - \beta^2\right)\left(x_t - \hat{x}_{t-1}(1)\right), \\
\hat{a}_2(t) &= \hat{a}_2(t-1) + (1 - \beta)^2\left(x_t - \hat{x}_{t-1}(1)\right),
\end{aligned}
\tag{2}
$$

where β is the smoothing parameter. On the other hand, the forecasting theory based on an $\mathrm{ARIMA}(p, d, q)$ process shows that

$$
\hat{x}_t(k) = \sum_{i=1}^{p+d} b_i(t) f_i(k), \quad \forall\, h > q - p + d,
\tag{3}
$$

where the $f_i(k)$ are the elementary solutions of the difference equation associated with $\Phi(L)$ and the $b_i(t)$ are determined writing (3) for $k = q, q - 1, \ldots, q - p - d + 1$. Let

$$
\mathbf{F}_k =
\begin{pmatrix}
f_1(k) & \cdots & f_{p+d}(k) \\
\vdots & \ddots & \vdots \\
f_1(k+p+d-1) & \cdots & f_{p+d}(k+p+d-1)
\end{pmatrix},
$$

$$
\mathbf{b}(t) =
\begin{pmatrix}
b_1(t) \\
\vdots \\
b_{p+d}(t)
\end{pmatrix},
\quad
\tilde{\mathbf{h}}_k =
\begin{pmatrix}
h_k \\
\vdots \\
h_{k+p+d-1}
\end{pmatrix}.
$$

(i)   Show that, $\forall\, k > q - p - d$

$$
\mathbf{b}(t) = \mathbf{F}_k^{-1}\mathbf{F}_{k+1}\mathbf{b}(t-1) + \mathbf{F}_k^{-1}\tilde{\mathbf{h}}_h \epsilon_t,
\tag{4}
$$

where $\{\epsilon_t\}$ is the noise innovation of the $\mathrm{ARIMA}(p, d, q)$ process, and the h_j's have the usual meaning.

(ii) Show that in order for (3) to be written as (1) we must have $\Phi(L) = (1 - L)^2$. Show that the formulae (2) and (4) coincide if and only if $\Theta(L) = (1 - \beta L)^2$.

(iii) Verify that the double exponential smoothing is optimal for $\{x_t\}$ satisfying

$$\Delta^2 x_t = (1 - \beta L)^2 \epsilon_t.$$

Exercise 6.6: For each of the models below, write the expressions of the forecast functions at time t, $\hat{x}_t(k)$. Show the pivotal elements as well, which will allow the derivation of the parameters.

$$(1 - L)(1 - \phi L)x_t = \epsilon_t,$$

$$(1 - L)(1 - \phi L)x_t = (1 - \theta_1 L - \theta_2 L^2 - \theta_3 L^3)\epsilon_t,$$

$$(1 - L)^2(1 - \phi L)x_t = \theta^* + \epsilon_t,$$

$$(1 - L)(1 - L^4)(1 - \phi L)x_t = \theta^* + (1 - \theta_1 L)\epsilon_t.$$

Exercise 6.7: Let us consider the model

$$(1 - L)(1 - 0.5L)x_t = (1 - 0.8L)\epsilon_t,$$

where ϵ_t is a zero mean white noise with variance $\sigma^2 = 0.25$. Let us assume that

$$x_T = 12 \quad \text{and} \quad \hat{x}_T(1) = 10.$$

Provide a forecast interval for x_{T+2} at 95%.

Exercise 6.8: Show that a confidence region for the parameter vector

$$\boldsymbol{\alpha} = (\phi_1, \ldots, \phi_p, \theta_1, \ldots, \theta_q)'$$

is given by

$$\frac{T}{S(\tilde{\boldsymbol{\alpha}}_T)}\left(S(\boldsymbol{\alpha}) - S(\tilde{\boldsymbol{\alpha}}_T)\right) \leq \chi^2_{0.95}(p + q),$$

where $\tilde{\boldsymbol{\alpha}}_T$ is the least squares estimator of α. The contours of this region are described by the equation

$$S(\boldsymbol{\alpha}) = S(\tilde{\boldsymbol{\alpha}}_T)\left(1 + \frac{1}{T}\chi^2_{0.95}(p + q)\right).$$

Exercise 6.9: Denoting by $\ln L_T^*$ the concentrated log-likelihood, obtained by replacing the parameter σ^2 in $\ln L_T$ by its expression as a function of $\boldsymbol{\alpha}$, that is, $\sigma^2 = \tilde{\sigma}_T^2(\boldsymbol{\alpha})$ derived from $\partial \ln L_T / \partial \sigma^2 = 0$. We have, then

$$\ln L_T^*(\boldsymbol{\alpha}) = \ln L_T\left(\boldsymbol{\alpha}, \tilde{\sigma}^2(\boldsymbol{\alpha})\right),$$

with

$$\frac{\partial \ln L_T\left(\boldsymbol{\alpha}, \tilde{\sigma}^2(\boldsymbol{\alpha})\right)}{\partial \sigma^2} = 0.$$

Compute

$$\frac{\partial^2 \ln L_T^*}{\partial \boldsymbol{\alpha} \partial \boldsymbol{\alpha}'},$$

and show that the matrix

$$\mathbf{A} = -\plim_{T \to +\infty} \left(\frac{1}{T} \frac{\partial^2 \ln L_T}{\partial \boldsymbol{\alpha} \partial \boldsymbol{\alpha}'}\right)^{-1}_{\hat{\alpha}_T, \hat{\sigma}_T^2},$$

can also be written as

$$\mathbf{A} = -\plim_{T \to +\infty} \left(\frac{1}{T} \frac{\partial^2 \ln L_T^*}{\partial \boldsymbol{\alpha} \partial \boldsymbol{\alpha}'}\right)^{-1}_{\hat{\alpha}_T}.$$

In the above expressions, $\hat{\boldsymbol{\alpha}}_T$ and $\hat{\sigma}^2$ denote the maximum likelihood estimators of $\boldsymbol{\alpha}$ and of σ^2.

Exercise 6.10: Show that

$$\frac{\partial^2 \ln L_T^*}{\partial \sigma^2} = \frac{T}{2\sigma^4} - \frac{S(\boldsymbol{\alpha})}{\sigma^6},$$

and

$$\hat{\sigma}_T^2 = \frac{S(\hat{\boldsymbol{\alpha}}_T)}{T}.$$

Show that b in expression (6.16)

$$b = -\plim_{T \to +\infty} \left(\frac{1}{T} \frac{\partial^2 \ln L_T}{\partial (\sigma^2)^2}\right)^{-1}$$

can also be written as

$$b = 2\plim_{T \to +\infty} \left(\frac{S(\hat{\boldsymbol{\alpha}}_T)}{T}\right)^2.$$

In the above expressions $\hat{\boldsymbol{\alpha}}_T$ and $\hat{\sigma}^2$ denote the maximum likelihood estimators of $\boldsymbol{\alpha}$ and of σ_T^2.

Exercise 6.11: Let us consider an ARIMA$(0,1,q)$ process x. Compute

$$\rho(h,t) = \frac{\text{cov}(x_t, x_{t+h})}{\sqrt{\text{var}(x_t), \text{var}(x_{t+h})}}.$$

Verify that $\rho(h,t)$ tends to 1 when $t \to +\infty$.

Table 6.11 *Values for Exercise 6.12*

h	1	2	3
$\hat{\rho}(h)$	0.56	0.26	0.08
$\hat{r}(h)$	0.56	-0.08	-0.05
$\hat{\rho}i(h)$	-0.47	0.03	0.02

Exercise 6.12: The identification phase of a series x_t provides the values for the estimated autocorrelations, partial autocorrelations, and inverse autocorrelations for $w_t = \Delta x_t$ reported in table 6.11.

The empirical value of the mean of w_t is 10. Which initial values would you suggest for the following models?

ARIMA(2,1,0) with constant term.

ARIMA(1,1,1) without constant term.

ARIMA(1,1,2) with constant term.

Exercise 6.13: $\{x_t\}$ is the first-order moving average process defined as

$$x_t = \epsilon_t - 2\epsilon_{t-1},$$

where $\{\epsilon_t\}$ is a white noise with variance 1.

(i)   What is the correlogram of $\{x_t\}$?

(ii) Express ϵ_t as a function of the x_{t-i}'s.

(iii) A statistician suggests we use the simple exponential method to forecast x_{t+k}. Not knowing which smoothing parameter to choose, he chooses the middle value $\beta = 0.5$. As a result the optimal forecast $\hat{x}_t(k)$ is equal to 10. Do you agree with the procedure?

(iv) Compute the values of var$(e_t(k))$ for all integer $k > 0$.

(v)   Assume that the process x_t is unobservable, and that what we observe is, in fact, the process y_t defined as

$$y_t = x_t + \xi_t,$$

where $\{\xi_t\}$ is a white noise with variance 0.8, representing measurement errors assumed uncorrelated with $\{\epsilon_t\}$ (i.e., $E(\epsilon_t\xi_s) = 0 \ \forall \ t, s$).

Show that $\{y_t\}$ is a moving average process of order 1 and write it in explicit form. (Hint: use spectral densities.)

(vi)   Knowing that with the smoothing parameter $\beta = 0.4$, the simple exponential smoothing of $\{y_t\}$ at time t is equal to 9, give for all k the numerical values of $\hat{y}_t(k)$ and of the forecast error variances.

Exercise 6.14: *Spatial Aggregation of Two Autoregressive Processes of Order 1* Let us consider two independent stationary processes $\{x_t\}$ and $\{y_t\}$ such that

$$(1 - \rho_1 L)x_t = u_t, \quad |\rho_1| < 1,$$

$$(1 - \rho_2 L)y_t = v_t, \quad |\rho_2| < 1,$$

with

$$E(u_t) = E(v_t) = 0, \ \forall \, t,$$

$$E(u_t u_s) = \sigma_u^2 \delta_{ts}, \ \forall \, t, s,$$

$$E(v_t v_s) = \sigma_v^2 \delta_{ts}, \ \forall \, t, s.$$

Let $z_t = x_t + y_t$.

(i)   Let us suppose that the x_t and the y_t are observed up to date T, and that we want to forecast z_{T+1}. What is the forecast error variance V_D if we use the optimal forecast based on the $\{x_t, y_t\}$, $t \leq T$?

(ii)   Show that the process $\{z_t\}$ is an ARMA(2,1) corresponding to an expression

$$\Phi(L)z_t = (1 - \theta L)\epsilon_t,$$

where

$$\Phi(L) = 1 - (\rho_1 + \rho_2)L + \rho_1 \rho_2 L^2,$$

and $\{\epsilon_t\}$ is a zero mean white noise. (Hint: Recall that the sum of two uncorrelated moving averages of order 1 is a moving average of order at most equal to 1.)

(iii) What relationship do ρ_1, ρ_2, σ_u^2, σ_v^2 have to satisfy, in order for the process $\{z_t\}$ to be an AR(2). Show that, if ρ_1 and ρ_2 have the same sign, $\{z_t\}$ cannot be an AR(2).

(iv)   Show that we cannot have $\theta = \pm 1$ and that we can always assume $|\theta| < 1$.

(v)   Show that we can write

$$\epsilon_t = u_t + \frac{(\theta - \rho_2)}{1 - \theta L} u_{t-1} + v_t + \frac{(\theta - \rho_1)}{1 - \theta L} v_{t-1}.$$

Derive an expression for $V_A - V_D$, where V_A is the forecast error variance for z_{T+1} when we use the optimal forecast based on the aggregated variables $\{z_t\}$. Verify that $V_A - V_D$ is greater than or equal to 0. When is it 0?

Exercise 6.15: *Temporal Aggregation of an AR(1) on Two Periods* Let us consider a stationary process $\{x_t\}$ such that

$$(1 - \rho L)x_t = u_t \qquad |\rho| < 1,$$

where u_t is a white noise with zero mean and unit variance. Let us also define the aggregate process

$$z_T = x_{2T} + x_{2T-1}.$$

Denoting

$$\tilde{L}z_T = z_{T-1},$$

note that

$$\tilde{L}z_T = x_{2T-2} + x_{2T-3}$$

$$= L^2(x_{2T} + x_{2T-1}).$$

(i)   Let us assume that the disaggregated process $\{x_t\}$ is known until $t = 2T$ and that we want to forecast z_{T+1}. Compute the error variance V_D of the optimal forecast based on the $\{x_t\}$, $t \le 2T$.

(ii) Express

$$v_T = (1 - \rho^2 L)z_T$$

as a function of $u_{2T}, u_{2T-1}, u_{2T-2}$. Compute the autocorrelation function of the process $\{v_T\}$. Recalling the result according to which a zero autocovariance function for $h > q$ characterizes an MA(q), show that $\{z_T\}$ can be written as an ARMA(1,1) of the type

$$(1 - \rho^2 L)z_T = (1 - \theta L)\epsilon_T,$$

where ϵ_t is a zero mean white noise with variance σ_ϵ^2.

(iii) Compute θ and σ_ϵ^2 as a function of ρ so as to have ϵ_T as the innovation of z_T.

(iv) Let us denote V_A the forecast error variance for z_{T+1} when we use the optimal forecast based on the aggregated variables $\{z_s\}$, $s \le T$. Compute the relative increase in variance due to aggregation as a function of ρ

$$a(\rho) = \frac{V_A - V_D}{V_D}.$$

Verify that $a(\rho)$ is greater than or equal to 0. What values of ρ correspond to $a(\rho) = 0$? What is the behavior of the function in a neighborhood of $\rho = 0$? What is its limit as $\rho \to 1$?

7

Multivariate Time Series

The notion of stationarity and the autoregressive-moving average representations can be easily extended to the multivariate time series. This generalization is important from a practical point of view, because the multivariate framework is needed to analyze the links among different time series. In this chapter we will restrict ourselves to the case of series which may be seen as a linear transformation of a white noise. The introduction of an initial date allows one to describe stationary and nonstationary series as well. Finally, we will introduce some formulas for forecasts in matrix form, which will be at the basis of the state-space representation studied in the following chapter.

7.1 Introduction

The set of variables of interest is summarized by a vector of size n which we will denote as $\mathbf{y}$; the values taken by this vector at the different dates $t \in \mathcal{T}$ are $\mathbf{y}_t$. The set of indices for the time $\mathcal{T}$ can be the set of the positive integers, or of all integers according to whether we introduce a starting time. We will generally omit the reference to such a set unless necessary.

Each component y_{jt}, $j = 1, \ldots, n$ is a real random variable. The complete sequence $\mathbf{y} = \{\mathbf{y}_t\}$ forms an n-dimensional process.

The distribution of a process can often be summarized by the first two moments (which we will assume exist).

(i)   The mean of the process is the n-dimensional sequence defined as

$$\mathbf{m}_t = E(\mathbf{y}_t). \qquad (7.1)$$

The j-th component of this sequence is the mean of the j-th component of $\mathbf{y}$: $m_{jt} = E(y_{jt})$. When $\mathbf{m}_t = \mathbf{0}$, the process is defined as *centered*.

(ii) The moments of order 2 are defined as *autocovariances*, collected in the $(n \times n)$ matrices $\boldsymbol{\Gamma}(t,h)$ with $\gamma_{j,l}(t,h) = \mathrm{cov}\,(y_{jt}, y_{l,t-h})$ as its generic element

$$
\begin{aligned}
\boldsymbol{\Gamma}(t,h) &= \mathrm{cov}\,(\mathbf{y}_t, \mathbf{y}_{t-h}) \\
&= E\left((\mathbf{y}_t - \mathbf{m}_t)(\mathbf{y}_{t-h} - \mathbf{m}_{t-h})'\right)
\end{aligned}
\qquad (7.2)
$$

The sequence of the autocovariances has a high informative content about the process. In fact, it gives an idea about the evolution of

(i)   the variability of each variable since

$$\gamma_{j,j}(t,0) = \mathrm{cov}\,(y_{jt}, y_{jt}) = \mathrm{var}\,(y_{jt});$$

(ii) the instantaneous links among two components of the process since the correlation between y_{jt} and y_{lt} is

$$\frac{\gamma_{j,l}(t,0)}{\sqrt{\gamma_{j,j}(t,0)\gamma_{l,l}(t,0)}};$$

(iii) the temporal links between two values of the same series associated to two different dates, since the correlation between $y_{j,t}$ and $y_{j,t-h}$ is

$$\frac{\gamma_{j,j}(t,h)}{\sqrt{\gamma_{j,j}(t,0)\gamma_{j,j}(t-h,0)}}.$$

More generally, it gives a measure of the temporal link among two different components.

7.2 Stationary Processes

7.2.1 Definitions

Let us start from the processes the properties of which are invariant with respect to time.

Definition 7.1: *A process* $\mathbf{y} = \{\mathbf{y}_t\}$ *is called* stationary *if the mean* $\mathbf{m}_t$ *and the autocovariances* $\boldsymbol{\Gamma}(t,h)$ *are independent of* t.

The first two moments are characterized by

(i)   a constant $\mathbf{m}$, being the common mean of the various variables $\mathbf{y}_t$;

(ii)   an autocovariance function

$$\mathbf{\Gamma}(h) = \text{cov}\,(\mathbf{y}_t, \mathbf{y}_{t-h}).$$

This function $\mathbf{\Gamma}$ must satisfy a number of conditions ensuring that $\mathbf{\Gamma}(h)$ can be interpreted as a covariance. In fact, we must have

$$\text{cov}\,(\mathbf{y}_t, \mathbf{y}_{t-h}) = \text{cov}\,(\mathbf{y}_{t-h}, \mathbf{y}_t)' = \text{cov}\,(\mathbf{y}_t, \mathbf{y}_{t+h})',$$

that is, in terms of autocovariances

$$\mathbf{\Gamma}(h) = \mathbf{\Gamma}(-h)'. \tag{7.3}$$

On the other hand, if α_k, $k = 1, \ldots, K$ is a sequence of n-dimensional vectors we have

$$\text{var}\left(\sum_{k=1}^{K} \alpha_k' \mathbf{y}_{t+k}\right) \geq 0, \quad \forall\, K,\ \forall\, \alpha_k,\ k = 1, \ldots, K$$

which can be rewritten as

$$\sum_{k=1}^{K}\sum_{l=1}^{K} \alpha_k' \text{cov}\,(\mathbf{y}_{t+k}, \mathbf{y}_{t+l})\, \alpha_l \geq 0, \quad \forall\, K,\ \forall\, \alpha_k,\ k = 1, \ldots, K$$

or, in terms of autocovariances

$$\sum_{k=1}^{K}\sum_{l=1}^{K} (\alpha_k' \mathbf{\Gamma}(k - l)\alpha_l) \geq 0, \quad \forall\, K,\ \forall\, \alpha_k,\ k = 1, \ldots, K. \tag{7.4}$$

Example 7.1: As in the univariate case, the simplest stationary processes are white noises. A white noise is a sequence of random vectors $\{\boldsymbol{\varepsilon}_t\}$ with zero mean $E(\boldsymbol{\varepsilon}_t) = \mathbf{0}$ and with the same variance $\text{var}\,(\boldsymbol{\varepsilon}_t) = \mathbf{\Omega}$, uncorrelated between themselves, $\text{cov}\,(\boldsymbol{\varepsilon}_t, \boldsymbol{\varepsilon}_\tau) = \mathbf{0}$, if $t \neq \tau$. Its autocovariance function is given by

$$\mathbf{\Gamma}(h) = \begin{cases} \mathbf{\Omega} & \text{if } h = 0, \\ \mathbf{0}, & \text{otherwise.} \end{cases}$$

7.2.2 Moving Average Representation

The white noise plays a special role in the analysis of stationary processes. We can in fact show that, under certain regularity conditions, any stationary process $\mathbf{y} = \{\mathbf{y}_t\}$ can be expressed as a function of a white noise $\{\boldsymbol{\varepsilon}_t\}$

$$\mathbf{y}_t = \sum_{j=0}^{+\infty} \mathbf{H}_j \boldsymbol{\varepsilon}_{t-j} + \mathbf{m}, \tag{7.5}$$

where the matrices $\mathbf{H}_j$ are of order $n \times n$ and $\mathbf{H}_0 = \mathbf{I}$. This expression goes under the name of *Wold Representation*.

Let us study the properties of such a process with possibly a noise with a different size.

Definition 7.2: *The process* $\mathbf{y} = \{\mathbf{y}_t\}$ *admits an infinite moving average representation if it can be written as*

$$\mathbf{y}_t = \sum_{j=0}^{+\infty} \mathbf{H}_j \boldsymbol{\varepsilon}_{t-j} + \mathbf{m},$$

where $\boldsymbol{\varepsilon}$ *is an* $\tilde{n}$-*dimensional process with a nonsingular variance–co-variance matrix* $\boldsymbol{\Omega}$ *and the matrices* $\mathbf{H}_j$ *are of order* $n \times \tilde{n}$.

In order to simplify the various computations of the sequence of coefficients $\mathbf{H}_j$, $j = 0, 1, \ldots$ (called *Markov coefficients*), we will impose that it be absolutely summable

$$\sum_{j=0}^{+\infty} \|\mathbf{H}_j\| < +\infty, \qquad (7.6)$$

where $\|\mathbf{A}\|^2$ indicates the largest eigenvalue of $\mathbf{A}\mathbf{A}'$ (or, equivalently, of $\mathbf{A}'\mathbf{A}$).

We can derive a direct computation of the expressions of the two first moments of $\mathbf{y}$ as a function of $\mathbf{m}, \boldsymbol{\Omega}$, and of the sequence $\mathbf{H} = \{\mathbf{H}_j, \ j = 0, 1, \ldots\}$. We have

$$E(\mathbf{y}_t) = \sum_{j=0}^{+\infty} \mathbf{H}_j E(\boldsymbol{\varepsilon}_{t-j}) + \mathbf{m} = \mathbf{m},$$

since $\boldsymbol{\varepsilon}$ has a zero mean, and

$$\mathrm{cov}\,(\mathbf{y}_t, \mathbf{y}_{t-h}) = \sum_{j=0}^{+\infty} \sum_{l=0}^{+\infty} \mathbf{H}_j \mathrm{cov}\,(\boldsymbol{\varepsilon}_{t-j}, \ \boldsymbol{\varepsilon}_{t-h-l}) \mathbf{H}_l'$$

$$= \sum_{j=0}^{+\infty} \mathbf{H}_j \boldsymbol{\Omega} \mathbf{H}_{j-h}',$$

where we used the convention $\mathbf{H}_j = 0$ if $j < 0$. Since the two first moments do not depend on time t we have found stationarity of the process again. The expression for the autocovariance function

$$\boldsymbol{\Gamma}_{\mathbf{y}}(h) = \sum_{j=0}^{+\infty} \mathbf{H}_j \boldsymbol{\Omega} \mathbf{H}_{j-h}', \qquad (7.7)$$

where we used the convention $\mathbf{H}_j = 0$ if $j < 0$, can be written in a simpler form if we use the generating functions associated to the sequences $\mathbf{H}_j$ and $\boldsymbol{\Gamma}(h)$.

Definition 7.3:

(i) *We define the* autocovariance generating function *the power series*

$$\mathbf{\Gamma}^{\mathbf{y}}(z) = \sum_{h=-\infty}^{+\infty} \mathbf{\Gamma_y}(h) z^h.$$

(ii) *We define the* generating function of **H** *the power series*

$$\mathbf{H}(z) = \sum_{j=0}^{+\infty} \mathbf{H}_j z^j.$$

These series provide a suitable notation to represent a sequence in short form. We can define various operations on these series which have their counterpart in terms of sequences (cf. the appendix). These operations are defined in a way as to be compatible with the usual operations on the integer series. Thus using expression (7.7) of the autocovariances we have

$$\mathbf{\Gamma}^{\mathbf{y}}(z) = \sum_{h=-\infty}^{+\infty} \mathbf{\Gamma_y}(h) z^h$$

$$= \sum_{h=-\infty}^{+\infty} \sum_{j=0}^{+\infty} \mathbf{H}_j \mathbf{\Omega} \mathbf{H}'_{j-h} z^h$$

$$= \sum_{h=-\infty}^{+\infty} \sum_{j=0}^{+\infty} \mathbf{H}_j z^j \mathbf{\Omega} \mathbf{H}'_{j-h} z^{h-j}$$

$$= \left(\sum_{j=0}^{+\infty} \mathbf{H}_j z^j \right) \mathbf{\Omega} \left(\sum_{l=0}^{+\infty} \mathbf{H}'_l z^{-l} \right),$$

changing the indices and using the convention $\mathbf{H}_j = 0$ if $j < 0$.

Finally, the expression (7.7) can be written as

$$\mathbf{\Gamma}^{\mathbf{y}}(z) = \mathbf{H}(z) \mathbf{\Omega} \mathbf{H} \left(\frac{1}{z} \right)'. \tag{7.8}$$

For the time being, we have a dummy argument z appearing in the definition of the series. We can however replace it with some operator or with complex numbers, which gives a fairly different meaning to the corresponding series. These replacements are possible since

$$\sum_{j=0}^{+\infty} \|\mathbf{H}_j\| < +\infty.$$

This, in turn, implies the absolute summability of the sequence of autocovariances, since

$$\sum_{h=-\infty}^{+\infty} \| \, \mathbf{\Gamma_y}(h) \, \| = \sum_{h=-\infty}^{+\infty} \| \sum_{j=0}^{+\infty} \mathbf{H}_j \mathbf{\Omega} \mathbf{H}'_{j-h} \, \|$$

$$\leq \sum_{h=-\infty}^{+\infty} \sum_{j=0}^{+\infty} \| \, \mathbf{H}_j \mathbf{\Omega} \mathbf{H}'_{j-h} \, \|$$

$$\leq \sum_{h=-\infty}^{+\infty} \sum_{j=0}^{+\infty} \| \, \mathbf{H}_j \, \| \, \| \, \mathbf{\Omega} \, \| \, \| \, \mathbf{H}'_{j-h} \, \|$$

$$= \left(\sum_{j=0}^{+\infty} \| \, \mathbf{H}_j \, \| \right) \| \, \mathbf{\Omega} \, \| \left(\sum_{j=0}^{+\infty} \| \, \mathbf{H}'_j \, \| \right)$$

$$< +\infty.$$

Thus, we may replace the argument z with a complex number equal to 1 in modulus, keeping the meaning of convergence for the series.

Definition 7.4:

(i)   The spectral density function *of the process* $\mathbf{y}$ *is a mapping from* $(-\pi, \pi)$ *to the set of the* $n \times n$ *matrices with complex coefficients. It is defined as*

$$f_{\mathbf{y}}(\omega) = \frac{1}{2\pi} \mathbf{\Gamma}^{\mathbf{y}} \left(\exp(i\omega) \right)$$

$$= \frac{1}{2\pi} \mathbf{H} \left(\exp(i\omega) \right) \mathbf{\Omega} \overline{\mathbf{H} \left(\exp(i\omega)' \right)}.$$

(ii) The transfer function *of the moving average* $\mathbf{H}$ *is the mapping transforming* $\omega \in (-\pi, \pi)$ *into* $\mathbf{H} \left(\exp(i\omega) \right)$.

The spectral density function and the transfer function (divided by 2π) are the Fourier transforms of the sequences $\{\mathbf{\Gamma_y}(h)\}$ and $\{\mathbf{H}_j\}$. They contain the same information as the initial sequences. In particular, we can get the autocovariances from the spectral density function using the expression

$$\mathbf{\Gamma_y}(h) = \int_{-\pi}^{\pi} \exp(-ih\omega) f_{\mathbf{y}}(\omega) \, d\omega. \tag{7.9}$$

Symmetry condition (7.3) and positiveness condition (7.4) satisfied by the autocovariance function have their analogs in terms of spectral density. Thus, using the symmetry $\Gamma(h) = \Gamma(-h)'$, we have

$$f_{\mathbf{y}}(\omega) = \frac{1}{2\pi} \sum_{h=-\infty}^{+\infty} \exp(ih\omega)\Gamma_{\mathbf{y}}(h)$$

$$= \frac{1}{2\pi} \sum_{h=-\infty}^{+\infty} \exp(ih\omega)\Gamma_{\mathbf{y}}(-h)'$$

$$= \frac{1}{2\pi} \sum_{h=-\infty}^{+\infty} \exp(-ih\omega)\Gamma_{\mathbf{y}}(h)'$$

$$= f_{\mathbf{y}}(-\omega)'$$

$$= \overline{f_{\mathbf{y}}(\omega)'}.$$

As far as positiveness is concerned, it is easy to extend condition (7.4) to the complex case. For any value of K and any family of n-dimensional vectors $\boldsymbol{\alpha}_k$, $k = 1, \ldots, K$ with complex elements, we have

$$\sum_{k=1}^{K}\sum_{l=1}^{K} \overline{\boldsymbol{\alpha}_k}'\Gamma_{\mathbf{y}}(k-l)\boldsymbol{\alpha}_l \geq 0.$$

Choosing $\boldsymbol{\alpha}_k = \boldsymbol{\alpha}\exp(i\omega k)$ with $\boldsymbol{\alpha}$ an n-dimensional vector of complex elements and $\omega \in [-\pi, \pi]$ we have

$$\overline{\boldsymbol{\alpha}}'\left(\sum_{k=1}^{K}\sum_{l=1}^{K} \exp\left(i\omega(k-l)\right)\Gamma_{\mathbf{y}}(k-l)\right)\boldsymbol{\alpha} \geq 0,$$

$\forall\, K, \boldsymbol{\alpha}, \omega$. Letting K tend to infinity we can show that

$$\overline{\boldsymbol{\alpha}}'\left(\sum_{j=1}^{+\infty} \exp(i\omega j)\Gamma_{\mathbf{y}}(j)\right)\boldsymbol{\alpha} \geq 0$$

$$\Leftrightarrow \overline{\boldsymbol{\alpha}}' f_{\mathbf{y}}(\omega)\boldsymbol{\alpha} \geq 0,$$

$\forall\, \boldsymbol{\alpha}, \omega$.

Theorem 7.1: *The spectral density function matrix is Hermitian positive*

(i) $f_{\mathbf{y}}(\omega) = \overline{f_{\mathbf{y}}(\omega)}'$,

(ii) $\overline{\boldsymbol{\alpha}}' f_{\mathbf{y}}(\omega)\boldsymbol{\alpha} \geq 0$, *for any* $\boldsymbol{\alpha}$, n-*dimensional vector of complex elements.*

As a consequence, the diagonal terms of $f_{\mathbf{y}}$ corresponding to the spectral densities of the elements of $\mathbf{y}$ are real and positive.

Example 7.2: In the case of a white noise $\boldsymbol{\varepsilon}$ with variance–covariance matrix $\boldsymbol{\Omega}$ we have $\boldsymbol{\Gamma}(0) = \boldsymbol{\Omega}$, $\boldsymbol{\Gamma}(h) = \mathbf{0}$ if h is different from 0. The spectral density function is thus equal to

$$f_\epsilon(\omega) = \frac{1}{2\pi}\boldsymbol{\Omega},$$

independent of ω. Conversely, through (7.9) we can easily verify that any stationary process with a constant spectral density function is necessarily a white noise.

Definition 7.5: *The lag operator denoted by L is the mapping transforming a (deterministic or random, uni- or multidimensional) sequence* $\mathbf{y} = \{\mathbf{y}_t\}$ *into the sequence* $\mathbf{y}^* = \{\mathbf{y}_t^*\}$ *with* $\mathbf{y}_t^* = L\mathbf{y}_t = \mathbf{y}_{t-1}$.

This notation was already used in the univariate case and has the same properties as before. If we apply this operator repeatedly we slide the time index toward the past

$$L^n\mathbf{y}_t = \mathbf{y}_{t-n}. \tag{7.10}$$

This operator is invertible. Its inverse denoted by $F = L^{-1}$ is called the *lead or forward operator*. Its effect on the series is

$$F\mathbf{y}_t = L^{-1}\mathbf{y}_t = \mathbf{y}_{t+1}. \tag{7.11}$$

We can show that the application of the lag operator to the stationary process has a unit norm (cf. exercise 7.1). This implies that the sum

$$\mathbf{H}(L) = \sum_{j=0}^{+\infty} \mathbf{H}_j L^j$$

is meaningful since

$$\sum_{j=0}^{+\infty} \parallel \mathbf{H}_j L^j \parallel \leq \sum_{j=0}^{+\infty} \parallel \mathbf{H}_j \parallel \parallel L^j \parallel = \sum_{j=0}^{+\infty} \parallel \mathbf{H}_j \parallel < +\infty.$$

The operator $\mathbf{H}(L)$ is called a *linear filter* or *moving average transformation*. The moving average representation of the process $\mathbf{y}$ can be written in the synthetic form

$$\mathbf{y}_t = \mathbf{H}(L)\boldsymbol{\varepsilon}_t + \mathbf{m}. \tag{7.12}$$

7.2.3 Autoregressive Representation

Whenever the noise and the process have the same dimension n and when $\mathbf{H}_0 = \mathbf{I}$, the power series $\mathbf{H}(z) = \sum_{j=0}^{+\infty} \mathbf{H}_j z^j$ is such that $\mathbf{H}(0) = \mathbf{H}_0$ is invertible. It is therefore possible to derive the inverse series (cf. the appendix)

$$\mathbf{\Pi}(z) = (\mathbf{H}(z))^{-1} = \mathbf{\Pi}_0 + \mathbf{\Pi}_1 z + \ldots + \mathbf{\Pi}_j z^j + \ldots \qquad (7.13)$$

such that $\mathbf{\Pi}(z)\mathbf{H}(z) = \mathbf{I}$.

When the series $\sum_{j=0}^{+\infty} \mathbf{\Pi}_j \left(\mathbf{y}_{t-j} - \mathbf{m} \right)$ converges in quadratic mean, we can write (7.12) in its equivalent form

$$\mathbf{\Pi}(L)\left(\mathbf{y}_t - \mathbf{m}\right) = \boldsymbol{\varepsilon}_t. \qquad (7.14)$$

Definition 7.6:

(i)   *The stationary process* $\mathbf{y}$ *defined by the moving average representation (7.12) is said to be* invertible *if the series* $\sum_{j=0}^{+\infty} \mathbf{\Pi}_j \left(\mathbf{y}_{t-j} - \mathbf{m} \right)$ *converges in quadratic mean.*

(ii)   *Expression (7.14) is called* infinite autoregressive form *of the process.*

Since $\left(\mathbf{y}_t - \mathbf{m}\right)$ is a stationary process, a sufficient condition for invertibility is that the sequence of the autoregressive coefficients $\mathbf{\Pi}_j$ be absolutely summable $\sum_{j=0}^{+\infty} \parallel \mathbf{\Pi}_j \parallel < +\infty$.

In the univariate case we have seen that, when it exists, the autoregressive form is well suited to the forecast calculations. This result is carried over to the general case. Since $\mathbf{\Pi}_0 = \mathbf{I}$, expression (7.14) can also be written as

$$\mathbf{y}_t = \mathbf{m} + \left(\mathbf{I} - \mathbf{\Pi}(L)\right)\left(\mathbf{y}_t - \mathbf{m}\right) + \boldsymbol{\varepsilon}_t.$$

Let us assume that the vectors $\boldsymbol{\varepsilon}_t$ are independent and let us denote by I_{t-1} the information contained in the past values $\mathbf{y}_{t-1}, \mathbf{y}_{t-2}, \ldots$. This information will be identified with the set of these variables $\mathbf{y}_{t-1}, \mathbf{y}_{t-2}, \ldots$. Noting that ϵ_t is independent of I_{t-1}, and that $\left(\mathbf{I} - \mathbf{\Pi}(L)\right)\left(\mathbf{y}_t - \mathbf{m}\right)$ depends just on the past values of the process, we have

$$E(\mathbf{y}_t \mid I_{t-1}) = \mathbf{m} + E\left(\left(\mathbf{I} - \mathbf{\Pi}(L)\right)\left(\mathbf{y}_t - \mathbf{m}\right) \mid I_{t-1}\right) + E\left(\boldsymbol{\varepsilon}_t \mid I_{t-1}\right),$$

$$= \mathbf{m} + \left(\mathbf{I} - \mathbf{\Pi}(L)\right)\left(\mathbf{y}_t - \mathbf{m}\right) + E\left(\boldsymbol{\varepsilon}_t\right),$$

$$= \mathbf{m} + \left(\mathbf{I} - \mathbf{\Pi}(L)\right)\left(\mathbf{y}_t - \mathbf{m}\right).$$

This forecast will be denoted by $_{t-1}\hat{\mathbf{y}}_t$ which contains the index of the variable to be forecast and the date at which the forecast is made.

Theorem 7.2: *If the vectors $\boldsymbol{\varepsilon}_t$ are independent:*

(i)   *The best forecast of $\mathbf{y}_t$ on the basis of the information set I_{t-1} is*

$$_{t-1}\hat{\mathbf{y}}_t = E(\mathbf{y}_t \mid I_{t-1}) = \mathbf{m} + (\mathbf{I} - \boldsymbol{\Pi}(L))(\mathbf{y}_t - \mathbf{m});$$

(ii) *The corresponding forecast error is*

$$\mathbf{y}_t - {}_{t-1}\hat{\mathbf{y}}_t = \boldsymbol{\varepsilon}_t.$$

The white noise can be interpreted as the sequence of the forecast errors. It constitutes the *innovation process* of the process $\mathbf{y}$.

7.3 Linear Processes

7.3.1 Definitions

The stationarity hypothesis is not always suited to the study of the available series. Therefore, we need a class of simple models which can describe certain cases of nonstationarity. By analogy with the infinite moving average representation, from now on we will consider processes defined as

$$\mathbf{y}_t = \sum_{j=0}^{t} \mathbf{H}_j \boldsymbol{\varepsilon}_{t-j} + \tilde{\mathbf{h}}(t)\mathbf{z}_{-1} \quad t \geq 0, \tag{7.15}$$

where the process $\boldsymbol{\varepsilon}$ is a white noise and the matrices $\mathbf{H}_j$ are Markov coefficients. This form differs from the one of the previous section for a number of reasons

(i)   the process is characterized by an index $t \geq 0$. The analysis of the nonstationary processes requires that an initial date be fixed (by convention equal to 0).

(ii) The values of the process depend on the past, prior to the initial date. We suppose here that all information relative to this past is summarized into a random vector $\mathbf{z}_{-1}$. This initial vector $\mathbf{z}_{-1}$ is called *initial condition* and is assumed to be uncorrelated with the future values of the noise $\boldsymbol{\varepsilon}_0, \boldsymbol{\varepsilon}_1, \boldsymbol{\varepsilon}_2, \ldots$. The coefficient matrix $\tilde{\mathbf{h}}(t)$ is deterministic and depends on time.

(iii) We do not formulate any *a priori* assumptions on the absolute summability of the sequence $\mathbf{H}_j$.

(iv) The sum $\sum_{j=0}^{t} \mathbf{H}_j \boldsymbol{\varepsilon}_{t-j}$ has a finite number of terms, function of the date t. This peculiarity is fairly unimportant. In fact, if we define the process *

$$\tilde{\boldsymbol{\varepsilon}}_t = \begin{cases} \boldsymbol{\varepsilon}_t & \text{if } t \geq 0, \\ \mathbf{0} & \text{if } t < 0, \end{cases} \tag{7.16}$$

we can write the expression (7.15) as

$$\mathbf{y}_t = \mathbf{H}(L)\tilde{\boldsymbol{\varepsilon}} + \tilde{\mathbf{h}}(t)\mathbf{z}_{-1}, \tag{7.17}$$

with $\mathbf{H}(L) = \sum_{i=0}^{+\infty} \mathbf{H}_i L^i$.

The two first-order moments of a process expressed as the linear representation (7.15) can be determined as follows

(i)   The mean is given by

$$\mathbf{m}_t = E(\mathbf{y}_t) = \tilde{\mathbf{h}}(t)E(\mathbf{z}_{-1}). \tag{7.18}$$

(ii)   The autocovariances can be derived from the assumptions of uncorrelation

$$\boldsymbol{\Gamma}(t, h) = \text{cov}(\mathbf{y}_t, \mathbf{y}_{t-h})$$

$$= \text{cov}\left(\sum_{j=0}^{t} \mathbf{H}_j \boldsymbol{\varepsilon}_{t-j} \sum_{l=0}^{t-h} \mathbf{H}_l \boldsymbol{\varepsilon}_{t-h-l} \right) +$$

$$+ \text{cov}\left(\tilde{\mathbf{h}}(t)\mathbf{z}_{-1}, \ \tilde{\mathbf{h}}(t)\mathbf{z}_{-1} \right)$$

$$= \sum_{j=0}^{t} \mathbf{H}_j \boldsymbol{\Omega} \mathbf{H}'_{j-h} + \tilde{\mathbf{h}}(t)\text{var}(\mathbf{z}_{-1})\tilde{\mathbf{h}}(t - h)'.$$

This representation allows one to consider fairly different cases:

(i)   Certain multivariate stationary processes can be easily written in this form. Thus, noting $\mathbf{A}$ an $n \times n$ matrix with norm strictly less than one, we know that the process

$$\mathbf{y}_t = \sum_{j=0}^{+\infty} \mathbf{A}^j \boldsymbol{\varepsilon}_{t-j}$$

is stationary. We can also write it as

$$\mathbf{y}_t = \sum_{j=0}^{t} \mathbf{A}^j \boldsymbol{\varepsilon}_{t-j} + \sum_{j=t+1}^{+\infty} \mathbf{A}^j \boldsymbol{\varepsilon}_{t-j}$$

$$= \sum_{j=0}^{t} \mathbf{A}^j \boldsymbol{\varepsilon}_{t-j} + \mathbf{A}^{t+1}\mathbf{y}_{-1}.$$

Note that the past prior to the initial date is summarized in $\mathbf{y}_{-1}$.

---

* The process $\tilde{\boldsymbol{\varepsilon}}$ is clearly not a white noise.

(ii)   A number of processes of the form (7.17), although nonstationary, can be close to a stationary process. Thus the process defined as

$$\tilde{\mathbf{y}}_t = \sum_{j=0}^{t} \mathbf{A}^j \boldsymbol{\varepsilon}_{t-j},$$

with $t \geq 0$ and $\parallel \mathbf{A} \parallel < 1$, is such that

$$\tilde{\mathbf{y}}_t - \sum_{j=0}^{+\infty} \mathbf{A}^j \boldsymbol{\varepsilon}_{t-j} = -\mathbf{A}^{t+1} \mathbf{y}_{-1}.$$

Since $E(\parallel \mathbf{y}_{-1} \parallel)^2 < +\infty$, and since $\parallel \mathbf{A} \parallel < 1$ we see that the square mean error between $\tilde{\mathbf{y}}_t$ and $\mathbf{y}_t$ tends to 0 as t goes to infinity.

Definition 7.7: *A process* $\tilde{\mathbf{y}} = \{\tilde{\mathbf{y}}_t\}$ *is said to be* asymptotically stationary *if there exists a stationary process* $\mathbf{y} = \{\mathbf{y}_t\}$ *such that*

$$\lim_{t \to +\infty} E \parallel \mathbf{y}_t - \tilde{\mathbf{y}}_t \parallel^2 = 0.$$

A sufficient condition for the process

$$\tilde{\mathbf{y}}_t = \sum_{j=0}^{t} \mathbf{H}_j \boldsymbol{\varepsilon}_{t-j} + \tilde{\mathbf{h}}(t)\mathbf{z}_{-1}$$

to be asymptotically stationary is that

$$\lim_{t \to +\infty} \tilde{\mathbf{h}}(t) = 0 \quad \text{and} \quad \sum_{j=0}^{+\infty} \parallel \mathbf{H}_j \parallel < +\infty. \qquad (7.19)$$

In this case $\tilde{\mathbf{y}}_t$ approximates $\mathbf{y}_t = \sum_{j=0}^{+\infty} \mathbf{H}_j \boldsymbol{\varepsilon}_{t-j}$.

(iii)   Finally, expression (7.17) allows us also to describe true nonstationary processes. The simplest example is the *random walk*

$$\mathbf{y}_t = \sum_{j=0}^{t} \boldsymbol{\varepsilon}_{t-j}. \qquad (7.20)$$

In this case we have $\mathbf{m}_t = E(\mathbf{y}_t) = \mathbf{0}$, and

$$\boldsymbol{\Gamma}(t,h) = \mathrm{cov}\,(\mathbf{y}_t, \mathbf{y}_{t-h}) = \min(t+1, t+1-h)\boldsymbol{\Omega}.$$

When t tends to infinity

$$\mathrm{var}\,(\mathbf{y}_t) = \boldsymbol{\Gamma}(0,h) = (t+1)\boldsymbol{\Omega}$$

tends also to infinity, which implies a tendency toward explosive paths. Moreover, we note that the temporal correlation of a component y_j is

$$\text{corr}\,(y_{jt}, y_{j,t-h}) = \frac{\text{cov}\,(y_{jt}, y_{j,t-h})}{\sqrt{\text{var}\,(y_{jt})}\sqrt{\text{var}\,(y_{j,t-h})}}$$

$$= \frac{\min(t+1, t+1-h)\omega_{jj}}{\sqrt{(t+1, t+1-h)\omega_{jj}}}$$

$$= \frac{\min(t+1, t+1-h)}{\sqrt{(t+1)(t+1-h)}},$$

which tends to 1 as t goes to infinity.

As in the stationary case, the sequence of the Markov coefficients $\mathbf{H}_j$ is characterized by the power series

$$\mathbf{H}(z) = \sum_{j=0}^{+\infty} \mathbf{H}_j z^j.$$

In general, the sequence of these coefficients is not absolutely summable and the sum of the series with general term $\mathbf{H}_j\,(\exp(i\omega j))$ may not exist. However, when the integer series has a radius of convergence equal to 1 we can sometimes define $\mathbf{H}\,(\exp(i\omega))$ by a continuity argument for almost all $\omega \in [-\pi, \pi]$. This happens for example for the series

$$\mathbf{H}(z) = \sum_{j=0}^{+\infty} z^j = \frac{1}{1-z}.$$

In this limit case, $\mathbf{H}\,(\exp(i\omega))$ is called *pseudo-transfer function* and

$$f(\omega) = \frac{1}{2\pi}\mathbf{H}\,(\exp(i\omega))\,\mathbf{\Omega}\overline{\mathbf{H}\,(\exp(i\omega))}'$$

is called *pseudo-spectrum*. Beware of not considering the function f as the Fourier transform of the autocovariance function, because the latter is not defined in the case of a nonstationary process.

7.3.2 Forecasts

System (7.17) can be written explicitly as

$$\mathbf{y}_t = \sum_{j=0}^{+\infty} \mathbf{H}_j \tilde{\boldsymbol{\varepsilon}}_{t-j} + \tilde{\mathbf{h}}(t)\mathbf{z}_{-1}$$

for various dates, for example those after t. Keeping separate the values of the noise for the past from those for the future (relative to t) we have

$$
\begin{pmatrix} \mathbf{y}_t \\ \mathbf{y}_{t+1} \\ \mathbf{y}_{t+2} \\ \vdots \end{pmatrix} = \begin{pmatrix} \mathbf{H}_0 & \mathbf{H}_1 & \mathbf{H}_2 & \cdots \\ \mathbf{H}_1 & \mathbf{H}_2 & \mathbf{H}_3 & \cdots \\ \mathbf{H}_2 & \mathbf{H}_3 & \mathbf{H}_4 & \cdots \\ \vdots & \vdots & \vdots & \end{pmatrix} \begin{pmatrix} \tilde{\boldsymbol{\varepsilon}}_t \\ \tilde{\boldsymbol{\varepsilon}}_{t-1} \\ \tilde{\boldsymbol{\varepsilon}}_{t-2} \\ \vdots \end{pmatrix}
$$

$$
+ \begin{pmatrix} \mathbf{0} & \mathbf{0} & \mathbf{0} & \cdots \\ \mathbf{H}_0 & \mathbf{0} & \mathbf{0} & \cdots \\ \mathbf{H}_1 & \mathbf{H}_0 & \mathbf{0} & \cdots \\ \vdots & \vdots & \vdots & \end{pmatrix} \begin{pmatrix} \tilde{\boldsymbol{\varepsilon}}_{t+1} \\ \tilde{\boldsymbol{\varepsilon}}_{t+2} \\ \tilde{\boldsymbol{\varepsilon}}_{t+3} \\ \vdots \end{pmatrix} + \begin{pmatrix} \tilde{\mathbf{h}}(t) \\ \tilde{\mathbf{h}}(t+1) \\ \tilde{\mathbf{h}}(t+2) \\ \vdots \end{pmatrix} \mathbf{z}_{-1}
$$

or, with synthetic notation

$$
\mathbf{y}_t^+ = \mathcal{H}\tilde{\boldsymbol{\varepsilon}}_t^- + \bar{\mathcal{T}}\tilde{\boldsymbol{\varepsilon}}_t^+ + \tilde{\mathbf{h}}_t^+ \mathbf{z}_{-1}, \tag{7.21}
$$

where $^+$ and $^-$ mean future and past (including the present) respectively. $\mathcal{H}$ and $\bar{\mathcal{T}}$ are infinite *Hankel* and *Toeplitz* matrices, the latter scaled down by one element (cf. the appendix).

The matrices $\mathcal{H}$ and $\bar{\mathcal{T}}$ are characterizations of the sequence of Markov coefficients. The usual operations on the sequences $\{\mathbf{H}_j\}$ may be translated to operations on these matrices (cf. the appendix). The decomposition (7.21) has an interpretation in terms of forecasts, when the matrix $\mathbf{H}_0$ is nonsingular. In this case, if the variables $\boldsymbol{\varepsilon}_0, \boldsymbol{\varepsilon}_1, \ldots,$ $\boldsymbol{\varepsilon}_t, \ldots, \mathbf{z}_{-1}$ are independent, and if I_t is the information contained in $\mathbf{y}_t, \mathbf{y}_{t-1}, \ldots, \mathbf{y}_0, \mathbf{z}_{-1}$ or, equivalently, in $\boldsymbol{\varepsilon}_t, \boldsymbol{\varepsilon}_{t-1}, \ldots, \boldsymbol{\varepsilon}_0, \mathbf{z}_{-1}$ we can determine the forecasts of the variables $\mathbf{y}_{t+h}$, $h \geq 0$.

The h-step ahead forecast made at time t is $_t\mathbf{y}_{t+h} = E(\mathbf{y}_{t+h} \mid I_t)$. We have that

$$
\begin{pmatrix} _t\hat{\mathbf{y}}_t \\ _t\hat{\mathbf{y}}_{t+1} \\ _t\hat{\mathbf{y}}_{t+2} \\ \vdots \end{pmatrix} = E(\mathbf{y}_t^+ \mid I_t) = \mathcal{H}\tilde{\boldsymbol{\varepsilon}}_t^- + \tilde{\mathbf{h}}_t^+ \mathbf{z}_{-1}. \tag{7.22}
$$

The rows of the matrix $\mathcal{H}$ represent the coefficients of the noise elements in the formulas for the forecasts. The forecast errors at the different horizons are given by

$$
\mathbf{y}_t^+ - E(\mathbf{y}_t^+ \mid I_t) = \bar{\mathcal{T}}\tilde{\boldsymbol{\epsilon}}_t^+. \tag{7.23}
$$

Note that considering the time t as part of the past and not of the future is just a convention. Had we chosen the opposite convention we would have had

$$
\begin{pmatrix} \mathbf{y}_t \\ \mathbf{y}_{t+1} \\ \mathbf{y}_{t+2} \\ \vdots \end{pmatrix} = \begin{pmatrix} \mathbf{H}_1 & \mathbf{H}_2 & \mathbf{H}_3 & \cdots \\ \mathbf{H}_2 & \mathbf{H}_3 & \mathbf{H}_4 & \cdots \\ \vdots & \vdots & \vdots & \end{pmatrix} \begin{pmatrix} \tilde{\boldsymbol{\varepsilon}}_{t-1} \\ \tilde{\boldsymbol{\varepsilon}}_{t-2} \\ \vdots \end{pmatrix}
$$

$$
+ \begin{pmatrix} \mathbf{H}_0 & \mathbf{0} & \mathbf{0} & \cdots \\ \mathbf{H}_1 & \mathbf{H}_0 & \mathbf{0} & \cdots \\ \vdots & \vdots & \vdots & \end{pmatrix} \begin{pmatrix} \tilde{\boldsymbol{\varepsilon}}_t \\ \tilde{\boldsymbol{\varepsilon}}_{t+1} \\ \tilde{\boldsymbol{\varepsilon}}_{t+2} \\ \vdots \end{pmatrix} + \begin{pmatrix} \tilde{\mathbf{h}}(t) \\ \tilde{\mathbf{h}}(t+1) \\ \tilde{\mathbf{h}}(t+2) \\ \vdots \end{pmatrix} \mathbf{z}_{-1},
$$

or

$$
\mathbf{y}_t^+ = \bar{\mathcal{H}} \tilde{\boldsymbol{\varepsilon}}_{t-1}^- + \mathcal{T} \tilde{\boldsymbol{\varepsilon}}_{t-1}^+ + \tilde{\mathbf{h}}_t^+ \mathbf{z}_{-1}. \tag{7.24}
$$

This time, the Hankel matrix is the scaled down one. Although in this decomposition the Toeplitz matrix appears in its usual form, note that this expression presents the inconvenience that the scaled down Hankel matrix does not characterize the sequence anymore (cf. the appendix). However, the interpretation for the forecasts rests since

$$
E(\mathbf{y}_t^+ \mid I_{t-1}) = \bar{\mathcal{H}} \tilde{\boldsymbol{\varepsilon}}_{t-1}^- + \tilde{\mathbf{h}}_t^+ \mathbf{z}_{-1}.
$$

7.3.3 Autoregressive Form

When a model is written in the form

$$
\mathbf{y}_t = \mathbf{H}(L)\tilde{\boldsymbol{\varepsilon}} + \tilde{\mathbf{h}}(t)\mathbf{z}_{-1}, \tag{7.25}
$$

with $\mathbf{H}_0 = \mathbf{I}$, it is always possible to provide an equivalent autoregressive form. This possibility is due to the existence of initial conditions. As $\mathbf{H}_0 = \mathbf{I}$ is invertible, we can divide $\mathbf{I}$ by $\mathbf{H}(z)$ according to increasing powers (cf. the appendix). We have

$$
\mathbf{I} = \mathbf{Q}_t(z)\mathbf{H}(z) + \mathbf{R}_t(z)z^{t+1}, \tag{7.26}
$$

in the case of the right division of $\mathbf{I}$ by $\mathbf{H}(z)$ where $\mathbf{Q}_t$ has degree t. Left multiplying by $\mathbf{Q}_t(L)$ the two members of (7.25), we get

$$
\mathbf{Q}_t(L)\mathbf{y}_t = \mathbf{Q}_t(L)\mathbf{H}(L)\tilde{\boldsymbol{\varepsilon}} + \mathbf{Q}_t(L)\tilde{\mathbf{h}}(t)\mathbf{z}_{-1} \quad \forall\, t \geq 0,
$$

$$
\mathbf{Q}_t(L)\mathbf{y}_t = \tilde{\boldsymbol{\varepsilon}}_t - \mathbf{R}_t(L)\tilde{\boldsymbol{\varepsilon}}_{-1} + \mathbf{Q}_t(L)\tilde{\mathbf{h}}(t)\mathbf{z}_{-1} \quad \forall\, t \geq 0.
$$

Since $\tilde{\boldsymbol{\varepsilon}}_{-1} = \boldsymbol{\varepsilon}_{-1}$ if $t \geq 0$ and $\tilde{\boldsymbol{\varepsilon}}_{-1} = 0 \ \forall\, t < 0$, we get

$$
\mathbf{Q}_t(L)\mathbf{y}_t = \boldsymbol{\varepsilon}_t - \mathbf{Q}_t(L)\tilde{\mathbf{h}}(t)\mathbf{z}_{-1}. \tag{7.27}
$$

The current value $\mathbf{y}_t$ of the variable is expressed as a function of the innovation $\boldsymbol{\varepsilon}_t$, of the past values $\mathbf{y}_{t-1}, \mathbf{y}_{t-2}, \ldots, \mathbf{y}_0$ and of initial conditions $\mathbf{z}_{-1}$.

Using the theorem 7.5 in the appendix we can say that
$$\mathbf{Q}_t(L) = \mathbf{I} + \mathbf{\Pi}_1 L + \mathbf{\Pi}_t L^t,$$
with
$$\mathbf{\Pi}(z) = \sum_{j=0}^{+\infty} \mathbf{\Pi}_j z^j = (\mathbf{H}(z))^{-1}.$$

Let us introduce the notations
$$\tilde{\mathbf{y}}_t = \begin{cases} \mathbf{y}_t & \text{if } t \geq 0, \\ 0, & \text{otherwise}, \end{cases}$$

$$\mathbf{h}^*(t) = \begin{cases} \tilde{\mathbf{h}}_t & \text{if } t \geq 0, \\ 0, & \text{otherwise}. \end{cases}$$

We can derive an autoregressive form equivalent to (7.27)
$$\mathbf{\Pi}(L)\tilde{\mathbf{y}}_t = \boldsymbol{\varepsilon}_t + (\mathbf{\Pi}(L)\mathbf{h}^*(t))\,\mathbf{z}_{-1} \quad t \geq 0. \tag{7.28}$$

Remark 7.1: If the initial condition $\mathbf{z}_{-1} = \mathbf{0}$ or if $\tilde{\mathbf{h}}(t)$ tends to 0 as $t \to +\infty$, and moreover, if the sequences associated with the power series $\mathbf{H}(z)$ and $\mathbf{\Pi}(z) = (\mathbf{H}(z))^{-1}$ are absolutely summable, the process $\{\tilde{\mathbf{y}}_t, t \geq 0\}$ is asymptotically stationary and the relationship (7.28) "tends" toward the autoregressive relationship
$$\mathbf{\Pi}(L)\mathbf{y}_t = \boldsymbol{\varepsilon}_t.$$

The common stationary case appears as a limit case of this formulation.

7.4 Appendix
Representation of Matrix Sequences

7.4.1 Operations on the Sequences

The set of sequences defined in $\mathbb{R}^{nK}$, indexed by j positive integer, can be identified with a set of sequences of matrices of size $n \times K$ with real coefficients. Such a sequence is denoted by
$$\mathbf{A} = \{\mathbf{A}_j\} = (\mathbf{A}_0, \mathbf{A}_1, \mathbf{A}_2, \ldots).$$
We can define a number of operations on this set, the definitions of which are provided below.

Addition If $\mathbf{A} = \{\mathbf{A}_j\}$ and $\mathbf{B} = \{\mathbf{B}_j\}$ are two sequences in $\mathbb{R}^{nK}$, their sum is defined by $\mathbf{A} + \mathbf{B} = \{\mathbf{A}_j + \mathbf{B}_j\}$, obtained summing $\mathbf{A}$ and $\mathbf{B}$ element by element.

Matrix Multiplication If $\mathbf{A} = \{\mathbf{A}_j\}$ is a sequence in $\mathbb{R}^{nK}$, and $\mathbf{Q}$ is a square matrix of size n, we can introduce the sequence "left product" of $\mathbf{Q}$ by $\mathbf{A}$. This sequence is defined by $\mathbf{QA} = \{\mathbf{QA}_j\}$ and is obtained by left multiplying each element of the sequence by the same matrix $\mathbf{Q}$.

The right multiplication by a matrix is defined in an analogous, symmetric manner. When the matrix $\mathbf{Q}$ is a scalar matrix, that is, $\mathbf{Q} = \lambda\mathbf{I}$, the operation boils down to a multiplication by a scalar. The joint properties of addition and multiplication by a scalar allow to show that the set of sequences in $\mathbb{R}^{nK}$ is a vector space on $\mathbb{R}$.

Convolution Product

Definition 7.8: *Given two sequences* $\mathbf{A} = \{\mathbf{A}_j\}$ *in* $\mathbb{R}^{nK}$ *(n rows, K columns) and* $\mathbf{B} = \{\mathbf{B}_j\}$ *in* $\mathbb{R}^{KH}$ *(K rows, H columns), the convolution of the sequences* $\mathbf{A}$ *and* $\mathbf{B}$ *is the sequence* $\mathbf{C}$ *in* $\mathbb{R}^{nH}$ *the general term of which is*

$$\mathbf{C}_j = \sum_{k=0}^{j} \mathbf{A}_k\mathbf{B}_{j-k} = \sum_{k=0}^{j} \mathbf{A}_{j-k}\mathbf{B}_k$$

noted as $\mathbf{C} = \mathbf{A} * \mathbf{B}$.

The operation convolution is

(i)   Associative
$$(\mathbf{A} * \mathbf{B}) * \mathbf{C} = \mathbf{A} * (\mathbf{B} * \mathbf{C}).$$

(ii)   Distributive to the left and to the right relative to the addition
$$\mathbf{A} * (\mathbf{B} + \mathbf{C}) = \mathbf{A} * \mathbf{B} + \mathbf{A} * \mathbf{C},$$
$$(\mathbf{A} + \mathbf{B}) * \mathbf{C} = \mathbf{A} * \mathbf{C} + \mathbf{B} * \mathbf{C}.$$

(iii)   It is not commutative in general
$$\mathbf{A} * \mathbf{B} \neq \mathbf{B} * \mathbf{A}.$$

This is a consequence of the noncommutativity of matrix multiplication. Note however that in the case of real sequences $a = \{a_j\}$, $b = \{b_j\}$, the convolution product is commutative.

Theorem 7.3: *If a and b are two real sequences,*
$$a * b = b * a.$$

(iv)   The operation convolution admits a neutral element to the left (respectively to the right). This sequence is of the form
$$e = (\mathbf{I}, 0, 0, 0, \ldots)$$

where the matrix size is $n \times n$ (respectively $K \times K$). In fact we have

$$(\mathbf{e} * \mathbf{A})_j = \sum_{j=0}^{j} e_k \mathbf{A}_{j-k} = \mathbf{e}_0 \mathbf{A}_j = \mathbf{A}_j.$$

(v)   The last operation to discuss is the invertibility of a sequence given by the product $*$. Let us limit ourselves to the case of square matrices $n = K$. In this case the neutral element to the left is equal to the neutral element to the right. We try to solve the equation

$$\mathbf{A} * \mathbf{B} = \mathbf{e}$$

with respect to $\mathbf{B}$. Writing this equation element by element we get

$$\mathbf{A}_0 \mathbf{B}_0 = \mathbf{I},$$

$$\mathbf{A}_0 \mathbf{B}_1 + \mathbf{A}_1 \mathbf{B}_0 = \mathbf{0},$$

$$\mathbf{A}_0 \mathbf{B}_2 + \mathbf{A}_1 \mathbf{B}_1 + \mathbf{A}_2 \mathbf{B}_0 = \mathbf{0},$$

$$\vdots$$

A necessary condition for the invertibility of the sequence is that $\mathbf{A}_0$ be nonsingular, since $\det \mathbf{A}_0 \det \mathbf{B}_0 = 1 \neq 0$. Under this condition we can solve recursively

$$\mathbf{B}_0 = \mathbf{A}_0^{-1},$$

$$\mathbf{B}_1 = -\mathbf{A}_0^{-1}\mathbf{A}_1\mathbf{B}_0 = -\mathbf{A}_0^{-1}\mathbf{A}_1\mathbf{A}_0^{-1},$$

$$\mathbf{B}_2 = -\mathbf{A}_0^{-1}\mathbf{A}_1\mathbf{B}_1 - \mathbf{A}_0^{-1}\mathbf{A}_2\mathbf{B}_0,$$

$$= \mathbf{A}_0^{-1}\left(\mathbf{A}_1\mathbf{A}_0^{-1}\mathbf{A}_1\mathbf{A}_0^{-1} - \mathbf{A}_2\right)\mathbf{A}_0^{-1},$$

$$\vdots$$

Therefore we have

Theorem 7.4: *A sequence* $\mathbf{A}$ *of square matrices* $n \times n$ *is invertible for a convolution product, if and only if the first term of the sequence* $\mathbf{A}_0$ *is invertible.*

7.4.2 Power Series

Definitions and Operations Other types of notation are often used to describe such sequences. Here we introduce the power series associated to the sequence **A** noted as

$$\mathbf{A}(z) = \sum_{j=0}^{+\infty} \mathbf{A}_j z^j. \tag{1}$$

This is just a useful notation; in particular the argument z in this expression should not be interpreted as a real number, nor as a complex number, nor as an operator. The notation here is meaningful independently of any notion of convergence of the series. The various operations introduced above for the sequences have their counterparts in terms of series. Thus

(i) The operation addition of the sequences translates into addition of the series. We can replace the notation $(\mathbf{A}+\mathbf{B})(z)$ with $\mathbf{A}(z)+\mathbf{B}(z)$ and simply write

$$\begin{aligned}
\mathbf{A}(z) + \mathbf{B}(z) &= \sum_{j=0}^{+\infty} \mathbf{A}_j z^j + \sum_{j=0}^{+\infty} \mathbf{B}_j z^j \\
&= \sum_{j=0}^{+\infty} (\mathbf{A}_j + \mathbf{B}_j) z^j \\
&= (\mathbf{A} + \mathbf{B})(z).
\end{aligned}$$

(ii) By the same token, the operation multiplication by a matrix $\mathbf{Q}$ is directly carried over

$$(\mathbf{Q}\mathbf{A})(z) = \mathbf{Q}\mathbf{A}(z)$$

that is

$$\sum_{j=0}^{+\infty} \mathbf{Q}\mathbf{A}_j z^j = \mathbf{Q} \sum_{j=0}^{+\infty} \mathbf{A}_j z^j.$$

(iii) Finally, we need to find a counterpart notation for the analog of the convolution product. By definition we have

$$(\mathbf{A} * \mathbf{B})(z) = \sum_{j=0}^{+\infty} \sum_{k=0}^{j} (\mathbf{A}_k \mathbf{B}_{j-k}) z^j.$$

Let us assume, for a moment, that z is a complex number and that the integer series $\mathbf{A}(z)$ and $\mathbf{B}(z)$ are convergent. We could write

$$\sum_{j=0}^{+\infty} \sum_{k=0}^{j} \left(\mathbf{A}_k \mathbf{B}_{j-k}\right) z^j = \sum_{j=0}^{+\infty} \left(\sum_{k=0}^{+\infty} \mathbf{A}_k z^k \mathbf{B}_{j-k} z^{j-k}\right)$$

$$= \left(\sum_{k=0}^{+\infty} \mathbf{A}_k z^k\right) \left(\sum_{j=0}^{+\infty} \mathbf{B}_j z^j\right)$$

$$= \mathbf{A}(z)\mathbf{B}(z).$$

We will denote as "multiplication" the isomorphic operation of the convolution product.

Theorem 7.5: *The operation multiplication is defined on the set of the series as*

$$\mathbf{A}(z)\mathbf{B}(z) = (\mathbf{A} * \mathbf{B})(z).$$

From the properties of the convolution products, we derive that the product of series of size $n \times n$ admits $\mathbf{I}$ as the neutral element, and that a series $\mathbf{A}(z)$ is invertible if and only if $\mathbf{A}_0 = A(0)$ is a nonsingular matrix. In this case the inverse is noted $(\mathbf{A}(z))^{-1}$ (or $\frac{1}{A(z)}$ in the scalar case).

Use of the Properties of the Polynomials The proposed notations for the series and for the analog of the convolution product allow us to use a large number of established results for the polynomials. Let us start by giving a definition of a polynomial.

Definition 7.9: *The series $\mathbf{A}(z)$ is a polynomial of degree p if and only if $\mathbf{A}_p \neq 0$ and $\mathbf{A}_j = 0$, $\forall j \geq p+1$.*

For our purposes, we need to derive the results about the divisions.

(i) Divisors Given two polynomials $\mathbf{A}(z)$ and $\mathbf{B}(z)$ of size $n \times n$ we say that $\mathbf{B}(z)$ divides $\mathbf{A}(z)$ to the left if there exists a polynomial $\mathbf{Q}(z)$ such that

$$\mathbf{A}(z) = \mathbf{B}(z)\mathbf{Q}(z).$$

If $\mathbf{B}(z)$ is nonsingular, that is if $\mathbf{B}_0$ is a nonsingular matrix, $\mathbf{B}(z)$ divides $\mathbf{A}(z)$ when the coefficients of the sequence associated to $\mathbf{B}(z)^{-1}\mathbf{A}(z)$

become 0 after a certain rank. The right division can be defined symmetrically.

(ii) Long Division It is useful to recall the main results related to the long division of a series. We present here the case of the left division, since the same result can be shown for the right division.

Let us consider two series $\mathbf{A}(z)$ and $\mathbf{B}(z)$, assuming $\mathbf{B}(z)$ nonsingular.

Theorem 7.6:

(i) *For all integer $k \geq 0$ there exists a polynomial $\mathbf{Q}_k(z)$ of degree k and a series $\mathbf{R}_k(z)$ such that*

$$\mathbf{A}(z) = \mathbf{B}(z)\mathbf{Q}_k(z) + z^{k+1}\mathbf{R}_k(z).$$

(ii) *The pair $(\mathbf{Q}_k(z), \mathbf{R}_k(z))$ is unique.*

PROOF:

(i) The existence of such a pair can be proved by induction. For $k = 0$ we can write $\mathbf{A}(z) = \mathbf{B}(z)\mathbf{Q}_0(z) + z\mathbf{R}_0(z)$ with $\mathbf{Q}_0(z) = \mathbf{B}_0^{-1}\mathbf{A}_0$ and $z\mathbf{R}_0(z) = \mathbf{A}(z) - \mathbf{B}(z)\mathbf{B}_0^{-1}\mathbf{A}_0$. If we assume that the result holds true for $k \leq K$, given, we can write

$$\mathbf{A}(z) = \mathbf{B}(z)\mathbf{Q}_K(z) + z^{K+1}\mathbf{R}_K(z),$$

$$\mathbf{R}_K(z) = \mathbf{B}(z)\tilde{\mathbf{Q}}_0(z) + z\mathbf{R}_0(z).$$

Thus

$$\mathbf{A}(z) = \mathbf{B}(z)\left(\mathbf{Q}_K(z) + z^{K+1}\tilde{\mathbf{Q}}_0(z)\right) + z^{K+2}\tilde{\mathbf{R}}_0(z).$$

We need just to choose

$$\mathbf{Q}_{K+1}(z) = \mathbf{Q}_K(z) + z^{K+1}\tilde{\mathbf{Q}}_0(z),$$

$$\mathbf{R}_{K+1}(z) = \tilde{\mathbf{R}}_0(z).$$

(ii) Uniqueness can be proved by noting that if

$$\mathbf{A}(z) = \mathbf{B}(z)\mathbf{Q}_k(z) + z^{k+1}\mathbf{R}_k(z)$$

$$= \mathbf{B}(z)\tilde{\mathbf{Q}}_k(z) + z^{k+1}\tilde{\mathbf{R}}_k(z)$$

are two decompositions of $\mathbf{A}(z)$ we have

$$\mathbf{B}(z)\left(\mathbf{Q}_k(z) - \tilde{\mathbf{Q}}_k(z)\right) = z^{k+1}\left(\mathbf{R}_k(z) - \tilde{\mathbf{R}}_k(z)\right).$$

Equating the coefficients of the zero degree term, we get

$$\mathbf{B}_0\left(\mathbf{Q}_{0k} - \tilde{\mathbf{Q}}_{0k}\right) = \mathbf{0}$$

$$\Leftrightarrow \left(\mathbf{Q}_{0k} - \tilde{\mathbf{Q}}_{0k}\right) = \mathbf{0}$$

since $\mathbf{B}_0$ is nonsingular. Equating next the coefficients of the first degree term

$$\mathbf{B}_0 \left(\mathbf{Q}_{1k} - \tilde{\mathbf{Q}}_{1k} \right) + \mathbf{B}_1 \left(\mathbf{Q}_{0k} - \tilde{\mathbf{Q}}_{0k} \right) = 0$$

$$\Leftrightarrow \mathbf{B}_0 \left(\mathbf{Q}_{1k} - \tilde{\mathbf{Q}}_{1k} \right) = 0$$

$$\Leftrightarrow \mathbf{Q}_{1k} = \tilde{\mathbf{Q}}_{1k}.$$

This procedure can be repeated up to the k-th degree term. We conclude then that $\mathbf{Q}_k(z) = \tilde{\mathbf{Q}}_k(z)$ and that $\mathbf{R}_k(z) = \tilde{\mathbf{R}}_k(z)$. □

The quotients $\mathbf{Q}_k(z)$ of the long division are easy to obtain in practice thanks to the following proposition.

Theorem 7.7: *Let*

$$\mathbf{B}(z)^{-1}\mathbf{A}(z) = \mathbf{\Pi}(z) = \sum_{j=0}^{+\infty} \mathbf{\Pi}_j z^j;$$

the left quotient $\mathbf{Q}_k(z)$ is given by

$$\mathbf{Q}_k(z) = \sum_{j=0}^{k} \mathbf{\Pi}_j z^j.$$

PROOF: We have
$$\mathbf{A}(z) = \mathbf{B}(z)\mathbf{\Pi}(z)$$

$$= \mathbf{B}(z) \sum_{j=0}^{k} \mathbf{\Pi}_j z^j + z^{k+1}\mathbf{B}(z) \sum_{j=k+1}^{+\infty} \mathbf{\Pi}_j z^{j-k-1},$$

and the result follows from the uniqueness of the pair $\mathbf{Q}_k(z), \mathbf{R}_k(z)$. □

Note that when $\mathbf{A}(z)$ and $\mathbf{B}(z)$ are polynomials of degree p, respectively q, the remainder $\mathbf{R}_k(z)$ is also a polynomial. The degree of the remainder $\mathbf{R}_k(z)$ is at most $\max(p, q+k) - k - 1$ and is equal to $q - 1 = \mathrm{degree}(\mathbf{B}) - 1$ when k is large enough.

Use of the Properties of Matrices   We can also extend various familiar matrix operations to the matrix series.

(i)   We can define the transposed series as

$$\mathbf{A}'(z) = \sum_{j=0}^{+\infty} \mathbf{A}'_j z^j.$$

Assuming the nonsingularity of **A**, we can easily verify that

$$(\mathbf{A}(z) + \mathbf{B}(z))' = \mathbf{A}'(z) + \mathbf{B}'(z),$$

$$(\mathbf{A}(z)\mathbf{B}(z))' = \mathbf{B}'(z)\mathbf{A}'(z),$$

$$(\mathbf{A}'(z))^{-1} = (\mathbf{A}^{-1}(z))'.$$

(ii) We can even write down the expressions in terms of single elements of the series $\mathbf{A}(z)$. Let $a_{kl,j}$ be the (k,l)-th element of $\mathbf{A}_j$ and $a_{kl}(z) = \sum_{j=0}^{+\infty} a_{kl,j} z^j$ the scalar series associated to the sequence of these elements. We can write

$$\mathbf{A}(z) = \begin{pmatrix} a_{11}(z) & a_{12}(z) & \dots & a_{1K}(z) \\ \vdots & \vdots & \ddots & \vdots \\ a_{n1}(z) & a_{n2}(z) & \dots & a_{nK}(z) \end{pmatrix}.$$

The various elements can be combined together by operations of the type: addition, product, multiplication by a scalar, etc.

(iii) We can define the determinant of $\mathbf{A}(z)$ through the usual formula. For any $n \times n$ matrix series we have

$$\det \mathbf{A}(z) = \sum_{\sigma \in \mathcal{S}} (-1)^{\epsilon(\sigma)} a_{1\sigma(1)}(z) \dots a_{n\sigma(n)}(z)$$

where $\mathcal{S}$ indicates the set of permutations of $\{1, \dots, n\}$ and $\epsilon(\sigma)$ the sign of the σ permutation. A direct computation shows that

$$(\det \mathbf{A}(z))_{z=0} = \det(\mathbf{A}_0).$$

The following theorem is a consequence of this result.

Theorem 7.8: *The series $\mathbf{A}(z)$ of size $n \times n$ is invertible if and only if the scalar series $\det \mathbf{A}(z)$ is invertible.*

(iv) Theorem 7.8 allows us to express the inversion of the matrix series $\mathbf{A}(z)$ in terms of one of the series $\det \mathbf{A}(z)$. We have

$$(\mathbf{A}(z))^{-1} = \frac{1}{\det \mathbf{A}(z)} \tilde{\mathbf{A}}(z), \tag{2}$$

where $\tilde{\mathbf{A}}(z)$ is the adjoint matrix of **A**.

Extensions to the Series Indexed in $(-\infty, +\infty)$ The notation for the series can be extended to the sequences indexed in $(-\infty, +\infty)$. Given such a series $\{\mathbf{A}_j\}$ we can associate to it the series

$$\mathbf{A}(z) = \sum_{j=-\infty}^{+\infty} \mathbf{A}_j z^j$$

$$= \ldots + \mathbf{A}_{-1}\frac{1}{z} + \mathbf{A}_0 + \mathbf{A}_1 z + \mathbf{A}_2 z^2 + \ldots \ .$$

The operations sum and multiplication by a scalar can be defined as previously. The convolution product needs some clarification. The sequence $\mathbf{C} = \mathbf{A} * \mathbf{B}$ should have

$$\mathbf{C}_j = \sum_{k=-\infty}^{+\infty} \mathbf{A}_k \mathbf{B}_{j-k}$$

as the general term. Since the sequence involves an infinite number of terms, it may not exist. It is therefore necessary to impose some conditions on the sequences $\mathbf{A}$ and $\mathbf{B}$ to give a meaning to the convolution product.

Theorem 7.9: *We can define the convolution product on the set of the abolutely summable sequences.*

PROOF: This is the result of the inequalities

$$\sum_{j=-\infty}^{+\infty} \| \mathbf{C}_j \| \leq \sum_{j=-\infty}^{+\infty} \sum_{k=-\infty}^{+\infty} \| \mathbf{A}_k \mathbf{B}_{j-k} \|$$

$$\leq \sum_{j=-\infty}^{+\infty} \sum_{k=-\infty}^{+\infty} \| \mathbf{A}_k \| \, \| \mathbf{B}_{j-k} \|$$

$$= \left(\sum_{j=-\infty}^{+\infty} \| \mathbf{A}_k \| \right) \left(\sum_{j=-\infty}^{+\infty} \| \mathbf{B}_j \| \right) < +\infty.$$

$\square$

Under these conditions, we may define the product of the associated series.

One transformation is common in the computations. Let $\bar{\mathbf{A}}$ be the sequence derived from $\mathbf{A}$ as $\bar{\mathbf{A}}_j = \mathbf{A}_{-j}$ then $\bar{\mathbf{A}}(z) = \mathbf{A}\left(\frac{1}{z}\right)$. Thus, under the hypothesis of absolute summability, the sequence $\mathbf{C}$ with general term

$$\mathbf{C}_j = \sum_{k=-\infty}^{+\infty} \mathbf{A}_k \mathbf{B}_{j+k}$$

is associated to the series

$$C(z) = A\left(\frac{1}{z}\right) B(z).$$

7.4.3 Hankel and Toeplitz Matrices

Definitions In the applications, it is fairly straightforward to represent the sequences through tables with an infinite number of rows and columns (*infinite size matrices*). Two types of matrices are used. Let $A = \{A_j\}$ be a sequence of matrices. We call the corresponding *infinite size Hankel matrix* the matrix defined as

$$\mathcal{H}(A) = \begin{pmatrix} A_0 & A_1 & A_2 & \dots \\ A_1 & A_2 & A_3 & \dots \\ A_2 & A_3 & A_4 & \dots \\ \vdots & \vdots & \vdots \end{pmatrix}.$$

This "matrix" shows the peculiarity of having equal blocks on the secondary diagonals.

By the same token we define the *Toeplitz Matrix* associated to the sequence as

$$\mathcal{T}(A) = \begin{pmatrix} A_0 & 0 & 0 & \dots \\ A_1 & A_0 & 0 & \dots \\ A_2 & A_1 & A_0 & \dots \\ \vdots & \vdots & \vdots \end{pmatrix}.$$

This is a lower block-triangular matrix with identical blocks on the diagonals.

Some Operations on the Infinite Matrices The operations addition and multiplication by a constant (possibly a matrix) are immediately translated to the infinite matrices. We get formulas of the type

$$\mathcal{H}(A + B) = \mathcal{H}(A) + \mathcal{H}(B)$$

and

$$\mathcal{H}(QA) = Q\mathcal{H}(A),$$

where A and B are sequences and Q a matrix of suitable size.

In certain cases we can extend the matrix product to infinite size matrices. The idea is to preserve the usual computation formula for the elements of the product matrix summing in this case over an infinite number of terms. To do that, we need the infinite sum to be meaningful.

For instance, we can perform matrix multiplication between two Toeplitz matrices

$$
\mathcal{T}(\mathbf{A})\mathcal{T}(\mathbf{B}) =
\begin{pmatrix}
\mathbf{A}_0 & 0 & 0 & \cdots \\
\mathbf{A}_1 & \mathbf{A}_0 & 0 & \cdots \\
\mathbf{A}_2 & \mathbf{A}_1 & \mathbf{A}_0 & \cdots \\
\vdots & \vdots & \vdots &
\end{pmatrix}
\begin{pmatrix}
\mathbf{B}_0 & 0 & 0 & \cdots \\
\mathbf{B}_1 & \mathbf{B}_0 & 0 & \cdots \\
\mathbf{B}_2 & \mathbf{B}_1 & \mathbf{B}_0 & \cdots \\
\vdots & \vdots & \vdots &
\end{pmatrix}
$$

$$
=
\begin{pmatrix}
\mathbf{A}_0\mathbf{B}_0 & 0 & 0 & \cdots \\
\mathbf{A}_1\mathbf{B}_0 + \mathbf{A}_0\mathbf{B}_1 & \mathbf{A}_0\mathbf{B}_0 & 0 & \cdots \\
\mathbf{A}_2\mathbf{B}_0 + \mathbf{A}_1\mathbf{B}_1 + \mathbf{A}_0\mathbf{B}_2 & \mathbf{A}_1\mathbf{B}_0 + \mathbf{A}_0\mathbf{B}_1 & \mathbf{A}_0\mathbf{B}_0 & \cdots \\
\vdots & \vdots & \vdots &
\end{pmatrix},
$$

that is to say

$$
\mathcal{T}(\mathbf{A})\mathcal{T}(\mathbf{B}) = \mathcal{T}(\mathbf{A} * \mathbf{B}). \tag{3}
$$

The convolution product of sequences is translated into a matrix product of the associated Toeplitz representations.

7.5 Exercises

Exercise 7.1: Given a unidimensional stationary process of order 2 with zero mean $\{x_t\}$ show that

$$\| Lx_t \| = \| x_t \|,$$

where $\| x \| = \sqrt{E(x^2)}$. Derive the expression for the norm of the operator L, that is

$$\| L \| = \sup_{k_0, k_1, \alpha} \frac{\| L \left(\sum_{k=k_0}^{k_1} \alpha_k x_{t-k} \right) \|}{\| \sum_{k=k_0}^{k_1} \alpha_k x_{t-k} \|}.$$

Exercise 7.2: Let us consider the right and left divisions of $\mathbf{I}$ by $\mathbf{H}(z)$

$$\mathbf{I} = \mathbf{Q}_t(z)\mathbf{H}(z) + \mathbf{R}_t(z)z^{t+1},$$

$$\mathbf{I} = \mathbf{H}(z)\bar{\mathbf{Q}}_t(z) + \bar{\mathbf{R}}_t(z)z^{t+1}.$$

Compute the product $\mathbf{Q}_t(z)\mathbf{H}(z)\bar{\mathbf{Q}}_t(z)$ in two different ways, and deduce that $\mathbf{Q}_t(z)$ and $\bar{\mathbf{Q}}_t(z)$ are equal.

Exercise 7.3: Derive the quotient and the remainder of the long division of 1 by $(1 - z)^p$ up to the order t.

Exercise 7.4: Let $\mathbf{A}(z)$ and $\mathbf{B}(z)$ be series of size $n \times K$ and $K \times H$ respectively. Let their product $\mathbf{A}(z)\mathbf{B}(z)$ be defined as in theorem 7.5 in the appendix. Verify that we can associate a scalar series to each element of $\mathbf{A}(z)\mathbf{B}(z)$, obtained by the usual rules of matrix multiplication from the elements of $\mathbf{A}(z)$ and $\mathbf{B}(z)$.

Exercise 7.5: Let us consider the $n \times n$ polynomial $\mathbf{A}(z) = \mathbf{I} - \mathbf{A}z$. Compute $(\mathbf{A}(z))^{-1}$. Under what conditions is the sequence of matrices associated with $(\mathbf{A}(z))^{-1}$ absolutely summable?

8

Time-series Representations

8.1 ARMA Representations

8.1.1 Stationary ARMA Processes

Definition 8.1: *A stationary process* $\{\mathbf{y}_t\}$ *admitting an infinite moving average representation*

$$\mathbf{y}_t = \sum_{j=0}^{+\infty} \mathbf{H}_j \boldsymbol{\varepsilon}_{t-j},$$

with $E(\boldsymbol{\varepsilon}_t) = \mathbf{0}$ *and* $\mathrm{var}\,(\boldsymbol{\varepsilon}_t) = \boldsymbol{\Omega}$ *nonsingular, is called ARMA*(p,q), *that is, Autoregressive–Moving Average of order* p *and* q, *if it satisfies a difference equation of the type*

$$\boldsymbol{\Phi}(L)\mathbf{y}_t = \boldsymbol{\Theta}(L)\boldsymbol{\varepsilon}_t,$$

where $\boldsymbol{\Phi}(L)$ *and* $\boldsymbol{\Theta}(L)$ *are matrix polynomials of order* p *and* q, *respectively, i.e.*

$$\boldsymbol{\Phi}(L) = \boldsymbol{\Phi}_0 + \boldsymbol{\Phi}_1 L + \ldots + \boldsymbol{\Phi}_p L^p,$$

$$\boldsymbol{\Theta}(L) = \boldsymbol{\Theta}_0 + \boldsymbol{\Theta}_1 L + \ldots + \boldsymbol{\Theta}_q L^q,$$

where $\boldsymbol{\Phi}_0 = \mathbf{I}$, $\boldsymbol{\Phi}_p \neq \mathbf{0}$, $\boldsymbol{\Theta}_0 = \mathbf{I}$, $\boldsymbol{\Theta}_q \neq \mathbf{0}$.

From this definition, $\boldsymbol{\varepsilon}$ and $\mathbf{y}$ are of the same size, and $\mathbf{H}_0 = \mathbf{I}$. In the limit case $q = 0$, the process can be written as $\boldsymbol{\Phi}(L)\mathbf{y}_t = \boldsymbol{\varepsilon}_t$ and is called *autoregressive of order p* – AR(p). When $p = 0$ $\mathbf{y}_t = \boldsymbol{\Theta}(L)\boldsymbol{\varepsilon}_t$ and is called *moving average of order q* – MA(q).

Nonuniqueness of the Representation. Note immediately that, for a given ARMA process, the pairs of polynomials $(\boldsymbol{\Phi}(L), \boldsymbol{\Theta}(L))$ and the orders p, q are not unique.

(i)   Thus, if $\boldsymbol{\Phi}(L)\mathbf{y}_t = \boldsymbol{\Theta}(L)\boldsymbol{\varepsilon}_t$ and if $\mathbf{A}(L)$ is another matrix polynomial of size $(n \times n)$, by premultiplying by $\mathbf{A}(L)$, we get

$$\mathbf{A}(L)\boldsymbol{\Phi}(L)\mathbf{y}_t = \mathbf{A}(L)\boldsymbol{\Theta}(L)\boldsymbol{\varepsilon}_t \Leftrightarrow \boldsymbol{\Phi}^*(L)\mathbf{y}_t = \boldsymbol{\Theta}^*(L)\boldsymbol{\varepsilon}_t,$$

with $\boldsymbol{\Phi}^*(L) = \mathbf{A}(L)\boldsymbol{\Phi}(L)$ and $\boldsymbol{\Theta}^*(L) = \mathbf{A}(L)\boldsymbol{\Theta}(L)$.

(ii) Independently of this "common factors" problem, other cases of multiplicity of the representation can exist. Let us consider, for example, a nilpotent matrix $\boldsymbol{\Theta}_1$, and the stationary MA(1) process

$$\mathbf{y}_t = \boldsymbol{\varepsilon}_t - \boldsymbol{\Theta}_1\boldsymbol{\varepsilon}_{t-1}.$$

Multiplying the two sides of the equation by $(\mathbf{I} + \boldsymbol{\Theta}_1 L)$ we get

$$(\mathbf{I} + \boldsymbol{\Theta}_1 L)\mathbf{y}_t = (\mathbf{I} - \boldsymbol{\Theta}_1^2 L^2)\boldsymbol{\varepsilon}_t \Leftrightarrow (\mathbf{I} + \boldsymbol{\Theta}_1 L)\mathbf{y}_t = \boldsymbol{\varepsilon}_t$$

since $\boldsymbol{\Theta}_1^2 = \mathbf{0}$. The process $\mathbf{y}_t$ admits an AR(1) and an MA(1) representation at the same time.

It is clear that we would need to introduce a concept of minimal representation ARMA(p, q), that is such that the process does not admit an ARMA(p', q') representation with $p \leq p'$, $q \leq q'$, one of the two inequalities being a strict one. These problems of minimality are complex from a mathematical point of view and will not be discussed in what follows, even if they should be kept present in many of the results of this chapter.

Restrictions on the Autoregressive Polynomial For a given choice of the polynomials $\boldsymbol{\Phi}(L)$, $\boldsymbol{\Theta}(L)$, there does not necessarily exist a stationary solution to the equation

$$\boldsymbol{\Phi}(L)\mathbf{y}_t = \boldsymbol{\Theta}(L)\boldsymbol{\varepsilon}_t.$$

Thus, the processes satisfying

$$(\mathbf{I} - L)\mathbf{y}_t = \mathbf{y}_t - \mathbf{y}_{t-1} = \boldsymbol{\varepsilon}_t$$

are such that

$$\mathbf{y}_t = \sum_{\tau=0}^{t} \boldsymbol{\varepsilon}_\tau + \mathbf{y}_{-1}.$$

We have seen that $\operatorname{var}(\mathbf{y}_t) = (t+1)\boldsymbol{\Omega} + \operatorname{var}(\mathbf{y}_{-1})$. As soon as $\boldsymbol{\Omega} \neq \mathbf{0}$, this form of variance is incompatible with stationarity.

We can easily find a set of restrictions on the autoregressive polynomials ensuring that the difference equation admits a stationary solution.

Theorem 8.1: *Let us consider a matrix polynomial* $\boldsymbol{\Phi}$ *such that the roots of the polynomial* $\det(\boldsymbol{\Phi}(z))$ *(z complex), be all outside the unit circle, that is, strictly greater than 1 in modulus. Then the equation* $\boldsymbol{\Phi}(L)\mathbf{y}_t = \boldsymbol{\Theta}(L)\boldsymbol{\varepsilon}_t$ *admits a stationary solution y and such a solution is unique.*

PROOF: The condition on the roots of $\det(\boldsymbol{\Phi}(z))$ allows us to write the coefficients of the series

$$\frac{1}{\det(\boldsymbol{\Phi}(z))} = \sum_{j=0}^{+\infty} \psi_j z^j,$$

in the form

$$\psi_j = \sum_{k=0}^{K} P_k(j)\lambda_k^j,$$

where λ_k is the inverse of a root of $\det(\boldsymbol{\Phi}(z))$, and $P_k(j)$ is a polynomial in j the degree of which depends on the order of multiplicity of this root. Since $|\lambda_k| < 1$, we conclude that the series with ψ_j as a general term is absolutely summable. This allows us to give a meaning to the operator $\frac{1}{\det(\boldsymbol{\Phi}(L))} = \psi(L)$ defined on the stationary processes. The equation $\boldsymbol{\Phi}(L)\mathbf{y}_t = \boldsymbol{\Theta}(L)\boldsymbol{\varepsilon}_t$ can be written as

$$\mathbf{y}_t = \frac{\tilde{\boldsymbol{\Phi}}(L)\boldsymbol{\Theta}(L)}{\det(\boldsymbol{\Phi}(L))}\boldsymbol{\varepsilon}_t = \mathbf{H}(L)\boldsymbol{\varepsilon}_t,$$

where $\tilde{\boldsymbol{\Phi}}(L)$ is the adjoint matrix of $\boldsymbol{\Phi}(L)$.

The moving average process $\mathbf{y}_t = \mathbf{H}(L)\boldsymbol{\varepsilon}_t = \boldsymbol{\Phi}(L)^{-1}\boldsymbol{\Theta}(L)\boldsymbol{\varepsilon}_t$ is stationary, given the absolute summability; it is also the only stationary solution of the ARMA model. $\square$

The condition on the roots of the determinant of the autoregressive polynomial in theorem 8.1 is not necessary. Thus the equation

$$\mathbf{y}_t - 2\mathbf{y}_{t-1} = \boldsymbol{\varepsilon}_t - 2\boldsymbol{\varepsilon}_{t-1}$$

in which the autoregressive polynomial has a root equal to 0.5, admits the stationary solution $\mathbf{y}_t = \boldsymbol{\varepsilon}_t$.

Existence of an Autoregressive Representation

Theorem 8.2: *Let* $y = \{y_t\}$ *a stationary process satisfying the* ARMA *representation*

$$\Phi(L)\mathbf{y}_t = \Theta(L)\boldsymbol{\varepsilon}_t.$$

If the polynomial $\det(\Theta(L))$ *has all its roots strictly outside the unit circle, then* y *admits the infinite autoregressive representation*

$$\Theta(L)^{-1}\Phi(L)\mathbf{y}_t = \boldsymbol{\varepsilon}_t.$$

PROOF: The condition on the roots of $\det(\Theta(z))$ implies the invertibility of the operator $\Theta(L)$ defined on the values of a stationary process, hence the result. $\square$

In the ARMA representation of a stationary process, in practice we often impose the two conditions

$$\det(\Phi(z)) = 0 \Rightarrow |z| > 1,$$

$$\det(\Theta(z)) = 0 \Rightarrow |z| > 1.$$

This allows us to use one or the other of the three equivalent representations

$$\text{ARMA}(p,q) \quad \Phi(L)\mathbf{y}_t = \Theta(L)\boldsymbol{\varepsilon}_t$$

$$\text{MA}(\infty) \quad \mathbf{y}_t = \mathbf{H}(L)\boldsymbol{\varepsilon}_t$$

$$= \Phi(L)^{-1}\Theta(L)\boldsymbol{\varepsilon}_t$$

$$\text{AR}(\infty) \quad \Pi(L)\mathbf{y}_t = \Theta(L)^{-1}\Phi(L)\mathbf{y}_t = \boldsymbol{\varepsilon}_t.$$

In this case $\boldsymbol{\varepsilon}$ is the innovation process of $\mathbf{y}$.

Some Examples of Paths

In order to illustrate the behavior of processes satisfying an ARMA representation, we give in this section some examples of paths corresponding respectively to an MA(1) and an AR(1) process.

Example 8.1: Let us consider a bivariate process $\mathbf{y}$ defined as

$$\mathbf{y}_t = \boldsymbol{\varepsilon}_t - \begin{pmatrix} 0.2 & 0.3 \\ -0.6 & 1.1 \end{pmatrix} \boldsymbol{\varepsilon}_{t-1}$$

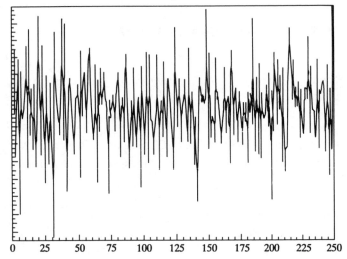

Figure 8.1 Simulated Path of y_1 from a Bivariate MA

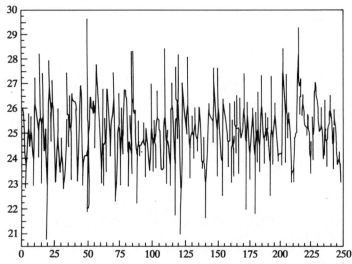

Figure 8.2 Simulated Path of y_2 from a Bivariate MA

with

$$\mathrm{var}\left(\boldsymbol{\varepsilon}_t\right) = \boldsymbol{\Omega} = \begin{pmatrix} 4 & 1 \\ 1 & 1 \end{pmatrix}.$$

The polynomial $\det(\mathbf{I} + \boldsymbol{\Theta}_1 z) = 1 - 1.3z - 0.4z^2$ has two distinct roots $\lambda_1 = \frac{1.3 + .03}{0.8}$ and $\lambda_2 = \frac{1.3 - .03}{0.8}$ both greater than 1.

Figures 8.1 and 8.2 give a simulated path of each of the components of $\mathbf{y}$.

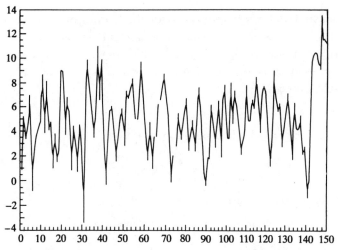

Figure 8.3   Simulated Path of y_1 from a Bivariate AR

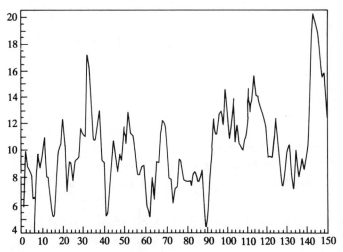

Figure 8.4   Simulated Path of y_2 from a Bivariate AR

Example 8.2: Analogously, figures 8.3 and 8.4 provide the graphical representations of the simulated paths of an AR(1) process defined as

$$\mathbf{y}_t - \begin{pmatrix} 0.2 & 0.3 \\ -0.6 & 1.1 \end{pmatrix} \mathbf{y}_{t-1} = \boldsymbol{\varepsilon}_t$$

with

$$\mathrm{var}\,(\boldsymbol{\varepsilon}_t) = \boldsymbol{\Omega} = \begin{pmatrix} 4 & 1 \\ 1 & 1 \end{pmatrix}.$$

Autocovariance and Spectral Density Functions In the case of
an ARMA process, the autocovariance function satisfies some linear difference equations, which can be determined to derive its form explicitly.
We can obtain such an equation in the following way. Let us consider
an ARMA process

$$\mathbf{\Phi}_0 \mathbf{y}_t + \mathbf{\Phi}_1 \mathbf{y}_{t-1} + \ldots + \mathbf{\Phi}_p \mathbf{y}_{t-p} = \mathbf{\Theta}_0 \boldsymbol{\varepsilon}_t + \mathbf{\Theta}_1 \boldsymbol{\varepsilon}_{t-1} + \ldots + \mathbf{\Theta}_q \boldsymbol{\varepsilon}_{t-q},$$

with $\mathbf{\Phi}_0 = \mathbf{\Theta}_0 = \mathbf{I}$. Its MA($\infty$) representation is

$$\mathbf{y}_t = \sum_{j=0}^{+\infty} \mathbf{H}_j \boldsymbol{\varepsilon}_{t-j}.$$

We can write, then, for $h \geq 0$

$$\text{cov}\ (\mathbf{\Phi}_0 \mathbf{y}_{t+h} + \mathbf{\Phi}_1 \mathbf{y}_{t+h-1} + \ldots + \mathbf{\Phi}_p \mathbf{y}_{t+h-p}, \mathbf{y}_t)$$

$$= \text{cov}\ (\mathbf{\Theta}_0 \boldsymbol{\varepsilon}_{t+h} + \mathbf{\Theta}_1 \boldsymbol{\varepsilon}_{t+h-1} + \ldots + \mathbf{\Theta}_q \boldsymbol{\varepsilon}_{t+h-q}, \mathbf{H}_0 \boldsymbol{\varepsilon}_t + \mathbf{H}_1 \boldsymbol{\varepsilon}_{t-1} + \ldots).$$

Expanding this equality we get

$$\mathbf{\Phi}_0 \mathbf{\Gamma}_h + \mathbf{\Phi}_1 \mathbf{\Gamma}_{h-1} + \ldots + \mathbf{\Phi}_p \mathbf{\Gamma}_{h-p} = \begin{cases} 0 & \text{if } h > q, \\ \sum_{j=0}^{q-h} \mathbf{\Theta}_{j+h} \mathbf{\Omega} \mathbf{H}'_j, & \text{if } h \leq q. \end{cases} \quad (8.1)$$

Theorem 8.3:

(i)   *An ARMA(p, q) process admits an autocovariance function satis-
       fying a linear homogeneous difference equation of order p starting
       from the rank $q + 1$.*

(ii) *In particular, the autocovariances of a pure MA(q) moving average
       process become zero starting from the rank $q + 1$.*

These properties of the sequence of the autocovariances characterize the
stationary processes admitting ARMA representations.

Theorem 8.4: *Let us consider a linear stationary process*

$$\mathbf{y}_t = \sum_{j=0}^{+\infty} \mathbf{H}_j \boldsymbol{\varepsilon}_{t-j},$$

*where $\mathbf{H}_0 = \mathbf{I}$ and ϵ is the innovation of the process such that the se-
quence of the autocovariances satisfies*

$$\mathbf{\Phi}_0 \mathbf{\Gamma}_h + \mathbf{\Phi}_1 \mathbf{\Gamma}_{h-1} + \ldots + \mathbf{\Phi}_p \mathbf{\Gamma}_{h-p} = \mathbf{0} \quad \forall\, h \geq q+1,$$

with $\mathbf{\Phi}_0 = \mathbf{I}$. Then $\mathbf{y}$ admits an ARMA(p, q) representation.

PROOF: The condition on the autocovariances means that

$$\text{cov}\left(\boldsymbol{\Phi}_0\mathbf{y}_{t+h} + \boldsymbol{\Phi}_1\mathbf{y}_{t+h-1} + \ldots + \boldsymbol{\Phi}_p\mathbf{y}_{t+h-p}, \mathbf{y}_t\right) = \mathbf{0} \quad \forall\, h \geq q+1,$$

$$\Leftrightarrow \quad \text{cov}\left(\boldsymbol{\Phi}_0\mathbf{y}_t + \boldsymbol{\Phi}_1\mathbf{y}_{t-1} + \ldots + \boldsymbol{\Phi}_p\mathbf{y}_{t-p}, \mathbf{y}_{t-h}\right) = \mathbf{0} \quad \forall\, h \geq q+1.$$

Therefore the vector

$$\boldsymbol{\Phi}_0\mathbf{y}_t + \boldsymbol{\Phi}_1\mathbf{y}_{t-1} + \ldots + \boldsymbol{\Phi}_p\mathbf{y}_{t-p},$$

uncorrelated with $\mathbf{y}_{t-q-1}, \mathbf{y}_{t-q-2}, \ldots$ is also uncorrelated with the innovations $\boldsymbol{\varepsilon}_{t-q-1}, \boldsymbol{\varepsilon}_{t-q-2}, \ldots$. The MA($\infty$) representation of $\boldsymbol{\Phi}_0\mathbf{y}_t + \boldsymbol{\Phi}_1\mathbf{y}_{t-1} + \ldots + \boldsymbol{\Phi}_p\mathbf{y}_{t-p}$ interpretable as the decomposition of this vector in the "orthogonal basis" $\boldsymbol{\varepsilon}_t, \boldsymbol{\varepsilon}_{t-1}, \ldots, \boldsymbol{\varepsilon}_{t-q}, \boldsymbol{\varepsilon}_{t-q-1}, \ldots$, admits zero components for the $\boldsymbol{\varepsilon}_{t-j}$, $j \geq q+1$. We have then

$$\boldsymbol{\Phi}_0\mathbf{y}_t + \boldsymbol{\Phi}_1\mathbf{y}_{t-1} + \ldots + \boldsymbol{\Phi}_p\mathbf{y}_{t-p} = \psi_0\boldsymbol{\varepsilon}_t + \psi_1\boldsymbol{\varepsilon}_{t-1} + \ldots + \psi_q\boldsymbol{\varepsilon}_{t-q},$$

that is, an ARMA(p, q) representation. $\square$

In particular, an infinite moving average process admits an MA(q) representation *if and only if* the sequence of autocovariances becomes zero starting from $q + 1$.

Example 8.3: Let us consider a stationary univariate process the autocovariance function of which satisfies

$$\gamma(h) = \sum_{j=1}^{p} a_j \lambda_j^h \quad \forall\, h \geq 0,$$

where the λ_j are real numbers smaller than 1 in modulus. We can easily see that

$$\prod_{j=1}^{p} (1 - \lambda_j L)\gamma(h) = 0 \quad \forall\, h \geq p,$$

where we have $L\gamma(h) = \gamma(h-1)$. The constraint $h \geq p$ comes from the fact that the particular form for $\gamma(h)$ is not satisfied but for positive values of h. We can conclude that the process y admits an ARMA $(p, p-1)$ representation.

The spectral density function of an ARMA process

$$\boldsymbol{\Phi}(L)\mathbf{y}_t = \boldsymbol{\Theta}(L)\boldsymbol{\varepsilon}_t,$$

with var $(\boldsymbol{\varepsilon}_t) = \boldsymbol{\Omega}$, can be obtained easily from definition 7.4

$$\mathbf{f}(\omega) = \frac{1}{2\pi}\boldsymbol{\Phi}^{-1}(\exp(i\omega))\boldsymbol{\Theta}(\exp(i\omega))\boldsymbol{\Omega}\overline{\boldsymbol{\Theta}(\exp(i\omega))}'\,\overline{\boldsymbol{\Phi}^{-1}(\exp(i\omega))}'.$$

$$(8.2)$$

This formula can be applied when $\det(\boldsymbol{\Phi}(z))$ has all its roots outside the unit circle. It has a meaning, however, so long as $\boldsymbol{\Phi}$ and $\boldsymbol{\Theta}$ have certain common roots smaller than 1 in modulus. In fact, some simplifications can be operated when we carry out the product

$$\boldsymbol{\Phi}^{-1}(\exp(i\omega))\boldsymbol{\Theta}(\exp(i\omega)).$$

The spectral density function can also be written as

$$\mathbf{f}(\omega) = \frac{1}{2\pi} \frac{\tilde{\boldsymbol{\Phi}}(\exp(i\omega))\boldsymbol{\Theta}(\exp(i\omega))\boldsymbol{\Omega}\overline{\boldsymbol{\Theta}(\exp(i\omega))}'\overline{\tilde{\boldsymbol{\Phi}}'(\exp(i\omega))}}{\mid \det \boldsymbol{\Phi}(\exp(i\omega)) \mid^2}. \qquad (8.3)$$

Written in this form $f(\omega)$ is a matrix the elements of which are rational fractions of $\exp(i\omega)$. This property is a characteristic of the ARMA process.

Theorem 8.5: *Any stationary process for which the spectral density function can be written as a matrix the elements of which are rational fractions of* $\exp(i\omega)$ *is an* ARMA *process.*

PROOF: cf. Azencott and Dacunha-Castelle (1984). □

Linear Transformation of an ARMA process

Theorem 8.6: *Let* $\mathbf{y} = \{\mathbf{y}_t\}$ *be a stationary process of size n admitting an* ARMA *representation*

$$\boldsymbol{\Phi}(L)\mathbf{y}_t = \boldsymbol{\Theta}(L)\boldsymbol{\varepsilon}_t,$$

where $\operatorname{var}(\boldsymbol{\varepsilon}_t) = \boldsymbol{\Omega}$, *and let* $\psi(L)$ *be a polynomial in L of size* $(m \times n)$. *The stationary process* $\mathbf{y}_t^* = \psi(L)\mathbf{y}_t$ *admits also an* ARMA *representation.*

PROOF: The spectral density function of y^* is

$$\mathbf{f}_{y^*}(\omega) = \boldsymbol{\psi}(\exp(i\omega))\mathbf{f}_y(\omega)\overline{\boldsymbol{\psi}(\exp(i\omega))}'$$

$$= \frac{1}{2\pi}\boldsymbol{\psi}(\exp(i\omega))\boldsymbol{\Phi}^{-1}(\exp(i\omega))\boldsymbol{\Theta}(\exp(i\omega))\boldsymbol{\Omega}$$

$$\times \overline{\boldsymbol{\Theta}(\exp(i\omega))}'\,\overline{\boldsymbol{\Phi}^{-1}(\exp(i\omega))}'\,\overline{\boldsymbol{\psi}(\exp(i\omega))}'.$$

Since its elements are rational fractions in $\exp(i\omega)$, the result is a direct consequence of theorem 8.5. □

The expressions of the polynomials $\boldsymbol{\Phi}^*$ and $\boldsymbol{\Theta}^*$ of the ARMA representation of the process y^* are often of difficult derivation. We give hereafter an example of such a derivation.

Example 8.4: Let y_1 and y_2 be two moving average processes of order 1, uncorrelated with each other. They are defined as

$$y_{1t} = \epsilon_{1t} - \theta_1 \epsilon_{1,t-1},$$

$$y_{2t} = \epsilon_{2t} - \theta_2 \epsilon_{2,t-1},$$

with var $(\epsilon_{1t}) = \sigma_1^2$ and var $(\epsilon_{2t}) = \sigma_2^2$ and the two white noises uncorrelated, cov $(\epsilon_{1t}, \epsilon_{2\tau}) = 0 \ \forall \ t, \tau$. The bidimensional process can be represented as

$$\mathbf{y}_t = \begin{pmatrix} y_{1t} \\ y_{2t} \end{pmatrix} = \boldsymbol{\epsilon}_t + \begin{pmatrix} -\theta_1 & 0 \\ 0 & -\theta_2 \end{pmatrix} \boldsymbol{\epsilon}_{t-1}$$

with

$$\text{var} \begin{pmatrix} \epsilon_{1t} \\ \epsilon_{2t} \end{pmatrix} = \begin{pmatrix} \sigma_1^2 & 0 \\ 0 & \sigma_2^2 \end{pmatrix}.$$

Let us examine now the process

$$y_t^* = \begin{pmatrix} 1 & 1 \end{pmatrix} \begin{pmatrix} y_{1t} \\ y_{2t} \end{pmatrix} = y_{1t} + y_{2t}.$$

On the basis of the theorem 8.6, we are dealing with a process admitting an ARMA representation. More precisely, noting that

$$\text{cov} \, (y_{1t}, y_{1,t+h}) = 0 \qquad \forall \, h \geq 2,$$

$$\text{cov} \, (y_{2t}, y_{2,t+h}) = 0 \qquad \forall \, h \geq 2,$$

$$\text{cov} \, (y_{1t}, y_{2\tau}) = 0 \qquad \forall \, t, \tau,$$

we have

$$\text{cov} \, (y_t^*, y_{t+h}^*) = \text{cov} \, (y_{1t} + y_{2t}, y_{1,t+h} + y_{2,t+h}) = 0 \quad \forall \, h \geq 2.$$

As a result of theorem 8.4 the process y^* admits an MA(1) representation, that is, it can be written as

$$y_t^* = \epsilon_t^* + \theta^* \epsilon_{t-1}^*$$

with var $(\epsilon_t^*) = \sigma^{*2}$. In order to find θ^* and σ^{*2} we can write the first two elements of the autocovariance function of y^*. We have

$$\gamma^*(0) = \text{var} \, (y_{1t}) + \text{var} \, (y_{2t}),$$

$$\gamma^*(1) = \text{cov} \, (y_{1t}, y_{1,t-1}) + \text{cov} \, (y_{2t}, y_{2,t-1}),$$

which implies

$$\sigma^{*2}(1 + \theta^{*2}) = \sigma_1^2(1 + \theta_1^2) + \sigma_2^2(1 + \theta_2^2),$$

$$\theta^* \sigma^{*2} = \theta_1 \sigma_1^2 + \theta_2 \sigma_2^2.$$

This system admits two pairs of solutions (θ^*, σ^{*2}). In fact if we look for the solution for θ^* we get

$$\theta^* + \frac{1}{\theta^*} = \frac{\sigma_1^2(1+\theta_1^2) + \sigma_2^2(1+\theta_2^2)}{\theta_1\sigma_1^2 + \theta_2\sigma_2^2}.$$

This second-order equation in θ^* admits two solutions, one of which is the inverse of the other. In order to obtain the representation which allows for an interpretation in terms of innovation, we will choose the value of θ^* smaller than 1 in modulus.

8.1.2 Nonstationary Processes Admitting an ARMA Representation

Definition 8.2: *More generally, we say that a process* $\mathbf{y} = \{\mathbf{y}_t\}$ *admits an* ARMA *representation if it satisfies a difference equation of the type*

$$\mathbf{\Phi}(L)\mathbf{y}_t = \mathbf{\Theta}(L)\boldsymbol{\varepsilon}_t,$$

with

$$\mathbf{\Phi}(L) = \mathbf{\Phi}_0 + \mathbf{\Phi}_1 L + \ldots + \mathbf{\Phi}_p L^p,$$

$$\mathbf{\Theta}(L) = \mathbf{\Theta}_0 + \mathbf{\Theta}_1 L + \ldots + \mathbf{\Theta}_q L^q.$$

$\mathbf{\Phi}_0 = \mathbf{I}$, $\mathbf{\Phi}_p \neq \mathbf{0}$, $\mathbf{\Theta}_0 = \mathbf{I}$, $\mathbf{\Theta}_q \neq \mathbf{0}$, *where the variables* $\mathbf{y}_{-1}, \ldots, \mathbf{y}_{-p}$, $\boldsymbol{\varepsilon}_{-1}, \ldots, \boldsymbol{\varepsilon}_{-p}$ *are assumed to be uncorrelated with* $\boldsymbol{\varepsilon}_0, \boldsymbol{\varepsilon}_1, \ldots, \boldsymbol{\varepsilon}_t, \ldots$, *and where* $\{\boldsymbol{\varepsilon}_t\}$ *is a white noise with nonsingular covariance matrix* $\mathbf{\Omega}$.

The previous relationship unambiguously defines the process $\mathbf{y}$. In fact, if we introduce the quotient of the long right-division of $\mathbf{I}$ by $\mathbf{\Phi(L)}$ we get

$$\mathbf{I} = \mathbf{Q}_t(L)\mathbf{\Phi(L)} + L^{t+1}\mathbf{R}_t(L),$$

with degree $(\mathbf{Q}_t(L)) = t$ and degree$(\mathbf{R}_t(L)) \leq p-1$. This division may be carried out since $\mathbf{\Phi}_0 = \mathbf{I}$ is invertible. Premultiplying by $\mathbf{Q}_t(L)$ the two sides of the difference equation, we get

$$\mathbf{y}_t = \mathbf{Q}_t(L)\mathbf{\Theta}(L)\boldsymbol{\varepsilon}_t + \mathbf{R}_t(L)\mathbf{y}_{-1}.$$

The result is an expression of the type

$$\mathbf{y}_t = \sum_{j=0}^{t} \mathbf{H}_j\boldsymbol{\varepsilon}_{t-j} + \sum_{j=1}^{q} \tilde{\mathbf{h}}_j(t)\boldsymbol{\varepsilon}_{-j} + \sum_{j=1}^{p} \mathbf{h}_j^*(t)\mathbf{y}_{-j},$$

with degree $(\mathbf{Q}_t(L)\mathbf{\Theta}(L)) \leq t+q$ and degree $(\mathbf{R}_t(L)) \leq p-1$. We find thus a (generally nonstationary) process admitting a linear representation, with a sequence of coefficients given by

$$\mathbf{H}(z) = (\mathbf{\Phi}(z))^{-1}\mathbf{\Theta}(z),$$

and by the initial values

$$\mathbf{z}_{-1} = \left(\boldsymbol{\varepsilon}_{-1}, \dots, \boldsymbol{\varepsilon}_{-q}, \mathbf{y}_{-1}, \dots, \mathbf{y}_{-p} \right).$$

Remark 8.1: Since the series $\mathbf{H}(z)$ has the form of a rational fraction in z, the sequence $\mathbf{H}_j$ $j \geq 0$ is completely characterized by the knowledge of this rational fraction for $z = \exp(i\omega)$, $\omega \in [-\pi, \pi] - W_d$, where W_d indicates a finite set of discontinuity points. Thus it is possible to define the pseudo-spectrum

$$\mathbf{f}(\omega) = \frac{1}{2\pi} \mathbf{H}(\exp(i\omega)) \boldsymbol{\Omega} \overline{\mathbf{H}(\exp(i\omega))}',$$

since it is also a rational fraction, and has a finite number of discontinuity points.

ARIMA Processes   Among all the nonstationary processes admitting an ARMA representation, generally special attention is given to the processes called ARIMA (i.e., Autoregressive Integrated Moving Average).

Definition 8.3: *A process* $\{y_t\}$ *admits an* ARIMA *representation if it satisfies a difference equation of the type*

$$\boldsymbol{\Phi}(L)\mathbf{y}_t = \boldsymbol{\Theta}(L)\boldsymbol{\varepsilon}_t,$$

where in addition to the conditions of definition 8.2 we impose

(i) $\det(\boldsymbol{\Theta}(z))$ has all its roots outside the unit circle;

(ii) $\det(\boldsymbol{\Phi}(z))$ has all its roots outside the unit circle but for some equal to 1.

Such processes are introduced especially for the following case. Let us consider the operator *first difference* $\Delta y_t = y_t - y_{t-1}$, and let us assume that the autoregressive polynomial can be written as $\boldsymbol{\Phi}(L) = \phi(L)\Delta^d$, where the matrix polynomial $\phi(L)$ is such that $\det(\phi(z))$ has all its roots outside the unit circle. The model becomes

$$\phi(L)\Delta^d \mathbf{y}_t = \boldsymbol{\Theta}(L)\boldsymbol{\varepsilon}_t. \tag{8.4}$$

If degree $(\phi(L)) = p$ and degree $(\boldsymbol{\Theta}(L)) = q$ we say that the model admits an ARIMA(p, d, q) representation.

The polynomial $\det(\phi(z))$ has all its roots strictly greater than 1 in modulus. Noting $\tilde{\boldsymbol{\varepsilon}}_t = \boldsymbol{\varepsilon}_t$ if $t \geq 0$ or 0 otherwise, we can then write the relationship under the form

$$\Delta^d \mathbf{y}_t = (\phi(L))^{-1}\boldsymbol{\Theta}(L)\tilde{\boldsymbol{\epsilon}}_t + \mathbf{R}_t(L)\Delta^d \mathbf{y}_{-1} + \sum_{j=1}^{q} \tilde{\mathbf{h}}_j(t)\boldsymbol{\varepsilon}_{-j},$$

where $\mathbf{R}_t(L)$ is the remainder of the long division of $\mathbf{I}$ by $\phi(L)$ up to the order t and where the $\tilde{\mathbf{h}}_j(t)$, $t = 1, \ldots, q$ are linear combinations of the coefficient of order $t, t - 1, \ldots, t - q - 1$ of the quotient of $\mathbf{I}$ by ϕ. When t tends to infinity $\mathbf{R}_t(L)\mathbf{y}_{-1}$ and $\tilde{\mathbf{h}}_j(t)$, $j = 1, \ldots, q$ tend to 0 and the process differenced d times tends to the stationary process $(\phi(L))^{-1}\mathbf{\Theta}(L)\tilde{\mathbf{\varepsilon}}_t$.

Note that all ARIMA processes do not necessarily appear in this form. Thus the autoregressive polynomial $\begin{pmatrix} 1 - L & 0 \\ 0 & 1 \end{pmatrix}$ is not divisible by $(1 - L)$ although its determinant is so. In this example the first and second components have different integration orders.

We can try to establish the *order of nonstationarity* of an ARIMA process. In order to simplify computations, let us consider a scalar ARIMA(0,d,0) process defined as

$$\Delta^d \mathbf{y}_t = \mathbf{\varepsilon}_t \qquad t \geq 0,$$

where the initial conditions $(\mathbf{y}_{-1}, \ldots, \mathbf{y}_{-d})$ are fixed. $\{\mathbf{y}_t\}$ can be written as

$$\mathbf{y}_t = \sum_{j=0}^{t} \pi_j \mathbf{\varepsilon}_{t-j} + \mathbf{m}_t,$$

where $\mathbf{m}_t$ indicates the mean of $\mathbf{y}_t$, and is a function of the initial values $\mathbf{y}_{-1}, \ldots, \mathbf{y}_{-d}$ and where $\pi(z) = (1 - z)^{-d}$.

Taking the expected value on the two sides of the difference equation we have $E(\Delta^d \mathbf{y}_t) = E(\mathbf{\varepsilon}_t) \Leftrightarrow \Delta^d \mathbf{m}_t = \mathbf{0}$.

The sequence $\{\mathbf{m}_t\}$ is solution of a difference equation admitting 1 as a root of multiplicity d. It can be written as a polynomial in t of degree smaller than or equal to $d - 1$. If now we consider the random part, we can write the coefficients π_j explicitly. Given that

$$(1 - z)^{-d} = \sum_{j=0}^{+\infty} C_{d+j-1}^j z^j = \sum_{j=0}^{+\infty} \frac{(j+1)\ldots(d+j-1)}{(d-1)!} z^j,$$

the variance of the purely random part is

$$\mathrm{var}\left(\sum_{j=0}^{t} \pi_j \mathbf{\varepsilon}_{t-j}\right) = \sigma^2 \sum_{j=0}^{t} \pi_j^2$$

$$= \sigma^2 \sum_{j=0}^{t} \left(\frac{(j+1)\ldots(d+j-1)}{(d-1)!}\right)^2.$$

This quantity is of the same order as $A \sum_{j=0}^{t} j^{2d-2}$ with $A > 0$, that is, of the same order as Bt^{2d-1}. The standard error is of the same order as $\sqrt{B}t^{d-1/2}$. Thus we see that the order d or, rather, $d - \frac{1}{2}$ can be interpreted as the degree of nonstationarity.

8.1.3 Characterization of the ARMA Representation through Markov Coefficients

Markov Coefficients Imposing that the stationary or nonstationary linear process admits an ARMA representation is equivalent to imposing some constraints on the sequence of the Markov coefficients. In order to simplify the notation, we consider the stationary case, but the results are rigorously the same in the nonstationary case. The process $\mathbf{y}_t = \mathbf{H}(L)\boldsymbol{\varepsilon}_t$ admits an ARMA representation if and only if there exist two matrix polynomials $\boldsymbol{\Phi}$ and $\boldsymbol{\Theta}$ of order $(n \times n)$ such that

$$\boldsymbol{\Phi}(L)\mathbf{y}_t = \boldsymbol{\Theta}(L)\boldsymbol{\varepsilon}_t \Leftrightarrow \boldsymbol{\Phi}(L)\mathbf{H}(L)\boldsymbol{\varepsilon}_t = \boldsymbol{\Theta}(L)\boldsymbol{\varepsilon}_t,$$

where degree $(\boldsymbol{\Phi}(L)) = p$ and degree $(\boldsymbol{\Theta}(L)) = q$. Since var $(\boldsymbol{\varepsilon}_t) = \boldsymbol{\Omega}$ is nonsingular, this condition is equivalent to

$$\boldsymbol{\Phi}(L)\mathbf{H}(L) = \boldsymbol{\Theta}(L).$$

Element by element this condition becomes

$$\sum_{j=0}^{\min(l,p)} \boldsymbol{\Phi}_j \mathbf{H}_{l-j} = \begin{cases} \boldsymbol{\Theta}_l & \text{if } l \leq q, \\ 0, & \text{otherwise.} \end{cases} \tag{8.5}$$

Theorem 8.7: *The process admits an ARMA representation if and only if the Markov coefficients sequence satisfies a homogeneous linear difference equation starting from a certain index.*

PROOF:

(i) *Necessary Condition* It is straightforward, as we have (cf. (8.5))

$$\sum_{j=0}^{p} \boldsymbol{\Phi}_j \mathbf{H}_{l-j} = 0 \qquad \forall\ l \geq \max(p, q+1).$$

(ii) *Sufficient Condition* Conversely, let us assume that the sequence $\{\mathbf{H}_j\}$ is such that

$$\sum_{j=0}^{p} \boldsymbol{\Phi}_j \mathbf{H}_{l-j} = 0 \qquad \forall\ l \geq r \geq p,$$

with $\boldsymbol{\Phi}_0 = \mathbf{I}$. The term $\sum_{j=0}^{p} \boldsymbol{\Phi}_j \mathbf{H}_{l-j}$ is the l-th coefficient of the convolution $\boldsymbol{\Phi} \cdot \mathbf{H}$ (with $\boldsymbol{\Phi} = (\boldsymbol{\Phi}_0, \boldsymbol{\Phi}_1, \ldots, \boldsymbol{\Phi}_p, \mathbf{0}\ldots)$). Thus $(\boldsymbol{\Phi} \cdot \mathbf{H})_l = 0\ \forall\ l \geq r$. This means that $\boldsymbol{\Phi}(z)\mathbf{H}(z)$ is a series not involving powers of z greater than or equal to r. $\Phi(z)\mathbf{H}(z)$ is a polynomial, and the process $\mathbf{y}_t = \mathbf{H}(L)\boldsymbol{\varepsilon}_t$ satisfies

$$\Phi(L)\mathbf{y}_t = \Phi(L)\mathbf{H}(L)\boldsymbol{\varepsilon}_t = \Theta(L)\boldsymbol{\varepsilon}_t.$$

$\square$

Example 8.5: The first-order autoregressive process

$$\mathbf{y}_t = \Phi\mathbf{y}_{t-1} + \boldsymbol{\varepsilon}_t$$

has a sequence of Markov coefficients

$$\mathbf{I}, \Phi, \Phi^2, \ldots, \Phi^j, \ldots$$

This sequence satisfies the relationship $\mathbf{H}_l - \Phi\mathbf{H}_{l-1} = 0$, for $l \geq 1$.

Characterization through the Hankel Matrix Rank The condition on the Markov coefficients can be rewritten in terms of the infinite Hankel matrix

$$\mathcal{H} = \begin{pmatrix} \mathbf{H}_0 & \mathbf{H}_1 & \mathbf{H}_2 & \ldots \\ \mathbf{H}_1 & \mathbf{H}_2 & \ldots & \ldots \\ \mathbf{H}_2 & \ldots & \ldots & \ldots \\ \vdots & & & \end{pmatrix}.$$

Note that there exist three different ways to define the rank of such an infinite matrix

(i)   the *column rank* of $\mathcal{H}$ is equal to the largest number of linearly independent (sequence) columns of $\mathcal{H}$;

(ii) the *row rank* of $\mathcal{H}$ is equal to the largest number of linearly independent (sequence) rows of $\mathcal{H}$;

(iii) the rank of $\mathcal{H}$ can also be defined as

$$\sup_{N,N'} \varrho(\mathcal{H})_{N,N'}$$

where $\varrho(\cdot)$ indicates the rank, with

$$\mathcal{H}_{N,N'} = \begin{pmatrix} \mathbf{H}_0 & \mathbf{H}_1 & \ldots & \mathbf{H}'_N \\ \mathbf{H}_1 & \mathbf{H}_2 & \ldots & \ldots \\ \vdots & \vdots & & \\ \mathbf{H}_N & \ldots & \ldots & \mathbf{H}_{N+N'} \end{pmatrix}.$$

We know that the three definitions coincide for finite size matrices. Hereafter we will see that this result carries over to the case of infinite Hankel matrices.

Theorem 8.8: *The process admits an* ARMA *representation if and only if the row rank of the Hankel matrix is finite.*

PROOF:

(i)   Note that the condition

$$\exists\ \boldsymbol{\Phi}_0 = \mathbf{I}, \boldsymbol{\Phi}_1, \ldots, \boldsymbol{\Phi}_p$$

such that

$$\sum_{j=0}^{p} \boldsymbol{\Phi}_j \mathbf{H}_{l-j} = \mathbf{0} \qquad \forall\, l \geq r \geq p$$

is equivalent to

$$(\mathbf{H}_r, \mathbf{H}_{r+1}, \ldots) = -\boldsymbol{\Phi}_1 (\mathbf{H}_{r-1}, \mathbf{H}_r, \mathbf{H}_{r+1}, \ldots) - \cdots$$
$$-\boldsymbol{\Phi}_p (\mathbf{H}_{r-p}, \mathbf{H}_{r-p+1}, \ldots).$$

This relationship means that the rows in

$$(\mathbf{H}_r, \mathbf{H}_{r+1}, \mathbf{H}_{r+2}, \ldots)$$

are linear combinations of the rows in

$$(\mathbf{H}_{r-1}, \mathbf{H}_r, \mathbf{H}_{r+1}, \ldots), \ldots, (\mathbf{H}_{r-p}, \mathbf{H}_{r-p+1}, \ldots).$$

(ii) Let us assume then that the matrix $\mathcal{H}$ has a finite rank r_0. There exists an index $r - 1$ such that the rows of

$$\begin{pmatrix} \mathbf{H}_0 & \mathbf{H}_1 & \cdots \\ \mathbf{H}_1 & \mathbf{H}_2 & \cdots \\ \vdots & \vdots & \\ \mathbf{H}_{r-1} & \mathbf{H}_r & \cdots \end{pmatrix}$$

contain a complete subsystem of rank r_0. In this case, the rows of $(\mathbf{H}_r, \mathbf{H}_{r+1}, \mathbf{H}_{r+2}, \ldots)$ are linear combinations of the preceding ones, that is, $\exists \boldsymbol{\Phi}_1, \ldots, \boldsymbol{\Phi}_r$ such that

$$(\mathbf{H}_r, \mathbf{H}_{r+1}, \mathbf{H}_{r+2}, \ldots)$$
$$= -\boldsymbol{\Phi}_1 (\mathbf{H}_{r-1}, \mathbf{H}_r, \mathbf{H}_{r+1}, \ldots) - \cdots - \boldsymbol{\Phi}_r (\mathbf{H}_0, \mathbf{H}_1, \ldots)$$

so that on the basis of (i) and of theorem 8.7, the process is ARMA.

(iii) Conversely, if the process is ARMA(p, q), from (i) we have that:

$$(\mathbf{H}_r, \mathbf{H}_{r+1}, \ldots) = -\boldsymbol{\Phi}_1 (\mathbf{H}_{r-1}, \mathbf{H}_r, \ldots) - \cdots - \boldsymbol{\Phi}_p (\mathbf{H}_{r-p}, \mathbf{H}_{r-p+1}, \ldots) \tag{8.6}$$

for an appropriately chosen r. This equality involves in particular that

$$(\mathbf{H}_{r+1}, \mathbf{H}_{r+2}, \ldots) = -\boldsymbol{\Phi}_1 (\mathbf{H}_r, \mathbf{H}_{r+1}, \ldots) \ldots - \boldsymbol{\Phi}_p (\mathbf{H}_{r-p+1}, \ldots).$$

Thus the $(r + 1)$-th row block is a combination of the p previous ones. Replacing $(\mathbf{H}_r, \mathbf{H}_{r+1}, \ldots)$ with its expression from (8.6), we see that the $(r+1)$-th row block is a linear function of the $(r-1)$-th, ..., $(r-p)$-th row blocks. We can follow an inductive approach. Any row block with indices $r+h$, $h \geq 0$ is a linear combination of the row blocks with indices $r-1, \ldots, r-p$. Thus the subspace spanned by the rows of the Hankel matrix coincides with the subspace spanned by those associated with the blocks with indices $0, 1, \ldots, (r-1)$. Hence $\mathcal{H}$ has a finite rank. □

We could even adopt the reverse approach and examine under what circumstances the Markov coefficients are such that two polynomials exist, $\mathbf{\Phi}^*(L)$ and $\mathbf{\Theta}^*(L)$ with $\mathbf{H}(L)\mathbf{\Phi}^*(L) = \mathbf{\Theta}^*(L)$. We would have obtained then the finiteness of the rank of $\mathcal{H}$ as a necessary and sufficient condition. This leads to

Theorem 8.9:   *The process admits an* ARMA *representation if and only if the column rank of the Hankel matrix is finite.*

PROOF: In fact, if the process is ARMA, we have

$$\mathbf{\Phi}(L)\mathbf{H}(L) = \mathbf{\Theta}(L)$$

$$\Rightarrow \det \mathbf{\Phi}(L)\mathbf{H}(L) = \tilde{\mathbf{\Phi}}(L)\mathbf{\Theta}(L)$$

$$\Rightarrow \mathbf{H}(L) \det \mathbf{\Phi}(L) = \tilde{\mathbf{\Phi}}(L)\mathbf{\Theta}(L),$$

since $\det(\mathbf{\Phi}(L))$ is a scalar. Hence the matrix $\mathcal{H}$ has a finite column rank.

Conversely, if $\mathcal{H}$ has a finite column rank we have

$$\mathbf{H}(L)\mathbf{\Phi}^*(L) = \mathbf{\Theta}^*(L)$$

$$\det \mathbf{\Phi}^*(L)\mathbf{H}(L) = \mathbf{\Theta}^*(L)\tilde{\mathbf{\Phi}}^*(L)$$

and the process admits an ARMA representation. □

Corollary: *The three definitions for the rank coincide for a Hankel matrix.*

PROOF: We have

$$\sup_{N,N'} \varrho(\mathcal{H}_{N,N'}) \geq \sup_{N} \varrho(\mathcal{H})_{N,\infty} = \text{row rank}.$$

Therefore, we can just restrict ourselves to the case where the row rank is finite (the column rank is finite as well on the basis of theorems 8.8 and 8.9). If this row rank r_0 is finite, we must have

$$\varrho(\mathcal{H}_{N,N'}) \leq r_0,$$

so that

$$\sup_{N,N'} \varrho(\mathcal{H}_{N,N'}) \leq r_0.$$

On the other hand, choosing N large enough to include the r_0 independent rows, then N' large enough, we see that it is possible to reach the value r_0. Thus, row rank $= \sup_{N,N'} \varrho(\mathcal{H}_{N,N'})$. Since the line of reasoning is symmetric for the column rank, the result follows. □

Predictor Space   We have seen in chapter 7 that successive forecasts can be expressed through the matrix $\mathcal{H}$

$$E\left(\mathbf{y}_{t+h} \mid I_t\right) = {}_t\hat{\mathbf{y}}_{t+h} = \sum_{j=0}^{+\infty} \mathbf{H}_{j+h}\boldsymbol{\varepsilon}_{t-j}, \ \forall \ h \geq 0.$$

Since the variance–covariance matrix of $\boldsymbol{\varepsilon}_t$ is nonsingular, it is equivalent to writing the linear independence conditions on the forecasts, or to write them on the components $\mathbf{H}_{j+h}$. Theorem 8.8 can then be expressed as

Theorem 8.10:   *The process admits an ARMA representation if and only if the space spanned by the forecasts ${}_t\hat{\mathbf{y}}_{t+h}$, $h \geq 0$ is of finite dimension. The dimension of this space is then equal to the rank of the Hankel matrix $\mathcal{H}$.*

Given the importance of the predictor space, it is interesting to explain how to find its bases.

Theorem 8.11:   *There exist bases for the predictor space in the form*

$${}_t\hat{\mathbf{y}}_t^1, \ldots, {}_t\hat{\mathbf{y}}_{t+r_1-1}^1,$$

$${}_t\hat{\mathbf{y}}_t^2, \ldots, {}_t\hat{\mathbf{y}}_{t+r_2-1}^2,$$

$$\cdots$$

$${}_t\hat{\mathbf{y}}_t^n, \ldots, {}_t\hat{\mathbf{y}}_{t+r_n-1}^n,$$

where $r_1, \ldots, r_n$ are positive or zero integers, the sum of which $r_1 + r_2 + \ldots + r_n = r$ and where $\hat{\mathbf{y}}^j$ indicates the forecast of the j-th component of $\mathbf{y}$.

We are adopting the convention that if $r_j = 0$ there is no forecast relative to the j-th component in the basis. The peculiarity of such a basis is that for each component it contains all the forecasts corresponding to a horizon smaller than a given value.

PROOF:

(i)   Let us consider the forecasts $_t\hat{\mathbf{y}}_{t+h}^1$ $h \geq 0$ relative to the first element. There exists a smallest integer r_1 (possibly 0) for which the forecasts $_t\hat{\mathbf{y}}_t^1, \ldots, {_t\hat{\mathbf{y}}}_{t+r_1}^1$ are linearly dependent. Since

$$\mathbf{y}_t^1 = \sum_{j=0}^{+\infty} \mathbf{H}_j^1 \boldsymbol{\varepsilon}_{t-j},$$

where $\mathbf{H}_j^1$ denotes the first row of $\mathbf{H}_j$, we have

$$_t\hat{\mathbf{y}}_{t+h}^1 = \sum_{j=0}^{+\infty} \mathbf{H}_{j+h}^1 \boldsymbol{\varepsilon}_{t-j}.$$

The condition of a linear relationship between $_t\hat{\mathbf{y}}_t^1, \ldots,$ and $_t\hat{\mathbf{y}}_{t+r_1}^1$ implies the existence of real numbers $a_{11}, \ldots, a_{1r_1}$ such that

$$_t\hat{\mathbf{y}}_{t+r_1}^1 = a_{1r_1}{_t\hat{\mathbf{y}}}_t^1 + \ldots + a_{11}{_t\hat{\mathbf{y}}}_{t+r_1-1}^1$$

$$\Rightarrow \mathbf{H}_{j+r_1}^1 = a_{1r_1}\mathbf{H}_j^1 + \ldots + a_{11}\mathbf{H}_{j+r_1-1}^1,$$

$\forall j \geq 0$. As in the proof for theorem 8.8, we can show that $_t\hat{\mathbf{y}}_{t+h}^1$, $h \geq r_1$ is linearly dependent on $_t\hat{\mathbf{y}}_t^1, \ldots, {_t\hat{\mathbf{y}}}_{t+r_1-1}^1$.

(ii)   The procedure for the construction of a basis is carried out considering the forecasts $_t\hat{\mathbf{y}}_{t+h}^2$, $h \geq 0$ linearly dependent on the second component. We define r_2 as the smallest integer (possibly 0) such that the system

$$_t\hat{\mathbf{y}}_t^1, \ldots, {_t\hat{\mathbf{y}}}_{t+r_1-1}^1, {_t\hat{\mathbf{y}}}_t^2, \ldots, {_t\hat{\mathbf{y}}}_{t+r_2-1}^1$$

be linearly dependent. We can show by moving average expansions that $_t\hat{\mathbf{y}}_{t+h}^2$, $h \geq r_2$ is linearly dependent on $_t\hat{\mathbf{y}}_t^1, \ldots, {_t\hat{\mathbf{y}}}_{t+r_2-1}^2$ for $h \geq r_2$.

(iii)   The line of reasoning is completed recursively for all components, up to index n. $\square$

The particular form of the previous basis leads to the decomposition of the dimension of the predictor space, showing the number of elements $(r_1, \ldots, r_n)$ corresponding to each component. This allows us to find the "maximum lags" associated with each variable, conditionally on the previous ones. It is clear, however, that a basis of the same type could have been built using a different order of the indices, for example starting from the n-th component, then the $(n-1)$-th, and so on. With a different ordering, we obtain a "decomposed dimension" $(r_1^* \ldots r_n^*)$ which is not necessarily the same as before (as shown in the Example 8.6).

Example 8.6: Let us consider a bivariate case. Let us assume that the predictor space is defined by the Hankel matrix

$$\mathcal{H} = \begin{pmatrix} \begin{pmatrix} 1 & 0 \\ 0 & 1 \end{pmatrix} & \begin{pmatrix} 0 & 1 \\ 0 & 0 \end{pmatrix} & \begin{pmatrix} 0 & 0 \\ 0 & 0 \end{pmatrix} & \cdots \\[1em] \begin{pmatrix} 0 & 1 \\ 0 & 0 \end{pmatrix} & \begin{pmatrix} 0 & 0 \\ 0 & 0 \end{pmatrix} & \begin{pmatrix} 0 & 0 \\ 0 & 0 \end{pmatrix} & \cdots \\[1em] \begin{pmatrix} 0 & 0 \\ 0 & 0 \end{pmatrix} & \begin{pmatrix} 0 & 0 \\ 0 & 0 \end{pmatrix} & \begin{pmatrix} 0 & 0 \\ 0 & 0 \end{pmatrix} & \cdots \\[1em] \vdots & \vdots & \vdots \end{pmatrix}.$$

The rank of the matrix $\mathcal{H}$ is equal to 2.

(i) Building the basis from the first component $\mathbf{y}^1$ we see that $_t\hat{\mathbf{y}}_t^1$, $_t\hat{\mathbf{y}}_{t+1}^1$, corresponding to the first and third row, are independent. Thus we have a "decomposed dimension" equal to $(2,0)$.

(ii) If we start to build from the second component, we keep $_t\hat{\mathbf{y}}_t^2$ (second row) and $_t\hat{\mathbf{y}}_t^1$ (first row). The new "decomposed dimension" is equal to $(1,1)$.

The particular bases in the predictor space just described, correspond to specific ARMA representations. To highlight them, we need to write the expansions of the links among the predictors. We have already presented those corresponding to the first component

$$\mathbf{H}_j^1 = a_{11}\mathbf{H}_{j-1}^1 + \ldots + a_{1r_1}\mathbf{H}_{j-r_1}^1,$$

for $j \geq r_1$. In terms of power series, this relationship can be written as

$$\mathbf{\Phi}_{11}(z)\mathbf{H}^1(z) = \mathbf{\Theta}^1(z),$$

where $\mathbf{\Phi}_{11}(z) = 1 - a_{11}z - \ldots - a_{1r_1}z^{r_1}$ and where $\mathbf{\Theta}^1(z)$ is a polynomial of size $(1,n)$ with elements $\mathbf{\Theta}_{1j}(z)$, $(j = 1, \ldots, n)$, at most of order $(r_1 - 1)$. Note that, since $_t\hat{\mathbf{y}}_t^1, \ldots, _t\hat{\mathbf{y}}_{t+r_1-1}^1$ are linearly independent, we have that the maximum common divisor (m.c.d.) of

$$\text{m.c.d.} \left(\mathbf{\Phi}_{11}(z), \mathbf{\Theta}_{11}(z), \ldots, \mathbf{\Theta}_{1n}(z) \right) = 1,$$

and

$$\max \left(\text{degree} \left(\mathbf{\Phi}_{11}(z) \right), \text{degree} \left(\mathbf{\Theta}_{11}(z) \right) + 1, \ldots, \right.$$

$$\left. \text{degree} \left(\mathbf{\Theta}_{1n}(z) \right) + 1 \right) = r_1.$$

At the second stage, r_2 is the minimal order for which $_t\hat{\mathbf{y}}_{t+h}$ is linearly dependent on

$$_t\hat{\mathbf{y}}_t^1, \ldots, _t\hat{\mathbf{y}}_{t+r_1-1}^1, _t\hat{\mathbf{y}}_t^2, \ldots, _t\hat{\mathbf{y}}_{t+r_2-1}^1$$

for $h \geq r_2$.

This condition can be expressed in terms of power series as

$$\mathbf{\Phi}_{21}(z)\mathbf{H}^1(z) + \mathbf{\Phi}_{22}(z)\mathbf{H}^2(z) = \mathbf{\Theta}^2(z)$$

with

$$\max\left(\text{degree}\left(\boldsymbol{\Phi}_{22}(z)\right), \text{degree}\left(\boldsymbol{\Theta}_{21}(z)\right)+1\ldots, \text{degree}\left(\boldsymbol{\Theta}_{2n}(z)\right)+1\right)=r_2$$

$$\text{degree}\left(\boldsymbol{\Phi}_{21}(z)\right)\le r_1$$

and the minimality condition for r_2 can be expressed as

$$\text{m.c.d.}\left(\boldsymbol{\Phi}_{22}(z), \boldsymbol{\Theta}_{21}(z), \ldots, \boldsymbol{\Theta}_{2n}(z)\right)=1,$$

and so on.

This allows us to state the following result

Theorem 8.12: *To a basis of the predictor space of the type*

$$_t\hat{\mathbf{y}}_t^1, \ldots, {}_t\hat{\mathbf{y}}_{t+r_1-1}^1, {}_t\hat{\mathbf{y}}_t^2, \ldots, {}_t\hat{\mathbf{y}}_{t+r_n-1}^n,$$

built according to the order $1, 2, \ldots, n$ *of the indices, corresponds an* ARMA *representation satisfying*

$$\boldsymbol{\Phi}(z)\mathbf{H}(z)=\boldsymbol{\Theta}(z),$$

with

(i)

$$\boldsymbol{\Phi}(z)=\begin{pmatrix}\boldsymbol{\Phi}_{11}(z) & 0 & \ldots & 0 \\ \boldsymbol{\Phi}_{21}(z) & \boldsymbol{\Phi}_{22}(z) & \ldots & 0 \\ \vdots & \vdots & \ddots & \vdots \\ \boldsymbol{\Phi}_{n1}(z) & \boldsymbol{\Phi}_{n2}(z) & \ldots & \boldsymbol{\Phi}_{nn}(z)\end{pmatrix},$$

$$\boldsymbol{\Theta}(z)=\begin{pmatrix}\boldsymbol{\Theta}^1(z) \\ \boldsymbol{\Theta}^1(z) \\ \vdots \\ \boldsymbol{\Phi}^n(z)\end{pmatrix}=\left(\boldsymbol{\Theta}_{ij}(z)\right),$$

(ii)

$$\text{degree } \boldsymbol{\Phi}_{ij}(z)\le r_j,$$

(iii)

$$\max\left(\text{degree }\left(\boldsymbol{\Phi}_{ii}(z)\right), \text{degree}\left(\boldsymbol{\Theta}_{ii}(z)\right)+1, \ldots,\right.$$
$$\left.\text{degree }\left(\boldsymbol{\Theta}_{in}(z)\right)+1\right)=r_i, \ \forall \ i,$$

(iv)

$$\text{m.c.d.}\left(\boldsymbol{\Phi}_{i1}(z), \boldsymbol{\Theta}_{ii}(z), \ldots, \boldsymbol{\Theta}_{in}(z)\right)=1, \ \forall \ i.$$

This ARMA representation appears in a very specific form since the autoregressive matrix is triangular.

8.2 State-space Representation

We have considered in the previous section the particular case of dynamic linear systems for which the Hankel matrix giving the predictors has a finite rank. We have seen that they could be translated into an autoregressive moving average representation. Under the same condition, we can show now the existence of another type of representation.

8.2.1 State-space Representation

The Form of the System Let us consider the evolution of a set of n real variables, denoted as a vector $\mathbf{y}$ and let us assume that the values taken by the various elements of $\mathbf{y}$ depend on the values taken by other variables $\mathbf{z}$. This dependency can be described by the equation system

$$
\begin{cases}
\mathbf{z}_{t+1} = \mathbf{A}\mathbf{z}_t + \mathbf{B}\mathbf{u}_t \\
\mathbf{y}_t = \mathbf{C}\mathbf{z}_t + \mathbf{D}\mathbf{u}_t
\end{cases}
\tag{8.7}
$$

for $t \geq 0$. In (8.7) $\mathbf{u}_t$ is $m \times 1$, $\mathbf{z}_t$ is $K \times 1$, $\mathbf{y}_t$ is $n \times 1$ and the matrices $\mathbf{A}$, $\mathbf{B}$, $\mathbf{C}$, $\mathbf{D}$ are, respectively, $K \times K$, $K \times m$, $n \times K$, $n \times m$. In the system theory terminology, the variables $\mathbf{u}$ are called *inputs*, the variables $\mathbf{y}$ are *outputs* or *observations*. The variables $\mathbf{z}$ which intuitively summarize the dynamic effect of $\mathbf{u}$ on $\mathbf{y}$ are called *state variables*. These variables are predetermined in that they depend only on the past values $\mathbf{u}_{t-1}, \mathbf{u}_{t-2}, \dots$.

System (8.7) implies two separate equations. The first one, called *state equation* explains how the state variable evolves according to the input. The second one, called *measurement equation*, determines the output as a function of the state of the system. The previous system gives a unique path for $\mathbf{y}$ for a given path of u, for given $\mathbf{A}$, $\mathbf{B}$, $\mathbf{C}$, $\mathbf{D}$ and for given initial state $\mathbf{z}_0$ of the system. This system can be seen as a linear mapping S of the space of the m-dimensional sequences into a space of n-dimensional sequences. This mapping is characterized by the given $\mathbf{A}$, $\mathbf{B}$, $\mathbf{C}$, $\mathbf{D}$ and $\mathbf{z}_0$ noted as

$$
S = S(\mathbf{A}, \mathbf{B}, \mathbf{C}, \mathbf{D}, \mathbf{z}_0).
\tag{8.8}
$$

In system theory reference is made to a *black-box representation*

$$
\xrightarrow{\mathbf{u}} \ S \ \xrightarrow{\mathbf{y}}
$$

in order to stress this interpretation of the system as a mapping, and the fact that this mapping is defined by a state variable.

8.2.2 Multiplicity of the Representations

Definition 8.4: *Given a system S_0, we define a system representation, any family $\mathbf{A}, \mathbf{B}, \mathbf{C}, \mathbf{D}, \mathbf{z}_0$ such that $S_0 = S(\mathbf{A}, \mathbf{B}, \mathbf{C}, \mathbf{D}, \mathbf{z}_0)$.*

A system S_0 admits many different representations. For any nonsingular matrix $\mathbf{Q}$ of order K, we can write the system (8.7) as

$$\begin{cases} \mathbf{z}_{t+1}^* = \mathbf{Q}\mathbf{A}\mathbf{Q}^{-1}\mathbf{z}_t^* + \mathbf{Q}\mathbf{B}\mathbf{u}_t, \\ \mathbf{y}_t = \mathbf{C}\mathbf{Q}^{-1}\mathbf{z}_t^* + \mathbf{D}\mathbf{u}_t, \end{cases}$$

with $t \geq 0$, and $\mathbf{z}_t^* = \mathbf{Q}\mathbf{z}_t$. This expression is similar to the one in (8.7) with $\mathbf{z}_t^*$ as a new state variable.

Theorem 8.13:

(i)   *For any nonsingular matrix $\mathbf{Q}$ of order K, we have*
$$S(\mathbf{A}, \mathbf{B}, \mathbf{C}, \mathbf{D}, \mathbf{z}_0) = S(\mathbf{Q}\mathbf{A}\mathbf{Q}^{-1}, \mathbf{Q}\mathbf{B}, \mathbf{C}\mathbf{Q}^{-1}, \mathbf{D}, \mathbf{Q}\mathbf{z}_0).$$

(ii) *Two representations $(\mathbf{A}, \mathbf{B}, \mathbf{C}, \mathbf{D}, \mathbf{z}_0)$ and $(\mathbf{A}^*, \mathbf{B}^*, \mathbf{C}^*, \mathbf{D}^*, \mathbf{z}_0^*)$ of the same system are said to be* equivalent *if there exists a nonsingular $\mathbf{Q}$ such that*
$$\mathbf{A}^* = \mathbf{Q}\mathbf{A}\mathbf{Q}^{-1}, \quad \mathbf{B}^* = \mathbf{Q}\mathbf{B},$$
$$\mathbf{C}^* = \mathbf{C}\mathbf{Q}^{-1}, \quad \mathbf{D}^* = \mathbf{D},$$
$$\mathbf{z}_0^* = \mathbf{Q}\mathbf{z}_0.$$

There exists a number of other representations which are not derived from (8.7) through a regular transformation. Thus the system

$$\begin{pmatrix} \mathbf{z}_{t+1} \\ \tilde{\mathbf{z}}_{t+1} \end{pmatrix} = \begin{pmatrix} \mathbf{A} & \mathbf{0} \\ \mathbf{A}_1 & \mathbf{A}_2 \end{pmatrix} \begin{pmatrix} \mathbf{z}_t \\ \tilde{\mathbf{z}}_t \end{pmatrix} + \begin{pmatrix} \mathbf{B} \\ \mathbf{B}_1 \end{pmatrix} \mathbf{u}_t$$

$$\mathbf{y}_t = (\mathbf{C}\ \mathbf{0}) \begin{pmatrix} \mathbf{z}_t \\ \tilde{\mathbf{z}}_t \end{pmatrix} + \mathbf{D}\mathbf{u}_t,$$

with $t \geq 0$, is also equivalent to the initial system. Intuitively, the representation (8.7) is preferable to this new representation; in fact, the variable $\tilde{z}_t$ does not exert any influence on the output and its consideration seems of little practical interest. This leads us to introduce the following definition

Definition 8.5:

(i)   The minimal size *of a system S_0 admitting a state-space representation is the smallest possible size of the state vector. It is denoted as $\underline{K}$.*

(ii) *A representation* $(\mathbf{A}, \mathbf{B}, \mathbf{C}, \mathbf{D}, \mathbf{z}_0)$ *of S_0 is called* minimal *if $\mathbf{A}$ is of order $\underline{K} \times \underline{K}$.*

We can notice that a minimal representation necessarily does exist; moreover, it is not unique, since any representation equivalent to a minimal representation is also minimal.

8.2.3 Expanded Expression for y

By successive substitutions in the first equation of the system (8.7) we get

$$\mathbf{z}_{t+1} = \mathbf{A}^{t+1}\mathbf{z}_0 + \sum_{j=0}^{t} \mathbf{A}^j \mathbf{B}\mathbf{u}_{t-j}$$

from which we derive the following expression of the output value at time t

$$\mathbf{y}_t = \mathbf{D}\mathbf{u}_t + \sum_{j=1}^{t} \mathbf{C}\mathbf{A}^{j-1}\mathbf{B}\mathbf{u}_{t-j} + \mathbf{C}\mathbf{A}^t\mathbf{z}_0. \qquad (8.9)$$

When the input $\mathbf{u}$ is an n-dimensional white noise, we see that the output has a moving average representation. By the same token, we call the *Markov coefficients* with index j the coefficients $\mathbf{H}_j$ of $\mathbf{u}_{t-j}$ in this expression. These coefficients are given by

$$\mathbf{H}_0 = \mathbf{D}, \qquad \mathbf{H}_j = \mathbf{C}\mathbf{A}^{j-1}\mathbf{B}, \quad j \geq 1. \qquad (8.10)$$

Remark 8.2: The expression (8.9) for the output value is obtained taking $t = 0$ as a starting date. This choice must be considered as a convention. Thus, taking successively $t = 0$ and $t = h$ as starting dates, we have

$$\mathbf{y}_{t+h} = \mathbf{C}\mathbf{A}^{t+h}\mathbf{z}_0 + \mathbf{D}\mathbf{u}_{t+h} + \mathbf{C}\mathbf{B}\mathbf{u}_{t+h-1} + \ldots + \mathbf{C}\mathbf{A}^{t+h-1}\mathbf{B}\mathbf{u}_0,$$

$$\mathbf{y}_{t+h} = \mathbf{C}\mathbf{A}^t\mathbf{z}_h + \mathbf{D}\mathbf{u}_{t+h} + \mathbf{C}\mathbf{B}\mathbf{u}_{t+h-1} + \ldots + \mathbf{C}\mathbf{A}^{t-1}\mathbf{B}\mathbf{u}_h.$$

These expressions show that the influence of the past previous to $h-1$ on $\mathbf{y}_{t+h}$, that is $\mathbf{CA}^{t+h}\mathbf{z}_0+\mathbf{CA}^t\mathbf{Bu}_{h-1}+\ldots+\mathbf{CA}^{t+h-1}\mathbf{Bu}_0$, is equal to $\mathbf{CA}^t\mathbf{z}_h$. It is perfectly summarized by the given state $\mathbf{z}_h$. We find once again the result that the state variable contains all the useful information about $\mathbf{y}$.

If now we write down the moving average expansions for successive values $\mathbf{y}_t, \mathbf{y}_{t+1}, \ldots$ of the output, we get

$$\begin{pmatrix} \mathbf{y}_t \\ \mathbf{y}_{t+1} \\ \vdots \end{pmatrix} = \begin{pmatrix} \mathbf{H}_1 & \mathbf{H}_2 & \mathbf{H}_3 & \cdots \\ \mathbf{H}_2 & \mathbf{H}_3 & \cdots & \cdots \\ \mathbf{H}_3 & \cdots & \cdots & \cdots \\ \vdots \end{pmatrix} \begin{pmatrix} \tilde{\mathbf{u}}_{t-1} \\ \tilde{\mathbf{u}}_{t-2} \\ \vdots \end{pmatrix}$$

$$+ \begin{pmatrix} \mathbf{H}_0 & \mathbf{0} & \mathbf{0} & \cdots \\ \mathbf{H}_1 & \mathbf{H}_0 & \cdots & \cdots \\ \mathbf{H}_2 & \cdots & \cdots & \cdots \\ \vdots \end{pmatrix} \begin{pmatrix} \tilde{\mathbf{u}}_t \\ \tilde{\mathbf{u}}_{t+1} \\ \vdots \end{pmatrix} + \begin{pmatrix} \tilde{\mathbf{h}}(t) \\ \tilde{\mathbf{h}}(t+1) \\ \vdots \end{pmatrix} \mathbf{z}_0,$$

with $\tilde{\mathbf{u}}_t = \mathbf{u}_t,\ \forall\ t \geq 0$, 0 otherwise. In matrix form, and using the notation of chapter 7, we have

$$\mathbf{y}_t^+ = \bar{\mathcal{H}}\tilde{\mathbf{u}}_{t-1}^- + \mathcal{T}\tilde{\mathbf{u}}_t^+ + \tilde{\mathbf{h}}^+(t)\mathbf{z}_0,$$

where, in particular

$$\bar{\mathcal{H}} = \begin{pmatrix} \mathbf{CB} & \mathbf{CAB} & \mathbf{CA}^2\mathbf{B} & \cdots \\ \mathbf{CAB} & \mathbf{CA}^2\mathbf{B} & \cdots & \cdots \\ \mathbf{CA}^2\mathbf{B} & \cdots & \cdots & \cdots \\ \vdots \end{pmatrix}.$$

The structure of this infinite Hankel matrix is fairly peculiar. In fact, using an infinite size matrix product, we can write

$$\bar{\mathcal{H}} = \begin{pmatrix} \mathbf{C} \\ \mathbf{CA} \\ \mathbf{CA}^2 \\ \vdots \end{pmatrix} (\mathbf{B} \quad \mathbf{AB} \quad \mathbf{A}^2\mathbf{B} \quad \cdots).$$

This expression leads us to introduce the two infinite matrices called *controllability* and *observability matrices*, which play an important role in what follows.

Definition 8.6:

(i) We call observability matrix *the infinite matrix*

$$\mathcal{O} = \begin{pmatrix} \mathbf{C} \\ \mathbf{CA} \\ \mathbf{CA}^2 \\ \vdots \end{pmatrix}.$$

(ii) The controllability matrix *is the infinite matrix*

$$\mathcal{C} = \begin{pmatrix} \mathbf{B} & \mathbf{AB} & \mathbf{A}^2\mathbf{B} & \cdots \end{pmatrix}$$

so that

$$\bar{\mathcal{H}} = \mathcal{O}\mathcal{C}. \tag{8.11}$$

Although the two matrices $\mathcal{O}$ and $\mathcal{C}$ have infinite size, it is not difficult to define their rank. In fact, since the observability matrix has a finite number of columns, a definition of rank based on the number of linearly independent columns gives a finite rank. We can say that this rank is equal to

$$\varrho(\mathcal{O}) = (\text{column rank}(\mathcal{O})) = \lim_{N\to\infty} \varrho(\mathcal{O}_N),$$

where $\mathcal{O}_N$ is made of the first N rows of $\mathcal{O}$. By the same token we have

$$\varrho(\mathcal{C}) = (\text{row rank}(\mathcal{C})) = \lim_{N\to\infty} \varrho(\mathcal{C}_{N'}).$$

Finally, we need to mention some conditions on the matrices $\mathcal{O}$ and $\mathcal{C}$ as they are to appear in the theorems which follow.

Definition 8.7: *The representation* $(\mathbf{A}, \mathbf{B}, \mathbf{C}, \mathbf{D}, \mathbf{z}_0)$ *of the system S where $\mathbf{A}$ is of order $K \times K$ is said to be*

(i) observable *if* $\varrho(\mathcal{O}) = K$;
(ii) controllable *if* $\varrho(\mathcal{C}) = K$.

8.2.4 Realization Theory

Let us consider a linear system written in a moving average form

$$\mathbf{y}_t = \sum_{j=0}^{t} \mathbf{H}_j \mathbf{u}_{t-j},$$

for $t \geq 0$.

The *realization theory* pertains to the existence conditions of a state-space representation of this system

$$\mathbf{z}_{t+1} = \mathbf{A}\mathbf{z}_t + \mathbf{B}\mathbf{u}_t,$$

$$\mathbf{y}_t = \mathbf{C}\mathbf{z}_t + \mathbf{D}\mathbf{u}_t,$$

for $t \geq 0$. In terms of Markov coefficients, we are looking for the conditions under which there exist some matrices $\mathbf{A}, \mathbf{B}, \mathbf{C}, \mathbf{D}$ such that

$$\mathbf{H}_0 = \mathbf{D} \quad \text{and} \quad \mathbf{H}_j = \mathbf{C}\mathbf{A}^{j-1}\mathbf{B} \quad j \geq 1.$$

Systems with finite rank Hankel matrices

Theorem 8.14: *The Hankel matrix $\bar{\mathcal{H}}$ of a system admitting a state-space representation has a finite rank smaller than or equal to the dimension of the state.*

PROOF: We have

$$\varrho(\bar{\mathcal{H}}) = \sup_{N,N'} \bar{\mathcal{H}}_{N,N'} \leq \sup_N \varrho(\mathcal{O}_N) \leq K.$$

$\square$

Since this theorem is valid for any representation of the system, we derive the following corollary

Corollary: *The Hankel matrix $\bar{\mathcal{H}}$ of a system admitting a state-space representation has a rank smaller than or equal to the smallest size $\underline{K}$.*

The following theorem is the dual of the one just proved.

Theorem 8.15: *A system with a finite rank Hankel matrix $\bar{\mathcal{H}}$ admits a state-space representation. This representation can be chosen with a size equal to the rank of the Hankel matrix. In particular we have*

$$\varrho(\bar{\mathcal{H}}) = \underline{K}.$$

PROOF: The proof is fairly long, but it is instructive, since it shows that suitable forecasts are an exhaustive summary of the past.

(i)   Since the matrix $\bar{\mathcal{H}}$ has a finite rank, we can make use of the interpretation in terms of predictors in theorem 8.11. We need to take into account the rescaling in the Hankel matrix, that is the fact that $\bar{\mathcal{H}}$ has replaced $\mathcal{H}$. If $\bar{\mathcal{H}}$ has finite rank (it is the same as $\mathcal{H}$), we can then find a predictor basis the elements of which are

$$_{t-1}\hat{\mathbf{y}}_t^1, \ldots, {}_{t-1}\hat{\mathbf{y}}_{t+r_1-1}^1, \ {}_{t-1}\hat{\mathbf{y}}_t^2, \ldots, {}_{t-1}\hat{\mathbf{y}}_{t+r_2-1}^2, \ldots,$$

$$_{t-1}\hat{\mathbf{y}}_t^n, \ldots, {}_{t-1}\hat{\mathbf{y}}_{t+r_n-1}^n,$$

where $r_1, \ldots, r_n$ are positive integers such that $\sum_i r_i = \varrho(\bar{\mathcal{H}})$. The elements of this basis should summarize the information contained in the past of u about the future of y. Let us write

$$\mathbf{z}_{t+1} = \begin{pmatrix} {}_t\hat{\mathbf{y}}_{t+1}^1 \\ \vdots \\ {}_t\hat{\mathbf{y}}_{t+r_1}^1 \\ \vdots \\ {}_t\hat{\mathbf{y}}_{t+r_n}^n \end{pmatrix}.$$

(ii) Let us examine if z satisfies a state-space equation. We have, for all positive k

$$_t\hat{\mathbf{y}}_{t+k}^1 = {}_{t-1}\hat{\mathbf{y}}_{t+k}^1 + \mathbf{H}_k\mathbf{u}_t,$$

from the moving average representation of the prediction function. This allows us to write

$$\mathbf{z}_{t+1} = \begin{pmatrix} {}_t\hat{\mathbf{y}}_{t+1}^1 \\ \vdots \\ {}_t\hat{\mathbf{y}}_{t+r_1}^1 \\ \vdots \\ {}_t\hat{\mathbf{y}}_{t+r_n}^n \end{pmatrix} = \begin{pmatrix} {}_{t-1}\hat{\mathbf{y}}_{t+1}^1 \\ \vdots \\ {}_{t-1}\hat{\mathbf{y}}_{t+r_1}^1 \\ \vdots \\ {}_{t-1}\hat{\mathbf{y}}_{t+r_n}^n \end{pmatrix} + \mathbf{B}\mathbf{u}_t, \qquad (8.12)$$

where $\mathbf{B}$ indicates a matrix whose rows are derived directly from the matrix $\bar{\mathcal{H}}$.

(iii) Moreover, in the proof of theorem 8.11 the constructed basis has the following property:

$_{t-1}\hat{\mathbf{y}}_{t+r_1}^1$ is a linear combination of $_{t-1}\hat{\mathbf{y}}_t^1, \ldots, {}_{t-1}\hat{\mathbf{y}}_{t+r_1-1}^1,$
$_{t-1}\hat{\mathbf{y}}_{t+r_2}^2$ is a linear combination of $_{t-1}\hat{\mathbf{y}}_t^1, \ldots, {}_{t-1}\hat{\mathbf{y}}_{t+r_1-1}^1,$
$\qquad\qquad\qquad\qquad {}_{t-1}\hat{\mathbf{y}}_t^2, \ldots, {}_{t-1}\hat{\mathbf{y}}_{t+r_2-1}^2,$

$\vdots$

$_{t-1}\hat{\mathbf{y}}_{t+r_n}^n$ is a linear combination of $_{t-1}\hat{\mathbf{y}}_t^1, \ldots, {}_{t-1}\hat{\mathbf{y}}_{t+r_1-1}^1,$

$$\cdots$$

$$_{t-1}\hat{\mathbf{y}}_t^n, \ldots, {}_{t-1}\hat{\mathbf{y}}_{t+r_n-1}^n.$$

We can take into account these relationships to write equation

(8.12) under the form

$$\mathbf{z}_{t+1} = \mathbf{A}\mathbf{z}_t + \mathbf{B}\mathbf{u}_t.$$

Matrix $\mathbf{A}$ admits a block decomposition of the form

$$\mathbf{A} = \begin{pmatrix} \mathbf{A}_{11} & \mathbf{A}_{12} & \cdots & \mathbf{A}_{1n} \\ \mathbf{A}_{21} & \mathbf{A}_{22} & \cdots & \mathbf{A}_{2n} \\ \vdots & \vdots & \ddots & \vdots \\ \mathbf{A}_{n1} & \mathbf{A}_{n2} & \cdots & \mathbf{A}_{nn} \end{pmatrix},$$

with blocks $\mathbf{A}_{ij}$ of order $(r_i \times r_j)$ such that

$$\mathbf{A}_{ii} = \begin{pmatrix} 0 & 1 & 0 & \cdots & 0 \\ 0 & 0 & 1 & \cdots & 0 \\ \vdots & \vdots & \vdots & \ddots & \vdots \\ 0 & 0 & 0 & \cdots & 1 \\ * & * & * & \cdots & 0 \end{pmatrix},$$

and

$$\mathbf{A}_{ij} = \begin{pmatrix} 0 & 0 & 0 & \cdots & 0 \\ 0 & 0 & 0 & \cdots & 0 \\ \vdots & \vdots & \vdots & \ddots & \vdots \\ 0 & 0 & 0 & \cdots & 0 \\ * & * & * & \cdots & * \end{pmatrix},$$

for $i > j$, and $\mathbf{A}_{ij} = \mathbf{0}$ if $i < j$. The $*$'s indicate the possibility of elements different from 0.

(iv) Let us examine now the measurement equation. We can always write the value $\mathbf{y}_t$ as the sum of the prediction and of the prediction error

$$\mathbf{y}_t =_{t-1} \hat{\mathbf{y}}_t + \mathbf{H}_0 \mathbf{u}_t.$$

This relationship can be rewritten in terms of the state vector $\mathbf{z}_t$ which (assuming, for simplicity, $r_1 > 0, \ldots, r_n > 0$) contains

$$_{t-1}\hat{\mathbf{y}}_t^1, \ldots, \,_{t-1}\hat{\mathbf{y}}_t^n$$

among its components. We have then

$$\mathbf{y}_t = \mathbf{C}\mathbf{z}_t + \mathbf{D}\mathbf{u}_t$$

with $\mathbf{D} = \mathbf{H}_0$ and $\mathbf{C} = (\mathbf{C}_1, \ldots, \mathbf{C}_n)$ where the block $\mathbf{C}_j$, of order

$(n \times r_j)$, can be written as

$$
\mathbf{C}_j = \begin{pmatrix}
0 & 0 & 0 & \dots & 0 \\
\vdots & \vdots & \vdots & \ddots & \vdots \\
0 & 0 & 0 & \dots & 0 \\
1 & 0 & 0 & \dots & 0 \\
\vdots & \vdots & \vdots & \ddots & \vdots \\
0 & 0 & 0 & \dots & 0
\end{pmatrix},
$$

with a unit element occurring at the j-th row of the first column.

(v)   We have shown how the initial system can be written in a state-space form. The order of this representation is the same as the size of $\mathbf{z}$, that is $\varrho(\bar{\mathcal{H}})$. In particular, $\varrho(\bar{\mathcal{H}}) \geq \underline{K}$, and therefore, given the corollary to theorem 8.13, $\varrho(\bar{\mathcal{H}}) = \underline{K}$. The representation thus constructed is therefore minimal. $\square$

8.2.5 Minimal Representations

Let us now look for simple characterizations of minimal representations. These will help us in constructing minimal representations different from the one just presented and easier to use in practice.

Theorem 8.16: *A representation of S is minimal if and only if it is observable and controllable.*

PROOF:

Necessary Condition For a minimal representation we have $\bar{\mathcal{H}} = \mathcal{O}\mathcal{C}$ where $\mathcal{O}$ has $\underline{K}$ columns and $\mathcal{C}$ has $\underline{K}$ rows. On the other hand, we know that

$$
\underline{K} = \varrho(\bar{\mathcal{H}}) \leq \inf(\varrho(\mathcal{O}), \varrho(\mathcal{C})) \leq \sup(\varrho(\mathcal{O}), \varrho(\mathcal{C})) \leq \underline{K}.
$$

This inequality can be derived from similar inequalities valid for finite dimension matrices. Thus, we have $\varrho(\mathcal{O}) = \varrho(\mathcal{C}) = \underline{K}$.

Sufficient Condition Let us now suppose that $\bar{H} = \mathcal{O}\mathcal{C}$ where $\mathcal{O}$ and $\mathcal{C}$ are $(\infty \times K)$, respectively, $(K \times \infty)$ of rank K. Then, for all values N and N' large enough we have

$$
\bar{\mathcal{H}}_{NN'} = \mathcal{O}_N \mathcal{C}_{N'},
$$

with $\varrho(\mathcal{O}_N) = \varrho(\mathcal{C}_{N'}) = K$. Since $\mathcal{O}_N$ has full column rank, $\mathcal{O}'_N \mathcal{O}_N$ is nonsingular and

$$(\mathcal{O}'_N \mathcal{O}_N)^{-1} \mathcal{O}'_N \bar{\mathcal{H}}_{NN'} = \mathcal{C}_{N'};$$

applying the inequalities on the ranks, we have

$$K \geq \varrho(\bar{\mathcal{H}}) \geq \varrho(\bar{\mathcal{H}}_{NN'}) \geq \varrho(\mathcal{C}_{N'}) = K.$$

Thus we have that $\varrho(\bar{\mathcal{H}}) = K$ which shows that the representation is minimal. $\square$

In order to derive the other properties, we will use the following lemma

Lemma: *If $\mathbf{H}$ is a matrix of size $(N \times N')$ with rank $\underline{K}$ which can be written as: $\mathbf{H} = \mathbf{PR} = \mathbf{P}^* \mathbf{R}^*$ with $\mathbf{P}$ and $\mathbf{P}^*$ of size $(N \times \underline{K})$, $\mathbf{R}$ and $\mathbf{R}^*$ of size $(\underline{K} \times N')$, then there exists a nonsingular matrix $\mathbf{Q}$ of size $\underline{K} \times \underline{K}$ such that $\mathbf{P} = \mathbf{P}^* \mathbf{Q}$ and $\mathbf{R} = \mathbf{Q}^{-1} \mathbf{R}^*$.*

PROOF: Cf. exercise 8.1. $\square$

Theorem 8.17: *If the Hankel matrix $\bar{\mathcal{H}}$ has a finite rank $\underline{K}$ and admits a decomposition*

$$\bar{\mathcal{H}} = \mathbf{PR},$$

where $\mathbf{P}$ includes $\underline{K}$ columns and $\mathbf{R}$ includes $\underline{K}$ rows, then there exists some unique matrices $\mathbf{A}$, $\mathbf{B}$, $\mathbf{C}$ such that

$$\mathbf{P} = \begin{pmatrix} \mathbf{C} \\ \mathbf{CA} \\ \mathbf{CA}^2 \\ \vdots \end{pmatrix}, \qquad \mathbf{R} = \begin{pmatrix} \mathbf{B} & \mathbf{AB} & \mathbf{A}^2\mathbf{B} & \cdots \end{pmatrix},$$

where $\mathbf{A}$ is of order $(\underline{K} \times \underline{K})$.

PROOF:

(i)   In the proof of theorem 8.15, we have stressed the existence of a minimal representation. Let us denote such a representation as $\mathbf{A}^*, \mathbf{B}^*, \mathbf{C}^*, \mathbf{D}^*$ and let us note $\mathcal{O}^*$ and $\mathcal{C}^*$ the associated controllability and observability matrices. From theorems 8.15 and 8.16 we have

$$\bar{\mathcal{H}} = \mathcal{O}^* \mathcal{C}^*,$$

where $\mathcal{O}^*$ is $(\infty \times \underline{K})$, $\mathcal{C}^*$ is $(\underline{K} \times \infty)$, $\varrho(\bar{\mathcal{H}}) = \varrho(\mathcal{O}^*) = \varrho(\mathcal{C}^*) = \underline{K}$. On the other hand, since $\bar{\mathcal{H}} = \mathbf{PR}$ with $\varrho(\bar{\mathcal{H}}) = \varrho(\mathbf{P}) = \varrho(\mathbf{R}) = \underline{K}$

we deduce from the lemma applied to truncated matrices that there exists a nonsingular matrix $\mathbf{Q}$ of order $(\underline{K} \times \underline{K})$ such that

$$\mathbf{P} = \mathcal{O}^*\mathbf{Q} \quad \text{and} \quad \mathbf{R} = \mathbf{Q}^{-1}\mathcal{C}^*.$$

Expanding these relationships we obtain

$$\mathcal{O}^*\mathbf{Q} = \begin{pmatrix} \mathbf{C}^*\mathbf{Q} \\ \mathbf{C}^*\mathbf{Q}\mathbf{Q}^{-1}\mathbf{A}^*\mathbf{Q} \\ \mathbf{C}^*\mathbf{Q}\mathbf{Q}^{-1}\mathbf{A}^{*2}\mathbf{Q} \\ \vdots \qquad \vdots \end{pmatrix}$$

$$\mathbf{R} = \left(\mathbf{Q}^{-1}\mathbf{B}^*, \mathbf{Q}^{-1}\mathbf{A}^*\mathbf{Q}\mathbf{Q}^{-1}\mathbf{B}^*, \ldots\right),$$

that is

$$\mathbf{P} = \begin{pmatrix} \mathbf{C} \\ \mathbf{CA} \\ \mathbf{CA}^2 \\ \vdots \end{pmatrix},$$

$$\mathbf{R} = \left(\mathbf{B}, \mathbf{AB}, \mathbf{A}^2\mathbf{B}, \ldots\right),$$

with $\mathbf{C} = \mathbf{C}^*\mathbf{Q}$, $\mathbf{B} = \mathbf{Q}^{-1}\mathbf{B}$, $\mathbf{A} = \mathbf{Q}^{-1}\mathbf{A}^*\mathbf{Q}$, which proves the existence.

(ii) We need now to show the uniqueness. This part of the proof is interesting because it will provide us with a simple way of computing $\mathbf{A}$, $\mathbf{B}$, and $\mathbf{C}$ starting from $\mathbf{P}$ and $\mathbf{R}$. Let us denote $\mathbf{P}_1$ the first n rows of $\mathbf{P}$ and $\mathbf{R}_1$ the first m columns of $\mathbf{R}$. We have $\mathbf{C} = \mathbf{P}_1$, $\mathbf{B} = \mathbf{R}_1$, so that $\mathbf{C}$ and $\mathbf{B}$ are defined without ambiguity. In order to show that $\mathbf{A}$ is also determined without ambiguity, let us consider the Hankel matrix $\bar{\mathcal{H}} = \mathbf{PR}$, and let us introduce a similar matrix scaled down by one element

$$\tau\bar{\mathcal{H}} = \begin{pmatrix} \mathbf{H}_2 & \mathbf{H}_3 & \mathbf{H}_4 & \cdots \\ \mathbf{H}_3 & \mathbf{H}_4 & \mathbf{H}_5 & \cdots \\ \vdots & \vdots & \vdots & \end{pmatrix} = \begin{pmatrix} \mathbf{CAB} & \mathbf{CA}^2\mathbf{B} & \cdots \\ \mathbf{CA}^2\mathbf{B} & \mathbf{CA}^3\mathbf{B} & \cdots \\ \vdots & \vdots & \end{pmatrix}.$$

This matrix can be written also as

$$\tau\bar{\mathcal{H}} = \mathbf{PAR}$$

Since $\mathbf{P}$ and $\mathbf{R}$ are of full column, respectively, row rank, upon truncation we can compute the left-inverse of $\mathbf{P}$ and the right-inverse of $\mathbf{R}$. For N large enough we have $\varrho(\mathbf{P}_N) = \varrho(\mathbf{R}_N) = \underline{K}$.

Thus

$$\tau\bar{\mathcal{H}}_{NN} = \mathbf{P}_N\mathbf{A}\mathbf{R}_N$$

$$\Rightarrow \mathbf{A} = (\mathbf{P}'_N\mathbf{P}_N)^{-1}\mathbf{P}'_N(\tau\bar{\mathcal{H}}_{NN})\mathbf{R}'_N(\mathbf{R}_N\mathbf{R}'_N)^{-1},$$

which shows how $\mathbf{A}$ can be calculated starting from $\mathbf{P}$ and $\mathbf{R}$. □

Corollary: *If the initial conditions are zero, i.e., $\mathbf{z}_0 = 0$, two minimal state-space representations of the same system are necessarily equivalent (cf. theorem 8.12).*

PROOF: It follows from the proof of theorem 8.16. □

8.2.6 Derivation of the Minimal Representations

The technique used for the proof of theorem 8.16 provides a simple way to find the minimal representations associated with a Hankel matrix with finite rank $\underline{K}$.

Algorithm   We can use the following iterative procedure
Step 1: Look for N and N' integer such that

$$\varrho(\bar{\mathcal{H}}) = \varrho(\bar{\mathcal{H}}_{NN'}) = \underline{K}.$$

Step 2: Factorize $\bar{\mathcal{H}}_{NN'}$ as $\bar{\mathcal{H}}_{NN'} = \mathbf{P}_N\mathbf{R}_{N'}$ where matrices $\mathbf{P}_N$ and $\mathbf{R}_{N'}$ have $\underline{K}$ columns, respectively, rows;
Step 3: Find the first n rows $\mathbf{P}_1$ of $\mathbf{P}$ and the first m columns $\mathbf{R}_1$ of $\mathbf{R}$;
Step 4: Compute the matrix

$$(\mathbf{P}'_N\mathbf{P}_N)^{-1}\mathbf{P}'_N\tau\bar{\mathcal{H}}_{NN'}\mathbf{R}'_{N'}(\mathbf{R}_{N'}\mathbf{R}'_{N'})^{-1}.$$

A minimal representation is

$$\mathbf{A} = (\mathbf{P}'_N\mathbf{P}_N)^{-1}\mathbf{P}'_N\tau\bar{\mathcal{H}}_{NN'}\mathbf{R}'_{N'}(\mathbf{R}_{N'}\mathbf{R}'_{N'})^{-1},$$

$$\mathbf{B} = \mathbf{R}_1, \qquad \mathbf{C} = \mathbf{P}_1, \qquad \mathbf{D} = \mathbf{H}_0.$$

Singular Value Decomposition   In order to perform step 2 we need to get a simple way of factorizing the matrix $\bar{\mathcal{H}}_{NN'}$. In order to simplify the notation, in what follows we will consider the case $m = n$ which is the only one used in this context. Let us take $N = N'$ as well. The truncated Hankel matrix $\bar{\mathcal{H}}_{NN}$ is a square matrix of order $(nN \times nN)$. We can obtain a factorization of this matrix starting from a Singular

Value Decomposition theorem (the proof of which is reported in the appendix).

Theorem 8.18: *Any square matrix* $\mathbf{M}$ *can be written in the form* $\mathbf{M} = \mathbf{U}\boldsymbol{\Lambda}\mathbf{V}'$ *where* $\boldsymbol{\Lambda}$ *is a diagonal matrix with positive elements and where* $\mathbf{U}$ *and* $\mathbf{V}$ *are orthogonal matrices.*

PROOF: Let us apply the singular value decomposition to the matrix $\bar{\mathcal{H}} = \mathbf{U}\boldsymbol{\Lambda}\mathbf{V}'$. Since we have chosen N large enough to have $\varrho(\bar{\mathcal{H}}_{NN}) = \underline{K} = \varrho(\bar{\mathcal{H}})$, it follows that $\varrho(\boldsymbol{\Lambda}) = \underline{K}$. Ordering the *singular values*, that is the diagonal elements of $\boldsymbol{\Lambda}$ in decreasing order we can write

$$
\bar{\mathcal{H}}_{NN} = \mathbf{U} \begin{pmatrix} \lambda_1 & 0 & \cdots & 0 & \cdots & 0 \\ 0 & \lambda_2 & \cdots & 0 & \cdots & 0 \\ \cdots & \cdots & \ddots & 0 & \cdots & 0 \\ 0 & 0 & \cdots & \lambda_{\underline{K}} & \cdots & 0 \\ \vdots & \vdots & & & \ddots & \vdots \\ 0 & 0 & & \cdots & & 0 \end{pmatrix} \mathbf{V}'.
$$

Indicating by $\underline{\mathbf{U}}$ the submatrix of $\mathbf{U}$ consisting of the first $\underline{K}$ columns and similarly for $\underline{\mathbf{V}}$, we have

$$
\bar{\mathcal{H}}_{NN} = \underline{\mathbf{U}} \begin{pmatrix} \lambda_1 & 0 & \cdots & 0 \\ 0 & \lambda_2 & \cdots & 0 \\ \vdots & \vdots & \ddots & 0 \\ 0 & 0 & \cdots & \lambda_{\underline{K}} \end{pmatrix} \underline{\mathbf{V}}'.
$$

Step 2 can be taken with

$$
\mathbf{P}_N = \underline{\mathbf{U}} \begin{pmatrix} \lambda_1 & 0 & \cdots & 0 \\ 0 & \lambda_2 & \cdots & 0 \\ \vdots & \vdots & \ddots & 0 \\ 0 & 0 & \cdots & \lambda_{\underline{K}} \end{pmatrix} \qquad \text{and } \mathbf{R}_N = \underline{\mathbf{V}}'.
$$

□

We could also use singular value decompositions where matrices $\mathbf{U}$ and $\mathbf{V}$ are orthogonal with respect to scalar products other than the identity matrix (cf. exercise 8.2).

8.2.7 ARMA Representation and State Representation

Comparison Given an n-dimensional process $\mathbf{y} = \{\mathbf{y}_t,\ t \geq 0\}$ defined as

$$\mathbf{y}_t = \sum_{j=0}^{t} \mathbf{H}_j \boldsymbol{\varepsilon}_{t-j}, \quad t \geq 0,$$

where $\boldsymbol{\varepsilon}$ is an n-dimensional white noise process $\boldsymbol{\varepsilon} = (\boldsymbol{\varepsilon}_t,\ t \geq 0)$ with $\mathbf{H}_0 = \mathbf{I}$, we have seen in theorem 8.9 that it admits an ARMA representation if and only if the Hankel matrix $\mathcal{H}$ has a finite rank. By the same token, we have just seen that it admits a state-space representation

$$\mathbf{z}_{t+1} = \mathbf{A}\mathbf{z}_t + \mathbf{B}\boldsymbol{\varepsilon}_t$$

$$\mathbf{y}_t = \mathbf{C}\mathbf{z}_t + \boldsymbol{\varepsilon}_t,$$

for $t \geq 0$ and $\mathbf{D} = \mathbf{H}_0 = \mathbf{I}$, if and only if the Hankel matrix $\mathcal{H}$ has a finite rank. The two matrices $\bar{\mathcal{H}}$ and $\mathcal{H}$ are different by n columns, so that it is the same to say that the rank of $\mathcal{H}$ is finite or the rank of $\bar{\mathcal{H}}$ is finite.

Theorem 8.19: *A process*

$$\mathbf{y}_t = \sum_{j=0}^{t} \mathbf{H}_j \epsilon_{t-j},$$

with $\mathbf{H}_0 = \mathbf{I}$, *admits an* ARMA *representation if and only if it admits a state-space representation.*

This equivalence can be expressed in terms of a transfer function. The transfer function of an ARMA process is

$$\Phi(L)\mathbf{y}_t = \Theta(L)\epsilon_t \quad \text{is} \quad \Phi(z)^{-1}\Theta(z).$$

The transfer function associated to a state-space representation is

$$\sum_{j=0}^{+\infty} \mathbf{H}_j z^j = \mathbf{I} + \sum_{j=0}^{+\infty} \mathbf{C}\mathbf{A}^{j-1}\mathbf{B}z^j = \mathbf{I} + \mathbf{C}\left(\mathbf{I} - \mathbf{A}z\right)^{-1}\mathbf{B}z.$$

Corollary:

(i)   *Any rational transfer function* $\Phi(z)^{-1}\Theta(z)$ *where* Φ *and* Θ *are square of order* n *can be written as*

$$\mathbf{I} + \mathbf{C}\left(\mathbf{I} - \mathbf{A}z\right)^{-1}\mathbf{B}z,$$

where $\mathbf{C}$, $\mathbf{A}$, *and* $\mathbf{B}$ *are of order* $(n \times K)$, $(K \times K)$ *and* $(K \times n)$, *respectively.* (ii)   *The reverse is also true.*

Unidimensional ARMA Process: Minimal Orders Some more precise results can be obtained in the unidimensional case $n = 1$. We know that a unidimensional ARMA process can be expressed in a variety of representations

$$\Phi(L)y_t = \Theta(L)\epsilon_t, \qquad \Phi^*(L)y_t = \Theta^*(L)\epsilon_t, \cdots$$

Given two such representations, we have the equality of the transfer functions

$$\frac{\Theta(z)}{\Phi(z)} = \frac{\Theta^*(z)}{\Phi^*(z)}.$$

Among all these representations, the one corresponding to the form of the rational fraction where no simplifications are possible gives the smallest possible values of p and q.

Definition 8.8: *The representation $\Phi(L)y_t = \Theta(L)\epsilon_t$ of the unidimensional process y is called* minimal ARMA $(\underline{p}, \underline{q})$ *if and only if $\phi_{\underline{p}} \neq 0$ and $\theta_{\underline{q}} \neq 0$ and if the polynomials Φ and Θ do not have common factors. The resulting orders $\underline{p}$ and $\underline{q}$ are called* minimal orders.

These orders can be expressed in terms of a difference equation on the Markov coefficients. Let

$$\begin{cases} \tilde{h}_j = h_j, & \text{if } j \geq 0, \\ \tilde{h}_j = 0, & \text{otherwise} \end{cases}$$

be the enlarged sequence of the Markov coefficients. We know (cf. chapter 5) that the minimal order $\underline{p}$ is the smallest order of the homogeneous linear difference equations satisfied after a certain rank by $\tilde{h}$. The smallest index from which this $\underline{p}$-th order equation is satisfied is then $\underline{q} + 1$.

Minimal Orders of ARMA Representations and Minimal Dimension of the State Representations We have just introduced the notion of minimal order $\underline{p}, \underline{q}$ of an ARMA process. Moreover, it admits state-space representations as well, some of which have minimal dimension $\underline{K}$.

Theorem 8.20: *We have $\underline{K} = \max(\underline{p}, \underline{q})$.*

PROOF: Recall that $\underline{K}$ is the dimension of the predictor space

$$_{t-1}\hat{y}_t, \, _{t-1}\hat{y}_{t+1}, \cdots, \, _{t-1}\hat{y}_{t+j}, \cdots,$$

and that $\underline{K}$ is also the first index k for which $_{t-1}\hat{y}_{t+k}$ is the linear combination of $_{t-1}\hat{y}_t, \ldots, {}_{t-1}\hat{y}_{t+k-1}$ (cf. the procedure shown in theorem 8.11). Let us rewrite this condition in an explicit way in terms of Markov coefficients. $\underline{K}$ is the first index k for which there exist $\phi_1, \ldots, \phi_k$ with

$$h_j + \phi_1 h_{j-1} + \ldots + \phi_k h_{j-k} = 0$$

for $j \geq k+1$. The result follows from the characterization of $\underline{p}, \underline{q}$ derived from the difference equations. $\square$

Example 8.7: For an AR(1) process

$$y_t = \rho y_{t-1} + \epsilon_t = \sum_{j=0}^{+\infty} \rho^j \epsilon_{t-j},$$

the predictors take the form

$$_{t-1}\hat{y}_{t+k} = \sum_{j=k+1}^{+\infty} \rho^j \epsilon_{t+k-j} = \rho^k \left(\rho \epsilon_{t-1} + \rho^2 \epsilon_{t-2} + \ldots \right) = \rho^k {}_{t-1}\hat{y}_t.$$

Since they are all proportional to $_{t-1}\hat{y}_t$, we have

$$\underline{K} = 1 = \max(\underline{p}, \underline{q}) = \max(1, 0).$$

Example 8.8: In the case of an MA(q) process, we have

$$y_t = \epsilon_t + \theta_1 \epsilon_{t-1} + \ldots + \theta_q \epsilon_{t-q},$$

and the predictors are

$$_{t-1}\hat{y}_t = \theta_1 \epsilon_{t-1} + \ldots + \theta_q \epsilon_{t-q},$$

$$_{t-1}\hat{y}_{t+1} = \theta_2 \epsilon_{t-1} + \ldots + \theta_q \epsilon_{t-q+1},$$

$$_{t-1}\hat{y}_{t+k} = 0 \qquad \forall\, k \geq q.$$

The predictor space has dimension

$$\underline{K} = q = \max(\underline{p}, \underline{q}) = \max(0, q).$$

Some State Representations of an ARMA Process

(i)   *Representation in terms of a predictor basis.* A minimal state-space representation was shown in theorem 8.15. We will determine it from a minimal ARMA representation of the univariate process

$$y_t + \phi_1 y_{t-1} + \ldots + \phi_{\underline{p}} y_{t-\underline{p}} = \epsilon_t + \theta_1 \epsilon_{t-1} + \ldots + \theta_{\underline{q}} \epsilon_{t-\underline{q}}.$$

If $\underline{K} = \max(\underline{p}, \underline{q})$, we know that the choice of the state vector is

$$
\mathbf{z}_t = \begin{pmatrix} {}_{t-1}\hat{y}_t \\ \vdots \\ {}_{t-1}\hat{y}_{t+\underline{K}-1} \end{pmatrix}.
$$

Moreover, we know that $\forall\ k \geq 0$, ${}_t\hat{y}_{t+k} = {}_{t-1}\hat{y}_{t+k} + h_k \epsilon_t$. Hence, the ARMA representation $\underline{K}$ periods ahead is

$$
y_{t+\underline{K}} + \phi_1 y_{t+\underline{K}-1} + \ldots + \phi_{\underline{p}} y_{t+\underline{K}-\underline{p}} = \epsilon_{t+\underline{K}} + \theta_1 \epsilon_{t-1} + \ldots + \theta_{\underline{q}} \epsilon_{t+\underline{K}-\underline{q}}.
$$

Taking the forecast of each member conditional on the past prior to $t-1$ and recalling that $\underline{K} - \underline{q} \geq 0$ we have the difference equation among predictors

$$
{}_{t-1}\hat{y}_{t+\underline{K}} + \phi_1 \ {}_{t-1}\hat{y}_{t+\underline{K}-1} + \ldots + \phi_{\underline{p}} \ {}_{t-1}\hat{y}_{t+\underline{K}-\underline{p}} = 0 \qquad \forall\ t.
$$

Then, letting

$$
\tilde{\phi}_j = \begin{cases} \phi_j, & \text{if } j \leq \underline{p}, \\ 0, & \text{otherwise}, \end{cases}
$$

the resulting state-space representation is

$$
\mathbf{z}_{t+1} = \begin{pmatrix} 0 & 1 & 0 & \cdots & 0 \\ 0 & 0 & 1 & \cdots & 0 \\ \vdots & \vdots & \ddots & \ddots & \vdots \\ 0 & 0 & \cdots & 0 & 1 \\ -\tilde{\phi}_{\underline{K}} & -\tilde{\phi}_{\underline{K}-1} & \cdots & \cdots & -\tilde{\phi}_1 \end{pmatrix} \mathbf{z}_t + \begin{pmatrix} h_1 \\ h_2 \\ \vdots \\ h_{\underline{K}} \end{pmatrix} \epsilon_t
$$

$$
\mathbf{y}_t = (\, 1 \quad 0 \quad \cdots \quad 0 \,)\, \mathbf{z}_t + \epsilon_t.
$$

(ii) *Representation in terms of an ARMA equation.* We have

$$
y_t = \left(-\phi_1 y_{t-1} + \ldots - \phi_{\underline{p}} y_{t-\underline{p}} + \theta_1 \epsilon_{t-1} + \ldots + \theta_{\underline{q}} \epsilon_{t-\underline{q}} \right) + \epsilon_t,
$$

so that we can summarize the past as

$$
\mathbf{z}_t = \begin{pmatrix} y_{t-1} \\ \vdots \\ y_{t-\underline{p}} \\ \epsilon_{t-1} \\ \vdots \\ \epsilon_{t-\underline{q}} \end{pmatrix}. \tag{8.13}
$$

The resulting state-space representation is

$$
\mathbf{z}_{t+1} =
\begin{pmatrix}
-\phi_1 & -\phi_2 & \cdots & -\phi_{p-1} & -\phi_p & \theta_1 & \cdots & \theta_{q-1} & \theta_q \\
1 & 0 & \cdots & 0 & 0 & 0 & \cdots & 0 & 0 \\
0 & 1 & \cdots & 0 & 0 & 0 & \cdots & 0 & 0 \\
\vdots & \vdots & \ddots & \vdots & \vdots & \vdots & & \vdots & \vdots \\
0 & 0 & \cdots & 1 & 0 & 0 & \cdots & 0 & 0 \\
0 & 0 & \cdots & 0 & 0 & 1 & \cdots & 0 & 0 \\
\vdots & \vdots & & \vdots & \vdots & \vdots & \ddots & \vdots & \vdots \\
0 & 0 & \cdots & 0 & 0 & 0 & \cdots & 1 & 0
\end{pmatrix}
\mathbf{z}_t
$$

$$
+
\begin{pmatrix}
1 \\
0 \\
\vdots \\
0 \\
1 \\
0 \\
\vdots \\
0
\end{pmatrix}
\epsilon_t
$$

$$
\mathbf{y}_t = \begin{pmatrix} -\phi_1 & \cdots & -\phi_p & \theta_1 & \cdots & \theta_q \end{pmatrix} \mathbf{z}_t + \epsilon_t.
$$

This representation of dimension $p+q$ is not minimal except in the case when $p+q = \max(p,q)$, that is in the case of pure AR or MA. For an AR(p), the state vector is made of the past values of the process. For an MA(q) it involves only past innovations.

8.3 Frequency Domain

In the previous sections, we have taken into consideration essentially the time series y by means of the autocovariance function or of the sequence of the Markov coefficients. The idea was to analyze the links between past and future, giving the spotlight to the time index t. This approach is called *time domain approach*.

Other approaches are possible. The spectral representation theorem introduced in this section, allows one to write the components $y_{j,t}$, $j = 1, \ldots, n$ of the process as "combinations with random coefficients" of periodic functions $\exp(it\omega)$. We can then study the importance of each frequency in the values taken by y_t, that is, how the correlations can be decomposed at each frequency. Such an approach is called *frequency domain approach*.

8.3.1 Spectral Representation Theorem: Univariate Case

The spectral representation theorem is based on the notions of *stochastic integrals and measures*. These notions are complex from a mathematical point of view, so that we will only outline their characteristics here, in that they are a good example of the calculations used in what follows.

Let $y = (y_t)$ be a zero mean stationary process, with autocovariance function $\gamma(h)$ and spectral density function (assuming that it exists) $f(\omega)$, $\omega \in [-\pi, +\pi]$. The links between the autocovariance and the spectral density functions are given by (cf. section 5.1.5)

$$f(\omega) = \frac{1}{2\pi} \sum_{-\infty}^{+\infty} \gamma(h) \exp(i\omega h),$$

$$\gamma(h) = \int_{-\pi}^{+\pi} \exp{-(ih\omega)} f(\omega) d\omega.$$

This last equality can be written as

$$E\left(y_t\, y_{t-h}\right) = \int_{-\pi}^{+\pi} \exp{-(it\omega)} \overline{\exp{-(i(t-h)\omega)}} f(\omega) d\omega, \qquad (8.14)$$

where the term on the left-hand side contains the scalar product between y_t and y_{t-h} in $L_C^2(P)$ and the term on the right-hand side the scalar product between $\exp{-(it\omega)}$ and $\exp{-(i(t-h)\omega)}$ in $L_C^2(f(\omega)\, d\omega)$. This leads us to introduce a mapping J which associates the variables y_t to the functions $\exp{-(it\omega)}$

$$y_t = J(\exp{-(it\omega)}).$$

Equation (8.14) shows that the mapping J is closed with respect to the scalar product. Then it is possible to show that J is an isometric map from the space generated by the functions $\exp{-(it\omega)}$, that is $L_C^2(f(\omega)d\omega)$, onto the space of the square integrable variables generated by $\{y_t\}$.

To better interpret this isometric mapping, we need to examine the possible transformations of the indicator functions for sets of $[-\pi, +\pi]$. Let us denote the image of such an indicator function as $J(\mathbb{1}_A) = \xi(A)$.

(i)   If A and $\tilde{A}$ are disjoint sets, the linearity of the mapping J implies that

$$\xi(A \cup \tilde{A}) = J(\mathbb{1}_{A \cup \tilde{A}}) = J(\mathbb{1}_A + \mathbb{1}_{\tilde{A}}) = J(\mathbb{1}_A) + J(\mathbb{1}_{\tilde{A}}) = \xi(A) + \xi(\tilde{A}).$$

The possibly complex valued random function ξ is therefore additive. We can then interpret ξ as a kind of measure; ξ is called a *stochastic measure* associated with y. Since J is the isometric mapping which extends ξ, we can denote and interpret it as an integral. From now on, we will denote

$$J(\cdot) = \int_{-\pi}^{+\pi} (\cdot)d\xi(\omega), \qquad (8.15)$$

and we will call it a *stochastic integral* with respect to ξ.

(ii)   Let us now analyze the closedness with respect to the scalar product. That can be written as

$$\text{cov} \left(\int_{-\pi}^{+\pi} A(\omega)d\xi(\omega), \int_{-\pi}^{+\pi} B(\omega)d\xi(\omega) \right)$$
$$= \int_{-\pi}^{+\pi} A(\omega)\overline{B(\omega)}f(\omega)d(\omega) \qquad (8.16)$$

for all square integrable functions A and B with respect to $f(\omega)d\omega$. In particular, choosing some indicator functions, we have

$$\text{cov}\ (\xi(A), \xi(B)) = E\left(\xi(A)\overline{\xi(B)} \right) = 0, \qquad (8.17)$$

if A and B are disjoint, and

$$\text{var}\ (\xi(A)) = E\left(|\xi(A)|^2 \right) = \int_A f(\omega)d\omega. \qquad (8.18)$$

These two expressions are often rewritten in terms of the process $\xi(\omega) = \xi\left((-\pi, \omega]\right)$ and the increment $d\xi(\omega) = \xi(\omega, \omega + d\omega)$. Let us then state the following theorem in a simplified form:

Theorem 8.21: Spectral Representation Theorem
Let $y = \{y_t\}$ be a univariate stationary process with spectral density function $f(\omega)$. We can then write

$$y_t = \int_{-\pi}^{+\pi} \exp -(it\omega)d\xi(\omega),$$

where the stochastic measure ξ is such that: (i) $E\left(d\xi(\omega)\right) = 0 \quad \forall\ \omega$.
(ii) $\text{cov}\ (d\xi(\omega), d\xi(\tilde{\omega})) = E\left(d\xi(\omega)\overline{d\xi(\tilde{\omega})} \right) = 0 \quad \forall\ \omega \neq \tilde{\omega}$.
(iii) $\text{var}\ (d\xi(\omega)) = f(\omega)d(\omega) \quad \forall\ \omega$.

y_t is then expressed as a linear combination of the single components $\exp -(it\omega)$ associated with each of the frequencies ω. The component with frequency ω has a "random weight" $d\xi(\omega)$. The average importance, so to speak, of this infinitesimal weight can be measured as

$$\frac{E \mid d\xi(\omega) \mid^2}{d\omega} \approx f(\omega).$$

Thus, if $f(\omega_1) > f(\omega_2)$, the frequency component ω_1 is more important than the frequency component ω_2 in the decomposition of y_t. Note that condition (ii) of uncorrelation between the various $d\xi(\omega)$ is essential for the interpretation (we say that $\xi(\omega)$ has *orthogonal increments*). It allows us to decompose a certain number of indices used in the time domain at each frequency. For instance, we know that

$$\text{var}\,(y_t) = \gamma(0) = \int_{-\pi}^{+\pi} f(\omega)d\omega = \int_{-\pi}^{+\pi} \text{var}\,(d\xi(\omega))$$

$$= \text{var}\left(\int_{-\pi}^{+\pi} d\xi(\omega)\right).$$

The total variance of the process is then obtained by summing all the variances at each frequency.

Finally, note that if the process y is normal, the space generated by the variables y_t is composed of normal variables only (combinations of the previous ones or limits in quadratic mean of such combinations).

Theorem 8.22: *If y is normal, the process $\{\xi(\omega)\}, \omega \in (-\pi, +\pi]$ is normal as well.*

8.3.2 Spectral Representation Theorem: Multivariate Case

The spectral representation theorem can be generalized to the multidimensional case. In order to write

$$\mathbf{y}_t = \int_{-\pi}^{+\pi} \exp -(it\omega)d\xi(\omega),$$

we need an n-dimensional stochastic measure ξ.

Theorem 8.23: *Let $\mathbf{y} = \{\mathbf{y}_t\}$ be a multivariate stationary process with spectral density function $f(\omega)$. We can write*

$$\mathbf{y}_t = \int_{-\pi}^{+\pi} \exp -(it\omega)d\xi(\omega)$$

where the n-dimensional stochastic measure is such that:

(i) $E\left(d\xi(\omega)\right) = 0 \quad \forall\, \omega.$

(ii) $\text{cov}\left(d\xi(\omega), d\xi(\tilde{\omega})\right) = E\left(d\xi(\omega), \overline{d\xi(\tilde{\omega})'}\right) = 0 \quad \forall\, \omega \neq \tilde{\omega}.$

(iii) $\text{var}\left(d\xi(\omega)\right) = f(\omega)d(\omega) \quad \forall\, \omega.$

In order to give the intuition behind the theorem, let us take into consideration the bivariate case. We can write the result for the two components of the process

$$y_{1t} = \int_{-\pi}^{+\pi} \exp -(it\omega)d\xi_1(\omega),$$

$$y_{2t} = \int_{-\pi}^{+\pi} \exp -(it\omega)d\xi_2(\omega).$$

We can derive that the components of $\xi(\omega)$ are the stochastic measures associated with each of the components of **y**. The stochastic weights $d\xi_1(\omega)$ and $d\xi_2(\omega)$ attached to the frequency ω can be correlated. In fact, from (iii) of theorem 8.23 we get

$$\text{cov}\left(d\xi_1(\omega), d\xi_2(\omega)\right) = f_{12}(\omega)d\omega.$$

Let us introduce an appropriate definition of correlation at each frequency to measure this link.

Definition 8.9: *The* coherence *between the components y_1 and y_2 is the function defined as*

$$K_{12}(\omega) = \frac{\mid \text{cov}\left(d\xi_1(\omega), d\xi_2(\omega)\right) \mid}{\sqrt{\text{var}\left(d\xi_1(\omega)\right)}\sqrt{\text{var}\left(d\xi_2(\omega)\right)}} = \frac{\mid f_{12}(\omega) \mid}{\sqrt{f_{11}(\omega)f_{22}(\omega)}}.$$

The modulus in the definition is needed since $f_{12}(\omega)$ is generally a complex number and in order to ensure the symmetry $K_{12} = K_{21}$.

Note that the decomposition of the variance by frequency is valid for the covariance as well. In fact

$$\text{cov}\left(y_{1t}, y_{2t}\right) = \int_{-\pi}^{+\pi} f_{12}(\omega)d\omega = \int_{-\pi}^{+\pi} \text{cov}\left(d\xi_1(\omega), d\xi_2(\omega)\right).$$

8.3.3 Linear Transformations in the Frequency Domain

On the basis of the spectral representation theorem we know that it is the same to work with the process y or with the stochastic measure $d\xi(\omega)$, $\omega \in [-\pi, +\pi]$. The results established in sections 8.1 and 8.2 can then be expressed in the frequency domain, that is, as a function of

ξ. Let us consider here the case of linear transformations of stationary processes.

Let $\{\mathbf{A}_j\}$ be a sequence of $(m \times n)$ matrices absolutely summable; we can then introduce the stationary process $\tilde{\mathbf{y}}$ defined as

$$\tilde{\mathbf{y}}_t = \sum_{j=-\infty}^{+\infty} \mathbf{A}_j \mathbf{y}_{t-j}. \tag{8.19}$$

Replacing $\mathbf{y}_{t-j}$ in (8.18) by its spectral expression, we get

$$\tilde{\mathbf{y}}_t = \sum_{j=-\infty}^{+\infty} \mathbf{A}_j \int_{-\pi}^{+\pi} \exp -(i(t-j)\omega)d\xi(\omega)$$

$$= \int_{-\pi}^{+\pi} \exp -(it\omega) \sum_{j=-\infty}^{+\infty} \mathbf{A}_j \exp(ij\omega)d\xi(\omega)$$

$$= \int_{-\pi}^{+\pi} \exp -(it\omega)\mathbf{A}\left(\exp(i\omega)\right) d\xi(\omega).$$

This is a spectral representation expression with stochastic measure $d\tilde{\xi}(\omega) = \mathbf{A}\left(\exp(i\omega)\right) d\xi(\omega)$.

Theorem 8.24: *The linear transformation $\tilde{\mathbf{y}}$ of $\mathbf{y}$ by the moving average $\mathbf{A}(L)$ has an associated stochastic measure*

$$d\tilde{\xi}(\omega) = \mathbf{A}\left(\exp(i\omega)\right) d\xi(\omega),$$

where $d\xi$ is the measure associated with $\mathbf{y}$.

From this relationship between stochastic measures we find the relationship among spectral densities

$$f(\omega)d\omega = \text{var}\left(d\tilde{\xi}(\omega)\right) = \text{var}\left(\mathbf{A}\left(\exp(i\omega)\right) d\xi(\omega)\right)$$

$$= \mathbf{A}\left(\exp(i\omega)\right) \text{var}\left(d\xi(\omega)\right) \overline{\mathbf{A}\left(\exp(i\omega)\right)}'$$

$$= \mathbf{A}\left(\exp(i\omega)\right) f(\omega)d\omega \overline{\mathbf{A}\left(\exp(i\omega)\right)}',$$

from which $\tilde{f}(\omega) = \mathbf{A}\left(\exp(i\omega)\right) f(\omega) \overline{\mathbf{A}\left(\exp(i\omega)\right)}'$.

8.3.4 Kolmogorov's Equality

Let $\mathbf{y} = \{\mathbf{y}_t\}$ be a stationary process, whose innovation process $\{\epsilon_t\}$ has a nonsingular variance–covariance matrix Ω. Kolmogorov's Equality establishes a relationship between this matrix and the spectral density function of the process $\mathbf{y}$

$$\ln \det \Omega = \frac{1}{2\pi} \int_{-\pi}^{+\pi} \ln \det\left(2\pi f(\omega)\right) d\omega. \tag{8.20}$$

In the univariate case, the forecast error variance results as the geometric average of $2\pi f(\omega)$

$$\sigma^2 = \exp\left(\frac{1}{2\pi} \int_{-\pi}^{+\pi} \ln\left(2\pi f(\omega)\right) d\omega\right). \qquad (8.21)$$

The Intuition behind the Equality The usual proof of the equality rests on some results of the analytical function theory; for this reason it presents little interest in this context. Rather, we will explain the intuition behind the equality. In order to simplify matters, let us consider the unidimensional case.

(i) Let us consider a random vector $\mathbf{y}$ which can be written in two different ways

$$\mathbf{y} = \mathbf{Q}_1 \boldsymbol{\varepsilon}_1 = \mathbf{Q}_2 \boldsymbol{\varepsilon}_2,$$

where $\mathbf{Q}_1$ and $\mathbf{Q}_2$ are two square matrices of order T with determinants $\det\left(\mathbf{Q}_1\right) = \det\left(\mathbf{Q}_2\right) = \pm 1$ and where $\boldsymbol{\varepsilon}_1$ and $\boldsymbol{\varepsilon}_2$ are two random vectors with diagonal variance–covariance matrices

$$\operatorname{var}\left(\boldsymbol{\varepsilon}_1\right) = \begin{pmatrix} \lambda_{11} & \cdots & 0 \\ \vdots & \ddots & \vdots \\ 0 & \cdots & \lambda_{1T} \end{pmatrix}, \quad \operatorname{var}\left(\boldsymbol{\varepsilon}_2\right) = \begin{pmatrix} \lambda_{21} & \cdots & 0 \\ \vdots & \ddots & \vdots \\ 0 & \cdots & \lambda_{2T} \end{pmatrix}.$$

We have

$$\operatorname{var}\left(\mathbf{y}\right) = \mathbf{Q}_1 \operatorname{var}\left(\boldsymbol{\varepsilon}_1\right) \mathbf{Q}_1' = \mathbf{Q}_2 \operatorname{var}\left(\boldsymbol{\varepsilon}_2\right) \mathbf{Q}_2'$$

$$\det\left(\operatorname{var}\left(\mathbf{y}\right)\right) = \det\left(\mathbf{Q}_1 \operatorname{var}\left(\boldsymbol{\varepsilon}_1\right) \mathbf{Q}_1'\right) = \det\left(\mathbf{Q}_2 \operatorname{var}\left(\boldsymbol{\varepsilon}_2\right) \mathbf{Q}_2'\right)$$

$$\Leftrightarrow \det\left(\operatorname{var}\left(\boldsymbol{\varepsilon}_1\right)\right) = \det\left(\operatorname{var}\left(\boldsymbol{\varepsilon}_2\right)\right)$$

$$\Leftrightarrow \frac{1}{T} \sum_{t=1}^{T} \ln \lambda_{1t} = \frac{1}{T} \sum_{t=1}^{T} \ln \lambda_{2t}.$$

Although in our case we are dealing with processes, that is with infinite-order vectors, we have available two expressions of the previous type.

(ii) We know that the moving average decomposition is

$$y_t = \epsilon_t + h_1 \epsilon_{t-1} + \ldots + h_j \epsilon_{t-j} + \ldots$$

and $\operatorname{var}\left(\epsilon_t\right) = \sigma^2$. In infinite matrix form this becomes

$$\mathbf{y} = \begin{pmatrix} \cdots & 1 & 0 & 0 & \cdots & 0 & \cdots \\ \cdots & h_1 & 1 & 0 & \cdots & 0 & \cdots \\ \cdots & h_2 & h_1 & 1 & \cdots & 0 & \cdots \\ & \vdots & \vdots & \vdots & \vdots & \ddots & \vdots \\ & \vdots & \vdots & \vdots & & 1 & \cdots \end{pmatrix} \boldsymbol{\varepsilon}.$$

The transformation matrix $\mathbf{Q}_1$ is triangular with 1's on the main diagonal. Its "determinant" is equal to $\det(\mathbf{Q}_1) = 1$. On the other hand, the components of $\boldsymbol{\epsilon}$ are uncorrelated, with the same variance σ^2. Therefore

$$\lim_{T \to +\infty} \frac{1}{T} \sum_{t=1}^{T} \ln \operatorname{var}(\epsilon_t) = \ln \sigma^2.$$

(iii) We have the spectral representation

$$\mathbf{y}_t = \int_{-\pi}^{+\pi} \exp -(it\omega) d\xi(\omega).$$

A difficulty with this representation is that the number of components of $\mathbf{y}$ is countable whereas $d\xi$ is continuous. To solve this difficulty, we can make the integral discrete. For $t = 1, \cdots, T$ we can partition the interval $(-\pi, +\pi)$ in T intervals of the same length. Let us set

$$\omega_j = -\pi + \frac{2\pi j}{T}, \quad j = 1, \ldots, T,$$

and let us approximate y_t as

$$y_t \approx \sum_{j=1}^{T} \exp -(it\omega_j) \left(\xi(\omega_j) - \xi(\omega_{j-1}) \right)$$

$$= \sum_{j=1}^{T} \frac{1}{\sqrt{T}} \exp(-it\omega_j) \sqrt{T} \left(\xi(\omega_j) - \xi(\omega_{j-1}) \right).$$

We have then for any t and τ

$$\sum_{j=1}^{T} \frac{1}{\sqrt{T}} \exp(-it\omega_j) \frac{1}{\sqrt{T}} \overline{\exp(-i\tau\omega_j)} = \frac{1}{T} \sum_{j=1}^{T} \exp(-i(t-\tau)\omega_j)$$

$$\approx \frac{1}{2\pi} \int_{-\pi}^{+\pi} \exp -(it\omega) \exp(i\tau\omega) d\omega = \delta_{t\tau}.$$

The coefficients $\frac{1}{\sqrt{T}} \exp(-it\omega_j)$, $j = 1, \ldots, T$, $t = 1, \ldots, T$ approximately form an orthogonal matrix $\mathbf{Q}_2$, and $|\det(\mathbf{Q}_2)| \approx 1$. Moreover, the variables $\sqrt{T}(\xi(\omega_j) - \xi(\omega_{j-1}))$ are uncorrelated with variance $T(F(\omega_j) - F(\omega_{j-1}))$, where F is the cumulative distribution function associated with f

$$T\left(F(\omega_j) - F(\omega_{j-1})\right) \approx Tf(\omega_j)(\omega_j - \omega_{j-1}) = 2\pi f(\omega_j).$$

We can then compute the average of the logarithms of the variances of the components of ϵ_2

$$\lim_{T \to +\infty} \frac{1}{T} \sum_{j=1}^{T} \ln\left(2\pi f(\omega_j)\right) = \frac{1}{2\pi} \int_{-\pi}^{+\pi} \ln\left(2\pi f(\omega)\right) d\omega.$$

(iv) Comparing the two geometric means, we have

$$\ln \sigma^2 = \frac{1}{2\pi} \int_{-\pi}^{+\pi} \ln\left(2\pi f(\omega)\right) d\omega.$$

□

We can give another interesting interpretation to Kolmogorov's equality in the univariate case. We have seen in the proof that if λ_{jT}, $j = 1, \ldots, T$ are the eigenvalues of the variance–covariance matrix

$$\Sigma_T = \text{var} \begin{pmatrix} y_1 \\ \vdots \\ y_T \end{pmatrix},$$

we have

$$\lim_{T \to +\infty} \frac{1}{T} \sum_{j=1}^{T} \ln \lambda_{jT} = \frac{1}{2\pi} \int_{-\pi}^{+\pi} \ln\left(2\pi f(\omega)\right) d\omega.$$

Let us introduce the uniform distribution μ on the interval $[-\pi, \pi]$. We have

$$\lim_{T \to +\infty} \frac{1}{T} \sum_{j=1}^{T} \ln \lambda_{jT} = \frac{1}{2\pi} \int_{-\pi}^{+\pi} \ln\left(2\pi f(\omega)\right) d\mu(\omega)$$

$$= \int_{0}^{+\infty} \ln \lambda \, d\mu^{2\pi f}(\lambda),$$

where $\mu^{2\pi f}$ indicates the transformed distribution of the uniform distribution through the mapping $2\pi f$.

We can then easily show (cf. Grenander and Szegö, 1958) that the same relationship exists whenever the function ln is replaced by any other bounded continuous function, say h

$$\lim_{T \to +\infty} \frac{1}{T} \sum_{j=1}^{T} h\left(\lambda_{jT}\right) = \int_{0}^{+\infty} h(\lambda) d\mu^{2\pi f}(\lambda), \quad \forall \text{ continuous bounded } h.$$

This theorem is equivalent to the convergence in distribution of the empirical distribution of the eigenvalues.

Theorem 8.25: *Let*

$$\Sigma_T = \text{var} \begin{pmatrix} y_1 \\ \vdots \\ y_T \end{pmatrix}.$$

The empirical distribution of the eigenvalues of Σ_T converges in distribution to the transformation of the uniform distribution on $[-\pi, +\pi]$ by the mapping $2\pi f$.

8.4 Appendix
Singular Value Decomposition Theorem

8.4.1 Some Notions

Let us recall some classic results of matrix theory. If $\mathbf{M}$ is a square matrix of order n, we can define its square both as the matrix $\mathbf{MM'}$ or as $\mathbf{M'M}$. These two matrices are symmetric, and positive definite. They have positive real eigenvalues and it is possible to choose for each of these matrices orthonormal bases of eigenvectors. Let us establish how this choice of basis can be done.

Theorem 8.26:

(i) *Let us note $\lambda_1^2 \geq \lambda_2^2 \geq \ldots \geq \lambda_J^2$ the strictly positive eigenvalues of $\mathbf{MM'}$ arranged in a decreasing order, and $\mathbf{u}_j$, $j = 1, \ldots, J$ an orthonormal system of associated eigenvectors. The system*

$$v_j = \frac{\mathbf{M'}u_j}{\lambda_j}, \ j = 1, \ldots, J,$$

is an orthonormal system of eigenvectors of $\mathbf{MM'}$ associated with the same set of eigenvalues.

(ii) *In particular $\mathbf{MM'}$ and $\mathbf{M'M}$ have the same set of eigenvalues with the same order of multiplicity.*

PROOF:

(i) We have, in fact

$$\mathbf{v}_k' \mathbf{v}_j = \frac{\mathbf{u}_k' \mathbf{MM'} \mathbf{u}_j}{\lambda_k \lambda_j} = \frac{\lambda_j}{\lambda_k} \mathbf{u}_k' \mathbf{u}_j = \delta_{kj},$$

where δ_{kj} is Kronecker's delta. Thus the system is orthonormal.

(ii)   We need to prove that $\mathbf{v}_j$ is just the eigenvector of $\mathbf{MM}'$ associated with λ_j^2. We have

$$\mathbf{MM}'\mathbf{v}_j = \frac{\mathbf{M}'\mathbf{MM}'\mathbf{u}_j}{\lambda_j} = \frac{\mathbf{M}'(\lambda_j^2\mathbf{u}_j)}{\lambda_j} = \lambda_j^2\mathbf{v}_j.$$

□

In matrix form we have

$$\mathbf{MM}' = \mathbf{U}\mathbf{\Lambda}^2\mathbf{U}',$$

$$\mathbf{M}'\mathbf{M} = \mathbf{V}\mathbf{\Lambda}^2\mathbf{V}',$$

$$\mathbf{U}'\mathbf{U} = \mathbf{I},$$

$$\mathbf{V}'\mathbf{V} = \mathbf{I},$$

$$\mathbf{M}'\mathbf{U} = \mathbf{V}\mathbf{\Lambda},$$

$$\mathbf{MV} = \mathbf{U}\mathbf{\Lambda},$$

where $\mathbf{U} = (\mathbf{u}_1,\ldots,\mathbf{u}_J)$, $V = (\mathbf{v}_1,\ldots,\mathbf{v}_J)$ and

$$\mathbf{\Lambda} = \begin{pmatrix} \lambda_1 & \cdots & 0 \\ \vdots & \ddots & \vdots \\ 0 & \cdots & \lambda_J \end{pmatrix}.$$

Corollary: Singular Value Decomposition *Any square matrix* $\mathbf{M}$ *can be written as:* $\mathbf{M} = \mathbf{U}\mathbf{\Lambda}\mathbf{V}'$, *where* $\mathbf{\Lambda}$ *is diagonal with strictly positive terms and* $\mathbf{U}$ *and* $\mathbf{V}$ *satisfy* $\mathbf{U}'\mathbf{U} = \mathbf{V}'\mathbf{V} = \mathbf{I}$.

PROOF: $\mathbf{V}$ can be completed by column vectors of the nullspace of $\mathbf{M}$, equal to the nullspace of $\mathbf{M}'\mathbf{M}$, so as to obtain an orthogonal matrix $\mathbf{V}^*$ satisfying $\mathbf{MV}^* = \mathbf{U}\mathbf{\Lambda}^*$, with $\mathbf{\Lambda}^* = (\mathbf{\Lambda},\mathbf{0})$. We deduce that $\mathbf{M} = \mathbf{U}\mathbf{\Lambda}^*\mathbf{V}^{-1} = \mathbf{U}\mathbf{\Lambda}^*\mathbf{V}^{*\prime} = \mathbf{U}\mathbf{\Lambda}\mathbf{V}$. □

This decomposition can be written in explicit form in terms of the vectors $\mathbf{u}_j$ and $\mathbf{v}_j$

$$\mathbf{M} = (\mathbf{u}_1,\ldots,\mathbf{u}_J)\begin{pmatrix} \lambda_1 & \cdots & 0 \\ \vdots & \ddots & \vdots \\ 0 & \cdots & \lambda_J \end{pmatrix}\begin{pmatrix} \mathbf{v}_1' \\ \vdots \\ \mathbf{v}_J' \end{pmatrix},$$

that is

$$\mathbf{M} = \sum_{j=1}^{J} \lambda_j\mathbf{u}_j\mathbf{v}_j'.$$

Note that the corollary can be used to find other types of decompositions.

Corollary: *Let* $\mathbf{Q}$ *and* $\mathbf{S}$ *be two symmetric and positive definite matrices of order n. Any matrix* $\mathbf{M}$ *can be written as*

$$\mathbf{M} = \mathbf{U\Lambda V'}$$

with $\mathbf{\Lambda}$ *diagonal with strictly positive terms,* $\mathbf{U'QU} = \mathbf{I}$, *and* $\mathbf{V'SV} = \mathbf{I}$.

It is possible to change the metrics on the spaces used, and these changes can be done independently one from the other.

PROOF: Applying the singular value decomposition to the matrix $\mathbf{Q}^{-1/2}\mathbf{M}\mathbf{S}^{-1/2}$ we can see that $\mathbf{Q}^{-1/2}\mathbf{M}\mathbf{S}^{-1/2} = \tilde{\mathbf{U}}\mathbf{\Lambda}\tilde{\mathbf{V}}'$, with $\tilde{\mathbf{U}}'\tilde{\mathbf{U}} = \mathbf{I}$, $\tilde{\mathbf{V}}'\tilde{\mathbf{V}} = \mathbf{I}$. Therefore $\mathbf{M} = \mathbf{Q}^{1/2}\tilde{\mathbf{U}}\mathbf{\Lambda}\tilde{\mathbf{V}}'\mathbf{S}^{1/2}$ and it suffices to pose $\mathbf{U} = \mathbf{Q}^{1/2}\tilde{\mathbf{U}}$ and $\mathbf{V} = \mathbf{S}^{1/2}\tilde{\mathbf{V}}$ to obtain the result. $\square$

8.5 Exercises

Exercise 8.1: Let us consider the hypotheses of the lemma preceding theorem 8.17.

(i)   Prove that $\varrho(\mathbf{P}) = \varrho(\mathbf{P}^*) = \varrho(\mathbf{R}) = \varrho(\mathbf{R}^*) = \underline{K}$;
(ii) Verify that $\mathbf{R} = (\mathbf{P}'\mathbf{P})^{-1} \mathbf{P}'\mathbf{P}^*\mathbf{R}^*$;
(iii) Show that $\varrho(\mathbf{P}'\mathbf{P}^*) = \underline{K}$ and derive the result of the Lemma.

Exercise 8.2: Develop an algorithm (as in section 8.2.6) by decomposing the matrix $\bar{\mathcal{H}}_{NN'}$ according to a singular value decomposition with a different metric from the identity (use the corollary in the appendix).

Exercise 8.3: Let us consider a real stationary process with spectral representation

$$y_t = \int_{-\pi}^{+\pi} \exp -(it\omega)d\xi(\omega).$$

Let us denote the real, respectively, imaginary parts of $\xi(\omega)$ as $u(\omega)$ and $v(\omega)$. Show that

$$y_t = \int_{-\pi}^{+\pi} cos(\omega t)du(\omega) + \int_{-\pi}^{+\pi} sin(\omega t)dv(\omega).$$

Let us denote by u_j, v_j, $j = 1, \ldots, n$ the components of $\mathbf{u}$ and $\mathbf{v}$. Show that

$$E\left(du_j^2(\omega)\right) = E\left(dv_j^2(\omega)\right) = \frac{1}{2}f_{jj}(\omega)d\omega,$$

and

$$E\left(du_j(\omega)dv_j(\omega)\right) = 0.$$

Exercise 8.4: Let us consider a bivariate stationary process

$$\mathbf{y}_t = \begin{pmatrix} y_{1t} \\ y_{2t} \end{pmatrix},$$

and let

$$y_{2t} = \sum_{-\infty}^{+\infty} a_j y_{1,t-j} + \epsilon_t,$$

where $\{\epsilon_t\}$ is a stationary process uncorrelated with the process $\{y_{1t}\}$.

Let us pose

$$y_{jt} = \int_{-\pi}^{+\pi} \exp -(itw) d\xi_j(w), \; j = 1, 2$$

$$\epsilon_t = \int_{-\pi}^{+\pi} \exp -(itw) d\xi_\epsilon(w).$$

Show that

$$d\xi_2(w) = a\left(\exp(iw)\right) d\xi_1(w) + d\xi_\epsilon(w),$$

with

$$a(\exp(iw)) = \sum_{h=-\infty}^{+\infty} a_h \exp(ihw).$$

Denoting the spectral density functions of y_1, y_2, and ϵ as f_{11}, f_{22}, and f_ϵ respectively, show that

$$f_{22}(w) = \mid a(\exp(iw)) \mid^2 f_{11}(w) + f_\epsilon(w).$$

Show also that

$$f_{21}(w) = a(\exp(iw)) f_{11}(w).$$

Derive from this result that the square of the coherence between y_{1t} and y_{2t} is

$$K_{12}^2(w) = \frac{\mid a\left(\exp(iw)\right) \mid^2 f_{11}(w)}{f_{22}(w)} = 1 - \frac{f_\epsilon(w)}{f_{22}(w)},$$

and that the coherence is equal to 1 if and only if y_{2t} is a linear function of the $y_{1,t-j}$'s.

Exercise 8.5: Let us consider a bivariate stationary moving average process

$$\begin{pmatrix} y_{1t} \\ y_{2t} \end{pmatrix} = \begin{pmatrix} \Theta_{11}(L) & \Theta_{12}(L) \\ \Theta_{21}(L) & \Theta_{22}(L) \end{pmatrix} \begin{pmatrix} \epsilon_{1t} \\ \epsilon_{2t} \end{pmatrix},$$

with var $\begin{pmatrix} \epsilon_{1t} \\ \epsilon_{2t} \end{pmatrix} = \mathbf{I}$. Let us consider the linear regression of y_{2t} on the $y_{1,t-h}$'s; this regression is denoted as $\sum_{h=-\infty}^{+\infty} a_h y_{1,t-h}$. Use the results of the previous exercise to compute the Fourier transform of the a_h

$$a(\exp(iw)) = \sum_{h=-\infty}^{+\infty} a_h(\exp(ihw))$$

as a function of

$$\Theta_{11}(\exp(iw)), \;\; \Theta_{22}(\exp(iw)), \;\; \Theta_{12}(\exp(iw)), \;\; \Theta_{21}(\exp(iw)).$$

9

Estimation and Testing
(Stationary Case)

In chapter 6, we have presented the approach proposed by Box and Jenkins to analyze univariate time-series. This consists in deriving an ARMA or ARIMA model compatible with the data, in order to perform a number of diagnostic checks concerning the estimated model and to forecast future values of the series. In this chapter we address the issues related to statistical inference in a more rigorous fashion. Since the main results available concern the asymptotic behavior of the estimators, in section 1 we present some limit theorems which generalize the law of large numbers and the central limit theorem to the case of stationary processes. It is then possible to derive the asymptotic behavior of the empirical means, of the periodogram, of the empirical autocovariances and partial autocovariances.

In section 2, we discuss the maximum likelihood estimation of the parameters in a univariate time-series model. We check whether the classical sampling theory results still hold, that is whether the estimator is consistent, asymptotically normal, and its asymptotic variance is the inverse of Fisher's Information Matrix associated to the model. We give various forms of this matrix according to the representation (time domain, frequency domain, etc.) chosen to describe the series.

In the third section, we recall the main testing procedures currently used in statistics: the likelihood ratio, Wald, Lagrange multiplier (or score) tests. We develop in greater detail the latter type of test, which is often the simplest to use. We give a complete description of how this testing procedure is used in order to verify the hypothesis of white noise.

Finally in the last section, we generalize these results to the case of multivariate time-series.

9.1 Limit Distributions of Empirical Moments

The first- and second-order moments of a stationary process, that is the mean, the autocovariance function, the spectral density function, and so on, are unknown in reality and have to be estimated from a sample of observations. A first suggestion is to estimate the theoretical moments by their empirical counterparts. In this section we provide the main asymptotic properties of empirical moments, and refer the reader to the proofs in Anderson (1971) and Fuller (1976).

9.1.1 Empirical Mean

Let us denote by $\mathbf{y}_1, \ldots, \mathbf{y}_T$ the available observations.

Theorem 9.1: *Let y be a stationary process having an infinite moving average representation*

$$\mathbf{y}_t = \sum_{j=0}^{\infty} \mathbf{H}_j \boldsymbol{\varepsilon}_{t-j}, \quad \sum_{j=0}^{\infty} \parallel \mathbf{H}_j \parallel^2 < +\infty.$$

Then $\bar{\mathbf{y}}_T = \frac{1}{T} \sum_{t=1}^{T} \mathbf{y}_t$ converges to 0 in quadratic mean.

The result can be easily extended to include processes of the form

$$\mathbf{y}_t^* = \mathbf{m} + \sum_{j=0}^{\infty} \mathbf{H}_j \boldsymbol{\varepsilon}_{t-j}.$$

It follows from theorem 9.1 that $\bar{\mathbf{y}}_T^*$ is a consistent estimator of the mean $\mathbf{m}$ of the process.

The inspection of the variance–covariance matrix of $\sqrt{T}\bar{\mathbf{y}}_T$ gives an idea of the speed of convergence. In fact, we have

$$\mathrm{var}\left(\sqrt{T}\bar{\mathbf{y}}_T\right) = \frac{1}{T}\mathrm{var}\left(\sum_{t=1}^{T} \mathbf{y}_t\right) = \frac{1}{T}\sum_{k=1-T}^{T-1}(T - \mid k \mid)\boldsymbol{\Gamma}(k)$$

$$= \sum_{k=1-T}^{T-1}(1 - \frac{\mid k \mid}{T})\boldsymbol{\Gamma}(k) \approx \sum_{k=-\infty}^{+\infty}\boldsymbol{\Gamma}(k) = 2\pi\mathbf{f}(0).$$

Now we are in the condition of understanding the more precise result below, which states the asymptotic normality of the empirical mean.

Theorem 9.2: *Let* $\mathbf{y}_t = \sum_{j=0}^{\infty} \mathbf{H}_j \boldsymbol{\epsilon}_{t-j}$ *be an infinite moving average stationary process based on a vector of independent white noise distur- bances; if the spectral density function* $\mathbf{f}$ *is bounded, continuous in 0, and such that* $\det \mathbf{f}(0) \neq 0$, *the variable* $\sqrt{T} \bar{\mathbf{y}}_T$ *is asymptotically normal*

$$\sqrt{T} \bar{\mathbf{y}}_T \xrightarrow{d} \mathcal{N}(0, 2\pi \mathbf{f}(0)) = \mathcal{N}(0, \sum_{k=-\infty}^{\infty} \mathbf{\Gamma}(k)).$$

Example 9.1: For an ARMA(p, q) process satisfying the relationship

$$\Phi(L)x_t = \Theta(L)\epsilon_t,$$

where ϵ is an independent white noise, we get

$$f(0) = \frac{\sigma^2}{2\pi} \frac{\Theta(1)^2}{\Phi(1)^2} = \frac{1}{2\pi} \sum_{k=-\infty}^{+\infty} \gamma(k).$$

Therefore

$$\sqrt{T} \bar{x}_T \xrightarrow{d} \mathcal{N}\left(0, \sigma^2 \frac{\Theta(1)^2}{\Phi(1)^2}\right).$$

9.1.2 The Periodogram

The periodogram is defined by

$$\mathbf{I}_T(\omega) = \frac{1}{2\pi} \frac{1}{T} (\sum_{t=1}^{T} \mathbf{y}_t \exp(i\omega t))(\sum_{t=1}^{T} \mathbf{y}_t' \exp -(i\omega t))$$

$$= \frac{1}{2\pi} \sum_{k=-(T-1)}^{(T-1)} (\frac{1}{T} \sum_t \mathbf{y}_t \mathbf{y}_{t-k}') \exp(i\omega k)$$

$$= \frac{1}{2\pi} \sum_{k=-(T-1)}^{T-1} \hat{\mathbf{\Gamma}}_T(k) \exp(i\omega k).$$

It is a natural estimator of the spectral density function

$$\mathbf{f}(\omega) = \frac{1}{2\pi} \sum_{k=-\infty}^{+\infty} \mathbf{\Gamma}(k) \exp(i\omega k).$$

However, when k is close to the boundaries $\pm(T-1)$ the estimated au- tocovariances $\hat{\mathbf{\Gamma}}_t(k)$ are computed from a small number of observations. Therefore, they are a bad estimate of the actual autocovariances. This explains the inconsistency result in theorem 9.3.

Theorem 9.3: *The periodogram* $\mathbf{I}_T(\omega)$ *is an asymptotically unbiased estimator of the spectral density function* $\mathbf{f}(\omega)$, *but it is not consistent.*

The inconsistency of the periodogram does not forbid its use. Given the estimator is unbiased, we could hope that although we are making a mistake on the value of the function f, we can have a good idea of its general form. But this is not true in practice. We can show that in the univariate case

$$\lim_{T \to +\infty} \text{var}\,(I_T(\omega)) = \begin{cases} f^2(\omega) & \text{if } \omega \neq 0, \pm\pi, \\ 2f^2(\omega) & \text{if } \omega = 0, \pm\pi, \end{cases}$$

$$\lim_{T \to +\infty} \text{cov}\,(I_T(\omega), I_t(\omega')) = 0, \quad \text{if } \omega \neq \omega'.$$

Since the periodogram values associated with different frequencies are not correlated, an irregular and erratic shape for the function I_T will result. Nevertheless, the periodogram is the basis on which to build consistent estimators. The idea is to suppress the erratic character of the function I_T by smoothing it. For example, this can be done by considering some integrals of continuous functions with respect to the measure of density $I_T(\omega)$ on $[-\pi, \pi]$.

The results below are given under the normality assumption for the white noise. Even though this condition is not necessary for consistency and for asymptotic normality, it intervenes in a crucial way in the determination of the asymptotic variance. Indeed, when normality is not satisfied, we have to add to the asymptotic variance expression a correction term which is a function of the kurtosis of the noise

$$\frac{E(\epsilon_t^4)}{E(\epsilon_t^2)^2}.$$

Theorem 9.4: *Let us denote by g a continuous bounded complex function defined on $(-\pi, \pi)$. We can write*

$$\mathbf{I}_T(g) = \int_{-\pi}^{\pi} g(\omega)\mathbf{I}_T(\omega)\,d\omega.$$

If $\mathbf{y}$ is a Gaussian stationary process having an infinite moving average representation, we have

$$\mathbf{I}_T(g) = \int_{-\pi}^{\pi} g(\omega)\mathbf{I}_T(\omega)\,d\omega \xrightarrow{a.s.} \mathbf{f}(g) = \int_{-\pi}^{\pi} g(\omega)\mathbf{f}(\omega)\,d\omega.$$

Moreover we obtain asymptotic normality. In order to keep the notation simple, we give the result for the univariate case only. The version for the multivariate case is obtained by applying the result on all the linear combinations of the coordinates of $\mathbf{y}$.

Theorem 9.5: *Let x be a unidimensional Gaussian stationary process, having an infinite moving average representation, and such that*

$$\sum_{k=-\infty}^{+\infty} \mid k\gamma(k) \mid < +\infty.$$

Then, for any $g_1,\ldots,g_p$, bounded continuous complex function on $(-\pi, \pi)$, we have

$$\sqrt{T} \begin{pmatrix} I_T(g_1) - f(g_1) \\ \vdots \\ I_T(g_p) - f(g_p) \end{pmatrix} \xrightarrow{d} \mathcal{N}(0, \Omega),$$

where

$$\omega_{hl} = \mathrm{acov}\left(\sqrt{T}(I_T(g_h) - f(g_h)), \sqrt{T}\,(I_t(g_l) - f(g_l))\right)$$

$$= 4\pi \int_{-\pi}^{\pi} g_h(w)\overline{g_l(\omega)}f^2(\omega)\,d\omega.$$

9.1.3 Empirical Autocovariances

The results concerning the periodogram apply directly to the study of the empirical autocovariances. Let us show the details for the univariate case. We have

$$\gamma(k) = \int_{-\pi}^{\pi} \cos(\omega k)f(\omega)\,d\omega,$$

$$\hat{\gamma}_T(k) = \int_{-\pi}^{\pi} \cos(\omega k)I_T(\omega)\,d\omega.$$

One just needs to perform the inverse Fourier transform of the relationship

$$I_T(\omega) = \frac{1}{2\pi} \sum_{k=-(T-1)}^{T-1} \hat{\gamma}_T(k) \exp(i\omega k).$$

From theorems 9.4 and 9.5, we then obtain

Theorem 9.6: *Under the same conditions of regularity as in theorems 9.4 and 9.5*

(i) $\hat{\gamma}_T(k)$ *is a consistent estimator of $\gamma(k)$;*
(ii)   *for all values of K*

$$\sqrt{T} \begin{pmatrix} \hat{\gamma}_T(1) - \gamma(1) \\ \vdots \\ \hat{\gamma}_T(K) - \gamma(K) \end{pmatrix} \xrightarrow{d} \mathcal{N}(0, \Omega),$$

where

$$\omega_{kl} = \text{acov}\left(\sqrt{T}(\hat{\gamma}_T(k) - \gamma(k)), \sqrt{T}(\hat{\gamma}_T(l) - \gamma(l))\right)$$

$$= 4\pi \int_{-\pi}^{\pi} \cos(\omega k) \cos(\omega l) f^2(\omega)\, d\omega.$$

The asymptotic variance is given here in the frequency domain, but its expression in the time domain follows quite easily.

Theorem 9.7:

$$\omega_{kl} = \text{acov}\left(\sqrt{T}(\hat{\gamma}_T(k) - \gamma(k)), \sqrt{T}(\hat{\gamma}_T(l) - \gamma(l))\right)$$

$$= \sum_{j=-\infty}^{+\infty} \gamma(j)\gamma(j + k + l) + \sum_{j=-\infty}^{+\infty} \gamma(j)\gamma(j + k - l).$$

PROOF: We have

$$\omega_{kl} = 2\pi \int_{-\pi}^{\pi} \left(\cos\left(\omega(k + l)\right) + \cos\left(\omega(k - l)\right)\right) f^2(\omega) d\omega.$$

Since $\int_{-\pi}^{\pi} \cos(\omega k) f^2(\omega) d\omega$ is the coefficient of $\exp(-ik\omega)$ in the Fourier series of $2\pi f^2(\omega)$ and is equal to $\frac{1}{2\pi}\sum_{j=-\infty}^{+\infty} \gamma(j)\gamma(j - k)$, the proof is trivial. $\square$

Example 9.2: In the case of the process $x_t = \epsilon_t$ (i.e., a white noise), we have

$$\omega_{kl} = \frac{\sigma^4}{2\pi} \int_{-\pi}^{\pi} \left(\cos\left(\omega(k + l)\right) + \cos\left(\omega(k - l)\right)\right) d\omega$$

$$= \frac{\sigma^4}{2\pi} \int_{-\pi}^{\pi} \cos\left(\omega(k - l)\right) d\omega$$

$$= \begin{cases} 0, & \text{if } k \neq l \\ \sigma^4, & \text{if } k = l. \end{cases}$$

In particular, for a white noise, the empirical autocovariances of various orders are asymptotically independent.

9.1.4 Application of Previous Results

From the asymptotic properties of the mean and empirical autocovariances we derive the limit theorems of a large number of other estimators.

Functions of Asymptotically Normal Estimators   Let $\hat{\boldsymbol{\theta}}_T$ be a consistent estimator of a parameter vector $\boldsymbol{\theta} \in \boldsymbol{R}^p$. We suppose that $\sqrt{T}(\hat{\boldsymbol{\theta}}_T - \boldsymbol{\theta})$ converges in distribution to a normal distribution $\mathcal{N}(\mathbf{0}, \boldsymbol{\Sigma})$. This implies in particular that $\hat{\boldsymbol{\theta}}_T$ converges in probability to $\boldsymbol{\theta}$. Let us then consider a function $\mathbf{g}$ defined from $\boldsymbol{R}^p$ to $\boldsymbol{R}^q$ and the problem of estimating $\mathbf{g}(\boldsymbol{\theta})$. A natural estimator of this function is $\mathbf{g}(\hat{\boldsymbol{\theta}}_T)$.

Theorem 9.8:   *If $\mathbf{g}$ is continuous, $\mathbf{g}(\hat{\boldsymbol{\theta}}_T)$ converges in probability to* $\mathbf{g}(\boldsymbol{\theta})$.

This property (see Monfort, 1980, chapter 23, theorem 8) shows that $\mathbf{g}(\hat{\boldsymbol{\theta}}_T)$ is a consistent estimator of $\mathbf{g}(\boldsymbol{\theta})$.

In order to study the asymptotic distribution of $\mathbf{g}(\hat{\boldsymbol{\theta}}_T)$, we assume $\mathbf{g}$ to be a continuously differentiable function, and we can expand (in probability) $\mathbf{g}(\hat{\boldsymbol{\theta}}_T)$ in a neighborhood of the value $\boldsymbol{\theta}$

$$\sqrt{T}\left(\mathbf{g}(\hat{\boldsymbol{\theta}}_T) - \mathbf{g}(\boldsymbol{\theta})\right) \approx \frac{\partial \mathbf{g}}{\partial \boldsymbol{\theta}'}(\boldsymbol{\theta})\sqrt{T}(\hat{\boldsymbol{\theta}}_T - \boldsymbol{\theta}).$$

Thus, the difference between the estimator and its limit is asymptotically similar to a linear transformation of a normal vector. This gives

Theorem 9.9:   *If $\mathbf{g}$ is continuously differentiable in a neighborhood of* $\boldsymbol{\theta}$, *we have*

$$\sqrt{T}\left(\mathbf{g}(\hat{\boldsymbol{\theta}}_T) - \mathbf{g}(\boldsymbol{\theta})\right) \overset{\mathrm{d}}{\to} \mathcal{N}\left(\mathbf{0}, \frac{\partial \mathbf{g}}{\partial \boldsymbol{\theta}'}(\boldsymbol{\theta})\boldsymbol{\Sigma}\frac{\partial \mathbf{g}'}{\partial \boldsymbol{\theta}}(\boldsymbol{\theta})\right).$$

Asymptotic Behavior of $\hat{\rho}_T(k) = \hat{\gamma}_T(k)/\hat{\gamma}_T(0)$ We have

$$\sqrt{T}\left(\hat{\rho}_T(k) - \rho(k)\right) = \sqrt{T}\left(\frac{\hat{\gamma}_T(k)}{\hat{\gamma}_T(0)} - \frac{\gamma(k)}{\gamma(0)}\right)$$

$$= \sqrt{T}\,\frac{\hat{\gamma}_T(k)\gamma(0) - \hat{\gamma}_T(0)\gamma(k)}{\hat{\gamma}_T(0)\gamma(0)}$$

$$\approx \sqrt{T}\,\frac{\gamma(0)\left(\hat{\gamma}_T(k) - \gamma(k)\right) - \gamma(k)\left(\hat{\gamma}_T(0) - \gamma(0)\right)}{\gamma(0)^2}$$

$$= \frac{1}{\gamma(0)}\sqrt{T}\left(\hat{\gamma}_T(k) - \gamma(k)\right) - \frac{1}{\gamma(0)}\rho(k)\sqrt{T}\left(\hat{\gamma}_T(0) - \gamma(0)\right).$$

Let $\omega_{k,l}$ be the asymptotic covariance between $\sqrt{T}\left(\hat{\gamma}_T(k) - \gamma(k)\right)$ and $\sqrt{T}\left(\hat{\gamma}_T(l) - \gamma(l)\right)$ given in theorem 9.7; we can easily derive the asymptotic behavior of empirical autocorrelations from theorems 9.8, 9.9, and from the expansion above.

Theorem 9.10:

(i) $\hat{\rho}_T(k)$ *is a consistent estimator of* $\rho(k)$.

(ii) *The vector* $\sqrt{T}\left(\hat{\rho}_T(1) - \rho(1), \ldots, \hat{\rho}_T(K) - \rho(K)\right)'$ *is asymptotically normal, with a variance–covariance matrix with entries*

$$\text{acov}\left(\sqrt{T}\left(\hat{\rho}_T(k) - \rho(k)\right), \sqrt{T}\left(\hat{\rho}_T(l) - \rho(l)\right)\right)$$

$$= \frac{1}{\gamma(0)^2}\omega_{kl} - \frac{1}{\gamma(0)^2}\rho(k)\omega_{0l} - \frac{1}{\gamma(0)^2}\rho(l)\omega_{0k}$$

$$+ \frac{1}{\gamma(0)^2}\rho(k)\rho(l)\omega_{00}.$$

We can write this expression in terms of correlations only as

$$\text{acov}\left(\sqrt{T}\left(\hat{\rho}_T(k) - \rho(k)\right), \sqrt{T}\left(\hat{\rho}_T(l) - \rho(l)\right)\right)$$

$$= \sum_{j=-\infty}^{+\infty}\left(\rho(j)\rho(j+k+l) + \rho(j)\rho(j+k-l)\right)$$

$$- 2\rho(k)\sum_{j=-\infty}^{+\infty}\rho(j)\rho(j+l) - 2\rho(l)\sum_{j=-\infty}^{+\infty}\rho(j)\rho(j+k)$$

$$+ 2\rho(k)\rho(l)\sum_{j=-\infty}^{+\infty}\rho(j)^2.$$

Example 9.3: Let us consider a pure moving average process $MA(q)$ $x_t = \epsilon_t + \theta_1\epsilon_{t-1}\ldots + \theta_q\epsilon_{t-q}$. We know that the correlations vanish after the order $q+1$. Then, if we examine the asymptotic variance of $\hat{\rho}_T(k)$, for $k > q+1$, we have

$$\text{avar}\left(\sqrt{T}\left(\hat{\rho}_T(k) - \rho(k)\right)\right)$$

$$= \sum_{j=-\infty}^{+\infty}\left(\rho(j)\rho(j+2k) + \rho(j)^2\right) - 4\rho(k)\sum_{j=-\infty}^{+\infty}\rho(j)\rho(j+k)$$

$$+ 2\rho(k)^2\sum_{j=-\infty}^{+\infty}\rho(j)^2.$$

Recalling that for $k \geq q+1$, we have $\rho(k) = 0$, $\rho(j)\rho(j+2k) = 0$ $\forall j$ and $\rho(j) = 0$, if $|j| \geq q+1$, the formula can be simplified to give

$$\text{avar}\left(\sqrt{T}\left(\hat{\rho}_T(k) - \rho_T(k)\right)\right) = \sum_{j=-q}^{q}\rho(j)^2 = 1 + 2\sum_{j=1}^{q}\rho(j)^2, \text{ if } k \geq q+1.$$

In particular, this expression does not depend on the index k. The expression above is useful especially when we need to determine the confidence intervals in the representation of the correlogram (cf. section 6.3).

Moving Average of Empirical Autocovariances   Let us consider a univariate stationary process $\{x\}$ and let us denote by $\hat{\gamma}_T(k)$ its empirical autocovariances. We now examine the moving averages of these autocovariances.

Let $a_1, \ldots, a_p$ be p real numbers. We define

$$\hat{\psi}_T(h) = \hat{\gamma}_T(h) + a_1 \hat{\gamma}_T(h-1) \ldots + a_p \hat{\gamma}_T(h-p).$$

The associated parameters are

$$\psi(h) = \gamma(h) + a_1 \gamma(h-1) \ldots + a_p \gamma(h-p).$$

We obtain directly from the asymptotic properties of the empirical autocovariances that $\hat{\psi}_T(h)$ converges to $\psi(h)$, and the vector

$$\sqrt{T} \left(\hat{\psi}_T(1) - \psi(1), \ldots, \hat{\psi}_T(H) - \psi(H) \right)'$$

has an asymptotically normal distribution. We still have to determine the form of the asymptotic covariances. We have (setting $a_0 = 1$)

$$\text{acov} \left(\sqrt{T} \left(\hat{\psi}_T(h) - \psi(h) \right), \sqrt{T} \left(\hat{\psi}_T(l) - \psi(l) \right) \right)$$

$$= \sum_{j=0}^{p} \sum_{k=0}^{p} a_j a_k \, \text{acov} \left(\sqrt{T} \left(\hat{\gamma}_T(h-j) - \gamma(h-j) \right), \sqrt{T} \left(\hat{\gamma}_T(l-k) - \gamma(l-k) \right) \right)$$

$$= 4\pi \sum_{j=0}^{p} \sum_{k=0}^{p} a_j a_k \int_{-\pi}^{\pi} \cos \left(\omega(h-j) \right) \cos \left(\omega(l-k) \right) f^2(\omega) \, d\omega$$

(from Theorem (9.6)),

$$= 2\pi \sum_{j=0}^{p} \sum_{k=0}^{p} a_j a_k \int_{-\pi}^{\pi} \left(\cos \left(\omega_1 \right) + \cos \left(\omega_2 \right) \right) f^2(\omega) \, d\omega$$

(where $\omega_1 = \omega(h+l-k-j)$ and $\omega_2 = \omega(h-l+k-j)$)

$$= 2\pi \sum_{j=0}^{p} \sum_{k=0}^{p} a_j a_k \int_{-\pi}^{\pi} \exp \left(i\omega(h+l) \right) \exp(-i\omega k) \exp(-i\omega j) f^2(\omega) \, d\omega$$

$$+ 2\pi \sum_{j=0}^{p} \sum_{k=0}^{p} a_j a_k \int_{-\pi}^{\pi} \exp \left(i\omega(h-l) \right) \exp(i\omega k) \exp(-i\omega j) f^2(\omega) \, d\omega$$

$$= 2\pi \int_{-\pi}^{\pi} \exp\left(i\omega(h+l)\right) A(\exp-(i\omega))^2 f^2(\omega) d\omega$$

$$+ 2\pi \int_{-\pi}^{\pi} \exp\left(i\omega(h-l)\right) \mid A(\exp-(i\omega)) \mid^2 f^2(\omega) d\omega$$

where $A(\exp(i\omega)) = \sum_{j=0}^{p} a_j \exp(i\omega j)$.

This formula can be simplified for some particular moving averages A.

Theorem 9.11: *Let x be a univariate* ARMA *process satisfying*

$$\Phi(L) x_t = \Theta(L)\epsilon_t,$$

where degree $(\Phi) = p$, degree $(\Theta) = q$.

$$\sqrt{T}\left(\hat{\psi}_T(h) - \psi(h)\right) = \sqrt{T}\Phi(L)\left(\hat{\gamma}_T(h) - \gamma(h)\right), \ h \geq q+1$$

is an asymptotically stationary Gaussian process with zero mean and admits an ARMA $(p, 2q)$ *representation*

$$\Phi(L)\sqrt{T}\left(\hat{\psi}_T(h) - \psi(h)\right) = \Theta^2(L)\eta_t,$$

with $\eta_t = \sigma^4$.

PROOF: Let us look at the form of the autocovariance function of the process

$$\sqrt{T}\left(\hat{\psi}_T(h) - \psi(h)\right).$$

Since

$$f(\omega) = \frac{\sigma^2}{2\pi} \frac{\mid \Theta(\exp(i\omega)) \mid^2}{\mid \Phi(\exp(i\omega)) \mid^2},$$

and

$$A(\exp(i\omega)) = \Phi(\exp(i\omega)),$$

we have

$$\text{acov}\left(\sqrt{T}\left(\hat{\psi}_T(h) - \psi(h)\right), \sqrt{T}\left(\hat{\psi}_T(l) - \psi(l)\right)\right)$$

$$= \frac{\sigma^4}{2\pi} \int_{-\pi}^{\pi} \exp(i\omega)(h+l)\frac{\mid \Theta(\exp(i\omega)) \mid^4}{\Phi^2(\exp(i\omega))} d\omega$$

$$+ \frac{\sigma^4}{2\pi} \int_{-\pi}^{\pi} \exp(i\omega)(h-l)\frac{\mid \Theta(\exp(i\omega)) \mid^4}{\mid \Phi(\exp(i\omega)) \mid^2} d\omega.$$

If h and l are greater than $q+1$, the function in the first integral has an expansion which contains only strictly positive powers of $\exp(i\omega)$.

Therefore the first integral is equal to zero and we have

$$\text{acov}\left(\sqrt{T}\left(\hat{\psi}_T(h) - \psi(h)\right), \sqrt{T}\left(\hat{\psi}_T(l) - \psi(l)\right)\right)$$

$$= \frac{\sigma^4}{2\pi}\int_{-\pi}^{\pi} \exp(i\omega)(h-l)\frac{|\Theta(\exp(i\omega))|^4}{|\Phi(\exp(i\omega))|^2}d\omega.$$

This covariance depends only on the difference between the indexes h and l, and the theorem 9.11 is a consequence of this expression. $\square$

Remark 9.1: Note that if $x_t = \epsilon_t$ is a white noise, the series of empirical autocovariances $\hat{\gamma}_T(h), h \geq 1$ is also asymptotically a white noise.

9.2 Maximum Likelihood Estimator

9.2.1 The Model

In this section and in the next one, we are interested in univariate stationary processes $x = \{x_t\}$, having both infinite moving average and infinite autoregressive representations based on an independent white noise with unknown variance σ^2. We assume that the coefficients of the moving-average and autoregressive processes are unknown, but they depend on a parameter $\boldsymbol{\theta} \in \boldsymbol{\Theta} \subset \boldsymbol{R}^K$. Therefore the model can be written in the moving average form

$$x_t = H_\theta(L)\epsilon_t = \sum_{j=0}^{\infty} h_j(\boldsymbol{\theta})\epsilon_{t-j} \tag{9.1}$$

with $h_0(\boldsymbol{\theta}) = 1$, $E(\epsilon_t) = 0$ and $\text{var}(\epsilon_t) = \sigma^2$, or in the autoregressive form

$$\Pi_\theta(L)x_t = \sum_{j=0}^{\infty} \pi_j(\boldsymbol{\theta})x_{t-j} = \epsilon_t, \tag{9.2}$$

with $\pi_0(\boldsymbol{\theta}) = 1$, $E(\epsilon_t) = 0$ var$(\epsilon_t) = \sigma^2$.

We can also describe it through the autocovariance function or the spectral density function. Since the parameters in $\boldsymbol{\theta}$ appear uniquely in H or Π, we can write

$$\gamma_{\theta,\sigma^2}(k) = \sigma^2 c_\theta(k), \tag{9.3}$$

and

$$f_{\theta,\sigma^2}(\omega) = \sigma^2 g_\theta(\omega). \tag{9.4}$$

Written in this way, the previous model is semi-parametric, since the distribution of the noise has not been specified. Most of the results that are presented below are valid in this setting: for example the consistency of estimators, their asymptotic normality, etc. Nevertheless, in order to simplify the presentation, we assume the noise to be Gaussian

$$\epsilon_t \sim \mathcal{N}\left(0, \sigma^2\right). \tag{9.5}$$

Moreover, these results are similar to those available in a sampling framework, and are valid as soon as the temporal links are not too large, for example if the correlations decrease in an exponential manner. This regularity condition is supposed to be satisfied for all possible values of the parameter and in particular in the case of the ARMA processes.

9.2.2 The Log-Likelihood and its Approximations

The Exact Log-Likelihood Function Let us denote by $x_1 \ldots x_T$ the successive observations on the process. The log-likelihood function is obtained directly by using the assumption of normality of the noise, which characterizes the distribution of the process $\{x\}$.

It is given by

$$L_T\left(\mathbf{x}_T; \boldsymbol{\theta}, \sigma^2\right) = -\frac{T}{2}\log 2\pi - \frac{1}{2}\log \det \boldsymbol{\Gamma}_T\left(\boldsymbol{\theta}, \sigma^2\right)$$
$$-\frac{1}{2}\mathbf{x}_T' \boldsymbol{\Gamma}_T\left(\boldsymbol{\theta}, \sigma^2\right)^{-1}\mathbf{x}_T, \tag{9.6}$$

where $\mathbf{x}_T = (x_1, \ldots, x_T)'$ and where $\boldsymbol{\Gamma}_T\left(\boldsymbol{\theta}, \sigma^2\right)$ is the variance–covariance matrix of $(x_1, \ldots, x_T)'$. Its generic element is

$$\gamma_{\boldsymbol{\theta}, \sigma^2}(i-j) = \sigma^2 c_{\boldsymbol{\theta}}(i-j), \ 1 \leq i, \ j \leq T.$$

This log-likelihood function can be rewritten by separating the two parameters $\boldsymbol{\theta}$ and σ^2. In order to do this, let us introduce the matrix

$$\mathbf{C}_T(\boldsymbol{\theta}) = \frac{1}{\sigma^2}\boldsymbol{\Gamma}_T(\boldsymbol{\theta}, \sigma^2).$$

We have

$$L_T\left(\mathbf{x}_T; \boldsymbol{\theta}, \sigma^2\right) = -\frac{T}{2}\log 2\pi - \frac{T}{2}\log \sigma^2 - \frac{1}{2}\log \det \mathbf{C}_T(\boldsymbol{\theta})$$
$$-\frac{1}{2\sigma^2}\mathbf{x}_T' \mathbf{C}_T(\boldsymbol{\theta})^{-1}\mathbf{x}_T. \tag{9.7}$$

We can notice that given that the matrix $\mathbf{C}_T(\boldsymbol{\theta})$ is a Toeplitz matrix (it has the same elements on the subdiagonals parallel to the main diagonal), the quadratic form $\mathbf{x}_T' \mathbf{C}_T(\boldsymbol{\theta})\mathbf{x}_T$ has a simple form. This result does not carry over to the quadratic form $\mathbf{x}_T' \mathbf{C}_T(\boldsymbol{\theta})^{-1}\mathbf{x}_T$ indeed, the inverse of a Toeplitz matrix is not in general Toeplitz itself (see the appendix to chapter 7). We can suggest various approximations to the exact log-likelihood function, when the number of observations T is large. We give below the two most typical ones: the approximation by conditional distributions and the approximation in the frequency domain.

Approximation by Conditional Distributions The distribution of the vector $\mathbf{x}_T = (x_1 \ldots x_T)'$ can be expressed by making explicit the successive conditional distributions. Let

$$l\left(x_t \mid x_{t-1}, \ldots, x_1; \boldsymbol{\theta}, \sigma^2\right)$$

be the density function of x_t conditional on $x_{t-1} \ldots x_1$. We have

$$l_T\left(\mathbf{x}_T; \boldsymbol{\theta}, \sigma^2\right) = \prod_{t=1}^{T} l\left(x_t \mid x_{t-1} \ldots x_1; \boldsymbol{\theta}, \sigma^2\right).$$

Each of these conditional distributions is normal, with mean

$$E\left(x_t \mid x_{t-1}, \ldots, x_1\right),$$

and variance

$$\text{var}\left(x_t \mid x_{t-1}, \ldots, x_1\right) = \text{var}\left(x_t - E\left(x_t \mid x_{t-1}, \ldots, x_1\right)\right).$$

When t goes to infinity, the expectation $E\left(x_t \mid x_{t-1}, \ldots, x_1\right)$ converges to the expectation based on the infinite past

$$E\left(x_t \mid x_{t-1}, \ldots, x_1\right) \approx E\left(x_t \mid x_{t-1}, \ldots, x_1, \ldots\right)$$

$$= -\sum_{j=1}^{\infty} \pi_j(\boldsymbol{\theta})x_{t-j} = -\left(\Pi_\theta(L) - 1\right)x_t.$$

By the same token, the conditional variance can be approximated by the quadratic error of the corresponding expectation, that is σ^2. Therefore a possible approximation to the log-likelihood function is

$$L_T^c(\mathbf{x}_T; \boldsymbol{\theta}, \sigma^2) = -\frac{T}{2}\log 2\pi - \frac{T}{2}\log \sigma^2 - \frac{1}{2\sigma^2}\sum_{t=1}^{T}\left(\Pi_\theta(L)x_t\right)^2. \quad (9.8)$$

This function is called *theoretical conditional log-likelihood function.* A shortcoming of this representation is that it does not depend on the observations $x_1, \ldots, x_T$ only, but on the whole past of the process. It can be modified to overcome this problem, for example, introducing *the conditional log-likelihood function*

$$\tilde{L}_T^c(\mathbf{x}_T; \boldsymbol{\theta}, \sigma^2) = -\frac{T}{2}\log 2\pi - \frac{T}{2}\log \sigma^2$$

$$- \frac{1}{2\sigma^2}\sum_{t=1}^{T}\left(x_t + \pi_1(\boldsymbol{\theta})x_{t-1} \ldots + \pi_{t-1}(\boldsymbol{\theta})x_1\right)^2. \quad (9.9)$$

Approximation in the Frequency Domain Another approximation introduced by Whittle (1951) is very useful. It is obtained by writing the log-likelihood function in the frequency domain. First of all let us remark that the approximation by conditional distributions calls for replacing $\log \det \mathbf{\Gamma}_T(\boldsymbol{\theta}, \sigma^2)$ by $T \log \sigma^2$. This approximation can be viewed also as a consequence of the Kolmogorov equality. On the other hand, if we consider the infinite Toeplitz matrix $\mathbf{\Gamma}_\infty(\boldsymbol{\theta}, \sigma^2)$, we can assimilate it to the series of coefficients $(\gamma_{\theta,\sigma^2}(h))$ of the Fourier transform

$$2\pi f_{\theta,\sigma^2}(\omega)$$

(cf. the appendix to chapter 7).

The "normalized" inverse spectral function

$$fi_{\theta,\sigma^2}(\omega) = \frac{1}{(2\pi)^2} \left(f_{\theta,\sigma^2}(\omega) \right)^{-1},$$

is then associated to the sequence of the "normalized" inverse autocovariances of the process $\left(\gamma i_{\theta,\sigma^2}(h) \right)$. This sequence is linked to the sequence of the direct autocovariances by

$$\gamma_{\theta,\sigma^2} * \gamma i_{\theta,\sigma^2} = e,$$

where $*$ is the convolution product and where e is the neutral element sequence for this product. Introducing the matrix $\mathbf{\Gamma i}_\infty(\boldsymbol{\theta}, \sigma^2)$ associated to the sequence $\{\gamma i_{\theta,\sigma^2}(h)\}$, the existing relation between the sequences is written in matrix form by (cf. the appendix to chapter 7)

$$\mathbf{\Gamma}_\infty(\boldsymbol{\theta}, \sigma^2)\mathbf{\Gamma i}_\infty(\boldsymbol{\theta}, \sigma^2) = \mathbf{I}_\infty$$

$$\Leftrightarrow \mathbf{\Gamma i}_\infty(\boldsymbol{\theta}, \sigma^2) = \mathbf{\Gamma}_\infty(\boldsymbol{\theta}, \sigma^2)^{-1}.$$

Therefore we can approximate the inverse $\mathbf{\Gamma}_T^{-1}(\boldsymbol{\theta}, \sigma^2)$ by a main submatrix of $\mathbf{\Gamma i}_\infty(\boldsymbol{\theta}, \sigma^2)$ of size T; thus, we get the approximation

$$\mathbf{x}_T' \mathbf{\Gamma}_T^{-1}(\boldsymbol{\theta}, \sigma^2)^{-1} \mathbf{x}_T \approx \mathbf{x}_T' \mathbf{\Gamma i}_T(\boldsymbol{\theta}, \sigma^2) \mathbf{x}_T.$$

We can then use the results concerning the quadratic forms based on the Toeplitz matrices. We see that

$$\mathbf{x}_T' \mathbf{\Gamma}_T(\boldsymbol{\theta}, \sigma^2)^{-1} \mathbf{x}_T \approx \mathbf{x}_T' \mathbf{\Gamma i}_T(\boldsymbol{\theta}, \sigma^2) \mathbf{x}_T$$

$$= \int_{-\pi}^{\pi} \left| \sum_{t=1}^{T} x_t \exp(-it\omega) \right|^2 fi_{\theta,\sigma^2}(\omega) \, d\omega$$

$$= \frac{1}{(2\pi)^2} \int_{-\pi}^{\pi} \left| \sum_{t=1}^{T} x_t \exp(-it\omega) \right|^2 \frac{1}{f_{\theta,\sigma^2}(\omega)} \, d\omega.$$

Let $I_T(\omega) = \frac{1}{2\pi T} \left| \sum_{t=1}^{T} x_t \exp(-it\omega) \right|^2$ be the periodogram of order T of the process x, we have

$$\mathbf{x}_T' \mathbf{\Gamma i}_T(\boldsymbol{\theta}, \sigma^2) \mathbf{x}_T = \frac{T}{2\pi} \int_{-\pi}^{\pi} \frac{I_T(\omega)}{f_{\theta,\sigma^2}(\omega)} \, d\omega = T \, E_\mu \left(\frac{I_T}{f_{\theta,\sigma^2}} \right),$$

where μ is the uniform distribution on $(-\pi, \pi]$.

Replacing it in the expression of the exact log-likelihood function, we get

$$\tilde{L}_T(\mathbf{x}_T; \boldsymbol{\theta}, \sigma^2) = -\frac{T}{2}\log 2\pi - \frac{T}{2}\log \sigma^2 - \frac{T}{2\sigma^2}E_\mu\left(\frac{I_T}{g_\theta}\right), \qquad (9.10)$$

where $f_{\theta,\sigma^2} = \sigma^2 g_\theta$.

9.2.3 Definition and Consistency of
Maximum Likelihood Estimators

Consistency Condition Having found several (exact or approximated) forms of the log-likelihood function, we can now define several maximum likelihood estimators by optimizing one or the other of these expressions. All of these estimators are solutions to a problem

$$\max_{\theta,\sigma^2} L_T^*(\mathbf{x}_T; \boldsymbol{\theta}, \sigma^2), \qquad (9.11)$$

where

$$L_T^* = L_T \text{ or } \tilde{L}_T^c \text{ or } \tilde{L}_T.$$

We denote these estimators by $(\hat{\boldsymbol{\theta}}_T, \hat{\sigma}_T^2)$.

In order to know whether such an estimator exists and converges to
the true value $(\boldsymbol{\theta}_0, \sigma_0^2)$ of the parameter, the standard approach is to
study the asymptotic behavior of the objective function $L_T^*(\mathbf{x}_T, \boldsymbol{\theta}, \sigma^2)$,
or, which is the same, that of

$$K_T^*(P \mid P_0) = \frac{1}{T}L_T^*(\mathbf{x}_T; \boldsymbol{\theta}_0, \sigma_0^2) - \frac{1}{T}L_T^*(\mathbf{x}_T; \boldsymbol{\theta}, \sigma^2). \qquad (9.12)$$

The problem of deriving the maximum likelihood estimator is equivalent
to the following one

$$\min_{\theta,\sigma^2} K_T^*(P \mid P_0). \qquad (9.13)$$

If the objective function $K_T^*(P \mid P_0)$ converges almost surely uniformly
in the $(\boldsymbol{\theta}, \sigma^2)$ space to a limit $K^*(P \mid P_0)$, and furthermore this limit
admits a unique minimum in the $(\boldsymbol{\theta}, \sigma^2)$ space at $(\boldsymbol{\theta}_0, \sigma_0^2)$, then the finite
sample problem (9.13) admits a solution for a large enough sample size T
and this solution converges to $(\boldsymbol{\theta}_0, \sigma_0^2)$, the solution of the limit problem

$$\min_{\theta,\sigma^2} K^*(P \mid P_0). \qquad (9.14)$$

We expand on this approach below. We can verify that the objective
function does not depend on the (exact or approximated) form of the
log-likelihood function. Therefore we can write it as $K(P \mid P_0)$. On the
other hand, the quantity $K(P \mid P_0)$ is interesting in itself. Indeed, it can
be interpreted as a measure of the proximity between the distributions
P_0 and P. The function K is called *Kullback contrast*.

Forms of the Kullback Contrast It is clear from the previous discussion, that a possible definition of $K\left(P\mid P_0\right)$ is

$$K\left(P\mid P_0\right) = \plim_{T\to+\infty}\left(\frac{1}{T}L_T^*(\mathbf{x}_T;\boldsymbol{\theta}_0,\sigma_0^2) - \frac{1}{T}L_T^*(\mathbf{x}_T;\boldsymbol{\theta},\sigma^2)\right). \quad (9.15)$$

Other expressions can be obtained from the various forms of the likelihood function.

(a)   Use of the Approximation in the Frequency Domain

We have

$$\tilde{K}_T\left(P\mid P_0\right) = \frac{1}{T}\left(-\frac{T}{2}\log 2\pi - \frac{T}{2}\log\sigma_0^2 - \frac{T}{2\sigma_0^2}E_\mu\left(\frac{I_T}{g_{\theta_0}}\right)\right)$$

$$-\frac{1}{T}\left(-\frac{T}{2}\log 2\pi - \frac{T}{2}\log\sigma^2 - \frac{T}{2\sigma^2}E_\mu\left(\frac{I_T}{g_\theta}\right)\right)$$

$$= \frac{1}{2}\log\frac{\sigma^2}{\sigma_0^2} - \frac{1}{2\sigma_0^2}E_\mu\left(\frac{I_T}{g_{\theta_0}}\right) + \frac{1}{2\sigma^2}E_\mu\left(\frac{I_T}{g_\theta}\right).$$

Although the periodogram does not converge to the exact spectral density function, we have seen that, for any bounded continuous function h, the integral $E_\mu(h\hat{I}_t)$ converges to $E_\mu(hf_{\theta_0,\sigma_0^2})$ (cf. theorem 9.4). Applying this result, we have

$$\plim_{T\to+\infty}\tilde{K}_T(P\mid P_0) = \frac{1}{2}\log\frac{\sigma^2}{\sigma_0^2} - \frac{1}{2\sigma_0^2}E_\mu\sigma_0^2 + \frac{1}{2\sigma^2}E_\mu\left(\sigma_0^2\frac{g_{\theta_0}}{g_\theta}\right).$$

After simplification, the expression of the contrast is given by the following

Theorem 9.12: *The contrast between P_0 and P is*

$$K\left(P\mid P_0\right) = \frac{1}{2}E_\mu\left(\log\frac{\sigma^2}{\sigma_0^2} - 1 + \frac{\sigma_0^2}{\sigma^2}\frac{g_{\theta_0}}{g_\theta}\right).$$

Remark 9.2: From Kolmogorov's inequality

$$\log\sigma^2 = E_\mu\left(\log 2\pi f_{\theta,\sigma^2}(\omega)\right),$$

one can obtain another equivalent expression of this contrast

$$K\left(P\mid P_0\right) = \frac{1}{2}E_\mu\left(\log\frac{f_{\theta,\sigma^2}}{f_{\theta_0,\sigma_0^2}} - 1 + \frac{f_{\theta_0,\sigma_0^2}}{f_{\theta,\sigma^2}}\right),$$

which has a simple interpretation.

Theorem 9.13: *The contrast between P_0 and P is the average of the measures of proximity frequency by frequency*

$$K\left(P \mid P_0\right) = E_\mu K(\omega),$$

where

$$K(\omega) = \frac{1}{2}\left(\log \frac{f_{\theta,\sigma^2}}{f_{\theta_0,\sigma_0^2}} - 1 + \frac{f_{\theta_0,\sigma_0^2}}{f_{\theta,\sigma^2}}\right).$$

(b)   Use of the Conditional Distributions

Another expression for the Kullback contrast is derived from the likelihood function written in terms of conditional distributions. We have

$$K(P \mid P_0) = \plim_{T \to +\infty} \left(\frac{1}{T}L_T^c(\mathbf{x}_T; \boldsymbol{\theta}_0, \sigma_0^2) - \frac{1}{T}L_T^c(\mathbf{x}_T; \boldsymbol{\theta}, \sigma^2)\right)$$

$$= \plim_{T \to +\infty} \frac{1}{T} \sum_{t=1}^{T} \left(\log l(x_t \mid \underline{\mathbf{x}}_{t-1}; \boldsymbol{\theta}_0, \sigma_0^2) - \log l(x_t \mid \underline{\mathbf{x}}_{t-1}; \boldsymbol{\theta}, \sigma^2)\right),$$

where

$$l(x_t \mid \underline{\mathbf{x}}_{t-1}; \boldsymbol{\theta}, \sigma^2)$$

is the conditional density function of x_t given $\underline{\mathbf{x}}_{t-1} = (x_{t-1}, x_{t-2}, \ldots)$. By using the stationarity property of the process and the convergence of the empirical mean to the theoretical expectation, we get

$$K\left(P \mid P_0\right) = E_0 \left(\log \frac{l(x_t \mid \underline{\mathbf{x}}_{t-1}; \boldsymbol{\theta}_0, \sigma_0^2)}{l(x_t \mid \underline{\mathbf{x}}_{t-1}; \boldsymbol{\theta}, \sigma^2)}\right),$$

$$K\left(P \mid P_0\right) = E_0 \ E_0 \left(\log \frac{l(x_t \mid \underline{\mathbf{x}}_{t-1}; \boldsymbol{\theta}_0, \sigma_0^2)}{l(x_t \mid \underline{\mathbf{x}}_{t-1}; \boldsymbol{\theta}, \sigma^2)} \mid \underline{\mathbf{x}}_{t-1}\right).$$

$$(9.16)$$

Introducing then the quantity

$$K\left(P \mid P_0; \underline{\mathbf{x}}_{t-1}\right) = E_0 \left(\log \frac{l(x_t \mid \underline{\mathbf{x}}_{t-1}; \boldsymbol{\theta}_0, \sigma_0^2)}{l(x_t \mid \underline{\mathbf{x}}_{t-1}; \boldsymbol{\theta}, \sigma^2)} \mid \underline{\mathbf{x}}_{t-1}\right),$$

which can be interpreted as the contrast conditional on the past values, we can notice that $K\left(P \mid P_0\right) = E_0 K\left(P \mid P_0; \underline{\mathbf{x}}_{t-1}\right)$. This formula gives a decomposition in the time domain which is similar to the one established in theorem 9.13 for the frequency domain.

Finally, substituting the conditional densities by their expressions, we have

$$K\left(P \mid P_0\right) = E_0 \frac{1}{2}\left(\log \frac{\sigma^2}{\sigma_0^2} - \frac{1}{\sigma_0^2}\left(\Pi_{\theta_0}(L)x_t\right)^2 + \frac{1}{\sigma^2}\left(\Pi_\theta(L)x_t\right)^2\right)$$

$$= \frac{1}{2}\left(\log \frac{\sigma^2}{\sigma_0^2} - \frac{1}{\sigma_0^2}\mathrm{var}_0\left(\Pi_{\theta_0}(L)x_t\right) + \frac{1}{\sigma^2}\mathrm{var}_0\left(\Pi_\theta(L)x_t\right)\right)$$

$$= \frac{1}{2}\left(\log \frac{\sigma^2}{\sigma_0^2} - 1 + \frac{1}{\sigma^2}\mathrm{var}_0\left(\Pi_\theta(L)x_t\right)\right).$$

$$(9.17)$$

Existence of a Unique Solution to the Minimization Problem
We still need to analyze under which conditions the problem

$$\min_{\theta,\sigma^2} K\left(P \mid P_0\right)$$

has the unique solution $\theta = \theta_0, \sigma^2 = \sigma_0^2$. In order to find this result, we can take one of the equivalent forms of the Kullback contrast. For example, let us take the formula in the frequency domain, and let us write

$$a(x) = -\log x - 1 + x.$$

We notice that the function a is continuous, positive, and is zero only for $x = 1$. Since the Kullback contrast is written as

$$K\left(P \mid P_0\right) = \frac{1}{2}E_\mu a\left(\frac{f_{\theta_0,\sigma_0^2}}{f_{\theta,\sigma^2}}\right),$$

it is always nonnegative and reaches its minimum of 0 for $f_{\theta,\sigma^2} = f_{\theta_0,\sigma_0^2}$.

Definition 9.1: *The parameter vector θ, σ^2 is identifiable if and only if $f_{\theta,\sigma^2} = f_{\theta_0,\sigma_0^2}$ which implies $\theta = \theta_0, \sigma^2 = \sigma_0^2$.*

We can easily verify (cf. exercise 9.1) that the previous condition, equivalent to $\Pi_\theta(L) = \Pi_{\theta_0}(L)$, gives $\theta = \theta_0$.

Theorem 9.14: *The maximum likelihood estimator exists asymptotically and is consistent if and only if the parameters are identifiable.*

9.2.4 Vector of Scores

If the actual value of (θ_0, σ_0^2) belongs to the set of possible values of the parameter, if the parameter is identifiable and if the likelihood function has first derivatives then the consistency of the maximum likelihood estimator guarantees that it satisfies asymptotically the first-order condition

$$\frac{\partial L_T^*}{\partial(\boldsymbol{\theta}', \sigma^2)'}(\mathbf{x}_T; \hat{\boldsymbol{\theta}}_T, \hat{\sigma}_T^2) = 0. \tag{9.18}$$

This leads us to write explicitly the vector of scores as

$$\frac{\partial L_T^*}{\partial(\boldsymbol{\theta}', \sigma^2)'}(\mathbf{x}_T; \boldsymbol{\theta}_0, \sigma_0^2)$$

for the various forms (exact or approximated) of the log-likelihood function.

Exact Score Let us start with the exact form given in (9.7). We have

$$\frac{\partial L_T}{\partial \sigma^2}(\mathbf{x}_T; \boldsymbol{\theta}, \sigma^2) = -\frac{T}{2\sigma^2} + \frac{1}{2\sigma^4}\mathbf{x}_T' \mathbf{C}_T(\boldsymbol{\theta})^{-1}\mathbf{x}_T,$$

and

$$\frac{\partial L_T}{\partial \theta_k}(\mathbf{x}_T; \boldsymbol{\theta}, \sigma^2)$$

$$= -\frac{1}{2}\frac{\partial}{\partial \theta_k}(\log \det \mathbf{C}(\boldsymbol{\theta})) - \frac{1}{2\sigma^2}\frac{\partial}{\partial \theta_k}\left(\mathbf{x}_T' \mathbf{C}_T(\boldsymbol{\theta})^{-1}\mathbf{x}_T\right)$$

$$= -\frac{1}{2}\mathrm{tr}\left(\mathbf{C}_T(\boldsymbol{\theta})^{-1}\frac{\partial \mathbf{C}_T(\boldsymbol{\theta})}{\partial \theta_k}\right) \tag{9.19}$$

$$+ \frac{1}{2\sigma^2}\mathbf{x}_T' \mathbf{C}_T(\boldsymbol{\theta})^{-1}\frac{\partial \mathbf{C}_T(\boldsymbol{\theta})}{\partial \theta_k}\mathbf{C}_T(\boldsymbol{\theta})^{-1}\mathbf{x}_T,$$

which can be found by using some classical formulae of matrix differentiation (cf. exercise 9.3).

Approximated Score Derived from the Conditional Expression From the conditional formula (9.8), we find

$$\frac{\partial L_T^c}{\partial \sigma^2}(\mathbf{x}_T; \boldsymbol{\theta}, \sigma^2) = -\frac{T}{2\sigma^2} + \frac{1}{2\sigma^4}\sum_{t=1}^{T}(\Pi_\theta(L)x_t)^2,$$

and

$$\frac{\partial L_T^c}{\partial \boldsymbol{\theta}}(\mathbf{x}_T; \boldsymbol{\theta}, \sigma^2) = -\frac{1}{\sigma^2}\sum_{t=1}^{T}\frac{\partial \Pi_\theta(L)}{\partial \boldsymbol{\theta}}x_t \Pi_\theta(L)x_t$$

$$= -\frac{1}{\sigma^2}\sum_{t=1}^{T}\left(\sum_{j=1}^{\infty}\frac{\partial \pi_j(\boldsymbol{\theta})}{\partial \boldsymbol{\theta}}x_{t-j}\right)\left(x_t + \sum_{j=1}^{\infty}\pi_j(\boldsymbol{\theta})x_{t-j}\right).$$

Under this infinite autoregressive form, we can give the usual interpretation in terms of nonlinear least squares. Thus the expression for the likelihood equation

$$\frac{\partial L_T^c}{\partial \boldsymbol{\theta}}(\mathbf{x}_T; \hat{\boldsymbol{\theta}}_T, \hat{\sigma}_T^2) = 0,$$

can be seen as an orthogonality condition between the residuals

$$\hat{\epsilon}_t = x_t + \sum_{j=1}^{\infty} \pi_j(\hat{\boldsymbol{\theta}}_T) x_{t-j},$$

and the "explanatory variables"

$$\sum_{j=1}^{\infty} \frac{\partial \pi_j(\hat{\boldsymbol{\theta}}_T)}{\partial \boldsymbol{\theta}_k} x_{t-j},$$

with k varying.

The other likelihood equation provides an estimator for the variance from the sum of squares of residuals

$$\hat{\sigma}_T^2 = \frac{1}{T} \sum_{t=1}^{T} \hat{\epsilon}_t^2.$$

Approximated Score in the Frequency Domain Finally, from expression (9.10) of the log-likelihood function, we get

$$\frac{\partial \tilde{L}_T}{\partial \sigma^2}(\mathbf{x}_T; \boldsymbol{\theta}, \sigma^2) = -\frac{T}{2\sigma^2} + \frac{T}{2\sigma^4} E_\mu \left(\frac{\hat{I}_T}{g_\theta} \right),$$

and

$$\frac{\partial \tilde{L}_T}{\partial \boldsymbol{\theta}}(\mathbf{x}_T; \boldsymbol{\theta}, \sigma^2) = \frac{T}{2\sigma^2} E_\mu \left(\hat{I}_T \frac{1}{g_\theta^2} \frac{\partial g_\theta}{\partial \boldsymbol{\theta}} \right). \tag{9.20}$$

Taking the derivatives of the Kolmogorov equality,

$$\log 2\pi + E_\mu \log g_\theta = 0,$$

with respect to the parameter $\boldsymbol{\theta}$, the second derivative above can also be written as

$$\frac{\partial \tilde{L}_T}{\partial \boldsymbol{\theta}}(\mathbf{x}_T; \boldsymbol{\theta}, \sigma^2) = \frac{T}{2\sigma^2} E_\mu \left(\left(\hat{I}_T - \sigma^2 g(\boldsymbol{\theta}) \right) \frac{1}{g_\theta^2} \frac{\partial g_\theta}{\partial \boldsymbol{\theta}} \right). \tag{9.21}$$

9.2.5 Asymptotic Distributions and Fisher's Information Matrix

Asymptotic Distribution of Scores In this subsection we show the main asymptotic properties of the score vector. These properties are summarized below and given without proof (cf. Gourieroux and Monfort, 1989, chapter 17).

Theorem 9.15:

(i)   The score vector divided by T

$$\frac{1}{T}\frac{\partial L_T^*}{\partial(\boldsymbol{\theta}',\sigma^2)'}(\mathbf{x}_T;\boldsymbol{\theta}_0,\sigma_0^2)$$

converges (almost surely) to 0.

(ii)   If L_T^* and L_T^{**} are two expressions for the likelihood function (exact or approximated), then

$$\frac{1}{\sqrt{T}}\frac{\partial L_T^*}{\partial(\boldsymbol{\theta}',\sigma^2)'}(\mathbf{x}_T;\boldsymbol{\theta}_0,\sigma_0^2) - \frac{1}{\sqrt{T}}\frac{\partial L_T^{**}}{\partial(\boldsymbol{\theta}',\sigma^2)'}(\mathbf{x}_T;\boldsymbol{\theta}_0,\sigma_0^2)$$

converges to 0 in probability.

(iii) Asymptotic normality holds

$$\frac{1}{\sqrt{T}}\frac{\partial L_T^*}{\partial(\boldsymbol{\theta}',\sigma^2)'}(\mathbf{x}_T;\boldsymbol{\theta}_0,\sigma_0^2) \xrightarrow{\mathrm{d}} \mathcal{N}\left(0,\mathbf{J}(\boldsymbol{\theta}_0,\sigma_0^2)\right).$$

Obviously, these properties are valid under certain regularity conditions, for example if $\{\epsilon_t\}$ is an independent white noise and if the moving average and autoregressive coefficients decrease in an exponential way. Result (ii) is more difficult to obtain. Since it implies that the asymptotic variance matrix $\mathbf{J}(\boldsymbol{\theta}_0,\sigma_0^2)$ does not depend on the choice of the likelihood function, we use it in order to derive many equivalent expressions for this matrix.

As in the sampling case, the matrix $\mathbf{J}(\boldsymbol{\theta}_0,\sigma_0^2)$ is called the *Fisher's information matrix*.

Use of the Score in the Frequency Domain   The score is written as an integral of the periodogram

$$\begin{pmatrix} \frac{\partial \tilde{L}_T}{\partial\theta}(\mathbf{x}_T;\boldsymbol{\theta}_0,\sigma_0^2) \\ \frac{\partial \tilde{L}_T}{\partial\sigma^2}(\mathbf{x}_T;\boldsymbol{\theta}_0,\sigma_0^2) \end{pmatrix} = \frac{T}{2\sigma_0^2}\begin{pmatrix} E_\mu\left(\left(\hat{I}_T - f_{\theta_0,\sigma_0^2}\right)\frac{1}{g_{\theta_0}^2}\frac{\partial g_{\theta_0}}{\partial\theta}\right) \\ E_\mu\left(\frac{\hat{I}_T - f_{\theta_0,\sigma_0^2}}{f_{\theta_0,\sigma_0^2}}\right) \end{pmatrix}.$$

We can now apply directly the asymptotic properties of the periodogram (cf. theorems 9.4 and 9.5). We have

$$\frac{1}{T}\begin{pmatrix} \frac{\partial \tilde{L}_T}{\partial\theta}(\mathbf{x}_T;\boldsymbol{\theta}_0,\sigma_0^2) \\ \frac{\partial \tilde{L}_T}{\partial\sigma^2}(\mathbf{x}_T;\boldsymbol{\theta}_0,\sigma_0^2) \end{pmatrix}$$

$$\xrightarrow{a.s.} \frac{1}{2\sigma_0^2}\begin{pmatrix} E_\mu\left(\left(f_{\theta_0,\sigma_0^2} - f_{\theta_0,\sigma_0^2}\right)\frac{1}{g_{\theta_0}^2}\frac{\partial g_{\theta_0}}{\partial\theta}\right) \\ E_\mu\left(\frac{f_{\theta_0,\sigma_0^2} - f_{\theta_0,\sigma_0^2}}{f_{\theta_0,\sigma_0^2}}\right) \end{pmatrix} = \mathbf{0}.$$

On the other hand

$$\frac{1}{\sqrt{T}} \begin{pmatrix} \frac{\partial \tilde{L}_T}{\partial \theta}(\mathbf{x}_T; \boldsymbol{\theta}_0, \sigma_0^2) \\ \frac{\partial \tilde{L}_T}{\partial \sigma^2}(\mathbf{x}_T; \boldsymbol{\theta}_0, \sigma_0^2) \end{pmatrix} \xrightarrow{\text{d}} \mathcal{N}\left(0, \mathbf{J}(\boldsymbol{\theta}_0, \sigma_0^2)\right),$$

with

$$\mathbf{J}(\boldsymbol{\theta}_0, \sigma_0^2) = \frac{2}{4\sigma_0^4} \begin{pmatrix} \sigma_0^4 E_\mu \left(\frac{\partial \log g_{\theta_0}}{\partial \theta} \frac{\partial \log g_{\theta_0}}{\partial \theta'} \right) & \sigma_0^2 E_\mu \left(\frac{\partial \log g_{\theta_0}}{\partial \theta} \right) \\ \sigma_0^2 E_\mu \left(\frac{\partial \log g_{\theta_0}}{\partial \theta'} \right) & \sigma_0^2 E_\mu \left(\frac{f_{\theta_0, \sigma_0^2}^2}{f_{\theta_0, \sigma_0^2}^2} \right) \end{pmatrix}.$$

Using Kolmogorov equality, which leads to

$$E_\mu \left(\frac{\partial \log g_{\theta_0}}{\partial \theta'} \right) = 0,$$

we see that the Fisher's information matrix is given by

$$\mathbf{J}(\boldsymbol{\theta}_0, \sigma_0^2) = \begin{pmatrix} \frac{1}{2} E_\mu \left(\frac{\partial \log g_{\theta_0}}{\partial \theta} \frac{\partial \log g_{\theta_0}}{\partial \theta'} \right) & 0 \\ 0 & 1/2\sigma_0^4 \end{pmatrix}. \tag{9.22}$$

Since this matrix is block-diagonal, we obtain right away the following theorem

Theorem 9.16: *The two components*

$$\frac{1}{\sqrt{T}} \frac{\partial \tilde{L}_T}{\partial \theta}(\mathbf{x}_T; \boldsymbol{\theta}_0, \sigma_0^2)$$

and

$$\frac{1}{\sqrt{T}} \frac{\partial \tilde{L}_T}{\partial \sigma^2}(\mathbf{x}_T; \boldsymbol{\theta}_0, \sigma_0^2)$$

of the score vector are asymptotically independent.

Use of the Conditional Score Let us consider now the conditional form

$$\frac{\partial L_T^c(\mathbf{x}_T; \boldsymbol{\theta}_0, \sigma_0^2)}{\partial(\boldsymbol{\theta}', \sigma^2)'} = \sum_{t=1}^{T} \frac{\partial \log l(x_t \mid \underline{\mathbf{x}}_{t-1}; \boldsymbol{\theta}_0, \sigma_0^2)}{\partial(\boldsymbol{\theta}', \sigma^2)'}.$$

The variables

$$z_t = \frac{\partial \log l(x_t \mid \underline{\mathbf{x}}_{t-1}; \boldsymbol{\theta}_0, \sigma_0^2)}{\partial(\boldsymbol{\theta}', \sigma^2)'}$$

present in the sum are such that

$$E_0(z_t \mid \underline{\mathbf{x}}_{t-1}) = E_0 \left(\frac{\partial \log l(x_t \mid \underline{\mathbf{x}}_{t-1}; \boldsymbol{\theta}_0, \sigma_0^2)}{\partial(\boldsymbol{\theta}', \sigma^2)'} \mid \underline{\mathbf{x}}_{t-1} \right) = 0.$$

Therefore they constitute a stationary sequence satisfying the martingale difference condition: $E_0(z_t \mid \underline{z}_{t-1}) = 0$, and therefore it is serially uncorrelated. Then, given the limit theorems in the time domain, we get

$$\frac{1}{T}\frac{\partial L_T^c(\mathbf{x}_T;\boldsymbol{\theta}_0,\sigma_0^2)}{\partial(\boldsymbol{\theta}',\sigma^2)'} \overset{a.s.}{\to} E_0\left(\frac{\partial \log l(x_t\mid\underline{\mathbf{x}}_{t-1};\boldsymbol{\theta}_0,\sigma_0^2)}{\partial(\boldsymbol{\theta}',\sigma^2)'}\right) = 0.$$

Furthermore, we obtain asymptotic normality

$$\frac{1}{\sqrt{T}}\frac{\partial L_T^c(\mathbf{x}_T;\boldsymbol{\theta}_0,\sigma_0^2)}{\partial(\boldsymbol{\theta}',\sigma^2)'} \overset{d}{\to} \mathcal{N}\left(0,\mathbf{J}(\boldsymbol{\theta}_0,\sigma_0^2)\right),$$

with

$$\mathbf{J}(\boldsymbol{\theta}_0,\sigma_0^2) = \operatorname{var}_0\left(\frac{\partial \log l(x_t\mid\underline{\mathbf{x}}_{t-1};\boldsymbol{\theta}_0,\sigma_0^2)}{\partial(\boldsymbol{\theta}',\sigma^2)'}\right). \tag{9.23}$$

Making this last formula explicit, we have

$$\mathbf{J}(\boldsymbol{\theta}_0,\sigma_0^2) = \operatorname{var}_0\begin{pmatrix} -\frac{1}{\sigma^2}\epsilon_t\sum_{j=1}^{\infty}\frac{\partial\pi_j}{\partial\theta}(\boldsymbol{\theta}_0)x_{t-j} \\ -\frac{1}{2\sigma_0^2}+\frac{1}{2\sigma_0^4}\epsilon_t^2 \end{pmatrix}.$$

Using the normality of ϵ_t, we have $E_0\epsilon_t^2 = \sigma_0^2, E_0\epsilon_t^3 = 0, E_0\epsilon_t^4 = 3\sigma_0^4$, and therefore

$$\mathbf{J}(\boldsymbol{\theta}_0,\sigma_0^2) = \begin{pmatrix} \frac{1}{\sigma^2}\operatorname{var}_0\left(\frac{\partial\Pi_{\theta_0}(L)}{\partial\theta}\right)x_t & 0 \\ 0 & 1/2\sigma_0^4 \end{pmatrix}. \tag{9.24}$$

An Alternative Expression for the Information Matrix   An equivalent form of the information matrix can be easily derived with the conditional approach. We have

$$\mathbf{J}(\boldsymbol{\theta}_0,\sigma_0^2) = \operatorname{var}_0\left(\frac{\partial \log l(x_t\mid\underline{\mathbf{x}}_{t-1};\boldsymbol{\theta}_0,\sigma_0^2)}{\partial(\boldsymbol{\theta}',\sigma^2)'}\right)$$

$$= E_0 E_0\left(\frac{\partial \log l(x_t\mid\underline{\mathbf{x}}_{t-1};\boldsymbol{\theta}_0,\sigma_0^2)}{\partial(\boldsymbol{\theta}',\sigma^2)'}\frac{\partial \log l(x_t\mid\underline{\mathbf{x}}_{t-1};\boldsymbol{\theta}_0,\sigma_0^2)}{\partial(\boldsymbol{\theta}',\sigma^2)}\mid\underline{\mathbf{x}}_{t-1}\right)$$

$$= E_0 E_0\left(-\frac{\partial^2 \log l(x_t\mid\underline{\mathbf{x}}_{t-1};\boldsymbol{\theta}_0,\sigma_0^2)}{\partial(\boldsymbol{\theta}',\sigma^2)'\partial(\boldsymbol{\theta}',\sigma^2)}\mid\underline{\mathbf{x}}_{t-1}\right)$$

$$= \operatorname*{plim}_{T\to+\infty}\left(-\frac{1}{T}\sum_{t=1}^{T}\frac{\partial^2 \log l(x_t\mid\underline{\mathbf{x}}_{t-1};\boldsymbol{\theta}_0,\sigma_0^2)}{\partial(\boldsymbol{\theta}',\sigma^2)'\partial(\boldsymbol{\theta}',\sigma^2)}\right),$$

$$\mathbf{J}(\boldsymbol{\theta}_0,\sigma_0^2) = \operatorname*{plim}_{T\to+\infty}-\frac{1}{T}\frac{\partial^2 L_T^c(x;\boldsymbol{\theta}_0,\sigma_0^2)}{\partial(\boldsymbol{\theta}',\sigma^2)'\partial(\boldsymbol{\theta}',\sigma^2)}. \tag{9.25}$$

9.2.6 Asymptotic Normality of Maximum Likelihood Estimators

The asymptotic distribution of the estimator $(\hat{\boldsymbol{\theta}}_T',\hat{\sigma}_T^2)$ is derived in the usual way from the one of the score. Performing an expansion in probability of the first-order conditions, we get

$$\frac{1}{\sqrt{T}} \frac{\partial L_T^*}{\partial(\boldsymbol{\theta}', \sigma^2)'}(\mathbf{x}_T; \hat{\boldsymbol{\theta}}_T', \hat{\sigma}_T^2) = 0$$

$$\Leftrightarrow \frac{1}{\sqrt{T}} \frac{\partial L_T^*(\mathbf{x}_T; \boldsymbol{\theta}_0, \sigma_0^2)}{\partial(\boldsymbol{\theta}', \sigma^2)'} + \frac{1}{T} \frac{\partial^2 L_T^*(\mathbf{x}_T; \boldsymbol{\theta}_0, \sigma_0^2)}{\partial(\boldsymbol{\theta}', \sigma^2)'\partial(\boldsymbol{\theta}', \sigma^2)} \sqrt{T} \begin{pmatrix} \hat{\boldsymbol{\theta}}_T - \boldsymbol{\theta}_0 \\ \hat{\sigma}_T^2 - \sigma_0^2 \end{pmatrix} \approx 0$$

$$\Leftrightarrow \sqrt{T} \begin{pmatrix} \hat{\boldsymbol{\theta}}_T - \boldsymbol{\theta}_0 \\ \hat{\sigma}_T^2 - \sigma_0^2 \end{pmatrix}$$

$$\approx \left(-\operatorname*{plim}_{T \to +\infty} \frac{1}{T} \frac{\partial^2 L_T^*(\mathbf{x}_T; \boldsymbol{\theta}_0, \sigma_0^2)}{\partial(\boldsymbol{\theta}', \sigma^2)'\partial(\boldsymbol{\theta}', \sigma^2)} \right)^{-1} \frac{1}{\sqrt{T}} \frac{\partial L_T^*(\mathbf{x}_T; \boldsymbol{\theta}_0, \sigma_0^2)}{\partial(\boldsymbol{\theta}', \sigma^2)'}$$

$$\Leftrightarrow \sqrt{T} \begin{pmatrix} \hat{\boldsymbol{\theta}}_T - \boldsymbol{\theta}_0 \\ \hat{\sigma}_T^2 - \sigma_0^2 \end{pmatrix}$$

$$\approx \mathbf{J}(\boldsymbol{\theta}_0, \sigma_0^2)^{-1} \frac{1}{\sqrt{T}} \frac{\partial L_T^*(\mathbf{x}_T; \boldsymbol{\theta}_0, \sigma_0^2)}{\partial(\boldsymbol{\theta}', \sigma^2)'}.$$

Since the asymptotic distribution of the score is normal with zero mean and variance–covariance matrix $\mathbf{J}(\boldsymbol{\theta}_0, \sigma_0^2)$, we obtain

Theorem 9.17: *The maximum likelihood estimator is asymptotically normal*

$$\sqrt{T} \begin{pmatrix} \hat{\boldsymbol{\theta}}_T - \boldsymbol{\theta}_0 \\ \hat{\sigma}_T^2 - \sigma_0^2 \end{pmatrix} \xrightarrow{\mathrm{d}} \mathcal{N}\left(0; \mathbf{J}(\boldsymbol{\theta}_0, \sigma_0^2)^{-1}\right).$$

Moreover, using the form of the information matrix, we get the following:

Corollary:

(i) *The estimators $\hat{\boldsymbol{\theta}}_T$ and $\hat{\sigma}_T^2$ are asymptotically independent.*

(ii) *The asymptotic precision of $\hat{\boldsymbol{\theta}}_T$ is independent of the value of the variance σ_0^2.*

It follows from the expression of the matrix $\mathbf{J}(\boldsymbol{\theta}_0, \sigma_0^2)$ that

$$\operatorname{avar}\left(\sqrt{T}(\hat{\boldsymbol{\theta}}_T - \boldsymbol{\theta}_0)\right) = 2 \left(E_\mu \left(\frac{\partial \log g_{\theta_0}}{\partial \boldsymbol{\theta}} \frac{\partial \log g_{\theta_0}}{\partial \boldsymbol{\theta}'} \right) \right)^{-1}$$

$$= \sigma_0^2 \left(\operatorname{var}_0 \left(\frac{\partial \Pi_{\theta_0}(L)}{\partial \boldsymbol{\theta}} x_t \right) \right)^{-1} \tag{9.26}$$

$$= \sigma_0^2 \left(\operatorname{var}_0 \left(\frac{\partial \log \Pi_{\theta_0}(L)}{\partial \boldsymbol{\theta}} \epsilon_t \right) \right)^{-1}.$$

Generally the matrix avar $\left(\sqrt{T}(\hat{\boldsymbol{\theta}}_T - \boldsymbol{\theta}_0)\right)$ must be estimated. A consistent estimator is, for example

$$\hat{\sigma}_T^2 \left(\frac{1}{T}\sum_{t=1}^T \frac{\partial \Pi_{\hat{\theta}_T}(L)}{\partial \boldsymbol{\theta}} \tilde{x}_t \frac{\partial \Pi_{\hat{\theta}_T}(L)}{\partial \boldsymbol{\theta}'} \tilde{x}_t\right)^{-1}$$

$$= \hat{\sigma}_T^2 \left(\frac{1}{T}\sum_{t=1}^T \frac{\partial \log \Pi_{\hat{\theta}_T}(L)}{\partial \boldsymbol{\theta}} \tilde{\epsilon}_t \frac{\partial \log \Pi_{\hat{\theta}_T}(L)}{\partial \boldsymbol{\theta}'} \tilde{\epsilon}_t\right)^{-1}, \tag{9.27}$$

with

$$\tilde{x}_t = \begin{cases} x_t, & \text{if } t \geq 1, \\ 0, & \text{otherwise,} \end{cases}$$

$$\tilde{\epsilon}_t = \Pi_{\hat{\theta}_T}^{-1}\tilde{x}_t,$$

$$\hat{\sigma}_T^2 = \frac{1}{T}\sum_{t=1}^T \tilde{\epsilon}_t^2.$$

9.2.7 Some Examples

Estimation of the Parameters of an AR(p) Process Let us consider the model

$$x_t + \varphi_1 x_{t-1} + \ldots + \varphi_p x_{t-p} = \epsilon_t,$$

with a parameter vector

$$\boldsymbol{\theta} = (\varphi_1 \ldots \varphi_p, \sigma^2)'.$$

We have

$$\text{var}_0 \left(\frac{\partial \Pi_{\theta_0}(L)}{\partial(\varphi_1,\ldots,\varphi_p)'} x_t\right)$$

$$= \text{var}_0 \begin{pmatrix} x_{t-1} \\ \vdots \\ x_{t-p} \end{pmatrix} = \begin{pmatrix} \gamma(0) & \cdots & \gamma(p-1) \\ \vdots & \ddots & \vdots \\ \gamma(p-1) & \cdots & \gamma(0) \end{pmatrix}.$$

Given expression (9.26), we obtain

$$\text{avar}\left(\sqrt{T}(\hat{\varphi}_T - \varphi)\right) = \frac{\sigma_0^2}{\gamma(0)} \begin{pmatrix} 1 & \rho(1) & \cdots & \rho(p-1) \\ \rho(1) & 1 & \cdots & \rho(p-2) \\ \vdots & \ddots & \ddots & \vdots \\ \rho(p-1) & \cdots & \rho(1) & 1 \end{pmatrix}^{-1}.$$

Estimation of the Parameters of an MA(1) Process Let us consider the model $x_t = \epsilon_t - \theta \epsilon_{t-1}$. We have

$$\Pi_\theta(L) = 1 + \theta L + \theta^2 L^2 + \ldots + \theta^j L^j + \ldots$$

$$\frac{\partial \Pi_\theta(L)}{\partial \theta} = L + 2\theta L^2 + \ldots + j\theta^{j-1} L^j + \ldots,$$

$$\text{var}_0 \left(\frac{\partial \Pi_{\theta_0}(L)\mathbf{x}_t}{\partial \theta} \right)$$

$$= \text{var}_0 \left(x_{t-1} + 2\theta_0 x_{t-2} + \ldots + j\theta_0^{j-1} x_{t-j} + \ldots \right)$$

$$= \gamma(0) \sum_{j=1}^{\infty} j^2 \theta_0^{2j-2} + 2\gamma(1) \sum_{j=1}^{\infty} j(j+1)\theta_0^{j-1} \theta_0^j$$

$$= (1 + \theta_0^2)\sigma_0^2 \sum_{j=1}^{\infty} j^2 \theta_0^{2j-2} - 2\theta_0 \sigma_0^2 \sum_{j=1}^{\infty} (j^2 + j)\theta_0^{2j-1}$$

$$= \sigma_0^2 \left(\sum_{j=1}^{\infty} j^2 \theta_0^{2j-2} + \sum_{j=1}^{\infty} (-j^2 + 2j)\theta_0^{2j} \right).$$

Therefore

$$\text{avar}\,(\sqrt{T}(\hat{\boldsymbol{\theta}}_T - \boldsymbol{\theta}_0)) = \left(\sum_{j=1}^{\infty} j^2 \theta_0^{2j-2} + \sum_{j=1}^{\infty} (-j^2 + 2j)\theta_0^{2j} \right)^{-1}.$$

We could go on computing the sum of the series appearing in this expression. However, it is clear that the precision of the components of the moving average part is more difficult to derive than the precision of the components of the autoregressive part.

9.3 Testing Procedures

9.3.1 Main Testing Procedures

Let us consider a stationary process x, whose distribution depends on a parameter vector $\boldsymbol{\gamma}$ of dimension K. We assume that this parameter vector $\boldsymbol{\gamma}$ can be decomposed in two subvectors

$$\boldsymbol{\gamma} = \begin{pmatrix} \boldsymbol{\alpha} \\ \boldsymbol{\beta} \end{pmatrix},$$

where $\boldsymbol{\beta}$ is of size r and $\boldsymbol{\alpha}$ of size $K - r$. In what follows, we test the hypothesis $H_0 : (\boldsymbol{\beta} = \mathbf{0})$ with a sample of T observations $x_1 \ldots x_T$ of the process. Let $L_T(\mathbf{x}_T; \boldsymbol{\alpha}, \boldsymbol{\beta})$ be the log-likelihood function associated with these T observations and let

$$\hat{\gamma}_T = \begin{pmatrix} \hat{\alpha}_T \\ \hat{\beta}_T \end{pmatrix}$$

be the maximum likelihood estimator (possibly computed from an approximated likelihood function); it is implicitly defined by

$$L_T(\mathbf{x}_T; \hat{\alpha}_T, \hat{\beta}_T) = \max_{\alpha, \beta} L_T(\mathbf{x}_T; \alpha, \beta).$$

Similarly, we introduce the restricted maximum likelihood estimator under the hypothesis H_0. We write $\hat{\gamma}_T^0 = \begin{pmatrix} \hat{\alpha}_T^0 \\ 0 \end{pmatrix}$ implicitly defined by

$$L_T(\mathbf{x}_T; \hat{\alpha}_T^0, 0) = \max_{\alpha} L_T(\mathbf{x}_T; \alpha, 0).$$

There are several asymptotic methods to test the null hypothesis

$$H_0 : (\beta = 0);$$

the best-known ones are the likelihood ratio test, the Wald test, and the Lagrange multiplier (or score) test. We quickly illustrate these approaches which are asymptotically equivalent under the null hypothesis. In the following sections, we look at the principle of the Lagrange multiplier in detail, since this approach is often easier to work out and to interpret.

Likelihood Ratio Test The idea behind this test is to accept the null hypothesis if the difference between the restricted and the nonrestricted maxima of the log-likelihood function is small enough. The test statistic is

$$\xi_T^{LR} = 2 \left(L_T(\mathbf{x}_T; \hat{\alpha}_T, \hat{\beta}_T) - L_T(\mathbf{x}_T; \hat{\alpha}_T^0, 0) \right), \qquad (9.28)$$

and is always nonnegative.

Under regularity conditions almost identical to the ones guaranteeing the asymptotic normality of the maximum likelihood estimator, it can be shown that under the null hypothesis

$$\xi_T^{LR} \xrightarrow{\text{d}} \chi^2(r), \qquad (9.29)$$

where r denotes the number of restrictions implied by H_0 (that is the number of elements of β). This gives the critical value against which the value of the test statistic is to be compared.

Theorem 9.18: *The* likelihood ratio test *of the hypothesis* $H_0 : (\beta = 0)$ *entails the following decision rule*

$$\begin{cases} \text{accept the null hypothesis,} & \text{if } \xi_T^{LR} \leq \chi_{95\%}^2(r), \\ \text{reject the null hypothesis,} & \text{otherwise,} \end{cases}$$

where $\chi^2_{95\%}(r)$ denotes the 95% percentile of the chi-square distribution with r degrees of freedom (the probability of Type I error has been fixed at 5%).

Wald Test The principle consists of accepting the null hypothesis if the unrestricted estimator of β is almost zero. In section 9.2, we derived the asymptotic normality of the maximum likelihood estimator. Let

$$\mathbf{J}_{\alpha\alpha}, \quad \mathbf{J}_{\alpha\beta}, \quad \mathbf{J}_{\beta\alpha}, \quad \mathbf{J}_{\beta\beta}$$

be the Fisher information matrix blocks associated with the subvectors of parameters and let $\hat{\mathbf{J}}$ be some estimators of these blocks under the null hypothesis; under H_0

$$\sqrt{T}\begin{pmatrix} \hat{\boldsymbol{\alpha}}_T - \boldsymbol{\alpha} \\ \hat{\boldsymbol{\beta}}_T \end{pmatrix} \overset{d}{\to} \mathcal{N}\left(\begin{pmatrix} 0 \\ 0 \end{pmatrix}, \begin{pmatrix} \mathbf{J}_{\alpha\alpha} & \mathbf{J}_{\alpha\beta} \\ \mathbf{J}_{\beta\alpha} & \mathbf{J}_{\beta\beta} \end{pmatrix}^{-1} \right).$$

Examining only the lower right block of the asymptotic variance–covariance matrix, we have

$$\sqrt{T}\hat{\boldsymbol{\beta}}_T \overset{d}{\to} \mathcal{N}\left(0; \left(\mathbf{J}_{\beta\beta} - \mathbf{J}_{\beta\alpha}(\mathbf{J}_{\alpha\alpha})^{-1}\mathbf{J}_{\alpha\beta}\right)^{-1} \right).$$

Finally, computing the associated quadratic form, after estimating the variances, we notice that under H_0

$$\xi_T^W = T\hat{\boldsymbol{\beta}}_T' \left(\hat{\mathbf{J}}_{\beta\beta} - \hat{\mathbf{J}}_{\beta\alpha}\hat{\mathbf{J}}_{\alpha\alpha}^{-1}\hat{\mathbf{J}}_{\alpha\beta} \right) \hat{\boldsymbol{\beta}}_T \overset{d}{\to} \chi^2(r). \tag{9.30}$$

The statistic ξ_T^W is called *Wald statistic*.

Theorem 9.19: *The Wald test of the hypothesis $H_0 : (\beta = 0)$ entails the following decision rule*

$$\begin{cases} \text{accept the null hypothesis}, & \text{if } \xi_T^W \le \chi^2_{95\%}(r), \\ \text{reject the null hypothesis}, & \text{otherwise}. \end{cases}$$

Lagrange Multiplier Test (or Score Test) Another idea is to accept the null hypothesis if the restricted score is almost 0. Since the score is

$$\begin{pmatrix} \frac{\partial L_T}{\partial \alpha}(\mathbf{x}_T; \hat{\boldsymbol{\alpha}}_T^0, 0) \\ \frac{\partial L_T}{\partial \beta}(\mathbf{x}_T; \hat{\boldsymbol{\alpha}}_T^0, 0) \end{pmatrix} = \begin{pmatrix} 0 \\ \frac{\partial L_T}{\partial \beta}(\mathbf{x}_T; \hat{\boldsymbol{\alpha}}_T^0, 0) \end{pmatrix},$$

it is enough to look at the second term.

To determine the critical value, we have to look at the asymptotic distribution of

$$\frac{1}{\sqrt{T}} \frac{\partial L_T}{\partial \beta}(\mathbf{x}_T; \hat{\boldsymbol{\alpha}}_T^0, 0),$$

under the null hypothesis. We know that the asymptotic relationship between the estimator $\hat{\boldsymbol{\alpha}}_T^0$ and the corresponding score is

$$\sqrt{T}(\hat{\boldsymbol{\alpha}}_T^0 - \boldsymbol{\alpha}) \approx (\mathbf{J}_{\alpha\alpha}^0)^{-1} \frac{1}{\sqrt{T}} \frac{\partial L_T}{\partial \boldsymbol{\alpha}}(\mathbf{x}_T; \boldsymbol{\alpha}, \mathbf{0}).$$

On the other hand, expanding around $\boldsymbol{\alpha}$, we get

$$\frac{1}{\sqrt{T}} \frac{\partial L_T}{\partial \boldsymbol{\beta}}(\mathbf{x}_T; \hat{\boldsymbol{\alpha}}_T^0, \mathbf{0}) \approx \frac{1}{\sqrt{T}} \frac{\partial L_T}{\partial \boldsymbol{\beta}}(\mathbf{x}_T; \boldsymbol{\alpha}, \mathbf{0}) + \frac{1}{T} \frac{\partial^2 L_T}{\partial \boldsymbol{\beta} \partial \boldsymbol{\alpha}'} \sqrt{T}(\hat{\boldsymbol{\alpha}}_T^0 - \boldsymbol{\alpha})$$

$$\approx \frac{1}{\sqrt{T}} \frac{\partial L_T}{\partial \boldsymbol{\beta}}(\mathbf{x}_T; \boldsymbol{\alpha}, \mathbf{0}) - \mathbf{J}_{\beta\alpha}^0 \left(\mathbf{J}_{\alpha\alpha}^0\right)^{-1} \frac{1}{\sqrt{T}} \frac{\partial L_T}{\partial \boldsymbol{\alpha}'}(\mathbf{x}_T; \boldsymbol{\alpha}, \mathbf{0}).$$

Then given the asymptotic normality of the score (cf. 9.17) we have under the null hypothesis

$$\frac{1}{\sqrt{T}} \frac{\partial L_T}{\partial \boldsymbol{\beta}}(\mathbf{x}_T; \hat{\boldsymbol{\alpha}}_T^0, \mathbf{0}) \xrightarrow{\text{d}} \mathcal{N}\left(\mathbf{0}; \mathbf{J}_{\beta\beta}^0 - \mathbf{J}_{\beta\alpha}^0 \left(\mathbf{J}_{\alpha\alpha}^0\right)^{-1} \mathbf{J}_{\alpha\beta}^0\right).$$

The associated quadratic form is

$$\xi_T^{LM} = \frac{1}{T} \frac{\partial L_T}{\partial \boldsymbol{\beta}'}(\mathbf{x}_T; \hat{\boldsymbol{\alpha}}_T^0, \mathbf{0}) \left(\hat{\mathbf{J}}_{\beta\beta}^0 - \hat{\mathbf{J}}_{\beta\alpha}^0 \left(\hat{\mathbf{J}}_{\alpha\alpha}^0\right)^{-1} \hat{\mathbf{J}}_{\alpha\beta}^0\right)^{-1} \frac{\partial L_T}{\partial \boldsymbol{\beta}}(\mathbf{x}_T; \hat{\boldsymbol{\alpha}}_T^0, \mathbf{0}).$$

$$(9.31)$$

Theorem 9.20: *The* Lagrange multiplier test *of the hypothesis* H_0 : $(\boldsymbol{\beta} = \mathbf{0})$ *entails the following decision rule*

$$\begin{cases} \text{accept the null hypothesis,} & \text{if } \xi_T^{LM} < \chi_{95\%}^2(r), \\ \text{reject the null hypothesis,} & \text{otherwise.} \end{cases}$$

We can notice that the matrix of the quadratic form is equal to the one appearing in the Wald statistic, apart from being computed under H_0.

Comparison of the Three Approaches The three previous approaches above give quite similar asymptotic results. This comes from the property below which is given without proof (cf. Gourieroux and Monfort, 1989, chapter 17).

Theorem 9.21: *Under the null hypothesis, the statistics* ξ_T^{LR}, ξ_T^W, *and* ξ_T^{LM} *are asymptotically equivalent.*

The choice between the three principles can then be based on their properties in small samples, but these properties are difficult to derive; it may also be based on simplicity of computation.

Since the likelihood ratio statistic requires the computation of the restricted and unrestricted estimators, the Wald test requires the unrestricted estimator and the Lagrange multiplier the restricted one, it is often the latter approach which is the simplest one, the null hypothesis being characterized by a smaller number of parameters than the maintained hypothesis.

In the next section we provide two simple ways of computing the statistic ξ_T^{LM} which only involve linear regressions.

9.3.2 Approximate Linear Model (Univariate Case)

The Model The Lagrange multiplier statistic can be simplified when the parameter of interest $\boldsymbol{\theta}$ restricted by the hypothesis H_0 concerns only the lag polynomial. Introducing the variance of the noise separately, and modifying the notations consequently, the model is defined by

$$\Pi_\theta(L)x_t = \epsilon_t \iff x_t = H_\theta(L)\epsilon_t,$$

where $\epsilon = \{\epsilon_t\}$ is a scalar Gaussian white noise, with variance σ^2. The parameter $\boldsymbol{\theta}$ is decomposed into $\boldsymbol{\theta} = \begin{pmatrix} \alpha \\ \beta \end{pmatrix}$ and the hypothesis to be tested is $H_0 : (\boldsymbol{\beta} = \mathbf{0})$.

Taking into account the change of notation, and letting

$$\mathbf{b} = \frac{\partial L_T}{\partial \boldsymbol{\beta}}(\mathbf{x}_T; \hat{\boldsymbol{\alpha}}_T^0, \mathbf{0}, \hat{\sigma}_T^{02}),$$

the Lagrange multiplier statistic is

$$\xi_T^{LM} = \frac{1}{T}\mathbf{b}'\left(\hat{\mathbf{J}}_{\beta\beta}^0 - \hat{\mathbf{J}}_{\beta(\alpha,\sigma^2)}^0 \left(\hat{\mathbf{J}}_{(\alpha,\sigma^2)(\alpha,\sigma^2)}^0\right)^{-1}\hat{\mathbf{J}}_{(\alpha,\sigma^2)\beta}^0\right)^{-1}\mathbf{b}.$$

Since the Fisher's information matrix of this model is block diagonal

$$\mathbf{J}^0 = \begin{pmatrix} \mathbf{J}_{\alpha\alpha}^0 & \mathbf{J}_{\alpha\beta}^0 & 0 \\ \mathbf{J}_{\beta\alpha}^0 & \mathbf{J}_{\beta\beta}^0 & 0 \\ 0 & 0 & \mathbf{J}_{\sigma^2\sigma^2} \end{pmatrix},$$

we can easily verify that the matrix in the quadratic form defining ξ_T^{LM} reduces to

$$\left(\hat{\mathbf{J}}_{\beta\beta}^0 - \hat{\mathbf{J}}_{\beta\alpha}^0 \left(\hat{\mathbf{J}}_{\alpha\alpha}^0\right)^{-1}\hat{\mathbf{J}}_{\alpha\beta}^0\right)^{-1},$$

and that

$$\xi_T^{LM} = \frac{1}{T}\mathbf{b}'\left(\hat{\mathbf{J}}_{\beta\beta}^0 - \hat{\mathbf{J}}_{\beta\alpha}^0(\hat{\mathbf{J}}_{\alpha\alpha}^0)^{-1}\hat{\mathbf{J}}_{\alpha\beta}^0\right)^{-1}\mathbf{b}. \tag{9.32}$$

The Linear Model Built from the Scores There exist several equivalent forms of the Lagrange multiplier statistics, depending on the likelihood function type used (exact or approximated) and on the choice

of the consistent estimator of the information matrix. Looking at the
conditional likelihood function, we have

$$\frac{\partial L_T^c}{\partial \boldsymbol{\theta}}(\mathbf{x}_T; \boldsymbol{\theta}, \sigma^2) = -\frac{1}{\sigma^2} \sum_{t=1}^{T} \frac{\partial \Pi_\theta(L)}{\partial \boldsymbol{\theta}} \tilde{x}_t \, \Pi_\theta(L)\tilde{x}_t$$

with $\tilde{x}_t = \begin{cases} x_t, \text{ if } t \geq 1, \\ 0, \text{ otherwise.} \end{cases}$

Let us define

$$\mathbf{z}_{1t} = \frac{\partial \Pi_{\hat{\theta}_T^0}(L)}{\partial \alpha} \tilde{x}_t, \quad \mathbf{z}_{2t} = \frac{\partial \Pi_{\hat{\theta}_T^0}(L)}{\partial \beta} \tilde{x}_t,$$

and let us denote the residual under the null hypothesis as

$$\tilde{\epsilon}_t^0 = \Pi_{\hat{\theta}_T^0}(L)\tilde{x}_t.$$

The restricted estimator of the variance is

$$\hat{\sigma}_T^{02} = \frac{1}{T} \sum_{t=1}^{T} \left(\tilde{\epsilon}_t^0\right)^2.$$

On the other hand, consistent estimators of the elements of the information matrix are

$$\hat{\mathbf{J}}_{\beta\alpha}^0 = \frac{1}{\hat{\sigma}_T^{02}} \frac{1}{T} \sum_{t=1}^{T} \mathbf{z}_{2t}\mathbf{z}_{1t}',$$

$$\hat{\mathbf{J}}_{\beta\beta}^0 = \frac{1}{\hat{\sigma}_T^{02}} \frac{1}{T} \sum_{t=1}^{T} \mathbf{z}_{2t}\mathbf{z}_{2t}',$$

$$\hat{\mathbf{J}}_{\alpha\alpha}^0 = \frac{1}{\hat{\sigma}_T^{02}} \frac{1}{T} \sum_{t=1}^{T} \mathbf{z}_{1t}\mathbf{z}_{1t}'.$$

Substituting them in the expression of the test statistic, we get the following result

Theorem 9.22: *A possible choice of the Lagrange multiplier statistic is*

$$\xi_T^{LM} = \frac{1}{\hat{\sigma}_T^{02}} (\sum_{t=1}^{T} \mathbf{z}_{2t}\tilde{\epsilon}_t^0)' \left(\sum_{t=1}^{T} \mathbf{z}_{2t}\mathbf{z}_{2t}' \right.$$

$$\left. - \sum_{t=1}^{T} \mathbf{z}_{2t}\mathbf{z}_{1t}'(\sum_{t=1}^{T} \mathbf{z}_{1t}\mathbf{z}_{1t}')^{-1} \sum_{t=1}^{T} \mathbf{z}_{1t}\mathbf{z}_{2t}' \right)^{-1} (\sum_{t=1}^{T} \mathbf{z}_{2t}\tilde{\epsilon}_t^0)$$

with

$$\mathbf{z}_{1t} = \frac{\partial \Pi_{\hat{\theta}_T^0}(L)}{\partial \boldsymbol{\alpha}} \tilde{x}_t, \quad \mathbf{z}_{2t} = \frac{\partial \Pi_{\hat{\theta}_T^0}(L)}{\partial \boldsymbol{\beta}} \tilde{x}_t,$$

$$\tilde{\epsilon}_t^0 = \Pi_{\hat{\theta}_T^0}(L) \tilde{x}_t, \hat{\sigma}_t^{02} = \frac{1}{T} \sum_{t=1}^{T} \left(\tilde{\epsilon}_t^0 \right)^2.$$

This expression for the statistic has a direct interpretation in terms of regression. Let us consider the auxiliary regression model

$$\tilde{\epsilon}_t^0 = \mathbf{z}'_{1t}\mathbf{a} + \mathbf{z}'_{2t}\mathbf{b} + e_t, \quad t = 1, \ldots, T, \tag{9.33}$$

and the corresponding null hypothesis $H_0^* : (\mathbf{b} = \mathbf{0})$.

If we write $\mathbf{Z}$ (resp.$\mathbf{Z}_1$) the matrices with rows $(\mathbf{z}'_{1t}, \mathbf{z}'_{2t})$ (resp. $\mathbf{z}'_{1t}$), and $\mathbf{M} = \mathbf{Z}(\mathbf{Z}'\mathbf{Z})^{-1}\mathbf{Z}'$, $\mathbf{M}_1 = \mathbf{Z}_1(\mathbf{Z}'_1\mathbf{Z}_1)^{-1}\mathbf{Z}'_1$, the respective projectors on the spaces spanned by the columns of $\mathbf{Z} = (\mathbf{Z}_1, \mathbf{Z}_2)$ and of $\mathbf{Z}_1$, from the likelihood equations we get

$$\mathbf{M}_1 \tilde{\boldsymbol{\varepsilon}}_0 = 0 \Leftrightarrow \mathbf{Z}'_1 \tilde{\boldsymbol{\varepsilon}}_0 = 0.$$

This restriction satisfied by the residuals leads to the following interpretation.

Theorem 9.23: *If SSR_U represents the sum of the square residuals of the unrestricted auxiliary model (9.33), and SSR_R represents the same sum under the null hypothesis H_0^*, we get*

$$\xi_T^{LM} = \frac{SSR_R - SSR_U}{\hat{\sigma}_T^{02}}.$$

PROOF: We have

$$SSR_R - SSR_U = \tilde{\boldsymbol{\varepsilon}}'^0(\mathbf{I} - \mathbf{M}_1)\tilde{\boldsymbol{\varepsilon}}^0 - \tilde{\boldsymbol{\varepsilon}}'^0(\mathbf{I} - \mathbf{M})\tilde{\boldsymbol{\varepsilon}}^0$$

$$= \tilde{\boldsymbol{\varepsilon}}'^0(\mathbf{M} - \mathbf{M}_1)\tilde{\boldsymbol{\varepsilon}}^0 = \tilde{\boldsymbol{\varepsilon}}'^0\mathbf{M}\tilde{\boldsymbol{\varepsilon}}^0$$

$$= \tilde{\boldsymbol{\varepsilon}}'^0\mathbf{Z}(\mathbf{Z}'\mathbf{Z})^{-1}\mathbf{Z}'\tilde{\boldsymbol{\varepsilon}}^0$$

$$= (0, \tilde{\boldsymbol{\varepsilon}}'^0\mathbf{Z}_2) \begin{pmatrix} \mathbf{Z}'_1\mathbf{Z}_1 & \mathbf{Z}'_1\mathbf{Z}_2 \\ \mathbf{Z}'_2\mathbf{Z}_1 & \mathbf{Z}'_2\mathbf{Z}_2 \end{pmatrix}^{-1} \begin{pmatrix} 0 \\ \mathbf{Z}'_2\tilde{\boldsymbol{\varepsilon}}^0 \end{pmatrix}$$

$$= \tilde{\boldsymbol{\varepsilon}}'^0\mathbf{Z}_2\{\mathbf{Z}'_2\mathbf{Z}_2 - \mathbf{Z}'_2\mathbf{Z}_1(\mathbf{Z}'_1\mathbf{Z}_1)^{-1}\mathbf{Z}'_1\mathbf{Z}_2\}^{-1}\mathbf{Z}'_2\tilde{\boldsymbol{\varepsilon}}^0$$

$$= \hat{\sigma}_T^{02}\xi_T^{LM}.$$

□

Locally Equivalent Alternatives Let us consider two models which are introduced to describe the evolution of the series and have the same types of parameters

$$\Pi_{\alpha,\beta}(L)x_t = \epsilon_t, \quad \epsilon_t \sim N(0,\sigma^2), \tag{9.34}$$

$$\Pi^*_{\alpha,\beta}(L)x_t = \eta_t, \quad \eta_t \sim N(0,\sigma^2), \tag{9.35}$$

keeping the same parameter notation for ease of reference.

Since the Lagrange multiplier test is based on the behavior of the derivative of the log-likelihood function in a null hypothesis neighborhood, it is therefore natural to study these models in such a neighborhood.

Definition 9.2: *The two models are said to provide* locally equivalent alternatives, *in a neighborhood of* $H_0 : (\boldsymbol{\beta} = \mathbf{0})$, *if the two following conditions are satisfied*

(i) $\Pi_{\alpha,0}(L) = \Pi^*_{\alpha,0}(L)$;

(ii) $\partial \Pi_{\alpha,0}(L)/\partial \beta = \mathbf{A}\left(\partial \Pi^*_{\alpha,0}(L)/\partial \beta\right)$ *for a nonsingular matrix* $\mathbf{A}$.

The first condition means that both hypothesis $H_0 : (\boldsymbol{\beta} = \mathbf{0})$, defined on the model (9.35), and $H^*_0 : (\boldsymbol{\beta} = \mathbf{0})$ defined on the model (9.36), correspond to the same set of distributions. The second equality deals with the alternatives $H_1 : (\boldsymbol{\beta} \neq \mathbf{0})$ and $H^*_1 : (\boldsymbol{\beta} \neq \mathbf{0})$ associated with both models. Restricting ourselves to the alternative hypotheses involving distributions corresponding to small values of the parameter $\boldsymbol{\beta}$, we conclude that these alternatives are first-order equivalent.

The condition (i) implies that the restricted estimators $\hat{\boldsymbol{\alpha}}^0_T$ and $\hat{\sigma}^{02}_T$ are the same ones for both models. It also leads to

$$\frac{\partial \Pi_{\alpha,0}(L)}{\partial \alpha} = \frac{\partial \Pi^*_{\alpha,0}(L)}{\partial \alpha};$$

the component vectors

$$\mathbf{z}_{1t} = \frac{\partial \Pi_{\hat{\alpha}^0_T,0}(L)}{\partial \boldsymbol{\alpha}}\tilde{x}_t \text{ and } \mathbf{z}^*_{1t} = \frac{\partial \Pi^*_{\hat{\alpha}^0_T,0}(L)}{\partial \boldsymbol{\alpha}}\tilde{x}_t$$

coincide. On the other hand, the condition (ii) implies that the vectors $\mathbf{z}_{2t}$ and $\mathbf{z}^*_{2t}$ are linked by a linear bijective function. We derive then the following theorem

Theorem 9.24: *If two models provide locally equivalent alternatives in a neighborhood of the null hypothesis, the Lagrange multiplier statistics computed from the conditional approach coincide*

$$\xi^{LM}_T = \xi^{*LM}_T.$$

This result may be used in two different ways

(i) When the test rejects the null hypothesis, it is obvious that there is a priori no reason to select H_1 rather than H_1^*.

(ii) The property may serve to determine more easily the statistic ξ_T^{LM} by substituting to the initial model another more convenient, locally equivalent model.

Decomposable Models In order to illustrate the approach of locally equivalent alternatives, we consider the usual case, where the autoregressive operator is decomposed into

$$\Pi_{\alpha,\beta}(L) = \Pi_\alpha^1(L)\Pi_\beta^2(L), \quad \text{with } \Pi_\alpha^1(0) = 1 \tag{9.36}$$

(and therefore also $\Pi_\beta^2(0) = 1$).

Expanding this operator in a neighborhood of $\beta = \mathbf{0}$, we get

$$\Pi_{\alpha,\beta}(L) \approx \Pi_\alpha^1(L)\left(\Pi_0^2(L) + \frac{\partial\Pi_0^2(L)}{\partial\beta'}\beta\right).$$

Since we can always choose by convention the decomposition so that $\Pi_0^2(L) = 1$, we have

$$\Pi_{\alpha,\beta}(L) \approx \Pi_\alpha^1(L) + \Pi_\alpha^1(L)\frac{\partial\Pi_0^2(L)}{\partial\beta'}\beta.$$

Therefore it is natural to consider both models

$$\Pi_\alpha^1(L)\Pi_\beta^2(L)x_t = \epsilon_t, \operatorname{var}(\epsilon_t) = \sigma^2, \tag{9.37}$$

$$\Pi_{\alpha,\beta}^*(L)x_t = \left(\Pi_\alpha^1(L) + \Pi_\alpha^1(L)\frac{\partial\Pi_0^2(L)}{\partial\beta'}\beta\right)x_t = \eta_t, \operatorname{var}(\eta_t) = \sigma^2. \tag{9.38}$$

We verify right away that

$$\Pi_{\alpha,0}(L) = \Pi_\alpha^1(L) = \Pi_{\alpha,0}^*(L),$$

and that

$$\frac{\partial\Pi_{\alpha,0}(L)}{\partial\beta} = \Pi_\alpha^1(L)\frac{\partial\Pi_0^2(L)}{\partial\beta} = \frac{\partial\Pi_{\alpha,0}^*(L)}{\partial\beta}.$$

Theorem 9.25: *To perform the Lagrange multiplier test of the hypothesis $H_0 : (\beta = 0)$, the decomposable model (9.36) can be replaced by*

$$\Pi_\alpha^1(L)x_t + \Pi_\alpha^1(L)\frac{\partial\Pi_0^2(L)}{\partial\beta'}x_t\beta = \eta_t, \quad \operatorname{var}(\eta_t) = \sigma^2,$$

which provides a locally equivalent alternative.

The advantage is obvious. We substitute the initial model, generally nonlinear in β, with another model, which is linear.

Another approximately linear model can easily be deduced from the model just obtained. Let us write

$$\mathbf{z}_t = \Pi^1_{\hat{\alpha}^0_T}(L)\frac{\partial \Pi^2_0(L)}{\partial \boldsymbol{\beta}}x_t, \tag{9.39}$$

and let us introduce the artificial model

$$\Pi^1_\alpha(L)x_t + \mathbf{z}'_t\boldsymbol{\beta} = \omega_t, \operatorname{var}(\omega_t) = \mu^2. \tag{9.40}$$

If we perform the Lagrange multiplier test of $H_0 : \{\boldsymbol{\beta} = \mathbf{0}\}$ as if the estimator $\hat{\alpha}^0_T$ in $\mathbf{z}_t$ were deterministic, we notice that the Lagrange multiplier test statistic coincides with the one of the initial model.

Theorem 9.26: *The statistic ξ^{LM}_T can be computed from the approximately linear model*

$$\Pi^1_\alpha(L)x_t + \mathbf{z}'_t\boldsymbol{\beta} = \omega_t, \ \operatorname{var}(\omega_t) = \mu^2,$$

with $\mathbf{z}_t = \Pi^1_{\hat{\alpha}^0_T}(L)\frac{\partial \Pi^2_0(L)}{\partial \boldsymbol{\beta}}x_t$, and considering $\hat{\boldsymbol{\alpha}}^0_T$ as deterministic.

This last approximation is very simple to use:

(i)   generally we start by estimating the model under the null hypothesis which provides the estimators $\hat{\alpha}^0_T, \hat{\sigma}^{02}_T$ and the restricted residuals $\tilde{\epsilon}^0_t, t = 1, \ldots, T$.

(ii) Then we get the statistic ξ^{LM}_T by testing $(\boldsymbol{\beta} = \mathbf{0})$ in the artificial model

$$\Pi^1_\alpha(L)x_t + \mathbf{z}'_t\boldsymbol{\beta} = \omega_t, \quad \text{with} \quad \mathbf{z}_t = \frac{\partial \Pi^2_0(L)}{\partial \boldsymbol{\beta}}\tilde{\epsilon}^0_t.$$

Thus, the test becomes a test of the omitted variables $\mathbf{z}_t$, which are easily computed from the restricted residuals.

Another interpretation of the test is deduced from the estimated score expression. Indeed, we get

$$\frac{\partial L^c_T}{\partial \boldsymbol{\beta}}(\mathbf{x}_T; \hat{\boldsymbol{\alpha}}^0_T, \mathbf{0}, \hat{\sigma}^{02}_T)$$

$$= -\frac{1}{\hat{\sigma}^{02}_T}\sum_{t=1}^T \left(\frac{\partial \Pi^2_0(L)}{\partial \boldsymbol{\beta}'}\Pi^1_{\hat{\alpha}^0_T}(L)x_t\right)\left(\Pi^2_0(L)\Pi^1_{\hat{\alpha}^0_T}(L)x_t\right)$$

$$= -\frac{1}{\hat{\sigma}^{02}_T}\sum_{t=1}^T \frac{\partial \Pi^2_0(L)}{\partial \boldsymbol{\beta}'}\tilde{\epsilon}^0_t\, \tilde{\epsilon}^0_t.$$

Therefore the test turns out to be a test of the orthogonality of the restricted residuals and the variables $\mathbf{z}_t$.

Inverse Models Given a decomposable model

$$\Pi^1_\alpha(L)\Pi^2_\beta(L)x_t = \epsilon_t, \ \operatorname{var}(\epsilon_t) = \sigma^2, \text{with } \Pi^2_0(L) = 1,$$

we can consider at the same time the partially inverted model

$$\Pi_\alpha^1(L) \frac{1}{\Pi_\beta^2(L)} x_t = \eta_t, \ \text{var}(\eta_t) = \sigma^2. \tag{9.41}$$

Theorem 9.27: *The decomposable model and the associated partially inverted model provide locally equivalent alternatives for the hypothesis* $H_0 : (\boldsymbol{\beta} = \mathbf{0})$.

PROOF: Let us write $\tilde{\Pi}_{\alpha,\beta}(L) = \Pi_\alpha^1(L)/\Pi_\beta^2(L)$. Then we can verify both conditions of definition 9.2

(i)

$$\tilde{\Pi}_{\alpha,0}(L) = \Pi_\alpha^1(L) \frac{1}{\Pi_0^2(L)} = \Pi_\alpha^1(L) = \Pi_{\alpha,0}(L);$$

(ii)

$$\frac{\partial \tilde{\Pi}_{\alpha,0}(L)}{\partial \beta} = -\frac{\Pi_\alpha^1(L)}{(\Pi_0^2(L))^2} \frac{\partial \Pi_0^2(L)}{\partial \beta} = -\frac{\partial \Pi_{\alpha,0}(L)}{\partial \beta}.$$

□

Example 9.4: For example let us suppose that the null hypothesis corresponds to an ARMA(p, q) representation

$$\Pi_{1,\alpha}^1(L) = \frac{\Phi(L)}{\Theta(L)}, \ \text{with degree}(\Phi) = p, \ \text{degree}(\Theta) = q,$$

and let us take a lag polynomial of degree r as the second factor

$$\Pi_\beta^2(L) = 1 + \beta_1 L + \ldots + \beta_r L^r.$$

The direct model $\Pi_\alpha^1(L)\Pi_\beta^2(L)$ corresponds to an ARMA$(p + r, q)$ representation and the inverse model

$$\Pi_\alpha^1(L) \frac{1}{\Pi_\beta^2(L)}$$

to an ARMA$(p, q + r)$ representation. Thus, from theorem 9.27, the Lagrange multiplier statistic to test an ARMA(p, q) representation against an ARMA$(p+r, q)$ representation is identical to the one obtained to test an ARMA(p, q) representation against an ARMA$(p, q + r)$ representation.

Moreover, we can easily derive an interpretation of the test statistic. We have

$$\Pi_{\alpha,\beta}(L) = \frac{\Phi(L)}{\Theta(L)}(1 + \beta_1 L + \ldots + \beta_r L^r),$$

$$\frac{\partial \Pi_{\alpha,\beta}(L)}{\partial \beta} = \frac{\Phi(L)}{\Theta(L)} \begin{pmatrix} L \\ L^2 \\ \vdots \\ L^r \end{pmatrix}.$$

The variables $\mathbf{z}_{2t}$ appearing in the expression of the Lagrange Multiplier statistic (cf. theorem 9.22) are

$$\mathbf{z}_{2t} = \frac{\hat{\Phi}_0(L)}{\hat{\Theta}_0(L)} \begin{pmatrix} L \\ L^2 \\ \vdots \\ L^r \end{pmatrix} x_t = \begin{pmatrix} L \\ L^2 \\ \vdots \\ L^r \end{pmatrix} \tilde{\epsilon}_t^0 = \begin{pmatrix} \tilde{\epsilon}_{t-1}^0 \\ \vdots \\ \tilde{\epsilon}_{t-r}^0 \end{pmatrix}.$$

Thus the product $\sum_{t=1}^{T} \mathbf{z}_{2t}\tilde{\epsilon}_t^0$ is equal to

$$\left(\sum_{t=1}^{T} \tilde{\epsilon}_t^0 \tilde{\epsilon}_{t-1}^0, \ldots, \sum_{t=1}^{T} \tilde{\epsilon}_t^0 \tilde{\epsilon}_{t-r}^0 \right)',$$

and the test statistic appears as a function of the first r sample covariances computed on restricted residuals.

9.3.3 White Noise Test

As an example let us examine the white noise hypothesis tests more closely. For simplification purposes, we limit ourselves to the statistic to be used when the parameter vector β contains just one element.

A Class of Tests Under the white noise hypothesis the components x_t of the process are not correlated. Thus, there is no correlation between the current value of the process at time t, x_t, and a linear combination of past values

$$A(L)x_t = (a_1 L + a_2 L^2 + \ldots + a_k L^K + \ldots)x_t.$$

It is natural to consider the statistic corresponding to the square empirical correlation between x_t and $A(L)x_t$

$$\xi_T(A) = \frac{\left(\sum_{t=1}^{T} x_t (A(L)x_t) \right)^2}{\sum_{t=1}^{T} x_t^2 \sum_{t=1}^{T} (A(L)x_t)^2}. \tag{9.42}$$

Under the null hypothesis, $\{x_t\}$ is an independent white noise and we can apply the standard limit theorems

$$\operatorname*{plim}_{T \to +\infty} \frac{1}{T} \sum_{t=1}^{T} x_t^2 = \operatorname{var}(x_t) = \sigma^2;$$

$$\operatorname*{plim}_{T \to +\infty} \frac{1}{T} \sum_{t=1}^{T} (A(L)x_t)^2 = \operatorname{var}(A(L)x_t) = \left(\sum_{k=1}^{\infty} a_k^2 \right) \sigma^2.$$

Moreover, asymptotic normality follows

$$\frac{1}{\sqrt{T}} \sum_{t=1}^{T} x_t (A(L)x_t) \xrightarrow{d} N \left(0, \sigma^4 \sum_{k=1}^{\infty} a_k^2 \right).$$

Indeed, the components $x_t, A(L)x_t$ are uncorrelated, since

$$E \left(x_t (A(L)x_t) \cdot x_{t+h} (A(L)x_{t+h}) \right)$$

$$= E(x_t) E \left((A(L)x_t) \, x_{t+h} \, (A(L)x_{t+h}) \right) = 0$$

for $h < 0$ and their common variance is

$$E \left(x_t^2 (A(L)x_t)^2 \right) = E(x_t^2) E (A(L)x_t)^2 = \sigma^4 \sum_{k=1}^{\infty} a_k^2.$$

Thus we have the following theorem

Theorem 9.28: *Under the white noise hypothesis, we have*

$$T\xi_T(A) \xrightarrow{d} \chi^2(1).$$

Therefore, a white noise test entails the following decision rule

$$\begin{cases} \text{accept the null hypothesis,} & \text{if } T\xi_T(A) \leq \chi^2_{95\%}(1), \\ \text{reject the null hypothesis,} & \text{otherwise.} \end{cases}$$

Distribution of the Test Statistic under Local Alternatives In order to get the form of the test, we have determined the distribution of $T\xi_T(A)$ under the null hypothesis. Now we are looking for this distribution under a *sequence of local alternatives*. We assume that the alternative model is

$$\Pi_{\boldsymbol{\theta}_T}(L)x_t = \epsilon_t, \qquad \Pi_{\boldsymbol{\theta}_T}(0) = 1, \tag{9.43}$$

where the parameter $\boldsymbol{\theta}_T$ is not fixed, but is a function of the number of observations. More precisely, we write

$$\boldsymbol{\theta}_T = \frac{\boldsymbol{\theta}^*}{\sqrt{T}}. \tag{9.44}$$

We have then the approximations

$$\left(1 + \frac{\partial \Pi_0(L)}{\partial \theta} \frac{\boldsymbol{\theta}^*}{\sqrt{T}}\right) x_t \approx \epsilon_t (\text{since } \Pi_0(L) = 1)$$

$$\Leftrightarrow x_t \approx \left(1 - \frac{\partial \Pi_0(L)}{\partial \theta} \frac{\boldsymbol{\theta}^*}{\sqrt{T}}\right) \epsilon_t.$$

Since $\Pi_\theta(0) = 1$, notice that we always have

$$\frac{\partial \Pi_0}{\partial \theta}(0) = 0.$$

We can then establish the asymptotic behavior of the test statistic (cf. exercise 9.7).

Theorem 9.29: *Under the sequence of local alternatives (9.44), $T\xi_T(A)$ converges in distribution to a noncentral chi-square distribution with one degree of freedom, and the noncentrality parameter*

$$\boldsymbol{\theta}^{*2} \frac{\left(\text{cov}\left(\frac{\partial \Pi_0(L)}{\partial \theta} \epsilon_t, A(L)\epsilon_t\right)\right)^2}{\text{var}(\epsilon_t) \, \text{var}(A(L)\epsilon_t)}.$$

Search for a Locally Optimal Test Let us then assume that the model

$$\Pi_\theta(L) x_t = \epsilon_t,$$

corresponds to the maintained hypothesis. It is interesting to examine whether there exists a test with the greatest power, among all the previous tests based on $\xi_T(A)$ with A varying. In fact, we cannot compare the power of the test for any value of the parameter in a uniform way, but we can do it in a neighborhood of $\boldsymbol{\theta} = \mathbf{0}$, for example for the local alternatives associated with $\boldsymbol{\theta}_T = \boldsymbol{\theta}^*/\sqrt{T}$. The asymptotic power of the test is

$$\lim_T P_{\boldsymbol{\theta}_T}\left(T\xi_T(A) > \chi^2_{95\%}(1)\right).$$

Since under $\boldsymbol{\theta}_T$, $T\xi_T(A)$ follows asymptotically a noncentral chi-square distribution, and since the quantity $\lim_T P_{\boldsymbol{\theta}_T}\left(T\xi_T(A) > \chi^2_{95\%}(1)\right)$ is an increasing function of the noncentrality parameter, the search for a locally optimal test comes down to the solution of the problem

$$\max_A \boldsymbol{\theta}^{*2} \frac{\left(\text{cov}\left(\frac{\partial \Pi_0(L)}{\partial \theta} \epsilon_t, A(L)\epsilon_t\right)\right)^2}{\text{var}(\epsilon_t) \, \text{var}(A(L)\epsilon_t)}$$

$$\Leftrightarrow \max_A \boldsymbol{\theta}^{*2} \frac{\left(\text{cov}\left(\frac{\partial \Pi_0(L)}{\partial \theta} \epsilon_t, A(L)\epsilon_t\right)\right)^2}{\text{var}\left(\frac{\partial \Pi_0(L)}{\partial \theta} \epsilon_t\right) \text{var}(A(L)\epsilon_t)}.$$

We know that the correlation between these zero-mean variables is the greatest when the variables are proportional; this provides the solutions

$$A^*(L) = a \frac{\partial \Pi_0(L)}{\partial \theta}.$$

Theorem 9.30: *The Lagrange multiplier test of the white noise hypothesis against the model $\Pi_\theta(L)x_t = \epsilon_t$, is optimal in the previous class.*

PROOF: By direct application of formulas in section 9.3.2, we have

$$\frac{\partial L_T}{\partial \theta}(\mathbf{x}_T; 0) = -\frac{1}{\sigma^2} \sum_{t=1}^{T} x_t \frac{\partial \Pi_0(L)}{\partial \theta} x_t.$$

This shows that the test is based on the empirical covariance between x_t and

$$A^*(L)x_t = -\frac{1}{\sigma^2} \frac{\partial \Pi_0(L)}{\partial \theta} x_t$$

(and the statistic is derived directly from the square correlation after reduction). □

9.4 Extensions to the Multivariate Case

The results in the previous sections can be extended to the multivariate case. We present such generalizations for (exact or approximated) likelihood function expressions, likelihood equations, and Fisher's information matrix. Moreover, we explain the estimation problem of a pure autoregressive model and describe one case where it is possible to treat it as a univariate model.

In this section, the observations $\mathbf{y}_1, \ldots, \mathbf{y}_T$ relate to an n-dimensional stationary process having an infinite autoregressive representation

$$\Pi_\theta(L)\mathbf{y}_t = \boldsymbol{\epsilon}_t, \quad \text{with } \Pi_\theta(0) = \mathbf{I}, \quad \text{var}(\boldsymbol{\epsilon}_t) = \boldsymbol{\Omega},$$

where the parameters $\boldsymbol{\theta}$ and $\boldsymbol{\Omega}$ are not related to each other.

9.4.1 Conditional Log-likelihood Function

It is easy to give a number of expressions for the conditional log-likelihood function

$$\log \left(\prod_{t=1}^{T} l(\mathbf{y}_t | \mathbf{y}_{t-l}; \boldsymbol{\theta}, \boldsymbol{\Omega}) \right),$$

recalling that in this expression the values of $\mathbf{y}_t$ associated with null or negative indexes t are put to zero.

Time Domain We have

$$L_T^c(\mathbf{y}; \boldsymbol{\theta}, \boldsymbol{\Omega}) = -\frac{nT}{2} \log 2\pi - \frac{T}{2} \log \det \boldsymbol{\Omega}$$

$$-\frac{1}{2} \sum_{t=1}^{T} (\Pi_\theta(L)\mathbf{y}_t)' \boldsymbol{\Omega}^{-1} (\Pi_\theta(L)\mathbf{y}_t),$$

This expression can also be written

$$L_T^c(\mathbf{y}; \boldsymbol{\theta}, \boldsymbol{\Omega}) = -\frac{nT}{2} \log 2\pi - \frac{T}{2} \log \det \boldsymbol{\Omega}$$

$$-\frac{1}{2} \sum_{t=1}^{T} \operatorname{tr} \left((\Pi_\theta(L)\mathbf{y}_t)' \boldsymbol{\Omega}^{-1} (\Pi_\theta(L)\mathbf{y}_t) \right).$$

Using the properties of the trace operator

$$\operatorname{tr}(\mathbf{AB}) = \operatorname{tr}(\mathbf{BA}),$$

we have

$$L_T^c(\mathbf{y}; \boldsymbol{\theta}, \boldsymbol{\Omega}) = -\frac{nT}{2} \log 2\pi - \frac{T}{2} \log \det \boldsymbol{\Omega}$$

$$-\frac{1}{2} \operatorname{tr} \left(\boldsymbol{\Omega}^{-1} \sum_{t=1}^{T} (\Pi_\theta(L)\mathbf{y}_t)(\Pi_\theta(L)\mathbf{y}_t)' \right).$$

Frequency Domain The log-likelihood function

$$L_T^c(\mathbf{y}; \boldsymbol{\theta}, \boldsymbol{\Omega}) = -\frac{nT}{2} \log 2\pi - \frac{T}{2} \log \det \boldsymbol{\Omega}$$

$$-\frac{T}{2} \operatorname{tr} \left(\boldsymbol{\Omega}^{-1} \frac{1}{T} \sum_{t=1}^{T} (\Pi_\theta(L)\mathbf{y}_t)(\Pi_\theta(L)\mathbf{y}_t)' \right)$$

depends on the observations through the empirical variances of the variables $\Pi_\theta(L)\mathbf{y}_t$. Switching to the Fourier transform and noticing that the periodogram associated with the process $\Pi_\theta(L)\mathbf{y}_t$ is

$$\Pi_\theta(\exp(i\omega)) I_T(\omega) \overline{(\Pi_\theta \exp i\omega)'},$$

where $I_T(\omega)$ is the periodogram of $\mathbf{y}_1, \ldots, \mathbf{y}_t$, we have

$$L_T^c(\mathbf{y}; \boldsymbol{\theta}, \boldsymbol{\Omega}) \approx -\frac{nT}{2} \log 2\pi - \frac{T}{2} \log \det \boldsymbol{\Omega}$$

$$- \frac{T}{2} \mathrm{tr} \left(\boldsymbol{\Omega}^{-1} \int_{-\pi}^{\pi} \Pi_\theta(\exp(i\omega)) I_T(\omega) \overline{(\Pi_\theta \exp i\omega)}' d\omega \right)$$

$$= -\frac{nT}{2} \log 2\pi - \frac{T}{2} \log \det \boldsymbol{\Omega}$$

$$- \frac{T}{2} \int_{-\pi}^{\pi} \mathrm{tr} \left(\overline{(\Pi_\theta \exp(i\omega))}' \boldsymbol{\Omega}^{-1} \Pi_\theta(\exp(i\omega)) I_T(\omega) \right) d\omega$$

$$= -\frac{nT}{2} \log 2\pi - \frac{T}{2} \log \det \boldsymbol{\Omega}$$

$$- \frac{T}{2} \int_{-\pi}^{\pi} \mathrm{tr} \left(\left(\Pi_\theta(\exp(i\omega))^{-1} \boldsymbol{\Omega} \left(\overline{(\Pi_\theta \exp(i\omega))}' \right)^{-1} \right)^{-1} I_T(\omega) \right) d\omega.$$

We recognize under the integral the expression of the spectral density function of the process y; moreover, using Kolmogorov's inequality, we have

$$L_T^c(\mathbf{y}; \boldsymbol{\theta}, \boldsymbol{\Omega}) \approx -\frac{nT}{2} \log 2\pi - \frac{T}{2} E_\mu \log \det(2\pi f(\omega))$$

$$- \frac{T}{2} E_\mu \mathrm{tr} \left(f(\omega)^{-1} \hat{I}_T(\omega) \right). \tag{9.45}$$

This formula generalizes (9.10).

9.4.2 First-order Conditions

The maximum likelihood estimators $\hat{\boldsymbol{\theta}}_T, \hat{\boldsymbol{\Omega}}_T$ are found when setting the derivatives of the log-likelihood function to zero.

Derivative w.r.t. $\boldsymbol{\theta}$ We have

$$\frac{\partial L_T^c}{\partial \theta_k}(\mathbf{y}; \hat{\boldsymbol{\theta}}_T, \hat{\boldsymbol{\Omega}}_T) = 0, \forall k$$

$$\Leftrightarrow \sum_{t=1}^{T} (\frac{\partial}{\partial \theta_k} \Pi_{\hat{\theta}_T}(L) \mathbf{y}_t)' \hat{\boldsymbol{\Omega}}_T^{-1} \tilde{\boldsymbol{\varepsilon}}_t = 0, \ \forall k.$$

This is an orthogonality condition for the scalar product $\hat{\boldsymbol{\Omega}}_T^{-1}$ between the residuals $\tilde{\boldsymbol{\varepsilon}}_t$ and the variables

$$\frac{\partial}{\partial \theta_k} \Pi_{\hat{\theta}_T}(L) \mathbf{y}_t.$$

Differential w.r.t. Ω To optimize with respect to Ω, it is easier to consider the differential. We have

$$dL_T^c = -\frac{T}{2}d(\log \det \Omega) - \frac{T}{2}\text{tr}\left(d(\Omega^{-1})\frac{1}{T}\sum_{t=1}^{T}(\Pi_\theta(L)\mathbf{y}_t)(\Pi_\theta(L)\mathbf{y}_t)'\right).$$

Then (cf. exercise 9.3), we see that

$$dL_T^c = -\frac{T}{2}\text{tr}\left(\Omega^{-1}d\Omega\right)$$

$$+ \frac{T}{2}\text{tr}\left(\Omega^{-1}d\Omega\Omega^{-1}\frac{1}{T}\sum_{t=1}^{T}(\Pi_\theta(L)\mathbf{y}_t)(\Pi_\theta(L)\mathbf{y}_t)'\right).$$

We notice that this differential is zero, for

$$\Omega = \frac{1}{T}\sum_{t=1}^{T}(\Pi_\theta(L)\mathbf{y}_t)(\Pi_\theta(L)\mathbf{y}_t)'.$$

Theorem 9.31: *The maximum likelihood estimators $\hat{\boldsymbol{\theta}}_T$ and $\hat{\Omega}_T$ are such that*

$$\hat{\Omega}_T = \frac{1}{T}\sum_{t=1}^{T}\tilde{\boldsymbol{\varepsilon}}_t\tilde{\boldsymbol{\varepsilon}}_t',$$

with

$$\tilde{\boldsymbol{\varepsilon}}_t = \Pi_{\hat{\theta}_T}(L)\mathbf{y}_t.$$

9.4.3 Fisher's Information Matrix

The information matrix is obtained by computing the expectation of the inverse of the second derivative of the log-likelihood function with respect to the parameters, with its sign changed.

Cross Terms Let us first consider an element of this matrix corresponding to one element of $\boldsymbol{\theta}$ and to one element of Ω (or, equivalently, of Ω^{-1}). We have

$$\frac{\partial L_T^c}{\partial \theta_j} = \sum_{t=1}^{T}\sum_{k}\sum_{l}\left(\frac{\partial}{\partial \theta_j}\Pi_\theta^k(L)\mathbf{y}_t\right)\omega^{kl}\left(\Pi_\theta^l(L)\mathbf{y}_t\right),$$

where $\Pi_\theta^k(L)$ denotes the k-th row of the matrix $\Pi_\theta(L)$ and ω^{kl} is the (k,l)-th element of the inverse matrix Ω^{-1}.

Taking into account the symmetry of the matrix $\boldsymbol{\Omega}^{-1}$, we have

$$\frac{\partial^2 L_T^c}{\partial \theta_j \partial \omega^{kl}} = \sum_{t=1}^{T} \left(\frac{\partial}{\partial \theta_j} \Pi_\theta^k(L) \mathbf{y}_t \right) \left(\Pi_\theta^l(L) \mathbf{y}_t \right)$$

$$+ \sum_{t=1}^{T} \left(\frac{\partial}{\partial \theta_j} \Pi_\theta^l(L) \mathbf{y}_t \right) \left(\Pi_\theta^k(L) \mathbf{y}_t \right)$$

for $k \neq l$, and

$$\frac{\partial^2 L_T^c}{\partial \theta_j \partial \omega^{kk}} = \sum_{t=1}^{T} \left(\frac{\partial}{\partial \theta_j} \Pi_\theta^k(L) \mathbf{y}_t \right) \left(\Pi_\theta^k(L) \mathbf{y}_t \right).$$

These two derivatives have a zero expected value. Indeed, let us consider for example the second one

$$E \left(\frac{\partial^2 L_T^c}{\partial \theta_j \partial \omega^{kk}} \right) = T E \left(\frac{\partial}{\partial \theta_j} \Pi_\theta^k(L) \mathbf{y}_t \; \boldsymbol{\epsilon}_t^k \right)$$

$$= T E \left(\frac{\partial}{\partial \theta_j} \Pi_\theta^k(L) \mathbf{y}_t \right) E(\boldsymbol{\epsilon}_t^k) = 0,$$

since $\partial \Pi_\theta^k(L) \mathbf{y}_t / \partial \theta_j$ does not depend on the current values of y and since the noise ϵ has a zero expected value. Thus, the information matrix and its inverse are block diagonal. Taking into account the asymptotic normality of these estimators we have the following theorem

Theorem 9.32: *The estimators $\hat{\boldsymbol{\theta}}_T$ and $\hat{\boldsymbol{\Omega}}_T$ are asymptotically independent.*

Square Term Relative to $\boldsymbol{\theta}$ The asymptotic precision of the estimator of the parameter $\boldsymbol{\theta}$ can be derived from the term $\mathbf{J}_{\theta\theta}$ of the information matrix, as shown in theorem 9.32. We have

$$\mathbf{J}_{\theta\theta} = \frac{1}{T} E \left(-\frac{\partial^2 \log L_T^c}{\partial \boldsymbol{\theta} \partial \boldsymbol{\theta}'} \right)$$

$$= \sum_k \sum_l E \left(\left(-\frac{\partial^2}{\partial \boldsymbol{\theta} \partial \boldsymbol{\theta}'} \Pi_\theta^k(L) \mathbf{y}_t \right) \omega_\theta^{kl} \left(\Pi_\theta^l(L) \mathbf{y}_t \right) \right)$$

$$+ \sum_k \sum_l E \left(\left(\frac{\partial}{\partial \boldsymbol{\theta}} \Pi_\theta^k(L) \mathbf{y}_t \right) \omega^{kl} \left(\frac{\partial}{\partial \boldsymbol{\theta}'} \Pi_\theta^l(L) \mathbf{y}_t \right) \right)$$

$$= \sum_k \sum_l E\left(\left(\frac{\partial}{\partial\boldsymbol{\theta}}\Pi_\theta^k(L)\mathbf{y}_t\right)\omega^{kl}\left(\frac{\partial}{\partial\boldsymbol{\theta}'}\Pi_\theta^l(L)\mathbf{y}_t\right)\right)$$

$$= \sum_k \sum_l \omega^{kl} E\left(\left(\frac{\partial}{\partial\boldsymbol{\theta}}\Pi_\theta^k(L)\mathbf{y}_t\right)\left(\frac{\partial}{\partial\boldsymbol{\theta}'}\Pi_\theta^l(L)\mathbf{y}_t\right)\right)$$

$$= E\left(\frac{\partial\Pi_\theta'(L)\mathbf{y}_t}{\partial\boldsymbol{\theta}}\boldsymbol{\Omega}^{-1}\frac{\partial\Pi_\theta(L)\mathbf{y}_t}{\partial\boldsymbol{\theta}'}\right).$$

9.4.4 Estimation of a Pure Autoregressive Process

The estimation is particularly simple in the case of pure autoregressive processes without restriction on the parameters. This explains in part the success of these models in the multivariate case. Let us assume that the process $\mathbf{y}_t$ can be written as

$$\mathbf{y}_t = \boldsymbol{\Phi}_1\mathbf{y}_{t-1} + \ldots + \boldsymbol{\Phi}_p\mathbf{y}_{t-p} + \boldsymbol{\varepsilon}_t,$$

where $\mathrm{var}\,(\boldsymbol{\varepsilon}_t) = \boldsymbol{\Omega}$, $t = 1,\ldots,T$ and the parameters $\boldsymbol{\Phi}_1,\ldots,\boldsymbol{\Phi}_p,\boldsymbol{\Omega}$ are not related to each other.

We can write this expression by separating the components of $\mathbf{y}$. With obvious notation, we get the so-called *seemingly unrelated regression model*

$$\mathbf{y}_{jt} = \left(\mathbf{y}_{t-1}',\ldots,\mathbf{y}_{t-p}'\right)\boldsymbol{\psi}_j + \epsilon_{jt}, \quad j = 1\ldots n, t = 1\ldots T,$$

where $\boldsymbol{\psi}_j$ is a vector of parameters of size pn.

Let us denote

$$\underline{\mathbf{y}}_j = \begin{pmatrix} y_{j1} \\ \vdots \\ y_{jT} \end{pmatrix}, \quad \underline{\underline{\mathbf{y}}} = \begin{pmatrix} \mathbf{y}_0' & \cdots & \mathbf{y}_{1-p}' \\ \vdots & & \vdots \\ \mathbf{y}_{T-1}' & \cdots & \mathbf{y}_{T-p}' \end{pmatrix}, \quad \underline{\boldsymbol{\varepsilon}}_j = \begin{pmatrix} \epsilon_{j1} \\ \vdots \\ \epsilon_{jT} \end{pmatrix}.$$

The previous system can be written as

$$\begin{pmatrix} \underline{\mathbf{y}}_1 \\ \vdots \\ \underline{\mathbf{y}}_n \end{pmatrix} = \begin{pmatrix} \underline{\underline{\mathbf{y}}} & & 0 \\ & \underline{\underline{\mathbf{y}}} & \\ 0 & & \underline{\underline{\mathbf{y}}} \end{pmatrix}\begin{pmatrix} \boldsymbol{\psi}_1 \\ \vdots \\ \boldsymbol{\psi}_n \end{pmatrix} + \begin{pmatrix} \underline{\boldsymbol{\varepsilon}}_1 \\ \vdots \\ \underline{\boldsymbol{\varepsilon}}_n \end{pmatrix},$$

with

$$\mathrm{var}\begin{pmatrix} \underline{\epsilon}_1 \\ \vdots \\ \underline{\epsilon}_n \end{pmatrix} = \begin{pmatrix} \omega_{11}\mathbf{I} & \omega_{12}\mathbf{I} & \cdots & \omega_{1n}\mathbf{I} \\ \cdots & \cdots & \cdots & \cdots \\ \omega_{n1}\mathbf{I} & \cdots & \cdots & \omega_{nn}\mathbf{I} \end{pmatrix}.$$

Introducing $(\mathbf{A} \otimes \mathbf{B})$ as the Kronecker product of matrices $\mathbf{A}$ and $\mathbf{B}$, the model can be written as

$$
\begin{pmatrix} \underline{\mathbf{y}}_1 \\ \vdots \\ \underline{\mathbf{y}}_n \end{pmatrix} = \left(\mathbf{I} \otimes \underline{\mathbf{y}} \right) \begin{pmatrix} \boldsymbol{\psi}_1 \\ \vdots \\ \boldsymbol{\psi}_n \end{pmatrix} + \begin{pmatrix} \underline{\boldsymbol{\varepsilon}}_1 \\ \vdots \\ \underline{\boldsymbol{\varepsilon}}_n \end{pmatrix},
$$

with

$$
\begin{pmatrix} \underline{\boldsymbol{\varepsilon}}_1 \\ \vdots \\ \underline{\boldsymbol{\varepsilon}}_n \end{pmatrix} \sim \mathcal{N}\left(\mathbf{0}, \boldsymbol{\Omega} \otimes \mathbf{I} \right)
$$

under the normality assumption. The first-order condition relative to

$$
\boldsymbol{\theta} = \begin{pmatrix} \boldsymbol{\psi}_1 \\ \vdots \\ \boldsymbol{\psi}_n \end{pmatrix}.
$$

gives the generalized least squares formula

$$
\begin{pmatrix} \hat{\boldsymbol{\psi}}_{1T} \\ \vdots \\ \hat{\boldsymbol{\psi}}_{nT} \end{pmatrix} = \left((\mathbf{I} \otimes \underline{\mathbf{y}})'(\hat{\boldsymbol{\Omega}}_T \otimes \mathbf{I})^{-1}(\mathbf{I} \otimes \underline{\mathbf{y}}) \right)^{-1} (\mathbf{I} \otimes \underline{\mathbf{y}})'(\hat{\boldsymbol{\Omega}}_T \otimes \mathbf{I})^{-1} \begin{pmatrix} \underline{\mathbf{y}}_1 \\ \vdots \\ \underline{\mathbf{y}}_n \end{pmatrix}
$$

$$
= \left((\mathbf{I} \otimes \underline{\mathbf{y}})'(\hat{\boldsymbol{\Omega}}_T^{-1} \otimes \mathbf{I})(\mathbf{I} \otimes \underline{\mathbf{y}}) \right)^{-1} (\mathbf{I} \otimes \underline{\mathbf{y}})'(\hat{\boldsymbol{\Omega}}_T^{-1} \otimes \mathbf{I}) \begin{pmatrix} \underline{\mathbf{y}}_1 \\ \vdots \\ \underline{\mathbf{y}}_n \end{pmatrix}
$$

$$
= \left(\hat{\boldsymbol{\Omega}}_T^{-1} \otimes \underline{\mathbf{y}}'\underline{\mathbf{y}} \right)^{-1} \left(\hat{\boldsymbol{\Omega}}_T^{-1} \otimes \underline{\mathbf{y}}' \right) \begin{pmatrix} \underline{\mathbf{y}}_1 \\ \vdots \\ \underline{\mathbf{y}}_n \end{pmatrix}
$$

$$
= \left(\hat{\boldsymbol{\Omega}}_T \otimes \left(\underline{\mathbf{y}}'\underline{\mathbf{y}} \right)^{-1} \right) \left(\hat{\boldsymbol{\Omega}}_T^{-1} \otimes \underline{\mathbf{y}}' \right) \begin{pmatrix} \underline{\mathbf{y}}_1 \\ \vdots \\ \underline{\mathbf{y}}_n \end{pmatrix}
$$

$$
= \left(\mathbf{I} \otimes \left(\underline{\mathbf{y}}'\underline{\mathbf{y}} \right)^{-1} \underline{\mathbf{y}} \right) \begin{pmatrix} \underline{\mathbf{y}}_1 \\ \vdots \\ \underline{\mathbf{y}}_n \end{pmatrix},
$$

using the formulae

$$(\mathbf{A} \otimes \mathbf{B})(\mathbf{C} \otimes \mathbf{D}) = \mathbf{A}\mathbf{C} \otimes \mathbf{B}\mathbf{D},$$

$$(\mathbf{A} \otimes \mathbf{B})^{-1} = \mathbf{A}^{-1} \otimes \mathbf{B}^{-1},$$

$$(\mathbf{A} \otimes \mathbf{B})' = \mathbf{A}' \otimes \mathbf{B}'.$$

We conclude that

$$\begin{pmatrix} \hat{\psi}_{1T} \\ \vdots \\ \hat{\psi}_{nT} \end{pmatrix} = \begin{pmatrix} (\underline{\underline{\mathbf{y}}}'\underline{\underline{\mathbf{y}}})^{-1}\underline{\underline{\mathbf{y}}}'\underline{\mathbf{y}}_1 \\ \vdots \\ (\underline{\underline{\mathbf{y}}}'\underline{\underline{\mathbf{y}}})^{-1}\underline{\underline{\mathbf{y}}}'\underline{\mathbf{y}}_n \end{pmatrix}.$$

This provides the following result:

Theorem 9.33: *In the case of a pure unrestricted autoregressive model, the autoregressive coefficients can be estimated by applying the method of ordinary least squares to each equation separately.*

Hence, it is possible to follow the univariate setup and obtain the maximum likelihood estimators $\mathbf{\Phi}_1 \ldots \mathbf{\Phi}_p$ without prior estimation of the variance–covariance matrix $\mathbf{\Omega}$.

The estimated variance–covariance matrix of the estimator is given by the usual formula

$$\widehat{\mathrm{var}} \begin{pmatrix} \hat{\psi}_{1T} \\ \vdots \\ \psi_{nT} \end{pmatrix} = \left(\left(\mathbf{I} \otimes \underline{\mathbf{y}} \right)' \left(\hat{\mathbf{\Omega}}_T \otimes \mathbf{I} \right)^{-1} \left(\mathbf{I} \otimes \underline{\mathbf{y}} \right) \right)^{-1}$$

$$(9.46)$$

$$= \left(\hat{\mathbf{\Omega}}_T \otimes \underline{\underline{\mathbf{y}}}'\underline{\underline{\mathbf{y}}} \right)^{-1}.$$

9.5 Exercises

Exercise 9.1: Verify that the following two conditions are equivalent

(i) $f_{\theta,\sigma^2} = f_{\theta_0,\sigma_0^2} \Rightarrow \boldsymbol{\theta} = \boldsymbol{\theta}_0, \ \sigma^2 = \sigma_0^2;$

(ii) $\Pi_\theta(L) = \Pi_{\theta_0}(L) \Rightarrow \boldsymbol{\theta} = \boldsymbol{\theta}_0.$

Exercise 9.2: Using the inverse Fourier transform show that

$$\operatorname{var}_0\left(\Pi_\theta(L)x_t\right) = \int_{-\pi}^{\pi} f_{\Pi_\theta(L)x_t}(\omega)d\omega = \sigma^2 E_\mu\left(\frac{f_{\theta_0,\sigma_0^2}}{f_{\theta,\sigma^2}}\right).$$

From it, give a straightforward proof of the equality of the expressions (9.12) and (9.13) for the Kullback contrast.

Exercise 9.3:

(i) Verify that

$$\left(\mathbf{C}_T(\boldsymbol{\theta}) + \frac{\partial \mathbf{C}_T(\boldsymbol{\theta})}{\partial \theta_k}d\theta_k\right)^{-1} - \mathbf{C}_T(\boldsymbol{\theta})^{-1}$$

$$\approx \left(\mathbf{I} + \mathbf{C}_T(\boldsymbol{\theta})^{-1}\frac{\partial \mathbf{C}_T(\boldsymbol{\theta})}{\partial \theta_k}d\theta_k\right)^{-1}\mathbf{C}_T(\boldsymbol{\theta})^{-1} - \mathbf{C}_T(\boldsymbol{\theta})^{-1}$$

$$\approx -\mathbf{C}_T(\boldsymbol{\theta})^{-1}\frac{\partial \mathbf{C}_T(\boldsymbol{\theta})}{\partial \theta_k}\mathbf{C}_T(\boldsymbol{\theta})^{-1}d\theta_k.$$

Prove that

$$\frac{\partial \left(\mathbf{C}_T(\boldsymbol{\theta})\right)^{-1}}{\partial \theta_k} = -\mathbf{C}_T(\boldsymbol{\theta})^{-1}\frac{\partial \mathbf{C}_T}{\partial \theta_k}(\boldsymbol{\theta})\mathbf{C}_T(\boldsymbol{\theta})^{-1}.$$

(ii) Verify that

$$\det\left(\mathbf{C}_T(\boldsymbol{\theta}) + \frac{\partial \mathbf{C}_T(\boldsymbol{\theta})}{\partial \theta_k}d\theta_k\right) - \det\mathbf{C}_T(\boldsymbol{\theta})$$

$$= \det\mathbf{C}_T(\boldsymbol{\theta})\det\left(\mathbf{I} + \mathbf{C}_T(\boldsymbol{\theta})^{-1}\frac{\partial \mathbf{C}_T(\boldsymbol{\theta})}{\partial \theta_k}d\theta_k\right) - \det\mathbf{C}_T(\boldsymbol{\theta})$$

$$\approx \det\mathbf{C}_T(\boldsymbol{\theta})\sum_{t=1}^{T}a_{tt}(\boldsymbol{\theta})d\theta_k,$$

where $a_{tt}(\boldsymbol{\theta})$ is the t-th diagonal element of the matrix

$$\mathbf{C}_T(\boldsymbol{\theta})^{-1}\frac{\partial \mathbf{C}_T(\boldsymbol{\theta})}{\partial \theta_k}.$$

Show that

$$\frac{\partial}{\partial \theta_k}\left(\log\det\mathbf{C}_T(\boldsymbol{\theta})\right) = \operatorname{tr}\left(\mathbf{C}_T(\boldsymbol{\theta})^{-1}\frac{\partial \mathbf{C}_T(\boldsymbol{\theta})}{\partial \theta_k}\right).$$

Exercise 9.4: From the expression of the score in the frequency domain and from the definition of the periodogram show that

$$\frac{\partial \log \tilde{L}_T}{\partial \boldsymbol{\theta}}(\mathbf{x}_T; \boldsymbol{\theta}, \sigma^2)$$

$$= \frac{T}{8\pi^2\sigma^2} \sum_{h=1-T}^{T-1} \hat{\gamma}_T(h) \int_{-\pi}^{\pi} \exp(ih\omega) \left(\frac{\partial g_\theta}{\partial \theta}(\omega)/g_\theta^2(\omega) \right) d\omega.$$

Exercise 9.5: Consider a white noise $x_t = \epsilon_t$ having a standard normal distribution $\epsilon_t \sim \mathcal{N}(0, 1)$.

(i)   Verify that, if $I_T(\omega) = \frac{1}{2\pi T} \left| \sum_{t=1}^{T} \epsilon_t \exp(it\omega) \right|^2$,

$$4\pi^2 E(I_T^2(\omega)) = \frac{1}{T^2} \sum_s E(\epsilon_s^4) + \frac{1}{T^2} \sum_s \sum_u E(\epsilon_s^2 \epsilon_u^2)$$

$$+ \frac{1}{T^2} \sum_s \sum_t \exp(-2i\omega s + 2i\omega t) E(\epsilon_s^2 \epsilon_t^2)$$

$$+ \frac{1}{T^2} \sum_s \sum_t E(\epsilon_s^2 \epsilon_t^2)$$

$$= \frac{3}{T} + 2 + \frac{1}{T^2} \frac{1 - \exp(-2i\omega T)}{1 - \exp(-2i\omega)} \frac{1 - \exp(2i\omega T)}{1 - \exp(2i\omega)}.$$

(ii)   Prove that

$$\lim_{T \to \infty} \text{var}(I_T(\omega)) = \begin{cases} f(\omega)^2 & \text{if } \omega \neq 0, \pm\pi \\ 2f(\omega)^2 & \text{if } \omega = 0, \pm\pi. \end{cases}$$

Exercise 9.6:

(i)   Write $\hat{\gamma}_T(h) = \frac{1}{T} \sum_{t=1}^{T-h} (x_t - \bar{x}_T)(x_{t+h} - \bar{x}_T)$ as an explicit function of $\hat{\gamma}_T(h)$ and of the empirical means of the values of x.

(ii)   Prove that if x is zero mean, $\tilde{\gamma}_T(h)$ has the same limiting distribution as $\hat{\gamma}_T(h)$.

Exercise 9.7: Under the same conditions as in section 3.2, verify that

$$\operatorname*{plim}_{T \to +\infty} \frac{1}{T} \sum_{t=1}^{T} x_t^2 = \sigma^2,$$

$$\operatorname*{plim}_{T \to +\infty} \frac{1}{T} \sum_{t=1}^{T} (A(L)x_t)^2 = \sigma^2 \sum_{k=1}^{\infty} a_k^2,$$

and

$$\frac{1}{\sqrt{T}} \sum_{t=1}^{T} x_t \left(A(L) x_t \right)$$

$$\xrightarrow{\mathrm{d}} \mathcal{N} \left(-\boldsymbol{\theta}^* \mathrm{cov} \left(\frac{\partial \Pi_0(L)}{\partial \theta} \epsilon_t, A(L) \epsilon_t \right), \ \mathrm{var}\left(\epsilon_t \right) \ \mathrm{var}\left(A(L) \epsilon_t \right) \right).$$

III
Time-series Econometrics:
Stationary and Nonstationary Models

10

Causality, Exogeneity, and Shocks

10.1 Dynamic Macroeconometric Models

10.1.1 General Aspects

Some Goals of Macroeconomic Modeling In this chapter and in the following ones, we are mainly interested in the use of time-series techniques in the domain of macroeconomics. The available data refer to variables which can be generally classified as quantities (production, consumption, investment, imports, money supply, total employment, unsatisfied employment demand, etc.) and as prices (prices of consumption goods, of investment goods, foreign prices, wages, interest rates, etc.). These quantities and prices are the result of aggregation procedures with respect to economic agents, goods, and time. For example, the term "price" should be interpreted as a price index relative to a certain period and to a certain category of goods. Macroeconomics studies how certain variables are related to each other.

In a macroeconomic study, we generally start by choosing the appropriate variables. These are then divided into two groups. Some are specific to the phenomenon under study, and the knowledge of their values at regular intervals allows one to follow its evolution. These are called *endogenous*. To consider only these endogenous variables translates into just a descriptive study and not an interpretive one. In order to be able to have some explanation for the phenomenon, we need to

take into consideration other variables as well which can possibly have
an influence on the endogenous variables, the values of which are fixed
outside the phenomenon. These variables are called *exogenous* (a more
precise definition will be given in section 10.3). The phenomenon and its
explanation are summarized in a macroeconometric model. If we limit
ourselves only to the case of a linear model, such a model takes the form
of a linear system linking current endogenous variables to the exogenous
variables and to the lagged values of the endogenous and exogenous variables. If we denote by $\mathbf{y}_t$ the vector of the n endogenous variables at
time t, $\mathbf{x}_t$ the vector of the m exogenous variables at time t, the system
can be written as

$$\mathbf{A}_0\mathbf{y}_t + \mathbf{A}_1\mathbf{y}_{t-1} + \ldots + \mathbf{A}_p\mathbf{y}_{t-p} + \mathbf{B}_0\mathbf{x}_t + \mathbf{B}_1\mathbf{x}_{t-1} + \ldots + \mathbf{B}_p\mathbf{x}_{t-p} + \mu = 0,$$
$$(10.1)$$

where $\mathbf{A}_j$, $j = 0, \ldots, p$ are (n, n) matrices, $\mathbf{B}_j$, $j = 0, \ldots, p$ are (n, m)
matrices, and μ is a $(n, 1)$ vector. The matrix $\mathbf{A}_0$ is supposed nonsingular, so that system (10.1) allows for a unique determination of the current
values of the endogenous variables. In order to illustrate this procedure,
let us introduce a simplified Keynesian model. This model was first
proposed to derive the impact on the economy of an autonomous expenditure policy, decided exogenously by the government. The endogenous
variables are:

Gross Domestic Product: GDP_t,

Consumption: C_t,

Investment: I_t.

There is just one exogenous variable, the autonomous public expenditure G_t. The system is made of three equations

$$\begin{cases} GDP_t = C_t + I_t + G_t, \\ \quad C_t = a\, GDP_{t-1}, \\ \quad I_t = b\,(GDP_{t-1} - GDP_{t-2}). \end{cases}$$

The first equation gives the equilibrium between total supply GDP_t and
total demand, represented by the sum of demand by consumers C_t, by
firms I_t, and by the government G_t. The second equation describes consumption behavior: consumption at time t is a function of the revenue
distributed at the previous date. The coefficient a is positive (consumption increases with revenue); on the other hand, it is likely to be less than
1 (since one cannot spend more than one earns for an extended time).
Finally, the last equation describes the propensity to invest ($b > 0$) in a

period of growth. The previous system can be written in vector form as

$$\begin{pmatrix} 1 & -1 & -1 \\ 0 & 1 & 0 \\ 0 & 0 & 1 \end{pmatrix} \begin{pmatrix} GDP_t \\ C_t \\ I_t \end{pmatrix} - \begin{pmatrix} 0 & 0 & 0 \\ a & 0 & 0 \\ b & 0 & 0 \end{pmatrix} \begin{pmatrix} GDP_{t-1} \\ C_{t-1} \\ I_{t-1} \end{pmatrix}$$

$$(10.2)$$

$$+ \begin{pmatrix} 0 & 0 & 0 \\ 0 & 0 & 0 \\ b & 0 & 0 \end{pmatrix} \begin{pmatrix} GDP_{t-2} \\ C_{t-2} \\ I_{t-2} \end{pmatrix} - \begin{pmatrix} 1 \\ 0 \\ 0 \end{pmatrix} G_t = \mathbf{0}.$$

Note that the matrices $\mathbf{A}_0$, $\mathbf{A}_1$, $\mathbf{A}_2$ are subject to a number of constraints; in particular a lot of their coefficients are equal to 0.

10.1.2 Introduction of the Random Disturbances

The dynamic model (10.2) is deterministic, which for the moment does not allow for comparisons with those models we used for time-series analysis. This difficulty is solved by introducing random disturbances in the various equations. If the whole dynamics has been correctly included in the initial specification of the model, these disturbances should be temporally independent. However, before introducing them, we need to give a more precise interpretation to the various equations. We usually make the distinction among three types of equations

(i) The *accounting identities* are equations defining certain variables. Thus in the Keynesian model there is an implicit definition of total demand TD_t

$$TD_t = C_t + I_t + G_t,$$

where the relationship is satisfied without error.

(ii) The *equilibrium conditions* express the equality between demand and supply. This equality is assumed to be the result of an adjustment in prices. The equation $GDP_t = TD_t$ is an example of such equilibrium equations. When we suppose that equilibrium takes place, there is no reason to introduce error terms in the corresponding equation.

(iii) The *behavioral equations* express the way in which economic agents determine certain variables conditionally on certain others. Thus

$$C_t = a \, GDP_{t-1}$$

describes a consumption behavior

$$I_t = b \, (GDP_{t-1} - GDP_{t-2})$$

an investment behavior.

In the previous example, these behaviors have been formalized in a very simplistic fashion; it is clear that consumption depends on factors other than revenue. Generally, it is in these behavioral equations that the error terms are introduced, in order to represent these "forgotten" effects or those thought of as secondary with respect to the problem of interest. With the introduction of a random disturbance term the initial model can be written as

$$
\begin{cases}
TD_t = C_t + I_t + G_t, \\
GDP_t = TD_t, \\
\quad C_t = a\, GDP_{t-1} + u_t, \\
\quad I_t = b\, (GDP_{t-1} - GDP_{t-2}) + v_t.
\end{cases}
$$

In order to obtain a more homogeneous specification, where the disturbances appear in all the retained equations, oftentimes we get rid of the accounting identities or the equilibrium relationships. Thus eliminating GDP_t and TD_t we get a model describing the evolution of the pair (C_t, I_T)

$$C_t = aC_{t-1} + aI_{t-1} + aG_{t-1} + u_t,$$

$$I_t = bC_{t-1} + bI_{t-1} + bG_{t-1} - bC_{t-2} - bI_{t-2} - bG_{t-2} + v_t,$$

or

$$
\begin{pmatrix} C_t \\ I_t \end{pmatrix} = \begin{pmatrix} a & a \\ b & b \end{pmatrix} \begin{pmatrix} C_{t-1} \\ I_{t-1} \end{pmatrix} + \begin{pmatrix} 0 & 0 \\ -b & -b \end{pmatrix} \begin{pmatrix} C_{t-2} \\ I_{t-2} \end{pmatrix}
$$

$$
+ \begin{pmatrix} a \\ b \end{pmatrix} G_{t-1} + \begin{pmatrix} 0 \\ -b \end{pmatrix} G_{t-2} + \begin{pmatrix} u_t \\ v_t \end{pmatrix}.
$$

This model contains the whole dynamics of the initial model. The value of GDP_t can be derived from the relationship $GDP_t = C_t + I_t + G_t$. The previous example shows that after the introduction of the additive disturbance terms in the behavioral equations and the elimination of the accounting identities and the equilibrium relationships the model can be expressed in the form

$$
\begin{aligned}
&\mathbf{A}_0 \mathbf{y}_t + \mathbf{A}_1 \mathbf{y}_{t-1} + \ldots + \mathbf{A}_p \mathbf{y}_{t-p} \\
&\quad + \mathbf{B}_0 \mathbf{x}_t + \mathbf{B}_1 \mathbf{x}_{t-1} + \ldots + \mathbf{B}_p \mathbf{x}_{t-p} + \boldsymbol{\mu} = \boldsymbol{\varepsilon}_t,
\end{aligned}
\tag{10.3}
$$

where $\boldsymbol{\varepsilon}_t$ is the vector of which the elements are the disturbances associated to the behavioral equations.

10.1.3 Control Variables and Environment Variables

In the previous sections we have made a distinction between endogenous and exogenous variables. Other distinctions are possible. We often observe that certain exogenous variables can be controlled, that is fixed to an arbitrary level by a policy maker. These are called *instruments* (of economic policy), *control variables*, or *decision variables*. The other exogenous variables have their own evolution on which we cannot easily intervene. They are called *environment variables*. These differences in interpretation between exogenous variables should show up in the expression of the model. We can therefore start by separating the two types of variables in expression (10.3). Keeping the same notation x for the environment exogenous variables, we can denote the control variables by z. We have

$$\mathbf{A}_0 \mathbf{y}_t + \mathbf{A}_1 \mathbf{y}_{t-1} + \ldots + \mathbf{A}_p \mathbf{y}_{t-p} + \mathbf{B}_0 \mathbf{x}_t + \mathbf{B}_1 \mathbf{x}_{t-1} + \ldots + \mathbf{B}_p \mathbf{x}_{t-p}$$
$$+ \mathbf{C}_0 \mathbf{z}_t + \mathbf{C}_1 \mathbf{z}_{t-1} + \ldots + \mathbf{C}_p \mathbf{z}_{t-p} + \boldsymbol{\mu} = \boldsymbol{\varepsilon}_t.$$

$$(10.4)$$

This expression is perfectly symmetric in x and z, so that the distinction between the two types will not appear unless we complete the model by describing the evolution of the exogenous variables.

Evolution of the Environment Variables As a first approximation, let us consider the control variables as fixed and let us describe the evolution of the environment variables. The latter, which influence the endogenous variables are assumed to be determined before the values $\mathbf{y}_t$. Choosing a linear model, we can describe this concept as

$$\mathbf{A}_0 \mathbf{y}_t + \mathbf{A}_1 \mathbf{y}_{t-1} + \ldots + \mathbf{A}_p \mathbf{y}_{t-p} + \mathbf{B}_0 \mathbf{x}_t + \mathbf{B}_1 \mathbf{x}_{t-1} + \ldots + \mathbf{B}_p \mathbf{x}_{t-p}$$
$$+ \mathbf{C}_0 \mathbf{z}_t + \mathbf{C}_1 \mathbf{z}_{t-1} + \ldots + \mathbf{C}_p \mathbf{z}_{t-p} + \boldsymbol{\mu} = \boldsymbol{\varepsilon}_t,$$
$$\mathbf{x}_t + \mathbf{D}_1 \mathbf{x}_{t-1} + \ldots + \mathbf{D}_p \mathbf{x}_{t-p} + \mathbf{E}_0 \mathbf{z}_t + \mathbf{E}_1 \mathbf{z}_{t-1} + \ldots + \mathbf{E}_p \mathbf{z}_{t-p}$$
$$+ \mathbf{F}_1 \mathbf{y}_{t-1} + \ldots \mathbf{F}_p \mathbf{y}_{t-p} + \boldsymbol{\nu} = \mathbf{u}_t,$$

$$(10.5)$$

where $\{\boldsymbol{\varepsilon}_t\}$ and $\{\mathbf{u}_t\}$ are two mutually uncorrelated white noises. Two hypotheses are behind the previous expression

(i)   The control variables can have an impact on the values of the endogenous variables, but also on the values of the environment variables. However, they do not influence directly the dynamics of the variables y and x, that is the coefficients $\mathbf{A}_j$, $\mathbf{B}_j$, $\mathbf{D}_j$, $\mathbf{F}_j$.

(ii)   The variables x are exogenous in the sense that the $\mathbf{x}_t$'s are fixed prior to the $\mathbf{y}_t$'s. This concept is translated into the constraints

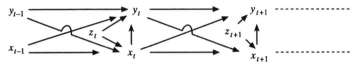

Figure 10.1   Causal Chain Scheme

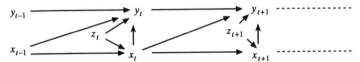

Figure 10.2   Modified Causal Chain Scheme

$\mathbf{F}_0 = \mathbf{0}$ and cov $(\mathbf{u}_t, \epsilon_t) = \mathbf{0}$. Fixing the values is performed according to the scheme represented in figure 10.1 (called *causal chain*) for the model

$$\mathbf{A}_0\mathbf{y}_t + \mathbf{A}_1\mathbf{y}_{t-1} + \mathbf{B}_0\mathbf{x}_t + \mathbf{C}_0\mathbf{z}_t + \boldsymbol{\mu} = \boldsymbol{\varepsilon}_t,$$

$$\mathbf{x}_t + \mathbf{D}_1\mathbf{x}_{t-1} + \mathbf{E}_0\mathbf{z}_t + \mathbf{F}_1\mathbf{y}_{t-1} + \boldsymbol{\nu} = \mathbf{u}_t.$$

Sometimes, model (10.5) is called *block-recursive* (determination of x and then of y). The recursive model (10.5) corresponds to a fairly weak notion of exogeneity. We could introduce a more restrictive notion assuming, for example, that the values of $\mathbf{x}_t$ are determined *autonomously*, that is, without a relationship to the lagged endogenous variables. This corresponds to imposing $\mathbf{F}_j = \mathbf{0}$, $\forall\, j$, and leads to a model of the type

$$\mathbf{A}_0\mathbf{y}_t + \mathbf{A}_1\mathbf{y}_{t-1} + \ldots + \mathbf{A}_p\mathbf{y}_{t-p} + \mathbf{B}_0\mathbf{x}_t + \mathbf{B}_1\mathbf{x}_{t-1} + \ldots + \mathbf{B}_p\mathbf{x}_{t-p}$$

$$+ \mathbf{C}_0\mathbf{z}_t + \mathbf{C}_1\mathbf{z}_{t-1} + \ldots + \mathbf{C}_p\mathbf{z}_{t-p} + \boldsymbol{\mu} = \boldsymbol{\varepsilon}_t,$$

$$\mathbf{x}_t + \mathbf{D}_1\mathbf{x}_{t-1} + \ldots + \mathbf{D}_p\mathbf{x}_{t-p}$$

$$+ \mathbf{E}_0\mathbf{z}_t + \mathbf{E}_1\mathbf{z}_{t-1} + \ldots + \mathbf{E}_p\mathbf{z}_{t-p} + \boldsymbol{\nu} = \mathbf{u}_t,$$

$$(10.6)$$

with cov $(\boldsymbol{\varepsilon}_t, \mathbf{u}_t) = \mathbf{0}$. As an illustrative example, let us consider the model

$$\mathbf{A}_0\mathbf{y}_t + \mathbf{A}_1\mathbf{y}_{t-1} + \mathbf{B}_0\mathbf{x}_t + \mathbf{C}_0\mathbf{z}_t + \boldsymbol{\mu} = \boldsymbol{\varepsilon}_t,$$

$$\mathbf{x}_t + \mathbf{D}_1\mathbf{x}_{t-1} + \mathbf{E}_0\mathbf{z}_t + \boldsymbol{\nu} = \mathbf{u}_t.$$

The modified causal chain appears in figure 10.2. The two types of exogeneity will be rigorously defined in section 10.3.

Characterization of Economic Policy   In order to have a certain effect on the evolution of the endogenous variables, a policy maker should intervene on the control variables $\mathbf{z}$. For example, he could fix the evolution of the control variables in a way that will lead to the desired evolutions of the endogenous variables. Taking the Keynesian model as an example, the government can affect consumption, gross domestic product, and investment through government expenditure. We can envisage various economic policies. For example, it could be decided to maintain a constant level of expenditure

$$G_t = G_{t-1},$$

or to modify government expenditure according to the observed evolution of investment

$$G_t - G_{t-1} = \lambda(I_{t-1} - I_{t-2}).$$

These simple examples show that a direct way of describing economic policy consists in explaining how the values of the control variables will be fixed, in terms of the main aggregates. This can be expressed by adding to (10.5) a new equation giving the determination of the variables z_t

$$\mathbf{A}_0\mathbf{y}_t + \mathbf{A}_1\mathbf{y}_{t-1} + \ldots + \mathbf{A}_p\mathbf{y}_{t-p} + \mathbf{B}_0\mathbf{x}_t + \mathbf{B}_1\mathbf{x}_{t-1} + \ldots + \mathbf{B}_p\mathbf{x}_{t-p}$$

$$+ \mathbf{C}_0\mathbf{z}_t + \mathbf{C}_1\mathbf{z}_{t-1} + \ldots + \mathbf{C}_p\mathbf{z}_{t-p} + \boldsymbol{\mu} = \boldsymbol{\varepsilon}_t,$$

$$\mathbf{x}_t + \mathbf{D}_1\mathbf{x}_{t-1} + \ldots + \mathbf{D}_p\mathbf{x}_{t-p} + \mathbf{E}_0\mathbf{z}_t + \mathbf{E}_1\mathbf{z}_{t-1} + \ldots + \mathbf{E}_p\mathbf{z}_{t-p}$$

$$+ \mathbf{F}_1\mathbf{y}_{t-1} + \ldots \mathbf{F}_p\mathbf{y}_{t-p} + \boldsymbol{\nu} = \mathbf{u}_t,$$

$$\mathbf{z}_t + \mathbf{G}_1\mathbf{z}_{t-1} + \ldots + \mathbf{G}_p\mathbf{z}_{t-p} + \mathbf{H}_1\mathbf{x}_{t-1} + \ldots + \mathbf{H}_p\mathbf{x}_{t-p}$$

$$+ \mathbf{I}_1\mathbf{y}_{t-1} + \ldots \mathbf{I}_p\mathbf{y}_{t-p} + \boldsymbol{\gamma} = \mathbf{v}_t,$$

$$(10.7)$$

with $\operatorname{cov}(\boldsymbol{\varepsilon}_t, \mathbf{u}_t) = \operatorname{cov}(\boldsymbol{\varepsilon}_t, \mathbf{v}_t) = \operatorname{cov}(\mathbf{u}_t, \mathbf{v}_t) = \mathbf{0}$. In this model there is an additional recursiveness: determination of $\mathbf{z}$, then of $\mathbf{x}$, then of $\mathbf{y}$. However the distinction between the two types of exogenous variables rests on a different level. While the first two equations describe the reactions of the environment, the last describes an economic policy possibly chosen by the policy maker. Thus, we can think that the decision maker may give the values he wants to the coefficients $\mathbf{G}_j$, $\mathbf{H}_j$, $\mathbf{I}_j$, whereas he does not have any influence on the other parameters of the model.

Equilibrium Relationships In the above framework, we stressed the idea of block recursiveness. We need, though, to give a possible interpretation for when this recursiveness is not satisfied. This leads us back to the notion of equilibrium and to a definition of an equilibrium relationship. Let us take the classical example of a model describing how the exchanged quantities and prices are fixed on the goods market. The model, called "tatonnement" model is constructed by analogy to certain markets where we see the evolution of the demanded and supplied quantities, as well as of the prices during the day. Let us denote by t the index of the day, and by $\tau = 1, 2, \ldots$ the successive instants of trading during the day. At any instant (t, τ), we have a price quotation $p_{t,\tau}$. The buyers attach a desired quantity to this price

$$D_{t,\tau} = a\, p_{t,\tau} + x_t b,$$

where $a < 0$, and x_t indicates the set of variables affecting behavior. At the same price, the sellers propose to sell a quantity

$$S_{t,\tau} = \alpha\, p_{t,\tau} + x_t \beta,$$

with $\alpha > 0$. In general, these two quantities are different: either we have an excess demand $D_{t,\tau} > S_{t,\tau}$ or we have an excess supply $S_{t,\tau} > D_{t,\tau}$. In the former case we would increase the price whereas in the latter we would decrease it. In a simplified fashion, we can consider that the next price quotation is fixed according to a price adjustment equation

$$p_{t,\tau+1} - p_{t,\tau} = \lambda\left(D_{t,\tau} - S_{t,\tau}\right),$$

with $\lambda \geq 0$. During the day, we have a succession of values for $p_{t,\tau}$, $D_{t,\tau}$, $S_{t,\tau}$. What is the path for the prices? Replacing the expressions for $D_{t,\tau}$ and $S_{t,\tau}$ in the adjustment equation we get

$$p_{t,\tau+1} - p_{t,\tau} = \lambda\left(a - \alpha\right) p_{t,\tau} + \lambda\left(x_t b - x_t \beta\right)$$

$$\Leftrightarrow p_{t,\tau+1} - \left(1 + \lambda\left(a - \alpha\right)\right) p_{t,\tau} = \lambda\left(x_t b - x_t \beta\right).$$

The price satisfies a linear difference equation. The coefficient $1 - \lambda(a-\alpha)$ is less than 1 by assumption (since $\lambda > 0$, $a < 0$, $\alpha > 0$). If it is greater than -1, the sequence of the prices $p_{t,\tau}$ will tend to a limit $p_t^* = p_{t,\infty}$ for which

$$p_t^* - p_t^* = \lambda\left(D_{t,\infty} - S_{t,\infty}\right)$$

$$\Leftrightarrow \quad D_{t,\infty} = S_{t,\infty}.$$

The limit p_t^* is called equilibrium price, and is characterized by the equality of demand and supply. The quantity exchanged at this equilibrium price is assumed equal to this common value

$$Q_t^* = D_{t,\infty} = S_{t,\infty}.$$

The macroeconomic models are aggregate models with respect to individuals, goods, but also with respect to time. Since the phase of price adjustment cannot be taken into consideration if it is quick enough, the used observations are relative just to the equilibrium values p_t^*, Q_t^* (if the equilibrium is reached). In order to provide an interpretation in terms of recursiveness, it is interesting to examine the causal chain during the phase of adjustment (figure 10.3).

Figure 10.3   Causal Chain Scheme for the Price Evolution

Figure 10.4   Limit Behavior for the Price Evolution

However, if we observe just the equilibrium, that is the limit behavior of this chain, we get the situation depicted in figure 10.4.

The prices look like they are determining the quantities which, in turn, seemingly determine the prices. Thus the recursive behavior is lost, and we say that there is a simultaneous determination of the variables p and Q.

10.1.4 Various Forms of a Dynamic Model

There exist various ways of writing a dynamic model, in which a distinction will be made between endogenous and exogenous variables. These different expressions are interesting for analyzing the models and for better understanding, for example, the links among the variables.

The Structural Form   The structural form corresponds to the initial equation (10.1). It is written as

$$\mathbf{A}_0\mathbf{y}_t + \mathbf{A}_1\mathbf{y}_{t-1} + \ldots + \mathbf{A}_p\mathbf{y}_{t-p} + \mathbf{B}_0\mathbf{x}_t + \mathbf{B}_1\mathbf{x}_{t-1} + \ldots + \mathbf{B}_p\mathbf{x}_{t-p} + \boldsymbol{\mu} = \boldsymbol{\varepsilon}_t,$$
(10.8)

where $\boldsymbol{\varepsilon}_t$ is a white noise. Each of these equations provides the value of one of the endogenous variables as a function of the current values of the other endogenous variables, of the past values of the endogenous and exogenous variables (we do not make a distinction here between control and environment variables) and of an error term. The matrix $\mathbf{A}_0$ is often expressed with unit elements along its main diagonal. Then the model can be written as

$$\mathbf{y}_t = (\mathbf{I} - \mathbf{A}_0)\,\mathbf{y}_t - \mathbf{A}_1\mathbf{y}_{t-1} - \ldots - \mathbf{A}_p\mathbf{y}_{t-p}$$

$$- \mathbf{B}_0\mathbf{x}_t - \mathbf{B}_1\mathbf{x}_{t-1} - \ldots - \mathbf{B}_p\mathbf{x}_{t-p} - \boldsymbol{\mu} + \boldsymbol{\varepsilon}_t,$$

where $\mathbf{I} - \mathbf{A}_0$ has zero elements on the main diagonal. Although it is derived from macroeconomic theory, such a system can be difficult to interpret without additional constraints. Thus the simultaneity among the variables can be introduced at the same time through the coefficients of $\mathbf{A}_0$ and through the nonzero contemporaneous correlations of the elements of the vector $\boldsymbol{\varepsilon}$. While the simultaneity appearing in $\mathbf{A}_0$ is easily interpretable in terms of equilibrium, the one appearing in var (ϵ) is not. Moreover (cf. exercise 10.7), it is easy to show that it is not possible to keep the two sources of simultaneity separate.

The Reduced Form The reduced form of the model is the expression in which each endogenous variable is expressed as a function of the lagged endogenous variables, of the exogenous variables, and of the disturbance term. Such a form can be written as

$$\mathbf{y}_t = -\mathbf{A}_0^{-1}(\mathbf{A}_1\mathbf{y}_{t-1} + \ldots + \mathbf{A}_p\mathbf{y}_{t-p}$$
$$+ \mathbf{B}_0\mathbf{x}_t + \mathbf{B}_1\mathbf{x}_{t-1} + \ldots + \mathbf{B}_p\mathbf{x}_{t-p} + \boldsymbol{\mu}) + \mathbf{A}_0^{-1}\boldsymbol{\varepsilon}_t. \tag{10.9}$$

We can simplify the notation by introducing the lag polynomials

$$\mathbf{A}(L) = \mathbf{A}_0 + \mathbf{A}_1 L + \ldots + \mathbf{A}_p L^p,$$

$$\mathbf{B}(L) = \mathbf{B}_0 + \mathbf{B}_1 L + \ldots + \mathbf{B}_p L^p.$$

We have then

$$\mathbf{y}_t = -\mathbf{A}(0)^{-1}\left((\mathbf{A}(L) - \mathbf{A}(0))\mathbf{y}_t + \mathbf{B}(L)\mathbf{x}_t + \boldsymbol{\mu}\right) + \mathbf{A}(0)^{-1}\boldsymbol{\varepsilon}_t. \tag{10.10}$$

The time independence of the elements of the error term vector $\mathbf{A}(0)^{-1}\boldsymbol{\varepsilon}_t$ shows that the whole dynamics of the system, that is the effect of the past on the present, is summarized in the functions $\mathbf{A}_0^{-1}\mathbf{A}_1, \ldots, \mathbf{A}_0^{-1}\mathbf{A}_p,$ $\mathbf{A}_0^{-1}\mathbf{B}_0, \ldots, \mathbf{A}_0^{-1}\mathbf{B}_p$. These transformations of the initial parameters of the system are often called *reduced form parameters*.

The Final Form We can also express the current value of the endogenous variables $\mathbf{y}_t$ as a function of the exogenous variables and of the disturbances $\boldsymbol{\varepsilon}_\tau$, $\tau \leq t$. This expression is called *final form*. When the polynomial $\mathbf{A}(L)$ is such that det $\mathbf{A}(L)$ has all its roots outside the unit circle, this form is expressed as

$$\mathbf{y}_t = -\mathbf{A}(L)^{-1}\mathbf{B}(L)\mathbf{x}_t - \mathbf{A}(L)^{-1}\boldsymbol{\mu} + \mathbf{A}(L)^{-1}\boldsymbol{\varepsilon}_t, \tag{10.11}$$

or

$$\mathbf{y}_t = -\mathbf{A}(L)^{-1}\mathbf{B}(L)\mathbf{x}_t - \mathbf{A}(L)^{-1}\boldsymbol{\mu} + \mathbf{A}(L)^{-1}\mathbf{A}_0\left(\mathbf{A}_0^{-1}\boldsymbol{\varepsilon}_t\right)$$

which allows us to separate the influence of the exogenous variables and of the disturbances on $\mathbf{y}$ (cf. section 10.3).

10.2 Causality

We have seen that in the macroeconometric practice we are used to a distinction between endogenous and exogenous variables and within the group of the exogenous, between control and environment variables. However, we can consider a different approach, consisting in analyzing the joint evolution of the various variables of interest, and in examining whether some of them are fixed before others. Such an approach can be developed only if we consider a model describing the joint determination of all variables. It can be applied to both endogenous and environment exogenous variables, or to the set of all variables when the policy is described as in (10.7). It will never allow one to know which variables can be used for control purposes. In order to simplify notation, we will introduce the main concept without considering the variables z. We have available then observations on the multivariate processes $\{\mathbf{x}_t\}, \{\mathbf{y}_t\}$.

10.2.1 Definitions

We can associate with each process the information contained in the past behavior of the process itself. Thus, for example, we can consider

$$\underline{\mathbf{x}}_t = (\mathbf{x}_t, \mathbf{x}_{t-1}, \ldots) = (\mathbf{x}_{t-i}, \ i \geq 0),$$

$$\underline{\mathbf{y}}_t = (\mathbf{y}_t, \mathbf{y}_{t-1}, \ldots) = (\mathbf{y}_{t-i}, \ i \geq 0),$$

$$(\underline{\mathbf{x}}_t, \underline{\mathbf{y}}_t) = (\mathbf{x}_{t-i}, \ i \geq 0, \ \mathbf{y}_{t-i}, \ i \geq 0).$$

This information can be used to forecast future values of the variables. In what follows, we will assume that the forecasts of the variables are obtained by the linear regression method. The best linear forecast of a vector $\mathbf{x}$ based on the information I is denoted by $E(\mathbf{x} \mid I)$. The corresponding forecast error is $\boldsymbol{\varepsilon}(\mathbf{x} \mid I) = \mathbf{x} - E(\mathbf{x} \mid I)$. The associated mean square error can be computed from the estimated residual variance–covariance matrix

$$\mathrm{var}\,(\boldsymbol{\varepsilon}(\mathbf{x} \mid I)).$$

Granger (1969) has suggested the introduction of the following definitions which involve the variable forecasts starting from their past.

Definition 10.1:

(i) $\mathbf{y}$ *causes* $\mathbf{x}$ *at time t if and only if*

$$E\left(\mathbf{x}_t \mid \underline{\mathbf{x}}_{t-1}, \underline{\mathbf{y}}_{t-1}\right) \neq E\left(\mathbf{x}_t \mid \underline{\mathbf{x}}_{t-1}\right).$$

(ii) $\mathbf{y}$ *causes* $\mathbf{x}$ *instantaneously at time t if and only if*

$$E\left(\mathbf{x}_t \mid \underline{\mathbf{x}}_{t-1}, \underline{\mathbf{y}}_t\right) \neq E\left(\mathbf{x}_t \mid \underline{\mathbf{x}}_{t-1}, \underline{\mathbf{y}}_{t-1}\right).$$

As a result of the properties of the linear regression, the variable forecast

based on more information is necessarily the best one. Thus we always
have

$$\text{var}\left(\boldsymbol{\varepsilon}(\mathbf{x}_t \mid \underline{\mathbf{x}}_{t-1}, \underline{\mathbf{y}}_{t-1})\right) \leq \text{var}\left(\boldsymbol{\varepsilon}(\mathbf{x}_t \mid \underline{\mathbf{x}}_{t-1})\right).$$

We can then present the condition of noncausality starting from the
forecast error (cf. the appendix).

Theorem 10.1:

(i)   **y** *does not cause* **x** *at time t if and only if*

$$\text{var}\left(\boldsymbol{\varepsilon}(\mathbf{x}_t \mid \underline{\mathbf{x}}_{t-1}, \underline{\mathbf{y}}_{t-1})\right) = \text{var}\left(\boldsymbol{\varepsilon}(\mathbf{x}_t \mid \underline{\mathbf{x}}_{t-1})\right).$$

(ii) **y** *does not cause* **x** *instantaneously at time t if and only if*

$$\text{var}\left(\boldsymbol{\varepsilon}(\mathbf{x}_t \mid \underline{\mathbf{x}}_{t-1}, \underline{\mathbf{y}}_t)\right) = \text{var}\left(\boldsymbol{\varepsilon}(\mathbf{x}_t \mid \underline{\mathbf{x}}_{t-1}, \underline{\mathbf{y}}_{t-1})\right).$$

Thus **y** causes **x** at time t if the past of **y** provides additional information
for the forecast of $\mathbf{x}_t$ with respect to considering the past of **x** alone.
The conditions of noncausality allow for an interpretation in terms of
partial uncorrelation. Let us recall that two vectors **x** and **y** are partially
uncorrelated with respect to an information set I (denoted $\mathbf{x} \perp \mathbf{y} \mid I$) if
and only if

$$\text{cov}\left(\mathbf{x} - E(\mathbf{x} \mid I),\ \mathbf{y} - E(\mathbf{y} \mid I)\right) = \text{cov}\left(\boldsymbol{\varepsilon}(\mathbf{x} \mid I),\ \boldsymbol{\varepsilon}(\mathbf{y} \mid I)\right) = 0.$$

Theorem 10.2: (i)   **y** *does not cause* **x** *at time t if and only if* $\mathbf{x}_t$
   and $\underline{\mathbf{y}}_{t-1}$ *are not partially correlated with respect to* $\underline{\mathbf{x}}_{t-1}$, *that is*

$$\mathbf{x}_t \perp (\underline{\mathbf{y}}_{t-1} \mid \underline{\mathbf{x}}_{t-1}).$$

   (ii) **y** *does not cause* **x** *instantaneously at time t if and only if*
   $\mathbf{x}_t$ *and* $\mathbf{y}_t$ *are not partially correlated with respect to* $(\underline{\mathbf{x}}_{t-1},\ \underline{\mathbf{y}}_{t-1})$,
   that is

$$\mathbf{x}_t \perp \mathbf{y}_t \mid (\underline{\mathbf{x}}_{t-1},\ \underline{\mathbf{y}}_{t-1}).$$

PROOF: In the appendix at the end of this chapter. $\square$

Under the latter characterization, note that the definition of instantaneous causality involves the two processes **x** and **y** in a symmetric
fashion. Thus, we have the following corollary.

Corollary: *The two following statements are equivalent*

(i)   **y** *does not cause* **x** *instantaneously at time t;*
(ii) **x** *does not cause* **y** *instantaneously at time t.*

The previous definitions of causality have been criticized (see, for example, Zellner, 1979) since they differ from others used by epistemologists. This type of critique can be applied to many mathematical definitions, and boils down to a matter of semantics. It is clear that definition 10.1 involves conditions on the forecast error only. It might be preferable, then, to use terms such as "predictability" and "instantaneous predictability" instead of "causality" and "instantaneous causality." We will use the latter terms, however, given their more frequent use. Nevertheless, we should keep constantly in mind the implications and the limits of the previous definitions, when we use them to describe a real-world phenomenon.

Example 10.1: Let us consider the process defined as

$$x_t = \epsilon_t + a\eta_t + b\eta_{t-1},$$

$$y_t = \eta_t,$$

where ϵ and η are independent white noises. We have

(i)

$$E\left(x_t \mid \underline{x}_{t-1}, \underline{y}_{t-1}\right) = b\eta_{t-1} = by_{t-1}.$$

Since the expression involves y_{t-1} we immediately see that y causes x at time t if and only if $b \neq 0$.

(ii)

$$E\left(x_t \mid \underline{x}_{t-1}, \underline{y}_t\right) = a\eta_t + b\eta_{t-1} = ay_t + by_{t-1}.$$

There is instantaneous causality of y to x at time t if and only if the term involving y_t is actually present in the expression, that is, if $a \neq 0$.

(iii) Note that from this example we conclude that there is no link between the two concepts of causality, since the parameters a and b of the example are not functionally related.

The definitions of causality proposed are valid for any time t. In reality, for certain phenomena we could observe a causality reversal. Thus **y** may cause **x**, and **x** not cause **y** before a certain date; after that date we might see **x** causing **y** and **y** not causing **x**. Definition 10.2 provides a definition applicable in the absence of such reversals.

Definition 10.2: **y** *does not cause* **x** *(instantaneously) if and only if* **y** *does not cause* **x** *(instantaneously) at time t for all possible times t.*

When the process $(\mathbf{x}, \mathbf{y})$ is stationary, it is apparent that the definitions for a certain date or for all dates coincide.

10.2.2 Other Characterizations of Causality

Two other characterizations of causality have been proposed in the literature and are valid for stationary regular processes $\mathbf{x}, \mathbf{y}$.

Theorem 10.3: **(Pierce-Haugh)** $\mathbf{y}$ *does not cause* $\mathbf{x}$ *if and only if*

$$\operatorname{cov}\left(\boldsymbol{\varepsilon}(\mathbf{x}_t \mid \underline{\mathbf{x}}_{t-1}), \ \boldsymbol{\varepsilon}(\mathbf{y}_{t-j} \mid \underline{\mathbf{y}}_{t-j-1})\right) = 0, \quad j \geq 1.$$

PROOF: Cf. the appendix. □

The previous result can be easily interpreted. In order to simplify matters, let us consider the case when x and y are univariate. We can express x_t and y_t as a function of their own past

$$x_t = \sum_{j=1}^{+\infty} a_j x_{t-j} + u_t,$$

$$y_t = \sum_{j=1}^{+\infty} b_j y_{t-j} + v_t.$$

The innovations correspond to

$$u_t = \boldsymbol{\varepsilon}(x_t \mid \underline{x}_{t-1}),$$

$$v_t = \boldsymbol{\varepsilon}(y_t \mid \underline{y}_{t-1}).$$

The condition proposed by Pierce and Haugh is a constraint of uncorrelation between the current innovation of x_t and all past innovations of y, namely $v_{t-1}, v_{t-2}, \ldots$. We can also introduce the notion of instantaneous noncausality in terms of these innovations.

Corollary: $\mathbf{y}$ *does not cause* $\mathbf{x}$ *and does not cause* $\mathbf{x}$ *instantaneously if and only if*

$$\operatorname{cov}\left(\boldsymbol{\varepsilon}(\mathbf{x}_t \mid \underline{\mathbf{x}}_{t-1}), \ \boldsymbol{\varepsilon}(\mathbf{y}_{t-j} \mid \underline{\mathbf{y}}_{t-j-1})\right) = 0, \quad j \geq 0.$$

Note however that instantaneous noncausality is not equivalent to the condition

$$\operatorname{cov}\left(\boldsymbol{\varepsilon}(\mathbf{x}_t \mid \underline{\mathbf{x}}_{t-1}), \ \boldsymbol{\varepsilon}(\mathbf{y}_t \mid \underline{\mathbf{y}}_{t-1})\right) = 0$$

(cf. Price, 1979).

Theorem 10.4: (Sims) $\mathbf{y}$ *does not cause* $\mathbf{x}$*, that is* $\mathbf{x}_t \perp \underline{\mathbf{y}}_{t-1} \mid \underline{\mathbf{x}}_{t-1}$ *if and only if* $\overline{\mathbf{x}}_{t+1} = (\mathbf{x}_{t+1}, \mathbf{x}_{t+2}, \ldots)$ *is partially uncorrelated with* $\mathbf{y}_t$ *with respect to* $\underline{\mathbf{x}}_t$

$$\overline{\mathbf{x}}_{t+1} \perp \mathbf{y}_t \mid \underline{\mathbf{x}}_t.$$

PROOF: Cf. the appendix. □

Limiting ourselves to univariate processes, the condition can be interpreted as follows: let us consider the regression of y_t on all values (past, current, and future) of x_t

$$y_t = \sum_{-\infty}^{+\infty} a_j x_{t-j} + \omega_t;$$

y does not cause x if and only if the future values of x cannot be used to predict y_t, that is, if and only if $a_j = 0, \ \forall \ j < 0$.

10.2.3 Causality and Multivariate Autoregressive Models

The definitions of causality can be simplified in the case of autoregressive stationary processes. Let us consider an expression of the type

$$\begin{pmatrix} \mathbf{\Phi}_y(L) & \mathbf{\Phi}_{yx}(L) \\ \mathbf{\Phi}_{xy}(L) & \mathbf{\Phi}_x(L) \end{pmatrix} \begin{pmatrix} \mathbf{y}_t \\ \mathbf{x}_t \end{pmatrix} = \begin{pmatrix} \mathbf{c}_y \\ \mathbf{c}_x \end{pmatrix} + \begin{pmatrix} \boldsymbol{\varepsilon}_{yt} \\ \boldsymbol{\varepsilon}_{xt} \end{pmatrix},$$

where the usual conditions on the roots of the autoregressive characteristic polynomial are satisfied. We can choose a normalization of the type

$$\mathbf{\Phi}(0) = \begin{pmatrix} \mathbf{\Phi}_y(0) & \mathbf{\Phi}_{yx}(0) \\ \mathbf{\Phi}_{xy}(0) & \mathbf{\Phi}_x(0) \end{pmatrix} = \mathbf{I},$$

so that $\begin{pmatrix} \boldsymbol{\varepsilon}_{yt} \\ \boldsymbol{\varepsilon}_{xt} \end{pmatrix}$ can be interpreted as the innovation of the process $\begin{pmatrix} \mathbf{y} \\ \mathbf{x} \end{pmatrix}$.

In this case, all simultaneous links between the two processes are summarized in the covariance $\mathrm{cov}\,(\boldsymbol{\varepsilon}_{yt}, \boldsymbol{\varepsilon}_{xt})$.

Theorem 10.5:

(i) $\mathbf{y}$ *does not cause* $\mathbf{x}$ *if and only if* $\mathbf{\Phi}_{xy}(L) = 0$.

(ii) $\mathbf{y}$ *and* $\mathbf{x}$ *do not instantaneously cause each other if and only if*
$\mathrm{cov}\,(\boldsymbol{\varepsilon}_{yt}, \boldsymbol{\varepsilon}_{xt}) = \mathbf{0}$.

PROOF: Let us prove, for instance, the first proposition. We have
$$E\left(\mathbf{x}_t \mid \underline{\mathbf{x}}_{t-1}, \underline{\mathbf{y}}_{t-1}\right) = -\left(\boldsymbol{\Phi}_x(L) - \mathbf{I}\right)\mathbf{x}_t - \boldsymbol{\Phi}_{xy}(L)\mathbf{y}_t + \mathbf{c}_x.$$
y does not cause **x** if and only if the past values of **y** do not appear in the expression for the forecast, that is if and only if $\boldsymbol{\Phi}_{xy}(L) = \mathbf{0}$.
□

Theorem 10.5 depends crucially upon the chosen normalization
$$\boldsymbol{\Phi}(0) = \mathbf{I}.$$
If we had an autoregressive model
$$\begin{pmatrix} \boldsymbol{\Phi}_y(L) & \boldsymbol{\Phi}_{yx}(L) \\ \boldsymbol{\Phi}_{xy}(L) & \boldsymbol{\Phi}_x(L) \end{pmatrix} \begin{pmatrix} \mathbf{y}_t \\ \mathbf{x}_t \end{pmatrix} = \begin{pmatrix} \mathbf{c}_y \\ \mathbf{c}_x \end{pmatrix} + \begin{pmatrix} \boldsymbol{\varepsilon}_{yt} \\ \boldsymbol{\varepsilon}_{xt} \end{pmatrix},$$
with $\boldsymbol{\Phi}(0) \neq \mathbf{I}$, the error term $\begin{pmatrix} \boldsymbol{\varepsilon}_{yt} \\ \boldsymbol{\varepsilon}_{xt} \end{pmatrix}$ cannot be interpreted as the innovation of the process. We would have to transform the model by premultiplying it by $\boldsymbol{\Phi}(0)^{-1}$. Introducing a partitioned inverse notation we have
$$\boldsymbol{\Phi}(0)^{-1} = \begin{pmatrix} \boldsymbol{\Phi}^y(0) & \boldsymbol{\Phi}^{yx}(0) \\ \boldsymbol{\Phi}^{xy}(0) & \boldsymbol{\Phi}^x(0) \end{pmatrix}.$$
The corresponding normalized model would be
$$\begin{pmatrix} \boldsymbol{\Phi}^y(0) & \boldsymbol{\Phi}^{yx}(0) \\ \boldsymbol{\Phi}^{xy}(0) & \boldsymbol{\Phi}^x(0) \end{pmatrix} \begin{pmatrix} \boldsymbol{\Phi}_y(L) & \boldsymbol{\Phi}_{yx}(L) \\ \boldsymbol{\Phi}_{xy}(L) & \boldsymbol{\Phi}_x(L) \end{pmatrix} \begin{pmatrix} \mathbf{y}_t \\ \mathbf{x}_t \end{pmatrix}$$
$$= \begin{pmatrix} \boldsymbol{\Phi}^y(0) & \boldsymbol{\Phi}^{yx}(0) \\ \boldsymbol{\Phi}^{xy}(0) & \boldsymbol{\Phi}^x(0) \end{pmatrix} \left(\begin{pmatrix} \mathbf{c}_y \\ \mathbf{c}_x \end{pmatrix} + \begin{pmatrix} \boldsymbol{\varepsilon}_{yt} \\ \boldsymbol{\varepsilon}_{xt} \end{pmatrix} \right).$$
We will have noncausality of y to x if and only if
$$\boldsymbol{\Phi}^{xy}(0)\boldsymbol{\Phi}_y(L) + \boldsymbol{\Phi}^x(0)\boldsymbol{\Phi}_{xy}(L) = \mathbf{0}.$$
We will have instantaneous noncausality of **y** to **x** if and only if
$$\boldsymbol{\Phi}^y(0)\mathrm{var}\left(\boldsymbol{\varepsilon}_{yt}\right)\boldsymbol{\Phi}^{xy}(0)'$$
$$+ \boldsymbol{\Phi}^{yx}(0)\mathrm{cov}\left(\boldsymbol{\varepsilon}_{xt}, \boldsymbol{\varepsilon}_{yt}\right)\boldsymbol{\Phi}^{xy}(0)'$$
$$+ \boldsymbol{\Phi}^y(0)\mathrm{cov}\left(\boldsymbol{\varepsilon}_{yt}, \boldsymbol{\varepsilon}_{xt}\right)\boldsymbol{\Phi}^x(0)'$$
$$+ \boldsymbol{\Phi}^{yx}(0)\mathrm{var}\left(\boldsymbol{\varepsilon}_{xt}\right)\boldsymbol{\Phi}^x(0)' = \mathbf{0}.$$
Evidently, an adequate normalization choice simplifies writing down the constraints. In particular, for instantaneous noncausality the choice $\boldsymbol{\Phi} = \mathbf{I}$ avoids introducing constraints where there appear both autoregressive parameters and elements of the error term variance–covariance

matrix. We will see in section 10.3.2 that a block-recursive normalization allows one to write this hypothesis of instantaneous noncausality without resorting to the variances and covariances of the error term.

10.2.4 Measures of Causality

In practice, the three types of causality, of **y** to **x**, of **x** to **y** and instantaneous, can coexist. It is necessary, then, to determine the relative importance of each type, i.e., to introduce *measures of causality*. These measures will have to satisfy certain properties which will translate into simple usage and interpretation. They will have to be positive, not to become 0 unless there is noncausality, and to be easy to determine, for example on the basis of regression results. Such measures can be defined from the characterization given in theorem 10.1. If **y** causes **x**, we have

$$\text{var}\left(\boldsymbol{\varepsilon}(\mathbf{x}_t \mid \underline{\mathbf{x}}_{t-1}, \underline{\mathbf{y}}_{t-1})\right) \neq \text{var}\left(\boldsymbol{\varepsilon}(\mathbf{x}_t \mid \underline{\mathbf{x}}_{t-1})\right).$$

On the other hand, the bigger the difference between the two matrices, the more information is contained in **y** about **x**. A suggestion is for a positive valued scalar function of these variance–covariance matrices which is an increasing function of the difference and is equal to zero if and only if the two matrices are equal to each other.

An example of such a function is

$$C_{y \to x} = \ln \left(\frac{\det \text{var}\left(\boldsymbol{\varepsilon}(\mathbf{x}_t \mid \underline{\mathbf{x}}_{t-1})\right)}{\det \text{var}\left(\boldsymbol{\varepsilon}(\mathbf{x}_t \mid \underline{\mathbf{x}}_{t-1}, \underline{\mathbf{y}}_{t-1})\right)} \right).$$

Definition 10.3: *The causality measures are defined as*

(i)   *causality of* **y** *to* **x**

$$C_{y \to x} = \ln \left(\frac{\det \text{var}\left(\boldsymbol{\varepsilon}(\mathbf{x}_t \mid \underline{\mathbf{x}}_{t-1})\right)}{\det \text{var}\left(\boldsymbol{\varepsilon}(\mathbf{x}_t \mid \underline{\mathbf{x}}_{t-1}, \underline{\mathbf{y}}_{t-1})\right)} \right);$$

(ii) *causality of* **x** *to* **y**

$$C_{x \to y} = \ln \left(\frac{\det \text{var}\left(\boldsymbol{\varepsilon}(\mathbf{y}_t \mid \underline{\mathbf{y}}_{t-1})\right)}{\det \text{var}\left(\boldsymbol{\varepsilon}(\mathbf{y}_t \mid \underline{\mathbf{x}}_{t-1}, \underline{\mathbf{y}}_{t-1})\right)} \right);$$

(iii) *instantaneous causality between* **x** *and* **y**

$$C_{x \leftrightarrow y} = \ln \left(\frac{\det \text{var}\left(\boldsymbol{\varepsilon}(\mathbf{x}_t \mid \underline{\mathbf{x}}_{t-1}, \underline{\mathbf{y}}_{t-1})\right)}{\det \text{var}\left(\boldsymbol{\varepsilon}(\mathbf{x}_t \mid \underline{\mathbf{x}}_{t-1}, \underline{\mathbf{y}}_t)\right)} \right).$$

All these measures are positive by construction and become 0 only when the corresponding noncausality occurs. Some of these measures admit other expressions. We provide alternative expressions of the instantaneous causality measure in theorem 10.6 (cf. the appendix).

Theorem 10.6:

$$C_{x \leftrightarrow y} = \ln \left(\frac{\det \operatorname{var} \left(\boldsymbol{\varepsilon}(\mathbf{x}_t \mid \underline{\mathbf{x}}_{t-1}, \underline{\mathbf{y}}_{t-1}) \right)}{\det \operatorname{var} \left(\boldsymbol{\varepsilon}(\mathbf{x}_t \mid \underline{\mathbf{x}}_{t-1}, \underline{\mathbf{y}}_t) \right)} \right)$$

$$= \ln \left(\frac{\det \operatorname{var} \left(\boldsymbol{\varepsilon}(\mathbf{y}_t \mid \underline{\mathbf{x}}_{t-1}, \underline{\mathbf{y}}_{t-1}) \right)}{\det \operatorname{var} \left(\boldsymbol{\varepsilon}(\mathbf{y}_t \mid \underline{\mathbf{x}}_t, \underline{\mathbf{y}}_{t-1}) \right)} \right)$$

$$= \ln \left(\frac{\det \operatorname{var} \left(\boldsymbol{\varepsilon}(\mathbf{x}_t \mid \underline{\mathbf{x}}_{t-1}, \underline{\mathbf{y}}_{t-1}) \right) \det \operatorname{var} \left(\boldsymbol{\varepsilon}(\mathbf{y}_t \mid \underline{\mathbf{x}}_{t-1}, \underline{\mathbf{y}}_{t-1}) \right)}{\det \operatorname{var} \left(\boldsymbol{\varepsilon}(\mathbf{x}_t, \mathbf{y}_t \mid \underline{\mathbf{x}}_{t-1}, \underline{\mathbf{y}}_{t-1}) \right)} \right).$$

The first equality comes from the symmetry of instantaneous causality with respect to $\mathbf{x}$ and $\mathbf{y}$. The second comes from the characterization of instantaneous causality in terms of uncorrelated innovations. Adding up the three causality measures we get

$$C_{y \to x} + C_{x \to y} + C_{x \leftrightarrow y}$$

$$= \ln \left(\frac{\det \operatorname{var} \left(\boldsymbol{\varepsilon}(\mathbf{x}_t \mid \underline{\mathbf{x}}_{t-1}) \right)}{\det \operatorname{var} \left(\boldsymbol{\varepsilon}(\mathbf{x}_t \mid \underline{\mathbf{x}}_{t-1}, \underline{\mathbf{y}}_{t-1}) \right)} \right)$$

$$+ \ln \left(\frac{\det \operatorname{var} \left(\boldsymbol{\varepsilon}(\mathbf{y}_t \mid \underline{\mathbf{y}}_{t-1}) \right)}{\det \operatorname{var} \left(\boldsymbol{\varepsilon}(\mathbf{y}_t \mid \underline{\mathbf{x}}_{t-1}, \underline{\mathbf{y}}_{t-1}) \right)} \right)$$

$$+ \ln \left(\frac{\det \operatorname{var} \left(\boldsymbol{\varepsilon}(\mathbf{x}_t \mid \underline{\mathbf{x}}_{t-1}, \underline{\mathbf{y}}_{t-1}) \right) \det \operatorname{var} \left(\boldsymbol{\varepsilon}(\mathbf{y}_t \mid \underline{\mathbf{x}}_{t-1}, \underline{\mathbf{y}}_{t-1}) \right)}{\det \operatorname{var} \left(\boldsymbol{\varepsilon}(\mathbf{x}_t, \mathbf{y}_t \mid \underline{\mathbf{x}}_{t-1}, \underline{\mathbf{y}}_{t-1}) \right)} \right)$$

$$= \ln \left(\frac{\det \operatorname{var} \left(\boldsymbol{\varepsilon}(\mathbf{x}_t \mid \underline{\mathbf{x}}_{t-1}) \right) \det \operatorname{var} \left(\boldsymbol{\varepsilon}(\mathbf{y}_t \mid \underline{\mathbf{y}}_{t-1}) \right)}{\det \operatorname{var} \left(\boldsymbol{\varepsilon}(\mathbf{x}_t, \mathbf{y}_t \mid \underline{\mathbf{x}}_{t-1}, \underline{\mathbf{y}}_{t-1}) \right)} \right).$$

By this quantity it is possible to know whether the two series should be studied jointly $\left[\text{the term} \det \operatorname{var} \left(\boldsymbol{\varepsilon}(\mathbf{x}_t, \mathbf{y}_t \mid \underline{\mathbf{x}}_{t-1}, \underline{\mathbf{y}}_{t-1}) \right) \right]$ or rather considered separately from each other

$$\left[\text{the term} \ \det \text{var} \left(\boldsymbol{\varepsilon}(\mathbf{x}_t \mid \underline{\mathbf{x}}_{t-1}) \right) \det \text{var} \left(\boldsymbol{\varepsilon}(\mathbf{y}_t \mid \underline{\mathbf{y}}_{t-1}) \right) \right].$$

This quantity can be interpreted as a measure of the dependence between the two processes.

Definition 10.4: *The dependence measure between the two processes* $\mathbf{x}$ *and* $\mathbf{y}$ *is defined as*

$$C_{x,y} = \ln \left(\frac{\det \text{var} \left(\boldsymbol{\varepsilon}(\mathbf{x}_t \mid \underline{\mathbf{x}}_{t-1}) \right) \det \text{var} \left(\boldsymbol{\varepsilon}(\mathbf{y}_t \mid \underline{\mathbf{y}}_{t-1}) \right)}{\det \text{var} \left(\boldsymbol{\varepsilon}(\mathbf{x}_t, \mathbf{y}_t \mid \underline{\mathbf{x}}_{t-1}, \underline{\mathbf{y}}_{t-1}) \right)} \right).$$

Theorem 10.7: *We have the following equality*

$$C_{x,y} = C_{y \to x} + C_{x \to y} + C_{x \leftrightarrow y}.$$

This equality establishes that the dependence measure = the unidirectional causality measure of $\mathbf{x}$ to $\mathbf{y}$ + the unidirectional causality measure of $\mathbf{y}$ to $\mathbf{x}$ + the instantaneous causality measure.

Since all measures are positive, we can show that the two processes do not have any link ($\text{cov}(\mathbf{x}_t, \mathbf{y}_\tau) = 0$, $\forall \ t \neq \tau$) if and only if $C_{x,y} = 0$, that is if there is no unidirectional causality (in either direction) nor instantaneous causality (cf. exercise 10.8). The convenience of the previous measures rests upon their derivability from regressions of the variables on their past.

Let us consider the following regressions

Regression of $\mathbf{x}_t$ on its own past

$$\mathbf{x}_t = \sum_{j=1}^{+\infty} \mathbf{A}_j^1 \mathbf{x}_{t-j} + \mathbf{a}^1 + \mathbf{u}_t^1, \quad \text{var}(\mathbf{u}_t^1) = \boldsymbol{\Omega}_1.$$

Regression of $\mathbf{y}_t$ on its own past

$$\mathbf{y}_t = \sum_{j=1}^{+\infty} \mathbf{A}_j^2 \mathbf{y}_{t-j} + \mathbf{a}^2 + \mathbf{u}_t^2, \quad \text{var}(\mathbf{u}_t^2) = \boldsymbol{\Omega}_2.$$

Regression of $\mathbf{x}_t$ on the past of $\mathbf{x}$ and $\mathbf{y}$

$$\mathbf{x}_t = \sum_{j=1}^{+\infty} \mathbf{A}_j^3 \mathbf{x}_{t-j} + \sum_{j=1}^{+\infty} \mathbf{A}_j^4 \mathbf{y}_{t-j} + \mathbf{a}^3 + \mathbf{u}_t^3, \quad \text{var}(\mathbf{u}_t^3) = \boldsymbol{\Omega}_3.$$

Regression of $\mathbf{y}_t$ on the past of x and y

$$\mathbf{y}_t = \sum_{j=1}^{+\infty} \mathbf{A}_j^5 \mathbf{x}_{t-j} + \sum_{j=1}^{+\infty} \mathbf{A}_j^6 \mathbf{y}_{t-j} + \mathbf{a}^4 + \mathbf{u}_t^4, \quad \mathrm{var}\left(\mathbf{u}_t^4\right) = \boldsymbol{\Omega}_4.$$

Regression of $\mathbf{x}_t$ on the past of x and y and on current y

$$\mathbf{x}_t = \sum_{j=1}^{+\infty} \mathbf{A}_j^7 \mathbf{x}_{t-j} + \sum_{j=0}^{+\infty} \mathbf{A}_j^8 \mathbf{y}_{t-j} + \mathbf{a}^5 + \mathbf{u}_t^5, \quad \mathrm{var}\left(\mathbf{u}_t^5\right) = \boldsymbol{\Omega}_5.$$

Regression of $\mathbf{y}_t$ on the past of x and y and on current x

$$\mathbf{y}_t = \sum_{j=0}^{+\infty} \mathbf{A}_j^9 \mathbf{x}_{t-j} + \sum_{j=1}^{+\infty} \mathbf{A}_j^{10} \mathbf{y}_{t-j} + \mathbf{a}^6 + \mathbf{u}_t^6, \quad \mathrm{var}\left(\mathbf{u}_t^6\right) = \boldsymbol{\Omega}_6.$$

Regression of $\mathbf{x}_t$, $\mathbf{y}_t$ on the past of x and y

$$\begin{pmatrix} \mathbf{x}_t \\ \mathbf{y}_t \end{pmatrix} = \sum_{j=1}^{+\infty} \mathbf{A}_j \begin{pmatrix} \mathbf{x}_{t-j} \\ \mathbf{y}_{t-j} \end{pmatrix} + \mathbf{a} + \mathbf{u}_t, \quad \mathrm{var}\left(\mathbf{u}_t\right) = \boldsymbol{\Omega}.$$

We have

$$C_{x \to y} = \ln \frac{\det \boldsymbol{\Omega}_2}{\det \boldsymbol{\Omega}_4},$$

$$C_{y \to x} = \ln \frac{\det \boldsymbol{\Omega}_1}{\det \boldsymbol{\Omega}_3},$$

$$C_{x \leftrightarrow y} = \ln \frac{\det \boldsymbol{\Omega}_3}{\det \boldsymbol{\Omega}_5} = \ln \frac{\det \boldsymbol{\Omega}_4}{\det \boldsymbol{\Omega}_6} = \ln \frac{\det \boldsymbol{\Omega}_1 \det \boldsymbol{\Omega}_2}{\det \boldsymbol{\Omega}}.$$

10.2.5 Decomposition of Causality Measures

The links between the two series **x** and **y** can be decomposed both in the time domain by specifying the lags needed for one variable to influence the other ones and in the frequency domain, by analyzing the links at each frequency.

Decomposition in the Time Domain The first decomposition proposed concerns the effect of $\mathbf{y}_{t-j}$ on $\mathbf{x}_t$ conditionally to the past $\underline{\mathbf{x}}_{t-1}$ and $\underline{\mathbf{y}}_{t-j-1}$. It can be measured as

$$C_{y \to x}^{(j)} = \ln \left(\frac{\det \mathrm{var}\left(\boldsymbol{\varepsilon}(\mathbf{x}_t \mid \underline{\mathbf{x}}_{t-1}, \underline{\mathbf{y}}_{t-j-1})\right)}{\det \mathrm{var}\left(\boldsymbol{\varepsilon}(\mathbf{x}_t \mid \underline{\mathbf{x}}_{t-1}, \underline{\mathbf{y}}_{t-j})\right)} \right), \quad j \geq 0.$$

As a consequence we have the decomposition

$$C_{x,y} = C_{x \leftrightarrow y} + \sum_{j=1}^{+\infty} C_{y \to x}^{(j)} + \sum_{j=1}^{+\infty} C_{x \to y}^{(j)}. \tag{10.12}$$

For instance such a decomposition can pinpoint the presence of a short-term causality of $\mathbf{y}$ to $\mathbf{x}$ – if the values $C_{y\rightarrow x}^{(j)}$ are fairly large for small j – with the absence of a long-term causality of $\mathbf{y}$ to $\mathbf{x}$ – if the values $C_{y\rightarrow x}^{(j)}$ are small for large j.

Let us provide, as an example of such a decomposition, the case of the evolution of German and French prices. After the abandonment of the gold-standard and the generalization of the floating exchange rates, the German and French prices have experienced two kinds of evolution. From 1978 to 1982 there has been an acceleration in inflation in both countries. After 1982, there has been a disinflation period. It is advisable, therefore to keep separate the two periods before and after 1982. This year was a year of changes for other reasons as well. In fact, during this year the monetary changes made during 1981 have shown their effects. Thus, the causality analysis has been conducted separately on the two sub-periods (January 1978–April 1982) and (May 1982–December 1985) on the monthly price indices published by the European Community. The measures have been computed on the price rates of change. The ratios (in percentage terms)

$$\frac{C_{x\rightarrow y}^{(j)}}{C_{x,y}}, \quad \frac{C_{y\rightarrow x}^{(j)}}{C_{x,y}}, \quad \frac{C_{x\leftrightarrow y}}{C_{x,y}},$$

estimated from the associated regression models with eleven lags, are given in the tables 10.1 (for the first period) and 10.2 (for the second period).

Note the marked difference of the causal shares between the two periods. On the first subperiod, the two unidirectional causalities are approximately of the same order of magnitude. In the disinflation period, the influence of French prices on German prices is stronger than the other way around. To be noted also is the increase in simultaneity (instantaneous causality) in the price formation. This latter phenomenon is to be connected to the values of the unidirectional mean lags. These are defined as

$$D_{x\rightarrow y} = \frac{\sum_{j=1}^{+\infty} j C_{x\rightarrow y}^{(j)}}{\sum_{j=1}^{+\infty} C_{x\rightarrow y}^{(j)}}, \tag{10.13}$$

$$D_{y\rightarrow x} = \frac{\sum_{j=1}^{+\infty} j C_{y\rightarrow x}^{(j)}}{\sum_{j=1}^{+\infty} C_{y\rightarrow x}^{(j)}}. \tag{10.14}$$

Analogously, we could define a mean causality lag taking into account

Table 10.1 *Causality Decomposition – Period 1978.01-1982.04*

Lag	Instantaneous causality	Causality French prices $\longrightarrow$ German prices	Causality German prices $\longrightarrow$ French prices	
0	2.4			
1		6.8	6.6	
2		≈ 0	2.3	
3		1.1	0.8	
4		0.9	5.4	
5		≈ 0	13.1	
6		14.0	3.5	
7		1.0	2.2	
8		0.5	2.1	
9		6.8	≈ 0	
10		5.7	15.1	
11		9.4	0.3	
Total	2.4	46.2	51.4	100

all possible directions. Referring to the causality of **x** to **y**, we have

$$D = \left(\frac{\sum_{j=1}^{+\infty} j C_{x \to y}^{(j)} + 0\ C_{x \leftrightarrow y} + \sum_{j=1}^{+\infty} (-j) C_{y \to x}^{(j)}}{C_{x,y}} \right). \tag{10.15}$$

The various mean lags are related to each other through

$$D = D_{x \to y} \frac{C_{x \to y}}{C_{x,y}} - D_{y \to x} \frac{C_{y \to x}}{C_{x,y}}. \tag{10.16}$$

The values of these lags on the price series are reported in table 10.3; they show a noticeable decrease in the unidirectional mean lag between the two periods, on average by two months.

The same phenomenon can be seen visually, when we represent the cumulated effects for each kind of causality and on each period (figures 10.5 and 10.6). These effects can be defined as

$$F_{x \to y}^{(j)} = \frac{\sum_{k=1}^{j} C_{x \to y}^{(k)} + C_{x \leftrightarrow y}/2}{C_{x \to y} + C_{x \leftrightarrow y}/2} \quad j = 1, 2 \ldots . \tag{10.17}$$

Table 10.2 *Causality Decomposition – Period 1982.05/1985.12*

Lag	Instantaneous causality	Causality French prices $\longrightarrow$ German prices	Causality German prices $\longrightarrow$ French prices	
0	8.9			
1		1.1	6.0	
2		8.0	9.9	
3		1.8	≈ 0	
4		7.6	0.5	
5		25.9	6.5	
6		5.9	≈ 0	
7		0.2	0.1	
8		1.6	1.1	
9		≈ 0	3.6	
10		9.3	0.5	
11		1.0	0.5	
Total 8.9		62.4	28.7	100

$F^{(j)}_{x \to y}$ gives the importance of the short-term causality, short-term being defined as the set of lags less than or equal to j.

The cumulative functions corresponding to the period 1978–82 are always less than the cumulative functions corresponding to the other period (but for the lag $j = 1$ and for one direction). Thus the short-term component appears proportionately stronger in the phase of disinflation, no matter what definition of short-term we adopt, namely for all values of j. Note that the previous discussion gives some ideas about the link between the two series, but does not provide any information about the autonomous evolution of each of the two series separately, that is the influence of the past values on the current value of the same series. For this purpose we can introduce a variance decomposition of x_t, separating the effects of the lagged values of x (i.e., effect of its own past), the lagged values effects of y and the residual effect. The decompositions for the example are given in tables 10.4 and 10.5.

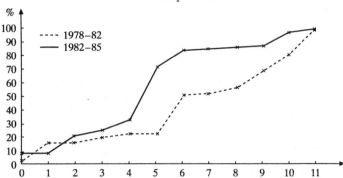

Figure 10.5 Cumulated Effects French Prices → German Prices

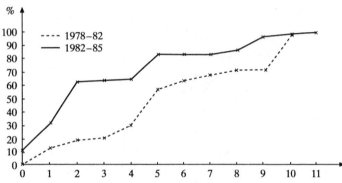

Figure 10.6 Cumulated Effects German Prices → French Prices

Table 10.3 *Mean Causality Lags*

Average lag	Unidirectional French prices ⟶ German prices	Unidirectional German prices ⟶ French prices	Global
1978-82	7.14	5.99	0.22
1982-5	5.38	3.92	2.23

Between the two periods we can observe a systematic decrease of the residual component, an increase in the own effect in the evolution of the French prices and an increase of the influence of French prices on German prices.

Table 10.4 *Decomposition for the French Prices*

	Effect from its own past	Effect from German prices	Residual effect	
1978-82	16	43	41	100
1982-5	48	26	26	100

Table 10.5 *Decomposition for the German Prices*

	Effect of its own past	Effect from German prices	Residual effect	
1978-82	44	25	31	100
1982-5	39	45	16	100

Frequency Domain Decomposition We can try to decompose the links between the two series as well, by showing the causality links at each frequency. We are looking for functions $g_{x,y}$, $g_{x \to y}$, $g_{y \to x}$, $g_{x \leftrightarrow y}$ defined on the frequency domain, corresponding to the intuition behind the procedure. They must be positive and admit the decomposition

$$g_{x,y} = g_{x \to y} + g_{y \to x} + g_{x \leftrightarrow y}, \qquad (10.18)$$

and such that

$$C_{x,y} = \frac{1}{2\pi} \int_{-\pi}^{+\pi} g_{x,y}(\omega) \, d\omega,$$

$$C_{y \to x} = \frac{1}{2\pi} \int_{-\pi}^{+\pi} g_{y \to x}(\omega) \, d\omega,$$

$$\qquad (10.19)$$

$$C_{x \to y} = \frac{1}{2\pi} \int_{-\pi}^{+\pi} g_{x \to y}(\omega) \, d\omega,$$

$$C_{x \leftrightarrow y} = \frac{1}{2\pi} \int_{-\pi}^{+\pi} g_{x \leftrightarrow y}(\omega) \, d\omega.$$

Such a decomposition for each frequency is easy to derive for the global link measure $C_{x,y}$. In fact, we know that

$$C_{x,y} = \ln \left(\frac{\det \text{var} \left(\boldsymbol{\varepsilon}(\mathbf{x}_t \mid \underline{\mathbf{x}}_{t-1}) \right) \det \text{var} \left(\boldsymbol{\varepsilon}(\mathbf{y}_t \mid \underline{\mathbf{y}}_{t-1}) \right)}{\det \text{var} \left(\boldsymbol{\varepsilon}(\mathbf{x}_t, \mathbf{y}_t \mid \underline{\mathbf{x}}_{t-1}, \underline{\mathbf{y}}_{t-1}) \right)} \right),$$

and, using the Kolmogorov equality (cf. 8.20), we can write

$$C_{x,y} = \frac{1}{2\pi} \int_{-\pi}^{+\pi} \ln \left(\frac{\det \left(2\pi \mathbf{f}_x(\omega) \right) \det \left(2\pi \mathbf{f}_y(\omega) \right)}{\det \left(2\pi \mathbf{f}_{x,y}(\omega) \right)} \right) d\omega$$

$$= \frac{1}{2\pi} \int_{-\pi}^{+\pi} \ln \left(\frac{\det \left(\mathbf{f}_x(\omega) \right) \det \left(\mathbf{f}_y(\omega) \right)}{\det \left(\mathbf{f}_{x,y}(\omega) \right)} \right) d\omega.$$

We can then choose

$$g_{x,y}(\omega) = \ln \left(\frac{\det \left(\mathbf{f}_x(\omega) \right) \det \left(\mathbf{f}_y(\omega) \right)}{\det \left(\mathbf{f}_{x,y}(\omega) \right)} \right). \tag{10.20}$$

Note also that when the two processes are univariate, this measure can be written also as

$$g_{x,y}(\omega) = -\ln \left(1 - K_{x,y}^2(\omega) \right),$$

where $K_{x,y}^2(\omega) = (f_{x,y}(\omega))^2 / f_x(\omega) f_y(\omega)$ is the square of the coherency. We see then that $g_{x,y}(\omega)$ can be interpreted as a measure of the link relative to the frequency ω. It is always positive; it becomes 0 when the coherency is 0, that is when the spectral measures are uncorrelated at this frequency

$$\text{cov} \left(d\xi_x(\omega), d\xi_y(\omega) \right) = 0 \Leftrightarrow g_{x,y}(\omega) = 0.$$

It attains its maximum when $d\xi_x(\omega)$ and $d\xi_y(\omega)$ are linearly related.

In order to get the decomposition of other causality measures, for example for $C_{x \to y}$, we can argue along the following steps. Let us consider the recursive form of the model where $\mathbf{x}_t$ is determined as a function of the past of the two processes $\mathbf{x}$ and $\mathbf{y}$, and where $\mathbf{y}_t$ is expressed as a function also of $\mathbf{x}_t$

$$\mathbf{x}_t = \sum_{j=1}^{+\infty} \mathbf{A}_j^3 \mathbf{x}_{t-j} + \sum_{j=1}^{+\infty} \mathbf{A}_j^4 \mathbf{y}_{t-j} + \mathbf{a}^3 + \mathbf{u}_t^3, \quad \text{var} \left(\mathbf{u}_t^3 \right) = \boldsymbol{\Omega}_3,$$

$$\mathbf{y}_t = \sum_{j=0}^{+\infty} \mathbf{A}_j^9 \mathbf{x}_{t-j} + \sum_{j=1}^{+\infty} \mathbf{A}_j^{10} \mathbf{y}_{t-j} + \mathbf{a}^6 + \mathbf{u}_t^6, \quad \text{var} \left(\mathbf{u}_t^6 \right) = \boldsymbol{\Omega}_6.$$

Introducing the lag polynomials, we can get an expression of the type

$$\begin{pmatrix} \mathbf{A}^3(L) & \mathbf{A}^4(L) \\ \mathbf{A}^9(L) & \mathbf{A}^{10}(L) \end{pmatrix} \begin{pmatrix} \mathbf{x}_t \\ \mathbf{y}_t \end{pmatrix} = \begin{pmatrix} \mathbf{a}^3 \\ \mathbf{a}^6 \end{pmatrix} + \begin{pmatrix} \mathbf{u}_t^3 \\ \mathbf{u}_t^6 \end{pmatrix},$$

with

$$\text{var} \begin{pmatrix} \mathbf{u}_t^3 \\ \mathbf{u}_t^6 \end{pmatrix} = \begin{pmatrix} \mathbf{\Omega}_3 & 0 \\ 0 & \mathbf{\Omega}_6 \end{pmatrix}.$$

Since the disturbances $\mathbf{u}_t^3$ and $\mathbf{u}_t^6$ are uncorrelated, all simultaneous effects have been combined with the effects of x to y in the second group of equations. Then the first group summarizes just the effects of $\mathbf{y}$ to $\mathbf{x}$. We can invert the previous expression to derive a moving average representation as a function of $\begin{pmatrix} \mathbf{u}_t^3 \\ \mathbf{u}_t^6 \end{pmatrix}$. Noting the elements of the inverse matrix with a subscript index we get

$$\begin{pmatrix} \mathbf{x}_t \\ \mathbf{y}_t \end{pmatrix} = \begin{pmatrix} \mathbf{A}_3(L) & \mathbf{A}_4(L) \\ \mathbf{A}_9(L) & \mathbf{A}_{10}(L) \end{pmatrix} \left(\begin{pmatrix} \mathbf{a}^3 \\ \mathbf{a}^6 \end{pmatrix} + \begin{pmatrix} \mathbf{u}_t^3 \\ \mathbf{u}_t^6 \end{pmatrix} \right).$$

In particular $\mathbf{x}_t$ can be decomposed as a function of the noises,

$$\mathbf{x}_t = \mathbf{A}_3(L) \left(\mathbf{a}^3 + \mathbf{u}_t^3 \right) + \mathbf{A}_4(L) \left(\mathbf{a}^6 + \mathbf{u}_t^6 \right).$$

Since these noises are uncorrelated, the spectral density of $\mathbf{x}$ can be written as

$$\begin{aligned} \mathbf{f}_x(\omega) &= \mathbf{A}_3 \left(\exp(i\omega) \right) \mathbf{\Omega}_3 \mathbf{A}_3 \left(\exp(-i\omega) \right)' \\ &+ \mathbf{A}_4 \left(\exp(i\omega) \right) \mathbf{\Omega}_6 \mathbf{A}_4 \left(\exp(-i\omega) \right)'. \end{aligned}$$

The second term of this decomposition provides a measure of the influence of $\mathbf{y}$ to $\mathbf{x}$. We can then choose

$$g_{y \to x}(\omega) = \ln \left(\frac{\det \mathbf{f}_x(\omega)}{\det \mathbf{A}_3 \left(\exp(i\omega) \right) \mathbf{\Omega}_3 \mathbf{A}_3 \left(\exp(-i\omega) \right)'} \right). \tag{10.21}$$

Analogously, taking the other recursive expression we get

$$g_{x \to y}(\omega) = \ln \left(\frac{\det \mathbf{f}_y(\omega)}{\det \mathbf{A}_8 \left(\exp(i\omega) \right) \mathbf{\Omega}_5 \mathbf{A}_8 \left(\exp(-i\omega) \right)'} \right). \tag{10.22}$$

The last function is obtained as a residual (to ensure the adding up constraint). We have

$$\begin{aligned} g_{x \leftrightarrow y}(\omega) &= \ln \left(\frac{\det \mathbf{A}_3 \left(\exp(i\omega) \right) \mathbf{\Omega}_3 \mathbf{A}_3 \left(\exp(-i\omega) \right)'}{\det \mathbf{f}_{x,y}(\omega)} \right) \\ &+ \ln \left(\det \mathbf{A}_8 \left(\exp(i\omega) \right) \mathbf{\Omega}_5 \mathbf{A}_8 \left(\exp(-i\omega) \right)' \right). \end{aligned} \tag{10.23}$$

We can establish the following result (cf. exercise 10.9).

Theorem 10.8:

(i)   We have

$$C_{y \to x} = \frac{1}{2\pi} \int_{-\pi}^{+\pi} g_{y \to x}(\omega) \, d\omega,$$

$$C_{x \to y} = \frac{1}{2\pi} \int_{-\pi}^{+\pi} g_{x \to y}(\omega) \, d\omega,$$

$$C_{x \leftrightarrow y} = \frac{1}{2\pi} \int_{-\pi}^{+\pi} g_{x \leftrightarrow y}(\omega) \, d\omega.$$

(ii)   The various functions g are positive valued.

10.3 Exogeneity

In the previous sections the concept of exogeneity has been presented in a very intuitive fashion. We need now to analyze it more rigorously so that we can work with definitions mathematically precise and statistically testable. In what follows, we will distinguish between those variables possibly responding to certain exogeneity properties (noted $\mathbf{x}$) and the others (noted $\mathbf{y}$).

10.3.1 Vector Autoregressive (VAR) Representations

Canonical Form Let us assume (in line with what has been mentioned previously) that the vector of the observations is partitioned in two sub-vectors $\begin{pmatrix} \mathbf{y}_t \\ \mathbf{x}_t \end{pmatrix}$ of size n, respectively m. Let this vector of observations form a stationary vector autoregressive process (VAR) of order p

$$\begin{pmatrix} \boldsymbol{\Phi}_y(L) & \boldsymbol{\Phi}_{yx}(L) \\ \boldsymbol{\Phi}_{xy}(L) & \boldsymbol{\Phi}_x(L) \end{pmatrix} \begin{pmatrix} \mathbf{y}_t \\ \mathbf{x}_t \end{pmatrix} = \begin{pmatrix} \mathbf{c}_y \\ \mathbf{c}_x \end{pmatrix} + \begin{pmatrix} \boldsymbol{\varepsilon}_{yt} \\ \boldsymbol{\varepsilon}_{xt} \end{pmatrix}. \tag{10.24}$$

We note

$$\mathrm{var} \begin{pmatrix} \boldsymbol{\varepsilon}_{yt} \\ \boldsymbol{\varepsilon}_{xt} \end{pmatrix} = \begin{pmatrix} \boldsymbol{\Sigma}_y & \boldsymbol{\Sigma}_{yx} \\ \boldsymbol{\Sigma}_{xy} & \boldsymbol{\Sigma}_x \end{pmatrix} = \boldsymbol{\Sigma}.$$

At this stage we do not impose any constraint on the parameters but those implied by the stationarity of the process and the positive definiteness of $\boldsymbol{\Sigma}$. We maintain the usual normalization

$$\boldsymbol{\Phi}_y(0) = \mathbf{I}, \quad \boldsymbol{\Phi}_{yx}(0) = \mathbf{0},$$

$$\boldsymbol{\Phi}_{xy}(0) = \mathbf{0}, \quad \boldsymbol{\Phi}_x(0) = \mathbf{I}.$$

With this normalization convention $\begin{pmatrix} \boldsymbol{\varepsilon}_{yt} \\ \boldsymbol{\varepsilon}_{xt} \end{pmatrix}$ can be interpreted as the innovation of $\begin{pmatrix} \mathbf{y}_t \\ \mathbf{x}_t \end{pmatrix}$. The expression (10.24) is called *canonical form.* Note that in this form the current value of $\mathbf{x}_t$ does not intervene in the first set of equations and $\mathbf{y}_t$ does not intervene in the second one.

Block-recursive Representation Other autoregressive representations, equivalent to the previous one, can be obtained by premultiplying (10.24) by a nonsingular matrix. Thus we can achieve a new representation in which the two new disturbance vectors are uncorrelated. In fact, the regression of $\boldsymbol{\varepsilon}_{yt}$ on $\boldsymbol{\varepsilon}_{xt}$ is $\Sigma_{yx}\Sigma_x^{-1}\boldsymbol{\varepsilon}_{xt}$. The residual of this regression is $\boldsymbol{\eta}_{yt} = \boldsymbol{\varepsilon}_{yt} - \Sigma_{yx}\Sigma_x^{-1}\boldsymbol{\varepsilon}_{xt}$. This residual is uncorrelated with $\boldsymbol{\varepsilon}_{xt}$. If we premultiply the two elements of equation (10.24) by the matrix

$$\begin{pmatrix} \mathbf{I} & -\Sigma_{yx}\Sigma_x^{-1} \\ \mathbf{0} & \mathbf{I} \end{pmatrix},$$

we get

$$\begin{pmatrix} \boldsymbol{\Phi}_y^+(L) & \boldsymbol{\Phi}_{yx}^+(L) \\ \boldsymbol{\Phi}_{xy}(L) & \boldsymbol{\Phi}_x(L) \end{pmatrix} \begin{pmatrix} \mathbf{y}_t \\ \mathbf{x}_t \end{pmatrix} = \begin{pmatrix} \mathbf{c}_y^+ \\ \mathbf{c}_x^+ \end{pmatrix} + \begin{pmatrix} \boldsymbol{\eta}_{yt} \\ \boldsymbol{\varepsilon}_{xt} \end{pmatrix}, \qquad (10.25)$$

with

$$\boldsymbol{\Phi}_y^+(L) = \boldsymbol{\Phi}_y(L) - \Sigma_{yx}\Sigma_x^{-1}\boldsymbol{\Phi}_{xy}(L) = \mathbf{I} - \sum_{i=1}^p \boldsymbol{\Phi}_{yi}^+ L^i,$$

$$\boldsymbol{\Phi}_{yx}^+(L) = \boldsymbol{\Phi}_{yx}(L) - \Sigma_{yx}\Sigma_x^{-1}\boldsymbol{\Phi}_x(L) = -\sum_{i=0}^p \boldsymbol{\Phi}_{yxi}^+ L^i, \qquad (10.26)$$

$$\mathbf{c}_y^+ = \mathbf{c}_y - \Sigma_{yx}\Sigma_x^{-1}\mathbf{c}_x.$$

The variance–covariance matrix of $\begin{pmatrix} \boldsymbol{\eta}_{yt} \\ \boldsymbol{\varepsilon}_{xt} \end{pmatrix}$ is then block-diagonal

$$\begin{pmatrix} \Sigma_y^+ & \mathbf{0} \\ \mathbf{0} & \Sigma_y \end{pmatrix},$$

with $\Sigma_y^+ = \Sigma_y - \Sigma_{yx}\Sigma_x^{-1}\Sigma_{xy}$. The representation (10.25) (equivalent to (10.23)), is called a *block-recursive* representation of the process. In this representation the correlation among the disturbances $\boldsymbol{\eta}_{yt}$ and $\boldsymbol{\varepsilon}_{xt}$ is 0. The current value $\mathbf{x}_t$ enters the first set of equations, whereas $\mathbf{y}_t$ never enters the second set of equations. The first set of equations provides the regressions of $\mathbf{y}_t$ on the past values of $\mathbf{y}$ and on the present and past values of $\mathbf{x}$

$$\mathbf{y}_t = \sum_{i=1}^{p} \boldsymbol{\Phi}_{yi}^{+} \mathbf{y}_{t-i} + \sum_{i=0}^{p} \boldsymbol{\Phi}_{yxi}^{+} \mathbf{x}_{t-i} + \mathbf{c}_y^{+} + \boldsymbol{\eta}_{yt}. \qquad (10.27)$$

The second set of equations provides the regressions of the components of $\mathbf{x}_t$ on the past values of $\mathbf{x}$ and $\mathbf{y}$

$$\mathbf{x}_t = \sum_{i=1}^{p} \boldsymbol{\Phi}_{xyi} \mathbf{y}_{t-i} + \sum_{i=1}^{p} \boldsymbol{\Phi}_{xi} \mathbf{x}_{t-i} + \mathbf{c}_x + \boldsymbol{\varepsilon}_{xt}. \qquad (10.28)$$

The uncorrelation of $\boldsymbol{\eta}_{yt}$ and $\boldsymbol{\varepsilon}_{xt}$ and the absence of the current value $\mathbf{y}_t$ in (10.28) are the conditions which led to a first intuitive notion of exogeneity ($\mathbf{x}_t$ being determined before $\mathbf{y}_t$). In the present context, we are verifying that this notion is meaningless because we can always find a representation, namely (10.24), satisfying these conditions. In fact, the notion of exogeneity becomes of interest only after having defined a structural form.

10.3.2 Linear Structural Form

Besides being represented as a VAR, let us suppose that the process $\begin{pmatrix} \mathbf{y}_t \\ \mathbf{x}_t \end{pmatrix}$ satisfies a model suggested by the economic theory. This model or *structural form* consists of a system of equations linking the various variables y and x, and of a separation between a group of variables x having certain "exogeneity" properties and other variables y.

The Equations   The relationships among the variables are of the type

$$\mathbf{A}_0 \mathbf{y}_t + \mathbf{A}_1 \mathbf{y}_{t-1} + \ldots + \mathbf{A}_p \mathbf{y}_{t-p} + \mathbf{B}_0 \mathbf{x}_t + \mathbf{B}_1 \mathbf{x}_{t-1} + \ldots + \mathbf{B}_p \mathbf{x}_{t-p} + \boldsymbol{\mu} = \boldsymbol{\varepsilon}_t. \qquad (10.29)$$

The matrix $\mathbf{A}_0$ is supposed nonsingular and $\{\boldsymbol{\varepsilon}_t\}$ is a white noise with a generic variance–covariance matrix $\mathbf{Q}$ and uncorrelated with the past values of $\mathbf{y}_t$. Since these relationships are derived from the economic theory, the parameters $\mathbf{A}_i$, $\mathbf{B}_i$, $i = 1, 2, \ldots, p$ and $\boldsymbol{\mu}$ are often interpretable. Thus they may be subject to a number of constraints. The most frequent constraints are (cf. 10.2):

the equality of certain parameters to 1 (normalization restriction);

the equality of certain parameters to 0 (zero restriction);

the equality of certain parameters among each other.

All these constraints can be expressed linearly with respect to the elements of the matrices $\mathbf{A}_i$, $\mathbf{B}_i$, and $\boldsymbol{\mu}$. Denoting by

$$\boldsymbol{\Gamma} = (\mathbf{A}_0, \mathbf{A}_1, \ldots, \mathbf{A}_p, \mathbf{B}_0, \mathbf{B}_1, \ldots, \mathbf{B}_p, \boldsymbol{\mu}),$$

and by vec $\mathbf{\Gamma}$ the vector obtained by stacking the elements of $\mathbf{\Gamma}$ starting from the first column of $\mathbf{A}_0$, then its second column, and so on, we can write the constraints as

$$\mathbf{R} \text{ vec } \mathbf{\Gamma} = \mathbf{r}, \qquad (10.30)$$

where $\mathbf{r}$ is a known vector of size q, $\mathbf{R}$ is a known matrix of size $(q \times n((n+m)(p+1)+1)$. We suppose that $\mathbf{R}$ has rank q. In practice, the set of restrictions can be partitioned into constraints relative to $\mathbf{A}_0$ and $\mathbf{B}_0$ and constraints relative to the other parameters. We will denote the constraints relative to $\mathbf{A}_0$ and $\mathbf{B}_0$ by

$$\mathbf{R}_0 \text{ vec } \mathbf{\Gamma}_0 = \mathbf{r}_0, \qquad (10.31)$$

with $\mathbf{\Gamma}_0 = (\mathbf{A}_0, \mathbf{B}_0)$. These constraints are particularly interesting because they define in which equations the current values of the variables intervene. We can refer to them as defining a *simultaneity structure*.

Weak Structural Form

Definition 10.5: *A weak structural form is made of*

(i)   *a system of equations*

$$\mathbf{A}_0 \mathbf{y}_t + \mathbf{A}_1 \mathbf{y}_{t-1} + \ldots + \mathbf{A}_p \mathbf{y}_{t-p}$$
$$+ \mathbf{B}_0 \mathbf{x}_t + \mathbf{B}_1 \mathbf{x}_{t-1} + \ldots + \mathbf{B}_p \mathbf{x}_{t-p} + \boldsymbol{\mu} = \boldsymbol{\varepsilon}_t, \qquad (\text{cf. } (10.29)),$$

where $\{\boldsymbol{\varepsilon}_t\}$ is a white noise with a generic variance–covariance matrix $\mathbf{Q}$ and uncorrelated with the past values of $\mathbf{y}_t$;

(ii)   *a number of restrictions on the coefficients*

$$\mathbf{R} \text{ vec } \mathbf{\Gamma} = \mathbf{r} \qquad (\text{cf. } (10.30));$$

(iii) *a condition called* predeterminedness

$$\text{cov} (\boldsymbol{\varepsilon}_t, \mathbf{x}_{t-k}) = 0, \ \ \forall \ k \geq 0. \qquad (10.32)$$

The coefficients $\mathbf{A}_i$, $\mathbf{B}_i$, and $\boldsymbol{\mu}$ of this form are called *structural coefficients* and the variable $\mathbf{x}$ is said *predetermined* with respect to the structural form. It is not trivial that such a weak structural form be compatible with a VAR model. This will be the case if the coefficients of the autoregressive polynomials $\mathbf{\Phi}_y^+, \mathbf{\Phi}_{yx}^+, \mathbf{c}_y^+$ called *reduced form coefficients* satisfy certain constraints.

Theorem 10.9: *The* VAR *model is compatible with a weak structural form satisfying (10.30) and (10.32) if and only if there exists*

$$\mathbf{\Gamma} = (\mathbf{A}_0, \mathbf{A}_1, \ldots, \mathbf{A}_p, \mathbf{B}_0, \mathbf{B}_1, \ldots, \mathbf{B}_p, \boldsymbol{\mu}),$$

such that

$$\mathbf{A}_0 \mathbf{\Phi}_{yxi}^+ + \mathbf{B}_i = \mathbf{0}, \quad i = 0, \dots, p,$$

$$\mathbf{A}_0 \mathbf{\Phi}_{yi}^+ + \mathbf{A}_i = \mathbf{0}, \quad i = 1, \dots, p,$$

$$\mathbf{A}_0 \mathbf{c}_y^+ + \boldsymbol{\mu} = \mathbf{0},$$

$$\mathbf{R} \text{ vec } \mathbf{\Gamma} = \mathbf{r}.$$

PROOF: From (10.29) we can write

$$\mathbf{y}_t + \mathbf{A}_0^{-1} \mathbf{A}_1 \mathbf{y}_{t-1} + \dots + \mathbf{A}_0^{-1} \mathbf{A}_p \mathbf{y}_{t-p}$$

$$+ \mathbf{A}_0^{-1} \mathbf{B}_0 \mathbf{x}_t + \dots + \mathbf{A}_0^{-1} \mathbf{B}_p \mathbf{x}_{t-p} + \mathbf{A}_0^{-1} \boldsymbol{\mu} = \mathbf{A}_0^{-1} \boldsymbol{\varepsilon}_t.$$

This form can be equated to the first subsystem of the block-recursive representation (10.27) since in both cases we are expressing the current value of $\mathbf{y}_t$ as a function of the past values of $\mathbf{y}_t$ and of the current and past values of $\mathbf{x}_t$.   □

If we have a weak structural form (10.29), and if we assume that the noise $\begin{pmatrix} \boldsymbol{\varepsilon}_{yt} \\ \boldsymbol{\varepsilon}_{xt} \end{pmatrix}$ is normally distributed, the conditional distribution of $\mathbf{y}_t$ given $\mathbf{y}_{t-1}, \dots, \mathbf{y}_{t-p}, \mathbf{x}_t, \mathbf{x}_{t-1}, \dots, \mathbf{x}_{t-p}$ is normal with expected value

$$-\mathbf{A}_0^{-1} \mathbf{A}_1 \mathbf{y}_{t-1} - \dots - \mathbf{A}_0^{-1} \mathbf{A}_p \mathbf{y}_{t-p} - \mathbf{A}_0^{-1} \mathbf{B}_0 \mathbf{x}_t - \dots - \mathbf{A}_0^{-1} \mathbf{B}_p \mathbf{x}_{t-p} - \mathbf{A}_0^{-1} \boldsymbol{\mu},$$

with variance–covariance matrix $\mathbf{A}_0^{-1} \mathbf{Q} \mathbf{A}_0^{-1}$. We can denote this conditional density as $f_t^y(\mathbf{y}_t; \mathbf{\Gamma}, \mathbf{Q})$. The conditional distribution of $\mathbf{x}_t$ given $\mathbf{y}_{t-1}, \dots, \mathbf{y}_{t-p}, \mathbf{x}_t, \mathbf{x}_{t-1}, \dots, \mathbf{x}_{t-p}$ is normal with expected value

$$\sum_{i=1}^{p} \mathbf{\Phi}_{xyi} \mathbf{y}_{t-i} + \sum_{i=1}^{p} \mathbf{\Phi}_{xi} \mathbf{x}_{t-i} + \mathbf{c}_x$$

(cf. (10.28)), and with variance–covariance matrix $\mathbf{\Sigma}_x$. The associated density function can be denoted by $f_t^x(\mathbf{x}_t; \ \boldsymbol{\phi})$, where $\boldsymbol{\phi}$ contains the parameters of the distribution. The likelihood of the T observations (conditional on the p initial observations) is

$$\prod_{t=1}^{T} (f_t^y(\mathbf{y}_t; \mathbf{\Gamma}, \mathbf{Q}) f_t^x(\mathbf{x}_t; \ \boldsymbol{\phi})) = \prod_{t=1}^{T} f_t^y(\mathbf{y}_t; \mathbf{\Gamma}, \mathbf{Q}) \prod_{t=1}^{T} f_t^x(\mathbf{x}_t; \ \boldsymbol{\phi}).$$

If we are interested in estimating the parameters of the weak structural form $\mathbf{\Gamma}, \mathbf{Q}$ by the maximum likelihood method, we can thus maximize $\prod_{t=1}^{T} f_t^y(\mathbf{y}_t; \mathbf{\Gamma}, \mathbf{Q})$, and ignore the other term. In other words, the knowledge of the structural form is sufficient, and we can neglect the set of equations (10.28). Note, however, that $\prod_{t=1}^{T} f_t^y(\mathbf{y}_t; \mathbf{\Gamma}, \mathbf{Q})$ is not, in general, a density function. If we want to simulate $\mathbf{y}_{T+1}, \dots, \mathbf{y}_{T+h}$ for fixed values of $\mathbf{x}_{T+1}, \dots, \mathbf{x}_{T+h}$, having observed $\mathbf{x}$ and $\mathbf{y}$ up to time

T, we need to determine the conditional distribution of $\mathbf{y}_{T+1}$ given $\mathbf{y}_1, \ldots \mathbf{y}_T, \mathbf{x}_1, \ldots, \mathbf{x}_{T+h}$. If the expression (10.29) is weak structural, $\boldsymbol{\varepsilon}_{T+1}$ is, in general, correlated with $\mathbf{x}_{T+2}, \ldots, \mathbf{x}_{T+h}$, and hence the conditional distribution cannot be derived on the basis of the structural form (10.29) only.

Strong Structural Form

Definition 10.6: *A strong structural form is made of*

(i)   a system of equations

$$\mathbf{A}_0 \mathbf{y}_t + \mathbf{A}_1 \mathbf{y}_{t-1} + \ldots + \mathbf{A}_p \mathbf{y}_{t-p}$$

$$+ \mathbf{B}_0 \mathbf{x}_t + \mathbf{B}_1 \mathbf{x}_{t-1} + \ldots + \mathbf{B}_p \mathbf{x}_{t-p} + \boldsymbol{\mu} = \boldsymbol{\varepsilon}_t \qquad \text{(cf. (10.29)),}$$

where $\{\boldsymbol{\varepsilon}_t\}$ is a white noise with a generic variance–covariance matrix $\mathbf{Q}$ and uncorrelated with the past values of $\mathbf{y}_t$; (ii)   a number of restrictions on the coefficients

$$\mathbf{R} \text{ vec } \boldsymbol{\Gamma} = \mathbf{r} \qquad \text{(cf. (10.30));}$$

(iii)   a condition called strict exogeneity

$$\operatorname{cov}\left(\boldsymbol{\varepsilon}_t, \mathbf{x}_{t-k}\right) = 0, \ \forall \ k. \tag{10.33}$$

The variable $\mathbf{x}$ is called *strictly exogenous* with respect to the strong structural form. On the other hand, we see that a strong structural form is also a weak structural form. The existence of a strong structural form implies some constraints also on the reduced form parameters.

Theorem 10.10: *The* VAR *model is compatible with a strong structural form satisfying (10.29) and (10.33) if and only if*

$$\mathbf{A}_0 \boldsymbol{\Phi}_{yxi}^+ + \mathbf{B}_i = \mathbf{0}, \quad i = 0, \ldots, p,$$

$$\mathbf{A}_0 \boldsymbol{\Phi}_{yi}^+ + \mathbf{A}_i = \mathbf{0}, \quad i = 1, \ldots, p,$$

$$\mathbf{A}_0 \mathbf{c}_y^+ + \boldsymbol{\mu} = \mathbf{0},$$

$$\mathbf{R} \text{ vec } \boldsymbol{\Gamma} = \mathbf{r},$$

$$\boldsymbol{\Phi}_{xyi} = \mathbf{0}, \quad i = 1, \ldots, p.$$

PROOF:

(i)   Let us assume that the VAR model is compatible with a strong structural form defined by (10.29), (10.30) and (10.33). Since this strong structural form is also weak, theorem 10.9 shows that the only condition to be verified is $\boldsymbol{\Phi}_{xyi} = \mathbf{0}$ $i = 1, \ldots, p$. Comparison of (10.27) and (10.29) implies that $\boldsymbol{\eta}_{yt} = \mathbf{A}_0^{-1}\boldsymbol{\varepsilon}_t$. Then equation (10.28) is written for time $t + 1$ as

$$\mathbf{x}_{t+1} = \sum_{i=1}^{p} \boldsymbol{\Phi}_{xyi}\mathbf{y}_{t+1-i} + \sum_{i=1}^{p} \boldsymbol{\Phi}_{xi}\mathbf{x}_{t+1-i} + \mathbf{c}_x + \boldsymbol{\varepsilon}_{x,t+1}.$$

On the basis of (10.33), we know that $\mathbf{x}_{t+1}$ and $\boldsymbol{\varepsilon}_t$ are uncorrelated. It is so also for $\mathbf{x}_{t+1}$ and $\boldsymbol{\eta}_{yt}$, and the previous equation implies

$$E(\mathbf{x}_{t+1}\boldsymbol{\eta}_{yt}') = \boldsymbol{\Phi}_{xy1}E(\mathbf{y}_t\boldsymbol{\eta}_{yt}')$$

$$= \boldsymbol{\Phi}_{xy1}\boldsymbol{\Sigma}_y^+$$

$$= \mathbf{0},$$

from which

$$\boldsymbol{\Phi}_{xy1} = \mathbf{0}.$$

By the same token

$$E(\mathbf{x}_{t+2}\boldsymbol{\eta}_{yt}') = \boldsymbol{\Phi}_{x1}E(\mathbf{x}_{t+1}\boldsymbol{\eta}_{yt}') + \boldsymbol{\Phi}_{xy1}E(\mathbf{y}_{t+1}\boldsymbol{\eta}_{yt}')$$

$$+ \boldsymbol{\Phi}_{xy2}E(\mathbf{y}_t\boldsymbol{\eta}_{yt}')$$

$$= \boldsymbol{\Phi}_{xy2}\boldsymbol{\Sigma}_y^+$$

$$= \mathbf{0},$$

from which $\boldsymbol{\Phi}_{xy2} = \mathbf{0}$, so that, by induction $\boldsymbol{\Phi}_{xyi} = \mathbf{0}$, $i = 1, \ldots, p$.
(ii)   Conversely, under the conditions of the theorem, the VAR model is compatible with the weak structural form (10.29), (10.30), (10.32) on the basis of theorem 10.9. Moreover, since we know that $\boldsymbol{\Phi}_{xyi} = \mathbf{0}$, $i = 1, \ldots, p$, we have

$$\mathbf{x}_{t+1} = \sum_{i=1}^{p} \boldsymbol{\Phi}_{xi}\mathbf{x}_{t+1-i} + \mathbf{c}_x + \boldsymbol{\varepsilon}_{x,t+1},$$

and

$$E(\mathbf{x}_{t+1}\boldsymbol{\varepsilon}_{yt}') = \sum_{i=1}^{p} \boldsymbol{\Phi}_{xi}E\left(\mathbf{x}_{t+1-i}\boldsymbol{\varepsilon}_t'\right) = \mathbf{0}.$$

By the same token, $E(\mathbf{x}_{t+i}\boldsymbol{\varepsilon}_{yt}') = 0$, $\forall\, i > 0$, which implies that the VAR model is compatible with the strong structural form (10.29), (10.30) and (10.33). $\square$

Now the conditions have implications also for the second subsystem of the block-recursive decomposition. This additional condition allows us to interpret the decomposition of the likelihood function given after theorem 10.9 in terms of marginal and conditional distributions. $\prod_{t=1}^{T} f_t^x$

is the marginal density of $\mathbf{x}_1, \ldots, \mathbf{x}_T$, and hence $\prod_{t=1}^{T} f_t^y$ is the conditional density of $\mathbf{y}_1, \ldots, \mathbf{y}_T$ given $\mathbf{x}_1, \ldots, \mathbf{x}_T$. Therefore, the conditional distribution of $\mathbf{y}_{T+1}$ given $\mathbf{y}_1, \ldots, \mathbf{y}_T, \mathbf{x}_1, \ldots, \mathbf{x}_{T+h}$ can be derived now from the structural form. This distribution is normal with mean

$$-\sum_{i=1}^{p} \mathbf{A}_0^{-1} \mathbf{A}_i \mathbf{y}_{T+1-i} - \sum_{i=0}^{p} \mathbf{A}_0^{-1} \mathbf{B}_i \mathbf{x}_{T+1-i} - \mathbf{A}_0^{-1} \boldsymbol{\mu},$$

and with a variance–covariance matrix $\mathbf{A}_0^{-1} \mathbf{Q} (\mathbf{A}_0^{-1})'$. We can predict $\mathbf{y}_{T+1}$ given $\mathbf{x}_1, \ldots, \mathbf{x}_{T+h}$ on the basis of the structural form; the same can be done for $\mathbf{y}_{T+2}, \ldots, \mathbf{y}_{T+h}$. The simulation of *scenarios*, imposing future values on the exogenous variables, can be done on the basis of a strong structural form (but not from a weak structural form).

10.3.3 Analysis of the Simultaneity Structure

We have seen that the constraints $\mathbf{R} \operatorname{vec} \boldsymbol{\Gamma} = \mathbf{r}$ can often be partitioned in restrictions relative to $\mathbf{A}_0$, $\mathbf{B}_0$ and restrictions relative to the other parameters. The restrictions on $\mathbf{A}_0$ and $\mathbf{B}_0$, that is $\mathbf{R}_0 \operatorname{vec} \boldsymbol{\Gamma}_0 = \mathbf{r}_0$ (cf. 10.31) define the simultaneity structure. It may be of interest, at least as a first step, to take into consideration these restrictions only, defining some concepts which involve them alone.

Definition 10.7: *The variable x is* predetermined *for the simultaneity structure (10.31)* $\mathbf{R}_0 \operatorname{vec} \boldsymbol{\Gamma}_0 = \mathbf{r}_0$ *if and only if*

$$\mathbf{A}_0 \boldsymbol{\Phi}_{yx0}^+ + \mathbf{B}_0 = \mathbf{0},$$

$$\mathbf{R}_0 \operatorname{vec} \boldsymbol{\Gamma}_0 = \mathbf{r}_0.$$

Definition 10.8: *The variable x is* strictly exogenous *for the simultaneity structure (10.31) if and only if*

$$\mathbf{A}_0 \boldsymbol{\Phi}_{yx0}^+ + \mathbf{B}_0 = \mathbf{0},$$

$$\mathbf{R}_0 \operatorname{vec} \boldsymbol{\Gamma}_0 = \mathbf{r}_0,$$

$$\boldsymbol{\Phi}_{xyi}^+ = \mathbf{0}, \quad i = 1, \ldots, p.$$

Definition 10.7, respectively 10.8, means that the VAR model is compatible with a weak (respectively, strong) structural form satisfying the simultaneity structure $\mathbf{R}_0 \operatorname{vec} \boldsymbol{\Gamma}_0 = \mathbf{r}_0$. The difference between the two systems of restrictions comes from the additional conditions $\boldsymbol{\Phi}_{xyi} = \mathbf{0}$, $i = 1, \ldots, p$ corresponding to the condition of noncausality of $\mathbf{y}$ to $\mathbf{x}$ (cf. theorem 10.5(i)). This concept of strict exogeneity corresponds to the restrictive notion of exogeneity introduced in section 10.1 in an intuitive fashion. Note also that the instantaneous noncausality between x and y defined by $\boldsymbol{\Sigma}_{yx} = \mathbf{0}$ is equivalent to $\boldsymbol{\Phi}_{yx0}^{+} = \mathbf{0}$ since from (10.26) $\boldsymbol{\Phi}_{yx0}^{+} = -\boldsymbol{\Sigma}_{yx}\boldsymbol{\Sigma}_{x}^{-1}$. In particular, we see that $\mathbf{x}$ can be predetermined or strictly exogenous even if there is a link of contemporaneous causality with $\mathbf{y}$, since this link translates into $\boldsymbol{\Phi}_{yx0}^{+} \neq \mathbf{0}$, that is, $\mathbf{B}_0 \neq 0$.

10.3.4 Identification

Until now we have discussed the compatibility conditions with a VAR model, ensuring the existence of a (weak or strong) structural form. We may also wonder whether the structural parameters

$$\boldsymbol{\Gamma} = (\mathbf{A}_0, \mathbf{A}_1, \dots, \mathbf{A}_p, \mathbf{B}_0, \mathbf{B}_1, \dots, \mathbf{B}_p, \boldsymbol{\mu}),$$

are uniquely determined as a function of the reduced-form parameters, $\boldsymbol{\Phi}_{yi}^{+}$, $i = 1, \dots, p$, $\boldsymbol{\Phi}_{yxi}^{+}$, $i = 0, \dots, p$ and $\mathbf{c}_{y}^{+}$ (cf. (10.27)), taking into consideration the constraints (10.30) $\mathbf{R} \operatorname{vec} \boldsymbol{\Gamma} = \mathbf{r}$. This is defined as the *first-order identification* problem.

Theorem 10.11: *The structural form (10.29), (10.30), and (10.32) is first-order identifiable if and only if the* rank condition

$$\varrho\left(\mathbf{R}\left(\boldsymbol{\Gamma}' \otimes \mathbf{I}\right)\right) = n^2$$

is satisfied where n is the number of endogenous variables $\mathbf{y}$.

PROOF: Let us suppose that we have another set of parameters

$$\boldsymbol{\Gamma}^* = \left(\mathbf{A}_0^*, \mathbf{A}_1^*, \dots, \mathbf{A}_p^*, \mathbf{B}_0^*, \mathbf{B}_1^*, \dots, \mathbf{B}_p^*, \boldsymbol{\mu}^*\right)$$

corresponding to the same reduced form. We would have

$$\boldsymbol{\Phi}_{yi}^* = -\mathbf{A}_0^{-1}\mathbf{A}_i = -\mathbf{A}_0^{*-1}\mathbf{A}_i^*, \quad i = 1, \dots, p,$$

$$\boldsymbol{\Phi}_{xyi}^* = -\mathbf{A}_0^{-1}\mathbf{B}_i = -\mathbf{A}_0^{*-1}\mathbf{B}_i^*, \quad i = 0, \dots, p,$$

$$\mathbf{c}_y^* = -\mathbf{A}_0^{-1}\boldsymbol{\mu} = -\mathbf{A}_0^{*-1}\boldsymbol{\mu}^*, \quad i = 1, \dots, p.$$

Posing $\mathbf{M} = \mathbf{A}_0^* \mathbf{A}_0^{-1}$ we see that we would have $\boldsymbol{\Gamma}^* = \mathbf{M}\boldsymbol{\Gamma}$. This set of parameters must satisfy the restrictions (10.30) as well. Hence,

$$\mathbf{R} \operatorname{vec} \mathbf{M}\boldsymbol{\Gamma} = \mathbf{R}\left(\boldsymbol{\Gamma}' \otimes \mathbf{I}\right) \operatorname{vec} \mathbf{M} = \mathbf{r}.$$

We know that this system admits $\text{vec}\,\mathbf{M} = \text{vec}\,\mathbf{I}$ as a unique solution if and only if the matrix $\mathbf{R}\,(\mathbf{\Gamma}' \otimes \mathbf{I})$ has full column rank (n^2). $\square$

Corollary: *A necessary condition for identification is the* order condition $q \geq n^2$.

PROOF: Note that the matrix $\mathbf{R}\,(\mathbf{\Gamma}' \otimes \mathbf{I})$ has q rows. $\square$

The difference $q - n^2$ is called the degree of overidentification of the structural form. We can even ask ourselves if the simultaneity structure, that is, the constraints $\mathbf{R}_0\,\text{vec}\,\mathbf{\Gamma}_0 = \mathbf{r}_0$ allow us to uniquely determine $\text{vec}\,\mathbf{\Gamma}_0 = (\mathbf{A}_0\ \mathbf{B}_0)$. This is the first-order *contemporaneous identification* problem. From theorem 10.11 we can conclude that this will happen if and only if

$$\text{rank}\,\mathbf{R}_0\,(\mathbf{\Gamma}_0' \otimes \mathbf{I}) = n^2. \qquad (10.34)$$

This condition implies the order condition $q_0 \geq n^2$, and $q_0 - n^2$ is called the *degree of contemporaneous overidentification*.

10.3.5 Nested Hypotheses Involving the Dynamic Structure

In the previous sections we have analyzed six hypotheses

H_V General VAR hypothesis (10.24),

H_P Hypothesis of predeterminedness of $\mathbf{x}$ (cf. definition 10.7),

H_E Hypothesis of strict exogeneity of $\mathbf{x}$ (cf. definition 10.8),

H_N Hypothesis of noncausality of $\mathbf{y}$ to $\mathbf{x}$ (cf. theorem 10.5.(i)),

H_W Hypothesis of existence of a weak structural form (cf. theorem 10.9),

H_S Hypothesis of existence of a strong structural form (cf. theorem 10.10).

Going from the most general to the most restrictive, these hypotheses can be nested in three different ways

$$H_V \supset H_P \supset H_W \supset H_S,$$

$$H_V \supset H_P \supset H_E \supset H_S, \qquad (10.35)$$

$$H_V \supset H_N \supset H_E \supset H_S.$$

These three paths can be visualized in figure 10.7.

Let us note that these hypotheses are restrictive in various degrees with respect to the structural form.

H_N does not impose anything on the structural form.

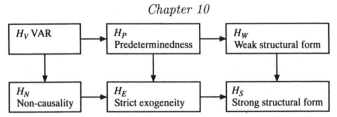

Figure 10.7   Nested hypotheses

H_P and H_E impose the definition of the simultaneity structure on the structural form.

H_W and H_S impose the set of restrictions on the structural form.

10.4 Shocks and Multipliers

10.4.1 Deterministic Control

The Keynesian Model Let us recall the Keynesian model introduced in (10.2). Let us suppose that there is a change in government expenditure by ΔG at a given date t_0. This change will exert its effects on the endogenous variables of the model. At time t these variables are changed by ΔGDP_t, ΔC_t and ΔI_t with

$$\Delta GDP_{t_0} = \Delta C_{t_0} + \Delta I_{t_0} + \Delta G,$$

$$\Delta C_{t_0} = 0,$$

$$\Delta I_{t_0} = 0,$$

which implies

$$\Delta GDP_{t_0} = \Delta G,$$

$$\Delta C_{t_0} = 0,$$

$$\Delta I_{t_0} = 0.$$

There is, therefore, an immediate effect on GDP and no immediate effect on consumption and investment. In fact, this effect starts at the next period due to the lag existing between the determination of GDP and of C and I. We have

$$\Delta GDP_{t_0+1} = \Delta C_{t_0+1} + \Delta I_{t_0+1},$$

$$\Delta C_{t_0+1} = a\Delta GDP_{t_0} = a\Delta G,$$

$$\Delta I_{t_0+1} = b\Delta GDP_{t_0} = b\Delta G,$$

which implies

$$\Delta GDP_{t_0+1} = (a+b)\Delta G,$$

$$\Delta C_{t_0+1} = a\Delta G,$$

$$\Delta I_{t_0+1} = b\Delta G.$$

Such effects will be exerted on future values of the endogenous variables. Their nature is the subject of this section.

Shocks on a Control Variable Let us consider the model with deterministic control defined in (10.5). Introducing the polynomials in the lag operator

$$\mathbf{A}(L) = \mathbf{A}_0 + \ldots + \mathbf{A}_p L^p, \qquad \mathbf{B}(L) = \mathbf{B}_0 + \ldots + \mathbf{B}_p L^p,$$

$$\mathbf{C}(L) = \mathbf{C}_0 + \ldots + \mathbf{C}_p L^p, \qquad \mathbf{D}(L) = \mathbf{I} + \ldots + \mathbf{D}_p L^p,$$

$$\mathbf{E}(L) = \mathbf{E}_0 + \ldots + \mathbf{E}_p L^p, \qquad \mathbf{F}(L) = \mathbf{F}_1 + \ldots + \mathbf{F}_p L^p.$$

This model appears in the form

$$\mathbf{A}(L)\mathbf{y}_t + \mathbf{B}(L)\mathbf{x}_t + \mathbf{C}(L)\mathbf{z}_t + \boldsymbol{\mu} = \boldsymbol{\varepsilon}_t,$$

$$\mathbf{D}(L)\mathbf{x}_t + \mathbf{E}(L)\mathbf{z}_t + \mathbf{F}(L)\mathbf{y}_t + \boldsymbol{\nu} = \mathbf{u}_t, \tag{10.36}$$

where $\mathbf{y}$ is the vector of endogenous variables, $\mathbf{x}$ is the vector of the exogenous environment variables, $\mathbf{z}$ is the vector of the exogenous control variables, and $(\boldsymbol{\varepsilon}_t)$ and $(\mathbf{u}_t)$ are two uncorrelated noises. From the previous model, we can derive the expressions for $\mathbf{x}_t$ and $\mathbf{y}_t$ as a function of the current and past values of the control variables and of the disturbances. We obtain

$$\begin{pmatrix} \mathbf{A}(L) & \mathbf{B}(L) \\ \mathbf{F}(L) & \mathbf{D}(L) \end{pmatrix} \begin{pmatrix} \mathbf{y}_t \\ \mathbf{x}_t \end{pmatrix} = - \begin{pmatrix} \mathbf{C}(L) \\ \mathbf{E}(L) \end{pmatrix} \mathbf{z}_t - \begin{pmatrix} \boldsymbol{\mu} \\ \boldsymbol{\nu} \end{pmatrix} + \begin{pmatrix} \boldsymbol{\varepsilon}_t \\ \mathbf{u}_t \end{pmatrix}.$$

Inverting

$$\begin{pmatrix} \mathbf{y}_t \\ \mathbf{x}_t \end{pmatrix} = - \begin{pmatrix} \mathbf{A}(L) & \mathbf{B}(L) \\ \mathbf{F}(L) & \mathbf{D}(L) \end{pmatrix}^{-1} \begin{pmatrix} \mathbf{C}(L) \\ \mathbf{E}(L) \end{pmatrix} \mathbf{z}_t$$

$$+ \begin{pmatrix} \mathbf{A}(L) & \mathbf{B}(L) \\ \mathbf{F}(L) & \mathbf{D}(L) \end{pmatrix}^{-1} \left(\begin{pmatrix} \boldsymbol{\varepsilon}_t \\ \mathbf{u}_t \end{pmatrix} - \begin{pmatrix} \boldsymbol{\mu} \\ \boldsymbol{\nu} \end{pmatrix} \right).$$

We can derive an expression of the type

$$\mathbf{y}_t = \mathbf{H}(L)\mathbf{z}_t + \boldsymbol{\varepsilon}_t^*,$$

$$\mathbf{x}_t = \mathbf{K}(L)\mathbf{z}_t + \mathbf{u}_t^*,$$

where $\boldsymbol{\varepsilon}_t^*$ and $\mathbf{u}_t^*$ are functions of current and past disturbances and of the constants, and where

$$\mathbf{H}(L) = \sum_{j=0}^{+\infty} \mathbf{H}_j L^j$$

$$= -\mathbf{A}(L)^{-1}\mathbf{C}(L) - \mathbf{A}(L)^{-1}\mathbf{B}(L)\left(\mathbf{D}(L) - \mathbf{F}(L)\mathbf{A}(L)^{-1}\mathbf{B}(L)\right)^{-1}$$

$$\left(\mathbf{F}(L)\mathbf{A}(L)^{-1}\mathbf{C}(L) - \mathbf{E}(L)\right),$$

$$\mathbf{K}(L) = \sum_{j=0}^{+\infty} \mathbf{K}_j L^j$$

$$= \left(\mathbf{D}(L) - \mathbf{F}(L)\mathbf{A}(L)^{-1}\mathbf{B}(L)\right)^{-1}\left(\mathbf{F}(L)\mathbf{A}(L)^{-1}\mathbf{C}(L) - \mathbf{E}(L)\right).$$

Thus we can apply various forms of shocks to the control variables. We will assume that such shocks can be applied without changes in the values of the disturbances $\boldsymbol{\epsilon}$ and $\boldsymbol{\eta}$. A shock is said to be *transitory* if it affects the value of the control variable corresponding to a given date t_0. If the extent of the shock is Δz_{t_0}, the effects on the variables $\mathbf{y}$ and $\mathbf{x}$ at time $t_0 + j$, $j \geq 0$ are given by

$$\Delta \mathbf{y}_{t_0+j} = \mathbf{H}_j \Delta z_{t_0}, \qquad \Delta \mathbf{x}_{t_0+j} = \mathbf{K}_j \Delta z_{t_0}.$$

The coefficients $\mathbf{H}_j$ and $\mathbf{K}_j$ of the polynomials $\mathbf{H}(L)$ and $\mathbf{K}(L)$ allow to measure the effects of the shocks. They are called *dynamic multipliers*. $\mathbf{H}_0$ and $\mathbf{K}_0$ are called *impact multipliers*; $\mathbf{H}_j$ and $\mathbf{K}_j$ are called *lagged multipliers*. Note that the effect of the shock on the endogenous variable can be decomposed into two parts; in fact, $\mathbf{H}(L)$ is the sum of

$$-\mathbf{A}(L)^{-1}\mathbf{C}(L),$$

which measures the direct effect of $\mathbf{z}$ on $\mathbf{y}$, and of

$$-\mathbf{A}(L)^{-1}\mathbf{B}(L)\mathbf{K}(L),$$

which gives the effect of $\mathbf{z}$ on $\mathbf{y}$ through the intermediate variable $\mathbf{x}$. Other shocks can be considered. Let us define, for example, a *permanent* or *sustained* shock, as a constant modification of the values of z after a certain date t_0. The corresponding changes in the other variables are obtained by cumulating the dynamic multipliers

$$\Delta \mathbf{y}_{t_0+j} = \left(\sum_{k=0}^{j} \mathbf{H}_k\right) \Delta z \qquad \Delta \mathbf{x}_{t_0+j} = \left(\sum_{k=0}^{j} \mathbf{K}_k\right) \Delta z.$$

In particular, we call *long-term* multipliers the limit of the cumulated multipliers as j tends to infinity. These multipliers are given by

$$\sum_{k=0}^{+\infty} \mathbf{H}_k = \mathbf{H}(1), \qquad \sum_{k=0}^{+\infty} \mathbf{K}_k = \mathbf{K}(1). \qquad (10.37)$$

Shocks on an Environment Variable In our model, the environment variables are different from the control variables in that they cannot be modified in an arbitrary way. We can however study the consequences of a shock on the environment at a given date t_0, represented by the innovation u_{t_0} associated with that date. The disturbances of the type $\mathbf{u}$ enter in the expressions of $\mathbf{x}_t$ and $\mathbf{y}_t$ through some lag operators given by

$$\mathbf{M}(L)\mathbf{u}_t = \left(\mathbf{D}(L) - \mathbf{F}(L)\mathbf{A}(L)^{-1}\mathbf{B}(L)\right)^{-1}\mathbf{u}_t$$

$$= \sum_{j=0}^{+\infty} \mathbf{M}_j \mathbf{u}_{t-j},$$

for the $\mathbf{x}$ and

$$\mathbf{N}(L)\mathbf{u}_t = -\mathbf{A}(L)^{-1}\mathbf{B}(L)\left(\mathbf{D}(L) - \mathbf{F}(L)\mathbf{A}(L)^{-1}\mathbf{B}(L)\right)^{-1}\mathbf{u}_t$$

$$= \sum_{j=0}^{+\infty} \mathbf{N}_j \mathbf{u}_{t-j}$$

for the $\mathbf{y}$, respectively. The effect of the shock at time t_0 can be measured by the innovation variance $\mathbf{\Omega} = \mathrm{var}\,(\mathbf{u}_{t_0})$. The total effect of the shocks on $\mathbf{u}$ on the endogenous variable variance can be measured by the sum

$$\sum_{j=0}^{+\infty} \mathbf{N}_j \mathbf{\Omega} \mathbf{N}_j',$$

each term of which represents the effect of the shock realized j periods before. The same line of reasoning applies to the environment variable, since the effects on $\mathbf{x}_t$ of the various shocks can be measured by $\mathbf{M}_j\mathbf{\Omega}\mathbf{M}_j'$. When the variable $\mathbf{y}_t$ or $\mathbf{x}_t$ considered is a single variable, the various measures $\mathbf{N}_j\mathbf{\Omega}\mathbf{N}_j'$ (or $\mathbf{M}_j\mathbf{\Omega}\mathbf{M}_j'$) have positive values. We can then associate with each lag j the variance share due to the innovation at that date, that is

$$\mu_j = \frac{\mathbf{N}_j\mathbf{\Omega}\mathbf{N}_j'}{\sum_{j=0}^{+\infty} \mathbf{N}_j\mathbf{\Omega}\mathbf{N}_j'}.$$

In such a way, we define a probability distribution on the lags which can be used as any probability distribution. Thus, we can define an *mean lag*

$$m = \sum_{j=0}^{+\infty} \frac{j\mathbf{N}_j\mathbf{\Omega}\mathbf{N}_j'}{\sum_{j=0}^{+\infty} \mathbf{N}_j\mathbf{\Omega}\mathbf{N}_j'},$$

which can be used as a synthetic characteristic of the polynomial $\mathbf{N}(L)$.

Example 10.2: In order to illustrate the previous definitions, let us consider the following dynamic model

$$\mathbf{y}_t = \mathbf{A}\mathbf{y}_{t-1} + \mathbf{B}\mathbf{x}_t + \mathbf{C}z_t + \boldsymbol{\varepsilon}_t,$$

$$\mathbf{x}_t = \mathbf{u}_t.$$

The only lags present in the model refer to the endogenous variables $\mathbf{y}$. To simplify matters, we have assumed z univariate.

(i)   A shock on the control variable z exerts its effect on $\mathbf{y}$ in the following way

$$\mathbf{y}_t = (\mathbf{I} - \mathbf{A}L)^{-1}(\mathbf{C}z_t + \mathbf{B}\mathbf{u}_t + \boldsymbol{\varepsilon}_t)$$

$$= \sum_{j=0}^{+\infty}\mathbf{A}^j\mathbf{C}z_{t-j} + (\mathbf{I} - \mathbf{A}L)^{-1}(\mathbf{B}\mathbf{u}_t + \boldsymbol{\varepsilon}_t).$$

The multipliers representing the impact on $\mathbf{y}$ of a transitory shock on z are given by

$$\Delta\mathbf{y}_{t_0+j} = \mathbf{A}^j\mathbf{C}\Delta z_{t_0}.$$

We see that the evolution of these multipliers as a function of j depends uniquely on $\mathbf{A}^j$. Thus, if the matrix $\mathbf{A}$ can be diagonalized with eigenvalues λ_j, $j = 1, 2, \ldots, n$, the effect on the i-th endogenous variable is of the kind

$$\frac{\Delta\mathbf{y}_{t_0+j}^{(i)}}{\Delta z_{t_0}} = \sum_{k=1}^{n}\gamma_{ik}\lambda_k^j,$$

that is, a combination of exponential functions.

(ii) Let us consider now an environment shock; to simplify the notation, let us assume x univariate. The effect on $\mathbf{y}_t$ of the innovations $\{u_{t-j}, \; j \geq 0\}$ is summarized by

$$(\mathbf{I} - \mathbf{A}L)^{-1}\mathbf{B}u_t = \sum_{j=0}^{+\infty}\mathbf{A}^j\mathbf{B}u_{t-j}.$$

The effect of u_{t-j} is measured by

$$\mathbf{A}^j\mathbf{B}\mathrm{var}\,(u_{t-j})\mathbf{B}'\mathbf{A}^{j'}.$$

Also in this case we could make explicit the role of the eigenvalues of the matrix $\mathbf{A}$.

10.4.2 Stochastic Control

In the previous section, we have derived the dynamic multipliers under the assumption that the control variable be deterministic and could be subject to an arbitrary shock at each date. Now, we are in a position to analyze the case of a control variable fixed on the basis of the values assumed by the various variables at previous times. Therefore, we will consider that during the period under consideration, an economic policy has been conducted through a control variable $\mathbf{z}$, and that this policy can be described through the dynamic equation

$$\mathbf{G}(L)\mathbf{z}_t + \mathbf{H}(L)\mathbf{x}_t + \mathbf{I}(L)\mathbf{y}_t + \boldsymbol{\gamma} = \mathbf{v}_t, \qquad (10.38)$$

with

$$\mathbf{G}(L) = \sum_{j=0}^{p} \mathbf{G}_j L^j, \qquad \mathbf{H}(L) = \sum_{j=1}^{p} \mathbf{H}_j L^j, \qquad \mathbf{I}(L) = \sum_{j=1}^{p} \mathbf{I}_j L^j,$$

where $\{\mathbf{v}_t\}$ is a white noise uncorrelated with $\{\boldsymbol{\varepsilon}_t\}$ and with $\{\mathbf{u}_t\}$.

Shocks Associated with the Control Variables and with the Environment Variables The variable $\mathbf{z}$ is ruled by the scheme given in (10.38). The impact of the shocks on this variable should be examined through the effects of the innovations $\mathbf{v}$ intervening in the definition of the variable $\mathbf{z}$. In order to determine this effect, we need to write the whole system. In matrix form we have

$$\begin{pmatrix} \mathbf{A}(L) & \mathbf{B}(L) & \mathbf{C}(L) \\ \mathbf{F}(L) & \mathbf{D}(L) & \mathbf{E}(L) \\ \mathbf{I}(L) & \mathbf{H}(L) & \mathbf{G}(L) \end{pmatrix} \begin{pmatrix} \mathbf{y}_t \\ \mathbf{x}_t \\ \mathbf{z}_t \end{pmatrix} + \begin{pmatrix} \boldsymbol{\mu} \\ \boldsymbol{\nu} \\ \boldsymbol{\gamma} \end{pmatrix} = \begin{pmatrix} \boldsymbol{\varepsilon}_t \\ \mathbf{u}_t \\ \mathbf{v}_t \end{pmatrix}.$$

By inverting the first matrix on the left, we can work with a moving average representation of the system

$$\begin{pmatrix} \mathbf{y}_t \\ \mathbf{x}_t \\ \mathbf{z}_t \end{pmatrix} = \begin{pmatrix} \mathbf{A}(L) & \mathbf{B}(L) & \mathbf{C}(L) \\ \mathbf{F}(L) & \mathbf{D}(L) & \mathbf{E}(L) \\ \mathbf{I}(L) & \mathbf{H}(L) & \mathbf{G}(L) \end{pmatrix}^{-1} \left(\begin{pmatrix} \boldsymbol{\varepsilon}_t \\ \mathbf{u}_t \\ \mathbf{v}_t \end{pmatrix} - \begin{pmatrix} \boldsymbol{\mu} \\ \boldsymbol{\nu} \\ \boldsymbol{\gamma} \end{pmatrix} \right).$$

We can then evaluate the effects of the innovations $\mathbf{v}_t$ on the future values of the various variables $\mathbf{y}_{t+j}$, $\mathbf{x}_{t+j}$ and $\mathbf{z}_{t+j}$. As in section 10.2.3, we consider, for example the moving average coefficient $\mathbf{P}_j$ of $\mathbf{y}_t$ associated with $\mathbf{v}_{t-j}$. The impact of the shock is measured by $\mathbf{P}_j \mathrm{var}\,(\mathbf{v}_t)\mathbf{P}_j'$. Note that the previous system can be used to measure the effects of shocks in the environment. We just examine the effect of $\mathbf{u}_t$ on the future values of the variables. We can see that, in general, the consequence of a shock is different from that obtained with a deterministic control. In fact, since the followed policy is fixed in terms of the values of $\mathbf{x}$ and $\mathbf{y}$, a shock on the environment generally implies a shock on the control variable $\mathbf{z}$, which is transmitted as a supplementary shock to $\mathbf{x}$, and so on.

Changes in Economic Policy Let us now examine the consequences of a change in economic policy. Such a change can be carried out taking different values of the parameters of economic policy, i.e., $\mathbf{I}(L)$, $\mathbf{H}(L)$, $\mathbf{G}(L)$, and $\text{var}(\mathbf{v}_t) = \mathbf{Q}$. We have seen that the impact of the shocks $\mathbf{v}_{t-j}$ on the endogenous variables $\mathbf{y}_t$ can be measured by $\mathbf{P}_j \text{var}(\mathbf{v}_t)\mathbf{P}_j' = \mathbf{P}_j \boldsymbol{\Omega} \mathbf{P}_j'$. It is clear that the matrices $\mathbf{P}_j$, $j = 0, 1, \ldots$ depend in particular on $\mathbf{I}(L)$, $\mathbf{H}(L)$, $\mathbf{G}(L)$, so that $\mathbf{P}_j = \mathbf{P}_j(\mathbf{I}(L), \mathbf{H}(L), \mathbf{G}(L))$. A change in the economic policy has an effect on the values of the multipliers. Finally, let us examine the case in which all variables $\mathbf{y}$, $\mathbf{x}$, $\mathbf{z}$ are univariate. We have then

$$P(L) = \sum_{j=0}^{+\infty} P_j L^j = \frac{\det \begin{pmatrix} B(L) & C(L) \\ D(L) & E(L) \end{pmatrix}}{\det \begin{pmatrix} A(L) & B(L) & C(L) \\ F(L) & D(L) & E(L) \\ I(L) & H(L) & G(L) \end{pmatrix}}.$$

P_j is for example, a nonlinear function of the coefficients I_k of the polynomial $I(L)$. As a result, the effect on P_j of a change in I_k depends on the values of I_j, $j \geq 0$, and these changes (also called *variations*) must be carried out for different values of I_j, $j \geq 0$. If the policy shock is not very strong, we can summarize the effects through the partial derivatives of P_j with respect to I_k.

10.5 Appendix
Partial Links among Random Vectors

10.5.1 Some Results on Linear Regression

Definition 10.9: *Given two square integrable random vectors* $\mathbf{x}$ *and* $\mathbf{y}$ *of size* m, *respectively,* n, *we can try to approximate the elements of* $\mathbf{y}$ *by affine linear functions of the elements of* $\mathbf{x}$. *We know that this optimal linear prediction exists and can be written in the form*

$$E(\mathbf{y} \mid \mathbf{x}) = E(\mathbf{y}) + \text{cov}(\mathbf{y}, \mathbf{x})\text{var}(\mathbf{x})^{-1}(\mathbf{x} - E(\mathbf{x})), \qquad (10.39)$$

since the variance–covariance matrix of $\mathbf{x}$ *is invertible. The corresponding forecast error (or regression residual) is written as*

$$\boldsymbol{\varepsilon}(\mathbf{y} \mid \mathbf{x}) = \mathbf{y} - E(\mathbf{y} \mid \mathbf{x}) = \mathbf{y} - E(\mathbf{y}) - \operatorname{cov}(\mathbf{y}, \mathbf{x}) \operatorname{var}(\mathbf{x})^{-1}(\mathbf{x} - E(\mathbf{x})).$$
(10.40)

The residual variance provides a good measure of the mean square error; it is given by

$$\operatorname{var}(\boldsymbol{\varepsilon}(\mathbf{y} \mid \mathbf{x})) = \operatorname{var}(\mathbf{y}) - \operatorname{cov}(\mathbf{y}, \mathbf{x}) \operatorname{var}(\mathbf{x})^{-1} \operatorname{cov}(\mathbf{x}, \mathbf{y}), \qquad (10.41)$$

$$\operatorname{var}(\boldsymbol{\varepsilon}(\mathbf{y} \mid \mathbf{x})) = \operatorname{var}(\mathbf{y}) - \operatorname{var}(E(\mathbf{y} \mid \mathbf{x})). \qquad (10.42)$$

Properties of Linear Regression Each element $E(y_j \mid \mathbf{x})$, $j = 1, \ldots, n$ can be interpreted as the orthogonal projection in L^2 of y_j on the subspace spanned by the elements of the vector $\mathbf{x}$ and the constant random variable 1. It has all the usual properties of such projections. Let us recall here some of them.

Theorem 10.12: (Iterated Regressions Theorem) *If* $\mathbf{x}$, $\mathbf{y}$ *and* $\mathbf{z}$ *are three random vectors,*

$$E\left(E(\mathbf{y} \mid \mathbf{x}, \mathbf{z}) \mid \mathbf{z}\right) = E(\mathbf{y} \mid \mathbf{z}) = E\left(E(\mathbf{y} \mid \mathbf{z}) \mid \mathbf{x}, \mathbf{z}\right).$$

Theorem 10.13: (Frisch–Waugh Theorem) *If* $\mathbf{x}$, $\mathbf{y}$ *and* $\mathbf{z}$ *are three square integrable random vectors, we have the decompositions*

$$E(\mathbf{y} \mid \mathbf{x}, \mathbf{z}) = E(\mathbf{y} \mid \mathbf{x}) + E\left(\mathbf{y} \mid \mathbf{z} - E(\mathbf{z} \mid \mathbf{x})\right) - E(\mathbf{y}),$$

$$\boldsymbol{\varepsilon}(\mathbf{y} \mid \mathbf{x}, \mathbf{z}) = \boldsymbol{\varepsilon}(\mathbf{y} \mid \mathbf{x}) - E\left(\mathbf{y} \mid \mathbf{z} - E(\mathbf{z} \mid \mathbf{x})\right) + E(\mathbf{y}),$$

$$\operatorname{var} E(\mathbf{y} \mid \mathbf{x}, \mathbf{z}) = \operatorname{var} E(\mathbf{y} \mid \mathbf{x}) + \operatorname{var} E\left(\mathbf{y} \mid \mathbf{z} - E(\mathbf{z} \mid \mathbf{x})\right),$$

$$\operatorname{var}(\boldsymbol{\varepsilon}(\mathbf{y} \mid \mathbf{x}, \mathbf{z})) = \operatorname{var}(\boldsymbol{\varepsilon}(\mathbf{y} \mid \mathbf{x})) - \operatorname{var} E\left(\mathbf{y} \mid \mathbf{z} - E(\mathbf{z} \mid \mathbf{x})\right).$$

In particular, the following corollary holds

Corollary:

$$\operatorname{var} E(\mathbf{y} \mid \mathbf{x}, \mathbf{z}) \geq \operatorname{var} E(\mathbf{y} \mid \mathbf{x}),$$

$$\operatorname{var}(\boldsymbol{\varepsilon}(\mathbf{y} \mid \mathbf{x}, \mathbf{z})) \leq \operatorname{var}(\boldsymbol{\varepsilon}(\mathbf{y} \mid \mathbf{x}))$$

with equality holding if and only if

$$E(\mathbf{y} \mid \mathbf{x}, \mathbf{z}) = E(\mathbf{y} \mid \mathbf{x}).$$

10.5.2 Partial Uncorrelation

Definition 10.10: *Two random vectors* $\mathbf{x}$ *and* $\mathbf{y}$ *are partially uncorrelated with a third vector* $\mathbf{z}$ *if and only if*

$$\mathrm{cov}\left(\boldsymbol{\varepsilon}(\mathbf{x}\mid\mathbf{z}),\,\boldsymbol{\varepsilon}(\mathbf{y}\mid\mathbf{z})\right)=\mathbf{0}.$$

In what follows, we will indicate this condition as $\mathbf{y}\perp\mathbf{x}\mid\mathbf{z}$. Two vectors $\mathbf{x}$ and $\mathbf{y}$ partially uncorrelated with $\mathbf{z}$ are vectors which are linearly unrelated, once the linear influence of $\mathbf{z}$ has been extracted from both vectors. The previous condition is equivalent to

$$\mathrm{cov}\left(\epsilon(x_i\mid\mathbf{z}),\,\epsilon(y_j\mid\mathbf{z})\right)=0,\quad\forall\ i=1,\ldots,m,\quad\forall\ j=1,\ldots,n.$$

Any combination of the elements of $\mathbf{x}$ is partially uncorrelated with any combination of the elements of $\mathbf{y}$. This shows that the partial uncorrelation is actually a property of the subspaces spanned by $(x_i,\ i=1,\ldots,m)$ respectively $(y_i,\ i=1,\ldots,n)$, and $(z_k,\ i=1,\ldots,K)$. The partial uncorrelation can be characterized in several ways.

Theorem 10.14: *There is equivalence among the following propositions*

(i)
$$\mathbf{y}\perp\mathbf{x}\mid\mathbf{z},$$

(ii)
$$\mathbf{x}\perp\mathbf{y}\mid\mathbf{z},$$

(iii)
$$\mathbf{y}\perp(\mathbf{x}-E(\mathbf{x}\mid\mathbf{z}))\mid\mathbf{z},$$

(iv)
$$E(\mathbf{y}\mid\mathbf{x},\mathbf{z})=E(\mathbf{y}\mid\mathbf{z}),$$

(v)
$$E(\mathbf{y}\mid(\mathbf{x}-E(\mathbf{x}\mid\mathbf{z})))=E(\mathbf{y}),$$

(vi)
$$\mathrm{var}\left(\boldsymbol{\varepsilon}(\mathbf{y}\mid\mathbf{x},\mathbf{z})\right)=\mathrm{var}\left(\boldsymbol{\varepsilon}(\mathbf{y}\mid\mathbf{z})\right),$$

(vii)
$$\mathrm{cov}\left(\mathbf{y},\mathbf{x}\right)=\mathrm{cov}\left(\mathbf{y},\mathbf{z}\right)\mathrm{var}\left(\mathbf{z}\right)^{-1}\mathrm{cov}\left(\mathbf{z},\mathbf{x}\right).$$

10.5.3 Recursive Properties of Partial Uncorrelation

Theorem 10.15: *We have the equivalence*

$$\mathbf{y} \perp (x_1, x_2, \ldots, x_n) \mid \mathbf{z} \Leftrightarrow \begin{cases} \mathbf{y} \perp x_1 \mid \mathbf{z} \\ \mathbf{y} \perp x_2 \mid (\mathbf{z}, x_1) \\ \ldots \\ \mathbf{y} \perp x_n \mid (\mathbf{z}, x_1, \ldots, x_{n-1}). \end{cases}$$

PROOF:

Necessary Condition: Partial uncorrelation is equivalent to

$$E\left(\mathbf{y} \mid \mathbf{z}, x_1, x_2, \ldots, x_n\right) = E(\mathbf{y} \mid \mathbf{z}).$$

Applying on each side the operator $E\left(\mathbf{y} \mid \mathbf{z}, x_1, x_2, \ldots, x_i\right)$ and using the property of iterated projections we obtain

$$E\left(\mathbf{y} \mid \mathbf{z}, x_1, x_2, \ldots, x_i\right) = E(\mathbf{y} \mid \mathbf{z}), \quad \forall\, i.$$

Thus we have

$$E\left(\mathbf{y} \mid \mathbf{z}, x_1, x_2, \ldots, x_i\right) = E\left(\mathbf{y} \mid \mathbf{z}, x_1, x_2, \ldots, x_{i-1}\right), \quad \forall\, i,$$

that is

$$\mathbf{y} \perp x_i \mid (\mathbf{z}, x_1, \ldots, x_{i-1}), \quad \forall\, i.$$

Sufficient Condition: Conversely, if we have

$$E\left(\mathbf{y} \mid \mathbf{z}, x_1, x_2, \ldots, x_i\right) = E\left(\mathbf{y} \mid \mathbf{z}, x_1, x_2, \ldots, x_{i-1}\right) \quad \forall\, i,$$

we also have

$$E\left(\mathbf{y} \mid \mathbf{z}, x_1, x_2, \ldots, x_n\right) = E\left(\mathbf{y} \mid \mathbf{z}\right),$$

which corresponds to the property of partial uncorrelation. □

10.5.4 Sims's Characterization of Noncausality

The equivalence between the definitions of noncausality suggested by Granger and by Sims can be shown using the theorem 10.16, which is just an extension of theorem 10.15. This extension is valid when the $\mathbf{x}$, $\mathbf{y}$, and $\mathbf{z}$ have an infinite order corresponding to successive values of stationary processes.

Theorem 10.16: *The Granger noncausality of* **y** *to* **x**

$$\mathbf{x}_t \perp \underline{\mathbf{y}}_{t-1} \mid \underline{\mathbf{x}}_{t-1},$$

is equivalent to the noncausality in the sense of Sims

$$\overline{\mathbf{x}}_{t+1} \perp \mathbf{y}_t \mid \underline{\mathbf{x}}_t,$$

when $\{\mathbf{x}_t, \mathbf{y}_t\}$ *is a stationary process.*

PROOF: From stationarity, we have

$$\mathbf{x}_t \perp \underline{\mathbf{y}}_{t-1} \mid \underline{\mathbf{x}}_{t-1}$$

$$\Leftrightarrow \mathbf{x}_t \perp \underline{\mathbf{y}}_{t-1} \mid \underline{\mathbf{x}}_{t-1}, \ \forall\, t$$

$$\Leftrightarrow \mathbf{x}_t \perp \mathbf{y}_{t-h} \mid \underline{\mathbf{x}}_{t-1} \ \forall\, t, \ \forall\, h > 0$$

$$\Leftrightarrow \mathbf{x}_{t+h} \perp \mathbf{y}_t \mid \underline{\mathbf{x}}_{t+h-1} \ \forall\, t, \ \forall\, h > 0$$

given the stationarity

$$\overline{\mathbf{x}}_{t+1} \perp \mathbf{y}_t \mid \underline{\mathbf{x}}_t$$

given the extension of (10.15).

□

10.5.5 Pierce and Haugh's Characterization of Noncausality

Theorem 10.17: *Let us consider a stationary process* $\{\mathbf{x}, \mathbf{y}\}$ *and let us denote the innovations associated with each process as*

$$\boldsymbol{\varepsilon}_t(\mathbf{x}) = \mathbf{x} - E(\mathbf{x}_t \mid \underline{\mathbf{x}}_{t-1}),$$

$$\boldsymbol{\varepsilon}_t(\mathbf{y}) = \mathbf{y} - E(\mathbf{y}_t \mid \underline{\mathbf{y}}_{t-1}).$$

There is noncausality of **y** *to* **x** *in the sense of Granger*

$$\mathbf{x}_t \perp \underline{\mathbf{y}}_{t-1} \mid \underline{\mathbf{x}}_{t-1}, \ \forall\, t,$$

if and only if

$$\mathrm{cov}\,(\boldsymbol{\varepsilon}_t(\mathbf{x}), \boldsymbol{\varepsilon}_\tau(\mathbf{y})) = \mathbf{0}, \ \forall\, t > \tau.$$

PROOF: We have previously noted that the property of partial uncorrelation is a property relative to vector subspaces spanned by the

components of $\underline{\mathbf{y}}_{t-1}$, respectively, $\underline{\mathbf{x}}_{t-1}$. We have then

$$\mathbf{x}_t \perp \underline{\mathbf{y}}_{t-1} \mid \underline{\mathbf{x}}_{t-1}$$

$$\Leftrightarrow \mathbf{x}_t \perp \underline{\boldsymbol{\varepsilon}}_{t-1}(\mathbf{y}) \mid \underline{\boldsymbol{\varepsilon}}_{t-1}(\mathbf{x}), \ \forall \, t$$

$$\Leftrightarrow \left(\mathbf{x}_t - E\left(\mathbf{x}_t \mid \underline{\boldsymbol{\varepsilon}}_{t-1}(\mathbf{x})\right)\right) \perp \underline{\boldsymbol{\varepsilon}}_{t-1}(\mathbf{y}) \mid \underline{\boldsymbol{\varepsilon}}_{t-1}(\mathbf{x}), \ \forall \, t$$

given theorem 10.14(iii)

$$\Leftrightarrow \boldsymbol{\varepsilon}_t(\mathbf{x}) \perp \underline{\boldsymbol{\varepsilon}}_{t-1}(\mathbf{y}) \mid \underline{\boldsymbol{\varepsilon}}_{t-1}(\mathbf{x}), \ \forall \, t,$$

$$\Leftrightarrow \operatorname{cov}\left(\boldsymbol{\varepsilon}_t(\mathbf{x}), \underline{\boldsymbol{\varepsilon}}_{t-1}(\mathbf{y})\right) = \operatorname{cov}\left(\boldsymbol{\varepsilon}_t(\mathbf{x}), \underline{\boldsymbol{\varepsilon}}_{t-1}(\mathbf{x})\right)$$

$$\operatorname{var}\left(\underline{\boldsymbol{\varepsilon}}_{t-1}(\mathbf{x})\right)^{-1} \operatorname{cov}\left(\underline{\boldsymbol{\varepsilon}}_{t-1}(\mathbf{x})\underline{\boldsymbol{\varepsilon}}_{t-1}(\mathbf{y})\right) \ \forall \ t$$

given theorem 10.14(vii)

$$\Leftrightarrow \operatorname{cov}\left(\boldsymbol{\varepsilon}_t(\mathbf{x}), \underline{\boldsymbol{\varepsilon}}_{t-1}(\mathbf{y})\right) = \mathbf{0} \ \forall t,$$

the last result being derived from the fact that $\boldsymbol{\varepsilon}_t(\mathbf{x})$ is an innovation process and hence $\operatorname{cov}\left(\boldsymbol{\varepsilon}_t(\mathbf{x}), \underline{\boldsymbol{\varepsilon}}_{t-1}(\mathbf{x})\right) = \mathbf{0}$. $\square$

10.5.6 Measures of Partial Links

Let us introduce now a measure of the link between two random vectors conditionally to a third one. This measure will be defined from the joint distribution of the three vectors. Applying the results to the case of the normal distribution, we will obtain measures of partial link based just on the linear predictions of the vectors. Let us consider three random vectors $(\mathbf{x}, \mathbf{y}, \mathbf{z})$, the joint probability density function (p.d.f.) of which is indicated by $l(\mathbf{x}, \mathbf{y}, \mathbf{z})$ with respect to a product measure. We can easily derive the marginal p.d.f. $l(\mathbf{x})$, $l(\mathbf{y})$, $l(\mathbf{z})$, $l(\mathbf{x}, \mathbf{y})$, $l(\mathbf{x}, \mathbf{z})$, $l(\mathbf{y}, \mathbf{z})$, and the conditional p.d.f. through a formula of the type

$$l(\mathbf{y} \mid \mathbf{x}, \mathbf{z}) = \frac{l(\mathbf{x}, \mathbf{y}, \mathbf{z})}{l(\mathbf{x}, \mathbf{z})}.$$

Theorem 10.18:

(i)   *The quantity*

$$K(\mathbf{y}, \mathbf{x} \mid \mathbf{z}) = E\left(\ln \frac{l(\mathbf{y} \mid \mathbf{x}, \mathbf{z})}{l(\mathbf{y} \mid \mathbf{z})}\right)$$

is always positive or 0. *(ii)*   *It becomes* 0 *if and only if*

$$l(\mathbf{y} \mid \mathbf{x}, \mathbf{z}) = l(\mathbf{y} \mid \mathbf{z}),$$

that is, if $\mathbf{x}$ *and* $\mathbf{y}$ *are independent conditionally to* $\mathbf{z}$.

PROOF: (i)   We have

$$E\left(\ln\frac{l\left(\mathbf{y}\mid\mathbf{x},\mathbf{z}\right)}{l\left(\mathbf{y}\mid\mathbf{z}\right)}\right) = E\left(E\left(\ln\frac{l\left(\mathbf{y}\mid\mathbf{x},\mathbf{z}\right)}{l\left(\mathbf{y}\mid\mathbf{z}\right)}\right)\mid\mathbf{x},\mathbf{z}\right)$$

$$= E\left(E\left(-\ln\frac{l\left(\mathbf{y}\mid\mathbf{z}\right)}{l\left(\mathbf{y}\mid\mathbf{x},\mathbf{z}\right)}\right)\mid\mathbf{x},\mathbf{z}\right)$$

$$\geq E\left(-\ln E\left(\frac{l\left(\mathbf{y}\mid\mathbf{z}\right)}{l\left(\mathbf{y}\mid\mathbf{x},\mathbf{z}\right)}\right)\mid\mathbf{x},\mathbf{z}\right)$$

given the convexity inequality

$$= E(-\ln(1)) = 0.$$

(ii)   On the other hand, the quantity becomes 0 if and only if there is an equality in the convexity inequality. This happens if and only if $l\left(\mathbf{y}\mid\mathbf{x},\mathbf{z}\right) = l\left(\mathbf{y}\mid\mathbf{z}\right)$. $\square$

It is possible to give other equivalent expressions to the previous quantity. In fact, we have

$$\frac{l\left(\mathbf{y}\mid\mathbf{x},\mathbf{z}\right)}{l\left(\mathbf{y}\mid\mathbf{z}\right)} = \frac{l\left(\mathbf{x},\mathbf{y},\mathbf{z}\right)}{l\left(\mathbf{y}\mid\mathbf{z}\right)l\left(\mathbf{x},\mathbf{z}\right)} = \frac{l\left(\mathbf{x},\mathbf{y},\mathbf{z}\right)/l(\mathbf{z})}{l\left(\mathbf{y}\mid\mathbf{z}\right)l\left(\mathbf{x},\mathbf{z}\right)/l(\mathbf{z})}$$

$$= \frac{l\left(\mathbf{x},\mathbf{y}\mid\mathbf{z}\right)}{l\left(\mathbf{y}\mid\mathbf{z}\right)l\left(\mathbf{x}\mid\mathbf{z}\right)}.$$

Theorem 10.19: *We have also the identities*

$$K\left(\mathbf{y},\mathbf{x}\mid\mathbf{z}\right) = E\left(\ln\frac{l\left(\mathbf{y}\mid\mathbf{x},\mathbf{z}\right)}{l\left(\mathbf{y}\mid\mathbf{z}\right)}\right) = E\left(\ln\frac{l\left(\mathbf{x},\mathbf{y}\mid\mathbf{z}\right)}{l\left(\mathbf{y}\mid\mathbf{z}\right)l\left(\mathbf{x}\mid\mathbf{z}\right)}\right)$$

$$= E\left(\ln\frac{l\left(\mathbf{x}\mid\mathbf{y},\mathbf{z}\right)}{l\left(\mathbf{x}\mid\mathbf{z}\right)}\right).$$

The quantity K measures the deviation between the distribution of the pair $\mathbf{x},\mathbf{y}$ conditional on $\mathbf{z}$, and the product of the marginal distributions $l\left(\mathbf{y}\mid\mathbf{z}\right)$, $l\left(\mathbf{x}\mid\mathbf{z}\right)$. It may be interpreted as a measure of partial link.

Let us consider now the particular case where the vectors $\mathbf{y},\mathbf{x},\mathbf{z}$ are normal, making explicit the expression of the measure of the link. The conditional distribution of $\mathbf{y}$ given $\mathbf{z}$, for example, is normal as well. If n indicates the size of the vector $\mathbf{y}$ we have

$$l\left(\mathbf{y}\mid\mathbf{z}\right) = \frac{1}{2\pi^{n/2}}\det\left(\text{var}\left(\mathbf{y}\mid\mathbf{z}\right)\right)^{-1/2}$$

$$\times\exp\left(-\frac{1}{2}\left(\mathbf{y}-E(\mathbf{y}\mid\mathbf{z})\right)'\text{var}\left(\mathbf{y}\mid\mathbf{z}\right)^{-1}\left(\mathbf{y}-E(\mathbf{y}\mid\mathbf{z})\right)\right),$$

from which

$$\ln l\,(\mathbf{y}\mid \mathbf{z}) = -\frac{n}{2}\ln(2\pi) - \frac{1}{2}\ln \det\,(\mathrm{var}\,(\mathbf{y}\mid \mathbf{z}))$$
$$-\frac{1}{2}Tr\,\left(\mathrm{var}\,(\mathbf{y}\mid \mathbf{z})^{-1}\,(\mathbf{y} - E(\mathbf{y}\mid \mathbf{z}))\,(\mathbf{y} - E(\mathbf{y}\mid \mathbf{z}))'\right).$$

Taking the conditional expectation with respect to $\mathbf{z}$ we get

$$E\,(\ln l\,(\mathbf{y}\mid \mathbf{z})\mid \mathbf{z}) = -\frac{n}{2}\ln(2\pi) - \frac{1}{2}\ln \det\,(\mathrm{var}\,(\mathbf{y}\mid \mathbf{z})) - \frac{n}{2},$$

and hence also

$$E\,(\ln l\,(\mathbf{y}\mid \mathbf{z})) = -\frac{n}{2}\ln(2\pi) - \frac{1}{2}\ln \det\,(\mathrm{var}\,(\mathbf{y}\mid \mathbf{z})) - \frac{n}{2},$$

since, in the normal case, the conditional variance–covariance matrix does not depend on the conditioning variable. We derive the following result

Theorem 10.20: *In the Gaussian case, we have*

$$K\,(\mathbf{x}, \mathbf{y}\mid \mathbf{z}) = \frac{1}{2}C\,(\mathbf{x}, \mathbf{y}\mid \mathbf{z}),$$

with

$$C\,(\mathbf{x}, \mathbf{y}\mid \mathbf{z}) = \ln \frac{\det \mathrm{var}\,(\mathbf{y}\mid \mathbf{z})}{\det \mathrm{var}\,(\mathbf{y}\mid \mathbf{x}, \mathbf{z})} = \ln \frac{\det \mathrm{var}\,(\boldsymbol{\varepsilon}(\mathbf{y}\mid \mathbf{z}))}{\det \mathrm{var}\,(\boldsymbol{\varepsilon}(\mathbf{y}\mid \mathbf{x}, \mathbf{z}))}.$$

The quantity

$$C\,(\mathbf{x}, \mathbf{y}\mid \mathbf{z}) = \ln \frac{\det \mathrm{var}\,(\boldsymbol{\varepsilon}(\mathbf{y}\mid \mathbf{z}))}{\det \mathrm{var}\,(\boldsymbol{\varepsilon}(\mathbf{y}\mid \mathbf{x}, \mathbf{z}))} \qquad (10.43)$$

can be computed even if the vectors are not normal. It may be interpreted as a measure of the partial linear link between $\mathbf{x}$ and $\mathbf{y}$ given $\mathbf{z}$. From theorem 10.19, we derive immediately that

$$C\,(\mathbf{x}, \mathbf{y}\mid \mathbf{z}) = \ln \frac{\det \mathrm{var}\,(\boldsymbol{\varepsilon}(\mathbf{y}\mid \mathbf{z}))}{\det \mathrm{var}\,(\boldsymbol{\varepsilon}(\mathbf{y}\mid \mathbf{x}, \mathbf{z}))} = \ln \frac{\det \mathrm{var}\,(\boldsymbol{\varepsilon}(\mathbf{x}\mid \mathbf{z}))}{\det \mathrm{var}\,(\boldsymbol{\varepsilon}(\mathbf{x}\mid \mathbf{y}, \mathbf{z}))}$$
$$= \ln \frac{\det \mathrm{var}\,(\boldsymbol{\varepsilon}(\mathbf{y}\mid \mathbf{z})) \det \mathrm{var}\,(\boldsymbol{\varepsilon}(\mathbf{x}\mid \mathbf{z}))}{\det \mathrm{var}\,(\boldsymbol{\varepsilon}(\mathbf{x}, \mathbf{y}\mid \mathbf{z}))}. \qquad (10.44)$$

The measure of the partial linear link can be seen as a generalization of the notion of partial correlation. In fact, if we consider the case of univariate variables, we have

$$C\left(x,y\mid z\right)$$

$$= \ln\left(\frac{\mathrm{var}\left(\boldsymbol{\varepsilon}(x\mid z)\right)\mathrm{var}\left(\boldsymbol{\varepsilon}(y\mid z)\right)}{\det\left(\begin{array}{cc}\mathrm{var}\left(\boldsymbol{\varepsilon}(x\mid z)\right) & \mathrm{cov}\left(\boldsymbol{\varepsilon}(x\mid z),\boldsymbol{\varepsilon}(y\mid z)\right)\\ \mathrm{cov}\left(\boldsymbol{\varepsilon}(x\mid z),\boldsymbol{\varepsilon}(y\mid z)\right) & \mathrm{var}\left(\boldsymbol{\varepsilon}(y\mid z)\right)\end{array}\right)}\right)$$

$$= -\ln\left(1 - \frac{\mathrm{cov}^2(\boldsymbol{\varepsilon}(x\mid z),\boldsymbol{\varepsilon}(y\mid z))}{\mathrm{var}\left(\boldsymbol{\varepsilon}(x\mid z)\right)\mathrm{var}\left(\boldsymbol{\varepsilon}(y\mid z)\right)}\right)$$

$$= -\ln\left(1 - \rho^2(x,y\mid z)\right),$$

which is an increasing function of the square of the partial correlation.

10.5.7 Application to Stationary Processes

The previous measures can be extended to the stationary processes, when the conditioning vectors are infinite sized, corresponding to the past of such a process. We can then define causality measures starting from the distributions of such processes.

(i) **Instantaneous causality**

$$K\left(x\leftrightarrow y\right) = E\ln\frac{l\left(\mathbf{y}_t\mid\underline{\mathbf{x}}_t,\underline{\mathbf{y}}_{t-1}\right)}{l\left(\mathbf{y}_t\mid\underline{\mathbf{x}}_{t-1},\underline{\mathbf{y}}_{t-1}\right)}$$

$$= E\ln\frac{l\left(\mathbf{x}_t,\mathbf{y}_t\mid\underline{\mathbf{x}}_{t-1},\underline{\mathbf{y}}_{t-1}\right)}{l\left(\mathbf{x}_t\mid\underline{\mathbf{x}}_{t-1},\underline{\mathbf{y}}_{t-1}\right)l\left(\mathbf{y}_t\mid\underline{\mathbf{x}}_{t-1},\underline{\mathbf{y}}_{t-1}\right)}$$

$$= E\ln\frac{l\left(\mathbf{x}_t\mid\underline{\mathbf{x}}_{t-1},\underline{\mathbf{y}}_t\right)}{l\left(\mathbf{x}_t\mid\underline{\mathbf{x}}_{t-1},\underline{\mathbf{y}}_{t-1}\right)}.$$

(ii) **Unidirectional causality of x to y**

$$K\left(x\rightarrow y\right) = E\ln\frac{l\left(\mathbf{y}_t\mid\underline{\mathbf{x}}_{t-1},\underline{\mathbf{y}}_{t-1}\right)}{l\left(\mathbf{y}_t\mid\underline{\mathbf{y}}_{t-1}\right)}.$$

(iii) **Unidirectional causality of y to x**

$$K\left(y\rightarrow x\right) = E\ln\frac{l\left(\mathbf{x}_t\mid\underline{\mathbf{x}}_{t-1},\underline{\mathbf{y}}_{t-1}\right)}{l\left(\mathbf{x}_t\mid\underline{\mathbf{x}}_{t-1}\right)}.$$

(iv) **Dependency**

$$K\left(y,x\right) = E\ln \frac{l\left(\mathbf{x}_t, \mathbf{y}_t \mid \underline{\mathbf{x}}_{t-1}, \underline{\mathbf{y}}_{t-1}\right)}{l\left(\mathbf{x}_t \mid \underline{\mathbf{x}}_{t-1}\right) l\left(\mathbf{y}_t \mid \underline{\mathbf{y}}_{t-1}\right)}.$$

We can see immediately that $K\left(y,x\right) = K\left(x \leftrightarrow y\right) + K\left(x \to y\right) + K\left(y \to x\right)$. Similar expressions for the linear causality measures can be derived directly considering the case of the normal distribution. For example,

$$C\left(\mathbf{x} \leftrightarrow \mathbf{y}\right) = \ln \frac{\det \mathrm{var}\left(\boldsymbol{\varepsilon}(\mathbf{y}_t \mid \underline{\mathbf{x}}_{t-1}, \underline{\mathbf{y}}_{t-1})\right)}{\det \mathrm{var}\left(\boldsymbol{\varepsilon}(\mathbf{y}_t \mid \underline{\mathbf{x}}_t, \underline{\mathbf{y}}_{t-1})\right)}$$

$$= \ln \frac{\det \mathrm{var}\left(\boldsymbol{\varepsilon}(\mathbf{y}_t \mid \underline{\mathbf{x}}_{t-1}, \underline{\mathbf{y}}_{t-1})\right) \det \mathrm{var}\left(\boldsymbol{\varepsilon}(\mathbf{x}_t \mid \underline{\mathbf{x}}_{t-1}, \underline{\mathbf{y}}_{t-1})\right)}{\det \mathrm{var}\left(\boldsymbol{\varepsilon}(\mathbf{x}_t, \mathbf{y}_t \mid \underline{\mathbf{x}}_{t-1}, \underline{\mathbf{y}}_{t-1})\right)}$$

and

$$C_{y,x} = C_{x \leftrightarrow y} + C_{x \to y} + C_{y \to x}.$$

10.6 Exercises

Exercise 10.1: Verify that y does not cause y.

Exercise 10.2: Show that the causality relationship is not transitive. [Hint: take $x_t = \epsilon_t$, $y_t = \epsilon_{t-1} + \eta_t$, $z_t = \eta_{t-1}$, where ϵ and η are independent white noises.]

Exercise 10.3: Show that the noncausality relationship is not transitive. [Hint: take $x_t = z_{t-1} = \epsilon_t$, $y_t = \eta_t$, where ϵ and η are independent white noises.]

Exercise 10.4: Show that x may cause y even if it does not cause (y, z). [Hint: take $y_t = z_{t-1} = \epsilon_t$, $x_{t-1} = \epsilon_t + \eta_t$, where ϵ and η are independent white noises.]

Exercise 10.5: Show that (x, z) does not cause y if and only if x does not cause y and z does not cause y.

Exercise 10.6: Let us consider the process $y_t = \epsilon_t + \eta_t$, $x_{t-1} = \epsilon_t - \eta_t$, $z_{t-1} = \eta_t$, where ϵ and η are independent white noises with the same variance. Verify that it is possible that x causes (y, z), even if it does not cause either y or z.

Exercise 10.7: A static simultaneous equation model is defined as

$$\mathbf{A}_0 \mathbf{y}_t + \mathbf{B}_0 \mathbf{x}_t = \boldsymbol{\varepsilon}_t,$$

where we suppose that the disturbance term follows a normal distribution with mean zero and variance–covariance matrix $\boldsymbol{\Omega}$. The diagonal elements of $\mathbf{A}_0$ are equal to one. Let us assume that there are no other constraints on $\mathbf{A}_0, \mathbf{B}_0$, and $\boldsymbol{\Omega}$.

(i)   Derive the distribution of $\mathbf{y}_t$.
(ii) Verify that it is not possible to derive the elements of $\mathbf{A}_0, \mathbf{B}_0$, and $\boldsymbol{\Omega}$ unambiguously as functions of this distribution.

Exercise 10.8: Let us consider a bivariate stationary Gaussian process (x, y). Use theorem 10.20 (in the appendix) relating the measures of the links based on the distributions and on the second-order moments to show that the two processes x and y are independent (i.e., uncorrelated in this case) if and only if the causality measures are all 0.

Exercise 10.9:

(i) Let $\mathbf{D}(L) = \mathbf{I} + \mathbf{D}_1 L + \mathbf{D}_2 L^2 + \dots$ a series with $\mathbf{I}$ as a constant term. From Kolmogorov's inequality show that

$$\int_{-\pi}^{+\pi} \ln \det \left(\mathbf{D}(\exp(i\omega)) \mathbf{D}(\exp-(i\omega)') \right) d\omega = 0.$$

(ii) Using the notation of section 10.2.5, let us consider the causality measure of y to x at each frequency (cf. (10.21))

(a) Verify that $\mathbf{A}_3(L)$ is such that $\mathbf{A}_3(0) = \mathbf{I}$.

(b) From (a) show that

$$C_{y \to x} = \frac{1}{2\pi} \int_{-\pi}^{+\pi} \ln \det \left(g_{y \to x}(\omega) \right) d\omega.$$

11

Trend Components

The starting point for the analysis of series of observations indexed by time $\{y_t,\, t \geq 0\}$ is to examine their graphical representations. Oftentimes it happens that the series exhibit an explosive pattern, that is, they give the impression of tending toward infinity with t. In such a case, the attention is focused on the dominant components of the series which are smoother than the original ones, but asymptotically equivalent to them. In this chapter we will mainly stress the importance of such components, which we will assume are diverging in a polynomial fashion. It is possible to obtain such a behavior through a nonlinear transformation of the original series most of the time. We can ask a number of questions about this trend component, according to whether we examine the series separately or jointly.

What is the rate of divergence of the various series? What are the differences among them?

What happens to the series once the dominant component is eliminated; are there still some diverging components and how important are they?

The joint plot of two series sometimes shows fairly strong links among the trend components of the series. Is it possible to make these links explicit, to study the cases where they are particularly strong, and to compare the strength of these links with those of other components of the series?

Such a study is interesting for a number of reasons:

(i)   Since it is regular and dominant, a trend is important for forecasting. In particular, to improve the forecasts, it seems important to detect relevant links among the trends of different series.

(ii) The statistical concept of trend can be put in relation with the economic concept of "equilibrium path," and the notion of a relationship among trends of different series can be put in relation with the concept of "long-term model."

As we have seen in previous chapters, a study of the trend component must be based on a model.

In the first section we examine in particular the ARIMA models where the trend is introduced by means of an autoregressive polynomial with some roots equal to 1. We show that such a model is well suited for a nonstationary series decomposition in components with smaller and smaller rates of divergence. This decomposition allows us also to study series whose dominant components are strongly linked (*cointegrated series*).

In section 11.2, we examine the links between the time-series models and the usual dynamic macroeconomic models. We recall some basic notions of macroeconomic model building – objective functions, partial adjustment, balanced growth – examining the constraints that they impose on the time-series models.

In section 11.3, we introduce a generalization of the ARIMA processes of the type

$$(1 - L)^d \Phi(L) y_t = \Theta(L) \tilde{\epsilon}_t,$$

where the power d is not necessarily an integer. Such processes are called "fractional processes." We give the main properties of such processes, stationarity and invertibility, the expressions of the spectral density and of the autocovariances, showing how they are produced by aggregation of autoregressive processes.

11.1 Decomposition of a Series with Polynomial Trend

11.1.1 Decomposition Formula

In this section, we consider a time series which can be represented as a multivariate ARIMA

$$\Phi(L)\mathbf{y}_t = \Theta(L)\tilde{\boldsymbol{\epsilon}}_t, \quad t \geq 0, \tag{11.1}$$

where the size of $\mathbf{y}_t$ is n, and where $\tilde{\boldsymbol{\epsilon}}_t$ is a white noise with a variance–covariance matrix $\boldsymbol{\Sigma}$.

Let us assume that the values of the white noise before the initial date t are 0, as are the corresponding values of the process. The autoregressive polynomial is such that $\det(\mathbf{\Phi}(L))$ has all roots outside the unit circle, apart from some equal to 1. We can then write the expression (11.1) as

$$\det(\mathbf{\Phi}(L))\mathbf{y}_t = \mathbf{\Phi}^*(L)\mathbf{\Theta}(L)\tilde{\boldsymbol{\varepsilon}}_t$$

indicating by $\mathbf{\Phi}^*(L)$ the adjoint of the matrix $\mathbf{\Phi}(L)$. Isolating the roots of $\det(\mathbf{\Phi}(L))$ equal to 1 from the others, we get an expression of the type

$$(1-L)^d \mathbf{y}_t = \mathbf{H}(L)\tilde{\boldsymbol{\varepsilon}}_t, \qquad (11.2)$$

where d is an integer number and where

$$\mathbf{H}(L) = \frac{\mathbf{\Phi}^*(L)\mathbf{\Theta}(L)}{(\det(\mathbf{\Phi}(L)))/(1-L)^d)}$$

is a rational fraction admitting a series expansion with exponentially decreasing coefficients.

As soon as the power d is strictly positive, the series in general includes nonstationary components. In the moving average representation of this series (cf. chapter 8)

$$\mathbf{y}_t = \frac{\mathbf{H}(L)}{(1-L)^d}\tilde{\boldsymbol{\varepsilon}}_t,$$

the coefficient of $\tilde{\boldsymbol{\varepsilon}}_{t-j}$ is of the same order as j^{d-1} for large j. This gives an idea of the magnitude of the nonstationarity: thus the variance of $\mathbf{y}_t$ is of the same order as $\sum_{j=1}^{t} j^{2d-2}$, that is of the same order as t^{2d-1} and the standard deviation of the same order as $t^{d-\frac{1}{2}}$. The number $d-\frac{1}{2}$ is called the *degree of nonstationarity of the series* ($d \geq 1$) (cf. section 8.1.2). This degree of nonstationarity also appears in the decomposition of the series based on Taylor's formula.

Theorem 11.1: **Taylor's Formula**

(i)   If $\mathbf{H}(L)$ *is a polynomial in the lag operator, we can write*

$$\mathbf{H}(L) = \sum_{k=0}^{p} \frac{\mathbf{H}^{(k)}(1)}{k!}(-1)^k(1-L)^k,$$

where p indicates the degree of the polynomial $\mathbf{H}$, and $\mathbf{H}^{(k)}(1)$ is the k-th derivative of $\mathbf{H}$ evaluated at 1. (ii)   If

$$\mathbf{H}(L) = \frac{\mathbf{A}(L)}{\mathbf{b}(L)}$$

is a rational fraction in the lag operator with a scalar denominator, we can write

$$\mathbf{H}(L) = \sum_{k=0}^{d-1} \frac{\mathbf{H}^{(k)}(1)}{k!}(-1)^k(1-L)^k + (1-L)^d\mathbf{R}(L),$$

where $\mathbf{R}(L)$ is a series with exponentially decreasing coefficients if $\mathbf{b}(L)$ has all roots outside the unit circle.

PROOF: The first part of the theorem is just Taylor's formula. In order to verify the second part, note that

$$\mathbf{A}(L) - \mathbf{b}(L) \sum_{k=0}^{d-1} \frac{\mathbf{H}^{(k)}(1)}{k!}(-1)^k(1-L)^k$$

$$= \mathbf{b}(L)\mathbf{H}(L) - \mathbf{b}(L) \sum_{k=0}^{d-1} \frac{\mathbf{H}^{(k)}(1)}{k!}(-1)^k(1-L)^k$$

is a polynomial in L with zero derivatives of order $1, \ldots, d-1$, when evaluated in 1. From (i) it follows that this polynomial is divisible by $(1-L)^d$, that is, can be written as $(1-L)^d\mathbf{B}(L)$, where $\mathbf{B}$ is a polynomial. The result is derived by setting

$$\mathbf{R}(L) = \frac{\mathbf{B}(L)}{\mathbf{b}(L)}.$$

The exponentially decreasing behavior of the coefficients of $\mathbf{R}(L)$ comes from this expression in a rational fraction form. □

Replacing $\mathbf{H}(L)$ in the moving average representation by its Taylor expansion, we get

$$\mathbf{y}_t = \mathbf{H}(1)(1-L)^{-d}\tilde{\boldsymbol{\varepsilon}}_t - \mathbf{H}^{(1)}(1)(1-L)^{-d+1}\tilde{\boldsymbol{\varepsilon}}_t + \ldots$$
$$\frac{\mathbf{H}^{(d-1)}(1)(-1)^{d-1}}{(d-1)!}(1-L)^{-1}\tilde{\boldsymbol{\varepsilon}}_t + \mathbf{R}(L)\tilde{\boldsymbol{\varepsilon}}_t, \tag{11.3}$$

which is an expression where $\mathbf{y}_t$ appears as the sum of various components

$$\mathbf{y}_t = \mathbf{y}_t^{(d)} + \mathbf{y}_t^{(d-1)} + \ldots + \mathbf{y}_t^{(1)} + \mathbf{y}_t^{(0)}$$

with

$$\mathbf{y}_t^{(k)} = \begin{cases} (-1)^{d-k}\frac{H^{(d-k)}(1)}{(d-k)!}(1-L)^{-k}\tilde{\boldsymbol{\varepsilon}}_t & \text{if } k \geq 1 \\ \mathbf{R}(L)\tilde{\epsilon}_t & \text{if } k = 0. \end{cases}$$

The component $\mathbf{y}_t^{(0)}$ is asymptotically stationary, because of the hypothesis made on $\det(\boldsymbol{\Phi}(L))$ which implies that $\mathbf{R}(L)$ has coefficients exponentially approaching 0. The other components $\mathbf{y}_t^{(k)}$ are in general nonstationary with a nonstationarity degree equal to $k - \frac{1}{2}$. Thus the larger k, the more rapidly the corresponding component diverges.

Remark 11.1: Such a decomposition of the series into components with different degrees of nonstationarity is not unique. Without modifying the degrees, we could have taken

$$\mathbf{y}_t = \left(\mathbf{y}_t^{(d)} + \frac{\mathbf{y}_t^{(d-1)}}{2}\right) + \frac{\mathbf{y}_t^{(d-1)}}{2} + \mathbf{y}_t^{(d-2)} + \ldots$$

The dominant component would have been

$$\tilde{\mathbf{y}}_t^{(d)} = \left(\mathbf{y}_t^{(d)} + \frac{\mathbf{y}_t^{(d-1)}}{2}\right) = \frac{\mathbf{H}(1) - \frac{1}{2}\mathbf{H}^{(1)}(1)(1-L)}{(1-L)^d}\tilde{\boldsymbol{\varepsilon}}_t.$$

We can verify that the decomposition chosen above is the one for which the dominant component admits an ARMA representation with the smallest autoregressive order (here d), and then conditional on the AR order, the smallest moving average order (here 0). In this *canonical decomposition* the components are chosen so as to obtain the most parsimonious dynamic representation.

Remark 11.2: The assumption on the initial values $\mathbf{y} : \mathbf{y}_t = 0 \ \forall \ t \leq 0$ is not neutral with respect to this decomposition. In fact, had we introduced nonzero initial conditions, their effect on the series would have corresponded to a solution of the homogeneous difference equation $\boldsymbol{\Phi}(L)\mathbf{y}_t = 0$. Since $\boldsymbol{\Phi}(L)$ admits d unit roots, this solution is in general of order $d - 1$. This effect can dominate all components $\mathbf{y}_t^{(d-1)}, \ldots, \mathbf{y}_t^{(1)}, \mathbf{y}_t^{(0)}$. Only the dominant component $\mathbf{y}_t^{(d)}$ is not sensitive to the choice of initial values. The same kind of remark can be done for the case where a constant term is introduced in the model (cf. exercise 11.4).

Note that so far we have supposed that the dominant component is the one of order d, i.e., we have assumed that $\mathbf{H}(1) \neq 0$, or that $1 - L$ cannot be factorized in $\mathbf{H}(L)$. This is not always the case, as shown in the following example.

Example 11.1: Let us consider a model of the type

$$(1 - L)\boldsymbol{\phi}(L)\mathbf{y}_t = \boldsymbol{\Theta}(L)\tilde{\boldsymbol{\varepsilon}}_t,$$

where $\det(\boldsymbol{\phi}(L))$ has all roots outside the unit circle. The direct application of the decomposition consists in computing the determinant of the autoregressive polynomial, which here contains a unit root with multiplicity n equal to the dimension of the series

$$\det\left((1-L)\phi(L)\right) = (1-L)^n \det(\phi(L)).$$

Thus we have a decomposition of the type

$$\mathbf{y}_t = \mathbf{y}_t^{(n)} + \mathbf{y}_t^{(n-1)} + \ldots + \mathbf{y}_t^{(1)} + \mathbf{y}_t^{(0)}.$$

However, in this simple case, we see that the first components $\mathbf{y}_t^{(n)}$, $\mathbf{y}_t^{(n-1)}$, ..., $\mathbf{y}_t^{(2)}$ are all 0. In fact, we can write

$$\mathbf{y}_t = \frac{1}{1-L}\phi(L)^{-1}\boldsymbol{\Theta}(L)\tilde{\boldsymbol{\epsilon}}_t$$

$$= \frac{\phi(1)^{-1}\boldsymbol{\Theta}(1)}{1-L}\tilde{\boldsymbol{\epsilon}}_t + \frac{\phi(L)^{-1}\boldsymbol{\Theta}(L) - \phi(1)^{-1}\boldsymbol{\Theta}(1)}{1-L}\tilde{\boldsymbol{\epsilon}}_t,$$

with only the components $\mathbf{y}_t^{(1)}$ and $\mathbf{y}_t^{(0)}$ appearing in the expression.

Example 11.2: The various coordinates of the series do not necessarily have the same rate of divergence. Let us consider a bivariate series of the type

$$(1-L)\begin{pmatrix} y_{1t} \\ y_{2t} \end{pmatrix} = \begin{pmatrix} 1-L & L \\ 0 & 1-L \end{pmatrix}\begin{pmatrix} \tilde{\epsilon}_{1t} \\ \tilde{\epsilon}_{2t} \end{pmatrix}.$$

We have

$$\begin{cases} y_{1t} = \tilde{\epsilon}_{1t} + \dfrac{L\tilde{\epsilon}_{2t}}{1-L} \\[2mm] y_{2t} = \tilde{\epsilon}_{2t} \end{cases} \Leftrightarrow \begin{cases} y_{1t} = \dfrac{\tilde{\epsilon}_{2t}}{1-L} + \tilde{\epsilon}_{1t} - \tilde{\epsilon}_{2t} \\[2mm] y_{2t} = \tilde{\epsilon}_{2t}. \end{cases}$$

The first coordinate is explosive, whereas the second is stationary. By the same token, we see from this example that the innovation in $\mathbf{y}_{1t}$, i.e., $\tilde{\epsilon}_{1t}$, does not coincide with the innovation $\tilde{\epsilon}_{2t}$ of its dominant part. In fact, the latter forms the innovation of the second component y_{2t}.

This aspect of the innovations of the various components can be studied from the decomposition formula (11.3). As soon as $\mathbf{H}(0) = \mathbf{I}$, the innovation of $\mathbf{y}_t$ is $\tilde{\epsilon}_t$. The innovations of the explosive components $\mathbf{y}_t^{(k)}$, $k = 1, \ldots, d$ are

$$(-1)^{d-k}\frac{\mathbf{H}^{(d-k)}(1)}{(d-k)!}\tilde{\boldsymbol{\epsilon}}_t = (1-L)^k\mathbf{y}_t^{(k)}.$$

The innovation of the stationary part is given by

$$\left(\mathbf{I} - \sum_{k=0}^{d-1}(-1)^k\frac{\mathbf{H}^{(k)}(1)}{k!}\right)\tilde{\boldsymbol{\epsilon}}_t.$$

11.1.2 Transformation of the Components by Filtering

Let us consider a series $\{y_t\}$, admitting a decomposition of the type
(11.3)

$$\mathbf{y}_t = \mathbf{H}(1)(1-L)^{-d}\tilde{\boldsymbol{\varepsilon}}_t + \ldots + (-1)^{d-1}\frac{\mathbf{H}^{(d-1)}(1)}{(d-1)!}(1-L)^{(-1)}\tilde{\boldsymbol{\varepsilon}}_t + \mathbf{R}(L)\tilde{\boldsymbol{\varepsilon}}_t.$$

Let us assume that we transform this series with a linear filter $\mathbf{A}(L)$,
with exponentially decreasing coefficients. The new series is defined as

$$\mathbf{y}_t^* = \mathbf{A}(L)\mathbf{y}_t.$$

Replacing $\mathbf{y}_t$ by its expression as a function of the noise, we obtain a
moving average representation of the transformed series

$$\mathbf{y}_t^* = \frac{\mathbf{H}^*(L)}{(1-L)^d}\tilde{\boldsymbol{\varepsilon}}_t,$$

with $\mathbf{H}^*(L) = \mathbf{A}(L)\mathbf{H}(L)$.

Let us consider the decomposition of the transformed series. We can
write

$$\mathbf{y}_t^* = \mathbf{H}^*(1)(1-L)^{-d}\tilde{\boldsymbol{\varepsilon}}_t + \ldots$$

$$+ (-1)^{d-1}\frac{\mathbf{H}^{*(d-1)}(1)}{(d-1)!}(1-L)^{(-1)}\tilde{\boldsymbol{\varepsilon}}_t + \mathbf{R}^*(L)\tilde{\boldsymbol{\varepsilon}}_t.$$

Since $\mathbf{H}^*(L) = \mathbf{A}(L)\mathbf{H}(L)$, the various derivatives can be written as

$$\mathbf{H}^{*(p)}(1) = \sum_{k=0}^{p}\mathbf{C}_p^k\mathbf{A}^{(p-k)}(1)\mathbf{H}^{(k)}(1).$$

The k-th component of $\mathbf{y}_t^*$ is given by

$$\mathbf{y}_t^{*(k)} = (-1)^{d-k}\frac{\mathbf{H}^{*(d-k)}(1)}{(d-k)!}(1-L)^{(-k)}\tilde{\boldsymbol{\varepsilon}}_t$$

$$= \frac{(-1)^{d-k}}{(d-k)!}\sum_{j=k}^{d}\mathbf{C}_{d-k}^{j-k}\mathbf{A}^{(j-k)}(1)\mathbf{H}^{(d-j)}(1)(1-L)^{-k}\tilde{\boldsymbol{\varepsilon}}_t$$

$$= \sum_{j=k}^{d}(-1)^{j-k}\frac{\mathbf{A}^{(j-k)}(1)}{(j-k)!}(-1)^{d-j}\frac{\mathbf{H}^{(d-j)}(1)}{(d-j)!}(1-L)^{j-k}(1-L)^{-j}\tilde{\boldsymbol{\varepsilon}}_t$$

$$= \sum_{j=k}^{d}(-1)^{j-k}\frac{\mathbf{A}^{(j-k)}(1)}{(j-k)!}(1-L)^{j-k}\mathbf{y}_t^{(j)}.$$

Theorem 11.2: *Given a filter* $\mathbf{A}(L)$ *with exponentially decreasing coefficients (toward 0) and* $\mathbf{y}^*$ *the transformed series of* $\mathbf{y}$ *through this filter, the components of the transformed series can be derived from the components of the initial one through*

$$\mathbf{y}_t^{*(k)} = \sum_{j=k}^{d}(-1)^{j-k}\frac{\mathbf{A}^{(j-k)}(1)}{(j-k)!}(1-L)^{j-k}\mathbf{y}_t^{(j)},$$

i.e., the k-th component of the transformed series depends on the components with index k or higher in the initial series.

Example 11.3: Let us consider the case $d = 1$. We have

$$\mathbf{y}_t = \frac{\mathbf{H}(L)}{1-L}\tilde{\boldsymbol{\varepsilon}}_t = \frac{\mathbf{H}(1)}{1-L}\tilde{\boldsymbol{\varepsilon}}_t + \frac{\mathbf{H}(L) - \mathbf{H}(1)}{1-L}\tilde{\boldsymbol{\varepsilon}}_t,$$

which gives the decomposition of $\mathbf{y}$. The decomposition of $\mathbf{y}^*$ is

$$\mathbf{y}_t^* = \frac{\mathbf{A}(1)\mathbf{H}(1)}{1-L}\tilde{\boldsymbol{\varepsilon}}_t + \frac{\mathbf{A}(L)\mathbf{H}(L) - \mathbf{A}(1)\mathbf{H}(1)}{1-L}\tilde{\boldsymbol{\varepsilon}}_t,$$

$$= \mathbf{A}(1)\mathbf{y}_t^{(1)} + \left(\left(\mathbf{A}(L) - \mathbf{A}(1)\right)\mathbf{y}_t^{(1)} + \mathbf{A}(L)\mathbf{y}_t^{(0)}\right).$$

Note that the last term is stationary, since $\mathbf{A}(L) - \mathbf{A}(1)$ contains the factor $1 - L$ which takes away the nonstationarity from $\mathbf{y}_t^{(1)}$.

11.1.3 Cointegration

Integrated Series of Order d Let us consider a multivariate time series where all components have the same degree of nonstationarity. This means that the decomposition of the series $\mathbf{y}_t$ is such that

$$\mathbf{y}_t = \mathbf{H}(1)(1-L)^{-d}\tilde{\boldsymbol{\varepsilon}}_t + \ldots + (-1)^{d-1}\frac{\mathbf{H}^{d-1}(1)}{(d-1)!}(1-L)^{-1}\tilde{\boldsymbol{\varepsilon}}_t + \mathbf{R}(L)\tilde{\boldsymbol{\varepsilon}}_t$$

with no row of $\mathbf{H}(1)$ equal to 0.

We say that the series is integrated of order d with the notation

$$\mathbf{y}_t \sim I(d). \tag{11.4}$$

We can easily see that if $\bar{\mathbf{y}}$ and $\bar{\bar{\mathbf{y}}}$ are two series of the same dimension and integrated of order $\bar{d}$ and $\bar{\bar{d}}$, with $\bar{d} \neq \bar{\bar{d}}$, subject to the same disturbances or to independent disturbances, their sum $\bar{\mathbf{y}} + \bar{\bar{\mathbf{y}}}$ is an integrated series of order $\max(\bar{d}, \bar{\bar{d}})$. Moreover, if $\bar{d} = \bar{\bar{d}}$, we can have simplifications among dominant components, which may lead to a decrease in the degree of nonstationarity of some components.

Cointegrated Series Although each component y_{jt}, $j = 1, \ldots, n$ has an explosive behavior with a nonstationarity degree $d - \frac{1}{2}$, it may happen that some of the explosive evolutions be strongly related to each other. In particular, it may happen that some linear combination of the components

$$\alpha' \mathbf{y}_t = \sum_{j=1}^{n} \alpha_j y_{jt}$$

have a "more stationary" behavior than each component.

Definition 11.1: *The series* $\{y_{jt}\}$, $j = 1, \ldots, n$, *where* $\mathbf{y}_t$ *is integrated of order* d, *are called* cointegrated *if and only if there exists a nontrivial linear combination of the components which is integrated of order strictly smaller than* d.

A linear combination of the components $\alpha' \mathbf{y}_t$ admits the decomposition

$$\alpha' \mathbf{y}_t = \alpha' \mathbf{H}(1)(1 - L)^{-d} \tilde{\boldsymbol{\varepsilon}}_t + \ldots$$

$$+ (-1)^{d-1} \alpha' \frac{\mathbf{H}^{d-1}(1)}{(d-1)!} (1 - L)^{(-1)} \tilde{\boldsymbol{\varepsilon}}_t + \alpha' \mathbf{R}(L) \tilde{\boldsymbol{\varepsilon}}_t.$$

The dominant component disappears if and only if $\alpha' \mathbf{H}(1) = 0$.

Theorem 11.3: *The series* $\{y_{jt}\}$, $j = 1, \ldots, n$ *are cointegrated if and only if the nullspace of* $\mathbf{H}(1)'$, $\mathcal{N}(\mathbf{H}(1)')$ *is not empty, that is if* $\mathbf{H}(1)$ *is singular. In this case, the linear combinations with smaller nonstationarity degrees are obtained for all nonzero vectors* α *belonging to* $\mathcal{N}(\mathbf{H}(1)')$. *These vectors are called* cointegrating *vectors.*

Remark 11.3: Note that in the presence of cointegration there is an infinity of cointegrating vectors.

Degree of Cointegration If the series $\{y_{jt}\}$, $j = 1, \ldots, n$, are cointegrated and if α is a cointegrating vector, the degree of nonstationarity of $\alpha' \mathbf{y}_t$ may, in principle, take different values. It may happen, in fact, that several dominant components of $\mathbf{y}_t$ are simultaneously put to 0 in the combination $\alpha' \mathbf{y}_t$. In order to clarify this concept, let us introduce some vector subspaces of $\mathbb{R}^n$

$$E_k = \cap_{j=k+1}^{d} \mathcal{N}\left(\mathbf{H}^{(d-j)}(1)' \right), \quad k = 0, 1, \ldots, d - 1. \tag{11.5}$$

These subspaces have the property

$$E_0 \subset E_1 \subset \ldots \subset E_{d-1}.$$

If a nonzero vector $\boldsymbol{\alpha}$ belongs to E_k, the combination $\boldsymbol{\alpha}'\mathbf{y}_t$ admits a dominant term with a nonstationarity degree smaller than or equal to $k - \frac{1}{2}$. Moreover if $\boldsymbol{\alpha}$ does not belong to E_{k-1}, the nonstationarity degree of $\boldsymbol{\alpha}'\mathbf{y}_t$ is exactly $k - \frac{1}{2}$. In particular the nonzero elements of E_0, if they exist, correspond to some stationary combinations $\boldsymbol{\alpha}'\mathbf{y}_t$ of the nonstationary series $\{y_{jt}\}$, $j = 1, \ldots, n$.

Definition 11.2: *The degree of cointegration of the vector* $\mathbf{y}$ *is equal to* b *(integer smaller than or equal to d) if and only if*

$$E_{d-b} \neq \{\mathbf{0}\} \quad \text{and} \quad E_{d-b-1} = \{\mathbf{0}\}.$$

A vector $\boldsymbol{\alpha} \neq \mathbf{0}$ *is called a cointegrating vector of degree* $b(\boldsymbol{\alpha})$ *if* $\boldsymbol{\alpha} \in E_{d-b(\alpha)}$ *and* $\boldsymbol{\alpha} \notin E_{d-b(\alpha)-1}$ *(it follows that it must be $b(\alpha) \leq b$). In this case, we can write*

$$\mathbf{y}_t \sim CI(d, b). \tag{11.6}$$

Relationships among Components It is interesting to stress the mathematical interpretation of the cointegration condition. $\boldsymbol{\alpha}$ is a cointegrating vector of degree 1 if $\boldsymbol{\alpha}'\mathbf{H}(1) = 0$ or, equivalently, if $\boldsymbol{\alpha}'\mathbf{y}_t^{(d)} = 0$. Thus, there is a static (i.e., without lagged variables) *deterministic relationship*, among the various dominant components of the various series. Let us consider a vector $\boldsymbol{\alpha}$ with the degree of cointegration equal to 2. We have at the same time $\boldsymbol{\alpha}'\mathbf{H}(1) = 0$, $\boldsymbol{\alpha}'\mathbf{H}^{(1)}(1) = 0$, that is $\boldsymbol{\alpha}'\mathbf{y}_t^{(d)} = 0$ and $\boldsymbol{\alpha}'\mathbf{y}_t^{(d-1)} = 0$. The static deterministic relationship exists simultaneously for the first two dominant components. We will see in section 11.2 that it is sometimes possible to give to these relationships a meaning of *long-term equilibrium*.

Dynamic Cointegration There is no a priori reason to look just for static links among dominant components. Analogously, we could be interested in dynamic links implying a small number of lags. To make this point clear, let us see under which conditions a combination of $\mathbf{y}_t$ and $\mathbf{y}_{t-1}$, or, which is the same, of $\mathbf{y}_t$ and $\Delta\mathbf{y}_t$, can decrease the degree of nonstationarity. Such a combination can be written as $\boldsymbol{\alpha}'\mathbf{y}_t + \boldsymbol{\beta}'\Delta\mathbf{y}_t$. By looking at the two first dominating components we have

$$\boldsymbol{\alpha}'\mathbf{y}_t + \boldsymbol{\beta}'\Delta\mathbf{y}_t = \frac{\boldsymbol{\alpha}'\mathbf{H}(1)}{(1-L)^d}\tilde{\epsilon}_t + \left(-\frac{\boldsymbol{\alpha}'\mathbf{H}^{(1)}(1)}{(1-L)^{d-1}}\tilde{\epsilon}_t + \frac{\boldsymbol{\beta}'\mathbf{H}(1)}{(1-L)^{d-1}}\tilde{\epsilon}_t \right) + \cdots$$

In order to eliminate the first component, we need $\boldsymbol{\alpha}$ to be a cointegrating vector. However, we see that if $\boldsymbol{\alpha}'\mathbf{H}^{(1)}(1) \neq 0$ that is if the cointegration degree associated with $\boldsymbol{\alpha}$ is equal to 1, it is sometimes possible to equate to 0 also the second component. In order to do that we need $\boldsymbol{\alpha}, \boldsymbol{\beta}$ to be such that

$$\boldsymbol{\alpha}'\mathbf{H}(1) = \mathbf{0}$$

$$-\boldsymbol{\alpha}'\mathbf{H}^{(1)}(1) + \boldsymbol{\beta}'\mathbf{H}(1) = \mathbf{0}.$$

The condition of dynamic cointegration with a single lag dynamics is

$$\mathcal{N} \begin{pmatrix} \mathbf{H}(1)' & \mathbf{0} \\ \mathbf{H}^{(1)}(1)' & \mathbf{H}(1)' \end{pmatrix} \neq \mathbf{0}. \qquad (11.7)$$

Example 11.4:

(i)   Let us consider a very simple model defined as

$$y_{1t} - y_{1,t-1} + y_{1t} + y_{2t} = \epsilon_{1t},$$

$$y_{1t} - y_{1,t-1} + y_{2t} - y_{2,t-1} = \epsilon_{2t}.$$

Using the lag polynomials, we have

$$\begin{pmatrix} 2-L & 1 \\ 1-L & 1-L \end{pmatrix} \mathbf{y}_t = \boldsymbol{\varepsilon}_t$$

$$\Leftrightarrow (1-L)^2 \mathbf{y}_t = \begin{pmatrix} 1-L & -1 \\ -(1-L) & 2-L \end{pmatrix} \boldsymbol{\varepsilon}_t,$$

$$\mathbf{y}_t = \begin{pmatrix} 0 & -1 \\ 0 & 1 \end{pmatrix} \frac{\boldsymbol{\varepsilon}_t}{(1-L)^2} + \begin{pmatrix} 1 & 0 \\ -1 & 1 \end{pmatrix} \frac{\boldsymbol{\varepsilon}_t}{(1-L)}.$$

The process is integrated of order 2. (ii)   We have

$$\mathcal{N} \begin{pmatrix} 0 & -1 \\ 0 & 1 \end{pmatrix}' = \mathcal{N} \begin{pmatrix} 0 & 0 \\ -1 & 1 \end{pmatrix},$$

which is spanned by the vector $\begin{pmatrix} 1 \\ 1 \end{pmatrix}$, so that a combination of the type $y_{1t} + y_{2t}$ has a smaller degree of nonstationarity. Moreover, we see that

$$(1 \ \ 1) \begin{pmatrix} 1 & 0 \\ -1 & 1 \end{pmatrix} \neq 0,$$

so that $y_{1t} + y_{2t} \sim I(1)$ and $\mathbf{y}_t \sim CI(2,1)$. (iii)   Let us examine now the possibility of a dynamic cointegration through the nullspace

$$\mathcal{N} \begin{pmatrix} 0 & 0 & 0 & 0 \\ -1 & 1 & 0 & 0 \\ 1 & -1 & 0 & 0 \\ 0 & 1 & -1 & 1 \end{pmatrix}.$$

An element of the nullspace must satisfy the relationships

$$-\alpha_1 + \alpha_2 = 0,$$

$$\alpha_1 - \alpha_2 = 0,$$

$$\alpha_2 - \beta_1 + \beta_2 = 0.$$

These vectors can be written as

$$\begin{pmatrix} \alpha \\ \alpha \\ \alpha + \beta \\ \beta \end{pmatrix}.$$

The corresponding dynamic combinations are

$$\alpha \left(y_{1t} + y_{2t} + \Delta y_{1t} \right) + \beta \Delta \left(y_{1t} + y_{2t} \right),$$

and are integrated of order 0, that is, are stationary.

11.1.4 Frequency Domain

The definition of cointegration refers mainly to the components associated with the autoregressive unit root, that is the components associated with low frequencies. This suggests characterization of the phenomenon in the frequency domain. Since the series are nonstationary, we cannot utilize the spectral representation theorem. However, we have seen that the concept of spectral density can be extended to the case of ARIMA models.

Pseudo-spectrum For notational convenience, we restrict ourselves to a model of the type

$$(1 - L)\phi(L)\mathbf{y}_t = \mathbf{\Theta}(L)\tilde{\boldsymbol{\varepsilon}}_t,$$

where $\det \phi(L)$ has all its roots outside the unit circle and the noise variance is $\mathrm{var}(\tilde{\boldsymbol{\varepsilon}}_t) = \mathbf{\Sigma}$.

The pseudo-spectrum is defined as

$$\mathbf{f}(\omega) = \frac{1}{2\pi} \frac{\phi(\exp(i\omega))^{-1}\mathbf{\Theta}(\exp(i\omega))\mathbf{\Sigma}\mathbf{\Theta}'(\exp(i\omega))\phi'(\exp(-i\omega))^{-1}}{\mid 1 - \exp(i\omega) \mid^2}.$$

This matrix, the elements of which are rational fractions in $\exp(i\omega)$, is defined for all ω's but $\omega = 0$. In this case, some elements are infinite because of the factor $\mid 1 - \exp(i\omega) \mid^{-2}$; this simply corresponds to the nonstationarity of the series $\mathbf{y}$. The series is cointegrated if and only if $\mathbf{H}(1) = \boldsymbol{\phi}(1)^{-1}\boldsymbol{\Theta}(1)$ is singular, or, equivalently, if and only if $\mathbf{H}(1)\boldsymbol{\Sigma}\mathbf{H}(1)'$ is singular.

Theorem 11.4: *The series* $\mathbf{y}$ *following an ARIMA process*

$$(1 - L)\boldsymbol{\phi}(L)\mathbf{y}_t = \boldsymbol{\Theta}(L)\tilde{\boldsymbol{\varepsilon}}_t$$

is cointegrated if and only if its pseudo-spectrum is such that

$$\lim_{\omega \to 0} \mid 1 - \exp(i\omega) \mid^2 \mathbf{f}(\omega)$$

has a 0 determinant.

Pseudo-coherence   This property can be described in an equivalent form by introducing the pseudo-coherences among the components of the series. By analogy with the stationary case, let us define the *pseudo-coherence* between y_i and y_j as

$$K_{ij}(\omega) = \frac{f_{ij}(\omega)}{\sqrt{f_{ii}(\omega)f_{jj}(\omega)}},$$

where $f_{ij}(\omega)$ is the i, j-th element of the pseudo-spectrum.

Let us set $\mathbf{f}^{(1)}(\omega) = \mid 1 - \exp(i\omega) \mid^2 \mathbf{f}(\omega)$ the spectral density of the differenced process $(1 - L)\mathbf{y}$ (which is asymptotically stationary) and

$$K_{ij}^{(1)}(\omega) = \frac{f_{ij}^{(1)}(\omega)}{\sqrt{f_{ii}^{(1)}(\omega)f_{jj}^{(1)}(\omega)}}$$

the coherence between the i-th and j-th components of the differenced process. Note that it is equivalent to evaluating the pseudo-coherences on the initial process or on the differenced process

$$K_{ij}(\omega) = K_{ij}^{(1)}(\omega).$$

Moreover, the theorem below expresses the existence of a strict link among the low frequency components, in the case of cointegration.

Theorem 11.5: *The components of the vector* $\mathbf{y}$ *following an ARIMA process are cointegrated if and only if the determinant of the matrix of the pseudo-coherences evaluated at 0 is 0 itself, that is*

$$\det(\mathbf{K}(0)) = 0.$$

Example 11.5: In the case $n = 3$, this condition can be written as

$$\det \begin{vmatrix} 1 & K_{12}(0) & K_{13}(0) \\ K_{21}(0) & 1 & K_{23}(0) \\ K_{31}(0) & K_{32}(0) & 1 \end{vmatrix}$$

$$= 1 - \mid K_{12}(0) \mid^2 - \mid K_{13}(0) \mid^2 - \mid K_{23}(0) \mid^2 +$$

$$- K_{12}(0)K_{23}(0)K_{31}(0) - K_{21}(0)K_{13}(0)K_{32}(0)$$

$$= 0.$$

11.1.5 Explanatory Models and Shock Transmission

A Recursive Model In practice, the explanatory models make a difference between the exogenous variables x and the endogenous ones y (cf. chapter 10). In the univariate case and for a strictly exogenous x the model may be written as

$$\begin{cases} a(L)y_t + b(L)x_t = \tilde{\epsilon}_{1t}, \\ (1 - L)c(L)x_t = \tilde{\epsilon}_{2t}, \end{cases}$$

where $a(L)$ and $c(L)$ are lag polynomials with roots strictly outside the unit circle, and $\tilde{\epsilon}_{1t}, \tilde{\epsilon}_{2t}$ represent uncorrelated noises.

The bivariate autoregressive representation of the model is

$$\begin{pmatrix} a(L) & b(L) \\ 0 & (1-L)c(L) \end{pmatrix} \begin{pmatrix} y_t \\ x_t \end{pmatrix} = \begin{pmatrix} \tilde{\epsilon}_{1t} \\ \tilde{\epsilon}_{2t} \end{pmatrix},$$

and its moving average representation can be written as

$$\begin{pmatrix} y_t \\ x_t \end{pmatrix} = \frac{1}{(1-L)a(L)c(L)} \begin{pmatrix} (1-L)c(L) & -b(L) \\ 0 & a(L) \end{pmatrix} \begin{pmatrix} \tilde{\epsilon}_{1t} \\ \tilde{\epsilon}_{2t} \end{pmatrix}.$$

We can easily isolate the dominant components, by introducing the polynomials $b^*(L), a^*(L)$ defined through the relationships

$$b(L) = b(1) + (1 - L)b^*(L),$$

$$a(L) = a(1) + (1 - L)a^*(L).$$

We have

$$\begin{pmatrix} y_t \\ x_t \end{pmatrix} = \frac{1}{(1-L)a(L)c(L)} \begin{pmatrix} 0 & -b(1) \\ 0 & a(1) \end{pmatrix} \begin{pmatrix} \tilde{\epsilon}_{1t} \\ \tilde{\epsilon}_{2t} \end{pmatrix}$$

$$+ \frac{1}{a(L)c(L)} \begin{pmatrix} c(L) & -b^*(L) \\ 0 & a^*(L) \end{pmatrix} \begin{pmatrix} \tilde{\epsilon}_{1t} \\ \tilde{\epsilon}_{2t} \end{pmatrix}.$$

Thus the recursive form of the model and the introduction of a non-stationarity in the process x imply that these processes x and y are cointegrated. Moreover, a stationary combination of these processes is

$$y_t + \frac{b(1)}{a(1)} x_t.$$

Sustained Shock on the Control Variable Let us assume that the variable x may be interpreted as a control variable and that the changes in y from changes in x may be calculated from the first equation of the system

$$a(L)y_t + b(L)x_t = \tilde{\epsilon}_{1t}.$$

A sustained shock of Δx on the variables x_t, $t \geq 0$ implies a long-term change in y equal to $-\frac{b(1)}{a(1)}\Delta x$. Therefore we see that the stationary combination of the process $y_t + \frac{b(1)}{a(1)} x_t$ can be interpreted as the deviation between the process y and the process $-\frac{b(1)}{a(1)} x$ representing the long-term effect of x on y.

Transitory Shock on the Innovation of the Explanatory Variable We may as well introduce other types of shocks (cf. section 10.3) on the explanatory variable, for example shocks on the innovation $\tilde{\epsilon}_2$. Let us assume that the innovation at time $t = 0$ is modified by $\Delta\epsilon_{20}$, so that it will have an effect on all the future values of the explanatory process. In fact, the moving average representation of x_t is of the form $x_t = \sum_{j=0}^{t} h_j \tilde{\epsilon}_{2,t-j}$, where the coefficients h_j, derived from the long division of 1 by $(1-L)c(L)$, tend asymptotically to a nonzero value h_∞. The long-term effect on x of a transitory change in $\tilde{\epsilon}_2$ is therefore nonzero. The same line of reasoning is valid for all combinations of x and y admitting a dominant nonstationary component.

On the other hand, the moving average representation of $y_t + \frac{b(1)}{a(1)}x_t$ involves moving average coefficients asymptotically tending to 0. Thus, a transitory shock on the innovation of the explanatory variable has a persistent effect on all the nonstationary combinations of x and y, but it has an asymptotically zero effect on the combination $y_t + \frac{b(1)}{a(1)}x_t$ corresponding to the cointegrating vector.

11.1.6 Steady Growth Path

The ideas of dominant components and of cointegration are strongly related to the practice by macroeconometricians of examining the steady state representation of a given model. The fact that this line of reasoning usually starts from a deterministic model does not prevent from drawing an analogy between the two approaches.

The Usual Approach Let us consider a dynamic macroeconometric model written as

$$\mathbf{y}(t) = f\left(\mathbf{y}(t), \mathbf{y}(t-1), \mathbf{x}(t)\right), \quad t \geq 0,$$

where $\mathbf{y}(t)$ is an $(n \times 1)$ vector of endogenous variables and $\mathbf{x}(t)$ is an $(m \times 1)$ vector of exogenous variables.

A solution $\{(\mathbf{x}(t), \mathbf{y}(t)), t \geq 0\}$ of this system is called a *steady growth path* solution if it has the form

$$\mathbf{x}_i^*(t) = \mathbf{x}_i^*(0)a_i^t, \ i = 1, \ldots, m, \ (a_i > 1),$$

$$\mathbf{y}_j^*(t) = \mathbf{y}_j^*(0)b_j^t, \ j = 1, \ldots, n, \ (b_j > 1).$$

It is common practice to investigate whether the model is compatible with these paths and possibly to modify its specification in order to achieve such a compatibility. With this respecification, we show that in the usual macroeconometric models all the growth rates of the endogenous variables $b_1, b_2, \ldots, b_n$ can be derived from some base rates. Oftentimes three exogenous growth rates are used, that is,

η the exogenous population growth rate,

γ the exogenous technological progress growth rate,

m the exogenous money supply growth rate or ρ_e the foreign price growth rate.

Generally, the endogenous variables corresponding to levels evolve following the same growth rate g such that $(1 + g) = (1 + \eta)(1 + \gamma)$.

The Relationship with Cointegration We can immediately see three differences with respect to the specification used until now:

(i)   The model is deterministic;

(ii)   The growth is assumed of an exponential and not a polynomial type;

(iii)   The solution has a simple form.

The choice of exponential evolution is to be interpreted as a convention, since a simple logarithmic transformation leads to linear evolutions. On the other hand, the choice of a strictly exponential form is not necessary to obtain the fundamental result about the links among growth rates. These results can also be obtained if we just assume that the variables have dominant components of an exponential type

$$\mathbf{x}_i(t) = \mathbf{x}_i^*(0)a_i^t + o(a_i^t), \ i = 1, \ldots, m,$$

$$\mathbf{y}_j(t) = \mathbf{y}_j^*(0)b_j^t + o(b_j^t), \ j = 1, \ldots, n.$$

In order to interpret the relationships among growth rates of the type $(1 + g) = (1 + \eta)(1 + \gamma)$, let us consider some variables such that

$$y_1(t) = y_1^*(0)(1 + g)^t + o\left((1 + g)^t\right),$$

$$x_1(t) = x_1^*(0)(1 + \eta)^t + o\left((1 + \eta)^t\right),$$

$$x_2(t) = x_2^*(0)(1 + \gamma)^t + o\left((1 + \gamma)^t\right).$$

We have

$$\log y_1(t) = t\log(1 + g) + o\left(t\right),$$

$$\log x_1(t) = t\log(1 + \eta) + o\left(t\right),$$

$$\log x_2(t) = t\log(1 + \gamma) + o\left(t\right).$$

The existence of the relationship $(1 + g) = (1 + \eta)(1 + \gamma)$ implies that some linear combinations of the variables expressed in logarithms have some dominant terms of order strictly smaller than t. Thus we have

$$\log y_1(t) - \log x_1(t) - \log x_2(t) = o(t),$$

providing a condition very similar to the one defining cointegration with cointegrating vectors given a priori.

11.2 Some Relationships with Macroeconometric Modeling: Error Correction Models and Cointegration

Although the ARIMA models were first introduced for forecasting purposes, we have already noted in chapter 10 that they may prove useful in order to understand the mechanisms ruling the dynamics of a macroeconometric model or to derive its specification. In this respect, we have examined the notions of causality and of shock transmission.

The presence of trending variables and the properties of cointegration can be examined in the perspective of explanatory model building. The model building process follows two steps:

(i)   economic theory or some intuitive line of reasoning is used to obtain some equations linking the variables of interest; the resulting system is basically static;

(ii) this system is augmented by considering the dynamic aspect, in order to capture a number of phenomena which should be modeled in a specific way: technological progress, expectations by the economic agents, behavioral changes, adjustment costs, learning, and so on.

The basic static model often allows for an interpretation in terms of long-run equilibrium, whereas the additional dynamics can be interpreted as the result of the adjustment around this equilibrium. The intuition behind a separation between short- and long-run is appealing: the aim of this section is to propose other representations for ARIMA models, where such a separation is made evident.

11.2.1 Error Correction Models (ECM)

A Model for Targets and Adjustment Costs Control theory is one of the tools used to specify models. It starts from the assumption that a decision maker wishes to fix the values of some economically important variables or to specify the relationship among them. Thus, for example, a government might decide to control the ratio of the budget deficit to GNP, to set the wage increase equal to inflation, and so on.

Let us denote by $\mathbf{y} = (y_1, y_2, \ldots, y_n)'$ the variables of interest on which we can define some objectives specified in the form of relationships (called *target* relationships) which these variables should satisfy. For the sake of simplicity, let us assume that these relationships are linear, so that the objectives can be written as

$$\boldsymbol{\alpha}'\mathbf{y}_t = \mathbf{0}. \tag{11.8}$$

Evidently, these target relationships will not be satisfied in practice because of adjustment or transaction costs, or because of a stochastic environment.

The adjustment costs are a function of the importance of the changes made to the variables. These changes can be measured in levels

$$\Delta \mathbf{y}_t = \mathbf{y}_t - \mathbf{y}_{t-1}$$

or in growth rates

$$\Delta^2 \mathbf{y}_t = \mathbf{y}_t - \mathbf{y}_{t-1} - (\mathbf{y}_{t-1} - \mathbf{y}_{t-2}).$$

The decision maker takes into account the desired objectives and the ensuing costs. In a simple formulation, we can assume that he fixes the values $\mathbf{y}_t$ which minimize the criterion function

$$\min \left(\boldsymbol{\alpha}'\mathbf{y}_t\right)' \boldsymbol{\Omega}_1 \left(\boldsymbol{\alpha}'\mathbf{y}_t\right) + \left(\Delta\mathbf{y}_t\right)' \boldsymbol{\Omega}_2 \left(\Delta\mathbf{y}_t\right) + \left(\Delta^2\mathbf{y}_t\right)' \boldsymbol{\Omega}_3 \left(\Delta^2\mathbf{y}_t\right),$$

where $\boldsymbol{\Omega}_j$, $j = 1, 2, 3$ are positive definite matrices of appropriate size.

The solution to this optimization problem is such that

$$\boldsymbol{\alpha}\boldsymbol{\Omega}_1\boldsymbol{\alpha}'\mathbf{y}_t + \boldsymbol{\Omega}_2\Delta\mathbf{y}_t + \boldsymbol{\Omega}_3\Delta^2\mathbf{y}_t = \mathbf{0}, \tag{11.9}$$

which is a relationship between the errors made on the objectives $\boldsymbol{\alpha}'\mathbf{y}_t$ (the so-called tracking errors, in general nonzero) and the adjustments

$\Delta \mathbf{y}_t$, $\Delta^2 \mathbf{y}_t$. This relationship is dynamic but deterministic. The introduction of a stochastic term can be done in two different ways. We can either add an error term to the deterministic equation (11.9), by changing it to

$$\alpha \mathbf{\Omega}_1 \alpha' \mathbf{y}_t + \mathbf{\Omega}_2 \Delta \mathbf{y}_t + \mathbf{\Omega}_3 \Delta^2 \mathbf{y}_t = \epsilon_t \qquad (11.10)$$

or we could start from a stochastic target equation $\alpha' \mathbf{y}_t = \epsilon_t$ in the place of $\alpha' \mathbf{y}_t = \mathbf{0}$ which would provide a similar result.

11.2.2 Definitions

By analogy with the equation (11.10) let us introduce the following definition:

Definition 11.3: *A dynamic linear system of the type*

$$\mathbf{C} \alpha' \mathbf{y}_t + \sum_{j=1}^{\infty} \mathbf{B}_j \Delta^j \mathbf{y}_t = \epsilon_t, \quad t \geq 0,$$

where α' is an $(r \times n)$ matrix of rank r and $\mathbf{C}$ is an $(n \times r)$ of rank r, is called an Error Correction Model – *ECM*.

The interest of such a representation is clear. Thinking of it as the outcome of an optimization process based on the concepts of targets and of adjustment costs, the parameters α', $\mathbf{C}$ and $\mathbf{B}_j$ have precise interpretations. α' provides the coefficients to the target equations, and the parameters $\mathbf{C}$ and $\mathbf{B}_j$ summarize the cost and the utility of the decision maker. It is then natural to introduce constraints on the coefficients through α, for example, rather than through the combined coefficients such as the coefficient on $\mathbf{y}_t$, i.e. $\mathbf{C} \alpha' + \sum_{j=1}^{\infty} \mathbf{B}_j$.

11.2.3 ECM Representation of a Dynamic Model

Let us consider the constraints imposed on a dynamic model in order for the ECM representation to exist. In fact, we will see that, in general, any model can be written in this form. It would be preferable, therefore, to talk about an error correction *form* or *representation*, rather than an error correction *model*.

The Case of an Autoregressive Model Let us consider an autoregressive process defined as

$$\Phi(L)\mathbf{y}_t = \tilde{\epsilon}_t, \qquad (11.11)$$

where $\Phi(L)$ is a matrix polynomial of degree p with $\Phi(0) = \mathbf{I}$ and where

$\mathbf{y}_t = 0$ if $t \leq 0$. Let us assume that the roots of $\det(\mathbf{\Phi}(L))$ are greater than or equal to 1 in modulus.

Theorem 11.6: *An autoregressive model admits an error correction representation*

$$\mathbf{\Phi}(1)\mathbf{y}_t + \sum_{j=1}^{p} \tilde{\mathbf{\Phi}}_j \Delta^j \mathbf{y}_t = \tilde{\boldsymbol{\varepsilon}}_t.$$

PROOF: The polynomial $\mathbf{\Phi}(L)$ can be written as

$$\mathbf{\Phi}(L) = \mathbf{\Phi}(1) + \sum_{j=1}^{p} \tilde{\mathbf{\Phi}}_j (1 - L)^j,$$

with

$$\tilde{\mathbf{\Phi}}_j = \frac{(-1)^j}{j!} \mathbf{\Phi}^{(j)}(1),$$

hence the result. □

We can then write the model in the error correction representation of definition 11.3 by posing $\mathbf{\Phi}(1) = \mathbf{C}\boldsymbol{\alpha}'$. It is apparent that this representation is not unique. However, the number of rows r of $\boldsymbol{\alpha}'$ (or of columns of $\mathbf{C}$) is clearly defined since it is equal to the rank of $\mathbf{\Phi}(1)$. The rank of $\mathbf{\Phi}(1)$ has a simple interpretation in terms of structural parameters, since it provides the number of underlying equilibrium relationships.

Let us consider in particular the case where $\mathbf{y}_t$ is integrated of order 1, which can be written as

$$(1 - L)\mathbf{y}_t = \mathbf{H}(L)\tilde{\boldsymbol{\varepsilon}}_t, \tag{11.12}$$

where $\mathbf{H}(L)$ is a matrix series in L (whose terms decrease exponentially) such that no row in $\mathbf{H}(1)$ is 0. This condition implies, in particular, that 1 is a root of $\det(\mathbf{\Phi}(L))$ with multiplicity order $d \geq 1$. Thus we have $\det(\mathbf{\Phi}(L)) = (1 - L)^d \phi(L)$, the roots of $\phi(L)$ being strictly greater than 1 in modulus; as a consequence, the model can also be written as

$$(1 - L)^d \mathbf{y}_t = \frac{\mathbf{\Phi}^*(L)}{\phi(L)} \tilde{\boldsymbol{\varepsilon}}_t, \tag{11.13}$$

where $\mathbf{\Phi}^*(L)$ is the adjoint of $\mathbf{\Phi}(L)$. By comparing (11.12) and (11.13) we get

$$\mathbf{\Phi}^*(L) = \phi(L)\mathbf{H}(L)(1 - L)^{d-1} = \bar{\mathbf{\Phi}}(L)(1 - L)^{d-1},$$

where

$$\bar{\mathbf{\Phi}}(L) = \phi(L)\mathbf{H}(L).$$

We have then $\bar{\mathbf{\Phi}}(1) = \phi(1)\mathbf{H}(1)$, and since $\phi(1)$ is a nonzero scalar, the nullspaces of $\bar{\Phi}'(1)$ and of $\mathbf{H}'(1)$ are the same. On this basis we can show the following

Theorem 11.7: **Engle–Granger Representation Theorem**
(Engle and Granger, 1987)

(i) *The series* **y** *is not cointegrated if and only if the model (11.11) can be written as*

$$\tilde{\Phi}(L)\Delta\mathbf{y}_t = \tilde{\boldsymbol{\varepsilon}}_t,$$

where $\tilde{\Phi}(L)$ is a matrix polynomial of degree $p-1$ such that the roots of $\det(\tilde{\Phi}(L))$ are strictly outside of the unit circle.

(ii) *If the series* **y** *is cointegrated and if $\boldsymbol{\alpha}'$ is a matrix $(r \times n)$ the rows of which are independent cointegrating vectors, the model (11.11) admits an error correction representation of the type*

$$\mathbf{D}\boldsymbol{\alpha}'\mathbf{y}_t + \tilde{\Phi}(L)\Delta\mathbf{y}_t = \tilde{\boldsymbol{\varepsilon}}_t,$$

where $\mathbf{D}$ is a matrix $(n \times r)$ and $\tilde{\Phi}(0) = \mathbf{I} - \mathbf{D}\boldsymbol{\alpha}'$ or, equivalently,

$$\mathbf{D}\boldsymbol{\alpha}'\mathbf{y}_{t-1} + \tilde{\tilde{\Phi}}(L)\Delta\mathbf{y}_t = \tilde{\boldsymbol{\varepsilon}}_t$$

with

$$\tilde{\tilde{\Phi}}(L) = \mathbf{I}.$$

PROOF: From the definition of an adjoint matrix we have

$$\Phi(L)\Phi^*(L) = \mathbf{I}\det(\Phi(L)),$$

$$\Phi(L)\bar{\Phi}(L)(1-L)^{d-1} = \mathbf{I}(1-L)^d\phi(L)$$

or, also,

$$\Phi(L)\bar{\Phi}(L) = \mathbf{I}(1-L)\phi(L).$$

This in turn implies

$$\Phi(1)\bar{\Phi}(1) = 0.$$

As a consequence, the rows of $\Phi(1)$ belong to the nullspace of $\bar{\Phi}'(1)$, which is also the nullspace of $\mathbf{H}'(1)$, i.e., the space of the cointegrating vectors (on the basis of theorem 11.3).

(i) If

$$\Phi(L) = \tilde{\Phi}(L)(1-L),$$

we have

$$\det(\Phi(L)) = \det(\tilde{\Phi}(L))(1-L)^n.$$

Moreover

$$\Phi(L)\bar{\Phi}(L) = \mathbf{I}(1-L)\phi(L)$$

implies

$$\det(\mathbf{\Phi}(L)) \det(\bar{\mathbf{\Phi}}(L)) = (1 - L)^n \phi^n(L),$$

so that

$$\det(\tilde{\mathbf{\Phi}}(L)) \det(\bar{\mathbf{\Phi}}(L)) = \phi^n(L)$$

and, in particular

$$\det(\tilde{\mathbf{\Phi}}(1)) \det(\bar{\mathbf{\Phi}}(1)) = \phi^n(1) \neq 0.$$

Thus $\bar{\mathbf{\Phi}}(1)$ is non singular, as well as $\mathbf{H}(1)$, and the space of cointegrating vectors is reduced to $\{0\}$. Conversely, if the series is not cointegrated, $\mathcal{N}(\mathbf{H}'(1)) = \{0\}$, we must have $\mathbf{\Phi}(1) = 0$ since the rows of $\mathbf{\Phi}(1)$ belong to $\mathcal{N}(\mathbf{H}'(1))$. As a consequence, $\mathbf{\Phi}(L)$ can be written as $\tilde{\mathbf{\Phi}}(L)(1 - L)$. Moreover, since $(1 - L)\mathbf{y}_t$ is stationary, $\det(\tilde{\mathbf{\Phi}}(L))$ has its roots outside the unit circle.

(ii) Let us assume now that the series is cointegrated. Since

$$\mathbf{\Phi}(1)\bar{\mathbf{\Phi}}(1) = 0,$$

the rows of $\mathbf{\Phi}(1)$ belong to $\mathcal{N}(\bar{\mathbf{\Phi}}'(1)) = \mathcal{N}(\mathbf{H}'(1))$. The rows of $\boldsymbol{\alpha}'$ form a basis of $\mathcal{N}(\mathbf{H}'(1))$ and this allows us to write $\mathbf{\Phi}(1)$ in the form $\mathbf{\Phi}(1) = \mathbf{D}\boldsymbol{\alpha}'$. Let us write, then, $\mathbf{\Phi}(L) = \mathbf{\Phi}(1) + (1-L)\tilde{\mathbf{\Phi}}(L)$. Then model (11.11) becomes

$$\mathbf{\Phi}(1)\mathbf{y}_t + \tilde{\mathbf{\Phi}}(L)\Delta\mathbf{y}_t = \tilde{\boldsymbol{\varepsilon}}_t,$$

where

$$\mathbf{D}\boldsymbol{\alpha}'\mathbf{y}_t + \tilde{\mathbf{\Phi}}(L)\Delta\mathbf{y}_t = \tilde{\boldsymbol{\varepsilon}}_t.$$

Since $\mathbf{\Phi}(0) = \mathbf{I}$, we have

$$\mathbf{I} = \mathbf{\Phi}(1) + \tilde{\mathbf{\Phi}}(0),$$

or $\tilde{\mathbf{\Phi}}(0) = \mathbf{I} - \mathbf{D}\boldsymbol{\alpha}'$. Replacing $\mathbf{y}_t$ by $\mathbf{y}_{t-1} + \Delta\mathbf{y}_t$, we get also

$$\mathbf{D}\boldsymbol{\alpha}'\mathbf{y}_{t-1} + \left(\tilde{\mathbf{\Phi}}(L) + \mathbf{D}\boldsymbol{\alpha}'\right)\Delta\mathbf{y}_t = \tilde{\epsilon}_t$$

or

$$\mathbf{D}\boldsymbol{\alpha}'\mathbf{y}_{t-1} + \tilde{\tilde{\mathbf{\Phi}}}(L)\Delta\mathbf{y}_t = \tilde{\epsilon}_t$$

with

$$\tilde{\tilde{\mathbf{\Phi}}}(L) = \tilde{\mathbf{\Phi}}(L) + \mathbf{D}\boldsymbol{\alpha}'.$$

It is readily seen that $\tilde{\tilde{\mathbf{\Phi}}}(0) = \mathbf{I}$. $\square$

The Case of an ARIMA Model Let us assume now that $\mathbf{y}_t$ is an ARIMA process defined as

$$\mathbf{\Phi}(L)\mathbf{y}_t = \mathbf{\Theta}(L)\tilde{\epsilon}_t \tag{11.14}$$

with $\mathbf{y}_t = 0$ if $t \leq 0$, $\mathbf{\Phi}(0) = \mathbf{\Theta}(0) = \mathbf{I}$ and where the roots of $\det(\mathbf{\Phi}(L))$ and $\det(\mathbf{\Theta}(L))$ are equal to 1 or outside the unit circle. The degree of the polynomials $\mathbf{\Phi}(L)$ and $\mathbf{\Theta}(L)$ is p, respectively, q.

General Result

Theorem 11.8: *An ARIMA model admits an error correction representation of the type*

$$\mathbf{\Phi}(1)\mathbf{y}_t + \sum_{j=1}^{p} \tilde{\mathbf{\Phi}}_j \Delta^j \mathbf{y}_t = \mathbf{\Theta}(L)\tilde{\epsilon}_t.$$

PROOF: The demonstration is the same as in theorem 11.6. □

Case of $\mathbf{y}_t$ integrated of order 1 Equation (11.13) becomes

$$(1 - L)^d \mathbf{y}_t = \frac{\mathbf{\Phi}^*(L)\mathbf{\Theta}(L)}{\phi(L)}\tilde{\boldsymbol{\varepsilon}}_t$$

from which, comparing it with the general result (11.12) we get

$$\mathbf{\Phi}^*(L)\mathbf{\Theta}(L) = \phi(L)\mathbf{H}(L)(1 - L)^{d-1}$$
$$= \bar{\mathbf{\Phi}}(L)(1 - L)^{d-1},$$

where $\bar{\mathbf{\Phi}}(L) = \phi(L)\mathbf{H}(L)$. We always have $\bar{\mathbf{\Phi}}(1) = \phi(1)\mathbf{H}(1)$ so that $\mathcal{N}(\bar{\mathbf{\Phi}}'(1)) = \mathcal{N}(\mathbf{H}'(1))$.

Theorem 11.9:

(i) Let us assume $\mathbf{\Theta}(L)$ nonsingular. $\mathbf{y}$ is not cointegrated if and only if the model (11.14) can be written as

$$\tilde{\mathbf{\Phi}}(L)\Delta\mathbf{y}_t = \mathbf{\Theta}(L)\tilde{\boldsymbol{\varepsilon}}_t,$$

   where $\tilde{\mathbf{\Phi}}(L)$ is a matrix polynomial of degree $p - 1$ such that the roots of $\det(\tilde{\mathbf{\Phi}}(L))$ are outside the unit circle.

(ii) If the series $\mathbf{y}$ is cointegrated and if $\boldsymbol{\alpha}'$ is a $(r \times n)$ matrix the rows of which are independent cointegrating vectors, the model (11.14) admits an error correction representation

$$\mathbf{D}\boldsymbol{\alpha}'\mathbf{y}_t + \tilde{\mathbf{\Phi}}(L)\Delta\mathbf{y}_t = \mathbf{\Theta}(L)\tilde{\boldsymbol{\varepsilon}}_t$$

   with $\tilde{\mathbf{\Phi}}(0) = \mathbf{I} - \mathbf{D}\boldsymbol{\alpha}'$ or, equivalently,

$$\mathbf{D}\boldsymbol{\alpha}'\mathbf{y}_{t-1} + \tilde{\tilde{\mathbf{\Phi}}}(L)\Delta\mathbf{y}_t = \mathbf{\Theta}(L)\tilde{\boldsymbol{\varepsilon}}_t$$

   with $\tilde{\tilde{\mathbf{\Phi}}}(0) = \mathbf{I}$.

PROOF: A line of reasoning similar to the one in the Engle–Granger Representation Theorem implies

$$\mathbf{\Phi}(L)\bar{\mathbf{\Phi}}(L) = \mathbf{\Theta}(L)(1 - L)\phi(L).$$

In particular

$$\mathbf{\Phi}(1)\bar{\mathbf{\Phi}}(1) = 0,$$

so that $\mathbf{\Phi}(1) = \mathbf{D}\boldsymbol{\alpha}'$.

If $\mathbf{\Phi}(L) = \tilde{\mathbf{\Phi}}(L)(1 - L)$, we get

$$\det(\mathbf{\Phi}(L))\det(\bar{\mathbf{\Phi}}(L)) = \det(\mathbf{\Theta}(L))(1 - L)^n \phi^n(L),$$

$$\det(\tilde{\mathbf{\Phi}}(L))\det(\bar{\mathbf{\Phi}}(L)) = \det(\mathbf{\Theta}(L))\phi^n(L).$$

Hence

$$\det(\tilde{\mathbf{\Phi}}(1))\det(\bar{\mathbf{\Phi}}(1)) = \det(\mathbf{\Theta}(1))\phi^n(1).$$

Since $\mathbf{\Theta}(L)$ is nonsingular, $\det(\mathbf{\Theta}(1))$ is nonzero, so that $\det(\bar{\mathbf{\Phi}}(1))$ is nonzero, which implies that $\mathcal{N}\,(\mathbf{H}'(1)) = \{0\}$ so that $\mathbf{y}$ is not cointegrated. The remainder of the proof is identical to that of theorem 11.7. □

The error correction representations proposed in the previous theorem are not unique. As an example we have also (cf. exercise 11.5)

$$\mathbf{D}_1\boldsymbol{\alpha}'\mathbf{y}_t + \tilde{\mathbf{\Phi}}_1(L)\Delta\mathbf{y}_t = \det(\mathbf{\Theta}(L))\tilde{\boldsymbol{\varepsilon}}_t,$$

$$\mathbf{D}_1\boldsymbol{\alpha}'\mathbf{y}_{t-1} + \tilde{\tilde{\mathbf{\Phi}}}_1(L)\Delta\mathbf{y}_t = \det(\mathbf{\Theta}(L))\tilde{\boldsymbol{\varepsilon}}_t \tag{11.15}$$

with $\tilde{\mathbf{\Phi}}_1(0) = \mathbf{I} - \mathbf{D}_1\boldsymbol{\alpha}'$ and $\tilde{\tilde{\mathbf{\Phi}}}_1(0) = \mathbf{I}$.

Example 11.6: Let us consider the bivariate autoregressive process

$$\begin{pmatrix} 1 - 0.9L & 0.1L \\ 0.4L & 1 - 0.6L \end{pmatrix} \begin{pmatrix} y_{1t} \\ y_{2t} \end{pmatrix} = \tilde{\boldsymbol{\varepsilon}}_t.$$

The determinant of the matrix $\mathbf{\Phi}(L)$ is

$$(1 - 0.9L)(1 - 0.6L) - 0.04L^2 = (1 - L)(1 - 0.5L).$$

We can write

$$(1 - L)\begin{pmatrix} y_{1t} \\ y_{2t} \end{pmatrix} = (1 - 0.5L)^{-1}\begin{pmatrix} 1 - 0.6L & -0.1L \\ -0.4L & 1 - 0.9L \end{pmatrix} \tilde{\boldsymbol{\varepsilon}}_t.$$

The process $\mathbf{y}_t$ is integrated of order 1. The matrix

$$\mathbf{H}(L) = (1 - 0.5L)^{-1}\begin{pmatrix} 1 - 0.6L & -0.1L \\ -0.4L & 1 - 0.9L \end{pmatrix}$$

is such that

$$\mathbf{H}(1) = 2 \begin{pmatrix} 0.4 & -0.1 \\ -0.4 & 0.1 \end{pmatrix}.$$

$\mathbf{H}'(1)$ has a rank equal to 1 and its nullspace is spanned by $\alpha = \begin{pmatrix} 1 \\ 1 \end{pmatrix}$, which is a cointegrating vector. The error correction representation

$$\mathbf{D}\alpha'\mathbf{y}_t + \tilde{\mathbf{\Phi}}(L)\Delta\mathbf{y}_t = \tilde{\boldsymbol{\varepsilon}}_t$$

of theorem 11.7 is written here as

$$\begin{pmatrix} 0.1 \\ 0.4 \end{pmatrix} (y_{1t} + y_{2t}) + \begin{pmatrix} 0.9 & -0.1 \\ -0.4 & 0.6 \end{pmatrix} \Delta\mathbf{y}_t = \tilde{\boldsymbol{\varepsilon}}_t.$$

The expression

$$\mathbf{D}\alpha'\mathbf{y}_{t-1} + \tilde{\mathbf{\Phi}}(L)\Delta\mathbf{y}_t = \tilde{\boldsymbol{\varepsilon}}_t$$

becomes

$$\begin{pmatrix} 0.1 \\ 0.4 \end{pmatrix} (y_{1,t-1} + y_{2,t-1}) + \Delta\mathbf{y}_t = \tilde{\boldsymbol{\varepsilon}}_t.$$

11.2.4 Explicit Representation of the Long-run Model

Let us consider now the possibility of introducing some error correction representations so that the long-run coefficients appear in an explicit way.

The first error correction representation (Davidson, Hendry, Srba, and Yeo, 1978) was based on this idea. The most classical application is the estimation of a consumption function. The two variables of interest are total consumption C_t and income X_t. If we assume that income has a dominating component evolving at an exponential rate, i.e., $X_t \approx X_0\rho^t$, it is natural to assume that consumption as well evolves at the same rate $C_t \approx C_0\rho^t$. In fact, if we had a faster rate of evolution $\tilde{\rho} > \rho$ so that $C_t \approx C_0\tilde{\rho}^t$, we would have C_t/X_t tending to infinity and implying that the consumers would consume infinitely more than their resources, which is unsustainable in the long run. If the rate of divergence were weaker $\tilde{\rho} < \rho$ so that $C_t \approx C_0\tilde{\rho}^t$, we would have C_t/X_t tending to 0 so that consumption could become negligible in the long run with respect to saving. Thus, most likely, the growth rate of the two variables must be the same (cf. the section on the steady growth paths). Turning to logarithms, we have

$$\log(C_t) = \log(X_t) + o(\log(X_t)).$$

Often we express the same concept by saying that the long-run elasticity of consumption with respect to income is unity. If we want to test this hypothesis, we should make explicit the coefficient expressing long-run elasticity. Denoting $c_t = \log(C_t)$ and $x_t = \log(X_t)$, let us assume that the dynamic relationship between c_t and x_t can be written as

$$a(L)c_t + b(L)x_t = \tilde{\epsilon}_t,$$

with $a(0) = 1$

$$c_t = -\sum_{j=1}^{r} a_j c_{t-j} - \sum_{j=0}^{s} b_j x_{t-j} + \tilde{\epsilon}_t.$$

This relationship can also be written as

$$\left(1 + \sum_{j=1}^{r} a_j\right) c_t = -\left(\sum_{j=0}^{s} b_j\right) x_t + \sum_{j=1}^{r} a_j \left(c_t - c_{t-j}\right)$$

$$+ \sum_{j=1}^{s} b_j \left(x_t - x_{t-j}\right) + \tilde{\epsilon}_t$$

$$\Leftrightarrow \quad c_t = -\frac{b(1)}{a(1)} x_t + \sum_{j=0}^{r-1} a_j^* \Delta c_{t-j} + \sum_{j=0}^{s-1} b_j^* \Delta x_{t-j} + \tilde{\epsilon}_t.$$

This expression contains the long-run coefficient $-\frac{b(1)}{a(1)}$ (which can be studied for its proximity to 1) and the *adjustments* Δc_{t-j} and Δx_{t-j}. This expression is very similar to the one given in definition 11.3 for the definition of an ECM. However, note that the two representations have different goals:

(i)   There is no preconceived idea about the equilibrium relationship in the previous approach, and how to approach this equilibrium. It is just a suitable expression to test the long-run behavior of the model.

(ii) This difference is apparent from the expression itself: in fact, here we consider a model conditional on y whereas before we considered unconditional models. Moreover, it would have been possible here to replace the form obtained with another expression which shows the long-run coefficient as well. For example, we could choose

$$c_{t-p} = -\frac{b(1)}{a(1)} x_{t-p} + \sum_{j=0}^{r-1} a_j^{**} \Delta c_{t-j} + \sum_{j=0}^{s-1} b_j^{**} \Delta x_{t-j} + \tilde{\epsilon}_t,$$

with $p \leq \min(r-1, s-1)$.

11.3 Fractional Processes

In the previous sections we have taken into consideration the trend components by considering an autoregressive polynomial the determinant of which admits 1 as a (possibly multiple) root. This leads us to write the process as

$$(1 - L)^d \mathbf{y}_t = \mathbf{H}(L)\tilde{\boldsymbol{\varepsilon}}_t,$$

with d positive integer and with $\mathbf{H}(L)$ a matrix series in L the terms of which decrease exponentially.

Choosing an integer degree of differencing involves a number of difficulties, both from the point of view of the specification and from the point of view of the statistical inference. Thus, we have seen in chapter 6 that d integer leads to separate the phase of estimation (identification) of d from the one of the other model parameters.

In this section, we will introduce a more general class of models in which d may be real, known as *fractional processes*. In order to make the presentation simple, we will refer to the univariate case, but it is easy to extend the results to the multivariate case.

11.3.1 Definition and Moving Average Representation

Definition 11.4: *A fractional process is a process y_t, $t \geq 0$ satisfying a system of difference equations of the type*

$$\Phi(L)(1 - L)^d y_t = \Theta(L)\tilde{\epsilon}_t$$

for $t \geq 0$ with initial conditions $y_t = 0$, if $t < 0$ and where

$$\tilde{\epsilon}_t = \begin{cases} \epsilon_t, & \text{white noise if } t \geq 0, \\ 0, & \text{otherwise}, \end{cases}$$

where $\Phi(L)$ and $\Theta(L)$ are two polynomials with roots strictly outside the unit circle, d is a real number and where

$$(1 - L)^d = 1 + \sum_{j=1}^{+\infty} \frac{d(d-1)\dots(d-j+1)}{j!}(-1)^j L^j.$$

The ARIMA (p, d, q) process corresponds to the special case where d is a positive integer. The proposed definition for $(1 - L)^d$ is based on the series expansion of the power function. This expansion admits a synthetic expression by introducing the notation

$$\Gamma(d) = \int_0^{+\infty} x^{d-1} \exp(-x) dx \qquad d \geq 0.$$

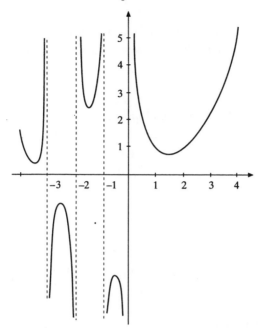

Figure 11.1 Behavior of the Gamma Function

The extension to the negative values of d is based on the formula $\Gamma(d) = \Gamma(d+1)/d$. The function Γ has the behavior shown in figure 11.1.

From the definition of $\Gamma(d)$ we derive

$$\frac{\Gamma(d+j)}{\Gamma(d)} = (d+j-1)\ldots(d+1)d.$$

We have also

$$(1-L)^d = 1 + \sum_{j=1}^{+\infty} \frac{(-d)(-d+1)\ldots(-d+j-1)L^j}{j!}$$

$$= \sum_{j=1}^{+\infty} \frac{\Gamma(-d+j)L^j}{\Gamma(-d)j!}.$$

The moving average representation of the process is obtained directly by inverting the autoregressive series. We have

$$y_t = (1-L)^{-d}\Phi(L)^{-1}\Theta(L)\tilde{\epsilon}_t$$

$$= (1-L)^{-d}A(L)\tilde{\epsilon}_t$$

with

$$A(L) = \Phi(L)^{-1}\Theta(L) = \sum_{j=0}^{+\infty} a_j L^j.$$

The asymptotic stationarity or nonstationarity properties of the model can be studied from the limit behavior of the coefficients h_j of the moving average representation of y_t.

Theorem 11.10: *A fractional process admits an infinite moving average representation with moving average coefficients such that*

$$h_j \approx \frac{\Theta(1)}{\Phi(1)\Gamma(d)} j^{d-1}.$$

as j tends to infinity.

PROOF: We have

$$y_t = H(L)\tilde{\epsilon}_t = (1-L)^{-d} A(L)\tilde{\epsilon}_t$$

$$= \sum_{j=0}^{+\infty} h_j \tilde{\epsilon}_{t-j} = \left(\sum_{j=0}^{+\infty} \frac{\Gamma(d+j)L^j}{\Gamma(d)j!} \right) \left(\sum_{j=0}^{+\infty} a_j L^j \right) \tilde{\epsilon}_t.$$

We can derive that

$$h_j = \sum_{k=0}^{j} a_{j-k} \frac{\Gamma(k+d)}{\Gamma(d)} \frac{1}{\Gamma(k+1)},$$

since $\Gamma(k+1) = k!$. From Stirling's formula we get

$$\frac{\Gamma(k+d)}{\Gamma(k+1)} \approx k^{d-1},$$

as k tends to ∞. We have then

$$\left| h_j - \frac{A(1)}{\Gamma(d)} j^{d-1} \right|$$

$$= \left| \sum_{k=0}^{j} a_{j-k} \frac{\Gamma(k+d)}{\Gamma(d)\Gamma(k+1)} - \frac{A(1)}{\Gamma(d)} j^{d-1} \right|$$

$$\leq |a_j| + \left| \sum_{k=1}^{j} a_{j-k} \left[\frac{\Gamma(k+d)}{\Gamma(d)\Gamma(k+1)} - \frac{k^{d-1}}{\Gamma(d)} \right] \right|$$

$$+ \left| \sum_{k=1}^{j} a_{j-k} \left(\frac{k^{d-1}}{\Gamma(d)} - \frac{j^{d-1}}{\Gamma(d)} \right) \right| + \left| \sum_{k=j}^{+\infty} a_k \frac{j^{d-1}}{\Gamma(d)} \right|.$$

Using the fact that the series with a_j as a general term decreases exponentially and the inequality

$$\exists \, c : \left| \frac{\Gamma(k+d)}{\Gamma(d)\Gamma(k+1)} - \frac{k^{d-1}}{\Gamma(d)} \right| \leq ck^{d-2}, \qquad \forall \, k \geq 1,$$

we can verify that each element on the right-hand side of the inequality tends to 0 when j tends to infinity (cf. Akonom and Gourieroux, 1988).

□

The knowledge of the asymptotic behavior of the moving average coefficients allows for a classification of the time series according to the following scheme

Definition 11.5: *The series*

$$y_t = \sum_{j=0}^{+\infty} h_j \tilde{\epsilon}_{t-j}$$

is:

(i) asymptotically stationary *if* $\sum_{j=0}^{+\infty} h_j^2 < +\infty$,

(ii) (asymptotically) nonstationary *if* $\sum_{j=0}^{+\infty} h_j^2 = +\infty$.

If it is asymptotically stationary it is defined as having:

(ia) short-memory *if* $\sum_{j=0}^{+\infty} |h_j| < +\infty$,

(ib) long-memory *if* $\sum_{j=0}^{+\infty} |h_j| = +\infty$.

Up to now the stationary series taken into consideration generally had ARMA representations with autoregressive and moving average polynomials with roots outside the unit circle. In such a case the coefficients of the infinite moving average representation decrease exponentially and, in particular, $\sum_{j=0}^{+\infty} |h_j| < +\infty$. The ARMA processes have short-memory.

Let us now consider a fractional process; on the basis of theorem 11.10

$$h_j \approx \frac{\Theta(1)}{\Phi(1)\Gamma(d)} j^{d-1}.$$

The series with the general term j^{d-1} can be summable, square-summable or nonsummable according to the values taken by the exponent d. We have then

Theorem 11.11:

(i) *The fractional process is asymptotically stationary if and only if* $d < \frac{1}{2}$.

(ii) *The fractional process is asymptotically stationary with short-memory if* $d \leq 0$, *with long-memory if* $0 < d < \frac{1}{2}$.

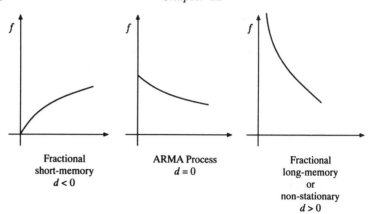

Figure 11.2   Pseudo-Spectrum of Fractional Processes

11.3.2 Second-Order Properties

Spectrum and Pseudo-Spectrum   We can define the pseudo-spectrum of the series irrespective of whether it is asymptotically stationary or not

$$f(\omega) = \frac{\sigma^2}{2\pi} \frac{|\Theta(\exp(i\omega))|^2}{|\Phi(\exp(i\omega))|^2} |1 - \exp(i\omega)|^{-2d} . \tag{11.16}$$

In a neighborhood of $\omega = 0$ we have

$$f(\omega) \approx \frac{\sigma^2}{2\pi} \left(\frac{\Theta(1)}{\Phi(1)}\right)^2 |1 - \exp(i\omega)|^{-2d} \approx \frac{\sigma^2}{2\pi} \left(\frac{\Theta(1)}{\Phi(1)}\right)^2 \omega^{-2d}. \tag{11.17}$$

A study of the function f at low frequencies allows to detect the differencing order d. Therefore the ratio

$$\frac{f(\omega)}{|1 - \exp(i\omega)|^{-2d}}$$

is only a function of f and k. Knowing the pseudo-spectrum, we can then determine the properties of

$$\frac{\sigma^2}{2\pi} \left(\frac{\Theta(\exp(i\omega))}{\Phi(\exp(i\omega))}\right)^2,$$

that is the second-order properties of the differenced process $(1 - L)^d y_t$ (for large t).

The behavior of the pseudo-spectrum near 0 allows one to understand the difference between short-memory and long-memory (or nonstationary) processes. For the latter ones, the pseudo-spectrum is, in fact, infinite for $\omega = 0$.

In particular, when d is positive, the longer is the memory, the more rapidly the pseudo-spectrum tends to infinity as ω tends to 0. Referring to (11.17) we note that $\log(f(\omega)) \approx$ constant $- 2d\log(\omega)$. Thus a logarithmic transformation expresses this rate directly to the exponent d.

Autocovariance Function The autocovariance function has a meaning in the asymptotically stationary case, that is, for $d < 1/2$. The autocovariances do not have simple expressions in the general case. However, we can establish the following

Theorem 11.12: *Let us consider a fractional process*

$$(1 - L)^d y_t = \tilde{\epsilon}_t$$

with $d < 1/2$. The covariance $\gamma(t, h) = \mathrm{cov}(y_t, y_{t+h})$ tends to

$$\gamma(h) = \sigma^2 \frac{\Gamma(h + d)}{\Gamma(h + 1 - d)} \frac{\Gamma(1 - 2d)}{\Gamma(d)\Gamma(1 - d)}$$

as t goes to infinity.

PROOF: The moving average representation of the process is

$$y_t = (1 - L)^{-d}\tilde{\epsilon}_t = \sum_{j=0}^{+\infty} \frac{\Gamma(j + d)}{\Gamma(j + 1)\Gamma(d)}\tilde{\boldsymbol{\epsilon}}_{t-j}.$$

We conclude that

$$\gamma(h) = \sigma^2 \sum_{j=0}^{+\infty} \frac{\Gamma(j + d)}{\Gamma(j + 1)\Gamma(d)} \frac{\Gamma(j + h + d)}{\Gamma(j + h + 1)\Gamma(d)}$$

$$= \sigma^2 \frac{\Gamma(h + d)}{\Gamma(h + 1)\Gamma(d)} \left(\frac{\Gamma(h + 1)}{\Gamma(h + d)\Gamma(d)} \sum_{j=0}^{+\infty} \frac{\Gamma(j + d) + \Gamma(j + h + d)}{\Gamma(j + h + 1)\, j!} \right)$$

$$= \sigma^2 \frac{\Gamma(h + d)}{\Gamma(h + 1)\Gamma(d)} F(d, d + h, h + 1; 1),$$

where

$$F(a, b, c; z) = \frac{\Gamma(c)}{\Gamma(a)\Gamma(b)} \sum_{j=0}^{+\infty} \frac{\Gamma(a + j)\Gamma(b + j)}{\Gamma(c + j)} \frac{z^j}{j!}$$

indicates the hypergeometric function. A classical formula for this function is (cf. Abramovitz and Stegun, 1985)

$$F(a, b, c; 1) = \frac{\Gamma(c)\Gamma(c - a - b)}{\Gamma(c - a)\Gamma(c - b)},$$

from which we get

$$\gamma(h) = \sigma^2 \frac{\Gamma(h+d)}{\Gamma(h+1)\Gamma(d)} \frac{\Gamma(h+1)\Gamma(1-2d)}{\Gamma(h+1-d)\Gamma(1-d)}$$

$$= \sigma^2 \frac{\Gamma(h+d)}{\Gamma(h+1-d)} \frac{\Gamma(1-2d)}{\Gamma(d)\Gamma(1-d)}.$$

□

Starting from this example we can study the rate of convergence to 0 of the autocovariances. For h large enough

$$\gamma(h) \approx \sigma^2 h^{2d-1} \frac{\Gamma(1-2d)}{\Gamma(d)\Gamma(1-d)}.$$

The autocovariances decrease at a smaller rate than the usual exponential rate. Moreover, we see that the correlation

$$\rho(h) = \frac{\gamma(h)}{\gamma(0)} \approx constant \times h^{2d-1}$$

tends to grow with the value of d for h large enough. From an intuitive point of view, this corresponds to the idea of long-memory. Since the correlations are stronger than the usual ARMA case, a shock to the innovation at time t will tend to have an impact on the future values y_{t+h} for a longer period. Let us remark also that, if d is a negative integer, y_t is a moving average process and that the equivalence for $\gamma(h)$ given above is not valid anymore since $\mid \Gamma(d) \mid = +\infty$; we have, though, $\gamma(h) = 0$ for h large enough.

11.3.3 Aggregation of First-order Autoregressive Processes

The presence of strong temporal correlations can be the outcome of aggregation. If a number of series $(y_{i,t}), i = 1, \ldots, n$ are correlated among each other, the computation of the mean $\bar{y}_{n,t} = \frac{1}{n} \sum_{i=1}^{n} y_{i,t}$ can introduce a temporal smoothing of the aggregated series and therefore a stronger dependence between successive values of the series.

The Principle Let us consider several time-series data

$$y_{i,t}, \ i = 1, \ldots, n, \ldots; \ t = 0, 1, \ldots, T, \ldots.$$

In order to simplify matters, let us assume that each series $(y_{i,t}, t \geq 0)$ $i = 1, \ldots, n, \ldots$ satisfies a first-order autoregressive representation with an adjustment coefficient depending on i. By the same token, let us take into consideration the possibility of a correlation among series by introducing an error decomposition in *time effect* and *cross effect*. More precisely, let us pose

$$y_{i,t} = \phi_i y_{i,t-1} + c_i \epsilon_t + \eta_{i,t},$$

for $t \geq 0$, $i = 1, 2, \ldots$ with $y_{i,-1} = 0$, $\forall\, i$. The noise terms ϵ_t, η_{1t}, $\eta_{2t}, \ldots$ are assumed pairwise independent, with zero mean and with variances $\mathrm{var}\,(\epsilon_t) = \sigma^2$, $\mathrm{var}\,(\eta_{it}) = \mu^2, \forall\, i$. We have retained the recursive relation only for positive indices. This allows us to treat simultaneously the case of asymptotically stationary processes ($|\phi_i| < 1$) and that of nonstationary processes ($|\phi_i| \geq 1$).

Let us complete the set of assumptions needed for the aggregation by formulating some hypotheses about the structural coefficients ϕ_i, c_i. Let us assume that these values can be considered as independently drawn according to the same density function, that they are independent of the values taken by the noise terms and that the variables ϕ and c are independent between each other. The parameter c is assumed to have a nonzero mean. The mean calculated on the first n series is

$$\bar{y}_{n,t} = \frac{1}{n} \sum_{i=1}^{n} y_{i,t}$$

$$= \frac{1}{n} \sum_{i=1}^{n} \sum_{k=0}^{t} \phi_i^k \left(c_i \epsilon_{t-k} + \eta_{i,t-k} \right)$$

$$= \sum_{k=0}^{t} \left(\frac{1}{n} \sum_{i=1}^{n} \phi_i^k c_i \right) \epsilon_{t-k} + \sum_{k=0}^{t} \left(\frac{1}{n} \sum_{i=1}^{n} \phi_i^k \eta_{i,t-k} \right).$$

As n goes to infinity, we get

$$\lim_{n \to \infty} \frac{1}{n} \sum_{i=1}^{n} \phi_i^k c_i = E(\phi^k c) = E(\phi_i^k) E(c),$$

$$\lim_{n \to \infty} \frac{1}{n} \sum_{i=1}^{n} \phi_i^k \eta_{i,t-k} = E(\phi^k \eta_{i,t-k}) = E(\phi^k) E(\eta_{i,t-k}) = 0.$$

We can see that at the limit the aggregated process

$$\bar{y}_t = \lim_{n} \bar{y}_{n,t}$$

satisfies a relationship such as

$$\bar{y}_t = \sum_{k=0}^{t} E(\phi^k) E(c) \epsilon_{t-k} = \sum_{k=0}^{t} E(\phi^k) \bar{\epsilon}_{t-k},$$

with $\bar{\epsilon}_t = E(c) \epsilon_t$. Thus, the temporal dependence of the process $\bar{y}$ is introduced by the terms $c_i \epsilon_t$ and comes into play only because of the contemporaneous correlation between the innovations of the various disaggregated series.

Effects of the Aggregation

Theorem 11.13: *If the density function of ϕ is defined over positive real numbers, and if the aggregated process is stationary, the autocorrelations for the aggregated series are greater than the means of the disaggregated autocorrelations.*

PROOF:

(i)   The disaggregated correlations are

$$\rho_i(h) = \phi_i^h,$$

and therefore their mean is $E(\rho(h)) = E(\phi^h)$.

(ii) The correlation of order h of the aggregated series can be obtained from the coefficients of its moving average representation. We have

$$\bar{\rho}(h) = \frac{\sum_{k=0}^{+\infty} E(\phi^k)E(\phi^{k+h})}{\sum_{k=0}^{+\infty} \left(E(\phi^k)\right)^2}.$$

(iii) We can then note that for h and k given, the mappings $\phi \mapsto \phi^h$ and $\phi \mapsto \phi^k$ are increasing. We conclude that (cf. exercise 11.1)

$$\mathrm{cov}\left(\phi^h, \phi^k\right) \geq 0,$$

or that $E(\phi^{k+h}) - E(\phi^k)E(\phi^h) \geq 0$.

(iv) Finally, we can establish the following inequality for $\bar{\rho}(h)$

$$\bar{\rho}(h) = \frac{\sum_{k=0}^{+\infty} E(\phi^k)E(\phi^{k+h})}{\sum_{k=0}^{+\infty} \left(E(\phi^k)\right)^2} \geq \frac{\sum_{k=0}^{+\infty} E(\phi^k)E(\phi^k)E(\phi^h)}{\sum_{k=0}^{+\infty} \left(E(\phi^k)\right)^2}$$

$$= E(\rho(h)).$$

□

Thus this effect leads to an increase in the autocorrelations, except in the limit case where ϕ is the same for the various series. In this case we have $\bar{\rho}(h) = E(\bar{\rho}(h))$.

Aggregation with a Beta Density   The increase in correlation can be sizeable. Thus the aggregation of a short-memory series can generate a long-memory stationary series or even nonstationary series. Let us illustrate this point by taking into consideration the autoregressive coefficient as being generated by a Beta distribution $B(p, 1-p)$, $0 < p < 1$. The density function can be written as

$$g(\phi) = \frac{\phi^{p-1}(1-\phi)^{-p}}{B(p, 1-p)} \mathbb{1}_{[0,1]}(\phi),$$

with $B(p, 1 - p) = \Gamma(p)\Gamma(1 - p)$. The moments of this distribution are

$$E(\phi^k) = \frac{\Gamma(p + k)}{\Gamma(p)} \frac{1}{\Gamma(1 + k)}.$$

The aggregated process admits the representation

$$\bar{y}_t = \sum_{k=0}^{+\infty} E(\phi^k)\tilde{\bar{\epsilon}}_{t-k},$$

with $\tilde{\bar{\epsilon}}_t = 0$ if $t \leq 0$

$$\bar{y}_t = \sum_{k=0}^{+\infty} E(\phi^k) L^k \tilde{\bar{\epsilon}}_t$$

$$= \left(\sum_{k=0}^{+\infty} \frac{\Gamma(p + k)}{\Gamma(p)} \frac{L^k}{k!} \right) \tilde{\bar{\epsilon}}_t$$

$$= (1 - L)^{-p} \tilde{\bar{\epsilon}}_t,$$

that is, a fractional aggregated series.

Theorem 11.14: *The aggregation of first-order autoregressive series associated with a Beta distribution $B(p, 1 - p)$, $0 < p < 1$ is a fractional process. In particular*

(i) *It is long-memory stationary if $p < \frac{1}{2}$.*
(ii) *It is nonstationary if $p \geq \frac{1}{2}$.*

11.3.4 Change in the Time or Measurement Units

The Principle If we represent a time series graphically, it may show a dominant polynomial component, which can be isolated by an appropriate choice of the units for the axes (time axis and axis for the values of the variable). The explosive characteristics can be eliminated by means of an adequate choice of the unit for the $y-$axis and the resulting curve can be smoothed by means of an appropriate choice of the time unit. This is the approach presented in this section.

Let us replace the initial series $y_1, \ldots, y_T$ with a concentrated series defined as

$$y_T(r) = \frac{y_{[Tr]}}{T^\alpha}, \tag{11.18}$$

for $\alpha > 0$ and $0 \leq r \leq 1$, and where $[x]$ indicates the integer part of x. These series are indexed by the same index $r \in [0, 1]$. On the other hand, the coefficient α will be chosen, whenever possible, in such

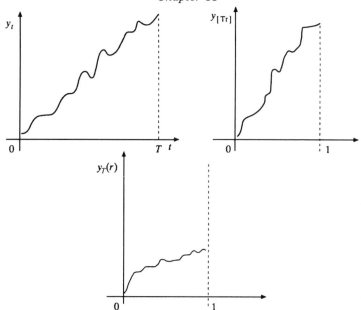

Figure 11.3   Steps of Transformation of a Series

a way as to make the resulting series $y_T(r)$ neither explosive nor close to 0. We can interpret α as the degree of nonstationarity of the series. The transformation of the original series into the concentrated series is described graphically in figure 11.3.

It is clear that, from a mathematical point of view, the concentrated series is a process $x(r)$ indexed by a continuous set $[0,1]$. The properties of such processes are fairly close to the ones of discrete-time processes. Thus we can define their distribution, their expected value (a function which maps $x(r)$ into $E(x(r))$), and their covariances (a function which maps $x(r_1), x(r_2)$ into $\operatorname{cov}(x(r_1), x(r_2)) = \phi(r_1, r_2)$).

Since the index set is continuous, it is also possible to introduce a concept of continuity of the process. Let us define the process as *continuous in quadratic mean* if

$$\forall \ r \quad \lim_{h \to 0} E\left(x(r+h) - x(r)\right)^2 = 0.$$

We can then provide the following definition

Definition 11.6: *The series y_t, $t \geq 0$ is asymptotically locally equivalent to a monomial of degree α if and only if the concentrated series converges in distribution to a continuous in quadratic mean, nontrivial second-order process*

$$y_T(r) = \frac{y_{[Tr]}}{T^\alpha} \quad \overset{\mathrm{d}}{\to} \quad W(r).$$

Intuitively, for T large enough, we can replace the concentrated series by $W\left(\frac{t}{T}\right)$ and the initial series by $T^\alpha W\left(\frac{t}{T}\right)$. The continuity of W implies that, in a neighborhood of a value r_0, we have $W(r) \approx W(r_0)$ and thus, in a neighborhood of $t_0 = r_0 T$, we have

$$y_t \approx T^\alpha W\left(\frac{t_0}{T}\right) \approx \left(\frac{t}{r_0}\right)^\alpha W\left(\frac{t_0}{T}\right).$$

The series can be approximated by a monomial of degree α in a neighborhood of $t_0 = r_0 T$. Obviously, a change in the value of r_0 modifies the leading coefficient of the monomial.

Note that the convergence in distribution intervening in the definition 11.5 involves random functions indexed by $[0, 1]$. In such a case, it does not suffice that there be convergence of any finite subfamily $[y_T(r_1), \ldots, y_T(r_n)]$ in order to have convergence in distribution of the random function itself. In addition, it is necessary that this random function be sufficiently smooth (*tightness condition*). In order to keep the presentation simple, let us not insist in what follows on this additional technical requirement, referring the interested reader to Billingsley (1968).

Donsker's Theorem The condition of convergence in distribution introduced in definition 11.6 is satisfied for the processes used so far to model the series with polynomial trends. Let us verify this for a univariate random walk by considering a univariate independent white noise (ϵ_t) with variance σ^2 and the process defined as

$$y_t - y_{t-1} = \epsilon_t,$$

for $t \geq 1$ and with $y_0 = 0$. We have

$$y_t = \sum_{\tau=1}^{t} \epsilon_\tau.$$

Changing the time units and assuming $\alpha = \frac{1}{2}$, since the random walk explodes at a rate of $\sqrt{T}$, we get

$$y_T(r) = \frac{y_{[Tr]}}{T^{\frac{1}{2}}} = \frac{1}{\sqrt{T}} \sum_{\tau=1}^{[Tr]} \epsilon_\tau.$$

From the central limit theorem we have that

$$\frac{1}{\sigma} y_T(r) \approx \frac{\sqrt{r}}{\sqrt{[Tr]}} \sum_{\tau=1}^{[Tr]} \frac{\epsilon_\tau}{\sigma}$$

is asymptotically distributed as a normal $\mathcal{N}(0, r)$. This provides the convergence in distribution of $y_T(r)$ for each value of r. Let us consider now several components associated with different values of r; we can always adopt a multivariate central limit theorem to derive similar results. Thus taking into account two components we have

$$\begin{pmatrix} \frac{1}{\sigma}y_T(r_1) \\ \frac{1}{\sigma}y_T(r_2) \end{pmatrix} \approx \begin{pmatrix} \frac{\sqrt{r_1}}{\sqrt{[Tr_1]}}\sum_{\tau=1}^{[Tr_1]}\frac{\epsilon_\tau}{\sigma} \\ \frac{\sqrt{r_2}}{\sqrt{[Tr_2]}}\sum_{\tau=1}^{[Tr_2]}\frac{\epsilon_\tau}{\sigma} \end{pmatrix}$$

$$\xrightarrow{d} \mathcal{N}\left(\begin{pmatrix} 0 \\ 0 \end{pmatrix}, \begin{pmatrix} r_1 & \min(r_1,r_2) \\ \min(r_1,r_2) & r_2 \end{pmatrix} \right).$$

This line of reasoning on a finite number of components can be extended to obtain the convergence in distribution of the concentrated process (cf. Billingsley, 1968).

The limit distribution thus obtained corresponds to a process $[B(r)]$ indexed by $r \in [0,1]$, normal with zero mean, and with variances and covariances given by $\mathrm{cov}\,(B(r_1), B(r_2)) = \min(r_1, r_2)$.

Definition 11.7: *The process $(B(r), r \in [0,1])$, normal with zero mean, and such that*

$$\mathrm{cov}\,(B(r_1), B(r_2)) = \min(r_1, r_2)$$

$\forall\, r_1,\, r_2\, \in [0,1]$ *is called* Brownian motion *on* $[0,1]$.

The result about the convergence in distribution can be expressed as follows

Theorem 11.15: Donsker's Theorem

If $(y_t, t \geq 0)$ is a random walk based on an independent white noise with variance σ^2 then

$$\frac{1}{\sigma}y_T(r) \xrightarrow{d} B(r),$$

where B is a Brownian motion on $[0,1]$ (cf. Billingsley, 1968).

Stochastic Integral with Respect to a Brownian Motion Let us consider a Brownian motion on $[0,1]$ and some values $r_1 < r_2 < r_3 < r_4$. We have

$$\mathrm{cov}\,(B(r_2) - B(r_1), B(r_4) - B(r_3))$$

$$= \mathrm{cov}\,(B(r_2), B(r_4)) - \mathrm{cov}\,(B(r_1), B(r_4))$$

$$- \mathrm{cov}\,(B(r_2), B(r_3)) + \mathrm{cov}\,(B(r_1), B(r_3))$$

$$= r_2 - r_1 - r_2 + r_1 = 0.$$

Thus, the Brownian motion has uncorrelated increments; since it is normally distributed the increments are independent. As a result, we can use it as a stochastic measure and construct the associated stochastic integral. Let us define $dB(r)$ the stochastic measure; the associated density function is

$$f(r)dr = \text{var } (dB(r)) \approx \text{var } (B(r+dr) - B(r)) = dr,$$

which corresponds to the uniform distribution on $[0, 1]$.

For any square integrable function g on $[0, 1]$

$$\int_0^1 g^2(r)dr < \infty,$$

we can introduce the stochastic integral

$$\int_0^1 g(r)dB(r).$$

Using the interpretation of the stochastic integral as being an isometry we get

$$E\left(\int_0^1 g(r)dB(r)\right) = \int_0^1 g(r)dE\left(B(r)\right) = 0,$$

and

$$\text{cov}\left(\int_0^1 g(r)dB(r), \int_0^1 h(r)dB(r)\right) = \int_0^1 g(r)h(r)dr.$$

Note that the stochastic integral can be seen also as a limit in quadratic mean of Riemann sums

$$\int_0^1 g(r)dB(r) = \lim_{T\to+\infty} \sum_{t=1}^T g\left(\frac{t-1}{T}\right)\left(B\left(\frac{t}{T}\right) - B\left(\frac{t-1}{T}\right)\right).$$

$$(11.19)$$

Asymptotic Behavior of Stationary Fractional Processes Let us now verify heuristically that the fractional processes are asymptotically locally approximated by monomials. For the sake of simplicity let us consider once again the univariate process y defined as

$$y_t = (1-L)^{-d}\Phi(L)^{-1}\Theta(L)\tilde{\epsilon}_t,$$

for $t \geq 0$, where

$$\tilde{\epsilon}_t = \begin{cases} \epsilon_t, & \text{if } t > 0, \\ 0, & \text{otherwise} \end{cases}$$

with ϵ an independent white noise with variance σ^2, Φ and Θ lag polynomials with roots outside the unit circle. The integration order d is greater than $1/2$ which involves the nonstationarity of the series.

Denoting the moving average representation of the process as

$$y_t = \sum_{k=1}^{t} h_{t-k}^{(d)} \epsilon_k,$$

we know from theorem 11.10 that the moving average coefficients are such that

$$h_t^{(d)} \approx \frac{\Theta(1)}{\Phi(1)\Gamma(d)} t^{d-1},$$

for t large enough. The concentrated process

$$y_T(r) = \frac{1}{T^{d-1/2}} y_{[Tr]}$$

can be approximated by

$$y_T(r) = \frac{1}{T^{d-1/2}} \sum_{k=1}^{[Tr]} h_{[Tr]-k}^{(d)} \epsilon_k$$

$$\approx \frac{1}{T^{d-1/2}} \sum_{k=1}^{[Tr]} \frac{\Theta(1)}{\Phi(1)\Gamma(d)} ([Tr] - k)^{d-1} \epsilon_k$$

$$\approx \sigma \frac{\Theta(1)}{\Phi(1)\Gamma(d)} \sum_{k=1}^{[Tr]} \left(r - \frac{k}{T} \right)^{d-1} \frac{1}{\sqrt{T}} \frac{\epsilon_k}{\sigma}$$

$$= \sigma \frac{\Theta(1)}{\Phi(1)\Gamma(d)} \sum_{k=1}^{[Tr]} \left(r - \frac{k}{T} \right)^{d-1}$$

$$\left(\frac{1}{\sqrt{T}} \frac{\epsilon_1 + \epsilon_2 + \ldots + \epsilon_k}{\sigma} - \frac{1}{\sqrt{T}} \frac{\epsilon_1 + \epsilon_2 + \ldots + \epsilon_{k-1}}{\sigma} \right).$$

Applying Donsker's Theorem which allows for the approximation in distribution of the sums

$$\frac{1}{\sqrt{T}} \frac{\epsilon_1 + \epsilon_2 + \ldots + \epsilon_k}{\sigma}$$

by $B\left(\frac{k}{T}\right)$ we have

$$y_T(r) \approx \sigma \frac{\Theta(1)}{\Phi(1)\Gamma(d)} \sum_{k=1}^{[Tr]} \left(r - \frac{k}{T} \right)^{d-1} \left(B\left(\frac{k}{T}\right) - B\left(\frac{k-1}{T}\right) \right),$$

which is a Riemann sum which asymptotically can be replaced by the corresponding stochastic integral

$$y_T(r) \approx \sigma \frac{\Theta(1)}{\Phi(1)\Gamma(d)} \int_0^r (r - s)^{d-1} dB(s).$$

Theorem 11.16: *Given a nonstationary fractional process*

$$y_t = (1 - L)^{-d} \Phi(L)^{-1} \Theta(L) \epsilon_t,$$

with $d > 1/2$, the concentrated process

$$y_T(r) = \frac{1}{T^{d-1/2}} y_{[Tr]}$$

is such that

$$y_T(r) \overset{d}{\to} \sigma \frac{\Theta(1)}{\Phi(1)\Gamma(d)} \int_0^r (r-s)^{d-1} dB(s).$$

Remark 11.4: As one would expect, the stationary part of the model, that is, $\Phi(L)^{-1}\Theta(L)$ appears only through the long-run multiplier $\frac{\Theta(1)}{\Phi(1)}$.

Remark 11.5: The previous theorem allows for the evaluation of the order of magnitude of the second-order moment of the process y_T. In fact, we have

$$y_T(1) = \frac{1}{T^{d-1/2}} y_T \approx \sigma \frac{\Theta(1)}{\Phi(1)\Gamma(d)} \int_0^1 (1-s)^{d-1} dB(s).$$

Thus

$$\text{var}\,(y_T(1)) = \frac{1}{T^{2d-1}} \text{var}\,(y_T) \approx \sigma^2 \frac{\Theta(1)^2}{\Phi(1)^2\Gamma(d)^2} \int_0^1 (1-s)^{2d-2} ds$$

$$= \sigma^2 \frac{\Theta(1)^2}{\Phi(1)^2\Gamma(d)^2} \frac{1}{2d-1}$$

so that

$$\text{var}\,(y_T) \approx \sigma^2 \frac{\Theta(1)^2}{\Phi(1)^2\Gamma(d)^2} \frac{1}{2d-1} T^{2d-1}.$$

11.4 Exercises

Exercise 11.1: Let x be a real-valued random variable and g, h two increasing functions. Let us consider two independent variables x_1 and x_2 with the same distribution as x.

(i)   Verify that $(g(x_1) - g(x_2))(h(x_1) - h(x_2))$ is always nonnegative.

(ii) Write

$$E\,(g(x_1) - g(x_2))\,(h(x_1) - h(x_2))$$

as a function of cov $(g(x), h(x))$. From (i) show that this covariance is positive.

Exercise 11.2: Let us consider the process $\mathbf{y}$ with $\mathbf{\Phi}(L)\mathbf{y}_t = \tilde{\boldsymbol{\varepsilon}}_t$ a bivariate autoregressive process of order 1. Which are the conditions on the coefficients of $\mathbf{\Phi}$ in order for $\mathbf{y}_t$ to be integrated of order 1? and in order for the components of $\mathbf{y}_t$ to be cointegrated?

Exercise 11.3: Under the assumptions of formulas 11.11 and 11.12, show that $\det(\bar{\mathbf{\Phi}}(L)) = (1 - L)^{n-d}\phi^{n-1}(L)$ by using the equality

$$\mathbf{\Phi}(L)\mathbf{\Phi}^*(L) = \det(\mathbf{\Phi}(L))\mathbf{I}.$$

Show that $d \leq n$ and that if $n = d$, $\mathbf{\Phi}(1)$ is invertible.

Exercise 11.4:

(i)   A nonstationary process y is defined by

$$(1 - L)^d(y_t - m) = \tilde{\epsilon}_t$$

for $t \geq 0$ and $y_t = 0$ if $t < 0$. Provide a canonical decomposition of y using components with different rates of divergence, and separating the deterministic and the stochastic terms.

(ii) Solve the same problem for a process defined as

$$(1 - L)^d y_t = \tilde{\epsilon}_t + m$$

and compare the rates of divergence of the deterministic and stochastic components.

Exercise 11.5: Show that the equation defining an ARIMA process $\mathbf{\Phi}(L)\mathbf{y}_t = \mathbf{\Theta}(L)\tilde{\boldsymbol{\varepsilon}}_t$ can also be written as

$$\mathbf{\Theta}^*(L)\mathbf{\Phi}(L)y_t = \det(\mathbf{\Theta}(L))\tilde{\boldsymbol{\varepsilon}}_t,$$

where $\boldsymbol{\Theta}^*(L)$ is the adjoint matrix of $\boldsymbol{\Theta}(L)$ or also as

$$\boldsymbol{\Phi}_1(L)y_t = \det(\boldsymbol{\Theta}(L))\tilde{\boldsymbol{\varepsilon}}_t$$

with $\boldsymbol{\Phi}_1(0) = \mathbf{I}$. Derive expression (11.15) applying theorem 11.9.

Exercise 11.6: Let us consider a univariate series y satisfying an autoregressive model of order 1

$$y_t = \rho(\theta)y_{t-1} + \epsilon_t,$$

with var $(\epsilon_t) = \sigma^2$, where the correlation coefficient depends on an unobservable heterogeneity factor θ. Let us assume that this factor is independent of the noise ϵ and has a continuous density function $\pi(\theta)$. We want to compare the first-order correlation obtained by integrating out the heterogeneity factor

$$\rho = \frac{E(y_t y_{t-1})}{E(y_t^2)}$$

with the mean of the correlations

$$\rho(\theta) = \frac{E(y_t y_{t-1}|\theta)}{E(y_t^2|\theta)}.$$

(i)   Let u and v be two random variables. Using the fact that

$$\frac{E(u)}{E(v)} - E\left(\frac{u}{v}\right) = \frac{1}{E(v)}\left(E\left(\frac{u}{v}v\right) - E\left(\frac{u}{v}\right)E(v)\right),$$

derive the result that the difference between the ratio of the expected values and the average of the ratios is equal to a covariance up to a factor.

(ii) Applying this result to the case of correlations prove that

$$\rho - \int \rho(\theta)\pi(\theta)d\theta = \frac{1}{E(y_t^2)}\text{cov}\,\left(\rho(\theta), E(y_t^2|\theta)\right)$$

$$= \frac{1}{E(y_t^2)}\text{cov}\,\left(\rho(\theta), \frac{\sigma^2}{1-\rho^2(\theta)}\right).$$

(iii) Deduce that if $\rho(\theta) \geq 0, \forall\,\theta$, then

$$\rho - \int \rho(\theta)\pi(\theta)d\theta \geq 0.$$

What happens if $\rho(\theta) \leq 0, \forall\,\theta$?

Exercise 11.7: Let us consider an autoregressive model of order 1, integrated of order 1, for which a basis of r cointegrating vectors is formed by the columns of a matrix $\boldsymbol{\alpha}$. This model admits an error correction representation

$$\mathbf{y}_t - \mathbf{y}_{t-1} = \mathbf{D}\boldsymbol{\alpha}'\mathbf{y}_{t-1} + \epsilon_t$$

with $\mathbf{D}$ a $(n \times r)$ matrix.

(i)   Let $\boldsymbol{\beta}$ be a matrix the columns of which together with those of $\boldsymbol{\alpha}$ form a basis in $\mathbb{R}^n$. Verify that

$$\boldsymbol{\alpha}'\mathbf{y}_t = (\mathbf{I} + \boldsymbol{\alpha}'\mathbf{D})\boldsymbol{\alpha}'\mathbf{y}_{t-1} + \boldsymbol{\alpha}'\epsilon_t,$$

$$\boldsymbol{\beta}'\mathbf{y}_t = \boldsymbol{\beta}'\mathbf{y}_{t-1} + \boldsymbol{\beta}'\mathbf{D}\boldsymbol{\alpha}'\mathbf{y}_{t-1} + \boldsymbol{\beta}'\epsilon_t.$$

Prove that the matrix $\mathbf{D}$ is necessarily subject to some constraints so that the first equation leads to a stationary process $\boldsymbol{\alpha}'\mathbf{y}_t$.

(ii) Let us denote $\operatorname{var}(\boldsymbol{\epsilon}_t) = \boldsymbol{\Omega}$. We can then choose $\boldsymbol{\alpha}$, $\boldsymbol{\beta}$ such that $\boldsymbol{\alpha}'\boldsymbol{\Omega}\boldsymbol{\beta} = 0$. Prove that the initial model admits a recursive form where the components $\boldsymbol{\alpha}'\mathbf{y}$ are determined first and then the components $\boldsymbol{\beta}'\mathbf{y}$ are derived.

12

Expectations

Most of the models and results described in the previous chapters are based on the notion of an optimal forecast of a variable given its past. For example, this notion has been useful to define the autoregressive form of a process, its innovation, and so on, but also to analyze in greater details the links between processes (partial correlation, causality measurement, etc.) or to develop estimation methods (maximum likelihood in conditional form).

In this chapter we are interested in a more practical aspect of this optimal forecast.

Economic agents, e.g., firms, financial operators, consumers, must in general decide their current behavior taking into consideration the ideas they have about the future. Since this future is partially unknown, they have to forecast it in a proper way. This leads us to study two questions which are linked to each other:

(i)   How do agents foresee their future?
(ii)   How do their expectations influence their current behavior?

In the first section we will start by recalling a number of results on forecasts which have been introduced in the previous chapters. We will treat the updating problem in great detail and specify the economic terminology which is slightly different from the probabilistic terminology used up to now.

The other sections are all related to the analysis of explanatory models containing expectations among the explanatory variables. More pre-

cisely, we will look at the properties of these models in the case of optimal
expectations (or *rational* in the economic terminology).

12.1 Review of the Expectation Schemes

12.1.1 Forecast Problem

When a variable of interest y is unknown, we can focus on some approximations $\tilde{y}$. These are called *forecasts* or *expectations*. In general they
are found using *the available information* on other variables x. Then a
forecast of y is of the form

$$\tilde{y} = f(x), \tag{12.1}$$

where f represents the computation method which allows one to go
from the observations x to the approximation $\tilde{y}$ of y. Thus, given an
information set $I = \{x\}$, there exist as many ways to obtain forecasts
as choices of the function f. The latter is often called an *expectation
scheme*.

Later on we will always consider that the variable to be approximated
y and the explanatory variables x are random. On the other hand, the
computation method f is assumed nonrandom. Since the forecast $\tilde{y}$ is a
nonrandom function of the random variables x, it is random as well.

The *expectation problem* is the problem of finding an "adequate" approximation $\tilde{y}$ of y. This approximation is in general different from y
and the corresponding *forecast error*: $e = y - \tilde{y}$, is also random. This
error may be summarized by means of the mean square error

$$Ee^2 = E(y - \tilde{y})^2.$$

12.1.2 Successive Forecasts

Later on we will often be led to consider forecasts made at different
dates. Thus we need to introduce processes $\{y_t\}$, $\{x_t\}$, instead of the
variables y_t and x_t only. Similarly, we have to introduce a sequence of
information sets; the set I_t is interpreted as the available information
at time t. This information is often built from observable variables
considering the current and past values of these variables

$$I_t = (x_t, x_{t-1} \ldots) = (\underline{x}_t)$$

(this information could also contain values of the process y).

Then the available information increases with time. At time $t + 1$,
this information is increased by $x_{t+1} : I_{t+1} = \{x_{t+1}, I_t\}$.

Nevertheless, notice (cf. exercise 12.2) that it is also possible to introduce nonincreasing information sets. If we just keep the last ten observations of x, we have

$$I_t = (x_t, x_{t-1}, \ldots, x_{t-9}).$$

The set I_{t+1} is derived from I_t adding the information in x_{t+1} and eliminating the one in x_{t-9}.

In this dynamic context, we can consider various forecasting problems. Thus, let us assume that we are at time t and that the information is I_t. This information can be used to forecast the different values y_{t+h} of the process y. A forecast of y_{t+h} done at time t is of the form

$$_t\tilde{y}_{t+h} = f_{t,h}(I_t)$$

so that we have a series of forecasts available with a double index t and h.

When $t + h = T$ is fixed and t varies, we get the series of successive forecasts of the variable $y_T = y_{t+h}$, made at various dates. We can then study the evolution of the forecasts when the information changes. The variation between two successive dates is

$$_t\tilde{y}_T - {}_{t-1}\tilde{y}_T = f_{t,T-t}(I_t) - f_{t-1,T-t+1}(I_{t-1}). \tag{12.2}$$

This difference represents the *updating* of forecasts.

12.1.3 The Main Expectation Schemes

In the previous chapters we encountered various expectation schemes. Let us briefly recall their definitions; the reader can refer to the appropriate chapters (4 and 6) for more details.

Adaptive Scheme It is the simple exponential model. The scheme is defined directly by the updating formula

$$_t\tilde{y}_{t+1} = (1 - \lambda)\,_{t-1}\tilde{y}_t + \lambda y_t, \tag{12.3}$$

with $\lambda \in [0, 1]$.

Solving iteratively we get the *extrapolative* form of this scheme

$$_t\tilde{y}_{t+1} = \lambda \sum_{j=0}^{\infty} (1 - \lambda)^j y_{t-j}, \tag{12.4}$$

as soon as the series of the second term in (12.4) exists. These two equivalent formulations show that there exist several couples (f_t, I_t) corresponding to this forecast scheme. From (12.4) we can take $I_t = (y_t, y_{t-1} \ldots)$ and (12.3) shows that this information can be summarized by $\tilde{I}_t = (y_t,\, {}_{t-1}\tilde{y}_t)$. Note that in both cases the corresponding functions f_t and $\tilde{f}_t$ are independent of time t. Then, we can say that the *expectation scheme is stationary*.

Naive Expectation Note that when $\lambda = 1$, the adaptive scheme forces us to choose the last observed value as a forecast

$$_t\tilde{y}_{t+1} = y_t$$

This expectation is called *naive*.

Rational Scheme Various criteria can be considered to choose among expectation schemes: the ease of computation, the possibility of reproducing the cycles present in the series (y_t), but above all accuracy of the proposed approximation. We have seen that, when this accuracy is measured by the mean square error, the best approximation of a variable y based on an information $I = \{x\}$ is computed as a conditional expectation (or as a linear regression). In the economic literature such an optimal forecast is called *rational*. It is written $E(y \mid I)$ as before.

12.1.4 Some Properties of Rational Expectations

We derive various properties of rational expectations from the well-known ones of conditional expectations.

Theorem 12.1: *The forecast error $e = y - E(y \mid I)$*

(i)   *has zero mean: $Ee = 0$,*
(ii)   *is uncorrelated with the forecast*

$$E\left(eE(y \mid I)\right) = cov\left(e, E(y, \mid I)\right) = 0,$$

(iii)   *is uncorrelated with any variable x in the information set*

$$E(ex) = cov\,(e, x) = 0,$$

$\forall\, x \in I$.

PROOF: Left as an exercise to the reader. □

The properties derived in a dynamic context and relative to forecast errors at multiple horizons and to the updating rules are more interesting.

Thus, let us consider a process $y = \{y_t\}$, and a sequence $\{I_t\}$ of information sets. This sequence is assumed to be increasing, and y_t is assumed to be in I_t.

The forecast errors at time t and horizon h are

$$v_{t,h} = y_{t+h} - E(y_{t+h} \mid I_t). \tag{12.5}$$

The *successive updates* are

$$\epsilon_t^h = E\left(y_{t+h} \mid I_t\right) - E(y_{t+h} \mid I_{t-1}). \tag{12.6}$$

The forecast errors can easily be expressed as functions of successive updates. We have

$$v_{t,h} = y_{t+h} - E\left(y_{t+h} \mid I_t\right)$$

$$= y_{t+h} - E\left(y_{t+h} \mid I_{t+h-1}\right)$$

$$+ E\left(y_{t+h} \mid I_{t+h-1}\right) - E\left(y_{t+h} \mid I_{t+h-2}\right)$$

$$\vdots$$

$$+ E\left(y_{t+h} \mid I_{t+1}\right) - E\left(y_{t+h} \mid I_t\right),$$

$$v_{t,h} = \sum_{i=0}^{h-1} \epsilon_{t+h-i}^i. \tag{12.7}$$

The updates have various martingale properties: some definitions are therefore in order.

Definition 12.1: *Consider an increasing sequence of information sets* $I = (I_t)$:

(i) *A process* $m = \{m_t\}$ *is a* martingale *if and only if*

$$E\left(m_{t+1} \mid I_t\right) = m_t$$

$\forall\, t$ *integer.*

(ii) *A process* $d = \{d_t\}$ *is a* martingale difference sequence *if and only if* $d_t \in I_t$ *and* $E(d_{t+1} \mid I_t) = 0$.

A martingale appears as a process for which the rational expectation and naive expectations coincide. A martingale difference sequence is such that each component is uncorrelated with the past. Note in particular that a martingale difference sequence is such that

$$Ed_t = EE(d_t \mid I_{t-1}) = 0,$$

$$E(d_t d_{t-i}) = E\left(d_{t-i} E(d_t \mid I_{t-1})\right) = 0, \quad \forall\, i > 0.$$

Therefore it has zero mean and no serial correlation.

Theorem 12.2:

(i) *The sequence* $\left\{\epsilon_t^h,\ t \text{ varying}\right\}$ *of updates at horizon* h *is a martingale difference sequence.*

(ii) *The sequence* $\{\epsilon_t^{T-t},\ t \text{ varying}\}$ *of updates is a martingale difference sequence.*

(iii) *The sequence* $\{E(y_T \mid I_t),\ t \text{ varying}\}$ *of rational forecasts of* y_T *is a martingale.*

PROOF: As an example let us check the second result. We have
$$\epsilon_t^{T-t} = E(y_T \mid I_t) - E(y_T \mid I_{t-1}).$$
We derive
$$E\left(\epsilon_t^{T-t} \mid I_{t-1}\right) = E\left(E(y_T \mid I_t) \mid I_{t-1}\right) - E\left(E(y_T \mid I_{t-1}) \mid I_{t-1}\right)$$
$$= E(y_T \mid I_{t-1}) - E(y_T \mid I_{t-1}) = 0.$$
□

In particular the third property was applied by Samuelson (1965) to the forward prices. If p_T is the price on the market at time T, if $_t\tilde{p}_T$ is the price to pay at time t to buy a unit of a good at time T (forward price), it may be possible to assume that $_t\tilde{p}_T$ coincides with $E(p_T \mid I_t)$ for an efficient market. Then the sequence of forward prices should be a martingale for such a market.

12.2 Model with Expectation of the Current Variable

12.2.1 Walrasian Equilibrium Model

Historically, the first rational expectation model was introduced by Muth (1961). It was an equilibrium model for an agricultural good market, where producers must decide their behavior without completely knowing the values of some variables of interest for the economy. Since we are particularly interested in the expectation patterns of the suppliers, we keep the whole demand function to a simple specification.

Let p_t be the price of the good at time t, let q_t be the demanded quantity, and let $\mathbf{z}_{1t}$ be some exogenous variables acting on the demand; the inverse demand function is
$$p_t = D(q_t, \mathbf{z}_{1t}).$$
Let us look now at the supply behavior assuming, for simplicity, the existence of a single firm. Let $\mathbf{z}_{2t}$ be the exogenous variables entering the production function, and let $C(q, \mathbf{z}_{2t})$ be the cost at time t of a production q. The corresponding profit is
$$p_t q - C(q, \mathbf{z}_{2t}).$$
When deciding on the quantity to produce, the producer does not necessarily know the exact value of the price p_t and of the exogenous variables $\mathbf{z}_{1t}, \mathbf{z}_{2t}$. On the basis of the available information set I_{t-1} we can, as a first approximation, consider that the producer will maximize the expected profit
$$E\left(p_t q - C(q, \mathbf{z}_{2t}) \mid I_{t-1}\right)$$
$$= E(p_t \mid I_{t-1})q - C^e(q, I_{t-1}),$$

where $C^e(q, I_{t-1}) = E\left(C(q, \mathbf{z}_{2t}) \mid I_{t-1}\right)$ is the expected cost function. The optimal quantity is then obtained by setting the expected cost equal to the marginal expected cost (C^e is assumed convex w.r.t. q)

$$E(p_t \mid I_{t-1}) = \frac{\partial}{\partial q} C^e(q_t, I_{t-1}).$$

It is derived from the expected price through the inverse function of the marginal expected cost

$$q_t = \left(\frac{\partial}{\partial q} C^e\right)^{-1} (E(p_t \mid I_{t-1}), I_{t-1}).$$

Finally in equilibrium, we have the equality of supply and demand

$$p_t = D(q_t, \mathbf{z}_{1t}),$$

$$q_t = \left(\frac{\partial}{\partial q} C^e\right)^{-1} (E(p_t \mid I_{t-1}), I_{t-1}).$$

We deduce an equilibrium price equation

$$p_t = D\left(\left(\frac{\partial}{\partial q} C^e\right)^{-1} (E(p_t \mid I_{t-1}), I_{t-1}), \mathbf{z}_{1t}\right). \tag{12.8}$$

The price is expressed as a function of the expected price, of the exogenous variables in the demand function and of the forecasts of exogenous variables in the supply equation (through expected cost).

Nevertheless, this form cannot be considered as a reduced form, since the price appears in the right hand side term through its expectation. It is possible here to derive from equation (12.8), the form of the expectation $E(p_t \mid I_{t-1})$. Indeed, introducing the function of expected inverse demand, we have

$$D^e(q_t, I_{t-1}) = E\left(D(q_t, \mathbf{z}_{1t}) \mid I_{t-1}\right).$$

Taking the expectation of each term in equation (12.8) conditional on I_{t-1}, we have

$$E(p_t \mid I_{t-1}) = D^e\left(\left(\frac{\partial}{\partial q} C^e\right)^{-1} (E(p_t \mid I_{t-1}), I_{t-1}), I_{t-1}\right). \tag{12.9}$$

It is an implicit relation in $E(p_t \mid I_{t-1})$. The equilibrium exists if this equation admits at least one solution, and, if it exists, the number of equilibria is equal to the number of solutions of this equation.

This relation provides the expected price as a function of the expectations of the transformed exogenous variables $\mathbf{z}_{1t}$, $\mathbf{z}_{2t}$ (through the expected cost and demand functions).

Solving in $E(p_t \mid I_{t-1})$ the equation (12.9) and putting it in the relation (12.8) gives the equilibrium price p_t as a function only of the exogenous variables and of their expectations.

Example 12.1: The model just described is customarily used with a linear demand function and a quadratic cost function. Moreover, the exogenous variables are introduced in order to make easy the derivation of the expected cost and demand functions.

Let us write

$$D(q, \mathbf{z}_{2t}) = aq + \mathbf{z}'_{1t}\mathbf{b}$$

and

$$C(q, \mathbf{z}_{2t}) = \frac{1}{2}\alpha q^2 + \mathbf{z}'_{2t}\boldsymbol{\beta}q + \varphi(\mathbf{z}_{2t}).$$

The expected cost is

$$C^e(q, \mathbf{z}_{2t}) = \frac{1}{2}\alpha q^2 + E(\mathbf{z}_{2t} \mid I_{t-1})'\boldsymbol{\beta}q + E(\varphi(\mathbf{z}_{2t}) \mid I_{t-1}).$$

The supply function is derived from the equation

$$E(p_t \mid I_{t-1}) = \frac{\partial}{\partial q}C^e(q_t, \mathbf{z}_{2t}) = \alpha q_t + E(\mathbf{z}_{2t} \mid I_{t-1})'\boldsymbol{\beta},$$

$$q_t = \frac{1}{\alpha}E(p_t \mid I_{t-1}) - \frac{1}{\alpha}E(\mathbf{z}_{2t} \mid I_{t-1})'\boldsymbol{\beta}.$$

We get the equation of price determination by equating supply and demand

$$p_t = a\left(\frac{1}{\alpha}E(p_t \mid I_{t-1}) - \frac{1}{\alpha}E(\mathbf{z}_{2t} \mid I_{t-1})'\boldsymbol{\beta}\right) + \mathbf{z}'_{1t}\mathbf{b}.$$

As in the general presentation, taking the expectation of each member conditional on I_{t-1}, we have

$$E(p_t \mid I_{t-1}) = a\left(\frac{1}{\alpha}E(p_t \mid I_{t-1}) - \frac{1}{\alpha}E(\mathbf{z}_{2t} \mid I_{t-1})'\boldsymbol{\beta}\right) + E(\mathbf{z}_{1t} \mid I_{t-1})'\mathbf{b}.$$

Usually the coefficient a is negative and the coefficient α is positive; therefore we have $(a/\alpha) \neq 1$ and the previous equation admits a unique solution. There is existence and uniqueness of the equilibrium. Also, we get the following expressions for the price expectation and for the price

$$E(p_t \mid I_{t-1}) = -\frac{a/\alpha}{1 - a/\alpha}E(\mathbf{z}_{2t} \mid I_{t-1})'\boldsymbol{\beta} + \frac{1}{1 - a/\alpha}E(\mathbf{z}_{1t} \mid I_{t-1})'\mathbf{b},$$

$$p_t = -\frac{a/\alpha}{1 - a/\alpha}E(\mathbf{z}_{2t} \mid I_{t-1})'\boldsymbol{\beta} + \frac{a/\alpha}{1 - a/\alpha}E(\mathbf{z}_{1t} \mid I_{t-1})'\mathbf{b}$$

$$+ \mathbf{z}'_{1t}\mathbf{b}.$$

12.3 Dynamic Properties of a Linear Model with Expectation of the Current Variable

12.3.1 Rational Expectation Model

Before eliminating the expectation and assuming linearity, the reduced form of the model is of the type

$$y_t = aE(y_t \mid I_{t-1}) + \mathbf{x}'_t \mathbf{b}. \tag{12.10}$$

Let y be the endogenous variable (e.g., the price in the previous example), let $\mathbf{x}$ be the vector of exogenous variables (including the constant term, in some cases the expected exogenous variables and the error term), let a and $\mathbf{b}$ be the reduced form parameters, in general nonlinear functions of the structural parameters. As seen previously, we derive from the previous equation

$$E(y_t \mid I_{t-1}) = aE(y_t \mid I_{t-1}) + E(\mathbf{x}_t \mid I_{t-1})' \mathbf{b}$$

and

$$y_t = \frac{a}{1-a} E(\mathbf{x}_t \mid I_{t-1})' \mathbf{b} + \mathbf{x}'_t \mathbf{b},$$

with $a \neq 1$.

A careful look at this equation shows that the dynamic aspect will be derived once the dependence of the exogenous variables with respect to the past is known. It is necessary to complete the model specifying

(i)   the available information I_{t-1};
(ii)   the temporal evolution of the exogenous variables and of the information.

In general, a different evolution of the endogenous process corresponds to each of these specifications.

Case of Perfect Foresight   Assume the available information I_{t-1} contains the current values $\mathbf{x}_t$ of the exogenous variables. They can be predicted without any error $E(\mathbf{x}_t \mid I_{t-1}) = \mathbf{x}_t$, and the equation giving the current value of the endogenous variable is written as

$$y_t = \frac{a}{1-a} \mathbf{x}'_t \mathbf{b} + \mathbf{x}'_t \mathbf{b} = \frac{1}{1-a} \mathbf{x}'_t \mathbf{b}.$$

It corresponds to the *perfect foresight* model

$$y_t = a y_t + \mathbf{x}'_t \mathbf{b},$$

which is without error. As we would expect, the perfect foresight hypothesis appears as a particular case of rational expectation corresponding to a large enough information set.

Future Partially Unknown The rational expectation model is nevertheless more interesting, when the future is only partially known. Assume that among the K independent variables $\mathbf{x}$, the first $\tilde{K}$, $\tilde{\mathbf{x}}_t$, are known at time $t-1$ and the $(K^\star = K - \tilde{K})$, $\mathbf{x}^\star$, are not. We have

$$y_t = \frac{a}{1-a} E(\tilde{\mathbf{x}}_t \mid I_{t-1})'\tilde{\mathbf{b}} + \frac{a}{1-a} E(\mathbf{x}_t^\star \mid I_{t-1})'\mathbf{b}^\star + \tilde{\mathbf{x}}_t'\tilde{\mathbf{b}} + \mathbf{x}_t^{\star'}\mathbf{b}^\star,$$

$$y_t = \frac{1}{1-a} \tilde{\mathbf{x}}_t'\tilde{\mathbf{b}} + \frac{a}{1-a} E(\mathbf{x}_t^\star \mid I_{t-1})'\mathbf{b}^\star + \mathbf{x}_t^\star \mathbf{b}^\star.$$

The model must then be completed by specifying the form of the forecasts of the exogenous variables $\mathbf{x}_t^\star$. Choosing a first-order autoregressive scheme, we have

$$E(\mathbf{x}_t^{\star'} \mid I_{t-1}) = \mathbf{H}_0 + \tilde{\mathbf{x}}_t'\mathbf{H}_1 + \tilde{\mathbf{x}}_{t-1}'\mathbf{H}_2 + \mathbf{x}_{t-1}^{\star'}\mathbf{H}_3 + y_{t-1}\mathbf{H}_4,$$

where $\mathbf{H}_0, \mathbf{H}_1, \mathbf{H}_2, \mathbf{H}_3$, and $\mathbf{H}_4$ are matrices of sizes, $(1 \times K^\star)$, $(\tilde{K} \times K^\star)$, $(\tilde{K} \times K^\star)$, $(K^\star \times K^\star)$, and $(1 \times K^\star)$, respectively. We get a dynamic model in the variables $y, \mathbf{x}$

$$y_t = \frac{a}{1-a} \mathbf{H}_0\mathbf{b}^\star + \frac{1}{1-a} \tilde{\mathbf{x}}_t'(\tilde{\mathbf{b}} + a\mathbf{H}_1\mathbf{b}^\star) + \mathbf{x}_t^{\star'}\mathbf{b}^\star + \frac{a}{1-a} \tilde{\mathbf{x}}_{t-1}'\mathbf{H}_2\mathbf{b}^\star$$

$$+ \frac{a}{1-a} \mathbf{x}_{t-1}^{\star'}\mathbf{H}_3\mathbf{b}^\star + \frac{a}{1-a} y_{t-1}\mathbf{H}_4\mathbf{b}^\star$$

$$\mathbf{x}_t^{\star'} = \mathbf{H}_0 + \tilde{\mathbf{x}}_t'\mathbf{H}_1 + \tilde{\mathbf{x}}_{t-1}'\mathbf{H}_2 + \mathbf{x}_{t-1}^{\star'}\mathbf{H}_3 + y_{t-1}\mathbf{H}_4 + \mathbf{v}_t,$$

$$(12.11)$$

with $E(\mathbf{v}_t \mid I_{t-1}) = \mathbf{0}$.

The model appears in an autoregressive form for $y, \mathbf{x}^\star$, conditional on the predetermined variables $\tilde{\mathbf{x}}$.

12.3.2 Comparison with the Unrestricted Reduced Form

The previous model (12.11) can be compared in a direct way with the unrestricted reduced form

$$y_t = \mathbf{\Pi}_0 + \tilde{\mathbf{x}}_t'\mathbf{\Pi}_1 + \mathbf{x}_t^{\star'}\mathbf{\Pi}_2 + \tilde{\mathbf{x}}_{t-1}'\mathbf{\Pi}_3 + \tilde{\mathbf{x}}_{t-1}'\mathbf{\Pi}_4 + y_{t-1}\mathbf{\Pi}_5,$$

$$(12.12)$$

$$\mathbf{x}_t^{\star'} = \mathbf{H}_0 + \tilde{\mathbf{x}}_t'\mathbf{H}_1 + \tilde{\mathbf{x}}_{t-1}'\mathbf{H}_2 + \mathbf{x}_{t-1}^{\star'}\mathbf{H}_3 + y_{t-1}\mathbf{H}_4 + \mathbf{v}_t.$$

The existence of a form involving rational expectations on the current variable y_t depends on the form of the reduced-form coefficients. It is possible if and only if it exists $a, \tilde{\mathbf{b}}, \mathbf{b}^\star$ with

$$\mathbf{\Pi}_0 = \frac{a}{1-a} \mathbf{H}_0\mathbf{b}^\star, \qquad \mathbf{\Pi}_1 = \frac{1}{1-a} \left(\tilde{\mathbf{b}} + a\mathbf{H}_1\mathbf{b}^\star\right), \qquad \mathbf{\Pi}_2 = \mathbf{b}^\star,$$

$$\mathbf{\Pi}_3 = \frac{a}{1-a} \mathbf{H}_2\mathbf{b}^\star, \qquad \mathbf{\Pi}_4 = \frac{a}{1-a} \mathbf{H}_3\mathbf{b}^\star, \qquad \mathbf{\Pi}_5 = \frac{a}{1-a} \mathbf{H}_4\mathbf{b}^\star.$$

Letting $c = (1-a)/a$, $\mathbf{d} = \tilde{\mathbf{b}}/a$ this system of constraints can also be written as

$$\exists\, c, \mathbf{d}, \mathbf{b}^\star : c\mathbf{\Pi}_0 = \mathbf{H}_0\mathbf{b}^\star, \qquad c\mathbf{\Pi}_1 = \mathbf{d} + \mathbf{H}_1\mathbf{b}^\star, \qquad \mathbf{\Pi}_2 = \mathbf{b}^\star,$$

$$c\mathbf{\Pi}_3 = \mathbf{H}_2\mathbf{b}^\star, \qquad c\mathbf{\Pi}_4 = \mathbf{H}_3\mathbf{b}^\star. \qquad (12.13)$$

Note that these constraints are linear both in the parameters $\mathbf{\Pi}_0$, $\mathbf{\Pi}_1$, $\mathbf{\Pi}_2$, $\mathbf{\Pi}_3$, $\mathbf{H}_0$, $\mathbf{H}_1$, $\mathbf{H}_2$, $\mathbf{H}_3$, and in the auxiliary parameters: $c, \mathbf{d}, \mathbf{b}^\star$. This particular form of the constraints will be used to build hypothesis testing procedures of the rational expectation hypothesis in chapter 13.

12.3.3 Comparison of Various Expectation Schemes

The model (12.10) summarizes in a single relation two quite different ideas. The expectation effect on the values of the variables is given by

$$y_t = a\,_{t-1}\hat{y}_t + \mathbf{x}_t'\mathbf{b},$$

where $_{t-1}\hat{y}_t$ stands for the expectation of the variable y_t at time $t-1$. On the other hand, we are assuming that the expectation is rational i.e.,

$$_{t-1}\hat{y}_t = E(y_t \mid I_{t-1}).$$

In this section we propose to modify this second part of the model and to discuss the consequences of such a modification over the evolution of the endogenous process. To simplify the discussion, we restrict ourselves to the case of a single independent variable x and we assume that it has an autoregressive representation

$$x_t = \rho x_{t-1} + \epsilon_t,$$

with $\mid \rho \mid < 1$.

Rational Expectation Model
When the expectation is rational based on the information

$$I_{t-1} = (x_{t-1}, y_{t-1}, x_{t-2}, y_{t-2} \ldots),$$

we have

$$_{t-1}\hat{y}_t = E(y_t \mid I_{t-1}) = \frac{b}{1-a}E(x_t \mid I_{t-1}) = \frac{b\rho}{1-a}x_{t-1}.$$

Hence

$$y_t = a\,_{t-1}\hat{y}_t + bx_t = \frac{ab\rho}{1-a}x_{t-1} + bx_t.$$

Introducing the lag operator L, we have the joint model

$$y_t = \left(\frac{ab\rho}{1-a}L + b\right)x_t,$$

$$(1 - \rho L)x_t = \epsilon_t.$$

The endogenous process can be expressed as a function of the innovation ϵ of the exogenous process

$$y_t = \left(\frac{ab\rho}{1-a} L + b \right) (1 - \rho L)^{-1} \epsilon_t. \qquad (12.14)$$

This process admits an ARMA(1,1) representation and in particular is stationary, whatever the values of the structural parameters a and b (with $a \neq 1$) are.

Moreover, it is worthwhile looking at the effect on the endogenous variable of a shock intervening on the exogenous process. It is customary to define such a shock as a change in the innovation process ϵ. A sustained shock of $\Delta \epsilon$ on the components ϵ_t of the noise leads to a modification $\Delta x = \frac{1}{1-\rho} \Delta \epsilon$ in the exogenous variable x_t, $\Delta \hat{y}_t = \frac{b\rho}{(1-a)(1-\rho)} \Delta \epsilon$ in the expectation $_{t-1}\hat{y}_t$ and

$$\Delta y = \frac{1}{1 - \rho} \left(\frac{ab\rho}{1-a} + b \right) \Delta \epsilon$$

in the endogenous variable y_t. Thus a modification of the evolution scheme of the exogenous process has a double effect on the endogenous process: direct, through the term bx_t and indirect through the expectation

$$\frac{\Delta y}{\Delta x} = \underset{\text{indirect effect}}{\underbrace{\frac{ab\rho}{1-a}}} \quad + \quad \underset{\text{direct effect}}{\underbrace{b}}. \qquad (12.15)$$

Moreover the size of the effect depends on the dynamics of the exogenous process due to the presence of the parameter ρ (see Lucas, 1972, 1973).

Adaptative Expectation Model Assume now that the expectation is defined through an adaptive scheme, so that the model becomes

$$y_t = a\,_{t-1}\hat{y}_t + x_t b,$$

$$_{t-1}\hat{y}_t = \lambda y_{t-1} + (1 - \lambda)\,_{t-2}\hat{y}_{t-1}, \qquad \text{with } \lambda \in [0,1],$$

$$x_t = \rho x_{t-1} + \epsilon_t.$$

From the first equation and the form of the expectations scheme, we deduce that

$$y_t - (1 - \lambda)y_{t-1} = a(\,_{t-1}\hat{y}_t - (1 - \lambda)\,_{t-2}\hat{y}_{t-1})$$

$$+ (x_t - (1 - \lambda)x_{t-1})b,$$

$$y_t - (1 - \lambda)y_{t-1} = a\lambda\, y_{t-1} + (x_t - (1 - \lambda)x_{t-1})b,$$

$$(1 - (1 - \lambda + a\lambda)L)\, y_t = b\,(1 - (1 - \lambda)L)\, x_t$$

$$= \frac{b}{1 - \rho L}\,(1 - (1 - \lambda)L)\, \epsilon_t.$$

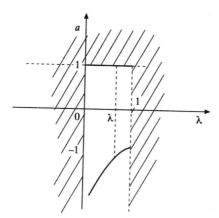

Figure 12.1 Parameter Region for a Stationary Solution

The equation just obtained is of the ARMA type, but does not always lead to a stationary solution y. For that the parameter $1 - \lambda + a\lambda$ must be strictly between -1 and +1. This condition is equivalent to

$$1 - \frac{2}{\lambda} < a < 1.$$

We give the area for which parameter values lead to a stationary solution in figure 12.1.

The larger the adaptation coefficient λ is, the smaller is the interval of values a leading to stationarity. In the presence of stationarity the effect on the endogenous variable of a sustained shock on the exogenous variable x is

$$\frac{\Delta y}{\Delta x} = \frac{b(1 - (1 - \lambda))}{1 - (1 - \lambda + a\lambda)} = \frac{b}{1 - a},$$

$$\frac{\Delta y}{\Delta x} = \frac{ab}{1 - a} \quad + \quad b. \tag{12.16}$$

$$\text{indirect effect} \quad \text{direct effect}$$

We find again a decomposition of the effect into a direct effect of x and an indirect effect through the expectation. Since the adaptative expectation scheme is chosen independently of the evolution of the exogenous process, we see that the indirect effect is independent of ρ. It is also independent of the adaptation coefficient λ.

12.4 Models with Future Variables Expectations

The original Muth model introduced in the previous section leads to an equation, where the endogenous variable y_t is a function of the expectation of its current value $E(y_t \mid I_{t-1})$ and of the values taken by various exogenous variables (observable or not). The fact that in general such an equation admits a unique solution simplifies its study. In this section, we consider a seemingly minor modification of the initial formulation, by replacing the rational expectation of the current variable $E(y_t \mid I_{t-1})$ by the expectation of the future variable $E(y_{t+1} \mid I_t)$. As we will see later on, this change has an important impact on the solutions of the model, since in this case the model has an infinity of solutions to be studied in detail.

12.4.1 An Example

A classical model with expectation of the future variable is used to describe the evolution of the price of a financial asset.

Let us first consider a deterministic environment and let p_t be the price of the asset at time t, let d_t be the dividend paid over the period $[t, t+1)$, and let η be the short-term interest rate (assumed constant). The condition of no dynamic arbitrage opportunity implies the equilibrium condition

$$p_t = \frac{1}{1+\eta}(p_{t+1} + d_t) \qquad (12.17)$$

with $t \geq 0$. This means that the dividend compensates exactly for the present discounted change in price.

Analogously, in an uncertain environment, a relationship of the same type is often written by replacing the future price by its expectation

$$p_t = \frac{1}{1+\eta}(E(p_{t+1} \mid I_t) + d_t) \qquad (12.18)$$

with $t \geq 0$. Thus, we implicitly assume that the dividend d_t and the interest rate η are known at time t. On the other hand, we have assumed that the equilibrium model in an uncertain environment is directly derived from the model in a certain environment by replacing some variables by their conditional means.

12.4.2 Description of the Solution Methods

In this section, let us consider a reduced form equation analogous to the price equation (12.18). Let y_t be the endogenous variable, I_t be the available information at time t. The equation is

$$y_t = aE(y_{t+1} \mid I_t) + u_t \qquad (12.19)$$

with $t \geq 0$.

Let us assume that the distribution of the residual term $(u_t, t \geq 0)$ is given. A *solution* of the equation (12.19) is a process $(y_t, t \geq 0)$

compatible with the relation. In order for the expectation of the variable to have a real effect on the realization we constrain the parameter a to be different from 0.

Forward-Backward Approaches A first suggestion consists in solving recursively the equation toward the future (*forward approach*) or toward the past (*backward approach*).

Forward approach

The recursive solution toward the future leads to

$$y_t = aE(y_{t+1} \mid I_t) + u_t$$

$$= a^2 E(y_{t+2} \mid I_t) + u_t + aE(u_{t+1-1} \mid I_t)$$

$$\vdots$$

$$= a^i E(y_{t+i} \mid I_t) + u_t + aE(u_{t+1} \mid I_t) + \ldots + a^{i-1}E(u_{t+i-1} \mid I_t).$$

If the series of general term $a^i E(u_{t+i} \mid I_t)$ converges, the equation (12.19) has the particular solution, called the *forward solution*

$$y_t^F = \sum_{i=0}^{\infty} a^i E(u_{t+i} \mid I_t). \tag{12.20}$$

Note that if the residual exogenous term u_t is stationary, we have

$$\text{var} \left(E(u_{t+i} \mid I_t) \right) \leq \text{var} \left(u_{t+i} \right) = \text{var} \left(u_t \right).$$

As soon as a is smaller than 1 in modulus, we have the convergence in quadratic mean of the series defining y_t^F.

Theorem 12.3: *A sufficient condition for the existence of the forward solution is the stationarity of the exogenous process and the restriction* $\mid a \mid < 1$.

Example 12.2: When the exogenous process is a first-order autoregressive process

$$u_t = \rho u_{t-1} + \epsilon_t,$$

with $\mid \rho \mid < 1$, we have

$$E(u_{t+i} \mid I_t) = \rho^i u_t,$$

$$y_t^F = \sum_{t=0}^{\infty} a^i (\rho^i u_t) = \frac{1}{1 - a\rho} u_t.$$

Note that the series converges if $\mid a\rho \mid < 1$.

Remark 12.1: In some applications the forward solution may have interesting economic interpretations. Consider equation (12.18) giving the evolution of an asset price. The forward solution provides the price

$$p_t^F = \sum_{i=0}^{\infty} \frac{1}{(1+\eta)^{i+1}} E(d_{t+i} \mid I_t) = E(V_t \mid I_t),$$

where $V_t = \sum_{i=0}^{\infty} \frac{1}{(1+\eta)^{i+1}} d_{t+i}$ is interpreted as the present discounted value of the sum of the dividends paid between t and ∞. p_t^{∞} is then the expectation of this discounted value.

Backward approach

To solve backward the equation (12.19), we need to be able to express the future value y_{t+1} as a function of the current value y_t. Therefore we need to extract the realization y_{t+1} from its expectation $E(y_{t+1} \mid I_t)$. As a first step, we often examine whether there exists a solution with perfect foresight, such that $y_{t+1} = E(y_{t+1} \mid I_t)$. The extraction problem is then solved right away and the equation becomes

$$y_t = a y_{t+1} + u_t$$

$$\Leftrightarrow y_{t+1} = \frac{1}{a} y_t - \frac{1}{a} u_t$$

$$\Leftrightarrow y_t = \frac{1}{a} y_{t-1} - \frac{1}{a} u_{t-1}.$$

It is an equation without expectation which can be directly analyzed. Assuming that the process $\{u_t\}$ exists also for negative indexes, by substitution we see that the series (if it exists)

$$y_t^B = -\sum_{i=1}^{\infty} \frac{1}{a^i} u_{t-i} \tag{12.21}$$

is a solution to the initial equation (12.19), since the information set I_t contains the current and past values of the exogenous variable appearing in the residual term u_t.

Theorem 12.4: *When the series of general term $\frac{1}{a^i} u_{t-i}$ converges (in quadratic mean) and when the information I_t contains $u_t, u_{t-1}, \ldots$ then*

$$y_t^B = -\sum_{i=1}^{\infty} \frac{1}{a^i} u_{t-i}$$

is a solution to the rational expectation model (12.19). It is called the backward solution.

This particular solution can be written in a synthetic form by introducing the lag operator L. We have

$$y_t^B = -\sum_{i=1}^{\infty} \frac{1}{a^i} L^i u_t = -\frac{L}{a-L} u_t. \tag{12.22}$$

When the process $\{u_t\}$ is stationary, we see right away that the backward solution exists if and only if the coefficient a is greater than 1 in modulus.

Linear Solutions

Exogenous Variable Dynamics

It is often convenient to complete the initial formulation by describing the dynamics of the exogenous variables $\{u_t, t \geq 0\}$. In a moving average framework, let us assume that

$$u_t = \sum_{j=0}^{t} \mathbf{h}_j \boldsymbol{\varepsilon}_{t-j} = \sum_{j=0}^{\infty} \mathbf{h}_j \tilde{\boldsymbol{\varepsilon}}_{t-j} = \mathbf{h}(L)\tilde{\boldsymbol{\varepsilon}}_t,$$

where $\boldsymbol{\varepsilon} = (\boldsymbol{\varepsilon}_t, t \geq 0)$ is a multidimensional white noise, $\tilde{\boldsymbol{\varepsilon}}_t = \boldsymbol{\varepsilon}_t$ if $t \geq 0$, $\tilde{\boldsymbol{\varepsilon}}_t = 0$ if $t < 0$, and $\mathbf{h}_j$, $j = 1, \ldots$, are row vectors.

Linear Solutions

Assume the available information at time t is made of current and past values of $\boldsymbol{\varepsilon}$. We can see if there exist some solutions y allowing for a similar expression as for u_t. This amounts to writing

$$y_t = \mathbf{c}(L)\tilde{\boldsymbol{\varepsilon}}_t = \sum_{j=0}^{\infty} \mathbf{c}_j \tilde{\boldsymbol{\varepsilon}}_{t-j}.$$

When this moving average form is imposed, we have

$$y_{t+1} = \mathbf{c}(L)\tilde{\boldsymbol{\varepsilon}}_{t+1} = \mathbf{c}_0 \tilde{\boldsymbol{\varepsilon}}_{t+1} + \frac{\mathbf{c}(L) - \mathbf{c}_0}{L} \tilde{\boldsymbol{\varepsilon}}_t,$$

$$E(y_{t+1} \mid I_t) = \mathbf{c}_0 E(\tilde{\boldsymbol{\varepsilon}}_{t+1} \mid I_t) + E\left(\frac{\mathbf{c}(L) - \mathbf{c}_0}{L} \tilde{\boldsymbol{\varepsilon}}_t \mid I_t\right)$$

$$= \frac{\mathbf{c}(L) - \mathbf{c}_0}{L} \tilde{\boldsymbol{\varepsilon}}_t.$$

Replacing it in the dynamic equation for y, we get

$$y_t = aE(y_{t+1} \mid I_t) + u_t$$

$$\Leftrightarrow \mathbf{c}(L)\tilde{\boldsymbol{\varepsilon}}_t = a\frac{\mathbf{c}(L) - \mathbf{c}_0}{L} \tilde{\boldsymbol{\varepsilon}}_t + \mathbf{h}(L)\tilde{\boldsymbol{\varepsilon}}_t$$

$$\Leftrightarrow \mathbf{c}(L) = a\frac{\mathbf{c}(L) - \mathbf{c}_0}{L} + \mathbf{h}(L)$$

$$\Leftrightarrow \mathbf{c}(L) = -\frac{a\mathbf{c}_0}{L-a} + \frac{L\mathbf{h}(L)}{L-a}.$$

This method is just an undetermined coefficient approach such as the one used by Muth (1961) or McCallum (1976). The use of polynomials in the lag operator simplifies this solution a lot. Note that the moving average operator obtained, $\mathbf{c}(L)$, depends not only on the dynamics of the exogenous variables $\mathbf{h}(L)$, and on the structural parameter of the conditional model a, but also on the auxiliary parameters in the row vector $\mathbf{c}_0$ the size of which is p.

Theorem 12.5: *Let us consider the model* $y_t = aE(y_{t+1} \mid I_t) + u_t$, *where the exogenous process satisfies*

$$u_t = \mathbf{h}(L)\tilde{\boldsymbol{\varepsilon}}_t$$

and where the information is

$$I_t = (\tilde{\boldsymbol{\varepsilon}}_t, \tilde{\boldsymbol{\varepsilon}}_{t-1}, \tilde{\boldsymbol{\varepsilon}}_{t-2}, \dots) .$$

This model admits an infinite number of linear solutions given by

$$y_t = \left(-\frac{a\mathbf{c}_0}{L - a} + \frac{Lh(L)}{L - a} \right) \tilde{\boldsymbol{\varepsilon}}_t,$$

where $\mathbf{c}_0 \in \mathbb{R}^p$ *(p being the size of* $\tilde{\boldsymbol{\varepsilon}}_t$).

In the present context, the backward solution always exists and is given by

$$y_t^B = \frac{L}{L - a} u_t = \frac{L\mathbf{h}(L)}{L - a}\tilde{\boldsymbol{\varepsilon}}_t.$$

Comparing this equation with the general expression for the linear solutions, we see that the latter can be expressed as functions of the backward solution

$$y_t = -\frac{a\mathbf{c}_0}{L - a}\tilde{\boldsymbol{\varepsilon}}_t + y_t^B .$$

The linear solutions span an affine space containing the backward solution and of dimension equal to the size p of the underlying noise.

Stationary Linear Solutions

The previous solution allows one to get the results relative to the asymptotically stationary case. Let us assume an asymptotically stationary exogenous process

$$u_t = \sum_{j=0}^{t} \mathbf{h}_j \boldsymbol{\varepsilon}_{t-j} = \sum_{j=0}^{\infty} \mathbf{h}_j \tilde{\boldsymbol{\varepsilon}}_{t-j},$$

with $\sum_{j=0}^{\infty} \mathbf{h}_j \mathbf{h}_j' < \infty$.

Among the linear solutions previously obtained, we can select the asymptotically stationary ones. We need to check if $\sum_{j=0}^{\infty} \mathbf{c}_j \mathbf{c}_j'$ is finite or not. Since

$$\mathbf{c}(L) = \frac{1}{L-a}\left(-a\mathbf{c}_0 + L\mathbf{h}(L)\right),$$

two cases have to be considered:

(i) If $\mid a \mid > 1$, the moving average representation of $\frac{1}{a-L}$ corresponds to a convergent series and the solution is asymptotically stationary for every choice of $\mathbf{c}_0$.

(ii) If $\mid a \mid \leq 1$, the representation of $\frac{1}{a-L}$ corresponds to a nonconverging series. The condition $\sum_{j=0}^{\infty}\mathbf{c}_j\mathbf{c}_j' < \infty$ can only be satisfied if a is a root of the numerator. The only possible choice of the auxiliary parameter is $\mathbf{c}_0 = \mathbf{h}(a)$.

Theorem 12.6: *Consider the model* $y_t = aE(y_{t+1} \mid I_t) + u_t$, *where the exogenous process is stationary and defined as*

$$u_t = \mathbf{h}(L)\boldsymbol{\varepsilon}_t, \qquad \sum_{j=0}^{\infty}\mathbf{h}_j\mathbf{h}_j' < \infty,$$

and where $I_t = (\boldsymbol{\varepsilon}_t, \boldsymbol{\varepsilon}_{t-1}, \dots)$.

(i) *If* $\mid a \mid > 1$, *the model admits an infinity of stationary solutions*

$$y_t = \left(-\frac{a\mathbf{c}_0}{L-a} + \frac{L\mathbf{h}(L)}{L-a}\right)\boldsymbol{\varepsilon}_t$$

with $\mathbf{c}_0 \in \mathbb{R}^p$.

(ii) *If* $\mid a \mid \leq 1$, *the model admits a unique stationary linear solution. It is given by*

$$y_t = \frac{L\mathbf{h}(L) - a\mathbf{h}(a)}{L-a}\boldsymbol{\varepsilon}_t.$$

When $\mid a \mid < 1$, we have seen that the forward solution exists. It coincides with the one derived in theorem 12.6

$$y_t^F = \frac{L\mathbf{h}(L) - a\mathbf{h}(a)}{L-a}\boldsymbol{\varepsilon}_t.$$

General Solution

Approach Based on the Homogeneous Equation

The equation to solve is a linear difference equation, up to the presence of the expectation term. This kind of linear difference equation is usually solved by searching for the solution of the corresponding homogeneous equation. The same steps can be followed in our context (see Gourieroux,

Laffont, and Monfort, 1982). Let (y_t^0) be a solution (called specific) to the equation and y_t be another solution to the same equation. We have at the same time

$$y_t = aE(y_{t+1} \mid I_t) + u_t,$$

$$y_t^0 = aE(y_{t+1}^0 \mid I_t) + u_t.$$

Taking the difference and using the linearity of the conditional expectation, we notice that the difference $z_t = y_t - y_t^0$ between the two solutions satisfies an homogeneous equation

$$z_t = aE(z_{t+1} \mid I_t)$$

$$\Leftrightarrow a^t z_t = a^{t+1} E(z_{t+1} \mid I_t).$$

The process $(m_t = a^t z_t)$ is such that the rational expectation

$$E(m_{t+1} \mid I_t)$$

coincides with the naive expectation m_t, i.e., it is a martingale.

Theorem 12.7: *If (y_t^0) is a specific solution of the equation, the other solutions are obtained by*

$$y_t = y_t^0 + \frac{1}{a^t} m_t,$$

where (m_t) is a martingale which can be arbitrarily chosen.

Introduction of the Forecast Errors
An approach which seems to extend easily to more general models was proposed by Broze, Gourieroux, and Szafarz (1985). The idea is to use the same steps as for the backward solution without assuming perfect foresight anymore. More precisely, by introducing the forecast error, we can always express the expectation as a function of the realizations

$$y_{t+1} = E(y_{t+1} \mid I_t) + \epsilon_{t+1}^0.$$

The process $\{\epsilon_t^0\}$ must have the properties of a forecast error process $E(\epsilon_t^0 \mid I_{t-1}) = 0$, thus must be a martingale difference sequence.

The initial equation $y_t = aE(y_{t+1} \mid I_t) + u_t$ can then be replaced by $y_t = a(y_{t+1} - \epsilon_{t+1}^0) + u_t$, or in an equivalent way

$$y_t = \frac{1}{a} y_{t-1} - \frac{u_{t-1}}{a} + \epsilon_t^0.$$

Of course, the possible choices for the forecast error are to be found.

Theorem 12.8:

(i)   *If y is a solution to the rational expectation model, then y satisfies the linear difference equation*

$$y_t = \frac{1}{a} y_{t-1} - \frac{u_{t-1}}{a} + \epsilon_t^0, \ \forall \ t,$$

where ϵ_t^0 is the forecast error on y_t.

(ii) *Conversely, let ϵ^0 be a random martingale difference sequence and let y be a solution to the difference equation*

$$y_t = \frac{1}{a} y_{t-1} - \frac{u_{t-1}}{a} + \epsilon_t^0, \ \forall \ t.$$

Then y is a solution to the rational expectation model.

PROOF: We just need to verify the second part of the proposition. For that, we can compute the forecast conditional on I_{t-1} for each of the elements of the difference equation

$$E(y_t \mid I_{t-1}) = \frac{1}{a} y_{t-1} - \frac{u_{t-1}}{a} + E(\epsilon_t^0 \mid I_{t-1})$$

$$= \frac{1}{a} y_{t-1} - \frac{u_{t-1}}{a},$$

since (ϵ_t^0) is a martingale difference sequence. We deduce that we have necessarily

$$\epsilon_t^0 = y_t - E(y_t \mid I_{t-1}).$$

Replacing ϵ_t^0 by this expression in the difference equation, we get

$$y_t = \frac{1}{a} y_{t-1} - \frac{u_{t-1}}{a} + y_t - E(y_t \mid I_{t-1})$$

$$\Leftrightarrow y_{t-1} = a E(y_t \mid I_{t-1}) + u_{t-1}, \ \forall \ t.$$

But this is the initial equation. □

12.4.3 Properties of the Solutions Set

Effect of a Terminal Condition   When the solution is known at a time t_0, from the equation we have that

$$y_{t_0 - 1} = a E(y_{t_0} \mid I_{t_0 - 1}) + u_{t_0 - 1},$$

i.e., $y_{t_0 - 1}$ is a function of the exogenous variables and of y_{t_0}, and therefore is also known. By backward substitution, once y_{t_0} is known, we see that the set of past values $y_{t_0 - 1}, y_{t_0 - 2}, \ldots$ is determined.

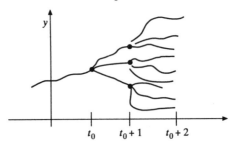

Figure 12.2   Multiple Solutions in the Future

Effect of an Initial Condition   On the other hand, the future value
is given by

$$y_{t_0+1} = \frac{1}{a}y_{t_0} - \frac{u_{t_0}}{a} + \epsilon^0_{t_0+1},$$

where $\epsilon^0_{t_0+1}$ is any variable orthogonal to I_{t_0}. Thus, there is an infinite
number of future values y_{t_0+1} compatible with a given value at time t_0.
Examining the value y_{t_0+2}, we have

$$y_{t_0+2} = \frac{1}{a}y_{t_0+1} - \frac{u_{t_0+1}}{a} + \epsilon^0_{t_0+2}$$

$$= \frac{1}{a^2}y_{t_0} - \frac{u_{t_0+1}}{a} - \frac{u_{t_0}}{a^2} + \epsilon^0_{t_0+2} + \frac{\epsilon^0_{t_0+1}}{a}.$$

This time, the multiplicity comes from two arbitrary variables

$$\epsilon^0_{t_0+1}, \epsilon^0_{t_0+2},$$

orthogonal to I_{t_0}, respectively, to I_{t_0+1}. Thus there is an increase of
the multiplicity as the horizon increases, for a given value y_{t_0} (cf. figure
12.2).

This multiplicity is specific to the expectation models and does not
exist in the corresponding deterministic models (that is, with perfect
foresight) $y_t = ay_{t+1} + u_t$.

Sunspots   Often we choose the information set as the one spanned by
the current and past values of the exogenous variables of the underlying
structural model. We could also extend the set I_t as to include some observations on some explanatory variables independent of the exogenous
disturbances. Such variables, "external" to the initial structural model,
are often called *sunspots*. To simplify matters, we consider only linear
cases; we can introduce the sunspots by writing

$$u_t = \mathbf{h}(L)\tilde{\boldsymbol{\varepsilon}}_t = \mathbf{h}_1(L)\tilde{\boldsymbol{\varepsilon}}_{1t} + \mathbf{h}_2(L)\tilde{\boldsymbol{\varepsilon}}_{2t} = \mathbf{h}_1(L)\tilde{\boldsymbol{\varepsilon}}_{1t}.$$

The residual variable depends only on the innovation variables $\boldsymbol{\varepsilon}_1$ and
does not depend on the outside innovation variables $\boldsymbol{\varepsilon}_2$. Moreover, we

impose the independence between $\boldsymbol{\varepsilon}_1$ and $\boldsymbol{\varepsilon}_2$. From theorem 12.5 the form of the linear solutions can be written as

$$y_t = \left(-\frac{a\mathbf{c}_{01}}{L-a}\tilde{\boldsymbol{\varepsilon}}_{1t} + \frac{L\mathbf{h}_1(L)}{L-a}\tilde{\boldsymbol{\varepsilon}}_{1t} \right) - \frac{a\mathbf{c}_{02}}{L-a}\tilde{\boldsymbol{\varepsilon}}_{2t}.$$

The solution may depend on these outside variables $\boldsymbol{\varepsilon}_2$ although the latter do not really enter the structural model which expresses the realization $y_t = a \,_t\hat{y}_{t+1} + u_t$ as a function of the expectation $_t\hat{y}_{t+1}$. Thus just thinking that sunspots may have an influence, say, on prices and taking into consideration these outside variables in the expectation formation can lead to a real effect on prices themselves, and reinforce the agents' idea that sunspots matter.

Moreover, using the independence of $\boldsymbol{\varepsilon}_1$ and $\boldsymbol{\varepsilon}_2$, note that

$$\mathrm{var}\,(y_t) = \mathrm{var}\,\left(-\frac{a\mathbf{c}_{01}}{L-a}\tilde{\boldsymbol{\varepsilon}}_{1t} + \frac{L\mathbf{h}_1(L)}{L-a}\tilde{\boldsymbol{\varepsilon}}_{1t} \right) + \mathrm{var}\,\left(\frac{a\mathbf{c}_{02}}{L-a}\tilde{\boldsymbol{\varepsilon}}_{2t} \right)$$

$$\geq \mathrm{var}\,\left(-\frac{a\mathbf{c}_{01}}{L-a}\tilde{\boldsymbol{\varepsilon}}_{1t} + \frac{L\mathbf{h}_1(L)}{L-a}\tilde{\boldsymbol{\varepsilon}}_{1t} \right).$$

The presence of these outside variables leads to a greater variability in the solution.

Variability of the Stationary Linear Solutions Restricting ourselves to the stationary linear solutions, and considering the case $\mid a \mid > 1$, we can write

$$y_t = \left(-\frac{a\mathbf{c}_0}{L-a} + \frac{L\mathbf{h}(L)}{L-a} \right)\boldsymbol{\varepsilon}_t,$$

with $\mathbf{c}_0 \in \mathbf{R}^p$.

Let us introduce the processes

$$y_t^0 = \frac{L\mathbf{h}(L)}{L-a}\boldsymbol{\varepsilon}_t, \qquad y_t^j = -\frac{a}{L-a}\boldsymbol{\varepsilon}_{jt},$$

with $j = 1,\ldots,p$, and where ϵ_{jt} indicates the j-th component of $\boldsymbol{\varepsilon}_t$. The general solution is written in the form of an affine linear combination

$$y_t = \sum_{j=1}^p c_j y_t^j + y_t^0.$$

The question is now whether there exists a choice of coefficients c_j, $j = 1,\ldots,p$, leading to a minimal variability of the solution (cf. Taylor, 1977). This is the same as solving the problem

$$\min_{c_j} Ey_t^2 = \min_{c_j} E(y_t^0 + \sum_{j=1}^p c_j y_t^j)^2.$$

The optimal choice $\hat{c}_j$ $j = 1, \ldots, p$ of the coefficients corresponds to the opposite of the regression coefficients of y_t^0 on y_t^j, $j = 1, \ldots, p$

$$\begin{pmatrix} \hat{c}_1 \\ \vdots \\ \hat{c}_p \end{pmatrix} = - \begin{pmatrix} \text{var } y_t^1 & \cdots & \text{cov}\,(y_t^1, y_t^p) \\ \vdots & & \vdots \\ \text{cov}\,(y_t^1, y_t^p) & \cdots & \text{var }(y_t^p) \end{pmatrix}^{-1} \begin{pmatrix} \text{cov}\,(y_t^1, y_t^0) \\ \vdots \\ \text{cov}\,(y_t^p, y_t^0) \end{pmatrix}$$

$$= -\,(\text{var}\,(\mathbf{y}_t))^{-1}\,\text{cov}\,(\mathbf{y}_t, y_t^0),$$

with $\mathbf{y}_t = (y_t^1, \ldots, y_t^p)'$.

The minimum variance solution is therefore

$$\hat{y}_t = y_t^0 + \sum_{j=1}^{p} \hat{c}_j y_t^j,$$

and is interpreted as the residual of the previous regression. In particular it is orthogonal to the variables y_t^j, $j = 1, \ldots, p$.

All the other solutions can then be written as

$$y_t = \hat{y}_t + \sum_{j=1}^{p} (c_j - \hat{c}_j) y_t^j.$$

The corresponding variance is

$$\text{var}\,(y_t) = \text{var}\,(\hat{y}_t) + (\mathbf{c} - \hat{\mathbf{c}})' Var(\mathbf{y}_t)(\mathbf{c} - \hat{\mathbf{c}}),$$

which is a variance decomposition into the minimum variance and the deviation with respect to it. The solution $\hat{y}_t$ plays an important role as it corresponds to a less erratic behavior. $\hat{y}$ is found in the literature as the *bubbleless solution*. The other solutions whose variance is greater are called *bubble solutions*; the importance of the bubble is measured by the additional term $(\mathbf{c} - \hat{\mathbf{c}})' \text{var}\,(\mathbf{y}_t)(\mathbf{c} - \hat{\mathbf{c}})$.

12.5 Models with Several Expectations

Some of the solution methods discussed in the previous sections can be extended to the case of an equation showing different types of expectations. Thus, following the martingale difference approach, we can transform the initial structural model into a dynamic equation with respect to y_t by simply rewriting the expectations as a function of the y_t's and the errors. This equation involves observable variables and is the basis for the solution. Let us start by studying some examples which will show that sometimes it is necessary to impose some constraints between successive forecast errors. Then we will describe the general result and its use in finding stationary solutions.

12.5.1 Some Examples

A Model with Several Expectations of the Current Variable

An extension of Muth's model consists in introducing in the equation current variable expectations at various past times. An example of such a model is

$$y_t = aE(y_t \mid I_{t-1}) + bE(y_t \mid I_{t-2}) + u_t. \qquad (12.23)$$

Taking the conditional expectation of the two terms of the equation with respect to the information set I_{t-1}, and then with respect to the information set I_{t-2}, we get

$$E(y_t \mid I_{t-1}) = aE(y_t \mid I_{t-1}) + bE(y_t \mid I_{t-2}) + E(u_t \mid I_{t-1}),$$

$$E(y_t \mid I_{t-2}) = aE(y_t \mid I_{t-2}) + bE(y_t \mid I_{t-2}) + E(u_t \mid I_{t-2}),$$

which allows one to write the expectations of the endogenous variable as a function of the expectations of the exogenous variables. We have

$$E(y_t \mid I_{t-1}) = \frac{b}{1-a} \frac{1}{1-a-b} E(u_t \mid I_{t-2}) + \frac{1}{1-a} E(u_t \mid I_{t-1}),$$

$$E(y_t \mid I_{t-2}) = \frac{1}{1-a-b} E(u_t \mid I_{t-2}).$$

Therefore, the model (12.23) admits a unique solution like Muth's model. This one is

$$y_t = \frac{b}{(1-a)(1-a-b)} E(u_t \mid I_{t-2}) + \frac{a}{1-a} E(u_t \mid I_{t-1}) + u_t.$$

Thus, if the exogenous process verifies a first-order autoregressive process $u_t = \rho u_{t-1} + \epsilon_t$, $\mid \rho \mid < 1$, and if the information set is made up of the current and past values of $y_t, u_t, y_{t-1}, u_{t-1}, \ldots$, we have

$$E(u_t \mid I_{t-1}) = \rho u_{t-1}, \qquad E(u_t \mid I_{t-2}) = \rho^2 u_{t-2}.$$

The solution is

$$y_t = \frac{b\rho^2 u_{t-2}}{(1-a)(1-a-b)} + \frac{a\rho}{1-a} u_{t-1} + u_t.$$

The dynamics of the exogenous variable has an impact on the dynamics of the endogenous one through the expectation mechanism.

A Generalization of the Model with Expectation of the Future Variable

An extension of the model studied in section 12.3 is

$$y_t = aE(y_{t+2} \mid I_t) + u_t. \qquad (12.24)$$

Writing this expectation as a function of the realization and of the forecast error, we get

$$y_t = a(y_{t+2} - v_{t,2}) + u_t,$$

with $v_{t,2} = y_{t+2} - E(y_{t+2} \mid I_t)$. Hence

$$y_t = a(y_{t+2} - \epsilon_{t+2}^0 - \epsilon_{t+1}^1) + u_t,$$

with

$$\epsilon_{t+2}^0 = y_{t+2} - E(y_{t+2} \mid I_{t+1}),$$

$$\epsilon_{t+1}^1 = E(y_{t+2} \mid I_{t+1}) - E(y_{t+2} \mid I_t).$$

Therefore we have

$$y_t = \frac{1}{a} y_{t-2} - \frac{1}{a} u_{t-2} + \epsilon_t^0 + \epsilon_{t-1}^1, \qquad (12.25)$$

where ϵ^0 and ϵ^1 are two martingale difference sequences.

Conversely, given any two martingale difference sequences ϵ^0 and ϵ^1 and a process y satisfying the equation (12.25), we can get

$$E(y_t \mid I_{t-2}) = \frac{1}{a} y_{t-2} - \frac{1}{a} u_{t-2} + E(\epsilon_t^0 \mid I_{t-2}) + E(\epsilon_t^1 \mid I_{t-2})$$

$$= \frac{1}{a} y_{t-2} - \frac{1}{a} u_{t-2},$$

by taking the conditional expectation of each term with respect to I_{t-2}. This equation coincides with the initial rational expectation model.

The solutions are thus all obtained considering the equation (12.25) with any ϵ^0 and ϵ^1. There is here an infinity of solutions "parameterized" by ϵ^0 and ϵ^1. We will say that the dimension of the solutions space is 2 with respect to the arbitrary martingale difference sequences.

A Model with Expectations of a Current and a Future Variable

Taylor (1977) has obtained the reduced form of a macroeconomic model with rational expectations as

$$y_t = aE(y_{t+1} \mid I_{t-1}) + bE(y_t \mid I_{t-1}) + u_t, \qquad (12.26)$$

containing both types of expectations previously examined. Introducing the forecast errors at horizons 1 and 2, we see that any solution to (12.26) satisfies

$$y_t = a(y_{t+1} - \epsilon_{t+1}^0 - \epsilon_t^1) + b(y_t - \epsilon_t^0) + u_t, \qquad (12.27)$$

where (ϵ_t^0) and (ϵ_t^1) are martingale difference sequences associated with the forecast updates.

Conversely, let us consider a solution of the equation (12.27), where ϵ^0 and ϵ^1 are martingale difference sequences and let us examine if they can be interpreted as forecast updates.

Computing the forecasts of each member of (12.27) with respect to I_t and I_{t-1}, we get

$$y_t = a(_t\hat{y}_{t+1} - \epsilon_t^1) + b(y_t - \epsilon_t^0) + u_t, \qquad (12.28)$$

and

$$t-1\hat{y}_t = a\,{}_{t-1}\hat{y}_{t+1} + b\,{}_{t-1}\hat{y}_t + {}_{t-1}\hat{u}_t. \tag{12.29}$$

Subtracting (12.28) from (12.27), we get

$$0 = a(y_{t+1} - {}_t\hat{y}_{t+1} - \epsilon^0_{t+1}),$$

which shows that the martingale difference sequence ϵ^0_t is to be interpreted as the sequence of forecast errors at horizon 1. Subtracting now (12.29) from (12.28), we have

$$y_t - {}_{t-1}\hat{y}_t = a\left({}_t\hat{y}_{t+1} - {}_{t-1}\hat{y}_{t+1} - \epsilon^1_t\right) + b\left(y_t - {}_{t-1}\hat{y}_t - \epsilon^0_t\right) + u_t - {}_{t-1}\hat{u}_t.$$

Taking into account the expression of ϵ^0_t, note that this equation can be written as

$$\epsilon^0_t = a\left({}_t\hat{y}_{t+1} - {}_{t-1}\hat{y}_{t+1} - \epsilon^1_t\right) + u_t - {}_{t-1}\hat{u}_t,$$

so that ϵ^1 can be interpreted as the update

$$\epsilon^1_t = {}_t\hat{y}_{t+1} - {}_{t-1}\hat{y}_{t+1},$$

if and only if $\epsilon^0_t = u_t - {}_{t-1}\hat{u}_t$.

Equation (12.27) provides a solution to the model (12.26) only if one of the martingale difference sequences is previously restricted. Here the forecast error on y at horizon 1 must coincide with the forecast error at horizon 1 on the exogenous term u. The equation in the observed variable which is equivalent to the initial model is

$$y_t = a\left(y_{t+1} - (u_{t+1} - {}_t\hat{u}_{t+1}) - \epsilon^1_t\right) + b\left(y_t - u_t - {}_{t-1}\hat{u}_t\right) + u_t,$$

$$\Leftrightarrow y_t = \frac{1-b}{a}y_{t-1} + u_t - E(u_t \mid I_{t-1}) + \frac{b-1}{a}u_{t-1}$$

$$- \frac{b}{a}E(u_{t-1} \mid I_{t-2}) + \epsilon^1_{t-1},$$

$$\tag{12.30}$$

where ϵ^1 is an arbitrary martingale difference sequence.

These few examples show that resorting to the introduction of updates will most probably allow us to find the solutions in a general model, provided that one examines the various restrictions satisfied by these updates. Moreover, the dimension of the set of solutions with respect to the arbitrary martingale difference sequences may vary according to the number and the type of expectations in the model.

12.5.2 General Cases

The Model The most general linear model with rational expectations is

$$y_t = \sum_{k=0}^{K}\sum_{h=1}^{H} a_{kh} E(y_{t+h-k} \mid I_{t-k}) + \sum_{k=1}^{K} a_{k0}y_{t-k} + u_t. \tag{12.31}$$

The endogenous variable depends on the lagged variables $y_{t-1} \ldots y_{t-K}$, on a synthesis of the exogenous term u_t and on a number of expectations. These can refer to the future $(h > k)$, current $(h = k)$, or past $(h < k)$ variables; they can be formulated at dates prior $(k > 0)$, or contemporary to the realization $(k = 0)$. h is interpreted as the forecast horizon, H as the largest horizon appearing in the model.

Expectations as a Function of the Realizations We can express each of the expectations as a function of the corresponding realization; we have

$$E(y_{t+h-k} \mid I_{t-k}) = y_{t+h-k} - \sum_{j=0}^{h-1} \epsilon_{t+h-k-j}^{j}.$$

Replacing it in the initial model, we get

$$y_t = \sum_{k=0}^{K} \sum_{h=1}^{H} a_{kh} \left(y_{t+h-k} - \sum_{j=0}^{h-1} \epsilon_{t+h-k-j}^{j} \right) + \sum_{k=1}^{K} a_{k0} y_{t-k} + u_t.$$

Introducing the sum of the structural coefficients associated with each realization

$$a_i^\star = \sum_{\substack{k \in \{0, \ldots, K\} \\ i+k \in \{0, \ldots, H\}}} a_{k,i+k}$$

(with $a_{00} = -1$), we get the equation

$$\sum_{i=I_0}^{I_1} a_i^\star y_{t+i} = \sum_{k=0}^{K} \sum_{h=1}^{H} a_{kh} \sum_{j=0}^{h-1} \epsilon_{t+h-k-j}^{j} - u_t, \tag{12.32}$$

where the two integers I_0 and I_1 are defined by

$$I_0 = \min(i : a_i^\star \neq 0), \qquad I_1 = \max(i : a_i^\star \neq 0). \tag{12.33}$$

This equation involves H martingale difference sequences, that is, the successive updates $\epsilon^0, \epsilon^1, \ldots, \epsilon^{H-1}$.

Restrictions on the Updates The previous result shows that every solution of the initial model satisfies the relation in (12.32) with the various updates as martingale difference sequences. Conversely, given arbitrary martingale difference sequences, we can analyze whether a solution y to the equation (12.32) will satisfy the initial structural model (12.31). Obviously, this is not always the case as we have seen in the example described in section 12.1.3. In fact, there is a general need for constraining the martingale difference sequences $\epsilon^0 \ldots \epsilon^{H-1}$, so they can in turn be interpreted as updates. These necessary and sufficient constraints are described below (see Broze, Gourieroux, and Szafarz, 1985, for a proof).

Theorem 12.9: *The solution to the model (12.32) satisfies the initial model with rational expectations if the martingale difference sequences satisfy the constraints*

$$\epsilon_t^i = \sum_{k=0}^{i} \sum_{h=0}^{H} a_{kh} \epsilon_t^{h-k+i} + E(u_{t+i} \mid I_t) - E(u_{t+i} \mid I_{t-1}),$$

$i = 0, \ldots, H - I_1 - 1$, *for* $H > I_1$.

If $H = I_1$, *the martingale difference sequences can be arbitrarily chosen.*

Some Consequences

(i) The previous proposition provides in particular the "dimension" of the solution set in terms of martingale difference sequences. Initially there are H martingale difference sequences constrained by $H - I_1$ linear relations. After solving, there remain I_1 arbitrary martingale difference sequences.

(ii) On the other hand, recall that in the case of the model with future variable expectation the multiplicity of solutions has two components: the first one comes from the dynamics inside the model with respect to perfect foresight, that is to the fact that y is allowed to interact with its lagged values. This happens when $I_1 \neq I_0$. Nevertheless, this multiplicity can be solved by imposing some restrictions on the initial conditions. The second cause of multiplicity comes from the possibility of arbitrarily choosing martingale difference sequences for $I_1 > 0$. We saw that this cause cannot be reduced by imposing initial conditions. It seems therefore advisable to look for models with a "small" number of solutions.

Theorem 12.10: *Rational expectation models whose solutions are characterized by the knowledge of a finite number of initial values correspond to the case* $I_1 = 0$.

For example, this is the case for models such as

$$y_t = \sum_{k=0}^{K} \sum_{h=1}^{k} a_{kh} E(y_{t+h-k} \mid I_{t-k}) + \sum_{k=1}^{K} a_{k0} y_{t-k} + u_t$$

which contain only expectations of the current or past values of the endogenous variable.

Theorem 12.11: *The rational expectation models admitting a unique solution are characterized by $I_0 = I_1 = 0$.*

These are models such as

$$y_t = \sum_{k=1}^{K} a_{kk} E(y_t \mid I_{t-k}) + u_t$$

which contain only expectations of the current variable and which can easily be solved recursively following the method used for (12.23).

(iii) We could also examine under which conditions a backward solution exists. Such a solution corresponds to the case where the rational expectations coincide with the perfect foresight, that is where the martingale difference sequences $\epsilon^0, \ldots, \epsilon^{H-1}$ are all equal to 0. It suffices to examine whether these zero conditions are compatible with the restrictions in theorem 12.10 on the updates. Note that if $H > I_1$ the constraints will be compatible when $E(u_{t+i} \mid I_t) = E(u_{t+i} \mid I_{t-1})$, $i = 0, \ldots, H - I_1 - 1$, which corresponds to the unlikely hypothesis of a predetermination of the exogenous process. Thus a backward solution can only exist when $H = I_1$.

Some Applications We have gathered in table 12.1 the reduced forms associated with the various rational expectation models ordered by value of the indexes H, K, I_1.

12.5.3 Linear Solutions

General Form of the Linear Solutions Let us assume that the exogenous process admits a moving average representation (possibly nonstationary)

$$u_t = \Theta(L)\tilde{\epsilon}_t,$$

where

$$\tilde{\epsilon}_t = \begin{cases} \epsilon_t, & \text{if } t \geq 0, \\ 0, & \text{otherwise,} \end{cases}$$

and ϵ is a white noise.

We might be interested in the existence of linear solutions, that is, admitting a similar moving average expression

$$y_t = A(L)\tilde{\epsilon}_t = a_0\epsilon_t + a_1\epsilon_{t-1} + \ldots a_t\epsilon_0.$$

The successive updates are then proportional to the innovation of the exogenous process

$$\epsilon_t^j = a_j \epsilon_t, \forall\ j. \tag{12.34}$$

Table 12.1 *Various R.E. Models with their Reduced Forms*

A $y_t = aE(y_t \mid I_{t-1}) + u_t \;\Rightarrow\; y_t = \dfrac{a}{1-a}E(u_t \mid I_{t-1}) + u_t$ (**Muth**)

     with $H=1,\; K=1,\; I_1=0$;

B $y_t = aE(y_{t+1} \mid I_t) + u_t \;\Rightarrow\; y_t = \dfrac{1}{a}y_{t-1} - \dfrac{1}{a}u_{t-1} + \epsilon_t^0$ (**Cagan**)

     with $H=1,\; K=0,\; I_1=1$;

C $y_t = aE(y_{t+1}|I_{t-1}) + u_t$

     $\Rightarrow\; y_t = \dfrac{1}{a}y_{t-1} - \dfrac{1}{a}u_{t-1} + u_t - E(u_t|I_{t-1}) + \epsilon_{t-1}^1$

     with $H=2,\; K=1,\; I_1=1$;

D $y_t = aE(y_{t+1}|I_t) + by_{t-1} + u_t \;\Rightarrow\; y_t = \dfrac{1}{a}y_{t-1} - \dfrac{b}{a}y_{t-2} - \dfrac{1}{a}u_{t-1} + \epsilon_t^0$

     with $H=1,\; K=1,\; I_1=1$;

E $y_t = aE(y_{t+1}|I_{t-1}) + bE(y_t|I_{t-1}) + u_t$ (**Taylor**)

$\Rightarrow\; y_t = \dfrac{1-b}{a}y_{t-1} + u_t - E(u_t|I_{t-1}) + \dfrac{b-1}{a}u_{t-1} - \dfrac{b}{a}E(u_{t-1}|I_{t-2}) + \epsilon_{t-1}^1$

     with $H=2,\; K=1,\; I_1=1$;

F $y_t = aE(y_{t+2}|I_t) + u_t \;\Rightarrow\; y_t = \dfrac{1}{a}y_{t-2} - \dfrac{1}{a}u_{t-2} + \epsilon_t^0 + \epsilon_{t-1}^1$

     with $H=2,\; K=0,\; I_1=2$;

G $y_t = aE(y_{t+2}|I_t) + bE(y_{t+1}|I_t) + u_t$

     $\Rightarrow\; y_t = -\dfrac{b}{a}y_{t-1} + \dfrac{1}{a}y_{t-2} - \dfrac{1}{a}u_{t-2} + \epsilon_t^0 - \dfrac{b}{a}\epsilon_{t-1}^0 + \epsilon_{t-1}^1$

     with $H=2,\; K=0,\; I_1=2$;

H $y_t = \displaystyle\sum_{h=1}^{H} a_h E(y_{t+h}|I_t) + u_t \;\Rightarrow\; y_t = -\dfrac{1}{a_H}\sum_{h=1}^{H} a_{H-h}y_{t-h} + \dfrac{1}{a_H}y_{t-H}$

     $+ \displaystyle\sum_{h=1}^{H} a_h \sum_{j=0}^{h-1} \epsilon_{t+h-j-H}^j - \dfrac{1}{a_H}u_{t-H}$

     with $H=H,\; K=0,\; I_1=H$.

Conversely, in order to obtain all the linear solutions, it will suffice to choose martingale difference sequences of this form such that they satisfy possible restrictions.

Asymptotic Stationarity of the Linear Solutions Let us assume now that the exogenous process is (asymptotically) stationary. The question is whether among the linear solutions there exist some which are (asymptotically) stationary, i.e., such that

$$\sum_{j=0}^{\infty} a_j^2 < \infty.$$

We can show that the restrictions on the martingale difference sequences in theorem 12.10 allow one to express the differences as a linear function of the last I_1 ones, i.e., $\epsilon^{H-I_1}, \ldots, \epsilon^{H-1}$. We can then express the former as a function of the latter and replace them in model (12.32) in terms of the realizations. The result is a relation of the type

$$\sum_{i=I_0}^{I_1} a_i^\star y_{t+i} = \sum_{j=H-I_1}^{H-1} \sum_{k=k_j}^{K_j} c_{jk} \epsilon_{t+I_1-k}^j + g_{t+I_1}(u),$$

where $g_t(u)$ is a linear stationary function of the process u as soon as u is linear and stationary $g_t(u) = \Omega(L)\epsilon_t$.

The linear solutions are then parameterized by the coefficients a_j, $j = H - I_1, \ldots, H - 1$ and are given by

$$\sum_{i=I_0}^{I_1} a_i^\star y_{t+i} = \sum_{j=H-I_1}^{H-1} \left(\sum_{k=k_j}^{K_j} c_{jk} a_j L^{k-I_1} \right) \tilde{\epsilon}_t + \Omega(L)\tilde{\epsilon}_{t+I_1},$$

$$\left(\sum_{i=0}^{I_1-I_0} a_{I_1-i}^\star L^i \right) y_t = \left(\sum_{j=H-I_1}^{H-1} \sum_{k=k_j}^{K_j} c_{jk} a_j L^k + \Omega(L) \right) \tilde{\epsilon}_t.$$

$$(12.35)$$

It is an ARMA representation of the linear solutions. Nonetheless, in order to know whether they correspond to asymptotically stationary solutions or not, we have to examine the roots of the autoregressive polynomial and their position with respect to the unit circle.

Let us assume that this autoregressive polynomial admits a root called λ_1 inside the unit circle. It is possible to get rid of this root by forcing it to be a root of the moving average polynomial as well. This implies the constraint

$$\sum_{j=H-I_1}^{H-1} \sum_{k=k_j}^{K_j} c_{jk} a_j \lambda_1^k + \Omega(\lambda_1) = 0,$$

on the parameters $a_{H-I_1}, \ldots, a_{H-1}$. We can of course follow this approach for the various roots misplaced in the autoregressive part. This brings us to the following theorem:

Theorem 12.12: *Let N be the number of roots of the polynomial*

$$\sum_{i=0}^{I_1-I_0} a^{\star}_{I_1-i} \lambda^i = 0$$

inside the unit circle.

If $I_1 - N > 0$, the general stationary linear solution involves $I_1 - N$ arbitrary scalar parameters.

If $I_1 = N$, there is a single stationary linear solution.

If $I_1 - N < 0$, there is no stationary linear solution.

An Example   Let us consider the model

$$y_t = a E(y_{t+2} \mid I_t) + b E(y_{t+1} \mid I_t) + \epsilon_t$$

with $a \neq 0$.

From table 12.1 we get that the general solution can be obtained from the model

$$y_t = -\frac{b}{a} y_{t-1} + \frac{1}{a} y_{t-2} - \frac{1}{a} \epsilon_{t-2} + \epsilon_t^0 - \frac{b}{a} \epsilon_{t-1}^0 + \epsilon_{t-1}^1.$$

The linear solutions can be derived by taking $\epsilon_t^0 = a_0 \epsilon_t$, $\epsilon_t^1 = a_1 \epsilon_t$. After replacing, we get

$$y_t = -\frac{b}{a} y_{t-1} + \frac{1}{a} y_{t-2} - \frac{1}{a} \epsilon_{t-2} + a_0 \epsilon_t - \frac{b}{a} a_0 \epsilon_{t-1} + a_1 \epsilon_{t-1},$$

$$(a + bL - L^2) y_t = (a a_0 + (a a_1 - b a_0)L - L^2) \epsilon_t.$$

Various cases must be taken into account depending on the position of the roots of $a + b\lambda - \lambda^2 = 0$.

(i)   If the two roots are outside the unit circle, there is a double infinity of stationary solutions, parameterized by a_0, a_1.

(ii)   If only one of the roots is outside the unit circle, there is a single infinity of stationary solutions. If λ_1 stands for the other root, the parameters a_0 and a_1 are restricted by

$$a a_0 + (a a_1 - b a_0)\lambda_1 - \lambda_1^2 = 0.$$

(iii) If the two roots are inside the unit circle there is a unique stationary solution coinciding with $y_t = \epsilon_t$.

12.6 Multivariate Models with Rational Expectations

12.6.1 A Canonical Form

The results of the previous sections can be extended to the case of multivariate endogenous variables. The model appears under the form

$$\mathbf{y}_t = \sum_{k=0}^{K} \sum_{h=1}^{H} \mathbf{A}_{kh} E(\mathbf{y}_{t+h-k} \mid I_{t-k}) + \sum_{k=1}^{K} \mathbf{A}_{k0} \mathbf{y}_{t-k} + \mathbf{u}_t,$$

where $\mathbf{y}_t, \mathbf{u}_t$ are vectors of size n and $\mathbf{A}_{kh}$ are square matrices of order n.

The first possible simplification of this expression has to be compared with the state space representation of an autoregressive model. The idea is to decrease the number of horizons and lags by considering a series $\mathbf{z}_t$ of greater dimension built from the original series and its expectations.

Theorem 12.13: *Every model with rational expectations can be rewritten in the equivalent form*

$$\mathbf{z}_t = \mathbf{A} E(\mathbf{z}_{t+1} \mid I_t) + \mathbf{B} \mathbf{z}_{t-1} + \mathbf{v}_t$$

which involves just an expectation on a future variable and a lagged variable.

PROOF:

(i)   We will examine whether the two transformations

$$\mathbf{y}_t \overset{\text{P}}{\to} E(\mathbf{y}_{t+1} \mid I_t)$$

and

$$\mathbf{y}_t \overset{\text{L}}{\to} \mathbf{y}_{t-1}$$

may be composed to recover all independent variables on the right-hand side of the structural equation.
We get $P^h \mathbf{y}_t = E(\mathbf{y}_{t+h} \mid I_t), h = 0, \dots, H$, by applying the theorem of iterated projections. Then we can write

$$L^k P^h \mathbf{y}_t = E(\mathbf{y}_{t+h-k} \mid I_{t-k}), k = 0, \dots, K.$$

(ii)   To build the underlying vector $\mathbf{z}$ it suffices to consider the various expectations $P^h \mathbf{y}_t = E(\mathbf{y}_{t+h} \mid I_t), h = 0, \dots, H$. For each horizon h we can determine the largest number of lags occurring in the structural equation $K_h = \max(k : A_{hk} \neq 0)$. The elements of the vector $\mathbf{z}_t$ are

$$\mathbf{z}_{k,h}(t) = L^k P^h \mathbf{y}_t = E(\mathbf{y}_{t+h-k} \mid I_{t-k}),$$

with $h = 0, \dots, H, k = 0, \dots, K_h - 1$.

(iii) The model describing the evolution of $\mathbf{z}_t$ is obtained by constructing the first equation as the one derived from the structural equation where all the variables are replaced as functions of the components of $\mathbf{z}$. The other equations are obtained using the relations

$$\mathbf{z}_{0,h}(t) = P\mathbf{z}_{0,h-1}(t) = E(\mathbf{z}_{0,h-1}(t+1) \mid I_t)$$

$$\mathbf{z}_{k,h}(t) = L\mathbf{z}_{k-1,h}(t) = \mathbf{z}_{k-1,h}(t-1)$$

with $h = 1, \ldots, H$ and $k = 1, \ldots, K_{h-1}$. $\square$

As an example, let us consider the following univariate model

$$y_t = a_{01}y_{t-1} + a_{02}y_{t-2} + a_{20}E(y_{t+2} \mid I_t) + a_{10}E(y_{t+1} \mid I_t)$$

$$+ a_{12}E(y_{t-1} \mid I_{t-2}) + a_{21}E(y_{t+1} \mid I_{t-1}) + u_t.$$

The largest horizon is $H = 2$. At each horizon the largest numbers of lags are $K_0 = 2, K_1 = 2, K_2 = 1$.

The underlying vector $\mathbf{z}_t$ is

$$\mathbf{z}_t = \begin{pmatrix} y_t \\ y_{t-1} \\ E(y_{t+1} \mid I_t) \\ E(y_t \mid I_{t-1}) \\ E(y_{t+2} \mid I_t) \end{pmatrix}.$$

The expectations $E(y_{t+1} \mid I_t) = z_{3t}$ and $E(y_{t+2} \mid I_t) = z_{5t}$ are recursively derived by writing

$$z_{3t} = E(z_{1,t+1} \mid I_t) \text{ and } z_{5t} = E(z_{3,t+1} \mid I_t).$$

The other components can then be derived taking lags $z_{2,t} = z_{1,t-1}$, $z_{4,t} = z_{3,t-1}$. Moreover, since $z_{2,t-1} = y_{t-2}$, $z_{4,t-1} = E(y_{t-1} \mid I_{t-2})$ and $z_{5,t-1} = E(y_{t+1} \mid I_{t-1})$, we get the following form which is equivalent to the initial structural model

$$\mathbf{z}_t = \begin{pmatrix} 0 & 0 & a_{10} & 0 & a_{20} \\ 0 & 0 & 0 & 0 & 0 \\ 1 & 0 & 0 & 0 & 0 \\ 0 & 0 & 0 & 0 & 0 \\ 0 & 0 & 1 & 0 & 0 \end{pmatrix} E(\mathbf{z}_{t+1} \mid I_t)$$

$$+ \begin{pmatrix} a_{01} & a_{02} & 0 & a_{12} & a_{21} \\ 1 & 0 & 0 & 0 & 0 \\ 0 & 0 & 0 & 0 & 0 \\ 0 & 0 & 1 & 0 & 0 \\ 0 & 0 & 0 & 0 & 0 \end{pmatrix} \mathbf{z}_{t-1} + \begin{pmatrix} u_t \\ 0 \\ 0 \\ 0 \\ 0 \end{pmatrix}.$$

The tradeoff for the decreased number of expectations appearing in the model is the increase in the dimension and the introduction of a large number of zeros or normalization constraints on the elements of the matrices $\mathbf{A}$ and $\mathbf{B}$.

12.6.2 Solution

At this stage we will only stress some of the new difficulties concerning the solution of these models referring for general results to Broze, Gourieroux, and Szafarz (1990). For this matter, we will solve just the canonical form.

Nonsingular Matrix A   Starting from the canonical form

$$\mathbf{z}_t = \mathbf{A}E(\mathbf{z}_{t+1} \mid I_t) + \mathbf{B}\mathbf{z}_{t-1} + \mathbf{v}_t, \tag{12.36}$$

we can introduce the forecast errors at horizon 1 on the transformed process $\mathbf{z}$. Let $\boldsymbol{\eta}_t^0$ be these errors. After substituting we get an equation necessarily satisfied by the solutions

$$\mathbf{z}_t = \mathbf{A}(\mathbf{z}_{t+1} - \boldsymbol{\eta}_{t+1}^0) + \mathbf{B}\mathbf{z}_{t-1} + \mathbf{v}_t, \tag{12.37}$$

where $\boldsymbol{\eta}_{t+1}^0$ is a process of dimension equal to the one of $\mathbf{z}$ and for which all components are martingale difference sequences. To examine whether we can choose this vector process arbitrarily, let us take a process satisfying (12.37) and compute the forecast of each element conditional on the information at date t. We get

$$\mathbf{z}_t = \mathbf{A}E(\mathbf{z}_{t+1} \mid I_t) + \mathbf{B}\mathbf{z}_{t-1} + \mathbf{v}_t,$$

and subtracting from (12.37), we see that

$$0 = \mathbf{A}(\mathbf{z}_{t+1} - E(\mathbf{z}_{t+1} \mid I_t) - \boldsymbol{\eta}_{t+1}^0).$$

Since $\mathbf{A}$ is assumed nonsingular, we see that the martingale difference must correspond to the forecast error on $\mathbf{z}$ and that the solution of (12.37) satisfies the initial structural model.

Example 12.3: Let us consider the model $y_t = \sum_{h=1}^{H} a_h E(y_{t+h} \mid I_t) + u_t$. Using the canonical form it can be written as

$$\mathbf{z}_t = \begin{pmatrix} a_1 & a_2 & \cdots & a_{H-1} & a_H \\ 1 & 0 & \cdots & 0 & 0 \\ 0 & 1 & \cdots & 0 & 0 \\ \vdots & \vdots & \ddots & \ddots & \vdots \\ 0 & 0 & \cdots & 1 & 0 \end{pmatrix} E(\mathbf{z}_{t+1} \mid I_t) + \begin{pmatrix} u_t \\ 0 \\ \vdots \\ \vdots \\ 0 \end{pmatrix}$$

with $\mathbf{z}_t = (y_t, E(y_{t+1} \mid I_t), \ldots, E(y_{t+H-1} \mid I_t))'$ (in this specific case it is not necessary to introduce $E(y_{t+H} \mid I_t))$. The matrix $\mathbf{A}$ is nonsingular since a_H is nonzero. We can then arbitrarily choose the elements of

$$\mathbf{z}_t - E(\mathbf{z}_t \mid I_{t-1}) = \left(\eta_t^0, \ldots, \eta_t^{H-1}\right)'$$

$$= (y_t - E(y_t \mid I_{t-1}), E(y_{t+1} \mid I_t) - E(y_{t+1} \mid I_{t-1}), \ldots,$$

$$E(y_{t+H} \mid I_t) - E(y_{t+H-1} \mid I_{t-1}))'$$

$$= \left(\epsilon_t^0, \ldots, \epsilon_t^{H-1}\right)'.$$

Thus we have the possibility of arbitrarily choosing the H-th first updates of the initial process y, since $H = I_1$ in this model.

Nilpotent Matrix A When the matrix $\mathbf{A}$ is singular, the martingale difference sequences intervening in η_t^0 cannot be chosen arbitrarily and would be subject to some constraints. The extreme case is when the matrix $\mathbf{A}$ is nilpotent and $\mathbf{B}$ is null; there exists an integer p such that $\mathbf{A}^p = \mathbf{0}$ or, equivalently, the matrix $\mathbf{A}$ has all its eigenvalues equal to 0. A forward solution can then be obtained

$$\mathbf{z}_t = \mathbf{v}_t + \mathbf{A}E(\mathbf{z}_{t+1} \mid I_t),$$

$$\mathbf{z}_t = \mathbf{v}_t + \mathbf{A}E(\mathbf{v}_{t+1} \mid I_t) + \mathbf{A}^2 E(\mathbf{z}_{t+2} \mid I_t),$$

$$\vdots \qquad \vdots$$

$$\mathbf{z}_t = \mathbf{v}_t + \mathbf{A}E(\mathbf{v}_{t+1} \mid I_t) + \ldots + \mathbf{A}^{p-1}E(\mathbf{v}_{t+p-1} \mid I_t) + \mathbf{A}^p E(\mathbf{z}_{t+p} \mid I_t).$$

Since $\mathbf{A}^p$ is nilpotent, the last term on the right-hand side is 0 and the model admits a unique solution

$$\mathbf{z}_t = \mathbf{v}_t + \mathbf{A}E(\mathbf{v}_{t+1} \mid I_t) + \ldots + \mathbf{A}^{p-1}E(\mathbf{v}_{t+p-1} \mid I_t).$$

Note that the occurrence of a nilpotent matrix is not only a theoretical one. In fact, it may arise when the initial model exhibits a recursivity of a certain type such as

$$y_{1t} = aE(y_{2t+1} \mid I_t) + by_{2t} + u_{1t},$$

$$y_{2t} = u_{2t}.$$

This simple case can be solved recursively: from the second equation, we derive the expectation $E(y_{2t+1} \mid I_t)$, which can then be substituted in the first one to get the expression of the first component.

12.7 Exercises

Exercise 12.1: Is the series $v_{t,h} = y_{t+h} - E(y_{t+h} \mid I_t)$, t varying, a martingale difference sequence? Is it a martingale? What about the series $(v_{T-t,t})$, t varying?

Exercise 12.2: Let us consider a first-order autoregressive process

$$y_t = \rho y_{t-1} + \epsilon_t, \qquad \mid \rho \mid < 1,$$

and the information set

$$I_t = (y_t, y_{t-1}, \ldots, y_{t-K}),$$

where K is a given positive integer.

(i)   Derive the rational expectation at the horizon h

$$_t\hat{y}_{t+h} = E(y_{t+h} \mid I_t) = E(y_{t+h} \mid y_t, y_{t-1}, \ldots, y_{t-K}).$$

(ii)   Derive the mean square forecast error

$$\sigma_{h,k}^2 = E(y_{t+h} - {_t\hat{y}_{t+h}})^2.$$

How does this error vary with h, with K?

Exercise 12.3: Let (m_t) be a martingale with respect to the sequence of information sets (I_t). Verify that $(d_t = m_t - m_{t-1})$, t varying is a martingale difference sequence.

Exercise 12.4: Let (m_t) be a martingale. Verify that

$$E(m_{t+1}) = E(m_t) \quad \text{and} \quad \text{var}(m_{t+1}) \geq \text{var}(m_t).$$

Can a martingale be second-order stationary?

Exercise 12.5: Consider the model

$$y_t = \sum_{l=0}^{M} a_l E(y_{t+l} \mid I_{t-1}) + \sum_{k=1}^{K} b_k y_{t-k} + u_t,$$

with $a_L \neq 0$ and where $u_t = \epsilon_t$ is a white noise.

(i)   Verify that there is a constraint on the updates, and that it takes the form

$$\epsilon_t^0 = \epsilon_t.$$

(ii) Let us assume that the roots of the characteristic equation

$$\sum_{l=0}^{M} a_{M-l}\lambda^l - \lambda^M + \sum_{k=1}^{K} b_k\lambda^{M+k} = 0$$

are outside the unit circle. Find the stationary linear solutions.

(iii) Show that the stationary linear solutions can all be represented as ARMA $(K + M, M)$ processes with an autoregressive polynomial common to every solution and given by

$$1 + \frac{a_{H-1}}{a_M}L + \ldots + \frac{a_1}{a_M}L^{M-1} + \frac{a_0 - 1}{a_M}L^M$$

$$+ \frac{b_1}{a_M}L^{M+1} + \ldots + \frac{b_K}{a_M}L^{M+K},$$

whereas the moving average polynomial can be arbitrarily chosen.

Exercise 12.6: Let us consider the model

$$y_t = aE(y_{t+1} \mid I_t) + by_{t-1} + cz_t + dE(z_{t+1} \mid I_t) + u_t,$$

where z_t is an exogenous variable and (u_t) a white noise. Verify that the solutions are obtained from

$$(a - L + bL^2)y_t = a\epsilon_t^0 - cz_{t-1} + dE(z_t \mid I_{t-1}) - u_{t-1},$$

where ϵ^0 is an arbitrary martingale difference sequence.

Exercise 12.7: Find the rational expectation model for which the canonical form given in theorem 12.13 can be written as

(i) $\mathbf{z}_t = \mathbf{A}E(\mathbf{z}_{t+1} \mid I_t) + \mathbf{v}_t,$

(ii) $\mathbf{z}_t = \mathbf{B}\mathbf{z}_{t-1} + \mathbf{v}_t.$

Exercise 12.8: We consider the linear rational expectation model

$$y_t = \sum_{k=0}^{K}\sum_{h=1}^{H} a_{kh}E(y_{t+h-k} \mid I_{t-k}) + \sum_{k=1}^{K} a_{k0}y_{t-k} + u_t.$$

Let us assume $H = I_1$ and take an ARMA (p_0, q_0) for the exogenous process. From equation (12.32) derive the maximum autoregressive and moving average orders of the ARMA solutions of the model.

13

Specification Analysis

13.1 General Remarks on Specification Search

13.1.1 Top–Down or Bottom–Up Approach

The classical econometric approach starts from the estimation of a model suggested by economic theory. The next step is the comparison of the model with a more general one to test the appropriateness of the restrictions. This approach is dubbed "bottom–up" in that it starts from a particular model which is extended toward a more general one. This kind of approach presents a number of advantages: the base model has a good economic interpretation by definition, the number of parameters is relatively small, and when the battery of tests for a correct specification is chosen to be of the Lagrange multiplier type, it is the only model to be estimated. By the same token, there are some disadvantages deriving from the fact that the model may be excessively restrictive, that some of the restrictions are not tested, and that the various hypothesis tests are not independent. In this chapter we will not follow the classical approach, which is described in the econometrics textbooks, but rather we will present a "top–down" approach. This approach starts from a general model, that is a VAR (Vector Autoregressive) model; an increasingly restrictive set of hypotheses is then tested. Let us start by recalling some concepts on the main testing procedures available, on the nested hypotheses, and on the various forms of null hypotheses.

13.1.2 The Various Testing Procedures

Let us consider a stationary dynamic model, the log-likelihood of which is $L_T(\boldsymbol{\theta})$, where T is the number of observations and $\boldsymbol{\theta}$ is the unknown k-vector of parameters. Let us denote the unconstrained maximum likelihood estimator as $\hat{\boldsymbol{\theta}}_T$ obtained through the maximization of $L_T(\boldsymbol{\theta})$. Let us consider a null hypothesis of the type

$$H_0 : \{\mathbf{g}(\boldsymbol{\theta}) = 0\},$$

where $\mathbf{g}$ is a vector function of size $r \leq k$ such that $\partial \mathbf{g}/\partial \boldsymbol{\theta}'$ has rank r. We know that there exist three types of asymptotically equivalent tests for this hypothesis: the Lagrange multiplier (or score) test, the Wald test, and the likelihood ratio test. These tests are based on the following statistics

$$
\begin{aligned}
\xi_T^{LM} &= \frac{1}{T} \frac{\partial L_T}{\partial \boldsymbol{\theta}'}(\hat{\boldsymbol{\theta}}_T^0) \hat{\mathcal{I}}^{-1} \frac{\partial L_T}{\partial \boldsymbol{\theta}}(\hat{\boldsymbol{\theta}}_T^0) \\
&= \frac{1}{T} \hat{\boldsymbol{\lambda}}_T' \frac{\partial \mathbf{g}}{\partial \boldsymbol{\theta}'}(\hat{\boldsymbol{\theta}}_T^0) \hat{\mathcal{I}}^{-1} \frac{\partial \mathbf{g}'}{\partial \boldsymbol{\theta}}(\hat{\boldsymbol{\theta}}_T^0) \hat{\boldsymbol{\lambda}}_T, \\
\xi_T^W &= T\mathbf{g}'(\hat{\boldsymbol{\theta}}_T) \left(\frac{\partial \mathbf{g}}{\partial \boldsymbol{\theta}'}(\hat{\boldsymbol{\theta}}_T^0) \hat{\mathcal{I}}^{-1} \frac{\partial \mathbf{g}'}{\partial \boldsymbol{\theta}}(\hat{\boldsymbol{\theta}}_T^0) \right)^{-1} \mathbf{g}(\hat{\boldsymbol{\theta}}_T), \\
\xi_T^{LR} &= 2 \left(L_T(\hat{\boldsymbol{\theta}}_T) - L_T(\hat{\boldsymbol{\theta}}_T^0) \right).
\end{aligned}
\tag{13.1}
$$

where $(\hat{\boldsymbol{\theta}}_T^0)$ is the maximum likelihood estimator under H_0, $(\hat{\boldsymbol{\lambda}}_T)$ is the Lagrange multiplier associated with the constraints $\mathbf{g}(\boldsymbol{\theta}) = 0$, and $\hat{\mathcal{I}}$ is a consistent estimator of the Fisher Information matrix under H_0

$$\mathcal{I}(\boldsymbol{\theta}) = E_\theta \left(-\frac{\partial^2 \log f_t(\boldsymbol{\theta})}{\partial \boldsymbol{\theta} \partial \boldsymbol{\theta}'} \right).$$

Given f_t the density function of the current observations conditional on the past, we could take

$$\hat{\mathcal{I}} = -\frac{1}{T} \sum_{t=1}^T \frac{\partial^2 \log f_t(\tilde{\boldsymbol{\theta}}_T)}{\partial \boldsymbol{\theta} \partial \boldsymbol{\theta}'} \tag{13.2}$$

or

$$\hat{\mathcal{I}} = -\frac{1}{T} \sum_{t=1}^T \frac{\partial \log f_t(\tilde{\boldsymbol{\theta}}_T)}{\partial \boldsymbol{\theta}} \frac{\partial \log f_t(\tilde{\boldsymbol{\theta}}_T)}{\partial \boldsymbol{\theta}'} \tag{13.3}$$

with $\tilde{\boldsymbol{\theta}}_T = \hat{\boldsymbol{\theta}}_T$ or $\hat{\boldsymbol{\theta}}_T^0$ (cf. Gourieroux and Monfort, 1989, chapter 17). These tests imply asymptotic critical regions at the significance level α

$$\{\xi_T \geq \chi_{1-\alpha}^2(r)\},$$

where ξ_T is one of the statistics above. They are asymptotically equivalent under the null hypothesis (and under a sequence of local alternatives). The Lagrange multiplier test statistic ξ_T^{LM} can be calculated only on the basis of the constrained estimator $\hat{\theta}_T^0$ of $\boldsymbol{\theta}$. Instead, the Wald statistic ξ_T^W can be calculated only on the basis of the unconstrained estimator ξ_T^W of θ. Hence, the former seems more suitable for a bottom–up approach and the latter for a top–down (or general to specific) approach.

13.1.3 Nested or Nonnested Hypotheses

Let us assume that in the unconstrained model we have defined a sequence of L nested hypotheses

$$H_0^L \supset \ldots \supset H_0^l \supset H_0^{l-1} \supset \ldots \supset H_0^1.$$

We can then choose the following strategy. We test the hypothesis H_0^L at the level α_L in the unconstrained model. If H_0^L is rejected, we stop the procedure, otherwise we test H_0^{L-1} in the model constrained by H_0^L and so forth until one hypothesis H_0^l is rejected, in which case H_0^{l+1} is the more restrictive hypothesis accepted, or H_0^1 is accepted. In practice, at each step we use one of the classical testing procedures: Lagrange multiplier or Wald or likelihood ratio tests. If ξ_T^l indicates the statistic used to test the hypothesis H_0^l in H_0^{l+1} and if the number of independent constraints needed to pass from H_0^{l+1} to H_0^l is r_l, the critical region of this test is

$$\{\xi_T^l \geq \chi_{1-\alpha_l}^2(r_l)\}.$$

The top–down approach is summarized in figure 13.1.

The sequence ξ_T^l, $l = 1, \ldots, L$ of the test statistics has some interesting independence properties. We can show (cf. Gourieroux and Monfort, 1989, chapter 19) that the statistics $\xi_T^l, \xi_T^{l+1}, \ldots, \xi_T^L$ are asymptotically independent under the null hypothesis H_0^l. This result allows us to compute the significance level of the top–down procedure to test the hypothesis H_0^l in the context of the general model. In fact, we reject H_0^l if at least one of the conditions

$$\xi_T^j \geq \chi_{1-\alpha_j}^2(r_j), \quad j = l, \ldots, L$$

is verified. Using the asymptotic independence, we see that the probability of such an event tends to $1 - \prod_{i=l}^L (1 - \alpha_i)$. Note that a statistic ξ_T^l can be obtained also by using the formula

$$\xi_T^l = \bar{\xi}_T^l - \bar{\xi}_T^{l+1} \tag{13.4}$$

where $\bar{\xi}_T^l$ is one of the statistics (Lagrange multiplier, Wald, likelihood ratio) used to test H_0^l in the unconstrained model. This remark is particularly interesting if we use the Wald statistic: the computation of the statistic $\bar{\xi}_T^l$ and therefore of the statistic ξ_T^l needs just the estimation of the unconstrained model. In a top–down strategy, therefore, the Wald tests are the easiest to use. The approach can be extended to the

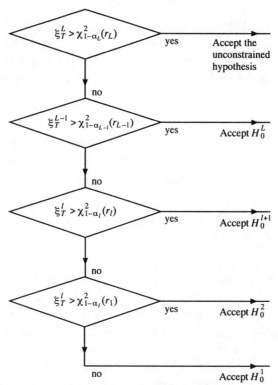

Figure 13.1 Top–down Strategy

case of nonnested hypotheses. Let us consider L nonnested hypotheses H_0^l, $l = 1, \ldots, L$ and let us consider the hypothesis testing for their intersection $H_0 = \cap_{l=1}^L H_0^l$. We can consider each hypothesis H_0^l in the unconstrained model by testing it at the significance level α_l, and accept H_0 if all hypotheses H_0^l are accepted. When H_0 is rejected, this approach allows one to isolate the hypotheses H_0^l responsible for the rejection. The test statistics are not independent under the null hypothesis H_0 anymore and we cannot compute the exact asymptotic significance level of the procedure. However, denoting by W_l, $l = 1, \ldots, L$ the critical regions of the various tests, the critical region for H_0 is $W = \cup_{l=1}^L W_l$ and therefore the significance level for the procedure is less than $\sum_{l=1}^L \alpha_l$.

Other Expressions for the Null Hypothesis Until now we have assumed that the null hypothesis was written as r constraints on the parameter $H_0 : \mathbf{g}(\boldsymbol{\theta}) = \mathbf{0}$. This is called *implicit form*. There are other expressions possible for the null hypothesis. In the *explicit form* the parameter $\boldsymbol{\theta}$ of size k can be expressed as a function of k_0 parameters $\boldsymbol{\lambda}$ chosen on the basis of the null hypothesis.

Then the hypothesis can be written as $H_0 : \{\boldsymbol{\theta} = \mathbf{h}(\boldsymbol{\lambda})\}$ where $\mathbf{h}$ is a function defined on $\mathbb{R}^{k_0}$. When the parameters (and the constraints) are independent, we have

$$r = k - k_0.$$

In the mixed form, the initial parameter $\boldsymbol{\theta}$ is related to some auxiliary parameters as well. The constraints are of the type

$$H_0 = \{\exists \mathbf{a} \in \mathbb{R}^{k_1} : \mathbf{g}(\boldsymbol{\theta}, \mathbf{a}) = \mathbf{0}\}, \tag{13.5}$$

where the function $\mathbf{g}$ is of size $r_1 \leq k$ and $\mathbf{a}$ is a vector of size $k_1 \leq r_1$. When the parameters (and the constraints) are functionally independent, the dimensions are related by

$$r = r_1 - k_1. \tag{13.6}$$

Note that the mixed form is the most general one, in that either an explicit form is a special case (with $r_1 = k$, $k_1 = k_0 = k - r$) or an implicit form can be obtained for the case without auxiliary parameters ($k_1 = 0$ and $r_1 = r$). The various testing procedures described before can be suitable for these new formulations of the null hypotheses. In particular it proves interesting for the top–down approach to describe the extension of the Wald procedure to the mixed forms. We can show that a test statistic which is asymptotically equivalent to the likelihood ratio test is given by

$$\xi_T^M = \min_a T\mathbf{g}'(\hat{\boldsymbol{\theta}}_T, \mathbf{a}) \left(\frac{\partial \hat{\mathbf{g}}}{\partial \boldsymbol{\theta}'} \hat{\mathcal{I}}^{-1} \frac{\partial \hat{\mathbf{g}}'}{\partial \boldsymbol{\theta}'} \right)^{-1} \mathbf{g}(\hat{\boldsymbol{\theta}}_T, \mathbf{a}), \tag{13.7}$$

where

$$\frac{\partial \hat{\mathbf{g}}}{\partial \boldsymbol{\theta}'} = \frac{\partial \mathbf{g}}{\partial \boldsymbol{\theta}'}(\hat{\boldsymbol{\theta}}_T, \tilde{\mathbf{a}}_T)$$

with $\tilde{\mathbf{a}}_T$ a consistent estimator of $\mathbf{a}$. Such an estimator may be obtained by minimizing $\mathbf{g}'(\hat{\boldsymbol{\theta}}_T, \mathbf{a})g(\hat{\boldsymbol{\theta}}_T, \mathbf{a})$. The critical region for this test is

$$\{\xi_T^M \geq \chi_{1-\alpha}^2(r_1 - k_1)\}. \tag{13.8}$$

The solution to (13.7) gives an estimator $\tilde{\mathbf{a}}_T$, called *asymptotic least squares estimator*, which can be shown to be asymptotically equivalent to the maximum likelihood estimator of $\mathbf{a}$ under the null hypothesis. Note that if $\mathbf{g}$ is linear in $\mathbf{a}$, the minimization is very simple, since it reduces to the computation of ordinary linear least squares or generalized least squares. Note also that in the explicit form case $\boldsymbol{\theta} = \mathbf{h}(\mathbf{a})$ which is a special case of the previous one, the computation of ξ_T^M simplifies to

$$\xi_t^M = \min_a T(\hat{\boldsymbol{\theta}}_T - \mathbf{h}(\mathbf{a}))' \hat{\mathcal{I}}(\hat{\boldsymbol{\theta}}_T - \mathbf{h}(\mathbf{a})), \tag{13.9}$$

where it is not necessary to compute an intermediate estimator $\tilde{\mathbf{a}}_T$ of $\mathbf{a}$.

The Framework of a VAR Model Let us assume that the process $(\mathbf{v}_t)$ of size ν of the variables of interest is autoregressive stationary of order p

$$\mathbf{\Phi}(L)\mathbf{v}_t = \mathbf{c} + \boldsymbol{\varepsilon}_t, \tag{13.10}$$

where $\boldsymbol{\varepsilon}_t$ is a normal white noise with a variance–covariance matrix $\boldsymbol{\Sigma}$ and where $\mathbf{\Phi}(0) = \mathbf{I}$. Since the parameters intervening in $\mathbf{\Phi}(L)$ are unconstrained, we know (cf. chapter 9) that they can be estimated by the least squares method equation by equation which, in this case, is equivalent to the maximum likelihood method. It is however clear that in order to estimate the parameters, we need to fix the order of the maximum lag p. A possible choice comes from fixing a sufficiently high order p_{max} and then testing a smaller order by one. It is a top–down procedure based on nested hypotheses. Here the estimation is particularly easy under any hypothesis. We can then use the likelihood ratio test which has a particularly simple expression. To test the null hypothesis for the order of the model equal to $i-1$ in the general model of order i, the likelihood ratio statistic is

$$\xi_T^{(LR)} = T \log \frac{\det \hat{\boldsymbol{\Sigma}}_{i-1}}{\det \hat{\boldsymbol{\Sigma}}_i}, \tag{13.11}$$

where $\hat{\boldsymbol{\Sigma}}_i$ is the estimated variance–covariance matrix from the OLS residuals in a model with i lags for each variable. The test has a critical region

$$\{\xi_T^{(LR)} \geq \chi_{1-\alpha}^2(\nu^2)\}$$

for an asymptotic significance level α. This result is a direct consequence of the following lemma which will be used often in what follows.

Lemma: *Let $\mathbf{z}_t = \mathbf{A}\mathbf{w}_t + \mathbf{u}_t$, $t = 1, \ldots, T$ a multivariate linear regression model where $\mathbf{z}_t$ is a vector of size s, $\mathbf{w}_t$ is a vector of size k, $\mathbf{A}$ is a $(s \times k)$ matrix of unknown parameters and $\mathbf{u}_t$ a normal white noise with unknown variance–covariance matrix $\boldsymbol{\Omega}$. Let H_0 be a hypothesis on $\mathbf{A}$. The likelihood ratio statistic is*

$$\xi_T^{(1)} = T \log \frac{\det \hat{\boldsymbol{\Omega}}_0}{\det \hat{\boldsymbol{\Omega}}},$$

where $\hat{\boldsymbol{\Omega}}_0$ and $\hat{\boldsymbol{\Omega}}$ are the constrained, respectively, unconstrained maximum likelihood estimators of $\boldsymbol{\Omega}$.

PROOF: The log-likelihood is

$$-\frac{Ts}{2}\log 2\pi - \frac{T}{2}\log\det(\mathbf{\Omega}) - \frac{1}{2}\sum_{t=1}^{T}\left(\mathbf{z}_t - \mathbf{A}\mathbf{w}_t\right)'\mathbf{\Omega}^{-1}\left(\mathbf{z}_t - \mathbf{A}\mathbf{w}_t\right)$$

or

$$-\frac{Ts}{2}\log 2\pi - \frac{T}{2}\log\det(\mathbf{\Omega}) - \frac{1}{2}\mathrm{tr}\left(\mathbf{\Omega}^{-1}\left(\mathbf{z}_t - \mathbf{A}\mathbf{w}_t\right)\left(\mathbf{z}_t - \mathbf{A}\mathbf{w}_t\right)'\right).$$

Taking the derivatives with respect to the elements of $\mathbf{\Omega}^{-1}$ we get

$$T\mathbf{\Omega} = \sum_{t=1}^{T}\left(\mathbf{z}_t - \mathbf{A}\mathbf{w}_t\right)\left(\mathbf{z}_t - \mathbf{A}\mathbf{w}_t\right)'.$$

The concentrated log-likelihood with respect to $\mathbf{\Omega}$ is

$$-\frac{Ts}{2}\log 2\pi - \frac{T}{2}\log\det\left(\frac{1}{T}\sum_{t=1}^{T}\left(\mathbf{z}_t - \mathbf{A}\mathbf{w}_t\right)\left(\mathbf{z}_t - \mathbf{A}\mathbf{w}_t\right)'\right) - \frac{1}{2}Ts.$$

The likelihood ratio statistic can be written as

$$2\left(-\frac{T}{2}\log\det\left(\frac{1}{T}\sum_{t=1}^{T}\left(\mathbf{z}_t - \hat{\mathbf{A}}\mathbf{w}_t\right)\left(\mathbf{z}_t - \hat{\mathbf{A}}\mathbf{w}_t\right)'\right)\right.$$

$$\left.+ \frac{T}{2}\log\det\left(\frac{1}{T}\sum_{t=1}^{T}\left(\mathbf{z}_t - \hat{\mathbf{A}}_0\mathbf{w}_t\right)\left(\mathbf{z}_t - \hat{\mathbf{A}}_0\mathbf{w}_t\right)'\right)\right)$$

$$= T\log\frac{\det\hat{\mathbf{\Omega}}_0}{\det\hat{\mathbf{\Omega}}}.$$

□

13.2 Causality Tests

13.2.1 Hypothesis Formulation

The first class of tests which can be implemented in an autoregressive model are the causality tests. Let us assume that the vector $\mathbf{v}_t$ is formed of two subvectors

$$\mathbf{v}_t = \begin{pmatrix}\mathbf{y}_t \\ \mathbf{x}_t\end{pmatrix}$$

of dimension n, respectively m. The autoregressive model (13.10) can then be written as

$$\begin{pmatrix}\mathbf{\Phi}_y(L) & \mathbf{\Phi}_{yx}(L) \\ \mathbf{\Phi}_{xy}(L) & \mathbf{\Phi}_x(L)\end{pmatrix}\begin{pmatrix}\mathbf{y}_t \\ \mathbf{x}_t\end{pmatrix} = \begin{pmatrix}\mathbf{c}_y \\ \mathbf{c}_x\end{pmatrix} + \begin{pmatrix}\boldsymbol{\varepsilon}_{yt} \\ \boldsymbol{\varepsilon}_{xt}\end{pmatrix} \qquad (13.12)$$

with

$$\operatorname{var}\begin{pmatrix} \boldsymbol{\varepsilon}_{yt} \\ \boldsymbol{\varepsilon}_{xt} \end{pmatrix} = \begin{pmatrix} \boldsymbol{\Sigma}_y & \boldsymbol{\Sigma}_{yx} \\ \boldsymbol{\Sigma}_{xy} & \boldsymbol{\Sigma}_x \end{pmatrix} = \boldsymbol{\Sigma}.$$

We know that an equivalent expression is the block-recursive form presented in (10.25)

$$\begin{pmatrix} \boldsymbol{\Phi}_y^+(L) & \boldsymbol{\Phi}_{yx}^+(L) \\ \boldsymbol{\Phi}_{xy}(L) & \boldsymbol{\Phi}_x(L) \end{pmatrix} \begin{pmatrix} \mathbf{y}_t \\ \mathbf{x}_t \end{pmatrix} = \begin{pmatrix} \mathbf{c}_y^+ \\ \mathbf{c}_x \end{pmatrix} + \begin{pmatrix} \boldsymbol{\eta}_{yt} \\ \boldsymbol{\varepsilon}_{xt} \end{pmatrix} \qquad (13.13)$$

with

$$\boldsymbol{\Phi}_y^+(L) = \boldsymbol{\Phi}_y(L) - \boldsymbol{\Sigma}_{yx}\boldsymbol{\Sigma}_x^{-1}\boldsymbol{\Phi}_{xy}(L) = \mathbf{I} - \sum_{i=1}^{p} \boldsymbol{\Phi}_{yi}^+ L^i,$$

$$\boldsymbol{\Phi}_{yx}^+(L) = \boldsymbol{\Phi}_{yx}(L) - \boldsymbol{\Sigma}_{yx}\boldsymbol{\Sigma}_x^{-1}\boldsymbol{\Phi}_x(L) = -\sum_{i=0}^{p} \boldsymbol{\Phi}_{yxi}^+ L^i,$$

$$\mathbf{c}_y^+ = \mathbf{c}_y - \boldsymbol{\Sigma}_{yx}\boldsymbol{\Sigma}_x^{-1}\mathbf{c}_x,$$

with

$$\operatorname{var}\begin{pmatrix} \boldsymbol{\eta}_{yt} \\ \boldsymbol{\varepsilon}_{xt} \end{pmatrix} = \begin{pmatrix} \boldsymbol{\Sigma}_y^+ & \mathbf{0} \\ \mathbf{0} & \boldsymbol{\Sigma}_x \end{pmatrix}$$

and

$$\boldsymbol{\Sigma}_y^+ = \boldsymbol{\Sigma}_y - \boldsymbol{\Sigma}_{yx}\boldsymbol{\Sigma}_x^{-1}\boldsymbol{\Sigma}_{xy}.$$

We have seen (cf. theorem 10.5) that $\mathbf{y}$ does not cause $\mathbf{x}$ instantaneously if and only if $\boldsymbol{\Sigma}_{yx} = \mathbf{0}$ or, which is the same, $\boldsymbol{\Phi}_{xy0}^+ = \mathbf{0}$. Moreover, $\mathbf{y}$ does not cause $\mathbf{x}$ if and only if $\boldsymbol{\Phi}_{xy}(L) = \mathbf{0}$ and $\mathbf{x}$ does not cause $\mathbf{y}$ if and only if $\boldsymbol{\Phi}_{yx}(L) = \mathbf{0}$. We can then test these various hypotheses. Let us start by examining the expression of the likelihood. The density function of $\mathbf{y}_t$ conditional on $\mathbf{y}_{t-1}, \ldots, \mathbf{y}_{t-p}, \mathbf{x}_t, \mathbf{x}_{t-1}, \ldots, \mathbf{x}_{t-p}$ is normal with mean

$$\mathbf{c}_y^+ + \sum_{i=1}^{p} \boldsymbol{\Phi}_{yi}^+ L^i \mathbf{y}_t + \sum_{i=0}^{p} \boldsymbol{\Phi}_{yxi}^+ L^i \mathbf{x}_t$$

and variance–covariance matrix $\boldsymbol{\Sigma}_y^+$. This density can be denoted by $f_t^{y|x}(\mathbf{y}_t; \boldsymbol{\phi}_y^+)$, where $\boldsymbol{\phi}_y^+$ collects the parameters of the distribution. By the same token, the distribution of $\mathbf{x}_t$ conditional on $\mathbf{y}_{t-1}, \ldots, \mathbf{y}_{t-p},$ $\mathbf{x}_{t-1}, \ldots, \mathbf{x}_{t-p}$ is normal with mean

$$\mathbf{c}_x + \boldsymbol{\Phi}_{xy}(L)\mathbf{y}_t - (\boldsymbol{\Phi}_x(L) - \mathbf{I})\mathbf{x}_t$$

and the density of which is denoted by $f_t^x(\mathbf{x}_t; \boldsymbol{\phi}_x)$. The likelihood (conditional on p initial observations) can then be written as

$$\prod_{t=1}^{T} f_t^{y|x}(\mathbf{y}_t; \boldsymbol{\phi}_y^+) f_t^x(\mathbf{x}_t; \boldsymbol{\phi}_x) \qquad (13.14)$$

and the log-likelihood is

$$L_T(\boldsymbol{\theta}) = \sum_{t=1}^{T} \log f_t^{y|x}(\mathbf{y}_t; \boldsymbol{\phi}_y^+) + \sum_{t=1}^{T} \log f_t^x(\mathbf{x}_t; \boldsymbol{\phi}_x), \qquad (13.15)$$

where $\boldsymbol{\theta}$ is the set of parameters of the model (i.e., $\boldsymbol{\phi}_y^+$ and $\boldsymbol{\phi}_x$). The log-likelihood is then formed of the sum of the two terms

$$L_T(\boldsymbol{\theta}) = L_T^{y|x}(\boldsymbol{\phi}_y^+) + L_T^x(\boldsymbol{\phi}_x). \qquad (13.16)$$

13.2.2 The Instantaneous Noncausality Test

The instantaneous noncausality between $\mathbf{y}$ and $\mathbf{x}$ (hypothesis H_1) is defined by the constraint $\boldsymbol{\Phi}_{yx0}^+ = \mathbf{0}$. This condition involves a subset of parameters of $\boldsymbol{\phi}_y^+$. From decomposition (13.16) the maximum likelihood estimator of $\boldsymbol{\phi}_x$ under the null hypothesis of instantaneous noncausality is identical to the unconstrained maximum likelihood estimator $\hat{\boldsymbol{\phi}}_x$. The likelihood ratio statistic is then

$$\begin{aligned}\xi_T^{(1)} &= 2\left(L_T(\hat{\boldsymbol{\theta}}_T) - L_T(\hat{\boldsymbol{\theta}}_T^0)\right) \\ &= 2\left(L_T^{y|x}(\hat{\boldsymbol{\phi}}_y^+) + L_T^x(\hat{\boldsymbol{\phi}}_x) - L_T^{y|x}(\hat{\boldsymbol{\phi}}_y^{+0}) - L_T^x(\hat{\boldsymbol{\phi}}_x)\right) \qquad (13.17) \\ &= 2\left(L_T^{y|x}(\hat{\boldsymbol{\phi}}_y^+) - L_T^{y|x}(\hat{\boldsymbol{\phi}}_y^{+0})\right).\end{aligned}$$

The estimator $\hat{\boldsymbol{\phi}}_y^+$ is obtained by regressing each component of $\mathbf{y}_t$ on the elements of $\mathbf{y}_{t-1}, \ldots, \mathbf{y}_{t-p}, \mathbf{x}_{t-1}, \ldots, \mathbf{x}_{t-p}$ plus a constant. In particular the estimator of $\boldsymbol{\Sigma}_y^+$ is the empirical variance–covariance matrix $\hat{\boldsymbol{\Sigma}}_y^+$ of the residuals in this regression. Analogously, the estimator $\boldsymbol{\phi}_y^{+0}$ is obtained by excluding the elements of $\mathbf{x}_t$ from the list of regressors. Also in this case, the estimator of $\boldsymbol{\Sigma}_y^{+0}$ is the empirical variance–covariance matrix $\hat{\boldsymbol{\Sigma}}_y^{+0}$ of the residuals in this regression. From lemma 13.1, the likelihood ratio statistic (13.17) is equal to

$$\xi_T^{(1)} = T \log \frac{\det \hat{\boldsymbol{\Sigma}}_y^{+0}}{\det \hat{\boldsymbol{\Sigma}}_y^+}. \qquad (13.18)$$

In 10.2.4 we have shown that a measure of instantaneous causality is

$$C_{x\leftrightarrow y} = \log \frac{\det \boldsymbol{\Sigma}_y^{+0}}{\det \boldsymbol{\Sigma}_y^+},$$

so that

$$\xi_T^{(1)} = T\hat{C}_{x\leftrightarrow y},$$

where

$$\hat{C}_{x\leftrightarrow y} = \log \frac{\det \hat{\boldsymbol{\Sigma}}_y^{+0}}{\det \hat{\boldsymbol{\Sigma}}_y^+}$$

is the empirical measure of instantaneous causality. The number of constraints implied by the noncausality hypothesis is equal to the number of elements in $\mathbf{\Phi}_{yx0}^{+}$, that is, nm. Therefore, the critical region at the asymptotic significance level α is

$$\{\xi_T^{(1)} \geq \chi_{1-\alpha}^2(nm)\}. \tag{13.19}$$

13.2.3 The Noncausality Tests of y to x and of x to y

The noncausality of $\mathbf{y}$ to $\mathbf{x}$ (hypothesis H_2) is characterized by the polynomial $\mathbf{\Phi}_{xy}(L)$ being equal to 0, that is by the fact that a subset of parameters in ϕ_x is equal to 0. By analogy to the previous section, we can use the decomposition (13.16) to show that the maximum likelihood estimator of ϕ_y^+ under a noncausality hypothesis is identical to the unconstrained maximum likelihood estimator. Therefore, the likelihood ratio statistic is

$$\xi_T^{(2)} = 2\left(L_T^x(\hat{\phi}_x) - L_T^x(\hat{\phi}_x^0)\right), \tag{13.20}$$

where $\hat{\phi}_x$ and ϕ_x^0 are the unconstrained, respectively, constrained maximum likelihood estimators of ϕ_x. From the lemma above we get

$$\xi_T^{(2)} = T \log \frac{\det \hat{\mathbf{\Sigma}}_x^0}{\det \hat{\mathbf{\Sigma}}_x}, \tag{13.21}$$

where $\hat{\mathbf{\Sigma}}_x$ (respectively, $\hat{\mathbf{\Sigma}}_x^0$) is the empirical variance–covariance matrix from the residuals in the regressions of the elements of $\mathbf{x}_t$ on the elements of $\mathbf{y}_{t-1}, \ldots, \mathbf{y}_{t-p}, \mathbf{x}_{t-1}, \ldots, \mathbf{x}_{t-p}$, respectively, $\mathbf{x}_{t-1}, \ldots, \mathbf{x}_{t-p}$. The number of parameters in $\mathbf{\Phi}_{xy}(L)$ is nmp, so that the critical region at the asymptotic level α is

$$\{\xi_T^{(2)} \geq \chi_{1-\alpha}^2(nmp)\} \tag{13.22}$$

From the results in section 10.2.4 we can also write

$$\xi_T^{(2)} = T\hat{C}_{y \to x},$$

where $\hat{C}_{y \to x}$ is the natural estimator of

$$C_{y \to x} = \log \frac{\det \mathbf{\Sigma}_x^{+0}}{\det \mathbf{\Sigma}_x}.$$

Obviously, we can invert the role of $\mathbf{x}$ and $\mathbf{y}$ so as to derive the expression for the likelihood ratio test for the null hypothesis of noncausality of $\mathbf{x}$ to $\mathbf{y}$ (hypothesis H_3)

$$\xi_T^{(3)} = T \log \frac{\det \hat{\mathbf{\Sigma}}_y^0}{\det \hat{\mathbf{\Sigma}}_y}, \tag{13.23}$$

where $\hat{\mathbf{\Sigma}}_y$ (respectively, $\hat{\mathbf{\Sigma}}_y^0$) is the empirical variance–covariance matrix from the residuals in the regressions of the elements of $\mathbf{y}_t$ on the elements of $\mathbf{y}_{t-1}, \ldots, \mathbf{y}_{t-p}, \mathbf{x}_{t-1}, \ldots, \mathbf{x}_{t-p}$, respectively, $\mathbf{y}_{t-1}, \ldots, \mathbf{y}_{t-p}$. Also

$$\xi_T^{(3)} = T\hat{C}_{x \to y}.$$

The critical region at the asymptotic level α is

$$\{\xi_T^{(3)} \geq \chi_{1-\alpha}^2(nmp)\}. \tag{13.24}$$

13.2.4 Test of Independence

The independence between the processes $\mathbf{y}$ and $\mathbf{x}$ (conditional on the p initial values) is denoted by H_4 and is characterized by

$$\mathbf{\Phi}_{yx0} = \mathbf{0} \qquad \mathbf{\Phi}_{xy}(L) = \mathbf{0} \qquad \mathbf{\Phi}_{yx}(L) = \mathbf{0}$$

that is, the intersection of the three noncausality hypotheses. By analogy, again, the statistic for the likelihood ratio test is

$$\xi_T^{(4)} = T \log \frac{\det \hat{\mathbf{\Sigma}}_x^0 \det \hat{\mathbf{\Sigma}}_y^0}{\det \hat{\mathbf{\Sigma}}}, \tag{13.25}$$

where $\hat{\mathbf{\Sigma}}$ is the empirical variance–covariance matrix of the residuals from the regression of the elements of $\mathbf{y}_t$ and $\mathbf{x}_t$ on the elements of $\mathbf{y}_{t-1}, \ldots, \mathbf{y}_{t-p}, \mathbf{x}_{t-1}, \ldots, \mathbf{x}_{t-p}$. The critical region at the asymptotic level α is

$$\{\xi_T^{(4)} \geq \chi_{1-\alpha}^2(nm(2p+1))\}. \tag{13.26}$$

Note that

$$\xi_T^{(4)} = T\hat{C}_{x,y}$$

and that

$$\xi_T^{(4)} = \xi_T^{(1)} + \xi_T^{(2)} + \xi_T^{(3)}.$$

13.2.5 The Order of Testing

The tests proposed in the previous sections refer to hypotheses H_i, $i = 1, \ldots, 4$ in the general unconstrained VAR model. In order to get back to a top–down procedure of the kind proposed in section 13.1, we can, for example, define the hypotheses

$$H_{12} = H_1 \cap H_2$$

$$H_{123} = H_1 \cap H_2 \cap H_3 = H_4$$

and examine the sequence of nested hypotheses

$$H_1 \supset H_{12} \supset H_{123} = H_4.$$

Let us denote $\xi_T^{(1)}$ the likelihood ratio statistic to test H_1 in the general model, $\xi_T^{(12)}$ the likelihood ratio statistic to test H_{12} in H_1, and $\xi_T^{(123)}$ the likelihood ratio statistic to test H_{123} in H_{12}.

We have the following:

Theorem 13.1:

$$\xi_T^{(12)} = \xi_T^{(2)}$$

$$\xi_T^{(123)} = \xi_T^{(3)}$$

PROOF: The decomposition (13.16) shows that the imposition of a constraint on ϕ_y^+, namely, $\Phi_{yx0}^+ = 0$ does not change either the unconstrained estimation of ϕ_x or the constrained estimation under H_2. Therefore $\xi_T^{(12)} = \xi_T^{(2)}$. By the same token, if we impose H_1 and H_2, the constrained log-likelihood can be written as

$$L_T^y(\phi_y) + L_T^x(\phi_x^0),$$

where ϕ_x^0 contains the elements of ϕ_x different from the coefficients of $\Phi_{xy}(L)$. The likelihood ratio statistic to test H_3 in this constrained model is therefore

$$\xi^{(123)} = 2\left(L_T^y(\hat{\phi}_y) - L_T^y(\hat{\phi}_y^0)\right).$$

Inverting the role of **x** and **y**, expression (13.20) shows that $\xi_T^{(123)} = \xi_T^{(3)}$. □

The general results recalled in section 13.1.3 show that, under H_{12}, the statistics $\xi_T^{(1)}$ and $\xi_T^{(12)}$ are asymptotically independent. From theorem 13.1, $\xi_T^{(1)}$ and $\xi_T^{(2)}$ are also asymptotically independent under H_{12}. Moreover, we see that under $H_{123} = H_4$ the statistics $\xi_T^{(1)}$, $\xi_T^{(12)}$, and $\xi_T^{(123)}$ and thus the statistics $\xi_T^{(1)}$, $\xi_T^{(2)}$, and $\xi_T^{(3)}$ are asymptotically independent. This remark allow us to test the hypothesis H_4 of independence by taking

$$\{\xi_T^{(1)} \geq \chi_{1-\alpha_1}^2(nm)\} \cup \{\xi_T^{(2)} \geq \chi_{1-\alpha_2}^2(nmp)\} \cup \{\xi_T^{(3)} \geq \chi_{1-\alpha_3}^2(nmp)\}$$

as the critical region.

The asymptotic significance level of this test is $1-(1-\alpha_1)(1-\alpha_2)(1-\alpha_3)$. The advantage of following this procedure relative to a test based on $\xi_T^{(4)}$ is that once the hypothesis is rejected, one can trace back the origin of this rejection. The order chosen, that is, $H_1 \supset H_{12} \supset H_{123}$, is not the only one which supplies test statistics suited to verify the validity of the unconstrained VAR model, i.e. $\xi_T^{(1)}$, $\xi_T^{(2)}$, $\xi_T^{(3)}$. In fact, we can verify that the only two cases where this is not true correspond to testing H_1 as the last one. This is a consequence of the fact that, if Σ_{yx} is not 0, the constraint $\Phi_{xy}(L) = 0$ modifies the estimation of $\Phi_y(L)$ and of $\Phi_{yx}(L)$ (and conversely, if we invert the role of **x** and **y**

– cf. exercise 13.3). Therefore, one should avoid testing instantaneous causality last.

13.3 Tests for Predeterminedness and Exogeneity and of Existence of a Structural Form

The concepts of predeterminedness and exogeneity are strictly related to the structural form (cf. chapter 10). Let us then consider a structural form expressed as

$$\mathbf{A}_0 \mathbf{y}_t + \ldots + \mathbf{A}_p \mathbf{y}_{t-p} + \mathbf{B}_0 \mathbf{x}_t + \ldots + \mathbf{B}_p \mathbf{x}_{t-p} + \boldsymbol{\mu} = \boldsymbol{\varepsilon}_t, \quad (13.27)$$

where $\mathbf{A}_0$ is nonsingular and where $(\boldsymbol{\varepsilon}_t)$ is a white noise with variance–covariance matrix $\mathbf{Q}$, uncorrelated with past values of $\mathbf{y}_t$. Let us denote

$$\boldsymbol{\Gamma} = (\mathbf{A}_0, \mathbf{A}_1, \ldots, \mathbf{A}_p, \mathbf{B}_0, \mathbf{B}_1, \ldots, \mathbf{B}_p, \boldsymbol{\mu})$$

$$\boldsymbol{\Gamma}_0 = (\mathbf{A}_0, \mathbf{B}_0).$$

These parameters are constrained by the relationship

$$\mathbf{R} \mathrm{vec}\, \boldsymbol{\Gamma} = \mathbf{r} \quad (13.28)$$

where $\mathbf{R}$ is a known matrix of rank q and of size $(q \times n((n+m)(p+1)+1))$ and r is a known vector of size q. Some of the constraints involve the parameter matrices $\mathbf{A}_0$ and $\mathbf{B}_0$. We will assume that $(\mathbf{A}_0, \mathbf{B}_0)$ only appear in the q_0 constraints

$$\mathbf{R}_0 \mathrm{vec}\, \boldsymbol{\Gamma}_0 = \mathbf{r}_0. \quad (13.29)$$

Finally, we will assume that the identifiability conditions of $\boldsymbol{\Gamma}$ (theorem 10.11) and of contemporaneous identifiability (10.34) are satisfied.

13.3.1 Test of Predeterminedness

We have previously seen (cf. definition 10.7) that the process $\mathbf{x}$ is predetermined for a structural form satisfying the simultaneity structure (13.29) if and only if there exists $\boldsymbol{\Gamma}_0 = (\mathbf{A}_0, \mathbf{B}_0)$ such that

$$\mathbf{R}_0 \mathrm{vec}\, \boldsymbol{\Gamma}_0 = \mathbf{r}_0$$

$$\mathbf{A}_0 \boldsymbol{\Phi}_{yx0}^+ + \mathbf{B}_0 \equiv \boldsymbol{\Gamma}_0 \begin{pmatrix} \boldsymbol{\Phi}_{yx0}^+ \\ \mathbf{I}_m \end{pmatrix} = \mathbf{0}.$$

The hypothesis of predeterminedness is of the mixed type presented in the previous section. Here the initial parameter $\boldsymbol{\theta}$ is made of the components of $\boldsymbol{\Phi}_{yx0}^+$ and the auxiliary parameter is equal to vec $\boldsymbol{\Gamma}_0$. The system of constraints defining the null hypothesis of predeterminedness (H_P) can be written as

$$\mathbf{R}_0 \mathrm{vec}\, \boldsymbol{\Gamma}_0 = \mathbf{r}_0$$

$$\left(\left(\boldsymbol{\Phi}_{yx0}^{+'} \quad \mathbf{I}_m \right) \otimes \mathbf{I}_n \right) \mathrm{vec}\, \boldsymbol{\Gamma}_0 = \mathbf{0}.$$

The procedure to obtain the test statistic here is very simple because of the linearity of the system in the auxiliary parameter $\mathbf{a} = \text{vec}\,\mathbf{\Gamma}_0$. The statistic ξ_t^P is obtained as follows:

(i) We estimate the auxiliary parameter $\text{vec}\,\mathbf{\Gamma}_0$ by OLS in the model

$$\left(\left(\,\hat{\mathbf{\Phi}}_{yx0}^{+\,'}\quad \mathbf{I}_m\,\right) \otimes \mathbf{I}_n\right) \text{vec}\,\mathbf{\Gamma}_0 = \mathbf{u}$$

subject to the constraints

$$\mathbf{R}_0 \text{vec}\,\mathbf{\Gamma}_0 = \mathbf{r}_0,$$

where $\hat{\mathbf{\Phi}}_{yx0}^{+\,'}$ is the OLS estimator of $\mathbf{\Phi}_{yx0}^{+\,'}$. Let us denote the estimator thus obtained as $\tilde{\mathbf{\Gamma}}_0 = \left(\tilde{\mathbf{A}}_0, \tilde{\mathbf{B}}_0\right)$.

(ii) We apply generalized least squares to the same model taking as the variance–covariance matrix of the error u

$$\widehat{\text{var}}\,(\mathbf{u}) = \widehat{\text{var}}\left(\text{vec}\,\left(\mathbf{A}_0\hat{\mathbf{\Phi}}_{yx0}^+ + \mathbf{B}_0\right)\right)$$

$$= \left(\mathbf{I}_m \otimes \tilde{\mathbf{A}}_0\right) \widehat{\text{var}}\,(\text{vec}\,\hat{\mathbf{\Phi}}_{yx0}^+) \left(\mathbf{I}_m \otimes \tilde{\mathbf{A}}_0\right)',$$

where $\text{var}\,(\text{vec}\,\hat{\mathbf{\Phi}}_{yx0}^+)$ is the estimated asymptotic variance–covariance matrix of

$$\sqrt{T}\left((\text{vec}\,\hat{\mathbf{\Phi}}_{yx0}^+) - (\text{vec}\,\mathbf{\Phi}_{yx0}^+)\right).$$

(iii) The test statistic ξ_T^P is equal to T times the minimized value of the loss function used at the second stage

$$\xi_T^P = T \min_{\mathbf{\Gamma}_0} \mathbf{u}'\,(\widehat{\text{var}}\,(\mathbf{u}))^{-1}\,\mathbf{u}.$$

The test has a critical region defined as

$$\{\xi_T^P \geq \chi_{1-\alpha}^2(q_0 - n^2)\}$$

since in this case the number of constraints is $r_1 = nm + q_0$, the number of auxiliary parameters is $k_1 = nm + n^2$, and thus $r_1 - k_1 = q_0 - n^2$. It corresponds to the degree of contemporaneous overidentification. Note that the previous test procedure, based on asymptotic least squares, needs some regularity conditions which are verified since the matrix $\mathbf{A}_0$ is nonsingular, and the contemporaneous identifiability condition is satisfied (cf. Monfort and Rabemananjara, 1990).

13.3.2 Tests of Strict Exogeneity

We have seen in definition 10.8 that the hypothesis of strict exogeneity of $\mathbf{x}$ corresponds to the intersection of the hypothesis H_P of predeterminedness and of the hypothesis H_2 of noncausality of $\mathbf{y}$ to $\mathbf{x}$. It can be characterized as

$$\mathbf{R}_0 \operatorname{vec} \boldsymbol{\Gamma}_0 = \mathbf{r}_0,$$

$$\mathbf{A}_0 \boldsymbol{\Phi}_{yx0}^+ + \mathbf{B}_0 = \mathbf{0},$$

$$\boldsymbol{\Phi}_{xyi} = \mathbf{0}, \qquad i = 1, \ldots, p.$$

First of all, it can be easily shown that the maximum likelihood estimators of the contemporaneous coefficient $\boldsymbol{\Phi}_{yx0}^+$, on the one hand, and of the lagged coefficients $\boldsymbol{\Phi}_{xyi}$, $i = 1, \ldots, p$, on the other, are asymptotically independent. In fact, the elements of the matrix $\boldsymbol{\Phi}_{yx0}^+$ belong to $\boldsymbol{\phi}_y^+$, those of the matrices $\boldsymbol{\Phi}_{xyi}$ belong to $\boldsymbol{\phi}_x$. On the basis of (13.16) we know that the corresponding Hessian matrix

$$\frac{\partial^2 L_T}{\partial \boldsymbol{\theta} \partial \boldsymbol{\theta}'}$$

is block-diagonal relative to $\boldsymbol{\phi}_y^+$ and $\boldsymbol{\phi}_x$. The statistic ξ_T^E for the test of strict exogeneity based on the asymptotic least squares (13.7) can be decomposed as

$$\xi_T^E = \xi_T^P + \xi_T^{(2)}, \tag{13.30}$$

where $\xi_T^{(2)}$ is the noncausality test from $\mathbf{y}$ to $\mathbf{x}$. Moreover, the two statistics ξ_T^P and $\xi_T^{(2)}$ are independent under the hypothesis of strict exogeneity. Therefore, to test the strict exogeneity hypothesis of $\mathbf{x}$ in the general model, there are two possibilities. First, it is possible to use the statistic ξ_T^E directly. The critical region at the asymptotic level α is then

$$\{\xi_T^E \geq \chi_{1-\alpha}^2(q_0 - n^2 + nmp)\}.$$

Second, it is possible to use a critical region of the type

$$\{\xi_T^P \geq \chi_{1-\alpha_1}^2(q_0 - n^2)\} \cup \{\xi_T^{(2)} \geq \chi_{1-\alpha_2}^2(nmp)\}.$$

Making use of the asymptotic independence just shown, we see that the asymptotic significance level of this test is $1 - (1 - \alpha_1)(1 - \alpha_2) = \alpha_1 + \alpha_2 - \alpha_1 \alpha_2$. The latter approach traces back the rejection of the null of strict exogeneity whether this is to be attributed to the rejection of predeterminedness and/or of noncausality.

13.3.3 Test of a Weak or Strong Structural Form

By definition, there exists a weak structural form (13.27) satisfying the constraints (13.28), if there exist some auxiliary parameters

$$\boldsymbol{\Gamma} = (\mathbf{A}_0, \ldots, \mathbf{A}_p, \mathbf{B}_0, \ldots, \mathbf{B}_p, \mu)$$

such that

$$\mathbf{A}_0\mathbf{\Phi}_{yxi}^+ + \mathbf{B}_i = \mathbf{0}, \qquad i = 0, \dots, p$$

$$\mathbf{A}_0\mathbf{\Phi}_{yi}^+ + \mathbf{A}_i = \mathbf{0}, \qquad i = 1, \dots, p$$

$$\mathbf{A}_0\mathbf{c}_y^+ + \boldsymbol{\mu} = \mathbf{0},$$

$$\mathbf{R}\mathrm{vec}\,\mathbf{\Gamma} = \mathbf{0}.$$

This is still a mixed-type hypothesis, linear in $\mathrm{vec}\,\mathbf{\Gamma}$. We can then use the same kind of procedure as for the test of predeterminedness, based on OLS and GLS. The conditions of validity of the test are satisfied given the nonsingularity of the matrix $\mathbf{A}_0$ and the identification condition. If we denote the obtained statistic as ξ_T^W the test has a critical region at the asymptotic significance level α

$$\{\xi_T^W \geq \chi_{1-\alpha}^2(q - n^2)\}$$

since in this case $r_1 = nm(p+1) + n^2p + n + q$, $k_1 = (p+1)(nm+n^2) + n$ and hence $r_1 - k_1 = q - n^2$; this is the order of overidentification. We also know that (cf. theorem 10.10) that the hypothesis of the existence of a strong structural form is identical to the intersection of the hypothesis of existence of a weak structural form and of noncausality from $\mathbf{y}$ to $\mathbf{x}$. If we denote ξ_T^S the corresponding test statistic of a strong structural form we have, for the same reasons as in the previous section

$$\xi_T^S = \xi_T^W + \xi_T^{(2)} \tag{13.31}$$

since ξ_T^W and $\xi_T^{(2)}$ are asymptotically independent under the null hypothesis H_S of the existence of a strong structural form. We can therefore test the hypothesis H_S in two ways: the critical regions are, respectively

$$\{\xi_T^S \geq \chi_{1-\alpha}^2(q - n^2 + nmp)\}$$

and

$$\{\xi_T^W \geq \chi_{1-\alpha_1}^2(q - n^2)\} \cup \{\xi_T^{(2)} \geq \chi_{1-\alpha_2}^2(nmp)\}$$

with $\alpha = \alpha_1 + \alpha_2 - \alpha_1\alpha_2$. Recall (cf. section 13.1.4) that, as a by-product, the previous testing procedures provide an estimator of $\mathbf{\Gamma}$ which is asymptotically equivalent to the full information maximum likelihood estimator and which can be obtained just using ordinary and generalized least squares.

13.3.4 Order of Testing

Summarizing, we have six hypotheses:

H_V General VAR hypothesis

H_P Hypothesis of predeterminedness of $\mathbf{x}$

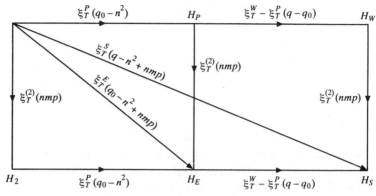

Figure 13.2   Ordering of the Tests

Table 13.1 *Values of Test Statistics*

Null Hypothesis	H_P	H_2	H_W
Test Statistic	1.3	72.7	39.8
Degrees of Freedom	4	60	44
Asymptotic p-value	0.86	0.13	0.64

H_E Hypothesis of strict exogeneity of $\mathbf{x}$

H_2 Hypothesis of noncausality from $\mathbf{y}$ to $\mathbf{x}$

H_W Hypothesis of a weak structural form

H_S Hypothesis of a strong structural form

In order to go from the less restrictive H_V to the most restrictive H_S there are three possible descending procedures. These paths are summarized in figure 13.2 where the test statistics are reported with the related degrees of freedom.

The three statistics ξ_T^P, $\xi_T^{(2)}$, $\xi_T^W - \xi_T^P$, used for no matter what path from H_V to H_S are asymptotically independent under H_S and therefore we can control the asymptotic significance level of such a top–down procedure.

13.3.5 An Example

Let us consider a model of the type wage-price loop in which the endogenous variables are the hourly wage W, the producer price PP and the consumer price CP. The potentially exogenous variables are IP import

Table 13.2 *Sequence*
$H_V \supset H_P \supset H_W \supset H_S$

Null Hypothesis	H_P	H_W	H_S
Test Statistic	1.3	38.8	75.4
Degrees of Freedom	4	40	60
Asymptotic p-value	0.86	0.52	0.09

prices, EP energy prices, AP agricultural prices, Q productivity, and U a measure of the excess labor supply (cf. Monfort and Rabemananjara, 1990). The series are seasonally adjusted quarterly series for the French economy between 1962Q2 and 1983Q4. After various tests on the number of lags, a block-recursive VAR model of order 4 was retained for the variables expressed in growth rates (approximated by a first difference on the variables in logs – denoted in small letters) except for the variable U. Constant terms and dummy variables (D1 for 1968Q2 and D2 for 1968Q3) have been added. The retained structural form is

$$\Delta w_t = \delta_1 + \sum_{i=1}^{4} \gamma_{11i}\Delta w_{t-i} + \sum_{i=0}^{4} \gamma_{13i}\Delta cp_{t-i} + \sum_{i=0}^{4} \gamma_{17i}\Delta q_{t-i} +$$

$$+ \sum_{i=0}^{4} \gamma_{18i}\Delta U_{t-i} + \alpha_1 D1 + \alpha_2 D2 + u_{1t},$$

$$\Delta pp_t = \delta_2 + \sum_{i=1}^{4} \gamma_{22i}\Delta pp_{t-i} + \sum_{i=0}^{4} \gamma_{21i}\Delta w_{t-i} + \sum_{i=0}^{4} \gamma_{24i}\Delta ip_{t-i} +$$

$$+ \sum_{i=0}^{4} \gamma_{25i}\Delta ep_{t-i} + \sum_{i=0}^{4} \gamma_{26i}\Delta ap_{t-i} + \sum_{i=0}^{4} \gamma_{27i}\Delta q_{t-i} +$$

$$+ \alpha_3 D1 + \alpha_4 D2 + u_{2t},$$

$$\Delta cp_t = \delta_3 + \sum_{i=1}^{4} \gamma_{33i}\Delta cp_{t-i} + \sum_{i=0}^{4} \gamma_{31i}\Delta pp_{t-i} + \sum_{i=0}^{4} \gamma_{35i}\Delta ep_{t-i} +$$

$$+ \sum_{i=0}^{4} \gamma_{36i}\Delta ap_{t-i} + \alpha_5 D1 + \alpha_6 D2 + u_{3t}.$$

The three statistics to test predeterminedness, strict exogeneity, and noncausality, the weak or strong structural form are ξ_T^P, $\xi_T^{(2)}$, ξ_T^W, using

Table 13.3 *Sequence*
$H_V \supset H_P \supset H_E \supset H_S$

Null Hypothesis	H_P	H_E	H_S
Test Statistic	1.3	67.6	43.1
Degrees of Freedom	4	60	40
Asymptotic p-value	0.86	0.23	0.34

Table 13.4 *Sequence*
$H_V \supset H_2 \supset H_E \supset H_S$

Null Hypothesis	H_2	H_E	H_S
Test Statistic	72.7	1.7	43.1
Degrees of Freedom	60	4	40
Asymptotic p-value	0.13	0.79	0.34

the notation of the previous section. These statistics are given in table 13.1, using the correction by Anderson (1958) to obtain a statistic with a finite sample distribution closer to the asymptotic distribution.

These statistics allow us to construct the three sequences of tests going from the most general H_V to the most restrictive H_S.

These tables show that the hypotheses of predeterminedness and of weak structural form are largely accepted by the data. On the contrary, the hypothesis of strict exogeneity and thus of strong structural form is much more uncertain. In particular the sequence $H_V \supset H_P \supset H_W \supset H_S$ shows an asymptotic p-value for the last test of 9%.

13.4 Tests on the Lag Structure

13.4.1 Common Factor Tests

The Hypothesis Let us consider an equation of the type

$$\sum_{i=1}^{p} \psi_i(L) z_{it} = \epsilon_t, \tag{13.32}$$

where ϵ_t is a white noise and the $\psi_i(L)$ are polynomials in the lag operator L of degree f_i. Let us suppose that $\psi_1(L)$ is normalized by imposing $\psi_1(0) = 1$. Equation (13.32) might correspond to one of the equations of a VAR model or of a structural form. The variables z_{it} are then endogenous, lagged endogenous, or exogenous variables. Let us examine now the null hypothesis H_R according to which the lag polynomials $\psi_i(L)$, $i = 1, \ldots, p$ have a common root. If this hypothesis is true, and if $1 + \rho L$ indicates the common factor to the various polynomials, we can simplify the lag structure and write the dynamic relationship

$$\sum_{i=1}^{p} \alpha_i(L) z_{it} = \eta_t, \tag{13.33}$$

where $\alpha_i(L)$ is now the polynomial of degree $f_i - 1$ defined as $\psi_i(L) = \alpha_i(L)(1 + \rho L)$ and where η_t is the autoregressive process of order 1 defined as $(1 + \rho L)\eta_t = \epsilon_t$. We say that a part of the dynamic structure of the model is driven by the disturbance η_t.

In order to understand the problems posed by the test of such hypothesis, let us start by examining the case of two polynomials of degree 2 and 1, that is, $p = 2$, $f_1 = 2$, $f_2 = 1$. These polynomials are $\psi_1(L) = 1 + \psi_{11}L + \psi_{12}L^2$ and $\psi_2(L) = \psi_{20} + \psi_{21}L$ and if they admit a common root, we have

$$1 + \psi_{11}L + \psi_{12}L^2 = (1 + \rho L)(1 + \beta_{11}L)$$

$$\psi_{20} + \psi_{21}L = (1 + \rho L)\beta_{20}.$$

We can write the hypothesis under an explicit form, that is, write the initial parameters as a function of $\rho, \beta_{11}, \beta_{20}$

$$\psi_{11} = \rho + \beta_{11} \quad \psi_{12} = \rho\beta_{11} \quad \psi_{20} = \beta_{20} \quad \psi_{21} = \rho\beta_{20}.$$

In this expression, though, the relationships are nonlinear in the parameters ρ, β_{20} and β_{11}. An alternative would be to show the relationship in an implicit form, obtaining a nonlinear relationship among the initial parameters

$$\psi_{11} = \frac{\psi_{21}}{\psi_{20}} + \frac{\psi_{12}\psi_{20}}{\psi_{21}}.$$

A last possibility is to write this hypothesis in a mixed form, using Bezout's Theorem as in Gourieroux, Monfort, and Renault (1989)

$$\exists \beta_{11}, \beta_{20} : (1 + \psi_{11}L + \psi_{12}L^2)\beta_{20} = (\psi_{20} + \psi_{21}L)(1 + \beta_{11}L).$$

Distributing the product we obtain

$$\exists \beta_{11}, \beta_{20} : \begin{cases} \beta_{20} = \psi_{20}, \\ \beta_{20}\psi_{11} = \beta_{11}\psi_{20} + \psi_{21}, \\ \beta_{20}\psi_{12} = \beta_{11}\psi_{21}. \end{cases} \tag{13.34}$$

This expression is linear in the auxiliary parameters β_{11}, β_{20} and in this case the test based on the asymptotic least squares (13.7) can be constructed from OLS and GLS.

The Test Procedure The details of the procedure are as follows: the constraints (13.34) are linear both in the original parameters ψ and the auxiliary parameters β. They can then be written in two different ways

$$\begin{pmatrix} \psi_{20} \\ \psi_{21} \\ 0 \end{pmatrix} = \begin{pmatrix} 0 & 1 \\ -\psi_{20} & \psi_{11} \\ -\psi_{21} & \psi_{12} \end{pmatrix} \begin{pmatrix} \beta_{11} \\ \beta_{20} \end{pmatrix}, \qquad (13.35)$$

or $h(\psi) = \mathbf{H}(\psi)\beta$, and

$$\begin{pmatrix} \beta_{20} \\ 0 \\ 0 \end{pmatrix} = \begin{pmatrix} 0 & 0 & 1 & 0 \\ -\beta_{20} & 0 & \beta_{11} & 1 \\ 0 & -\beta_{20} & 0 & \beta_{11} \end{pmatrix} \begin{pmatrix} \psi_{11} \\ \psi_{12} \\ \psi_{20} \\ \psi_{21} \end{pmatrix}, \qquad (13.36)$$

or $a(\beta) = \mathbf{A}(\beta)\psi$. Let us denote a consistent estimator of ψ as $\hat{\psi}$ which is asymptotically normal $\sqrt{T}(\hat{\psi} - \psi) \overset{d}{\rightarrow} \mathcal{N}(\mathbf{0}, \mathbf{V})$ and a consistent estimator of the matrix $\mathbf{V}$ as $\hat{\mathbf{V}}$. In this autoregressive case these estimators are obtained by OLS. The test procedure is articulated in three steps:

(i)   We estimate β_{11}, β_{20} by OLS in the system (13.35) by replacing ψ_{ij} by their estimates $\hat{\psi}_{ij}$. Let us denote the result $\tilde{\beta}_{11}, \tilde{\beta}_{20}$.

(ii) We estimate β_{11} and β_{20} by GLS in the same system using as a variance–covariance matrix of the disturbances $\mathbf{A}(\tilde{\beta})\hat{\mathbf{V}}\mathbf{A}'(\tilde{\beta})$.

(iii) The test statistic ξ_T^R is equal to T times the value of the objective function used in the second step. The critical region of the test at the asymptotic level α is then $\{\xi_T^R \geq \chi_{1-\alpha}^2(1)\}$.

General Case The procedure just described can be extended to the general case considered at the beginning of this section (Gourieroux, Monfort and Renault, 1989). Bezout's Theorem can be written as:

Theorem 13.2: *If the polynomials $\psi_i(L)$, $i = 1, \ldots, p$ have at most s roots in common, a necessary and sufficient condition for having exactly s of them, is that there exist p polynomials $\beta_i(L)$ of degree $f_i - s$ verifying $\beta_1(0) = 1$ and such that*

$$\psi_i(L)\beta_{i+1}(L) = \psi_{i+1}(L)\beta_i(L) \quad i = 1, \ldots, p - 1.$$

It is necessary to note, though, that the matrix $\mathbf{A}(\boldsymbol{\beta})$, obtained by writing the constraints as in (13.36), is not always a full row rank matrix. In fact, it can be shown that this matrix has

$$q = \sum_{i=1}^{p} (f_i + 1) - 1$$

columns, and

$$k = \sum_{i=1}^{p-1} (f_i + f_{i+1} - s + 1)$$

rows and that its rank is $q - s \leq k$. In the case just examined, we had $q = 4$, $k = 3$, $s = 1$, so that $q - s = k$ and $\mathbf{A}(\boldsymbol{\beta})$ was of full row rank. If we take the case of three polynomials of degree 2, though, having a common root (cf. exercise 13.5), we have $p = 3$, $f_1 = f_2 = f_3 = 2$, $q = 8$, $k = 8$, $s = 1$, and therefore $q - s = 7$. If $\mathbf{A}(\boldsymbol{\beta})$ is not of full row rank, the test statistic is obtained as

$$\xi_T^R = T \min_{\beta} \left(h(\hat{\psi}) - \mathbf{H}(\hat{\psi})\boldsymbol{\beta} \right)' \left(\mathbf{A}(\tilde{\beta})\hat{\mathbf{V}}\mathbf{A}'(\tilde{\beta}) \right)^{+} \left(h(\hat{\psi}) - \mathbf{H}(\hat{\psi})\boldsymbol{\beta} \right),$$

where the superscript $+$ denotes the Moore–Penrose generalized inverse. In either case the critical region of asymptotic size α is

$$\{\xi_T^R \geq \chi_{1-\alpha}^2(s(k-1))\}.$$

13.4.2 Rational Distributed Lags

Hypothesis and Test Procedure In the previous sections we showed an easy testing procedure for the case of a mixed-type hypothesis

$$\exists \mathbf{a} : g(a, \theta)$$

when the g function is bilinear in θ and a (cf. Gourieroux, Monfort, and Renault, 1990, for further details). The hypothesis of a rational distributed lag is also of this form. Indeed, let us consider a polynomial in the lag operator of degree f

$$\psi(L) = \sum_{i=0}^{f} \psi_i L^i.$$

We want to test the hypothesis H_{RD} according to which $\psi(L)$ corresponds to the first $f+1$ terms of the integer series expansion of a rational fraction of the type

$$\frac{C(L)}{B(L)},$$

where

$$C(L) = c_0 + c_1 L + \ldots c_s L^s,$$

$$B(L) = 1 + b_1 L + \ldots b_q L^q,$$

with s and q integers such that $s + q < f$. This condition can be written as

$$(1 + b_1 L + \ldots b_q L^q)\left(\psi_0 + \psi_1 L + \ldots + \psi_f L^f + \psi_{f+1} L^{f+1} + \ldots\right)$$

$$= (c_0 + c_1 L + \ldots c_s L^s).$$

By equating the terms with the same exponent we get

$$\exists\, c_0, \ldots, c_s, b_1, \ldots, b_q, \text{ such that}$$

$$c_0 = \psi_0,$$

$$c_1 = \psi_1 + b_1 \psi_0,$$

$$\ldots$$

$$c_s = \psi_s + b_1 \psi_{s-1} + \ldots + b_q \psi_{s-q},$$

$$0 = \psi_{s+1} + b_1 \psi_s + \ldots + b_q \psi_{s-q+1},$$

$$\ldots$$

$$0 = \psi_f + b_1 \psi_{f-1} + \ldots + b_q \psi_{f-q},$$

with the convention $\psi_i = 0$ if $i < 0$. Let us assume that for any polynomial satisfying these constraints, the last $f - s$ equations determine $b_1, \ldots, b_q$ uniquely. The $s + 1$ first equations are automatically verified and can be omitted. Finally, the constraints are

$$\exists\, b_1, \ldots, b_q \text{ such that}$$

$$0 = \psi_i + b_1 \psi_{i-1} + \ldots + b_q \psi_{i-q}$$

for $i = s+1, \ldots, f$, with the convention $\psi_i = 0$ if $i < 0$. The constraints are bilinear with respect to the initial parameters ψ_j, $j = 0, \ldots, f$ and to the auxiliary parameters b_i, $i = 1, \ldots, q$. If we have available consistent and asymptotically normal estimators $\hat{\psi}_j$, we can easily apply the test based on the asymptotic least squares. Denoting by ξ_T^{RD} the test statistic, the critical region at the asymptotic level α is

$$\{\xi_T^{RD} \geq \chi_{1-\alpha}^2(f - s - q)\}.$$

Examples Let us examine some special cases:

(i) $s = 0, q = 1$ The constraints can be written as

$$\exists\, b \text{ such that}$$

$$0 = \psi_1 - b\psi_0$$

$$\ldots$$

$$0 = \psi_f - b\psi_{f-1}.$$

Solving these various relationships, we can express the initial parameters as a function of b and $a = \psi_0/(1 - b)$. We get

$$\psi_0 = a(1 - b), \;\; \psi_1 = a(1 - b)b, \ldots, \psi_f = a(1 - b)b^f.$$

Such a lag structure is called *exponential* or *Koyck distributed lags*. It appears in the models implying adaptive expectation variables (cf. chapter 12). The asymptotic distribution of ξ_T^{RD} under the null hypothesis is $\chi^2(f - 1)$.

(ii) $s = q = 1$ The constraints can be written as

$$\exists\, b \text{ such that}$$

$$0 = \psi_2 - b\psi_1,$$

$$\ldots$$

$$0 = \psi_f - b\psi_{f-1}.$$

The expression for the initial parameters is once again of an exponential type $\psi_i = a(1-b)b^j$, but only starting from the index $i = 1$. The asymptotic distribution of ξ_T^{RD} under the null hypothesis is $\chi^2(f - 2)$.

(iii) $s = 1, q = 2$ The constraints can be written as

$$\exists\, b_1, b_2 \text{ such that}$$

$$0 = \psi_2 - b_1\psi_1 + b_2\psi_0,$$

$$\ldots$$

$$0 = \psi_f - b_1\psi_{f-1} + b_2\psi_{f-1}.$$

The asymptotic distribution of ξ_T^{RD} under the null hypothesis is $\chi^2(f - 3)$. Note that the structure of this type associated to the values $b_1 = -2$ and $b_2 = 1$ corresponds to the Almon specification of order 1. The initial values of the parameters satisfy the recursive equation $\psi_j - 2\psi_{j-1} + \psi_{j-2} = 0$. They can be written as a polynomial of degree 1, that is, $\psi_j = \alpha j + \beta$. A test for these constraints allows for the test of the Almon specification.

13.5 Tests of Rational Expectations

The hypothesis about the expectation formation by economic agents can be examined following two routes.

(i)   Sometimes we have data on the realizations of a variable y_t, $t = 1, \ldots, T$ and on the expectations (one step-ahead, for example) $\hat{y}_t$ that are formed on them. We can then examine these data directly in order to link the expectations to the current and past realizations in order to derive the underlying prediction function. Such tests are called *direct*.

(ii) Often the expectations are unobservable. However, we can try and obtain some information about them, if they affect other variables which, in turn, are observable. Then we need to resort to a model containing some expectation terms, for example of the type

$$y_t = a\hat{y}_t + \mathbf{x}_t b + u_t,$$

where y_t and $\mathbf{x}_t$ are observable, while $\hat{y}_t$ and u_t are not. The next step is to analyze whether a given expectation formation scheme leads to a good fit of the model or not on the basis of the empirical evidence. Such an approach, which considers simultaneously the expectation formation scheme and the structural model linking the endogenous variable to the exogenous variables and to the expectation is called *indirect test*.

The two approaches, direct and indirect can be followed in order to test a number of expectation schemes: naïve, perfect, adaptive, and rational. In this section we will examine mainly the rational scheme (cf. exercises 13.6 and 13.7 for the adaptive case). We will be led to test the hypothesis of optimal determination of the forecasts, and to examine the question of the information sets on the basis of which expectations are formed.

13.5.1 Direct Tests

Let us assume that the available information concerns the realizations y_t, $t = 1, \ldots, T$ of a variable and the measurements of the related expectations y_t^*, $t = 1, \ldots, T$. In what follows we will consider a measurement error scheme such as

$$y_t^* = \hat{y}_t + \eta_t,$$

where $\hat{y}_t$ is the expectation and η_t is the measurement error. To simplify matters, we will assume that the measurement error process η is independent of the processes y and $\hat{y}$, that η is a white noise and that y and

$\hat{y}$ are stationary, but not necessarily with zero mean. The null hypothesis is for example one of rational expectations based on the information contained in the past values of the variable

$$H_0 : \hat{y}_t = E\left(y_t | \underline{y}_{t-1}\right), \qquad (13.36)$$

with $\underline{y}_{t-1} = (y_{t-1}, y_{t-2}, \ldots)$.

Test of Unbiasedness A first approach can be one of not testing the hypothesis itself, but its consequences. Thus, under the hypothesis of rationality we know that the forecasts are unbiased, that is

$$E(\hat{y}_t) = E(y_t)$$

and that the forecast error is uncorrelated with the forecast itself

$$\text{cov}\left(y_t - \hat{y}_t, \hat{y}_t\right) = 0.$$

Let us consider then the regression model

$$y_t = a y_t^* + b + u_t. \qquad (13.37)$$

The theoretical regression coefficients are given by

$$a = \frac{\text{cov}\left(y_t, y_t^*\right)}{\text{var}\left(y_t^*\right)} = \frac{\text{cov}\left(y_t, \hat{y}_t\right)}{\text{var}\left(\hat{y}_t\right) + \text{var}\left(\eta\right)}$$

and

$$b = E(y_t) - aE(y_t^*) = E(y_t) - aE(\hat{y}_t).$$

We can then distinguish between two cases:

(i)   If the measurement error is not present, we have under the rationality hypothesis

$$a = \frac{\text{cov}\left(y_t, y_t^*\right)}{\text{var}\left(y_t^*\right)} = \frac{\text{var}\left(\hat{y}_t\right)}{\text{var}\left(\hat{y}_t\right)} = 1$$

and

$$b = E(y_t) - aE(\hat{y}_t) = 0.$$

Since the error term $u_t = y_t - \hat{y}_t$ is orthogonal to the explanatory variable $\hat{y}_t$, serially uncorrelated and homoskedastic, we can directly test the consequence of the rationality hypothesis H_0^* : $a = 1$, $b = 0$ by estimating by OLS a and b, and then building a Fisher-type test on the joint hypothesis H_0^*. This is a test called in the literature *unbiasedness test*. It is clear that it relates not only to the unbiasedness condition, but also to the one of orthogonality.

(ii) If a measurement error is present, then under the hypothesis of rational expectations we have

$$a = \frac{\text{var}\left(\hat{y}_t\right)}{\text{var}\left(\hat{y}_t\right) + \text{var}\left(\eta_t\right)} \leq 1$$

and $b = (1 - a)E(y_t)$. The equalities are lost, and we would be tempted to think of analyzing whether the OLS estimator of a is less than 1 and whether the estimator of b has the same sign as the mean of the realizations. However such a procedure is incorrect since we have

$$u_t = y_t - ay_t^* - b = y_t - a\hat{y}_t - b - a\eta_t$$

and this error term is correlated to the explanatory variable $y_t^* = \hat{y}_t + \eta_t$. The OLS estimators are then inconsistent. Thus we see that the unbiasedness test is simple to implement, but not so robust with respect to measurement errors in the expectations.

Optimality Test Another approach was proposed by Pesando (1975) and is based on a VAR representation of the bivariate process $\{y, y^*\}$. Under the rational expectation hypothesis, we have

$$E(y_t | \underline{y}_{t-1}, \underline{y}_{t-1}^*) = E(y_t | \underline{y}_{t-1}, \underline{\eta}_{t-1}).$$

Moreover, since y and η are independent

$$E(y_t | \underline{y}_{t-1}, \underline{y}_{t-1}^*) = E(y_t | \underline{y}_{t-1}) = \hat{y}_t.$$

Analogously

$$E(y_t^* | \underline{y}_{t-1}, \underline{y}_{t-1}^*) = E(y_t^* | \underline{y}_{t-1}, \underline{\eta}_{t-1})$$

$$= E(\hat{y}_t | \underline{y}_{t-1}, \underline{\eta}_{t-1}) + E(\eta_t | \underline{y}_{t-1}, \underline{\eta}_{t-1}) = \hat{y}_t.$$

Thus y_t and y_t^* share the same forecast as a function of the information $\underline{y}_{t-1}$. We can then write an autoregressive representation

$$y_t = a_0 + \sum_{j=1}^{p} a_j y_{t-j} + \sum_{j=1}^{p} b_j y_{t-j}^* + \epsilon_{1t},$$

$$y_t^* = c_0 + \sum_{j=1}^{p} c_j y_{t-j} + \sum_{j=1}^{p} d_j y_{t-j}^* + \epsilon_{2t},$$

then test the hypothesis $H_0 : a_j = c_j, j = 0, \dots, p, b_j = d_j, j = 1, \dots, p$ using one of the classical test statistics.

13.5.2 Indirect Tests

Muth's Model The approach is similar to the one described for testing the existence of a structural form. Here the problem relates to the existence of a structural form involving rational expectation terms. Let us assume that the model contains an expectation term related to the current endogenous variables and that it can be written as

$$\mathbf{y}_t = \mathbf{A}E(\mathbf{y}_t|I_{t-1}) + \sum_{k=1}^{p} \mathbf{A}_k \mathbf{y}_{t-k} + \sum_{k=1}^{p} \mathbf{B}_k \mathbf{x}_{t-k} + \mathbf{u}_t, \qquad (13.38)$$

where $\mathbf{y}_t$ and $\mathbf{x}_t$ are of size n, respectively, m and the error $\mathbf{u}_t$ is assumed independent of $\underline{\mathbf{y}}_{t-1}$ and $\underline{\mathbf{x}}_t$. We focus on the information set I_{t-1} as the one based on the past values of the various processes and the current value of the exogenous $I_{t-1} = \{\underline{\mathbf{y}}_{t-1}, \underline{\mathbf{x}}_t\}$. The structural coefficients

$$\mathbf{\Gamma} = (\mathbf{A}, \mathbf{A}_1, \ldots, \mathbf{A}_p, \mathbf{B}_0, \ldots, \mathbf{B}_p)$$

are subject to a number of linear constraints of the type $\mathbf{R}\,\text{vec}\,\mathbf{\Gamma} = \mathbf{r}$ and the structural form is assumed to be identified. If the series under analysis are compatible with an autoregressive representation, we can consider the regression of $\mathbf{y}_t$ on $\underline{\mathbf{y}}_{t-1}$ and $\underline{\mathbf{x}}_t$. It is given by

$$\mathbf{y}_t = \mathbf{\Phi}_{yx0}^+ \mathbf{x}_t + \sum_{k=1}^{p} \mathbf{\Phi}_{yxk}^+ \mathbf{x}_{t-k} + \sum_{k=1}^{p} \mathbf{\Phi}_{yk}^+ \mathbf{y}_{t-k} + \boldsymbol{\varepsilon}_t.$$

If the rational expectation model (13.38) is valid, the reduced form coefficients are restricted by

$$\exists \mathbf{A}, \mathbf{A}_k, k = 1, \ldots, p, \mathbf{B}_k, k = 0, \ldots, p$$

$$(\mathbf{I} - \mathbf{A})\mathbf{\Phi}_{yxk}^+ = \mathbf{B}_k, \quad k = 0, \ldots, p$$

$$(\mathbf{I} - \mathbf{A})\mathbf{\Phi}_{yk}^+ = \mathbf{A}_k, \quad k = 1, \ldots, p \qquad (13.39)$$

$$\mathbf{R}\,\text{vec}\,\mathbf{\Gamma} = \mathbf{r}$$

which are the constraints in a mixed form, where the auxiliary parameters are the structural parameters of the model (13.38). We could then apply directly a test procedure based on an estimation of the auxiliary parameters by OLS and then apply GLS from (13.39). As a by-product we would get estimators of $\mathbf{A}, \mathbf{A}_k$, and $\mathbf{B}_k$.

Generalization When the rational expectation model involves expectation terms with an horizon greater than 1 or expectations made at the current date, it is not possible to study the hypothesis on the basis of the model for $\mathbf{y}_t$ given $\underline{\mathbf{y}}_{t-1}$ and $\underline{\mathbf{x}}_t$. A joint study of the two processes y and x is needed. Moreover, the implied constraints for the parameters do not have a similarly simple form. They might involve nonlinearities and lead to a joint process without a VAR representation.

In fact, in order to illustrate what kind of difficulties arise, let us consider the following model

$$y_t = aE(y_{t+1}|I_t) + x_t b + u_t,$$

$$x_t = \rho x_{t-1} + \epsilon_t,$$

where ϵ and u are two independent white noises and where $|a| > 1$ and $|\rho| < 1$. The stationary solutions admitting an infinite moving average representation are such that

$$y_t = a(y_{t+1} - c\epsilon_{t+1} - du_{t+1}) + x_t b + u_t$$

$$x_t = \rho x_{t-1} + \epsilon_t$$

$$\Leftrightarrow$$

$$y_t = \frac{1}{a}y_{t-1} - \frac{b}{a}x_{t-1} - \frac{1}{a}u_{t-1} + c\epsilon_t + du_t$$

$$x_t = \rho x_{t-1} + \epsilon_t$$

$$\Leftrightarrow$$

$$y_t = \frac{1}{a}y_{t-1} - \frac{b}{a}x_{t-1} - \frac{1}{ad}\eta_{t-1} + \frac{c}{ad}\epsilon_{t-1} + \eta_t$$

$$x_t = \rho x_{t-1} + \epsilon_t$$

with $c \in \mathbb{R}$, $d \in \mathbb{R}$, and $\eta_t = c\epsilon_t + du_t$. Thus the rational expectation model leads to an ARMA representation which cannot be converted into a VAR expression. Using one of the classical procedures (Lagrange multiplier, Wald, likelihood ratio) we could test this ARMA representation versus a more general one involving higher orders. Note that if such a hypothesis is accepted, we can estimate the various parameters by maximum likelihood, namely, ρ describing the evolution of the exogenous variable, and a and b appearing in the structural equation, but also the additional parameters c and d which characterize the solution corresponding to the data in the set of possible solutions.

13.6 Exercises

Exercise 13.1: Let us consider the multivariate regression model

$$y_{1t} = \mathbf{a}_1 \mathbf{x}_t + u_{1t},$$

$$y_{2t} = \mathbf{a}_2 \mathbf{x}_t + u_{2t},$$

$$\ldots$$

$$y_{nt} = \mathbf{a}_n \mathbf{x}_t + u_{nt},$$

where $\mathbf{x}_t$ is a vector of exogenous variables and $\mathbf{u}_t = (u_{1t}, \ldots, u_{nt})$ is a Gaussian white noise with any instantaneous variance–covariance matrix. Show that the maximum likelihood estimators of the $\mathbf{a}_i$'s are the same as the OLS.

Exercise 13.2: Let us consider the multivariate regression model

$$y_{1t} = \mathbf{a}_1 \mathbf{x}_{1t} + u_{1t},$$

$$y_{2t} = \mathbf{a}_2 \mathbf{x}_{2t} + u_{2t},$$

$$\ldots$$

$$y_{nt} = \mathbf{a}_n \mathbf{x}_{nt} + u_{nt},$$

where $\mathbf{x}_{it}$ are vectors of exogenous variables and $\mathbf{u}_t = (u_{1t}, \ldots, u_{nt})$ is a Gaussian white noise with a diagonal instantaneous variance–covariance matrix. Show that the maximum likelihood estimators of the $\mathbf{a}_i$'s are the same as the OLS.

Exercise 13.3: Let us consider the regression model

$$y_{1t} = a_{11} x_{1t} + a_{12} x_{2t} + u_{1t},$$

$$y_{2t} = a_{21} x_{1t} + a_{22} x_{2t} + u_{2t},$$

where

$$\begin{pmatrix} u_{1t} \\ u_{2t} \end{pmatrix} \sim \mathcal{N}\left(\begin{pmatrix} 0 \\ 0 \end{pmatrix}, \begin{pmatrix} \sigma_1^2 & \sigma_{12} \\ \sigma_{12} & \sigma_2^2 \end{pmatrix} \right).$$

(i)   Show that we can write

$$y_{2t} = \alpha_0 y_{1t} + \alpha_1 x_{1t} + \alpha_2 x_{2t} + v_{2t}$$

with

$$\alpha_0 = \frac{\sigma_{12}}{\sigma_1^2}, \quad \alpha_1 = a_{21} - \frac{\sigma_{12}}{\sigma_1^2} a_{11}, \quad \alpha_2 = a_{22} - \frac{\sigma_{12}}{\sigma_1^2} a_{12}$$

and

$$\text{cov}\,(u_{1t}, v_{2t}) = 0 \quad \text{var}\,(v_{2t}) = s_2^2 = \sigma_2^2 - \frac{\sigma_{12}^2}{\sigma_1^2}.$$

(ii) We impose the constraint $a_{11} = 0$. Show that the maximum likelihood estimators of $\alpha_0, \alpha_1, \alpha_2$, and s_2^2 remain unchanged. Show that the constrained estimator of a_{21} is equal to the estimator of α_1 and that it is different from the unconstrained estimator, that is the OLS estimator.

Exercise 13.4: Let us consider a regression model

$$y_{1t} = \mathbf{a}_1 \mathbf{x}_t + u_{1t},$$

$$y_{2t} = \mathbf{a}_2 \mathbf{z}_t + u_{2t},$$

where

$$\begin{pmatrix} u_{1t} \\ u_{2t} \end{pmatrix} \sim \mathcal{N}\left(\begin{pmatrix} 0 \\ 0 \end{pmatrix}, \begin{pmatrix} \sigma_1^2 & \sigma_{12} \\ \sigma_{12} & \sigma_2^2 \end{pmatrix} \right)$$

and $\mathbf{x}_t, \mathbf{z}_t$ are two vectors of exogenous variables. Show that if the elements of $\mathbf{x}_t$ are included among those of $\mathbf{z}_t$, the maximum likelihood estimator of $\mathbf{a}_1$ is equal to the ordinary least squares and that that is not the same for $\mathbf{a}_2$. (Hint: follow the same approach as for exercise 13.3.)

Exercise 13.5: In the case of three polynomials of degree 2, i.e., $\psi_1(L)$, $\psi_2(L), \psi_3(L)$, with $\psi_1(0) = 1$ write the matrices $\mathbf{h}(\boldsymbol{\psi})$, $\mathbf{H}(\boldsymbol{\psi})$, $\mathbf{a}(\boldsymbol{\beta})$ and $\mathbf{A}(\boldsymbol{\beta})$ given in section 4.1. Verify that $\mathbf{A}(\boldsymbol{\beta})$ is a matrix (8×8) of rank 7.

Exercise 13.6: The adaptive expectation scheme links expectations and realizations through the expression

$$\hat{y}_t - \hat{y}_{t-1} = \mu(y_{t-1} - \hat{y}_{t-1}).$$

Let us assume that we have available joint observations on y_t and $y_t^* = \hat{y}_t + \eta_t$, where η denotes a measurement error independent of y and $\hat{y}$. Let us consider also the regression by ordinary least squares of y_t^* on the lagged values y_{t-1} and y_{t-1}^*

$$y_t^* = ay_{t-1} + by_{t-1}^* + u_t$$

and the Fisher test of the hypothesis $H_0 : a + b = 1$. Discuss the validity of this procedure as a test of the adaptive scheme.

Exercise 13.7: Let us consider a bivariate process (x_t, y_t) admitting a VAR representation. Find the relationship among the reduced-form coefficients of such a representation, when the series can be represented by a structural model with expectations

$$y_t = a\hat{y}_t + \sum_{k=1}^{p} a_k y_{t-k} + \sum_{k=1}^{p} b_k x_{t-k} + u_t,$$

where the expectation is assumed adaptive (cf. exercise 13.6) truncated at p lags. Study an indirect test procedure of the adaptive expectation hypothesis, which involves the linear constraints appearing in the structural model.

Exercise 13.8: Let us assume that we have available joint observations on realizations y_t and expectations $\hat{y}_t$. The expectation is assumed rational $\hat{y}_t = E(y_t | I_t)$ and we would like to determine whether a variable x_t can be considered as part of the information set.

(i)   Verify that, if x_t belongs to I_t

$$E\left((y_t - \hat{y}_t) x_t\right) = 0.$$

(ii)   We regress y_t on $\hat{y}_t$ and on x_t. What should the value of the theoretical regression coefficients be? Derive a test procedure for the hypothesis $H_0 : x_t \in I_t$.

14

Statistical Properties of Nonstationary Processes

14.1 Introduction

Econometricians have limited their analysis just to stationary processes for a long time, adopting some transformation of the data such as the deviation around a deterministic trend or first- (or higher-) order differencing. This practice can be justified on the basis of the fact that the classic econometric methods (built for a stationary framework) show bizarre properties when they are applied to nonstationary series. In this introduction we will show some of these unexpected properties using some simulations. In what follows we will suggest some of the mathematical tools which allow for the theoretical analysis of these properties.

14.1.1 The Spurious Regressions

It is well known that a regression applied to nonstationary variables can result in strange outcomes called spurious regressions (Granger and Newbold, 1974; Phillips, 1986).

To introduce the problem, let us consider two independent random walks $\{y_t\}$ and $\{x_t\}$, that is two processes defined as

$$y_t = y_{t-1} + \epsilon_t$$
$$x_t = x_{t-1} + \eta_t, \tag{14.1}$$

where $\{\epsilon_t\}$ and $\{\eta_t\}$ are independent white noises with the same variance. Since the process $\{x_t\}$ is independent of $\{y_t\}$, we would expect

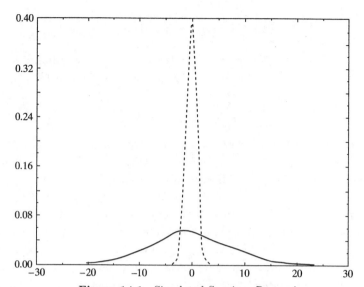

Figure 14.1 Simulated Spurious Regression
Comparison between a $\mathcal{N}(0,1)$ (– – –) and the Simulated Density of τ (——)

that, in the regression of $\{y_t\}$ on $\{x_t\}$

$$y_t = \hat{a} + \hat{\beta} x_t + \hat{w}_t, \quad t = 1, ..., T, \tag{14.2}$$

the ordinary least squares estimator $\hat{\beta}$ converges to 0 when T tends to infinity, and the probability of the critical region $W = \{|\tau| \geq 1.96\}$ where τ is the Student's t-ratio associated to $\hat{\beta}$ tends to 0.05. On the contrary, it can be shown (Phillips, 1986) that $\hat{\beta}$ has a nontrivial limit distribution, and that $T^{-1/2}\tau$ has a nontrivial limit distribution, which implies that the limit probability of W is 1. These results imply, for example, that the mechanical application of the testing procedures built for the stationary case often lead to rejecting the hypothesis of the β coefficient being equal to 0, with the implication that $\{x_t\}$ influences $\{y_t\}$, whereas the two processes are independent.

To measure the order of magnitude of this phenomenon, we have derived the distribution of τ by simulation when T is equal to 100 and we have compared it with the standard normal distribution (which the usual test is based on – cf. also Granger and Newbold, 1974). Figure 14.1 shows that these two distributions are very different. In particular, the distribution of τ is much more dispersed than the $\mathcal{N}(0,1)$ and gives for the region W a probability equal to 0.76. In this example we would conclude that $\{x_t\}$ influences $\{y_t\}$ three out of four times.

14.1.2 Disappearing Biases

As a second example, let us consider the estimation by ordinary least squares (OLS) of the coefficient ρ in the autoregressive model

$$y_t = \rho y_{t-1} + \epsilon_t, \tag{14.3}$$

where $\{\epsilon_t\}$ is a stationary process.

Let us consider first the case where ϵ_t is a white noise. Assuming that the true value of ρ is 1, that is $\{y_t\}$ is a random walk, it can be shown (cf. section 14.2) that the OLS estimator $\hat{\rho}$ is such that $\hat{\rho} - 1$ converges to 0 as $\frac{1}{T}$ and not as $\frac{1}{\sqrt{T}}$ as in the stationary case. We say that if $\rho = 1$, $\hat{\rho}$ is *superconsistent*. This superconsistency implies in particular that $\hat{\rho}$ stays consistent even if ϵ_t is an autocorrelated stationary process, which is not the case when $|\rho| < 1$. Figure 14.2 shows the evolution of the mean bias of the OLS estimator in the regression of y_t on y_{t-1} as a function of the number of observations. The comparison is between two models

$$y_t = y_{t-1} + \epsilon_t \qquad \epsilon_t = 0.7\epsilon_{t-1} + u_t,$$

and

$$y_t = 0.9 y_{t-1} + \epsilon_t \qquad \epsilon_t = 0.7\epsilon_{t-1} + u_t,$$

u_t being in both cases a Gaussian white noise.

In the first case (nonstationary) the bias tends to 0 rapidly whereas in the second (stationary) case this bias tends to 0.082.

14.1.3 Unusual Asymptotic Distributions

The kind of consistency just examined coexists in the nonstationary case with other nonstandard, but less appealing properties. Thus the Student's test statistic τ associated with the test of $\rho = 1$ does not converge to a $\mathcal{N}(0, 1)$, so that the usual test procedures must be changed. Although the asymptotic distribution of τ will be studied in section 14.3 from a theoretical point of view, it will suffice here to show some simulations of its behavior.

Figure 14.3 shows the density of τ for $T = 100$ and $\rho = 1$ obtained by 3000 replications with a normal white noise. We can see that this density is shifted to the left with respect to a $\mathcal{N}(0, 1)$. In particular, if we refer to the standard critical region $\{\tau < -1.64\}$ to test $\rho = 1$ versus $\rho < 1$ at the 5% significance level we reject twice too often the null hypothesis when it is true, since the probability of this region is about 10% when $\rho = 1$.

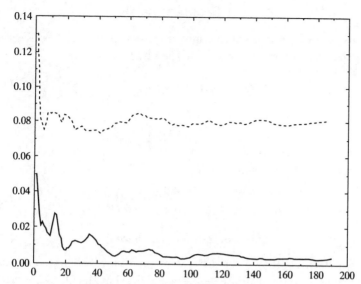

Figure 14.2 Regression of y_t on y_{t-1} with Autocorrelated Disturbances
Comparison between the Average Bias
for $\rho = 0.9$ $(- - -)$ and for $\rho = 1$ $(\!\!-\!\!-\!\!)$, 50 Replications

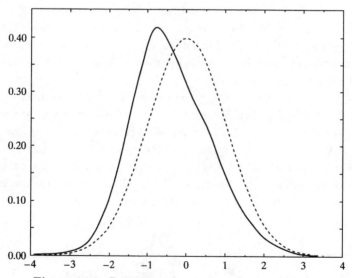

Figure 14.3 Regression of y_t on y_{t-1} (Random Walk)
Comparison between a $\mathcal{N}(0,1)$ $(- - -)$ and the
Simulated Density of τ (100 Observations, 3000 Replications) $(\!\!-\!\!-\!\!)$

14.1.4 Reappearing Biases

Let us consider now a multivariate regression problem. Let us assume that the data generating process is the bivariate process

$$\mathbf{y}_t = \mathbf{y}_{t-1} + \boldsymbol{\varepsilon}_t, \qquad \text{with } \mathbf{y}_t = \begin{pmatrix} y_{1t} \\ y_{2t} \end{pmatrix} \qquad (14.4)$$

and

$$\boldsymbol{\varepsilon}_t = \begin{pmatrix} \epsilon_{1t} \\ \epsilon_{2t} \end{pmatrix}$$

is a moving average defined as

$$\boldsymbol{\varepsilon}_t = \begin{pmatrix} \epsilon_{1t} \\ \epsilon_{2t} \end{pmatrix} = \begin{pmatrix} u_{1t} \\ u_{2t} \end{pmatrix} + \begin{pmatrix} -0.8 & 0.4 \\ 0.2 & -0.6 \end{pmatrix} \begin{pmatrix} u_{1,t-1} \\ u_{2,t-1} \end{pmatrix}, \qquad (14.5)$$

where $\mathbf{u}_t = \begin{pmatrix} u_{1t} \\ u_{2t} \end{pmatrix}$ is a standard normal white noise.

Since the process $\{\mathbf{y}_t\}$ is nonstationary, one may be tempted to extend the results for the univariate case, concluding that the OLS estimator of the regression of $\mathbf{y}_t$ on $\mathbf{y}_{t-1}$ is going to converge to the identity matrix, which is not the case. For example, figure 14.4 shows the density of the estimator of the coefficient of $y_{1,t-1}$ in a regression of y_{1t} on $y_{1,t-1}$ and $y_{2,t-1}$.

Since the first equation of (14.4) is $y_{1t} = y_{1,t-1} + \epsilon_t$, we might conjecture that, in spite of the time correlation of the ϵ_{1t}, this estimator is going to be close to 1. Now, from figure 14.4 we can see that this estimator is, in general, much smaller than 1. In particular the mode of its distribution is close to 0.4.

An intuitive explanation for this phenomenon can be obtained by verifying that, in spite of the nonstationarity of the process $\mathbf{y}_t$, there exists a linear combination of the two component processes y_{1t} and y_{2t} which is stationary. In such a case we say that the processes are cointegrated (cf. section 14.5). It is not surprising, therefore, to find the same problems as in a regression when the variables are stationary and the errors are autocorrelated. To verify that y_{1t} and y_{2t} are cointegrated we can write

$$(1 - L)\mathbf{y}_t = (\mathbf{I} + \boldsymbol{\Theta}L)\mathbf{u}_t, \qquad (14.6)$$

with

$$\boldsymbol{\Theta} = \begin{pmatrix} -0.8 & 0.4 \\ 0.2 & -0.6 \end{pmatrix}.$$

In fact, premultiplying both expressions of (14.6) by the vector $(1, -1)$, and posing $z_t = y_{1t} - y_{2t}$, we get

$$(1 - L)z_t = (1 - L, \ -1 + L)\mathbf{u}_t = (1 - L)(u_{1t} - u_{2t}),$$

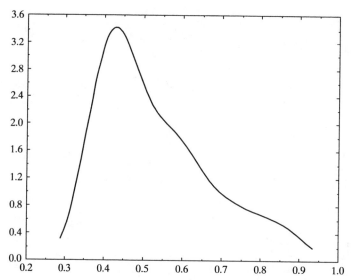

Figure 14.4 Density Estimation of the OLS Coefficient of $y_{1,t-1}$
in a Regression of y_{1t} on $y_{1,t-1}$ and $y_{2,t-1}$
Cointegrated Case – 500 Observations, 500 Replications

and

$$z_t = u_{1t} - u_{2t}.$$

Another way to write (14.6) is

$$(1 - L)\mathbf{y}_t = (1 - L)\mathbf{u}_t + (\mathbf{I} + \mathbf{\Theta})L\mathbf{u}_t$$

$$= (1 - L)\mathbf{u}_t + \begin{pmatrix} 1 \\ 1 \end{pmatrix} (0.2u_{1,t-1} + 0.4u_{2,t-1}).$$

Taking f_t such that $(1 - L)f_t = (0.2u_{1,t-1} + 0.4u_{2,t-1})$ we get

$$\mathbf{y}_t = \mathbf{u}_t + \begin{pmatrix} 1 \\ 1 \end{pmatrix} f_t,$$

or

$$y_{1t} = u_{1t} + f_t$$

$$y_{2t} = u_{2t} + f_t.$$

Thus, y_{1t} and y_{2t} are decomposed as sums of two independent white noises u_{1t} and u_{2t} and of a common nonstationary factor f_t (random walk). Evidently, this common factor is eliminated when taking differences.

From model (14.6) we can also investigate whether the practice of writing a stationary VAR model for $(1 - L)\mathbf{y}_t$ is an appropriate one. We see that in the case of model (14.6) this procedure is not valid because

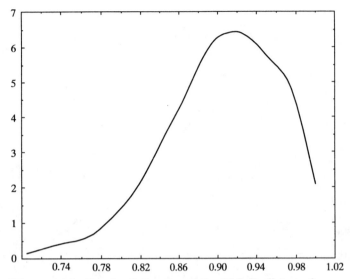

Figure 14.5 Density Estimation of the OLS Coefficient of $y_{1,t-1}$
in a Regression of y_{1t} on $y_{1,t-1}$ and $y_{2,t-1}$
Noncointegrated Case - 500 Observations, 500 Replications

the determinant of $(\mathbf{I} + \boldsymbol{\Theta} L)$ admits a unit root, so that it is not possible to invert this matrix to obtain an autoregressive representation. We will show in what follows that a VAR model on first differences will not be a valid one if there exists a cointegration relationship.

Finally, we can show that if $\boldsymbol{\Theta}$ is modified as to have -0.8 replaced by -0.4, we do not have a cointegration relationship, and that, in such a case, the estimator of the coefficient of $y_{1,t-1}$ in a regression of y_{1t} on $y_{1,t-1}$ and $y_{2,t-1}$ takes values close to 1 (figure 14.5).

This list of unexpected properties cannot be considered exhaustive. We could, for example, add that if a constant is present in (14.3), the Student's test statistic for the null hypothesis $\rho = 1$ has again a normal distribution (cf. section 14.3) under the null. We could also note that if we regress a process like (14.3) with $\rho = 1$ on time to eliminate the trend, the residuals could exhibit some spurious cyclical properties (Nelson and Kang, 1981).

14.2 Limit Properties of Some Relevant Statistics

Let us consider now a fractional process defined as

$$y_t = (1 - L)^{-d} \Phi(L)^{-1} \Theta(L) \tilde{\epsilon}_t, \ t \geq 0, \tag{14.7}$$

where $\{\epsilon_t\}$ is an independent white noise with variance σ^2, where $\tilde{\epsilon}_t = \epsilon_t$

if $t \geq 0$ and $\tilde{\epsilon}_t = 0$ if $t < 0$, and where the exponent d is greater than $1/2$ so that y_t is nonstationary. Recall that in chapter 11 we have shown that the transformed process

$$\tilde{y}_T(r) = \frac{1}{T^{d-1/2}} y_{[Tr]}$$

converges in distribution to

$$y_\infty(r) = \frac{\sigma\Theta(1)}{\Phi(1)\Gamma(d)} \int_0^r (r-s)^{d-1} dB(s), \qquad (14.8)$$

where B indicates a Brownian motion on $[0,1]$ such that $\text{var}\,(B(1)) = 1$.

The constant $\sigma\Theta(1)/\Phi(1)$ in the previous expression will be noted ω. We can see that the square of this constant

$$\omega^2 = \frac{\sigma^2\Theta^2(1)}{\Phi^2(1)}$$

is equal to $2\pi f(0)$, where $f(\cdot)$ is the spectral density of the stationary process $\Phi(L)^{-1}\Theta(L)\epsilon_t$ asymptotically equal to $(1-L)^d y_t$. The constant ω^2 can be written also as

$$\sum_{h=-\infty}^{\infty} \gamma(h),$$

where $\gamma(h)$ is the autocovariance function of the same process.

We will often make reference to the case of an integrated process of order 1, that is $d = 1$. In this case we have

$$(1-L)y_t = \Phi(L)^{-1}\Theta(L)\tilde{\epsilon}_t,$$

$$\tilde{y}_T(r) = \frac{1}{\sqrt{T}} y_{[Tr]},$$

$$y_\infty(r) = \omega B(r).$$

Taking $\Phi(L) = \Theta(L) = 1$ we get the random walk $(1-L)y_t = \tilde{\epsilon}_t$ obtaining $y_\infty(r) = \sigma B(r)$.

14.2.1 Sample Mean

Theorem 14.1: *Let $\{y_t, \ t \geq 0\}$ be a fractional process. The sample mean $\bar{y}_T = \frac{1}{T}\sum_{t=1}^{T} y_t$ is such that*

$$\frac{1}{T^{d-1/2}} \bar{y}_T \xrightarrow{\text{d}} \int_0^1 y_\infty(r)dr,$$

with

$$y_\infty(r) = \frac{\omega}{\Gamma(d)} \int_0^r (r-s)^{d-1} dB(s).$$

SKETCH OF THE PROOF: We have

$$\frac{1}{T^{d-1/2}}\bar{y}_T = \frac{1}{T}\frac{1}{T^{d-1/2}}\sum_{t=1}^{T} y_{[tT/T]}$$

$$= \frac{1}{T}\sum_{t=1}^{T}\tilde{y}_T\left(\frac{t}{T}\right)$$

$$\approx \frac{1}{T}\sum_{t=1}^{T} y_\infty\left(\frac{t}{T}\right).$$

This Riemann sum can then be approximated by the corresponding integral

$$\frac{1}{T^{d-1/2}}\bar{y}_T \xrightarrow{\text{d}} \int_0^1 y_\infty(r)dr.$$

□

Since $d > \frac{1}{2}$, we see right away that the sample mean tends to become infinite and in particular that it does not converge toward the corresponding theoretical mean, that is, 0. Although consistency is not satisfied, the asymptotic normality is preserved after an appropriate normalization. In fact, the limit is a linear transformation of the Brownian motion B, which is Gaussian.

In the special case of an integrated process of order 1, we get the following result

Corollary: *Let* $\{y_t, \ t \geq 0\}$ *be an integrated process of order 1, the sample mean is such that*

$$\frac{1}{T^{1/2}}\bar{y}_T \xrightarrow{\text{d}} \omega \int_0^1 B(r)dr,$$

with $\omega = \sigma$ *in the case of a random walk.*

Note that the rate of divergence $\sqrt{T}$ of the sample mean coincides with the one of the series y_t itself.

14.2.2 Sample Second-order Moments

A similar approach allows immediately to derive the limit behavior of the second-order moment.

Theorem 14.2: *Let $\{y_t,\, t \geq 0\}$ be a fractional process. Then*

$$\frac{1}{T^{2d}} \sum_{t=1}^{T} y_t^2 \;\overset{d}{\to}\; \int_0^1 y_\infty^2(r)dr.$$

In the special case $d = 1$ we get

$$\frac{1}{T^2} \sum_{t=1}^{T} y_t^2 \;\overset{d}{\to}\; \omega^2 \int_0^1 B^2(r)dr,$$

with $\omega^2 = \sigma^2$ in the case of a random walk. Also in this case there is divergence of the sample moment

$$\frac{1}{T} \sum_{t=1}^{T} y_t^2.$$

14.2.3 First-order Autocovariances

The analysis of the cross-moments of order 1 is easy to carry out by considering the cross-moment

$$\sum_{t=1}^{T} y_t(y_t - y_{t-1}).$$

It is clear that a number of cases should be analyzed according to the value of the exponent d. In fact, the differenced series can be stationary or nonstationary, which modifies the limit behavior. In particular, we have the following results.

Theorem 14.3: *Let $\{y_t,\; t \geq 0\}$ be a fractional process. Then:*

(i) *If $d > 1$*

$$\frac{1}{T^{2d-1}} \sum_{t=1}^{T} y_t(y_t - y_{t-1}) \;\overset{d}{\to}\; \frac{1}{2} y_\infty^2(1).$$

(ii) *If $d = 1$*

$$\frac{1}{T} \sum_{t=1}^{T} y_t(y_t - y_{t-1}) \;\overset{d}{\to}\; \frac{1}{2} y_\infty^2(1) + \frac{1}{2}\mathrm{var}\,(y_t - y_{t-1}).$$

(iii) *If $d < 1$*

$$\frac{1}{T} \sum_{t=1}^{T} y_t(y_t - y_{t-1}) \;\overset{d}{\to}\; \frac{1}{2}\mathrm{var}\,(y_t - y_{t-1}).$$

PROOF: Cf. the appendix. □

It is useful to examine how this result is modified if we focus our attention on

$$\frac{1}{T}\sum_{t=1}^{T} y_{t-1}(y_t - y_{t-1}).$$

Theorem 14.4: *Let $\{y_t,\ t \geq 0\}$ be a fractional process. Then:*

(i)   If $d > 1$

$$\frac{1}{T^{2d-1}}\sum_{t=1}^{T} y_{t-1}(y_t - y_{t-1}) \xrightarrow{d} \frac{1}{2}y_\infty^2(1).$$

(ii) If $d = 1$

$$\frac{1}{T}\sum_{t=1}^{T} y_{t-1}(y_t - y_{t-1}) \xrightarrow{d} \frac{1}{2}y_\infty^2(1) - \frac{1}{2}\mathrm{var}\,(y_t - y_{t-1}).$$

(iii) If $d < 1$

$$\frac{1}{T}\sum_{t=1}^{T} y_{t-1}(y_t - y_{t-1}) \xrightarrow{d} -\frac{1}{2}\mathrm{var}\,(y_t - y_{t-1}).$$

PROOF: We have

$$\sum_{t=1}^{T} y_{t-1}(y_t - y_{t-1}) = \sum_{t=1}^{T} y_t(y_t - y_{t-1}) - \sum_{t=1}^{T}(y_t - y_{t-1})^2.$$

The result follows from the fact that in the case $d > 1$, $\sum_{t=1}^{T}(y_t - y_{t-1})^2$ has a rate of divergence always smaller than $2d - 1$ (in fact, equal to $2d - 2$ if $d > 3/2$ and 1 if $d \leq 3/2$).

Moreover, if $d \leq 1$, $\frac{1}{T}\sum_{t=1}^{T}(y_t - y_{t-1})^2$ tends to $\mathrm{var}\,(y_t - y_{t-1})$. □

Note that in any case

$$\frac{1}{T^{2d}}\sum_{t=1}^{T} y_t y_{t-1} = \frac{1}{T^{2d}}\left(\sum_{t=0}^{T-1} y_t^2 + \sum_{t=1}^{T}(y_t - y_{t-1})y_{t-1}\right)$$

is equivalent to

$$\frac{1}{T^{2d}}\sum_{t=1}^{T} y_t^2.$$

14.2.4 Behavior of the Periodogram at Low Frequencies

In spite of the fact that the nonstationary process y does not admit spectral density, we can define the periodogram

$$I_T(\omega) = \frac{1}{2\pi T}|J_T(\omega)|^2,$$

where

$$J_T(\omega) = \sum_{t=1}^{T} y_t \exp(it\omega).$$

Theorem 14.5: *When the number of observations tends to infinity, we have*

$$\frac{1}{T^{d+\frac{1}{2}}} J_T\left(\frac{\omega}{T}\right) \overset{d}{\to} \int_0^1 \exp(i\omega r) y_\infty(r) dr.$$

SKETCH OF THE PROOF: We have

$$\frac{1}{T^{d+\frac{1}{2}}} J_T\left(\frac{\omega}{T}\right) = \frac{1}{T^{d+\frac{1}{2}}} \sum_{t=1}^{T} y_t \exp(i\frac{t}{T}\omega) = \frac{1}{T} \frac{1}{T^{d-\frac{1}{2}}} \sum_{t=1}^{T} y_{[Tt/T]} \exp(i\frac{t}{T}\omega)$$

$$\approx \frac{1}{T} \sum_{t=1}^{T} y_\infty(t/T) \exp(i\frac{t}{T}\omega) \overset{d}{\to} \int_0^1 \exp(i\omega r) y_\infty(r) dr.$$

□

14.2.5 Empirical Autocorrelations

In the Box–Jenkins approach, it is common to compute the empirical autocorrelation of order 1, for example through the formula

$$\hat{\rho}_T = \frac{\sum_{t=1}^{T} y_t y_{t-1}}{\sum_{t=1}^{T} y_{t-1}^2}.$$

This formula coincides with the one of the regression coefficient of the y_t on the y_{t-1}. We have seen that a value of $\hat{\rho}_T$ close to 1 can be used as an indicator of nonstationarity of the series (cf. section 6.3). This concept is going to be expanded in this section, analyzing the asymptotic behavior of $\hat{\rho}_T$ first.

Theorem 14.6: *Let $\{y_t,\ t \geq 0\}$ be a fractional process. We have:*

(i)   If $d > 1$

$$T(1 - \hat{\rho}_T) \overset{d}{\to} -\frac{y_\infty^2(1)}{2\int_0^1 y_\infty^2(r)dr}$$

(ii) If d=1

$$T(1 - \hat{\rho}_T) \xrightarrow{\mathrm{d}} \frac{1/2 \left(\frac{\nu^2}{\omega^2} - B^2(1) \right)}{\int_0^1 B^2(r) dr},$$

with $\nu^2 = \mathrm{var}\,(y_t - y_{t-1})$.

(iii) If $\frac{1}{2} < d < 1$

$$T^{2d-1}(1 - \hat{\rho}_T) \xrightarrow{\mathrm{d}} \frac{\nu^2}{2 \int_0^1 y_\infty^2(r) dr}.$$

PROOF: We have

$$1 - \hat{\rho}_T = 1 - \frac{\sum_{t=1}^T y_t y_{t-1}}{\sum_{t=1}^T y_{t-1}^2} = -\frac{\sum_{t=1}^T y_{t-1}(y_t - y_{t-1})}{\sum_{t=1}^T y_{t-1}^2},$$

so that the result follows from theorem 14.4 and from theorem 14.2. □

We note that the support of the limit distribution of $T(1 - \hat{\rho}_T)$ is $\mathbb{R}^-$ if $d > 1$, $\mathbb{R}^+$ if $1/2 < d < 1$ and contains positive and negative values if $d = 1$. Thus in the case of a random walk, we have $\nu^2 = \omega^2$ and the probability of $\mathbb{R}^-$ for the limit distribution is

$$P(B^2(1) > 1) = P(\chi^2(1) > 1) = P(|N(0,1)| > 1) = 0.32.$$

We can verify as well that if we had taken the quantity

$$\tilde{\rho}_T = \frac{\sum_{t=1}^T y_t y_{t-1}}{\sum_{t=1}^T y_t^2}$$

as empirical autocorrelation of order 1, instead of $\hat{\rho}_T$, the asymptotic behavior would have stayed unchanged for $1/2 < d < 1$. By the same token, for $d = 1$ the limit distribution of $T(1 - \tilde{\rho}_T)$ would be

$$\frac{1/2 \left(\frac{\nu^2}{\omega^2} + B^2(1) \right)}{\int_0^1 B^2(r) dr},$$

the support of which does not include negative values and for $d > 1$ the limit distribution would be

$$\frac{y_\infty^2(1)}{2 \int_0^1 y_\infty^2(r) dr},$$

the support of which is also $\mathbb{R}^+$.

14.3 Unit Root Tests

14.3.1 Dickey–Fuller Tests

Let us assume that y_t is a first-order autoregressive process

$$y_t = \rho y_{t-1} + \epsilon_t,$$

with $|\rho| \leq 1$, and ϵ_t is a white noise of variance σ_ϵ^2. We want to test the null hypothesis of a random walk $H_0 : (\rho = 1)$. We know that $\hat{\rho}_T$ is a consistent estimator of ρ and theorem 14.6 (with $\nu^2 = \omega^2$) gives the limit distribution of $T(1 - \hat{\rho}_T)$ under H_0

$$\frac{1 - B^2(1)}{2 \int_0^1 B^2(r)dr}.$$

Therefore, we can propose a test of asymptotic size α and with critical region $\{T(1-\hat{\rho}_T) > c_\alpha\}$, where c_α is determined on the basis of the limit distribution. This test was first proposed by Dickey and Fuller (1979, 1981) and the distribution of $T(1 - \hat{\rho}_T)$ has been tabulated by Fuller (1976, p. 371). Thus for $\alpha = 1\%$, 5%, and 10% the values of c_α are, respectively, 13.8, 8.1, 5.7. Other values of c_α, as well as critical values when T is finite and ϵ_t is Gaussian are given in table 7 at the end of the book.

Another procedure is based on a Student's t-ratio

$$\hat{t} = \frac{1 - \hat{\rho}_T}{\left(\hat{\sigma}_\epsilon^2 / \sum_{t=1}^T y_{t-1}^2\right)^{1/2}}$$

$$= \frac{T(1 - \hat{\rho}_T) \sum_{t=1}^T (y_{t-1}^2/T^2)^{\frac{1}{2}}}{\hat{\sigma}_\epsilon},$$

with $\hat{\sigma}_\epsilon^2 = \frac{1}{T} \sum_{t=1}^T (y_t - y_{t-1})^2$, or $\frac{1}{T} \sum_{t=1}^T (y_t - \hat{\rho}_T y_{t-1})^2$ which under H_0 converges to σ^2 $(= \nu^2 = \omega^2$ in this case). This statistic $\hat{t}$ is the opposite of the usual Student statistic to test the significance of the parameter a in the model $\Delta y_t = a y_{t-1}$ with $\Delta y_t = y_t - y_{t-1}$; also note that this opposite statistic was used in section 14.1.3. This other way of computing $\hat{t}$ is interesting because it is done automatically in the regression programs of Δy_t on y_{t-1}. Theorem 14.2 shows immediately that $\hat{t}$ converges in distribution to

$$\frac{\left(1 - B^2(1)\right)}{2 \left(\int_0^1 B^2(r)dr\right)^{1/2}}.$$

This distribution has been studied by Fuller (1976). We can therefore propose a test with asymptotic size α with critical region $(\hat{t} > t_\alpha)$. We have for $\alpha = 1\%$, 5%, 10%, $t_\alpha = 2.58, 1.95, 1.62$. These values are to be compared with the values of a standard normal distribution in the univariate case, that is 2.32, 1.64, 1.28. A test based on the usual values would tend to reject H_0 too often. Other values of t_α, as well as critical values when T is finite and ϵ_t is Gaussian are given in table 8 at the end of the book.

Fuller (1976) has studied the asymptotic behavior of similar statistics under the same null hypothesis $H_0 : y_t = y_{t-1} + \tilde{\epsilon}_t$ using a different estimated model. Thus, we have

$$\text{Regression Model} : y_t = \mu + \rho y_{t-1} + \epsilon_t,$$

$$\text{Statistics} : \quad T(1 - \hat{\rho}'_T), \quad \hat{t}',$$

$$\text{Regression Model} : y_t = \mu_1 + \mu_2 t + \rho y_{t-1} + \epsilon_t,$$

$$\text{Statistics} : \quad T(1 - \hat{\rho}''_T), \quad \hat{t}'',$$

where $\hat{\rho}'_T$ and $\hat{\rho}''_T$ are the OLS estimators of ρ for the two regression models, and $\hat{t}'$, $\hat{t}''$ are the associated Student's t-ratios. The corresponding asymptotic distributions for $T(1 - \rho''_T)$ and $\hat{t}''$ are fixed under a generic family of hypotheses $y_t = \mu + y_{t-1} + \tilde{\epsilon}_t$, for any μ.

The asymptotic tests at the level $\alpha = 1\%, 5\%, 10\%$ are then the tests with critical regions

$$\{T(1 - \hat{\rho}'_T) > c'_\alpha\} \text{ with } \quad c'_\alpha = 20.7, \ 14.1, \ 11.3,$$

$$\{\hat{t}' > t'_\alpha\} \text{ with } \quad t'_\alpha = 3.43, \ 2.86, \ 2.57,$$

$$\{T(1 - \hat{\rho}''_T) > c''_\alpha\} \text{ with } \quad c''_\alpha = 29.5, \ 21.8, \ 18.3,$$

$$\{\hat{t}'' > t''_\alpha\} \text{ with } \quad t''_\alpha = 3.96, \ 3.41, \ 3.12.$$

Other values of $c'_\alpha, c''_\alpha, t'_\alpha, t''_\alpha$, as well as critical values when T is finite and ϵ_t is Gaussian are given in Tables 7 and 8 at the end of the book.

Note now that if we want to test the null hypothesis $H_0^* : \rho = 1$ in the model

$$y_t = \mu + \rho y_{t-1} + \tilde{\epsilon}_t$$

(with $\mu \neq 0$ and $\tilde{\epsilon}_t$ a white noise of variance σ^2) against the alternative $|\rho| < 1$ we can use the usual unilateral Student's procedure because, under H_0^*, the limit distribution of the Student's ratio is $\mathcal{N}(0, 1)$. Indeed, under the hypothesis $H_0^* : y_t = \mu + y_{t-1} + \tilde{\epsilon}_t$ called *random walk with drift* we have

$$y_t = \mu t + y_0 + \tilde{y}_t,$$

where $\tilde{y}_t = \sum_{i=1}^{t} \epsilon_i$ is a random walk without drift. As a consequence, letting $\bar{y} = \frac{1}{T}\sum_{t=1}^{T} y_{t-1}$

$$\hat{\rho}_T - 1 = \frac{\sum_{t=1}^{T} \epsilon_t(y_{t-1} - \bar{y})}{\sum_{t=1}^{T}(y_{t-1} - \bar{y})^2}$$

$$= \frac{\sum_{t=1}^{T} \epsilon_t \left((t-1)\mu + \tilde{y}_{t-1} - \mu\frac{(T-1)}{2} - \tilde{\bar{y}}\right)}{\sum_{t=1}^{T} \left((t-1)\mu + \tilde{y}_{t-1} - \mu\frac{(T-1)}{2} - \tilde{\bar{y}}\right)^2}$$

$$= \frac{\sum_{t=1}^{T} \epsilon_t \left(\mu\frac{(2t-1-T)}{2} + \tilde{y}_{t-1} - \tilde{\bar{y}}\right)}{\sum_{t=1}^{T} \left(\mu\frac{(2t-1-T)}{2} + \tilde{y}_{t-1} - \tilde{\bar{y}}\right)^2}.$$

The term $\frac{\mu}{2}\sum_{t=1}^{T} \epsilon_t(2t-1-T)$ of the numerator is of the same order of magnitude as $T^{3/2}$ and the order of magnitude of the other terms is equal to T. Therefore the numerator is equivalent to $\frac{\mu}{2}\sum_{t=1}^{T} \epsilon_t(2t-1-T)$. By the same token the denominator is equivalent to $\frac{\mu^2}{4}\sum_{t=1}^{T}(2t-1-T)^2$. Thus we have

$$T^{3/2}(1-\hat{\rho}_T) \approx -\frac{T^{-3/2}\sum_{t=1}^{T} \epsilon_t(2t-1-T)}{\frac{\mu}{2}T^{-3}\sum_{t=1}^{T}(2t-1-T)^2}.$$

It can be easily verified that the numerator converges in distribution to a $\mathcal{N}\left(0, \sigma_\epsilon^2/3\right)$ while the denominator converges to $\frac{\mu}{6}$. Finally

$$T^{3/2}(1-\hat{\rho}_T) \xrightarrow{\text{d}} \mathcal{N}\left(0, \frac{12\sigma_\epsilon^2}{\mu^2}\right).$$

The Student's ratio can be written as

$$\frac{1-\hat{\rho}_T}{\left(\hat{\sigma}_\epsilon^2/\sum_{t=1}^{T}(y_{t-1}-\bar{y})^2\right)^{1/2}} = \frac{T^{3/2}(1-\hat{\rho}_T)}{\left(\hat{\sigma}_\epsilon^2 T^3/\sum_{t=1}^{T}(y_{t-1}-\bar{y})^2\right)^{1/2}}.$$

The denominator tends to $\sigma_\epsilon\sqrt{12}/\mu$ so that the Student's ratio converges in distribution to a $\mathcal{N}(0,1)$. Thus if we use the critical values t'_α given above instead of the standard normal values, we will accept H_0 too often.

By the same token, if we want to test $\rho = 1$ in $y_t = \mu_1 + \mu_2 t + \rho y_{t-1} + \epsilon_t$ (or $a = 0$ in $\Delta y_t = \mu_1 + \mu_2 t + a y_{t-1} + \epsilon_t$) for any μ_1 and $\mu_2 \neq 0$ we can use the usual one-sided Student's procedure.

14.3.2 Generalizations of the Dickey–Fuller Tests

In the previous section we have seen that under the null hypothesis of random walk $y_t - y_{t-1} = \tilde{\epsilon}_t$ the asymptotic distribution of $T(1-\hat{\rho}_T)$ is

$$\frac{\frac{1}{2}\left(1 - B^2(1)\right)}{\int_0^1 B^2(r)dr}, \tag{14.9}$$

and that of the Student's $\hat{t}$

$$\frac{\frac{1}{2}\left(1 - B^2(1)\right)}{\left(\int_0^1 B^2(r)dr\right)^{1/2}}. \tag{14.10}$$

Let us assume now that the process y_t is such that $y_t - y_{t-1} = \tilde{\eta}_t$, where $\tilde{\eta}_t$ is equal for $t \geq 0$ to an ARMA process η_t defined as $\Phi(L)\eta_t = \Theta(L)\epsilon_t$, with ϵ_t a white noise of variance σ_ϵ^2, which is the same as saying that y_t is an ARIMA process, integrated of order 1. Theorem 14.6 shows that the limit distribution of $T(1 - \hat{\rho}_T)$ is then

$$\frac{\frac{1}{2}\left((\nu^2/\omega^2) - B^2(1)\right)}{\int_0^1 B^2(r)dr,} \tag{14.11}$$

where

$$\omega^2 = \frac{\sigma_\epsilon^2 \Theta^2(1)}{\Phi^2(1)} = 2\pi f(0) = \sum_{h=-\infty}^{+\infty} \gamma(h)$$

$$\nu^2 = \operatorname{var}(y_t - y_{t-1}) = \gamma(0).$$

By the same reasoning we find that the limit distribution of $\hat{t}$ is

$$\frac{\omega\left((\nu^2/\omega^2) - B^2(1)\right)}{2\nu\left(\int_0^1 B^2(r)dr\right)^{1/2}}. \tag{14.12}$$

These limit distributions depend on an unknown nuisance parameter ν/ω and cannot be used as such. This problem can be solved in two different manners: by the first method we are looking for a transformation of the statistics $T(1 - \hat{\rho}_T)$ and $\hat{t}$ still having (14.9) and (14.10) respectively as limit distributions (Phillips, 1987; Phillips and Perron, 1988). By the second approach we consider the coefficients of y_{t-1} and the associated Student's t in a larger regression than the simple one of y_t on y_{t-1} so that, again, the limit distributions are (14.9) and (14.10), and we obtain the so-called *Augmented Dickey–Fuller tests*.

Transformation of the Statistics The limit distribution (14.11) of $T(1 - \hat{\rho}_T)$ can be written as

$$\frac{\frac{1}{2}\left(1 - B^2(1)\right)}{\int_0^1 B^2(r)dr} + \frac{\frac{1}{2}(\nu^2 - \omega^2)}{\omega^2 \int_0^1 B^2(r)dr},$$

so that the variable

$$T(1 - \hat{\rho}_T) - \frac{\frac{1}{2}(\nu^2 - \omega^2)}{\omega^2 \int_0^1 B^2(r)dr}$$

converges in distribution to the Dickey–Fuller distribution (14.9) for which we know the quantiles. An asymptotically equivalent variable is (cf. theorem 14.2)

$$T(1 - \hat{\rho}_T) - \frac{T^2 \left(\nu^2 - \omega^2\right)}{2 \sum_{t=1}^{T} y_{t-1}^2}.$$

This variable depends upon two unknown parameters, ν^2 and ω^2. The parameter ν^2 is consistently estimated by

$$\hat{\nu}_T^2 = \frac{1}{T} \sum_{t=1}^{T} (y_t - y_{t-1})^2.$$

For this estimator one does not need the order of the polynomials $\Phi(L)$ and $\Theta(L)$.

To estimate

$$\omega^2 = \frac{\sigma_\epsilon^2 \Theta^2(1)}{\Phi^2(1)} = 2\pi f(0),$$

we can use either some estimators of σ_ϵ^2, Θ, and Φ, once the orders of Θ and Φ are given, or use some nonparametric methods (cf. Phillips, 1987; Phillips and Perron, 1988); in particular a consistent and always positive estimator of ω^2 was proposed by Newey and West (1987) as

$$\hat{\omega}_{TK}^2 = \frac{1}{T} \sum_{t=1}^{T} \Delta y_t^2 + \frac{2}{T} \sum_{k=1}^{K} w_k \sum_{t=k+1}^{T} \Delta y_t \Delta y_{t-k},$$

where $w_k = 1 - \frac{k}{K+1}$, $\Delta y_t = y_t - y_{t-1}$, and K is of a smaller order of magnitude than $T^{1/4}$.

We will use then the transformed statistic

$$S_\rho = T(1 - \hat{\rho}_T) - \frac{T^2 \left(\hat{\nu}_T^2 - \hat{\omega}_T^2\right)}{2 \sum_{t=1}^{T} y_{t-1}^2},$$

where $\hat{\omega}_T^2$ is a consistent estimator of ω^2 (for instance, $\hat{\omega}_{TK}^2$) and compare its values against the critical values c_α mentioned above.

By the same line of reasoning we can show that the statistic

$$S_\tau = \frac{\hat{\nu}_T \hat{t}}{\hat{\omega}_T} - \frac{T \left(\hat{\nu}_T^2 - \hat{\omega}_T^2\right)}{2 \left(\sum_{t=1}^{T} y_{t-1}^2\right)^{1/2}}$$

converges in distribution to (14.10), the critical values of which, t_α, were presented above.

These two statistics (denoted as $-Z_\alpha$ and $-Z_t$ in Phillips, 1987) can be replaced by the statistics $\hat{S}_\rho$ and $\hat{S}_\tau$ derived from the former ones by replacing Δy_t by $y_t - \hat{\rho} y_{t-1}$ in the computation of $\hat{\nu}_T^2$ and $\hat{\omega}_{TK}^2$. The latter statistic seems preferable to the former on the basis of test power considerations.

Note also that by analogy to what was discussed before, if the null hypothesis is an ARIMA process, integrated of order 1 with a constant

$y_t - y_{t-1} = \mu + \tilde{\epsilon}_t$, $\mu \neq 0$, the Student ratio of the coefficient of y_{t-1} in the regression of y_t on a constant and y_{t-1} converges asymptotically to a normal distribution with mean 0. However, the variance is not unity, but ω^2/ν^2. Therefore, multiplying the Student ratio by $\hat{\nu}_T/\hat{\omega}_T$ we can go back to the standard case.

Augmented Dickey–Fuller Tests   Let us consider an ARIMA $(p, 1, 0)$, that is $y_t - y_{t-1}$ follows (asymptotically) an autoregressive process of order p. We have

$$y_t - y_{t-1} = \sum_{i=1}^{p} a_i(y_{t-i} - y_{t-i-1}) + \tilde{\epsilon}_t$$

$$y_t = y_{t-1} + \sum_{i=1}^{p} a_i(y_{t-i} - y_{t-i-1}) + \tilde{\epsilon}_t.$$

An AR$(p+1)$ can always be written as

$$y_t = a_0 y_{t-1} + \sum_{i=1}^{p} a_i(y_{t-i} - y_{t-i-1}) + \tilde{\epsilon}_t; \qquad (14.13)$$

this process has a unit root if and only if $a_0 = 1$.

Fuller (1976) has shown that, under the hypothesis that y_t follows an ARIMA$(p, 1, 0)$ the Student's ratio associated with the estimator of a_0 in the regression (14.13) converges in distribution to (14.10). We can perform the unit root test using the estimated ratio and comparing it to the critical values t_α seen above. As for the plain Dickey–Fuller test, this statistic is the opposite to the Student's statistic associated with the test $a = 0$ in the regression $\Delta y_t = a y_{t-1} + \sum_{i=1}^{p} a_i \Delta y_{t-1} + \tilde{\epsilon}_t$ and this statistic is a standard output of any regression routine.

When we introduce a constant term (or a constant and a trend) in the regression, the test of the null hypothesis $\Delta y_t = \sum_{i=1}^{p} a_i \Delta y_{t-1} + \tilde{\epsilon}_t$ can be performed starting from the opposite of the Student's statistic associated with the coefficient of y_{t-1} in the regression using the asymptotic critical values t'_α (respectively t''_α) mentioned before.

Note also that Dickey and Fuller (1981) have suggested other tests of the Fisher-type to test joint hypotheses on the coefficients. Thus we can use the Fisher's statistic to test the null hypothesis $\mu_2 = 0$ and $\rho = 1$ in the model

$$y_t = \mu_1 + \mu_2 t + \rho y_{t-1} + \epsilon_t.$$

The critical values at the asymptotic level $1\%, 5\%$, and 10% are, respectively, $8.27, 6.25$, and 5.34. The latter test allows one to suggest a simple testing strategy. If this test results in the acceptance of the null hypothesis $\mu_2 = 0$ and $\rho = 1$, we can then test $\mu_1 = 0$ by the classical procedure, that is the usual two-sided Student's test in $\Delta y_t = \mu_1 + \epsilon_t$. If the null hypothesis $\mu_2 = 0$ and $\rho = 1$ is rejected, we can test $\mu_2 = 0$ (and, therefore, $|\rho| < 1$) by the usual two-sided Student's test and $\rho = 1$ (and, therefore, $\mu_2 \neq 0$) by the usual one-sided Student's test.

When $\{y_t\}$ follows an ARIMA$(p, 1, q)$ with $q \neq 0$ we can go back to the previous case approximating the process $\{y_t\}$ by an ARIMA$(p', 1, 0)$ with p' large enough.

Schmidt-Phillips Tests The tests by Dickey and Fuller are simple, but they present some disadvantages. First of all, they are not asymptotically similar, that is, their asymptotic distribution under the null hypothesis depends on the value taken by some parameters. We have seen for example that the Student's statistic to test $a = 0$ in $\Delta y_t = \mu + a y_{t-1} + \epsilon_t$ does not have the same asymptotic distribution whether μ is 0 or not. Moreover, a model of the type $y_t = \mu_1 + \mu_2 t + \rho y_{t-1} + \epsilon_t$ has a polynomial deterministic trend the degree of which depends on the coefficient of the random variable y_{t-1}, that is, degree 1 if $|\rho| < 1$, degree 2 if $\rho = 1$.

These problems are addressed by Schmidt and Phillips (1992) who have suggested another reference model, that is

$$y_t = \psi_1 + \psi_2 t + z_t,$$
$$z_t = \rho z_{t-1} + \epsilon_t, \tag{14.14}$$

where ϵ_t is a white noise with variance σ_ϵ^2.

In this type of model the deterministic trend is linear for any ρ. Moreover, the test for $\rho = 1$ is based on asymptotically similar statistics. The method, inspired by the Lagrange Multiplier procedure, is the following:

(i)   Compute $\hat{\psi}_2 = (y_T - y_1)/(T - 1)$, $\hat{\psi}_1 = y_1 - \hat{\psi}_2$.
(ii) Compute the "residuals" $\hat{s}_{t-1} = y_{t-1} - \hat{\psi}_1 - \hat{\psi}_2(t - 1)$.
(iii) Perform the regression

$$\Delta y_t = a + b\hat{s}_{t-1} + u_t.$$

(iv) Derive the OLS estimator $\hat{b}$ of b and $\hat{t}$ the opposite of the Student's statistic corresponding to the test $b = 0$.

The critical regions of the tests of $\rho = 1$ are $\{-T\hat{b} > b_\alpha\}$ or $\{\hat{t} > t_\alpha\}$ where the values of b_α and t_α for $\alpha = 1\%, 5\%, 10\%$ are, respectively

$$b_\alpha : 25.2, \ 18.1, \ 15.0,$$

$$t_\alpha : 3.56, \ 3.02, \ 2.75.$$

If we do not assume that $\{\epsilon_t\}$ is a white noise but just a stationary process, it is enough to replace $T\hat{b}$ by $T\hat{b}/\hat{\lambda}^2$ and $\hat{t}$ by $\hat{t}/\hat{\lambda}$ with

$$\hat{\lambda}^2 = \frac{\hat{\sigma}_\epsilon^2}{\hat{\omega}_{TK}^2}$$

$$\hat{\sigma}_\epsilon^2 = \frac{1}{T} \sum_{t=1}^{T} \hat{\epsilon}_t^2$$

$$\hat{\omega}_{TK}^2 = \frac{1}{T} \sum_{t=1}^{T} \hat{\epsilon}_t^2 + \frac{2}{T} \sum_{k=1}^{K} \left(1 - \frac{k}{K+1}\right) \sum_{t=k+1}^{T} \hat{\epsilon}_t \hat{\epsilon}_{t-k},$$

where the $\hat{\epsilon}_t$ are the residuals in the regression of y_t on a constant, a time trend, and y_{t-1}.

14.4 Regression with Nonstationary Explanatory Variables

14.4.1 Description of the Model

In this section, we want to analyze whether the classical results about the OLS estimator, usually shown assuming the stationarity of the observations remain valid when the variables are nonstationary. As an example, let us consider a model with a single explanatory variable and a single lag on this variable. This model can be written as

$$y_t = ax_t + bx_{t-1} + \eta_t,$$

where $\{x_t\}$ is a fractional process defined as

$$x_t = (1-L)^{-d}\Phi(L)^{-1}\Theta(L)\tilde{\epsilon}_t,$$

where $\{\eta_t\}$ is a white noise with variance σ_η^2 assumed independent of the white noise ϵ_t associated with the explanatory variable, and $d > 1/2$.

We can reparameterize the initial dynamic equation as an error correction model so as to express a long-run coefficient a_1. A possibility is

$$y_t = a_1 x_t + a_2(x_t - x_{t-1}) + \eta_t, \qquad (14.15)$$

with $a_2 = -b$ and $a_1 = a + b$. Let us now consider the static model associated with (14.15), that is the model

$$y_t = \alpha x_t + u_t. \qquad (14.16)$$

The OLS estimator of α from such a static model is

$$\hat{\alpha}_T = \frac{\sum_{t=1}^{T} x_t y_t}{\sum_{t=1}^{T} x_t^2}. \qquad (14.17)$$

The question then becomes whether such an estimator is consistent for $a_1 = a + b$ and then, if so, whether it has the same asymptotic distribution as the OLS estimator of a_1 computed from equation (14.15), that is taking into account the dynamics of the system. The latter estimator is

$$\hat{a}_{1T} = \frac{\sum_{t=1}^{T} x_t y_t - \sum_{t=1}^{T} \Delta x_t x_t \left(\sum_{t=1}^{T} \Delta x_t^2 \right)^{-1} \sum_{t=1}^{T} \Delta x_t y_t}{\sum_{t=1}^{T} x_t^2 - \left(\sum_{t=1}^{T} \Delta x_t x_t \right)^2 \left(\sum_{t=1}^{T} \Delta x_t^2 \right)^{-1}}. \quad (14.18)$$

14.4.2 Limit Properties of the OLS Estimator Computed on the Static Model

By expanding the expression for the estimator $\hat{\alpha}_T$ we obtain

$$\hat{\alpha}_T = \frac{\sum_T x_t y_t}{\sum_{t=1}^{T} x_T^2} = \frac{\sum_{t=1}^{T} x_t \left(a_1 x_t + a_2 \Delta x_t + \eta_t \right)}{\sum_{t=1}^{T} x_t^2}$$

$$= a_1 + a_2 \frac{\sum_{t=1}^{T} x_t \Delta x_t}{\sum_{t=1}^{T} x_t^2} + \frac{\sum_{t=1}^{T} x_t \eta_t}{\sum_{t=1}^{T} x_t^2}.$$

The limit properties of the difference between the estimator and the long term coefficient $\hat{\alpha}_T - a_1$ can be deduced from those of the various empirical moments. In fact, the properties of $\sum_{t=1}^{T} x_t \Delta x_t$ and of $\sum_{t=1}^{T} x_t^2$ are given in theorems 14.2 and 14.3. Those of $\sum_T x_t \eta_t$ are established in the appendix. By denoting $W(r)$, $r \in [0,1]$ the Brownian motion associated with $\{\eta_t\}$

$$\frac{1}{T^d} \sum_{t=1}^{T} x_t \eta_t \xrightarrow{d} \sigma_\eta \int_0^1 x_\infty(r) dW(r).$$

Let us distinguish among the following cases according to the value of d:

(i) $d > 1$

$$\hat{\alpha}_T \approx a_1 + a_2 \frac{T^{2d-1}}{T^{2d}} \frac{\frac{1}{2} x_\infty^2(1)}{\int_0^1 x_\infty^2(r) dr} + \frac{T^d}{T^{2d}} \frac{\sigma_\eta \int_0^1 x_\infty(r) dW(r)}{\int_0^1 x_\infty^2(r) dr},$$

$$\hat{\alpha}_T \approx a_1 + \frac{a_2}{T} \frac{\frac{1}{2} x_\infty^2(1)}{\int_0^1 x_\infty^2(r) dr}.$$

(ii) $d = 1$

$$\hat{\alpha}_T \approx a_1 + a_2 \frac{T}{T^2} \frac{\frac{1}{2}x_\infty^2(1) + \frac{1}{2}\mathrm{var}\,(x_t - x_{t-1})}{\int_0^1 x_\infty^2(r)dr} + \frac{T}{T^2} \frac{\sigma_\eta \int_0^1 x_\infty(r)dW(r)}{\int_0^1 x_\infty^2(r)dr},$$

$$\hat{\alpha}_T \approx a_1 + \frac{1}{T} \left(a_2 \frac{\frac{1}{2}x_\infty^2(1) + \frac{1}{2}\mathrm{var}\,(x_t - x_{t-1})}{\int_0^1 x_\infty^2(r)dr} + \frac{\sigma_\eta \int_0^1 x_\infty(r)dW(r)}{\int_0^1 x_\infty^2(r)dr} \right).$$

(iii) $d < 1$

$$\hat{\alpha}_T \approx a_1 + a_2 \frac{T}{T^{2d}} \frac{\frac{1}{2}\mathrm{var}\,(x_t - x_{t-1})}{\int_0^1 x_\infty^2(r)dr} + \frac{T^d}{T^{2d}} \frac{\sigma_\eta \int_0^1 x_\infty(r)dW(r)}{\int_0^1 x_\infty^2(r)dr},$$

$$\hat{\alpha}_T \approx a_1 + a_2 \frac{1}{T^{2d-1}} \frac{\frac{1}{2}\mathrm{var}\,(x_t - x_{t-1})}{\int_0^1 x_\infty^2(r)dr}.$$

In summary we have:

Theorem 14.7: *The OLS estimator $\hat{\alpha}_T$ computed on the static model is a consistent estimator of the long-run coefficient $a_1 = a + b$. Its convergence rate is $1/T^{2d-1}$ if $d < 1$ and is $1/T$ if $d \geq 1$.*

Thus not taking the dynamics into account does not affect the consistency of the estimator.

14.4.3 Comparison with the OLS Estimator Computed on the Dynamic Model

The same kind of approach can be pursued to determine the asymptotic properties of $\hat{a}_{1T}$. The details of the computations are left to the reader as an exercise (exercise 14.4). There are two cases according to whether the exponent is bigger or smaller than $\frac{3}{2}$:

(i)   If $\frac{1}{2} < d < \frac{3}{2}$

$$\hat{a}_{1T} \approx a_1 + \frac{1}{T^d} \frac{\sigma_\eta \int_0^1 x_\infty(r)dW(r)}{\int_0^1 x_\infty^2(r)dr}.$$

(ii)   If $d > \frac{3}{2}$

$$\hat{a}_{1T} \approx a_1 + \frac{\sigma_\eta}{T^d}$$

$$\times \frac{\int_0^1 x_\infty(r)dW(r) \int_0^1 \Delta x_\infty^2(r)dr - \int_0^1 \Delta x_\infty(r)dW(r) \int_0^1 x_\infty \Delta x_\infty(r)dr}{\int_0^1 x_\infty^2(r)dr \int_0^1 \Delta x_\infty^2(r)dr - \left(\int_0^1 x_\infty(r)\Delta x_\infty(r)dr \right)^2}.$$

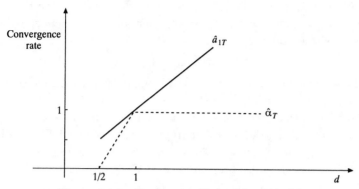

Figure 14.6 Convergence Rate of $\hat{\alpha}_T$ and of $\hat{a}_{1T}$

The behavior of the convergence of the two estimators $\hat{\alpha}_T$ and $\hat{a}_{1T}$ is described graphically in figure 14.6.

We can see that the estimator based on the dynamic model converges infinitely faster than the estimator based on the static model, except in the limit case $d = 1$. In the latter case, taking into consideration the expansions of $\hat{\alpha}_T$ and $\hat{a}_{1T}$ we see that they do not have the same asymptotic distribution. In summary we have:

Theorem 14.8: *Although the estimator $\hat{\alpha}_T$ is always consistent, the estimator $\hat{a}_{1T}$ is always preferable. It is infinitely preferable in the sense that*

$$\lim_{T \to +\infty} \frac{\mathrm{var}\,(\hat{a}_{1T} - a_1)}{\mathrm{var}\,(\hat{\alpha}_T - a_1)} = 0$$

whenever $d \neq 1$.

14.5 Cointegration

14.5.1 Analysis Based on the Empirical Covariance Matrix

Let us consider a nonstationary series y integrated of order 1. This series admits the expression

$$(1 - L)\mathbf{y}_t = \mathbf{H}(L)\tilde{\boldsymbol{\varepsilon}}_t, \tag{14.19}$$

where $\boldsymbol{\varepsilon}$ indicates an n-dimensional white noise (and $\tilde{\boldsymbol{\varepsilon}}_t = \boldsymbol{\varepsilon}_t$ if $t \geq 0$ and $\tilde{\boldsymbol{\varepsilon}}_t = \mathbf{0}$ if $t < 0$). We want to establish whether the components of this series are cointegrated, and, if so, determine the cointegrating vectors. Let us consider the case where the order of the subspace of the cointegrating vectors is r. Then, by definition, there exist r independent vectors of size n noted $\boldsymbol{\alpha}_1, \ldots, \boldsymbol{\alpha}_r$ such that

$$\boldsymbol{\alpha}_1'\mathbf{H}(1) = \ldots = \boldsymbol{\alpha}_r'\mathbf{H}(1) = 0,$$

and the vectors $\boldsymbol{\beta}$ in $\mathbb{R}^n$ which do not belong to the subspace of cointegrating vectors are such that $\boldsymbol{\beta}'\mathbf{H}(1) \neq 0$.

The cointegrating vectors can be derived directly from the analysis of the asymptotic properties of the empirical covariance matrix. Let us introduce the n-dimensional nonstandardized Brownian motion associated with the noise $\boldsymbol{\varepsilon}$. This process, denoted by $\mathbf{W}$, is defined as

$$\frac{1}{\sqrt{T}} \sum_{t=1}^{[Tr]} \boldsymbol{\varepsilon}_t \xrightarrow{\mathrm{d}} \mathbf{W}(r) \tag{14.20}$$

for $r \in [0, 1]$. Applying to any combination of the components of the process $\mathbf{y}$ the results in theorem 14.2, we get immediately the limit behavior of the variance–covariance matrix of $\mathbf{y}$.

Theorem 14.9: *We have*

$$\frac{1}{T^2} \sum_{t=1}^{T} \mathbf{y}_t\mathbf{y}_t' \xrightarrow{\mathrm{d}} \mathbf{H}(1) \left(\int_0^1 \mathbf{W}(r)\mathbf{W}'(r)dr \right) \mathbf{H}(1)'$$

where $\mathbf{H}(1)$ is the long-run coefficient matrix.

If we move to consider the empirical variance of a combination of the components we must distinguish two cases:

(i) If this combination $\boldsymbol{\beta}'\mathbf{y}$ is such that the vector $\boldsymbol{\beta}$ does not lie in the subspace spanned by the cointegrating vectors we have

$$\frac{1}{T^2} \sum_{t=1}^{T} (\boldsymbol{\beta}'\mathbf{y}_t)^2 \xrightarrow{\mathrm{d}} \boldsymbol{\beta}'\mathbf{H}(1) \left(\int_0^1 \mathbf{W}(r)\mathbf{W}'(r)dr \right) \mathbf{H}(1)'\boldsymbol{\beta} \neq 0.$$

The empirical variance $\frac{1}{T} \sum_{t=1}^{T} (\boldsymbol{\beta}'\mathbf{y}_t)^2$ is of the same order as T.

(ii) If this combination corresponds to a cointegrating vector $\boldsymbol{\alpha}$ we have

$$\frac{1}{T^2} \sum_{t=1}^{T} (\boldsymbol{\alpha}'\mathbf{y}_t)^2 \xrightarrow{\mathrm{d}} \boldsymbol{\alpha}'\mathbf{H}(1) \left(\int_0^1 \mathbf{W}(r)\mathbf{W}'(r)dr \right) \mathbf{H}(1)'\boldsymbol{\alpha} = 0.$$

In fact, since the process $\boldsymbol{\alpha}'\mathbf{y}$ is stationary, we know that the empirical variance converges to the corresponding moment

$$\frac{1}{T} \sum_{t=1}^{T} (\boldsymbol{\alpha}'\mathbf{y}_t)^2 \xrightarrow{\mathrm{d}} E(\boldsymbol{\alpha}'\mathbf{y}_t)^2.$$

Thus the empirical variance is $O_p(1)$.

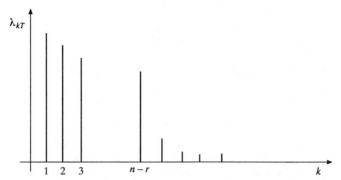

Figure 14.7 Graphical Detection of the Order of Cointegration

The modification of the rate of convergence for the cointegrating vectors allows us to examine the problem in a complete fashion:

(i) As a first step we can compute the empirical covariance matrix divided by T, that is,

$$\mathbf{M}_T = \frac{1}{T^2} \sum_{t=1}^{T} \mathbf{y}_t \mathbf{y}_t'.$$

This symmetric positive semidefinite matrix admits real eigenvalues, which can be presented in a decreasing order

$$\lambda_{1T} \geq \lambda_{2T} \geq \ldots \geq \lambda_{nT} \geq 0.$$

We know also that the k-th eigenvalue λ_{kT} is such that

$$\lambda_{kT} = \min_{\mathcal{E}_{n-k+1}} \max_{x \in \mathcal{E}_{n-k+1}} \frac{\mathbf{x}' \mathbf{M}_T \mathbf{x}}{\mathbf{x}' \mathbf{x}}$$

$$= \max_{\mathcal{E}_k} \min_{x \in \mathcal{E}_k} \frac{\mathbf{x}' \mathbf{M}_T \mathbf{x}}{\mathbf{x}' \mathbf{x}}$$

where $\mathcal{E}_k$ (respectively $\mathcal{E}_{n-k+1}$) denotes all subspaces of dimension k (respectively $n - k + 1$). We conclude that $\lambda_{1T}, \ldots, \lambda_{n-r,T}$ are of order 1 and that $\lambda_{n-r+1,T}, \ldots, \lambda_{nT}$ tend to 0.

(ii) We can then examine the eigenvalues of $\mathbf{M}_T$. Plotting them on a diagram, if the dimension of the subspace of the cointegrating vectors is r, we should see r eigenvalues close to 0, that is a break after the $(n-r)$-th largest eigenvalue. This gives an empirical tool to determine the order r and, in particular, to know whether r is different from 0, that is, if there is cointegration.

(iii) Finally, we can analyze the eigenvectors associated with the eigenvalues close to 0. These eigenvectors converge to the eigenvectors of the limit matrix

$$\mathbf{H}(1)\Big(\int_0^1 \mathbf{W}(r)\mathbf{W}'(r)dr\Big)\mathbf{H}(1)',$$

associated with the zero eigenvalues, that is to the cointegrating vectors.

This very simple approach is essentially descriptive. However, these three steps can be set up in an inference framework. We would need then:

(i)   to derive the limit distributions of the eigenvalues of the matrix $\mathbf{M}_T$ and to derive the critical threshold under which they are considered insignificant;

(ii) by the same token, we could examine not only the consistency of the cointegrating vectors, but also determine their rate of convergence and their limit distributions.

Such an analysis is a difficult one and has been only partially examined in the literature.

14.5.2 A Two-step Procedure

Engle and Granger (1987) have derived an estimation procedure in two steps for the coefficients of an error correction representation. Let us assume, for example, that $\mathbf{y}_t$ satisfies not only equation (14.19) (see also 11.12), but also an autoregressive relationship $\mathbf{\Phi}(L)\mathbf{y}_t = \tilde{\boldsymbol{\varepsilon}}_t$ and that the subspace of the cointegrating vectors is of order 1 (cf. exercise 14.1). The corresponding error correction model (cf. theorem 11.8) can be written as

$$\mathbf{D}\boldsymbol{\alpha}'\mathbf{y}_{t-1} + \tilde{\tilde{\mathbf{\Phi}}}(L)\Delta\mathbf{y}_t = \tilde{\boldsymbol{\varepsilon}}_t,$$

with $\tilde{\tilde{\mathbf{\Phi}}}(0) = \mathbf{I}$ and $\boldsymbol{\alpha}' = (-1, \alpha_2, \dots, \alpha_n)$. One equation of such a system (for instance the first one) can be written as

$$\Delta y_{1t} = (1 - \phi_{11}(L))\Delta y_{1t} - \dots - \phi_{1n}(L)\Delta y_{nt} - D_1\boldsymbol{\alpha}'\mathbf{y}_{t-1} + \tilde{\epsilon}_{1t}, \quad (14.21)$$

where $\phi_{1i}(L)$, $i = 1, \dots, n$ are the elements of the first row of $\tilde{\tilde{\mathbf{\Phi}}}(L)$ and D_1 is the first element of the vector $\mathbf{D}$.

The first step of the Engle and Granger procedure consists of estimating $\boldsymbol{\alpha}$ by minimizing

$$\sum_{t=1}^T (\boldsymbol{\alpha}'\mathbf{y}_t)^2$$

that is, regressing by ordinary least squares y_{1t} on $y_{2t}, \dots, y_{nt}$. This regression is called a *cointegrating regression*.

The minimization problem can be also written as

$$\min_{\alpha} \frac{1}{T^2} \sum_{t=1}^{T} (\alpha' \mathbf{y}_t)^2$$

or

$$\min_{\alpha} \alpha' \mathbf{M}_T \alpha.$$

The limit problem is (cf. theorem 14.9)

$$\min_{\alpha} \alpha' \mathbf{H}(1) \left(\int_0^1 \mathbf{W}(r) \mathbf{W}'(r) dr \right) \mathbf{H}(1)' \alpha,$$

the solution to which is α_0, the normalized cointegrating vector. The estimation procedure of α_0 is thus consistent and a slight modification to theorem 14.7 shows that the rate of convergence is $\frac{1}{T}$.

The second step consists of replacing in (14.21) α with the estimator $\hat{\alpha}_T$ obtained in the first step, in order to estimate the parameters in $\phi_{11}(L), \ldots, \phi_{1n}(L)$, and D_1 by OLS. Since the rate of convergence of $\hat{\alpha}_T$ is high, this second-step estimator has the same asymptotic properties as the "pseudo-estimator" obtained by taking α equal to its true value α_0, and the usual testing procedures are still valid (however, cf. Gourieroux, Maurel, and Monfort, 1987, for a limitation of this two-step procedure).

Another estimation procedure of equation (14.21) consists of applying nonlinear least squares (Stock, 1987). The estimator of α_0 thus obtained is also superconsistent. The estimators of the other parameters have the usual asymptotic properties and are asymptotically equivalent to the estimators of the second step in the Engle–Granger procedure. Note that, among the parameters having the usual behavior, there is also the coefficient D_1 of $y_{1,t-1}$. If we change the normalization for α, we can see that the coefficients $D_1 \alpha_i$ of $y_{i,t-1}$, $i = 2, \ldots, n$ also belong to the same category. We can then perform the usual inference procedures on the coefficients of $y_{i,t-1}$, $i = 1, \ldots, n$ taken individually.

We may also want to test whether there exists a cointegrating relationship. Such a test can be based on the residual $\hat{u}_t$ of the cointegrating regression, that is, the regression of y_{1t} on $y_{2t}, \ldots, y_{nt}$. Under the null hypothesis of no cointegration, $\alpha_0' \mathbf{y}_t = u_t$ is nonstationary and therefore it is natural to test such a null hypothesis with a unit root test on $\hat{u}_t$. Such a test has been proposed by Engle and Yoo (1987) and Phillips and Ouliaris (1988). In particular we can propose the augmented Dickey–Fuller tests and the statistics $S_\rho, S_\tau, \hat{S}_\rho, \hat{S}_\tau$ described in 14.3 (by replacing y_t with $\hat{u}_t$). However note that these statistics do not have the same asymptotic distribution as when they are computed on directly observable variables (and not on regression residuals). The tests

Table 14.1 *Critical Values for $\hat{S}_\rho$ with or without Constant Term*

	$\alpha = 1\%$		$\alpha = 5\%$		$\alpha = 10\%$	
n	NC	C	NC	C	NC	C
2	22.83	28.32	15.63	20.49	12.54	17.04
3	29.27	34.17	21.48	26.09	18.18	22.19
4	36.16	41.13	27.86	32.06	23.92	27.58
5	42.87	47.51	33.48	37.15	28.85	32.74
6	48.52	52.17	38.09	41.94	33.80	37.01

based on S_ρ and S_τ should be avoided because they are not consistent (cf. Phillips and Ouliaris, 1988). Under the null hypothesis of no cointegration of y_t and Δy_t stationary with zero mean (thus not necessarily VAR), the ADF statistic of Dickey–Fuller and $\hat{S}_\tau$ have the same asymptotic distribution. For the Augmented Dickey–Fuller test, though, we need to make the hypothesis that the number p of lags included in the regression tends to infinity with the number of observations, in such a way that $p = o(T^{1/3})$. Under the alternative hypothesis of cointegration we have $\hat{S}_\rho = O_p(T)$, $\hat{S}_\tau = O_p(T^{1/2})$, $ADF = O_p(T^{1/2})$. Therefore $\hat{S}_\rho$ seems preferable to the other statistics; since it diverges more rapidly under the alternative, the power for finite samples is probably higher. The critical values for the tests based on $\hat{S}_\rho$ on the one hand, and for $\hat{S}_\tau$ and ADF on the other, correspond to the values beyond which the null hypothesis of no cointegration is rejected. Tables 14.1 and 14.2 are taken from Phillips and Ouliaris (1988) and distinguish between the two cases when $\hat{u}_t$ is obtained in a regression of y_{1t} on $y_{2t}, \ldots, y_{nt}$ with (columns C) or without (NC) the constant term. In the former case the values can be found also in Engle and Yoo (1987).

14.5.3 Likelihood Ratio Test

We can easily perform a test about the dimension of the subspace of the cointegrating vectors. Let us consider a series $\{\mathbf{y}_t\}$ the components of which are nonstationary integrated of order 1 and which admit a finite autoregressive expression

$$\mathbf{y}_t + \mathbf{\Phi}_1 \mathbf{y}_{t-1} + \ldots + \mathbf{\Phi}_p \mathbf{y}_{t-p} = \boldsymbol{\varepsilon}_t$$

Table 14.2 *Critical Values for $\hat{S}_\tau$ and ADF with or without Constant Term*

| | $\alpha = 1\%$ | | $\alpha = 5\%$ | | $\alpha = 10\%$ | |
n	NC	C	NC	C	NC	C
2	3.386	3.962	2.762	3.365	2.450	3.066
3	3.839	4.308	3.267	3.767	2.987	3.449
4	4.304	4.732	3.737	4.112	3.445	3.833
5	4.672	5.073	4.126	4.454	3.807	4.156
6	4.990	5.281	4.400	4.710	4.142	4.431

for $t \geq 0$, and where $\boldsymbol{\varepsilon}$ is a white noise with variance–covariance matrix $\boldsymbol{\Omega}$.

Let us consider the null hypothesis

H_0 : the dimension of the subspace of the cointegrating vectors is r.

$$(14.22)$$

Constrained Maximum Likelihood Estimators Let us start by constructing the parameter estimators constrained by the cointegration hypothesis. In order to make this constraint apparent, let us start by rewriting the model in an error correction form. A suitable expression for the problem at hand, which can be derived from the theorem 11.7, is

$$\Delta \mathbf{y}_t = \boldsymbol{\Gamma}_1 \Delta \mathbf{y}_{t-1} + \ldots + \boldsymbol{\Gamma}_{p-1} \Delta \mathbf{y}_{t-p+1} - \mathbf{D}\boldsymbol{\alpha}' \mathbf{y}_{t-p} + \boldsymbol{\varepsilon}_t, \quad (14.23)$$

where $\boldsymbol{\Gamma}_1, \ldots, \boldsymbol{\Gamma}_{p-1}$ are square matrices $n \times n$, $\mathbf{D}$ is an $n \times r$ matrix and $\boldsymbol{\alpha}$ a matrix $n \times r$, the columns of which are independent cointegrating vectors (cf. exercise 14.3).

Under the assumption of normality of the errors, the conditional log-likelihood can be written as

$$\log L = -n\frac{T}{2}\log 2\pi - \frac{T}{2}\log \det \boldsymbol{\Omega}$$

$$-\frac{1}{2}\sum_{t=1}^{T}(\Delta \mathbf{y}_t - \boldsymbol{\Gamma}_1 \Delta \mathbf{y}_{t-1} - \ldots + \mathbf{D}\boldsymbol{\alpha}'\mathbf{y}_{t-p})'\boldsymbol{\Omega}^{-1}$$

$$(\Delta \mathbf{y}_t - \boldsymbol{\Gamma}_1 \Delta \mathbf{y}_{t-1} - \ldots + \mathbf{D}\boldsymbol{\alpha}'\mathbf{y}_{t-p}).$$

Concentrated Log-likelihood Let us start by concentrating the log-likelihood with respect to the parameters $\boldsymbol{\Gamma}_1, \ldots, \boldsymbol{\Gamma}_{p-1}$. This is equivalent to considering the regression of $\mathbf{R}_{0t}$ on $\mathbf{R}_{pt}$, where $\mathbf{R}_{0t}$ indicates the residual in the regression of $\Delta\mathbf{y}_t$ on $\Delta\mathbf{y}_{t-1}, \ldots, \Delta\mathbf{y}_{t-p+1}$, and $\mathbf{R}_{pt}$ the residual from the regression of $\mathbf{y}_{t-p}$ on $\Delta\mathbf{y}_{t-1}, \ldots, \Delta\mathbf{y}_{t-p+1}$. The concentrated model is

$$\mathbf{R}_{0t} = -\mathbf{D}\boldsymbol{\alpha}'\mathbf{R}_{pt} + \boldsymbol{\varepsilon}_t^* \tag{14.24}$$

with var $(\boldsymbol{\varepsilon}_t^*) = \boldsymbol{\Omega}$. Taking $\boldsymbol{\alpha}$ as fixed, we can concentrate the log-likelihood with respect to $\mathbf{D}$ and $\boldsymbol{\Omega}$. Since the model appears in the Seemingly Unrelated Regression form with the same set of explanatory variables $\boldsymbol{\alpha}'\mathbf{R}_{pt}$, we know that the generalized least squares estimator of $\mathbf{D}$ is the same as the OLS estimator. Then the solutions for $\mathbf{D}$ and $\boldsymbol{\Omega}$ are

$$\hat{\mathbf{D}}(\boldsymbol{\alpha}) = -\mathbf{S}_{0p}\boldsymbol{\alpha}\left(\boldsymbol{\alpha}'\mathbf{S}_{pp}\boldsymbol{\alpha}\right)^{-1},$$

$$\hat{\boldsymbol{\Omega}}(\boldsymbol{\alpha}) = \mathbf{S}_{00} - \mathbf{S}_{0p}\boldsymbol{\alpha}\left(\boldsymbol{\alpha}'\mathbf{S}_{pp}\boldsymbol{\alpha}\right)^{-1}\boldsymbol{\alpha}'\mathbf{S}_{p0},$$

with

$$\mathbf{S}_{ij} = \frac{1}{T}\sum_{t=1}^{T}\mathbf{R}_{it}\mathbf{R}_{jt}', \quad i, j = 0, \ p. \tag{14.25}$$

The concentrated log-likelihood is

$$\log L_c(\boldsymbol{\alpha}) = -\frac{T}{2}\log\det\left(\hat{\boldsymbol{\Omega}}(\boldsymbol{\alpha})\right) - \frac{nT}{2} - \frac{nT}{2}\log 2\pi. \tag{14.26}$$

Constrained Maximum Likelihood Estimator of the Cointegrating Vectors
The problem to be solved is then

$$\min_{\boldsymbol{\alpha}}\det\left(\mathbf{S}_{00} - \mathbf{S}_{0p}\boldsymbol{\alpha}\left(\boldsymbol{\alpha}'\mathbf{S}_{pp}\boldsymbol{\alpha}\right)^{-1}\boldsymbol{\alpha}'\mathbf{S}_{p0}\right).$$

On the basis of the formulas for the determinant of a block-partitioned matrix we have

$$\det\mathbf{S}_{00}\det\left(\boldsymbol{\alpha}'\mathbf{S}_{pp}\boldsymbol{\alpha} - \boldsymbol{\alpha}'\mathbf{S}_{p0}\mathbf{S}_{00}^{-1}\mathbf{S}_{0p}\boldsymbol{\alpha}\right)$$

$$= \det\left(\boldsymbol{\alpha}'\mathbf{S}_{pp}\boldsymbol{\alpha}\right)\det\left(\mathbf{S}_{00} - \mathbf{S}_{0p}\boldsymbol{\alpha}\left(\boldsymbol{\alpha}'\mathbf{S}_{pp}\boldsymbol{\alpha}'\right)^{-1}\boldsymbol{\alpha}'\mathbf{S}_{p0}\right).$$

The problem to be solved then is the same as

$$\min_{\boldsymbol{\alpha}}\frac{\det\left(\boldsymbol{\alpha}'\mathbf{S}_{pp}\boldsymbol{\alpha} - \boldsymbol{\alpha}'\mathbf{S}_{p0}\mathbf{S}_{00}^{-1}\mathbf{S}_{0p}\boldsymbol{\alpha}\right)}{\det\left(\boldsymbol{\alpha}'\mathbf{S}_{pp}\boldsymbol{\alpha}\right)}.$$

Moreover, the cointegrating vectors $\boldsymbol{\alpha}$ being defined up to a change in basis, we can always choose a normalization corresponding to a particular basis. For example, we can normalize $\boldsymbol{\alpha}$ so that $\boldsymbol{\alpha}'\mathbf{S}_{pp}\boldsymbol{\alpha} = \mathbf{I}$. The problem is then

$$\min_{\alpha} \det \left(\mathbf{I} - \boldsymbol{\alpha}' \mathbf{S}_{p0} \mathbf{S}_{00}^{-1} \mathbf{S}_{0p} \boldsymbol{\alpha} \right),$$

$$\text{s.t. } \boldsymbol{\alpha}' \mathbf{S}_{pp} \boldsymbol{\alpha} = \mathbf{I}.$$

(14.27)

The solution to the latter problem is a standard one (cf. Anderson, 1984), and it reduces to a problem of eigenvalues and eigenvectors. More precisely, let us denote by $\hat{\lambda}_1 > \ldots > \hat{\lambda}_n$ the solutions to the equation

$$\det \left(\lambda \mathbf{S}_{pp} - \mathbf{S}_{p0} \mathbf{S}_{00}^{-1} \mathbf{S}_{0p} \right) = 0,$$

(14.28)

and by $\hat{\mathbf{e}}_k$, $k = 1, \ldots, n$ the associated eigenvectors

$$\mathbf{S}_{p0} \mathbf{S}_{00}^{-1} \mathbf{S}_{0p} \hat{\mathbf{e}}_k = \hat{\lambda}_k \mathbf{S}_{pp} \hat{\mathbf{e}}_k$$

(14.29)

for $k = 1, \ldots, n$, normalized as

$$\hat{\mathbf{e}}_k' \mathbf{S}_{pp} \hat{\mathbf{e}}_j = \begin{cases} 0, & \text{if } k \neq j, \\ 1, & \text{if } k = j. \end{cases}$$

(14.30)

It can be shown that the eigenvalues $\hat{\lambda}_i$ are between 0 and 1, and that we have the following result:

Theorem 14.10: *The constrained maximum likelihood estimators of the cointegrating vectors are the eigenvectors $\hat{\mathbf{e}}_1, \ldots, \hat{\mathbf{e}}_r$ associated with the r largest eigenvalues solution to the equation*

$$\det \left(\lambda \mathbf{S}_{pp} - \mathbf{S}_{p0} \mathbf{S}_{00}^{-1} \mathbf{S}_{0p} \right) = 0$$

with $\hat{\mathbf{e}}_k \mathbf{S}_{pp} \hat{\mathbf{e}}_j = \delta_{kj}$ (Kronecker delta).

This result is clearly close to the descriptive procedure described before, based on the empirical variance–covariance matrix. However, note that in order to estimate the cointegrating vectors, it looks advisable not to take into consideration just the static relationships, but also the dynamics of adjustment. This result is in line with theorem 14.8 where we have seen that the estimator of the long-run parameter based on the dynamic relationship was preferable to the one computed on the basis of the static model.

The maximum likelihood estimators of $\boldsymbol{\Gamma}_1, \ldots, \boldsymbol{\Gamma}_{p-1}$ and of $\mathbf{D}$ are obtained by ordinary least squares applied to the equations (14.23) where $\boldsymbol{\alpha}$ has been replaced by the estimator $\hat{\boldsymbol{\alpha}}$ just derived.

Likelihood Ratio Test We can now derive the Likelihood Ratio statistic. The maximum of the log-likelihood under the null hypothesis is

$$\log L_c(\hat{\boldsymbol{\alpha}}) = -\frac{T}{2}\log\det\left(\hat{\boldsymbol{\Omega}}(\hat{\boldsymbol{\alpha}})\right) - \frac{nT}{2} - \frac{nT}{2}\log 2\pi$$

$$= -\frac{T}{2}\log\left(\frac{\det\mathbf{S}_{00}\det\left(\hat{\boldsymbol{\alpha}}'\mathbf{S}_{pp}\hat{\boldsymbol{\alpha}} - \hat{\boldsymbol{\alpha}}'\mathbf{S}_{p0}\mathbf{S}_{00}^{-1}\mathbf{S}_{0p}\hat{\boldsymbol{\alpha}}\right)}{\det\left(\hat{\boldsymbol{\alpha}}'\mathbf{S}_{pp}\hat{\boldsymbol{\alpha}}\right)}\right)$$

$$\quad - \frac{nT}{2} - \frac{nT}{2}\log 2\pi$$

$$= -\frac{T}{2}\log\det\mathbf{S}_{00} - \frac{T}{2}\log\left(\prod_{k=1}^{r}(1-\hat{\lambda}_k)\right) - \frac{nT}{2} - \frac{nT}{2}\log 2\pi.$$

Under the general hypothesis, where the coefficient of $\mathbf{y}_{t-p}$ in the regression is unconstrained, we have $\hat{\boldsymbol{\Omega}} = \mathbf{S}_{00} - \mathbf{S}_{0p}\mathbf{S}_{pp}^{-1}\mathbf{S}_{p0}$ and thus the maximum value of the unconstrained log-likelihood is

$$\log\hat{L} = -\frac{T}{2}\log\det\mathbf{S}_{00} - \frac{T}{2}\log\left(\prod_{k=1}^{n}(1-\hat{\lambda}_k)\right) - \frac{nT}{2} - \frac{nT}{2}\log 2\pi.$$

The form of the test statistic is derived then from theorem 14.11.

Theorem 14.11: *The Likelihood Ratio statistic of the null hypothesis H_0: the subspace of the cointegrating vectors is of size r, is*

$$\xi = 2\left(\log\hat{L} - \log L_c(\hat{\boldsymbol{\alpha}})\right) = -T\sum_{k=r+1}^{n}\log(1-\hat{\lambda}_k),$$

where the $\hat{\lambda}_k$, $k = r+1,\ldots,n$ are the $n-r$ smallest eigenvalues, roots of the equation

$$\det\left(\lambda\mathbf{S}_{pp} - \mathbf{S}_{p0}\mathbf{S}_{00}^{-1}\mathbf{S}_{0p}\right) = 0.$$

In order to apply the test, we need to know the distribution of the test statistic under the null hypothesis, derived by Johansen (1988).

Theorem 14.12: *Under the null hypothesis H_0: the subspace of the cointegrating vectors is of order r, the Likelihood Ratio statistic converges in distribution to the distribution of*

$$\mathrm{tr}\left(\int_0^1 \mathbf{W}(r)d\mathbf{W}'(r)\left(\int_0^1 \mathbf{W}(r)\mathbf{W}'(r)dr\right)^{-1}\int_0^1 d\mathbf{W}(r)\mathbf{W}'(r)\right),$$

where $\mathbf{W}$ is a Brownian motion of size $n-r$ with the variance–covariance matrix equal to the identity matrix.

Table 14.3 *Likelihood Ratio Test:* *Critical Values*

$n - r$	1	2	3	4	5
99%	6.51	16.31	29.75	45.58	66.52
95%	3.84	12.53	24.31	39.89	59.46
90%	2.86	10.47	21.63	36.58	55.44

Table 14.4 *Test: Order r vs. Order* *r + 1. Critical Values*

$n - r$	1	2	3	4	5
99%	6.51	15.69	22.99	28.82	35.17
95%	3.84	11.44	17.89	23.80	30.04
90%	2.86	9.52	15.59	21.58	27.62

The 99%, 95%, and 90% quantiles of this distribution can be computed by simulation. These quantiles correspond respectively to the critical values of the tests at the levels 1%, 5%, and 10%. They are given in table 14.3.

Another interesting test is formulated for a null hypothesis formulated as the cointegration subspace is of order r versus order $r + 1$. The likelihood ratio statistic is then

$$-T \log(1 - \hat{\lambda}_{r+1})$$

which, under the null hypothesis has an asymptotic distribution the quantiles of which are given in table 14.4.

Let us assume now that we introduce a constant term in model (14.23). The model becomes

$$\Delta \mathbf{y}_t = \boldsymbol{\mu} + \boldsymbol{\Gamma}_1 \Delta \mathbf{y}_{t-1} + \ldots + \boldsymbol{\Gamma}_{p-1} \Delta \mathbf{y}_{t-p+1} - \mathbf{D}\boldsymbol{\alpha}' \mathbf{y}_{t-p} + \boldsymbol{\varepsilon}_t. \quad (14.31)$$

If we want to test whether the order of the cointegration subspace is r against the general model we can again use the likelihood ratio statistic given by theorem 14.13.

Table 14.5 *Model with a Constant*
(Case A): Critical Values

$n-r$	1	2	3	4	5
99%	6.65	20.04	35.65	54.46	76.07
95%	3.76	15.41	29.68	47.21	68.52
90%	2.69	13.33	26.79	43.95	64.84

Theorem 14.13: *The Likelihood Ratio statistic of the null hypothesis H_0: the subspace of cointegration is of order r versus the general model, is*

$$\xi^* = -T \sum_{k=r+1}^{n} \log(1 - \lambda_k^*),$$

where the λ_k^*, $k = r + 1, \ldots, n$ are the $n - r$ smallest eigenvalues, roots of the equation

$$\det \left(\lambda \mathbf{S}_{pp}^* - \mathbf{S}_{p0}^* \mathbf{S}_{00}^{*-1} \mathbf{S}_{0p}^* \right) = 0,$$

the matrices $\mathbf{S}_{ij}^*$, $(i, j = 0, p)$ being constructed as the $\mathbf{S}_{ij}$ from the residuals $\mathbf{R}_{ij}^*$ of the regressions of the components of $\Delta \mathbf{y}_t$ on the components of $\Delta \mathbf{y}_{t-1}, \ldots, \Delta \mathbf{y}_{t-p+1}$ and a constant (for $\mathbf{R}_{0t}^*$) and of the components of $\mathbf{y}_{t-p}$ on the same variables (for $\mathbf{R}_{pt}^*$).

The problem with this new statistic ξ^* is that it is not asymptotically similar under the null hypothesis. In fact, its asymptotic distribution is not the same according to whether the constant $\boldsymbol{\mu}$ belongs to the image of $\mathbf{D}$ or not. If it does not, the quantiles of the asymptotic distribution under the null hypothesis are given in the table 14.5. If $\boldsymbol{\mu}$ belongs to the image of $\mathbf{D}$ we can write $\boldsymbol{\mu} = -\mathbf{D}\boldsymbol{\alpha}^*$, where $\boldsymbol{\alpha}^*$ is a vector of size r, and the model (14.31) can be written as

$$\Delta \mathbf{y}_t = \boldsymbol{\Gamma}_1 \Delta \mathbf{y}_{t-1} + \ldots + \boldsymbol{\Gamma}_{p-1} \Delta \mathbf{y}_{t-p+1} - \mathbf{D} \left(\boldsymbol{\alpha}^* + \boldsymbol{\alpha}' \mathbf{y}_{t-p} \right) + \boldsymbol{\varepsilon}_t. \quad (14.32)$$

In the latter case the asymptotic quantiles are given in table 14.6.

As in the case without a constant, we may also want to test the null hypothesis according to which the subspace of cointegration is of order r versus an alternative of it being of order $r + 1$. The likelihood ratio statistic is then $-T \log(1 - \lambda_{r+1}^*)$ and the quantiles of this statistic under the null hypothesis are given in table 14.7 when the constant does not belong to the cointegration subspace, and in table 14.8 for the case in which it does.

Table 14.6 *Model with a Constant (Case B): Critical Values*

$n - r$	1	2	3	4	5
99%	12.97	24.60	41.07	60.16	84.15
95%	9.24	19.96	34.91	53.12	76.07
90%	7.52	17.85	32.00	49.65	71.86

Table 14.7 *Test: Order r vs. Order r + 1 (Case A): Critical Values*

$n - r$	1	2	3	4	5
99%	6.65	18.63	25.52	32.24	38.77
95%	3.76	14.07	20.97	27.07	33.46
90%	2.69	12.07	18.60	24.73	30.90

Table 14.8 *Test: Order r vs. Order r + 1 (Case B): Critical Values*

$n - r$	1	2	3	4	5
99%	12.97	20.20	26.81	33.24	39.79
95%	9.24	15.67	22.00	28.14	34.40
90%	7.52	13.75	19.77	25.56	31.66

Note, in particular, that for the two types of tests, the quantiles of the statistics corresponding to the case where the constant belongs to the cointegration subspace are greater than in the opposite case. As a consequence if we do not want to make any assumptions on the constant, and we want a test with a smaller asymptotic size than α ($\alpha = 1\%, 5\%$ *or* 10%), we must use either table 14.6 or table 14.8.

For r chosen, the maximum likelihood estimator of the matrix $\boldsymbol{\alpha}$ appearing in (14.31) can be obtained by taking as an estimator of the i-th column of $\boldsymbol{\alpha}$ the eigenvector $\hat{\mathbf{e}}_i^*$ defined as

$$\mathbf{S}_{p0}^*(\mathbf{S}_{00}^*)^{-1}\mathbf{S}_{0p}^*\hat{\mathbf{e}}_i^* = \lambda_i^*\mathbf{S}_{pp}^*\hat{\mathbf{e}}_i^*, \qquad i = 1,\ldots,r.$$

These vectors correspond to the normalization $\hat{\mathbf{e}}_k'^*\mathbf{S}_{pp}^*\hat{\mathbf{e}}_j^* = \delta_{kj}$ (Kronecker delta).

The estimators of the other parameters of (14.31) are obtained by replacing $\boldsymbol{\alpha}$ by its estimated matrix $\hat{\boldsymbol{\alpha}}$ and by applying ordinary least squares. The usual tests can be applied for these parameters.

If we want to estimate the matrix $\tilde{\boldsymbol{\alpha}} = \begin{pmatrix} \boldsymbol{\alpha} \\ \boldsymbol{\alpha}^* \end{pmatrix}$ of order $(n+1) \times r$ under the assumption of model (14.32) we can take the eigenvectors $\tilde{\mathbf{e}}_i$ defined as

$$\tilde{\mathbf{S}}_{p0}\mathbf{S}_{00}^{-1}\tilde{\mathbf{S}}_{0p}\tilde{\mathbf{e}}_i = \tilde{\lambda}_i\tilde{\mathbf{S}}_{pp}\tilde{\mathbf{e}}_i, \qquad i = 1,\ldots,r,$$

and where the matrices $\tilde{\mathbf{S}}_{p0}$ and $\tilde{\mathbf{S}}_{pp}$ are computed as in (14.25) once the vectors of the residuals $\mathbf{R}_{pt}$ are replaced by the vectors obtained by regressing $\begin{pmatrix} \mathbf{y}_{t-p} \\ 1 \end{pmatrix}$ on the components of $\Delta\mathbf{y}_{t-1},\ldots,\Delta\mathbf{y}_{t-p+1}$. Also, the $\tilde{\lambda}_i$, for $i = 1,\ldots,r$ are the r largest eigenvalues. Note that the new vectors of residuals $\mathbf{R}_{pt}$ are of order $n+1$ (not n), and that the smallest eigenvalue is $\tilde{\lambda}_{n+1} = 0$ given that the matrix $\tilde{\mathbf{S}}_{p0}\mathbf{S}_{00}^{-1}\tilde{\mathbf{S}}_{0p}$ is singular.

Once r is given, if we want to test whether the constant is of the form $-\mathbf{D}\boldsymbol{\alpha}_0$, we can use the likelihood ratio test

$$-T \sum_{k=r+1}^{n} \log\left(\frac{1-\tilde{\lambda}_k}{1-\lambda_k^*}\right),$$

and this statistic is asymptotically distributed under the null hypothesis as a $\chi^2(n-r)$.

Finally, we can use different likelihood ratio tests on the matrix $\boldsymbol{\alpha}$ appearing in (14.31), without questioning the dimension r, and apply the classical asymptotic theory. Thus we may test whether the subspace of cointegration belongs to a given subspace of dimension $s \geq r$, i.e., that we have $\boldsymbol{\alpha} = \mathbf{H}\boldsymbol{\gamma}$, where $\mathbf{H}$ is a matrix $n \times s$ known and of rank s, and $\boldsymbol{\gamma}$ is an $s \times r$ matrix of parameters. The likelihood ratio statistic is then

$$-T \sum_{i=1}^{r} \log\frac{1-\bar{\lambda}_i}{1-\lambda_i^*},$$

where the $\bar{\lambda}_i$, $i = 1,\ldots,r$ are the r largest eigenvalues given by

$$\det\left(\lambda\mathbf{H}'\mathbf{S}_{pp}^*\mathbf{H} - \mathbf{H}'\mathbf{S}_{p0}^*\mathbf{S}_{00}^{-1*}\mathbf{S}_{0p}^*\mathbf{H}\right) = 0.$$

Such a statistic is asymptotically distributed as a $\chi^2(r(n-s))$ under the null hypothesis $\boldsymbol{\alpha} = \mathbf{H}\boldsymbol{\gamma}$.

14.6 Determination of the Order of Integration

One of the most important problems in the theory of nonstationary processes (ARIMA or fractional) is the determination of the order of integration d. Until now there does not exist an estimation method for this order with satisfactory asymptotic properties (distribution and possible optimality). However, we can suggest several approaches which intuitively lead to consistent results.

14.6.1 Estimation Based on the Empirical Mean

We have seen that if the process y is fractional

$$y_t = (1 - L)^{-d} \Phi(L)^{-1} \Theta(L) \tilde{\epsilon}_T$$

for $t \geq 0$, the empirical mean is such that

$$\frac{1}{T^{d-1/2}} \bar{y}_T \approx \int_0^1 y_\infty(r) dr.$$

We have then

$$\log |\bar{y}_T| \approx (d - 1/2) \log T + \log \left| \int_0^1 y_\infty(r) dr \right|.$$

Since the second term on the right-hand side is negligible with respect to the first, we can immediately propose as consistent estimator

$$\hat{d}_T^{(1)} = \frac{\log |\bar{y}_T|}{\log T} + \frac{1}{2}.$$

Since

$$\hat{d}_T^{(1)} - d \approx \frac{\log | \int_0^1 y_\infty dr |}{\log T},$$

we know the limit distribution of this estimator, and the rate of convergence $(1/\log T)$ which is fairly slow.

14.6.2 Estimation Based on the Periodogram

A fractional process admits as its pseudo-spectrum the expression

$$f(\omega) = \frac{\sigma^2}{2\pi} \frac{|\Theta(exp(i\omega))|^2}{|1 - exp(i\omega)|^{2d} |\Phi(exp(i\omega))|^2}.$$

At low frequencies, that is for ω tending toward 0, this pseudo-spectrum is equivalent to

$$f(\omega) \approx \frac{\sigma^2}{2\pi} \frac{\Theta(1)^2}{\Phi(1)^2} \frac{1}{\omega^{2d}}.$$

Thus the exponent d gives the rate of divergence of the pseudo-spectrum at the origin. Taking the logarithm we see that for ω small, we have approximately a linear relationship between the logarithm of the pseudo-spectrum and the logarithm of the frequency

$$\log f(\omega) \approx -2d \log(\omega) + constant.$$

The estimation of the parameter d by this approach consists of replacing the pseudo-spectrum with the periodogram $I_T(\omega)$ and then regressing $\log(I_T(\omega))$ on $\log(\omega)$ for some small values of ω.

Let us consider some values of the periodogram associated with frequencies tending to 0 such as $I\left(\frac{\omega}{T}\right)$. We know then that $J_T(\omega)$, linked to $I_T(\omega)$ by $I_T(\omega) = \frac{1}{2\pi T}|J_T(\omega)|^2$, verifies (cf. theorem 14.5)

$$\frac{1}{T^{d+1/2}} J_T\left(\frac{\omega}{T}\right) \approx \int_0^1 exp(i\omega r) y_\infty(r) dr,$$

$$\log J_T\left(\frac{\omega}{T}\right) \approx (d+1/2)\log T + \log\left(\int_0^1 exp(i\omega r) y_\infty(r) dr\right).$$

We have, then

$$\log\left(2\pi T I_T\left(\frac{\omega}{T}\right)\right) = \log J_T\left(\frac{\omega}{T}\right) + \log \bar{J}_T\left(\frac{\omega}{T}\right)$$

$$\approx (2d+1)\log T + 2\log\left|\int_0^1 exp(i\omega) y_\infty(r) dr\right|$$

$$= (2d+1)\log T + m(\omega, d) + u(\omega, d),$$

with $E(u(\omega, d)) = 0$. The function

$$m(\omega, d) = 2E\left(\log\left|\int_0^1 exp(i\omega) y_\infty(r) dr\right|\right)$$

might be computed by using the expression for $y_\infty(r)$, allowing us to derive a consistent estimator of d, $\hat{d}^{(2)}$ by minimizing

$$\sum_{j=1}^J \left(\log\left(2\pi I_T\left(\frac{\omega_j}{T}\right)\right) - (2d+1)\log T - m(\omega_j, d)\right)^2.$$

14.6.3 Analysis of the Variance–covariance Matrix

In the Box and Jenkins approach, the empirical variance–covariance matrix of the observations is usually computed. The question is whether such a matrix can help in identifying the order d of integration. To simplify matters, let us consider the case $d = 1$. Let the process be defined as

$$y_t = (1-L)^{-1} \nu_t,$$

with $\nu_t = \Phi(L)^{-1}\Theta(L)\epsilon_t$. Let us pose $\gamma(h) = \text{cov}(\nu_t, \nu_{t-h})$. We know that

$$\frac{1}{T^2}\sum_{t=1}^{T} y_t^2 \xrightarrow{\text{d}} \omega^2 \int_0^1 B(r)^2 dr.$$

In the appendix it is shown that

$$\frac{1}{T}\sum_{t=1}^{T} y_t(y_t - y_{t-h}) \xrightarrow{\text{d}} \frac{h}{2}\left(\omega^2 B(1)^2 + \gamma(0)\right) + \sum_{j=1}^{h}(h-j)\gamma(j).$$

Thus the various coefficients of the covariance matrix

$$\hat{\mathbf{\Gamma}}_T(H) = \begin{pmatrix} \frac{1}{T}\sum_{t=1}^{T} y_t^2 & \cdots & \frac{1}{T}\sum_{t=1}^{T} y_t y_{t-H} \\ \vdots & \ddots & \vdots \\ \frac{1}{T}\sum_{t=1}^{T} y_t y_{t-H} & \cdots & \frac{1}{T}\sum_{t=1}^{T} y_{t-H}^2 \end{pmatrix},$$

are of order T. Normalizing the coefficient differently, we can compute

$$\frac{1}{T}\hat{\mathbf{\Gamma}}_T(H) = \begin{pmatrix} \frac{1}{T^2}\sum_{t=1}^{T} y_t^2 & \cdots & \frac{1}{T^2}\sum_{t=1}^{T} y_t y_{t-H} \\ \vdots & \ddots & \vdots \\ \frac{1}{T^2}\sum_{t=1}^{T} y_t y_{t-H} & \cdots & \frac{1}{T^2}\sum_{t=1}^{T} y_{t-H}^2 \end{pmatrix}.$$

This matrix admits as a limit

$$\omega^2 \int_0^1 B(r)^2 dr \begin{pmatrix} 1 & \cdots & 1 \\ \vdots & \ddots & \vdots \\ 1 & \cdots & 1 \end{pmatrix}.$$

At this stage we have simply used the same approach as the one based on the empirical mean in order to obtain a limit. However, since we have here various statistics, i.e., elements of the matrix, we can exploit the particular structure of the limiting matrix.

Theorem 14.14: *In the case $d = 1$ the matrix $\frac{1}{T}\hat{\mathbf{\Gamma}}_T(H)$ admits H eigenvalues $\lambda_{H,T} \leq \ldots \leq \lambda_{1,T}$ such that $\lambda_{2,T}, \ldots, \lambda_{H,T}$ tend to 0 and $\lambda_{1,T}$ tends in distribution to a nondegenerate random variable.*

In the general case of an ARIMA(p, d, q) with d integer, $d \geq 1$, we could follow the same approach. We get theorem 14.15.

Theorem 14.15: *If $d \geq 1$, the matrix $\frac{1}{T}\hat{\mathbf{\Gamma}}(H)$ admits H eigenvalues $\lambda_{H,T} \leq \ldots \leq \lambda_{1,T}$ such that $\lambda_{d+1,T}, \ldots, \lambda_{H,T}$ tend to 0 and $\lambda_{d,T}$ tends in distribution to a nondegenerate random variable, and the others diverge.*

Thus it seems possible to determine d by using a descriptive approach similar to the correlogram, which would consist in plotting on a diagram the eigenvalues $\lambda_{1,T}, \dots, \lambda_{H,T}$ and to detecting which is the index from which these eigenvalues can be considered equal to 0.

14.7 Appendix
Asymptotic Approximation of Cross Moments

Let us denote by y_t the fractional process $(1-L)^{-d}\Phi(L)^{-1}\Theta(L)\tilde{\epsilon}_t$ of order d and by

$$y_\infty(r) = \frac{\sigma\Theta(1)}{\Phi(1)\Gamma(d)}\int_0^r (r-s)^{d-1}dB(s)$$

the limit in distribution of the associated transformed process

$$\tilde{y}_T(r) = \frac{1}{T^{d-1/2}}y_{[Tr]}.$$

Behavior of $\sum_{t=1}^T y_t(y_t - y_{t-1})$ Let us write

$$\sum_{t=1}^T y_t(y_t - y_{t-1}) = \sum_{t=1}^T y_t^2 - \sum_{t=1}^T y_t y_{t-1}$$

$$= \sum_{t=1}^T y_t^2 + \frac{1}{2}\left(\sum_{t=1}^T (y_t - y_{t-1})^2 - \sum_{t=1}^T y_t^2 - \sum_{t=1}^T y_{t-1}^2\right)$$

$$= \frac{1}{2}\sum_{t=1}^T (y_t - y_{t-1})^2 + \frac{1}{2}\left(\sum_{t=1}^T y_t^2 - \sum_{t=1}^T y_{t-1}^2\right)$$

$$= \frac{1}{2}\sum_{t=1}^T (y_t - y_{t-1})^2 + \frac{1}{2}\left(y_T^2 - y_0^2\right).$$

Thus the cross moment can be expressed as a function of the two values of the process y_T^2 and y_0^2 and of the second moment of the differenced process.

We know that

$$\frac{1}{T^{2d-1}}y_T^2 \xrightarrow{\text{d}} y_\infty^2(1).$$

On the other hand, if the differenced series $(y_t - y_{t-1})$ is stationary, that is if

$$\frac{1}{2} < d < \frac{3}{2},$$

we have

$$\frac{1}{T}\sum_{t=1}^T (y_t - y_{t-1})^2 \xrightarrow{\text{d}} \text{var}(y_t - y_{t-1}).$$

If it is nonstationary, we know that $\sum_{t=1}^{T}(y_t - y_{t-1})^2$ is of order T^{2d-2} smaller than that of y_T^2. Putting these results together, we can distinguish among three cases:

(i) If $d > 1$

$$\frac{1}{T^{2d-1}} \sum_{t=1}^{T} y_t(y_t - y_{t-1}) \overset{d}{\to} \frac{1}{2} y_\infty^2(1).$$

(ii) If $d = 1$

$$\frac{1}{T} \sum_{t=1}^{T} y_t(y_t - y_{t-1}) \overset{d}{\to} \frac{1}{2} y_\infty^2(1) + \text{var}\,(y_t - y_{t-1}).$$

(iii) If $d < 1$

$$\frac{1}{T} \sum_{t=1}^{T} y_t(y_t - y_{t-1}) \overset{d}{\to} \frac{1}{2}\text{var}\,(y_t - y_{t-1}).$$

Behavior of $\frac{1}{T^d}\sum_{t=1}^{T} y_t \eta_t$ when y and η are independent and η is a white noise We have

$$\frac{1}{T^d} \sum_{t=1}^{T} y_t \eta_t$$

$$= \frac{1}{T^{d-1/2}} y_{[Tt/T]} \sigma_\eta \left(\tilde{W}_T(\frac{t}{T}) - \tilde{W}_T(\frac{t-1}{T}) \right),$$

with $\tilde{W}_T(r) = \frac{1}{\sigma_\eta \sqrt{T}} \sum_{t=1}^{[Tr]} \eta_t$.

$$\frac{1}{T^d} \sum_{t=1}^{T} y_t \eta_t \approx \sum_{t=1}^{T} y_\infty \left(\frac{t}{T} \right) \sigma_\eta \left(W(\frac{t}{T}) - W(\frac{t-1}{T}) \right)$$

$$\approx \sigma_\eta \int_0^1 y_\infty(r) dW(r),$$

since, in this special case, $y_\infty(t/T)$ can be replaced by $y_\infty((t-1)/T)$ in the sum over t, giving a Stieltjes interpretation of the Ito integral.

Behavior of $\sum_{t=1}^{T} y_t(y_t - y_{t-h})$ when $d = 1$ Let us reason by induction. We have

$$\frac{1}{T} \sum_{t=1}^{T} y_t(y_t - y_{t-h-1}) = \frac{1}{T} \sum_{t=1}^{T} y_t(y_t - y_{t-h}) + \frac{1}{T} \sum_{t=1}^{T} y_t \nu_{t-h}.$$

By the same token, noting that

$$y_t = y_{t-h-1} + \nu_{t-h} + \nu_{t-h+1} + \ldots + \nu_t$$

we have

$$\frac{1}{T}\sum_{t=1}^{T} y_t \nu_{t-h} = \frac{1}{T}\sum_{t=1}^{T} y_{t-h-1}\nu_{t-h} + \sum_{j=0}^{h}\frac{1}{T}\sum_{t=1}^{T}\nu_{t-j}\nu_{t-h}$$

$$= \frac{1}{T}\sum_{t=1}^{T} y_{t-h-1}(y_{t-h} - y_{t-h-1}) + \sum_{j=0}^{h}\frac{1}{T}\sum_{t=1}^{T}\nu_{t-j}\nu_{t-h}$$

$$= \frac{1}{T}\sum_{t=1}^{T} y_{t-h}(y_{t-h} - y_{t-h-1}) - \frac{1}{T}\sum_{t=1}^{T}(y_{t-h} - y_{t-h-1})^2$$

$$+ \sum_{j=0}^{h}\frac{1}{T}\sum_{t=1}^{T}\nu_{t-j}, \nu_{t-h}$$

$$\approx \left(\frac{1}{2}y_\infty^2(1) - \frac{1}{2}\mathrm{var}\,(\nu_t)\right) + \sum_{j=0}^{h}\mathrm{cov}\,(\nu_{t-j}, \nu_{t-h})$$

$$= \frac{1}{2}y_\infty^2(1) - \frac{1}{2}\gamma(0) + \sum_{j=0}^{h}\gamma(j)$$

$$= \frac{1}{2}y_\infty^2(1) + \frac{1}{2}\gamma(0) + \sum_{j=1}^{h}\gamma(j).$$

Noting that $y_\infty^2(1) = \omega^2 B^2(1)$ we have then by induction

$$\frac{1}{T}\sum_{t=1}^{T} y_t(y_t - y_{t-h}) \xrightarrow{\mathrm{d}} \frac{h}{2}\left(\omega^2 B^2(1) + \gamma(0)\right) + \sum_{j=1}^{h}(h-j)\gamma(j).$$

14.8 Exercises

Exercise 14.1: Let us consider a nonstationary series $\mathbf{y}_t$ integrated of order 1

$$(1 - L)\mathbf{y}_t = \mathbf{H}(L)\tilde{\boldsymbol{\varepsilon}}_t.$$

Let also

$$\mathbf{M}_T = \frac{1}{T^2} \sum_{i=1}^{T} \mathbf{y}_t \mathbf{y}_t'.$$

Let us assume that the series is cointegrated, that the subspace of the cointegrating vectors is of order 1, and that it is spanned by a vector of the form $(-1, \alpha_2, \ldots, \alpha_n)' = \boldsymbol{\alpha}$.

Let us define the solution $\tilde{\boldsymbol{\alpha}}_T$ of the problem

$$\min_{\alpha_2, \ldots, \alpha_n} (-1, \alpha_2, \ldots, \alpha_n)' \mathbf{M}_T \begin{pmatrix} -1 \\ \alpha_2 \\ \vdots \\ \alpha_n \end{pmatrix}.$$

(i)   Show that this problem is equivalent to performing ordinary least squares on the static model

$$y_{1t} = \alpha_2 y_{2t} + \ldots + \alpha_n y_{nt} + u_t.$$

(ii) Verify that the estimator $\tilde{\boldsymbol{\alpha}}_T$ is a consistent estimator of the cointegrating vector, in which the first component is equal to -1.

(iii) Using the result of section 14.5, discuss its asymptotic distribution.

Exercise 14.2: Let us assume now that the series defined in exercise 14.1 is cointegrated, that the subspace of the cointegrating vectors is of order r and that it is spanned by vectors of the form

$$(1, 0, \ldots, 0, \alpha_{r+1}^1, \ldots, \alpha_n^1)',$$

$$(0, 1, \ldots, 0, \alpha_{r+1}^2, \ldots, \alpha_n^2)',$$

$$\ldots$$

$$(0, 0, \ldots, 1, \alpha_{r+1}^r, \ldots, \alpha_n^r)'.$$

Let $\mathbf{A}$ be an $r \times n$ matrix

$$\mathbf{A} = \left(\mathbf{I}, \tilde{\mathbf{A}} \right).$$

Let us define the solution $\mathbf{A}_T$ of the problem

$$\min_{A} \operatorname{tr} \left(\mathbf{A} \mathbf{M}_T \mathbf{A}' \right).$$

Verify that the rows of $\mathbf{A}_T$ converge to cointegrating vectors.

570

Exercise 14.3: Verify that the error correction system (cf. theorem 11.7)

$$\mathbf{D\alpha'y}_{t-1} + \tilde{\tilde{\boldsymbol{\Phi}}}(L)\Delta\mathbf{y}_t = \tilde{\boldsymbol{\varepsilon}}_t,$$

with $\tilde{\tilde{\boldsymbol{\Phi}}}(0) = \mathbf{I}$ can also be written as

$$\Delta\mathbf{y}_t = \Gamma_1\Delta\mathbf{y}_{t-1} + \ldots + \Gamma_{p-1}\mathbf{y}_{t-p+1} - \mathbf{D\alpha'y}_{t-p} + \tilde{\boldsymbol{\varepsilon}}_t,$$

and express the matrices $\Gamma_1, \ldots, \Gamma_{p-1}$ as a function of the coefficients of the autoregressive operator $\tilde{\tilde{\boldsymbol{\Phi}}}(L)$.

Exercise 14.4: Let us consider the regression model (14.15) and the ordinary least squares estimator $\hat{a}_{1T}$ of a_1. Show that the estimator $\hat{a}_{1T}$ is equal to

$$\hat{a}_{1T} = \frac{\sum_{t=1}^T x_t y_t - \sum_{t=1}^T x_t\Delta x_t \left(\sum_{t=1}^T (\Delta x_t)^2\right)^{-1}\sum_{t=1}^T \Delta x_t y_t}{\sum_{t=1}^T x_t^2 - \left(\sum_{t=1}^T x_t\Delta x_t\right)^2 \left(\sum_{t=1}^T (\Delta x_t)^2\right)^{-1}}.$$

Show that:

(i) If $\frac{1}{2} < d < \frac{3}{2}$

$$\hat{a}_{1T} \approx a_1 + \frac{1}{T^d}\frac{\sigma_\eta \int_0^1 x_\infty(r)dW(r)}{\int_0^1 x_\infty^2(r)dr}.$$

(ii) If $d > \frac{3}{2}$

$$\hat{a}_{1T} \approx a_1$$

$$+ \frac{1}{T^d}\sigma_\eta \frac{\int_0^1 x_\infty(r)dW(r)\int_0^1 \Delta x_\infty^2(r)dr}{\int_0^1 x_\infty^2(r)dr\int_0^1 \Delta x_\infty^2(r)dr - \left(\int_0^1 x_\infty(r)\Delta x_\infty(r)dr\right)^2}$$

$$- \frac{1}{T^d}\sigma_\eta \frac{\int_0^1 \Delta x_\infty(r)dW(r)\int_0^1 x_\infty(r)\Delta x_\infty(r)dr}{\int_0^1 x_\infty^2(r)dr\int_0^1 \Delta x_\infty^2(r)dr - \left(\int_0^1 x_\infty(r)\Delta x_\infty(r)dr\right)^2}.$$

Exercise 14.5: Let us consider again the regression model (14.15) and the ordinary least squares estimator $\hat{a}_{2T}$ of a_2. Show that the estimator $\hat{a}_{2T}$ is always consistent. Show that:

(i) If $\frac{1}{2} < d < \frac{3}{2}$

$$\sqrt{T}(\hat{a}_{2T} - a_2) \xrightarrow{d} \mathcal{N}\left(0, \sigma_\eta^2/\mathrm{var}\left(X_t - X_{t-1}\right)\right).$$

(ii) If $d > \frac{3}{2}$

$$T^{d-1}(\hat{a}_{2T} - a_2)$$

$$\xrightarrow{\text{d}} \sigma_\eta^2 \frac{\int_0^1 \Delta x_\infty(r)dW(r) \int_0^1 x_\infty^2(r)dr}{\int_0^1 x_\infty^2(r)dr \int_0^1 \Delta x_\infty^2(r)dr - \left(\int_0^1 x_\infty(r)\Delta x_\infty(r)dr\right)^2}$$

$$- \sigma_\eta^2 \frac{\int_0^1 x_\infty(r)dW(r) \int_0^1 x_\infty(r)\Delta x_\infty(r)dr}{\int_0^1 x_\infty^2(r)dr \int_0^1 \Delta x_\infty^2(r)dr - \left(\int_0^1 x_\infty(r)\Delta x_\infty(r)dr\right)^2}.$$

IV
State-space Models

15

State-space Models and the Kalman Filter

15.1 State-space Models

In chapter 8, we have seen that some multivariate processes $\{y_t, t \geq 0\}$ have a state-space representation, that is, verify equation systems of the type

$$\mathbf{z}_{t+1} = \mathbf{A}\mathbf{z}_t + \mathbf{B}\mathbf{u}_t,$$

$$\mathbf{y}_t = \mathbf{C}\mathbf{z}_t + \mathbf{D}\mathbf{u}_t, \qquad t \geq 0, \tag{15.1}$$

where $\{u_t\}$ is a white noise, $\mathbf{z}_t$ a random vector called a *state vector* and $\mathbf{A}$, $\mathbf{B}$, $\mathbf{C}$, $\mathbf{D}$ are nonrandom matrices.

In this chapter we will generalize this type of representation and will analyze state-space models.

Definition 15.1: *A* state-space model *is defined by the equation system*

$$(a) \quad \mathbf{z}_{t+1} = \mathbf{A}_t\mathbf{z}_t + \boldsymbol{\varepsilon}_t,$$

$$(b) \quad \mathbf{y}_t = \mathbf{C}_t\mathbf{z}_t + \boldsymbol{\eta}_t, \quad t \geq 0,$$

where $\left\{ \begin{pmatrix} \boldsymbol{\varepsilon}_t \\ \boldsymbol{\eta}_t \end{pmatrix} \right\}, t \geq 0$ *is a Gaussian white noise, the* $\mathbf{A}_t$'s *(resp.* $\mathbf{C}_t$'s) *are nonrandom matrices of order* $(K \times K)$ *(resp.* $(n \times K)$*), and* $\mathbf{z}_0$ *is a random vector distributed* $\mathcal{N}(m, P)$, *independent of* $\begin{pmatrix} \boldsymbol{\varepsilon}_t \\ \boldsymbol{\eta}_t \end{pmatrix}$, $t \geq 0$.

The equation system in the definition is more general than the system (15.1), as long as the matrices $\mathbf{A}_t$ and $\mathbf{C}_t$ may depend on time. On the other hand, we have imposed normality on the noise $\begin{pmatrix} \boldsymbol{\varepsilon}_t \\ \boldsymbol{\eta}_t \end{pmatrix}$ and the initial state z_0. Nevertheless, note that this assumption can be weakened and replaced by an existence condition of the second-order moments, as long as the conditional expectation is replaced by the affine regression.

The variance–covariance matrix of $\begin{pmatrix} \boldsymbol{\varepsilon}_t \\ \boldsymbol{\eta}_t \end{pmatrix}$ is written as

$$\boldsymbol{\Omega} = \begin{pmatrix} \mathbf{Q} & \mathbf{S} \\ \mathbf{S}' & \mathbf{R} \end{pmatrix}. \tag{15.2}$$

To simplify matters, this matrix is assumed to be independent of time; nevertheless the following results can easily be generalized in the case where $\boldsymbol{\Omega}$ is time-dependent. The partition of $\boldsymbol{\Omega}$ was conformable to $\begin{pmatrix} \boldsymbol{\varepsilon}_t \\ \boldsymbol{\eta}_t \end{pmatrix}$ so that $\mathbf{Q} = \mathrm{var}\,(\boldsymbol{\varepsilon}_t), \mathbf{R} = \mathrm{var}\,(\boldsymbol{\eta}_t)$ and $\mathbf{S} = \mathrm{cov}\,(\boldsymbol{\varepsilon}_t, \boldsymbol{\eta}_t)$. In order to introduce some terminology, the random vector $\mathbf{z}_t$, of size K, is called *the state* (of the system) at time t; generally, it is partially or completely unobservable.

The random vector $\mathbf{y}_t$, of size n, is the vector of *observations*, of *measurements*, or of *outputs* (of the system) at time t and it is observable.

The random vector $\boldsymbol{\varepsilon}_t$, of size K, is the vector of *innovations*, or of *perturbations*, or of *inputs* at time t; it is not observable.

The random vector $\boldsymbol{\eta}_t$, of size n, is the *measurement error* or *noise* vector at time t; it is not observable.

The matrices $\mathbf{A}_t$ and $\mathbf{C}_t$ are respectively the *transition* and *measurement* matrices, at time t. The vector $\mathbf{C}_t \mathbf{z}_t$ is called the *signal* at time t.

Finally, the equations in (15.1) are called *state*, respectively, *measurement* equations.

The assumptions in the definition provide the distribution of the process $\left\{ \begin{pmatrix} \mathbf{z}_t \\ \mathbf{y}_t \end{pmatrix}, t \geq 0 \right\}$; in particular note that this process is Gaussian.

Then the normality of the process $\left\{ \begin{pmatrix} \mathbf{z}_t \\ \mathbf{y}_t \end{pmatrix}, t \geq 0 \right\}$ allows one to compute the various conditional expectations by theoretical linear regression. In the following sections we will be interested in recursive derivations of conditional expectations.

First of all, we can look for the best approximation to the state $\mathbf{z}_t$ of the system at time t, knowing the present and past observations $\mathbf{y}_0, \mathbf{y}_1, \ldots, \mathbf{y}_t$. This approximation is given by $E(\mathbf{z}_t \mid \mathbf{y}_0, \ldots, \mathbf{y}_t)$ and the corresponding problem is called the *filtering problem*.

Of course this approximation can be improved if we consider more observations. This brings us to introduce the optimal approximation of

$\mathbf{z}_t$ given $\mathbf{y}_0, \ldots, \mathbf{y}_s$, where s is an index greater than t. It is given by $E(\mathbf{z}_0 \mid \mathbf{y}_0, \ldots, \mathbf{y}_s), s > t$. The problem is called the *smoothing problem*.

In the same way we can look at the forecasts of future variables. It is the same as computing $E(\mathbf{z}_t \mid \mathbf{y}_0, \ldots, \mathbf{y}_s), E(\mathbf{y}_t \mid \mathbf{y}_0, \ldots, \mathbf{y}_s)$ for $s < t$ and the problems are called *forecast problems*.

15.2 Kalman Covariance Filter

We want to compute recursively

$$ {}_t\hat{\mathbf{z}}_t = E(\mathbf{z}_t \mid \mathbf{y}_0, \ldots, \mathbf{y}_t), \tag{15.3} $$

by means of an algorithm based on simple operations: this simplicity is reached by updating not only ${}_t\hat{\mathbf{z}}_t$ but also the variance–covariance matrices of some other quantities which are interpreted as forecasts or errors. These quantities are:

the mean square filtering error on $\mathbf{z}_t$ at time t

$$ {}_t\boldsymbol{\Sigma}_t = E\left((\mathbf{z}_t - {}_t\hat{\mathbf{z}}_t)(\mathbf{z}_t - {}_t\hat{\mathbf{z}}_t)'\right) = \text{var}\left(\mathbf{z}_t - {}_t\hat{\mathbf{z}}_t\right), \tag{15.4} $$

the forecast $\mathbf{z}_t$ at time $t-1$

$$ {}_{t-1}\hat{\mathbf{z}}_t = E\left(\mathbf{z}_t \mid \mathbf{y}_0, \ldots, \mathbf{y}_{t-1}\right), \tag{15.5} $$

the corresponding mean square forecast error

$$ {}_{t-1}\boldsymbol{\Sigma}_t = E\left((\mathbf{z}_t - {}_{t-1}\hat{\mathbf{z}}_t)(\mathbf{z}_t - {}_{t-1}\hat{\mathbf{z}}_t)'\right) = \text{var}\left(\mathbf{z}_t - {}_{t-1}\hat{\mathbf{z}}_t\right). \tag{15.6} $$

15.2.1 Definition of the Filter when $\mathbf{S} = \mathbf{0}$

Let us first assume that the innovation $\boldsymbol{\varepsilon}$ and the measurement error $\boldsymbol{\eta}$ are not correlated $\text{cov}\left(\boldsymbol{\varepsilon}_t, \boldsymbol{\eta}_t\right) = \mathbf{S} = \mathbf{0}$. The computation algorithm is given by the Kalman Covariance Filter.

Theorem 15.1: **Covariance Filter** *For $t \geq 0$ we have the following relationships*

$$ (a) \qquad {}_t\hat{\mathbf{z}}_t = {}_{t-1}\hat{\mathbf{z}}_t + \mathbf{K}_t\left(\mathbf{y}_t - \mathbf{C}_t {}_{t-1}\hat{\mathbf{z}}_t\right) $$

with $\mathbf{K}_t = {}_{t-1}\boldsymbol{\Sigma}_t\mathbf{C}_t'\left(\mathbf{C}_t {}_{t-1}\boldsymbol{\Sigma}_t\mathbf{C}_t' + \mathbf{R}\right)^{-1}$;

$$ (a') \qquad {}_t\boldsymbol{\Sigma}_t = \left(\mathbf{I} - \mathbf{K}_t\mathbf{C}_t\right) {}_{t-1}\boldsymbol{\Sigma}_t; $$

$$ (b) \qquad {}_t\hat{\mathbf{z}}_{t+1} = \mathbf{A}_t {}_t\hat{\mathbf{z}}_t; $$

$$ (b') \qquad {}_t\boldsymbol{\Sigma}_{t+1} = \mathbf{A}_t {}_t\boldsymbol{\Sigma}_t\mathbf{A}_t' + \mathbf{Q}. $$

The matrix $\mathbf{K}_t$ is called the filter gain at time t.

PROOF: Let us introduce the forecast error at horizon 1 on $\mathbf{y}_t$

$$\tilde{\mathbf{y}}_t = \mathbf{y}_t - {}_{t-1}\hat{\mathbf{y}}_t = \mathbf{y}_t - E(\mathbf{y}_t \mid \mathbf{y}_0, \ldots, \mathbf{y}_{t-1}) = \mathbf{y}_t - C_{t\ t-1}\hat{\mathbf{z}}_t$$
$$= C_t(\mathbf{z}_t - {}_{t-1}\hat{\mathbf{z}}_t) + \boldsymbol{\eta}_t.$$

Formula (a) We have

$${}_t\hat{\mathbf{z}}_t = E(\mathbf{z}_t \mid \mathbf{y}_0, \ldots, \mathbf{y}_t)$$
$$= E(\mathbf{z}_t \mid \mathbf{y}_0, \ldots, \mathbf{y}_{t-1}, \tilde{\mathbf{y}}_t)$$
$$= E(\mathbf{z}_t \mid \mathbf{y}_0, \ldots, \mathbf{y}_{t-1}) + E(\mathbf{z}_t \mid \tilde{\mathbf{y}}_t) - E(\mathbf{z}_t),$$

since $\tilde{\mathbf{y}}_t$ is not correlated with $\mathbf{y}_0, \ldots, \mathbf{y}_{t-1}$.

Moreover the forecast $E(\mathbf{z}_t \mid \tilde{\mathbf{y}}_t)$ can be written as

$$E(\mathbf{z}_t \mid \tilde{\mathbf{y}}_t) - E(\mathbf{z}_t) = \text{cov}(\mathbf{z}_t, \tilde{\mathbf{y}}_t)\text{var}(\tilde{\mathbf{y}}_t)^{-1}\tilde{\mathbf{y}}_t$$
$$= \text{cov}(\mathbf{z}_t, C_t(\mathbf{z}_t - {}_{t-1}\hat{\mathbf{z}}_t) + \boldsymbol{\eta}_t)$$
$$Var[C_t(\mathbf{z}_t - {}_{t-1}\hat{\mathbf{z}}_t) + \boldsymbol{\eta}_t]^{-1}(\mathbf{y}_t - C_{t\ t-1}\hat{\mathbf{z}}_t)$$
$$= {}_{t-1}\Sigma_t C_t' \left(C_{t\ t-1}\Sigma_t C_t' + R\right)^{-1}\left(\mathbf{y}_t - C_{t\ t-1}\hat{\mathbf{z}}_t\right)$$
$$= \mathbf{K}_t \left(\mathbf{y}_t - C_{t\ t-1}\hat{\mathbf{z}}_t\right).$$

By substituting in the expression of ${}_t\hat{\mathbf{z}}_t$, we get *formula (a)*

$${}_t\hat{\mathbf{z}}_t = {}_{t-1}\hat{\mathbf{z}}_t + \mathbf{K}_t\left(\mathbf{y}_t - C_{t\ t-1}\hat{\mathbf{z}}_t\right).$$

Formula (a') The corresponding error is

$$\mathbf{z}_t - {}_t\hat{\mathbf{z}}_t = \mathbf{z}_t - {}_{t-1}\hat{\mathbf{z}}_t - \mathbf{K}_t\tilde{\mathbf{y}}_t.$$

Since $\mathbf{z}_t - {}_t\hat{\mathbf{z}}_t$ is not correlated with $\mathbf{y}_0, \mathbf{y}_1, \ldots, \mathbf{y}_t$, it is not correlated with $\tilde{\mathbf{y}}_t$. Then

$${}_t\Sigma_t = \text{var}(\mathbf{z}_t - {}_t\hat{\mathbf{z}}_t)$$
$$= \text{var}(\mathbf{z}_t - {}_{t-1}\hat{\mathbf{z}}_t) - \text{var}(\mathbf{K}_t\tilde{\mathbf{y}}_t)$$
$$= {}_{t-1}\Sigma_t - \mathbf{K}_t\text{var}(\tilde{\mathbf{y}}_t)\mathbf{K}_t'$$
$$= {}_{t-1}\Sigma_t - \mathbf{K}_t\left(C_{t\ t-1}\Sigma_t C_t' + R\right)\mathbf{K}_t'$$
$$= {}_{t-1}\Sigma_t - {}_{t-1}\Sigma_t C_t'\left(C_{t\ t-1}\Sigma_t C_t' + R\right)^{-1}C_{t\ t-1}\Sigma_t$$
$$= (\mathbf{I} - \mathbf{K}_t C_t){}_{t-1}\Sigma_t.$$

Formula (b) We have $\mathbf{z}_{t+1} = \mathbf{A}_t\mathbf{z}_t + \boldsymbol{\varepsilon}_t$.

Computing the conditional expectation for each element with respect to $\mathbf{y}_0, \ldots, \mathbf{y}_t$ and using the fact that the innovation and the measurement errors are uncorrelated, we get

$${}_t\hat{\mathbf{z}}_{t+1} = \mathbf{A}_t\ {}_t\hat{\mathbf{z}}_t.$$

Formula (b') The corresponding error is

$$\mathbf{z}_{t+1} - {}_t\hat{\mathbf{z}}_{t+1} = \mathbf{A}_t(\mathbf{z}_t - {}_t\hat{\mathbf{z}}_t) + \boldsymbol{\varepsilon}_t.$$

We can derive

$$
{}_t\boldsymbol{\Sigma}_{t+1} = \mathrm{var}\left(\mathbf{z}_{t+1} - {}_t\hat{\mathbf{z}}_{t+1}\right) = \mathrm{var}\left(\mathbf{A}_t\left(\mathbf{z}_t - {}_t\hat{\mathbf{z}}_t\right) + \boldsymbol{\varepsilon}_t\right)
$$
$$
= \mathbf{A}_t\, {}_t\boldsymbol{\Sigma}_t\mathbf{A}_t' + \mathbf{Q}.
$$

$\square$

The equations (a) and (a') are called the *measurement updating equations*. They allow one to modify the approximation of $\mathbf{z}_t$ and the corresponding precision for any new observation $\mathbf{y}_t$.

The equations (b) and (b') are called *time updating equations*: they explain how to compute the forecast of $\mathbf{z}_{t+1}$ from the filtering of $\mathbf{z}_t$ and provide the associated modifications to the variance–covariance matrices of the errors.

We can notice that the formulae (a') and (b') relative to the variance–covariance matrices ${}_t\boldsymbol{\Sigma}_t$, ${}_t\boldsymbol{\Sigma}_{t+1}$ do not use the observations $\mathbf{y}_0 \ldots \mathbf{y}_t \ldots$. Therefore they can be used independently of the two other formulae (a) and (b) and before having access to the observations (or *off line*).

Some formulae for the computation of forecasts at horizon 1 can be derived from the covariance filter.

Corollary: *Let us write*

$$_{t-1}\hat{\mathbf{y}}_t = E(\mathbf{y}_t \mid \mathbf{y}_0, \ldots, \mathbf{y}_{t-1})$$

and

$$_{t-1}\mathbf{M}_t = \mathrm{var}\left(\mathbf{y}_t - {}_{t-1}\hat{\mathbf{y}}_t\right).$$

We get

$$(c) \qquad {}_t\hat{\mathbf{y}}_{t+1} = \mathbf{C}_{t+1}\, {}_t\hat{\mathbf{z}}_{t+1};$$
$$(c') \qquad {}_t\mathbf{M}_{t+1} = \mathbf{C}_{t+1}\, {}_t\boldsymbol{\Sigma}_{t+1}\mathbf{C}_{t+1}' + \mathbf{R}. \qquad (15.7)$$

PROOF:

(i) From the measurement equation $\mathbf{y}_{t+1} = \mathbf{C}_{t+1}\mathbf{z}_{t+1} + \boldsymbol{\eta}_{t+1}$, taking the forecast of each element given $\mathbf{y}_0 \ldots \mathbf{y}_t$, we derive

$$_t\hat{\mathbf{y}}_{t+1} = \mathbf{C}_{t+1}\, {}_t\hat{\mathbf{z}}_{t+1}$$

which is formula (c).

(ii) The associated forecast error is

$$\mathbf{y}_{t+1} - {}_t\hat{\mathbf{y}}_{t+1} = \mathbf{C}_{t+1}(\mathbf{z}_{t+1} - {}_t\hat{\mathbf{z}}_{t+1}) + \boldsymbol{\eta}_{t+1}.$$

Taking the variance of each element, we get the formula (c')

$$_tM_{t+1} = \mathbf{C}_{t+1}\,_t\mathbf{\Sigma}_{t+1}\mathbf{C}'_{t+1} + \mathbf{R}.$$

□

Example 15.1: As an example, let us consider a regression model having one independent variable

$$y_t = x_t b + \eta_t, t \geq 0.$$

This model can also be written as

$$b_{t+1} = b_t, \quad y_t = x_t b_t + \eta_t, \qquad t \geq 0.$$

It has thus a state-space form with $n = K = 1, \mathbf{C}_t = x_t, \mathbf{A}_t = 1, \mathbf{Q} = 0, \mathbf{z}_t = b_t$.

The recursive formulae for the variances give

$$_t\mathbf{\Sigma}_t = (\mathbf{I} - \mathbf{K}_t\mathbf{C}_t)\,_{t-1}\mathbf{\Sigma}_t, \text{ with } \mathbf{K}_t = \,_{t-1}\mathbf{\Sigma}_t\mathbf{C}'_t(\mathbf{C}_t\,_{t-1}\mathbf{\Sigma}_t\mathbf{C}'_t + \mathbf{R})^{-1}$$

$$_t\mathbf{\Sigma}_{t+1} = \,_t\mathbf{\Sigma}_t.$$

Taking into account the last equality and the univariate nature of $\mathbf{y}_t$ and of $\mathbf{C}_t = x_t$, we get

$$_t\mathbf{\Sigma}_t = \left(1 - \frac{_{t-1}\mathbf{\Sigma}_{t-1}x_t^2}{x_t^2\,_{t-1}\mathbf{\Sigma}_{t-1} + R}\right)\,_{t-1}\mathbf{\Sigma}_{t-1},$$

$$\Leftrightarrow\,_t\mathbf{\Sigma}_t = \frac{R\,_{t-1}\mathbf{\Sigma}_{t-1}}{x_t^2\,_{t-1}\mathbf{\Sigma}_{t-1} + R},$$

$$\Leftrightarrow\frac{1}{_t\mathbf{\Sigma}_t} = \frac{x_t^2}{R} + \frac{1}{_{t-1}\mathbf{\Sigma}_{t-1}},$$

$$_t\mathbf{\Sigma}_t = \left(\frac{1}{R}\sum_{\tau=0}^{t}x_\tau^2 + \frac{1}{_{-1}\mathbf{\Sigma}_{-1}}\right)^{-1}.$$

On the other hand, $_t\hat{\mathbf{z}}_t$ is the best linear forecast of the parameter b when the observations $y_0, \ldots, y_t$ are known and for a given a priori distribution of b_0. We know that when this distribution is a priori chosen "diffuse on $\mathbf{R}$", that is when $_{-1}\hat{\mathbf{\Sigma}}_0^{-1} = \mathbf{P}^{-1} = \mathbf{0}$, $_t\hat{\mathbf{z}}_t$ is equal to the OLS estimator of b (see exercise 15.6 and section 16.1.1). We have the same result for the mean square errors. When $_{-1}\mathbf{\Sigma}_{-1}^{-1} = \,_{-1}\mathbf{\Sigma}_0^{-1} = 0$, we get $_t\mathbf{\Sigma}_t = \text{var}(\eta_t)\left(\sum_{\tau=0}^{t}x_\tau^2\right)^{-1}$, which is the variance of the ordinary least square estimator of b. The Kalman filter is interpreted here as a recursive computation of the OLS estimator (for $_t\hat{\mathbf{z}}_t$) and of its precision (for $_t\mathbf{\Sigma}_t$).

On the other hand, the filter can be written in a simpler form if we update the inverse of the matrices $_t\Sigma_t$ rather than the matrices themselves; this idea will be exploited later on (see section 15.4).

15.2.2 The Stationary Case

A particular case of the state-space model is when the matrices $\mathbf{A}_t$ and $\mathbf{C}_t$ are time independent

$$\mathbf{z}_{t+1} = \mathbf{A}\mathbf{z}_t + \boldsymbol{\varepsilon}_t,$$

$$\mathbf{y}_t = \mathbf{C}\mathbf{z}_t + \boldsymbol{\eta}_t, \qquad t \geq 0.$$

Moreover, if the matrix $\mathbf{A}$ has all its eigenvalues strictly smaller than 1 in modulus, we know that the process $\{\mathbf{z}\}$ is asymptotically stationary, with a first-order autoregressive representation. The process $\{\mathbf{y}\}$ obtained as a linear combination of $(\mathbf{z}, \boldsymbol{\eta})$ with time independent coefficients, is also asymptotically stationary. Therefore for t large enough $(t \to \infty)$, we can approximate the mean square errors with the ones of the associated stationary processes. More precisely, if $(\mathbf{z}_t^\star, \mathbf{y}_t^\star)$ represents the stationary process which $(\mathbf{z}_t, \mathbf{y}_t)$ tends to, we have

$$_t\Sigma_t = \text{var}\left(\mathbf{z}_t - E(\mathbf{z}_t \mid \mathbf{y}_t \ldots \mathbf{y}_0)\right)$$

$$\approx \text{var}\left(\mathbf{z}_t^\star - E(\mathbf{z}_t^\star \mid \mathbf{y}_t^\star \ldots \mathbf{y}_0^\star)\right)$$

$$\approx \text{var}\left(\mathbf{z}_t^\star - E(\mathbf{z}_t^\star \mid \mathbf{y}_t^\star \ldots \mathbf{y}_0^\star, \mathbf{y}_{-1}^\star, \ldots)\right).$$

This last expression is independent of the index t. The various matrices $_t\Sigma_t$, $_t\Sigma_{t+1}$, $_t\mathbf{M}_{t+1}$ converge to the limits $\overline{\Sigma}^\star, \overline{\Sigma}, \overline{M}$ when t goes to infinity.

This convergence can be used in practice to simplify the Kalman algorithm. If T is large enough, we can replace the initial filter (cf. theorem 15.1) by the *limit filter*.

$$\text{a)} \quad _t\hat{\mathbf{z}}_t = {}_{t-1}\hat{\mathbf{z}}_t + \overline{\mathbf{K}}(\mathbf{y}_t - \mathbf{C}\,_{t-1}\hat{\mathbf{z}}_t),$$

$$\text{b)} \quad _t\hat{\mathbf{z}}_{t+1} = \mathbf{A}\,_t\hat{\mathbf{z}}_t, \tag{15.8}$$

where the *limit gain* is the limit of $\mathbf{K}_t$

$$\overline{\mathbf{K}} = \overline{\Sigma}\mathbf{C}' \left(\mathbf{C}\overline{\Sigma}\mathbf{C}' + \mathbf{R}\right)^{-1} \tag{15.9}$$

which can be used after the distance between $\mathbf{K}_t$ and its limit can be considered numerically small.

15.2.3 Initialization of the Filter

In order to apply the covariance filter of theorem 15.1, we need the initial values $_{-1}\hat{\mathbf{z}}_0$ and $_{-1}\Sigma_0$.

Intuitively, we can think that $_{-1}\hat{\mathbf{z}}_0$ is the best approximation of $\mathbf{z}_0$ when no information is given, i.e., $_{-1}\hat{\mathbf{z}}_0 = E\mathbf{z}_0 = \mathbf{m}$. We would have then $_{-1}\Sigma_0 = \text{var}(\mathbf{z}_0) = \mathbf{P}$. We can formally prove this result by computing $_0\hat{\mathbf{z}}_0$ and $_0\Sigma_0$ directly, and by verifying their equality with the values obtained from the formulae (a) and (a') using $_{-1}\hat{\mathbf{z}}_0 = \mathbf{m}$ and $_{-1}\Sigma_0 = \mathbf{P}$.

Theorem 15.2: *We have*

$$_0\hat{\mathbf{z}}_0 = \mathbf{m} + \mathbf{K}_0(\mathbf{y}_0 - \mathbf{C}_0\mathbf{m}), \text{ with } \quad \mathbf{K}_0 = \mathbf{P}\mathbf{C}_0'\left(\mathbf{C}_0\mathbf{P}\mathbf{C}_0' + \mathbf{R}\right)^{-1},$$

$$_0\Sigma_0 = (\mathbf{I} - \mathbf{K}_0\mathbf{C}_0)\,\mathbf{P}.$$

PROOF: The pair

$$\begin{pmatrix} \mathbf{z}_0 \\ \mathbf{y}_0 \end{pmatrix} = \begin{pmatrix} \mathbf{z}_0 \\ \mathbf{C}_0\mathbf{z}_0 + \boldsymbol{\eta}_0 \end{pmatrix}$$

is Gaussian with mean

$$\begin{pmatrix} \mathbf{m} \\ \mathbf{C}_0\mathbf{m} \end{pmatrix}$$

and variance–covariance matrix

$$\begin{pmatrix} \mathbf{P} & \mathbf{P}\mathbf{C}_0' \\ \mathbf{C}_0\mathbf{P} & \mathbf{C}_0\mathbf{P}\mathbf{C}_0' + \mathbf{R} \end{pmatrix}.$$

We have then

$$_0\hat{\mathbf{z}}_0 = E(\mathbf{z}_0 \mid \mathbf{y}_0) = E\mathbf{z}_0 + \text{cov}(\mathbf{z}_0, \mathbf{y}_0)(\text{var}\,\mathbf{y}_0)^{-1}(\mathbf{y}_0 - E\mathbf{y}_0),$$

$$_0\hat{\mathbf{z}}_0 = \mathbf{m} + \mathbf{K}_0(\mathbf{y}_0 - \mathbf{C}_0 m).$$

By the same token

$$_0\Sigma_0 = \text{var}\,(\mathbf{z}_0 - E(\mathbf{z}_0 \mid \mathbf{y}_0))$$

$$= \text{var}\,\mathbf{z}_0 - \text{cov}\,(\mathbf{z}_0, \mathbf{y}_0)(\text{var}\,\mathbf{y}_0)^{-1}\text{cov}\,(\mathbf{y}_0, \mathbf{z}_0)$$

$$= (\mathbf{I} - \mathbf{K}_0\mathbf{C}_0)\,\mathbf{P}.$$

Obviously, these results are only valid if the matrix $\mathbf{C}_0\mathbf{P}\mathbf{C}_0' + \mathbf{R}$ is non-singular. □

The mechanism of the filter for $t = 0, \ldots, T$ (theorem 15.1 and corollary) is summarized in figure 15.1.

15.2.4 Direct Updating of the Filters
(Respectively of the Forecasts)

The algorithmic formulae given in theorem 15.1 update simultaneously the filters $_t\hat{\mathbf{z}}_t$ and the forecasts $_t\hat{\mathbf{z}}_{t+1}$. If we are only interested in the

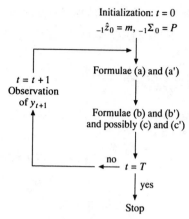

Figure 15.1 Flowchart for the Filter

filters (respectively in the forecasts), we can derive just the updating formulae which do not need the intermediate computations of the forecasts (respectively of the filters).

Filter Updating We have to eliminate

$$_t\hat{\mathbf{z}}_{t+1} \quad \text{and} \quad _t\boldsymbol{\Sigma}_{t+1}$$

in the equations of theorem 15.1. From formula (b') we have

$$_{t-1}\boldsymbol{\Sigma}_t = \mathbf{A}_{t-1}\,_{t-1}\boldsymbol{\Sigma}_{t-1}\mathbf{A}'_{t-1} + \mathbf{Q}.$$

Therefore the filter gain is

$$\begin{aligned}
\mathbf{K}_t &= \left(\mathbf{A}_{t-1}\,_{t-1}\boldsymbol{\Sigma}_{t-1}\mathbf{A}'_{t-1} + \mathbf{Q}\right)\mathbf{C}'_t \\
&\quad [\mathbf{C}_t(\mathbf{A}_{t-1}\,_{t-1}\boldsymbol{\Sigma}_{t-1}\mathbf{A}'_{t-1} + \mathbf{Q})\mathbf{C}'_t + \mathbf{R}]^{-1}.
\end{aligned} \tag{15.10}$$

The formulae (a) and (a') can be rewritten as

$$\begin{aligned}
_t\hat{\mathbf{z}}_t &= \mathbf{A}_{t-1}\,_{t-1}\hat{\mathbf{z}}_{t-1} + \mathbf{K}_t\left(\mathbf{y}_t - \mathbf{C}_t\mathbf{A}_{t-1}\,_{t-1}\hat{\mathbf{z}}_{t-1}\right), \\
_t\boldsymbol{\Sigma}_t &= (\mathbf{I} - \mathbf{K}_t\mathbf{C}_t)\left(\mathbf{A}_{t-1}\,_{t-1}\boldsymbol{\Sigma}_{t-1}\mathbf{A}'_{t-1} + \mathbf{Q}\right).
\end{aligned} \tag{15.11}$$

Forecast Updating In the same way we get a direct updating of the forecasts. It is given by

$$\begin{aligned}
_t\hat{\mathbf{z}}_{t+1} &= \mathbf{A}_t\,_{t-1}\hat{\mathbf{z}}_t + \mathbf{A}_t\mathbf{K}_t(\mathbf{y}_t - \mathbf{C}_t\,_{t-1}\hat{\mathbf{z}}_t), \\
_t\boldsymbol{\Sigma}_{t+1} &= \mathbf{A}_t(\mathbf{I} - \mathbf{K}_t\mathbf{C}_t)\,_{t-1}\boldsymbol{\Sigma}_t\mathbf{A}'_t + \mathbf{Q},
\end{aligned} \tag{15.12}$$

with $\mathbf{K}_t = {}_{t-1}\boldsymbol{\Sigma}_t\mathbf{C}'_t(\mathbf{C}_t\,_{t-1}\boldsymbol{\Sigma}_t\mathbf{C}'_t + \mathbf{R})^{-1}$. In the stationary case ($\mathbf{A}_t$ and $\mathbf{C}_t$ are time independent, $\mathbf{A}$ has eigenvalues strictly smaller than 1 in modulus) we have seen that $_t\boldsymbol{\Sigma}_{t+1}$ converges to a limit $\overline{\boldsymbol{\Sigma}}$. It results from (15.12) that this limit satisfies the *Riccati equation*

$$\overline{\Sigma} = \mathbf{A} \left(\overline{\Sigma} - \overline{\Sigma}\mathbf{C}' \left(\mathbf{C}\overline{\Sigma}\mathbf{C}' + \mathbf{R} \right)^{-1} \mathbf{C}\overline{\Sigma} \right) \mathbf{A}' + \mathbf{Q}. \qquad (15.13)$$

15.2.5 Generalizations of the Filter

Introduction of an Input in the Transition Equation or in the Measurement Equation

(i)   Let us assume that the initial model is replaced by

$$\mathbf{z}_{t+1} = \mathbf{A}_t \mathbf{z}_t + \mathbf{G}_t \mathbf{v}_t + \boldsymbol{\varepsilon}_t,$$

$$\mathbf{y}_t = \mathbf{C}_t \mathbf{z}_t + \boldsymbol{\eta}_t,$$

where $\mathbf{G}_t$ is a nonrandom matrix of size $(K \times m)$ and $\mathbf{v}_t$ is a vector of size m, which is either nonrandom, or a function of $\mathbf{y}_0 \ldots \mathbf{y}_t$. If we still assume that $\boldsymbol{\varepsilon}_t$ and $\boldsymbol{\eta}_t$ are not correlated, we see that $\mathbf{v}_t$ is predetermined, in the sense that it is independent of $\boldsymbol{\varepsilon}_t, \boldsymbol{\varepsilon}_{t+1} \cdots$. All the formulae of the filter remain valid with the exception of formula (b) of theorem 15.1

$$_t\hat{\mathbf{z}}_{t+1} = \mathbf{A}_t \,_t\hat{\mathbf{z}}_t$$

which should be replaced by

$$_t\hat{\mathbf{z}}_{t+1} = \mathbf{A}_t \,_t\hat{\mathbf{z}}_t + \mathbf{G}_t \mathbf{v}_t. \qquad (15.14)$$

(ii)   Similarly let us consider the introduction of an input in the measurement equation. The model is now

$$\mathbf{z}_{t+1} = \mathbf{A}_t \mathbf{z}_t + \boldsymbol{\varepsilon}_t,$$

$$\mathbf{y}_t = \mathbf{C}_t \mathbf{z}_t + \mathbf{H}_t \mathbf{w}_t + \boldsymbol{\eta}_t,$$

where $\mathbf{H}_t$ is a nonrandom matrix of size $(n \times p)$ and $\mathbf{w}_t$ is a vector of size p that is either nonrandom or a function of $(\mathbf{y}_0, \mathbf{y}_1 \ldots \mathbf{y}_{t-1})$. The only modified equations of the filter correspond to the equations where the vector $\mathbf{y}_t$ is explicit. It should be replaced by $\mathbf{y}_t - \mathbf{H}_t \mathbf{w}_t$. The formula (a) in theorem 15.1 is replaced by

$$_t\hat{\mathbf{z}}_t = \,_{t-1}\hat{\mathbf{z}}_t + \mathbf{K}_t \left(\mathbf{y}_t - \mathbf{C}_t \,_{t-1}\hat{\mathbf{z}}_t - \mathbf{H}_t \mathbf{w}_t \right).$$

The equation (15.6c) is replaced by

$$_t\hat{\mathbf{y}}_{t+1} = \mathbf{C}_{t+1} \,_t\hat{\mathbf{z}}_{t+1} + \mathbf{H}_{t+1} w_{t+1}. \qquad (15.15)$$

Note that under the normality assumption for the noises $\boldsymbol{\varepsilon}_t, \boldsymbol{\eta}_t$, and of the initial value $\mathbf{z}_0$, the processes $\mathbf{y}_t, \mathbf{z}_t$ remain Gaussian only if v_t (respectively w_t) is a linear function of $(\mathbf{y}_0, \ldots, \mathbf{y}_t)$ (respectively $(\mathbf{y}_0 \cdots \mathbf{y}_{t-1})$).

Case where the Noises are Correlated When the innovation $\boldsymbol{\varepsilon}_t$ and the measurement error $\boldsymbol{\eta}_t$ are correlated $\mathrm{cov}\,(\boldsymbol{\varepsilon}_t, \boldsymbol{\eta}_t) = \mathbf{S} \neq 0$, we can easily go back to the previous cases. For example, we can introduce the residual of the regression of $\boldsymbol{\varepsilon}_t$ on $\boldsymbol{\eta}_t$

$$\boldsymbol{\varepsilon}_t^\star = \boldsymbol{\varepsilon}_t - \mathbf{S}\mathbf{R}^{-1}\boldsymbol{\eta}_t.$$

We have then $E(\boldsymbol{\varepsilon}_t^\star \boldsymbol{\eta}_t') = \mathrm{cov}\,(\boldsymbol{\varepsilon}_t^\star, \boldsymbol{\eta}_t) = 0$, and var $\boldsymbol{\varepsilon}_t^\star = \mathbf{Q} - \mathbf{S}\mathbf{R}^{-1}\mathbf{S}'$. The transition equation is written as

$$\mathbf{z}_{t+1} = \mathbf{A}_t \mathbf{z}_t + \boldsymbol{\varepsilon}_t = \mathbf{A}_t \mathbf{z}_t + \mathbf{S}\mathbf{R}^{-1}\boldsymbol{\eta}_t + \boldsymbol{\varepsilon}_t^\star$$

or

$$\mathbf{z}_{t+1} = \mathbf{A}_t \mathbf{z}_t + \mathbf{S}\mathbf{R}^{-1}(\mathbf{y}_t - \mathbf{C}_t \mathbf{z}_t) + \boldsymbol{\varepsilon}_t^\star$$

$$= (\mathbf{A}_t - \mathbf{S}\mathbf{R}^{-1}\mathbf{C}_t)\mathbf{z}_t + \mathbf{S}\mathbf{R}^{-1}\mathbf{y}_t + \boldsymbol{\varepsilon}_t^\star.$$

In this new equation $\boldsymbol{\varepsilon}_t^\star$ is not correlated with $\boldsymbol{\eta}_t$, $\mathbf{A}_t$ has been replaced by $\mathbf{A}_t - \mathbf{S}\mathbf{R}^{-1}\mathbf{C}_t$ and the inputs $\mathbf{S}\mathbf{R}^{-1}\mathbf{y}_t$ have been added. The result of the previous section shows that the filter remains valid replacing $\mathbf{A}_t$ by $\mathbf{A}_t - \mathbf{S}\mathbf{R}^{-1}\mathbf{C}_t$ in formulae (b) and (b') of theorem 15.1, and adding $\mathbf{S}\mathbf{R}^{-1}\mathbf{y}_t$ to the second term of formula (b) and rewriting $\mathbf{Q}$ as $\mathbf{Q} - \mathbf{S}\mathbf{R}^{-1}\mathbf{S}'$ in formula (b').

Since the input $\mathbf{S}\mathbf{R}^{-1}\mathbf{y}_t$ is a linear function of $\mathbf{y}_t$, the normality is preserved.

Cases where the Transition and Measurement Matrices are Random Let us assume that the matrix $\mathbf{A}_t$ is a function of the observations $\mathbf{y}_0, \ldots, \mathbf{y}_t$ or that the matrix $\mathbf{C}_t$ is a function of $\mathbf{y}_0 \ldots \mathbf{y}_{t-1}$. Under the normality assumption, we can prove by induction (exercise 15.1) that the conditional distribution of the triplet $\mathbf{z}_t, \mathbf{z}_{t+1}, \mathbf{y}_{t+1}$ given $\mathbf{y}_0 \ldots \mathbf{y}_t$ is Gaussian and we can show (exercise 15.2) that the covariance filter (theorem 15.1) remains valid if the various variance–covariance matrices of the errors are interpreted as variance matrices *conditional* on the information used for the computation of the approximation.

Note also that, in spite of the existence of conditional Gaussian distributions, the process $\begin{pmatrix} \mathbf{z}_t \\ \mathbf{y}_t \end{pmatrix}$ is not Gaussian anymore. Indeed, the conditional expectation of $\mathbf{z}_t$ given $\mathbf{y}_0 \ldots \mathbf{y}_t$, for example, is a nonlinear function of $\mathbf{y}_0 \ldots \mathbf{y}_t$ and the conditional variance–covariance matrix depends on $\mathbf{y}_0 \ldots \mathbf{y}_t$.

15.3 Forecast

Let us assume once again the uncorrelation between $\boldsymbol{\varepsilon}_t$ and $\boldsymbol{\eta}_t$, $\mathbf{S} = 0$. We are interested in the forecasts of the variables $\mathbf{y}_{t+h}, \mathbf{z}_{t+h}, h =$

$1, \ldots, H$ conditional on $\mathbf{y}_0 \ldots \mathbf{y}_t$. Therefore we have to compute

$$_t\hat{\mathbf{y}}_{t+h} = E(\mathbf{y}_{t+h} \mid \mathbf{y}_0, \ldots, \mathbf{y}_t), \qquad _t\hat{\mathbf{z}}_{t+h} = E(\mathbf{z}_{t+h} \mid \mathbf{y}_0 \ldots \mathbf{y}_t),$$

and the variance–covariance matrices of the associated errors

$$_t\mathbf{M}_{t+h} = \text{var}\,(\mathbf{y}_{t+h} - {}_t\hat{\mathbf{y}}_{t+h}), \qquad _t\boldsymbol{\Sigma}_{t+h} = \text{var}\,(\mathbf{z}_{t+h} - {}_t\hat{\mathbf{z}}_{t+h}).$$

The covariance filters in theorem 15.1 and in the corollary following it provide the answer for $h = 1$. It is therefore sufficient to provide a recursive algorithm in the index h of these quantities.

Theorem 15.3: *If* $\mathbf{S} = \mathbf{0}$, *we have the recursive formulae*

$$_t\hat{\mathbf{z}}_{t+h} = \mathbf{A}_{t+h-1}\, {}_t\hat{\mathbf{z}}_{t+h-1},$$

$$_t\hat{\mathbf{y}}_{t+h} = \mathbf{C}_{t+h}\, {}_t\hat{\mathbf{z}}_{t+h},$$

and

$$_t\boldsymbol{\Sigma}_{t+h} = \mathbf{A}_{t+h-1}\, {}_t\boldsymbol{\Sigma}_{t+h-1}\mathbf{A}'_{t+h-1} + \mathbf{Q},$$

$$_t\mathbf{M}_{t+h} = \mathbf{C}_{t+h}\, {}_t\boldsymbol{\Sigma}_{t+h}\mathbf{C}'_{t+h} + \mathbf{R},$$

for all values of $h \geq 1$.

PROOF:

(i)   The space-state model provides the relations

$$\mathbf{z}_{t+h} = \mathbf{A}_{t+h-1}\mathbf{z}_{t+h-1} + \boldsymbol{\varepsilon}_{t+h-1},$$

$$\mathbf{y}_{t+h} = \mathbf{C}_{t+h}\mathbf{z}_{t+h} + \boldsymbol{\eta}_{t+h}.$$

Taking the conditional expectation given $\mathbf{y}_0, \ldots, \mathbf{y}_t$, we get

$$_t\hat{\mathbf{z}}_{t+h} = \mathbf{A}_{t+h-1}\, {}_t\hat{\mathbf{z}}_{t+h-1},$$

$$_t\hat{\mathbf{y}}_{t+h} = \mathbf{C}_{t+h}\, {}_t\hat{\mathbf{z}}_{t+h}.$$

(ii)   Subtracting, we get

$$\mathbf{z}_{t+h} - {}_t\hat{\mathbf{z}}_{t+h} = \mathbf{A}_{t+h-1}(\mathbf{z}_{t+h-1} - {}_t\hat{\mathbf{z}}_{t+h-1}) + \boldsymbol{\varepsilon}_{t+h-1},$$

$$\mathbf{y}_{t+h} - {}_t\hat{\mathbf{y}}_{t+h} = \mathbf{C}_{t+h}(\mathbf{z}_{t+h} - {}_t\hat{\mathbf{z}}_{t+h}) + \boldsymbol{\eta}_{t+h},$$

so that

$$_t\boldsymbol{\Sigma}_{t+h} = \mathbf{A}_{t+h-1}\, {}_t\boldsymbol{\Sigma}_{t+h-1}\mathbf{A}'_{t+h-1} + \mathbf{Q},$$

$$_t\mathbf{M}_{t+h} = \mathbf{C}_{t+h}\, {}_t\boldsymbol{\Sigma}_{t+h}\mathbf{C}'_{t+h} + \mathbf{R}.$$

$\square$

The formulae in theorem 15.3 show that several forecasts and the corresponding variance–covariance matrices can be easily obtained from the Kalman filter of theorem 15.1. After a first pass at time t on the filter formulae, we just have to go back to the stage of formula (b) and make

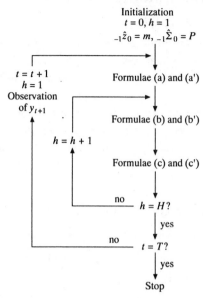

Initialization
$t = 0, h = 1$
$_{-1}\hat{z}_0 = m,\ _{-1}\hat{\Sigma}_0 = P$

$t = t + 1$
$h = 1$
Observation
of y_{t+1}

Formulae (a) and (a')

$h = h + 1$

Formulae (b) and (b')

Formulae (c) and (c')

no — $h = H$?

yes

no — $t = T$?

yes

Stop

Figure 15.2   Use of the Filter for Forecasting

$H - 1$ iterations following the formulae in theorem 15.3, that is, iterating formulae (b), (b'), (c), (c'). Of course, in order to be able to use the filter at time $t + 1$ the values $_t\hat{z}_{t+1}$ and $_t\Sigma_{t+1}$ have to be saved. This procedure is summarized in figure 15.2.

In the case of a nonzero matrix $\mathbf{S}$, let us remark that each formula of theorem 15.3 remains valid, except those providing $_t\hat{z}_{t+1}$ and $_t\Sigma_{t+1}$ which have to be modified, as mentioned in 15.2.5.

When $\mathbf{A}_t$ depends on $(\mathbf{y}_0, \ldots, \mathbf{y}_t)$ or $\mathbf{C}_t$ depends on $(\mathbf{y}_0, \ldots, \mathbf{y}_{t-1})$, the formulae for the forecast at the horizon 1 remain valid, as we have already seen, if the variance–covariance matrices have a conditional meaning. On the other hand, as soon as $h \geq 2$, the formulae are not valid anymore. This is apparent in the transition equation for $t + 2$, for example

$$\mathbf{z}_{t+2} = \mathbf{A}_{t+1}\mathbf{z}_{t+1} + \boldsymbol{\varepsilon}_{t+1}.$$

In this equation, $\mathbf{A}_{t+1}$ depends on $(\mathbf{y}_0, \ldots, \mathbf{y}_{t+1})$, so that if we condition on $(\mathbf{y}_0, \ldots, \mathbf{y}_t)$ this matrix remains stochastic and the conditional expectation of $\mathbf{A}_{t+1}\mathbf{z}_{t+1}$ is not anymore $\mathbf{A}_{t+1}\,_t\hat{\mathbf{z}}_{t+1}$.

15.4 Information Filter

In the first example of this chapter we have seen that sometimes the recursive relationships forming the Kalman filter can be expressed in a simpler form, when we consider the evolution of the inverse of the variance–covariance matrices rather than the matrices themselves. In such a case the relevant matrices are interpreted as information matrices, which explains the use of the term information filter. To obtain the information filter we need to express the Kalman filter as a function of the new quantities ${}_t\mathbf{\Sigma}_t^{-1}$, ${}_t\mathbf{\Sigma}_{t+1}^{-1}$. We also need to introduce the variables ${}_t\hat{\mathbf{U}}_t = {}_t\mathbf{\Sigma}_t^{-1}\,{}_t\hat{\mathbf{z}}_t$, ${}_t\hat{\mathbf{U}}_{t+1} = {}_t\mathbf{\Sigma}_{t+1}^{-1}\,{}_t\hat{\mathbf{z}}_{t+1}$.

Theorem 15.4: Information Filter *If* $\mathbf{S} = \mathbf{0}$, *we get*

$$(\alpha) \qquad {}_t\hat{\mathbf{U}}_t = {}_{t-1}\hat{\mathbf{U}}_t + \mathbf{C}_t'\mathbf{R}^{-1}\mathbf{y}_t;$$

$$(\alpha') \qquad {}_t\mathbf{\Sigma}_t^{-1} = {}_{t-1}\mathbf{\Sigma}_t^{-1} + \mathbf{C}_t'\mathbf{R}^{-1}\mathbf{C}_t;$$

$$(\beta) \qquad {}_t\hat{\mathbf{U}}_{t+1} = (\mathbf{I} - \mathbf{M}_t)\mathbf{A}_t'^{-1}\,{}_t\hat{\mathbf{U}}_t,$$

with

$$\mathbf{M}_t = \mathbf{N}_t(\mathbf{N}_t + \mathbf{Q}^{-1})^{-1}$$

$$\mathbf{N}_t = \mathbf{A}_t'^{-1}\,{}_t\mathbf{\Sigma}_t^{-1}\mathbf{A}_t^{-1};$$

$$(\beta') \qquad {}_t\mathbf{\Sigma}_{t+1}^{-1} = (\mathbf{I} - \mathbf{M}_t)\mathbf{N}_t.$$

(In these formulae we assume that $\mathbf{A}_t$ *and* $\mathbf{Q}$ *are invertible.)*

PROOF: We will use several times the following lemma on matrix inversion (see exercise 15.3).

Lemma:

$$(\mathbf{D} - \mathbf{C}\mathbf{A}^{-1}\mathbf{B})^{-1} = \mathbf{D}^{-1} + \mathbf{D}^{-1}\mathbf{C}(\mathbf{A} - \mathbf{B}\mathbf{D}^{-1}\mathbf{C})^{-1}\mathbf{B}\mathbf{D}^{-1}.$$

Formula (α') The formula (a') of theorem 15.1 can be written as

$$_t\mathbf{\Sigma}_t = {}_{t-1}\mathbf{\Sigma}_t - {}_{t-1}\mathbf{\Sigma}_t\mathbf{C}_t'(\mathbf{C}_t\,{}_{t-1}\mathbf{\Sigma}_t\mathbf{C}_t' + \mathbf{R})^{-1}\mathbf{C}_t\,{}_{t-1}\mathbf{\Sigma}_t.$$

The lemma implies (with $\mathbf{D}^{-1} = {}_{t-1}\mathbf{\Sigma}_t, \mathbf{C} = -\mathbf{C}_t', \mathbf{A} = \mathbf{R}$, and $\mathbf{B} = \mathbf{C}_t$)

$$_t\mathbf{\Sigma}_t = ({}_{t-1}\mathbf{\Sigma}_t^{-1} + \mathbf{C}_t'\mathbf{R}^{-1}\mathbf{C}_t)^{-1},$$

or

$$_t\mathbf{\Sigma}_t^{-1} = {}_{t-1}\mathbf{\Sigma}_t^{-1} + \mathbf{C}_t'\mathbf{R}^{-1}\mathbf{C}_t.$$

Formula (β') The formula (b') of theorem 15.1 can be written as

$$_t\mathbf{\Sigma}_{t+1} = \mathbf{A}_t\,{}_t\mathbf{\Sigma}_t\mathbf{A}_t' + \mathbf{Q} = \mathbf{N}_t^{-1} + \mathbf{Q},$$

therefore

$$_t\Sigma_{t+1}^{-1} = (N_t^{-1} + Q)^{-1}$$
$$= (I + N_tQ)^{-1}N_t.$$

Using the lemma (with $D = I, B = I, C = -N_t, A = Q^{-1}$), we get

$$(I + N_tQ)^{-1} = I - M_t,$$

with: $M_t = N_t(N_t + Q^{-1})^{-1}$. The required formula is

$$_t\Sigma_{t+1}^{-1} = (I - M_t)N_t.$$

Formula (β)

$$_t\hat{U}_{t+1} = {}_t\Sigma_{t+1}^{-1}\,_t\hat{z}_{t+1}$$
$$= (I - M_t)N_t\,_t\hat{z}_{t+1}$$
$$= (I - M_t)A_t'^{-1}\,_t\Sigma_t^{-1}A_t^{-1}\,_t\hat{z}_{t+1}$$
$$= (I - M_t)A_t'^{-1}\,_t\Sigma_t^{-1}\,_t\hat{z}_t$$
$$= (I - M_t)A_t'^{-1}\,_t\hat{U}_t.$$

Formula (α) The formula (a) in theorem 15.1 is written as

$$_t\hat{z}_t = {}_{t-1}\Sigma_t\,_{t-1}\hat{U}_t + {}_{t-1}\Sigma_tC_t'(C_t\,_{t-1}\Sigma_tC_t'+R)^{-1}(y_t - C_t\,_{t-1}\Sigma_t\,_{t-1}\hat{U}_t).$$

Using the expression of $_t\Sigma_t$, we get

$$_t\hat{z}_t = {}_t\Sigma_t\,_{t-1}\hat{U}_t + {}_{t-1}\Sigma_tC_t'(C_t\,_{t-1}\Sigma_tC_t' + R)^{-1}y_t,$$

or

$$_t\hat{U}_t = {}_{t-1}\hat{U}_t + {}_t\Sigma_t^{-1}\,_{t-1}\Sigma_tC_t'(C_t\,_{t-1}\Sigma_tC_t' + R)^{-1}y_t.$$

We have then to verify that

$$_{t-1}\Sigma_tC_t'(C_t\,_{t-1}\Sigma_tC_t' + R)^{-1} = {}_t\Sigma_tC_t'R^{-1}.$$

Multiplying formula (a') on the right by $C_t'R^{-1}$, we get

$$_t\Sigma_tC_t'R^{-1} = {}_{t-1}\Sigma_tC_t'R^{-1}$$
$$- {}_{t-1}\Sigma_tC_t'(C_t\,_{t-1}\Sigma_tC_t' + R)^{-1}C_t\,_{t-1}\Sigma_tC_t'R^{-1}$$
$$= {}_{t-1}\Sigma_tC_t'(R^{-1} - (C_t\,_{t-1}\Sigma_tC_t' + R)^{-1}C_t\,_{t-1}\Sigma_tC_t'R^{-1})$$
$$= {}_{t-1}\Sigma_tC_t'(C_t\,_{t-1}\Sigma_tC_t' + R)^{-1}$$
$$((C_t\,_{t-1}\Sigma_tC_t' + R)R^{-1} - C_t\,_{t-1}\Sigma_tC_t'R^{-1})$$
$$= {}_{t-1}\Sigma_tC_t'(C_t\,_{t-1}\Sigma_tC_t' + R)^{-1}.$$

□

Remark 15.1: The formulae of the information filter require the non-singularity of $\mathbf{Q}$. Nevertheless, we can verify that, in the case $\mathbf{Q} = \mathbf{0}$, the formulae (α), (α') still hold while the formulae (β), (β') are replaced by $_t\hat{\mathbf{U}}_{t+1} = \mathbf{A}_t'^{-1}{}_t\hat{\mathbf{U}}_t$ and $_t\mathbf{\Sigma}_{t+1}^{-1} = \mathbf{N}_t$ which correspond to the limit case $\mathbf{M}_t = \mathbf{0}$ implied by $\mathbf{Q} = \mathbf{0}$.

Remark 15.2: When little information is available on the initial variable $\mathbf{z}_0$, we have to consider a variance–covariance matrix $\mathbf{P} = {}_{-1}\mathbf{\Sigma}_0$, which is "large" in all directions, that is a matrix with large eigenvalues. The matrix $\mathbf{P}^{-1}$ is then close to $\mathbf{0}$. In the information filter, we can consider the limit case of the diffuse prior, where the initial values are $_{-1}\mathbf{\Sigma}_0^{-1} = \mathbf{0}$ and $_{-1}\hat{\mathbf{U}}_0 = {}_{-1}\mathbf{\Sigma}_0^{-1}{}_{-1}\hat{\mathbf{z}}_0 = 0$. The notation $_{t-1}\mathbf{\Sigma}_t^{-1}$ is misleading since it seems to imply that this matrix admits an inverse, which is impossible, at least for the first values of t, if $_{-1}\mathbf{\Sigma}_0 = \mathbf{0}$. The equivalence with the covariance filter works only when $_{t-1}\mathbf{\Sigma}_t^{-1}$ and $_t\mathbf{\Sigma}_t^{-1}$ are invertible.

15.5 Fixed Interval Smoothing

We consider the general state-space model

$$\mathbf{z}_{t+1} = \mathbf{A}_t\mathbf{z}_t + \boldsymbol{\varepsilon}_t,$$

$$\mathbf{y}_t = \mathbf{C}_t\mathbf{z}_t + \boldsymbol{\eta}_t, \qquad t \geq 0.$$

The matrix $\mathbf{S} = E(\boldsymbol{\varepsilon}_t\,\boldsymbol{\eta}_t')$ is in particular not constrained to be $\mathbf{0}$. Let us assume that $\mathbf{y}_0, \ldots, \mathbf{y}_T$ have been observed and the optimal approximation of $\mathbf{z}_t$ is to be computed, that is

$$_T\hat{\mathbf{z}}_t = E(\mathbf{z}_t \mid \mathbf{y}_0, \ldots, \mathbf{y}_T)$$

and

$$_T\mathbf{\Sigma}_t = \operatorname{var}(\mathbf{z}_t - {}_T\hat{\mathbf{z}}_t)$$

for $t \in \{0, \ldots, T\}$.

This is called a smoothing problem on a fixed time interval $\{0, \ldots, T\}$. As for the filtering and forecast aspects we can proceed recursively.

Theorem 15.5: Smoothing *We have for $t = 1, \ldots, T-1$*

$$(d) \quad _T\hat{\mathbf{z}}_t = {}_t\hat{\mathbf{z}}_t + \mathbf{F}_t({}_T\hat{\mathbf{z}}_{t+1} - {}_t\hat{\mathbf{z}}_{t+1})$$

with $\mathbf{F}_t = {}_t\mathbf{\Sigma}_t\mathbf{A}_t'\,{}_t\mathbf{\Sigma}_{t+1}^{-1}$

$$(d') \quad _T\mathbf{\Sigma}_t = {}_t\mathbf{\Sigma}_t + \mathbf{F}_t({}_T\mathbf{\Sigma}_{t+1} - {}_t\mathbf{\Sigma}_{t+1})\mathbf{F}_t'.$$

PROOF:

Formula (d):

(i) We have to compute $_T\hat{\mathbf{z}}_t = E(\mathbf{z}_t \mid \mathbf{y}_0, \ldots, \mathbf{y}_T)$. To this purpose let us consider the set of variables

$$I_t = \{\mathbf{y}_0, \ldots, \mathbf{y}_t, \mathbf{z}_{t+1} - {}_t\hat{\mathbf{z}}_{t+1}, \mathbf{w}_{t+1}, \ldots, \mathbf{w}_T\}$$

with $\mathbf{w}_t = \begin{pmatrix} \boldsymbol{\varepsilon}_t \\ \boldsymbol{\eta}_t \end{pmatrix}$. We can easily see that the variables $\mathbf{y}_{t+1}, \ldots, \mathbf{y}_T$ are functions of the variables in I_t (i.e., belong to I_t). Indeed, we have

$$\mathbf{z}_{t+1} = (\mathbf{z}_{t+1} - {}_t\hat{\mathbf{z}}_{t+1}) + {}_t\hat{\mathbf{z}}_{t+1},$$

and, by repeated substitution

$$\mathbf{z}_{t+i} = \mathbf{A}_{t+i-1} \ldots \mathbf{A}_{t+1}\mathbf{z}_{t+1}$$
$$+ \boldsymbol{\varepsilon}_{t+i-1} + \mathbf{A}_{t+i-1}\boldsymbol{\varepsilon}_{t+i-2} + \ldots + \mathbf{A}_{t+i-1} \ldots \mathbf{A}_{t+2}\boldsymbol{\varepsilon}_{t+1},$$

for $i \geq 1$.

Therefore the variables $\mathbf{z}_{t+i}, i \geq 0$ belong to I_t. Since

$$\mathbf{y}_{t+i} = \mathbf{C}_{t+i}\mathbf{z}_{t+i} + \boldsymbol{\eta}_{t+i}$$

we have the same property for $\mathbf{y}_{t+i}, i \geq 1$.

From iterated projections, we get

$$_T\hat{\mathbf{z}}_t = E(\mathbf{z}_t \mid \mathbf{y}_0, \ldots, \mathbf{y}_T) = E(E(\mathbf{z}_t \mid I_t) \mid \mathbf{y}_0, \ldots, \mathbf{y}_T).$$

(ii) We start by computing $E(\mathbf{z}_t \mid I_t)$. First note that the three subspaces of L_2 spanned respectively by

$$\{1, \mathbf{y}_0, \ldots, \mathbf{y}_t\}, \ \{\mathbf{z}_{t+1} -_t \hat{\mathbf{z}}_{t+1}\}, \ \text{and} \ \{\mathbf{w}_{t+1}, \ldots, \mathbf{w}_T\}$$

are orthogonal to each other since $(\mathbf{z}_{t+1} - {}_t\hat{\mathbf{z}}_{t+1})$ and $\mathbf{w}_{t+i}, i = 1, \ldots, T$ are zero–mean, have zero cross correlation and are also uncorrelated with $\mathbf{y}_j, j = 0, \ldots, t$. We can decompose the orthogonal projection on the subspace spanned by I_t, that is $E(\mathbf{z}_t \mid I_t)$, in three components corresponding to the orthogonal projections on these three orthogonal subspaces. These three components are

$$_t\hat{\mathbf{z}}_t, E(\mathbf{z}_t \mid \mathbf{z}_{t+1} - {}_t\hat{\mathbf{z}}_{t+1}) - E\mathbf{z}_t, E(\mathbf{z}_t \mid \mathbf{w}_{t+1}, \ldots, \mathbf{w}_T) - E\mathbf{z}_t.$$

The last component is zero and the second one is equal to

$$E(\mathbf{z}_t \mid \mathbf{z}_{t+1} - {}_t\hat{\mathbf{z}}_{t+1}) - E\mathbf{z}_t$$
$$= \text{cov}(\mathbf{z}_t, \mathbf{z}_{t+1} - {}_t\hat{\mathbf{z}}_{t+1}) {}_t\boldsymbol{\Sigma}_{t+1}^{-1}(\mathbf{z}_{t+1} - {}_t\hat{\mathbf{z}}_{t+1})$$
$$= \text{cov}(\mathbf{z}_t, \mathbf{A}_t(\mathbf{z}_t - {}_t\hat{\mathbf{z}}_t) + \boldsymbol{\varepsilon}_t) {}_t\boldsymbol{\Sigma}_{t+1}^{-1}(\mathbf{z}_{t+1} - {}_t\hat{\mathbf{z}}_{t+1})$$
$$= {}_t\boldsymbol{\Sigma}_t\mathbf{A}_t' {}_t\boldsymbol{\Sigma}_{t+1}^{-1}(\mathbf{z}_{t+1} - {}_t\hat{\mathbf{z}}_{t+1}).$$

Finally, we get

$$E(\mathbf{z}_t \mid I_t) = {}_t\hat{\mathbf{z}}_t + {}_t\boldsymbol{\Sigma}_t\mathbf{A}_t' {}_t\boldsymbol{\Sigma}_{t+1}^{-1}(\mathbf{z}_{t+1} - {}_t\hat{\mathbf{z}}_{t+1})$$

and, taking conditional expectation with respect to $\mathbf{y}_0, \ldots, \mathbf{y}_T$

$$_T\hat{\mathbf{z}}_t = {}_t\hat{\mathbf{z}}_t + {}_t\mathbf{\Sigma}_t\mathbf{A}_t'\,{}_t\mathbf{\Sigma}_{t+1}^{-1}({}_T\hat{\mathbf{z}}_{t+1} - {}_t\hat{\mathbf{z}}_{t+1})$$

$$= {}_t\hat{\mathbf{z}}_t + \mathbf{F}_t({}_T\hat{\mathbf{z}}_{t+1} - {}_t\hat{\mathbf{z}}_{t+1}).$$

Formula (d'): The formula (d) implies

$$\mathbf{z}_t - {}_T\hat{\mathbf{z}}_t + \mathbf{F}_t\,{}_T\hat{\mathbf{z}}_{t+1} = \mathbf{z}_t - {}_t\hat{\mathbf{z}}_t + \mathbf{F}_t\,{}_t\hat{\mathbf{z}}_{t+1}$$

$\mathbf{z}_t - {}_T\hat{\mathbf{z}}_t$ is uncorrelated with $\mathbf{y}_0, \mathbf{y}_1, \ldots, \mathbf{y}_T$ and therefore with ${}_T\hat{\mathbf{z}}_{t+1}$, for the same reason, $\mathbf{z}_t - {}_t\hat{\mathbf{z}}_t$ and ${}_t\hat{\mathbf{z}}_{t+1}$ are uncorrelated, so that

$$_T\mathbf{\Sigma}_t + \mathbf{F}_t\mathrm{var}\,({}_T\hat{\mathbf{z}}_{t+1})\mathbf{F}_t' = {}_t\mathbf{\Sigma}_t + \mathbf{F}_t\mathrm{var}\,({}_t\hat{\mathbf{z}}_{t+1})\mathbf{F}_t',$$

$$_T\mathbf{\Sigma}_t = {}_t\mathbf{\Sigma}_t + \mathbf{F}_t[\mathrm{var}\,({}_t\hat{\mathbf{z}}_{t+1}) - \mathrm{var}\,({}_T\hat{\mathbf{z}}_{t+1})]\mathbf{F}_t'.$$

Moreover, taking the noncorrelation into account, the equality

$$\mathbf{z}_{t+1} - {}_t\hat{\mathbf{z}}_{t+1} + {}_t\hat{\mathbf{z}}_{t+1} = \mathbf{z}_{t+1} - {}_T\hat{\mathbf{z}}_{t+1} + {}_T\hat{\mathbf{z}}_{t+1}$$

implies that

$$_t\mathbf{\Sigma}_{t+1} + \mathrm{var}\,({}_t\hat{\mathbf{z}}_{t+1}) = {}_T\mathbf{\Sigma}_{t+1} + \mathrm{var}\,({}_T\hat{\mathbf{z}}_{t+1}),$$

$$\mathrm{var}\,({}_t\hat{\mathbf{z}}_{t+1}) - \mathrm{var}\,({}_T\hat{\mathbf{z}}_{t+1}) = {}_T\mathbf{\Sigma}_{t+1} - {}_T\mathbf{\Sigma}_{t+1}.$$

Finally we have

$$_T\mathbf{\Sigma}_t = {}_t\mathbf{\Sigma}_t + \mathbf{F}_t({}_T\mathbf{\Sigma}_{t+1} - {}_t\mathbf{\Sigma}_{t+1})\mathbf{F}_t'.$$

□

The smoothing formulae of theorem 15.5 can be used in the following way. We first apply the covariance or information filter until the final time T. This gives ${}_T\hat{\mathbf{z}}_T$ and ${}_T\mathbf{\Sigma}_T$. The formulae (d) and (d') of the smoothing algorithm use these quantities as initial conditions (for $t = T - 1$) and provide recursively with t decreasing the quantities ${}_T\hat{\mathbf{z}}_t$ and ${}_T\mathbf{\Sigma}_t, t = T - 1, \ldots, 0$. Note that, in order to apply this procedure, the values ${}_t\hat{\mathbf{z}}_t$, ${}_t\hat{\mathbf{\Sigma}}_t$ and, possibly,

$$_t\hat{\mathbf{z}}_{t+1} = \mathbf{A}_t\,{}_t\hat{\mathbf{z}}_t \text{ and } {}_t\mathbf{\Sigma}_{t+1} = \mathbf{A}_t\,{}_t\mathbf{\Sigma}_t\mathbf{A}_t' + \mathbf{Q}$$

should be stored from the filtering stage. This process is summarized in the figure 15.3.

15.6 Estimation

15.6.1 Computation of the Log-Likelihood Function

The computations in the previous section assume that the various matrices $\mathbf{m}, \mathbf{P}, \mathbf{Q}, \mathbf{R}, \mathbf{S}, \mathbf{A}_t, \mathbf{C}_t$ are known. In practice, some of these matrices are often unknown and have therefore to be estimated from the observations $\mathbf{y}_0, \mathbf{y}_1, \ldots, \mathbf{y}_T$. In this section, we intend to consider the *maximum*

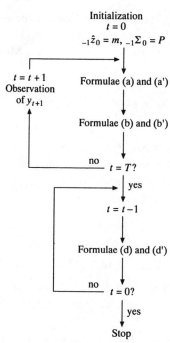

Figure 15.3 Smoothing Algorithm

likelihood method and to examine how the Kalman filter can be used for the numerical computation of this likelihood function.

Let θ be the vector of the unknown parameters, which various matrices depend on; the parameter θ is assumed identifiable. The likelihood function of the state-space model is given from the density of the observations $\mathbf{y}_0, \ldots, \mathbf{y}_T$. The density function is decomposed in a product of conditional density functions

$$l(y; \theta) = f(\mathbf{y}_0; \theta) f(\mathbf{y}_1 \mid \mathbf{y}_0; \theta) \ldots f(\mathbf{y}_T \mid \mathbf{y}_0, \ldots, \mathbf{y}_{T-1}; \theta). \qquad (15.16)$$

Under the assumption that $(\epsilon'_t, \boldsymbol{\eta}'_t)'$ is Gaussian these conditional density functions are Gaussian. The general term $f(\mathbf{y}_t \mid \mathbf{y}_0 \ldots \mathbf{y}_{t-1}; \theta)$ is the density function of the Gaussian distribution with mean $_{t-1}\hat{\mathbf{y}}_t(\theta)$ (i.e., the value of $_{t-1}\hat{\mathbf{y}}_t$ associated with θ, the value of the parameter) and the variance–covariance matrix $_{t-1}\mathbf{M}_t(\theta)$.

For each fixed value of θ, we can find $_{t-1}\hat{\mathbf{y}}_t(\theta)$ and $_{t-1}\hat{M}_t(\theta)$ from the Kalman filter (formulae (c) and (c') of (15.7)).

Therefore we can use the filter to compute the log-likelihood function for a fixed θ. This log-likelihood function is expressed as

$$
L_T(\theta) = -\frac{n\,(T+1)}{2}\ln 2\pi - \frac{1}{2}\sum_{t=0}^{T}\ln\det({}_{t-1}\mathbf{M}_t(\theta))
$$

$$
-\frac{1}{2}\sum_{t=0}^{T}(\mathbf{y}_t - {}_{t-1}\hat{\mathbf{y}}_t(\theta))'\,({}_{t-1}\mathbf{M}_t(\theta))^{-1}\,(\mathbf{y}_t - {}_{t-1}\hat{\mathbf{y}}_t(\theta)),
$$

(15.17)

with ${}_{-1}\hat{\mathbf{y}}_0(\theta) = E_\theta \mathbf{y}_0, {}_{-1}\mathbf{M}_0(\theta) = \operatorname{var}_\theta(\mathbf{y}_0)$.

The value of the likelihood function computed with the Kalman filter can be used in an optimization algorithm of L_T in order to provide the maximum likelihood estimator.

Remark 15.3: Note that the quantities

$$
{}_{-1}\hat{\mathbf{y}}_0 = \mathbf{C}_0\mathbf{m} \quad \text{and} \quad {}_{-1}\mathbf{M}_0 = \mathbf{C}_0\mathbf{P}\mathbf{C}_0' + \mathbf{R}
$$

are given by the Kalman filter provided that the formulae (c) and (c') in (15.7) start at $t = -1$ with the usual initial values ${}_{-1}\hat{\mathbf{z}}_0 = \mathbf{m}$, and ${}_{-1}\Sigma_0 = \mathbf{P}$.

We just have discussed the computation from the Kalman filter of the log-likelihood function associated with $\mathbf{y}_0 \ldots \mathbf{y}_T$. Similarly, we can derive other marginal or conditional log-likelihood functions. We just have to modify the initialization of the filter accordingly.

(i)   *Conditional Log-likelihood Function*

If in the formula (15.17), the sum does not start at $t = 0$ but at a time $\tau > 0$, we get the conditional log-likelihood function given $\mathbf{y}_0, \ldots, \mathbf{y}_{\tau-1}$ up to a change in the constant term. In particular if we start the Kalman filter with the formula (a) of theorem 15.1 at $t = 0$, with the initial values ${}_{-1}\hat{\mathbf{z}}_0 = \mathbf{m}$ and ${}_{-1}\Sigma_0 = \mathbf{P}$, we can compute the sum only starting from $t = 1$ and therefore we derive the conditional log-likelihood function of $\mathbf{y}_1 \ldots \mathbf{y}_T$ given the initial value $\mathbf{y}_0$.

(ii)   *Marginal Log-likelihood Function of* $\mathbf{y}_1, \ldots, \mathbf{y}_T$

If we start the Kalman filter with the equation (b) of theorem 15.1 at $t = 0$ with

$$
{}_0\hat{\mathbf{z}}_0 = \mathbf{m}, \qquad {}_0\Sigma_0 = \mathbf{P}
$$

we get

$$
{}_0\hat{\mathbf{y}}_1 = \mathbf{C}_1\mathbf{A}_0\mathbf{m} = E\mathbf{y}_1 \text{ and } {}_0\mathbf{M}_1 = \mathbf{C}_1(\mathbf{A}_0\mathbf{P}\mathbf{A}_0' + \mathbf{Q})\mathbf{C}_1' + \mathbf{R} = \operatorname{var}(\mathbf{y}_1)
$$

in (c) and (c') of (15.7). As a consequence, the formula (15.17) with the sums starting at $t = 1$ provides, up to an additive constant, the marginal log-likelihood of $\mathbf{y}_1, \ldots, \mathbf{y}_T$.

(iii) *Log-likelihood Function of* $\mathbf{y}_1 \ldots \mathbf{y}_T$ *Conditional on* $\mathbf{z}_0 = \mathbf{z}_0^*$
It is obtained when the filter is started with the formula (b) of theorem 15.1, for $t = 0$ with $_0\hat{\mathbf{z}}_0 = \mathbf{z}_0^*$, $_0\boldsymbol{\Sigma}_0 = \mathbf{0}$, and when the sums in (15.17) start at $t = 1$.

Example 15.2: Let us consider a first-order moving average model
$$y_t = u_t + \alpha u_{t-1},$$
where (u_t) is a Gaussian white noise, of variance σ^2.

1st Method It is possible to put this model in the state-space form using the state vector
$$\mathbf{z}_t = \begin{pmatrix} y_t \\ \alpha u_t \end{pmatrix}.$$
Indeed, we have
$$\mathbf{z}_{t+1} = \begin{pmatrix} 0 & 1 \\ 0 & 0 \end{pmatrix} \mathbf{z}_t + \begin{pmatrix} u_{t+1} \\ \alpha u_{t+1} \end{pmatrix},$$
$$y_t = (1,0)\mathbf{z}_t.$$
Here the vector θ of the unknown parameters is $\begin{pmatrix} \alpha \\ \sigma^2 \end{pmatrix}$ and we can use the Kalman filter to compute the model likelihood function.

In this case, the initial values $\mathbf{m} = {}_{-1}\hat{\mathbf{z}}_0 = E\mathbf{z}_0$ and $\mathbf{P} = {}_{-1}\boldsymbol{\Sigma}_0 = \text{var}(\mathbf{z}_0)$ are
$$\mathbf{m} = E(\mathbf{z}_0) = \begin{pmatrix} 0 \\ 0 \end{pmatrix}, \qquad \mathbf{P} = \text{var}(\mathbf{z}_0) = \sigma^2 \begin{pmatrix} 1+\alpha^2 & \alpha \\ \alpha & \alpha^2 \end{pmatrix}.$$
Moreover, $\tilde{y}_0 = y_0 - E(y_0) = y_0$ and $_{-1}M_0 = \text{var}(y_0) = \sigma^2(1+\alpha^2)$.

The formula of direct forecast updating (15.12) allows one to write
$$_t\hat{\mathbf{z}}_{t+1} = \begin{pmatrix} 0 & 1 \\ 0 & 0 \end{pmatrix} {}_{t-1}\hat{\mathbf{z}}_t + \begin{pmatrix} 0 & 1 \\ 0 & 0 \end{pmatrix} \mathbf{K}_t(y_t - (1,0)\,_{t-1}\hat{\mathbf{z}}_t) \qquad (15.18)$$
with
$$\mathbf{K}_t = {}_{t-1}\boldsymbol{\Sigma}_t \begin{pmatrix} 1 \\ 0 \end{pmatrix} \left((1,0)\,_{t-1}\boldsymbol{\Sigma}_t \begin{pmatrix} 1 \\ 0 \end{pmatrix} \right)^{-1}.$$
From the particular form of $\mathbf{z}_t = \begin{pmatrix} y_t \\ \alpha u_t \end{pmatrix}$, we derive that
$$_{t-1}\hat{\mathbf{z}}_t = \begin{pmatrix} {}_{t-1}\hat{y}_t \\ 0 \end{pmatrix}, \qquad \mathbf{z}_t - {}_{t-1}\hat{\mathbf{z}}_t = \begin{pmatrix} y_t - {}_{t-1}\hat{y}_t \\ \alpha u_t \end{pmatrix}.$$
Therefore we have
$$_{t-1}\boldsymbol{\Sigma}_t = \text{var}(\mathbf{z}_t - {}_{t-1}\hat{\mathbf{z}}_t) = \text{var}\begin{pmatrix} y_t - {}_{t-1}\hat{y}_t \\ \alpha u_t \end{pmatrix} = \begin{pmatrix} {}_{t-1}M_t & \alpha\sigma^2 \\ \alpha\sigma^2 & \alpha^2\sigma^2 \end{pmatrix}.$$

The filter gain is equal to

$$\mathbf{K}_t = \frac{1}{{}_{t-1}M_t} \begin{pmatrix} {}_{t-1}M_t \\ \alpha\sigma^2 \end{pmatrix} = \begin{pmatrix} 1 \\ \alpha\sigma^2/({}_{t-1}M_t) \end{pmatrix}.$$

Considering the various results obtained, it is seen that the forecast updating formula is

$${}_t\hat{y}_{t+1} = \frac{\alpha\sigma^2}{{}_{t-1}M_t}(y_t - {}_{t-1}\hat{y}_t). \tag{15.19}$$

Similarly, the formula of direct updating of the corresponding variance–covariance matrices (15.11) becomes

$${}_t\Sigma_{t+1} = \begin{pmatrix} 0 & 1 \\ 0 & 0 \end{pmatrix}(\mathbf{I} - \mathbf{K}_t(0,1))\, {}_{t-1}\Sigma_t \begin{pmatrix} 0 & 0 \\ 1 & 0 \end{pmatrix} + \sigma^2 \begin{pmatrix} 1 & \alpha \\ \alpha & \alpha^2 \end{pmatrix}.$$

Considering the first diagonal element of the matrix ${}_t\Sigma_{t+1}$, we then derive the updating formula for the variance ${}_{t-1}M_t$. We have

$${}_tM_{t+1} = (0,1) \begin{pmatrix} 0 & 0 \\ \frac{-\alpha\sigma^2}{{}_{t-1}M_t} & 1 \end{pmatrix} \begin{pmatrix} {}_{t-1}M_t & \alpha\sigma^2 \\ \alpha\sigma^2 & \alpha^2\sigma^2 \end{pmatrix} \begin{pmatrix} 0 \\ 1 \end{pmatrix} + \sigma^2,$$

$${}_tM_{t+1} = \left(\frac{-\alpha\sigma^2}{{}_{t-1}M_t}, 1\right) \begin{pmatrix} \alpha\sigma^2 \\ \alpha^2\sigma^2 \end{pmatrix} + \sigma^2, \tag{15.20}$$

$${}_tM_{t+1} = \frac{-\alpha^2\sigma^4}{{}_{t-1}M_t} + \alpha^2\sigma^2 + \sigma^2.$$

The formulae (15.19) and (15.20) allow one to compute recursively

$${}_t\hat{y}_{t+1} = E(y_{t+1} \mid y_0 \ldots y_t)$$

and the associated error variance in a simple way.

The convenience of the recursive computation is apparent from the example. Indeed, the explicit computation of ${}_t\hat{y}_{t+1}$ and of ${}_tM_{t+1}$ would have been difficult, even though equation (15.20) can be fully solved in this example (see exercise 15.4).

2nd Method The representation of state that we have considered is not minimal; indeed for a process $MA(1)$ the minimal size of the state vector is 1. We can then start again the analysis from another representation satisfying the minimality condition. We have retained the one in which the state vector is

$$z_t = ({}_{t-1}\hat{y}_t) = \alpha u_{t-1}$$

and the corresponding state-space representation is

$$z_{t+1} = \mathbf{0}\, z_t + \alpha u_t,$$

$$y_t = z_t + u_t.$$

The two error terms $\epsilon_t = \alpha u_t$ and $\eta_t = u_t$ are correlated. First we have to eliminate this correlation (cf. 15.2.5). This is equivalent to writing the model under the form

$$z_{t+1} = -\alpha z_t + \alpha y_t,$$

$$y_t = z_t + u_t.$$

Taking into account the existence of an input in the state equation, the updating formulae of the Kalman filter are:

$$(a) \qquad {}_t\hat{z}_t = {}_{t-1}\hat{z}_t + K_t(y_t - {}_{t-1}\hat{y}_t)$$

with $K_t = {}_{t-1}\Sigma_t / \left({}_{t-1}\Sigma_t + \sigma^2\right)$,

$$(a') \qquad {}_t\Sigma_t = (1 - K_t)\,{}_{t-1}\Sigma_t,$$

$$(b) \qquad {}_t\hat{z}_{t+1} = -\alpha\,{}_t\hat{z}_t + \alpha y_t,$$

$$(b') \qquad {}_t\Sigma_{t+1} = \alpha^2\,{}_t\Sigma_t,$$

$$(c) \qquad {}_t\hat{y}_{t+1} = {}_t\hat{z}_{t+1},$$

$$(c') \qquad {}_tM_{t+1} = {}_t\Sigma_{t+1} + \sigma^2$$

from which the recursive formulae (15.19) and (15.20) can be derived (see exercise 15.5).

15.7 Exercises

Exercise 15.1: Let us consider the case (discussed in section 15.2.5) where the transition and the measurement matrices are stochastic.

(i)   Assuming C_0 nonrandom, prove that the conditional distribution of z_0 given y_0 is normal.

(ii) Verify that the conditional distribution of

$$z_{t+1} \mid z_t, y_0, \ldots, y_t$$

is the distribution

$$\mathcal{N}(A_t z_t, Q)$$

and that the conditional distribution of

$$y_{t+1} \mid z_t, z_{t+1}, y_0, \ldots, y_t.$$

is the distribution

$$\mathcal{N}(C_{t+1} z_{t+1}, R).$$

(iii) Using the results in (ii), prove that if the conditional distribution of

$$z_t \mid y_0, \ldots, y_t$$

is a normal distribution written as

$$\mathcal{N}(\,_t\hat{z}_t,\,_t\Sigma_t)$$

then the conditional distribution of

$$(z_t, z_{t+1}, y_{t+1}) \mid y_0, \ldots, y_t$$

is a normal distribution and the conditional distribution of z_{t+1} given $y_0, \ldots, y_{t+1}$ is a normal distribution as well.

Exercise 15.2: Let us consider the same hypotheses as in the previous exercise.

(i)   Derive the conditional distribution of

$$(z_t, z_{t+1})$$

given $(y_0, \ldots, y_t)$ as a function of $_t\hat{z}_t$ and $_t\Sigma_t$. Show that the equations (b) and (b') of the covariance filter are valid for the conditional expectations and for the conditional variance–covariance matrices.

(ii) Make explicit the conditional distribution of the triplet

$$(z_t, z_{t+1}, y_{t+1})$$

given $y_0, \ldots, y_t$ as a function of $_t\hat{z}_t$, $_t\hat{z}_{t+1}$, $_t\Sigma_t$, $_t\Sigma_{t+1}$. Deduce that the equations (a) and (a') of the covariance filter (taken at $t+1$) are satisfied by the conditional expectations and the conditional variance–covariance matrices.

Exercise 15.3: (Lemma of Matrix Inversion) Let us consider the nonsingular square matrix $\begin{pmatrix} \mathbf{A} & \mathbf{B} \\ \mathbf{C} & \mathbf{D} \end{pmatrix}$, where $\mathbf{A}$ and $\mathbf{D}$ are nonsingular square matrices.

Let us write the inverse matrix as $\begin{pmatrix} \mathbf{P} & \mathbf{Q} \\ \mathbf{R} & \mathbf{S} \end{pmatrix}$. Prove that

$$\mathbf{S} = (\mathbf{D} - \mathbf{C}\mathbf{A}^{-1}\mathbf{B})^{-1},$$

$$\mathbf{S} = \mathbf{D}^{-1} + \mathbf{D}^{-1}\mathbf{C}(\mathbf{A} - \mathbf{B}\mathbf{D}^{-1}\mathbf{C})^{-1}\mathbf{B}\mathbf{D}^{-1}.$$

Derive the matrix inversion lemma used in the proof of theorem 15.4.

Exercise 15.4: Let us write

$$N_{t+1} = \frac{1}{_tM_{t+1} - \sigma^2} + \frac{1}{\sigma^2(1 - \alpha^2)}.$$

Prove that the equation (15.19) can be written as

$$N_{t+1} = \frac{1}{\alpha^2}N_t$$

then show that

$$_tM_{t+1} = \sigma^2 + \sigma^2\frac{(1 - \alpha^2)\alpha^{2(t+1)}}{1 - \alpha^{2(t+1)}}.$$

Exercise 15.5: Let us consider the same hypotheses as in the second method of estimation of example 15.2. Prove that

$$_t\hat{y}_{t+1} = \alpha(y_t - {}_{t-1}\hat{y}_t)(1 - K_t),$$

and

$$_tM_{t+1} = \alpha^2(1 - K_t)_{t-1}\Sigma_t + \sigma^2.$$

Prove the formulae (15.18) and (15.19).

Exercise 15.6: Let us consider the model

$$y_t = \mathbf{x}_t'\mathbf{b} + \eta_t, \quad t = 0, \ldots, T,$$

where $\mathbf{x}_t'$ is a row vector and $\mathbf{b}$ follows a normal distribution $\mathcal{N}(\mathbf{0}, \mathbf{P})$, and where the errors η_t $t = 0, \ldots, T$ are independent, with the same distribution $\mathcal{N}(0, \sigma^2)$;

(i)   How is the vector $(b, y_0, \ldots, y_T)'$ distributed?

(ii) Derive the expression of the best linear forecast of b

$$E(\mathbf{b} \mid y_0, \ldots, y_T).$$

Verify that this forecast admits a simple expression as a function of the ordinary least squares estimator

$$\hat{\mathbf{b}}_T = \left(\sum_{t=1}^{T} \mathbf{x}_t' \mathbf{x}_t \right)^{-1} \left(\sum_{t=1}^{T} \mathbf{x}_t' y_t \right)$$

and that this expression appears as a "convex combination" of this estimator and zero.

(iii) How can this forecast be written when the matrix $\mathbf{P}^{-1}$ tends to the zero matrix? Give an interpretation of this hypothesis about the matrix $\mathbf{P}$ in terms of available a priori information on the parameter $\mathbf{b}$.

16

Applications of the State-space Model

16.1 Application to Linear Models

16.1.1 The Standard Linear Model

The Model The standard linear model is written as

$$y_t = \mathbf{x}_t \boldsymbol{\beta} + \eta_t$$

with $t = 0, \ldots, T$, and where $\mathbf{x}_t$ is a nonrandom row vector of size K, $\boldsymbol{\beta}$ is a column vector of K unknown parameters, and $\{\eta_t\}$ is a Gaussian white noise of variance σ^2. This model has for state-space representation

$$\boldsymbol{\beta}_{t+1} = \boldsymbol{\beta}_t (= \boldsymbol{\beta}_0 = \boldsymbol{\beta}) \quad t \geq 0,$$

$$y_t = \mathbf{x}_t \boldsymbol{\beta}_t + \eta_t, \quad t = 0, \ldots, T,$$

where $\boldsymbol{\beta}$ is independent of the η_t's.

Thus we have

$$\mathbf{z}_{t+1} = \boldsymbol{\beta}, \mathbf{A}_t = \mathbf{I}, \epsilon_t = 0, \mathbf{C}_t = \mathbf{x}_t, \mathbf{Q} = \mathbf{0}, \mathbf{S} = \mathbf{0}, \mathbf{R} = \sigma^2, n = 1.$$

The information filter with $\mathbf{Q} = \mathbf{0}$ (see remark 15.1) is written as:

(α) $_t\hat{\mathbf{u}}_t = {}_{t-1}\hat{\mathbf{u}}_t + \mathbf{x}_t' y_t / \sigma^2,$
(α') $_t\boldsymbol{\Sigma}_t^{-1} = {}_{t-1}\boldsymbol{\Sigma}_t^{-1} + \mathbf{x}_t' \mathbf{x}_t / \sigma^2,$
(β) $_t\hat{\mathbf{u}}_{t+1} = {}_t\hat{\mathbf{u}}_t,$
(β') $_t\boldsymbol{\Sigma}_{t+1}^{-1} = {}_t\boldsymbol{\Sigma}_t^{-1}.$

Using formulae (β) and (β'), the notation can be simplified by letting $\hat{\mathbf{u}}_t = {}_t\hat{\mathbf{u}}_t = {}_t\hat{\mathbf{u}}_{t+1}$ and $\boldsymbol{\Sigma}_t^{-1} = {}_t\boldsymbol{\Sigma}_t^{-1} = {}_t\boldsymbol{\Sigma}_{t+1}^{-1}$; we have then

$$\hat{\mathbf{u}}_t = \hat{\mathbf{u}}_{t-1} + \frac{\mathbf{x}_t' y_t}{\sigma^2},$$

$$\boldsymbol{\Sigma}_t^{-1} = \boldsymbol{\Sigma}_{t-1}^{-1} + \frac{\mathbf{x}_t'\mathbf{x}_t}{\sigma^2}. \tag{16.1}$$

Diffuse Prior and OLS Updating Formula If we use the diffuse prior $\boldsymbol{\Sigma}_{-1}^{-1} = \mathbf{0}$ and $\hat{\mathbf{u}}_{-1}^{-1} = \mathbf{0}$, we get

$$\boldsymbol{\Sigma}_T^{-1} = \sum_{t=0}^{T} \frac{\mathbf{x}_t'\mathbf{x}_t}{\sigma^2} = \frac{\mathbf{X}_T'\mathbf{X}_T}{\sigma^2},$$

$$\hat{\mathbf{u}}_T = \frac{1}{\sigma^2} \sum_{t=0}^{T} \mathbf{x}_t' y_t = \frac{1}{\sigma^2}\mathbf{X}_T'\mathbf{y}_T, \tag{16.2}$$

where $\mathbf{X}_T$ is the matrix whose rows are $\mathbf{x}_t', t = 0, \ldots, T$ and $\mathbf{y}_T$ is the vector of components $y_t, t = 0, \ldots, T$. If the matrix $\mathbf{X}_T'\mathbf{X}_T$ is nonsingular, by noting $\hat{\boldsymbol{\beta}}_t = {}_t\hat{\mathbf{z}}_t = {}_t\hat{\mathbf{z}}_{t+1} = \boldsymbol{\Sigma}_t\hat{\mathbf{u}}_t$ we have

$$\hat{\boldsymbol{\beta}}_T = (\mathbf{X}_T'\mathbf{X}_T)^{-1}\mathbf{X}_T'\mathbf{y}_T$$

which is the ordinary least squares formula.

We also know that the Kalman covariance filter is equivalent to the information filter when $\boldsymbol{\Sigma}_t^{-1}$ is nonsingular. In the information filter with a diffuse prior

$$\boldsymbol{\Sigma}_t^{-1} = \sum_{i=0}^{t} \frac{\mathbf{x}_i'\mathbf{x}_i}{\sigma^2},$$

and generally this matrix is nonsingular for t greater or equal to $K - 1$. The information filter with a diffuse prior is then equivalent to the covariance filter initialized at $t = K$ with initial values $\boldsymbol{\Sigma}_{K-1} = \sigma^2(\mathbf{X}_{K-1}'\mathbf{X}_{K-1})^{-1}$ and $\hat{\boldsymbol{\beta}}_{K-1}$, the OLS estimator based on the observations $t = 0, \ldots, K - 1$ (we will show that σ^2 does not occur in the computation of $\hat{\boldsymbol{\beta}}_t$).

Note that the updating formulae (a) and (a') of the covariance filter in theorem 15.1 are written as

$$\hat{\boldsymbol{\beta}}_t = \hat{\boldsymbol{\beta}}_{t-1} + \mathbf{K}_t\tilde{y}_t = \hat{\boldsymbol{\beta}}_{t-1} + K_t(y_t - \mathbf{x}_t\hat{\boldsymbol{\beta}}_{t-1}),$$

$$\boldsymbol{\Sigma}_t = (\mathbf{I} - \mathbf{K}_t\mathbf{x}_t)\boldsymbol{\Sigma}_{t-1}.$$

with, using (a')

$$\mathbf{K}_t = \mathbf{\Sigma}_{t-1}\mathbf{x}_t'(\mathbf{x}_t\mathbf{\Sigma}_{t-1}\mathbf{x}_t' + \sigma^2)^{-1} = \frac{\mathbf{\Sigma}_t\mathbf{x}_t'}{\sigma^2}.$$

These equations allow one to find the standard *updating of ordinary least squares* formulae

$$\hat{\beta}_t = \hat{\beta}_{t-1} + \frac{\mathbf{\Sigma}_t\mathbf{x}_t'}{\sigma^2}\left(y_t - {}_{t-1}\hat{y}_t\right)$$

or

$$\hat{\beta}_t = \hat{\beta}_{t-1} + (\mathbf{X}_t'\mathbf{X}_t)^{-1}\mathbf{x}_t'(y_t - \mathbf{x}_t\hat{\beta}_{t-1}). \qquad (16.3)$$

Note that (a') provides an updating formula for $(\mathbf{X}_t'\mathbf{X}_t)^{-1}$

$$(\mathbf{X}_t'\mathbf{X}_t)^{-1} = \left(\mathbf{I} - \frac{(\mathbf{X}_{t-1}'\mathbf{X}_{t-1})^{-1}\mathbf{x}_t'\mathbf{x}_t}{\mathbf{x}_t(\mathbf{X}_{t-1}'\mathbf{X}_{t-1})^{-1}\mathbf{x}_t' + 1}\right)(\mathbf{X}_{t-1}'\mathbf{X}_{t-1})^{-1}.$$

Recursive Residuals The *recursive residual* at time t is the quantity

$$w_t = \frac{y_t - \mathbf{x}_t\hat{\beta}_{t-1}}{\left(1 + \mathbf{x}_t(\mathbf{X}_{t-1}'\mathbf{X}_{t-1})^{-1}\mathbf{x}_t'\right)^{1/2}},$$

for $t \geq K - 1$.

By construction, the distribution of w_t conditional on β is $\mathcal{N}(0, \sigma^2)$ which corresponds to its nonconditional distribution as well. Note that the covariance between w_t and w_s, $r < s$, is zero

$$E(\eta_r - \mathbf{x}_r(\mathbf{X}_{r-1}'\mathbf{X}_{r-1})^{-1}\sum_{i=1}^{r-1}\mathbf{x}_i'\eta_i)(\eta_s - \mathbf{x}_s(\mathbf{X}_{s-1}'\mathbf{X}_{s-1})^{-1}\sum_{j=1}^{s-1}\mathbf{x}_j'\eta_j)$$

$$= \sigma^2(-\mathbf{x}_s(\mathbf{X}_{s-1}'\mathbf{X}_{s-1})^{-1}\mathbf{x}_r'$$

$$+ \mathbf{x}_r(\mathbf{X}_{r-1}'\mathbf{X}_{r-1})^{-1}(\mathbf{X}_{r-1}'\mathbf{X}_{r-1})(\mathbf{X}_{s-1}'\mathbf{X}_{s-1})^{-1}\mathbf{x}_s')$$

$$= 0.$$

The recursive residuals are independent of each other and have the same distribution $\mathcal{N}(0, \sigma^2)$. The usual estimator of the variance

$$s_T^2 = \frac{1}{T + 1 - K}\sum_{t=0}^{T}(y_t - \mathbf{x}_t\hat{\beta}_T)^2$$

converges to this variance σ^2. We derive the asymptotic distribution of the sum of the standardized recursive residuals

$$W_t = \sum_{j=K}^{t}\frac{w_j}{s_T} \xrightarrow{\mathrm{d}} \mathcal{N}(0, t - K + 1) \quad \forall\, t \geq K.$$

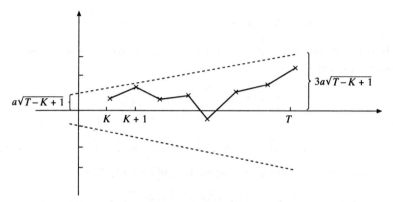

Figure 16.1   CUSUM Test

Using this result, Brown, Durbin, and Evans (1975) have proposed a
stability test of the coefficients of the model called *CUSUM test*, with a
critical region of asymptotic size α

$$\{\exists t, \ K \le t \le T,$$

$$\mid W_t \mid > a\sqrt{T - K + 1} + 2a(t - K + 1)/\sqrt{T - K + 1}\}, \qquad (16.4)$$

with $a = 0.95$, if $\alpha = 5\%$ and $a = 1.14$ if $\alpha = 1\%$.

We accept the hypothesis of coefficient stability if for $t \in \{K, \ldots, T\}$
the points in the plane (t, W_t) remain between the lines going through
the points $\{K - 1, \pm a\sqrt{T - K + 1}\}$ and $\{T, \pm 3a\sqrt{T - K + 1}\}$ (cf. figure
16.1).

16.1.2 Linear Model with Time-varying Coefficients

Let us consider the linear model

$$y_t = \mathbf{x}_t \boldsymbol{\beta}_t + \eta_t, t = 0, \ldots, T, \qquad (16.5)$$

where the coefficients $\boldsymbol{\beta}_t$ follow the equation

$$\boldsymbol{\beta}_{t+1} = \mathbf{A}\boldsymbol{\beta}_t + \boldsymbol{\mu} + \boldsymbol{\varepsilon}_t. \qquad (16.6)$$

The processes $\{\eta_t\}, \{\boldsymbol{\varepsilon}_t\}$ are independent white noises with var $(\eta_t) =$
σ^2, var $(\boldsymbol{\varepsilon}_t) = \mathbf{Q}$. Equations (16.5) and (16.6) form a particular state-
space model, in which the transition matrix is fixed and the correlation
between η_t and $\boldsymbol{\varepsilon}_t$ is zero. The methods described previously apply
directly, making use of the provisos introduced in section 15.2.5 when a
constant $\boldsymbol{\mu}$ is present.

The model depends on the unknown parameters $\boldsymbol{\theta}$ in $\mathbf{A}, \boldsymbol{\mu}, \sigma^2, \mathbf{Q}$. Assuming that the process $\boldsymbol{\beta}_t$ is stationary (i.e., the eigenvalues of $\mathbf{A}$ are

smaller than 1 in modulus) corresponds to imposing the initial conditions

$$_{-1}\hat{\boldsymbol{\beta}}_0 = E(\boldsymbol{\beta}_0) = (\mathbf{I} - \mathbf{A})^{-1}\boldsymbol{\mu}$$

and

$$_{-1}\boldsymbol{\Sigma}_0 = \text{var}\,(\boldsymbol{\beta}_0) = \sum_{i=0}^{\infty} \mathbf{A}^i \mathbf{Q} \mathbf{A}'^i.$$

The estimation of $\boldsymbol{\theta}$ can be done by maximum likelihood using the Kalman filter to compute the value of the log-likelihood function for a given $\boldsymbol{\theta}$.

When the estimation phase has been performed we can replace $\boldsymbol{\theta}$ by the estimated $\hat{\boldsymbol{\theta}}$ in $\mathbf{A}, \boldsymbol{\mu}, \sigma^2, \mathbf{Q}$ and use the smoothing algorithm to compute $_T\hat{\boldsymbol{\beta}}_t = E(\boldsymbol{\beta}_t \mid y_0, \ldots, y_T)$ and $_T\boldsymbol{\Sigma}_t = \text{var}\,(\boldsymbol{\beta}_t - {}_T\hat{\boldsymbol{\beta}}_t)$. Thus we get an estimation of the path of the time-varying coefficients $\boldsymbol{\beta}_t$.

16.2 Applications to the ARMA and ARIMA Models

16.2.1 Stationary Case

To simplify the notation, we only consider the univariate case, but the following results can be immediately generalized to the multivariate case. We have seen in chapter 8 that the ARMA process defined by

$$y_t + \varphi_1 y_{t-1} + \ldots + \varphi_p y_{t-p} = \epsilon_t + \theta_1 \epsilon_{t-1} + \ldots + \theta_q \epsilon_{t-q} \qquad (16.7)$$

with $\text{var}\,(\epsilon_t) = \sigma^2$ can be written as a state-space model. Denoting $K = \max(p, q)$, we have a minimal representation provided by

$$\mathbf{z}_{t+1} = \begin{pmatrix} 0 & 1 & \ldots & 0 \\ \vdots & \vdots & \ddots & \vdots \\ 0 & 0 & \ldots & 1 \\ -\varphi_K & -\varphi_{K-1} & \ldots & -\varphi_1 \end{pmatrix} \mathbf{z}_t + \begin{pmatrix} h_1 \\ \vdots \\ \vdots \\ h_K \end{pmatrix} \epsilon_t, \qquad (16.8)$$

$$y_t = (1, 0, \ldots, 0)\mathbf{z}_t + \epsilon_t,$$

where $\varphi_i = 0$, if $i > p$ and where the h_i are Markov coefficients.

In this representation the state vector is

$$\mathbf{z}_t = \begin{pmatrix} _{t-1}\hat{y}_t \\ \vdots \\ _{t-1}\hat{y}_{t+K-1} \end{pmatrix}. \qquad (16.9)$$

Another possible representation is

$$
\mathbf{z}_{t+1} =
\begin{pmatrix}
-\varphi_1 & \cdots & \cdots & -\varphi_{p-1} & -\varphi_p & \theta_1 & \cdots & \cdots & \theta_{q-1} & \theta_q \\
1 & 0 & \cdots & 0 & 0 & 0 & \cdots & \cdots & \cdots & 0 \\
0 & 1 & \cdots & 0 & 0 & 0 & \cdots & \cdots & \cdots & 0 \\
\vdots & \vdots & \ddots & \vdots & \vdots & \vdots & \cdots & \cdots & \cdots & \vdots \\
0 & 0 & \cdots & 1 & 0 & 0 & \cdots & \cdots & \cdots & 0 \\
0 & 0 & \cdots & 0 & 0 & 0 & \cdots & \cdots & \cdots & 0 \\
0 & \cdots & \cdots & 0 & 0 & 1 & 0 & \cdots & 0 & 0 \\
\vdots & \cdots & \cdots & \vdots & \vdots & 0 & 1 & \cdots & 0 & 0 \\
\vdots & \cdots & \cdots & \vdots & \vdots & \vdots & \vdots & \ddots & \vdots & \vdots \\
0 & \cdots & \cdots & 0 & 0 & 0 & 0 & \cdots & 1 & 0
\end{pmatrix}
\mathbf{z}_t
$$

$$
+
\begin{pmatrix}
1 \\ 0 \\ \vdots \\ \vdots \\ 0 \\ 0 \\ 1 \\ 0 \\ \vdots \\ \vdots \\ 0
\end{pmatrix}
\epsilon_{t+1},
$$

$$
y_t = (1, 0, \ldots, 0)\mathbf{z}_t
$$

$$(16.10)$$

with

$$
\mathbf{z}_t =
\begin{pmatrix}
y_t \\
\vdots \\
y_{t-p+1} \\
\epsilon_t \\
\vdots \\
\epsilon_{t-q+1}
\end{pmatrix}.
$$

This representation is not in general minimal (except in the cases of a pure AR or a pure MA). Note that there is no measurement error and therefore there is no correlation between the measurement error and the transition equation disturbance, which is not the case for the representation (16.8). Nevertheless, (16.8) can be slightly modified to avoid this correlation. For example, taking $K = \max(p, q+1)$ and the state vector

$$
\mathbf{z}_t = \begin{pmatrix} y_t \\ {}_t\hat{y}_{t+1} \\ \vdots \\ {}_t\hat{y}_{t+K-1} \end{pmatrix},
$$

we have

$$
\mathbf{z}_{t+1} = \begin{pmatrix} 0 & 1 & 0 & \cdots & 0 \\ \vdots & 0 & 1 & \ddots & \vdots \\ \vdots & \vdots & 0 & \ddots & \vdots \\ 0 & 0 & \cdots & \cdots & 1 \\ -\varphi_K & -\varphi_{K-1} & \cdots & \cdots & -\varphi_1 \end{pmatrix} \mathbf{z}_t + \begin{pmatrix} 1 \\ h_1 \\ \vdots \\ \vdots \\ h_{K-1} \end{pmatrix} \epsilon_{t+1},
$$

$$
y_t = (1, 0, \ldots, 0)\,\mathbf{z}_t.
$$

$$(16.11)$$

This representation is not minimal if $q + 1 > p$. Of course there exist other representations (cf. exercises 16.3 and 16.4).

The computation of the log-likelihood function proceeds as presented in chapter 15. One just needs to find out the starting values. We have

$$
\mathbf{m} = E(\mathbf{z}_0) = \mathbf{0}
$$

for the above representations. Moreover, since the process is stationary we can compute the quantity $\mathbf{P} = \mathrm{var}\,(\mathbf{z}_0)$, as a known function of the parameters $\varphi_1, \ldots, \varphi_p, \theta_1, \ldots, \theta_q, \sigma^2$.

Another possibility is to compute the log-likelihood function of the observations $y_1, \ldots, y_T$ knowing $\mathbf{z}_0 = \boldsymbol{\zeta}_0$, where $\boldsymbol{\zeta}_0$ is a fixed value; this method avoids the computation of $\mathrm{var}\,(\mathbf{z}_0)$ since the initial values of the filter are

$$
{}_0\hat{\mathbf{z}}_0 = \boldsymbol{\zeta}_0 \quad \text{and} \quad {}_0\boldsymbol{\Sigma}_0 = \mathbf{0}.
$$

If, for example, we use the representation (16.10), one possibility is to index the observations y_t starting from $t = -p + 1$ and to use

$$\zeta_0 = \begin{pmatrix} y_0 \\ \vdots \\ y_{-p+1} \\ 0 \\ \vdots \\ 0 \end{pmatrix}.$$

For practical purposes, one could use the information filter with a diffuse prior or the covariance filter with $\mathbf{m} = 0$, $\mathbf{P} = \lambda \mathbf{I}$ (where λ is a large scalar) and compute the likelihood function starting from the index after which the computation of ${}_t\hat{\mathbf{z}}_{t+1}$, ${}_t\mathbf{\Sigma}_{t+1}\,{}_t\hat{y}_{t+1}$ and ${}_t\mathbf{M}_{t+1}$ is possible.

When these parameters have been estimated we can use the forecasting algorithm to compute the ${}_t\hat{y}_{t+h}$ and ${}_t\mathbf{M}_{t+h}$.

16.2.2 Nonstationary Case

Let us consider an ARIMA process defined by

$$\phi(L)(1 - L)^d y_t = \Theta(L)\epsilon_t$$

for $t \geq 1$, and where

$$\phi(L) = 1 + \phi_1 L + \ldots + \phi_p L^p,$$

$$\Theta(L) = 1 + \theta_1 L + \ldots + \theta_q L^q$$

are polynomials with roots bigger than 1 in modulus, where the initial conditions $(y_0, \ldots, y_{-p-d+1}, \epsilon_0, \ldots, \epsilon_{-q+1})$ are not correlated with $\epsilon_1, \ldots, \epsilon_t, \ldots$, and where the process $\epsilon = (\epsilon_t, t \geq -q + 1)$ is a white noise of variance σ^2.

The representation (16.10) remains valid provided that $\phi_1, \ldots, \phi_p$ are replaced by the $p + d$ coefficients of $\Phi(L) = \phi(L)(1 - L)^d$. The vector $\mathbf{z}_0$ is

$$\mathbf{z}_0 = \begin{pmatrix} y_0 \\ y_{-p-d+1} \\ \epsilon_0 \\ \vdots \\ \epsilon_{-q+1} \end{pmatrix}.$$

Contrary to the stationary case the quantities $E(\mathbf{z}_0)$ and $\mathrm{var}\,(\mathbf{z}_0)$ cannot be computed from the parameters $\phi_1, \ldots, \phi_p, \theta_1, \ldots, \theta_q, \sigma^2$, and we can compute the likelihood function of the model only if we introduce more hypotheses on $E(\mathbf{z}_0)$ and $\mathrm{var}\,(\mathbf{z}_0)$. On the other hand, it is always possible to compute the log-likelihood function of $y_1, \ldots, y_T$ knowing $\mathbf{z}_0 = \zeta_0$.

Upon appropriate indexing of the observations, a possible value of ζ_0 is

$$
\mathbf{z}_0 = \begin{pmatrix} y_0 \\ \vdots \\ y_{-p-d+1} \\ 0 \\ \vdots \\ 0 \end{pmatrix}.
$$

If we write $w_t = (1 - L)^d y_t$, this log-likelihood is also the conditional log-likelihood function of $w_1, \ldots, w_T$ conditional on

$$
w_0, \ldots, w_{-p+1}, \quad \epsilon_0 = 0, \ldots, \epsilon_{-q+1} = 0,
$$

that is the log-likelihood function of an asymptotically stationary process. To compute this likelihood function, an alternative would be to work directly with the (asymptotically) ARMA series $w_1, \ldots, w_T$ and to use the described methods for the ARMA models. However this method does not allow to use the same representation for the further computation of the forecasts $_T\hat{y}_{T+h}$ and it cannot be used for a model with unobserved components, the components of which are ARIMA.

16.3 Unobserved Components Models

The state-space representation is often more suited to the analysis of the aggregation problems. The observed series (y_t) is then defined as the sum of various *components* $(u_t^i)\, i = 1 \ldots I$, generally unobserved. The model appears in the form

$$
y_t = \sum_{i=1}^{I} u_t^i \tag{16.12}
$$

and is called an *unobserved components* model.

We usually assume that the subprocesses $(u_t^i)i = 1, \ldots, I$ are independent of each other and we specify their marginal distributions or at least the two first moments of these distributions.

16.3.1 Seasonal Adjustment in ARIMA Components Models

ARMA or ARIMA Components When the components u^i admit ARMA or ARIMA representations, they can also be put in state-space form of the type

$$\mathbf{z}_{t+1}^i = \mathbf{A}_i \mathbf{z}_t^i + \boldsymbol{\varepsilon}_t^i,$$
$$u_t^i = (1, 0, \ldots, 0) \mathbf{z}_t^i, \tag{16.13}$$

where the errors ϵ^i are independent.

We derive a state-space representation of the observed process by taking the set of state variables associated to various components as state variable

$$\mathbf{z}_{t+1} = \begin{pmatrix} \mathbf{z}_{t+1}^1 \\ \vdots \\ \mathbf{z}_{t+1}^I \end{pmatrix} = \begin{pmatrix} \mathbf{A}_1 & \cdots & 0 \\ \vdots & \ddots & \vdots \\ 0 & \cdots & \mathbf{A}_I \end{pmatrix} \mathbf{z}_t + \begin{pmatrix} \boldsymbol{\varepsilon}_t^1 \\ \vdots \\ \boldsymbol{\varepsilon}_t^I \end{pmatrix}, \tag{16.14}$$

$$y_t = (1, 0, \ldots, 0, 1, 0, \ldots, 1, 0, \ldots, 0) \, \mathbf{z}_t.$$

We can use this form for estimation. Once we specify the way the matrices $\mathbf{A}_i$ and $\mathrm{var}\,(\epsilon_t^i)$ depend on the underlying parameters $\boldsymbol{\theta}$, we can use the Kalman filter to compute the likelihood function. When the components are all stationary, the initialization of the filter is easily done; if some components are ARIMA we can compute the conditional likelihood function for an initial value of the state vector or we can use the information algorithm with a diffuse prior.

Another approach is a priori possible. Since a sum of independent ARMA processes is still an ARMA process, we could derive the ARMA form of the observed process directly. Unfortunately the latter form depends in a complex way on the parameters $\mathbf{A}_i$, $\mathrm{var}\,(\epsilon_t^i)$, which makes its use for the computation of the likelihood function difficult in practice. Moreover, note that the Kalman smoothing applied to the model (16.14) provides also some approximations of the state variables such as, for example, $E(\mathbf{z}_t \mid y_t, \ldots, y_T), t = 1, \ldots, T$. Since the unobserved components are coordinates of this state vector, the smoothing provides some approximation of the various components

$$\hat{u}_T^i = E(u_t^i \mid y_1, \ldots, y_T).$$

We can therefore obtain a disaggregation of the initial series at each date

$$y_t = \sum_{i=1}^{I} \hat{u}_t^i.$$

Application to Seasonal Adjustment The approach of the seasonal adjustment problem by regression (recall Buys-Ballot's model in chapter 2) is based on a decomposition of the original series into three components: trend, seasonal, and noise. The first one is often described by a polynomial while the second one by a strictly periodical series. We already noted that this type of decomposition is in fact not very simple to use since the way the trend and seasonal components are modeled is restrictive. Starting from the original idea of the decomposition, we can follow a more symmetrical approach for the various components (Nerlove, Grether, Carvalho, and Diebold, 1994, Hillmer and Tiao, 1982, Maravall, 1985), decomposing the series into three independent random terms

$$y_t = u_t^\tau + u_t^s + u_t^I \tag{16.15}$$

for $t \geq 0$, which represent respectively the trend, the seasonal, and the irregular part. Moreover, each component is assumed to admit a suitable ARIMA representation.

To model the trend we can take a representation with a unit root in the autoregressive part

$$(1 - L)^d u_t^\tau = \frac{\Theta_\tau(L)}{\phi_\tau(L)} \tilde{\epsilon}_t^\tau, \tag{16.16}$$

where Θ_τ and ϕ_τ have roots outside of the unit circle and where the noise is of variance σ_τ^2.

In order to model the seasonal component of period S, we can take an autoregressive part divisible by $S(L) = 1 + L + \dots L^{S-1} = \frac{1-L^S}{1-L}$

$$S(L) u_t^s = \frac{\Theta_s(L)}{\phi_s(L)} \tilde{\epsilon}_t^s, \qquad \text{var}\,(\epsilon_t^s) = \sigma_s^2. \tag{16.17}$$

Finally the irregular part can be modeled by a stationary ARMA

$$u_t^I = \frac{\Theta_I(L)}{\phi_I(L)} \tilde{\epsilon}_t^I, \qquad \text{var}\,(\epsilon_t^I) = \sigma_I^2. \tag{16.18}$$

The overall model relative to the initial series is

$$y_t = \frac{1}{(1-L)^d} \frac{\Theta_\tau(L)}{\phi_\tau(L)} \tilde{\epsilon}_t^\tau + \frac{1}{S(L)} \frac{\Theta_s(L)}{\phi_s(L)} \tilde{\epsilon}_t^s + \frac{\Theta_I(L)}{\phi_I(L)} \tilde{\epsilon}_t^I. \tag{16.19}$$

The ARIMA representation of the series y is deduced from the pseudo-spectrum

$$f_y(\omega) = \frac{\sigma_\tau^2}{2\pi} \frac{\mid \Theta_\tau(\exp(i\omega)) \mid^2}{\mid 1 - \exp(i\omega) \mid^{2d} \mid \phi_\tau \exp(i\omega) \mid^2}$$

$$+ \frac{\sigma_s^2}{2\pi} \frac{\mid \Theta_s(\exp(i\omega)) \mid^2}{\mid S(\exp(i\omega)) \mid^2 \mid \phi_s(\exp(i\omega)) \mid^2} \tag{16.20}$$

$$+ \frac{\sigma_I^2}{2\pi} \frac{\mid \Theta_I(\exp(i\omega)) \mid^2}{\mid \phi_I(\exp(i\omega)) \mid^2}.$$

This can always be written as

$$f_y(\omega) = \frac{\sigma^2}{2\pi} \frac{\mid G(\exp i\omega) \mid^2}{\mid H(\exp i\omega) \mid^2},$$

but the derivation of the variance of the noise σ^2 and of the moving average polynomial G is difficult; their expressions depend in a complex way on the initial parameters $\sigma_\tau^2, \sigma_s^2, \sigma_I^2, \Theta_\tau, \Theta_s, \Theta_I, \phi_\tau, \phi_s, \phi_I$. This explains why the use of the state-space representation for the estimation simplifies this process.

This representation is particularly well-suited for the estimation of the components, i.e., of the trend, the seasonal, and the irregular part. For instance, the Kalman smoother provides right away the SA (seasonally adjusted) series

$$y_t - E\left(u_t^s \mid y_1 \dots y_T\right) = E\left(u_t^\tau \mid y_1 \dots y_T\right) + E\left(u_t^I \mid y_1 \dots y_T\right). \quad (16.21)$$

Optimal Moving Average We can analyze the issue of seasonal adjustment in more detail. Assuming that the initial series satisfies an unobserved component model with stationary components, the best estimator of $y_t - u_t^s$ is a linear function of the observations because of model linearity

$$y_t^{SA} = E\left(y_t - u_t^s \mid y_1, \dots, y_T\right) = \sum_{j=1-t}^{T-t} a_{j,t,T} y_{t+j}.$$

An approximate solution can be obtained by replacing $(y_1 \dots y_T)$ by $(y_t,\, t = -\infty, \dots, +\infty)$

$$y_t^{SA} \approx \sum_{j=-\infty}^{+\infty} a_j y_{t+j},$$

where this time the coefficients are independent of the indexes t and T. Thus the optimal determination of the seasonal adjustment is done through the application of a moving average $\sum_{j=-\infty}^{+\infty} a_j L^j$. The way to compute the coefficients a_j is given by the following theorem.

Theorem 16.1: *Let*

$$\mathbf{y}_t = \begin{pmatrix} \mathbf{y}_{1t} \\ \mathbf{y}_{2t} \end{pmatrix}$$

be a multivariate zero-mean stationary process admitting an infinite moving average representation. Let

$$\mathbf{f}_y = \begin{pmatrix} \mathbf{f}_{y_1} & \mathbf{f}_{y_1 y_2} \\ \mathbf{f}_{y_2 y_1} & \mathbf{f}_{y_2} \end{pmatrix}$$

be its spectral density matrix with $\det(\mathbf{f}_{y2}) \neq 0$. *Then the optimal forecast of* $\mathbf{y}_{1t}$ *conditional on* $\mathbf{y}_{2,t+j}, j$ *integer, is of the form*

$$E\left(\mathbf{y}_1 \mid \mathbf{y}_{2,t+j}, j = -\infty, \dots, +\infty\right) = \sum_{j=-\infty}^{+\infty} \mathbf{A}_j \mathbf{y}_{2,t+j}$$

with

$$A(\exp(-i\omega)) = \sum_{j=-\infty}^{+\infty} A_j \exp(-i\omega j) = f_{y_1 y_2}(\omega) f_{y_2}(\omega)^{-1}.$$

PROOF: The conditional expectation is characterized by the orthogonality between the forecast error and the conditioning variables.
We have

$$E\left(\left(y_{1t} - \sum_{j=-\infty}^{+\infty} A_j y_{2,t+j}\right) y'_{2,t+h}\right) = 0, \ \forall \ h$$

$$\Leftrightarrow E\left(y_1 y'_{2,t+h}\right) - \sum_{j=-\infty}^{+\infty} A_j E\left(y_{2t+j} y'_{2t+h}\right) = 0, \ \forall \ h.$$

Introducing the autocovariances, we get

$$\Gamma^{(h)}_{y_1,y_2} - \sum_{j=-\infty}^{+\infty} A_j \Gamma^{(h-j)}_{y2} = 0, \forall \ h$$

$$\Leftrightarrow \Gamma_{y_1,y_2} = A \star \Gamma_{y_2},$$

where $\star$ indicates the convolution product. It is sufficient then to transpose this equality to the frequency domain. $\square$

We can show that this property remains valid in the cases of ARIMA and SARIMA processes (Cleveland and Tiao, 1976; Pierce, 1979b). Applying this property to unobserved components, we have

$$y_t^{SA} \approx E\left(u_t^\tau \mid y_{t+j}, j = -\infty, \ldots, +\infty\right) + E\left(u_t^I \mid y_{t+j}\right)$$

$$= \sum_{j=-\infty}^{+\infty} a_j y_{t+j},$$

with $j = -\infty, \ldots, +\infty$ and where the coefficients a_j are such that

$$A(\exp(-i\omega)) = \frac{B_\tau + B_I}{B_\tau + B_S + B_I}, \tag{16.22}$$

where

$$B_\tau = \frac{\sigma_\tau^2}{2\pi} \frac{\mid \Theta_\tau(\exp(i\omega)) \mid^2}{\mid 1 - \exp(i\omega) \mid^{2d} \mid \phi_\tau(\exp(i\omega)) \mid^2},$$

$$B_I = \frac{\sigma_I^2}{2\pi} \frac{\mid \Theta_I(\exp(i\omega)) \mid^2}{\mid \phi_I(\exp(i\omega)) \mid^2},$$

$$B_S = \frac{\sigma_S^2}{2\pi} \frac{\mid \Theta_S(\exp(i\omega)) \mid^2}{\mid S(\exp(i\omega)) \mid^2 \mid \phi_s(\exp(i\omega)) \mid^2}.$$

Note that the optimal moving average has some properties that were found desirable for seasonal adjustment.

(i)   We have

$$A(\exp(-i\omega)) = A(\exp(i\omega))$$

which means that the moving average is symmetric: $a_{-j} = a_j$.

(ii) If the frequency tends to 0, we have

$$\lim_{\omega \to 0} A(\exp(-i\omega)) = 1.$$

In coefficient terms this can be written as $\sum_{j=-\infty}^{+\infty} a_j = 1$ and corresponds to the conservation of constant sequences (and polynomials of degree 1, cf. theorem 3.5).

(iii) If ω goes to one of the seasonal frequencies $\frac{2\pi l}{S}$, $l = 1, \ldots, S - 1$, we see that $A(\exp(-i\omega))$ goes to 0. This implies that

$$\sum_{j=-\infty}^{+\infty} a_j \exp \frac{2\pi i j l}{S} = 0,$$

that is, strictly periodic series of period S become 0.

16.3.2 "Structural" Models

Harrison and Stevens's Models Harrison and Stevens (1976) have proposed forecast methods based on unobserved components models in which each component has an intuitive interpretation. This allows us to use "subjective" information in order to modify the automatic procedure for the forecast of each component; hence the name of "Bayesian" forecast for these methods.

The most standard model among those proposed by Harrison and Stevens, is the *stochastic linear growth model* defined by

$$y_t = \mu_t + \eta_t,$$

$$\mu_{t+1} = \mu_t + \theta_t + u_t, \tag{16.23}$$

$$\theta_{t+1} = \theta_t + v_t$$

with

$$\text{var}(\eta_t) = \sigma_\eta^2,$$

$$\text{var}(u_t) = \sigma_u^2,$$

$$\text{var}(v_t) = \sigma_v^2.$$

In this model $\{\eta_t\}, \{u_t\}, \{v_t\}$ are independent Gaussian white noises. The variable μ_t is interpreted as a "random level" and the variable θ_t as a "random slope"; when μ_t and θ_t have nonzero initial values and when

$\sigma_u^2 = \sigma_v^2 = 0$, μ_t and θ_t become deterministic and the model is reduced to the deterministic linear trend $y_t = at + b + \mu_t$.

The model can be written in the state-space form, by posing

$$\mathbf{z}_t = \begin{pmatrix} \mu_t \\ \theta_t \end{pmatrix}.$$

We have

$$\mathbf{z}_{t+1} = \begin{pmatrix} 1 & 1 \\ 0 & 1 \end{pmatrix} \mathbf{z}_t + \begin{pmatrix} u_t \\ v_t \end{pmatrix},$$

(16.24)

$$y_t = (1, 0)\mathbf{z}_t + \eta_t.$$

The general techniques of filtering, estimation, and smoothing previously described can then be used.

Note that the process $\{y\}$ is the sum of the various independent components. Indeed, we have

$$\mu_t = \frac{L}{1-L}\theta_t + \frac{L}{1-L}u_t$$

and

$$\theta_t = \frac{L}{1-L}v_t.$$

Therefore

$$y_t = \mu_t + \eta_t$$

$$= \frac{L}{1-L}\theta_t + \frac{L}{1-L}u_t + \eta_t,$$

$$y_t = \frac{L^2}{(1-L)^2}v_t + \frac{L}{1-L}u_t + \eta_t.$$

The first two components correspond to independent explosive (at different rates) terms.

Hence the initial process admits an ARIMA(0, 2, 2) representation. In fact, we have

$$\Delta^2 y_t = L^2 v_t + L(1-L)u_t + (1-L)^2\eta_t$$

$$= v_{t-2} + u_{t-1} - u_{t-2} + \eta_t - 2\eta_{t-1} + \eta_{t-2}.$$

We obtain

$$\text{cov}\,(\Delta^2 y_t, \Delta^2 y_{t+h}) = 0, \forall\, h > 2,$$

therefore $\Delta^2 y_t$ is an MA(2) process.

The other autocovariances of the process $\Delta^2 y_t$ are

$$\gamma(0) = \sigma_v^2 + 2\sigma_u^2 + 6\sigma_\eta^2,$$

$$\gamma(1) = -\sigma_u^2 - 4\sigma_\eta^2,$$

$$\gamma(2) = \sigma_\eta^2.$$

Note that y_t is not any ARIMA(0, 2, 2) process since the signs of $\gamma(1), \gamma(2)$ are constrained. The equations providing $\gamma(0)$, $\gamma(1)$, $\gamma(2)$ can be used to compute consistent estimators of the noise variances, since

$$\sigma_\eta^2 = \gamma(2), \ \sigma_u^2 = -\gamma(1) - 4\gamma(2), \ \sigma_v^2 = \gamma(0) + 2\gamma(1) - 2\gamma(2).$$

We just have to replace in these relations the theorical autocovariances by their empirical counterpart. These estimators can be used as the initial values of parameters in the likelihood function maximization.

Harvey's Models   Harvey (1984, 1989) has proposed an extension of the Harrison and Stevens models allowing to consider the case of seasonal series (see also Harvey and Todd, 1983). These models have been dubbed "structural," although there is no explicative aspect as in the usual macroeconomic models.

The simplest model of this type is the following

$$y_t = \mu_t + \gamma_t + \eta_t,$$

$$\mu_{t+1} = \mu_t + \theta_t + u_t,$$

$$\theta_{t+1} = \theta_t + v_t, \qquad\qquad (16.25)$$

$$\gamma_{t+1} = -\sum_{j=1}^{S-1} \gamma_{t+1-j} + w_t,$$

where $(\eta_t), (u_t), (v_t), (w_t)$ are independent Gaussian white noise and

$$\mathrm{var}\,(\eta_t) = \sigma_\eta^2,$$

$$\mathrm{var}\,(u_t) = \sigma_u^2,$$

$$\mathrm{var}\,(v_t) = \sigma_v^2,$$

$$\mathrm{var}\,(w_t) = \sigma_w^2.$$

The new term appearing in the decomposition of y_t is the component $\gamma_t = w_t/S(L)$ which can be interpreted as a seasonal component. The first component can be interpreted as a trend term and decomposed according to its dominating components of various orders.

This model provides a simple example of decomposition for the seasonal analysis of the type given in (16.19). We have

$$y_t = \frac{L^2}{(1-L)^2}v_t + \frac{L}{1-L}u_t + \frac{L}{S(L)}w_t + \eta_t, \qquad (16.26)$$

where the first two terms on the right-hand side represent the trend, the third represents the seasonal component, and the last the irregular part.

As an example, let us consider the case $S = 4$ (quarterly series) and a state-space representation by taking as the state vector

$$\mathbf{z}_t' = (\mu_t, \theta_t, \gamma_t, \gamma_{t-1}, \gamma_{t-2}).$$

We have

$$\mathbf{z}_{t+1} = \begin{pmatrix} 1 & 1 & 0 & 0 & 0 \\ 0 & 1 & 0 & 0 & 0 \\ 0 & 0 & -1 & -1 & -1 \\ 0 & 0 & 1 & 0 & 0 \\ 0 & 0 & 0 & 1 & 0 \end{pmatrix} \mathbf{z}_t + \begin{pmatrix} u_t \\ v_t \\ w_t \\ 0 \\ 0 \end{pmatrix},$$

$$y_t = (\, 1 \quad 0 \quad 1 \quad 0 \quad 0\,)\, \mathbf{z}_t + \eta_t.$$

Model (16.26) depends only on the various noise variances $\sigma_v^2, \sigma_u^2, \sigma_w^2$, and σ_η^2 only. It is therefore of interest to derive the estimators of these variances. We can generalize the approach of the previous section.

Let us write $\Delta = (1 - L)$, $\Delta_S = 1 - L^S = (1 - L)S(L)$, so that

$$\Delta\Delta_S y_t = S(L)v_{t-2} + \Delta_S u_{t-1} + \Delta^2 w_{t-1} + \Delta\Delta_S \eta_t.$$

The second term is a moving average of order $S + 1$ and the initial process has therefore a SARIMA form. We verify also that for $S = 4$ the autocovariance function of $\Delta\Delta_S \, y_t$ is

$$\gamma(0) = 2\sigma_u^2 + 4\sigma_v^2 + 6\sigma_w^2 + 4\sigma_\eta^2,$$

$$\gamma(1) = 3\sigma_v^2 - 4\sigma_w^2 - 2\sigma_\eta^2,$$

$$\gamma(2) = 2\sigma_v^2 + \sigma_w^2,$$

$$\gamma(3) = \sigma_v^2 + \sigma_\eta^2,$$

$$\gamma(4) = -\sigma_u^2 - 2\sigma_\eta^2,$$

$$\gamma(5) = \sigma_\eta^2,$$

$$\gamma(h) = 0, \ \forall \, h > 5.$$

We have six equations linking the four parameters σ_u^2, σ_v^2, σ_w^2, and σ_η^2. From the empirical autocovariances we can derive various consistent estimators of these parameters, the optimal estimation being achieved through asymptotic least squares (see Gourieroux, Monfort, and Trognon, 1985). These estimators can be used as initial values of the parameters in the likelihood function maximization.

16.3.3 Linear Models with Stochastic Trend

Another possible domain of application of the techniques of this chapter are linear models with stochastic trend

$$y_t = \mu_t + \mathbf{x}_t\boldsymbol{\beta} + \eta_t,$$

where $\mathbf{x}_t$ is a row vector of K observed deterministic variables, $\boldsymbol{\beta}$ an unknown parameter vector, η_t a white noise of variance σ_η^2, and μ_t a stochastic trend which can be modeled, for example, as in Harrison and Stevens

$$\mu_{t+1} = \mu_t + \theta_t + u_t,$$

$$\theta_{t+1} = \theta_t + v_t.$$

This model can be written in state-space form by letting, for instance

$$\mathbf{z}_t' = (\mu_t, \theta_t, \boldsymbol{\beta}_t'),$$

$$\mathbf{z}_{t+1} = \begin{pmatrix} 1 & 1 & 0 \\ 0 & 1 & 0 \\ 0 & 0 & \mathbf{I} \end{pmatrix} \mathbf{z}_t + \begin{pmatrix} u_t \\ v_t \\ 0 \end{pmatrix}, \tag{16.27}$$

$$y_t = (1, 0, \mathbf{x}_t)\mathbf{z}_t + \eta_t.$$

The methods described in the previous chapter allow for the estimation of the parameters, but also the extraction of a stochastic trend $\hat{\mu}_t$ using the smoothing technique (cf. Harvey *et al.*, 1985) for an application.

16.4 Missing Data

16.4.1 The Example of an AR(1) Process

Complete Data Let us consider an autoregressive process of order 1

$$y_t = \rho y_{t-1} + \epsilon_t,$$

with var $(\epsilon_t) = \sigma^2$, $|\rho| < 1$.

When the available observations refer to $T+1$ successive values of the process $y_0, y_1, \ldots, y_T$, the log-likelihood function conditional on the first observation y_0 is

$$L_T(\rho, \sigma^2) = -\frac{T}{2}\log 2\pi - \frac{T}{2}\log \sigma^2 - \frac{1}{2\sigma^2}\sum_{t=1}^{T}(y_t - \rho y_{t-1})^2.$$

The maximum likelihood estimators of the parameters can be easily derived. For example, the estimator of ρ is

$$\hat{\rho}_T = \frac{\sum_{t=1}^{T} y_t y_{t-1}}{\sum_{t=1}^{T} y_{t-1}^2},$$

which is consistent and has an approximate variance

$$\mathrm{var}\,(\hat{\rho}_T) \approx \frac{1 - \rho^2}{T}.$$

16.4.2 Systematically Missing Data

Now let us assume that only one out of two data on the process are available. The observed process corresponds for example to $(\tilde{y}_t = y_{2t})$ and the observations are

$$\tilde{y}_0 = y_0, \ \tilde{y}_1 = y_2, \ldots, \tilde{y}_{[T/2]} = y_{2[T/2]},$$

where [.] designates the integer part.

The new process admits again an autoregressive expression since

$$y_t = \rho y_{t-1} + \epsilon_t = \rho^2 y_{t-2} + \epsilon_t + \rho \epsilon_{t-1}, \forall \ t \text{ integer},$$

which leads to

$$\tilde{y}_t = \rho^2 \tilde{y}_{t-1} + \tilde{\epsilon}_t,$$

where

$$\text{var}(\tilde{\epsilon}_t) = \sigma^2(1 + \rho^2).$$

The maximum likelihood estimator of ρ^2 is now given by

$$\tilde{\rho}_T^2 = \frac{\sum_{t=1}^{[T/2]} \tilde{y}_t \tilde{y}_{t-1}}{\sum_{t=1}^{[T/2]} \tilde{y}_{t-1}^2}.$$

with an approximate variance

$$\text{var}(\tilde{\rho}_T^2) \approx \frac{1 - \rho^4}{T/2} = \frac{2(1 - \rho^4)}{T}.$$

Assuming, for example a positive ρ, we can derive an estimator of ρ, $\tilde{\rho}_T = \sqrt{\tilde{\rho}_T^2}$ the asymptotic variance of which is

$$\text{var}(\tilde{\rho}_T) \approx \frac{2(1 - \rho^4)}{T} \frac{1}{(2\sqrt{\rho^2})^2} = \frac{1 - \rho^4}{2T\rho^2}.$$

The asymptotic variance ratio between $\tilde{\rho}_T$ and $\hat{\rho}_T$ is therefore

$$\frac{1 - \rho^4}{2T\rho^2} \frac{T}{1 - \rho^2} = \frac{1 + \rho^2}{2\rho^2} = \frac{1}{2} + \frac{1}{2\rho^2}$$

which is, not surprisingly, always greater than 1.

16.4.3 Irregularly Missing Data

In practice, however, the data are often missing in an irregular fashion. Let us assume for illustration purposes that the missing data are those indexed by 1, 3, and 4. The autoregressive representation written on the available data is

$$y_2 = \rho^2 y_0 + \epsilon_2 + \rho \epsilon_1,$$

$$y_5 = \rho^3 y_2 + \epsilon_5 + \rho \epsilon_4 + \rho^2 \epsilon_3,$$

$$y_t = \rho y_{t-1} + \epsilon_t \ t \geq 6.$$

It is apparent that the stationarity of the observed process is lost in this case. The regression coefficients depend on time, since they are $\rho^2, \rho^3, \rho, \ldots, \rho$. By the same token the variance of the innovations is equal to $\sigma^2(1 + \rho^2)$, $\sigma^2(1 + \rho^2 + \rho^4)$, $\sigma^2, \ldots, \sigma^2$. The log-likelihood function can be written as

$$L_T^m(\rho, \sigma^2) = -\frac{T-3}{2}\log 2\pi - \frac{T-3}{2}\log \sigma^2 +$$

$$- \frac{1}{2}\log(1 + \rho^2) - \frac{1}{2}\log(1 + \rho^2 + \rho^4) +$$

$$- \frac{1}{2\sigma^2}\left(\frac{(y_2 - \rho^2 y_0)^2}{1 + \rho^2} + \frac{(y_5 - \rho^3 y_2)^2}{1 + \rho^2 + \rho^4} + \sum_{t=6}^{T}(y_t - \rho y_{t-1})^2\right).$$

A direct maximization of this log-likelihood function does not give first-order conditions leading to a closed expression for the estimator of ρ. Therefore, we must resort to an estimation algorithm exploiting the model linearity.

An intuitive way to solve this problem is to treat the missing data as unknown parameters which should be estimated along with the coefficients ρ and σ. According to this approach we would maximize the log-likelihood function on the complete set of data with respect to ρ, σ^2, y_1, y_3, and y_4. Let us start with the missing datum y_1. We should maximize with respect to y_1 the quantity

$$-\frac{1}{2\sigma^2}\left((y_2 - \rho y_1)^2 + (y_1 - \rho y_0)^2\right).$$

The first-order condition gives

$$-\rho(y_2 - \rho\hat{y}_1) + (\hat{y}_1 - \rho y_0) = 0 \quad \Leftrightarrow \quad \hat{y}_1 = \frac{\rho(y_0 + y_2)}{1 + \rho^2}.$$

Hence

$$\hat{y}_1 - \rho y_0 = \frac{\rho y_2 - \rho^3 y_0}{1 + \rho^2} = \frac{\rho}{1 + \rho^2}(y_2 - \rho^2 y_0)$$

and

$$y_2 - \rho\hat{y}_1 = \frac{1}{1 + \rho^2}(y_2 - \rho^2 y_0) = \frac{\hat{y}_1 - \rho y_0}{\rho}.$$

The value of the log-likelihood function after concentrating out is therefore obtained by replacing

$$-\frac{1}{2\sigma^2}\left((y_2 - \rho y_1)^2 + (y_1 - \rho y_0)^2\right)$$

with

$$-\frac{1}{2\sigma^2}\left((y_2 - \rho\hat{y}_1)^2 + (\hat{y}_1 - \rho y_0)^2\right)$$

$$= -\frac{1}{2\sigma^2}\left(\frac{1}{(1+\rho^2)^2}(y_2 - \rho^2 y_0)^2 + \frac{\rho^2}{(1+\rho^2)^2}(y_2 - \rho^2 y_0)^2\right)$$

$$= -\frac{1}{2\sigma^2}\frac{(y_2 - \rho^2 y_0)^2}{1 + \rho^2}.$$

Thus we find again one of the terms of the log-likelihood function associated to the model with missing data. The same type of result is valid for the second term provided that the optimization is performed with respect to y_3 and y_4. Therefore up to the terms

$$-\frac{T-3}{2}\log\sigma^2 - \frac{1}{2}\log(1+\rho^2) - \frac{1}{2}\log(1+\rho^2+\rho^4)$$

the log-likelihood function L_T^m can be derived from the log-likelihood function L_T by concentrating out the missing data. Let us remark that such an approach leads not only to the estimation of ρ and σ^2, but also to the missing data forecast. Since the process is autoregressive of order 1, we can see that the best forecast of y_1 based on $y_0, y_2, y_5, y_6, \ldots$ coincides with the best forecast of y_1 based on y_0, y_2. This one is given by

$$E(y_1 \mid y_0, y_2) = (\text{cov}\,(y_1, y_0), \text{cov}\,(y_1, y_2))\left(\text{var}\begin{pmatrix} y_0 \\ y_2 \end{pmatrix}\right)^{-1}\begin{pmatrix} y_0 \\ y_2 \end{pmatrix}$$

$$= (\rho, \rho)\begin{pmatrix} 1 & \rho^2 \\ \rho^2 & 1 \end{pmatrix}^{-1}\begin{pmatrix} y_0 \\ y_2 \end{pmatrix}$$

$$= (\rho, \rho)\frac{1}{1 - \rho^4}\begin{pmatrix} 1 & -\rho^2 \\ -\rho^2 & 1 \end{pmatrix}\begin{pmatrix} y_0 \\ y_2 \end{pmatrix}$$

$$= \rho\frac{(1 - \rho^2)}{1 - \rho^4}(y_0 + y_2)$$

$$= \frac{\rho}{1 + \rho^2}(y_0 + y_2).$$

The optimal forecast formula coincides with the one obtained for $\hat{y}_1$ after the concentration.

16.4.4 Use of the Kalman Filter

The results just presented as examples can be generalized, provided that the data are missing in an exogenous way, that is, provided that the distribution of the observed data conditional on the fact that data are missing is identical to the unconditional distribution. They are implicitly obtained by applying the Kalman filter appropriately, which allows to simultaneously estimate the unknown parameters and forecast the missing data. The idea is the following: we use the filter as usual until the first missing data are encountered; at this stage we have available future data forecasts and variance–covariance matrices of forecast errors. These forecasts can be used for the evaluation of the missing data. The filter is considered again when the next data are available, taking as initial values the previously derived forecasts.

Let us assume that the datum at time $s - 1$ is the only one missing. If we have developed the filter equations up to the time $s - 2$ and if we start the filter equations in expression (b) of theorem 15.1 for the time $s - 1$, the properties of forecasting show that the filter is computing

$$_{s-2}\hat{\mathbf{z}}_s, \quad _{s-2}\mathbf{\Sigma}_s, \quad _{s-2}\hat{y}_s, \quad _{s-2}\hat{\mathbf{M}}_s.$$

If at time s, we consider again the filter in expression (a) of theorem 15.1 with $_{s-2}\hat{\mathbf{z}}_s, \,_{s-2}\mathbf{\Sigma}_s$ as values of $_{s-1}\hat{\mathbf{z}}_s, \,_{s-1}\mathbf{\Sigma}_s$, the formula of the filter provides similar quantities as the ones of the complete filter, the main difference being that the information implicitly used at time s is now $(y_0, y_1 \ldots y_{s-2}, y_s)$. The same results hold for the following time periods, since y_{s-1} does not appear anymore in the information set and the equations (c) and (c') in (15.6) give the expressions

$$_t\hat{y}_{t+1} = E(y_{t+1} \mid y_0, \ldots, y_{s-2}, y_s, \ldots, y_t),$$

$$_tM_{t+1} = \text{var}\,(y_{t+1} \mid y_0, \ldots, y_{s-2}, y_s, \ldots, y_t), \quad \forall \; t \geq s.$$

Having access to these various forecasts, we can derive directly the numerical value of the log-likelihood function associated with $y_0, \ldots, y_{s-2}, y_s, \ldots, y_T$.

When several subsequent observations are missing, it is enough to apply several times the equations (b), (b'), (c), and (c') of the filter which allows to obtain $_{s-2}\hat{\mathbf{z}}_{s+h}, _{s-2}\mathbf{\Sigma}_{s+h}$, where $h - 1$ is the number of consecutive missing data.

16.5 Rational Expectations Models

16.5.1 State-space Representation of a R.E. Model

Some rational expectations models can easily be written in the state-space form. The standard idea is to choose the unobserved expectations as state variables and, for symmetry reasons, to introduce expectations about the endogenous variables as well as about the exogenous variables. For example, let us consider the model with future variable expectation

$$\mathbf{y}_t = \mathbf{A}E(\mathbf{y}_{t+1} \mid I_t) + \mathbf{B}\mathbf{x}_t, \tag{16.28}$$

where I_t contains the present and past values of $\mathbf{x}$ and $\mathbf{y}$ and where the exogenous variables are assumed to satisfy an autoregressive model of order 1

$$\mathbf{x}_t = \boldsymbol{\Phi}\mathbf{x}_{t-1} + \boldsymbol{\varepsilon}_t^x. \tag{16.29}$$

Introducing the innovation $\boldsymbol{\varepsilon}_t^y$ of $\mathbf{y}$, we can write the relationship between realizations and forecasts

$$\mathbf{y}_t = E(\mathbf{y}_t \mid I_{t-1}) + \boldsymbol{\varepsilon}_t^y,$$
$$\mathbf{x}_t = E(\mathbf{x}_t \mid I_{t-1}) + \boldsymbol{\varepsilon}_t^x. \tag{16.30}$$

On the other hand, by replacing in the structural equations (16.28) and (16.29) the realizations as a function of the expectations, we get a dynamical model for the expectations

$$E(\mathbf{y}_t \mid I_{t-1}) + \boldsymbol{\varepsilon}_t^y = \mathbf{A}E(\mathbf{y}_{t+1} \mid I_t) + \mathbf{B}(E(\mathbf{x}_t \mid I_{t-1}) + \boldsymbol{\varepsilon}_t^x),$$
$$E(\mathbf{x}_t \mid I_{t-1}) = \boldsymbol{\Phi}(E(\mathbf{x}_{t-1} \mid I_{t-2}) + \boldsymbol{\varepsilon}_{t-1}^x). \tag{16.31}$$

If the matrix $\mathbf{A}$ is nonsingular, this last system is equivalent to

$$E(\mathbf{y}_{t+1} \mid I_t) = \mathbf{A}^{-1}E(\mathbf{y}_t \mid I_{t-1}) - \mathbf{A}^{-1}\mathbf{B}E(\mathbf{x}_t \mid I_{t-1})$$
$$+ \mathbf{A}^{-1}\boldsymbol{\varepsilon}_t^y - \mathbf{A}^{-1}\mathbf{B}\boldsymbol{\varepsilon}_t^x, \tag{16.32}$$

$$E(\mathbf{x}_{t+1} \mid I_t) = \boldsymbol{\Phi}E(\mathbf{x}_t \mid I_{t-1}) + \boldsymbol{\Phi}\boldsymbol{\varepsilon}_t^x.$$

This is a system describing the expectation updating mechanism. We can then choose as state variables

$$\mathbf{z}_t = \begin{pmatrix} E(\mathbf{y}_t \mid I_{t-1}) \\ E(\mathbf{x}_t \mid I_{t-1}) \end{pmatrix}.$$

The system for expectation updating provides the state equations

$$\mathbf{z}_{t+1} = \begin{pmatrix} \mathbf{A}^{-1} & -\mathbf{A}^{-1}\mathbf{B} \\ 0 & \boldsymbol{\Phi} \end{pmatrix} \mathbf{z}_t + \begin{pmatrix} \mathbf{A}^{-1} & -\mathbf{A}^{-1}\mathbf{B} \\ 0 & \boldsymbol{\Phi} \end{pmatrix} \boldsymbol{\varepsilon}_t. \tag{16.33}$$

Then the system (16.30) provides the measurement equations

$$\begin{pmatrix} \mathbf{y}_t \\ \mathbf{x}_t \end{pmatrix} = \mathbf{z}_t + \boldsymbol{\varepsilon}_t \tag{16.34}$$

with $\boldsymbol{\varepsilon}_t' = (\boldsymbol{\varepsilon}_t^{y\prime}, \boldsymbol{\varepsilon}_t^{x\prime})$.

Note that the practical usefulness for the state-space representation needs the introduction of new parameters through the innovation $\boldsymbol{\varepsilon}_t^y$. This one is zero mean, temporally uncorrelated with $\boldsymbol{\varepsilon}_\tau^y$ and $\boldsymbol{\varepsilon}_\tau^x$, $(\tau \neq t)$. However, it can be instantaneously correlated with $\boldsymbol{\varepsilon}_t^x$ and moreover its variance is a priori unconstrained. Limiting ourselves to the case of a linear stationary relationship between the innovations, we have

$$\boldsymbol{\varepsilon}_t^y = \boldsymbol{\pi}\boldsymbol{\varepsilon}_t^x + \mathbf{u}_t,$$

with

$$\text{cov}\,(\boldsymbol{\varepsilon}_t^x, \mathbf{u}_t) = \mathbf{0}, \quad \text{var}\,(\mathbf{u}_t) = \boldsymbol{\Omega}.$$

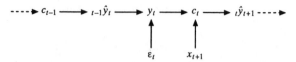

Figure 16.2   Determination of the Transition Equation

If we constrain the solutions $\mathbf{y}_t$ to depend only on present and past values of the exogenous $\mathbf{x}$, we have $\mathbf{\Omega} = \mathbf{0}$ and we are left with a multiplicity of solutions deriving from the arbitrary choice of $\boldsymbol{\pi}$. When this restriction is not imposed, there can be effects on $\mathbf{y}_t$ from variables not taking part explicitly in the initial structural form; these "sunspots" are summarized here by the residual term $\mathbf{u}_t$.

The state-space form can be also interesting for the estimation of parameters stressing the existence of an underlying linear model with respect to some of these parameters. Suitable parameters for the problem are $\mathbf{C} = \mathbf{A}^{-1}, \mathbf{D} = -\mathbf{A}^{-1}\mathbf{B}$ so that the underlying model is linear in $\mathbf{C}, \mathbf{D}, \boldsymbol{\Phi}$.

16.5.2 Learning

Preliminary Result   While studying the state-space models we have introduced autoregressive equations in which coefficients could be time dependent. The type of the transition equation is

$$\mathbf{z}_t = \mathbf{A}_{t-1}\mathbf{z}_{t-1} + \mathbf{B}_{t-1}\mathbf{u}_{t-1},$$

where $\mathbf{u}_t$ is white noise.

Often this time dependence is achieved through a function $\boldsymbol{\alpha}(t-1)$ of observations prior to time $t - 1$. We have a double recurrence. At time $t - 1$, we determine $\boldsymbol{\alpha}(t-1)$, which leads to the derivation of the coefficients $\mathbf{A}_{t-1}, \mathbf{B}_{t-1}$, then we determine $\mathbf{z}_t$. We can then update the value of $\boldsymbol{\alpha}$ and so on (see figure 16.2).

Moreover there exist many cases where the series $\boldsymbol{\alpha}(t)$ converges to a limit, say, $\boldsymbol{\alpha}^{\star}$. If the coefficients $\mathbf{A}_t, \mathbf{B}_t$ are continuous functions of $\boldsymbol{\alpha}(t)$, they will also tend toward limit values $\mathbf{A}^{\star}, \mathbf{B}^{\star}$. The process behind the observations $(\mathbf{z}_t)$, in general nonstationary, will normally converge to the stationary solution of the equation

$$\mathbf{z}_t^{\star} = \mathbf{A}^{\star}\mathbf{z}_{t-1}^{\star} + \mathbf{B}^{\star}\mathbf{u}_{t-1}$$

whenever the eigenvalues of $\mathbf{A}^{\star}$ are strictly less than 1 in modulus.

Several conditions have to be satisfied in order for a process with time dependent transition equation to get closer to a stationary model.

Hereafter, we describe a result by Ljung (1977) and we apply it to the learning problem in rational expectation models.

Let us consider a system of two difference equations

$$\mathbf{z}_t = \mathbf{A}\left(\boldsymbol{\alpha}(t-1)\right)\mathbf{z}_{t-1} + \mathbf{B}\left(\boldsymbol{\alpha}(t-1)\right)\mathbf{u}_{t-1},$$

$$\boldsymbol{\alpha}(t) = \boldsymbol{\alpha}(t-1) + \frac{1}{t}g\left(\boldsymbol{\alpha}(t-1), \mathbf{z}_t\right). \tag{16.35}$$

$\mathbf{z}_t$ and $\boldsymbol{\alpha}(t)$ are vectors of size n and m respectively, $\mathbf{u}_t$ is a white noise, possibly multivariate.

The existence of the factor $\frac{1}{t}$ in the second equation foreshadows the consistency of the series $\boldsymbol{\alpha}(t)$, since the successive growth $\boldsymbol{\alpha}(t) - \boldsymbol{\alpha}(t-1)$ is affected by a term going to 0.

To study the asymptotic behavior of the previous system, we should first associate it with the corresponding stationary system in replacing $\boldsymbol{\alpha}(t)$ by its possible limit $\boldsymbol{\alpha}^\star$, $\mathbf{z}_t$ by its stationary approximation $\mathbf{z}_t^\star$ and the function g by its certain equivalent, that is by its expectation

$$f(\boldsymbol{\alpha}^\star) = E\left(g(\boldsymbol{\alpha}^\star, \mathbf{z}_t^\star)\right).$$

This limit stationary model is written as

$$\mathbf{z}_t^\star = \mathbf{A}(\boldsymbol{\alpha}^\star)\mathbf{z}_{t-1}^\star + \mathbf{B}(\boldsymbol{\alpha}^\star)\mathbf{u}_{t-1},$$

$$f(\boldsymbol{\alpha}^\star) = E\,g(\boldsymbol{\alpha}^\star, \mathbf{z}_t^\star) = 0. \tag{16.36}$$

This system provides the possible limits $\boldsymbol{\alpha}^\star$ looking for the roots of $f(\boldsymbol{\alpha}^\star) = \mathbf{0}$.

If we want to refine this study we have to know how the series $\boldsymbol{\alpha}(t)$ will approach these possible limits. For that, we can introduce the deterministic differential equation associated with the updating formula of $\boldsymbol{\alpha}(t)$. It is given by

$$\frac{d\boldsymbol{\alpha}}{dt} = f(\boldsymbol{\alpha}). \tag{16.37}$$

Ljung's result (1977) can be summarized in the following way:

Theorem 16.2: *Let $\boldsymbol{\alpha}^\star$ be a solution to $f(\boldsymbol{\alpha}^\star) = \mathbf{0}$ for which $\mathbf{A}_{(}\boldsymbol{\alpha}^\star)$ has eigenvalues less than one in modulus. Let $\mathbf{D}_{\boldsymbol{\alpha}^\star}$ be the attraction domain of $\boldsymbol{\alpha}^\star$ for the differential equation (16.37). Then if the series $\boldsymbol{\alpha}(t)$ belongs to this attraction domain, this series converges to $\boldsymbol{\alpha}^\star$, and $\boldsymbol{\alpha}(t)$ tends to a deterministic path solution of the differential equation.*

Several other regularity conditions are also necessary, but they need not be introduced for the sake of understanding the results. They relate to some continuity conditions for the various functions which are generally satisfied in practice.

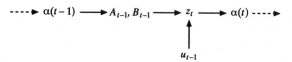

Figure 16.3   Expectation Computation Process by the Agents

Learning in Muth's Model   Let us consider a model where the realization y_t of the variable is a function of the expectation of this variable done at the previous date $_{t-1}\hat{y}_t$, of an exogenous x_t, and of a white noise ϵ_t. In order to simplify matters, let us assume that the exogenous variable satisfies an autoregressive process of order 1, we get a model

$$y_t = a\,_{t-1}\hat{y}_t + x_t b + \epsilon_t,$$
$$x_t = \rho x_{t-1} + \eta_t, \tag{16.38}$$

where $\mid \rho \mid < 1$.

The noises are such that var $(\epsilon_t) = \sigma_\epsilon^2$, var $(\eta_t) = \sigma_\eta^2$, cov $(\epsilon_t, \eta_t) = 0$.

We still have to specify the way the agents compute their expectation. We do not assume here the hypothesis of rational expectation, but we suppose that their forecast rule is regression based using past observed correlation between the variables x and y. More precisely their expectation is given by

$$_{t-1}\hat{y}_t = c_{t-1}x_t$$

with

$$c_t = \frac{\sum_{\tau=1}^{t} y_\tau x_\tau}{\sum_{\tau=1}^{t} x_\tau^2}.$$

Therefore at the beginning of the period t, the agents have computed their expectation $_{t-1}\hat{y}_t$, which, in turn, will affect the realization y_t of the endogenous variable. In the next period they will have one more observation x_{t+1}, y_t which allows them to update the regression coefficient, that is to compute c_t, and then the new expectation $_t\hat{y}_{t+1}$ (see figure 16.3).

The continuous modification of the coefficient c_t implies that the series (y_t) is nonstationary. Nevertheless, we can think that under some conditions, the series c_t will converge to a limit $c^\star$, the series (y_t) will get closer to a stationary process path, and in the limit this way of computing the expectation term will correspond to rationality.

Theorem 16.3: *If $a < 1$, the learning by regression is consistent and in the limit the expectation is the rational expectation based on the information $I_{t-1} = \{x_t\}$.*

PROOF:

(i) **Expression for the Double Recursion** Let us introduce the quantities

$$\gamma(t) = \frac{1}{t}\sum_{\tau=1}^{t} x_\tau y_\tau, \quad \delta(t) = \frac{1}{t}\sum_{\tau=1}^{t} x_\tau^2,$$

and let us write $\boldsymbol{\alpha}(t) = \begin{pmatrix} \gamma(t) \\ \delta(t) \end{pmatrix}$. We have

$$\boldsymbol{\alpha}(t) = \begin{pmatrix} \gamma(t) \\ \delta(t) \end{pmatrix} = \boldsymbol{\alpha}(t-1) + \frac{1}{t}\begin{pmatrix} x_t y_t - \gamma(t-1) \\ x_t^2 - \delta(t-1) \end{pmatrix}. \quad (16.39)$$

On the other hand, the observations x_t, y_t are such that

$$y_t = ac_{t-1}x_t + x_t b + \epsilon_t$$

$$= \left(a\frac{\gamma(t-1)}{\delta(t-1)} + b\right)x_t + \epsilon_t$$

$$= \left(a\frac{\gamma(t-1)}{\delta(t-1)} + b\right)\rho x_{t-1} + \epsilon_t + \left(a\frac{\gamma(t-1)}{\delta(t-1)} + b\right)\eta_t.$$

Let us write $\mathbf{z}_t = \begin{pmatrix} x_t \\ y_t \end{pmatrix}$; we have

$$\mathbf{z}_t = \begin{pmatrix} x_t \\ y_t \end{pmatrix} = \begin{pmatrix} \rho & 0 \\ \rho(a\gamma(t-1)/\delta(t-1)+b) & 0 \end{pmatrix}\begin{pmatrix} x_{t-1} \\ y_{t-1} \end{pmatrix}$$
$$+ \begin{pmatrix} 1 & 0 \\ a\gamma(t-1)/\delta(t-1)+b & 1 \end{pmatrix}\begin{pmatrix} \eta_t \\ \epsilon_t \end{pmatrix}. \quad (16.40)$$

The equations (16.39) and (16.40) provide the double recursion.

(ii) **Derivation of the function f** Let $\gamma^\star, \delta^\star$ be possible limits of $\gamma(t)$ and of $\delta(t)$. We have

$$y_t^\star = a\frac{\gamma^\star}{\delta^\star}x_t + x_t b + \epsilon_t,$$

$$x_t = \rho x_{t-1} + \eta_t.$$

The function f is given by

$$f(\alpha^\star) = E\left(\begin{array}{c} x_t y_t^\star - \gamma^\star \\ x_t^2 - \delta^\star \end{array}\right)$$

$$= \left(\begin{array}{c} (a\frac{\gamma^\star}{\delta^\star} + b)\mathrm{var}\,(x_t) - \gamma^\star \\ \mathrm{var}\,(x_t) - \delta^\star \end{array}\right)$$

$$= \left(\begin{array}{c} (a\frac{\gamma^\star}{\delta^\star} + b)\frac{\sigma_\eta^2}{1-\rho^2} - \gamma^\star \\ \frac{\sigma_\eta^2}{1-\rho^2} - \delta^\star \end{array}\right).$$

(iii) **Derivation of the Stationary Points** The solution of the system $f(\alpha^\star) = 0$ is unique and given by

$$\gamma^\star = \frac{b}{1-a}\frac{\sigma_\eta^2}{1-\rho^2}, \qquad \delta^\star = \frac{\sigma_\eta^2}{1-\rho^2}.$$

For this solution, the eigenvalues of $\mathbf{A}(\alpha^\star)$, that is ρ and 0, are actually less than 1 in modulus. We conclude that $c^\star = \frac{\gamma^\star}{\delta^\star} = \frac{b}{1-a}$, and we verify that this value corresponds to the rational expectation case.

Indeed, if we solve the rational expectation model, we have

$$y_t = aE(y_t \mid x_t) + x_t b + u_t$$

with $E(y_t \mid x_t) = cx_t$.

By taking the linear forecast of the two members involving x_t, we have

$$E(y_t \mid x_t) = aE(y_t \mid x_t) + x_t b$$

$$\text{and} \qquad E(y_t \mid x_t) = x_t \frac{b}{1-a}.$$

Therefore we find

$$c = \frac{b}{1-a} = c^\star.$$

(iv) **Analysis of the Associated Differential Equation** The associated differential equation is written as

$$\frac{d\gamma}{dt} = (a\frac{\gamma}{\delta} + b)\delta^\star - \gamma,$$

$$\frac{d\delta}{dt} = \delta^\star - \delta.$$

We deduce from the second part of the system that

$$\delta(t) = \delta^\star + K\exp(-t)$$

with K real.

Substituting in the first equation, we have

$$\frac{d\gamma}{dt} = \left(\frac{a\gamma}{\delta^\star + K\exp(-t)} + b\right)\delta^\star - \gamma,$$

$$\frac{d\gamma}{dt} = b\delta^\star + \gamma\left(\frac{(a-1)\delta^\star - K\exp(-t)}{\delta^\star + K\exp(-t)}\right).$$

For any initial condition, the solution for the component δ converges to $\delta^\star$ so that the attraction domain is $\mathbb{R}$. For the other component the attraction domain is $\mathbb{R}$ as well, if for t large enough, the coefficient

$$\frac{(a-1)\delta^\star - K\exp(-t)}{\delta^\star + K\exp(-t)}$$

is strictly negative. This provides the condition $a - 1 < 0 \Leftrightarrow a < 1$. $\square$

Learning in the Hyperinflation Model A similar approach can be used when the model has an expectation of a future variable. This example is interesting, since the consistency condition implies a different constraint on the structural parameters. The model is now given by

$$y_t = a_t\hat{y}_{t+1} + x_t b + \epsilon_t,$$

$$x_t = \rho x_{t-1} + \eta_t.$$

The expectations are computed by regression taking into consideration the lag between the expectation date and the date of the variable to forecast

$$_t\hat{y}_{t+1} = c_{t-1}x_t,$$

with

$$c_t = \frac{\sum_{\tau=1}^t y_\tau x_{\tau-1}}{\sum_{\tau=1}^t x_{\tau-1}^2}.$$

Letting $\gamma(t) = \frac{1}{t}\sum_{\tau=1}^t y_\tau x_{\tau-1}$ and $\delta(t) = \frac{1}{t}\sum_{\tau=1}^t x_{\tau-1}^2$, we get the system of difference equations

$$\gamma(t) = \gamma(t-1) + \frac{1}{t}\left(y_t x_{t-1} - \gamma(t-1)\right),$$

$$\delta(t) = \delta(t-1) + \frac{1}{t}\left(x_{t-1}^2 - \delta(t-1)\right),$$

$$\begin{pmatrix} y_t \\ x_t \\ x_{t-1} \end{pmatrix} = \begin{pmatrix} 0 & \rho\left(a\gamma(t-1)/\delta(t-1)+b\right) & 0 \\ 0 & \rho & 0 \\ 0 & 1 & 0 \end{pmatrix}\begin{pmatrix} y_{t-1} \\ x_{t-1} \\ x_{t-2} \end{pmatrix} + $$

$$\begin{pmatrix} 1 & \left(a\gamma(t-1)/\delta(t-1)+b\right) \\ 0 & 1 \\ 0 & 0 \end{pmatrix}\begin{pmatrix} \epsilon_t \\ \eta_t \end{pmatrix}.$$

The function f is given here by

$$f(\alpha^\star) = E\left(\begin{matrix} y_t^\star x_{t-1} - \gamma^\star \\ x_{t-1}^2 - \gamma^\star \end{matrix}\right) = \left(\begin{matrix} (a\gamma^\star/\delta^\star + b)\,\rho\sigma^2/(1-\rho^2) - \gamma^\star \\ \sigma^2/(1-\rho^2) - \delta^\star \end{matrix}\right).$$

There exists a unique stationary point solution of $f(\alpha^\star) = 0$. It is given by

$$\gamma^\star = \frac{b\rho\sigma^2}{(1-\rho^2)}\frac{1}{1-a\rho}, \qquad \delta^\star = \frac{\sigma^2}{1-\rho^2}.$$

It corresponds to an expectation of the type $c^\star x_t = b\rho x_t/(1-a\rho)$. We can directly verify that this expectation scheme corresponds to the rational expectation model

$$y_t = aE(y_{t+1} \mid x_t) + x_t b + \epsilon_t, \qquad E(y_{t+1} \mid x_t) = cx_t.$$

Indeed, we have $y_t = (ac + b)x_t + \epsilon_t$. We deduce that

$$E(y_t \mid x_{t-1}) = (ac + b)E(x_t \mid x_{t-1}) = (ac + b)\rho x_{t-1} = cx_{t-1}.$$

Therefore

$$(ac + b)\rho = c \Leftrightarrow c = \frac{b\rho}{1 - a\rho} = c^\star.$$

Finally, the associated system of differential equations is

$$\frac{d\gamma}{dt} = \left(a\frac{\gamma}{\delta} + b\right)\rho\delta^\star - \gamma,$$

$$\frac{d\delta}{dt} = \delta^\star - \delta.$$

In the second relation, we get $\delta = \delta^\star + K\exp(-t)$, which, substituted in the first one, produces

$$\frac{d\gamma}{dt} = b\rho\delta^\star + \gamma\left(\frac{(a\rho - 1)\delta^\star - K\exp(-t)}{\delta^\star + K\exp(-t)}\right).$$

The attraction domain is the entire space if the coefficient of γ in the previous equation is strictly negative for t large enough, that is if $a\rho < 1$.

Theorem 16.4: *In the model with a future expectation variable, the learning process converges to a rational scheme based on the information $I_t = \{x_t\}$, if the structural parameters are such that $a\rho < 1$.*

Since a priori the value of ρ is unknown and can be equal to any value less than 1 in modulus, the consistency is ensured uniformly in ρ, if the parameter a is such that $\mid a \mid < 1$. This condition on a is more restrictive than the one for Muth's model.

Muth's Model with Forecast Based on Lagged Endogenous Variable

(i)   Let us consider Muth's model

$$y_t = a\,_{t-1}\hat{y}_t + \epsilon_t,$$

where ϵ is a white noise.

Let us refer to the information contained in the last observed value y_{t-1} and forecast by the empirical formula

$$_{t-1}\hat{y}_t = c_{t-1}y_{t-1},$$

with

$$c_t = \frac{\sum_{\tau=1}^{t} y_\tau y_{\tau-1}}{\sum_{\tau=1}^{t} y_{\tau-1}^2}.$$

We denote $\gamma(t) = \frac{1}{t}\sum_{\tau=1}^{t} y_\tau y_{\tau-1}$, $\delta(t) = \frac{1}{t}\sum_{\tau=1}^{t} y_\tau^2$.

It can be seen that we obtain the system of difference equations

$$\gamma(t) = \gamma(t-1) + \frac{1}{t}\left(y_t y_{t-1} - \gamma(t-1),\right)$$

$$\delta(t) = \delta(t-1) + \frac{1}{t}\left(y_t^2 - \delta(t-1)\right),$$

$$\begin{pmatrix} y_t \\ y_{t-1} \end{pmatrix} = \begin{pmatrix} ac_{t-1} & 0 \\ 1 & 0 \end{pmatrix}\begin{pmatrix} y_{t-1} \\ y_{t-2} \end{pmatrix} + \begin{pmatrix} 1 \\ 0 \end{pmatrix}\epsilon_t.$$

(ii)   The function f is then given by

$$f(\boldsymbol{\alpha}^\star) = \begin{pmatrix} (a\gamma^\star\delta^\star\sigma^2)/(\delta^{\star 2} - a^2\gamma^{\star 2}) - \gamma^\star \\ \sigma^2/(1 - a^2c^{\star 2}) - \delta^\star \end{pmatrix}$$

with $c^\star = \gamma^\star/\delta^\star$.

We deduce that the equilibrium values can only be $\gamma^\star = 0$, $\delta^\star = \sigma^2$ or $\gamma^\star = 0$, $\delta^\star = 0$. The first couple corresponds to a rational expectation solution $_{t-1}\hat{y}_t = E(y_t \mid y_{t-1})$.

(iii)   The associated differential system is

$$\frac{d\gamma}{dt} = \frac{\gamma a\sigma^2/\delta}{1 - a^2\gamma^2/\delta^2} - \gamma,$$

$$\frac{d\delta}{dt} = \frac{\sigma^2}{1 - a^2\gamma^2/\delta^2} - \delta.$$

Moreover, let $u = c^2$, with $c = \gamma/\delta$; we notice that the previous system implies the system in u, δ

$$\frac{du}{dt} = \frac{2(a-1)u}{1 - a^2u}\frac{\sigma^2}{\delta},$$

$$\frac{d\delta}{dt} = \frac{\sigma^2}{1 - a^2u} - \delta.$$

(iv)   We know that $\delta(t)$ is always positive and $\mid a \mid < 1$. Hence du/dt is negative; the function u is therefore decreasing. Since it is positive, it converges to a limit. This one can only be 0. We conclude that every point (c, δ) of $(-1, 1) \times \mathbf{R}^{+\star}$ is attracted by the semi-line $c = 0$.

(v)   We have now to look at the second component δ. Let $\theta = 1 - \delta/\sigma^2$, we have

$$\frac{d\theta}{dt} = \frac{a^2 u}{1 - a^2 u} - \theta = -\theta - f(t),$$

where the function $f(t)$ converges to 0 when t goes to infinity. The resolution of this equation by the method of the variation of the constant gives

$$\theta(t) = K \exp(-t) - \left(\int_{t_0}^{t} f(u) \exp(u) du \right) \exp(-t).$$

Thus we have

$$\mid \theta(t) \mid \leq \mid K \mid \exp(-t) + \sup_{[t_0, \infty]} \mid f(u) \mid (\exp(t) - \exp(t_0)) \exp(-t),$$

and so

$$\limsup \mid \theta(t) \mid < \sup_{[t_0, \infty]} \mid f(u) \mid .$$

Since the inequality is valid for every value t_0 and since the function f tends to 0 as t goes to infinity, we conclude that θ goes to 0, that is δ tends to σ^2.

16.6 Exercises

Exercise 16.1: Prove directly the updating formula of the ordinary least squares (16.3), starting from the equality $(\mathbf{X}'_t \mathbf{X}_t)\hat{\beta}_t = \mathbf{X}'_t \mathbf{y}_t$, where $\mathbf{y}_t$ is the vector of the observations $y_0, \ldots, y_t$.

Exercise 16.2: Let the linear system be

$$y_t = \mathbf{x}_t \beta$$

with $t = 0, \ldots, K - 1$ and where β is an unknown vector of size K.

Show that the Kalman covariance filter can be used to solve this system. Interpret geometrically the filter mechanism when

$$_{-1}\hat{\beta}_0 = \mathbf{0} \quad \text{and} \quad _{-1}\Sigma_0 = \mathbf{I}.$$

Exercise 16.3: Show that the ARMA process given in (16.7) admits the minimal state-space representation (called the "innovation" representation)

$$\mathbf{z}_{t+1} = \mathbf{A}\mathbf{z}_t + \mathbf{b}\epsilon_t,$$

$$y_t = \mathbf{c}\mathbf{z}_t + \epsilon_t$$

with

$$\mathbf{A} = \begin{pmatrix} -\phi_1 & 1 & 0 & \ldots & 0 \\ -\phi_2 & 0 & 1 & \ldots & 0 \\ \vdots & \vdots & \vdots & \ddots & \vdots \\ -\phi_{K-1} & 0 & 0 & \ldots & 1 \\ -\phi_K & 0 & 0 & \ldots & 0 \end{pmatrix} \quad \mathbf{b} = \begin{pmatrix} \theta_1 - \phi_1 \\ \vdots \\ \theta_K - \phi_K \end{pmatrix}$$

and

$$\mathbf{c} = (1, 0, \ldots, 0),$$

$K = \max(p, q)$, $\phi_i = 0$, if $i > p$, $\theta_i = 0$, if $i > q$, the j-th component of $\mathbf{z}_{t+1}$ being

$$z^j_{t+1} = -\phi_j y_t - \ldots - \phi_K y_{t-K+j} + \theta_j \epsilon_t + \ldots + \theta_K \epsilon_{t-K+j}.$$

Exercise 16.4: Show that the ARMA process given in (16.7) admits the following state-space representation

$$\mathbf{z}_{t+1} = \mathbf{A}\mathbf{z}_t + \mathbf{b}\epsilon_{t+1},$$

$$y_t = \mathbf{c}\mathbf{z}_t$$

with

$$\mathbf{A} = \begin{pmatrix} -\phi_1 & 1 & 0 & \cdots & 0 \\ -\phi_2 & 0 & 1 & \cdots & 0 \\ \vdots & \vdots & \vdots & \ddots & \vdots \\ -\phi_{K-1} & 0 & 0 & \cdots & 1 \\ -\phi_K & 0 & 0 & \cdots & 0 \end{pmatrix} \qquad \mathbf{b} = \begin{pmatrix} 1 \\ \theta_1 \\ \vdots \\ \theta_{K-1} \end{pmatrix}$$

and

$$\mathbf{c} = (1, 0, \ldots, 0).$$

$K = \max(p, q+1)$, $\phi_i = 0$, if $i > p$, $\theta_i = 0$, if $i > q$, the j-th component of $\mathbf{z}_{t+1}$ being

$$z_{t+1}^j = -\phi_j y_t - \ldots - \phi_K y_{t-K+j} + \theta_{j-1}\epsilon_{t+1} + \ldots + \theta_{K-1}\epsilon_{t-K+j+1}$$

(with the convention $\theta_0 = 1$).

Exercise 16.5: Let us consider a series y_t which can be decomposed as $y_t = n_t + s_t$, where (n_t) and (s_t) are two independent stationary processes and where (s_t) is supposed to satisfy $s_t = \alpha s_{t-12} + \epsilon_t$, with $0 < \alpha < 1$ and where $\{\epsilon_t\}$ is a white noise.

(i) Find the spectral density f_{ss} of the process (s_t). Verify that $f_{ss}(\omega) > 0$ for any value of (ω) and find the frequencies for which this density is maximal.

(ii) Derive that the spectral densities f_{yy} and f_{nn} of y_t and n_t are such that $f_{yy}(\omega) > f_{nn}(\omega)$ and that the gap between these two functions is greatest for $\omega = \frac{k\pi}{12}$, $k = \ldots, -1, 0, +1, \ldots$.

Exercise 16.6: Let (y_t) be a time series and (y_t^{SA}) be a seasonally adjusted series. Give your opinion on the following statements about the relationship which should exist between these two series if the initial series has been adequately adjusted.

(i) "The pseudo-coherence between the two series should be high at all frequencies, except perhaps at seasonal frequencies."

(ii) "The seasonal adjustment method should flatten the maxima of the spectral density of y corresponding to the seasonal frequencies and, when possible, leave unchanged this density for other frequencies." [Hint: these statements are wrong to a large extent; to show it, one could, for example, use the exercise 16.5 or an unobserved components model.]

Exercise 16.7: Let us consider the rational expectation model

$$_t y_{t+r} = \sum_{i=1}^{r-1} \mu_i \, _t y_{t+r-i} + \sum_{j=0}^{p} \mu_{j+r} y_{t-j} + \mathbf{x}_t \boldsymbol{\beta} + u_t,$$

where $\mathbf{x}_t$ is a row vector and y_t is an unidimensional endogenous variable

$$_t y_{t+r} = E(y_{t+r} \mid I_t),$$

and where the information set contains the current and past values of the various variables.

Moreover, we assume the explanatory variables are generated by a first-order autoregressive process

$$\begin{pmatrix} \mathbf{x}'_t \\ u_t \end{pmatrix} = \begin{pmatrix} \boldsymbol{\Phi}_{11} & \boldsymbol{\Phi}_{12} \\ \boldsymbol{\Phi}_{21} & \boldsymbol{\Phi}_{22} \end{pmatrix} \begin{pmatrix} \mathbf{x}'_{t-1} \\ u_{t-1} \end{pmatrix} + \begin{pmatrix} \boldsymbol{\varepsilon}^x_t \\ \epsilon^u_t \end{pmatrix}.$$

(i)   Verify that the model can be written as

$$_t y_{t+k} = _{t-1} y_{t+k} + \epsilon_{t,k}, \quad k = 0, \dots, r-1,$$

$$\mathbf{x}'_t = _{t-1} \mathbf{x}'_t + \boldsymbol{\varepsilon}^x_t,$$

$$u_t = _{t-1} u_t + \epsilon^u_t,$$

$$\begin{pmatrix} _t \mathbf{x}'_{t+1} \\ _t u_{t+1} \end{pmatrix} = \begin{pmatrix} \boldsymbol{\Phi}_{11} & \boldsymbol{\Phi}_{12} \\ \boldsymbol{\Phi}_{21} & \boldsymbol{\Phi}_{22} \end{pmatrix} \begin{pmatrix} _{t-1} \mathbf{x}_t \\ _{t-1} u_t \end{pmatrix}$$

$$+ \begin{pmatrix} \boldsymbol{\Phi}_{11} & \boldsymbol{\Phi}_{12} \\ \boldsymbol{\Phi}_{21} & \boldsymbol{\Phi}_{22} \end{pmatrix} \begin{pmatrix} \boldsymbol{\varepsilon}^x_t \\ \epsilon^u_t \end{pmatrix},$$

$$_t y_{t+r} = \sum_{i=1}^{r+p} \mu_i \, _{t-1} y_{t+r-i} + _{t-1} \mathbf{x}_t \boldsymbol{\beta} + _{t-1} u_t$$

$$+ \sum_{i=1}^{r} \mu_i \epsilon_{t,t-i} + \boldsymbol{\beta}' \epsilon^x_t + \epsilon^u_t.$$

(ii)   Derive a state-space representation of this rational expectation model.

Exercise 16.8: We consider a multivariate model with future variable expectation

$$\mathbf{y}_t = \mathbf{A} E(\mathbf{y}_{t+1} \mid I_t) + \mathbf{u}_t$$

with $\mathbf{u}_t = \boldsymbol{\Phi} \mathbf{u}_{t-1} + \boldsymbol{\varepsilon}_t$, $(\boldsymbol{\varepsilon}_t)$ white noise.

Discuss the existence of a state-space form, when the matrix $\mathbf{A}$ is nonzero, but singular.

Exercise 16.9: Let us consider the process

$$y_t = s_t + u_t,$$

where s_t is an autoregressive process $s_t = \phi s_{t-1} + \epsilon_t$ and where ϵ and u are independent noises.

(i)   Verify that the process y satisfies an ARMA(1,1) model

$$(1 - \phi L)y_t = (1 - \beta L)\eta_t$$

and explain how to find β and $V(\eta_t) = \sigma_\eta^2$.

(ii) Prove that the best forecast of s_t based on the values $y_t, y_{t-1}, \ldots$ is given by $\hat{s}_t = \frac{1-\frac{\beta}{\phi}}{1-\beta L} y_t$. Derive the variance of the corresponding forecast error.

(iii) The previous model is directly in a state-space form when taking s_t as state variable, $s_t = \phi s_{t-1} + \epsilon_t$ as the transition equation, and $y_t = s_t + u_t$ as the measurement equation.

From the updating formula of the variance of the forecast error for s_t derive a second-degree equation satisfied asymptotically by this variance. Then show that the expectation updating is

$$\hat{s}_t = \frac{\phi \sigma_u^2 \hat{s}_{t-1} + (\phi^2 P + \sigma_\epsilon^2)y_t}{\phi^2 P + \sigma_\epsilon^2 + \sigma_u^2},$$

where $P = \text{var}(s_t)$.

(iv) Compare the results obtained by the two approaches.

Exercise 16.10: Let us consider the structural model introduced in (16.26)

$$y_t = \frac{L^2}{(1 - L)^2}v_t + \frac{L}{1 - L}u_t + \frac{L}{S(L)}w_t + \eta_t.$$

(i)   Find the best forecast of the seasonal component $Lw(t)/S(L)$ based on $(y_t, t = -\infty, \ldots, -1, 0, +1, \ldots, +\infty)$.

(ii) Write the coefficients of the corresponding moving average and discuss this representation.

References

Abramovitz, M. and I. Stegun (1985), *Handbook of mathematical functions*, New York: Dover.

Aitchison, J. and D. Silvey (1958), Maximum likelihood estimation of parameters subject to restraints, *The Annals of Mathematical Statistics*, 29, 813–28.

Akaike, H. (1969), Fitting autoregressive models for prediction, *Annals of the Institute of Statistical Mathematics*, 21, 243–7.

Akaike, H. (1977), On entropy maximization principle, in K. Krishnaiah (ed.) *Applications of statistics*, Amsterdam: North Holland, pp. 27–41.

Akonom, J. and C. Gourieroux (1988), A functional limit theorem for fractional processes, CEPREMAP Discussion Paper.

Ali, M. (1977), Analysis of ARMA models: estimation and prediction, *Biometrika*, 64, 535–45.

Ali, M. (1978), Correction to: Analysis of ARMA models: estimation and prediction, *Biometrika*, 65, 677.

Anderson, B. and J. Moore (1979a), *Linear optimal control*, Prentice Hall.

Anderson, B. and J. Moore (1979b), *Optimal filtering*, Prentice Hall.

Anderson, T.W. (1971), *The statistical analysis of time series*, New York: J.Wiley.

Anderson, T.W. (1984), *An introduction to multivariate statistical analysis*, New York: J.Wiley.

Anderson, T.W. and A. Walker (1964), On the asymptotic distribution of the autocorrelations of a sample from a linear stochastic process, *Annals of Mathematical Statistics*, 35, 1296–303.

Andrews, D. and D. Pregibon (1978), Finding the outliers that matter, *Journal of the Royal Statistical Society*, Series A, 140, 85–93.

Ansley, C. (1979), An algorithm for the exact likelihood of a mixed ARMA process, *Biometrika*, 66, 59–65.

Ansley, C. and P. Newbold (1981), On the bias in estimates of forecast mean squared error, *Journal of the American Statistical Association*, 76, 569–78.

Ansley, C., W. Spivey, and W. Wrobelski (1977a), On the structure of MA processes, *Journal of Econometrics*, 6, 121–34.

Ansley, C., W. Spivey, and W. Wrobelski (1977b), A class of transformations for Box–Jenkins seasonal models, *Applied Statistics*, 26, 173–78.

Aoki, M. (1986), *State space modelling of time series*, Berlin: Springer Verlag.

Arrow, K.J. (1959), Towards a theory of price adjustment, in M. Abramowitz et al. (eds.), *The allocation of economic resources*, Palo Alto: Stanford University Press, pp. 49–51.

Azencott, R. and D. Dacunha-Castelle (1984), *Séries d'observations irréguliéres*, Paris: Masson.

Balk, B. (1980), A method for constructing price indices for seasonal components, *Journal of the Royal Statistical Society*, Series A, 142, 68–75.

Bartlett, M. (1955), *Stochastic processes*, Cambridge: Cambridge University Press.

Basawa, I. and B. Prakasa-Rao (1980), *Statistical inference for stochastic processes*, London: Academic Press.

Beguin, J.M., C. Gourieroux, and A. Monfort (1980), Identification of an ARIMA process: the corner method, in T. Anderson (ed.), *Time Series*, Amsterdam: North Holland.

Billingsley, P. (1968), *Convergence of probability measures*, New York: J.Wiley.

Blanchard, O.J. (1978), Backward and forward solutions for economics with rational expectations, *American Economic Review*, 69, 114–8.

Blanchard, O.J. and C.M. Kahn (1980), The solution of linear difference models under rational expectations, *Econometrica*, 48, 1305–12.

Bongard, J. (1962), Quelques remarques sur les moyennes mobiles, Paris: OECD, pp. 389–427.

Bouissou, M., J.-J. Laffont, and Q. Vuong (1986), Tests of noncausality under Markov assumptions for qualitative panel data, *Econometrica*, 54, 395–414.

Box, G.E.P. and D. Cox (1964), An analysis of transformations, *Journal of the Royal Statistical Society*, Series B, 26, 211–43.

Box, G.E.P. and G. Jenkins (1970), *Time series analysis: forecasting and control*, San Francisco: Holden Day.

Box, G.E.P. and D. Pierce (1970), Distribution of residual autocorrelation in autoregressive integrated moving average time series models, *Journal of the American Statistical Association*, 65, 1509–29.

Box, G.E.P. and G. Tiao (1975), Intervention analysis with applications to economic and environmental problems, *Journal of the American Statistical Association*, 70, 70–9.

Branson, R. (1991), *Matrix Method: an Introduction*, London: Academic Press.

Bray, M. and N. Savin (1986), Rational expectation equilibria, learning and model specification, *Econometrica*, 54, 1129-60.

Brewer, K. (1973), Some consequences of temporal aggregation and systematic sampling for ARMA or ARMAX models, *Journal of Econometrics*, 1, 133–54.

Brillinger, D. (1975), *Time series: data analysis and theory*, Holt, Rinehart and Winston.

Brown, R.L. (1962), *Smoothing, forecasting and prediction*, Prentice Hall.

Brown, R.L., J. Durbin, and J.M. Evans (1975), Techniques for testing the constancy of regression relationship over time (with comments), *Journal of the Royal Statistical Society*, Series B, 37, 149–92.

Broze, L., C. Gourieroux, and A. Szafarz (1985), Solutions of linear rational expectations models, *Econometric Theory*, 1, 341–68.

Broze, L., C. Gourieroux, and A. Szafarz (1990), *Reduced forms of rational expectations models*, vol 42 of *Fundamentals of pure and applied economics*, Chur: Harwood Academic Publishers.

Burmeister, W. and K.F. Wallis (1982), Kalman filtering estimation of unobserved rational expectations with an application to German hyperinflation, *Journal of Econometrics*, 10, 255–84.

Buys–Ballot, C. (1847), *Les changements périodiques de la température*, Utrecht.

Cagan, P. (1956), The monetary dynamics of hyperinflation, in M. Friedman (ed.), *Studies in the quantity theory of money*, Chicago: Chicago University Press.

Campbell, N. (1978), The influence function as an aid in outlier detection in discriminant analysis, *Applied Statistics*, 27, 251–8.

Carlson, J. (1977), A study of price forecasts, *Annals of Economic and Social Measurement*, 27, 5–6.

Chamberlain, G. (1982), The general equivalence of Granger and Sims causality, *Econometrica*, 50, 569–91.

Chatfield, C. (1975), *The analysis of time series: theory and practice*, London: Chapman and Hall.

Chatfield, C. (1979), Inverse autocorrelations, *Journal of the Royal Statistical Society*, Series A, 142, 363–7.

Christ, C. (1975), Judging the performance of econometric models of the US economy, *International Economic Review*, 16, 54–74.

Cleveland, W. (1972), The inverse autocorrelations of time series and their applications, *Technometrics*, 14, 277–93.

Cleveland, W. and G. Tiao (1976), Decomposition of seasonal time series: a model for the Census X11 program, *Journal of the American Statistical Association*, 71, 5–81.

Cochrane, W.J. and G. Orcutt (1949), Application of least squares regressions to relationships containing autocorrelated error terms, *Journal of the American Statistical Association*, 44, 32–61.

Cogger, K. (1974), The optimality of general order exponential smoothing, *Operational Research*, 22, 858–67.

Cooper, R. (1972), The predictive performance of quarterly econometric models of the United States, in B. Hickman (ed.), *Econometric models of cyclical behavior*, New York: Columbia University Press.

Cox, D. (1961), Prediction by exponentially weighted moving average and related methods, *Journal of the Royal Statistical Society*, Series B, 23, 414–22.

Currie, D. (1986), Some long run features of dynamic time series models, *Economic Journal*, 363, 704–15.

Dagum, E.B. (1979), The X11 ARIMA seasonal adjustment method: outline of the methodology, Catalog 12, 564 E, Statistics Canada.

Davidson, J., D. Hendry, F. Srba, and S. Yeo (1978), Econometric modelling of the aggregate time series relationship between consumer's expenditure and income in the United Kingdom, *Economic Journal*, 88, 661–92.

Davies, N., M. Pate, and M. Frost (1974), Maximum autocorrelation for moving average processes, *Biometrika*, 61, 199–200.

Davies, N., C. Triggs, and P. Newbold (1977), Significance levels of the Box–Pierce portmanteau statistics in finite samples, *Biometrika*, 64, 517–22.

Deleau, M. and P. Malgrange (1978), *L'analyse des modéles macroéconomiques quantitatifs*, Paris: Economica.

Deleau, M., P. Malgrange, and P.-A. Muet (1984), A study of short–run and long–run properties of dynamic models by means of an aggregative core model, in P. Malgrange and P.-A. Muet (eds.), *Contemporary macroeconomic modelling*, Oxford: Basil Blackwell.

Dickey, D. and W. Fuller (1979), Distribution of the estimators for autoregressive time series with a unit root, *Journal of the American Statistical Association*, 74, 427–31.

Dickey, D. and W. Fuller (1981), Likelihood ratio statistics for autoregressive time series with a unit root, *Econometrica*, 49, 1057–72.

Doob, J. (1953), *Stochastic processes*, New York: J.Wiley.

Dunsmuir, W. and P. Robinson (1981), Estimation of time series models in the presence of missing data, *Journal of the American Statistical Association*, 74, 560–8.

Durbin, J. (1959), Efficient estimation of parameters in moving average models, *Biometrika*, 46, 306–16.

Durbin, J. (1960), The fitting of time series models, *International Statistical Institute Review*, 28, 233.

Durbin, J. and G.S. Watson (1950), Testing for serial correlation in least squares regression I, *Biometrika*, 37, 409–28.

Durbin, J. and G.S. Watson (1951), Testing for serial correlation in least squares regression II, *Biometrika*, 38, 159–78.

Eisenpress, H. (1956), Seasonal adjustment of economic time series and multiple regression analysis, *Journal of the American Statistical Association*, 51, 615–21.

Engle, R.F. and C.W.J. Granger (1987), Cointegration and error correction: representation, estimation and testing, *Econometrica*, 55, 251–76.

Engle, R.F., D. Hendry, and J.-F. Richard (1983), Exogeneity, *Econometrica*, 51, 277–304.

Engle, R.F., and B.S. Yoo (1987), Forecasting and testing in cointegrating systems, *Journal of Econometrics*, 35, 143–59.

Evans, G. and S. Honkapohja (1986), A complete characterization of ARMA solutions to linear rational expectations models, *Review of Economic Studies*, 173, 227–40.

Evans, G. and E. Savin (1981), Testing for unit roots 1, *Econometrica*, 49, 753–79.

Evans, G. and E. Savin (1984), Testing for unit roots 2, *Econometrica*, 52, 1241–69.

Evans, M., Y. Haitovsky, and G. Treyz (1972), An analysis of the forecasting properties of US econometric models, in B. Hickman (ed.), *Econometric models of cyclical behavior*, New York: Columbia University Press.

Fair, R. (1984), *Specification, estimation and analysis of macroeconometric models*, Cambridge, Mass.: Harvard University Press.

Fernandez-Macho, F., A. Harvey, and J. Stock (1987), Forecasting and interpolation using vector autoregressions with common trends, *Annales d'Economie et de Statistique*, 6/7, 279–88.

Fisher, I. (1930), *The theory of interest as determined by impatience to spend income and the opportunity to invest it*, New York: MacMillan.

Fishman, G. (1969), *Spectral methods in econometrics*, Cambridge, Mass.: Harvard University Press.

Flood, R. and P. Garber (1980), Market fundamentals versus price level bubbles: the first tests, *Journal of Political Economy*, 88, 745–70.

Florens, J.-P. and M. Mouchart (1985), A linear theory for non causality, *Econometrica*, 53, 157–175.

Fourgeaud, C., C. Gourieroux, and J. Pradel (1986), Learning procedures and convergence to rationality, *Econometrica*, 54, 845–68.

Friedman, B. (1980), Survey evidence on the rationality of interest rate expectations, *Journal of Monetary Economics*, 6, 453–65.

Fuller, W. (1976), *Introduction to statistical time series*, New York: J. Wiley.

Gantmacher, F.R. (1959), *The theory of matrices*, vols. I and II, New York: Chelsea.

Geweke, J. (1982), Measurement of linear dependence and feedback between multiple time series, *Journal of the American Statistical Association*, 77, 304–13.

Geweke, J., R. Meese, and W. Dent (1983), Comparing alternative tests of causality in temporal systems, *Journal of Econometrics*, 21, 161–94.

Geweke, J. and S. Porter-Hudak (1982), The estimation and application of long memory time series models, *Journal of Time Series Analysis*, 4, 221–38.

Gilchrist, W. (1976), *Statistical forecasting*, New York: J.Wiley.

Glasbey, C.A. (1982), A generalization of partial autocorrelations useful in identification of ARMA models, *Technometrics*, 24, 223–8.

Godfrey, L. (1979), Testing the adequacy of a time series model, *Biometrika*, 64, 67–72.

Godfrey, L. (1981), On the invariance of Lagrange multiplier test with respect to certain changes in the alternative hypothesis, *Econometrica*, 49, 1443–55.

Godolphin, E. (1977), A procedure for estimating seasonal moving average models based on efficient estimation of the correlogram, *Journal of the Royal Statistical Society*, Series B, 238–47.

References 643

Gonçalves, E. (1987), Une géneralisation des processus ARMA, *Annales d'Economie et de Statistique*, 5, 109–46.

Gonçalves, E. and C. Gourieroux (1987), Agrégation de processus auto-régressifs d'ordre 1, *Annales d'Economie et de Statistique*, 12, 127–47.

Goodwin, G.L. and K.S. Sin (1984), *Adaptive filtering, prediction and control*, Prentice–Hall.

Gourieroux, C. (1988), Une approche gèometrique des processus ARMA, *Annales d'Economie et de Statistique*, 8, 135–59.

Gourieroux, C., J.-J. Laffont, and A. Monfort (1982), Rational expectations in dynamic linear models, *Econometrica*, 50, 409–25.

Gourieroux, C., F. Maurel, and A. Monfort (1987), Regression and non-stationarity, CREST document no. 8708.

Gourieroux, C. and A. Monfort (1981), On the problem of missing data in linear models, *Review of Economic Studies*, 48, 579–83.

Gourieroux, C. and A. Monfort (1989), *Statistique et modéles économétriques* (2 volumes), Paris: Economica.

Gourieroux, C., A. Monfort, and E. Renault (1987), Kullback causality measures, *Annales d'Economie et de Statistique*, 6/7, 369–410.

Gourieroux, C., A. Monfort, and E. Renault (1989), Testing for common roots, *Econometrica*, 57, 171–185.

Gourieroux, C., A. Monfort, and E. Renault (1990), Bilinear constraints, estimation and tests in *Essays in honor of E. Malinvaud*, vol. III, Cambridge, Mass.: The MIT Press.

Gourieroux, C., A. Monfort, and A. Trognon (1985), Moindres carrés asymptotiques, *Annales de l'INSEE*, 58, 91–122.

Gourieroux, C. and I. Peaucelle (1987), Vérification empirique de la rationalité des anticipations de la demande par les entreprises, *Recherches Economiques de Louvain*, 53, 223–46.

Gourieroux, C. and J. Pradel (1986), Direct test of the rational expectation hypothesis, *European Economic Review*, 30, 265–84.

Granger, C.W.J. (1969), Investigating causal relations by econometric models and cross spectral methods, *Econometrica*, 37, 424–39.

Granger, C.W.J. (1978), New classes of time series models, *Statistician*, 27, 237–53.

Granger, C.W.J. (1980a), Testing for causality: a personal viewpoint, *Journal of Economic Dynamics and Control*, 2, 329–52.

Granger, C.W.J. (1980b), Long memory relationships and the aggregation of dynamic models, *Journal of Econometrics*, 14, 227–38.

Granger, C.W.J. (1986), Developments in the study of cointegrated economic variables, *Oxford Bulletin of Economics and Statistics*, 48, 213–28.

Granger, C.W.J. and M. Hatanaka (1964), *Spectral analysis of economic time series*, Princeton: Princeton University Press.

Granger, C.W.J. and R. Joyeux (1989), An introduction to long memory time series models and fractional differencing, *Journal of Time Series Analysis*, 1, 15–29.

Granger, C.W.J. and P. Newbold (1974), Spurious regressions in econometrics, *Journal of Econometrics*, 2, 111–20.

Granger, C.W.J. and P. Newbold (1976), Forecasting transformed series, *Journal of the Royal Statistical Society*, Series B, 38, 189–203.

Granger, C.W.J. and P. Newbold (1986), *Forecasting Economic Time Series*, New York: Academic Press.

Graupe, D. (1984), *Time series analysis, identification and adaptive filtering*, Miami: Krieger Publishing Co.

Grenander, U. and M. Rosenblatt (1956), *Statistical analysis of stationary time series*, New York: J.Wiley.

Grenander, U. and G. Szegö (1958), *Toeplitz forms and their applications*, University of California Press.

Grossman, S. (1981), An introduction to the theory of rational expectations under asymmetric information, *Review of Economic Studies*, 48, 541–59.

Hall, R. (1978), A stochastic life cycle model of aggregate consumption, *Journal of Political Economy*, 86, 971–87.

Hamilton, D. and D. Watts (1978), Interpreting partial autocorrelation functions of seasonal time series models, *Biometrika*, 65, 135–40.

Hannan, E. (1969a), The estimation of mixed moving average autoregressive systems, *Biometrika*, 56, 579–93.

Hannan, E. (1969b), The identification problem of vector mixed ARMA systems, *Biometrika*, 56, 223–5.

Hannan, E.(1970), *Multiple time series*, New York: J.Wiley.

Hannan, E. (1971), The identification problem for multiple equation systems with moving average errors, *Econometrica*, 39, 751–65.

Hannan, E. (1973), The asymptotic theory of linear time series, *Journal of Applied Probability*, 10, 130–45.

Hannan, E. (1980), The estimation of the order of an ARMA process, *Annals of Statistics*, 8, 1071–81.

Hannan, E. and B. Quinn (1979), The determination of the order of an autoregression, *Journal of the Royal Statistical Society*, Series B, 41, 190–5.

Harrison, P. (1967), Exponential smoothing and short term sales forecasting, *Management Science*, 13, 821–42.

Harrison, P.J. and C.F. Stevens (1976), Bayesian forecasting, *Journal of the Royal Statistical Society*, Series B, 38, 205–47.

Harvey, A.C. (1984), A unified view of statistical forecasting procedures, *Journal of Forecasting*, 3, 245–75.

Harvey, A.C. (1989), *Forecasting, structural time series and the Kalman Filter*, Cambridge: Cambridge University Press.

Harvey, A.C. (1990), *The econometric analysis of time series*, Cambridge, Mass.: MIT Press.

Harvey, A.C. (1990), *Time series models*, New York: Phillip Allan.

Harvey, A.C. and J. Durbin (1986), The effects of seat belt legislation on British road casualties: a case study in structural time series modelling, *Journal of the Royal Statistical Society*, Series A, 149, 187–227.

Harvey, A.C., S.G.B. Henry, S. Peters, and S. Wren-Lewis (1985), Stochastic trends in dynamic regression models: an application to the employment–output equation, London School of Economics.

Harvey, A.C. and G. Phillips (1979), The estimation of regression models with ARMA disturbances, *Biometrika*, 66, 49–58.

Harvey, A.C. and P. Todd (1983), Forecasting economic time series with structural and Box–Jenkins models: a case study, *Journal of Business and Economic Statistics*, 1, 299–307.

Hasza, D. (1980), The asymptotic distribution of the sample autocorrelation for an ARIMA process, *Journal of the American Statistical Association*, 75, 602–8.

Hendry, D. (1986), Econometric modelling with cointegrated variables: an overview, *Oxford Bulletin of Economics and Statistics*, 48, 201–12.

Hendry, D., A. Pagan, and J.D. Sargan (1984), Dynamic specification, Ch. 18 in Z. Griliches and M. Intriligator (eds.), *Handbook of econometrics*, Amsterdam: North Holland.

Henshaw, R. (1966), Application of the general linear model to seasonal adjustment of economic time series, *Econometrica*, 34, 381–95.

Herrndorf, N. (1984), A functional central limit theorem for weakly dependent sequences of random variables, *Annals of Probability*, 12, 141–53.

Hillmer, S.C. and G.C. Tiao (1982), An ARIMA model-based approach to seasonal adjustment, *Journal of the American Statistical Association*, 77, 63–70.

Hosoya, Y. (1977), On the Granger condition for noncausality, *Econometrica*, 45, 1735–6.

Hosking, J.R. (1980), Lagrange multiplier tests of time series models, *Journal of the Royal Statistical Society*, Series B, 42, 170–81.

Jazwinski, A. (1970), *Stochastic processes and filtering theory*, New York: Academic Press.

Jenkins, G. and D. Watts (1968), *Spectral analysis and its applications*, Holden Day.

Jennrich, R. (1969), Asymptotic properties of nonlinear least squares estimators, *The Annals of Mathematical Statistics*, 40, 633–43.

Johansen, S. (1988), Statistical analysis of cointegration vectors, *Journal of Economic Dynamics and Control*, 12, 231–54.

Johnston, J. (1972), *Econometric methods*, New York: J. Wiley.

Jonacek, G. (1982), Determining the degree of differencing for time series via the long spectrum, *Journal of Time Series Analysis*, 3, 177–83.

Jorgenson, D. (1964), Minimum variance, linear unbiased seasonal adjustment of economic time series, *Journal of the American Statistical Association*, 59, 681–724.

Kailath, T. (1980), *Linear system theory*, Prentice Hall.

Kalman, R.E. (1960), A new approach to linear filtering and prediction problem, *Journal of Basic Engineering*, 82, 34–45.

Kalman R.E. (1963), Mathematical description of linear dynamical systems, *SIAM Journal of Control*, 1, 152–92.

Kalman, R.E. and R.S. Bucy (1961), New results in linear filtering and prediction theory, *Journal of Basic Engineering*, 83, 95–108.

Kendall, G. (1973), *Time series*, London: Griffin.

Kendall, G. and A. Stuart (1968), *The advanced theory of statistics*, vol. III, London: Griffin.

Kiviet, J. (1980), Effects of ARMA errors on tests for regression coefficients: comments on Vinod's article, *Journal of the American Statistical Association*, 75, 353–8.

Kloek, T. (1985), Dynamic adjustment when the target is non stationary, *International Economic Review*, 25, 315–24.

Koopmans, L. (1964a), On the coefficient of coherence for weakly stationary stochastic processes, *Annals of Mathematical Statistics*, 35, 532–49.

Koopmans, L. (1964a), On the multivariate analysis of weakly stationary stochastic processes, *Annals of Mathematical Statistics*, 35, 1765–80.

Koopmans, L. (1974), *The spectral analysis of time series*, New York: Academic Press.

Kramer, W. (1984), On the consequence of trend for simultaneous equation estimation, *Economic Letters*, 14, 23–30.

Kuh, E., J. Neese and P. Hollinger (1985), *Structural sensitivity in econometric models*, New York: J.Wiley.

Ladd, G. (1964), Regression analysis of seasonal data, *Journal of the American Statistical Association*, 59, 402–21.

Laroque, G. (1977), Analyse d'une méthode de désaisonnalisation: le programme X11, version trimestrielle, *Annales de l'INSEE*, 28, 105–26.

Leong, Y. (1962), The use of an iterated moving average in measuring seasonal variations, *Journal of the American Statistical Association*, 57, 149–71.

Li, W. and A. McLeod (1986), Fractional time series modelling, *Biometrika*, 73, 217–21.

Little, R. and D. Rubin (1987), *Statistical analysis with missing data*, New York: J.Wiley.

Ljung, G., and G.E.P. Box (1978), On a measure of lack of fit in time series models, *Biometrika*, 65, 297–303.

Ljung, L. (1977), Analysis of recursive stochastic algorithms, *IEEE Transactions on Automatic Control*, 22, 551–75.

Ljung, L. and T. Soderstrom (1983), *Theory and practice of recursive identification*, Cambridge, Mass.: MIT Press.

Lovell, M. (1963), Seasonal adjustment of economic time series and multiple regression analysis, *Journal of the American Statistical Association*, 58, 993–1010.

Lovell, M. (1966), Alternative axiomatizations of seasonal adjustment, *Journal of the American Statistical Association*, 61, 374–8.

Lovell, M. (1986), Tests of the rational expectations hypothesis, *American Economic Review*, 76, 110-24.

Lucas, R.E. (1972), Expectations and the neutrality of money, *Journal of Economic Theory*, 4, 103–24.

Lucas, R.E. (1973), Some international evidence on output inflation trade-offs, *American Economic Review*, 63, 326–64.

Macaulay, F. (1931), *The smoothing of time series*, NBER.

MacClave, J. (1974), Estimating the order of moving average models: the maximum χ^2 method, *Journal of the American Statistical Association*, 73, 122–8.

Major, P. (1976), The approximation of partial sums of independent R.V.'s, *Zeitschrift für Wahrscheinlichkeitstheorie*, 35, 213–20.

Malgrange, P. (1985), Sentiers stationnaires des modéles macroéconomiques: Leçons de la maquette du CEPREMAP, in G. Ritschard and M. Boyer (eds.), *Optimalité et structures*, Paris: Economica.

Malinvaud, E. (1981), *Théorie macroéconomique*, Paris: Dunod.

Mandelbrot, B. (1971), A fast fractional Gaussian noise generator, *Water Resources Research*, 7, 543–53.

Mandelbrot, B. and J. Van Ness (1968), Fractional Brownian motions, fractional noises and applications, *SIAM Review*, 10, 422–37.

Mann, H. and A. Wald (1943), On the statistical treatment of linear stochastic difference equations, *Econometrica*, 11, 173–220.

Maravall, A. (1985), On structural time series models and the characterization of components, *Journal of Business and Economic Statistics*, 3, 350–5.

Marcet, A. and T. Sargent (1989), Convergence of least squares learning mechanisms in self referential linear stochastic models, *Journal of Economic Theory*, 48, 337-68.

McCallum, B.T. (1976), Rational expectations and the estimation of econometric models: an alternative procedure, *International Economic Review*, 17, 484–90.

McLeod, A. (1977), Improved Box–Jenkins estimators, *Biometrika*, 64, 531–4.

McLeod, A. (1978), On the distribution of residual autocorrelation Box–Jenkins models, *Journal of the Royal Statistical Society*, Series B, 40, 296–302.

McLeod, A. and W. Li (1983), Diagnostic checking for ARMA time series models using squared residual autocorrelations, *Journal of Time Series Analysis*, 4, 269–73.

Mizon, G.E. (1977), Model selection procedures in M.J. Artis and A.R. Nobay (eds.), *Studies in Modern Economic Analysis*, London: Basil Blackwell.

Monfort, A. (1980), *Cours de probabilités*, Paris: Economica.

Monfort, A. (1982), *Cours de statistique*, Paris: Economica.

Monfort, A. and R. Rabemananjara (1990), From a VAR model to a structural model, with an application to the wage price spiral, *Journal of Applied Econometrics*, 5, 203–27.

Mullineaux, D. (1978), On testing for rationality: another look at the Livingstone price expectations data, *Journal of Political Economy*, 86, 329–36.

Muth, J.R. (1960), Optimal properties of exponentially weighted forecasts, *Journal of the American Statistical Association*, 55, 299–305.

Muth, J.R. (1961), Rational expectations and the theory of price movements, *Econometrica*, 24, 315–35.

Nelson, C.R. (1974), The first order moving average process, *Journal of Econometrics*, 2, 121–41.

Nelson, C.R. and H. Kang (1981), Spurious periodicity in inappropriately detrended time series, *Econometrica*, 49, 741–51.

Nerlove, M. (1958), Adaptive expectations and cobweb phenomena, *Quarterly Journal of Economics*, 73, 227–40.

Nerlove, M., D. Grether, J. Carvalho, and F.X. Diebold (1994), *Analysis of economic time series*, New York: Academic Press.

Nerlove, M. and S. Wage (1964), On the optimality of adaptive forecasting, *Management Science*, 10, 198–206.

Newbold, P. (1974), The exact likelihood function for a mixed autoregressive moving average process, *Biometrika*, 61, 423–6.

Newey, W.K. and K.D. West (1987), A simple positive definite heteroskedasticity and autocorrelation consistent covariance matrix, *Econometrica*, 55, 703–8.

Nickell, S. (1985), Error correction, partial adjustment and all that: an expository note, *Oxford Bulletin of Economics and Statistics*, 47, 119–29.

Nijman, T. and F. Palm (1986), The construction and use of approximation for missing quarterly observations: a model based approach, *Journal of Business and Economic Statistics*, 4, 47–58.

Osborn, D. (1976), Maximum likelihood estimation of moving average processes, *Annals of Economic and Social Measurement*, 5, 75–87.

Osterwald–Lenum, M. (1992), A Note with Quantiles of the Asymptotic Distribution of the Maximum Likelihood Cointegration Rank Test Statistics, *Oxford Bulletin of Economics and Statistics*, 54, 461–71.

Otter, P.W. (1985), *Dynamic feature space modelling, filtering and self–tuning control of stochastic systems*, Berlin: Springer Verlag.

Ozaki, T. (1977), On the order determination of ARIMA models, *Applied Statistics*, 26, 290–301.

Palm, F. and T. Nijman (1984), Missing observations in the dynamic regression model, *Econometrica*, 52, 1415–35.

Park, J. and P.C.B. Phillips (1988), Statistical inference in regressions with integrated processes: part I, *Econometric Theory*, 4, 468–97.

Park, J. and P.C.B. Phillips (1989), Statistical inference in regressions with integrated processes: part II, *Econometric Theory*, 5, 95–131.

Parzen, E. (1962), *Stochastic processes*, San Francisco: Holden Day.

Pesando, J.E. (1975), A note on the rationality of the Livingstone price expectations, *Journal of Political Economy*, 83, 849–58.

Pesaran, H.M. (1981), Identification of rational expectations models, *Journal of Econometrics*, 16, 375–98.

Pesaran, H.M. (1987), *The limits to rational expectations*, Oxford: Basil Blackwell.

Pham Dinh, T. (1984), A note on some statistics useful in identifying the order of autoregressive moving average models, *Journal of Time Series Analysis*, 5, 273–9.

Phillips, P.C.B. (1986), Understanding spurious regressions in econometrics, *Journal of Econometrics*, 33, 311–40.

Phillips, P.C.B. (1987), Time series regression with a unit root, *Econometrica*, 55, 277–301.

Phillips, P.C.B. (1991), Optimal inference in cointegrated systems, *Econometrica*, 59, 283-306.

Phillips, P.C.B. and S. Durlauf (1986), Multiple time series regression with integrated processes, *Review of Economic Studies*, 53, 473–95.

Phillips, P.C.B. and S. Ouliaris (1990), Asymptotic properties of residual based tests for cointegration, *Econometrica*, 58, 165–93.

Phillips, P.C.B. and P. Perron (1988), Testing for a unit root in time series regression, *Biometrika*, 75, 335–46.

Pierce, D. (1970), A duality between AR and MA processes concerning their least squares estimates, *Annals of Mathematical Statistics*, 41, 422–6.

Pierce, D. (1971), Least squares estimation in the regression model with autoregressive-moving average errors, *Biometrika*, 58, 299–312.

Pierce, D. (1979a), R^2 measures for time series, *Journal of the American Statistical Association*, 74, 901–10.

Pierce, D. (1979b), Signal extraction error in nonstationary time series, *Annals of Statistics*, 7, 1303–20.

Pierce, D. and L. Haugh (1977), Causality in temporal systems, *Journal of Econometrics*, 5, 265–94.

Pierce, D. and L. Haugh (1979), The characterization of instantaneous causality: a comment, *Journal of Econometrics*, 10, 257–9.

Poskitt, D. and A. Tremayne (1981), An approach to testing linear time series models, *Annals of Statistics*, 9, 974–86.

Price, J. (1979), The characterization of instantaneous causality: a correction, *Journal of Econometrics*, 10, 253–6.

Priestley, M. (1981), *Spectral analysis and time series*, New York: Academic Press.

Prothero, D. and K. Wallis (1976), Modelling macroeconomic time series, *Journal of the Royal Statistical Society*, Series A, 468–500.

Quenouille, M. (1949a), Notes on the calculation of autocorrelations of linear autoregressive schemes, *Biometrika*, 34, 365–7.

Quenouille, M. (1949b), Approximate tests of correlation in time series, *Journal of the Royal Statistical Society*, Series B, 11, 68–84.

Quenouille, M. (1957), *The analysis of multiple time series*, London: Griffin.

Rao, C.R. (1973), *Linear statistical inference and its applications*, New York: J.Wiley.

Rissanen, J. and P. Caines (1979), The strong consistency of maximum likelihood estimators for ARMA processes, *Annals of Statistics*, 7, 297–315.

Rose, D. (1977), Forecasting aggregates of independent ARIMA processes, *Journal of Econometrics*, 5, 323–46.

Rosenblatt, M. (1963), *Time series analysis*, New York: J.Wiley.

Rosenblatt, M. (1976), Fractional integrals of stationary processes and the central limit theorem, *Journal of Applied Probability*, 13, 723–32.

Rosenblatt, M. (1985), *Stationary sequences and random fields*, Frankfurt: Birkhäuser.

Rozanov, Y. (1967), *Stationary random processes*, San Francisco: Holden Day.

Rudin, W. (1966), *Real and complex analysis*, New York: McGraw–Hill.

Saïd, S. and D. Dickey (1984), Testing for unit roots in ARMA of unknown order, *Biometrika*, 71, 599–607.

Salazar, D. (1982), Structure changes in time series models, *Journal of Econometrics*, 19, 147–63.

Salmon, M. (1982), Error correction mechanisms, *Economic Journal*, 92, 615–29.

Samuelson, P. (1965), Proof that properly anticipated prices fluctuate randomly, *Industrial Management Review*, 6, 41–9.

Sargan, J.D. (1980), Some tests of dynamic specification for a single equation, *Econometrica*, 48, 879–98.

Sargan, J.D. (1984), Alternative models for rational expectations in some simple irregular cases, Discussion Paper, London School of Economics.

Sargan, J.D. and E. Drettakis (1974), Missing data in an autoregressive model, *International Economic Review*, 13, 39–58.

Sargan, J.D. and F. Mehta (1983), A generalisation of the Durbin significance test and its application to dynamic specification, *Econometrica*, 51, 1551–68.

Sargent, T. (1985), *Macroeconomic Theory*, New York: Academic Press.

Sargent, T. and N. Wallace (1973), Rational expectations and the dynamics of hyperinflation, *International Economic Review*, 328–50.

Savin, N. and K. White (1978), Testing for autocorrelation with missing observations, *Econometrica*, 46, 59–67.

Schlicht, E. (1981), A seasonal adjustment principle and a seasonal adjustment method derived from this principle, *Journal of the American Statistical Association*, 76, 374–8.

Schmidt, P. and P.C.B. Phillips (1992), LM test for a unit root in the presence of deterministic trends, *Oxford Bulletin of Economics and Statistics*, 54, 257–87.

Schwartz, G. (1978), Estimating the dimension of a model, *Annals of Statistics*, 6, 461–4.

Shaman, P. (1975), An approximate inverse for the covariance matrix of moving average and autoregressive processes, *Annals of Statistics*, 3, 532–8.

Sheffrin, S. (1983), *Rational expectations*, Cambridge: Cambridge University Press.

Shibata, R. (1976), Selection of the order of an autoregressive model by Akaike's information criterion, *Biometrika*, 63, 117–26.

Shiller, R. (1978), Rational expectations and the dynamic structure of macroeconomic models, *Journal of Monetary Economics*, 4, 1–44.

Shiskin, J. and H. Eisenpress (1957), Seasonal adjustment by electronic computer methods, *Journal of the American Statistical Association*, 52, 415–49.

Shiskin, J, A. Young, and J. Musgrave (1965), The X11 variant of the Census method X11 seasonal adjustment program, Technical paper 15, Bureau of the Census.

Silvey, S. (1959), The Lagrangian multiplier test, *Annals of Mathematical Statistics*, 30, 389–407.

Sims, C. (1972), Money, income and causality, *American Economic Review*, 62, 540–52.

Sims, C. (1980), Macroeconomics and reality, *Econometrica*, 48, 1–48.

Sims C., J. Stock, and M. Watson (1990), Inference in linear time series models with some unit roots, *Econometrica*, 58, 113–44.

Slutsky, E. (1937), The summation of random causes as the source of cyclic processes, *Econometrica*, 5, 105–46.

Stock, J.H. (1987), Asymptotic properties of least squares estimates of cointegrating vectors, *Econometrica*, 55, 1035–56.

Tamhane, A. (1982), A note on the use of residuals for detecting an outlier in linear regression, *Biometrika*, 69, 488–91.

Taylor, J. (1977), Conditions for a unique solution in stochastic macroeconomic models with rational expectations, *Econometrica*, 45, 1377–87.

Theil, H. and S. Wage (1964), Some observations on adaptive forecasting, *Management Science*, 6, 324–42.

Tiao, G. and G.E.P. Box (1981), Modelling multiple time series with applications, *Journal of the American Statistical Association*, 76, 802–16.

Turnovsky, S. (1977), *Macroeconomic analysis and stabilization policy*, Cambridge: Cambridge University Press.

Turnovsky, S. and M. Wachter (1972), A test of the expectations hypothesis using directly observed wage and price expectations, *Review of Economics and Statistics*, 54, 47–54.

Vinod, H. (1976), Effects of ARMA errors on the significance tests for regression coefficients, *Journal of the American Statistical Association*, 71, 929–33.

Walker, A. (1961), Large sample estimation of parameters for moving average models, *Biometrika*, 48, 343–57.

Walker, A. (1984), Asymptotic properties of least squares estimators of parameters of the spectrum of a stationary nondeterministic time series, *Journal of the Australian Mathematical Society*, 4, 363–84.

Wallis, K. (1977), Multiple time series analysis and the final form of econometric models, *Econometrica*, 45, 1481–98.

Wallis, K. (1980), Econometric implications of the rational expectations hypothesis, *Econometrica*, 48, 49–73.

Wallis, K. (1982), Seasonal adjustment and revision of current data: linear filters for the X11 method, *Journal of the Royal Statistical Society*, Series A, 145, 74–85.

Watson, G.(1955), Serial correlation in regression analysis I, *Biometrika*, 42, 327–41.

Watson, G. and E.J. Hannan (1956), Serial correlation in regression analysis II, *Biometrika*, 43, 436–48.

Watson, M. (1985), Recursive solution methods for dynamic linear rational expectation models, Discussion Paper, Harvard University.

White, J. (1958), The limiting distribution of the serial correlation coefficient in the explosive case, *Annals of Mathematical Statistics*, 29, 1188–97.

Whiteman, C.H. (1983), *Linear rational expectations models: a user's guide*, Minneapolis: University of Minneapolis Press.

Whittle, P. (1951), *Hypothesis testing in time series analysis*, New York: Hafarer.

Whittle, P. (1953), The analysis of multiple time series, *Journal of the Royal Statistical Society*, Series B, 15, 125–39.

Whittle, P. (1963), *Prediction and regulation*, London: The English Universities Press.

Wickens, M. and T. Breusch (1986), Dynamic specification, the long run and the estimation of transformed regression models, Discussion Paper Queen's University.

Wilson, G. (1969), Factorization on the generating function of a pure moving average process, *SIAM Journal of Numerical Analysis*, 6, 1–7.

Winters, P. (1960), Forecasting sales by exponentially weighted moving averages, *Management Science*, 6, 324–42.

Woodward, W. and H. Gray (1981), On the relationship between the S-array and the Box–Jenkins method of ARMA model identification, *Journal of the American Statistical Association*, 76, 579–87.

Yoo, S. (1985), Multi-cointegrated time series and generalized error correction models, Discussion Paper, University of California at San Diego.

Yule, G. (1921), On the time correlation problem, *Journal of the Royal Statistical Society*, Series A, 84, 497–526.

Yule, G. (1927), On a method of investigating periodicities in disturbed series with special reference to Wolfer's sunspot numbers, *Phil. Trans. Royal Society*, London, A 226, 267–98.

Zellner, A. (1979), Causality and econometrics, in A. Brunner and K. Meltzer (eds.), *Three aspects of policy and policymaking: knowledge, data, and Institutions*, Carnegie-Rochester Conference Series on Public Policy, n.8, Amsterdam: North Holland.

Table 1 Normal distribution - A

$$F(x) = \frac{1}{\sqrt{2\pi}} \int_{-\infty}^{x} e^{-u^2/2}\,du$$

x	0.00	0.01	0.02	0.03	0.04	0.05	0.06	0.07	0.08	0.09
0.0	0.50000	0.50399	0.50798	0.51197	0.51595	0.51994	0.52392	0.52790	0.53188	0.53586
0.1	0.53983	0.54380	0.54776	0.55172	0.55567	0.55962	0.56356	0.56750	0.57142	0.57535
0.2	0.57926	0.58317	0.58706	0.59095	0.59484	0.59871	0.60257	0.60642	0.61026	0.61409
0.3	0.61791	0.62172	0.62552	0.62930	0.63307	0.63683	0.64058	0.64431	0.64803	0.65173
0.4	0.65542	0.65910	0.66276	0.66640	0.67003	0.67365	0.67724	0.68082	0.68439	0.68793
0.5	0.69146	0.69497	0.69847	0.70194	0.70540	0.70884	0.71226	0.71566	0.71904	0.72240
0.6	0.72575	0.72907	0.73237	0.73565	0.73891	0.74215	0.74537	0.74857	0.75175	0.75490
0.7	0.75804	0.76115	0.76424	0.76731	0.77035	0.77337	0.77637	0.77935	0.78230	0.78524
0.8	0.78814	0.79103	0.79389	0.79673	0.79955	0.80234	0.80511	0.80785	0.81057	0.81327
0.9	0.81594	0.81859	0.82121	0.82381	0.82639	0.82894	0.83147	0.83398	0.83646	0.83891
1.0	0.84134	0.84375	0.84614	0.84850	0.85083	0.85314	0.85543	0.85769	0.85993	0.86214
1.1	0.86433	0.86650	0.86864	0.87076	0.87286	0.87493	0.87698	0.87900	0.88100	0.88298
1.2	0.88493	0.88686	0.88877	0.89065	0.89251	0.89435	0.89617	0.89796	0.89973	0.90147
1.3	0.90320	0.90490	0.90658	0.90824	0.90988	0.91149	0.91309	0.91466	0.91621	0.91774
1.4	0.91924	0.92073	0.92220	0.92364	0.92507	0.92647	0.92786	0.92922	0.93056	0.93189
1.5	0.93319	0.93448	0.93574	0.93699	0.93822	0.93943	0.94062	0.94179	0.94295	0.94408
1.6	0.94520	0.94630	0.94738	0.94845	0.94950	0.95053	0.95154	0.95254	0.95352	0.95449
1.7	0.95543	0.95637	0.95728	0.95818	0.95907	0.95994	0.96080	0.96164	0.96246	0.96327
1.8	0.96407	0.96485	0.96562	0.96638	0.96712	0.96784	0.96856	0.96926	0.96995	0.97062
1.9	0.97128	0.97193	0.97257	0.97320	0.97381	0.97441	0.97500	0.97558	0.97615	0.97670
2.0	0.97725	0.97778	0.97831	0.97882	0.97932	0.97982	0.98030	0.98077	0.98124	0.98169
2.1	0.98214	0.98257	0.98300	0.98341	0.98382	0.98422	0.98461	0.98500	0.98537	0.98574
2.2	0.98610	0.98645	0.98679	0.98713	0.98745	0.98778	0.98809	0.98840	0.98870	0.98899
2.3	0.98928	0.98956	0.98983	0.99010	0.99036	0.99061	0.99086	0.99111	0.99134	0.99158
2.4	0.99180	0.99202	0.99224	0.99245	0.99266	0.99286	0.99305	0.99324	0.99343	0.99361
2.5	0.99379	0.99396	0.99413	0.99430	0.99446	0.99461	0.99477	0.99492	0.99506	0.99520
2.6	0.99534	0.99547	0.99560	0.99573	0.99585	0.99598	0.99609	0.99621	0.99632	0.99643
2.7	0.99653	0.99664	0.99674	0.99683	0.99693	0.99702	0.99711	0.99720	0.99728	0.99736
2.8	0.99744	0.99752	0.99760	0.99767	0.99774	0.99781	0.99788	0.99795	0.99801	0.99807
2.9	0.99813	0.99819	0.99825	0.99831	0.99836	0.99841	0.99846	0.99851	0.99856	0.99861

Table 2 *Normal distribution - B*

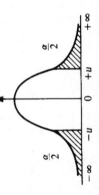

α	0.00	0.01	0.02	0.03	0.04	0.05	0.06	0.07	0.08	0.09
0.0	∞	2.5758	2.3263	2.1701	2.0537	1.9600	1.8808	1.8119	1.7507	1.6954
0.1	1.6449	1.5982	1.5548	1.5141	1.4758	1.4395	1.4051	1.3722	1.3408	1.3106
0.2	1.2816	1.2536	1.2566	1.2004	1.1750	1.1503	1.1264	1.1031	1.0803	1.0581
0.3	1.0364	1.0152	0.9945	0.9741	0.9542	0.9346	0.9154	0.8965	0.8779	0.8596
0.4	0.8416	0.8239	0.7892	0.8064	0.7722	0.7554	0.7388	0.7255	0.7063	0.6903
0.5	0.6745	0.6588	0.6433	0.6280	0.6128	0.5978	0.5828	0.5681	0.5534	0.5388
0.6	0.5244	0.5101	0.4959	0.4817	0.4677	0.4538	0.4399	0.4261	0.4125	0.3989
0.7	0.3853	0.3719	0.3585	0.3451	0.3319	0.3186	0.3000	0.2924	0.2793	0.2663
0.8	0.2533	0.2404	0.2275	0.2147	0.2019	0.1819	0.1764	0.1637	0.1510	0.1383
0.9	0.1257	0.1130	0.1004	0.0878	0.0753	0.0627	0.0502	0.0376	0.0251	0.0125

ν	α								
	0.990	0.975	0.950	0.900	0.100	0.050	0.025	0.010	0.001
1	0.000 2	0.0010	0.0039	0.0158	2.71	3.84	5.02	6.63	10.83
2	0.02	0.05	0.10	0.21	4.61	5.99	7.38	9.21	13.82
3	0.12	0.22	0.35	0.58	6.25	7.81	9.35	11.34	16.27
4	0.30	0.48	0.71	1.06	7.78	9.94	11.14	13.28	18.47
5	0.55	0.83	1.15	1.61	9.24	11.07	12.83	15.09	20.52
6	0.87	1.24	1.64	2.20	10.64	12.59	14.45	16.81	22.46
7	1.24	1.69	2.17	2.83	12.02	14.07	16.01	18.47	24.32
8	1.65	2.18	2.73	3.49	13.36	15.51	17.53	20.09	26.13
9	2.09	2.70	3.33	4.17	14.68	16.92	19.02	21.67	27.88
10	2.56	3.25	3.94	4.87	15.99	18.31	20.48	23.21	29.59
11	3.05	3.82	4.57	5.58	17.27	19.67	21.92	24.72	31.26
12	3.57	4.40	5.23	6.30	18.55	21.03	23.34	26.22	32.91
13	4.11	5.01	5.89	7.04	19.81	22.36	24.74	27.69	34.53
14	4.66	5.63	6.57	7.79	21.06	23.68	26.12	29.14	36.12
15	5.23	6.26	7.26	8.55	22.31	25.00	27.49	30.58	37.70
16	5.81	6.91	7.96	9.31	23.54	26.30	28.84	32.00	39.25
17	6.41	7.56	8.67	10.08	24.77	27.59	30.19	33.41	40.79
18	7.01	8.23	9.39	10.86	25.99	28.87	31.53	34.80	42.31
19	7.63	8.91	10.12	11.65	27.20	30.14	32.85	36.19	43.82
20	8.26	9.59	10.85	12.44	28.41	31.41	34.17	37.57	45.32
21	8.90	10.28	11.59	13.24	29.61	32.67	35.48	38.93	46.80
22	9.54	10.98	12.34	14.04	30.81	33.92	36.78	40.29	48.27
23	10.20	11.69	13.09	14.85	32.01	35.17	38.08	41.64	49.73
24	10.86	12.40	13.85	15.66	33.20	36.41	39.37	42.98	51.18
25	11.52	13.12	14.61	16.47	34.38	37.65	40.65	44.31	52.62
26	12.20	13.84	15.38	17.29	35.56	38.88	41.92	45.64	54.05
27	12.88	14.57	16.15	18.11	36.74	40.11	43.19	46.96	55.48
28	13.57	15.31	16.93	18.94	37.92	41.34	44.46	48.28	56.89
29	14.26	16.05	17.71	19.77	39.09	42.56	45.72	49.59	58.30
30	14.95	16.79	18.49	20.60	40.26	43.77	46.98	50.89	59.70

when $\nu > 30$, then $\sqrt{2\chi^2} - \sqrt{2\nu - 1}$ is approximately $N(0,1)$.

Table 4 Student's t distribution

ν \ α	0.90	0.80	0.70	0.60	0.50	0.40	0.30	0.20	0.10	0.05	0.02	0.01	0.001
1	0.158	0.325	0.510	0.727	1.000	1.376	1.963	3.078	6.314	12.706	31.821	63.657	636.619
2	0.142	0.289	0.445	0.617	0.816	1.061	1.386	1.886	2.920	4.303	6.965	9.925	31.598
3	0.137	0.277	0.424	0.584	0.765	0.978	1.250	1.638	2.353	3.182	4.541	5.841	12.929
4	0.134	0.271	0.414	0.569	0.741	0.941	1.190	1.533	2.132	2.776	3.747	4.604	8.610
5	0.132	0.267	0.408	0.559	0.727	0.920	1.156	1.476	2.015	2.571	3.365	4.032	6.869
6	0.131	0.265	0.404	0.553	0.718	0.906	1.134	1.440	1.943	2.447	3.143	3.707	5.959
7	0.130	0.263	0.402	0.549	0.711	0.896	1.119	1.415	1.895	2.365	2.998	3.499	5.408
8	0.130	0.262	0.399	0.546	0.706	0.889	1.108	1.397	1.860	2.306	2.896	3.355	5.041
9	0.129	0.261	0.398	0.543	0.703	0.883	1.100	1.383	1.833	2.262	2.821	3.250	4.781
10	0.129	0.260	0.397	0.542	0.700	0.879	1.093	1.372	1.812	2.228	2.764	3.169	4.587
11	0.129	0.260	0.396	0.540	0.697	0.876	1.088	1.363	1.796	2.201	2.718	3.106	4.437
12	0.128	0.259	0.395	0.539	0.695	0.873	1.083	1.356	1.782	2.179	2.681	3.055	4.318
13	0.128	0.259	0.394	0.538	0.694	0.870	1.079	1.350	1.771	2.160	2.650	3.012	4.221
14	0.128	0.258	0.393	0.537	0.692	0.868	1.076	1.345	1.761	2.145	2.624	2.977	4.140
15	0.128	0.258	0.393	0.536	0.691	0.866	1.074	1.341	1.753	2.131	2.602	2.947	4.073
16	0.128	0.258	0.392	0.535	0.690	0.865	1.071	1.337	1.746	2.120	2.583	2.921	4.015
17	0.128	0.257	0.392	0.534	0.689	0.863	1.069	1.333	1.740	2.110	2.567	2.898	3.965
18	0.127	0.257	0.392	0.534	0.688	0.862	1.067	1.330	1.734	2.101	2.552	2.878	3.922
19	0.127	0.257	0.391	0.533	0.688	0.861	1.066	1.328	1.729	2.093	2.539	2.861	3.883
20	0.127	0.257	0.391	0.533	0.687	0.860	1.064	1.325	1.725	2.086	2.528	2.845	3.850
21	0.127	0.257	0.391	0.532	0.686	0.859	1.063	1.323	1.721	2.080	2.518	2.831	3.819
22	0.127	0.256	0.390	0.532	0.686	0.858	1.061	1.321	1.717	2.074	2.508	2.819	3.792
23	0.127	0.256	0.390	0.532	0.685	0.858	1.060	1.319	1.714	2.069	2.500	2.807	3.767
24	0.127	0.256	0.390	0.531	0.685	0.857	1.059	1.318	1.711	2.064	2.492	2.797	3.745
25	0.127	0.256	0.390	0.531	0.684	0.856	1.058	1.316	1.708	2.060	2.485	2.787	3.725
26	0.127	0.256	0.390	0.531	0.684	0.856	1.058	1.315	1.706	2.056	2.479	2.779	3.707
27	0.127	0.256	0.389	0.531	0.684	0.855	1.057	1.314	1.703	2.052	2.473	2.771	3.690
28	0.127	0.256	0.389	0.530	0.683	0.855	1.056	1.313	1.701	2.048	2.467	2.763	3.674
29	0.127	0.256	0.389	0.530	0.683	0.854	1.055	1.311	1.699	2.045	2.462	2.756	3.659
30	0.127	0.256	0.389	0.530	0.683	0.854	1.055	1.310	1.697	2.042	2.457	2.750	3.646
40	0.126	0.255	0.388	0.529	0.681	0.851	1.050	1.303	1.684	2.021	2.423	2.704	3.551
80	0.126	0.254	0.387	0.527	0.679	0.848	1.046	1.296	1.671	2.000	2.390	2.660	3.460
120	0.126	0.254	0.386	0.526	0.677	0.845	1.041	1.289	1.658	1.980	2.358	2.617	3.373

ν_2	$\nu_1 = 1$		$\nu_1 = 2$		$\nu_1 = 3$		$\nu_1 = 4$		$\nu_1 = 5$	
	$P = 0.05$	$P = 0.01$	$P = 0.05$	$P = 0.01$	$P = 0.05$	$P = 0.01$	$P = 0.05$	$P = 0.01$	$P = 0.05$	$P = 0.01$
1	161.4	4052	199.5	4999	215.7	5403	224.6	5625	230.2	5764
2	18.51	98.49	19.00	99.00	19.16	99.17	19.25	99.25	19.30	99.30
3	10.13	34.12	9.55	30.81	9.28	29.46	9.12	28.71	9.01	28.24
4	7.71	21.20	6.94	18.00	6.59	16.69	6.39	15.98	6.26	15.52
5	6.61	16.26	5.79	13.27	5.41	12.06	5.19	11.39	5.05	10.97
6	5.99	13.74	5.14	10.91	4.76	9.78	4.53	9.15	4.39	8.75
7	5.59	12.25	4.74	9.55	4.35	8.45	4.12	7.85	3.97	7.45
8	5.32	11.26	4.46	8.65	4.07	7.59	3.84	7.01	3.69	6.63
9	5.12	10.56	4.26	8.02	3.86	6.99	3.63	6.42	3.48	6.06
10	4.96	10.04	4.10	7.56	3.71	6.55	3.48	5.99	3.33	5.64
11	4.84	9.65	3.98	7.20	3.59	6.22	3.36	5.67	3.20	5.32
12	4.75	9.33	3.88	6.93	3.49	5.95	3.26	5.41	3.11	5.06
13	4.67	9.07	3.80	6.70	3.41	5.74	3.18	5.20	3.02	4.86
14	4.60	8.86	3.74	6.51	3.34	5.56	3.11	5.03	2.96	4.69
15	4.54	8.68	3.68	6.36	3.29	5.42	3.06	4.89	2.90	4.56
16	4.49	8.53	3.63	6.23	3.24	5.29	3.01	4.77	2.85	4.44
17	4.45	8.40	3.59	6.11	3.20	5.18	2.96	4.67	2.81	4.34
18	4.41	8.28	3.55	6.01	3.16	5.09	2.93	4.58	2.77	4.25
19	4.38	8.18	3.52	5.93	3.13	5.01	2.90	4.50	2.74	4.17
20	4.35	8.10	3.49	5.85	3.10	4.94	2.87	4.43	2.71	4.10
21	4.32	8.02	3.47	5.78	3.07	4.87	2.84	4.37	2.68	4.04
22	4.30	7.94	3.44	5.72	3.05	4.82	2.82	4.31	2.66	3.99
23	4.28	7.88	3.42	5.66	3.03	4.76	2.80	4.26	2.64	3.94
24	4.26	7.82	3.40	5.61	3.01	4.72	2.78	4.22	2.62	3.90
25	4.24	7.77	3.38	5.57	2.99	4.68	2.76	4.18	2.60	3.86
26	4.22	7.72	3.37	5.53	2.98	4.64	2.74	4.14	2.59	3.82
27	4.21	7.68	3.35	5.49	2.96	4.60	2.73	4.11	2.57	3.70
28	4.20	7.64	3.34	5.45	2.95	4.57	2.71	4.07	2.56	3.75
29	4.18	7.60	3.33	5.42	2.93	4.54	2.70	4.04	2.54	3.73
30	4.17	7.56	3.32	5.39	2.92	4.51	2.69	4.02	2.53	3.70
40	4.08	7.31	3.23	5.18	2.84	4.31	2.61	3.83	2.45	3.51
60	4.00	7.08	3.15	4.98	2.76	4.13	2.52	3.65	2.37	3.34
120	3.92	6.85	3.07	4.79	2.68	3.95	2.45	3.48	2.29	3.17
∞	3.84	6.64	2.99	4.60	2.60	3.78	2.37	3.32	2.21	3.02

Table 5 *Continued*

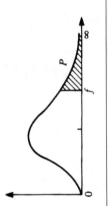

ν_2	$\nu_1 = 6$ $P = 0.05$	$P = 0.01$	$\nu_1 = 8$ $P = 0.05$	$P = 0.01$	$\nu_1 = 12$ $P = 0.05$	$P = 0.01$	$\nu_1 = 24$ $P = 0.05$	$P = 0.01$	$\nu_1 = \infty$ $P = 0.05$	$P = 0.01$
1	234.0	5 859	238.9	5 981	243.9	6 106	249.0	6 234	254.3	6 366
2	19.33	99.33	19.37	99.36	19.41	99.42	19.45	99.46	19.50	99.50
3	8.94	27.91	8.84	27.49	8.74	27.05	8.64	26.60	8.53	26.12
4	6.61	15.21	6.04	14.80	5.91	14.37	5.77	13.93	5.63	13.46
5	4.95	10.67	4.82	10.27	4.68	9.89	4.53	9.47	4.36	9.02
6	4.28	8.47	4.15	8.10	4.00	7.72	3.84	7.31	3.67	6.88
7	3.87	7.19	3.73	6.84	3.57	6.47	3.41	6.07	3.23	5.65
8	3.58	6.37	3.44	6.03	3.28	5.67	3.12	5.28	2.93	4.86
9	3.37	5.80	3.23	5.47	3.07	5.11	2.90	4.73	2.71	4.31
10	3.22	5.39	3.07	5.06	2.91	4.71	2.74	4.33	2.54	3.91
11	3.09	5.07	2.95	4.74	2.79	4.40	2.61	4.02	2.40	3.60
12	3.00	4.82	2.85	4.50	2.69	4.16	2.50	3.78	2.30	3.36
13	2.92	4.62	2.77	4.30	2.60	3.96	2.42	3.59	2.21	3.16
14	2.85	4.46	2.70	4.14	2.53	3.80	2.35	3.43	2.13	3.00
15	2.79	4.32	2.64	4.00	2.48	3.67	2.29	3.29	2.07	2.87
16	2.74	4.20	2.59	3.89	2.42	3.55	2.24	3.18	2.01	2.75
17	2.70	4.10	2.55	3.79	2.35	3.45	2.19	3.08	1.96	2.65
18	2.66	4.01	2.51	3.71	2.34	3.37	2.15	3.00	1.92	2.57
19	2.63	3.94	2.48	3.63	2.31	3.30	2.11	2.92	1.88	2.49
20	2.60	3.87	2.45	3.56	2.28	3.23	2.08	2.86	1.84	2.42
21	2.57	3.81	2.42	3.51	2.25	3.17	2.05	2.80	1.81	2.36
22	2.55	3.76	2.40	3.45	2.23	3.12	2.03	2.75	1.78	2.31
23	2.53	3.71	2.38	3.41	2.20	3.07	2.00	2.70	1.76	2.26
24	2.51	3.67	2.36	3.36	2.18	3.03	1.98	2.66	1.73	2.21
25	2.49	3.63	2.34	3.32	2.16	2.99	1.96	2.62	1.71	2.17
26	2.47	3.59	2.32	3.29	2.15	2.96	1.95	2.58	1.69	2.13
27	2.46	3.56	2.30	3.26	2.13	2.93	1.93	2.55	1.67	2.10
28	2.44	3.53	2.29	3.23	2.12	2.90	1.91	2.52	1.65	2.06
29	2.43	3.50	2.28	3.20	2.10	2.87	1.90	2.49	1.64	2.03
30	2.42	3.47	2.27	3.17	2.09	2.84	1.89	2.47	1.62	2.01
40	2.34	3.29	2.18	2.99	2.00	2.66	1.79	2.29	1.51	1.80
60	2.25	3.12	2.10	2.82	1.92	2.50	1.70	2.12	1.39	1.60
120	2.17	2.96	2.01	2.66	1.83	2.34	1.61	1.95	1.25	1.38

Table 6 *Durbin–Watson test: critical values* ($\alpha = 5\%$)

T	$k' = 1$		$k' = 2$		$k' = 3$		$k' = 4$		$k' = 5$	
	d_l	d_u	d_l	d_u	d_l	d_u	d_l	d_u	d_l	d_u
15	1.08	1.36	0.95	1.54	0.82	1.75	0.69	1.97	0.56	2.21
16	1.10	1.37	0.98	1.54	0.86	1.73	0.74	1.93	0.62	2.15
17	1.13	1.38	1.02	1.54	0.90	1.71	0.78	1.90	0.67	2.10
18	1.16	1.39	1.05	1.53	0.93	1.69	0.82	1.87	0.71	2.06
19	1.18	1.40	1.08	1.53	0.97	1.68	0.86	1.85	0.75	2.02
20	1.20	1.41	1.10	1.54	1.00	1.68	0.90	1.83	0.79	1.99
21	1.22	1.42	1.13	1.54	1.03	1.67	0.93	1.81	0.83	1.96
22	1.24	1.43	1.15	1.54	1.05	1.66	0.96	1.80	0.86	1.94
23	1.26	1.44	1.17	1.54	1.08	1.66	0.99	1.79	0.90	1.92
24	1.27	1.45	1.19	1.55	1.10	1.66	1.01	1.78	0.93	1.90
25	1.29	1.45	1.21	1.55	1.12	1.66	1.04	1.77	0.95	1.89
26	1.30	1.46	1.22	1.55	1.14	1.65	1.06	1.76	0.98	1.88
27	1.32	1.47	1.24	1.56	1.16	1.65	1.08	1.76	1.01	1.86
28	1.33	1.48	1.26	1.56	1.18	1.65	1.10	1.75	1.03	1.85
29	1.34	1.48	1.27	1.56	1.20	1.65	1.12	1.74	1.05	1.84
30	1.35	1.49	1.28	1.57	1.21	1.65	1.14	1.74	1.07	1.83
31	1.36	1.50	1.30	1.57	1.23	1.65	1.16	1.74	1.09	1.83
32	1.37	1.50	1.31	1.57	1.24	1.65	1.18	1.73	1.11	1.82
33	1.38	1.51	1.32	1.58	1.26	1.65	1.19	1.73	1.13	1.81
34	1.39	1.51	1.33	1.58	1.27	1.65	1.21	1.73	1.15	1.81
35	1.40	1.52	1.34	1.58	1.28	1.65	1.22	1.73	1.16	1.80
36	1.41	1.52	1.35	1.59	1.29	1.65	1.22	1.73	1.18	1.80
37	1.42	1.53	1.36	1.59	1.31	1.66	1.25	1.72	1.19	1.80
38	1.43	1.54	1.37	1.56	1.32	1.66	1.26	1.72	1.21	1.79
39	1.43	1.54	1.38	1.60	1.33	1.66	1.27	1.72	1.22	1.79
40	1.44	1.54	1.39	1.60	1.34	1.66	1.29	1.72	1.23	1.79
45	1.48	1.57	1.43	1.62	1.38	1.67	1.34	1.72	1.29	1.78
50	1.50	1.59	1.46	1.63	1.42	1.67	1.38	1.72	1.34	1.77
55	1.53	1.60	1.49	1.64	1.45	1.68	1.41	1.72	1.38	1.77
60	1.55	1.62	1.51	1.65	1.48	1.69	1.44	1.73	1.41	1.77
65	1.57	1.63	1.54	1.66	1.50	1.70	1.47	1.73	1.44	1.77
70	1.58	1.64	1.55	1.67	1.52	1.70	1.49	1.74	1.46	1.77
75	1.60	1.65	1.57	1.68	1.54	1.71	1.51	1.74	1.49	1.77
80	1.61	1.66	1.59	1.69	1.56	1.72	1.53	1.74	1.51	1.77
85	1.62	1.67	1.60	1.70	1.57	1.72	1.55	1.75	1.52	1.77
90	1.63	1.68	1.61	1.70	1.59	1.73	1.57	1.75	1.54	1.78
95	1.64	1.69	1.62	1.71	1.60	1.73	1.58	1.75	1.56	1.78
100	1.65	1.69	1.63	1.72	1.61	1.74	1.59	1.76	1.57	1.78

Note: T is the number of observations, k' is the number of regressors excluding the constant.

Table 7 *Distribution of* $T(1 - \hat{\rho}_T)$ *for* $\rho = 1$

Sample Size	Probability α of larger value							
T	0.01	0.025	0.05	0.10	0.90	0.95	0.975	0.99
					c_α			
25	11.9	9.3	7.3	5.3	-1.01	-1.40	-1.79	-2.28
50	12.9	9.9	7.7	5.5	-0.97	-1.35	-1.70	-2.16
100	13.3	10.2	7.9	5.6	-0.95	-1.31	-1.65	-2.09
250	13.6	10.3	8.0	5.7	-0.93	-1.28	-1.62	-2.04
500	13.7	10.4	8.0	5.7	-0.93	-1.28	-1.61	-2.04
∞	13.8	10.5	8.1	5.7	-0.93	-1.28	-1.60	-2.03
					c'_α			
25	17.2	14.6	12.5	10.2	0.76	-0.01	-0.65	-1.40
50	18.9	15.7	13.3	10.7	0.81	0.07	-0.53	-1.22
100	19.8	16.3	13.7	11.0	0.83	0.10	-0.47	-1.14
250	20.3	16.6	14.0	11.2	0.84	0.12	-0.43	-1.09
500	20.5	16.8	14.0	11.2	0.84	0.13	-0.42	-1.06
∞	20.7	16.9	14.1	11.3	0.85	0.13	-0.41	-1.04
					c''_α			
25	22.5	19.9	17.9	15.6	3.66	2.51	1.53	0.43
50	25.7	22.4	19.8	16.8	3.71	2.60	1.66	0.65
100	27.4	23.6	20.7	17.5	3.74	2.62	1.73	0.75
250	28.4	24.4	21.3	18.0	3.75	2.64	1.78	0.82
500	28.9	24.8	21.5	18.1	3.76	2.65	1.78	0.84
∞	29.5	25.1	21.8	18.3	3.77	2.66	1.79	0.87

Source: Fuller (1976) p. 371

Table 8 *Distribution of $\hat{t}$ for $\rho = 1$*

Sample Size	Probability α of larger value							
T	0.01	0.025	0.05	0.10	0.90	0.95	0.975	0.99
					t_α			
25	2.66	2.26	1.95	1.60	−0.92	−1.33	−1.70	−2.16
50	2.62	2.25	1.95	1.61	−0.91	−1.31	−1.66	−2.08
100	2.60	2.24	1.95	1.61	−0.90	−1.29	−1.64	−2.03
250	2.58	2.23	1.95	1.62	−0.89	−1.29	−1.63	−2.01
500	2.58	2.23	1.95	1.62	−0.89	−1.28	−1.62	−2.00
∞	2.58	2.23	1.95	1.62	−0.89	−1.28	−1.62	−2.00
					t_α'			
25	3.75	3.33	3.00	2.63	0.37	−0.00	−0.34	−0.72
50	3.58	3.22	2.93	2.60	0.40	0.03	−0.29	−0.66
100	3.51	3.17	2.89	2.58	0.42	0.05	−0.26	−0.63
250	3.46	3.14	2.88	2.57	0.42	0.06	−0.24	−0.62
500	3.44	3.13	2.87	2.57	0.43	0.07	−0.24	−0.61
∞	3.43	3.12	2.86	2.57	0.44	0.07	−0.23	−0.60
					t_α''			
25	4.38	3.95	3.60	3.24	1.14	0.80	0.50	0.15
50	4.15	3.80	3.50	3.18	1.19	0.87	0.58	0.24
100	4.04	3.73	3.45	3.15	1.22	0.90	0.62	0.28
250	3.99	3.69	3.43	3.13	1.23	0.92	0.64	0.31
500	3.98	3.68	3.42	3.13	1.24	0.93	0.65	0.32
∞	3.96	3.66	3.41	3.12	1.25	0.94	0.66	0.33

Source: Fuller (1976) p. 373

Index